360-0838

PRINCIPLES OF

MARKETING

THE PRENTICE HALL SERIES IN MARKETING
Philip Kotler, Series Editor

FIFTH EDITION

PRINCIPLES OF
MARKETING

Philip Kotler

Northwestern University

Gary Armstrong

University of North Carolina

PRENTICE HALL, Englewood Cliffs, New Jersey 07632

Library of Congress Cataloging-in-Publication Data

Kotler, Philip.
    Principles of marketing/Philip Kotler, Gary Armstrong.—5th
  ed.
      p. cm.—(The Prentice Hall series in marketing)
    Includes bibliographical references and indexes.
    ISBN 0-13-691247-8
    1. Marketing. I. Armstrong, Gary. II. Title. III. Series:
Prentice-Hall series in marketing.
HF5415.K636 1991
658.8—dc20   90-25245
                                            CIP

Principles of Marketing, fifth edition: Philip Kotler and Gary Armstrong
Editorial/production supervision: **Esther S. Koehn**
Interior design and cover design: **Suzanne Behnke**
Photo research: **Chris Pullo**
Photo editor: **Rona Tuccillo**
Manufacturing buyer: **Trudy Pisciotti/Robert Anderson**

 © 1991, 1989, 1986, 1983, 1980 by Prentice-Hall, Inc.
A Division of Simon & Schuster
Englewood Cliffs, New Jersey 07632

Printed in the United States of America
10 9 8 7 6 5 4 3 2 1

ISBN 0-13-691247-8

Prentice-Hall International (UK) Limited, *London*
Prentice-Hall of Australia Pty. Limited, *Sydney*
Prentice-Hall Canada Inc., *Toronto*
Prentice-Hall Hispanoamericana, S.A., *Mexico City*
Prentice-Hall of India Private Limited, *New Delhi*
Prentice-Hall of Japan, Inc., *Tokyo*
Simon & Schuster Asia Pte. Ltd., *Singapore*
Editora Prentice-Hall do Brasil, Ltda., *Rio de Janeiro*

To Nancy, Amy, Melissa, and Jessica Kotler

Kathy, Mandy, and K. C. Armstrong

About the Authors

Philip Kotler

Gary Armstrong

As a team, Philip Kotler and Gary Armstrong provide a blend of skills uniquely suited to writing an introductory marketing text. Professor Armstrong is one of the world's leading authorities on marketing. Professor Armstrong is an award-winning teacher of undergraduate business students. Together they make the complex world of marketing practical, approachable, and enjoyable.

Philip Kotler is S. C. Johnson & Son Distinguished Professor of International Marketing at the Kellogg Graduate School of Management, Northwestern University. He received his master's degree at the University of Chicago and his Ph.D. at M.I.T., both in economics. Dr. Kotler is author of *Marketing Management*: *Analysis*, *Planning*, *Implementation, and Control* (Prentice Hall), now in its seventh edition and the most widely used marketing textbook in graduate schools of business. He has written several other successful books and more than ninety articles for leading journals. He is the only three-time winner of the coveted Alpha Kappa Psi award for the best annual article in the *Journal of Marketing*. Dr. Kotler's numerous major honors include the *Paul D. Converse Award* given by the American Marketing Association to honor "outstanding contributions to science in marketing" and the *Steuart Henderson Britt Award* as Marketer of the Year. In 1985, he was the recipient of two new major awards: the *Distinguished Marketing Educator of the Year Award*, given by the American Marketing Association, and the *Philip Kotler Award for Excellence in Health Care Marketing*, presented by the Academy for Health Care Services Marketing. In 1989, he received the *Charles Coolidge Parlin Award* which annually honors an outstanding leader in the field of marketing. Dr. Kotler has served as chairman of the College on Marketing of the Institute of Management Sciences (TIMS) and as a director of the American Marketing Association. He has consulted with many major U.S. and foreign companies on marketing strategy.

Gary Armstrong is Professor and Chair of Marketing in the Graduate School of Business Administration at the University of North Carolina at Chapel Hill. He holds undergraduate and masters degrees in business from Wayne State University in Detroit, and he received his Ph.D. in marketing from Northwestern University. Dr. Armstrong has contributed numerous articles to leading business journals; his doctoral dissertation received the American Marketing Association's first-place award. As a consultant and researcher, he has worked with many companies on marketing research, sales management, and marketing strategy, but Professor Armstrong's first love is teaching. He has been very active in the teaching and administration of North Carolina's undergraduate business program. His recent administrative posts include Associate Director of the Undergraduate Business Program, Director of the Business Honors Program, and others. He works closely with business student groups and has received several campus-wide and School of Business teaching awards. He is the only two-time recipient of school's Award for Excellence in Undergraduate Teaching.

Contents

Part II
Analyzing Market
Opportunities

17   PROMOTING PRODUCTS: ADVERTISING, SALES PROMOTION, AND PUBLIC RELATIONS   442

18   PROMOTING PRODUCTS: PERSONAL SELLING AND SALES MANAGEMENT   476

Part V
Managing the Marketing Effort

19   COMPETITOR ANALYSIS AND COMPETITIVE MARKETING STRATEGIES   508

20   PLANNING, IMPLEMENTING, ORGANIZING, AND CONTROLLING MARKETING PROGRAMS   536

Part VI
Extending Marketing

Preface

"Marketing is too important to be left to the marketing department," states David Packard of Hewlett-Packard. Professor Stephen Burnett of Northwestern adds: "In a truly great marketing organization, you can't tell who's in the marketing department. Everyone in the organization has to make decisions based on the impact on the consumer."

Marketing is the business function that identifies customer needs and wants, determines which target markets the organization can best serve, designs appropriate products, services, and programs to serve these markets, and calls upon everyone in the organization to "think and serve customers." From a societal viewpoint, marketing links a society's material requirements and its economic patterns of response.

Yet, many people see marketing narrowly as the art of finding clever ways to dispose of a company's products. They see marketing only as advertising or selling. But real marketing does not involve the art of selling what you make so much as knowing *what* to make! Organizations gain market leadership by understanding consumer needs and finding solutions that satisfy these needs through product innovation, product quality, and customer service. If these are absent, no amount of advertising or selling can compensate.

Principles of Marketing is designed to help students learn about the basic concepts and practices of modern marketing in an enjoyable and practical way. Marketing is all around us, and we all need to know something about it. Most students are surprised to discover that marketing is so widely used. Marketing is used not only by manufacturing companies, wholesalers, and retailers, but by all kinds of individuals and organizations. Lawyers, accountants, and doctors use marketing to manage demand for their services; so do hospitals, museums, and performing arts groups. No politician can get the needed votes, and no resort the needed tourists, without developing and carrying out marketing plans.

People throughout these organizations need to know how to define and segment a market and develop need-satisfying products and services for chosen target segments. They must know how to price their offerings to make them attractive and affordable, and how to choose distribution channels to make their products available to customers. And they need to know how to advertise and promote products so that customers will know about and want them. Clearly, marketers need a broad range of skills in order to sense, serve, and satisfy consumer needs.

Students also need to know marketing in their roles as consumers and citizens. Someone is always trying to sell us something, so we need to recognize the methods they use. And when students enter the job market, they must do "marketing research" to find the best opportunities and the best ways to "market themselves" to prospective employers. Many will start their careers with marketing jobs in salesforces, in retailing, in advertising, in research, or in one of a dozen other marketing areas.

APPROACH AND OBJECTIVES

Principles of Marketing is designed to present the complex and fascinating world of marketing in an easy to grasp, lively, and enjoyable way. The book is *comprehensive* and *innovative*. It covers all of the basics of marketing and provides fresh insights into the latest marketing developments. It applies marketing thinking to products and services, consumer and industrial markets, profit and nonprofit organizations, domestic and international companies, and small and large firms. It covers important marketing principles and concepts that are supported by research and evidence from economics, the behavioral sciences, and modern management theory.

In addition to its comprehensive and innovative coverage, *Principles of Marketing* takes a *practical*, *managerial* approach to marketing. It provides a rich depth of practical examples and applications, showing the major decisions that marketing managers face in their efforts to balance the organization's objectives and resources against needs and opportunities in the marketplace. Each chapter opens with a major example describing an actual company situation. Boxed Marketing Highlights, short examples, cases, and color illustrations highlight high-interest ideas, stories, and marketing strategies.

Finally, *Principles of Marketing* makes learning marketing *easy* and *enjoyable*. Its writing style and level are well suited to the beginning marketing student. It tells the stories that reveal the drama of modern marketing: Kellogg's abrupt repositioning to meet changing baby-boomer life styles; the rise and fall of New Coke, the Edsel of the eighties; why Greyhound sold its bus line; how Oshkosh found a niche with "designer trucks;" 3M's legendary emphasis on new product development; tiny Vernor's success in the shadows of giants Coke and Pepsi; Procter & Gamble's fight to hold a share in the diaper and toothpaste markets; how Revlon sells not merely products, but hopes and dreams; giant Sears' failed attempt to convince consumers that it offers "your money's worth and a whole lot more;" Caterpillar's price war with Komatsu and Kodak's attack on Fuji Film in Japan; Gerber's difficult social responsibility decisions following a product-tampering scare. These and dozens of other examples and illustrations throughout each chapter reinforce key concepts and bring marketing to life.

Thus, *Principles of Marketing* gives the marketing student a comprehensive and innovative, managerial and practical introduction to marketing. Its style and extensive use of examples and illustrations make the book straight-forward, easy to read, and enjoyable.

CHANGES IN THE FIFTH EDITION

The fifth edition of *Principles of Marketing* offers several improvements in content and style. The fifth edition has been thoroughly edited to improve readability. It contains more illustrations—dozens of new color photos and advertisements have been added to illustrate key points and make the text more effective and appealing. Many new chapter-opening examples and Marketing Highlights illustrate important new concepts with actual business applications. All tables, facts, figures, and references have been thoroughly updated. Dozens of new examples have been added within the text materials. The text also offers an expanded list of real-life cases. A company case appears at the end of each chapter and a comprehensive case concludes each part. Three-quarters of these cases are new to this edition. In addition, twenty video cases—new to the fifth edition— are supported by the ABC NEWS/ PH VIDEO LIBRARY for *Principles of Marketing*. These cases and the quality videos that accompany them can bring the real world into the classroom.

The fifth edition of *Principles of Marketing* offers substantial new or improved material on several important topics: finding competitive advantage and differentiating the marketing offer, global marketing, the impact of Europe 1992, service marketing strategy, integrated direct marketing and database marketing, micromarketing, speed as strategy (turbo marketing), geodemographic segmentation, product quality and design, simultaneous product development, brand and category management, new consumer values and life styles, post-purchase satisfaction, the battle of advertising versus sales promotion, single-source data systems, relationship marketing, strategic alliances, cause marketing, the new environmentalism and "green marketing" and marketing ethics and social responsibility.

LEARNING AIDS

Many aids are provided within this book to help students learn about marketing. The main ones are:

- *Chapter Objectives*. Each chapter begins with objectives that prepare the student for the chapter material and point out learning goals.
- *Opening Examples*. Each chapter starts with a dramatic marketing story that introduces the chapter material and arouses student interest.
- *Full-Color Figures, Photographs, and Illustrations*. Throughout each chapter, important concepts and applications are illustrated with strong, full-color visual materials.
- *Marketing Highlights*. Additional examples and important information are highlighted in Marketing Highlight exhibits throughout the text.
- *Summaries*. Each chapter ends with a summary which wraps up the main points and concepts.
- *Review Questions*. Each chapter has a set of review questions covering the main chapter points.
- *Key Terms*. Key terms are highlighted within each chapter, and a list of key term definitions is provided at the end of each chapter.
- *Case Studies*. Forty-nine cases for class or written discussion are provided in this edition. These carefully developed cases challenge students to apply marketing principles in real situations.
- *Appendixes*. Two appendixes, "Marketing Arithmetic" and "Careers in Marketing," provide additional, practical information for students.
- *Glossary*. At the end of the book, an extensive glossary provides quick reference to the key terms found in the book.
- *Indexes*. Subject, company, and author indexes help students quickly find information and examples in the book.

SUPPLEMENTS

A successful marketing course requires more than a well-written book. It requires a dedicated teacher and a complete set of supplemental learning and teaching aids. The following aids support *Principles of Marketing*:

- **Annotated Instructor's Edition.** This volume, prepared by Richard G. Starr Jr. of the University of North Carolina, Chapel Hill, is an innovative teaching resource that combines the student text with a new set of teaching materials. Prepared especially for the instructor, it contains chapter summaries and comprehensive answers to the end-of-chapter discussion questions. Every page includes annotations that provide teaching tips and real-world examples.
- **Company Case & Case Video Commentaries.** This manual begins with an introduction

that suggests ways of teaching the introductory course using cases. For each company and video case in *Principles of Marketing* you will find:

* A synopsis of the case
* Teaching notes that outline how to use the case in class
* Discussion questions that focus students on the situations presented in the case

- **Instructor's Resource Manual.** This new teaching resource includes an overview of the text and suggested syllabi. Coverage of each chapter includes a chapter overview, annotated lecture outlines and applied learning exercises. In addition, the manual includes coverage for an additional video case that is applicable to the chapter. These videos are part of the package that is free to adopters.

- **Study Guide.** Prepared by Thomas J. Paczkowski of Cayuga Community College, this comprehensive study guide includes for each chapter a chapter overview, chapter objectives, a chapter outline, a concept review, mini-cases with questions for analysis, and multiple-choice and true/false questions.

- **Test Item File.** Prepared by Robert F. Gwinner, Arizona State University, the Test Item File is extensively revised. It provides 2300 items including multiple-choice, true/false and essay questions. Each chapter also includes a mini-case with application questions. It is available in a computerized version for IBM PC and compatible formats.

- **Full-Color Transparencies.** Over 140 full-color transparencies are offered—some of important figures and illustrations from the book, others of advertisements and illustrations from a variety of sources.

- **Marketing Today: Successes, Failures, and Turnarounds.** 2nd edition by John B. Clark. This casebook delves into the promotion strategy, marketing mix, and market forces at work in fifteen highly visible companies—five success stories, five failures, and five that have made remarkable turnarounds. An instructor's manual is available.

- **ABC NEWS/PH VIDEO LIBRARY for *Principles of Marketing*.** Prentice Hall and ABC News have joined forces to create the best and most comprehensive set of video materials available for any introductory marketing text. From its wide range of award-winning news programs—*Nightline, Business World, On Business, This Week with David Brinkley, World News Tonight,* and *Health Show*—ABC has assembled a selection of over 40 high-quality, relevant, and entertaining feature and documentary videos related to important text concepts and applications in *Principles of Marketing*. Twenty of these videos are accompanied by written video cases at the end of the text's chapters. All of the videos are supported by case commentaries and teaching suggestions in the *Instructor's Resource Manual* to help instructors to effectively integrate the videos into their lectures.

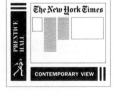

- **The New York Times/Prentice Hall Contemporary View Program.** Prentice Hall and *The New York Times* have joined to provide this 16 to 32 page ''mini-newspaper'' containing recent *NYT* articles carefully selected to bring the tempo of today's marketing world into the classroom. These fresh articles on important marketing topics to help to link the text and classroom sessions with what is happening in the world around us. To make *The New York Times* even more available on a daily basis, a reduced subscription rate is also available.

ACKNOWLEDGMENTS

No book is the work only of its authors. We owe much to the pioneers of marketing who first identified its major issues and developed its concepts and techniques. Our thanks also go to our colleagues at the J. L. Kellogg Graduate School of Management, Northwestern University, and the Graduate School of Business Administration, University of North Carolina at Chapel Hill, for ideas and suggestions. We owe special thanks to Richard G. Starr, Jr. of UNC-Chapel Hill, who prepared the *Annotated Instructor's Edition*. We also thank Lew Brown, of the UNC-Greensboro, and Michele Bunn, of SUNY-Buffalo, for their valuable work in preparing timely, lively, and company cases for the text. We also want to acknowledge the work of Martha R. McEnally, UNC-Greensboro, and Tom Paczkowski in preparing the video cases. Our thanks, too, to Robert Gwinner for updating the Test Item File. Sarah Woods provided valuable research and development assistance.

Many reviewers at other colleges provided valuable comments and suggestions. We are indebted to the following colleagues:

Gerald Albaum
University of Oregon

David Anderson
Wheaton College

David L. Appel
University of Notre Dame

Boris W. Becker
Oregon State University

Robert L. Berl
Memphis State University

Paul N. Bloom
University of North Carolina

Robert Boris
Bryant and Stratton Business Institute

Jane Bradlee-Durfee
Mankato State University

Austin Byron
Northern Arizona University

Helen Caldwell
Providence College

Paul Cohen
CUNY of Staten Island—Sunnyside

Keith Cox
University of Houston

Robert Dalton
Russell Sage College

Ronald Decker
University of Wisconsin—Eau Claire

Rohit Deshpande
Dartmouth College

Thomas Falcone
Indiana University of Penna.

David Georgoff
Florida Atlantic University

Thomas J. Hickey
SUNY-Oswego

Ralph Jackson
University of Tulsa

Raymond F. Keyes
Boston College

Irene Lange
California State University at Fullerton

Frederick Langrehr
University of Nebraska—Omaha

Charlotte Mason
University of North Carolina— Chapel Hill

Douglas W. Mellott, Jr.
Radford University

Ronald Michaels
University of Kansas

Chem Narayana
University of Illinois at Chicago

Christopher P. Puto
University of Michigan

David R. Rink
Northern Illinois University

Dean Siewers
Rochester Institute of Technology

Clint B. Tankersley
Syracuse University

Robert E. Thompson
Indiana State University

We also owe a great deal to the people at Prentice Hall who helped develop this book. Chris Treiber, marketing editor, provided solid advice and fresh insights. Esther Koehn, production editor, skillfully guided the book through production.

Finally, we owe many thanks to our families—Nancy, Amy, Melissa, and Jessica Kotler; and Kathy, Mandy, and K. C. Armstrong for their constant understanding, support, and encouragement.

Philip Kotler
Gary Armstrong

PRINCIPLES OF
MARKETING

1

Social Foundations of Marketing: Meeting Human Needs

Marketing touches all of us every day of our lives. We wake up to a Sears radio alarm clock playing an American Airlines commercial advertising a Bahamas vacation. Then we brush our teeth with Crest, shave with a Gillete Sensor razor, gargle with Scope, and use other toiletries and appliances produced by manufacturers around the world. Then we put on our Guess jeans and Nike shoes and head for the kitchen, where we drink Minute Maid orange juice and pour Borden milk over a bowl of Kellogg's Cracklin' Oat Bran. Later, we drink a cup of Maxwell House coffee with two teaspoons of Domino sugar while munching on a slice of Sara Lee coffee cake.

We consume oranges grown in California and coffee imported from Brazil, read a newspaper made of Canadian wood pulp, and tune into radio news coming from as far away as Australia. We fetch our mail to find a Metropolitan Museum of Art catalog, a letter from a Prudential insurance agent, and coupons offering discounts on an array of our favorite brands. We step out the door and drive our car to the Northbrook Court Shopping Center with its Neiman-Marcus, Lord & Taylor, Sears, and hundreds of other stores filled with goods from floor to ceiling. Later, we exercise at a Nautilus Fitness Center, have our hair trimmed at Super Cuts, grab a McDLT at McDonald's, and plan a trip to Disney World at a Thomas Cook travel agency.

The *marketing system* has made all this possible with little effort on our part. It has given us a standard of living that our ancestors could not have imagined.

After reading this chapter, you should be able to:

1. Define *marketing* and discuss its role in the economy.
2. Compare the five marketing management philosophies.
3. Identify the goals of the marketing system.
4. Explain how marketing can be used by different kinds of business and nonbusiness organizations.

The marketing system that delivers our high standard of living consists of many large and small companies, all seeking success. Two business researchers, Tom Peters and Robert Waterman, studied many successful companies—companies like Hewlett-Packard, Frito-Lay (PepsiCo), Procter & Gamble, 3M, McDonald's, and Marriott—to find out what made them tick. They reported the results in what became the best selling business book of all time, *In Search of Excellence*.[1] They found that these companies shared a set of basic marketing principles: Each boasted a keen understanding of its customers, strongly defined markets, and the ability to motivate its employees to produce high quality and value for its customers.

In his later books, Peters offers further stories about companies doing smart and wonderful things to improve their customers' satisfaction.[2] He describes how IBM collects customer ratings of its sales and service people and gives awards to employees who best satisfy customers. He explains how The Limited studies women's clothing needs and creates the right store systems for different market segments (The Limited, Limited Express, Victoria's Secret, Sizes Unlimited). He tells of Stew Leonard's supermarket in Norwalk, Connecticut, where Stew sits down with eight customers for a few hours each Saturday to talk about how he can improve customer service. And he describes how J. Willard Marriott, Sr. continued for 57 years to personally read guest complaint cards so that he could perfect the service in his Marriott Hotels.

Other business writers have presented their views of the attitudes and strategies that make companies great in books bearing such titles as *The Customer is Key*, *Service America!*, and *The Winning Performance*.[3] Although they suggest many factors that make a business successful—great strategy, dedicated employees, good information systems, excellent implementation—each author emphasizes the central importance of dedicating the business to sensing, serving, and satisfying the needs of customers in a well-understood target market.

The critical need for marketing in today's companies is dramatically documented in a recent study in which senior managers of major American companies identified their foremost problem as "developing, improving, and implementing competitive marketing strategies."[4] As a further sign, executive recruiting firms report a large increase in demand for top marketing executives. One such firm found that of current top executives more have come from marketing than any other field—31 percent of the chief executives of the *Fortune* 1000 companies had mostly marketing backgrounds, up 28 percent from four years earlier.[5]

Thus, marketing is a key factor in business success. The term *marketing* must be understood not in the old sense of making a sale—"selling"—but rather in the new sense of *satisfying customer needs*. Today's companies face increasingly stiff competition, and the rewards will go to those who can best read customer wants and deliver the greatest value to their target consumers. In the marketplace, marketing skills will separate the amateurs from the professionals.

In this chapter, we define marketing and its core concepts, describe the major philosophies of marketing thinking and practice, discuss the goals of the marketing system, and explain how marketing is used by different kinds of organizations.

WHAT IS MARKETING?

What does the term *marketing* mean? Many people mistakenly think of marketing only as selling and promotion. And no wonder—every day, Americans are bombarded with television commercials, newspaper ads, direct mail, and sales calls. Someone is always trying to sell us something. It seems that we cannot escape death, taxes, or selling.

Therefore, many students are surprised to learn that selling is only the tip of the marketing iceberg: It is but one of several marketing functions—and often not the most important one. If the marketer does a good job of identifying consumer needs, developing good products, and pricing, distributing, and promoting them effectively, these goods will sell very easily.

Everyone knows something about "hot" products. When Polaroid designed its Spectra camera, when Coleco first sold Cabbage Patch dolls, and when Ford introduced its Taurus model, these manufacturers were swamped with orders. They had designed the "right" products—not "me-too" products, but ones offering new benefits. Peter Drucker, a leading management thinker, has put it this way: "The aim of marketing is to make selling superfluous. The aim is to know and understand the customer so well that the product or service fits . . . and sells itself."[6]

This does not mean that selling and promotion are unimportant, but rather that they are part of a larger "marketing mix"—a set of marketing tools that work together to affect the marketplace. We define **marketing** as a social and managerial process by which individuals and groups obtain what they need and want through creating and exchanging products and value with others.[7] To explain this definition, we examine the following important terms: *needs, wants, demands, products, exchange, transactions,* and *markets.* These concepts are shown in Figure 1-1 and explained in the following discussion. As the figure shows, these core marketing concepts are linked, with each concept building on the one before it.

Needs   The most basic concept underlying marketing is that of human needs. A **human need is a state of felt deprivation.** Humans have many complex needs. They include basic *physical* needs for food, clothing, warmth, and safety; *social* needs for belonging and affection; and *individual* needs for knowledge and self-expression. These needs are not invented on Madison Avenue: They are a basic part of the human makeup.

When a need is not satisfied, a person will do one of two things—look for an object that will satisfy it or try to reduce the need. People in industrial societies may try to find or develop objects that will satisfy their desires. People in less developed societies may try to reduce their desires and satisfy them with what is available.

FIGURE 1-1
Core marketing concepts

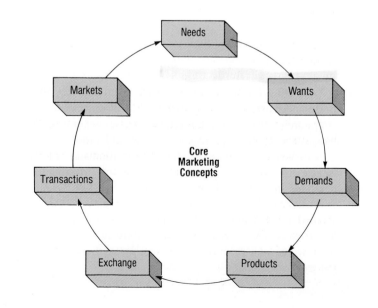

Kaiser Sand & Gravel Company's marketing mission is to "find a need and fill it."

Wants

A second basic concept in marketing is that of **human wants**—the form taken by human needs as they are shaped by culture and individual personality. A hungry person in Bali may want mangoes, suckling pig, and beans. A hungry person in the United States may want a hamburger, French fries, and a Coke. Wants are described in terms of objects that will satisfy needs. As a society evolves, the wants of its members expand. As people are exposed to more objects that arouse their interest and desire, producers try to provide more want-satisfying products and services.

Many sellers confuse wants and needs. A manufacturer of drill bits may think that the customer needs a drill bit, but what the customer really needs is a hole. These sellers may suffer from "marketing myopia."[8] They are so taken with their products that they focus only on existing wants and lose sight of underlying customer needs. They forget that a physical product is only a tool to solve a consumer problem. These sellers have trouble if a new product comes along that serves the need better or cheaper. The customer with the same *need* will *want* the new product. As a classic example, Hollywood fell on hard times because it concentrated on its products (movies) rather than underlying consumer needs (entertainment). The television industry grew rapidly at Hollywood's expense because it found a new and better way to serve consumers' entertainment needs.

Demands

People have almost unlimited wants but limited resources. Thus, they want to choose products that provide the most satisfaction for their money. When backed by buying power, wants become **demands**.

Listing the demands in a society at a given time is easy. In a single year, 246 million Americans may purchase 61 billion eggs, 200 million chickens, 29 million telephones, 341 billion domestic air-passenger miles, and more than 20 million lectures by college English professors. These and other consumer goods and services lead in turn to a demand for more than 100 million tons of steel, 38 million tons of paper, 4 billion tons of cotton, and many other industrial goods. These are but a few of the demands in a $5.3 trillion economy.

Consumers view products as bundles of benefits and choose products that give them the best bundle for their money. Thus, a Ford Escort means basic transportation, a low price, and fuel economy. A Mercedes means comfort, luxury, and status. Given their wants and resources, people choose the product with the benefits that add up to the most satisfaction.

MONTY, PYTHON.

Utah's **HOGLE ZOO**

Products do not have to be physical objects. Here, the "product" is a trip to the zoo.

Products

Human needs, wants, and demands suggest that products are available to satisfy them. A **product** is anything that can be offered to a market for attention, acquisition, use, or consumption and that might satisfy a need or want.

Suppose a person feels the need to be more attractive. We will call all the products that can satisfy this need the *product choice set*. This set may include new clothes, hair-styling services, a Caribbean suntan, exercise classes, and many other items or services. These products are not all equally desirable. Those that are more available and less expensive, such as clothing and a new haircut, are likely to be purchased first. Moreover, the closer products come to matching consumers' wants, the more successful they will be. Thus, producers must know what consumers want and must provide products that come as close as possible to satisfying those wants.

The concept of *product* is not limited to physical objects. Anything capable of satisfying a need can be called a product. In addition to goods and services, products include *persons*, *places*, *organizations*, *activities*, and *ideas*. A consumer decides which entertainers to watch on television, which places to go on a vacation, which organizations to contribute to, and which ideas to support. To the consumer, these are all products. If at times the term *product* does not seem to fit, we could substitute such terms as "satisfier," "resource," or "offer." All describe something of value to someone.

Exchange

Marketing occurs when people decide to satisfy needs and wants through exchange. **exchange** is the act of obtaining a desired object from someone by offering something in return. Exchange is only one of many ways people can obtain a desired object. For example, hungry people can find food by hunting, fishing, or gathering fruit. They could beg for food or take food from someone else. Finally, they could offer money, another good, or a service in return for food.

As a means of satisfying needs, exchange has much in its favor. People do not have to prey on others or depend on donations. Nor must they possess the skills to produce every necessity for themselves. They can concentrate on making things they are good at making and trade them for needed items made by others. Thus, the society produces much more than with any alternative system.

Exchange is the core concept of marketing.[9] For an exchange to take place, several conditions must be satisfied. Of course, at least two parties must participate, and each must have something of value to the other. Each party must want to deal with the other party; each must be free to accept or reject the other's offer. Finally, each party must be able to communicate and deliver.

These conditions simply make exchange *possible*. Whether exchange actually *takes place* depends on the parties' coming to an agreement. If they agree, we must conclude that the act of exchange has left both of them better off (or at least not worse off):

After all, each was free to reject or accept the offer. In this sense, just as production creates value, exchange creates value: It gives people more consumption possibilities.

Transactions   Whereas exchange is the core concept of marketing, a transaction is marketing's unit of measurement. A **transaction** consists of a trade of values between two parties. In a transaction, we must be able to say that A gives X to B and gets Y in return. For example, you pay Sears $400 for a television set. This is a classic **monetary transaction.** But not all transactions involve money. In a **barter transaction,** you might trade your old refrigerator in return for a neighbor's second-hand television set. A barter transaction can also involve services as well as goods—for example, when a lawyer writes a will for a doctor in return for a medical exam (see Marketing Highlight 1-1). A transaction involves at least two things of value, conditions that are agreed upon, a time of agreement, and a place of agreement.

In this broadest sense, the marketer tries to bring about a response to some offer. And the response may be more than simply "buying" or "trading" goods and services in the narrow sense. A political candidate, for instance, wants a response called "votes," a church wants "membership," a social-action group wants "idea acceptance." Marketing consists of actions taken to obtain a desired response from a target audience toward some product, service, idea, or other object.

Markets   The concept of transactions leads to the concept of a market. A **market** is the set of actual and potential buyers of a product. To understand the nature of a market, imagine a primitive economy consisting of only four people: a fisherman, a hunter, a potter, and a farmer. Figure 1-2 shows the three different ways in which these traders could meet their needs. In the first case, *self-sufficiency*, they gather the needed goods for themselves. Thus, the hunter spends most of the time hunting, but also must take time to fish, make pottery, and farm to obtain the other goods. The hunter is thereby less efficient at hunting, and the same is true of the other traders.

In the second case, *decentralized exchange*, each person sees the other three as potential "buyers" who make up a market. Thus the hunter may make separate trips to trade meat for the goods of the fisherman, the potter, and the farmer.

In the third case, *centralized exchange*, a new person called a *merchant* appears and locates in a central area called a *marketplace*. Each trader brings goods to the

---

MARKETING HIGHLIGHT 1–1

GOING BACK TO BARTER

With today's high prices, many companies are returning to the primitive but time-honored practice of barter—trading goods and services that they make or provide for other goods and services that they need. Currently, companies barter more than $275 billion worth of goods and services a year worldwide, and the practice is growing rapidly.

Companies use barter to increase sales, unload extra goods, and save cash. For example, when Climaco Corporation was overstocked with bubble bath, it swapped the excess for $300,000 worth of advertising space for one of its other products. McDonnell Douglas traded planes to Yugoslavia for hams and tools, and Pierre Cardin served as a consultant to China in exchange for silks and cashmeres. The cash-poor U.S. Olympics Committee bartered the promotional use of its Olympic logo for products and services needed by its staff and athletes. It obtained free transportation from United Airlines, 500 cars from Buick, clothing from Levi Strauss, and shoes from Nike. The committee even traded the logo for a swimming pool built by McDonald's.

As a result of this increase in barter activity, many kinds of specialty companies have appeared to help other companies with their bartering. Retail-trade exchanges and trade clubs arrange barter for small retailers. Larger corporations use trade consultants and brokerage firms. Media brokerage houses provide advertising in exchange for products, and international barter is often handled by countertrade organizations. One trading company, Barter Systems, Inc., operates sixty-two trading centers around the United States. A letter it recently sent to some of its 25,000 clients stated: "Wanted: $300,000 worth of dried milk or cornflakes in exchange for an airplane of equal value."

Sources: See Linda A. Dickerson, "Barter to Gain a Competitive Edge in a Cash-Poor Economy, *Marketing News*, March 16, 1984, pp. 1–2; and Arthur Bragg, "Bartering Comes of Age," *Sales & Marketing Management*, January 1988, pp. 61–63.

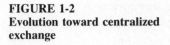

FIGURE 1-2
Evolution toward centralized exchange

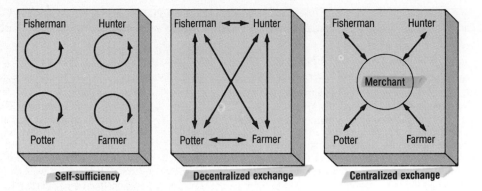

merchant and trades for other needed goods. Thus, rather than transacting with the other providers, the hunter transacts with one "market" to obtain all the needed goods. Merchants and central marketplaces greatly reduce the total number of transactions needed to accomplish a given volume of exchange.[10]

As the number of persons and transactions increases in a society, the number of merchants and marketplaces also increases. In advanced societies, markets need not be physical locations where buyers and sellers interact. With modern communications and transportation, a merchant can easily advertise a product on late-evening television, take orders from hundreds of customers over the phone, and mail the goods to the buyers on the following day without having had any physical contact with them.

A market can grow up around a product, a service, or anything else of value. For example, a *labor market* consists of people who are willing to offer their work in return for wages or products. In fact, various institutions, such as employment agencies and job-counseling firms, will grow up around a labor market to help it function better. The *money market* is another important market that emerges to meet the needs of people so that they can borrow, lend, save, and protect money. The *donor market* has emerged to meet the financial needs of nonprofit organizations.

Marketing   The concept of markets finally brings us full circle to the concept of marketing. Marketing means working with markets to bring about exchanges for the purpose of satisfying human needs and wants. Thus we return to our definition of marketing as a process by which individuals and groups obtain what they need and want by creating and exchanging products and value with others.

Exchange processes involve work. Sellers must search for buyers, identify their needs, design good products, promote them, store and deliver them, and set prices for them. Such activities as product development, research, communication, distribution, pricing, and service are core marketing activities.

Although we normally think of marketing as being carried on by sellers, buyers also carry on marketing activities. Consumers do "marketing" when they search for the goods they need at prices they can afford. Company purchasing agents do "marketing" when they track down sellers and bargain for good terms. A *seller's market* is one in which sellers have more power and buyers must be the more active "marketers." In a *buyer's market*, buyers have more power and sellers have to be more active "marketers."

During the early 1950s the supply of goods began to grow faster than the demand. Most markets became buyers' markets, and marketing became identified with sellers trying to find buyers. This book examines the marketing problems of sellers in a buyers' market.

MARKETING MANAGEMENT

Most people think of marketing management as finding enough customers for the company's current output, but this is too limited a view. The organization has a desired level of demand for its products. At any time, there may be no demand, adequate

VARIOUS STATES OF DEMAND

Marketing managers in different organizations might face any of the following states of demand. The marketing task is to manage demand effectively.

Negative Demand. A major part of the market dislikes the product and may even pay to avoid it. Examples are vaccinations, dental work, and seat belts. Marketers must analyze why the market dislikes the product, and whether product redesign, lower prices, or more positive promotion can change the consumer attitudes.

No Demand. Target consumers may be uninterested in the product. Thus farmers may not care about a new farming method, and college students may not be interested in taking foreign language courses. The marketer must find ways to connect the product's benefits with the market's needs and interests.

Latent Demand. Consumers have a want that is not satisfied by any existing product or service. Strong latent demand exists for nonharmful cigarettes, safer neighborhoods, biodegradable packages, and more fuel-efficient cars. The marketing task is to measure the size of the potential market and develop effective goods and services that will satisfy the demand.

Falling Demand. Sooner or later, every organization faces falling demand for one of its products. Churches have suffered membership decline, and private colleges have received fewer applications. The marketer must find the causes of market decline and restimulate demand by finding new markets, changing product features, or creating more effective communications.

Irregular Demand. Demand varies on a seasonal, daily, or even hourly basis, causing problems of idle or overworked capacity. In mass transit, much equipment is idle during slow travel hours and too little is available during peak hours. Museums are undervisited during weekdays and overcrowded during weekends. Marketers must find ways to change the time pattern of demand through flexible pricing, promotion, and other incentives.

Full Demand. The organization has just the amount of demand it wants and can handle. The marketer works to maintain the current level of demand in the face of changing consumer preferences and increasing competition. The organization maintains quality and continually monitors consumer satisfaction to make sure it is doing a good job.

Overfull Demand. Demand is higher than the company can or wants to handle. Thus the Golden Gate Bridge carries more traffic than is safe; and Yellowstone National Park is overcrowded in the summertime. Utilities, bus companies, restaurants, and other businesses often face overfull demand at peak times. The marketing task, called DEMARKETING, is to find ways to reduce the demand temporarily or permanently. Demarketing involves such actions as raising prices and reducing promotion and service. Demarketing does not aim to destroy demand, but only to reduce it.

---

demand, irregular demand, or too much demand, and marketing management must find ways to deal with these different demand states (see Marketing Highlight 1–2). Marketing management is concerned not only with finding and increasing demand, but also with changing or even reducing it. Thus marketing management seeks to affect the level, timing, and nature of demand in a way that will help the organization achieve its objectives. Simply put, marketing management is *demand management*.

We define **marketing management** as the analysis, planning, implementation, and control of programs designed to create, build, and maintain beneficial exchanges with target buyers for the purpose of achieving organizational objectives. Marketing managers include sales managers and salespeople, advertising executives, sales-promotion people, marketing researchers, product managers, pricing specialists, and others. We discuss these marketing jobs more in Chapters 2 and 20 and in Appendix B, "Careers in Marketing."

MARKETING MANAGEMENT PHILOSOPHIES

We have described marketing management as carrying out tasks to achieve desired exchanges with target markets. What *philosophy* should guide these marketing efforts? What weight should be given to the interests of the organization, customers, and society? Very often these interests conflict.

There are five alternative concepts under which organizations conduct their marketing activities: the *production*, *product*, *selling*, *marketing*, and *societal marketing* concepts.

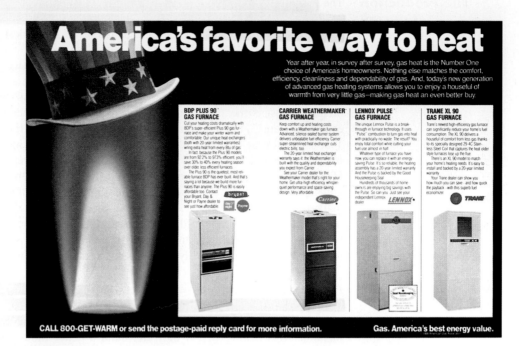

Managing demand: During the gas shortages of the 1970s, the American Gas Association demarketed natural gas by telling people how to conserve. Then when gas supplies grew in the 1980s, the AGA ran ads to stimulate sales while continuing to emphasize energy efficiency.

The Production Concept

The **production concept** holds that consumers favor products that are available and highly affordable and that management should therefore focus on improving production and distribution efficiency. This concept is one of the oldest philosophies that guides sellers.

The production concept is a useful philosophy in two types of situations. The first occurs when the demand for a product exceeds the supply. Here, management should look for ways to increase production. The second situation occurs when the product's cost is too high and improved productivity is needed to bring it down. For example, Henry Ford's whole philosophy was to perfect the production of the Model T so that its cost could be reduced and more people could afford it. He joked about offering people a car of any color as long is it was black. Today Texas Instruments (TI) follows this philosophy of increased production and lower costs in order to bring down prices. The company won a major share of the American hand-held calculator market with this philosophy. But when it used the same strategy in the digital watch market, TI failed. Although they were priced low, customers did not find TI's watches very attractive. In its drive to bring down prices, TI lost sight of something else that its customers wanted—namely, *attractive*, affordable digital watches.

The Product Concept

Another major concept guiding sellers, the **product concept**, holds that consumers favor products that offer the most quality, performance, and features, and that an organization should thus devote energy to making continuous product improvements. Some manufacturers believe that if they can build a better mousetrap, the world will beat a path to their door.[11] But they are often rudely shocked. Buyers may well be looking for a better solution to a mouse problem, but not necessarily for a better mousetrap. The solution might be a chemical spray, an exterminating service, or something that works better than a mousetrap. Furthermore, a better mousetrap will not sell unless the manufacturer designs, packages, and prices it attractively, places it in convenient distribution channels, brings it to the attention of people who need it, and convinces them that it is a better product.

The product concept can also lead to "marketing myopia." For instance, railroad management once thought that users wanted *trains* rather than *transportation* and overlooked the growing challenge of airlines, buses, trucks, and automobiles. Many colleges have assumed that high school graduates want a liberal arts education and have thus overlooked the increasing challenge of vocational schools.

The Selling Concept

Many organizations follow the **selling concept**, which holds that consumers will not buy enough of the organization's products unless it undertakes a large selling and promotion effort. The concept is typically practiced with *unsought goods*—those which buyers do not normally think of buying, say encyclopedias and funeral plots. These industries must be good at tracking down prospects and selling them on product benefits.

The selling concept is also practiced in the nonprofit area. A political party, for example, will vigorously sell its candidate to voters as a fantastic person for the job. The candidate works in voting precincts from dawn to dusk, shaking hands, kissing babies, meeting donors, making speeches. Much money is spent on radio and television advertising, posters, and mailings. Candidate flaws are hidden from the public because the aim is to get the sale, not worry about consumer satisfaction afterward.

The Marketing Concept

The **marketing concept** holds that achieving organizational goals depends on determining the needs and wants of target markets and delivering the desired satisfactions more effectively and efficiently than competitors. Surprisingly, this concept is a relatively recent business philosophy. The marketing concept has been stated in such colorful ways as "Find a need and fill it" (Kaiser Sand & Gravel); "To fly, to serve" (British Airways); and "We're not satisfied until you are" (GE). J. C. Penney's motto also summarizes the marketing concept: "To do all in our power to pack the customer's dollar full of value, quality, and satisfaction."

The selling concept and the marketing concept are frequently confused. Figure

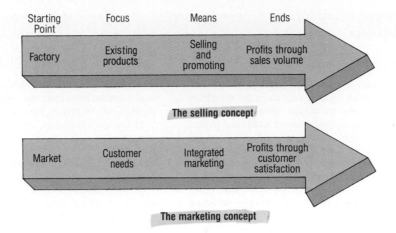

Starting Point	Focus	Means	Ends

Factory | Existing products | Selling and promoting | Profits through sales volume

The selling concept

Market | Customer needs | Integrated marketing | Profits through customer satisfaction

The marketing concept

FIGURE 1-3
The selling and marketing concepts contrasted

1-3 compares the two concepts. The selling concept takes an *inside-out* perspective. It starts with the factory, focuses on the company's existing products, and calls for heavy selling and promotion to obtain profitable sales. By contrast, the marketing concept takes an *outside-in* perspective. It starts with a well-defined market, focuses on customer needs, coordinates all the marketing activities affecting customers, and makes profits by creating customer satisfaction. Under the marketing concept, companies produce what consumers want, thereby satisfying consumers and making profits.

Many successful and well-known companies have adopted the marketing concept. Procter & Gamble, IBM, Disney, Marriott, and McDonald's follow it faithfully (see Marketing Highlight 1–3). L. L. Bean, the highly successful catalog retailer of clothing and outdoor sporting equipment, was founded on the marketing concept. In 1912, in his first circulars, L. L. Bean included the following notice:

The marketing concept: GE promises consumer satisfaction.

McDONALD'S APPLIES THE MARKETING CONCEPT

McDonald's Corporation, the fast-food hamburger retailer, is a master marketer. With 11,000 outlets in 50 countries and more than $17.5 billion in annual sales, McDonald's doubles the sales of its nearest rival, Burger King, and triples those of third-place Wendy's. Nineteen million customers pass through the famous golden arches each day, and an astounding 96 percent of all Americans eat at McDonald's each year. McDonald's now serves 145 hamburgers per second. Credit for this performance belongs to a strong marketing orientation: McDonald's knows how to serve people and adapt to changing consumer wants.

Before McDonald's appeared, Americans could get hamburgers in restaurants or diners. But consumers often encountered poor hamburgers, slow and unfriendly service, unattractive decor, unclean conditions, and a noisy atmosphere. In 1955 Ray Kroc, a 52-year-old salesman of milkshake-mixing machines, became excited about a string of seven restaurants owned by Richard and Maurice McDonald. Kroc liked their fast-food restaurant concept and bought the chain for $2.7 million. He decided to expand the chain by selling franchises, and the number of restaurants grew rapidly. As times changed, so did McDonald's. It expanded its sit-down sections, improved the decor, launched a breakfast menu, added new food items, and opened new outlets in high-traffic areas.

Kroc's marketing philosophy is captured in McDonald's motto of "Q.S.C. & V.," which stands for *q*uality, *s*ervice, *c*leanliness, and *v*alue. Customers enter a spotlessly clean restaurant, walk up to a friendly counterperson, quickly receive a good-tasting meal, and eat it there or take it out. There are no jukeboxes or telephones to create a teen-age hangout. Nor are there any cigarette machines or newspaper racks—McDonald's is a family affair, appealing strongly to children.

McDonald's has mastered the art of serving consumers, and it carefully teaches the basics to its franchisees and employees, all of whom take training courses at McDonald's "Hamburger University" in Elk Grove Village, Illinois. They emerge with a degree in "Hamburgerology" and a minor in french fries. McDonald's monitors product and service quality through continuous customer surveys and puts great energy into improving hamburger production methods in order to simplify operations, bring down costs, speed up service, and bring greater value to customers. Beyond these efforts, each McDonald's restaurant works to become a part of its neighborhood through community-involvement and service projects.

In 2,700 restaurants outside of the United States, McDonald's carefully customizes its menu and service to local tastes and customs. It serves corn soup and teriaki burgers in Japan, pasta salads in Rome, and wine and live piano music with its McNuggets in Paris. When McDonald's recently opened its first restaurant in Moscow, it quickly won the hearts of Soviet consumers. However, the company had to overcome some monstrous hurdles in order to meet its high standards for consumer satisfaction in this new market. It had to educate suppliers, employees, and even consumers about the time-tested, McDonald's way of doing things. Technical experts with special strains of disease resistant seed were brought in from Canada to teach Soviet farmers how to grow russet Burbank potatoes for french fries, and the company built its own pasteurizing plant to ensure a plentiful supply of fresh milk. It trained Soviet managers at Hamburger University and subjected each of 630 new employees (most of whom didn't know a Chicken McNugget from an Egg McMuffin) to 16–20 hours of training on such essentials as cooking meat patties, assembling Filet-O-Fish sandwiches, and giving service with a smile. McDonald's even had to

---

> I do not consider a sale complete until goods are worn out and the customer still satisfied. We will thank anyone to return goods that are not perfectly satisfactory. . . . Above all things we wish to avoid having a dissatisfied customer.

Today, L. L. Bean dedicates itself to giving "perfect satisfaction in every way." To inspire its employees to practice the marketing concept, it displays posters around its offices which proclaim the following:

> What is a customer? A customer is the most important person ever in this company—in person or by mail. A customer is not dependent on us, we are dependent on him. A customer is not an interruption of our work, he is the purpose of it. We are not doing a favor by serving him, he is doing us a favor by giving us the opportunity to do so. A customer is not someone to argue or match wits with—nobody ever won an argument with a customer. A customer is a person who brings us his wants—it is our job to handle them profitably to him and to ourselves.

On the other hand, many companies claim to practice the marketing concept but do not. They have the *forms* of marketing—such as a marketing vice-president, product managers, marketing plans, marketing research—but not the *substance*. Several years of hard work are needed to turn a sales-oriented company into a market-oriented company.[12]

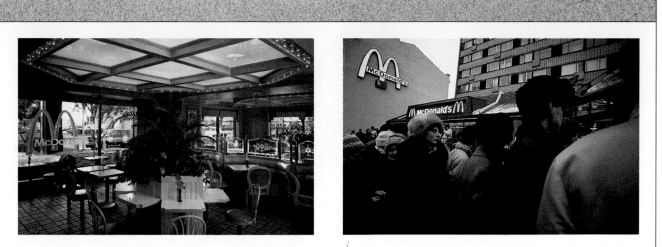

McDonald's delivers "quality, service, cleanliness, and value" here in the United States and around the world.

train consumers—most Muscovites had never seen a fast-food restaurant. Customers waiting in line were shown videos telling them everything from how to order and pay at the counter to how to handle a Big Mac. And in its usual way, McDonald's began immediately to build community involvement. On opening day, it held a kick-off party for 700 Muscovite orphans, and it donated all opening-day proceeds to the Moscow Children's Fund. As a result, the new Moscow restaurant got off to a very successful start. About 50,000 customers swarmed the restaurant during its first day of business.

The McDonald's focus on consumers has made it the world's largest food-service organization. It now captures about 20 percent of America's fast-food business. The company's huge success has also been reflected in the increased value of its stock over the years: 250 shares of McDonald's stock purchased for less than $6,000 in 1965 would be worth more than a million dollars today!

Sources: Penny Moser, "The McDonald's Mystique," *Fortune*, July 4, 1988; Scott Hume, "McDonald's Fred Turner: Making All the Right Moves, *Advertising Age*, January 1, 1990, pp. 6, 17; Gail McKnight, "Here Comes Bolshoi Mac," *USA Today Weekend*, January 26–28, 1990, pp. 4–5; and Rosemarie Boyle, "McDonald's Gives Soviets Something Worth Waiting For," *Advertising Age*, March 19, 1990, p. 61.

The Societal Marketing Concept

The **societal marketing concept** holds that the organization should determine the needs, wants, and interests of target markets. It should then deliver the desired satisfactions more effectively and efficiently than competitors in a way that maintains or improves the consumer's *and the society's* well-being. The societal marketing concept is the newest of the five marketing management philosophies.

The societal marketing concept questions whether the pure marketing concept is adequate in an age of environmental problems, resource shortages, rapid population growth, worldwide inflation, and neglected social services. It asks if the firm that senses, serves, and satisfies individual wants is always doing what's best for consumers and society in the long run. According to the societal marketing concept, the pure marketing concept overlooks possible conflicts between short-run consumer *wants* and long-run consumer *welfare*.

Consider the Coca-Cola Company. Most people see it as a highly responsible corporation producing fine soft drinks that satisfy consumer tastes. Yet certain consumer and environmental groups have voiced concerns that Coke has little nutritional value, can harm people's teeth, contains caffeine, and adds to the litter problem with disposable bottles and cans.

Such concerns and conflicts led to the societal marketing concept. As Figure 1-4

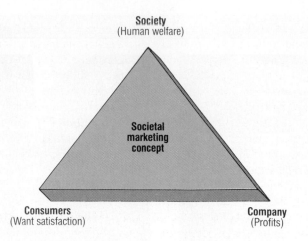

Society
(Human welfare)

Societal
marketing
concept

Consumers
(Want satisfaction)

Company
(Profits)

FIGURE 1-4
Three considerations
underlying the societal
marketing concept

shows, the societal marketing concept calls upon marketers to balance three considerations in setting their marketing policies: company profits, consumer wants, and society's interests. Originally, most companies based their marketing decisions largely on short-run company profit. Eventually, they began to recognize the long-run importance of satisfying consumer wants, and the marketing concept emerged. Now many companies are beginning to think of society's interests when making their marketing decisions.

One such company is Johnson & Johnson, rated recently in a *Fortune* magazine poll as America's most admired company for community and environmental responsibility.[13] J&J's concern for societal interests is summarized in a company document called "The Credo," which stresses honesty, integrity, and putting people before profits. Under this credo, Johnson & Johnson would rather take a big loss than ship a bad batch of one of its products. And the company supports many community and employee programs that benefit its consumers, workers, and the environment. J&J's chief executive puts it this way: "If we keep trying to do what's right, at the end of the day we believe the marketplace will reward us."

The company backs these words with actions. Consider the tragic tampering case in which eight people died from swallowing cyanide-laced capsules of Tylenol, a Johnson & Johnson brand. Although J&J believed that the pills had been altered in only a few stores, not in the factory, it quickly recalled all of its product. The recall cost the company $240 million in earnings. In the longer-run, however, the company's swift recall of Tylenol strengthened consumer confidence and loyalty, and Tylenol remains the nation's leading brand of pain reliever. In this and other cases, J&J management has found that doing what's right benefits both consumers and the company. Says the chief executive: "The Credo should not be viewed as some kind of social welfare program . . . it's just plain good business." Thus, over the years, Johnson & Johnson's dedication to consumers and community service has made it one of America's most admired companies, *and* one of the most profitable.

THE GOALS OF THE MARKETING SYSTEM

Our marketing system consists of the collective marketing activities of tens of thousands of profit and nonprofit organizations. This marketing system affects everyone—buyers, sellers, and many public groups with common characteristics. And the goals of these groups may conflict. *Buyers* want good-quality products at reasonable prices in convenient locations. They want wide brand and feature assortments; helpful, pleasant, and honest salespeople; and strong warranties backed by good follow-up service. The marketing system can greatly affect buyer satisfaction.

Sellers face many challenging decisions when preparing an offer for the market. What consumer groups should be targeted? What do target consumers need, and how should products be designed and priced to meet these needs? What wholesalers and retailers should be used? And what advertising, personal selling, and sales promotion would help sell the product? The market demands a lot. Sellers must apply modern marketing thinking to develop an offer that attracts and satisfies customers.

Legislators, public interest groups, and other *publics* have a strong interest in the marketing activities of business. Do manufacturers make safe and reliable products? Do they describe their products accurately in ads and packaging? Is competition working in the market to provide a reasonable range of quality and price choice? Are manufacturing and packaging activities hurting the environment? The marketing system has a major impact on the quality of life, and various groups of citizens want to make the system work as well as possible. They act as watchdogs of consumer interests and favor consumer education, information, and protection.

The marketing system affects so many people in so many ways that it inevitably stirs controversy. Some people intensely dislike modern marketing activity, charging it with ruining the environment, bombarding the public with senseless ads, creating unnecessary wants, teaching greed to youngsters, and committing several other sins. Consider the following:

> For the past 6,000 years the field of marketing has been thought of as made up of fast-buck artists, con-men, wheeler-dealers, and shoddy-goods distributors. Too many of us have been "taken" by the touts or con-men; and all of us at times have been prodded into buying all sorts of "things" we really did not need, and which we found later on we did not even want.[14]

Others vigorously defend marketing:

> Aggressive marketing policies and practices have been largely responsible for the high material standard of living in America. Today through mass, low-cost marketing we enjoy products which once were considered luxuries, and which still are so classified in many foreign countries.[15]

What should a society seek from its marketing system? Four alternative goals have been suggested: maximize *consumption*, maximize *consumer satisfaction*, maximize *choice*, and maximize *quality of life*.

Maximize Consumption

Many business executives believe that marketing's job should be to stimulate maximum consumption, which will in turn create maximum production, employment, and wealth. This view is promoted by such slogans as "Who says you can't have it all?" (Michelob), or "The costliest perfume in the world" (Joy), or "Greed is good" (from the movie "Wall Street"). The assumption is that the more people spend, buy, and consume, the happier they are. "More is better" is the war cry. Yet some people doubt that increased material goods mean more happiness. They see too many affluent people leading unhappy lives. Their philosophy is "less is more" and "small is beautiful."

Maximize Consumer Satisfaction

Another view holds that the goal of the marketing system is to maximize consumer satisfaction, not simply the quantity of consumption. Buying a new car or owning more clothes counts only if this adds to the buyer's satisfaction.

Unfortunately, consumer satisfaction is difficult to measure. First, nobody has discovered how to measure the total satisfaction created by a particular product or marketing activity. Second, the satisfaction that some individual consumers get from the "goods" of a product or service must be offset by the "bads," such as pollution and environmental damage. Third, the satisfaction that some people get from consuming certain goods, such as status goods, depends on the fact that few other people have these goods. Thus, evaluating the marketing system in terms of how much satisfaction it delivers is difficult.

Maximize Choice

Some marketers believe that the goal of a marketing system should be to maximize product variety and consumer choice. The system would enable consumers to find goods that exactly satisfy their tastes. Consumers would be able to fully realize their lifestyles and, therefore, maximize their overall satisfaction.

Unfortunatcly, maximizing consumer choice comes at a cost. First, the price of goods and services rises because producing great variety increases production and inventory costs. In turn, higher prices reduce consumers' real income and consumption. Second, the increase in product variety requires greater consumer search and effort. Consumers spend more time learning about and evaluating the different products. Third, more products do not necessarily increase the consumer's real choice; for example, hundreds of brands of beer are sold in the United States, but most taste the same. Thus, when a product category contains many brands with few differences, consumers face a choice that is really no choice at all. Finally, not all consumers welcome great product variety. For some consumers, too much choice leads to confusion and frustration.

Maximize Life Quality   Many people believe that the goal of a marketing system should be to improve the *quality of life*. This includes not only the quality, quantity, availability, and cost of goods, but the quality of the physical and cultural environments. Advocates of this view would judge marketing systems not just by the amount of direct consumer satisfaction but also by the impact of marketing on the quality of the environment. Most people would agree that quality of life is a worthwhile goal for the marketing system. But they would also agree that "quality" is hard to measure and that it means different things to different people.

THE RAPID ADOPTION OF MARKETING

Most people think that only large companies operating in capitalistic countries use marketing, but marketing actually occurs both inside and outside the business sector and in all kinds of countries.

In the Business Sector   In the business sector, different companies become interested in marketing at different times. General Electric, General Motors, Sears, Procter & Gamble, and Coca-Cola saw marketing's potential almost immediately. Marketing spread most rapidly in consumer packaged-goods companies, consumer durables companies, and industrial equipment companies—roughly in that order. Producers of such commodities as steel, chemicals, and paper adopted marketing later, and many still have a long way to go.

Within the past few decades, consumer service firms, especially airlines and banks, have adopted modern marketing practices. Marketing has also attracted the interest of insurance and financial services companies. The latest business groups to take an interest in marketing are professionals such as lawyers, accountants, physicians, and architects. Until recently, professional associations have not allowed their members to engage in price competition, client solicitation, and advertising. But the U.S. antitrust division has ruled that such restraints are illegal. Accountants, lawyers, and other professional people quickly moved to advertise and to price aggressively.

In the Nonprofit Sector   Marketing is also attracting the interest of *nonprofit* organizations such as colleges, hospitals, museums, symphonies, and even police departments. Consider the following developments:

Facing low enrollments and rising costs, many private colleges are using marketing to attract students and funds. St. Joseph's College in Renssalaer, Indiana, obtained a 40 percent increase in freshman enrollments by advertising in *Seventeen* and on several rock radio stations.

As hospital costs and room rates soar, many hospitals face underutilization, especially in their maternity and pediatrics sections. Many are taking steps toward marketing. A Philadelphia hospital, competing for maternity patients, offered a steak and champagne dinner with candlelight for new parents. St. Mary's Medical Center in Evanston, Indiana, uses innovative billboards to promote its emergency care service. Other hospitals, in an effort to attract physicians, have installed services such as saunas, chauffeurs, and private tennis courts.[16]

An example of innovative hospital advertising.

These organizations have marketing problems. Their administrators are struggling to keep them alive in the face of changing consumer attitudes and smaller financial resources. Many such institutions have turned to marketing as a possible answer to their problems.

In addition, U.S. government agencies are showing an increased interest in marketing. For example, the U.S. Postal Service and Amtrak have marketing plans for their operations. The U.S. Army has a marketing plan to attract recruits and is in fact one of the top advertising spenders in the country. Various government agencies and private nonprofit agencies are now designing *social marketing campaigns* to encourage energy conservation and concern for the environment, or to discourage smoking, excessive drinking, and hard drug use.[17]

In the International Sector

Marketing is practiced not only in the United States, but also in the rest of the world. In fact, several European and Japanese multinationals—companies such as Nestlé, Siemens, Toyota, and Sony—often outperform their U.S. competitors. Multinationals have spread modern marketing practices throughout the world. As a result, management in smaller countries is beginning to ask: Just what is marketing? How does it differ from plain selling? How can we introduce marketing into our firm? How will it make a difference and how much?

In socialist countries, marketing has traditionally had a bad name, even though limited marketing activities were employed in these countries. However, long-endured economic stagnation has caused many socialist countries to move toward more market-oriented economies. Such political and social changes have left business and government leaders in most socialist countries eager to learn everything they can about Western marketing practices. For example, in the USSR, two revolutionary policies—*peristroika* (economic restructuring) and *glastnost* (political democracy)— have opened new doors to the use of modern marketing. As one Russian leader states, the goal is to "create conditions under which enterprises will compete for better satisfaction of consumer needs and become more flexible to market developments."[18] However, changing from a centrally planned economy to a market-driven economy presents enormous problems, and the adoption of marketing and other Western business practices will take years if not decades to complete.

■ SUMMARY

Marketing touches everyone's life. It is the means by which a standard of living is developed and delivered to a people. Many people confuse marketing with *selling*, but in fact marketing occurs both before and after the selling event. Marketing actually combines many activities—marketing research, product development, distribution, pricing, advertising, personal selling, and others—designed to sense, serve, and satisfy consumer needs while meeting the organization's goals.

Marketing is human activity directed at satisfying needs and wants through *exchange processes*. The core concepts of marketing are *needs*, *wants*, *demands*, *products*, *exchange*, *transactions*, and *markets*.

Marketing management is the analysis, planning, implementation, and control of programs designed to create, build, and maintain beneficial exchanges with target markets in order to achieve organizational objectives. Marketers must be good at managing the level, timing, and composition of demand, because actual demand can be different from what the organization wants.

Marketing management can be guided by five different philosophies. The *production concept* holds that consumers favor products that are available at low cost and that management's task is to improve production efficiency and bring down prices. The *product concept* holds that consumers favor quality products, and that little promotional effort is thus required. The *selling concept* holds that consumers will not buy enough of the company's products unless they are stimulated through heavy selling and promotion. The *marketing concept* holds that a company should research the needs and wants of a well-defined target market and deliver the desired satisfactions. The *societal marketing concept* holds that the company should generate customer satisfaction and long-run societal well-being as the key to achieving both its goals and its responsibilities.

Marketing practices have a major impact on people in our society. Different goals have been proposed for a marketing system, such as maximizing *consumption*, *consumer satisfaction*, *consumer choice*, or *quality of life*. Interest in marketing is growing as more organizations in the business, nonprofit, and international sectors recognize the ways in which marketing can improve performance.

■ QUESTIONS FOR DISCUSSION

1. Why should *you* study marketing?

2. *In Search of Excellence* describes marketing principles practiced by many top companies. How can you apply these principles to market yourself and improve your chances of landing the job you want after graduation?

3. What is the greatest single difference between the marketing concept and, respectively, the production, product, and selling concepts? Which concepts are easiest to apply in the short run? Which concept offers the best long-term success?

4. Historian Arnold Toynbee and Economist John Kenneth Galbraith have argued that the desires stimulated by marketing efforts are not genuine: "A man who is hungry need never be told of his need for food." Is this a valid criticism of marketing? Why or why not?

5. Describe how the concepts of products, exchanges, and transactions apply when you buy a soft drink from a vending machine. Do they also apply when you vote for a political candidate?

6. Many people dislike or fear some products and would not "demand" them at any price. How might a health-care marketer manage the *negative* demand for such products as mammograms?

7. Identify organizations in your town that practice the production concept, the product concept, and the selling concept. How could these organizations become more marketing oriented? Give examples.

8. The headline for a Merrill Lynch ad says, "The reason we're a leader in so many areas isn't how much we talk but how attentively we listen." In what ways can companies "listen" to consumers? How does this help them practice the marketing concept?

9. According to economist Milton Friedman, "Few trends could so thoroughly undermine the very foundations of our free society as the acceptance by corporate officials of a social responsibility other than to make as much money for their stockholders as possible." Do you agree or disagree? What are some drawbacks of the societal marketing concept?

10. Florida and other states have attempted to tax advertising, many proposals have been made to end advertising for cigarettes, and the Supreme Court in 1986 upheld a ban on advertising for a legal service. Do these efforts conflict with the goals of our marketing system? Does your answer depend upon which goal you think is appropriate for our society?

11. Why have many nonprofit organizations adopted marketing techniques in recent years? How does your school market itself to attract new students?

12. Changes in the Soviet Union and Eastern Europe are leading to smaller U.S. military budgets. Before these changes, defense contractors followed the product concept and focused on high technology. Will military suppliers now need to change to the marketing concept? Who are their customers?

■ KEY TERMS

Barter transaction. A marketing transaction in which goods or services are traded for other goods or services.

Demands. Human wants that are backed by buying power.

Demarketing. Marketing in which the task is to temporarily or permanently reduce demand.

Exchange. The act of obtaining a desired object from someone by offering something in return.

Human need. A state of felt deprivation.

Human want. The form that a human need takes as shaped by culture and individual personality.

Market. The set of actual and potential buyers of a product.

Marketing. A social and managerial process by which individuals and groups obtain what they need and want through creating and exchanging products and value with others.

Marketing concept. The marketing management philosophy which holds that achieving organizational goals depends on determining the needs and wants of target markets and delivering the desired satisfactions more effectively and efficiently than competitors.

Marketing management. The analysis, planning, implementation, and control of programs designed to create, build, and maintain beneficial exchanges with target buyers for the purpose of achieving organizational objectives.

Monetary transaction. A marketing transaction in which goods or services are exchanged for money.

Product. Anything that can be offered to a market for attention, acquisition, use, or consumption and that may satisfy a need or want.

Product concept. The idea that consumers favor products that offer the most quality, performance, and features and that the organization should therefore devote its energy to making continuous product improvements.

Production concept. The philosophy that consumers favor products that are available and highly affordable and that management should therefore focus on improving production and distribution efficiency.

Selling concept. The idea that consumers will not buy enough of the organization's products unless the organization undertakes a large-scale selling and promotion effort.

Societal marketing concept. The idea that the organization should determine the needs, wants, and interests of target markets and deliver the desired satisfactions more effectively and efficiently than competitors in a way that maintains or improves the consumer's and society's well-being.

Transaction. A trade between two parties that involves at least two things of value, agreed-upon conditions, a time of agreement, and a place of agreement.

■ REFERENCES

1. Thomas J. Peters and Robert H. Waterman, Jr., *In Search of Excellence*: *Lessons from America's Best-Run Companies* (New York: Harper & Row, 1982).

2. See Thomas J. Peters and Nancy Austin, *A Passion for Excellence*: *The Leadership Difference* (New York: Random House, 1985); and Thomas J. Peters, *Thriving on Chaos* (New York: Alfred A. Knopf, 1987).

3. See Milind M. Lele with Jagdish Sheth, *The Customer is Key*: *Gaining an Unbeatable Advantage Through Customer Satisfaction* (New York: John Wiley & Sons, 1987); Karl Albrecht and Ron Zemke, *Service America!* (Homewood, Il.: Dow-Jones Irwin, 1985); and Donald K. Clifford, Jr. and Richard E. Cavanaugh, *The Winning Performance*: *How America's High-Growth Midsize Companies Succeed* (New York: Bantam Books, 1985).

4. "Business Planning in the Eighties: The New Competitiveness of American Corporations," a study conducted by Yankelovich, Skelly, & White for Coopers and Lybrand, 1984.

5. See E. S. Ely, "Room at the Top: American Companies Turn to Marketers to Lead Them Through the '80s," *Madison Avenue*, September 1984, p. 57.

6. Peter F. Drucker, *Management*: *Tasks, Responsibilities, Practices* (New York: Harper & Row, 1973), pp. 64–65.

7. Here are some other definitions: "Marketing is the performance of business activities that direct the flow of goods and services from producer to consumer or user." "Marketing is getting the right goods and services to the right people at the right place at the right time at the right price with the right communication and promotion." "Marketing is the creation and delivery of a standard of living." In 1985, the American Marketing Association approved this definition: "Marketing is the process of planning and executing the conception, pricing, promotion, and distribution of ideas, goods, and services to create exchanges that satisfy individual and organizational objectives."

8. See Theodore Levitt's classic article, "Marketing Myopia," *Harvard Business Review*, July–August 1960, pp. 45–56.

9. For more discussion on marketing as an exchange process, see Franklin S. Houston and Jule B. Gassenheimer, "Marketing and Exchange," *Journal of Marketing*, October 1987, pp. 3–18.

10. The number of transactions in a decentralized exchange system is given by $N(N-1)/2$. With four persons, this means $4(4-1)/2 = 6$ transactions. In a centralized exchange system, the number of transactions is given by N, here 4. Thus a centralized exchange system reduces the number of transactions needed for exchange.

11. Ralph Waldo Emerson offered this advice: "If a man . . . makes a better mousetrap . . . the world will beat a path to his door." Several companies, however, have built better mousetraps yet failed. One was a laser mousetrap costing $1,500. Contrary to popular assumptions, people do not automatically learn about new products, believe product claims, or willingly pay higher prices.

12. For more on the marketing concept, see Theodore Levitt, "Marketing and Its Discontents," *Across the Board*, February 1984, pp. 42–48; and Franklin S. Houston, "The Marketing Concept: What It Is and What It Is Not," *Journal of Marketing*, April 1986, pp. 81–87.

13. See "Leaders of the Most Admired," *Fortune*, January 29, 1990, pp. 40–54.

14. Richard N. Farmer, "Would You Want Your Daughter to Marry a Marketing Man?" *Journal of Marketing*, January 1967, p. 1.

15. William J. Stanton and Charles Futrell, *Fundamentals of Marketing*, 8th ed. (New York: McGraw-Hill, 1987), p. 7.

16. For other examples, and for a good review of nonprofit marketing, see Philip Kotler and Alan R. Andreasen, *Strategic Marketing for Nonprofit Organizations* (Englewood Cliffs, NJ: Prentice Hall, 1987).

17. See Philip Kotler and Eduardo Roberto, *Social Marketing*: *Strategies for Changing Public Behavior* (New York: The Free Press, 1990).

18. Wolfgang J. Koschnick, "Russian Bear Bullish on Marketing," *Marketing News*. November 21, 1988, p. 1.

THE ELECTRIC FEATHER PIROGUE: GOING WITH THE MARKETING FLOW

The Fin and Feather Products Company of Marshall, Texas, produces a line of small, versatile, lightweight boats called the Electric Feather Pirogue (pronounced pē rō). The term "feather" was chosen to emphasize the light weight of the boat and "electric" because it is propelled by an electric trolling motor. The name *Pirogue* refers to the historic small riverboats used on the Louisiana bayous. The kayak-shaped boat is 12 feet long, 38 inches wide, and 12 inches deep. It comes complete with motor and has a load capacity of about 540 pounds. Power is provided by a standard 12-volt automotive-type storage battery. The built-in Shakespeare motor is available with 18-pound or 24-pound thrust. The hull is handcrafted fiberglass, sturdily constructed by a hand-layup process.

The stable, flat-bottomed Pirogue can operate in very shallow water, so it is ideally suited for fishing, duck hunting, bird watching, or just leisure stream cruising. The propeller is protected from submerged objects by specially engineered motor guards on each side of the exposed drive unit. A 1½-inch sheet of polyurethane foam is built into the bottom to provide flotation. The boat is extremely simple to operate. A panel just below the wraparound gunwale contains two control switches—a forward-off-reverse switch and a low-medium-high speed switch. A horizontal lever just above the panel provides steering control. There is only one moving part in the entire control system. The 3-speed, 18-pound thrust motor has a maximum speed of 10 miles an hour, and the 4-speed, 24-pound thrust motor can attain a speed of 14 miles an hour. The company furnishes a one-year unlimited warranty on the boat, and the Shakespeare Company provides a similar warranty on the motor.

The company produced only one basic model of the boat but offered optional equipment that provided some variation within the product line. Retail prices ranged from approximately $490 to $650, depending on motor size and optional equipment. Although designed to accommodate two people, the standard model has only one molded plastic seat. The second seat, deluxe swivel seats, marine carpeting, and tonneau cover are the major optional items. No trailer is required because the boat fits nicely on the roof of even the smallest car or in the back of a station wagon or pickup truck. Without battery, the Pirogue weighs only about 80 pounds and can easily be handled by one person.

In Year 1 (the base year), Bill Wadlington purchased controlling interest in, and assumed managerial control of, the seven-year-old Fin and Feather Products Company. One of Mr. Wadlington's first moves was to adopt strict pay-as-you-go and cash-and-carry policies. Supplies and equipment were paid for at the time of purchase, and all sales were for cash prior to shipment whether shipment was to a dealer or directly to a customer. All shipments were F.O.B. the factory in Marshall, Texas. As a result of this policy, the firm has no accounts receivable and virtually no accounts payable. Mr. Wadlington anticipated sales of between 800 and 1000 units in Year 1. This volume approaches plant capacity and produce a wholesale dollar volume of approximately $350,000 to $400,000. After only six months of operation, Mr. Wadlington would not predict an exact annual net-profit figure, but he was very optimistic about the first year's profit. It was also difficult to predict future volume, but sales had shown a steady increase throughout the first half of the year. Inquiries from around the United States and from several foreign countries made the future look bright.

The company used a variety of methods to sell the Piroque. There were 15 independent dealers around the country who bought at wholesale and assumed a standard markup. There was no formal agreement or contract between the company and the dealers, but to qualify as a dealer, an individual or firm's initial order had to be for at least five boats. Subsequent orders could be for any quantity desired. Dealers' orders had to be accompanied by a check for the entire amount of the purchase. The dealers were assigned a specific territory in which they could sell the boats.

In addition to the dealers, the company had 20 agents who were authorized to take orders in areas outside dealer territories. These agents accepted orders for direct shipment to customers and were paid a commission for the boats they sold. As with all sales, agent orders had to be prepaid.

The company hired no outside salespeople, and Mr. Wadlington was the only in-house salesman. Direct orders from individuals were accepted at the factory when the customer lived outside a dealer territory. Most direct sales were the result of the company's advertisements in such magazines as *Ducks Unlimited*, *Outdoor Life*, *Argosy*, *Field and Stream*, and *Better Homes and Gardens*.

Mr. Wadlington had not established a systematic promotional program. The services of an out-of-state advertising agency were used to develop and place ads and to help with brochures and other promotional materials. The amount of advertising done at any time depended on existing sales volume. As sales declined, advertising was increased; when orders approached plant capacity, advertising was curtailed. Magazines were the primary advertising medium. The dealers and agents were provided with attractive, professionally prepared brochures. The company had exhibited, or had plans to exhibit, at boat shows in Texas, Ohio, and Illinois. Arrangements had been completed for Pirogues to be used as prizes on one of the more popular network game shows.

A detailed analysis of sales, in terms of who was buying the boats and for what purpose, had not been made. However, Mr. Wadlington did not know that one of the most successful ads was in *Better Homes and Gardens*. An examination of orders produced by the ad indicated that they were primarily from women who were buying the boat for family use. There had been reports of the boats being used as utility boats for large houseboats and yachts, but the extent of such use was unknown. Although orders had been coming in from all parts of the country, the best sales areas had been in the eastern and southeastern parts of the United States. Mr. Wadlington attributed this, at least in part, to the fact that the company's past sales efforts had been concentrated almost exclusively in the southern and southwestern areas of the country. After the company began using national media, totally new markets were tapped. The Pirogue had virtually no direct competition, particularly outside the Texas-Louisiana area.

QUESTIONS

1. Is Mr. Wadlington practicing the marketing concept? If not, which of the marketing philosophies does he follow?
2. What are the characteristics of the people who make up the market for the Electric Feather Pirogue? Describe the needs and wants that are satisfied by the product.
3. Mr. Wadlington seems to be opposed to changing his present marketing system. Apparently, he believes that his plan is working because sales are strong and profits are satisfactory. He would ask, "Why not stick with a winner?" How would you respond to Mr. Wadlington's assumptions?
4. What recommendations would you make to Mr. Wadlington if he wanted to adopt the marketing concept?

Source: This case was prepared by Robert H. Solomon and Janelle C. Ashley of Stephen F. Austin State University as a basis for class discussion. Used with permission.

SHOPPING IN THE USSR

The shortages of consumer goods in the Soviet Union are legendary. Meat, poultry, detergents, toilet paper, razor blades, gasoline, automobiles, fashionable clothing, and decent housing are in chronic short supply. An ordinary Soviet citizen waits in line an average of two hours each day to buy what is available. Over a lifetime, that amounts to five years wasted standing in lines. The Soviet currency (the ruble), is suspect at home and virtually worthless in international trade because it is not freely exchangeable with world currencies. This, along with restrictive trade policies, has severely limited the average Soviet citizen's access to foreign goods.

It is easy to assume that the reason for the paucity of consumer goods is that Soviet leaders simply decided to devote more of the nation's resources to military production and less to the production of consumer goods. But the problem is more complex than that and is partly based on the way decisions are made in the USSR.

In our capitalistic society with its market-directed economy, the public has the major say about what gets produced because they "vote" with their dollars. If people like a product, they will buy more of it. The manufacturers will quickly make more of it because they want to make money, and the only way to make money is to give the public what it wants.

Things haven't worked that way in the Soviet Union. The Soviets have a planned economy, which means that central planners in Moscow decide what it is that the people want—or should want—and order it produced. Decisions that are made in the marketplace in the United States are made by central planners in the Soviet Union. Sometimes the central planners are right; more often they are wrong. When they are wrong, shortages occur and a black market often arises to allocate the scarce goods and services.

Mikhail Gorbachev has instituted two revolutionary policies, *perestroika* (economic restructuring) and *glasnost* (openness or political democracy), in an effort to address certain problems in the Soviet Union. Glasnost has allowed Soviet citizens the opportunity to say what is on their minds, while perestroika has allowed (some) economic reform.

Government officials now realize that the satisfaction of consumer needs, wants, and desires and the flexibility to accommodate changing market conditions are critical to raising the standard of living of the Soviet people. One bold new proposal calls for a selloff of state-owned property and the means of production, as well as a decentralization of economic power from Moscow to the Soviet republics and the creation of a stock market. The doors have been opened to the use of modern marketing techniques, including branding, advertising, and demand-oriented pricing.

Gorbachev's proposals have been less thoroughgoing than some reformers would like. He wants to adopt some market devices in an economy that remains communistic. He also wants a multiparty political system—albeit one dominated by the Communist Party. But even this much change will not come easy. The average Soviet citizen has long had considerable security: guaranteed employment, health care, schooling, and housing. Sweeping change will exact a considerable price in the form of lower security, higher inflation, unemployment, and crime, and the need to institute unemployment and welfare programs.

QUESTIONS

1. What are the main characteristics of a market-directed economy? What role does marketing play in providing customer satisfaction in a market-directed economy?

2. How does a market-directed economy differ from a planned economy?

3. Not all decisions in a market-directed economy are made in the marketplace. Some critical decisions are made by government officials elected by the people. Identify the types of goods and services resulting from these decisions and explain why they cannot easily be made in the marketplace.

Source: "Holding a Bad Hand," *Newsweek* June 4, 1990, pp. 16–17; "Why He's Failing," *Newsweek* June 4, 1990, pp. 18–21; "Too Little and Too Late?" *Newsweek* June 4, 1990, pp. 22–23; and "Gorbachev Turns Radical, Endorses Capitalistic Reforms, *The Post Standard* September 12, 1990, p. A5.

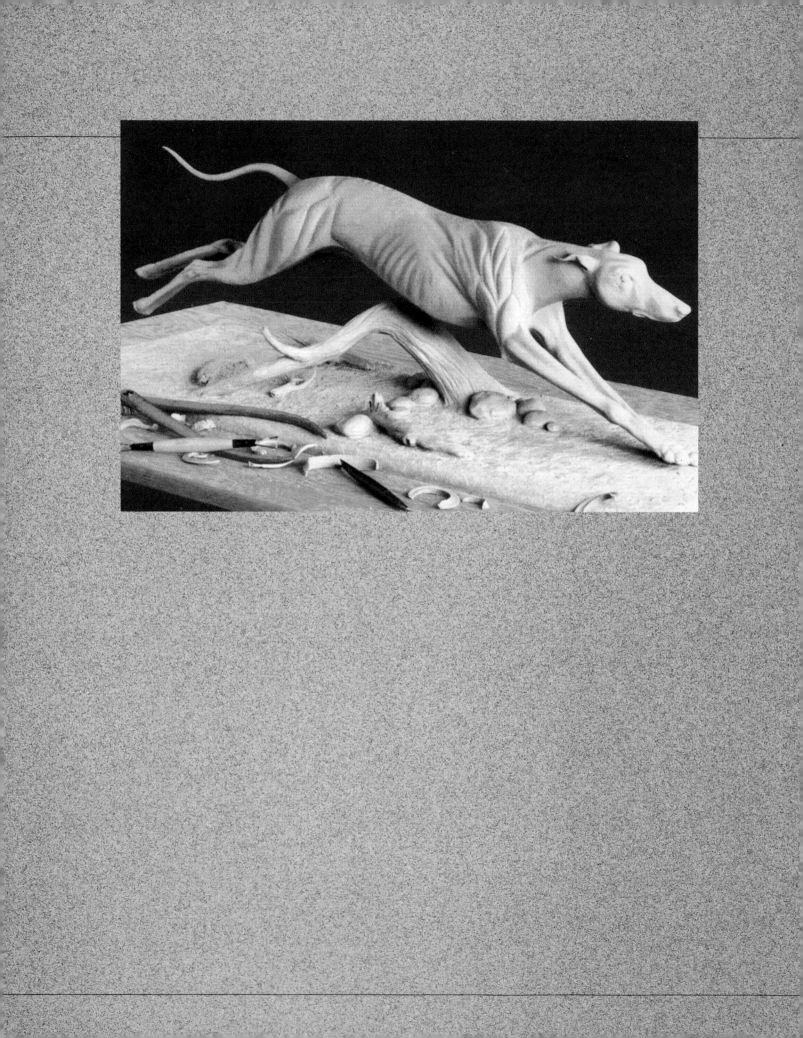

2

Strategic Planning and Marketing's Role in the Organization

Most people think they know a lot about Greyhound Corporation. Over the decades, Greyhound has become an American institution, with its buses cruising the nation's highways and connecting our cities and towns with convenient, inexpensive transportation. Surveys show that the venerable Greyhound name finishes second only to Coca-Cola in consumer recognition tests. In fact, however, consumers know very little about Greyhound Corporation. For example, most people would be startled to learn that this company no longer operates buses in the U.S. In 1987, facing industry deregulation, a deteriorating market, rising costs, stiff airline competition, and severe labor problems, the company made a profound and wrenching decision: It sold Greyhound Lines, the business upon which its history and culture had been built. The buses still carry the "Greyhound" name, but the Greyhound Corporation no longer owns the line.

What then, you may ask, *does* Greyhound Corporation do? The answer—lots of things, some familiar, some not. The sale of the bus line was just part of a sweeping program to restructure a struggling Greyhound Corporation. In the early 1980s, following 20 years of poorly planned diversification, Greyhound management set out to turn its hodgepodge of businesses into a leaner, more sharply focused, more profitable company. It sold off dozens of businesses which had poor growth potential or which no longer fit its growth strategy, ultimately shedding companies totaling $3 billion dollars in annual sales. Gone,

among others, are its meatpacking operation, mortgage insurance unit, computer leasing company, knitting supplies business, and, of course, the bus line. At the same time, Greyhound adopted a strategy of "growth by design." Building on its trimmer, more clearly focused base, it expanded its remaining businesses through internal growth and careful acquisition.

Today, the Greyhound Corporation operates four major business groups—consumer products, services, transportation manufacturing, and financial services. Its *consumer products* group (contributing about 29 percent of total company revenues) markets many familiar brands, but few consumers would connect them with Greyhound. The best known include Dial, Tone, and Pure&Natural hand soaps, Armour Star canned meats, Lunch Bucket microwave meals, Purex laundry products, StaPuf fabric softener, Sno Bol toilet bowl cleaner, and Brillo scouring pads.

Greyhound's greatest recent growth has been in its *services* group, which now contributes about 50 percent of company revenues. It consists of such diverse businesses as Traveler's Express, the nation's largest issuer of money orders, Premier Cruise Lines, the "official cruise line of Walt Disney World," and Greyhound Food Management, which operates restaurants (including 38 Burger King franchises) and factory cafeterias. However, almost half of Greyhound's services revenue derives from businesses that serve airlines and air travelers. Greyhound Airport Services provides baggage handling, fueling, and other ground services to airlines; the recently acquired Dobbs food services prepares some 200,000 in-flight meals daily for more than 60 airlines and also operates restaurants, lounges, gift shops, newstands, and duty-free shops at major airports and hotels.

Two other business groups provide Greyhound with smaller but still substantial revenues. Its *transportation manufacturing* groups (about 13 percent of sales) is the nation's largest bus producer and bus parts supplier. Greyhound recently expanded this group by purchasing General Motors' bus building and parts business. By contrast, Greyhound has recently scaled down and redirected its *financial services* business (about 8 percent of company revenues), selling off its computer leasing and mortgage insurance units and focusing on special market niches, mostly providing commercial and real estate financing for mid-size companies.

Thus, Greyhound isn't Greyhound buses anymore. Instead, it has been transformed into a modern, vigorous consumer products and services company. During the past several years, through a series of dramatic strategic planning actions, management has forced a new, streamlined Greyhound Corporation—one better matched to its changing market opportunities. In fact, the company has even changed its name—to Greyhound Dial—to better reflect its new direction and focus.

Although it still has a ways to go in making sense out of its portfolio and fully meeting its financial goals, most analysts believe that Greyhound is on the right track. But continuing to keep this large and diversified collection of businesses on track will be no easy task. Strategic planning is a never-ending process. and Greyhound management will continue to face many difficult questions. What new businesses should be added to the company and which old ones should be dropped? Which current businesses should receive more emphasis and which should be scaled back? How can management best position the company for success in its fact-changing environment? According to Greyhound Chairman John Teets, "No company can wholly [shape] the environment in which it will operate, but it *can* exploit circumstances, wringing from them the best alternatives and opportunities. . . . The job of management always has been to see the company not as it is, but as it can grow to be. Change is inevitable, and management must guide the forces of change to create value for shareholders. At Greyhound, we believe in renewing the company day-by-day."[1]

CHAPTER OBJECTIVES

After reading this chapter, you should be able to:

1. Explain company-wide strategic planning and its four steps.
2. Describe how companies develop mission statements and objectives.
3. Explain how companies evaluate and develop their "business portfolios."
4. Explain marketing's role in strategic planning.
5. Describe the marketing management process and the forces that influence it.

All companies must look ahead and develop long-term strategies to meet the changing conditions in their industries. No one strategy is best for all companies. Each company must find the game plan that makes the most sense given its situation, opportunities, objectives, and resources. The hard task of selecting an overall company strategy for long-run survival and growth is called *strategic planning*.

Marketing plays an important role in strategic planning. It provides information and other inputs to help prepare the strategic plan. In turn, strategic planning defines marketing's role in the organization. Guided by the strategic plan, marketing works with other departments in the organization to achieve overall strategic objectives.

In this chapter, we look first at the organization's overall strategic planning. Next, we discuss marketing's role in the organization as it is defined by the overall strategic plan. Finally we explain the marketing management process—the process that marketers undertake to carry out their role in the organization.

OVERVIEW OF PLANNING

Benefits of Planning Many companies operate without formal plans. In new companies, managers are so busy they often have no time for planning. In mature companies, many managers argue that they have done well without it and, therefore, formal planning cannot be too important. They may resist taking the time to prepare a written plan. They may argue that the marketplace changes too fast for a plan to be useful—that it would end up collecting dust.

Yet formal planning can yield many benefits. It encourages management to systematically think ahead and improves interactions between company executives. It forces the company to sharpen its objectives and policies, leads to better coordination of company efforts, and provides clearer performance standards for control. And the argument that planning is less useful in a fast-changing environment makes little sense. In fact, the opposite is true: Sound planning helps the company to anticipate and respond quickly to environmental changes and to better prepare for sudden developments.

Approaches to Planning Management can adopt one of three possible approaches to planning. In the first approach, *top-down planning,* top management sets goals and plans for all the lower levels of management. It assumes that employees cannot or will not take responsibility and prefer to be directed. In the opposite approach, *bottom-up planning,* the various organizational units prepare their own goals and plans and send them on to higher management levels for approval. This approach assumes that employees like responsibility, and that they will be more creative and committed if they participate in the planning. Most companies use a third approach known as *goals down-plans up planning.* In this approach, top management looks at the company's opportunities and requirements and sets corporate goals for the year. The various company units then develop plans to help the company reach the corporate goals. These plans, when approved by top management, become the final plan.

Kinds of Plans Companies usually prepare annual plans, long-range plans, and strategic plans. The **annual plan** describes the current marketing situation, company objectives, the marketing strategy for the year, the action program, budgets, and controls. Top management approves this plan and uses it to coordinate marketing activities with production, finance, and other areas of the company.

The **long-range plan** describes the major factors and forces expected to affect the organization during the next several years. It includes long-term objectives, the major marketing strategies that will be used to attain them, and the resources required. This long-range plan is reviewed and updated each year so that the company always has a current long-range plan. For example, American Hospital Supply has a "rolling" five-year plan. Its annual plan is a detailed version of the first year of the long-range plan. Managers prepare a five-year plan for each product early in the year and an annual plan later in the year. The five-year plan is revised each year because the environment changes and planning assumptions need to be reviewed.

The company's annual and long-range plans deal with current businesses and how to keep them going. Management must also plan which businesses the company should stay in or drop and which new ones it should pursue. The environment is full of surprises, and management must design the company to withstand shocks. *Strategic planning* involves adapting the firm to take advantage of opportunities in its constantly changing environment.

STRATEGIC PLANNING

Strategic planning sets the stage for the rest of the planning in the firm. We define **strategic planning** as the process of developing and maintaining a strategic fit between the organizations' goals and capabilities and its changing marketing opportunities. It

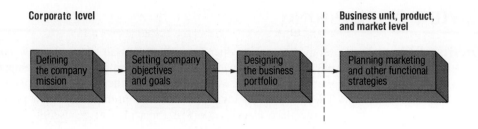

FIGURE 2-1
Steps in strategic planning

relies on developing a clear company mission, supporting objectives, a sound business portfolio, and coordinated functional strategies.

The steps in the strategic planning process are shown in Figure 2-1. At the corporate level, the company first defines its overall purpose and mission. This mission is then turned into detailed supporting objectives that guide the whole company. Next, headquarters decides what portfolio of businesses and products is best for the company and how much support to give each one. Each business and product unit must in turn develop detailed marketing and other departmental plans that support the company-wide plan. Thus marketing planning occurs at the business-unit, product, and market levels. It supports company strategic planning with more detailed planning for specific marketing opportunities.

Defining the Company Mission

An organization exists to accomplish something. At first, it has a clear purpose or mission, but over time its mission may become unclear as the organization grows and adds new products and markets. Or the mission may remain clear, but some managers may no longer be committed to it. Or the mission may remain clear but may no longer be the best choice given new conditions in the environment.

When management senses that the organization is drifting, it must renew its search for purpose. It is time to ask: What is our business? Who is the customer? What do consumers value? What will our business be? What should our business be? These simple-sounding questions are among the most difficult the company will ever have to answer. Successful companies continuously raise these questions and answer them carefully and completely.

Many organizations develop formal mission statements that answer these questions. A **mission statement** is a statement of the organization's purpose—what it wants to accomplish in the larger environment. Writing a formal company mission statement is not easy. Some organizations will spend a year or more trying to prepare a good statement of their firm's purpose. In the process they will discover a lot about themselves and their potential opportunities. A clear mission statement acts as an "invisible hand" that guides people in the organization so that they can work independently and yet collectively toward overall organizational goals.

Companies traditionally defined their business in product terms, such as "We manufacture furniture," or in technological terms, such as "We are a chemical-processing firm." But market definitions of a business are better than product or technological definitions. Products and technologies eventually become out-of-date, but basic market needs may last forever. A market-oriented mission statement defines the business in terms of satisfying basic customer needs. Thus AT&T is in the communications business, not the telephone business. Visa defines its business not as credit cards, but as allowing customers to exchange value—to exchange such assets as cash on deposit or equity in a home for virtually anything, anywhere in the world. And Sears' mission is not to run department stores but to provide a wide range of products and services that deliver value to middle-class home-owning American families.

Management should avoid making its mission too narrow or too broad. A lead pencil manufacturer that says it is in the communication equipment business is stating its mission too broadly. Mission statements should be specific and realistic. Many mission statements are written for public relations purposes and lack specific, workable guidelines.

Company mission: Visa defines its mission not as credit cards, but as allowing customers to exchange their assets for virtually anything, anywhere in the world.

The statement "We want to become the leading company in this industry by producing the highest-quality products with the best service at the lowest prices" sounds good but is full of generalities and contradictions. It will not help the company make tough decisions.

Many companies draft very detailed mission statements that define the company's goals and values in relation to its markets and consumers, employees, stockholders, and other publics. In addition, these mission statements often outline the company's standards of societal responsibility and ethical conduct in the broader marketing environment. To be meaningful, such statements must be backed by specific objectives and strategies.[2]

Setting Company Objectives and Goals

The company's mission needs to be turned into detailed supporting objectives for each level of management. Each manager should have objectives and be responsible for reaching them.

As an illustration, the International Minerals and Chemical Corporation is in many businesses, including the fertilizer business. The fertilizer division does not say that its mission is to produce fertilizer. Instead, it says that its mission is to "increase agricultural productivity." This mission leads to a hierarchy of objectives: business objectives, marketing objectives, and, finally, a marketing strategy (see Figure 2-2). The mission of increasing agricultural productivity leads to the company's business objective of researching new fertilizers that promise higher yields. But research is expensive and requires improved profits to plow back into research programs. So another major objective becomes "to

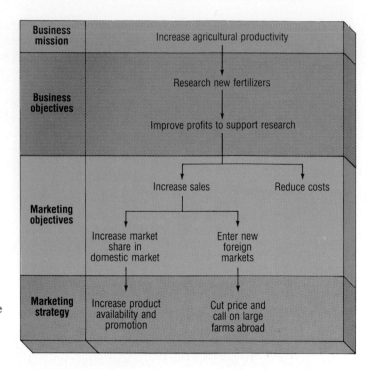

FIGURE 2-2
Hierarchy of objectives for the International Minerals and Chemical Corporation, Fertilizer Division

improve profits.'' Profits can be improved by increasing sales or reducing costs. Sales can be increased by increasing the company's share of the U.S. market, by entering new foreign markets, or both. These goals become the company's current marketing objectives.

Marketing strategies must be developed to support these marketing objectives. To increase its U.S. market share, the company may increase its product's availability and promotion. To enter new foreign markets, the company may cut prices and target large farms abroad. These are the broad marketing strategies.

Each marketing strategy must then be spelled out in greater detail. For example, increasing the product's promotion may require more salespeople and more advertising; if so, both requirements will have to be spelled out. In this way, the firm's mission is translated into a set of objectives for the current period. The objectives should be as specific as possible. The objective to ''increase our market share'' is not as useful as the objective to ''increase our market share to 15 percent by the end of the second year.''

Designing the Business Portfolio

Guided by the company's mission statement and objectives, management must now plan its business portfolio. A company's **business portfolio** is the collection of businesses and products that make up the company. The best business portfolio is the one which best fits the company's strengths and weaknesses to opportunities in the environment. The company must (1) analyze its *current* business portfolio and decide which businesses should receive more, less, or no investment, and (2) develop growth strategies for adding *new* products or businesses to the portfolio.

Analyzing the Current Business Portfolio

The major tool in strategic planning is business **portfolio analysis,** whereby management evaluates the businesses making up the company. The company will want to put strong resources into its more profitable businesses and phase down or drop its weaker businesses. For example, in recent years, Kraft has strengthened its portfolio by selling off many less attractive nonfood businesses while adding such promising ones as Lender's Bagel Bakery, Frusen Gladje and Charl's ice creams, Tombstone frozen pizza, and All-American Gourmet frozen foods.

Management's first step is to identify the key businesses making up the company. These can be called the strategic business units. A **strategic business unit (SBU)** is a unit of the company that has a separate mission and separate objective and that can be planned independently from other company businesses. An SBU can be a company division, a product line within a division, or sometimes a single product or brand.

Identifying SBUs can be difficult. In a large corporation, should SBUs be defined at the level of companies, divisions, product lines, or brands? At Greyhound, is the Consumer Products Division an SBU or is the Dial brand an SBU? Defining basic business units for portfolio analysis is often a complex task.

The next step in business portfolio analysis calls for management to assess the attractiveness of its various SBUs and decide how much support each deserves. In some companies, this is done informally. Management looks at the company's collection of businesses or products and uses judgment to decide how much each SBU should contribute and receive. Other companies use formal portfolio-planning methods.

The purpose of strategic planning is to find ways in which the company can best use its strengths to take advantage of attractive opportunities in the environment. So most standard portfolio-analysis methods evaluate SBUs on two important dimensions—the attractiveness of the SBU's market or industry and the strength of the SBU's position in that market or industry. The two best-known of these portfolio planning methods are those developed by the Boston Consulting Group, a leading management consulting firm, and by General Electric.[3]

THE BOSTON CONSULTING GROUP APPROACH. Using the Boston Consulting Group (BCG) approach, a company classifies all its SBUs according to the **growth-share matrix** shown in Figure 2-3. On the vertical axis, *market growth rate* provides a measure of market attractiveness. On the horizontal axis, *relative market share* serves as a measure of company strength in the market. By dividing the growth-share matrix as indicated, four types of SBUs can be distinguished.

- **Stars.** Stars are high-growth, high-share businesses or products. They often need heavy investment to finance their rapid growth. Eventually their growth will slow down, and they will turn into cash cows.
- **Cash cows.** Cash cows are low-growth, high-share businesses or products. These established and successful SBUs need less investment to hold their market share. Thus, they produce a lot of cash that the company uses to pay its bills and to support other SBUs that need investment.
- **Question marks.** Question marks are low-share business units in high-growth markets. They require a lot of cash to hold their share, let alone increase it. Management has to

FIGURE 2-3
The BCG growth-share matrix

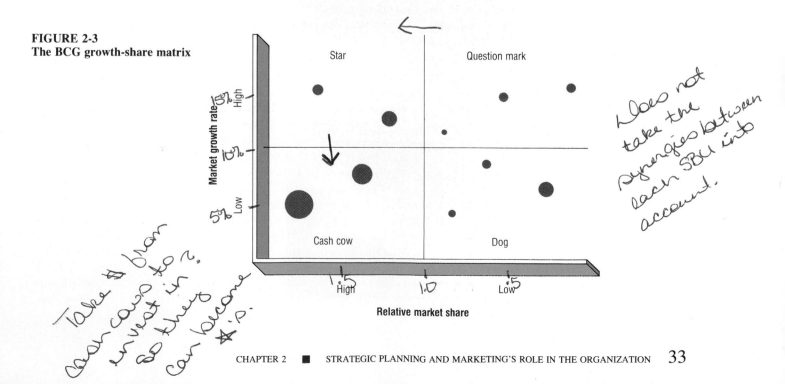

think hard about which question marks it should try to build into stars and which should be phased out.

- **Dogs.** Dogs are low-growth, low-share businesses and products. They may generate enough cash to maintain themselves, but do not promise to be large sources of cash.

The ten circles in the growth-share matrix represent a company's ten current SBUs. The company has two stars, two cash cows, three question marks, and three dogs. The areas of the circles are proportional to the SBU's dollar sales. This company is in fair shape, although not in good shape. Fortunately it has two good-sized cash cows, whose income helps finance the company's question marks, stars, and dogs. The company should take some decisive action concerning its dogs and its question marks. The picture would be worse if the company had no stars, or had too many dogs, or had only one weak cash cow.

Once it has classified its SBUs, the company must determine what role each will play in the future. One of four strategies can be pursued for each SBU. The company can invest more in the business unit in order to *build* its share. Or it can invest just enough to *hold* the SBU's share at the current level. It can *harvest* the SBU, milking its short-term cash flow regardless of the long-term effect. Finally, the company can *divest* the SBU by selling it or phasing it out and using the resources elsewhere.

As time passes, SBUs change their positions in the growth-share matrix. Each SBU has a lifecycle. Many SBUs start out as question marks, and move into the star category if they succeed. They later become cash cows as market growth falls, then finally die off or turn into dogs toward the end of their life cycle. The company needs to add new products and units continuously so that some of them will become stars and, eventually, cash cows to help finance other SBUs.

THE GENERAL ELECTRIC APPROACH. General Electric introduced a comprehensive portfolio planning tool called a **strategic business-planning grid** (see Figure 2-4). Like the BCG approach, it uses a matrix with two dimensions—one represents industry attractiveness (the vertical axis) and one represents company strength in the industry (the horizontal axis). The best businesses are those located in highly attractive industries where the company has high business strength.

The GE approach considers many factors besides market growth rate as part of industry attractiveness. It uses an industry attractiveness index made up of market size, market growth, industry profit margin, amount of competition, seasonality and cyclicality of demand, and industry cost structure. Each of these factors is rated and combined in an index of industry attractiveness. For our purposes, an industry's attractiveness is described as high, medium, or low. As an example, Kraft has identified numerous highly attractive industries—natural foods, specialty frozen foods, physical fitness products, and others. It has withdrawn from less attractive industries such as bulk oils and cardboard packaging.

FIGURE 2-4
General Electric's strategic business-planning grid

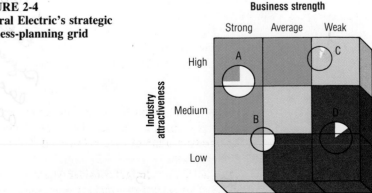

For *business strength,* the GE approach again uses an index rather than simply a measure of relative market share. The business strength index includes such factors as the company's relative market share, price competitiveness, product quality, customer and market knowledge, sales effectiveness, and geographic advantages. These factors are rated and combined in an index of business strength. Business strength can be described as strong, average, or weak. Thus Kraft has substantial business strength in food and related industries but is relatively weak in the home appliances industry.

The grid is divided into three zones. The green cells at the upper left show strong SBUs in which the company should invest and grow. The yellow diagonal cells contain SBUs that are medium in overall attractiveness. The company should maintain its level of investment in these SBUs. The three red cells at the lower right indicate SBUs that are low in overall attractiveness. The company should give serious thought to harvesting or divesting them.

The circles represent four company SBUs; the areas of the circles are proportional to the sizes of the industries in which these SBUs compete. The pie slices within the circles represent each SBU's market share. Thus, circle A represents a company SBU with a 75-percent market share in a good-sized, highly attractive industry in which the company has strong business strength. Circle B represents an SBU that has a 50-percent market share, but the industry is not very attractive. Circles C and D represent two other company SBUs in industries where the company has small market shares and not much business strength. Altogether, the company should build A, maintain B, and make some hard decisions about C and D.

Management would also plot the projected positions of the SBUs with and without changes in strategies. By comparing current and projected business grids, management can identify the major strategic issues and opportunities it faces.

PROBLEMS WITH MATRIX APPROACHES. The BCG, GE, and other formal methods developed during the 1970s revolutionized strategic planning. But such approaches have limitations. They can be difficult, time-consuming, and costly to implement. Management may find it difficult to define SBUs and measure market share and growth. In addition, these approaches focus on classifying *current* businesses, but provide little advice for *future* planning. Management must still rely on its own judgment to set the business objectives for each SBU, to determine what resources each will be given, and to decide which new businesses should be added.

Formal approaches can also lead the company to place too much emphasis on market-share growth or growth through entry into attractive new markets. Using these approaches, many companies plunged into unrelated and new high-growth businesses that they did not know how to manage—with very bad results. At the same time, they were often too quick to abandon, sell, or milk to death their healthy mature businesses. Despite these and other problems, and although many companies have dropped formal matrix methods in favor of more customized approaches better suited to their situations, most companies remain firmly committed to strategic planning. Roughly 75 percent of the *Fortune* 500 companies practice some form of portfolio planning.[4]

Such analysis is no cure-all for finding the best strategy. But it can help management to understand the company's overall situation, to see how each business or product contributes, to assign resources to its businesses, and to orient the company for future success. When used properly, strategic planning is just one important aspect of overall strategic management, a way of thinking about how to manage a business.[5]

Developing Growth Strategies

Beyond evaluating current businesses, designing the business portfolio involves finding future businesses and products the company should consider. One useful device for identifying growth opportunities is the **product/market expansion grid.**[6] This grid is shown in Figure 2-5. Below, we apply it to Kraft.

MARKET PENETRATION. First, Kraft management might consider whether the company's major brands can achieve deeper **market penetration**—making more sales to present

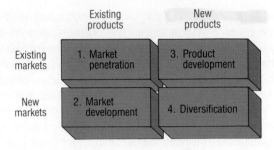

FIGURE 2-5
Market opportunity identification through the product/market expansion grid

customers without changing products in any way. For example, to increase its dairy-case sales, Kraft might cut prices, increase advertising, gets its products into more stores, or obtain better shelf positions for them. Basically, Kraft management would like to increase usage by current customers and attract customers of other brands to Kraft.

MARKET DEVELOPMENT. Second, Kraft management might consider possibilities for **market development**—identifying and developing new markets for current products. For example, managers at Kraft review *demographic markets*—infants, preschoolers, teenagers, young adults, senior citizens—to see if any of these groups can be encouraged to buy, or buy more, Kraft products. The managers also look at *institutional markets*—restaurants, food services, hospitals—to see if sales to these buyers can be increased.

Market development: Jockey enters the women's market.

And managers could review *geographical markets*—France, Thailand, India—to see if these markets can be developed. All these are market development strategies.

PRODUCT DEVELOPMENT. Third, management could consider **product development—offering modified or new products to current markets.** Kraft products could be offered in new sizes, or with new ingredients, or in new packaging, all representing possible product modifications. Kraft could also launch new brands to appeal to different users, or it could launch other food products that its current customers might buy. All these are product development strategies.

DIVERSIFICATION. Fourth, Kraft might consider **diversification.** It could start up or buy businesses entirely outside of its current products and markets. For example, the company's recent moves into such "hot" industries as fitness equipment, health foods, and frozen foods represent diversification. Some companies try to identify the most attractive emerging industries. They feel that half the secret of success is to enter attractive industries instead of trying to be efficient in an unattractive industry. But many companies that diversified too broadly in the 1960s and 1970s are now narrowing their market focus and getting back to the basics of serving one or a few industries that they know best (see Marketing Highlight 2–1).

Planning Functional Strategies

The company's strategic plan establishes what kinds of businesses the company will be in and its objectives for each. Then, more detailed planning must take place within each business unit. Each functional department—marketing, finance, accounting, purchasing, manufacturing, personnel, and others—plays an important role in the strategic-planning process. First, each department provides information for strategic planning. Then, management in each business unit prepares a plan that states the role each department will play. The plan shows how all the functional areas will work together to accomplish strategic objectives.

Each functional department deals with different publics to obtain inputs into business needs—inputs such as cash, labor, raw materials, research ideas, and manufacturing processes. For example, marketing brings in revenues by negotiating exchanges with consumers. Finance arranges exchanges with lenders and stockholders to obtain cash. Thus, the marketing and finance departments must work together to obtain needed funds. Similarly, the personnel department supplies labor, and purchasing obtains materials needed for operations and manufacturing.

Marketing's Role in Strategic Planning

There is much overlap between overall company strategy and marketing strategy. Marketing looks at consumer needs and the company's ability to satisfy them; these same factors guide the company mission and objectives. Most company strategy planning deals with marketing variables—market share, market development, growth—and it is sometimes hard to separate strategic planning from marketing planning. In fact, in some companies, strategic planning is called "strategic marketing planning."

Marketing plays a key role in the company's strategic planning in several ways. First, marketing provides a guiding *philosophy*—company strategy should revolve around serving the needs of important consumer groups. Second, marketing provides *inputs* to strategic planners by helping to identify attractive market opportunities and to assess the firm's potential for taking advantage of them. Finally, within individual business units, marketing designs *strategies* for reaching the unit's objectives.[7]

Within each business unit, marketing management must determine the best way to help achieve strategic objectives. Some marketing managers will find that their objective is not necessarily to build sales. It may be to hold existing sales with a smaller marketing budget, or it may actually be to reduce demand. Thus, marketing management must manage demand to the level decided upon by the strategic planning prepared at headquarters. Marketing helps to assess each business unit's potential, but once the unit's objective is set, marketing's task is to carry it out profitably.

AMERICAN BUSINESS GETS BACK TO THE BASICS

During the 1960s and 1970s, strategic planners in many American companies got expansion fever. It seemed that everyone wanted to get bigger and grow faster by broadening their business portfolios. Companies milked their stodgy but profitable core businesses to get the cash needed to acquire glamorous, faster-growing businesses in more attractive industries. It didn't seem to matter that many of the acquired businesses fit poorly with old ones, or that they operated in markets unfamiliar to company management.

Thus, many firms exploded into huge conglomerates, sometimes containing hundreds of unrelated products and businesses operating in a dozen diverse industries. Managing these "smorgasbord" portfolios often proved difficult. The conglomerate managers soon learned that it was tough to run businesses in industries they knew little about. Many newly acquired businesses bogged down under added layers of corporate management and increased administrative costs. Meanwhile, the profitable core businesses that had financed the acquisitions withered from lack of investment and management attention.

By the mid-1980s, as attempt after attempt at scattergun diversification foundered, acquisition fever gave way to a new philosophy—getting back to the basics. The new trend has many names—"narrowing the focus," "sticking to your knitting," "the contraction craze," "the urge to purge." They all mean narrowing the company's market focus and returning to the ideal of serving the one or the few core industries that it knows best. The company sheds businesses that don't fit its narrowed focus and rebuilds by concentrating resources on other businesses that do. The result is a smaller but more focused company, a more muscular firm serving fewer markets but serving them much better.

Today, companies in all industries are getting back in focus and shedding unrelated operations. According to one survey, 56 percent of all *Fortune* 500 companies have begun the slimming-down process during the past five years. Some companies have taken drastic steps. For example, during the 1970s, huge Gulf & Western acquired businesses in dozens of diverse industries ranging from auto products and industrial equipment to apparel and furniture, from cement and cigars to racetracks and video games. But since 1983, it has focused on entertainment, information, and financial services, purging the company of more than 50 operations that made up nearly half its sales. Similarly, ITT, after diversifying wildly during the 1960s and 1970s, is divesting $1.7 billion worth of businesses that don't fit its new focus.

Several food companies have also made strong moves back to the bread-and-butter basics. Quaker Oats sold off its specialty retailing businesses—Jos. A. Banks (clothing), Brookstone (tools), and Eyelab (optical)—and will probably sell its profitable Fisher-Price toy operation. It used the proceeds to strengthen current food brands and to acquire the Golden Grain Macaroni Company (Rice-a-Roni and Noodle-a-Roni) and Gaines Foods (pet foods), whose products strongly complement Quaker's. General Mills ended 20 years of diversification by lopping off most of its nonfood businesses and moving back to the kitchen. It sold such companies as Izod (fashions), Monet (jewelry), Parker Brothers (games), Kenner (toys), and Eddie Bauer and Talbots (specialty retailers) while increasing investment in its basic consumer food brands (Wheaties and other cereals, Betty Crocker cake mixes, Gorton's seafoods, Gold Medal flour) and restaurants (Red Lobster, Darryl's).

These and other companies have concluded that bigger is not always better and that fast-growing businesses in attractive industries are not good investments if they spread the company's resources too thin, or if the company's managers can't run them properly. They have learned that a company without market focus—one that tries to serve too many diverse markets—might end up serving few markets well.

Sources: See Thomas Moore, "Old-Line Industry Shapes Up," *Fortune*, April 27, 1987, pp. 23–32; David Lieberman and Joe Weber, "Gulf & Western: From Grab Bag to Lean, Mean, Marketing Machine," *Business Week*, September 14, 1987, pp. 152–156; and Walter Kiechel III, "Corporate Strategy for the 1990s," *Fortune*, February 29, 1988, pp. 34–42.

Marketing and the Other Business Functions

Confusion persists about marketing's importance in the firm. In some firms, it is just another function—all functions count in the company and none takes leadership (see Figure 2-6A). If the company faces slow growth or a sales decline, marketing may temporarily become more important (see Figure 2-6B).

Some marketers claim that marketing is the major function of the firm. They quote Drucker's statement: "The aim of the business is to create customers." They say it is marketing's job to define the company's mission, products, and markets and to direct the other functions in the task of serving customers (see Figure 2-6C).

More enlightened marketers prefer to put the customer at the center of the company. They argue that all functions should work together to sense, serve, and satisfy the customer (see Figure 2-6D).

Finally, some marketers say that marketing still needs to be in a central position to be certain that customers' needs are understood and satisfied (see Figure 2-6E). These marketers argue that the firm cannot succeed without customers, so the crucial task is to attract and hold customers. Customers are attracted by promises and held

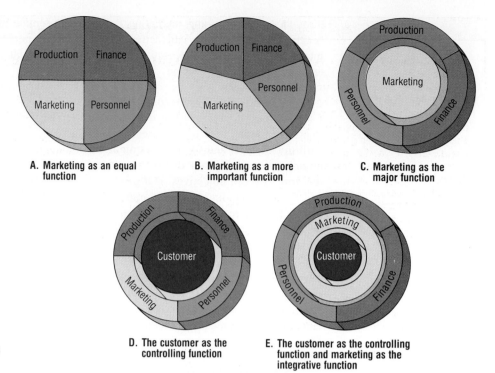

A. Marketing as an equal function

B. Marketing as a more important function

C. Marketing as the major function

D. The customer as the controlling function

E. The customer as the controlling function and marketing as the integrative function

FIGURE 2-6
Alternate views of marketing's role in the company

A Du Pont worker visits customers regularly then represents that customer on Du Pont's factory floor.

through satisfaction, and marketing defines the promise and ensures its delivery. But because actual consumer satisfaction is affected by the performance of other departments, marketing must play an integrative role to help ensure that all departments work together toward consumer satisfaction.

Conflict between Departments

Each business function has a different view of which publics and activities are most important. Manufacturing focuses on suppliers and production; finance is concerned with stockholders and sound investment; marketing emphasizes consumers and products, pricing, promotion, and distribution. Ideally, all the functions should blend to reach the firm's overall objectives. But in practice, departmental relations are full of conflicts and misunderstandings. Some conflicts result from differences of opinion as to what is in the best interest of the firm. Some result from real tradeoffs between departmental well-being and company well-being. And some conflicts result from unfortunate departmental stereotypes and biases.

Under the marketing concept, the company wants to blend all the different functions toward consumer satisfaction. The marketing department takes the consumer's point of view. But other departments stress the importance of their own tasks, and they may resist bending their efforts to the will of the marketing department. Because departments tend to define company problems and goals from their own points of view, conflicts are inevitable. Table 2-1 shows the main point-of-view-differences between marketing and other departments.

When marketing tries to develop customer satisfaction, it often causes other departments to do a poorer job *in their terms*. Marketing department actions can increase purchasing costs, disrupt production schedules, increase inventories, and create budget

**TABLE 2-1
Point of View
Differences between
Marketing and Other
Departments**

DEPARTMENT	EMPHASIS	MARKETING EMPHASIS
R&D (Research & Development)	Basic research Intrinsic quality Functional features	Applied research Perceived quality Sales features
Engineering	Long design lead time Few models Standard components	Short design lead time Many models Custom components
Purchasing	Narrow product line Standard parts Price of material Economical lot sizes Purchasing at infrequent intervals	Broad product line Nonstandard parts Quality of material Large lot sizes to avoid stockouts Immediate purchasing for customer needs
Manufacturing	Long production lead time Long runs with few models No model changes Standard orders Ease of fabrication Simple quality control	Short production lead time Short runs with many models Frequent model changes Custom orders Aesthetic appearance Tight quality control
Inventory	Fast-moving items, narrow product line Economical level of stock	Broad product line High level of stock
Finance	Strict rationales for spending Hard and fast budgets Pricing to cover costs	Intuitive arguments for spending Flexible budgets to meet changing needs Pricing to further market development
Accounting	Standrad transactions Few reports	Special terms and discounts Many reports
Credit	Full financial disclosures by customers Low credit risks Tough credit terms Tough collection procedures	Minimum credit examination of customers Medium credit risks Easy credit terms Easy collection procedures

headaches. Yet marketers must get all departments to "think consumer," to look through the customer's eyes, and to put the consumer at the center of company activity.

The DuPont "Adopt a Customer" program recognizes the importance of having people in all areas be "close to the customer." Through this program, DuPont encourages blue-collar workers at many of its plants to visit a customer once a month to learn about the customer's needs. The worker then represents that customer on the factory floor. If quality or delivery problems arise, the worker is more likely to see the adopted customer's point of view and to make decisions that will keep the customer happy.[8]

Marketing management can best gain support for its goal of consumer satisfaction by working to understand the company's other departments. Marketing managers must work closely with managers of other functions to develop a system of functional plans under which the different departments can work together to accomplish the company's overall strategic objectives.[9]

THE MARKETING MANAGEMENT PROCESS

The strategic plan defines the company's overall mission and objectives. Within each business unit, marketing helps accomplish the overall strategic objectives. Alert companies rely on marketing as the main system for monitoring and adapting to the changing marketplace. Marketing is not simply selling or advertising, but rather a whole process for matching the company to its best opportunities. We define the marketing management process as follows:

> The **marketing management process** consists of (1) analyzing marketing opportunities, (2) selecting target markets, (3) developing the marketing mix, and (4) managing the marketing effort.

These steps, along with the chapters that address each step, are shown in Figure 2-7. The rest of this chapter summarizes the entire process; later chapters discuss each step in detail.

FIGURE 2-7
The marketing management process

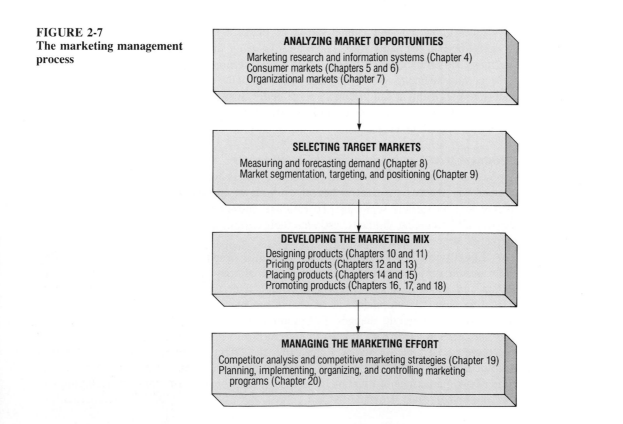

ANALYZING MARKET OPPORTUNITIES

Marketing research and information systems (Chapter 4)
Consumer markets (Chapters 5 and 6)
Organizational markets (Chapter 7)

SELECTING TARGET MARKETS

Measuring and forecasting demand (Chapter 8)
Market segmentation, targeting, and positioning (Chapter 9)

DEVELOPING THE MARKETING MIX

Designing products (Chapters 10 and 11)
Pricing products (Chapters 12 and 13)
Placing products (Chapters 14 and 15)
Promoting products (Chapters 16, 17, and 18)

MANAGING THE MARKETING EFFORT

Competitor analysis and competitive marketing strategies (Chapter 19)
Planning, implementing, organizing, and controlling marketing
  programs (Chapter 20)

Analyzing Market Opportunities

Every company needs to be able to identify new market opportunities. No company can depend on its present products and markets to last forever. The complex and changing environment constantly offers new opportunities and threats. The company must carefully analyze its consumers and the environment so that it can avoid the threats and take advantage of the opportunities. To survive, it must continually seek new ways to offer value to consumers.

Companies may think that they have few opportunities, but this belief is only a failure to think strategically about what business they are in and what strengths they have. Every company faces many opportunities. Companies can search for new opportunities casually or systematically. Many companies find new ideas by simply keeping their eyes and ears open to the changing marketplace. Other organizations use formal methods for analyzing the marketing environment.

Not all opportunities are right for a given company. A marketing opportunity must fit the company's objectives and resources. Cellular phones, facsimile machines, high-definition televisions and VCRs, laptop computers, and home satellite dishes are all highly attractive markets, but not for every company. For example, we sense that such markets would not be right for McDonald's. McDonald's seeks a high level of sales, growth, and profits from the fast-food business. And even though McDonald's has very large resources, it lacks the technical know-how, industrial marketing experience, and special distribution channels needed to sell such high-tech electronics products successfully.

When analyzing market opportunities—in fact, throughout the marketing management process—managers need a plentiful supply of information. They need information about consumers and how they make buying decisions. The managers need to know about the important actors in the marketing environment—competitors, suppliers, resellers, and publics. They also need to know about broader environmental forces that affect the company and its consumers—demographic, economic, natural, technological, political, and cultural. The marketing information system assesses the information needs of marketing managers and obtains the needed information from several sources—internal records, marketing intelligence, and marketing research. It then distributes this information to the right managers, in the right form, at the right time.

Selecting Target Consumers

Companies know that they cannot satisfy all consumers in a given market, at least not all consumers in the same way. There are too many different kinds of consumers with too many different kinds of needs. And some companies are in a better position to serve certain segments of the market. Each company must study the total market and choose the segments it can profitably serve better than its competitors can. This involves four steps: demand measurement and forecasting, market segmentation, market targeting, and market positioning.

Demand Measurement and Forecasting

Suppose a company is considering possible markets for a potential new product. The company first needs to make a careful estimate of the current and future size of the market and its various segments. To estimate current market size, the company must identify all competing products, estimate their current sales, and determine whether the market is large enough.

Equally important is future market growth. Companies want to enter markets that show strong growth prospects. Growth potential may depend on the growth rate of certain age, income, or nationality groups that favor the product. Growth may also be related to larger developments in the environment, such as economic conditions, the crime rate, and life style changes. For example, the future market for quality children's toys and clothing is strongly related to current birth rates, trends in consumer affluence, and projected family life styles. Forecasting the effects of these environmental forces is difficult, but it must be done in order to make decisions about the market. The company's marketing information specialists will probably use complex techniques to measure and forecast demand.

Market Segmentation

Suppose the demand forecast looks good. The company now has to decide how to enter the market. The market consists of many types of customers, products, and needs, and the marketer's task is to determine which segments offer the best chance to achieve company objectives. Consumers can be grouped in various ways based on geographic factors (regions, cities), demographic factors (sex, age, income, education), psychographic factors, (social classes, life styles) and behavioral factors (purchase occasions, benefits sought, usage rates). The process of classifying customers into groups with different needs, characteristics, or behavior is called **market segmentation.**

Every market is made up of market segments, but not all ways of segmenting the market are equally useful. For example, Tylenol would gain little by distinguishing between male and female users of pain relievers if both respond the same way to marketing stimuli. A **market segment** consists of consumers who respond in a similar way to a given set of marketing stimuli. In the car market, consumers who choose the biggest, most comfortable car no matter what its price make up one market segment. Other segments include buyers who care mainly about price and operating economy, those looking for style and status, those wanting high performance and sportiness, or those wanting safety and durability. It would be very difficult to make one model of car that would be the first choice of buyers in each of these segments. Companies are wise to focus their efforts on meeting the distinct needs of one or more market segments. Thus, they study the geographic, demographic, behavioral, and other characteristics of each market segment to evaluate its attractiveness as a marketing opportunity.

Market Targeting

After a company has evaluated market segments, it can enter one or many segments of a given market. A company with limited skills or resources might decide to serve only one or a few special segments. This strategy limits sales but can be very profitable (see Marketing Highlight 2–2). Or a company might choose to serve several related segments, perhaps those that have different kinds of customers but with the same basic wants. Or a large company might decide to offer a complete range of products to serve all the market segments.

Most companies enter a new market by serving a single segment, and if this proves successful, they add segments. Honda, Toyota, and Nissan first entered the U.S. market successfully with small economy cars, then added mid-price and higher-price cars. Large companies eventually seek full market coverage. They want to be the "General Motors" of their industry. GM says that it makes a car for every "person, purse, and personality." The leading company normally has different products designed to meet the special needs of each segment.

Market Positioning

Once a company has decided which market segments to enter, it must decide what "positions" it wants to occupy in those segments. A product's *position* is the place the product occupies in consumers' minds relative to competitors. If a product is perceived to be exactly like another product on the market, consumers would have no reason to buy it.

Market positioning is arranging for a product to occupy a clear, distinctive, and desirable place relative to competing products in the minds of target consumers. Thus, marketers plan positions that distinguish their products from competing products and that give them the greatest strategic advantage in their target markets. For example, the Hyundai automobile is positioned on low price as "the car that makes sense." Chrysler offers the "best built, best backed American cars"; Pontiac says "we build excitement"; and at Ford "quality is job one." Jaguar is positioned as "a blending of art and machine," while Saab is "the most intelligent car ever built." Mercedes is "engineered like no other car in the world"; the luxurious Bentley is "the closest a car can come to having wings." Such deceptively simple statements form the backbone of a product's marketing strategy.

MARKET SEGMENTATION AND TARGETING: "DESIGNER TRUCKS" BY OSHKOSH

Have you ever heard of the Oshkosh Truck Corporation? Perhaps not. But chances are good that you've seen some Oshkosh trucks around without realizing it. Oshkosh is the world's largest producer of crash, fire, and rescue trucks for airports. It also makes those "forward placement" concrete carriers—the ones that pour conveniently from the front but look as though they were put together backwards. In an environment where large, diversified truck manufacturers are having trouble, the smaller and more focused Oshkosh is thriving. The reason: smart market segmentation and targeting.

Oshkosh produces specialized heavy-duty trucks for customers who need unique, innovative designs for specific uses in adverse operating conditions. "Oshkosh is to trucks what Armani is to clothes. It builds designer trucks: heavy-

duty, off-road, all-wheel drive, frequently custom-designed vehicles that sell for anywhere from $36,000 to $750,000." Until the early 1980s, Oshkosh focused on special municipal and commercial segments with its unique concrete carriers and crash, fire, and rescue vehicles. But then, in 1981, it added a new target—the U.S. military. It began with a contract for 2,450 Heavy Expanded Mobility Tactical Trucks (HEMTT). The $120,000 HEMTT, an eight-wheel drive, all-terrain vehicle that carries up to 11 tons, quickly won the respect of military users and buyers. Since 1982, Oshkosh's defense business has soared, with contracts totaling more than $1.5 billion. Military orders now account for 84 percent of total Oshkosh sales.

Oshkosh's focused segmentation and targeting strategy has produced spectacular sales and profit results. The compa-

Oshkosh Trucking specializes in "designer trucks" for use in adverse operating conditions.

In positioning its product, the company first identifies possible competitive advantages upon which to build the position. To gain competitive advantage, the company must offer greater value to choosen target segments, either by charging lower prices than competitors or by offering more benefits to justify higher prices. But if the company positions the product as *offering* greater value, it must then *deliver* that greater value. Thus, effective positioning begins with actually *differentiating* the company's marketing offer so that it gives consumers more value than competitors' offer them.

The company might differentiate its offer in any of several ways. It can differentiate its *physical product* by providing more features, improved performance, or better styling and design. It can differentiate the *services* that accompany the product, or it can hire and train better customer-contact *people*. Finally, it can establish a brand or company image that differentiates its offer.

Not all differentiating factors are worth establishing. Marketers want to choose differences that are important to consumers, differences that distinguish the company from competitors. Marketers also look for differences that cannot be easily copied by competitors, that buyers can afford, and that the company can introduce profitably. The company can position a product on only one major differentiating factor or on several. However, positioning on too many factors can result in consumer confusion or disbelief. Once the company has chosen a desired position, it must take strong steps to deliver and communicate that position to target consumers. The company's entire marketing program should support the chosen positioning strategy.

ny's sales jumped from $72 million in 1981 to more than $400 million by 1987. During the past five years, profits have grown an average 64 percent per year; return on equity last year reached 38 percent. In fact, Oshkosh has been so successful that numerous competitors have begun to invade its snug specialty truck niche, hoping to share in the sumptuous returns.

With competition increasing rapidly in current segments, Oshkosh is developing new ones. For example, it's targeting municipal markets with new crash, fire, and rescue vehicles modified for emergency snow removal. And Oshkosh is working to establish itself in international specialty truck segments. "It built a set of powerful low-gear trucks to haul a 3,000-ton Saudi desalinization plant from the sea to the sands miles inland. For a Brazilian job, it created another set of monsters to carry 18 massive turbine generators, each weighing in at over six million pounds, at three miles an hour for 90 days"—a feat that won Oshkosh a mention in

The Guiness Book of World Records. Such projects testify to the company's versatility in meeting the needs of the special segments it serves. Says one Oshkosh executive, "We can build [a vehicle] in volumes of as low as one and as high as a thousand and still make money on it."

Thus, Oshkosh has built a strong position in a number of small, highly specialized market segments. Compared with truck industry giants such as General Motors, Ford, and Navistar, Oshkosh is a fairly small operator. But it is faster-growing and more profitable than its larger, less-focused competitors. And in its designer-truck segments, Oshkosh is the major player. Through smart market segmentation and targeting, Oshkosh has proven that small can be beautiful.

Sources: See Stuart Gannes, "The Riches in Market Niches," *Fortune*, April 27, 1987, p. 228. Extracts from Jagannath Dubashi, "Designer Trucks," *Financial World*, May 19, 1987, pp. 35–36.

Developing the Marketing Mix

Once the company has decided upon its positioning strategy, it is ready to begin planning the details of the marketing mix. The marketing mix is one of the major concepts in modern marketing. We define the **marketing mix** as the set of controllable marketing variables that the firm blends to produce the response it wants in the target market. The marketing mix consists of everything the firm can do to influence the demand for its product. The many possibilities can be collected into four groups of variables known as the "four Ps:" *product, price, place*, and *promotion*.[10] The particular marketing variables under each P are shown in Figure 2-8.

Product stands for the "goods-and-service" combination the company offers to the target market. Thus a Ford Taurus automobile "product" consists of nuts and bolts, sparkplugs, pistons, headlights, and thousands of other parts. Ford offers several Taurus styles and dozens of optional features. The car comes fully serviced, with a comprehensive warranty that is as much a part of the product as the tailpipe.

Price stands for the amount of money customers have to pay to obtain the product. Ford calculates suggested retail prices that its dealers might charge for each Taurus. But Ford dealers rarely charge the full sticker price. Instead, they negotiate the price with each customer, offering discounts, trade-in allowances, and credit terms to adjust for the current competitive situation and to bring the price into line with the buyer's perceptions of the car's value.

Place stands for company activities that make the product available to target consumers. Ford maintains a large body of independently owned dealerships that sell the compa-

Positioning: Here Embassy Suites positions itself on price/value with "You don't have to be a fat cat to enjoy the Suite Life." Alternatively, Westin Hotels and Resorts positions itself as "caring, comfortable, and civilized."

ny's many different car models. Ford selects its dealers carefully and supports them strongly. The dealers keep an inventory of Ford automobiles, demonstrate them to potential buyers, negotiate prices, close sales, and service the cars after the sale.

Promotion stands for activities that communicate the merits of the product and persuade target customers to buy it. Ford spends more than $600 million each year on advertising to tell consumers about the company and its products. Dealership salespeople assist potential buyers and persuade them that Ford is the best car for them. Ford and its dealers offer special promotions—sales, cash rebates, low financing rates—as added purchase incentives.

FIGURE 2-8
The four Ps of the marketing mix

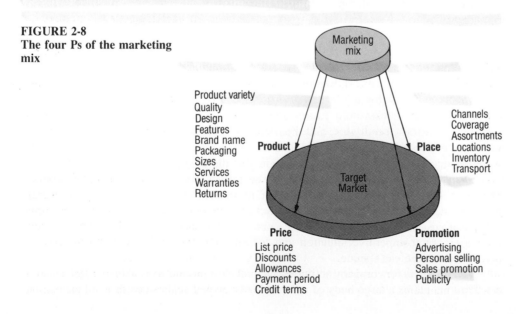

Marketing mix

Product
Product variety
Quality
Design
Features
Brand name
Packaging
Sizes
Services
Warranties
Returns

Place
Channels
Coverage
Assortments
Locations
Inventory
Transport

Target Market

Price
List price
Discounts
Allowances
Payment period
Credit terms

Promotion
Advertising
Personal selling
Sales promotion
Publicity

An effective marketing program blends all of the marketing mix elements into a coordinated program designed to achieve the company's marketing objectives.[11]

So far, we have looked at how the company analyzes consumers and selects target markets, and at the marketing mix tools the company can use to meet consumer needs. But when developing a marketing strategy, managers must consider more than consumer needs—they must also consider the company's industry position relative to competitors. Marketing managers must design competitive marketing strategies that match the company's position and resources against those of competitors, then effectively manage and adapt these strategies to meet changing conditions.

Competitive Marketing Strategies

To be successful, the company must do a better job than its competitors of satisfying target consumers. Thus, marketing strategies must be adapted to the needs of consumers and also to the strategies of competitors. Based on its size and industry position, the company must find the strategy that gives it the strongest possible competitive advantage.

Designing competitive marketing strategies begins with thorough analysis of competitors. The company constantly compares its products, prices, channels, and promotion with those of its close competitors. In this way it can discern areas of potential advantage and disadvantage. The company must formally or informally monitor the competitive environment to answer these and other important questions: Who are our competitors? What are their objectives and strategies? What are their strengths and weaknesses? How will they react to different competitive strategies we might use?

Which competitive marketing strategy a company adopts depends on its industry position. A firm that dominates a market can adopt one or more of several *market-leader* strategies. General Motors is the automobile industry leader. Other well-known leaders include IBM (computers), Caterpillar (large construction equipment), Kodak (photographic film), Sears (retailing), and Boeing (aircraft). Leaders can try to expand the total market by looking for new users and more use from current customers. Because the leader has the largest market share, it gains the most when the total market is expanded. Or the leader might try to increase its market share by investing heavily to attract customers away from competitors. The dominant company can also design strategies to defend its current business against competitor attacks. It can lead the industry in innovation, competitive effectiveness, and value to consumers. It can carefully assess potential threats, counterattacking when necessary. Or the market leader may launch new products or marketing programs to strike down competitors before they become major threats.

Market challengers are runner-up companies that aggressively attack competitors to get more market share. Ford and Toyota are among the challengers in the automobile industry. The challenger might attack the market leader, other firms its own size, or smaller local and regional competitors. Challengers can choose from several *market-challenger* strategies. If the challenger is strong enough, it can pit its resources directly against those of competitors. A weaker challenger can concentrate its strengths against the competitor's weaknesses. Or the challenger can bypass the competitor and develop new products, new markets, or new technologies. In the automobile industry in recent years, Ford and several Japanese challengers have eaten heavily into General Motors' industry lead.

Some runner-up firms will choose to follow rather than challenge the market leader. Firms using *market-follower* strategies seek stable market shares and profits by following competitor's product offers, prices, and marketing programs. They may follow closely or at a distance, or they may follow closely in some ways and sometimes go their own ways. The market follower's goal is to keep current customers and to attract a fair share of new ones without drawing retaliation from the market leader or other competitors. Many market followers are more profitable than the leaders in their industries. They can wait for the leader to develop the market for new products, learn from the leader's experiences, and then introduce products with equal or even superior designs and marketing programs.[12] For many years, Ford and Chrysler were content to follow General Motors. But recently, slow sales and increasing foreign competition have forced these companies into more aggressive strategies.

Smaller firms in a market, or even larger firms that lack established positions, often adopt *market-nicher* strategies. They specialize in serving market niches that major competitors overlook or ignore. "Nichers" avoid direct confrontations with the majors by specializing along market, customer, product, or marketing-mix lines. Through smart "niching," low-share firms in an industry can be as profitable as their larger competitors. In the auto industry, Hyundai niches in the very-low-price segment, Mercedes in the luxury segment, and Porsche in the high-performance, high-price segment.

Thus the company must choose its competitive marketing strategies based on its industry position and its strengths and weaknesses relative to competitors. And strategy must change to meet changes in the competitive situation.

The Marketing Management Functions

Marketing management's job is to field effective marketing programs which will give the company a strong competitive advantage in its target markets. This involves four key marketing management functions—analysis, planning, implementation, and control.

Marketing *analysis* and *planning*, discussed earlier in this chapter, involve examining the company's markets and marketing environment to find attractive opportunities, then deciding on marketing strategies that will help the company attain its overall strategic objectives. Good marketing analysis and planning are only a start toward successful company performance—the marketing plans must also be implemented well. Designing good marketing strategies is often easier than putting them into action.

People at all levels of the marketing system must work together to *implement* marketing strategies and plans. People in marketing must work closely with people in finance, purchasing, manufacturing, and other company departments. And many outside people and organizations must help with implementation—suppliers, resellers, advertising agencies, research firms, the advertising media. To successfully implement its marketing plans and strategies, the company must blend all elements into a cohesive program.

Many surprises are likely to occur as marketing plans are being implemented. The company needs *control* procedures to make sure that its objectives will be achieved. Companies want to make sure that they are achieving the sales, profits, and other goals set in their annual plans. This involves measuring ongoing market performance, determining the causes of any serious gaps in performance, and determining the best corrective action to close the gaps. Corrective action may call for improving the ways in which the plan is being implemented, or may even require changing the goals.

Also, every company should stand back from time to time and review its overall approach to the marketplace. The purpose is to make certain that the company's mission, objectives, policies, strategies, and programs remain appropriate in the face of rapid environmental changes. Giant companies such as Chrysler, International Harvester, Singer, and A&P all fell on hard times because they did not watch the changing marketplace and make the proper adaptations. A major tool used for such strategic control is the *marketing audit*, which is described in Chapter 20.

Figure 2-9 summarizes the entire marketing management process and the forces influencing company marketing strategy. Target consumers stand in the center. The company identifies the total market, divides it into smaller segments, selects the most promising segments, and focuses on serving and satisfying these segments. It designs a marketing mix made up of factors under its control—product, price, place, and promotion. To find the best marketing mix and put it into action, the company engages in marketing analysis, planning, implementation, and control. Through these activities, the company watches and adapts to the actors and forces in the marketing environment.

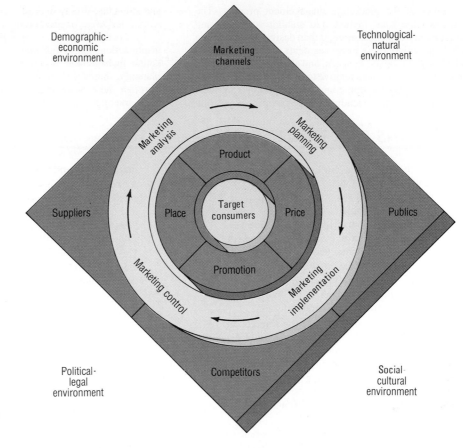

FIGURE 2-9
Factors influencing company marketing strategy

■ SUMMARY

Strategic planning involves developing a strategy for long-run survival and growth. Marketing helps in strategic planning, and the overall strategic plan defines marketing's role in the company. Marketers undertake the marketing management process to carry out their roles in the organization.

Some companies do not use formal planning; some use it but not well. Yet formal planning offers several benefits, including systematic thinking, better coordination of company efforts, sharper objectives, and improved performance measurement, all of which can lead to improved sales and profits. Companies develop three kinds of plans—*annual plans*, *long-range plans*, and *strategic plans*.

Strategic planning sets the stage for the rest of company planning. The strategic planning process consists of developing the company's mission, objectives and goals, business portfolio, and functional plans.

Developing a sound *mission statement* is a challenging undertaking. The mission statement should be market-oriented, feasible, motivating, and specific if it is to direct the firm to its best opportunities. The mission statement then leads to supporting objectives and goals.

Strategic planning calls for analyzing the company's *business portfolio* and deciding which businesses should receive more or less resources. The company might use a formal portfolio planning method such as the *BCG growth-share matrix* or the *General Electric strategic business grid*. But most companies are now designing more customized portfolio planning approaches that better suit their unique situations.

Beyond evaluating current strategic business units, management must plan for growth into new businesses and products. The *product-market expansion grid* shows four avenues for growth. *Market penetration* involves more sales of current products to current customers. *Market development* involves identifying new markets for current products. *Product development* involves offering new or modified products to current markets. Finally, *diversification* involves starting businesses entirely outside of current products and markets.

Each of the company's functional departments provides inputs for strategic planning. Once strategic objectives have been defined, management within each business must prepare a set of *functional plans* that coordinates the activities of the marketing, finance, manufacturing, and other departments. Each department has a different idea about which objectives and activities are most important. The marketing department stresses the consumer's point of view. Other departments stress different things, and this generates conflict between departments. Marketing managers must understand the points of view of the other functions and work with other functional managers to develop a system of plans that will best accomplish the firm's overall strategic objectives.

To fulfill their role in the organization, marketers engage in the *marketing management process*, which consists of analyzing marketing opportunities, selecting target markets, developing the marketing mix, and managing the market effort. The company first carefully analyzes consumers and the environment, looking for threats to avoid and opportunities to exploit. Consumers are at the center of the marketing management process. The marketer divides the total market into smaller segments and selects the segments it can best serve. It then designs its *marketing mix* to attract and satisfy these target segments. Marketing strategies must be based on consumer needs, and also on the company's industry position and resources relative to competitors. The company must continually monitor competitors' products, prices, channels, and promotion. Depending on the company's position and strengths, it may choose *market-leader*, *market-challenger*, *market-follower*, or *market-nicher* strategies and programs.

To find the best *competitive marketing strategy* and put it into action, marketing managers perform four important marketing management functions—marketing analysis, marketing planning, marketing implementation, and marketing control. Through these activities, the company watches and adapts to the marketing environment.

■ QUESTIONS FOR DISCUSSION

1. What are the benefits of a "rolling" five-year plan—that is, why should managers take time to write a five-year plan that will be changed every year?

2. In a series of job interviews, you ask three recruiters to describe the missions of their companies. One says, "To make profits." Another says, "To create customers." The third says, "To fight world hunger." What do these mission statements tell you about the companies?

3. Choose a local radio station and describe what its mission, objectives, and strategies appear to be. What other things could the station do to accomplish its mission?

4. An electronics manufacturer obtains the semiconductors it uses in production from a company-owned subsidiary that also sells to other manufacturers. The subsidiary is smaller and less profitable than competing producers and its growth rate has been below the industry average during the past five years. Into what cell of the BCG growth-share matrix does this strategic business unit fall? What should the parent company do with this SBU?

5. What market opportunities has Pizza Hut pursued in each of the four cells of the product/market expansion grid? What future opportunities would you suggest to Pizza Hut?

6. As companies become more customer and marketing oriented, many departments find that they must change their traditional way of doing business. How can a company's finance, accounting, and engineering departments help the company become more marketing oriented? Give examples.

7. The General Electric strategic business-planning grid provides a broad overview that can be very helpful in strategic decision making. For what types of decisions would this grid be helpful? For what types, if any, would it not be useful?

8. Assume you are considering starting a business after graduation. What is the opportunity for a new music store selling records, tapes, and compact discs in your town? Briefly describe the target market or markets you would pursue and the marketing mix you would develop for such a store.

9. Blockbuster Video is the market leader in home video rentals. It offers two-night rentals, large attractive stores, and wide variety at a moderately high price. Discuss how you would use market challenger, market follower, and market nicher strategies to compete with Blockbuster.

■ KEY TERMS

Annual plan. A short-range marketing plan that describes the current marketing situation, company objectives, the marketing strategy for the year, the action program, budgets, and controls.

BCG growth-share matrix. A portfolio planning method that evaluates a company's strategic business units in terms of their market growth rate and relative market share. SBUs are classified as stars, cash cows, question marks, or dogs.

Business portfolio. The collection of businesses and products that make up the company.

Cash cows. Low-growth, high-share businesses or products—established and successful units that generate cash which the company uses to pay its bills and support other business units that need investment.

Diversification. A strategy for company growth by starting up or acquiring businesses outside the company's current products and markets.

Dogs. Low-growth, low-share businesses and products that may generate enough cash to maintain themselves, but do not promise to be a large source of cash.

GE strategic business-planning grid. A portfolio planning method that evaluates a company's strategic business units using indexes of industry attractiveness and the company's strength in the industry.

Long-range plan. A marketing plan that (1) describes the major factors and forces expected to affect the organization during the next several years and (2) outlines long-term objectives, the major marketing strategies that will be used to attain them, and the resources required.

Market development. A strategy for company growth by identifying and developing new market segments for current company products.

Market penetration. A strategy for company growth by increasing sales of current products to current market segments without changing the product in any way.

Market positioning. Arranging for a product to occupy a clear, distinctive, and desirable place relative to competing products in the minds of target consumers.

Market segment. A group of consumers who respond in a similar way to a given set of marketing stimuli.

Market segmentation. The process of classifying customers into groups with different needs, characteristics, or behavior.

Marketing management process. The process of (1) analyzing marketing opportunities, (2) selecting target markets, (3) developing the marketing mix, and (4) managing the marketing effort.

Marketing mix. The set of controllable marketing variables that the firm blends to produce the response it wants in the target market.

Mission statement. A statement of the organization's purpose; what it wants to accomplish in the larger environment.

Portfolio analysis. A tool by which management identifies and evaluates the various businesses that make up the company.

Product development. A strategy for company growth by offering modified or new products to current market segments.

Product/market expansion grid. A portfolio planning tool for identifying company growth opportunities through market penetration, market development, product development, or diversification.

Question marks. Low-share business units in high-growth markets which require a lot of cash to hold their share or build into stars.

Stars. High-growth, high-share businesses or products which often require heavy investment to finance their rapid growth.

Strategic business unit (SBU). A unit of the company that has a separate mission and separate objectives and that can be planned independently of other company businesses. An SBU can be a company division, a product line within a division, or sometimes a single product or brand.

Strategic planning. The process of developing and maintaining a strategic fit between the organization's goals and capabilities and its changing marketing opportunities. It relies on developing a clear company mission, supporting objectives, a sound business portfolio, and coordinated functional strategies.

■ REFERENCES

1. See Marc Beauchamp, "Under the Gun," *Forbes*, June 13, 1988, pp. 90–92; Stewart Toy, "Can Greyhound Leave the Dog Days Behind?" *Business Week*, June 8, 1987, pp. 72–74; Eric Schine, "The Other Greyhound Isn't Winning Any Races," *Business Week*, June 19, 1989, p. 53; and "Greyhound Freshens Up Its Name, *Business Week*, March 12, 1990, p. 48.

2. For more on mission statements, see David A. Aaker, *Strategic Market Management*, 2nd ed. (New York: John Wiley and Sons, 1988), Chap. 3; Laura Nash, "Mission Statements—Mirrors and Windows," *Harvard Business Review*, March–April 1988, pp. 155–56; and Fred R. David, "How Companies Define Their Missions Statements," *Long Range Planning*, Vol. 22, No. 1, 1989, pp. 90–97.

3. For additional reading on these and other portfolio analysis approaches, see Philippe Haspeslagh, "Portfolio Planning: Limits and Uses," *Harvard Business Review*, January–February 1982, pp. 58–73; and Yoram Wind, Vijay Mahajan, and Donald J. Swire, "An Empirical Comparison of Standardized Portfolio Models," *Journal of Marketing*, Spring 1983, pp. 89–99.

4. Richard G. Hamermesh, "Making Planning Strategic," *Harvard Business Review*, July–August 1986, pp. 115–20.

5. See Daniel H. Gray, "Uses and Misuses of Strategic Planning," *Harvard Business Review*, January–February 1986, pp. 89–96.

6. H. Igor Ansoff, "Strategies for Diversification," *Harvard Business Review*, September–October 1957, pp. 113–24.

7. For more reading on marketing's role, see Paul F. Anderson, "Marketing, Strategic Planning and the Theory of the Firm," *Journal of Marketing*, Spring 1982, pp. 15–26; and Yoram Wind and Thomas S. Robertson, "Marketing Strategy: New Directions for Theory and Research," *Journal of Marketing*, Spring 1983, pp. 12–25.

8. Brian Dumaine, "Creating a New Company Culture," *Fortune*, January 15, 1990, p. 128.

9. For more reading, see Yoram Wind, "Marketing and the Other Business Functions," in *Research in Marketing*, Vol. 5, Jagdish N. Sheth, ed. (Greenwich, CT: JAI Press, 1981), pp. 237–56; Robert W. Ruekert and Orville C. Walker, Jr., "Marketing's Interaction with Other Functional Units: A Conceptual Framework and Empirical Evidence," *Journal of Marketing*, January 1987, pp. 1–19.

10. The four-P classification was first suggested by E. Jerome McCarthy, *Basic Marketing*: *A Managerial Approach*, (Homewood, IL: Irwin, 1960).

11. See Benson P. Shapiro, "Rejuvenating the Marketing Mix," *Harvard Business Review*, September–October 1985, pp. 28–34.

12. For more on follower strategies, see Daniel W. Haines, Rajan Chandran, and Arvind Parkhe, "Winning by Being First to Market . . . or Second?" *Journal of Consumer Marketing*, Winter, 1989, pp. 63–69.

TRAP-EASE AMERICA: THE BIG CHEESE OF MOUSETRAPS

On a spring morning in April, 1987, Martha House, President of Trap-Ease America, entered her office in Costa Mesa, California. She paused for a moment to contemplate the Ralph Waldo Emerson quote which she had framed and hung near her desk.

"If a man [can] . . . make a better mousetrap than his neighbor . . . the world will make a beaten path to his door."

Perhaps, she mused, Emerson knew something that she didn't. She *had* the better mouse trap—Trap-Ease—but the world didn't seem all that excited about it.

Martha had just returned from the National Hardware Show in Chicago. Standing in the trade show display booth for long hours and answering the same questions hundreds of times had been tiring. Yet, this show had excited her. Each year, National Hardware Show officials hold a contest to select the best new product introduced at the show. Of the more than 300 new products introduced at that year's show, her mousetrap had won first place. Such notoriety was not new for the Trap-Ease mousetrap. It had been featured in *People* magazine and had been the subject of numerous talk shows and articles in various popular press and trade publications. Despite all of this attention, however, the expected demand for the trap had not materialized. Martha hoped that this award might stimulate increased interest and sales.

Trap-Ease America had been formed in January, 1987, by a group of investors who had obtained worldwide rights to market the innovative mousetrap. In return for marketing rights, the group agreed to pay the inventor and patent holder, a retired rancher, a royalty fee for each trap sold. The group then hired Martha to serve as President and to develop and manage the Trap-Ease America organization.

The Trap-Ease, a simple yet clever device, is manufactured by a plastics firm under contract with Trap-Ease America. It consists of a square, plastic tube measuring about 6 inches long and 1 and ½ inches square. The tube bends in the middle at a 30-degree angle, so that when the front part of the tube rests on a flat surface, the other end is elevated. The elevated end holds a removable cap into which the user places bait (cheese, dog food, or some other tidbit). A hinged door is attached to the front end of the tube. When the trap is "open," this door rests on two narrow "stilts" attached to the two bottom corners of the door.

The trap works with simple efficiency. A mouse, smelling the bait, enters the tube through the open end. As it walks up the angled bottom towards the bait, its weight makes the elevated end of the trap drop downward. This elevates the open end, allowing the hinged door to swing closed, trapping the mouse. Small teeth on the ends of the stilts catch in a groove on the bottom of the trap, locking the door closed. The mouse can be disposed of live, or it can be left alone for a few hours to suffocate in the trap.

Martha felt the trap had many advantages for the consumer when compared with traditional spring-loaded traps or poisons. Consumers can use it safely and easily with no risk of catching their fingers while loading it. It poses no injury or poisoning threat to children or pets. Further, with Trap-Ease, consumers can avoid the unpleasant "mess" they encounter with the violent sprint-loaded traps—it creates no "clean-up" problem. Finally, the trap can be reused or simply thrown away.

Martha's early research suggested that women are the best target market for the Trap-Ease. Men, it seems, are more willing to buy and use the traditional, spring-loaded trap. The targeted women, however, do not like the traditional trap. They often stay at home and take care of their children. Thus, they want a means of dealing with the mouse problem that avoids the unpleasantness and risks that the standard trap creates in the home.

To reach this target market, Martha decided to distribute Trap-Ease through national grocery, hardware, and drug chains such as Safeway, K mart, Hechingers, and CB Drug. She sold the trap directly to these large retailers, avoiding any wholesalers or other middlemen.

The traps sold in packages of two, with a suggested retail price of $2.49. Although this price made the Trap-Ease about five to ten times more expensive than smaller, standard traps, consumers appeared to offer little initial price resistance. The manufacturing cost for the Trap-Ease, including freight and packaging costs, was about $.31 per unit. The company paid an additional 8.2 cents per unit in royalty fees. Martha priced the traps to retailers at $.99 per unit and estimated that after sales and volume discounts, Trap-Ease would realize net revenues from retailers of 75 cents per unit.

To promote the product, Martha had budgeted approximately $60,000 for the first year. She planned to use $50,000 of this amount for travel costs to visit trade shows and to make sales calls on retailers. She would use the remaining $10,000 for advertising. So far, however, because the mousetrap had generated so much publicity, she had not felt that she needed to do much advertising. Still, she had placed some advertising in *Good Housekeeping* and in other "home and shelter" magazines. Martha currently was the company's only "salesperson," but she intended to hire more salespeople soon.

Martha had initially forecasted Trap-Ease's first-year sales at five million units. Through April, however, the company had sold only several hundred thousand units.

Martha wondered if most new products got off to such a slow start, or if she was doing something wrong. She had detected some problems, although none seemed overly serious. For one, there had not been enough repeat buying. For another, she had noted that many of the retailers upon whom she called kept their sample mousetraps on their desks as conversation pieces—she wanted the traps to be used and demonstrated. Martha wondered if consumers were also buying the traps as novelties rather than as solutions to their mouse problems.

Martha knew that the investor group believed that Trap-Ease America had a "once-in-a-lifetime chance" with its innovative mousetrap. She sensed the group's impatience. She had budgeted approximately $250,000 in administrative and fixed costs for the first year (not including marketing costs). To keep the investors happy, the company needed to sell enough traps to cover those costs and make a reasonable profit.

In these first few months, Martha had learned that marketing a new product is not an easy task. Some customers were very demanding. For example, one national retailer had placed a large order with instructions that the order was to be delivered to the loading dock at one of its warehouses between 1:00 and 3:00 PM on a specified day. When the truck delivering the order had arrived late, the retailer had refused to accept the shipment. The retailer had told Martha it would be a year before she got another chance. Perhaps, Martha thought, she should send the retailer and other customers a copy of Emerson's famous quote.

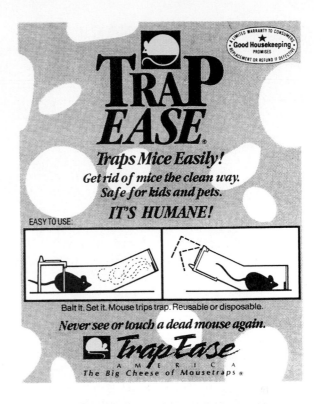

QUESTIONS

1. Martha and the Trap-Ease America investors feel they face a "once-in-a-lifetime" opportunity. What information do they need to evaluate this opportunity? How do you think the group would write its "mission statement"? How would *you* write it?

2. Has Martha identified the best target market for Trap-Ease? What other market segments might the firm target?

3. How has the company positioned the Trap-Ease relative to the chosen target market? Could it position the product in other ways?

4. Describe the current marketing mix for Trap-Ease. Do you see any problems with this mix?

5. Who is Trap-Ease America's competition?

6. How would you change Trap-Ease's marketing strategy? What kinds of control procedures would you establish for this strategy?

3

The Marketing Environment

In 1894, vegetarian Will Keith Kellogg of Battle Creek, Michigan, found a way to make nutritious wheat meal more appealing to patients in his brother's sanitarium. He invented a process to convert the unappetizing wheat meal into attractive, tasty little cereal flakes. The crunchy flakes quickly became popular. In 1906, W. K. founded the Kellogg Company to sell his cereal to the world at large, and the breakfast table would never again be the same. W. K. Kellogg's modest invention spawned the giant ready-to-eat cereal industry, in which half a dozen large competitors now battle for shares of $6 billion in yearly sales. Since the very beginning, the Kellogg Company has been atop the heap, leading the industry with innovative technology and marketing.

During the 1950s and 1960s, Kellogg and other cereal makers prospered. The post-World-War-II baby boom created lots of kids, and kids eat lots of cereal. As the baby boom generation passed through its childhood and teen years, cereal sales grew naturally with increases in the child population. Kellogg and its competitors focused heavily on the glut of young munchers. They offered presweetened cereals in fetching shapes and colors, pitched by memorable animated characters. Remember Tony the Tiger, Toucan Sam, and Snap, Crackle, and Pop?

But by 1980, the marketing environment had changed. The aging baby boomers, concerned about their spreading waistlines and declining fitness, launched a national obsession with clean living and good nutrition. They began giving up the cereals they'd loved as kids, and

industry sales growth flattened. After decades of riding natural market growth, Kellogg and its competitors now had to fight for profitable shares of a stagnant market. But through the good years, Kellogg had grown complacent and sluggish. The company stumbled briefly in the early 1980s and its market share dropped off. Some analysts claimed that Kellogg was a company "past its prime."

To counter slow cereal industry growth, most of Kellogg's competitors—General Mills, General Foods, Quaker Oats, Ralston-Purina—diversified broadly into faster-growing nonfood businesses. But Kellogg chose a different course. It implemented an aggressive marketing strategy to revive industry sales by persuading the nations eighty million baby boomers to eat cereal again.

Kellogg advertised heavily to reposition its old products and bring them more in line with changing adult life styles. New ad campaigns for the company's old brands stressed taste and nutrition. For example, a Kellogg's Corn Flakes ad shows adults discussing professional athletes who eat the cereal. In another spot, a young medical student tells his mom that Rice Krispies have more vitamins and minerals than her oatmeal. In a Frosted Flakes ad, consumers sitting at a breakfast table, their features obscured by shadows, confess that they still eat the Frosted Flakes they loved as kids. "That's okay," they're told, "Frosted Flakes have the taste adults have grown to love."

Beyond repositioning the old standards, Kellogg invested heavily in new brands aimed at adult taste buds and life styles. Crispix, Raisin Squares, the Nutri-Grain line, Mueslix, and many other innovative adult Kellogg brands sprouted on grocers' shelves. But the heart of Kellogg's push to capture the adult market was its growing line of high-fiber bran cereals—All-Bran, 40 Percent Bran Flakes, Bran Buds, Raisin Bran, Cracklin' Oat Bran, and Common Sense Oat Bran. Kellogg's advertising made some serious health pitches for these brands, tying them to high-fiber, low-fat diets and healthy living. One long-running ad campaign even linked Kellogg's All-Bran with reduced risks of cancer. The controversial campaign drew sharp criticism from competitors, strong praise from the National Cancer Institute, and sales from consumers. Kellogg continued the health claims controversy with the introduction of Heartwise, containing a cholesterol reducer. Kellogg did not make such strong claims, however, for all of its bran products. For example, one advertisement asked "Is your diet too fat for your own good?" and suggested that consumers eat Kellogg cereals to "get a taste for the healthy life." Another ad for Bran Flakes stated simply: "You take care of the outside; Kellogg's 40 Percent Bran Flakes will help you take care of the inside."

Kellogg's aggressive reaction to its changing marketing environment paid off handsomely. The company's high-powered marketing attack more than doubled the growth rate for the entire cereal industry. And while diversified competitors are now spending time and money fixing or unloading their nonfood businesses, Kellogg remains sharply focused on cereals. In only four years, Kellogg's overall market share grew from 35 percent to 42 percent, and the company's share of the fast-growing bran segment exceeds 50 percent. Four of the nation's five best-selling cereals are Kellogg brands, and Kellogg is once again one of America's most profitable companies. As Tony the Tiger would say, at Kellogg things are going G-r-r-reat![1]

CHAPTER OBJECTIVES

After reading this chapter, you should be able to:

1. Describe the environmental forces that affect the company's ability to serve its customers.
2. Explain how changes in the demographic and economic environments affect marketing decisions.
3. Identify the major trends in the firm's natural and technological environments.
4. Explain the key changes that occur in the political and cultural environments.

A company's **marketing environment** consists of the actors and forces outside marketing that affect marketing management's ability to develop and maintain successful transactions with its target customers. To be successful, a company must adapt its marketing mix to trends and developments in this environment.

The changing and uncertain marketing environment deeply affects the company. Instead of changing slowly and predictably, the environment can produce major surprises and shocks. How many managers at Gerber Foods foresaw the end of the baby boom? Which auto companies foresaw the huge impact that consumerism and environmentalism would have on their business decisions? Who in the American electronics industry foresaw the dominance of Japanese and other foreign competitors in world markets? The marketing environment offers both opportunities and threats, and the company must use its marketing research and marketing intelligence systems to watch the changing environment.

The marketing environment is made up of a *microenvironment* and a *macroenvironment*. The **microenvironment** consists of the forces close to the company that affect its ability to serve its customers—the company, marketing channel firms, customer markets, competitors, and publics. The **macroenvironment** consists of the larger societal forces that affect the whole microenvironment—demographic, economic, natural, technological, political, and cultural forces. We look first at the company's microenvironment and then at its macroenvironment.

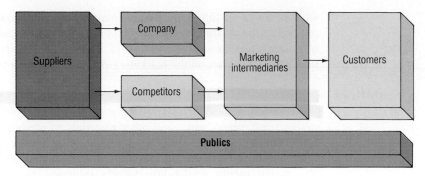

FIGURE 3-1
Major actors in the company's microenvironment

THE COMPANY'S MICROENVIRONMENT

The job of marketing management is to create attractive offers for target markets. However, marketing management's success is affected by the rest of the company, and by middlemen, competitors, and various publics. These actors in the company's microenvironment are shown in Figure 3-1. Marketing managers cannot simply focus on the target market's needs: They must also watch all actors in the company's microenvironment. We illustrate the role and impact of the company, suppliers, middlemen, customers, competitors, and publics by using as an example the Schwinn Bicycle Company, a major U.S. bicycle producer.

The Company   In making marketing plans, marketing management at Schwinn takes other company groups into account—groups such as top management, finance, research and development (R&D), purchasing, manufacturing, and accounting. All these interrelated groups form Schwinn's internal environment (see Figure 3-2).

Top management at Schwinn consists of the bicycle division's general manager, the executive committee, the chief executive officer, the chairman of the board, and the board of directors. These higher levels of management set the company's mission, objectives, broad strategies, and policies. Marketing managers must make decisions within the plans made by top management. And marketing plans must be approved by top management before they can be implemented.

Marketing managers must also work closely with other company departments. Finance is concerned with finding and using funds to carry out the marketing plan. R&D focuses on the problems of designing safe and attractive bicycles. Purchasing

FIGURE 3-2
Company's internal environment

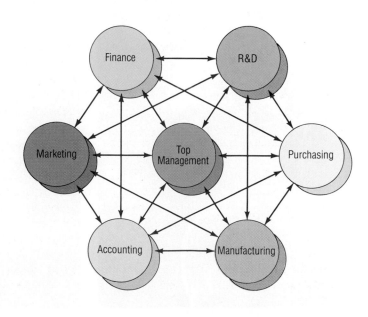

worries about getting supplies and materials, while manufacturing is responsible for producing the desired number of bicycles. Accounting measures revenues and costs to help marketing know how well it is achieving its objectives. All these departments thus have an impact on the marketing department's plan and actions.

Suppliers

Suppliers are firms and individuals that provide the resources needed by the company to produce its goods and services. For example, Schwinn must obtain steel, aluminum, rubber tires, gears, seats, and other materials to produce bicycles. It also must obtain labor, equipment, fuel, electricity, computers, and other factors of production.

Supplier developments can seriously affect marketing. Marketing managers must also watch supply availability. Supply shortages or delays, labor strikes, and other events can cost sales in the short run and damage customer goodwill in the long run. Marketing managers also monitor the price trends of their key inputs. Rising supply costs may force price increases that can harm the company's sales volume.

Marketing Intermediaries

Marketing intermediaries are firms that help the company to promote, sell, and distribute its goods to final buyers. They include *middlemen*, *physical distribution firms*, *marketing service agencies*, and *financial intermediaries*.

Middlemen

Middlemen are distribution channel firms that help the company find customers or make sales to them. These include wholesalers and retailers who buy and resell merchandise (they are often called *resellers*). Schwinn's primary method of marketing bicycles is to sell them to hundreds of independent dealers who resell them at a profit.

Why does Schwinn use middlemen? Middlemen perform important functions more cheaply than Schwinn can by itself. They stock bicycles where customers are located. They show and deliver bicycles when consumers want them. They advertise the bikes and negotiate terms of sale. Schwinn finds it better to work through independent middlemen than to own and operate its own massive system of outlets.

Middlemen perform important functions for Schwinn. They stock, display, promote, sell, service, and deliver Schwinn's bicycles.

Selecting and working with middlemen is not easy. No longer do manufacturers have many small, independent middlemen from which to choose. They now face large and growing middlemen organizations. More and more bicycles are being sold through large corporate chains (such as Sears and K mart) and large wholesaler, retailer, and franchised-sponsored voluntary chains. These groups often have enough power to dictate terms or even shut the manufacturer out of large markets. Manufacturers must work hard to get shelf space.

Physical Distribution Firms

Physical distribution firms help the company stock and move goods from their points of origin to their destinations. Warehouses are firms that store and protect goods before they move to the next destination. Transportation firms include railroads, trucking companies, airlines, barge companies, and others that specialize in moving goods from one location to another. A company must determine the best ways to store and ship goods, balancing such factors as cost, delivery, speed, and safety.

Marketing Services Agencies

Marketing services agencies are the marketing research firms, advertising agencies, media firms, and marketing consulting firms that help the company target and promote its products to the right markets. When the company decides to use one of these agencies, it must choose carefully because these firms vary in creativity, quality, service, and price. The company has to review the performance of these firms regularly and consider replacing those that no longer perform well.

Financial Intermediaries

Financial intermediaries include banks, credit companies, insurance companies, and other businesses that help finance transactions or insure against the risks associated with the buying and selling of goods. Most firms and customers depend on financial intermediaries to finance their transactions. The company's marketing performance can be seriously affected by rising credit costs, limited credit, or both. For this reason, the company has to develop strong relationships with important financial institutions.

Customers

The company must study its customer markets closely. The company can operate in five types of customer markets. These are shown in Figure 3-3 and defined below:

- *Consumer markets*: individuals and households that buy goods and services for personal consumption.
- *Industrial markets*: organizations that buy goods and services for further processing or for use in their production process.
- *Reseller markets*: organizations that buy goods and services in order to resell them at a profit.
- *Government markets*: government agencies that buy goods and services in order to produce public services or transfer these goods and services to others who need them.
- *International markets*: foreign buyers, including consumers, producers, resellers, and governments.

FIGURE 3-3
Types of customer markets

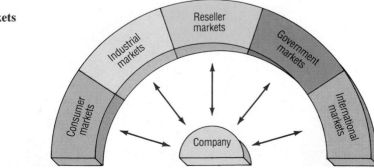

Schwinn sells bicycles in all these markets. It sells some bicycles directly to consumers through factory outlets. It sells bicycles to producers who use them to deliver goods or to get from one place to another in their large plant complexes. It sells bicycles to wholesalers and retailers who resell them to consumer and producer markets. It sells bicycles to government agencies. And it sells bicycles to foreign consumers, producers, resellers, and governments. Each market type has special characteristics that call for careful study by the seller.

Competitors

Every company faces a wide range of competitors. The marketing concept states that to be successful, a company must satisfy the needs and wants of consumers better than its competitors do. Thus, marketers must do more than simply adapt to the needs of target consumers. They must also adapt to the strategies of competitors who are serving the same target consumers. Companies must gain strategic advantage by strongly positioning their offerings against competitors' offerings in the minds of consumers.

No single competitive marketing strategy is best for all companies. Each firm should consider its own size and industry position compared to those of its competitors. Large firms with dominant positions in an industry can use certain strategies that smaller firms cannot afford. But being large is not enough. There are winning strategies for large firms, but there are also losing strategies. And small firms can find strategies that give them better rates of return than large firms. Both large and small firms must find marketing strategies that best position them against competitors in their markets.

Publics

The company's marketing environment also includes various publics. A **public** is any group that has an actual or potential interest in or impact on an organization's ability to achieve its objectives. Every company is surrounded by seven types of publics (see Figure 3-4):

- *Financial publics*: Financial publics influence the company's ability to obtain funds. Banks, investment houses, and stockholders are the major financial publics. Schwinn seeks the goodwill of these groups by issuing annual reports and showing the financial community that its house is in order.
- *Media publics*: Media publics are those that carry news, features, and editorial opinion. They include newspapers, magazines, and radio and television stations. Schwinn is interested in getting more and better media coverage.
- *Government publics*: Management must take government developments into account. Schwinn's marketers consult the company's lawyers on issues of product safety, truth-in-advertising, dealers' rights, and other matters. Schwinn may consider joining with other bicycle manufacturers to lobby for better laws.
- *Citizen-action publics*: A company's marketing decisions may be questioned by consumer organizations, environmental groups, minority groups, and others. For example, parent groups are lobbying for greater safety in bicycles, which are the nation's number-one hazardous product. Schwinn has the opportunity to be a leader in product-safety design. Schwinn's public relations department can help it to stay in touch with consumer groups.
- *Local publics*: Every company has local publics such as neighborhood residents and community organizations. Large companies usually appoint a community-relations officer to deal with the community, attend meetings, answer questions, and contribute to worthwhile causes.

FIGURE 3-4
Types of publics

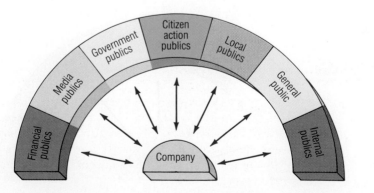

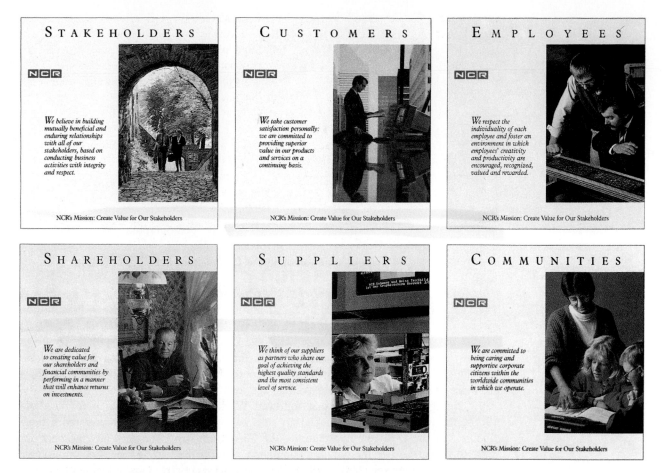

In these corporate image ads, NCR communicates with its customer, employee, shareholder, supplier, and community publics (which it calls stakeholders).

- *General publics*: A company needs to be concerned about the general public's attitude toward its products and activities. The public's image of the company affects its buying. To build a strong "corporate citizen" image, Schwinn will lend its officers to community fund drives, make large contributions to charity, and set up systems for consumer-complaint handling.
- *Internal publics*: A company's internal publics include blue-collar workers, white-collar workers, volunteers, managers, and the board of directors. Large companies use newsletters and other means to inform and motivate their internal publics. When employees feel good about their company, this positive attitude spills over to external publics.

A company can prepare marketing plans for its major publics as well as its customer markets. Suppose the company wants a specific response from a particular public, such as goodwill, favorable word of mouth, or donations of time or money. The company would have to design an offer to this public attractive enough to produce the desired response.

THE COMPANY'S MACROENVIRONMENT

The company and its suppliers, marketing intermediaries, customers, competitors, and publics all operate in a larger macroenvironment of forces that shape opportunities and pose threats to the company. The company must carefully watch and respond to these forces. The macroenvironment consists of the six major forces shown in Figure 3-5. The remaining sections of this chapter examine these forces and show how they affect marketing plans.

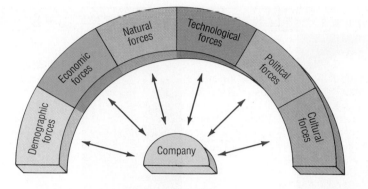

FIGURE 3-5
Major forces in the company's macroenvironment

Demographic Environment

Demography is the study of human populations in terms of size, density, location, age, sex, race, occupation, and other statistics. The demographic environment is of major interest to marketers because it involves people, and people make up markets. The most important demographic trends in the United States are described below.

Changing Age Structure of the U.S. Population

The U.S. population stood at almost 250 million in 1990 and may reach 300 million by the year 2020. The most important demographic trend in the United States is the changing *age structure* of the population. The U.S. population is getting *older* for two reasons. First, there is a slowdown in the birthrate, so there are fewer young people to pull the population's average age down. Second, life expectancy is increasing, so there are more older people to pull the average age up.

During the **baby boom** that followed World War II and lasted until the early 1960s, the annual birthrate reached an all-time high. The baby boom created a huge "bulge" in the U.S. age distribution—the 75 million baby boomers now account for more than one-third of the nation's population. And as the baby-boom generation ages, the nation's average age climbs with it. Because of its sheer size, most major demographic and socioeconomic changes occurring during the next half decade will be tied to the baby-boom generation (see Marketing Highlight 3–1).

The baby boom was followed by a "birth dearth," and by the mid-1970s the birthrate had fallen sharply. This decrease was caused by smaller family sizes resulting from Americans' desire to improve their personal living standards, from the increasing desire of women to work outside the home, and from improved birth control. Although family sizes are expected to remain smaller, the birthrate is climbing again as the baby-boom generation moves through the childbearing years and creates a second but smaller baby boom (the "echo boom"). The birth rate will then decline in the 1990s.[2]

The second factor in the general aging of the population is increased life expectancy. Current average life expectancy is 76 years—a 27-year increase since 1900. Increasing life expectancy and the declining birthrate are producing an aging population. The U.S. median age is now 32 and is expected to reach 36 by the year 2000 and the mid-40s by 2050.[3]

The changing age structure of the population will result in different growth rates for various age groups during the decade, and these differences will strongly affect marketers' targeting strategies. Growth trends for six age groups are summarized below:[4]

- *Children.* The number of preschoolers has increased to more than 19 million in 1990, creating an under-age-five market estimated at $6 billion per year. This market will taper off only slightly through the 1990s as the baby boomers move out of childbearing years. Markets for children's toys and games, clothes, furniture, and food are enjoying a short "boom" after years of "bust." For example, Sony and other electronics firms are now offering products designed for children. And many retailers are opening separate children's clothing chains, such as GapKids, Kids 'R' Us, and Esprit Kids. Such markets will continue to grow through the coming decade but will again decrease as the century closes.[5]

- *Youths.* The number of 10- to 19-year-olds will drop through the early 1990s, then begin to increase again at the end of the century. This age group consists of almost 30 million

THE BABY BOOMERS

The postwar baby boom, which began in 1946 and ran through the early 1960s, produced 75 million babies. Since then, the baby boomers have become one of the biggest forces shaping the marketing environment. The boomers have presented a moving target, creating new markets as they grew through infancy, preadolescent, teen-age, young-adulthood, and now middle-age years. They created markets for baby products and toys in the 1950s; jeans, records, and cosmetics in the 1960s; fun and informal fashions in the 1970s; and fitness, new homes, and childcare in the 1980s.

Today, the baby boomers are starting to gray at the temples and spread at the waist. And they are reaching their peak earning and spending years—the boomers account for a third of the population but make up 40 percent of the work force and earn more than half of all personal income. They are moving to the suburbs, settling into home-ownership, starting to raise families, and maturing into the most affluent generation in history. Thus, they constitute a lucrative market for housing, furniture and appliances, low-cal foods and beverages, physical fitness products, high-priced cars, convenience products, and financial services.

Baby boomers cut across all walks of life. But marketers have typically paid the most attention to the small upper crust of the boomer generation—its more educated, mobile, and wealthy segments. These segments have gone by many names. In the early to mid-1980s, they were called "yuppies" (young urban professionals), "yumpies" (young upwardly mobile professionals), "bumpies" (black upwardly mobile professionals), and "yummies" (young upwardly mobile mommies). These groups were replaced by the "DINKs"—dual-income, no-kids couples. Typically, DINKs worked long hours, made hefty incomes, spent money to save time, and bought lavishly:

> The members of this . . . species can best be spotted after 9 P.M. in gourmet groceries, their Burberry-clothed arms reaching for arugula or a Le Menu frozen flounder dinner. In the parking lot, they slide into their BMWs and lift cellular phones to their ears before zooming off to their architect-designed homes in the exurbs. . . . Then they consult the phone-answering machine, pop dinner into the microwave and finally sink into their Italian leather sofa to watch a videocassette of, say, last week's *L.A. Law* or *Cheers* on their high-definition, large-screen stereo television.

As we move into the 1990s, however, the yuppies and DINKs are giving way to a new breed. The boomers are evolving from the "youthquake generation" to the "backache generation"—they're slowing up, having children, and settling down. They are approaching life with a new stability and reasonableness in the way they live, think, eat, and spend. They have shifted their focus from the outside world to the inside world. Staying home with the family and being "couch potatoes" is becoming their favorite way to spend an evening. Community and family values have become more important. The upscale boomers still exert their affluence, but they indulge themselves in more subtle and sensible ways. They spend heavily on convenience and high quality products, but they have less of a taste for lavish or conspicuous buying.

Some marketers think that upscale boomers are tiring of all the attention or that focusing on affluent boomer groups is diverting companies from other profitable segments. Some are using subtler approaches that avoid stereotyping these consumers or tagging them as yuppies, or DINKs, or something else. But whatever you call them, you can't ignore them. The baby boomers have been the most potent market force for the past 40 years, and they will continue to be for the next 40.

Sources: See Elizabeth Ehrlich, "Boomers at Fortysomething," *Business Week*, September 25, 1989, pp. 142–43; Anne B. Fisher, "What Consumers Want in the 1990s," *Fortune*, January 29, 1990, pp. 108–12; and Jeremy Schlosberg, "Sitting Pretty," *American Demographics*, May 1988, pp. 24–27. The quoted material is from Martha Smilgis, "Here Come the DINKs," *Time*, April 20, 1987, p. 75.

The baby boomers: A prime target for marketers.

consumers who buy or strongly influence $250 billion purchases of products ranging from health and beauty aids, clothing, and food to stereo equipment, autos, family travel, entertainment, and college educations.[6]

- *Young adults*. This group will decline during the 1990s as the ''birth dearth'' generation moves in. Marketers who sell to the 20 to 34 age group—furniture makers, life insurance companies, sports equipment manufacturers—can no longer rely on increasing market size for increases in sales. They will have to work for bigger shares of smaller markets.
- *Early middle age*. The baby-boom generation will continue to move into the 35 to 49 age group, creating huge increases. For example, the number of 40- to 44-year-olds will increase by 50 percent. This group is a major market for larger homes, new automobiles, clothing, entertainment, and investments.
- *Late middle age*. The 50 to 64 age group will continue to shrink until the end of the century. Then it will begin to increase as the baby boomers move in. This group is a major market for eating out, travel, clothing, recreation, and financial services.
- *Retirees*. In 1990, this group included almost 13 percent of all Americans. By 2030, it will make up almost 21 percent of the population—there will be about as many people 65 and older as they are people 18 and younger. This group has a demand for retirement communities, quieter forms of recreation, single-portion food packaging, life-care and health-care services, and leisure travel.[7]

Thus the changing age structure of the U.S. population will strongly affect future marketing decisions. In particular, the baby boom generation will continue to be a prime target for marketers.

The Changing American Family

The American ideal of the two children, two car suburban family has lately been losing some of its luster. Despite the recent ''echo boom,'' the number of married couples with children will continue to decline through the 1990s. There are many forces at work.[8] People are marrying later and having fewer children. Although 96 percent of all Americans will marry, the average age of couples marrying for the first time has been rising. Couples with no children under 18 make up almost half of all families. And of those families that have children, the average number of children is less than 2, down from 3.5 in 1955.

Also, the number of working mothers has increased. The percentage of mothers of children younger than 18 who hold some kind of job has increased since 1960, from about 25 percent to more than 64 percent. Their incomes contribute 40 percent of their household incomes and influence the purchase of higher-quality goods and services. Marketers of tires, automobiles, insurance, travel, and financial services are increasingly directing their advertising to working women. All this activity is accompanied by a shift in the traditional roles and values of husbands and wives, with the husband assuming more domestic functions such as shopping and child care. As a result, husbands are becoming more of a target market for food and household appliance marketers.

Finally, the number of non-family households is increasing. Many young adults leave home and move into apartments. Other adults choose to remain single. Still others are divorced or widowed people living alone. By the year 2000, 47 percent of all households will be non-family or single-parent households—the fastest-growing categories of households. These groups have their own special needs. For example, they need smaller apartments; inexpensive and smaller appliances, furniture, and furnishings; and food that is packaged in smaller sizes.

Geographic Shifts in Population

Americans are a mobile people, with about 18 percent, or 43 million people, moving each year. Among the major trends are the following:[9]

- *Movement to the Sunbelt states*. During the 1980s, the populations in the West and South grew. On the other hand, many of the Midwest and Northeast states lost population. These shifts will continue through the 1990s (see Figure 3-6). These population shifts interest marketers because people in different regions buy differently. For example, the movement to the Sunbelt states will lessen the demand for warm clothing and home heating equipment and increase the demand for air conditioning.

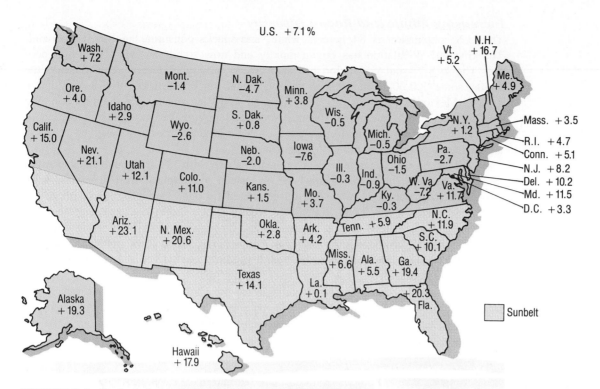

FIGURE 3-6 Projected population growth rates: 1990–2000 *Source*: U.S. Department of Commerce, Bureau of Census.

- *Movement from rural to urban areas.* Except for a short period during the early 1970s, Americans have been moving from rural to metropolitan areas for more than a century. The metropolitan areas show a faster pace of living, more commuting, higher incomes, and greater variety of goods and services than can be found in the small towns and rural areas that dot America. The largest cities, such as New York, Chicago, and San Francisco, account for most of the sales of expensive furs, perfumes, luggage, and works of art. These cities also support the opera, ballet, and other forms of "high culture."

- *Movement from the city to the suburbs.* In the 1950s, Americans made a massive exit from the cities to the suburbs. Big cities became surrounded by even bigger suburbs. The U.S. Census Bureau calls sprawling urban areas *MSAs* (Metropolitan Statistical Areas).[10] Companies use MSAs in researching the best geographical segments for their products and in deciding where to buy advertising time. MSA research shows, for example, that people in Seattle buy more toothbrushes per capita than any other U.S. city, people in Salt Lake City eat more candy bars, folks from New Orleans use more ketchup, and those in Miami drink more prune juice.[11]

Americans living in the suburbs engage in more casual, outdoor living, greater neighbor interaction, higher incomes, and younger families. Suburbanites buy station wagons, home workshop equipment, garden furniture, lawn and gardening tools, and outdoor cooking equipment.

A Better-Educated and More White-Collar Population

The population is becoming better educated. The percentage of Americans completing high school rose from only 34 percent in 1950 to 74 percent by 1985. And by 1990 more than 20 percent of Americans older than 24 had completed college. The rising number of educated people will increase the demand for quality products, books, magazines, and travel. It suggests a decline in television viewing, because college-educated consumers watch less TV than the population at large.

The workforce is also becoming more white-collar. Between 1950 and 1985, the proportion of white-collar workers rose from 41 to 54 percent, that of blue-collar workers declined from 47 to 33 percent, and that of service workers increased from 12 to 14 percent. Through 1995, most growth will come in the following occupational categories: computers, engineering, science, medicine, social service, buying, selling, secretarial, construction, refrigeration, health service, personal service, and protection.[12]

Increasing Ethnic and Racial Diversity

The U.S. population is 84 percent white, and blacks constitute another 12 percent. The Hispanic population has grown rapidly and now stands at over 21 million people. The U.S. Asian population has also grown rapidly in recent years. During the 1980s, some 500,000 immigrants a year accounted for one-fifth of all U.S. population growth. Mexicans, Filipinos, Chinese, Koreans, and Vietnamese were the most common new arrivals. Each group has specific wants and buying habits. Many marketers of food, clothing, furniture, and other products have targeted specially designed products and promotions to one or more of these groups.[13]

All of these demographic developments, along with life-style and other changes in the population, have transformed the American marketplace from a *mass market* into more fragmented *micromarkets* differentiated by age, sex, geography, life style, ethnic background, education, and other factors. Each group has strong preferences and consumer characteristics and can be reached through more narrowly focused media. Many companies are abandoning "shotgun" approaches aimed at the mythical "average American consumer" and are instead designing products and marketing programs targeting specific micromarkets.[14]

Demographic trends are highly reliable for the short and intermediate run. There is little excuse for a company's being suddenly surprised by a demographic development. Companies can easily list the major demographic trends and then spell out what the trends mean for them.

Economic Environment

The **economic environment** consists of factors that affect consumer purchasing power and spending patterns. Markets require buying power as well as people. Total buying power depends on current income, prices, savings, and credit. Marketers should be aware of major trends in income and of changing consumer spending patterns.

Changes in Income

Real income per capita declined during the past decade, as inflation, high unemployment, and increased taxes reduced the amount of money people had to spend. As a result, many Americans turned to more cautious buying. For example, they bought more store brands and fewer national brands to save money. Many companies introduced economy versions of their products and turned to price appeals in their advertising. Some consumers postponed purchases of durable goods, while others purchased them out of fear that prices would be 10 percent higher the next year. Many families began to believe that a large home, two cars, foreign travel, and private higher education were beyond their reach.

In the mid-1980s, however, economic conditions improved. And current projections suggest that real income will rise modestly through the mid-1990s. This will largely result from rising income in certain important segments.[15] The baby-boom generation will be moving into its prime wage-earning years, and the number of small families headed by dual-career couples will increase greatly. These more affluent groups will demand higher quality and better service—and they will be willing and able to pay for it. They will spend more on time-saving products and services, travel and entertainment, physical fitness products, cultural activities, and continuing education.

Marketers should pay attention to *income distribution* as well as average income. Income distribution in the United States is still very skewed. At the top are *upper-class* consumers, whose spending patterns are not affected by current economic events and who are a major market for luxury goods. There is a comfortable *middle class* that is somewhat careful about its spending but can still afford the good life some of the time. The *working class* must stick close to the basics of food, clothing, and shelter and must try hard to save. Finally, the *underclass* (persons on welfare and many retirees) must count their pennies when making even the most basic purchases.

Changing Consumer Spending Patterns

Table 3-1 shows the proportion of total expenditures that households at different income levels spend on major categories of goods and services. Food, housing, and transportation

TABLE 3-1
Distribution of Consumer Spending for Different Income Levels

	INCOME LEVEL		
EXPENDITURE	$10,000–15,000	$20,000–30,000	Over 40,000
Food	16.1%	15.2%	12.1%
Housing	18.0	17.2	17.9
Utilities	8.8	6.7	4.8
Clothing	5.4	5.5	6.0
Transportation	19.5	20.9	19.7
Health Care	6.8	4.9	3.4
Housekeeping Supplies	1.6	1.5	1.1
Household furnishings	3.5	3.8	5.1
Entertainment	4.0	4.6	5.1
Personal Care	1.5	1.3	1.2
Reading	.6	.6	.6
Education	1.2	.8	1.8
Tobacco	1.5	1.0	.5
Alcohol	1.2	1.2	1.1
Contributions	2.8	3.5	4.4
Insurance and Pensions	5.2	9.1	13.0
Other	2.3	2.2	2.2

Source: *Consumer Expenditure Survey: Integrated Survey Data, 1984–86*, U.S. Department of Labor, Bureau of Labor Statistics, Bulletin 2333, August 1989, pp. 164–66.

use up most household income. However, consumers at different income levels have different spending patterns. Some of these differences were noted more than a century ago by Ernst Engel, who studied how people shifted their spending as their incomes rose. He found that as family income rises, the percentage spent on food declines, the percentage spent on housing remains constant (except for such utilities as gas, electricity, and public services, which decrease), and both the percentage spent on other categories and that devoted to savings increase. "Engel's laws" have generally been supported by later studies.

Changes in such major economic variables as income, cost of living, interest rates, and savings and borrowing patterns have a large impact on the marketplace. Companies watch these variables using economic forecasting. Businesses do not have to be wiped out by an economic downturn or caught short in a boom. With adequate warning, they can take advantage of changes in the economic environment.

Natural Environment

The **natural environment** involves natural resources that are needed as inputs by marketers or which are affected by marketing activities. During the 1960s, public concern about damage to the natural environment began to grow. Popular books raised concerns about shortages of natural resources and about the damage to water, earth, and air caused by the industrial activities of modern nations. Watchdog groups such as the Sierra Club and Friends of the Earth sprang up, and legislators proposed measures to protect the environment.

These concerns have continued to grow during the past two decades. Some trend analysts believe that the 1990s will be the "Earth Decade" in which protection of the natural environment will be the major worldwide issue facing business and the public. In many world cities, air and water pollution have reached dangerous levels. Concern continues to mount about the depletion of the earth's ozone layer and the resultant "greenhouse effect," a dangerous warming of the earth. And many American's fear that we will soon be buried in our own trash. Marketers should be aware of four trends in the natural environment.

Shortages of Raw Materials

Air and water may seem to be infinite resources, but some groups see a long-run danger. Environmental groups have lobbied for a ban on certain propellants used in aerosol cans because of their potential damage to the ozone layer. Water shortage is already a big problem in some parts of the United States and the world.

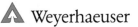
The natural environment: Weyerhaeuser recognizes that renewable resources have to be used wisely.

Renewable resources, such as forests and food, have to be used wisely. Companies in the forestry business are required to reforest timberlands in order to protect the soil and to ensure enough wood supplies to meet future demand. Food supply can be a major problem because the amount of farmable land is limited and because more and more of it is being developed for urban areas.

Nonrenewable resources, such as oil, coal, and various minerals, pose a serious problem. Firms making products that require these increasingly scarce minerals face large cost increases even if the materials do remain available; these firms may not find it easy to pass these costs on to the consumer. However, firms engaged in research and development and in exploration can help by developing new sources and materials.

Increased Cost of Energy

One nonrenewable resource, oil, has created the most serious problem for future economic growth. The major industrial economies of the world depend heavily on oil, and until economical energy substitutes can be developed, oil will continue to dominate the world political and economic picture. Large increases in the price of oil during the 1970s (from $2 per barrel in 1970 to $34.00 per barrel in 1982) created a frantic search for alternative forms of energy. Although oil prices have now dropped to less than $20 per barrel, coal is again popular, and many companies are searching for practical ways to harness solar, nuclear, wind, and other forms of energy. In fact, hundreds of firms are already offering products that use solar energy for heating homes and other uses.

Increased Levels of Pollution

Industry will almost always damage the quality of the natural environment. Consider the disposal of chemical and nuclear wastes, the dangerous mercury levels in the ocean, the quantity of DDT and other chemical pollutants in the soil and food supply, and the littering of the environment with nonbiodegradable bottles, plastics, and other packaging materials.

On the other hand, public concern creates a marketing opportunity for alert companies. It creates a large market for pollution control solutions such as scrubbers, recycling centers, and landfill systems. It leads to a search for new ways to produce and package goods that do not cause environmental damage. Concern for the natural environment has recently spawned the so-called "Green movement." Increasing numbers of consumers have begun doing more business with ecologically responsible companies and avoiding those whose actions harm the environment. They buy "environmentally friendly" products, even if these products cost more. Many companies are responding to such consumer demands with ecologically safer products, recyclable or biodegradable packaging, better pollution controls, and more energy-efficient operations.[16]

Government Intervention in Natural Resource Management

Various government agencies play an active role in environmental protection. For example, the Environmental Protection Agency (EPA) was created in 1970 to deal with pollution. The EPA sets and enforces pollution standards and conducts research on the causes and effects of pollution.

Marketing management must pay attention to the natural environment. In the future, business can expect strong controls from government and pressure groups. Instead of opposing regulation, marketers should help develop solutions to the material and energy problems facing the nation.

Technological Environment

Perhaps the most dramatic force now shaping our destiny is technology. The **technological environment** consists of forces which affect new technology, creating new product and market opportunities. Technology has released such wonders as penicillin, organ transplants, and supercomputers. It has also released such horrors as the hydrogen bomb, nerve gas, and the submachine gun. It has released such mixed blessings as the automobile, television, and credit cards. Our attitude toward technology depends on whether we are more impressed with its wonders or its blunders.

Every new technology replaces an older technology. Transistors hurt the vacuum-tube industry, xerography hurt the carbon-paper business, the auto hurt the railroads, and television hurt the movies. When old industries fought or ignored new technologies, their businesses declined.

New technologies create new markets and opportunities. The marketer should watch the following trends in technology.

Faster Pace of Technological Change

Many of today's common products were not available even a hundred years ago. Abraham Lincoln did not know about automobiles, airplanes, phonographs, radios, or the electric light. Woodrow Wilson did not know about television, aerosol cans, home freezers, automatic dishwashers, room air conditioners, antibiotics, or electronic computers. Franklin Delano Roosevelt did not know about xerography, synthetic detergents, tape recorders, birth control pills, or earth satellites. And John F. Kennedy did not know about personal computers, compact disk players, digital watches, VCRs, or facsimile machines. Companies that do not keep up with technological change will soon find their products out-of-date. And they will miss new product and market opportunities.

Unlimited Opportunities

Scientists today are working on a wide range of new technologies that will revolutionize our products and production processes. The most exciting work is being done in biotechnol-

Technology brings exciting new products and services.

ogy, miniature electronics, robotics, and materials science.[17] Scientists today are working on the following promising new products and services:

Practical solar energy	Commercial space shuttle	Effective superconductors
Cancer cures	Tiny but powerful supercomputers	Electric cars
Chemical control of mental health	Household robots that do cooking and cleaning	Electronic anesthetic for pain killing
Desalinization of seawater	Nonfattening, tasty, nutritious foods	Voice and gesture-controlled computers

Scientists also speculate on fantasy products, such as small flying cars, three-dimensional televisions, space colonies, and human clones. The challenge in each case is not only technical but commercial—to make *practical*, *affordable* versions of these products.

High R&D Budget

The United States leads the world in research and development spending. In 1987, R&D expenditures exceeded $123 billion and have been increasing rapidly in recent years. The federal government supplied almost half of total R&D funds. Government research can be a rich source of new product and service ideas (see Marketing Highlight 3–2).

Some companies also spend heavily on R&D. For example, General Motors spends a whopping $4.8 billion a year; IBM spends $4.4 billion; Ford spends $2.9 billion; and AT&T spends about $2.6 billion.[18] Today's research is usually carried out by research

NASA: AN IMPORTANT SOURCE OF TECHNOLOGY FOR BUSINESS

Since 1958, the National Aeronautics and Space Administration (NASA) has sponsored billions of dollars' worth of aerospace research that has brought us thousands of new products. In 1962, NASA set up a program to help pass its aerospace technology along to other state and federal government agencies, public institutions, and private industry. Nine NASA applications centers across the country provide information about existing NASA technology and help in applying it.

NASA-backed aerospace research has had a great impact on industrial and consumer products. For example, NASA's need for small space systems resulted in startling advances in microcircuitry, which in turn revolutionized consumer and industrial electronics with new products ranging from home computers and video games to computerized appliances and medical systems. NASA was the first to develop communications satellites, which now carry over two-thirds of all overseas communications traffic. Here are just a few of countless other applications.

- NASA's need for lightweight and very thin reflective materials led to research that changed the previously small-scale plastics metalization business into a flourishing industry. Using such technology, the Metalized Products Division of King-Seeley Thermos Company now makes a large line of consumer and industrial products ranging from "insulated outdoor garments to packaging materials for frozen foods, from wall coverings to aircraft covers, from bedwarmers to window shades, labels to candy wrappings, reflective blankets to photographic reflectors."

- NASA's efforts to develop tasty, nutritional, lightweight, compactly packaged, nonperishable food for astronauts in outer space have found many applications in the food industry. Many commercial food firms are now producing astronaut-type meals for public distribution—freeze-dried foods and "retort-pouch" meals that can be used for a number of purposes.

- NASA's need for a superstrong safety net to protect people working high in the air on space shuttles led to a new fiber. A relatively small net made of this fiber's twine can support the average-size automobile. The twine is now used to make fishing nets more than a mile long and covering more than 86 acres. The twine is thinner and denser than nylon cord, so the new nets offer less water resistance, sink faster, go deeper, and offer 30 percent productivity gains.

- A portable X-ray machine developed by NASA uses less than 1 percent of the radiation required by conventional X-ray devices. About the size of a thermos, the unit gives instant images and is ideal for use in emergency field situations such as on-the-spot scanning for bone injuries to athletes. It can also be used for instant detection of product flaws or for security uses such as examining parcels in mailrooms and business entrances.

- Special high-intensity lights developed by NASA to simulate the effect of sunlight on spacecraft resulted in several types of flashlights for professional and home use. One such hand-held light, which operates on a 12-volt auto or boat battery, is 50 times brighter than a car's high-beam headlights and projects a beam of light more than a mile. As a signal, it can be seen for over 30 miles.

- Bioengineering and physiological research to design cooling systems for astronaut space clothing has led to numerous commercial and consumer products—cooler athletic clothing, lightweight and heat-resistant clothing for firefighters, survival gear for hikers and campers, and dozens of others.

- While searching for a new material to be used in infrared tracking of heat-seeking missiles, Ceradyne developed a substance called translucent polycrystalline alumina (TPA). Ceradyne now uses TPA to make Transcend ceramic orthodontic braces, which are extremely strong yet virtually invisible during normal social interactions.

- Technology developed for the environmental control systems on the Apollo lunar landing spacecraft is now being used to reduce energy consumption in homes and commercial buildings. A company called Guaranteed Watt Savers now uses the technology in aluminized heat shields that keep heat, cold, and water vapor out or in as necessary. GWS calls its system "Smart House."

Source: Based on information found in *Spinoff* (Washington, DC: U.S. Government Printing Office), various issues between 1977 and 1989.

teams rather than by lone inventors like Thomas Edison, Samuel Morse, or Alexander Graham Bell. Managing company scientists is a major challenge. They often resent too much cost control. They are often more interested in solving scientific problems than in creating marketable products. Companies are adding marketing people to R&D research teams to try to obtain a stronger marketing orientation.

Concentration on Minor Improvements

As a result of the high cost of developing and introducing new technologies and products, many companies are making minor product improvements instead of gambling on major innovations. Even basic research companies like Du Pont, Bell Laboratories, and Pfizer are being cautious. Most companies are content to put their money into copying competitors' products, making minor feature and style improvements, or offering simple extensions of current brands. Much research is thus defensive rather than offensive.

As products become more complex, the public needs to know that they are safe. Thus government agencies investigate and ban potentially unsafe products. The Food and Drug Administration has set up complex regulations for testing new drugs. The Consumer Product Safety Commission sets safety standards for consumer products and penalizes companies that fail to meet them. Such regulations have resulted in much higher research costs and in longer times between new product ideas and their introductions. Marketers should be aware of these regulations when seeking and developing new products.

Technological change faces opposition from those who see it as threatening nature, privacy, simplicity, and even the human race. Various groups have opposed the construction of nuclear plants, high-rise buildings, and recreational facilities in national parks.

Marketers need to understand the changing technological environment and the varying ways new technologies can serve human needs. They need to work closely with R&D people to encourage more market-oriented research. And they must be alert to the possible negative aspects of any innovation that might harm users or arouse opposition.

Political Environment

Marketing decisions are strongly affected by developments in the political environment. The **political environment** consists of laws, government agencies, and pressure groups that influence and limit various organizations and individuals in a given society.

Legislation Regulating Business

Legislation affecting business has increased steadily over the years. This legislation has been enacted for many reasons. The first is to *protect companies* from each other. Business executives all praise competition but try to neutralize it when it threatens them:

> Until recently, antitrust worries kept IBM from playing too rough in the computer industry. Through the sixties and seventies the company had fought off antitrust suits and federal attempts to break it up. IBM took it easy on competitors by selling a product for four or five years and holding prices stable. This let competitors survive profitably against the industry giant. "As long as they came out with products fairly soon after IBM did, they could look forward to a few years of easy money." But in the late seventies, a more favorable regulatory climate let IBM flex its marketing muscle. IBM flooded the market with new products and made deep price cuts in all major market segments. The result was devastating to many of IBM's big, traditional rivals. Fearing total domination by IBM, competitors screamed loudly. Charging IBM with harmful competitive practices, they filed antitrust suits and urged federal regulators to step in and restore industry competitive balance.[19]

So laws are passed to define and prevent unfair competition. These laws are enforced by the Federal Trade Commission and the Antitrust Division of the U.S. Attorney General's office.

The second purpose of government regulation is to *protect consumers* from unfair business practices. Some firms, if left alone, would make poor products, tell lies in their advertising, and deceive consumers through their packaging and pricing. Unfair consumer practices have been defined and are enforced by various agencies. Many managers see purple with the passing of each new consumer law. Others welcome consumer protection and look for the opportunities it presents.

The third purpose of government regulation is to *protect the interests of society* against unrestrained business behavior. Profitable business activity does not always create a better quality of life. Regulation arises to make certain that firms take responsibility for the social costs of their production or products.

New laws and their enforcement will continue or increase. Business executives must watch these developments when planning their products and marketing programs. Marketers need to know about the major laws protecting competition, consumers, and society. The main federal laws are listed in Table 3-2. Marketers should also know the state and local laws that affect their local marketing activity.[20]

TABLE 3-2
Milestone U.S.
Legislation Affecting
Marketing

Sherman Antitrust Act (1890)
Prohibits (a) "monopolies or attempts to monopolize" and (b) "contracts, combinations, or conspiracies in restraint of trade" in interstate and foreign commerce.

Federal Food and Drug Act (1906)
Forbids the manufacture, sale, or transport of adulterated or fraudulently labeled foods and drugs in interstate commerce. Supplanted by the Food, Drug, and Cosmetic Act, 1938; amended by Food Additives Amendment in 1958 and the Kefauver-Harris Amendment in 1962. The 1962 amendment deals with pretesting of drugs for safety and effectiveness and labeling of drugs by generic name.

Meat Inspection Act (1906)
Provides for the enforcement of sanitary regulations in meat-packing establishments and for federal inspection of all companies selling meats in interstate commerce.

Federal Trade Commission Act (1914)
Establishes the commission, a body of specialists with broad powers to investigate and to issue cease-and-desist orders to enforce Section 5, which declares that "unfair methods of competition in commerce are unlawful."

Clayton Act (1914)
Supplements the Sherman Act by prohibiting certain specific practices (certain types of price discrimination, tying clauses and exclusive dealing, intercorporate stockholdings, and interlocking directorates) "where the effect . . . may be to substantially lessen competition or tend to create a monopoly in any line of commerce." Provides that violating corporate officials can be held individually responsible; exempts labor and agricultural organizations from its provisions.

Robinson-Patman Act (1936)
Amends the Clayton Act. Adds the phrase "to injure, destroy, or prevent competition." Defines price discrimination as unlawful (subject to certain defenses) and provides the FTC with the right to establish limits on quantity discounts, to forbid brokerage allowances except to independent brokers, and to prohibit promotional allowances or the furnishing of services or facilities except where made available to all "on proportionately equal terms."

Miller-Tydings Act (1937)
Amends the Sherman Act to exempt interstate fair-trade (price fixing) agreements from antitrust prosecution. (The McGuire Act, 1952, reinstates the legality of the nonsigner clause.)

Wheeler-Lea Act (1938)
Prohibits unfair and deceptive acts and practices regardless of whether competition is injured; places advertising of foods and drugs under FTC jurisdiction.

Lanham Trademark Act (1946)
Requires that trademarks must be distinctive and makes it illegal to make any false representation of goods or services entering interstate commerce.

Antimerger Act (1950)
Amends Section 7 of the Clayton Act by broadening the power to prevent intercorporate acquisitions where the acquisition may have a substantially adverse effect on competition.

Automobile Information Disclosure Act (1958)
Prohibits car dealers from inflating the factory price of new cars.

National Traffic and Safety Act (1958)
Provides for the creation of compulsory safety standards for automobiles and tires.

Fair Packaging and Labeling Act (1966)
Provides for the regulation of the packaging and labeling of consumer goods. Requires manufacturers to state what the package contains, who made it, and how much it contains. Permits industries' voluntary adoption of uniform packaging standards.

Child Protection Act (1966)
Bans sale of hazardous toys and articles. Amended in 1969 to include articles that pose electrical, mechanical, or thermal hazards.

Federal Cigarette Labeling and Advertising Act (1967)
Requires that cigarette packages contain the following statement: "Warning: The Surgeon General Has Determined That Cigarette Smoking is Dangerous to Your Health."

Truth-in-Lending Act (1968)
Requires lenders to state the true costs of a credit transaction, outlaws the use of actual or threatened violence in collecting loans, and restricts the amount of garnishments. Established a National Commission on Consumer Finance.

National Environmental Policy Act (1969)
Establishes a national policy on the environment and provides for the establishment of the Council on Environmental Quality. The Environmental Protection Agency was established by Reorganization Plan No. 3 of 1970.

Fair Credit Reporting Act (1970)
Ensures that a consumer's credit report will contain only accurate, relevant, and recent information and will be confidential unless requested for an appropriate reason by a proper party.

Consumer Product Safety Act (1972)
Establishes the Consumer Product Safety Commission and authorizes it to set safety standards for consumer products as well as exact penalties for failure to uphold the standards.

TABLE 3-2 (Continued)

Consumer Goods Pricing Act (1975)
Prohibits the use of price maintenance agreements among manufacturers and resellers in interstate commerce.

Magnuson-Moss Warranty/FTC Improvement Act (1975)
Authorizes the FTC to determine rules concerning consumer warranties and provides for consumer access to means of redress, such as the "class action" suit. Also expands FTC regulatory powers over unfair or deceptive acts or practices.

Equal Credit Opportunity Act (1975)
Prohibits discrimination in a credit transaction because of sex, marital status, race, national origin, religion, age, or receipt of public assistance.

Fair Debt Collection Practice Act (1978)
Makes it illegal to harass or abuse any person and make false statements or use unfair methods when collecting a debt.

FTC Improvement Act (1980)
Provides the House of Representatives and Senate jointly with veto power over FTC Trade Regulation Rules. Enacted to limit FTC's powers to regulate "unfairness" issues.

Toy Safety Act (1984)
Gives the government the power to recall dangerous toys quickly when they are found.

Changing Government Agency Enforcement

To enforce the laws, Congress established several federal regulatory agencies—the Federal Trade Commission, the Food and Drug Administration, the Interstate Commerce Commission, the Federal Communications Commission, the Federal Power Commission, the Civil Aeronautics Board, the Consumer Products Safety Commission, the Environmental Protection Agency, and the Office of Consumer Affairs. These agencies can have a major impact on a company's marketing performance. Government agencies have some discretion in enforcing the laws. From time to time, they appear to be overly eager and unpredictable. They are dominated by lawyers and economists who often lack a practical sense of how business and marketing work. In recent years, the Federal Trade Commission has added staff marketing experts to better understand complex business issues. The degree of enforcement lessened during the 1980s under the Reagan administration, which initiated a strong trend toward deregulation.

Growth of Public Interest Groups

The number and power of public interest groups have increased during the past two decades. The most successful is Ralph Nader's Public Citizen group, which watchdogs consumer interests. Nader lifted **consumerism** into a major social force, first with his successful attack on unsafe automobiles (resulting in the passage of the National Traffic and Motor Vehicle Safety Act of 1962) and then through investigations into meat processing (resulting in the passage of the Wholesome Meat Act of 1967), truth-in-lending, auto repairs, insurance, and X-ray equipment. Hundreds of other consumer interest groups—private and governmental—operate at the national, state, and local levels. Other groups that marketers need to consider are those seeking to protect the environment and to advance the rights of women, blacks, senior citizens, and others.

Cultural Environment

The **cultural environment** is made up of institutions and other forces that affect society's basic values, perceptions, preferences, and behaviors. People grow up in a particular society that shapes their basic beliefs and values. They absorb a world view that defines their relationships to themselves and others. The following cultural characteristics can affect marketing decisions.

Persistence of Cultural Values

People in a given society hold many beliefs and values. Their core beliefs and values have a high degree of persistence. For example, most Americans believe in working, getting married, giving to charity, and being honest. These beliefs shape more specific attitudes and behaviors found in everyday life. *Core* beliefs and values are passed on from parents to children and are reinforced by schools, churches, business, and government.

Secondary beliefs and values are more open to change. Believing in marriage is a core belief; believing that people should get married early is a secondary belief. Marketers have some chance of changing secondary values but little chance of changing core values. For example, family-planning marketers could argue more effectively that people should get married later than that they should not get married at all.

Subcultures

Each society contains subcultures—groups of people with shared value systems based on common life experiences or situations. Episcopalians, teenagers, and working women all represent separate subcultures whose members share common beliefs, preferences, and behaviors. To the extent that subcultural groups show different wants and buying behavior, marketers can choose subcultures as target markets.

Shifts in Secondary Cultural Values

Although core values are fairly persistent, cultural swings do take place. Consider the impact of popular music groups, movie personalities, and other celebrities on young people's hair styling, clothing, and sexual norms. Marketers want to predict cultural shifts in order to spot new opportunities or threats. Several firms offer "futures" forecasts in this connection. For example, the Yankelovich marketing research firm tracks forty-one cultural values, such as "anti-bigness," "mysticism," "living for today," "away from possessions," and "sensuousness." The firm describes the percentage of the population who share the attitude as well as the percentage who are antitrend. For example, the percentage of people who value physical fitness and well-being has risen steadily over the years. Marketers will want to cater to this trend with appropriate products and communication appeals.

Secondary cultural values: The shift toward physical fitness and well-being has created a need for new products and services.

CAUSE-RELATED MARKETING: DOING WELL BY DOING GOOD

These days, every product seems to be tied to some cause. Buy Hellman's mayonnaise or Skippy peanut butter and help Keep America Beautiful. Drink Tang and earn money for Mothers Against Drunk Driving. Or, if you want to help the Leukemia Society of America, buy Helping Hand trash bags or toilet paper. Pay for these purchases with the right charge card and you can help fight cancer or heart disease.

Cause-related marketing has become one of the hottest forms of corporate giving. It lets companies "do well by doing good" by linking purchases of the company's products or services with fund raising for worthwhile causes or charitable organizations. Cause-related marketing has grown rapidly since the early 1980s, when American Express offered to donate 1 cent to the restoration of the Statue of Liberty for each use of its charge card. American Express ended up having to contribute $1.7 million, but the cause-related campaign produced a 28 percent increase in card usage.

Companies now sponsor dozens of cause-related marketing campaigns each year. Many are backed by large budgets and a full complement of marketing activities. Here are recent examples:

- Continental Airlines sponsored its FlyAmerica campaign as a companion to the annual March of Dimes WalkAmerica fund-raiser. To participate in FlyAmerica, a sort of "fly-athon," consumers pledged to fly a certain number of miles on Continental and signed up sponsors who made donations based on the miles actually flown.. Continental promoted the campaign with in-flight videos, brochures, and a $2-million advertising campaign which invited consumers to "Join us to help the March of Dimes work for healthier arrivals every day." Last year, WalkAmerica raised $37 million for the March of Dimes. With FlyAmerica, Continental hopes to double that amount.

- Procter & Gamble has sponsored many cause-related marketing campaigns. For example, during the past many years, P&G has mailed out billions of coupons on behalf of the Special Olympics for retarded children, helping make the event a household word. P&G supports its Special Olympics efforts with national advertising and public relations, and its salespeople work with local volunteers to encourage retailers to build point-of-purchase displays. In another recent cause-related marketing effort, Procter & Gamble set up the Jif Children's Education Fund. For every pound of Jif peanut butter sold during the three-month promotion, P&G donates 10 cents to the fund, which will be distributed to parent-teacher groups at registered elementary schools in America. The program is designed to raise more than $4 million for U.S. elementary education.

- Johnson & Johnson has teamed with the Children's Hospital Medical Center and the National Safety Council to sponsor a five-year cause-related marketing campaign to reduce preventable children's injuries, the leading killer of children. Some 43 other nonprofit groups are helping to promote the campaign, including the American Red Cross, National Parent Teachers Association, and the Boy and Girl Scouts of America. The campaign offers consumers a free Safe Kids safety kit for children in exchange for proofs-of-purchase. Consumers can also buy a Child's Safety Video for $9.95—the video features a game show format that makes learning about safety entertaining as well as educational. To promote the campaign, J&J is distributing almost 50 million advertising inserts in daily newspapers and has developed a special information kit for retailers containing posters, floor displays, and other in-store promotion materials. Safe Kids Safety Tip Sheets and emergency phone stickers are also available as free consumer handouts.

The major cultural values of a society are expressed in people's views of themselves and others, of organizations, society, nature, and the universe.

PEOPLE'S VIEWS OF THEMSELVES.   People vary in their emphasis on serving themselves versus serving others. In the 1960s and 1970s, many people focused on self-satisfaction. In the 1980s, personal ambition and materialism increased dramatically. Some people sought only personal pleasure, wanting fun, change, and escape. Others sought self-realization, through religion, recreation, or the avid pursuit of careers or other life goals.

The marketing implications of a "me-society" are many. People use products, brands, and services as a means of self-expression. They buy their "dream cars" and take their "dream vacations." They spend more time in outdoor health activities (jogging, tennis), in thought, and on arts and crafts. The leisure industry (camping, boating, arts and crafts, sports) faces good growth prospects in a society where people seek self-fulfillment.

PEOPLE'S VIEWS OF OTHERS.   More recently, observers have noted a shift from a "me-society" to a "we-society" in which more people want to be with and serve others. Flashy spending and self indulgence appear to be on the way out, while saving, family, and helping others are on the rise. A recent survey showed that more people are becoming involved in charity, volunteer work, and social service activities.[21] This suggests a bright future for "social support" products and services that improve direct

The more you buy, the more we'll give to America's schools.

We at Jif know education takes money. Which is why we have created the Jif Children's Education Fund.

From February 1st through April 30th, every time you buy Jif® peanut butter, we'll make a donation to elementary schools across America. It's that simple. Our goal is to raise at least $4,000,000. And the more Jif you buy, the more we'll give. There's no limit!

Every elementary school has been invited to participate in this important program. Check with your parent-teacher group to see if your school has enrolled.

Remember, by choosing Jif, you'll be choosing to help America's kids.

Choose to help America's kids. Choose Jif.

Jif children's education fund

Cause marketing: Doing well by doing good—linking purchases of company products with fund raising for worthwhile projects.

Cause-related marketing has stirred some controversy. Critics are concerned that cause-related marketing might eventually undercut traditional "no-strings" corporate giving, as more and more companies grow to expect marketing benefits from their contributions. And they worry that cause-related marketing will cause a shift in corporate charitable support toward more visible, popular, and low-risk charities—those with more certain and substantial marketing appeal. For example, MasterCard's Choose to Make a Difference campaign raises money for six charities, each selected in part because of its popularity in a consumer poll. Finally, critics worry that cause-related marketing is more a strategy for selling than a strategy for giving—that "cause-related" marketing is really "cause-exploitative" marketing. They fear that companies are simply trying to buy better images by trading on the good works and hard-won reputations of the charitable organizations. Thus, companies using cause-related marketing might find themselves walking a fine line between increased sales and an improved image, and charges of exploitation.

However, if handled well, cause-related marketing can greatly benefit both the company and the charitable organization. The company gains an effective marketing tool while building a more positive public image, and promoting a cause can make the company's offer stand out from the clutter of competing products and promotions. The charitable organization gains greater visibility and important new sources of funding. This additional funding can be substantial. For example, by 1993, the American Red Cross plans to raise $10 million each year, or 10 percent of its annual national disaster relief budget, through cause-related marketing. In total, such campaigns now contribute some $100 million annually to the coffers of charitable organizations, and surveys show that these cause-related contributions usually add to, rather than undercut, direct company contributions. Thus, when cause marketing works, everyone wins.

Sources: See P. Rajan Varadarajan and Anil Menon, "Cause-Related Marketing: A Coalignment of Marketing Strategy and Corporate Philanthropy," *Journal of Marketing*, July 1988, pp. 58–74; Zachary Schiller, "Doing Well by Doing Good," *Business Week*, December 5, 1988, pp. 53–57; Cyndee Miller, "Drug Company Begins Its Own Children's Crusade," *Marketing News*, June 6, 1988, pp. 1, 2; Jennifer Lawrence, "Continental Rolls with Cause Effort," *Advertising Age*, March 6, 1989, p. 51; and "School Kids Snack for Cash," *Advertising Age*, February 2, 1990, p. 36.

communication between people, such as health clubs, vacations, and games. It also suggests a growing market for "social substitutes"—things that allow people who are alone to feel that they are not, such as VCRs and computers.

PEOPLE'S VIEWS OF ORGANIZATIONS. People vary in their attitudes toward corporations, government agencies, trade unions, universities, and other organizations. Most people accept these organizations, although some people are highly critical of particular ones. By and large, people are willing to work for major organizations and expect them, in turn, to carry out society's work. There has been, however, a decline in organizational loyalty. People are giving a little less to these organizations and are trusting them less.

Several marketing implications follow. Organizations need to find new ways to win consumer confidence. They need to review their advertising communications to make sure their messages are honest. They need to review their various activities to make sure that they are coming across as "good corporate citizens." More companies are linking themselves to worthwhile causes, measuring their images among important publics, and using public relations to build more positive images (see Marketing Highlight 3–3).

PEOPLE'S VIEWS OF SOCIETY. People vary in their attitudes toward their society, from patriots who defend it, to reformers who want to change it, to discontents who want to leave it. The trend through the 1960s and 1970s was toward declining patriotism

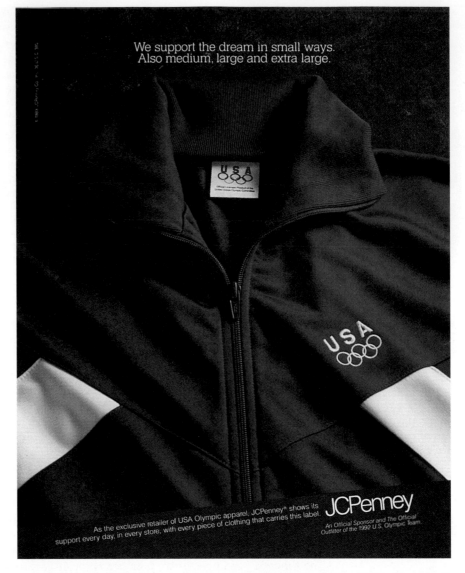

We support the dream in small ways.
Also medium, large and extra large.

As the exclusive retailer of USA Olympic apparel, JCPenney® shows its support every day, in every store, with every piece of clothing that carries this label. **JCPenney**

An Official Sponsor and The Official Outfitter of the 1992 U.S. Olympic Team.

J. C. Penney responds to renewed consumer patriotism with its "USA Olympics" theme.

and more criticism of the country's direction. The 1980s, however, saw an increase in patriotism. People's orientation to their society influences their consumption patterns, levels of savings, and attitudes toward the marketplace.

Marketers need to watch consumers' changing social orientations and adapt their strategies accordingly. Many U.S. companies have responded to renewed consumer patriotism with "made in America" themes and flag-waving promotions. For example, Chevrolet is "the heartbeat of America." On a recent catalog cover, Sears featured a picture of the Statue of Liberty and the message, "Thank You, America." And for the past several years, the American textile industry has blitzed consumers with its "Crafted with Pride in the USA" advertising campaign featuring Bob Hope, Diann Carroll, Cathy Lee Crosby, and other celebrities insisting that "made in USA" matters.[22]

PEOPLE'S VIEWS OF NATURE.   People vary in their attitudes toward the natural world. Some feel ruled by it, others feel in harmony with it, and still others seek to master it. A long-term trend has been people's growing mastery over nature through technology and the belief that nature is bountiful. More recently, however, people have recognized that nature is finite and fragile—that it can be destroyed or spoiled by human activities.

Love of nature is leading to more camping, hiking, boating, fishing, and other outdoor activity. Business has responded with hiking gear, camping equipment, better insect repellents, and other products for nature enthusiasts. Tour operators are offering more tours to wilderness areas. Food producers have found growing markets for "natural" products such as natural cereal, natural ice cream, and health foods. Marketing communicators are using appealing natural backgrounds in advertising their products.

PEOPLE'S VIEWS OF THE UNIVERSE.   Finally, people vary in their beliefs about the origin of the universe and their place in it. Although most Americans practice religion, religious conviction and practice have been dropping off through the years, and church attendance has fallen steadily. As people lose their religious orientation, they seek to enjoy life on earth as fully as possible. They seek goods and experiences with more immediate satisfactions. Some futurists, however, have noted an emerging renewal of interest in religion, perhaps as a part of a broader search for a new inner purpose. In the nineties, they believe, people will move away from materialism and dog-eat-dog ambition to seek more permanent values and a more certain grasp of right and wrong.

> The Nineties will be a far less cynical decade than the Eighties. Yes, we will still care what things cost. But we will seek to value only those things—family, community, earth, faith—that will endure.[23]

RESPONDING TO THE MARKETING ENVIRONMENT

Many companies view the marketing environment as an "uncontrollable" element to which they must adapt. They passively accept the marketing environment and do not try to change it. They analyze the environmental forces and design strategies which will help the company avoid the threats and take advantage of the opportunities the environment provides.

Other companies take an **environmental management perspective**.[24] Rather than simply watching and reacting, these firms take aggressive actions to affect the publics and forces in their marketing environment. Thus, companies hire lobbyists to influence legislation affecting their industries and stage media events to gain favorable press coverage. They run "advertorials" (ads expressing editorial points of view) to shape public opinion. They press law suits and file complaints with regulators to keep competitors in line. And they form contractual agreements to better control their distribution channels. The following example shows how one company overcame a seemingly uncontrollable environmental constraint:

> Citicorp, the U.S. banking giant, had been trying for years to start full-service banking in Maryland. It had only credit card and small service operations in the state. Under Maryland law, out-of-state banks could provide only certain services and were barred from advertising, setting up branches, and other types of marketing. In March 1985, Citicorp offered to build a major credit card center in Maryland that would create 1,000 white-collar jobs and further offered the state $1 million in cash for the property where it would locate. By imaginatively designing a proposal to benefit Maryland, Citicorp became the first out-of-state bank to provide full banking services there.[25]

Marketing management cannot always affect environmental forces—in many cases, it must settle for simply watching and reacting to the environment. For example, a company would have little success trying to influence geographic population shifts, the economic environment, or major cultural values. But whenver possible, rather than taking a *reactive* approach to the marketing environment, smart marketing managers take a *proactive* approach.

■ SUMMARY

The company must start with the *marketing environment* in searching for opportunities and monitoring threats. The marketing environment consists of all the actors and forces that affect the company's ability to transact effectively with the target market. The company's marketing environment can be divided into the microenvironment and the macroenvironment.

The *microenvironment* consists of five components. The first is the company's *internal environment*—its several departments and management levels—as it affects marketing management's decision making. The second component includes the *marketing channel firms* that cooperate to create value: the suppliers and marketing intermediaries (middlemen, physical distribution firms, marketing-service agencies, financial intermediaries). The third component consists of the five types of *markets* in which the company can sell: the consumer, producer, reseller, government, and international markets. The fourth component consists of the *competitors* facing the company. The fifth component consists of all the *publics* that have an actual or potential interest in or impact on the organization's ability to achieve its objectives: financial, media, government, citizen action, and local, general, and internal publics.

The company's *macroenvironment* consists of major forces that shape opportunities and pose threats to the company: demographic, economic, natural, technological, political, and cultural.

The *demographic environment* shows a changing age structure in the U.S. population, a changing American family, geographic population shifts, a better-educated and more white-collar population, and increasing ethnic and racial diversity. The *economic environment* shows changing real income and changing consumer spending patterns. The *natural environment* shows coming shortages of certain raw materials, increased energy costs, increased pollution levels, and increasing government intervention in natural-resource management. The *technological environment* shows rapid technological change, unlimited innovational opportunities, high R&D budgets, concentration on minor improvements rather than major discoveries, and increased regulation of technological change. The *political environment* shows increasing business regulation, strong government agency enforcement, and the growth of public-interest groups. The *cultural environment* shows long-run trends toward a "we-society," decreasing organizational loyalty, increasing patriotism, an increasing appreciation for nature, and a search for more meaningful and enduring values.

■ QUESTIONS FOR DISCUSSION

1. Some companies purchase in such large volumes that they have the power to dictate terms to their suppliers. What are the advantages and disadvantages of marketing to companies that can "make or break" you as a supplier?

2. In the 1930s President Franklin Roosevelt used his cigarette holder as a personal "trademark." Would a president be seen smoking today? How has the cultural environment changed? How might a cigarette manufacturer market its products differently to meet this new environment?

3. You are the communications director for a small regional airline. What publics might be affected by a news report that your company had a considerably less frequent maintenance schedule than competing airlines? How would you respond to this report?

4. What environmental trends will affect the success of Walt Disney Company during the 1990s? If you were in charge of marketing at Disney, what plans would you make to deal with these trends?

5. Immigration is an important component of U.S. population growth. Currently, there is one legal immigrant for every six or seven people born in the U.S., twice the ratio of twenty years ago. How will this trend affect marketing during the next five years? During the next fifty years?

6. Recent life-style studies have identified a growing attitude that "meal preparation should take as little time as possible." What products and businesses are being affected by this trend? What future marketing opportunities does this trend suggest?

7. If Union Carbide developed a battery that made practical electric cars feasible, how do you think U.S. auto manufacturers would respond? What kind of company do you think would be the first to market an electric car to the general public?

8. A major alcoholic beverage marketer is planning to introduce an "adult soft drink"—a socially acceptable substitute for stronger drinks that would be cheaper and lower in alcohol than wine coolers. What cultural and other factors might affect the success of this product?

9. Americans are becoming more concerned about the natural environment. How might this trend affect a company that markets plastic sandwich bags? Discuss some effective responses to this trend.

10. Some marketing goals, such as improved quality, require strong support from an internal public, a company's own employees. But surveys show that employees increasingly distrust management and that company loyalty is eroding. How can a company market internally to help meet its goals?

■ KEY TERMS

Baby boom. The major increase in the annual birthrate following World War II and lasting until the early 1960s. The "baby boomers," now moving into middle age, are a prime target for marketers.

Consumerism. An organized movement of citizens and government to strengthen the rights and power of buyers in relation to sellers.

Cultural environment. Institutions and other forces that affect society's basic values, perceptions, preferences, and behaviors.

Demography. The study of human populations in terms of size, density, location, age, sex, race, occupation, and other statistics.

Economic environment. Factors that affect consumer buying power and spending patterns.

Engel's laws. Differences noted more than a century ago by Ernst Engel regarding family spending patterns in response to increased income; categories studied included food, housing, transportation, health care, and other goods and services.

Environmental management perspective. A management perspective in which the firm takes aggressive actions to affect the publics and forces in its marketing environment rather than simply watching and reacting to it.

Financial intermediaries. Banks, credit companies, insurance companies, and other businesses that help finance transactions or insure against the risks associated with the buying and selling of goods.

Macroenvironment. The larger societal forces that affect the whole microenvironment—demographic, economic, natural, technological, political, and cultural forces.

Marketing environment. The actors and forces outside marketing that affect marketing management's ability to develop and maintain successful transactions with its target customers.

Marketing intermediaries. Firms that help the company to promote, sell, and distribute its goods to final buyers; they include middlemen, physical distribution firms, marketing-service agencies, and financial intermediaries.

Marketing services agencies. Marketing research firms, advertising agencies, media firms, marketing consulting firms, and other service providers that help a company target and promote its products to the right markets.

Microenvironment. The forces close to the company that affect its ability to serve its customers—the company, market channel firms, customer markets, competitors, and publics.

Middlemen. Distribution channel firms that help the company find customers or make sales to them.

Natural environment. Natural resources which are needed as inputs by marketers or which are affected by marketing activities.

Physical distribution firms. Warehouse, transportation, and other firms that help a company stock and move goods from their points of origin to their destinations.

Political environment. Laws, government agencies, and pressure groups that influence and limit various organizations and individuals in a given society.

Public. Any group that has an actual or potential interest in or impact on an organization's ability to achieve its objectives.

Suppliers. Firms and individuals that provide the resources needed by the company and its competitors to produce goods and services.

Technological environment. Forces that create new technologies, creating new product and market opportunities.

■ REFERENCES

1. For more information, see "Kellogg: Snap, Crackle, Profits," *Dun's Business Month*, December 1985, pp. 32–33; Russell Mitchell, "The Health Craze Has Kellogg Feeling G-r-r-reat," *Business Week*, March 30, 1987, pp. 52–53; Patricia Sellers, "How King Kellogg Beat the Blahs, *Fortune*, August 19, 1988, pp. 54–64; and Julie Liesse Erickson, "Kellogg Pours It On," *Advertising Age*, August 28, 1989, pp. 1, 30.

2. See "The Mommy Boom," *Sales & Marketing Management*, April 1988, p. 10.

3. See James Gollub and Harold Javitz, "Six Ways to Age," *American Demographics*, June 1989, pp. 28–35.

4. See Richard Kern, "USA 2000," *Sales & Marketing Management*, October 27, 1986, pp. 10–12.

5. See Jonathan B. Levine and Amy Dunkin, "Toddlers in $90 Suits? You Gotta Be Kidding," *Business Week*, September 21, 1987, pp. 52–54; Horst H. Stipp, "Children as Consumers," *American Demographics*, February 1988, pp. 27–32; and "Boomlet Market," *American Demographics*, March 1989, pp. 14–15.

6. See Patricia Sellers, "The ABC's of Marketing to Kids," *Fortune* May 8, 1989, pp. 114–20.

7. See Walecia Konrad and Gail DeGeorge, "U.S. Companies Go for the Gray," *Business Week*, April 3, 1989, pp. 64–67; and Melinda Beck, "The Geezer Boom," in "The 21st Century Family," a special issue of *Newsweek*, Winter/Spring 1990, pp. 62–67.

8. For more reading, see "The 21st Century American Family," 1990; Judith Waldrop, "America's Households," *American Demographics*, March 1989, pp. 20–32; and Thomas Exter, "Demographic Forecasts: Married with Kids," *American Demographics*, February 1990, p. 55.

9. See Joe Schwartz, "On the Road Again," *American Demographics*, April 1987, pp. 39–42; "Americans Keep Going West—And South," *Business Week*, May 16, 1988, p. 30; and Judith Waldrop, "2010," *American Demographics*, February 1989, pp. 18–21.

10. The MSA (Metropolitan Statistical Area) concept classifies heavily populated areas as MSAs or PMSAs (Primary Metropolitan Statistical Areas). MSAs and PMSAs are defined in the same way, except that PMSAs are also components of larger "megalopolies" called CMSAs (Consolidated Metropolitan Statistical Areas). MSAs and PMSAs are areas consisting of (1) a city of at least 50,000 in population, or (2) an urbanized area of at least 50,000 with a total metropolitan area of at least 100,000. See Richard Kern, "You Say Potato and I Say ADIMSADMAPMSA," *Sales & Marketing Management*, December 1988, p. 8.

11. See Thomas Moore, "Different Folks, Different Strokes," *Fortune*, September 16, 1985, pp. 65–68.

12. See Fabian Linden, "In the Rearview Mirror," p. 4. For more reading, see Bryant Robey and Cheryl Russell, "A Portrait of the American Worker," *American Demographics*, March 1984, pp. 17–21.

13. See Judith Waltrop and Thomas Exter, "What the 1990 Census Will Show," *American Demographics*, January 1990, p. 25.

14. See Zachary Schiller, "Stalking the New Consumer: As Markets Fracture, P&G and Others Sharpen 'Micro Marketing,' " *Business Week*, August 28, 1989, pp. 54–62.

15. See Thomas G. Exter, "Where the Money Is," *American Demographics*, March 1987, pp. 26–32; and Bickley Townsend, "Dollars and Dreams," *American Demographics*, December 1987, pp. 10, 55.

16. For more discussion, see the "Environmentalism" section in Chapter 23. Also see David Kirkpatrick, "Environmentalism: The New Crusade," *Fortune*, February 12, 1990, pp. 44–52; Shawn Tully, "What the 'Greens' Mean for Business, *Fortune*, October 23, 1989, pp. 159–64; and Brian Bremmer, "The New Sales Pitch: The Environment," *Business Week*, July 24, 1989, p. 50.

17. See Gene Bylinsky, "Technology in the Year 2000, *Fortune*, July 18, 1988, pp. 92–98.

18. See Stuart Gannes, "The Good News About U.S. R&D," *Fortune*, February 1, 1988, pp. 48–56: and "How R&D Pays Off," in a special "Innovation 1989" issues of *Business Week*, June 1989, pp. 178–79.

19. See Bro Uttal, "Is IBM Playing Too Rough?" *Fortune*, December 10, 1984, pp. 34–37; and "Personal Computers: IBM Will Keep Knocking Heads?" *Business Week*, January 10, 1985, p. 67.

20. For a summary of legal developments in marketing, see Louis W. Stern and Thomas L. Eovaldi, *Legal Aspects of Marketing Strategy: Antitrust and Consumer Protection Issues* (Englewood Cliffs, NJ: Prentice-Hall, 1984).

21. See Bill Barol, "The Eighties are Gone," *Newsweek*, January 14, 1988, p. 48; Natalie de Combray, "Volunteering in America," *American Demographics*, March 1987, pp. 50–52; Annetta Miller, "The New Volunteerism," *Newsweek*, February 8, 1988, pp. 42–43; and Ronald Henkoff, "Is Greed Dead?" *Fortune*, August 14, 1989, pp. 40–41.

22. See Kenneth Dreyfack, "Draping Old Glory Around Just About Everything," *Business Week*, October 27, 1986, pp. 66–67; and Pat Sloan, "Ads Go All-American," *Advertising Age*, July 28, 1986, pp. 3, 52.

23. Anne B. Fisher, "What Consumers Want in the 1990s," *Fortune*, January 21, 1990, p. 112.

24. See Carl P. Zeithaml and Valerie A. Zeithaml, "Environmental Management: Revising and Marketing Perspective," *Journal of Marketing*, Spring 1984, pp. 46–53.

25. Philip Kotler, "Megamarketing," *Harvard Business Review*, March–April 1986, p. 117.

CAMPBELL: RESPONDING TO A SOUPED-UP MARKETING ENVIRONMENT

Campbell has marketed canned soup under its familiar red-and-white label for almost 100 years. Although Campbell's share of the $2.2 billion total soup market has shrunk from about 80 percent in the early 1970s to about 60 percent, the company remains strong in the canned soup segment, with an 84-percent share. Recognizing that environmental and competitive changes may cause a decline in both the size of the overall canned soup market and the company's share of it, Campbell's new marketing-minded management is seeking both new market opportunities and new marketing approaches for old product lines. Although Campbell markets brands in other food categories—for example, its Pepperidge Farm, Vlasic, Prego, and LeMenu product lines—the soup business remains of special interest because of its historical importance to the company.

At many Campbell Soup factories, soup is still cooked the old-fashioned way. Sightseers peeking through factory windows might see workers pushing large trays of carrots to be dumped into big kettles—much as they did back in 1910. This is not to say, of course, that Campbell is not moving to retool plants and develop more efficient ways to make soup. But although the old-fashioned way of cooking soup may be growing out of date, Americans' affection for and loyalty to the Campbell name is not—Campbell is the second most powerful brand name in America (behind only Coca-Cola). However, despite this continuing consumer love affair with its name, Campbell faces stiff challenges in the 1990s. Increased competition, shifting demographics, and changing consumer lifestyles provide constant opportunities for and threats to Campbell's market share.

The mushrooming number of new soup products—170 in 1987 alone—and the rising importance of Progresso, Lipton, and the Japanese noodle makers Marachun and Nissan Foods provide evidence of increased competition. In the growing soup war, the weapon of choice has been line extensions—product variations retaining an established brand name. For example, to compete with Lipton, Campbell introduced a dehydrated soup under its own brand name rather than develop a separate brand name. With this strategy, companies try to thwart competition by attempting to satisfy every imaginable customer preference.

In addition to line extensions, the industry has created new categories of soups. Originally, there was canned soup, which was eventually followed by dehydrated soup. Although canned soup still accounts for 75 percent of the total market, excitement in the dehydrated category has been renewed with the startling growth of Japanese ramen noodle-style soups. More recently, microwavable soups (such as Campbell's Chunky Microwavable Soups and Fantastic Foods' "Fantastic Noodles") and new frozen/refrigerated soups (such as Chef San Francisco's Chilled Soups and Seatech's California Style Clam Chowder) have grown in popularity.

Changes in American lifestyles and other significant environmental changes have sparked this renewed interest in the soup market. The three most important trends affecting the soup market are the aging of the population, its evolving ethnic composition, and its various lifestyle changes. The aging of the population will strongly influence American food-consumption patterns. By the year 2000, the average age of the population will jump to about 37—up from an average age of 28 in 1970. Baby boomers will continue to be the biggest demographic group, and their impact will be enormous. For one thing, with fewer opportunities to job-hop in middle age, they will settle down. In addition, their tastes will change with age, and they will be increasingly concerned with health and fitness.

The ethnic composition of the U.S. population is also changing. For example, the number of Hispanics—primarily Mexican—is growing at five times the national rate.

In addition to the shifting demographic characteristics of the U.S. market, profound changes in lifestyle are occurring. The increasing number of dual-career and single-parent households has raised the demand for convenience products and packaging. For example, analysts predict that the $50-billion market for takeout foods will double during the next decade.

These and other trends present new challenges to Campbell's soup business. Campbell's short-run problem is how to make soup more attractive in the current environment. Toward this end, Campbell has recently characterized itself as the "well-being company" and promoted its foods as conducive to good health: One campaign even presented soup as health insurance. The slogan "Soup is Good Food" has also become a familiar part of the company's advertising. Efforts by Campbell to increase the consumption of soup also include promoting it for different occasions (eating it for breakfast), other uses (cooking sauces), and creative cookery (mixing two or more soups). And although most of Campbell's soups are condensed and must be diluted, the company created the ready-to-eat Chunky Soup line for people who want to make soup an entire meal.

In keeping with the changing times, Campbell has also developed many other new products. In fact, Campbell introduced more new products between 1982 and 1987 than any other food company. In addition to the classic red-and-white labeled soups and Campbell's Chunky Soup (introduced in 1970), other entries include:

- *Canned Soups*
  "Cooking Soups"—ingredient soups for recipes packaged with the traditional red and white label
  Golden Classics—restaurant-style soups for the premium-price segment
  Special Request—soups with one-third less salt for those interested in reduced sodium
  Creamy Natural—upscale, creamy condensed soups with no additives
  Home Cookin'—hearty soups for the ready-to-eat category

- *Dehydrated Soups*
  Quality Soup & Recipe Mix—dry soups and recipe mixes to compete with the Lipton classic
  Noodle Nest—ramen-style noodle soups
  Campbell's Cup—individual servings of instant soup

- *Microwavable Soups*
  Chunky Microwavable
  Soup—shelf-stable microwavable soups in plastic bowls
  Souper-Combos—frozen, single-serve combinations of soups and sandwiches

Recently, Campbell broke with industry tradition and introduced new soup products under some of its brand names in other food categories. For example, to meet the challenge from Progresso, Campbell introduced a ready-to-serve soup under the Prego name. Under its Pepperidge Farm label, it now sells a line of ultrafancy soups starting at $2 per can. Finally, under the *Casera* brand name (which means "home cooked" in Spanish), Campbell now markets 50 food products—including soups—aimed at Hispanics of Caribbean origin.

Campbell believed it could no longer ignore Hispanics, the second fastest growing consumer group. Further, Hispanics spent $47 billion in 1987 on food and other nondurables and their spending is growing 6% per year.

However, to serve this market, Campbell must go head-to-head with Goya Foods, Inc., the Secaucus, N.J.-based, family-owned company that dominates the Hispanic market. Goya had 1987 sales of about $275 million, many of them in corner grocery stores known as *bodegas*. Compared with Campbell's 1987 sales of $4.5 billion, Goya may look like small potatoes; but Goya is a formidable competitor. The company makes 700 items which com-

mand their market niche on the East Coast and in parts of the Midwest. As one industry observer noted, "Goya is at war every day. They take no prisoners."

To increase its chances for success, Campbell targets Casera to the younger, more affluent Hispanic segment, one that has yet to develop the stubborn brand loyalty of older generations. But, Campbell will spend less than $1 million in 1988 to promote Casera as compared with estimated Goya advertising spending of $5 million. Goya's newest commercials portray older generations passing their favorite Goya recipes to younger kin.

Campbell has also started an aggressive price war, pricing Casera items in some stores at two for $1 as compared with similar Goya items which sell for 69 cents each. However, this price competition does not seem to have been very effective to date.

Campbell realizes that it must learn quickly about the Hispanic market and build from the bottom up. Its efforts to understand the market start right in the bodegas—Goya's strongholds. Edwin Lopez is a Casera brand sales manager and front-line soldier in Campbell's assault on Goya. He frequents the bodegas in New York City's Hispanic neighborhoods shaking hands, giving out T-shirts, and chatting in Spanish. He also does most of the recruiting for the sales force, assigning new recruits to routes near their own neighborhoods. But progress is slow and difficult. "We still have a lot to learn, but we have no plans to pull out," says an official of Campbell U.S.A. "We're in this for the long haul."

QUESTIONS

1. Assess Campbell's recent responses to environmental forces affecting the market for soup. How has Campbell changed its marketing strategy and the positioning of its products?
2. Is there a market for "well-being" products? To develop the "well-being" strategy, how should new and existing product opportunities be evaluated?
3. What challenges does Campbell face in marketing its Casera line to the Hispanic Segment? What opportunities does it face?
4. What marketing lessons can one learn from Campbell's experience to date in trying to target the Hispanic market?
5. Are there other environmental trends to which Campbell should respond?

U.S. Auto Companies: Embittered, Embattled, and Bewildered

From the end of World War II until the 1960s, the U.S. auto industry experienced a sales boom. As sales escalated, the automakers added more chrome, more options, and higher and lower tailfins on their cars. Times were good in Detroit, and the automakers grew fat.

In the 1960s, European imports such as MG, Fiat, and Volkswagen invaded the United States. At first, their market share was small but annoying. Detroit responded to the threat by producing small cars such as the Falcon and the Corvair. Unfortunately, the Corvair had a serious handling problem—it flipped over on some curves. When owners of Corvairs that had overturned sued GM, consumer action groups used the negative publicity to get Congress to pass the Auto Safety Act. Since then, Detroit has had to install safety devices such as seat belts, shock-absorbing bumpers, and collapsible steering columns—all of which result in higher prices.

American automakers had not yet recovered from the safety issue when the 1974 energy crisis struck. As oil supplies dwindled and rationing produced 300 percent increases in gasoline prices, consumers became more concerned about fuel efficiency.

The stage was set for the entrance of the Japanese with their small, nimble, fuel-efficient cars. Japanese imports went from zero in the late 1960s to 23 percent in 1989, and experts believe that they will reach 35 or 40 percent in the 1990s. Why do consumers prefer Japanese cars? Initially, cost was a major factor: They sold for $1,500 to $2,000 less than American cars. But as the price differential declined, sales of Japanese cars grew, so continued consumer preference must be based on factors other than price.

One major factor is quality. Studies by J. D. Powers and Associates indicate that many Americans have formed such a strong perception of the superior quality of Japanese cars that they won't even consider buying a U.S. car. Reinforcing the perception are the lower repair ratings for Japanese cars in *Consumer Reports*. For American auto buyers who are disgruntled about the cost and poor service at dealerships, these ratings are highly appealing—particularly if they are pressed for time, as so many are in today's typical household where all the adults work. For people who have neither the time nor the willingness to take a car in for repeated service, quality may be buying motive number one.

Detroit responded to these price and quality issues by developing better designs and more efficient production procedures. Between 1975 and 1985, U.S. automakers spent nearly $80 billion to retool and rebuild their plants, and they may spend another $80 billion by the mid-1990s.

They have also instituted production teams and quality circles to increase workers' morale, productivity, and work quality. Further, they have succeeded in getting the United Auto Workers Union to accept lower wages and have reduced the number of managers—two moves that have held down prices.

Detroit has also improved its supplier relationships. While automakers once bought from numerous suppliers on the basis of price, they now have only one or a few suppliers for each needed part. This practice establishes long-run relationships with suppliers, which results in better terms and higher-quality parts.

To improve their relationship with consumers, U.S. automakers introduced many exciting new models in the 1980s, such as the Taurus, Probe, Reatta, Lumina, and the minivan. Unfortunately, they still have trouble gauging American tastes and responding quickly, so some of these innovations were not successful. The Japanese are faster at redesigning and developing models.

U.S. auto companies have tried to improve their marketing skills by introducing rebates, the zero-percent solution (no finance charge), computer disks as selling tools, and stronger advertising campaigns such as Chevrolet's "Heartbeat of America" campaign. But they have failed to improve the quality of thier dealerships, which is a source of continuing frustration to consumers.

Detroit is no longer seeking protection from abroad by asking the U.S. government to enforce lower import quotas. Instead, American car makers are actively entering into joint ventures with foreign companies to produce new models. For example, Chrysler has joined with Maserati and Mitsubishi, Ford with Nissan and Mazda, and GM with Opel and Toyota. These ventures tie the companies together through ownership and financial agreements; increase the flow of design and production technology; and move the industry toward a world car—designed in Japan, made in the United States or Europe, and sold everywhere in the world.

QUESTIONS

1. What are the major factors in the auto companies' microenvironment? How do they affect the companies?
2. What are the major factors in the auto companies' macroenvironment? How do they affect the companies?
3. What major trends or factors are likely to have the greatest impact on the auto companies in the future? How will they affect the automakers?

Sources: "Detroit's Merry-Go-Round," *Business Week*, September 12, 1983, pp. 72–76; "The All-American Small Car Is Fading," *Business Week*, March 12, 1984, p. 92; "Downsizing Detroit: The Big Three's Strategy for Survival," *Business Week*, April 14, 1986, pp. 86–88; "Detroit Tries to Rev Up," *Business Week*, June 12, 1989, pp. 78–81; "Why U.S. Carmakers Are Losing Ground," *Fortune*, October 23, 1989, pp. 96–98; Ken Gross, "Making the Right Moves," *Automotive Industries*, November 1988, pp. 32–33; "Driving Toward a World Car?" *Newsweek*, May 1, 1989, pp. 48–49; and "Can the Big Three Get Back in Gear?" *Newsweek*, January 22, 1990.

MAYTAG CORPORATION: EXPANDING THE APPLIANCE PORTFOLIO

"Ol Lonely," the famous Maytag Company repairman, may not have enough to do, but his employer's parent, Maytag Corporation, has been quite busy. Always one of the most profitable firms in an industry dominated by giant companies, Maytag often earns a higher return on stockholder's equity (for example, 27 percent in 1988) than any other company in its industry. For the five-year period from 1983 to 1987, Maytag's sales grew at an annual rate of more than 5 percent while its net income grew at almost 9 percent. Maytag achieved record sales of $1.9 billion in 1987. Facing the 1990s, Maytag is acquiring new product lines and adjusting its portfolio in response to a changing environment.

Traditionally, Maytag manufactured a limited line of appliances and marketed its washers, dryers, and dishwashers under a family name. Its strategy has simply been to make the best products and charge accordingly: thus, the company slogan—"Built to Last Longer." Maytag's products generally cost more than competitors' machines—roughly $100 more on average. With its reputation for making trouble-free appliances, Maytag has always targeted the upscale end of the market. In addition, by offering premium-priced products, Maytag has typically catered to second-time buyers. This replacement market slowed in the later 1970s but was strong again starting in 1982-1983: Even Maytag's appliances wear out—typically after 10 to 12 years.

Maytag shied away from the cyclical home-builders' segment—tough negotiators who, in the past, wanted well-known brands at low prices—and the new-household segment—always price-conscious because of the multitude of products customers need to buy in a relatively short time period. Since the early 1980s, however, changing conditions in the appliance market have made Maytag consider whether it should change its traditional high-quality, high-priced strategy.

Consumers and retailers have regarded Maytag's laundry appliances as top-of-the-line. But the premium-quality niche for laundry and kitchen appliances targeted by both Maytag and competitor KitchenAid (long the market leader in the high-quality, high-price segment) may be eroding. Although there is no solid evidence of this trend, many people involved in the appliance market and many consumers believe that although the *quality* difference between high-priced and medium-priced laundry and kitchen appliances is becoming smaller, the *price* difference is becoming larger.

Competition, always a major factor in the appliance industry, has become even keener in recent years. A recent wave of mergers and acquisitions has dramatically changed the structure of the industry, with a few large, full-line companies accounting for most of the industry's production. For example, Whirlpool, the biggest washer maker, increased its share to nearly 50 percent when it acquired KitchenAid dishwashers from Dart & Kraft.

Other trends are also reshaping the industry. First, a significant portion of each major company's output is supplied to other companies for sale under their own brand names. For example, White Consolidated Industries manufactures dryers for General Electric, Montgomery Ward, and Sears. Second, heavy investments in factory automation are being made by two of the largest appliance manufacturers, General Electric and Whirlpool, to bring down costs and increase competitiveness. Meanwhile, already low-cost producers, such as White Consolidated Industries, continue to drive for lower costs through more efficient operations. Third, appliance companies have intensified their marketing efforts, with greater emphasis being placed on short-term sales stimulants such as factory rebates, special factory-authorized sales, and additional incentives for consumers, dealers, and salespeople. Finally, foreign competition poses a serious threat.

In response to these changing market conditions, cash-rich Maytag has made several acquisitions, gambling that some of its success in washers, dryers, and dishwashers will rub off on products other than those with which it has been traditionally associated. First came the 1981 acquisition of Hardwick Stove Company—a 105-year-old manufacturer of gas and electric ranges and microwave ovens. These products are sold through conventional outlets in the medium- and low-price brackets. The following year, Maytag acquired Jenn-Aire Company, known for its down-draft grill range, introduced in 1961. The range permits year-round indoor grilling by sucking fumes into a surface ventilation system. In 1986, Magic Chef, Inc., the appliance industry's fourth largest firm, joined the Maytag portfolio. With this acquisition came a variety of products, including Magic Chef cooking equipment, Admiral refrigerators, Norge laundry equipment, and other appliances such as microwave ovens. The new product lines overlapped with Maytag's kitchen ranges, washers, and dryers.

The cooking equipment market differs markedly from the washer and dryer business. The industry is fragmented, with no brand clearly recognized as a premium product. Commenting on the acquisitions, Maytag Corporation's president explained that although "cooking equipment is a mature market, it is an exciting one because product innovation is changing the traditional way people cook and broadening sales opportunities."

For example, the microwave oven industry is a relatively new area of the cooking equipment market, and the product is now one of the hottest items in the appliance business. Microwave ovens first caught on during the 1950s, but their growth was slow until the early 1970s. At that time, microwaves had several problems. Cooking was uneven, meats would not brown, foil-wrapped foods could not be put in the oven, few cookbooks were available, and real or imagined radiation dangers were associated with the appliance. When such problems were overcome, sales took off. By the late 1970s, countertop microwave ovens were no longer considered a luxury. With more and more women working in the 1980s, the microwave oven's appeal has become even stronger. Sixty-five percent of U.S. households now contain microwave ovens, as compared to a 45-percent penetration for dishwashers. Industry analysts foresee an eventual penetration by microwaves comparable to that of color televisions.

Five of the forty or so producers of microwave ovens have well over 50 percent of the consumer market. Samsung, Sanyo, Goldstar, Sharp, and Matsushita are the industry's largest. Meanwhile, long-time market leaders Litton and Amana have fallen behind. Price competition and discounting are widespread, and premium prices are difficult to maintain. The microwave industry differs from Maytag's more familiar business arenas, and the acquisitions of Hardwick and Magic Chef provided only a minor position in the fast-moving microwave market.

As Maytag has continued to assimilate these new but related businesses into its portfolio of strategic business units, a recent merger has signaled a new strategic direction for the company. In 1988, Maytag Corporation merged with Chicago Pacific Corporation, best known for its Hoover vacuum cleaners and Pennsylvania House furniture lines. Hoover is an acknowledged leader in the U.S. vacuum cleaner industry, commanding a 32-percent share of the 10 million vacuum cleaners sold in this country each year. The combined sales of the two companies will exceed $3 billion per year.

Maytag, however, had a special interest in Hoover: Sixty-five percent of Hoover's revenues are generated *abroad*. Globalization in the appliance industry is a concept whose time is just arriving. Prior to its merger with Chicago Pacific, Maytag had almost no presence in overseas appliance markets. Most appliances built by Maytag and other U.S. companies are too large or use too much water for typical international markets. Hoover, however, has for years been producing and distributing washers, dryers, refrigerators, dishwashers, and microwave ovens in foreign markets—it now operates 13 plants in eight countries. Thus, through its merger with Chicago Pacific, Maytag Corporation has taken a first major step toward globalization.

QUESTIONS

1. Assess Maytag Corporation's portfolio of businesses, classifying each business unit or product line. Which units should receive more emphasis, which should receive less? What other new products might Maytag add?

2. Develop a formal mission statement for Maytag that will help to guide the company and all of its units of the future.

3. Why has Maytag been so successful in the past in marketing its laundry appliances? Should it use its traditional strategy for its new product lines? Why or why not?

4

Marketing Research and Information Systems

In 1985 the Coca-Cola Company made a spectacular marketing blunder. After 99 successful years, it set aside its long-standing rule—"don't mess with Mother Coke"—and dropped its original formula Coke! In its place came *New* Coke with a sweeter, smoother taste. The company boldly announced the new taste with a flurry of advertising and publicity.

At first, amid the introductory fanfare, New Coke sold well. But sales soon went flat as a stunned public reacted. Coke began receiving sacks of mail and more than 1,500 phone calls each day from angry consumers. A group called "Old Cola Drinkers" staged protests, handed out T-shirts, and threatened a class-action suit unless Coca-Cola brought back the old formula. Most marketing experts predicted that New Coke would be the "Edsel of the Eighties."

After just three months, the Coca-Cola Company brought old Coke back. Now called "Coke Classic," it sold side-by-side with New Coke on supermarket shelves. The company said that New Coke would remain its "flagship" brand, but consumers had a different idea. By the end of 1985, Classic was outselling New Coke in supermarkets by two to one. By mid-1986, the company's two largest fountain accounts, McDonald's and Kentucky Fried Chicken, had returned to serving Coke Classic in their restaurants.

Quick reaction saved the company from potential disaster. It stepped up efforts for Coke Classic and slotted New Coke into a supporting role. By 1987, Coke Classic was again the company's main brand—and the country's leading soft drink. New Coke became the company's "attack brand"—its Pepsi stopper. With computer-enhanced star Max Headroom leading the charge, company ads boldly compared New Coke's taste with Pepsi's. Still, New Coke managed only a 2 percent market share. By 1989, Coke Classic was outselling New Coke ten to one. In spring 1990, the company repackaged New Coke and relaunched it with a new name—Coke II. Most experts, however, are predicting that the company will eventually allow the brand to simply fade away.

Why was New Coke introduced in the first place? What went wrong? Many analysts blame the blunder on poor marketing research.

In the early 1980s, although Coke was still the leading soft drink, it was slowly losing market share to Pepsi. For years, Pepsi had successfully mounted the "Pepsi Challenge," a series of televised taste tests showing that consumers preferred the sweeter taste of Pepsi. By early 1985, although Coke led in the overall market, Pepsi led in share of supermarket sales by 2 percent. (That doesn't sound like much, but 2 percent of the huge soft-drink market amounts to $600 million in retail sales!) Coca-Cola had to do something to stop the loss of its market share—the solution appeared to be a change in Coke's taste.

Coca-Cola began the largest new product research project in the company's history. It spent more than two years and $4 million on research before settling on a new formula. It conducted some 200,000 taste tests—30,000 on the final formula alone. In blind tests, 60 percent of consumers chose New Coke over the old, and 52 percent chose it over Pepsi. Research showed that New Coke would be a winner and the company introduced it with confidence. So what happened?

Looking back, we can see that Coke's marketing research was too narrowly focused. The research looked only at taste; it did not explore consumers feelings about dropping the old Coke and replacing it with a new version. It took no account of the *intangibles*—Coke's name, history, packaging, cultural heritage, and image. But to many people, Coke stands alongside baseball, hotdogs, and apple pie as an American institution; it represents the very fabric of America. Coke's symbolic meaning turned out to be more important to many consumers than its taste. More complete marketing research would have detected these strong emotions.

Coke's managers may also have used poor judgment in interpreting the research and planning strategies around it. For example, they took the finding that 60 percent of consumers preferred New Coke's taste to mean that the new product would win in the marketplace—as when a political candidate wins with 60 percent of the vote. But it also meant that 40 percent still liked the old Coke. By dropping the Old Coke, the company trampled the taste buds of the large core of loyal Coke drinkers who didn't want a change. The company might have been wiser to leave the old Coke alone and introduce New Coke as a brand extension, as was later done successfully with Cherry Coke.

The Coca-Cola Company has one of the largest, best managed, and most advanced marketing research operations in America. Good marketing research has kept the company atop the rough-and-tumble soft-drink market for decades. But marketing research is far from an exact science. Consumers are full of surprises and figuring them out can be awfully tough. If Coca-Cola can make a large marketing research mistake, any company can.[1]

CHAPTER OBJECTIVES

After reading this chapter, you should be able to:

1. Explain the importance of information to the company.
2. Define the marketing information system and discuss its parts.
3. Describe the four steps in the marketing research process.
4. Identify the different kinds of information a company might use.
5. Compare the advantages and disadvantages of various methods of collecting information.

In carrying out marketing analysis, planning, implementation, and control, marketing managers need information at almost every turn. They need information about customers, competitors, dealers, and other forces in the marketplace. One marketing executive put it this way: "To manage a business well is to manage its future; and to manage the future is to manage information."[2]

During the past century, most companies were small and knew their customers firsthand. Managers picked up marketing information by being around people, observing them, and asking questions. During this century, however, many factors have increased the need for more and better information. As companies become national or international in scope, they need more information on larger, more distant markets. As incomes increase and buyers become more selective, sellers need better information about how buyers respond to different products and appeals. As sellers use more complex marketing approaches and face more competition, they need information on the effectiveness of their marketing tools. Finally, in today's more rapidly changing environments, managers need more up-to-date information to make timely decisions.

The supply of information has also increased greatly. John Naisbitt suggests that the United States is undergoing a "megashift" from an industrial to an information-based economy.[3] He found that more than 65 percent of the U.S. work force is now employed in producing or processing information, compared to only 17 percent in 1950. Using improved computer systems and other technologies, companies can now provide information in great quantities. In fact, today's managers sometimes receive too much information. For example, one study found that with all the companies offering data, and with all the information now available through supermarket scanners, a packaged-goods brand manager is bombarded with one million to one *billion* new numbers each week.[4] As Naisbitt points out: "Running out of information is not a problem, but drowning in it is."[5]

Yet marketers frequently complain that they lack information of the *right* kind or have too much of the *wrong* kind. Or marketing information is so widely spread throughout the company that it takes great effort to locate even simple facts. Subordinates may withhold information they believe will reflect badly on their performance. Important information often arrives too late to be useful or on-time information is not accurate. So marketing managers need more and better information. Companies have greater capacity to provide managers with information but often have not made good use of it. Many companies are now studying their managers' information needs and designing information systems to meet those needs.

THE MARKETING INFORMATION SYSTEM

A **marketing information system (mis)** consists of people, equipment, and procedures to gather, sort, analyze, evaluate, and distribute needed, timely, and accurate information to marketing decision makers. The marketing information system concept is illustrated in Figure 4-1. The MIS begins and ends with marketing managers. First, it interacts with these managers to assess their information needs. Next, it develops the needed information from internal company records, marketing intelligence activities, and the marketing research process. Information analysis processes the information to make it more useful. Finally, the MIS distributes information to managers in the right form and at the right time to help them in marketing planning, implementation, and control.

ASSESSING INFORMATION NEEDS

A good marketing information system balances the information managers would *like* to have against what they really *need* and what is *feasible* to offer. The company begins by interviewing managers to find out what information they would like. Table 4-1 lists a useful set of questions. But managers do not always need all the information they

FIGURE 4-1 The marketing information system

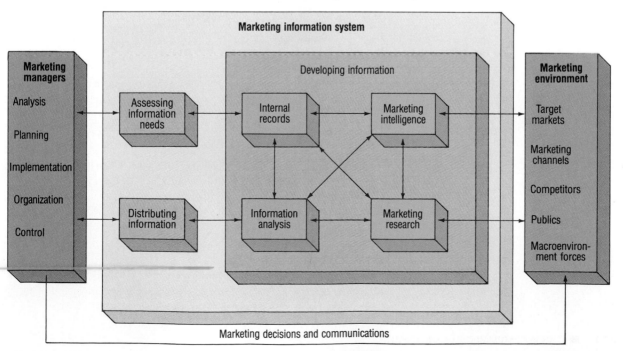

TABLE 4-1
Questions for Assessing
Marketing Information Needs

1. What types of decisions are you regularly called upon to make?
2. What types of information do you need to make these decisions?
3. What types of information do you regularly get?
4. What types of special studies do you periodically request?
5. What types of information would you like to get that you are not now getting?
6. What information would you want daily? Weekly? Monthly? Yearly?
7. What magazine and trade reports would you like to see routed to you on a regular basis?
8. What specific topics would you like to be kept informed of?
9. What types of data analysis programs would you like to see made available?
10. What do you think would be the four most helpful improvements that could be made in the present marketing information system?

ask for, and they may not ask for all they really need. Moreover, the MIS cannot always supply all the information managers request.

Some managers will ask for whatever information they can get without thinking carefully about what they really need. With today's information technology, most companies can provide much more information than managers can actually use. Too much information can be as harmful as too little.

Other managers may omit things they ought to know. Or managers may not know to ask for some types of information they should have. For example, managers might need to know that a competitor plans to introduce a new product during the coming year. Because they do not know about the new product, they do not think to ask about it. The MIS must watch the marketing environment and provide decision makers with information they should have to make key marketing decisions.

Sometimes the company cannot provide the needed information because it is not available or because of MIS limitations. For example, a brand manager might want to know how much competitors will change their advertising budgets next year and how these changes will affect industry market shares. The information on planned budgets is probably not available. Even if it is, the company's MIS may not be advanced enough to forecast resulting changes in market shares.

Finally, the company must decide whether the benefits of having an item of information are worth the costs of providing it, and both value and cost are often hard to assess. By itself, information has no worth—its value comes from its *use*. Although methods have been developed for calculating the value of information,[6] decision makers must often rely on subjective judgment. Similarly, although a company can total the

Information abounds—the problem is to give managers the *right information* at the *right time*.

costs of a marketing information system or the costs of a marketing research project, figuring the cost of a specific information item may be difficult.

The costs of obtaining, processing, storing, and delivering information can mount quickly. In many cases, additional information will do little to change or improve a manager's decision, or the costs of the information will exceed the returns from the improved decision. For example, suppose a company estimates that launching a new product without any further information will yield a profit of $500,000. The manager believes that additional information will improve the marketing mix and allow the company to make $525,000. Paying $30,000 for the extra information would be foolish.

DEVELOPING INFORMATION

The information needed by marketing managers can be obtained from *internal company records, marketing intelligence,* and *marketing research.* The information analysis system then processes this information to make it more useful for managers.

Internal Records   Most marketing managers use **internal records information** and reports regularly, especially for making day-to-day planning, implementation, and control decisions. The company's accounting department prepares financial statements and keeps detailed records of sales and orders, costs, and cash flows. Manufacturing reports on production schedules, shipments, and inventories. The salesforce reports on reseller reactions and competitor activities. Information on customer satisfaction or service problems is reported by the Customer Service Department. Research studies done for one department may provide useful information for several others. Managers can use information gathered from these and other sources within the company to evaluate performance and to detect problems and opportunities.

Here are examples of how companies use internal records information in making marketing decisions:[7]

- *American Hospital Supply.* AHS supplied hospital purchasing departments with computers so that the hospitals could submit orders and other information directly to the AHS sales department. As a result, the timely arrival of orders and the speedy analysis of sales data allowed AHS to cut inventories, improve customer service, and obtain better terms on larger volumes from its suppliers. Thus, AHS achieved a sizable advantage over competitors and its market share soared.

- *Sears.* Sears uses internal records as a powerful marketing tool. Marketing managers use computerized information on Sears' 40 million customers to promote special product and service offers to such diverse target segments as gardeners, appliance buyers, and expectant mothers. For example, Sears keeps track of the appliance purchases of each customer and promotes special service-package deals to customers who have bought several appliances but have not purchased maintenance contracts for them. Soon managers at other Sears subsidiaries—Allstate Insurance, Dean Witter Reynolds, and Coldwell Banker (real estate brokers)—will be able to develop sales leads using the same data.

- *Mead Paper.* Mead salespeople can obtain on-the-spot answers to customers' questions about paper availability by dialing Mead Paper's computer center. The computer determines whether paper is available at the nearest warehouse and when it can be shipped. If it is not in stock, the computer checks the inventory at other nearby warehouses until one is located. If the paper is nowhere in stock, the computer determines where and when it can be produced. The salespeople get an answer in seconds and thus have an advantage over competitors.

Information from internal records can usually be obtained more quickly and cheaply than information from other sources, but it also presents some problems. Because it was collected for other purposes, the information may be incomplete or in the wrong form for making marketing decisions. For example, accounting department sales and cost data used for preparing financial statements must be adapted for use in evaluating product, salesforce, or channel performance. In addition, the many different areas of a large company produce great amounts of information; keeping track of it all is difficult. The marketing information system must gather, organize, process, and index this mountain of information so that managers can find it easily and get it quickly.

INTELLIGENCE GATHERING: SNOOPING ON COMPETITORS

Competitive intelligence gathering has grown dramatically as more and more companies need to know what their competitors are doing. Such well-known companies as Ford, Motorola, Westinghouse, General Electric, Gillette, Revlon, Del Monte, Kraft, Marriott, and J.C. Penney are known to be busy snooping on their competitors.

Techniques companies use to collect their own intelligence fall into four major groups.

Getting Information from Recruits and Competitors' Employees

Companies can obtain intelligence through job interviews or from conversations with competitors' employees. According to *Fortune*:

When they interview students for jobs, some companies pay special attention to those who have worked for competitors, even temporarily. Job seekers are eager to impress and often have not been warned about divulging what is proprietary. They sometimes volunteer valuable information.

Companies send engineers to conferences and trade shows to question competitors' technical people. Often conversations start innocently—just a few fellow technicians discussing processes and problems . . . [yet competitors'] engineers and scientists often brag about surmounting technical challenges, in the process divulging sensitive information.

Companies sometimes advertise and hold interviews for jobs that don't exist in order to entice competitors' employees to spill the beans . . . Often applicants have toiled in obscurity or feel that their careers have stalled. They're dying to impress somebody.

Getting Information from People Who Do Business with Competitors

Key customers can keep the company informed about competitors and their products:

For example, a while back Gillette told a large Canadian account the date on which it planned to begin selling its new Good News disposable razor in the United States. The Canadian distributor promptly called Bic and told it about the impending product launch. Bic put on a crash program and was able to start selling its razor shortly after Gillette did.

Intelligence can also be gathered by infiltrating customers' business operations:

Companies may provide their engineers free of charge to customers . . . The close, cooperative relationship that the engineers on loan cultivate with the customers' design staff often enables them to learn what new products competitors are pitching.

Getting Information from Published Materials and Public Documents

Keeping track of seemingly meaningless published information can provide competitor intelligence. For example, the types of people sought in help wanted ads can indicate something about a competitor's new strategies and products. Government agencies are another good source. For example:

Although it is often illegal for a company to photograph a competitor's plant from the air, there are legitimate ways to get the photos . . . Aerial photos often are on file with the U.S. Geological Survey or Environmental Protection Agency. These are public documents, available for a nominal fee.

Zoning and tax assessment offices often have tax information on local factories and even blueprints of the facility, showing square footage and types of machinery. It's all publicly available.

Getting Information by Observing Competitors or Analyzing Physical Evidence

Companies can get to know competitors better by buying their products or examining other physical evidence:

Marketing Intelligence

Marketing intelligence is everyday information about developments in the marketing environment that helps managers prepare and adjust marketing plans. The marketing intelligence system determines what intelligence is needed, collects it by searching the environment, and delivers it to marketing managers who need it.

Marketing intelligence can be gathered from many sources. Much intelligence can be collected from the company's own personnel—executives, engineers and scientists, purchasing agents, and the salesforce. But company people are often busy and fail to pass on important information. The company must "sell" its people on their importance as intelligence gatherers, train them to spot new developments, and urge them to report intelligence back to the company.

The company must also get suppliers, resellers, and customers to pass along important intelligence. Information on competitors can be obtained from what they say about themselves in annual reports, speeches and press releases, and advertisements. The company can also learn about competitors from what others say about them in business publications and at trade shows. Or the company can watch what competitors do—including buying and analyzing their products, monitoring their sales, and checking for new patents (see Marketing Highlight 4–1).

Perhaps the most thorough form of competitive intelligence is benchmarking, the art of taking apart a rival's product, learning everything possible about it, and then beating it component by component. Popular since the early 1980s, benchmarking has helped Xerox turn around its copying business and Ford develop the successful Taurus and Sable.

A wine cooler Coors introduced in 1985 quickly failed. But management still wanted into the business, so an intelligence task force of five started digging. Working closely with the product developers, the team decided to find out what kind of profit margins Gallo was making on its wine coolers. Coors bought the products and through chemical analysis determined what wine and flavorings were inside . . . then went to suppliers and got the price of the ingredients. The investigation revealed that because Gallo was vertically integrated—it grew its own grapes and made its own labels—Coors could not compete on price. Coors management reluctantly decided in 1986 not to reenter the market.

Beyond looking at competitors' products, companies can examine many other types of physical evidence:

In the absence of better information on market share and the volume of products competitors are shipping, companies have measured the rust on rails of railroad sidings to their competitors' plants or have counted the tractor-trailers leaving loading bays.

Some companies even buy their competitors' garbage:

Once it has left the competitors' premises, refuse is legally considered abandoned property. While some companies now shred the paper coming out of their design labs, they often neglect to do this for almost-as-revealing refuse from the marketing or public relations departments.

Although most of these techniques are legal and some are considered shrewd competitiveness, many involve question-

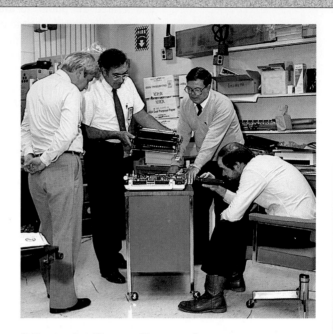

Collecting intelligence: Xerox engineers tear apart a competitor's product to assess its design and to estimate cost.

able ethics. The company should take advantage of publicly available information but avoid practices that might be considered illegal or unethical. A company does not have to break the law or accepted codes of ethics to get good intelligence information.

Companies also buy intelligence information from outside suppliers. The A. C. Nielsen Company sells data on brand shares, retail prices, and percentages of stores stocking different brands. The Market Research Corporation of America sells reports on weekly movements of brand shares, size, prices, and deals. For a fee, companies can subscribe to any of more than 3,000 online databases or information search services. For example, the *Adtrack* online database tracks all the advertisements of a quarter-page or larger from 150 major consumer and business publications. Companies can use these data to assess their own and competitors' advertising strategies and styles, shares of advertising space, media usage, and ad budgets. The *Donnelly Demographics* database provides demographic data from the U.S. census plus Donnelly's own demographic projections by state, city, or zip code. Companies can use it to measure markets and develop segmentation strategies. The *Electronic Yellow Pages,* containing listings from nearly all the nation's 4,800 phone books, is the largest directory of American companies available. A firm such as Burger King might use this database to count McDonald's restaurants in different geographic locations. A readily available online database exists to fill almost any marketing information need.[8]

Marketing intelligence can work in two directions, so companies must sometimes take steps to protect themselves from the snooping of competitors. For example, Kellogg had treated the public to tours of its Battle Creek plant since 1906 but recently closed its newly upgraded plant to outsiders to prevent competitors from getting any intelligence on its high-tech equipment. In its corporate offices, Du Pont displays a poster showing two people at a lunch table and warns, "Be careful in casual conversation. Keep security in mind."[9]

Some companies set up an office to collect and circulate marketing intelligence. The staff scans major publications, summarizes important news, and sends news bulletins to marketing managers. It develops a file of intelligence information and helps managers evaluate new information. These services greatly improve the quality of information available to marketing managers.

Marketing Research

Managers cannot always wait for information to arrive in bits and pieces from the marketing intelligence system. They often require formal studies of specific situations. For example, Compaq wants to know how many and what kinds of people or companies will buy its new ultralight personal computer. Or Barat College in Lake Forest, Illinois, needs to know what percentage of its target market has heard of Barat, what they know, how they heard about Barat, and how they feel about Barat. In such situations, the marketing intelligence system will not provide the detailed information needed, and managers normally do not have the skill or time to obtain the information on their own. They need formal marketing research.

We define **marketing research** as the function that links the consumer, customer, and public to the marketer through information—information used to identify and define marketing opportunities and problems; to generate, refine, and evaluate marketing actions; to monitor marketing performance; and to improve understanding of the marketing process.[10] Marketing research specifies the information needed to address marketing issues, designs the method for collecting information, manages and implements the data-collection process, analyzes the results, and communicates the findings and their implications.

A recent survey found that marketing researchers engage in a wide variety of activities, ranging from analyses of sales and market shares to studies of social values and policies (see Table 4-2). The ten most common activities are measurement of market

TABLE 4-2   Research Activities of 599 Companies

TYPE OF RESEARCH	PERCENTAGE DOING IT	TYPE OF RESEARCH	PERCENTAGE DOING IT
Advertising research		**Product research**	
1. Advertising motivation research	47%	1. New product acceptance and potential	76
2. Advertising copy research	61	2. Competitive product studies	87
3. Media research	68	3. Testing of existing products	80
4. Studies of ad effectiveness	76	4. Packaging research: design or physical	65
5. Studies of competitive advertising	67	characteristics	
Business economics and corporate research		**Sales and market research**	
1. Short-range forecasting (up to 1 year)	89	1. Measurement of market potentials	97
2. Long-range forecasting (over 1 year)	87	2. Market share analysis	97
3. Studies of business trends	91	3. Determination of market characteristics	97
4. Pricing studies	83	4. Sales analysis	92
5. Plant and warehouse location studies	68	5. Establishment of sales quotas, territories	78
6. Acquisition studies	73	6. Distribution channel studies	71
7. Export and international studies	49	7. Test markets, store audits	59
8. MIS (Marketing Information System)	80	8. Consumer panel operations	63
9. Operations Research	65	9. Sales compensation studies	60
10. Internal company employees	76	10. Promotional studies of premiums, coupons,	58
Corporate responsibility research		sampling, deals, etc.	
1. Consumer "right to know" studies	18		
2. Ecological impact studies	23		
3. Studies of legal constraints on advertising and promotion	46		
4. Social values and policies studies	39		

Source: Dik Warren Twedt, ed., *1983 Survey of Marketing Research* (Chicago: American Marketing Association, 1983), p. 41.

potentials, market-share analysis, the determination of market characteristics, sales analysis, studies of business trends, short-range forecasting, competitive product studies, long-range forecasting, marketing information systems studies, and pricing studies.

Every marketer needs research. A company can do marketing research in its own research department or have some or all of it done outside. Whether a company uses outside firms depends on the skills and resources within the company. Most large companies have their own marketing research departments. A company with no research department will have to buy the services of research firms. But even large companies with their own departments often use outside firms to do special research tasks or special studies.

Many people think of marketing research as a lengthy, formal process carried out by large marketing companies. But many small businesses and nonprofit organizations also use marketing research. Almost any organization can find informal, low-cost alternatives to the formal and complex marketing research techniques used by research experts in large firms (see Marketing Highlight 4–2).

The Marketing Research Process

The marketing research process (see Figure 4-2) consists of these four steps: *defining the problem and research objectives*, *developing the research plan*, *implementing the research plan*, and *interpreting and reporting the findings*.

Defining the Problem and Research Objectives

The marketing manager and the researcher must work closely together to define the problem carefully and agree on the research objectives. The manager best understands

---

MARKETING HIGHLIGHT 4—2

MARKETING RESEARCH IN SMALL BUSINESSES AND NONPROFIT ORGANIZATIONS

Managers of small businesses and nonprofit organizations often think that marketing research can be done only by experts in large companies with big research budgets. But many of the marketing research techniques discussed in this chapter can also be used less formally by smaller organizations—and at little or no expense.

Managers of small businesses and nonprofit organizations can obtain good marketing information simply by *observing* things around them. For example, retailers can evaluate new locations by observing vehicle and pedestrian traffic. They can visit competing stores to check on facilities and prices. They can evaluate their customer mix by recording how many and what kinds of customers shop in the store at different times. Competitor advertising can be monitored by collecting advertisements from local media.

Managers can conduct informal *surveys* using small convenience samples. The director of an art museum can learn what patrons think about new exhibits by conducting informal "focus groups"—inviting small groups to lunch and having discussions on topics of interest. Retail salespeople can talk with customers visiting the store; hospital officials can interview patients. Restaurant managers might make random phone calls during slack hours to interview consumers about where they eat out and what they think of various restaurants in the area.

Managers can also conduct their own simple *experiments*. For example, by changing the themes in regular fund-raising mailings and watching results, a nonprofit manager can find out much about which marketing strategies work

best. By varying newspaper advertisements, a store manager can learn the effects of things such as ad size and position, price coupons, and media used.

Small organizations can obtain most of the secondary data available to large businesses. In addition, many associations, local media, chambers of commerce, and government agencies provide special help to small organizations. The U.S. Small Business Administration offers dozens of free publications giving advice on topics ranging from planning advertising to ordering business signs. Local newspapers often provide information on local shoppers and their buying patterns.

Sometimes volunteers and colleges are willing to help carry out research. Nonprofit organizations can often use volunteers from local service clubs and other sources. Many colleges are seeking small businesses and nonprofit organizations to serve as cases for projects in marketing research classes.

Thus, secondary data collection, observation, surveys, and experiments can all be used effectively by small organizations with small budgets.

Although such informal research is less complex and costly, it must still be conducted carefully. Managers must carefully think through the objectives of the research, formulate questions in advance, recognize the biases introduced by smaller samples and less-skilled researchers, and conduct the research systematically. If carefully planned and implemented, such low-cost research can provide reliable information for improving marketing decision making.

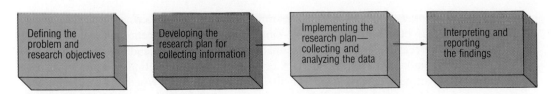

FIGURE 4-2
The marketing research process

the decision for which information is needed; the researcher best understands marketing research and how to obtain the information.

Managers must know enough about marketing research to help in the planning and to interpret research results. If they know little about marketing research, they may obtain the wrong information, accept wrong conclusions, or ask for information that costs too much. Experienced marketing researchers who understand the manager's problem should also be involved at this stage. The researcher must be able to help the manager define the problem and to suggest ways that research can help the manager make better decisions.

Defining the problem and research objectives is often the hardest step in the research process. The manager may know that something is wrong without knowing the specific causes. For example, managers of a discount retail store chain hastily decided that falling sales were caused by poor advertising and ordered research to test the company's advertising. When this research showed that current advertising was reaching the right people with the right message, the managers were puzzled. It turned out that the chain was not delivering what the advertising promised. Careful problem definition would have avoided the cost and delay of advertising research and would have suggested research on the real problem—consumer reactions to the products, services, and prices offered in the chain's stores.

When the problem has been carefully defined, the manager and researcher must set the research objectives. A marketing research project might have one of three types of objectives. Sometimes the objective is **exploratory**—to gather preliminary information that will help define the problem and suggest hypotheses. Sometimes the objective is **descriptive**—to describe things such as the market potential for a product or the demographics and attitudes of consumers who buy the product. Sometimes the objective is **causal**—to test hypotheses about cause-and-effect relationships. For example, would a 10-percent decrease in tuition at a private college result in an enrollment increase sufficient to offset the reduced tuition? Managers often start with exploratory research and later follow with descriptive or causal research.

The statement of the problem and research objectives will guide the entire research process. The manager and researcher should put the statement in writing to be certain that they agree on the purpose and expected results of the research.

Developing the Research Plan

The second step of the marketing research process calls for determining the information needed, developing a plan for gathering it efficiently, and presenting the plan to marketing management. The plan outlines sources of secondary data and spells out the specific research approaches, contact methods, sampling plans, and instruments that researchers will use to gather primary data.

DETERMINING SPECIFIC INFORMATION NEEDS.   Research objectives must be translated into specific information needs. For example, suppose Campbell decides to do research to find out how consumers would react to the company replacing its familiar red and white can with new bowl-shaped plastic containers that cost more but allow consumers to heat the soup in a microwave oven and eat it without using dishes. This research might call for the following specific information:

- The demographic, economic, and life-style characteristics of current soup users. (Busy working couples might find the convenience of the new packaging worth the price; families with children might want to pay less and wash the pan and bowls.)

- Consumer-usage patterns for soup—how much soup they eat, where, and when. (The new packaging might be ideal for adults eating lunch on the go but less convenient for parents feeding lunch to several children.)
- The number of microwave ovens in consumer and commercial markets. (The number of microwaves in homes and business lunchrooms will limit the demand for the new containers.)
- Retailer reactions to the new packaging. (Failure to get retailer support could hurt sales of the new package.)
- Consumer attitudes toward the new packaging. (The red and white Campbell can has become an American Institution—will consumers accept the new packaging?)
- Forecasts of sales of both new and current packages. (Will the new packaging increase Campbell's profits?)

Campbell managers will need these and many other types of information to decide whether or not to introduce the new packaging.

GATHERING SECONDARY INFORMATION. To meet the manager's information needs, the researcher can gather secondary data, primary data, or both. **Secondary data** consist of information that already exists somewhere, having been collected for another purpose. **Primary data** consist of information collected for the specific purpose at hand.

Researchers usually start by gathering secondary data. Table 4-3 shows the many

TABLE 4-3 **Sources of Secondary Data**	

A. Internal sources

Internal sources include company profit and loss statements, balance sheets, sales figures, sales call reports, invoices, inventory records, and prior research reports.

B. Government publications

Statistical Abstract of the U.S., updated annually, provides summary data on demographic, economic, social, and other aspects of the American economy and society.

County and City Data Book, updated every three years, presents statistical information for counties, cities, and other geographical units on population, education, employment, aggregate and median income, housing, bank deposits, retail sales, etc.

U.S. Industrial Outlook provides projections of industrial activity by industry and includes data on production, sales, shipments, employment, etc.

Marketing Information Guide provides a monthly annotated bibliography of marketing information. Other government publications include the *Annual Survey of Manufacturers*; *Business Statistics*; *Census of Manufacturers*; *Census of Population*; *Census of Retail Trade*, *Wholesale Trade*, and *Selected Service Industries*; *Census of Transportation*; *Federal Reserve Bulletin*; *Monthly Labor Review*; *Survey of Current Business*; and *Vital Statistics Report*.

C. Periodicals and books

Business Periodicals Index, a monthly, lists business articles appearing in a wide variety of business publications.

Standard and Poor's Industry Surveys provide updated statistics and analyses of industries.

Moody's Manuals provide financial data and names of executives in major companies.

Encyclopedia of Associations provides information on every major trade and professional association in the United States.

Marketing journals include the *Journal of Marketing*, *Journal of Marketing Research*, and *Journal of Consumer Research*.

Useful trade magazines include *Advertising Age*, *Chain Store Age*, *Progressive Grocer*, *Sales and Marketing Management*, *Stores*.

Useful general business magazines include *Business Week*, *Fortune*, *Forbes*, and *Harvard Business Review*.

D. Commercial data

Here are just a few of the dozens of commercial research houses selling data to subscribers:

A. C. Nielsen Company provides data on household purchasing (NPD/Nielsen Electronic Household Panel), supermarket scanner data (Scantrack), data on television audiences (Media Research Services), and others.

Arbitron/SAMI/Burke provides television and radio audience data (Arbitron), product movement reports based on warehouse withdrawals data from supermarkets, drugstores, and mass merchandisers (SAMI reports), and supermarket scanner data (Samscan).

Information Resources, Inc. provides supermarket scanner data for test marketing purposes (BehaviorScan) and for tracking grocery product movement (InfoScan).

MRB Group (Simmons Market Research Bureau) provides annual reports covering television markets, sporting goods, and proprietary drugs, giving VALS and geodemographic data by sex, income, age and brand preferences (selective markets and media reaching them).

I.M.S. International provides reports on the movements of pharmaceuticals, hospital laboratory supplies, animal health products, and personal care products.

MRCA Information Services provides data on weekly family purchases of consumer products (National Consumer Panel) and data on home food consumption (National Menu Census).

NFO Research provides data for the beverage industry (SIPS), mail order (MOMS), carpet and rug industries (CARS), and a mail panel for concept and product testing, attitudes and usage studies, and tracking and segmentation (Analycor).

secondary data sources, including *internal* and *external* sources.[11] Seconday data can usually be obtained more quickly and at a lower cost than primary data. For example, a visit to the library might provide all the information Campbell needs on microwave oven usage at almost no cost. A study to collect primary information might take weeks or months and cost thousands of dollars. Also, secondary sources can sometimes provide data an individual company cannot collect on its own information that is not directly available or would be too expensive to collect. For example, it would be too expensive for Campbell to conduct a continuing retail store audit to find out about the market shares, prices, and displays of competitors' brands. But it can buy the Nielsen Retail Index, which provides this information from regular audits of 1,300 supermarkets, 700 drug stores, and 150 mass merchandisers.

Secondary data also present problems. The needed information may not exist— researchers can rarely obtain all the data they need from secondary sources. For example, Campbell will not find existing information about consumer reactions to new packaging that it has not yet placed on the market. Even when data can be found, they might not be very usable. The researcher must evaluate secondary information carefully to make certain it is *relevant*, (fits research project needs), *accurate*, (reliably collected and reported), *current*, (up to date enough for current decisions), and *impartial* (objectively collected and reported).

Secondary data provide a good starting point for research and often help to define problems and research objectives. In most cases, however, secondary sources cannot provide all the needed information, and the company must collect primary data.

PLANNING PRIMARY DATA COLLECTION. Good decisions require good data. Just as researchers must carefully evaluate the quality of secondary information they obtain, they must also take great care in collecting primary data to assure that they provide marketing decision makers with relevant, accurate, current, and unbiased information. Table 4-4 shows that designing a plan for primary data collection calls for a number of decisions on *research approaches*, *contact methods*, *sampling plan*, and *research instruments*.

RESEARCH APPROACHES. **Observational research** is the gathering of primary data by observing relevant people, actions, and situations. For example:

- A food-products manufacturer sends researchers into supermarkets to find out the prices of competing brands or how much shelf space and display support retailers give its brands.
- A bank evaluates possible new branch locations by checking traffic patterns, neighborhood conditions, and the locations of competing branches.
- A maker of personal care products pretests its ads by showing them to people and measuring eye movements, pulse rates, and other physical reactions.
- A department store chain sends observers posing as customers to its stores to check on store conditions and customer service.
- A museum checks the popularity of various exhibits by noting the amount of floor wear around them.

Several companies sell information collected through *mechanical* observation. For example, the A.C. Nielsen Company attaches "*people meters*" to television sets in selected homes to record who watches which programs. Nielsen then provides summaries of the size and demographic makeup of audiences for different television programs. The television networks use these ratings to judge program popularity and to set charges for advertising time. Advertisers use the ratings when selecting programs for their commercials. *Checkout scanners* in retail stores also provide mechanical observation data. These laser scanners record consumer purchases in detail. Consumer products companies and

TABLE 4-4 Planning Primary Data Collection	RESEARCH APPROACHES	CONTACT METHODS	SAMPLING PLAN	RESEARCH INSTRUMENTS
	Observation	Mail	Sampling unit	Questionnaire
	Survey	Telephone	Sample size	Mechanical instruments
	Experiment	Personal	Sampling procedure	

retailers use scanner information to assess and improve product sales and store performance.[12] Some marketing research firms now offer **single-source data systems** that electronically monitor both consumers' purchases and their exposure to various marketing efforts in an effort to better evaluate the link between the two (see Marketing Highlight 4–3).

Observational research can be used to obtain information that people are unwilling or unable to provide. In some cases, observation may be the only way to obtain the needed information. On the other hand, some things simply cannot be observed—things such as feelings, attitudes, motives, or private behavior. Long-term or infrequent behavior is also difficult to observe. Because of these limitations, researchers often use observation along with other data collection methods.

Survey research is the approach best suited for gathering *descriptive* information. A company that wants to know about people's knowledge, attitudes, preferences, or buying behavior can often find out by asking them directly. Survey research can be structured or unstructured. *Structured* surveys use formal lists of questions asked of all respondents in the same way. *Unstructured* surveys let the interviewer probe respondents and guide the interview according to their answers.

MARKETING HIGHLIGHT 4–3

SINGLE-SOURCE DATA SYSTEMS: A POWERFUL NEW WAY TO MEASURE MARKETING IMPACT

Information Resources, Inc. knows all there is to know about the members of its panel households—what they eat for lunch, what they put in their coffee, and what they use to wash their hair, quench their thirsts, or make up their faces. The research company electronically monitors the television programs they watch and tracks the brands they buy, the coupons they use, where they shop, and what newspapers and magazines they read. These households are a part of IRI's Behavior-Scan service, a *single-source data system* that links consumers' exposure to television advertising, sales promotion, and other marketing efforts with their store purchases. Behavior-Scan and other single-source data systems have revolutionized the way consumer products companies measure the impact of their marketing activities.

The basics of single-source research are straightforward, and the IRI BehaviorScan system provides a good example. IRI maintains a panel of 70,000 households in 27 markets. The company meters each home's TV set to track who watches what and when, and it quizzes family members to find out what they read. It carefully records important facts about each household, such as family income, age of children, life style, and product and store buying history.

IRI also employs a panel of retail stores in each of its markets. For a fee, these stores agree to carry new products that IRI wishes to test and allow IRI to control such factors as shelf location, stocking, point-of-purchase displays, and pricing for these products.

Each BehaviorScan household receives an identification number. When household members shop for groceries in IRI panel stores, they give their identification number to the store check-out clerk. All the information about the family's purchases—brands bought, package sizes, prices paid—is recorded by the store's electronic scanner and immediately entered by computer into the family's purchase file. The system also records any other in-store factors that might affect purchase decisions, such as special competitor price promotions or shelf displays.

Thus, IRI builds a complete record of each household's demographic and psychographic make-up, purchasing behavior, media habits, and the conditions surrounding purchase. But IRI takes the process a step further. Through cable television, IRI controls the advertisements being sent to each household. It can beam different ads and promotions to different panel households, and then use the purchasing information obtained from scanners to assess which ads had more or less impact and how various promotions affected different kinds of consumers. Thus, from a single source, marketers can obtain information that links their marketing efforts directly with consumer buying behavior.

BehaviorScan and other single-source systems have their drawbacks, and some researchers are skeptical. One hitch is that such systems produce truckloads of data, more than most companies can handle. Another problem is cost: single-source data can cost marketers hundreds of thousands of dollars a year per brand. And because such systems are set up in only a relatively few market areas, usually small cities, the marketing often finds it difficult to generalize from the measures and results. Finally, although single-source systems provide important information for assessing the impact of promotion and advertising, they shed little light on the affects of other key marketing actions.

Despite these drawbacks, more and more companies are relying on single-source data systems to test new products and marketing strategies. Properly used, such systems can provide marketers with fast and detailed information about how their products are selling, who is buying them, and what factors affect purchase.

Sources: See Joanne Lipman, "Single-Source Ad Research Heralds Detailed Look at Household Habits," *Wall Street Journal*, February 16, 1988, p. 39; Joe Schwartz, "Back to the Source," *American Demographics*, January 1989, pp. 22–26; Thomas Exter, "Advertising and Promotion: The One-Two Punch," *American Demographics*, March 1990, pp. 18–21; and Magid M. Abraham and Leonard M. Lodish, "Getting the Most Out of Advertising and Promotion," *Harvard Business Review*, May–June 1990, pp. 50–60.

Survey research may be direct or indirect. In the *direct* approach, the research asks direct questions about behavior or thoughts—for example, "Why don't you buy clothes at K mart?" By contrast, the researcher might use the *indirect* approach by asking, "What kinds of people buy clothes at K mart?" From the response to this indirect question, the researcher may be able to discover why the consumer avoids K mart clothing—in fact, it may suggest reasons the consumer is not consciously aware of.

Survey research is the most widely used method for primary data collection, and it is often the only method used in a research study. The major advantage of survey research is its flexibility. It can be used to obtain many different kinds of information in many different marketing situations. Depending on the survey design, it may also provide information more quickly and at lower cost than observational or experimental research.

However, survey research also presents some problems. Sometimes people are unable to answer survey questions because they cannot remember or never thought about what they do and why. Or people may be unwilling to respond to unknown interviewers or about things they consider private. Busy people may not take the time. Respondents may answer survey questions even when they do not know the answer in order to appear smarter or more informed. Or they may try to help the interviewer by giving pleasing answers. Careful survey design can help to minimize these problems.

Whereas observation is best suited for exploratory research and surveys for descriptive research, **experimental research** is best suited for gathering *causal* information. Experiments involve selecting matched groups of subjects, giving them different treatments, controlling unrelated factors, and checking for differences in group responses. Thus, experimental research tries to explain cause-and-effect relationships. Observation and surveys may be used to collect information in experimental research.

Researchers at McDonald's might use experiments before adding a new sandwich to the menu to answer such questions as the following:

- How much will the new sandwich increase McDonald's sales?
- How will the new sandwich affect the sales of other menu items?
- Which advertising approach would have the greater effect on sales of the sandwich?
- How would different prices affect the sales of the product?
- Should the new item be targeted toward adults, children, or both?

For example, to test the effects of two different prices, McDonald's could set up the following simple experiment. It could introduce the new sandwich at one price in its restaurants in one city and at another price in restaurants in another city. If the cities are similar, and if all other marketing efforts for the sandwich are the same, then differences in sales in the two cities could be related to the price charged. More complex experiments could be designed to include other variables and other locations.

CONTACT METHODS.   Information can be collected by mail, telephone, or personal interview. Table 4-5 shows the strengths and weaknesses of each of these contact methods.

TABLE 4-5 Strengths and Weaknesses of the Three Contact Methods	MAIL	TELEPHONE	PERSONAL
1. Flexibility	Poor	Good	Excellent
2. Quantity of data that can be collected	Good	Fair	Excellent
3. Control of interviewer effects	Excellent	Fair	Poor
4. Control of sample	Fair	Excellent	Fair
5. Speed of data collection	Poor	Excellent	Good
6. Response rate	Poor	Good	Good
7. Cost	Good	Fair	Poor

Source: Adapted with permission of Macmillan Publishing Company from *Marketing Research: Measurement and Method*, 4th ed., by Donald S. Tull and Del I. Hawkins. Copyright © 1987 by Macmillan Publishing Company.

Mail questionnaires have many advantages. They can be used to collect large amounts of information at a low cost per respondent. Respondents may give more honest answers to more personal questions on a mail questionnaire than to an unknown interviewer in person or over the phone. No interviewer is involved to bias the respondent's answers.

However, mail questionnaires also have some disadvantages. They are not very flexible—they require simple and clearly worded questions; all respondents answer the same questions in a fixed order; and the researcher cannot adapt the questionnaire based on earlier answers. Mail surveys usually take longer to complete, and the response rate—the number of people returning completed questionnaires—is often very low. Finally, the researcher often has little control over the mail questionnaire sample—even with a good mailing list, it is often hard to control *who* at the mailing address fills out the questionnaire.

Telephone interviewing is the best method for gathering information quickly, and it provides greater flexibility than mail questionnaires. Interviewers can explain questions that are not understood. Depending on the respondent's answers, they can skip some questions or probe further on others. Telephone interviewing also allows greater sample control. Interviewers can ask to speak to respondents with the desired characteristics or even by name, and response rates tend to be higher than with mail questionnaires.

But telephone interviewing also has drawbacks. The cost per respondent is higher than with mail questionnaires, and people may not want to discuss personal questions with an interviewer. Using an interviewer increases flexibility but also introduces interviewer bias. The way interviewers talk, small differences in how they ask questions, and other differences may affect respondents' answers. Finally, different interviewers may interpret and record responses differently, and under time pressures some interviewers might even cheat by recording answers without asking questions.

Personal interviewing takes two forms—individual and group interviewing. *Individual interviewing* involves talking with people in their homes or offices, on the street, or in shopping malls. The interviewer must gain their cooperation, and the time involved can range from a few minutes to several hours. Sometimes a small payment is given to people in return for their time.

Group interviewing consists of inviting six to ten people to gather for a few hours with a trained interviewer to talk about a product, service, or organization. The interviewer needs objectivity, knowledge of the subject and industry, and some understanding of group and consumer behavior. The participants are normally paid a small sum for attending. The meeting is held in a pleasant place and refreshments are served to

Researchers watch a focus group session.

foster an informal setting. The interviewer starts with broad questions before moving to more specific issues and encourages free and easy discussion, hoping that group interactions will bring out actual feelings and thoughts. At the same time, the interviewer "focuses" the discussion—hence the name *focus-group interviewing*. The comments are recorded through written notes or on videotapes that are studied later. Focus-group interviewing is becoming one of the major marketing research tools for gaining insight into consumer thoughts and feelings.

Personal interviewing is quite flexible and can be used to collect large amounts of information. Trained interviewers can hold a respondent's attention for a long time and can explain difficult questions. They can guide interviews, explore issues, and probe as the situation requires. Personal interviews can be used with any type of questionnaire. Interviewers can show subjects actual products, advertisements, or packages and observe reactions and behavior. In most cases, personal interviews can be conducted fairly quickly.

The main drawbacks of personal interviewing are costs and sampling problems. Personal interviews may cost three to four times as much as telephone interviews. Group interview studies usually use small sample sizes to keep time and costs down, and it may be hard to generalize from the results. Because interviewers have more freedom in personal interviews, the problem of interviewer bias is greater.

Which contact method is best depends on what information the researcher wants and on the number and type of respondents to be contacted. Advances in computers and communications have had an impact on methods of obtaining information. For example, most research firms now do Computer Assisted Telephone Interviewing (CATI) using a combination of WATS (Wide Area Telephone Service) lines and data entry terminals. The interviewer reads a set of questions from a video screen and types the respondent's answers directly into the computer. Although this procedure requires a large investment in computer equipment and interviewer training, it eliminates data editing and coding, reduces errors, and saves time. Other research firms set up terminals in shopping centers—respondents sit down at a terminal, read questions from a screen, and type their own answers into the computer.[13]

Computer assisted telephone interviewing (CATI): The interviewer enters respondent's answers directly into the computer.

SAMPLING PLAN.   Marketing researchers usually draw conclusions about large groups of consumers by studying a small sample of the total consumer population. A **sample** is a segment of the population selected to represent the population as a whole. Ideally, the sample should be representative so that the researcher can make accurate estimates of the thoughts and behaviors of the larger population.

Designing the sample requires three decisions. First, *who* is to be surveyed (what *sampling unit*)? The answer to this question is not always obvious. For example, to study the decision-making process for a family automobile purchase, should the researcher interview the husband, wife, other family members, dealership salespeople, or all of these? The researcher must determine what information is needed and who is most likely to have it.

Second, *how many* people should be surveyed (what *sample size*)? Large samples give more reliable results than small samples. However, it is not necessary to sample the entire target market or even a large portion to get reliable results. If well-chosen, samples of less than one percent of a population can often give good reliability.

Third, *how* should the people in the sample be *chosen* (what *sampling procedure*)? Table 4-6 describes different types of samples. To obtain a representative sample, the researchers should draw one of the three types of *probability samples*. But when probability sampling costs too much or takes too much time, marketing researchers often take *nonprobability samples*. Nonprobability samples can serve well in many research situations, even though the sampling error cannot be measured. These varied ways of drawing samples have different costs and time limitations, as well as different accuracy and statistical properties. Which method is best depends on the needs of the research project.

RESEARCH INSTRUMENTS.   In collecting primary data, marketing researchers have a choice of two main research instruments—the *questionnaire* and *mechanical devices*.

The *questionnaire* is by far the most common instrument. Broadly speaking, a questionnaire consists of a set of questions presented to a respondent for his or her answers. The questionnaire is very flexible—there are many ways to ask questions. Questionnaires must be carefully developed and tested before they can be used on a large scale. A carelessly prepared questionnaire usually contains several errors (see Marketing Highlight 4–4).

In preparing a questionnaire, the marketing researcher must decide what questions to ask, the form of the questions, the wording of the questions, and the ordering of the questions. Questionnaires frequently leave out questions that should be answered and include questions that cannot be answered, will not be answered, or need not be answered. Each question should be checked to see that it contributes to the research objectives.

The *form* of the question can influence the response. Marketing researchers distinguish between closed-end and open-end questions. **Closed-end questions** include all the possible answers, and subjects make choices among them. Table 4-7A shows the most common forms of closed-end questions as they might appear in a Delta Airlines survey of airline users. **Open-end questions** allow respondents to answer in their own

TABLE 4-6 Types of Samples	**Probability sample**	
	Sample random sample	Every member of the population has a known and equal chance of selection.
	Stratified random sample	The population is divided into mutually exclusive groups (such as age groups), and random samples are drawn from each group.
	Cluster (area) sample	The population is divided into mutually exclusive groups (such as blocks), and the researcher draws a sample of the groups to interview.
	Nonprobability sample	
	Convenience sample	The researcher selects the easiest population members from which to obtain information.
	Judgment sample	The researcher uses his or her judgment to select population members who are good prospects for accurate information.
	Quota sample	The researcher finds and interviews a prescribed number of people in each of several categories.

A "QUESTIONABLE" QUESTIONNAIRE

Suppose that a summer camp director had prepared the following questionnaire to use in interviewing the parents of prospective campers. How would you assess each question?

1. What is your income to the nearest hundred dollars?

   People don't usually know their incomes to the nearest hundred dollars nor do they want to reveal their income that closely. Moreover, a researcher should never open a questionnaire with such a personal question.

2. Are you a strong or weak supporter of overnight summer camping for your children?

   What do "strong" and "weak" mean?

3. Do your children behave themselves well at a summer camp?
   Yes ( )   No ( )

   "Behave is a relative term. Furthermore, are "yes" and "no" the best responses to allow for this question?

Besides, will people want to answer this? Why ask the question in the first place?

4. How many camps mailed literature to you last April? This April?

   Who can remember this?

5. What are the most salient and determinant attributes in your evaluation of summer camps?

   What are "salient" and "determinant" attributes? Don't use big words on me!

6. Do you think it is right to deprive your child of the opportunity to grow into a mature person through the experience of summer camping?

   A loaded question. Given the bias, how can any parent answer "yes"?

---

words. The main forms are shown in Table 4-7B. Open-end questions often reveal more than closed-end questions because respondents are not limited in their answers. Open-end questions are especially useful in exploratory research in which the researcher is trying to find out what people think but not measuring how many people think in a certain way. Closed-end questions, on the other hand, provide answers that are easier to interpret and tabulate.

Care should also be used in the *wording* of questions. The researcher should use simple, direct, unbiased wording. The questions should be pretested before they are widely used. Care should also be used in the *ordering* of questions. The first question should create interest if possible. Difficult or personal questions should be asked last so that respondents do not become defensive. The questions should be arranged in a logical order.

Although questionnaires are the most common research instrument, *mechanical instruments* are also used. We discussed two mechanical instruments—people meters and supermarket scanners—earlier in the chapter. Another group of mechanical devices measures subjects' physical responses. For example, a galvanometer measures the strength of interest or emotions aroused by a subject's exposure to different stimuli, for example, an ad or picture. The galvanometer detects the minute degree of sweating that accompanies emotional arousal. The tachistoscope flashes an ad to a subject at an exposure range from less than one-hundredth of a second to several seconds. After each exposure, the respondents describe everything they recall. Eye cameras are used to study respondents' eye movements to determine at which points their eyes first focus and how long they linger on a given item.

PRESENTING THE RESEARCH PLAN.   At this stage, the marketing researcher should summarize the plan in a *written proposal*. A written proposal is especially important when the research project will be large and complex or when an outside firm carries it out. The proposal should cover the management problems addressed and the research objectives, the information to be obtained, the sources of secondary information or methods for collecting primary data, and the way the results will help management decision making. The proposal should also include research costs. A written research plan or proposal makes sure that the marketing manager and researchers have considered all the important aspects of the research and that they agree on why and how the research will be done.

TABLE 4-7 Types of Questions

A. CLOSED-END QUESTIONS

Name	Description	Example
Dichotomous	A question offering two answer choices.	"In arranging this trip, did you personally phone Delta?" Yes ☐ No ☐
Multiple choice	A question offering three or more answer choices.	"With whom are you traveling on this flight?" No one ☐ Children only ☐ Spouse ☐ Business associates/friends/relatives ☐ Spouse and children ☐ An organized tour group ☐
Likert scale	A statement with which the respondent shows the amount of agreement/disagreement.	"Small airlines generally give better service than large ones." Strongly disagree — Disagree — Neither agree nor disagree — Agree — Strongly agree 1 ☐ 2 ☐ 3 ☐ 4 ☐ 5 ☐
Semantic differential	A scale is inscribed between two bipolar words, and the respondent selects the point that represents the direction and intensity of his or her feelings.	*Delta Airlines* Large X :__:__:__:__:__ Small Experienced __:__:__:__: X :__ Inexperienced Modern __:__:__: X :__:__ Old-fashioned
Importance scale	A scale that rates the importance of some attribute from "not at all important" to "extremely important."	"Airline food service to me is" Extremely Important — Very important — Somewhat important — Not very important — Not at all important 1 __ 2 __ 3 __ 4 __ 5 __
Rating scale	A scale that rates some attribute from "poor" to "excellent."	"Delta's food service is" Excellent — Very good — Good — Fair — Poor 1 __ 2 __ 3 __ 4 __ 5 __
Intention-to-buy scale	A scale that describes the respondent's intentions to buy	"If in-flight telephone service were available on a long flight, I would" Definitely buy — Probably buy — Not certain — Probably not buy — Definitely not buy 1 __ 2 __ 3 __ 4 __ 5 __

B. OPEN-END QUESTIONS

Name	Description	Example
Completely unstructured	A question that respondents can answer in an almost unlimited number of ways.	"What is your opinion of Delta Airlines?"
Word association	Words are presented, one at a time, and respondents mention the first word that comes to mind.	"What is the first word that comes to your mind when you hear the following?" Airline _____ Delta _____ Travel _____
Sentence completion	Incomplete sentences are presented, one at a time, and respondents complete the sentence.	"When I choose an airline, the most important consideration in my decision is _____"
Story completion	An incomplete story is presented, and respondents are asked to complete it.	"I flew Delta a few days ago. I noticed that the exterior and interior of the plane had very bright colors. This aroused in me the following thoughts and feelings." *Now complete the story.*
Picture completion	A picture of two characters is presented, with one making a statement. Respondents are asked to identify with the other and fill in the empty balloon.	 Fill in the empty balloon.
Thematic Apperception Tests (TAT)	A picture is presented, and respondents are asked to make up a story about what they think is happening or may happen in the picture.	 Make up a story about what you see.

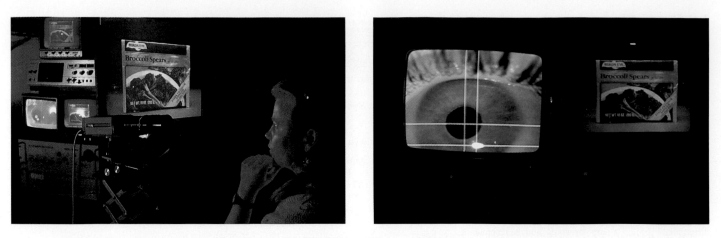

Mechanical research instruments: Eye cameras determine where eyes land and how long they linger on a given item.

Implementing the Research Plan

The researcher next puts the marketing research plan into action. This involves collecting, processing, and analyzing the information. Data collection can be carried out by the company's marketing research staff or by outside firms. The company keeps more control over the collection process and data quality by using its own staff. However, outside firms that specialize in data collection can often do the job more quickly and at lower cost.

The data-collection phase of the marketing research process is generally the most expensive and the most subject to error. The researcher should watch fieldwork closely to make sure that the plan is correctly implemented; developments to guard against include problems with contacting respondents, respondents who refuse to cooperate or who give biased or dishonest answers, and interviewers who make mistakes or take shortcuts.

The collected data must be processed and analyzed to isolate important information and findings. Data from questionnaires are checked for accuracy and completeness and coded for computer analysis. The researcher then applies standard computer programs to tabulate the results and to compute averages and other statistical measures.

Interpreting and Reporting the Findings

The researcher must now interpret the findings, draw conclusions, and report them to management. The researcher should not try to overwhelm managers with numbers and fancy statistical techniques. Rather, the researcher should present major findings that are useful in the major decisions faced by management.

However, interpretation should not be left only to the researchers. They are often experts in research design and statistics, but the marketing manager knows more about the problem and the decisions that must be made. In many cases, findings can be interpreted in different ways, and discussions between researchers and managers will help point to the best interpretations. The manager will also want to check that the research project was properly carried out and that all the necessary analysis was completed. Or, after seeing the findings, the manager may have additional questions that can be answered through further sifting of the data. Finally, the manager is the one who must ultimately decide what action the research suggests. The researchers may even make the data directly available to marketing managers so that they can perform new analyses and test new relationships on their own.

Interpretation is an important phase of the marketing process. The best research is meaningless if the manager blindly accepts wrong interpretations from the researcher. Similarly, managers may have biased interpretations—they tend to accept research results

DELICARE: A CASE OF RESEARCH MALPRACTICE?

In early 1986, Beecham Products launched Delicare, its new cold-water detergent for delicate fabrics, with much confidence. Yankelovich Clancy Shulman, a large research firm, had conducted simulated test market research and predicted that Delicare would quickly surpass market-leader Woolite, capturing a 45- to 52-percent market share. Beecham paid $75,000 for the research and spent over $6 million on introductory advertising for the product. Yet in the end, Delicare leveled off at less than 20 percent of the market, far short of the 30 percent Beecham needed to recoup its investment. Beecham claimed that Yankelovich's faulty forecasts had caused it to suffer huge losses. In a move that rocked the marketing research industry, Beecham sued Yankelovich for negligence and marketing malpractice, seeking $24 million in damages.

Simulated test markets like the one used in the Delicare research provide a quick and inexpensive method for estimating consumer responses to a new product. Sample consumers view ads for the new product and others, then shop in a simulated store containing a variety of products. The researcher keeps track of how many consumers buy the new product being tested and how many buy competing products. The data are fed into a sophisticated computer model which projects national sales from the results of the simulated test market. The Yankelovich model based its Delicare prediction on an important underlying statistic obtained from Beecham—the percentage of all U.S. homes that use a delicate-fabric detergent. Beecham claims it told Yankelovich to use a 30 percent figure but that the research firm used 75 percent. Yankelovich, however, claims that Delicare failed because Beecham provided inaccurate information, stopped advertising too soon, and ran ads different from those used in the research.

The Delicare case was eventually settled out of court. Although no details of the settlement were revealed, the Delicare case makes an important point for marketing managers and researchers—*both* must be closely involved in the entire research process. Beecham and Yankelovich managers share the blame for the Delicare research failure. If, as Yankelovich claims, Beecham provided inaccurate information, the researchers should have checked the data more carefully. And Beecham's marketers, rather than simply accepting the highly optimistic Delicare forecasts, should have reviewed the research outcomes and interpretations more critically. Ultimately, Beecham must take responsibility for its own marketing decisions. But if the company had worked more closely with Yankelovich throughout the research process, it might have avoided its Delicare fiasco.

Sources: See Matt Rothman, "A Case of Malpractice—in Marketing Research?" *Business Week*, August 10, 1987, pp. 28–29; Ted Knutson, "Marketing Malpractice Causes Concern," *Marketing News*, October 10, 1988, pp. 1, 7; and "AMA Attorneys Draft Sample Research Contract," *Marketing News*, September 11, 1989, pp. 12–13.

that show what they expected and to reject those that they did not expect or hope for. Thus, managers and researchers must work together closely when interpreting research results, and both share responsibility for the research process and resulting decisions (see Marketing Highlight 4–5).

Information Analysis Information gathered by the company's marketing intelligence and marketing research systems often requires more analysis, and sometimes managers may need more help to apply it to marketing problems and decisions. This help may include more advanced statistical analysis to learn more about both the relationships within a set of data and their statistical reliability. Such analysis allows managers to go beyond means and standard deviations in the data and to answer such questions as the following:

- What are the major variables affecting my sales and how important is each one?
- If I raised my price 10 percent and increased my advertising expenditures 20 percent, what would happen to sales?
- What are the best predictors of consumers who are likely to buy my brand versus my competitor's brand?
- What are the best variables for segmenting my market, and how many segments exist?

Information analysis might also involve a collection of mathematical models that will help marketers made better decisions. Each model represents some real system, process, or outcome. These models can help answer the questions of *what if* and *which is best*. During the past 20 years, marketing scientists have developed numerous models to help marketing managers make better marketing-mix decisions, design sales territories and sales-call plans, select sites for retail outlets, develop optimal advertising mixes, and forecast new-product sales.[14]

DISTRIBUTING INFORMATION

Marketing information has no value until managers use it to make better marketing decisions. The information gathered through marketing intelligence and marketing research must be distributed to the right marketing managers at the right time. Most companies have centralized marketing information systems that provide managers with regular performance reports, intelligence updates, and reports on the results of studies. Managers need these routine reports for making regular planning, implementation, and control decisions. But marketing managers may also need nonroutine information for special situations and on-the-spot decisions. For example, a sales manager having trouble with a large customer may want a summary of the account's sales and profitability over the past year. Or a retail store manager who has run out of a best-selling product may want to know the current inventory levels in the chain's other stores. In companies with centralized information systems, these managers must request the information from the MIS staff and wait; often, the information arrives too late to be useful.

Recent developments in information handling have caused a revolution in information distribution. With recent advances in microcomputers, software, and communications, many companies are decentralizing their marketing information systems. They are giving

MARKETING HIGHLIGHT 4–6

INFORMATION NETWORKS: DECENTRALIZING THE MARKETING INFORMATION SYSTEM

New information technologies are helping managers obtain, process, and send information directly through machines rather than relying on the services of information specialists. In our new "electronic society," the last decade's centralized information systems are giving way to systems that take information management out of the hands of staff specialists and put it into the hands of managers. Many companies are developing *information networks* that link separate technologies such as word processing, data processing, voice processing, and image processing into a single system.

For example, envision the working day of a future marketing manager. He awakes at 6:00 A.M. in his suburban Chicago home when his personal computer, programmed to sound an alarm when emergency messages arrive, tells him that the Marketing Vice President has hastily arranged a mid-morning meeting to discuss problems with an important customer in Pittsburgh. Checking his fax machine, he finds a copy of the meeting's agenda and a summary of key issues. He quickly showers and dresses, wolfs down breakfast, and departs for the office. During the thirty-minute commute, using the cellular phone in his car, he places a conference call to his assistant in the Chicago office and the Pittsburgh sales representative to find out more about the customer problem.

On arriving at work, the manager turns on his personal computer, ties into the company's information network, and reads the messages that arrived during the night, reviews the day's schedule, checks the status of an ongoing computer conference, reads several intelligence alerts, and browses through abstracts of relevant articles from the previous day's business press. To prepare for the morning meeting, the manager taps into the company's internal records system and retrieves information about the Pittsburgh customer—facts

about its operations and performance, key decision makers, recent sales history, and previous problems. The meeting runs smoothly, thanks to the wealth of information at hand. The meeting ends with a video conference in which the manager, vice president, Pittsburgh rep, and customer agree on steps to be taken to resolve the problem.

Before going to lunch, the manager prepares for an early afternoon meeting of the new products committee. He uses his PC to call up a recent marketing research report from microfilm storage, reviews relevant sections, edits them into a short report, sends copies electronically to other committee members who are also connected to the information network, and has the computer file a copy on microfilm.

The late afternoon is spent preparing sales and profit forecasts for the new product discussed at the earlier meeting. The manager obtains test-market data from company data banks and information on market demand, sales of competing products, and expected economic conditions from external data bases to which the company subscribes. These data are used as inputs for the sales-forecasting model stored in the company's model bank. The manager "plays" with the model to see how different assumptions affect predicted results.

Before leaving for home, the manager uses the computer to buy airline tickets for next week's trip to San Francisco and to make lunch reservations at a favorite restaurant there. At home that evening, the manager uses his laptop computer to contact the network, prepare a report on the product, and send copies to the computers of other involved managers, who can read them first thing in the morning. When the manager logs off, the computer automatically sets the alarm clock and puts out the cat.

managers direct access to information stored in the system.[15] In some companies, marketing managers can use a microcomputer to tie into the company's information network. From any location, they can obtain information from internal records or outside information services, analyze the information using statistical packages and models, prepare reports on a word processor, and communicate with others in the network through telecommunications (see Marketing Highlight 4–6).

Such systems offer exciting prospects. They allow the managers to get the information they need directly and quickly and to tailor it to their own needs. As more managers develop the skills needed to use such systems—and as improvements in the technology make them more economical—more and more marketing companies will use decentralized marketing information systems.

■ SUMMARY

In carrying out their marketing responsibilities, marketing managers need a great deal of information. Despite the growing supply of information, managers often lack enough information of the right kind or have too much of the wrong kind. To overcome these problems, many companies are taking steps to improve their marketing information systems.

A well-designed *marketing information system* begins and ends with the user. It first *assesses information needs* by interviewing marketing managers and surveying their decision environment to determine what information is desired, needed, and feasible to offer.

The MIS next *develops information* and helps managers to use it more effectively. *Internal records* provide information on sales, costs, inventories, cash flows, and accounts receivable and payable. Such data can be obtained quickly and cheaply, but must often be adapted for marketing decisions. The *marketing intelligence system* supplies marketing executives with everyday information about developments in the external marketing environment. Intelligence can be collected from company employees, customers, suppliers, and resellers, or by monitoring published reports, conferences, advertisements, competitor actions, and other activities in the environment.

Marketing research involves collecting information relevant to a specific marketing problem facing the company. Every marketer needs marketing research, and most large companies have their own marketing research departments. Marketing research involves a four-step process. The first step consists of the manager and researcher carefully *defining the problem and setting the research objectives*. The objective may be *exploratory*, *descriptive*, or *causal*. The second step consists of developing the *research plan* for collecting data from primary and secondary sources. *Primary data collection* calls for: choosing a *research approach* (observation, survey, experiment); choosing a *contact method* (mail, telephone, personal); designing a *sampling plan* (whom to survey, how many to survey, and how to choose them); and developing *research instruments* (questionnaire, mechanical). The third step consists of *implementing the marketing research plan* by collecting, processing, and analyzing the information. The fourth step consists of *interpreting and reporting the findings*. Further information analysis helps marketing managers to apply the information and provides advanced statistical procedures and models to develop more rigorous findings from the information.

Finally, the marketing information system distributes information gathered from internal sources, marketing intelligence, and marketing research to the right managers at the right times. More and more companies are decentralizing their information systems through *distributed processing networks* that allow managers to have direct access to information.

■ QUESTIONS FOR DISCUSSION

1. What are some kinds of information that managers would *like* to have? What kinds of information is a marketing information system likely to provide?

2. As a salesperson calling on industrial accounts, you would learn a lot that would help decision makers in your company. What kinds of information would you pass on to your company? How would you decide whether something is worth reporting?

3. Companies often test new products in plain white packages with no brand name or other marketing information. What does this "blind" testing really measure? Does applying these results to the "real" world raise any issues?

4. Companies often face quickly changing environments. Can market research information "go stale?" What issues does a manager face in using these research results?

5. The president of a campus organization has asked you to investigate why membership in the organization is declining. Discuss how you would apply the steps in the marketing research process to this project.

6. You are a research supplier, designing and conducting studies for a variety of companies. What is the *most* important thing you can do to ensure that your clients will get their money's worth from your services?

7. What research problem did the Coca-Cola company appear to be investigating prior to the introduction of New Coke? What problem *should* Coke have investigated instead?

8. What type of research would be appropriate in the following situations? Why?
   a. Kellogg wants to investigate the impact young children have on parents' decisions to buy breakfast foods.
   b. Your college bookstore wants to learn more about student perceptions of the store's merchandise, prices, and service.
   c. McDonald's is considering where to locate a new outlet in a fast-growing suburb.
   d. Gillette wants to determine whether a new line of deodorant for children will be profitable.

9. Focus-group interviewing is a widely-used and widely criticized research technique in marketing. What are the advantages and disadvantages of focus groups? What are some kinds of questions that focus groups can be used to investigate?

10. A recently completed study shows that most customers use more of your company's brand of shampoo than they need to get their hair clean. Company advertising encourages this overuse, which wastes customers' money but increases sales. You talked with the product manager and suggested that the advertising be modified, but no changes were made. Assuming that you are in the research department, what should you do now?

11. The IRI data system (Marketing Highlight 4-3) gets its information from panels of volunteers with cable television who live in small cities. Are these people typical? Does this make a difference in how a marketer should interpet this data?

■ KEY TERMS

Causal research. Marketing research to test hypotheses about cause-and-effect relationships.

Closed-end questions. Questions that include all the possible answers and allow subjects to make choices among them.

Descriptive research. Marketing research to better describe marketing problems, situations, or markets—such as the market potential for a product or the demographics and attitudes of consumers.

Experimental research. The gathering of primary data by selecting matched groups of subjects, giving them different treatments, controlling related factors, and checking for differences in group responses.

Exploratory research. Marketing research to gather preliminary information that will help to better define problems and suggest hypotheses.

Focus group interviewing. Personal interviewing which consists of inviting six to ten people to gather for a few hours with a trained interviewer to talk about a product, service, or organization. The interviewer "focuses" the group discussion on important issues.

Internal records information. Information gathered from sources within the company to evaluate marketing performance and to detect marketing problems and opportunities.

Marketing information system (MIS). People, equipment, and procedures to gather, sort, analyze, evaluate, and distribute needed, timely, and accurate information to marketing decision makers.

Marketing intelligence. Everyday information about developments in the marketing environment that helps managers prepare and adjust marketing plans.

Marketing research. The function that links the consumer, customer, and public to the marketer through information—information used to identify and define marketing opportunities and problems; to generate, refine, and evaluate marketing actions; to monitor marketing performance; and to improve understanding of the marketing process.

Observational research. The gathering of primary data by observing relevant people, actions, and situations.

Open-end questions. Questions that allow respondents to answer in their own words.

Primary data. Information collected for the specific purpose at hand.

Sample. A segment of the population selected for marketing research to represent the population as a whole.

Secondary data. Information that already exists somewhere, having been collected for another purpose.

Single-source data systems. Electronic monitoring systems that link consumers' exposure to television advertising and promotion (measured using television meters) with what they buy in stores (measured using store checkout scanners).

Survey research. The gathering of primary data by asking people questions about their knowledge, attitudes, preferences, and buying behavior.

■ REFERENCES

1. Based on numerous sources, including "Coke 'Family' Sales Fly as New Coke Stumbles," *Advertising Age*, January 17, 1986, p. 1; Jack Honomichl, "Missing Ingredients in 'New' Coke's Research," *Advertising Age*, July 22, 1985, p. 1; and Patricia Winters, "For New Coke, 'What Price Success?'" *Advertising Age*, March 20, 1989, pp. S1–S2.

2. Marion Harper, Jr., "A New Profession to Aid Management," *Journal of Marketing*, January 1961, p. 1.

3. John Naisbitt, *Megatrends: Ten New Directions Transforming Our Lives* (New York: Warner Books, 1984).

4. "Harnessing the Data Explosion," *Sales and Marketing Management*, January 1987, p. 31.

5. Naisbitt, *Megatrends*, p. 16.

6. Donald S. Tull and Del I. Hawkins, *Marketing Research: Measurement and Method*, 4th ed. (New York: MacMillan, 1987), pp. 40–41, 750–60.

7. See "Business Is Turning Data into a Potent Strategic Weapon," *Business Week*, August 22, 1983, p. 92; Catherine L. Harris, "Information Power: How Companies Are Using New Technologies to Gain a Competitive Edge," *Business Week*, October 14, 1985, pp. 108–14; and "Decision Systems for Marketers," *Marketing Communications*, March 1986, pp. 163–90.

8. See Tim Miller, "Focus: Competitive Intelligence," *Online Access Guide*, March/April 1987, pp. 43–57.

9. Ibid, p. 46.

10. The American Marketing Association officially adopted this definition in 1987.

11. For an excellent annotated reference to major secondary sources of business and marketing data, see Thomas C. Kinnear and James R. Taylor, *Marketing Research: An Applied Approach* (New York: McGraw-Hill, 1983), pp. 146–56, 169–84. Also see "Top 50 Research Companies Profiles," *Advertising Age*, June 5, 1989, pp. S2–S19; and *The Best 100 Sources of Marketing Information*, a supplement to *American Demographics*, 1989.

12. See Wayne Walley, "Meters Set New TV Ground Rules," *Advertising Age*," October 30, 1989, p. 12; and Zachary

Schiller, "Thanks to the Checkout Scanner, Marketing Is Losing Some of Its Mystery," *Business Week*, August 28, 1989, p. 57.

13. Selwyn Feinstein, "Computers Replacing Interviewers for Personnel and Marketing Tasks," *Wall Street Journal*, October 9, 1986, p. 35; and Diane Crispell, "People Talk, Computers Listen," *American Demographics*, October 1989, p. 8.

14. For more on statistical analysis, consult Tull and Hawkins, *Marketing Research*. For a review of marketing models, see Gary L. Lilien and Philip Kotler, *Marketing Decision Making: A Model Building Approach* (New York: Harper & Row, 1983); also see John D. C. Little, "Decision Support Systems for Marketing Managers," *Journal of Marketing*, Summer 1979, pp. 9–26.

15. See Peter Nulty, "How Personal Computers Change Managers' Lives," *Fortune*, September 3, 1984, pp. 38–48; "Marketing Managers No Stranger to the PC," *Sales & Marketing Management*, May 13, 1985; and "Make Way for the Salesman's Best Friend," *Sales & Marketing Management*, February 1988, pp. 53–56.

FAMILY SERVICE, INC.: MARKETING RESEARCH IN A SOCIAL SERVICE AGENCY

Family Service was established in 1941 as a private, non-profit organization. In 1942, the agency obtained United Way funding for the addition of a school lunch program. Since that time, the agency has undergone a series of name changes in an attempt to reflect changes in its service offerings. In 1983, the agency once again operated under the name of Family Service, Inc., and its service included counseling, family-life education, and home health care.

During 1983, Ann Marek, director of community affairs, became concerned about the community's lack of knowledge regarding available services. However, before embarking on an awareness campaign, she felt it necessary to assess the community's perceptions of Family Service and other agencies offering similar services.

Marek arranged for a local graduate student in marketing to assist with the project. Since the home health market was extremely competitive, the project involved a market-research survey of the general public with emphasis on home health services. Marek felt it was also important to survey physicians because many of Family Service's home health clients were referred by their doctors.

Telephone interviewing yielded 184 completed interviews from a random sample of 400 names drawn from the residential listings in the telephone directory. Respondents were first asked how they would rate the services provided by voluntary organizations in general. Ratings were on a scale of 1 to 5, 5 being high and 1 low. The results are shown in Table 1.

Respondents were then asked if they were aware of several specific organizations. Awareness did not mean knowledge of services—only that respondents were aware of the organization's existence. Respondents were then asked to rate (on a scale of 1 to 5) the overall performance of all organizations of which they were aware. The results are shown in Table 2. The 75 respondents aware of Family Service were also asked what they considered to be the most important criterion in selecting a provider of counseling, home health, and educational services. The results are shown in Table 3.

Telephone interviewing produced 102 completed interviews from a random list of 350 physicians. Each doctor was asked first to rate the efforts of home health organizations in general (scales of 1 to 5). The mean response was 3.82, with 80 no responses.

Physicians were then asked if they were aware of several specific organizations. If aware of an organization, he or she was also asked to rate the performance of that organization. The results are shown in Table 4.

The interviewer noted that although several doctors had heard of an organization, they did not know enough about it to rate it. Others, however, said that although they knew of an organization and had actually referred patients to it, they were unable to give a rating because they did not know how well the organization had served the patients.

TABLE 1 Overall Rating of Voluntary Organization

Rating	Number
Excellent (5)	38
Good (4)	87
Fair (3)	14
Poor (2)	1
Very Poor (1)	1
No rating	43
Mean = 4.13	
Standard deviation = .781	

TABLE 2 Awareness and Ratings of Specific Organizations

Organization	No. Aware	No. Rated	Mean Rating
United Way	160	128	3.70
North Texas Home Health Services	36	23	4.00
Crisis Intervention	118	79	3.84
Family Service	75	48	3.90
Meals on Wheels	170	138	4.59
Parenting Guidance Center	100	69	4.12
Visiting Nurses Association	107	72	4.31
Mental Health/Mental Retardation	154	108	4.11
Home Health Services of Tarrant County	69	41	3.93

TABLE 3 Criteria for Selecting Provider of Services

Criteria	No. of Responses
Quality	5
Accreditation	3
Cost	5
Recommendations*	23
Image/reputation	8
Credentials/knowledge of staff	9
Supportive staff	1
Success rate	2
Needs/benefits	2
Tradition	1
Confidentiality	1
Communication	1
Christian organization	1
Don't know	13

* Many respondents specified recommendations from doctors, ministers, school counselors, friends, and relatives.

Doctors were also asked to which home health organizations they usually referred their patients. Of the 102 interviewed physicians, 15 reported that they never referred to home health agencies. Of the remaining 87, 25 could not name any specific agency. Several of these 25 stated that they did not make the actual referral—that although they prescribed the needed services, a nurse or the hospital discharge planner actually selected the provider.

QUESTIONS

1. How does the general public view Family Service and the other agencies?
2. What are the marketing implications of Table 3?
3. How do physicians view Family Service and other similar agencies?
4. What is the importance of the discrepancy between the number of physicians who were aware of an organization and the number who rated the organization?
5. What are the marketing implications of the 25 doctors who could not name the agency or agencies to which their patients were referred?
6. What recommendations would you make to Family Service?

Source: This case was prepared by Donna Legg, Texas Christian University. Used with permission.

TABLE 4 Physicians' Awareness and Ratings of Specific Organizations

Organization	No. Aware	No. Rated	Mean Rating
United Way	94	75	3.68
North Texas Home Health Services	52	35	3.86
Crisis Intervention	65	35	4.03
Family Service	50	38	3.71
Meals on Wheels	89	68	4.25
Parenting Guidance Center	50	28	4.00
Visiting Nurses Association	78	61	3.95
Mental Health/Mental Retardation	91	64	3.63
Home Health Services of Tarrant County	57	41	3.76

5

Consumer Markets: Influences on Consumer Behavior

op managers at Porsche spend a great deal of time thinking about customers. They want to know who their customers are, what they think and how they feel, and why they buy a Porsche rather than a Jaguar, a Ferrari, or a big Mercedes coupe. These are difficult questions—even Porsche owners themselves don't know exactly what motivates their buying. But Porsche management needs to put top priority on understanding customers and what makes them tick.

Porsche appeals to a very narrow segment of financially successful people—achievers who set very high goals for themselves and then work doggedly to meet them. They expect no less from "their hobbies, or the clothes they wear, or the restaurants they go to, or the cars they drive." These achievers see themselves not as a regular part of the larger world, but as exceptions. They buy Porsches because the car mirrors their self-image—it stands for the things owners like to see in themselves and in their lives.

Most of us buy what Porsche executives call utility vehicles—"cars to be used: to go to work, to deliver the kids, to go shopping." We base buying decisions on facts like price, size, function, fuel economy, and other practical considerations. But a Porsche is a non-utility car—one to be enjoyed, not just used. Porsche buyers are moved not by facts, but by feelings. They are trying to match their dreams. To most Porsche owners, a car is more than mere transportation. It's like a piece of clothing, "something the owner actually wears and is seen in. . . . It's a very personal relationship, one that has to do with

the way the car sounds, the way it vibrates, the way it feels." People buy Porsches because they enjoy driving the car, just being in it. "Just to get there, they could do it a lot less expensively. The car is an expression of themselves." Surprisingly, many Porsche owners are not car enthusiasts; they are not interested in racing or learning how to drive a high-performance car. They simply like the way a Porsche makes them feel or what the car tells others about their achievements, life styles, and stations in life.

A Porsche costs a lot of money, but price isn't much of an issue with most buyers. The company deals often with people who can buy anything they want. To many Porsche owners, the car is a hobby. In fact, Porsche's competition comes not just from other cars, but from such things as sailboats, summer homes, and airplanes. But "most of those objects require a lot of one thing these folks don't have, and that's time. If you have a Porsche and make *it* your hobby, you can enjoy it every day on your way to work and on your way to the airport, something you can't do with a sailboat or summer home."

Porsche has traditionally worked hard to meet its buyers' expectations. But in the mid-1980s, the company made a serious marketing blunder—it shifted toward *mass* rather than *class* marketing. It increased its sales goal by nearly 50 percent, to 60,000 cars a year. To meet this volume goal, Porsche emphasized lower-priced models that sold for as little as $20,000. Moreover, after decades of priding itself on progressive engineering, high performance, and tasteful, timeless styling, the company allowed its models to grow out-of-date. These moves tarnished Porsche's exclusive image and confused its loyal but demanding customers. At the same time, Porsche was battered by a falling U.S. dollar and increasingly fierce competition from Nissan, Toyota, BMW, and other rivals pushing new luxury sports cars. As a result, Porsche's sales plunged by 51 percent in 1988.

Porsche then fought to rebuild its damaged image and to regain rapport with its customers. It revamped its model lines, once again targeting the high end of the market—the 1989 models ranged from $40,000 to $75,000. It set sales goal at a modest 40,000 cars a year, less than a month's production at Chevrolet. The company now looks for only moderate but profitable growth; it wants to make one less Porsche than the demand. According to one executive, "we aren't looking for volume . . . we're searching for exclusivity." Porsche does all it can to make Porsche ownership very special. It has even hired a representative to sell its cars to celebrities, executives of large companies, top athletes, and other notables. Having high-profile individuals driving Porsches and talking to their friends about them at cocktail parties is the best advertising the company could get.

Thus, understanding Porsche buyers is an essential but difficult task—the company must carefully craft the car and its image to match buyer needs and desires. But buyers are moved by a complex set of deep and subtle motivations. Their behavior springs from deeply held values and attitudes, from their view of the world and their place in it, from what they think of themselves and what they want others to think of them, from rationality and common sense and from whimsy and impulse. The chief executive at Porsche summed it up this way: ". . . If you really want to understand our customers, you have to understand the phrase, 'if I were going to be a car, I'd be a Porsche.' "[1]

CHAPTER OBJECTIVES

After reading this chapter, you should be able to:

1. Define the consumer market and construct a simple model of consumer buying behavior.
2. Name the four major factors that influence consumer buying behavior.
3. List the stages in the buyer decision process.
4. Describe the adoption process for new products.

The Porsche example shows that many different factors affect consumer buying behavior. Buying behavior is never simple, yet understanding it is the essential task of marketing management.

This chapter and the next explore the dynamics of consumer behavior and the consumer market. The **consumer market** consists of all the individuals and households who buy or acquire goods and services for personal consumption. The American consumer market consists of about 250 million people who consume more than $3 trillion of goods and services—that's more than $12,000 worth for every man, woman, and child. Each year this market grows by several million persons and more than $100 billion, making it one of the most attractive consumer markets in the world.

American consumers vary tremendously in age, income, education level, and tastes. And they buy an incredible variety of goods and services. How consumers make their choices among these products embraces a fascinating array of personal, cultural, and social factors.

MODEL OF CONSUMER BEHAVIOR

In earlier times, marketers could understand consumers well through the daily experience of selling to them. But as firms and markets have grown in size, many marketing decision makers have lost direct contact with their customers. Most marketers have had to turn to consumer research. They are spending more money than ever to study consumers, trying to learn more about consumer behavior. Who buys? How do they buy? When do they buy? Where do they buy? Why do they buy?

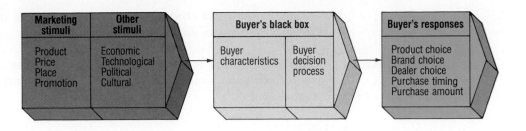

FIGURE 5-1
Model of buyer behavior

The central question is this: How do consumers respond to various marketing stimuli the company might use? The company that really understands how consumers will respond to different product features, prices, and advertising appeals has a great advantage over its competitors. Therefore, companies and academics have heavily researched the relationship between marketing stimuli and consumer response. Their starting point is the stimulus-response model of buyer behavior shown in Figure 5-1. This figure shows that marketing and other stimuli enter the consumer's "black box" and produce certain responses. Marketers must figure out what is in the buyer's "black box."[2]

On the left, marketing stimuli consist of the four Ps—product, price, place, and promotion. Other stimuli include major forces and events in the buyer's environment—economic, technological, political, and cultural. All these stimuli enter the buyer's black box, where they are turned into a set of observable buyer responses shown on the right—product choice, brand choice, dealer choice, purchase timing, and purchase amount.

The marketer wants to understand how the stimuli are changed into responses inside the consumer's black box. The black box has two parts. First, the buyer's characteristics influence how he or she perceives and reacts to the stimuli. Second, the buyer's decision process itself affects the buyer's behavior. In this chapter, we look at buyer characteristics as they affect buying behavior. In the next chapter, we look at the buyer decision process.

PERSONAL CHARACTERISTICS AFFECTING CONSUMER BEHAVIOR

Consumer purchases are strongly influenced by cultural, social, personal, and psychological characteristics. These factors are shown in Figure 5-2. For the most part, although they cannot be controlled by the marketer, they must be taken into account. We illustrate these characteristics for the case of a hypothetical consumer named Jennifer Smith. Jennifer Smith is a married college graduate who works as a brand manager in a leading consumer packaged-goods company. She wants to find a new leisure-time activity that will provide contrast to her working day. She is considering buying a camera and taking up photography. Many characteristics in her background will affect the way she

FIGURE 5-2
Factors influencing behavior

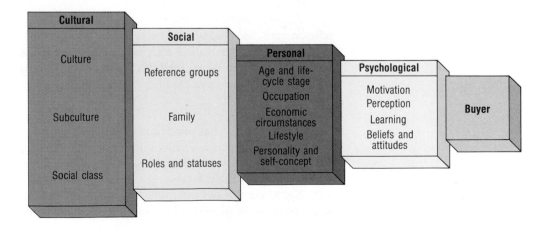

evaluates cameras and chooses a brand. The remainder of the chapter examines the personal characteristics that affect a consumer's behavior.

Cultural Factors

Cultural factors exert the broadest and deepest influence on consumer behavior. The marketer needs to understand the roles played by the buyer's *culture*, *subculture*, and *social class*.

Culture

Culture is the most basic cause of a person's wants and behavior. Human behavior is largely learned. Growing up in a society, a child learns basic values, perceptions, wants, and behaviors from the family and other important institutions. An American child normally learns or is exposed to the following values: achievement and success, activity and involvement, efficiency and practicality, progress, material comfort, individualism, freedom, external comfort, humanitarianism, youthfulness, and fitness and health.[3]

Jennifer Smith's wanting a camera is a result of being raised in a modern society in which camera technology and a whole set of consumer learnings and values have developed. Jennifer knows what cameras are. She knows how to read instructions, and her society has accepted the idea of women photographers. In another culture—say, a primitive tribe in central Australia—a camera may mean nothing. It may simply be a curiosity.

Marketers are always trying to spot *cultural shifts* in order to imagine new products that might be wanted. For example, the cultural shift toward greater concern about health and fitness has created a huge industry for exercise equipment and clothing, lighter and more natural foods, and health and fitness services. The shift toward informality has resulted in more demand for casual clothing, simpler home furnishings, and lighter entertainment. And the increased desire for leisure time has resulted in more demand for convenience products and services such as microwave ovens and fast food. It has also created a huge catalog-shopping industry. More than 6,500 catalog companies—ranging from giant retailers like Sears and Spiegel to specialty retailers like L. L. Bean, Sharper Image, Royal Silk, and Lands' End—bombard American households with 8.5 billion catalogs each year.

Subculture

Each culture contains smaller **subcultures,** or groups of people with shared value systems based on common life experiences and situations. Nationality groups such as the Irish, Polish, Italians, and Hispanics are found within larger communities and have distinct ethnic tastes and interests. Religious groups such as Catholics, Mormons, Presbyterians, and Jews are subcultures with their own preferences and taboos. Racial groups such as the blacks and Asians have distinct culture styles and attitudes. Geographical areas such as the South, California, and New England are distinct subcultures with characteristic life styles. Many of these subcultures make up important market segments, and marketers often design products and marketing programs tailored to the needs of these segments (see Marketing Highlight 5–1).[4]

Jennifer Smith's interest in various goods will thus be influenced by her nationality, religion, race, and geographical background. These factors will affect her food preferences, clothing choices, recreation activities, and career goals. Subcultures attach different meanings to picture taking, and this could affect not only Jennifer's interest in cameras but in the brand she buys.

Social Class

Almost every society has some form of social class structure. **Social classes** are relatively permanent and ordered divisions in a society whose members share similar values, interests, and behaviors. Social scientists have identified the seven American social classes shown in Table 5-1.

Social class is not determined by a single factor such as income but is measured as a combination of occupation, income, education, wealth, and other variables. In

TABLE 5-1
Characteristics of Seven Major American Social Classes

Upper uppers (less than 1 percent)
Upper uppers are the social elite who live on inherited wealth and have well-known family backgrounds. They give large sums to charity, run debutante balls, own more than one home, and send their children to the finest schools. They are a market for jewelry, antiques, homes, and vacations. They often buy and dress conservatively rather than showing off their wealth. While small in number, upper uppers serve as a reference group for others to the extent that their consumption decisions trickle down and are imitated by the other social classes.

Lower uppers (about 2 percent)
Lower uppers have earned high income or wealth through exceptional ability in the professions or business. They usually begin in the middle class. They tend to be active in social and civic affairs and buy for themselves and their children the symbols of status, such as expensive homes, schools, yachts, swimming pools, and automobiles. They include the new rich who consume conspicuously to impress those below them. They want to be accepted in the upper-upper stratum, a status more likely to be achieved by their children than by themselves.

Upper middles (12 percent)
Upper middles possess neither family status nor unusual wealth. They are primarily concerned with ''career.'' They have attained positions as professionals, independent businesspersons, and corporate managers. They believe in education and want their children to develop professional or administrative skills so that they will not drop into a lower stratum. Members of this class like to deal in ideas and ''high culture.'' They are joiners and highly civic-minded. They are the quality market for good homes, clothes, furniture, and appliances. They seek to run a gracious home, entertaining friends and clients.

Middle class (32 percent)
The middle class is made up of average-pay white- and blue-collar workers who live on ''the better side of town'' and try to ''do the proper things.'' To keep up with the trends, they often buy products that are popular. Twenty-five percent own imported cars, and most are concerned with fashion, seeking the better brand names. Better living means owning a nice home in a nice neighborhood with good schools. The middle class believes in spending more money on worthwhile experiences for their children and aiming them toward a college education.

Working class (38 percent)
The working class consists of average-pay blue-collar workers and those who lead a ''working class life style,'' whatever their income, school background, or job. The working class depends heavily on relatives for economic and emotional support, for tips on job opportunities, for advice on purchases, and for assistance in times of trouble. The working class maintains sharper sex role divisions and stereotyping. Car preferences include standard size and larger cars, rejecting domestic and foreign compacts.

Upper lowers (9 percent)
Upper lowers are working (are not on welfare), although their living standard is just above poverty. They perform unskilled work for very poor pay although they strive toward a higher class. Often, upper lowers are educationally deficient. Although they fall near the poverty line financially, they manage to ''present a picture of self-discipline'' and ''maintain some effort at cleanliness.''

Lower lowers (7 percent)
Lower lowers are on welfare, visibly poverty stricken, and usually out of work or have ''the dirtiest jobs.'' Often they are not interested in finding a job and are permanently dependent on public aid or charity for income. Their homes, clothes, and possessions are ''dirty,'' ''raggedy,'' and ''broken-down.''

Source: See Richard P. Coleman, ''The Continuing Significance of Social Class to Marketing,'' *Journal of Consumer Research*, December, 1983, pp. 265–280; and Richard P. Coleman and Lee P. Rainwater, *Social Standing in America: New Dimension of Class* (New York: Basic Books, 1978).

some social systems, members of different classes are reared for certain roles and cannot change their social positions. But in the United States, the lines between social classes are not fixed and rigid; people can move to a higher social class or drop into a lower one. Marketers are interested in social class because people within a given social class tend to exhibit similar behavior, including buying behavior.

Social classes show distinct product and brand preferences in such areas as clothing, home furnishings, leisure activity, and automobiles. Jennifer Smith's social class may affect her camera decision. She may have come from a higher social class background. In this case, her family probably owned an expensive camera and may have dabbled in photography. The fact that she thinks about ''going professional'' is also in line with a higher social class background.

Social Factors

A consumer's behavior is also influenced by social factors, such as the consumer's *small groups*, *family*, and *social roles and status*. Because these social factors can strongly affect consumer responses, companies must take them into account when designing their marketing strategies.

MARKETERS TARGET IMPORTANT SUBCULTURE GROUPS

When subcultures grow large and affluent enough, companies often design special marketing programs to serve their needs. Here are examples of three such important subculture groups.

Hispanic consumers. For years marketers have viewed the Hispanic market—Americans of Mexican, Cuban, and Puerto Rican descent—as small and poverty-stricken, but these perceptions are badly out of date. Expected to number 40 million by the year 2000, Hispanics are the second largest and fastest-growing U.S. minority. Annual Hispanic purchasing power totals $134 billion. More than half of all Hispanics live in one of six metropolitan areas—Los Angeles, New York, Miami, San Antonio, San Francisco, and Chicago. They are easy to reach through the growing selection of Spanish-language broadcast and print media that cater to Hispanics. Hispanics have long been a target for marketers of food, beverages, and household care products. But as the segment's buying power increases, Hispanics are now emerging as an attractive market for pricier products such as computers, financial services, photography equipment, large appliances, life insurance, and automobiles. Hispanic consumers tend to be brand-conscious and quality-conscious—generics don't sell well to Hispanics. Perhaps more important, Hispanics are very brand-loyal, and they favor companies who show special interest in them. Many companies are devoting larger ad budgets and preparing special appeals to woo Hispanics. Because of the segment's strong brand loyalty, companies that get the first foothold have an important head start in this fast-growing market.

Black consumers. If the U.S. Population of 30 million black Americans—with a total purchasing power of $218 billion annually—were a separate nation, their buying power would rank twelfth in the free world. The black population in the U.S. is growing in affluence and sophistication. Blacks spend relatively more than whites on clothing, personal care, home furnishings, and fragrances; and relatively less on food, transportation, and recreation. Although more price conscious, blacks are also strongly motivated by quality and selection. They place more importance than other groups on brand names, are more brand loyal, do less "shopping around," and shop more at neighborhood stores. In recent years, many large companies—Sears, McDonald's, Procter & Gamble, Coca-Cola—have stepped up their efforts to tap this lucrative market. They employ black-owned advertising agencies, use black models in their ads, and place ads in black consumer magazines. Some companies develop special

Marketers target important subculture groups such as Hispanic, black, and senior consumers.

products, packaging, and appeals for the black consumer market.

Mature consumers. As the U.S. population ages, "mature" consumers—those 65 and older—are becoming a very attractive market. The seniors market will grow to more than 40 million consumers by the year 2000. Seniors are better off financially—they spend about $200 billion each year, and they average twice the disposable income of consumers in the under-35 group. Mature consumers have long been the target of the makers of laxatives, tonics, and denture

Groups

A person's behavior is influenced by many small groups. Groups which have a direct influence and to which a person belongs are called **membership groups.** Some are *primary groups* with whom there is regular but informal interaction, such as family, friends, neighbors, and co-workers. Some are *secondary groups*, which are more formal and have less regular interaction. They include organizations such as religious groups, professional associations, and trade unions.

Reference groups are groups that serve as direct (face-to-face) or indirect points of comparison or reference in the forming of a person's attitudes or behavior. People are often influenced by reference groups to which they do not belong. For example, an **aspirational group** is one to which the individual wishes to belong, as when a teenage

products. But many marketers know that not all seniors are poor and feeble. Most are healthy and active, and they have many of the same needs and wants as younger consumers. Because seniors have more time and money, they are an ideal market for exotic travel, restaurants, high-tech home entertainment products, leisure goods and services, designer furniture and fashions, financial services, and life- and health-care services. Their desire to look as young as they feel makes seniors good candidates for specially designed cosmetics and personal-care products, health foods, home physical fitness products, and other products that combat aging. Several companies are hotly pursuing the seniors market. For example, Sears' 40,000-member "Mature Club" offers older consum-

ers 25 percent discounts on everything from eyeglasses to lawnmowers. Southwestern Bell publishes the "Silver Pages," crammed full of ads offering discounts and coupons to 20 million seniors in 90 markets. To appeal more to mature consumers, McDonald's employs older folks as hosts and hostesses in its restaurants and casts them in its ads. And GrandTravel of Chevy Chase, Maryland, sponsors barge trips through Holland, safaris to Kenya, and other exotic vacations for grandparents and their grandchildren. As the seniors segments grows in size and buying power, and as the stereotypes of seniors as doddering, creaky, impoverished shut-ins fade, more and more marketers will develop special strategies for this important market.

football player aspires to play someday for the Dallas Cowboys. He identifies with this group although there is no face-to-face contact.

Marketers try to identify the reference groups of their target markets. Reference groups influence a person in at least three ways. They expose the person to new behaviors and life styles. They influence the person's attitudes and self-concept because he or she wants to "fit in." And they create pressures to conform that may affect the person's product and brand choices. (See Marketing Highlight 5–2).

The importance of group influence varies across products and brands, but it tends to be strongest for conspicuous purchases.[5] A product or brand can be conspicuous for one of two reasons. First, it may be noticeable because the buyer is one of few people who owns it—luxuries are more conspicuous than necessities because fewer people

USING REFERENCE GROUPS TO SELL: HOME-PARTY AND OFFICE-PARTY SELLING

Many companies capitalize on reference-group influence to sell their products. Home-party and office-party selling involve throwing sales parties in homes or workplaces and inviting friends and neighbors or coworkers to see products demonstrated. Companies such as Mary Kay Cosmetics, Avon, and Tupperware are masters at this form of selling.

Mary Kay Cosmetics provides a good example of home-party selling. A Mary Kay beauty consultant (of which there arc 170,000) asks different women to host small beauty shows in their homes. Each hostess invites her friends and neighbors for a few hours of refreshments and informal socializing. Within this congenial atmosphere, the Mary Kay representative gives a two-hour beauty plan and free makeup lessons to the guests, hoping that many of them will buy some of the demonstrated cosmetics. The hostess receives a commission on sales plus a discount on personal purchases. Usually, about 60 percent of the guests buy something, partly because of the influence of the hostess and the other women attending the party.

In recent years, changing demographics have adversely affected home-party selling. An increasing proportion of women are working, which leaves fewer women with the time for shopping and fewer women at home to host or attend home sales parties. To overcome this problem, most party-plan sellers have followed their customers into the workplace with office-party selling. For example, Avon now trains its 400,000 salespeople to sell through office parties during coffee and lunch breaks and after hours. The company once sold only door-to-door but currently picks up a quarter of its sales from buyers at businesses. The well-known suburban Tupperware party has also invaded the office, in the form of Tupperware "rush-hour parties" held at the end of the workday in business offices around the country. At these parties, office workers meet in comfortable, familiar surroundings, look through Tupperware catalogs, watch product demonstrations, and discuss Tupperware products with their friends and associates. Tupperware's 85,000 sales representatives now make about 20 percent of their sales outside the home.

Home-party and office-party selling are now being used to market everything from cosmetics, kitchenware, and lingerie to exercise instruction and handmade suits. Such selling requires a sharp understanding of reference groups and how people influence each other in the buying process.

Sources: See Shannon Thurman, "Mary Kay Still in the Pink," *Advertising Age*, January 4, 1988, p. 32; Len Strazewski, "Tupperware Locks in a New Strategy," *Advertising Age*, February 8, 1988, p. 30; and Kate Ballen, "Get Ready for Shopping at Work," *Fortune*, February 15, 1988, pp. 95–98.

Reference group selling: Tupperware office-party selling and Mary Kay home-party selling.

own the luxuries. Second, a brand can be conspicuous because it is consumed in public where it can be seen by others. Figure 5-3 shows how group influence might affect product and brand choices for four types of products—public luxuries, private luxuries, public necessities, and private necessities.

A person considering the purchase of a public luxury such as a sailboat will be strongly influenced by others. Many people will notice the sailboat because few people own one. They will notice the brand because the boat is used in public. Both the product and the brand will be conspicuous, and the opinions of others will strongly

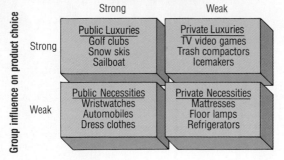

FIGURE 5-3
Extent of group influence on product and brand choice

Source: Adapted from William O. Bearden and Michael J. Etzel, "Reference Group Influence on Product and Brand Purchase Decisions," *The Journal of Consumer Research*, September 1982, p. 185.

influence decisions about whether to own a boat and what brand to buy. At the other extreme, group influences do not much affect decisions for private necessities because neither the product nor the brand will be noticed by others.

Manufacturers of products and brands subject to strong group influence must figure out how to reach the opinion leaders in the relevant reference groups. OPINION LEADERS are people within a reference group who, because of special skills, knowledge, personality, or other characteristics, exert influence on others. At one time, sellers thought that opinion leaders were primarily community social leaders whom the mass market imitated because of "snob appeal." But opinion leaders are found in all strata of society, and one person may be an opinion leader in certain product areas and an opinion follower in others. Marketers try to identify the personal characteristics of opinion leaders for their products, determine what media they use, and direct messages at them.

If Jennifer Smith buys a camera, both the product and the brand will be visible to others she respects, and her decision to buy the camera and her brand choice may be strongly influenced by some of her groups. Friends who belong to a photography club may influence her to buy a good camera.

Family

Family members can strongly influence buyer behavior. We can distinguish between two families in the buyer's life. The buyer's parents make up the *family of orientation*. From parents a person acquires an orientation toward religion, politics, and economics and a sense of personal ambition, self-worth, and love. Even if the buyer no longer interacts very much with his or her parents, the parents can still significantly influence the buyer's unconscious behavior. In countries where parents continue to live with their children, their influence can be crucial.

The *family of procreation*—the buyer's spouse and children—exert a more direct influence on everyday buying behavior. The family is the most important consumer-buying organization in society, and it has been researched extensively. Marketers are interested in the roles and relative influence of the husband, wife, and children on the purchase of a large variety of products and services.

Husband-wife involvement varies widely by product category and by stage in the buying process. And buying roles change with evolving consumer life styles. The wife has traditionally been the main purchasing agent for the family, especially in the areas of food, household products, and clothing. But this is changing with the increased number of working wives and the willingness of husbands to do more of the family purchasing. For example, women now buy about 45 percent of all cars and men account for about 40 percent of food-shopping dollars.[6]

In the case of expensive products and services, husbands and wives engage more in joint decision making. And their joint decisions often differ from those they would make as individuals. The marketer needs to determine how family members interact to reach decisions and how much influence each has on the purchase of a particular product or service. Understanding the dynamics of husband-wife decision making can help marketers to aim the best marketing strategies toward the right family members.

Family buying decisions: Depending on the product and situation, individual family members exert different amounts of influence.

In the case of Jennifer Smith buying a camera, her husband will play an influencer role. He may have an opinion about her buying a camera and the kind of camera to buy although she will be the primary decider, purchaser, and user.[7]

Roles and Status

A person belongs to many groups—family, clubs, organizations. The person's position in each group can be defined in terms of both *role* and *status*. With her parents, Jennifer Smith plays the role of daughter; in her family, she plays the role of wife; in her company, she plays the role of brand manager. A **role** consists of the activities people are expected to perform according to the persons around them. Each of Jennifer's roles will influence some of her buying behavior.

Each role carries a **status** reflecting the general esteem given to it by society. For example, the role of brand manager has more status in our society than the role of daughter. As a brand manager, Jennifer will buy the kind of clothing that reflects her role and status. People often choose products that show their status in society: A company president might drive a Mercedes or Cadillac, wear expensive clothes, and vacation in Europe; an office worker might drive a Taurus or Toyota, wear less expensive clothes, and take camping vacations.

Personal Factors A buyer's decisions are also influenced by personal characteristics such as the buyer's *age and life-cycle stage*, *occupation*, *economic situation*, *life style*, and *personality and self-concept*.

Age and Life-Cycle State

People change the goods and services they buy over their lifetimes. For instance, they eat baby food in their early years, most foods in their growing and mature years, and special diets in their later years. Their taste in clothes, furniture, and recreation is also age-related.

Buying is also shaped by the stage of the **family life cycle**—the stages through which families might pass as they mature over time. The stages of the family life

TABLE 5-2
Family Life-Cycle Stages

YOUNG	MIDDLE-AGED	OLDER
Single	Single	Older married
Married without children	Married without children	Older unmarried

Married with children
  Infant children
  Young children
  Adolescent children
	Married with children
	  Young children
	  Adolescent children	

Divorced with children	Married without dependent children	
	Divorced without children	

	Divorced with children
	  Young children
	  Adolescent children	

	Divorced without depen- dent children	

Sources: Adapted from Patrick E. Murphy and William A. Staples, "A Modernized Family Life Cycle," *Journal of Consumer Research*, June 1979, p. 16. Also see Janet Wagner and Sherman Hanna, "The Effectiveness of Family Life Cycle Variables in Consumer Expenditure Research," *Journal of Consumer Research*, December 1983, pp. 281–91.

cycle are listed in Table 5-2. Marketers often define their target markets in terms of life-cycle stage and develop appropriate products and marketing plans.

Psychological life-cycle stages have also been identified.[8] Adults experience certain passages or transformations as they go through life. Thus Jennifer Smith may move from being a satisfied brand manager and wife to being an unsatisfied person searching for a new way to fulfill herself. In fact, such a change may have stimulated her strong interest in photography. Marketers should pay attention to the changing buying interests that might be associated with these adult passages.

Occupation

A person's occupation affects the goods and services bought. A blue-collar worker will buy work clothes, work shoes, lunch boxes, and bowling recreation. A company president will buy expensive clothes, air travel, country club membership, and a large sailboat. Marketers try to identify the occupational groups that have an above-average interest in their products and services. A company can even specialize in making products needed by a given occupational group. Thus, computer software companies will design products for brand managers, accountants, engineers, lawyers, and doctors.

Economic Situation

A person's economic situation will greatly affect product choice. Jennifer Smith can consider buying an expensive Nikon if she has enough spendable income, savings, or borrowing power. Marketers of income-sensitive goods closely watch trends in personal income, savings, and interest rates. If economic indicators point to a recession, marketers can take steps to redesign, reposition, and reprice their products.

Life Style

People coming from the same subculture, social class, and even occupation may have quite different life styles. **Life style** is a person's pattern of living as expressed in his or her activities, interests, and opinions. Life style captures something more than the person's social class or personality. It profiles a person's whole pattern of acting and interacting in the world.

The technique of measuring life styles is known as **psychographics.**[9] It involves measuring the major dimensions shown in Table 5-3. The first three are known as the *AIO dimensions* (activities, interests, opinions). Consumer life styles are measured using long questionnaires—sometimes as long as twenty-five pages—that ask people how strongly they agree or disagree with such statements as:

- I am the kind of person who plans whatever I do very carefully.
- For fun, I would rather go out than stay home.

TABLE 5-3
Life Style Dimensions

ACTIVITIES	INTERESTS	OPINIONS	DEMOGRAPHICS
Work	Family	Themselves	Age
Hobbies	Home	Social issues	Education
Social events	Job	Politics	Income
Vacation	Community	Business	Occupation
Entertainment	Recreation	Economics	Family size
Club membership	Fashion	Education	Dwelling
Community	Food	Products	Geography
Shopping	Media	Future	City size
Sports	Achievements	Culture	Stage in life cycle

Source: Joseph T. Plummer, "The Concept and Application of Life-Style Segmentation," *Journal of Marketing*, January 1974, p. 34.

- I usually dress for fashion, not for comfort.
- I enjoy watching sports on television.

The data are then analyzed to find distinctive life style groups. Marketers often design marketing programs or appeals to fit specific life style groups.

Several research firms have developed life style classifications. The most widely used is the SRI *Values and Life Styles* (*VALS*) typology. The original VALS typology, introduced in 1978, classified consumers into nine life style groups according to whether they were inner-directed (for example, "Experientials"), outer-directed ("Achievers," "Belongers"), or need-driven ("Survivors"). The more recent version, VALS 2, classifies consumers into eight groups based on two major dimensions: self-orientation and resources. The *self-orientation* dimension captures three different buying approaches: Principle-oriented consumers base their buying on their views of how the world is or should be; status-oriented buyers on the actions and opinions of others; and action-oriented buyers on their desires for activity, variety, and risk-taking. Consumers within each orientation are further classified into one of two *resource* segments, depending on whether they have high or low levels of income, education, health, self-confidence, energy level, and other factors. Consumers with either very high or very low levels of resources are classified into separate groups without regard to their self-orientations. The eight VALS 2 life-style groups are described in Table 5-4. A person may progress through several of these life styles over the course of a lifetime. People's life styles affect their buying behavior.[10]

Several companies have used the VALS typologies to improve their marketing strategies. For example, based on the original version of VALS, Merrill Lynch changed its ad theme from "Bullish on America" (with ads showing a herd of bulls) to "A Breed Apart" (with ads showing a single bull taking its own lead). VALS analysis showed that the original ads attracted "belongers," traditional people who are content to follow the lead of others. But the heavy investors Merrill Lynch wanted to reach are "achievers," hard-working, successful people who do not want to be part of the crowd—they want to stand out. Thus, the "breed apart" theme, featuring a single, independent bull, had a greater impact on Merrill Lynch's target market.[11] In another example, Bank of America found that the businessmen they were targeting consisted mainly of "achievers" who were strongly competitive individualists. The bank designed highly successful ads showing men taking part in solo sports such as sailing, jogging, and water skiing.[12]

The life-style concept, when used carefully, can help the marketer gain an understanding of changing consumer values and how they affect buying behavior.[13] Jennifer Smith, for example, can choose to live the role of a capable homemaker, a career woman, or a free spirit—or all three. She plays several roles, and the way she blends them expresses her life style. If she becomes a professional photographer, this would change her life style, in turn changing what and how she buys.

TABLE 5-4
VALS 2: Eight American Life
Styles

Actualizers

People with the highest incomes and so many resources that they can indulge in any or all self-orientations. Image is important to them, not as evidence of status or power, but as an expression of their taste, independence, and character. Because of their wide range of interests and openness to change, they tend to buy "the finer things in life."

Principle-Oriented

Fulfilleds

Mature, responsible, well-educated professionals. Their leisure activities center on their homes, but they are well-informed about what goes on in the world, and they are open to new ideas and social change. They have high incomes, but they are practical, value-oriented consumers.

Believers

Principle-oriented consumers with more modest incomes. They are conservative and predictable consumers who favor American products and established brands. Their lives are centered on family, church, community, and nation.

Status-Oriented

Achievers

Successful, work-oriented people who get their satisfaction from their jobs and their families. They are politically conservative and respect authority and the status quo. They favor established products and services that show off their success.

Strivers

People with values similar to those of achievers but fewer economic, social, and psychological resources. Style is extremely important to them as they strive to emulate consumers in other, more resourceful groups.

Action-Oriented

Experiencers

People who like to affect their environment in tangible ways. They are the youngest of all groups. They have a lot of energy, which they pour into physical exercise and social activities. They are avid consumers, spending heavily on clothing, fast food, music, and other youthful favorites. They especially like new things.

Makers

People who like to affect their environment, but in more practical ways. They value self-sufficiency. They are focused on the familiar—family, work, and physical recreation—and have little interest in the broader world. As consumers, they are unimpressed by material possessions other than those with a practical or functional purpose.

Strugglers

People with the lowest incomes and too few resources to be included in any consumer orientation. With their limited means, they tend to be brand-loyal consumers.

Source: See Martha Farnsworth Riche, "Psychographics for the 1990s," *American Demographics*, July 1989, pp. 25–31.

Personality and Self-Concept

Each person's distinct personality will influence his or her buying behavior. **Personality** refers to the unique psychological characteristics that lead to relatively consistent and lasting responses to one's own environment. Personality is usually described in terms of such traits as the following:[14]

Self-confidence	Ascendancy	Emotional stability
Dominance	Sociability	Achievement
Autonomy	Defensiveness	Order
Change	Affiliation	Adaptability
Deference	Aggressiveness	Creativity

Personality can be useful in analyzing consumer behavior for some product or brand choices. For example, coffee makers have discovered that heavy coffee drinkers tend to be high on sociability. Thus, Maxwell House ads show people relaxing and socializing over a cup of steaming coffee.

Many marketers use a concept related to personality—a person's **self-concept** (also called self-image). The basic premise is that people's possessions contribute to and reflect their identities: that is, "we are what we have." Thus, to understand consumer

Life style: This Bank of America ad targets achievers.

behavior, the marketer must first understand the relationship between consumer self-concept and possessions. All of us have a complex mental picture of ourselves. For example, Jennifer Smith may see herself as outgoing, creative, and active. Thus, she will favor a camera that projects the same qualities. If the Nikon is promoted as a camera for outgoing, creative, and active people, then its brand image will match her self-image.[15]

The theory, admittedly, is not that simple. What if Jennifer's *actual self-concept* (how she views herself) differs from her *ideal self-concept* (how she would like to view herself) and from her *others self-concept* (how she thinks others see her). Which self will she try to satisfy when she buys a camera? Some marketers think that buyers' choices will result more from their actual self-concept; others from the ideal self-concept; and still others from the others self-concept. Thus self-concept theory has met with mixed success in predicting consumer responses to brand images.

Psychological Factors

A person's buying choices are also influenced by four major psychological factors— *motivation*, *perception*, *learning*, and *beliefs and attitudes*.

Motivation

We know that Jennifer Smith is interested in buying a camera. Why? What is she *really* seeking? What *needs* is she trying to satisfy?

A person has many needs at any given time. Some needs are *biological*, arising from states of tension such as hunger, thirst, or discomfort. Other needs are *psychological*, arising from the need for recognition, esteem, or belonging. Most of these needs will not be strong enough to motivate the person to act at a given point in time. A need becomes a *motive* when it is aroused to a sufficient lever of intensity. A **motive** (or *drive*) is a need that is sufficiently pressing to direct the person to seek satisfaction. Psychologists have developed theories of human motivation. Two of the most popular—the theories of Sigmund Freud and Abraham Maslow—have quite different meanings for consumer analysis and marketing.

FREUD'S THEORY OF MOTIVATION. Freud assumes that people are largely unconscious about the real psychological forces shaping their behavior. He sees the person as growing up and repressing many urges. These urges are never eliminated or under perfect control; they emerge in dreams, in slips of the tongue, in neurotic and obsessive behavior, or ultimately in psychoses.

Thus, a person does not fully understand his or her motivation. If Jennifer Smith wants to purchase an expensive camera, she may describe her motive as wanting a hobby or career. At a deeper level, she may be purchasing the camera to impress others with her creative talent. At a still deeper level, she may be buying the camera to feel young and independent again.

Motivation researchers collect in-depth information from small samples of consumers to uncover the deeper motives for their product choices. They use non-directive depth interviews and various ''projective techniques'' to throw the ego off guard—techniques such as word association, sentence completion, picture interpretation, and role playing. Motivation researchers have reached some interesting and sometimes odd conclusions about what may be in the buyer's mind regarding certain purchases. For example:

- Consumers resist prunes because they are wrinkled-looking and remind people of sickness and old age.
- Men smoke cigars as an adult version of thumbsucking
- People prefer vegetable shortening to animal fats because the latter arouse a sense of guilt over killing animals.
- A woman is very serious when baking a cake because, unconsciously, she is going through the symbolic act of giving birth.

Despite its sometimes unusual conclusions, motivation research remains a useful tool for marketers seeking a deeper understanding of consumer behavior (see Marketing Highlight 5–3).[16]

MASLOW'S THEORY OF MOTIVATION. Abraham Maslow sought to explain why people are driven by particular needs at particular times.[17] Why does one person spend much time and energy on personal safety and another on gaining the esteem of others? Maslow's answer is that human needs are arranged in a hierarchy, from the most pressing to the least pressing. Maslow's hierarchy of needs is shown in Figure 5-4. In order of importance, they are *physiological* needs, *safety* needs, *social* needs, *esteem* needs, and *self-actualization* needs. A person tries to satisfy the most important need first. When that important need is satisfied, it ceases to act as a motivator and the person will try to satisfy the next most important need.

For example, a starving man (Need 1) will not take an interest in the latest happenings in the art world (Need 5), nor in how he is seen or esteemed by others (Need 3 or 4), nor even in whether he is breathing clean air (Need 2). But as each important need is satisfied, the next most important need will come into play.

What light does Maslow's theory throw on Jennifer Smith's interest in buying a camera? We can guess that Jennifer has satisfied her physiological, safety, and social needs; they do not motivate her interest in cameras. Her camera interest might come from a strong need for more esteem from others. Or it might come from a need for self-actualization—she wants to be a creative person and express herself through photography.

Perception

A motivated person is ready to act. *How* the person acts is influenced by his or her *perception* of the situation. Two people with the same motivation and in the same

"TOUCHY-FEELY" RESEARCH INTO CONSUMER MOTIVATIONS

The term *motivational research* refers to qualitative research designed to probe consumers' hidden, subconscious motivations. Because consumers often don't know or can't describe just why they act as they do, motivation researchers use a wide variety of non-directive and projective techniques to uncover underlying emotions and attitudes towards brands and buying situations. The techniques range from sentence completion, word association, and inkblot or cartoon interpretation tests to having consumers describe typical brand users or form daydreams and fantasies about brands or buying situations. Some of these techniques verge on the bizarre. One writer offers the following tongue-in-cheek summary of a motivation research session:

> Good morning, ladies and gentlemen. We've called you here today for a little consumer research. Now, lie down on the couch, toss your inhibitions out the window and let's try a little free association. First, think about brands as if they were your *friends.* Imagine you could talk to your TV dinner. What would he say? And what would you say to him? . . . Now, think of your shampoo as an animal. Go on, don't be shy. Would it be a panda or a lion? A snake or a wooly worm? For our final exercise, let's all sit up and pull out our magic markers. Draw a picture of a typical cake-mix user. Would she wear an apron or a negligee? A business suit or a can-can dress?

Such projective techniques seem pretty goofy. But more and more, marketers are turning to these touchy-feely, motivation research approaches to help them probe consumer psyches and develop better marketing strategies.

Many advertising agencies employ teams of psychologists, anthropologists, and other social scientists to carry out their motivation research. Says the research director of one large agency, "We believe people make choices on a basic primitive level . . . we use the probe to get down to the unconscious." This agency routinely conducts one-on-one, therapy-like interviews to delve into the inner workings of consumers. Another agency asks consumers to describe their favorite brands as animals or cars (say, Cadillacs vs. Chevrolets) in order to assess the prestige associated with various brands. Still another agency has consumers draw figures of typical brand users:

> In one instance the agency asked 50 interviewees to sketch likely buyers of two different brands of cake mixes. Consistently, the group portrayed Pillsbury cus-

tomers as apron-clad, grandmotherly types, while they pictured Duncan Hines purchasers as svelte, contemporary women.

In a similar study, American Express had people sketch likely users of its gold card versus its green card. Respondents depicted gold card holders as active, broad-shouldered men; green card holders were perceived as "couch potatoes" lounging in front of a television sets. Based on these results, the company positioned its gold card as a symbol of responsibility for people capable of controlling their lives and finances.

Some motivation research studies employ more basic techniques, such as simply mingling with consumers to find out what makes them tick:

> Saatchi & Saatchi [an advertising agency] recently hired anthropologist Joe Lowe to spend a week in Texas sidling up to wearers of Wranglers blue jeans at rodeos and barbecues. His findings reinforced what the jeans company suspected: buyers associated Wranglers with cowboys. The company responded by running ads with plenty of Western touches. For a consumer-goods manufacturer, Lowe went to health clubs where he observed patrons applying deodorant. And for shampoo maker Helene Curtis, he spent three days in salons before coming to a somewhat predictable conclusion—going to the beauty shop makes women feel good.

Some marketers dismiss such motivation research as just so much mumbo-jumbo. And these approaches do present some problems: They use small samples and researcher interpretation of results is often highly subjective, sometimes leading to rather exotic explanations of otherwise ordinary buying behavior. However, others believe strongly that these approaches can provide interesting nuggets of insight into the relationships between consumers and the brands they buy. To marketers who use them, motivation research techniques provide a flexible and varied means of gaining insights into deeply held and often mysterious motivations behind consumer buying behavior.

Sources: Excerpts from Annetta Miller and Dody Tsiantar, "Psyching Out Consumers," *Newsweek*, February 27, 1989, pp. 46–47. Also see Sidney J. Levy, "Dreams, Fairy Tales, Animals, and Cars," *Psychology and Marketing*, Summer 1985, pp. 67–81; Ronald Alsop, "Advertisers Put Consumers on the Couch," *Wall Street Journal*, May 13, 1988, p. 21; and Rich Thomas, "You are What You Buy," *Newsweek*, June 4, 1990, pp. 59–60.

situation may act quite differently because they perceive the situation differently. Jennifer Smith might consider a fast-talking camera salesperson loud and phony. Another camera buyer might consider the same salesperson intelligent and helpful.

Why do people have different perceptions of the same situation? All of us learn by the flow of information through our five senses: sight, hearing, smell, touch, and taste. However, each of us receives, organizes, and interprets this sensory information in an individual way. **Perception** is the process by which people select, organize, and interpret information to form a meaningful picture of the world.

People can form different perceptions of the same stimulus because of three perceptual processes: *selective exposure, selective distortion,* and *selective retention.*

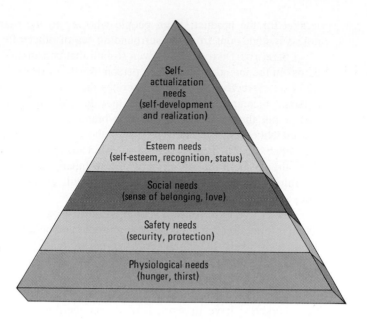

FIGURE 5-4
Maslow's hierarchy of needs

Adapted from Motivation and Personality, 2nd ed., by Abraham H. Maslow. Copyright © 1970 by Abraham H. Maslow. Reprinted by permission of Harper & Row, Publishers, Inc.

SELECTIVE EXPOSURE.   People are exposed to a great number of stimuli every day. For example, the average person may be exposed to more than 1,500 ads a day. It is impossible for a person to pay attention to all these stimuli; most will be screened out. The real challenge is to explain which stimuli people will notice. Research has shown that people are more likely to notice stimuli that relate to a current need. Jennifer Smith will suddenly notice all kinds of ads about cameras because she wants to buy one. People are also more likely to notice stimuli that they expect. Jennifer Smith is more likely to notice cameras than radios in a camera store, because she did not expect the store to carry radios. Finally, people are more likely to notice stimuli that deviate markedly from the normal. Jennifer Smith will notice an ad offering $100 off the list price of a Nikon before noticing one that offers $5 off the list price.

SELECTIVE EXPOSURE means that marketers must work especially hard to attract the consumer's attention. Their offer will be lost on most people who are not in the

The average person is exposed to over 1,500 ads per day—in magazines and newspapers, on radio and TV, and all around them on signs and billboards.

market for the product. Even people who are in the market may not notice the offer unless it stands out from the surrounding sea of other offers.

SELECTIVE DISTORTION. Even stimuli that consumers do notice do not always come across in the intended way. Each person tries to fit incoming information into an existing mind-set. **Selective distortion** describes the tendency of people to adapt information to personal meanings. Jennifer Smith may hear the salesperson mention some good and bad points about a competing camera brand. Because she already has a strong leaning toward Nikon, she is likely to distort those points in order to conclude that Nikon is the better camera. People tend to interpret information in a way that will support what they already believe. Selective distortion means that marketers must try to understand the mind-sets of consumers and how they will affect interpretations of advertising and sales information.

SELECTIVE RETENTION. People will also forget much that they learn. They tend to retain information that supports their attitudes and beliefs. Because of **selective retention,** Jennifer is likely to remember good points made about the Nikon and forget good points made about competing cameras. She remembers Nikon's good points because she "rehearses" them more whenever she thinks about choosing a camera.

These three perceptual factors—selective exposure, distortion, and retention—mean that marketers have to work hard to get their messages through. This explains why marketers use so much drama and repetition in sending messages to their market. Interestingly, although most marketers worry about whether their offers will be perceived at all, some consumers are worried that they will be affected by marketing messages without even knowing it (see Marketing Highlight 5–4).

Learning

When people act, they learn. **Learning** describes changes in an individual's behavior arising from experience. Learning theorists say that most human behavior is learned. Learning occurs through the interplay of *drives*, *stimuli*, *cues*, *responses*, and *reinforcement*.

We saw that Jennifer Smith has a drive for self-actualization. A *drive* is a strong internal stimulus that calls for action. Her drive becomes a *motive* when it is directed toward a particular *stimulus object*, in this case a camera. Jennifer's response to the idea of buying a camera is conditioned by the surrounding cues. *Cues* are minor stimuli that determine when, where, and how the person responds. Seeing cameras in a shop window, hearing of a special sales price, and being encouraged by her husband are all cues that can influence Jennifer's *response* to the impulse to buy a camera.

Suppose Jennifer buys the Nikon. If the experience is *rewarding*, the probability is that she will use the camera more and more. Her response to cameras will be *reinforced*. Then the next time she buys a camera, or binoculars, or similar product, the probability is greater that she will buy a Nikon. We say that she *generalizes* her response to similar stimuli.

The reverse of generalization is *discrimination*. When Jennifer examines binoculars made by Olympus, she sees that they are lighter and more compact than Nikon's binoculars. Discrimination means that she has learned to recognize differences in sets of products and can adjust her response accordingly.

The practical significance of learning theory of marketers is that they can build demand for a product by associating it with strong drives, using motivating cues, and providing positive reinforcement. A new company can enter the market by appealing to the same drives as competitors and providing similar cues because buyers are more likely to transfer loyalty to similar brands then to dissimilar ones (generalization). Or it may design its brand to appeal to a different set of drives and offer strong cue inducements to switch (discrimination).

Beliefs and Attitudes

Through acting and learning, people acquire their beliefs and attitudes. These in turn influence their buying behavior. A **belief** is a descriptive thought that a person has

SUBLIMINAL PERCEPTION: CAN CONSUMERS BE AFFECTED WITHOUT KNOWING IT?

In 1957, the words "Eat popcorn" and "Drink Coca-Cola" were flashed on a screen in a New Jersey movie theater every five seconds for one three-hundredths of a second. The researchers reported that although the audience did not consciously recognize these messages, viewers absorbed them subconsciously and bought 58 percent more popcorn and 18 percent more Coke. Suddenly advertising agencies and consumer-protection groups became intensely interested in *subliminal perception*. People voiced fears of being brainwashed, and California and Canada declared the practice illegal. The controversy cooled when scientists failed to replicate the original results, but the issue did not die. In 1974, Wilson Bryan Key claimed in his book *Subliminal Seduction* that consumers were still being manipulated by advertisers in print ads and television commercials.

Subliminal perception has since been studied by many psychologists and consumer researchers. None has been able to show that subliminal messages have any effect on consumer behavior. It appears that subliminal advertising simply doesn't have the power attributed to it by its critics. Most advertisers scoff at the notion of an industry conspiracy to manipulate consumers through "invisible" messages. As one advertising agency executive put it, "We have enough trouble persuading consumers using a series of up-front thirty-second ads—how could we do it in 1/300th of a second?"

While advertisers may avoid outright subliminal advertising, some critics claim that television advertising employs techniques approaching the subliminal. With more and more viewers reaching for their remote controls to avoid ads by switching channels or fast-forwarding through VCR tapes, advertisers are using new tricks to grab viewer attention and to affect consumers in ways they may not be aware of. Many ad agencies employ psychologists and neurophysiologists to help develop subtle psychological advertising strategies.

For example, some advertisers purposely try to confuse viewers, throw them off balance, or even make them uncomfortable:

[They use] film footage that wouldn't pass muster with a junior-high film club. You have to stare at the screen just to figure out what's going on—and that, of course, is the idea. Take the ads for Wang computers. In these hazy, washed-out spots, people walk partially in and out of the camera frame talking in computer jargon. But the confusion grabs attention. . . . Even people who don't understand a word are riveted to the screen.

Other advertisers use the rapid-fire technique. Images flash by so quickly you can barely register them. Pontiac used such "machine-gun editing" in recent ads—the longest shot flashed by in one and one-half seconds, the shortest in one-quarter of a second. The ads scored high in viewer recall.

Some advertisers go after our ears as well as our eyes, taking advantage of the powerful effects some sounds have on human brain waves:

Advertisers are using sounds to take advantage of the automatic systems built into the brain that force you to stop what you're doing and refocus on the screen. . . . You can't ignore these sounds. That's why commercials are starting off with noises ranging from a baby crying (Advil) to a car horn (Hertz) to a factory whistle (Almond Joy). In seeking the right sound . . . advertisers can be downright merciless. . . . Ads for Nuprin pain reliever kick off by assaulting viewers with the whine of a dentist's drill . . . to help the viewer recall the type of pain we've all experienced. Hey, thanks.

A few experts are concerned that new high-tech advertising might even hypnotize consumers, whether knowingly or not. They suggest that several techniques—rapid scene changes, pulsating music and sounds, repetitive phrases, and flashing logos—might actually start to put some viewers under.

Some critics think that such subtle, hard-to-resist psychological techniques are unfair to consumers—that advertisers can use these techniques to bypass consumers' defenses and affect them without their being aware of it. The advertisers who use these techniques, however, view them as innovative, creative approaches to advertising.

Sources: See Wilson Bryan Key, *Subliminal Seduction* (New York: NAL, 1974); Timothy E. Moore, "Subliminal Advertising: What You See Is What You Get," *Journal of Marketing*, Spring 1982, pp. 38–47; and Walter Weir, "Another Look at Subliminal 'Facts,'" *Advertising Age*, October 15, 1984, p. 46. Excerpts from David H. Freedman, "Why You Watch Commercials—Whether You Mean To Or Not," *TV Guide*, February 20, 1988, pp. 4–7.

about something. Jennifer Smith may believe that a Nikon takes great pictures, stands up well under hard use, and costs $550. These beliefs may be based on real knowledge, opinion, or faith. They may or may not carry an emotional charge. For example, Jennifer Smith's belief that a Nikon camera is heavy may or may not matter to her decision.

Marketers are interested in the beliefs that people formulate about specific products and services. These beliefs embrace products and brand images, and people do tend to act on their beliefs. If some of the beliefs are wrong and prevent purchase, the marketer will want to launch a campaign to correct them.

People have attitudes regarding religion, politics, clothes, music, food, and almost everything else. An **attitude** describes a person's relatively consistent evaluations, feelings, and tendencies toward an object or idea. Attitudes put people into a frame of

Attitudes are hard to change, but it can be done. Honda's "You meet the nicest people on a Honda" campaign changed people attitudes about who rides motorcycles.

mind of liking or disliking things, moving toward or away from them. Thus, Jennifer Smith may hold such attitudes as "Buy the best," "The Japanese make the best products in the world," and "Creativity and self-expression are among the most important things in life." The Nikon camera, therefore, fits well into Jennifer's existing attitudes. A company would benefit greatly from researching the various attitudes that might bear on its product.

Attitudes are difficult to change. A person's attitudes fit into a pattern, and to change one attitude may require difficult adjustments in many others. Thus, a company should usually try to fit its products into existing attitudes rather than to try to change them. There are exceptions, of course, in which the great cost of trying to change attitudes may pay off. For example:

> In the late 1950s, Honda entered the U.S. motorcycle market facing a major decision. It could either sell its motorcycles to the small but already established motorcycle market or try to increase the size of this market by attracting new types of consumers. Increasing the size of the market would be more difficult and expensive because many people had negative attitudes toward motorcycles. They associated motorcycles with black leather jackets, switchblades, and outlaws. Despite these adverse attitudes, Honda took the second course of action. It launched a major campaign to position motorcycles as good clean fun. Its theme "You meet the nicest people on a Honda" worked well, and many people adopted a new attitude toward motorcycles. Going into the 1990s, however, Honda faces a similar problem. With the aging of the baby boomers, the market has once again shifted toward only hard-core motorcycling enthusiasts. So Honda has again set out to change consumer attitudes. It is spending $75 million on its new "Come Ride With Us" campaign to reestablish the wholesomeness of motorcycling and to position it as fun and exciting for everyone.[18]

We can now appreciate the many individual characteristics and forces acting on consumer behavior. The person's choice is the result of the complex interplay of cultural, social, personal, and psychological factors. Many of these factors cannot be influenced by the marketer. However, they are useful in identifying interested buyers and shaping products and appeals to better serve their needs.

■ SUMMARY

Markets must be understood before marketing strategies can be developed. The consumer market buys goods and services for personal consumption. Consumers vary tremendously in age, income, education, tastes and other factors. Marketers must understand how consumers transform marketing and other inputs into buying responses. Consumer behavior is influenced by the buyer's characteristics and by the buyer's decision process. Buyer characteristics include four major factors: cultural, social, personal, and psychological.

Culture is the most basic determinant of a person's wants and behavior. It includes basics values, perceptions, preferences, and behaviors that a person learns from family and other important institutions. Marketers try to track cultural shifts that might suggest new ways to serve consumers. Subcultures are "cultures within cultures" that have distinct values and life styles. Social classes are subcultures whose members have similar social prestige based on occupation, income, education, wealth, and other variables. People with different cultural, subcultural, and social class characteristics develop different product and brand preferences. Marketers may want to focus their marketing programs on the special needs of certain groups.

Social factors also influence a buyer's behavior. A person's reference groups—family, friends, social organizations, professional associations—strongly affect product and brand choices. The person's position within each group can be defined in terms of role and status. A buyer chooses products and brands that reflect his or her role and status.

The buyer's age, life-cycle stage, occupation, economic circumstances, life style, personality, and other personal characteristics influence buying decisions. Young consumers have different needs and wants from older consumers; the needs of young married couples differ from those of retirees; consumers with

higher incomes buy differently from those who have less to spend. Consumer life styles—the whole pattern of acting and interacting in the world—are also an important influence of buyers' choices.

Finally, consumer buying behavior is influenced by four major psychological factors—motivation, perception, learning, and attitudes. Each of these factors provides a different perspective for understanding the workings of the buyer's "black box."

A person's buying behavior is the result of the complex interplay of all these cultural, social, personal, and psychological factors. Many of these factors cannot be controlled by marketers, but they are useful in identifying and understanding the consumers that marketers are trying to influence.

■ QUESTIONS FOR DISCUSSION

1. What factors could you add to the model shown in Figure 5-1 to make it a better description of consumer behavior?

2. A new method of packaging wine in plastic-lined cardboard boxes offers more consumer convenience than traditional bottles. Instead of a cork, an airtight dispenser is used that allows servings of the desired amount while keeping the remaining wine fresh for weeks. How will the factors shown in Figure 5-2 work for or against the success of this packaging method?

3. What do these phrases mean to marketers? (a) "If I were going to be a car, I'd be a Porsche." (b) "If my mother were a car, she'd be a Chevrolet." (c) "If my daughter were a car, she'd be a BMW."

4. What does each part of the following pairs tell you about a person's social class?
   a. Annual income of $30,000/annual income of $40,000.
   b. Floors are covered with Oriental rugs/house has wall-to-wall carpeting.
   c. Shops at Sears/shops at Nieman-Marcus.
   d. College graduate/high-school graduate

5. Ads sponsored by Rockers Against Drunk Driving feature popular recording artists telling listeners not to drink and drive. What social factors would you expect to contribute to the success or failure of this campaign?

6. In designing the advertising for a soft drink, which would you find more helpful: information about consumer demographics or consumer life styles? Give examples of how you would use each type of information.

7. Think about a very good or very bad experience you have had with a product. Did this shape your beliefs about this product? How long will these beliefs last?

8. What different levels of Maslow's hierarchy could be appealed to in marketing the following: (a) popcorn, (b) the armed forces, and (c) a college education?

9. One advertising agency president says, "Perception is reality." What does he mean by this? How is perception important to marketers?

10. How can an understanding of *attitudes* be used in designing marketing strategies? Give examples.

11. Would you buy a new American car? Why or why not? What would change your attitude?

■ KEY TERMS

Aspirational group. A group to which an individual wishes to belong.

Attitude. A person's consistently favorable or unfavorable evaluations, feelings, and tendencies toward an object or idea.

Belief. A descriptive thought that a person holds about something.

Consumer market. All the individuals and households who buy or acquire goods and services for personal consumption.

Culture. The set of basic values, perceptions, wants, and behaviors learned by a member of society from family and other important institutions.

Family life cycle. The stages through which families might pass as they mature.

Learning. Changes in an individual's behavior arising from experience.

Life style. A person's pattern of living as expressed in his or her activities, interests, and opinions.

Membership groups. Groups that have a direct influence on a person's behavior and to which a person belongs.

Motive (or drive). A need that is sufficiently pressing to direct the person to seek satisfaction of the need.

Opinion leaders. People within a reference groups who, because of special skills, knowledge, personality, or other characteristics, exert influence on others.

Perception. The process by which people select, organize, and interpret information to form a meaningful picture of the world.

Personality. A person's distinguishing psychological characteristics that lead to relatively consistent and lasting responses to his or her own environment.

Psychographics. The technique of measuring life styles and developing life-style classifications; it involves measuring the major AIO dimensions (activities, interests, opinions).

Reference groups. Groups that have a direct (face-to-face) or indirect influence on the person's attitudes or behavior.

Role. The activities a person is expected to perform according to the people around him or her.

Self-concept. Self-image, or the complex mental pictures people have of themselves.

Selective distortion. The tendency of people to adapt information to personal meanings.

Selective exposure. The tendency of people to screen most of the information to which they are exposed.

Selective retention. The tendency of people to retain certain parts of the information to which they are exposed, usually information that supports their attitudes and beliefs.

Social classes. Relatively permanent and ordered divisions in a society whose members share similar values, interests, and behaviors.

Status. The general esteem given to a role by society.

Subculture. A group of people with shared value systems based on common life experiences and situations.

■ REFERENCES

1. Excerpts from Peter Schutz and Jack Cook, "Porsche on Nichemanship," *Harvard Business Review*, March–April 1986, pp. 98–106. Copyright (c) 1986 by the President and Fellows of Harvard College; all rights reserved. Also see Cleveland Horton, "Porsche's Ads Get Racy in '88 with Tie to Indy," *Advertising Age*, November 2, 1987, p. 34; and Mark Maremont, "Europe's Long, Smooth Ride in Luxury Cars Is Over," *Business Week*, March 17, 1988, p. 57.

2. Several models of the consumer buying process have been developed by marketing scholars. The most prominent models are those of Howard and Sheth, *The Theory of Buyer Behavior* (New York: John Wiley and Sons, 1969); James F. Engel, Roger D. Blackwell, and Paul W. Miniard, *Consumer Behavior*, 5th ed. (New York: Holt, Rinehart and Winston, 1986); and James R. Bettman, *An Information Processing Theory of Consumer Choice* (Reading, MA: Addison-Wesley, 1979).

3. See Leon G. Schiffman and Leslie Lazar Kanuk, *Consumer Behavior*, 4th ed. (Englewood Cliffs, NJ: Prentice Hall, 1991), Chapter 14.

4. For more on marketing to Hispanics, blacks, mature consumers, and Asians, see Pete Engardio, "Fast Times on Avenida Madison," *Business Week*, June 6, 1988, pp. 62–67; Chester Swenson, "How to Speak to Hispanics," *American Demographics*, February 1990, pp. 40–41; Julia Lieblich, "If you Want a Big, New Market," *Fortune*, November 21, 1988, pp. 181–88; George Sternlieb and James W. Hughes, "Black Households: The $100 Billion Potential," *American Demographics*, April 1988, pp. 35–37; "Black Pride Plays a Role in Buying Goods," *Marketing News*, February 19, 1990, p. 11; Jeff Ostroff, "An Aging Market," *American Demographics*, May 1989, pp. 26–33; Walecia Konrad and Gail DeGeorge, "U.S. Companies Go for the Gray," *Business Week*, April 3, 1989, pp. 64–67. Milinda Beck, "The Geezer Boom," in "The 21st Century American Family," a special issue of *Newsweek*, Winter/Spring 1990, pp. 62–67; and "The Asian Market: Too Good to be True?" *Sales & Marketing Management*, May 1988, pp. 39–42.

5. William O. Bearden and Michael J. Etzel, "Reference Group Influence on Product and Brand Purchase Decisions," *Journal of Consumer Research*, September 1982, p. 185.

6. "Do Real Men Shop?" *American Demographics*, May 1987, p. 14; and Raymond Serafin, "Carmakers Step Up Chase for Women, *Advertising Age*, May 16, 1988, p. 76.

7. For more on family decision making see Schiffman and Kanuk, *Consumer Behavior*, Ch. 12; Rosann L. Spiro, "Persuasion in Family Decision Making," *Journal of Consumer Research*, March 1983, pp. 393–402; and Michael B. Menasco and David J. Curry, "Utility and Choice: An Empirical Study of Husband/Wife Decision Making," *Journal of Consumer Research*, June 1989, pp. 87–97.

8. See Lawrence Lepisto, "A Life Span Perspective of Consumer Behavior," in Elizabeth Hirshman and Morris Holbrook, *Advances in Consumer Research*, Vol. 12 (Provo, Utah: Association for Consumer Research, 1985), p. 47.

9. See William D. Wells, "Psychographics: A Critical Review," *Journal of Marketing Research*, May 1975, pp. 196–213; Bickley Townsend, "Psychographic Glitter and Gold," *American Demographics*, November 1985, pp. 22–29; and Martha Farnsworth Riche, "Psychographics for the 1990s," *American Demographics*, July 1989, pp. 25–31.

10. See Arnold Mitchell, *The Nine American Lifestyles* (New York: Macmillan, 1983); Riche, "Psychographics for the 1990s"; and Judith Graham, "New VALS 2 Takes the Psychological Route," *Advertising Age*, February 13, 1989, p. 24.

11. See Schiffman and Kanuk, *Consumer Behavior*, Ch. 5; and "Emotions Important for Successful Advertising," *Marketing News*, April 12, 1985, p. 18.

12. Kim Foltz, "Wizards of Marketing," *Newsweek*, July 22, 1985, p. 44.

13. For more on the pros and cons of using VALS and other life style approaches, see Lynn R. Kahle, Sharon E. Beatty, and Pamela Homer, "Alternative Measurement Approaches to Consumer Values: The List of Values (LOV) and Values and Life Styles (VALS)," *Journal of Consumer Research*, December 1986, pp. 405–409; and "Lifestyle Roulette," *American Demographics*, April 1987, pp. 24–25.

14. See Raymond L. Horton, "Some Relationships between Personality and Consumer Decision-Making," *Journal of Marketing Research*, May 1979, pp. 244–45. Also see Harold H. Kassarjian and Mary Jane Sheffet, "Personality in Consumer Behavior: An Update," in *Perspectives in Consumer Behavior*, Harold H. Kassarjian and Thomas S. Robertson, eds. (Glenview, IL: Scott Foresman, 1981), pp. 160–180; and Joseph T. Plummer, "How Personality Can Make a Difference," *Marketing News*, March–April 1984, pp. 17–20.

15. See M. Joseph Sirgy, "Self-Concept in Consumer Behavior: A Critical Review," *Journal of Consumer Research*, December 1982, pp. 287–300; and Russel W. Belk, "Possessions and the Extended Self," *Journal of Consumer Research*, September 1988, pp. 139–59.

16. See Annetta Miller and Dody Tsiantar, "Psyching Out Consumers," *Newsweek*, February 27, 1989, pp. 46–47.

17. Abraham H. Maslow, *Motivation and Personality*, 2nd ed. (New York: Harper & Row, 1970), pp. 80–106.

18. See "Honda Hopes to Win New Riders by Emphasizing 'Fun' of Cycles," *Marketing News*, August 28, 1989, p. 6.

RJR's PREMIER: WHERE THERE IS *NO* SMOKE, ARE THERE CUSTOMERS?

How would the average smoker feel about buying a pack of cigarettes that came with a four page instruction booklet? That's what happened when RJR/Nabisco launched its new smokeless cigarette, Premier, in St. Louis, Phoenix, and Tucson in late 1988. RJR used "The Cleaner Smoke" as Premier's advertising slogan. Instead of the glitzy, image-oriented advertising that typically accompanies a new cigarette, Premier featured a just-the-facts marketing message: a cigarette with no sidestream smoke, less nicotine than 97 percent of the brands on the market, and significant reductions in what RJR called "controversial compounds," such as tar.

RJR selected the initial markets with its targeted audience of older (over 25), urbanite smokers in mind. The Arizona cities in particular are skewed toward older smokers, many of whom are trying to quit and are looking for an alternative. And although Premier's ad campaign clearly lacked the pizazz of the Marlboro man or Benson and Hedges' yuppies, it was tailor-made for the targeted consumers. RJR appealed on a rational basis to people hooked on smoking.

To attract these upscale smokers, RJR positioned the smokeless cigarette as a "technological breakthrough" and used ads that were less image-oriented and more "copy-oriented" than typical cigarette ads. It named the innovative new brand Premier because it represented "the beginning of a whole new era of smoking enjoyment—cleaner enjoyment than you may have thought possible. The essential theme [was to be] the totality of its attributes, so that the product [would] be recognized as . . . a remarkable discovery."

But the company's marketing strategy was a risky one. For one thing, the firm priced Premier substantially higher than ordinary cigarettes. For another, by targeting older, better-educated smokers, RJR ran the risk of hurting its own brands in the low-tar market. Further, some saw the smokeless cigarette as hostile to smoking. Just as decaffeinated coffee helped accelerate the decline of coffee consumption, so might Premier speed the decline in cigarette smoking, which was already falling at 2 percent per year.

The marketing strategy, however, may have reflected the constraints imposed by the new product more than anything else. Premier needed lots of explanation, and hence, more ad copy. The higher costs of making the product forced a higher price tag—about 25 percent above ordinary cigarette brands—which also meant targeting more affluent customers. Beyond that, RJR had to walk a fine line in pitching the product as "cleaner" without representing it as "healthier."

Because of these problems, some skeptics questioned whether RJR's strategy would work. They noted, for instance, that cigarette ads usually try to push powerful images and simple themes: too many facts might only reinforce the negative impression people have of smoking. One advertising executive observed that cigarettes are a "very personal, image-driven product," and that RJR's approach would only work "if it's a terrific product."

The just-the-facts approach also contained special risks because the facts in this case were quite complex. One consultant, a former RJR employee, believed Premier had strong potential as a second brand for smokers who are reluctant to light up in restaurants and other public places. However, he added that the smokeless cigarette is kind of a "Rube Goldberg" contraption, with a carbon tip on one end and flavor beads, which provide most of the cigarette's nicotine, in an aluminum casing inside the cigarette. He concluded that all this could be a lot for people to get used to, and too much to explain in a single ad. One initial ad, for instance, even explained how to light the smokeless cigarette. "Hold the flame to Premier a second or two longer than you normally would, until an ash begins to form," the ads says. It went on to say that car lighters won't work and that "for best results, we recommend using a good quality butane lighter." Another consultant felt that this is too much for people to *want* to understand. "My own feeling is that it's going to bomb," he noted, adding that, "It sounds like it's too mechanical." RJR tried to overcome this complexity by taking a "Try it, you'll like it" approach in its ad campaign. "One week will convince you," a spot proclaimed. "If all this sounds too good to be true, prove it to yourself."

According to RJR, consumers gave Premier generally high marks in taste tests—they found it to be roughly comparable to that of Winston Lights, one of the company's low-tar brands. However, to independently test smokers' reactions to Premier, a *Wall Street Journal* reporter conducted a survey of about two dozen smokers at Atlanta's Hartsfield International Airport. Although unscientific, the survey indicated what some smokers thought about the cigarette and pointed up some marketing problems RJR would face.

Many smokers in the survey said they disliked Premier because of its taste and strangeness. Some who reacted favorably said they might buy Premier as a second brand for use where sidestream smoke isn't acceptable; others liked it as a step away from smoking. Overall, nearly twice as many smokers panned Premier as praised it. RJR officials cautioned against drawing conclusions from this sample, noting that for many of the 2000-plus people who test-smoked Premier in their research, it "did take some getting used to." But, they claimed, once many of the first-time skeptics got used to it, they liked it.

So, RJR needed to get smokers to try lots of Premiers. To encourage extended trial the lead markets, the company gave away two packs when smokers bought two—four packs at a time in some outlets. The company believed that many smokers would be attracted enough by the reduced tar and decreased offensiveness that they would stick with Premier and learn to like it. Just how many people would stay with it that long? One smoker in the airport survey discarded his Premier after only two puffs. "That taste doesn't get it," he observed.

Premier's complexity presented a problem in the airport survey also. Nearly all the smokers had trouble lighting the cigarette, most needing two or three tries. The carbon tip, which heats air to pass through the cigarette rather than burning tobacco, also makes the nonfilter part of the cigarette hot—leaving some people suspicious about just what is going on in there. One two-pack-a-day, 45-year-old smoker claimed that Premier tasted like her Now 100s, but she listened with growing horror to a description of the contents of the cigarette. "Carbon and metal?" she asked. "I'd rather smoke good old tobacco leaf. I know what I'm getting."

The fact that Premier doesn't burn down also baffled smokers. "I've been smoking the hell out of this, and it won't go away," exclaimed a lumber salesman. The cigarette remains lit until the carbon tip expires, after about eight to 10 puffs for the average smoker and about the same as for a king-sized cigarette. But Premier keeps smokers in suspense about how much they have left.

Other Premier properties also run counter to some deeply ingrained routines. A Merit-smoking management consultant in the survey laughed at himself as he kept trying to flick nonexistent ashes into an ashtray. "This is going to require some new habits," he said. Nor were he and others certain just what to do with the cigarette when they were finished. They tried to crush it into an ashtray, something the stiff-papered outer casing resists and, according to RJR, that isn't necessary.

Still, some smokers who were not enthusiastic about Premier said that they might try it to avoid offending nonsmokers. The chairman of an Atlanta billboard company noted that he didn't like the taste much but stated, "I'd smoke it to get rid of the nagging at home. You could use it as a substitute there, then use the high-octane stuff outside." An auditorium manager offered only faint praise for Premier but said he would consider switching because he was in a minority of smokers at work. He felt obliged to snuff out his cigarette when other people entered his office. But, due to Premier's lack of sidestream smoke, "I wouldn't be embarrassed to keep this going."

RJR needed to make Premier successful. It had worked on the cigarette since 1981, and estimates are that it had invested several hundred million dollars in the product so far. Further, RJR's share of the U.S. cigarette market had slid to 34 percent as compared with arch rival Philip Morris' 39 percent. RJR hoped that "no smoke" would attract customers and reverse this decline.

QUESTIONS

1. Make a list of the words and phrases used in the case to describe Premier's target market. Did RJR define Premier's target market well?

2. What cultural, social, personal, and psychological factors affect a consumer's decision to smoke? Did RJR effectively address these factors with Premier?

3. Given the consumer's decision making process, did RJR properly shape its marketing mix? What assumptions did RJR make about the consumer decision-making process?

4. What do the comments of the consumers surveyed in the Atlanta Airport suggest about the consumer learning process?

5. In what alternative ways could RJR position Premier?

Source: Adapted from John Helyar, "RJR Plans to Market Smokeless Cigarette as Breakthrough with Hefty Price Tag," *The Wall Street Journal*, September 30, 1988; and "RJR Smokeless Cigarette Encounters Skeptical Public," *The Wall Street Journal*, September 8, 1988.

② reference groups, peer pressure, stress, addiction

Marketing Mix
Instruction manual
Technological
Bad Taste
Main benefit went to
Non-Smokers
$ → 25% higher than
regular brands
Promotion → buy 2 get 2 free

JAPANESE CARS: REALLY BETTER?

By any measure, the Japanese pose the greatest threat domestic auto manufacturers have ever faced.

Consider the 1989 sales performance of Detroit's Big Three: Chrysler down 14 percent, Ford down 4 percent, General Motors down 10 percent. In the same year, Nissan was up 8 percent, Toyota up 6 percent, and Honda up 8 percent. In 1982, the Big Three controlled 73 percent of the U.S. car market. Today they control 67 percent, and their share could drop below 60 percent by the mid-1990s. Toyota, with 8.8 percent of the market, could soon overtake Chrysler at 8.9 percent, meaning that for the first time the Big Three would include a foreign-based manufacturer.

In 1989, Honda was the best-selling automobile in the United States. Of the top 20 models listed in a J. D. Power and Associates Initial Quality Survey, only 4 were American nameplates, while 14 were Japanese and 2 were German.

How do Japanese automobiles, even those produced in the United States, differ from automobiles produced by the Big Three? Customers speak of superior styling, reliability, and durability; fair price and better assembly; good trade-in value, and relatively few problems. In a word, the issue is quality. Many consumers are firmly convinced that Japanese vehicles are better all around than domestic automobiles. For example, one of Honda's strengths, according to some analysts, is its ability to *exceed* customers' expectations.

The superiority of Japanese cars has been attributed to both the management process and the production process the Japanese manufacturers employ.

On the management side, the Japanese believe in operation by consensus. While it takes them longer to make a decision, they display greater commitment to a decision once it is made. The Japanese also think and plan long term. In addition, they think and plan in terms of improving customer satisfaction. Finally, management has forged close links with suppliers in order to lower costs and speed production.

On the production side, there is a greater sense of team spirit and worker involvement in decision making than is found at the Big Three. Inspection takes place at every stage of production. The Japanese have also made effective use of robotics and automation, allowing for faster, more flexible, and more efficient production. And the closer tie to suppliers has enabled them to use just-in-time inventory control.

As ABC correspondent James Walker points out, the U.S. car industry is fighting more than just a "perception problem." The industry is also fighting its own short-comings. The work force at Japanese companies is younger and therefore requires less expensive health care and other benefits. Also, the Japanese built eight assembly plants in the United States during the 1980s, creating tens of thousands of jobs and faithful supporters. That is why many U.S. auto buyers no longer perceive Japanese automobiles as "foreign."

But haven't American automakers implemented many of these same ideas? Haven't they improved? The answer to both these questions is a resounding yes. But as the Americans got better, so did the Japanese. Even the industry leader, General Motors, has found it hard to beat a moving target.

When GM Chairman Roger Smith promised that his Saturn Division would build a top-quality small car using the "magic bullet" of technology to solve its competitiveness problem, it took over seven years and more than $3.5 billion to accomplish the goal. If the Saturn had been introduced in 1987 or 1988, it would have been ahead of the competition. But while GM improved, so did the Japanese. Where it took GM seven years to bring its new car to market, it takes the Japanese half that time to introduce a new automobile.

Interestingly, while GM is building the Saturn for the small-car market, many Japanese firms are adding upscale automobiles such as the Acura, the Infiniti, and the Lexus, which are capturing more and more of the high-profit-margin part of the car market. In another ominous trend, while only Nissan builds trucks here now, Toyota and other Japanese firms plan to start making trucks in the United States within a few years. Since trucks make up about one-third of U.S. vehicle sales, the Big Three can expect to see their share of the market decline further.

QUESTIONS

1. Explain how opinion leaders may influence the purchase of a Japanese vehicle over an American automobile.
2. Explain how the perceptive processes of selective distortion and selective retention might cause the satisfied owner of a Japanese automobile to disregard claims made by Lee Iacocca comparing the quality of American and Japanese automobiles.
3. Explain how the learning process might influence the satisfied owner of a Japanese automobile to purchase another Japanese automobile when it is time to trade.

Sources: "Overtaking the Big Three on Their Turf," *USA Today*, September 11, 1990, pp. B1 & B2; "GM's Plan for Saturn to Beat Small Imports Trails Original Goals," *The Wall Street Journal*, July 9, 1990, pp. A1 & A4; "Japanese Gain Record Share of Auto Sales," *USA Today*, September 7, 1990, p. B1; "Hands Across America: The Rise of Mitsubishi," *Business Week*, September 24, 1990, pp. 102–113.

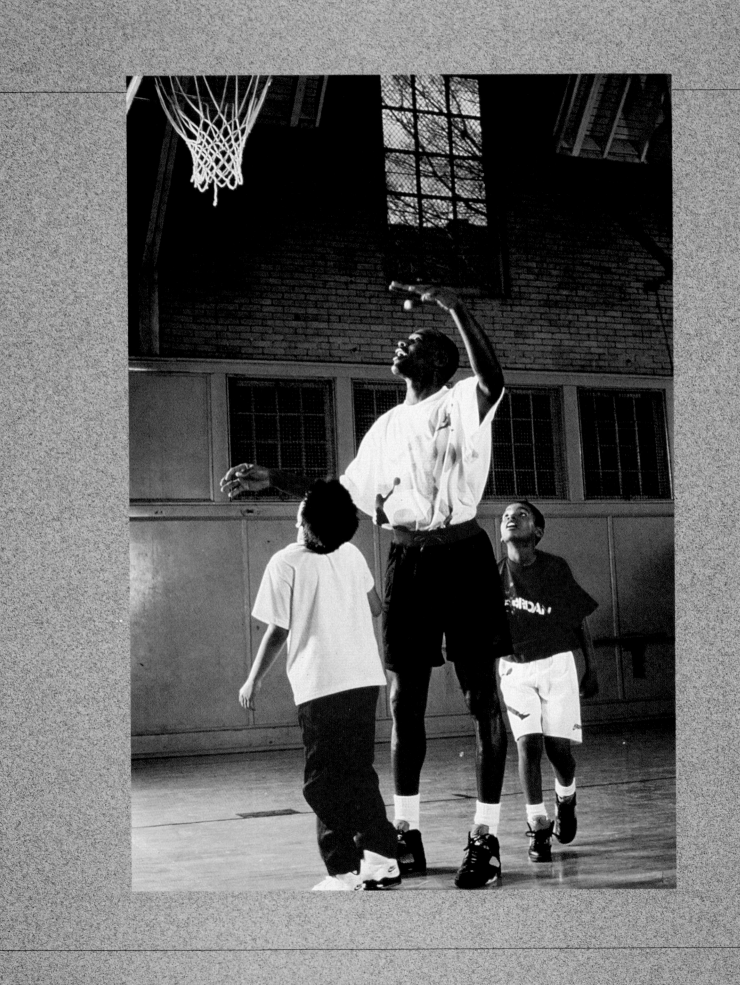

6

Consumer Markets: Buyer-Decision Processes

In the early 1980s, Nike won the opening battle in what many now call the "great sneaker wars." Based on the power of its running shoes—which were designed for fitness but used mostly for fun—Nike unseated Adidas and sprinted into the lead in the $5 billion U.S. athletic shoe market. But fashion is fickle, and Nike's lead was short-lived. In 1986, upstart Reebok caught Nike from behind with its new soft leather aerobics shoe. It turned sweaty sneakers into fashion statements and zoomed to the front. By 1987, Reebok had captured more than 30 percent of the market, while Nike's share had slumped to 18 percent.

In 1988, however, Nike retaliated. It targeted the reemerging "performance" market with the hard-hitting $20 million "Just Do It" advertising campaign featuring football and baseball star Bo Jackson. The company also introduced dozens of new products aimed at narrow segments in the rapidly fragmenting athletic shoe market. By 1990, Nike was selling footwear for almost every conceivable sport: hiking, walking, cycling, even cheerleading and windsurfing. The numbers attest to the rejuvenated Nike: its market share is now 25 percent and growing; Reebok's share has fallen dramatically to less than 24 percent.

But the sneaker wars are far from over. Reebok is already counterattacking with new products and marketing programs. And in a volatile industry that has seen many leaders—from venerable Converse in the 1970s to Adidas and Nike in the 1980s—first soar to the top and then plunge abruptly, both Nike and Reebok are watching their flanks for new competitors. For example, the success story of 1989 was neither Nike nor Reebok, but Number 3, L.A. Gear, which came from nowhere to grab $600 million in sales (triple its 1988 sales) and an 11 percent market share.

Winning in the sneaker wars, or even just surviving, requires a keen understanding of consumer behavior. But because sneakers can be a major means of self-expression, people's choices are usually shaped by a rich mix of influences. Thus, understanding consumer behavior in this seesaw market can be extremely difficult; trying to predict behavior can be even more difficult. The shoe companies introduce scores of new styles and colors every year chasing fads that often fade at blinding speed. One day salespeople will sell all they can get of a new style; the next day they can't discount it enough.

The fickle youth market is the biggest battleground in the sneaker wars, and the inner city is at the center. Consumers between 15 and 22 years old buy 30 percent of all sneakers and influence an additional 10 percent through word-of-mouth. Many trends start in the nation's inner cities and spread to suburbia and the rest of middle America. Urban kids represent authenticity to kids in the suburbs, so trends that catch on in the inner city often spread quickly to the rest of the country. It isn't surprising, then, that sneaker makers openly court inner-city shoe-store owners and kids. Nike and the other shoe manufacturers often give free sneakers to trend-setting teens whom the masses copy. Reebok even rebuilds inner-city playgrounds and repaves basketball courts to woo this constituency. And companies often launch new sneakers first in the inner city to see how they catch on before going national.

Those in the know, of course, don't call them sneakers. Instead, they're known as Alphas, Revolutions, 830s, Air Jordans—their model names and numbers. The shoes are the first and foremost fashion statement. Gone are the days when sneakers were mostly cheap, functional, and drab, when the choices were white or black canvas, low top or high top, with maybe a variation or two for avid runners. Now, sneakers are a status symbol, a subculture. Sneaker prices start at around $50 a pair and run to more than $180. You can get good sneakers for less, but nobody who is anybody would be caught dead in them.

Sneaker crazes are often hard to explain. For example, the fad of wearing sneakers with the laces untied apparently began because proud owners wanted to keep their shoes looking factory fresh. Pretty soon, everyone was doing it, and that was just the beginning. Next, some wearers untied the lace on one shoe only; then, they removed the laces completely. Soon after that, wearers switched back to tying their shoes, but with laces from a different shoe. Now many are wearing sneakers that don't match—say, a white Chuck Taylor Converse on one foot and a Black Cons Converse on the other—but brands can't be mixed. Another unwritten rule: When it comes to dates, Nikes don't mix with Reeboks, or Converse with Adidas. In some neighborhoods, teen-age girls report that the first thing they look at when a boy asks them out is his choice of sneakers. Teen-age romances have been thwarted by brand differences.

There are regional—and even local—preferences, too. Adidas is the "in" brand in Philadelphia, home of Temple University, whose basketball team wears Adidas shoes. Chicago is a Nike town because Chicago basketball star Michael Jordan endorses the shoes. (Celebrity endorsements are key: Nike pays Mr. Jordan more than $2.5 million over five years to wear the shoes.) In Boston, there are Nike streets and Adidas streets, and woe to anyone caught wearing the wrong brand on the wrong street.

When it comes to sneakers, some people get a little carried away. For example, Brian Washington has 150 pairs of sneakers scattered around his two-bedroom apartment in Harlem. For all-night dancing, he has the bright red and black Nike Airwalkers. For "impressing the ladies," there are the chartreuse and gold Adidas shoes with purple stripes. The black and sky-blue Evolvo low-tops are for Saturdays at the park. For just hanging out, he prefers ink-blue Nikes. "The fact is, in the inner city, you are what you wear—on your feet," he explains. Of course, owning too many pairs of shoes can be a problem. For one thing, it's hard to decide what is the moment's socially hip attire. Heading out for the playground one recent afternoon for a pickup basketball game, Mr. Washington stepped into a pair of white Nike Air Jordans. Under his arm, he put a brown leather basketball, and over his shoulder he carried a white pair of Avia 830s—just in case he changed his mind on his walk to the playground. Says Mr. Washington, ever fashion-conscious, "It's a jungle out there." Nike and the other sneaker wars combatants couldn't agree more.[1]

CHAPTER OBJECTIVES

After reading this chapter, you should be able to:

1. Identify the different roles people might play in making a buying decision.
2. Discuss how consumer decision making varies with the type of buying decision.
3. Explain the five stages of the buyer decision process.
4. Describe the consumer adoption process for new products.

Marketers must be extremely careful in analyzing consumer behavior. Consumers often turn down what appears to be a winning offer. If they do not endorse a product, the product loses. The new plant and equipment might as well have been built on quicksand. Polaroid learned this when it lost $170 million on its Polarvision instant home movie system. So did Ford when it launched the famous (or infamous) Edsel, losing a cool $350 million in the process. And so did RCA when it swallowed a huge $580 million loss on its SelectaVision videodisc player.

The preceding chapter examines the influences—cultural, social, personal, and psychological—that affect buyers. In this chapter we look at how consumers make buying decisions. First, we examine consumer buying roles and the types of decisions consumers face. Next we look at the main steps in the buyer decision process. Then we explore the process by which consumers learn about and buy new products.

CONSUMER BUYING ROLES

The marketer needs to know which people are involved in the buying decision and what role each person plays. Identifying the decision maker in many transactions is fairly easy. Men normally choose their own shoes and women choose their own pantyhose. Other products, however, involve group decisions. Consider the selection of a family automobile. The suggestion to buy a new car might come from the oldest child. A friend might advise the family on the kind of car to buy. The husband might choose the make. The wife might have a definite opinion regarding the car's style. The husband and wife might then make the final decision jointly. And the wife might end up using the car more than her husband.

Figure 6-1 shows that people might play any of several roles in a buying decision:

- **Initiator:** the person who first suggests or thinks of the idea of buying a particular product or service
- **Influencer:** a person whose views or advice carries some weight in making the final buying decision
- **Decider:** the person who ultimately makes a buying decision or any part of it—whether to buy, what to buy, how to buy, or where to buy
- **Buyer:** the person who makes an actual purchase
- **User:** the person who consumes or uses a product or service

A company needs to identify who occupies these roles because they affect product design and advertising message decisions. If Chevrolet finds that husbands make buying decisions for the family station wagon, it will direct most of its advertising for these models toward husbands. But Chevy ads will include wives, children, and others who might initiate or influence the buying decision. And Chevrolet will design its station wagons with features that meet the needs of those buying decision participants. Knowing the main participants and the roles they play helps the marketer fine-tune the marketing program.

FIGURE 6-1
Consumer buying roles

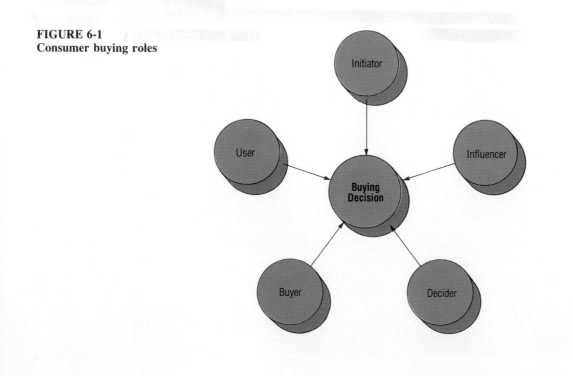

TYPES OF BUYING DECISION BEHAVIOR

Consumer decision making varies with the type of buying decision. There are great differences between buying toothpaste, a tennis racket, an expensive camera, and a new car. The more complex decisions are likely to involve more buying participants and more buyer deliberation. Figure 6-2 identifies three types of buying behavior.[2]

Routine Response Behavior

Routine response behavior, the simplest type of buying behavior, occurs when consumers buy low-cost, frequently purchased items. These buyers have very few decisions to make—they know a lot about the product class and major brands available, and they have fairly clear preferences among the brands. However, they do not always buy the same brand; stockouts, special deals, or simply a wish for variety may override any brand loyalty. In general, buyers do not give much thought, search, or time to the purchase. The goods in this class are often called *low-involvement goods*. For example, you don't spend a lot of time and effort choosing your laundry detergent, or your gas station. You usually just pick one of the brands or places you use regularly.

Marketers of products that consumers buy routinely have two tasks. First, they must satisfy current customers by maintaining consistent quality, service, and value. Second, they must try to attract new buyers—to break them out of the routine of buying competing products—by introducing new features and using point-of-purchase displays, price specials, and premiums.

Limited Problem Solving

Buying is more complex when buyers confront an unfamiliar brand in a familiar product class. For example, people thinking about buying a new tennis racket may be shown a new brand with a new shape or one made of a new material. They may ask questions and watch ads to learn more about the new brand. This is described as **limited problem solving** because buyers are fully aware of the product class, but are not familiar with all the brands and their features.

The marketer recognizes that consumers are trying to reduce risk by gathering information. Marketers must design a communication program that helps buyers understand the company's brand and give them confidence in it.

Extensive Problem Solving

Sometimes buyers face complex buying decisions for more expensive, less frequently purchased products in a less familiar product class. For these products, buyers often do not know about available brands or what factors to consider when they evaluate different brands. In these situations, people use **extensive problem solving.** For example, suppose you want to buy an expensive new stereo components system. You would probably spend time visiting different stores, collecting information, and comparing various brands before making the final decision.

Marketers of products in this class must understand the information-gathering and evaluation activities of prospective buyers. They need to help buyers learn about important

FIGURE 6-2   Types of buying decision behavior

ROUTINE RESPONSE BEHAVIOR ⟶	LIMITED PROBLEM SOLVING ⟶	EXTENSIVE PROBLEM SOLVING
Low-cost products	⟶	More expensive products
Frequent purchasing	⟶	Infrequent purchasing
Low consumer involvement	⟶	High consumer involvement
Familiar product class and brands	⟶	Unfamiliar product class and brands
Little thought, search, or time given to purchase	⟶	Extensive thought, search, and time given to purchase

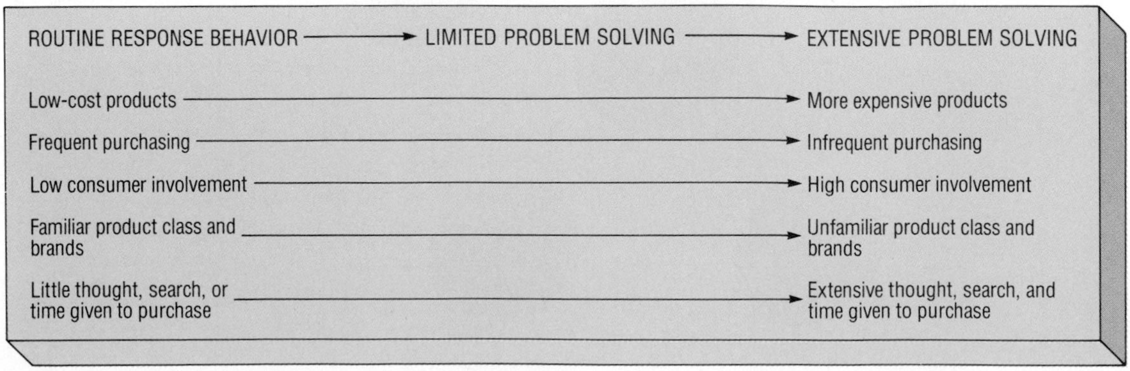

Extensive problem solving: Consumers shop different stores, collect information, and compare various brands before buying.

buying criteria and persuade buyers that their brands rate high on important attributes compared with competing products.

STAGES IN THE BUYER-DECISION PROCESS

Consumers make many buying decisions every day. Most large companies research consumer buying decisions in great detail. They want to answer questions about what consumers buy, where they buy, how and how much they buy, when they buy, and why they buy (see Marketing Highlight 6–1). Marketers can study consumer purchases to find answers to questions about what they buy, where, and how much. But learning about the *whys* of consumer buying behavior and buying decision process is not so easy—the answers are often locked deep within the consumer's head.

We can now examine the stages buyers pass through to reach a buying decision. As Figure 6-3 shows, the consumer passes through five stages: problem recognition, information search, evaluation of alternatives, purchase decision, and postpurchase behavior. This model emphasizes that the buying process starts long before the actual purchase and continues after the purchase. It encourages the marketer to focus on the entire buying process, rather than just the purchase decision.[3]

THE WHATS AND WHYS OF CONSUMER BUYING

No one knows better than Mom, right? But does she know how much underwear you own? Jockey International does. Or the number of ice cubes you put in a glass? Coca-Cola knows that one. Or how about which pretzels you usually eat first, the broken ones or the whole ones? Try asking Frito-Lay. Big companies know the whats, wheres, hows, and whens of their consumers. They figure out all sorts of things about us that we don't even know ourselves. To marketers, this isn't trivial pursuit—knowing all about the customer is the cornerstone of effective marketing. Most companies research us in detail and amass mountains of facts.

Coke knows that we put 3.2 ice cubes in a glass, see 69 of its commercials every year, and prefer cans to pop out of vending machines at a temperature of 35 degrees. One million of us drink Coke with breakfast every day. Kodak knows that amateur photographers muff more than two billion pictures every year. This fact led to the disk camera, which helped eliminate almost half of our out-of-focus and overexposed shots and became one of the most successful cameras in Kodak's history.

Each new day brings piles of fresh research reports detailing our buying habits and preferences. Did you know that 38 percent of Americans would rather have a tooth pulled than take their car to a dealership for repairs? We each spend $20 a year on flowers; Arkansas has the lowest consumption of peanut butter in the U.S.; 51 percent of all males put their pants on left-leg-first whereas 65 percent of women start with the right leg; if you send a husband and a wife to the store separately to buy beer, there is a 90 percent chance they will return with different brands.

Nothing about our behavior is sacred. Procter & Gamble once conducted a study to find out whether most of us fold or crumple our toilet paper; another study showed that 68 percent of consumers prefer their toilet paper to unwind over the spool rather than under. Abbott Laboratories figured out that one in four of us has "problem" dandruff, and Kimberly Clark, which makes Kleenex, has calculated that the average person blows his or her nose 256 times a year.

It's not that Americans are all that easy to figure out.

A few years ago, Campbell Soup gave up trying to learn our opinions about the ideal-sized meatball after a series of tests showed us preferring one so big it wouldn't fit in the can.

Hoover hooked up timers and other equipment to vacuum cleaners in people's homes and learned that we spend about 35 minutes each week vacuuming, sucking up about eight pounds of dust each year and using six bags to do so. Banks know that we write about 24 checks a month, and pharmaceutical companies know that all of us together take 52 million aspirins and 30 million sleeping pills a year. In fact, almost everything we swallow is closely monitored by someone. Each year we consume 156 hamburgers, 95 hot dogs, 283 eggs, five pounds of yogurt, nine pounds of cereal, two pounds of peanut butter, and 46 quarts of popcorn. We spend 90 minutes a day preparing our food and 40 minutes a day munching it. Then we down $650 million of antacid a year to help digest it.

Of all businesses, however, the prize for research thoroughness may go to toothpaste makers. Among other things, they know that our favorite toothbrush color is blue and that only 37 percent of us are using one that's more than six months old. About 47 percent of us put water on our brush before we apply the paste, 15 percent of us put water on after the paste, and 24 percent of us do both. Fourteen percent don't wet the brush at all.

Thus, most big marketing companies have answers to all the what, where, when, and how questions about their consumers' buying behavior. Seemingly trivial facts add up quickly and provide important input for designing marketing strategies. But to influence consumer behavior, marketers need the answer to one more question: Beyond knowing the whats and wherefores of behavior, they need to know the *whys*—what *causes* our buying behavior? That's a much harder question to answer.

Sources: John Koten, "You Aren't Paranoid If You Feel Someone Eyes You Constantly," *The Wall Street Journal*, March 29, 1985, pp. 1, 22; and "Offbeat Marketing," *Sales & Marketing Management*, January 1990, p. 35.

This model seems to imply that consumers pass through all five stages with every purchase. But in more routine purchases, consumers skip or reverse some stages. A woman buying her regular brand of toothpaste would recognize the need and go right to the purchase decision, skipping information search and evaluation. However, we use the model in Figure 6-3 because it shows all the considerations that arise when a consumer faces a new and complex purchase situation.

To illustrate this model, we again follow Jennifer Smith and try to understand how she became interested in buying an expensive camera and the stages she went through to make the final choice.

FIGURE 6-3 Buyer decision process

Problem Recognition The buying process starts with **problem recognition.** The buyer recognizes a problem or need. The buyer senses a difference between his or her *actual* state and some *desired* state. The need can be triggered by *internal stimuli*. One of the person's normal needs— hunger, thirst, sex—rises to a level high enough to become a drive. From previous experience, the person has learned how to cope with this drive and is motivated toward objects that he or she knows will satisfy it.

Or a need can be triggered by *external stimuli*. Jennifer Smith passes a bakery and the sight of freshly baked bread stimulates her hunger; she admires a neighbor's new car; or she watches a television commercial for a Jamaican vacation. All of these can lead her to recognize a problem or need. At this stage, the marketer needs to determine the factors and situations that usually trigger consumer problem recognition. The marketer should research consumers to find out what kinds of needs or problems arise, what brings them about, and how they lead the consumer to a particular product.

Jennifer Smith might answer that she felt the need for a new hobby when her busy season at work slowed down, and she thought of cameras after talking to a friend about photography. By gathering such information, the marketer can identify the stimuli that most often trigger interest in the product and can develop marketing programs which involve these stimuli.

Information Search An aroused consumer may or may not search for more information. If the consumer's drive is strong and a satisfying product is near at hand, the consumer is likely to buy it then. If not, the consumer may simply store the need in memory or undertake an **information search** bearing on the need.

At one level, the consumer may simply enter *heightened attention*. For example, Jennifer Smith becomes more receptive to information about cameras. She pays attention to camera ads, cameras used by friends, and camera conversations. Or Jennifer may go into *active information search*, in which she looks for reading material, phones friends, and gathers information in other ways. How much searching she does will depend upon the strength of her drive, the amount of information she starts with, the ease of obtaining more information, the value she places on additional information, and the satisfaction she gets from searching. Normally the amount of consumer search activity increases as the consumer moves from decisions that involve limited problem solving to those that involve extensive problem solving. The consumer can obtain information from any of several sources. The marketer must know about these sources and the influence each exerts on buying decisions. Consumer information sources include:

- *Personal sources*: family, friends, neighbors, acquaintances
- *Commercial sources*: advertising, salespeople, dealers, packaging, displays
- *Public sources*: mass media, consumer-rating organizations
- *Experiential sources*: handling, examining, using the product

The relative influence of these information sources varies with the product and the buyer. Generally, the consumer receives the most information about a product from commercial sources—those controlled by the marketer. The most effective sources, how-ever, tend to be personal. Commercial sources normally *inform* the buyer, but personal sources *legitimize* or *evaluate* products for the buyer. For example, doctors normally learn of new drugs from commercial sources but turn to other doctors for evaluation information.

As more information is obtained, the consumer's awareness and knowledge of available brands and features increases. In her information search, Jennifer Smith learned about the many camera brands available. The information also helped her drop certain brands from consideration. A company must design its marketing mix to make prospects aware of and knowledgeable about its brand. If it fails to do this, the company has lost its opportunity to sell to the customer. The company must also learn which other brands customers consider, so that it knows its competition and can plan its own appeals.

The marketer should carefully identify consumers' sources of information and

Information sources: People usually receive the most information about a product from marketer controlled sources.

the importance of each source. Consumers should be asked how they first heard about the brand, what information they received, and the importance they place on different information sources. This information is critical in preparing effective communication to target markets.

Evaluation of Alternatives

We have seen how the consumer uses information to arrive at a set of final brand choices. Now the question is: How does the consumer choose among the alternative brands? The marketer needs to know about **alternative evaluation**—that is, how the consumer processes information to arrive at brand choices. Unfortunately, no simple, single evaluation process is used by all consumers—nor even by one consumer in all buying situations. Instead, several evaluation processes are at work.

Certain basic concepts will help explain consumer evaluation processes. First, we assume that each consumer is trying to satisfy some need. The consumer is looking for certain *benefits* that can be acquired by buying a product or service. Further, each consumer sees a product as a bundle of *product attributes* with varying capacities for delivering these benefits and satisfying the need. For cameras, product attributes include picture quality, ease of use, camera size, price, and other features. Consumers will vary as to which of these attributes they consider relevant. Consumers will pay the most attention to those attributes connected with their needs.

TABLE 6-1
A Consumer's Brand
Beliefs about Cameras

CAMERA	ATTRIBUTE			
	Picture Quality	Ease of Use	Camera Size	Price
A	10	8	6	4
B	8	9	8	3
C	6	8	10	5
D	4	3	7	8

Note: The number 10 represents the highest desirable score on that attribute. In the case of price, a high number means a low cost, which makes the camera more desirable.

Second, the consumer will attach different *degrees of importance* to each attribute. A distinction can be drawn between the importance of an attribute and its salience.[4] *Salient attributes* are those that come to a consumer's mind when he or she is asked to think of a product's characteristics. But these are not necessarily the most important attributes to the consumer. Some of them may be salient because the consumer has just seen an advertisement mentioning them or has had a problem with them, making these attributes "top-of-the-mind." The consumer may have forgotten other attributes but recognize their importance once mentioned. Marketers should be more concerned with attribute importance than attribute salience.

Third, the consumer is likely to develop a set of *brand beliefs* about each brand's ranking for each attribute. The set of beliefs held about a particular brand is known as the **brand image.** The consumer's beliefs may vary from true attributes because of his or her experience and the effect of selective perception, selective distortion, and selective retention.

Fourth, the consumer is assumed to have a *utility function* for each attribute. The utility function shows how the consumer expects total product satisfaction to vary with different levels of different attributes. For example, Jennifer Smith may expect her satisfaction from a camera to increase with better picture quality; to peak with a medium-weight camera as opposed to a very light or very heavy one; to be higher for a 35-mm camera than for a 110-mm camera. If we combine the attribute levels at which her utilities are highest, they make up Jennifer's ideal camera. The camera would also be her preferred camera if it were available and affordable.

Fifth, the consumer arrives at attributes toward the different brands through some *evaluation procedure*. Consumers have been found to use one or more of several evaluation procedures, depending on the consumer and the buying decision.

For example, suppose Jennifer has narrowed her choice set to four cameras: A, B, C, and D. Assume that she is primarily interested in four attributes—picture quality, ease of use, camera size, and price. Table 6-1 shows her ratings of each brand's attributes on a 10-point scale. Jennifer believes that brand A deserves the highest rating in picture quality, 10; is easy to use, 8; is medium size, 6; and is fairly expensive, 4. Similarly, she has beliefs about how the other cameras rate on these attributes. The marketer would like to be able to predict which camera Jennifer will buy. Clearly, if one camera rated best on all the attributes, we could predict that Jennifer would choose it.

However, the brands vary in appeal. Some buyers base their buying decision on only one attribute, and their choices are easy to predict. If Jennifer wants picture quality above everything, she should buy A; if she wants the camera that is easiest to use, she should buy B; if she wants the best camera size, she should buy C; if she wants the lower-price camera, she should buy D.

Most buyers consider several attributes, but assign different importance to each. If we knew the importance weights Jennifer assigns to the four attributes, we could predict her camera choice more reliably. Suppose Jennifer assigns 40 percent of the importance to the camera's picture quality, 30 percent to ease of use, 20 percent to its size, and 10 percent to its price. To find Jennifer's perceived value for each camera, we can multiply her importance weights by her beliefs about each camera. This gives us the following perceived values:

$$\text{Camera A} = .4(10) + .3(8) + .2(6) + .1(4) = 8.0$$
$$\text{Camera B} = .4(8) + .3(9) + .2(8) + .1(3) = 7.8$$
$$\text{Camera C} = .4(6) + .3(8) + .2(10) + .1(5) = 7.3$$
$$\text{Camera D} = .4(4) + .3(3) + .2(7) + .1(8) = 4.7$$

We would predict that Jennifer will favor camera A.

This model is called the *expectancy value model* of consumer choice.[5] It is one of several possible models describing how consumers go about evaluating alternatives. Consumers might evaluate a set of alternatives in other ways. For example, Jennifer might decide that she should consider only cameras that satisfy a set of minimum attribute levels. She might decide a camera would have to offer a picture quality greater than 7 *and* ease of use greater than 8. In this case, we would predict that she would choose camera B because only camera B satisfies the minimum requirements. This is called the *conjunctive model* of consumer choice. Or Jennifer might decide that she would settle for a camera that had a picture quality greater than 7 *or* ease of use greater than 8. In this case, A and B both meet the requirements. This is called the *disjunctive model* of consumer choice.

How consumers go about evaluating purchase alternatives depends on the individual consumer and the specific buying situation. In some cases, consumers use careful calculations and logical thinking. At other times, the same consumers do little or no evaluating, instead buying on impulse and relying on intuition. Sometimes consumers make buying decisions on their own; sometimes they turn to friends, consumer guides, salespeople, or even computers for buying advice (see Marketing Highlight 6–2).

Marketers should study buyers to find out how they actually evaluate brand alternatives. If they know what evaluative processes go on, marketers can take steps to influence the buyer's decision. Suppose Jennifer is inclined to buy a Nikon camera because she rates it high on picture quality and ease of use. What strategies might another camera maker, say Minolta, use to influence people like Jennifer? There are several. Minolta could modify its camera so that it delivers better pictures or other features that consumers like Jennifer want. It could try to change buyers' beliefs about how its camera rates on important attributes, especially if consumers currently underestimate the camera's qualities. It could try to change buyers' beliefs about Nikon and other competitors. Finally, it could try to change the list of attributes that buyers consider, or the importance attached to these attributes. For example, it might advertise that all good cameras have about equal picture quality, and that its lighter-weight, lower-priced camera is a better buy for people like Jennifer.

Purchase Decision
In the evaluation stage, the consumer ranks brands and forms purchase intentions. Generally, the consumer's **purchase decision** will be to buy the most preferred brand, but two factors can come between the purchase *intention* and the purchase *decision*. These factors are shown in Figure 6-4.[6]

MARKETING HIGHLIGHT 6–2

THIS COMPUTER GIVES SHOPPERS CUSTOM-MADE ADVICE

Some people break out in a cold sweat when they have to shop. Others get cross-eyed from scanning the ratings in *Consumer Reports*. That consumers are befuddled doesn't surprise Thomas A. Williams. The Rochester Institute of Technology professor of decision sciences says he has been swamped with requests from friends who need help. So Williams is working on a high-tech solution: expert-system programs to help confused consumers shop.

Williams has tried his computerized advisers for such products as running shoes, washing machines, touring bikes, and cars. The systems grill shoppers about their preferences, personal characteristics, and price ranges. Then they watch the data with available products. If you wanted new running shoes, a system would base its recommendation on answers to questions about the anatomy of your feet, the terrain you run on, and how long and how often you run.

Williams is scouting stores that will let customers try his systems for microcomputers and cameras. He's still not sure shoppers will welcome the electronic adviser. "The typical consumer does not approach a purchasing decision in a logical fashion," he says.

Source: Reprinted from the December 7, 1987, issue of *Business Week* by special permission. Copyright 1987 by McGraw-Hill, Inc.

To rate higher with consumers, Minolta added autofocus, motorized film control, and other features. It took major competitor Canon three years to catch up.

The first factor is the *attitudes of others.* Suppose Jennifer Smith's husband feels strongly that Jennifer should buy the lowest-priced camera. Then the chances of Jennifer buying a more expensive camera will be reduced. How much another person's attitudes will affect Jennifer's choices depends both on the strength of the other person's attitudes toward her buying decision and on Jennifer's motivation to comply with that person's wishes. The more intense the other person's attitudes and the closer the other person is to Jennifer, the greater the effect the other person will have.

Purchase intention is also influenced by *unexpected situational factors.* The consumer forms a purchase intention based on such factors as expected family income, expected price, and expected benefits from the product. When the consumer is about to act, unexpected situational factors may arise to change the purchase intention. Jennifer Smith may lose her job, some other purchase may become more urgent, or a friend may report being disappointed in her preferred camera.

FIGURE 6-4
Steps between evaluation of alternatives and a purchase decision

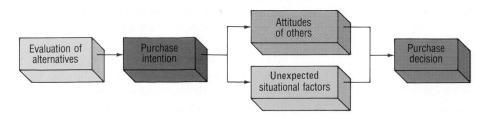

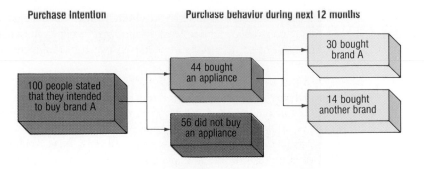

100 people stated that they intended to buy brand A

44 bought an appliance

56 did not buy an appliance

30 bought brand A

14 bought another brand

FIGURE 6-5
Results of purchase intentions and purchase decisions

Thus, preferences and even purchase intentions do not always result in actual purchase choice. They may direct purchase behavior, but may not fully determine the outcome. Figure 6-5 shows a fairly typical outcome. In a study of one hundred people who stated an intention to buy brand A of an appliance within the next twelve months, only forty-four ended up buying the particular appliance, and only thirty purchased brand A.

A consumer's decision to change, postpone, or avoid a purchase decision is heavily influenced by *perceived risk*. Many purchases involve some risk taking.[7] Consumers cannot be certain about the purchase outcome. This produces anxiety. The amount of perceived risk varies with the amount of money at stake, the amount of purchase uncertainty, and the amount of consumer self-confidence. A consumer takes certain actions to reduce risk, such as avoiding purchase decisions, gathering more information, and looking for national brand names and products with warranties. The marketer must understand the factors that provoke feelings of risk in consumers and must respond with information and support that will reduce the perceived risk.

Postpurchase Behavior

The marketer's job does not end when the product is bought. After purchasing the product, the consumer will be satisfied or dissatisfied and will engage in **postpurchase behavior** of interest to the marketer.

Postpurchase Satisfaction

What determines whether the buyer is satisfied or dissatisfied with a purchase? The answer lies in the relationship between the *consumer's expectations* and the product's *perceived performance*.[8] If the product falls short of expectations, the consumer is disappointed; if it meets expectations, the consumer is satisfied; if it exceeds expectations, the consumer is delighted.

Consumers base their expectations on messages they receive from sellers, friends, and other information sources. If the seller exaggerates the product's performance, consumer expectations will not be met, a situation that leads to dissatisfaction. The larger the gap between expectation and performance, the greater the consumer's dissatisfaction. This fact suggests that the seller should make product claims that faithfully represent the product's performance so that buyers are satisfied.

Some sellers might even understate performance levels to boost consumer satisfaction with the product. For example, Boeing sells aircraft, each worth tens of millions of dollars—consumer satisfaction is important for repeat purchases and the company's reputation. Boeing's salespeople sell their products with facts and knowledge, not with inflated promises. In fact, the salespeople tend to be conservative when they estimate their product's potential benefits. They almost always underestimate fuel efficiency—they promise a five percent savings that turns out to be eight. Customers are delighted with better-than-expected performance; they buy again and tell other potential customers that Boeing lives up to its promises.[9]

Almost all major purchases result in **cognitive dissonance**, or discomfort caused by post-purchase conflict. Consumers are satisfied with the benefits of the chosen brand and glad to avoid the drawbacks of the brands not purchased. On the other hand, every purchase involves compromise. Consumers feel uneasy about acquiring the drawbacks of the chosen brand and about losing the benefits of the brands not purchased. Thus, consumers feel at least some post-purchase dissonance for every purchase. And they will often take steps after the purchase to reduce dissonance.[10]

Postpurchase Actions

Why is it so important to satisfy the customer? Because a company's sales come from two basic groups—*new customers* and *repeat customers*. It usually costs more to attract new customers than to retain current ones. Thus, keeping current customers is often more critical than attracting new ones. And the key to keeping current customers is customer satisfaction. A satisfied customer buys a product again, talks favorably to others about the product, pays less attention to competing brands and advertising, and buys other products from the company. Many marketers go beyond merely *meeting* the expectations of customers—they aim to *delight* the customer. A delighted customer is even more likely to purchase again and to talk favorably about the product and company.

A dissatisfied consumer responds differently. Whereas, on average, a satisfied customer tells three people about a good product experience, a dissatisfied customer gripes to eleven people. In fact, one study showed that 13 percent of the people who had a problem with an organization complained about the company to more than 20 people.[11] Clearly, bad word-of-mouth travels farther and faster than good word-of-mouth and can quickly damage consumer attitudes about a company and its products.

Marketers should be aware of the many ways consumers might handle dissatisfaction. Figure 6-6 outlines these ways.[12] Consumers have a choice between taking and not taking any action. If they act, they can take public action or private action. Public actions include complaining to the company, going to a lawyer, or complaining to other groups such as consumer protection agencies that might help the buyer get satisfaction. Or the buyer may simply stop buying the product or warn friends not to buy it. In all these cases, the seller loses something.

Thus, a company would be wise to regularly measure customer satisfaction. It cannot simply rely on dissatisfied customers to volunteer their complaints. In fact, 96 percent of unhappy customers never tell the company about their problem. Companies should set up suggestion systems to *encourage* customers to complain (see Marketing Highlight 6–3). In this way, the company can learn how well it is doing and how it can do better. The 3M Company claims that more than two-thirds of its new product

FIGURE 6-6   How customers handle dissatisfaction

Source: Ralph L. Day and E. Laird Landon, Jr., "Toward a Theory of Consumer Complaining Behavior," in *Consumer and Industrial Buying Behavior*, ed. Arch G. Woodside, Jagdish N. Sheth, and Peter D. Bennett (New York: Elsevier North-Holland, 1977), p. 432.

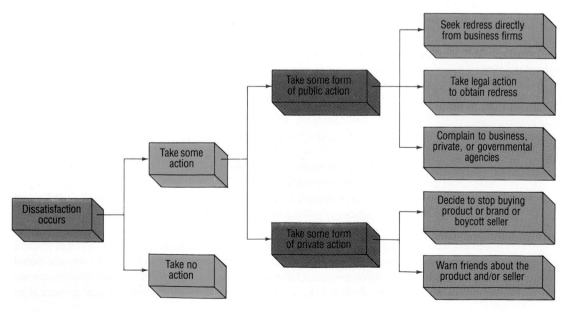

POST-PURCHASE SATISFACTION: TURNING COMPANY CRITICS INTO LOYAL CUSTOMERS

What should companies do with dissatisfied customers? Everything they can! Studies show that customers tell twice as many other people about bad experiences as they do good ones. Thus, unhappy customers not only stop buying, but also can quickly damage the company's image. On the other hand, dealing effectively with gripes can actually boost customer loyalty and the company's image. According to one study, 54 to 70 percent of consumers who register complaints will again do business with the company if their complaint is resolved. That figure jumps to a whopping 95 percent if the complaint is handled quickly. Moreover, customers whose complaints have been satisfactorily resolved tell an average of five other people about the good treatment they received. Thus, enlightened companies don't try to hide from dissatisfied customers or to dodge responsibility. To the contrary, they go out of their way to *encourage* customers to complain, then bend over backwards to make disgruntled buyers happy again.

The first opportunity to handle gripes often comes at the point of purchase. Thus, many retailers and other service firms teach their customer-contact people how to resolve problems and diffuse customer anger. They arm their customer-service representatives with liberal return and refund policies and other damage-control tools. Some companies go to extremes to see things the customer's way and to reward complaining, seemingly without regard for profit impact. For example, Hechinger, the large hardware and garden products retailer, accepts returns of items even when customers have obviously abused them. In other cases, it sends a dozen roses to purchasers who are particularly upset. Specialty retailer Neiman-Marcus is equally gracious with complainers. "We're not just looking for today's sale. We want a long-term relationship with our customers," says Gwen Baum, the chain's director of customer satisfaction. "If that means taking back a piece of Baccarat crystal that isn't from one of our stores, we'll do it." This generosity appears to help profits more than harm them—both Hechinger and Neiman-Marcus enjoy earnings well above industry averages. Such actions create tremendous buyer loyalty and goodwill, and for most retailers, customers who return items that they bought elsewhere or have already used account for less than 5 percent of all returns.

Many companies have also set up toll-free 800-number systems to better coax out and deal with consumer problems. Today, more than half of all companies with more than $10 million in sales use 800 numbers to handle complaints, inquiries, and orders. Last year these companies spent about $4.5 billion on more than eight billion 800 number calls. For example, Coca-Cola set up its 1-800-GET-COKE lines in late 1983 after studies showed that only one unhappy person in 50 bothers to complain. "The other 49 simply switch brands," explains the company's director of consumer affairs, "so it just makes good sense to seek them out." Consumers made good use of the 800 number some years ago when Coca-Cola tried to replace old Coke with new. Following the introduction of New Coke, the company received as many as 12,000 calls a day, most from unhappy coke drinkers. However, on the day after it returned Coke Classic to the shelves, Coca-Cola received 18,000 calls saying thank you.

Since 1979, Procter & Gamble has put an 800 number on every consumer product it sells in the U.S. P&G now receives about 800,000 mail and phone contacts about its products each year—mostly complaints, requests for information, and testimonials. The 800 number system serves as an early warning signal for product and customer problems. So far, the system has resulted in hundreds of actions and improvements ranging from tracking down batches of defective packages to putting instructions for baking at high altitudes on the Duncan Hines brownies package.

General Electric's Answer Center may be the most extensive 800 number system in the nation. It handles 3 million calls a year, 15 percent of them complaints. At the heart of the system is a giant database that provides the center's service reps with instant access to 750,000 answers concerning 8,500 models in 120 product lines. The center receives some unusual calls, as when a submarine off the Connecticut coast requested help fixing a motor, or when technicians on a James Bond film couldn't get their underwater lights working. Still, according to GE, its people resolve 90 percent of complaints or inquiries on the first call, and complainers often become even more loyal customers. Although the company may spend an average of $3.50 per call, it reaps two or three times that much in new sales and warranty savings.

In some companies, responsibility for assuring customer satisfaction goes all the way to the top. For example, J. W. Marriott Jr., chairman of Marriott hotels, "reads about 10 percent of the 8,000 letters and 2 percent of the 750,000 guest comment cards the company receives each year. When Marriott was president in the late 1960s, some 30,000 hotel guests submitted comments each year. He read every one."

The best way to keep customers happy is to provide

ideas come from listening to customer complaints. But listening is not enough—the company must also respond constructively to the complaints it receives.

Thus, in general, dissatisfied consumers may try to reduce their dissonance by taking any of several actions. In the case of Jennifer Smith's Nikon purchase, she may return the camera, or look at Nikon ads that tell of the camera's benefits, or talk with friends who will tell her how much they like her new camera.

Beyond seeking out and responding to complaints, marketers can take additional steps to reduce consumer post-purchase dissatisfaction and to help customers feel good about their purchases. Automobile companies can write or phone new car owners with

P&G puts an 800 number for customer service on every product it sells in the United States. Coca-Cola set up its 1–800–GET–COKE lines after studies showed that only one unhappy person in 50 bothers to complain.

good products and services in the first place. Short of that, however, a company must develop a good system for ferreting out and handling consumer problems. Such a system can be much more than a necessary evil—customer happiness usually shows up on the company's bottom line. One recent study found that dollars invested in complaint-handling and inquiry systems yield an average return of 100 to 200 percent. Maryanne Rasmussen, vice president of worldwide quality at American Express, offers this formula: ''Better complaint handling equals higher customer satisfaction equals higher brand loyalty equals higher performance.''

Sources: Quotes from Patricia Sellers, ''How to Handle Consumer Gripes,'' Fortune, October 24, 1988, pp. 88–100. Also see Karl Albrect and Ron Zemke, ServiceAmerica! (Homewood, IL: Dow-Jones Irwin, 1985, pp. 6–7; Mary C. Gilley and Richard W. Hansen, ''Consumer Complaint Handling As a Strategic Marketing Tool,'' Journal of Consumer Marketing, Fall 1985, pp. 5–16; and Henry Vanderleest and Shaheen Borna, ''A Structured Approach to Handling Customer Complaints,'' Retail Control, October 1988, pp. 14–19.

congratulations for having selected a fine car. They can place ads showing satisfied owners driving their new cars. They can obtain customer suggestions for improvements and list the location of available services. They can write instruction booklets that reduce dissatisfaction. They can send owners magazines full of articles describing the pleasures of owning the new car.[13] Post-purchase communications to buyers have been shown to result in fewer product returns and order cancellations.

Understanding the consumer's needs and buying process is the foundation of successful marketing. By understanding how buyers go through problem recognition, information search, evaluation of alternatives, the purchase decision, and post-purchase behavior, the marketer can pick up many clues about meeting the buyer's needs. By understanding the various participants in the buying process and the major influences on their buying behavior, the marketer can develop an effective marketing program to support an attractive offer to the target market.

BUYER-DECISION PROCESS FOR NEW PRODUCTS

We have looked at the stages buyers go through in trying to satisfy a need. Buyers may pass quickly or slowly through these stages, and some of the stages may even be reversed. Much depends on the nature of the buyer, the product, and the buying situation.

But how do buyers approach the purchase of new products? We define **new product** as a good, service, or idea that is perceived by some potential customers as new. The new product may have been around for a while, but our interest is in how consumers learn about products for the first time and make decisions on whether to adopt them. We define **adoption process** as "the mental process through which an individual passes from first learning about an innovation to final adoption."[14] We define **adoption** as the decision by an individual to become a regular user of the product.

Stages in the Adoption Process

Consumers go through five stages in the process of adopting a new product:

1. *Awareness*: The consumer becomes aware of the new product but lacks information about it.
2. *Interest*: The consumer is stimulated to seek information about the new product.
3. *Evaluation*: The consumer considers whether trying the new product makes sense.
4. *Trial*: The consumer tries the new product on a small scale to improve his or her estimate of its value.
5. *Adoption*: The consumer decides to make full and regular use of the new product.

This model suggests that the new-product marketer should think about how to help consumers move through these stages. A manufacturer of microwave ovens may discover that many consumers in the interest stage do not move to the trial stage because of uncertainty and the large investment. If these same consumers would be willing to use a microwave oven on a trial basis for a small fee, the manufacturer should consider offering a trial-use plan with an option to buy.

Individual Differences in Innovativeness

People differ greatly in their readiness to try new products. In each product area, there are "consumption pioneers" and early adopters. Other individuals adopt new products much later. This has led to a classification of people into the adopter categories shown in Figure 6-7.

After a slow start, an increasing number of people adopt the new product. The number of adopters reaches a peak and then drops off as fewer non-adopters remain. Innovators are defined as the first 2.5 percent of the buyers to adopt a new idea; the early adopters are the next 13.5 percent; and so forth.

The five adopter groups have different values. *Innovators* are venturesome—they try new ideas at some risk. *Early adopters* are guided by respect—they are opinion leaders in their community and adopt new ideas early but carefully. The *early majority* are deliberate—although they rarely are leaders, they adopt new ideas before the average person. The *late majority* are skeptical—they adopt an innovation only after a majority of people have tried it. Finally, *laggards* are tradition-bound—they are suspicious of changes and adopt the innovation only when it has become something of a tradition itself.

This adopter classification suggests that an innovating firm should research the characteristics of innovators and early adopters and direct marketing efforts to them. For example, home computer innovators have been found to be middle-aged and higher in income and education than noninnovators, and they tend to be opinion leaders. They also tend to be more rational, more introverted, and less social.[15] In general, innovators

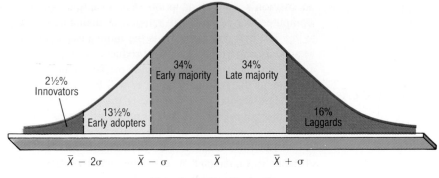

FIGURE 6-7
Adopter categorization on the basis of relative time of adoption of innovations
Source: Redrawn from Everett M. Rogers, *Diffusion of Innovations*, 3rd ed. (New York: 1983), p. 247. Adapted with permission of Macmillan Publishing Company, Inc. Copyright © 1962, 1971, 1983 by The Free Press.

2½% Innovators

13½% Early adopters

34% Early majority

34% Late majority

16% Laggards

$\overline{X} - 2\sigma$ $\overline{X} - \sigma$ $\overline{X}$ $\overline{X} + \sigma$

Time of adoption of innovations

tend to be relatively younger, better educated, and higher in income than later adopters and nonadopters. They are more receptive to unfamiliar things, rely more on their own values and judgment, and are more willing to take risks. They are less brand loyal and more likely to take advantage of special promotions such as discounts, coupons, and samples.[16]

Role of Personal Influence

Personal influence plays a major role in the adoption of new products. **Personal influence** describes the effect of statements made by one person on another's attitude or probability of purchase. Consumers consult each other for opinions about new products and brands, and the advice of others can strongly influence buying behavior.

Personal influence is more important in some situations and for some individuals than for others. Personal influence is more important in the evaluation stage of the adoption process than in the other stages. It has more influence on later adopters than early adopters. And it is more important in risky buying situations than in safe situations.

Influence of Product Characteristics on Rate of Adoption

The characteristics of the new product affect its rate of adoption. Some products catch on almost overnight (Frisbees), whereas others take a long time to gain acceptance (personal computers). Five characteristics are especially important in influencing an

Product characteristics affect the rate of adoption—products like home computers take a long time to gain wide acceptance.

innovation's rate of adoption. For example, consider the characteristics of personal computers for home use in relation to their rate of adoption.

The first characteristic is the innovation's *relative advantage*—the degree to which it appears superior to existing products. The greater the perceived relative advantage of using a personal computer—say, in preparing income taxes and keeping financial records—the sooner the personal computer will be adopted.

The second characteristic is the innovation's *compatibility*—the degree to which it fits the values and experiences of potential consumers. Personal computers, for example, are highly compatible with the life styles found in upper-middle-class homes.

The third characteristic is the innovation's *complexity*—the degree to which it is difficult to understand or use. Personal computers are complex and will therefore take a longer time to penetrate U.S. homes.

The fourth characteristic is the innovation's *divisibility*—the degree to which it may be tried on a limited basis. To the extent that people can rent personal computers with an option to buy, the product's rate of adoption will increase.

The fifth characteristic is the innovation's *communicability*—the degree to which the results can be observed or described to others. Because personal computers lend themselves to demonstration and description, their use will spread faster among consumers.

Other characteristics influence the rate of adoption, such as initial and ongoing costs, risk and uncertainty, and social approval. The new product marketer must research all these factors when developing the new product and its marketing program.

■ SUMMARY

Before planning its marketing strategy, a company needs to identify its target consumers and the types of decision processes they go through. Although many buying decisions involve only one decision maker, other decisions may involve several participants who play such roles as initiator, influencer, decider, buyer, and user. The marketer's job is to identify the other buying participants, their buying criteria, and their level of influence on the buyer. The marketing program should be designed to appeal to and reach the other key participants as well as the buyer.

The number of buying participants and the amount of buying effort increase with the complexity of the buying situation. There are three types of buying decision behavior: routine response behavior, limited problem solving, and extensive problem solving.

In buying something, the buyer goes through a decision process consisting of problem recognition, information search, evaluation of alternatives, purchase decision, and postpurchase behavior. The marketer's job is to understand the buyer's behavior at each stage and what influences are operating. This understanding allows the marketer to develop a significant and effective marketing program for the target market.

With regard to new products, consumers respond at different rates, depending on the consumer's characteristics and the product's characteristics. Manufacturers try to bring their new products to the attention of potential early adopters, particularly those with opinion leader characteristics.

■ QUESTIONS FOR DISCUSSION

1. What people played the different buying decision roles that led to the choice of the school you are attending?

2. Describe the five stages of your own buyer decision process for a major purchase such as a camera, stereo, or car. How does your decision process differ for a minor purchase such as a candy bar or a soda?

3. When you are planning to go to a movie, what information sources do you use in deciding which one to see? Do you use the same sources to help you decide which videotape to rent for watching at home?

4. For many Americans, changing to a healthier lifestyle would be an innovation. Doing so might require changes in diet, exercise, smoking and drinking. Discuss this innovation in terms of its relative advantage, compatibility, complexity, divisibility, and communicability. Is a healthy life-style likely to be adopted quickly by most Americans?

5. What factors do you think would be very important to most consumers in deciding where to do their grocery shopping?

Using these factors, discuss how the expectancy-value, conjunctive, and disjunctive models of consumer choice could explain a shopper's choice of a supermarket.

6. What kinds of risk are involved in purchasing a lawnmower? Compare these risks with the risk of hiring a service to fertilize your lawn and eliminate weeds and insects. What steps could marketers take to reduce these risks?

7. Why is the postpurchase behavior stage included in the model of the buying process? What relevance does this stage have for marketers?

8. Describe how cents-off coupons, sweepstakes, bonus-size packs, and other forms of sales promotion can help move consumers through the stages of the adoption process. Are there any drawbacks to using these techniques to promote product adoption?

9. Consumers play many different roles in the buying process: initiator, influencer, decider, buyer, and user. Who plays these roles when a mother is buying Teenage Mutant Ninja

Turtles Breakfast Cereal? L'Eggs pantyhose? Purina Dog Chow? A New VCR?

10. The recently developed home digital audiotape recorders (DATs) offer near-perfect fidelity in recording music and in playing prerecorded tapes. They are not compatible with existing cassette recorders, cost $1,000 to $2,000 or more, and the few available prerecorded tapes sell for more than $20. How will this innovation's characteristics affect its rate of adoption in the consumer market?

■ KEY TERMS

Adoption. The decision by an individual to become a regular user of the product.

Adoption process. The mental process through which an individual passes from first hearing about an innovation to final adoption.

Alternative evaluation. The stage of the buyer decision process in which the consumer uses information to evaluate alternative brands in the choice set.

Brand image. The set of beliefs consumers hold about a particular brand.

Buyer. The person who makes an actual purchase.

Cognitive dissonance. Buyer discomfort caused by post-purchase conflict.

Decider. The person who ultimately makes a buying decision or any part of it—whether to buy, what to buy, how to buy, or where to buy.

Extensive problem solving. Buyer behavior in cases in which buyers face complex buying decisions for more expensive, less frequently purchased products in an unfamiliar product class. Buyers engage in extensive information search and evaluation.

Influencer. A person whose views or advice carries some weight in making a final buying decision.

Information search. The stage of the buyer decision process in which the consumer is aroused to search for more information;

the consumer may simply have heightened attention or may go into active information search.

Initiator. The person who first suggests or thinks of the idea of buying a particular product or service.

Limited problem solving. Buying behavior in cases in which buyers are aware of the product class but not familiar with all the brands and their features. Buyers engage in limited information search and evaluation.

New product. A good, service, or idea that is perceived by some potential customers as new.

Personal influence. The effect of statements made by one person on another's attitude or probability of purchase.

Postpurchase behavior. The stage of the buyer decision process in which consumers take further action after the purchase, based on their satisfaction or dissatisfaction.

Problem recognition. The first stage of the buyer decision process in which the consumer recognizes a problem or need.

Purchase decision. The stage of the buyer decision process in which the consumer actually buys the product.

Routine response behavior. Buying behavior in cases in which buyers face simple buying decisions for low-cost, low-involvement, frequently purchased items in familiar product classes. Buyers do not give much thought, search, or time to the purchase.

User. The person who consumes or uses a product or service.

■ REFERENCES

1. Portions adapted from Joseph Pereira, "The Well-Healed: Pricey Sneakers Worn In Inner City Help Set Nation's Fashion Trend," *The Wall Street Journal*, December 1, 1988, pp. 1, 6. Also see Marcy Magiera, "Nike Edges Reebok; L. A. Gear Sprinting," *Advertising Age*, September 26, 1989, p. 93; Pat Sloan, "Reebok Chief Looks Beyond Nike," *Advertising Age*, January 29, 1990, pp. 16, 57; and Laura Jereski, "Can Paul Fireman Put the Bounce Back in Reebok?" *Business Week*, June 18, 1990, pp. 181–82.

2. See John A. Howard and Jagdish N. Sheth, *The Theory of Buyer Behavior* (New York: Wiley, 1969), pp. 27–28.

3. Several models of the consumer buying process have been developed by marketing scholars. The most prominent models are those of Howard and Sheth, *The Theory of Buyer Behavior*; Francesco M. Nicosia, *Consumer Decision Processes* (Englewood Cliffs, NJ: Prentice Hall, 1966); James F. Engel, Roger D. Blackwell, and Paul W. Miniard, *Consumer Behavior*, 5th ed. (New York: Holt, Rinehart and Winston, 1986); and James R. Bettman, *An Information Processing Theory of Consumer Choice* (Reading, MA: Addison-Wesley, 1979). For a summary, see Leon G. Schiffman and Leslie Lazar Kanuk, *Consumer Behavior*, 4th ed. (Englewood Cliffs, NJ: Prentice Hall, 1991), Chapter 20.

4. James H. Myers and Mark L. Alpert, "Semantic Confusion in Attitude Research: Salience vs. Importance vs. Determinance," in *Advances in Consumer Research* (Association for Consumer Research, 1976), IV, pp. 106–10.

5. This model was developed by Martin Fishbein. See Martin Fishbein and Icek Ajzen, *Belief, Attitude, Intention, and Behavior* (Reading, MA: Addison-Wesley, 1975). For a critical review of this model, see Paul W. Miniard and Joel B. Cohen, "An Examination of the Fishbein-Ajzen Behavioral Intentions Model's Concepts and Measures," *Journal of Experimental Social Psychology*, May 1981, pp. 309–99.

6. See Jagdish N. Sheth, "An Investigation of Relationships among Evaluative Beliefs, Affect, Behavioral Intention, and Behavior," in *Consumer Behavior: Theory and Application*, John U. Farley, John A. Howard, and L. Winston Ring, eds. (Boston: Allyn & Bacon, 1974), pp. 89–114.

7. See Raymond A. Bauer, "Consumer Behavior as Risk Taking," in *Risk Taking and Information Handling in Consumer Behavior*, Donald F. Cox, ed. (Boston: Division of Research, Harvard Business School, 1967); John W. Vann, "A Multi-Distributional Conceptual Framework for the Study of Perceived Risk," in Thomas C. Kinnear, ed., *Advance in Consumer Research* (Association for Consumer Research, 1983), XI, pp. 442–46; and Robert B. Settle and Pamela L. Alreck, "Reducing Buyers' Sense of Risk," *Marketing Communications*, January 1989, pp. 19–24.

8. See Priscilla A. LaBarbara and David Mazursky, "A Longitudinal Assessment of Consumer Satisfaction/Dissatisfaction: The Dynamic Aspect of the Cognitive Process," *Journal of Marketing Research*, November 1983, pp. 393–404.

9. See Bill Kelley, "How to Sell Airplanes, Boeing-Style, *Sales and Marketing Management*, December 9, 1985, p. 34.

10. See Leon Festinger, *A Theory of Cognitive Dissonance* (Stanford, CA: Stanford University Press, 1957); and Leon G. Schiffman and Leslie Lazar Kanuk, *Consumer Behavior*, Ch. 9.

11. See Karl Albrecht and Ron Zemke, *Service America!* (Homewood, IL: Down-Jones Irwin, 1985), pp. 6–7.

12. For more discussion, see Jagdip Singh, "Consumer Complaint Intentions and Behavior: Definitional and Taxonomical Issues," *Journal of Marketing*, January 1988, pp. 93–117.

13. See Thomas Moore, "Would You Buy a Car From This Man?" *Fortune*, April 11, 1988, pp. 72–74.

14. The following discussion draws heavily from Everett M. Rogers, *Diffusion of Innovations*, 3rd ed. (New York: Free Press, 1983). Also see Hubert Gatignon and Thomas S. Robertson, "A Propositional Inventory for New Diffusion Research," *Journal of Consumer Research*, March 1985, pp. 849–67.

15. Mary Lee Dickerson and James W. Gentry, "Characteristics of Adopters and Non-Adopters of Home Computers," *Journal of Consumer Research*, September 1983, pp. 225–35.

16. See Schiffman and Kanuk, *Consumer Behavior*, Ch. 18.

GILLETTE VERSUS BIC: DISPOSING OF DISPOSABLES

Half of all U.S. men get up each morning, confront their stubble in the bathroom mirror, and reach for a $.30 disposable plastic razor. Schick, Bic, Gillette, or whatever—most men figure that one brand does about as well as the next. And the razor makers seem to always have them on sale, so you can scoop up a dozen of them for next to nothing.

Gillette Company doesn't like this sort of thinking. Of course, women also use Gillette's razors, but Gillette is particularly concerned with the growing number of men who use disposables. The company makes about three times more money per unit on cartridge refills for its Atra and Trac II razor systems than it does on its Good News! disposables. However, since the first disposables appeared in 1975, their sales have grown faster than those of system razors. By 1988, disposables accounted for 40 percent of shaving-product dollar sales and more than 50 percent of unit sales.

GILLETTE AND THE WET-SHAVE MARKET

Gillette dominates the wet-shave industry with a 62 percent share of the $700 million U.S. market and 60 percent world-wide. Schick (with a 16.2 percent share), Bic (9.3 percent), and others, including Wilkinson, account for most of the rest of the market. Gillette's blades and razors produced 32 percent of its $3.5 billion sales in 1988 and 61 percent of its $268 million net income.

Gillette earned its dominant position in the market, especially with men, through large investments in research and development and through careful consumer research. Every day, about 10,000 men carefully record the results of their shaves for Gillette. Five hundred of these men shave in special in-plant cubicles under carefully controlled and monitored conditions, including observation through two-way mirrors and video cameras. Shavers record the precise number of nicks and cuts. In certain cases, researchers even collect sheared whiskers to weigh and measure. As a result, Gillette scientists know that an average man's beard grows 15/1000 of an inch a day (5.5 inches per year) and contains 15,500 hairs. During an average lifetime, a man will spend 3,350 hours scraping 27.5 feet of whiskers from his face. Gillette even uses electron microscopes to study blade surfaces and miniature cameras to analyze the actual shaving process.

Armed with its knowledge of shavers and shaving, Gillette prides itself in staying ahead of the competition. Just when competitors adjust to one shaving system, Gillette introduces yet another advance. In 1971 Gillette introduced the Trac II, the first razor system featuring two parallel blades mounted in a cartridge. In 1977, following $8 million in R&D expenditures, the company introduced Atra, a twin-blade cartridge which swivels during shaving to follow the face's contours. In 1985, Gillette launched the Atra Plus, which added a lubricating strip to the Atra cartridge to make shaving even smoother.

Although the company's founder, King Gillette, was interested in developing a disposable product, one that would be used and then thrown away, Gillette's marketing strategy has focused on developing products that use refill blades on a permanent handle. Gillette works to give its blades, and especially its handles, an aura of class and superior performance. By promoting new captive systems, in which blade cartridges fit only a certain razor handle, Gillette raises price and profit margins with each new technological leap. Thus, because Atra cartridges do not fit the Trac II handle, men had to buy a new handle to allow them to use the Atra blades when that system was introduced.

Gillette has never been concerned with the low end of the market—cheap, private-label blades. Status-seeking men, it believes, will always buy a classy product. Most men see shaving as a serious business and their appearance as a matter of some importance. Therefore, most men will not skimp and settle for an ordinary shave when, for a little more money, they can feel confident that they are getting the best shave from Gillette.

BIC AND THE RISE OF DISPOSABLES

The rapid rise of the disposable razor has challenged Gillette's view of men's shaving philosophy. Bic first introduced the disposable shaver in 1975 in Europe and then a year later in Canada. Realizing that the U.S. would be next, Gillette actually introduced the first disposable razor to the U.S. market in 1976—the blue plastic Good News! which used a Trac II blade. Despite its defensive reaction, however, Gillette predicted that the disposable would be used only for trips and locker rooms and when the real razor had been forgotten. Disposables would never capture more than 7 percent of the market, Gillette asserted.

Marcel Bich, Bic's founder and the force behind Bic's challenge to Gillette is, like King Gillette, devoted to disposability. Bich made his money by developing the familiar ballpoint pen. He pursues a strategy of turning status products into commodities. Often a product has status because it is difficult to make and must sell at a high price. But if a manufacturer develops ways to mass produce the product at low cost with little loss of functional quality, its status and allure will disappear. Consumers then will not feel embarrassed to buy and be seen using the new, cheaper version of the product. Thus, Bich brands his products, strips them of their glamour, distributes them widely, and sells them cheaply. His marketing strategy is simple: maximum service, minimum price.

Located in Milford, Connecticut, Bic attacks the

shaving business in a very different manner than Gillette. It does not assign anyone to regularly explore the fringes of shaving technology—it does not even own an electron microscope and it does not know or care how many hairs the average man's beard contains. It maintains only a small shave-testing panel consisting of about one hundred people. The Bic shaver has only one blade mounted on a short, hollow handle which sells for $.25 or less. Still, the Bic disposable razor presents Gillette with its most serious challenge since the company's early days. In 1988, Bic's shaving products achieved $52 million in sales with a net income of $9.4 million and held a 22.4 percent share of the disposable market.

GILLETTE VERSUS BIC

In their separate pursuits of disposability, Gillette and Bic have clashed before on other product fronts. First, beginning in the 1950s, they fought for market share in the writing pen market. Gillette's Paper Mate products, however, were no match for Bic's mass market advertising and promotion skills. The two firms met again in the 1970s in the disposable cigarette lighter arena, where they again made commodities of what had once been prestigious and sometimes expensive items. Although Gillette did better in disposable lighters than it had in pens, Bic's lighter captured the dominant market share.

In the most recent skirmish, however, Gillette's Good News! brand is winning with a 58 percent market share in the disposable razor market. But the victory is a bitter-sweet one. The problem? Good News! sells for a lot less than any of Gillette's older products. The key to commodity competition is price. To stay competitive with the 25-cent Bic razor and with other disposables, Gillette has to sell Good News! for much less than the retail price of an Atra or Trac II cartridge. As many Trac II and Atra users have concluded, although a twin-blade refill cartridge from Gillette costs as much as 56 cents, you can get precisely the same blade mounted on a plastic handle for as little as 25 cents. Good News! not only produces less revenue per blade sold, it also costs more because Gillette has to supply the handle as well as the cartridge. Each time Good News! gains a market share point, Gillette loses millions of dollars in sales and profits from its Atra and Trac II products.

THE PSYCHOLOGY OF SHAVING

The battle between Bic and Gillette represents more than a simple contest over what kinds of razors people want to use—it symbolizes a clash over one of the most enduring daily male rituals. Before King Gillette invented the safety razor, men found shaving a tedious, difficult, time-consuming, and often bloody task that they endured at most twice a week. Only the rich could afford to have a barber shave them daily.

Gillette patented the safety razor in 1904, but it was not until World War I that the product gained wide

consumer acceptance. Gillette had the brilliant idea of giving a free Gillette razor to every soldier. In this manner, millions of men just entering the shaving age were introduced to the daily, self-shaving habit.

The morning shaving ritual continues to occupy a very special place in most men's lives—it affirms their masculinity. The first shave remains a rite of passage into manhood. A survey by New York psychologists reported that although men complain about the bother of shaving, 97 percent of the sample would not want to use a cream, were one to be developed, that would permanently rid them of all facial hair. Gillette once introduced a new razor that came in versions for heavy, medium, and light beards. Almost no one bought the light version, because few men wanted to publically acknowledge their modest beard production.

Although shaving may require less skill and involve less danger than it once did, many men still want the razors they use to reflect their beliefs that shaving remains serious business. A typical man regards his razor as an important personal tool, a kind of extension of self, like an expensive pen, cigarette lighter, attache case, or set of golf clubs.

GILLETTE'S CHALLENGE

For more than 80 years Gillette's perception of the men's shaving market and the psychology of shaving has been perfect. Its products hold a substantial 62 percent share, and its technology and marketing philosophy have held sway over the entire industry. Gillette has worked successfully to maintain the razor's masculine look, heft, and feel as well as its status as an item of personal identification. Now, however, millions of men are scraping their faces each day with small, nondescript, passionless pieces of plastic costing 25 cents—an act that seems to be the ultimate denial of the shaving ritual.

Thus, Good News! is really bad news for Gillette. Gillette must find a way to dispose of the disposables.

QUESTIONS

1. Who is involved in a man's decision to buy a disposable razor and what roles do various participants play? Do these participants and roles differ for the decision to buy a system razor?

2. What types of buying decision behavior do men exhibit when purchasing razors?

3. Examine a man's decision process for purchasing a wet-shave razor. How have Gillette and Bic pursued different strategies with respect to this process?

4. What marketing strategy should Gillette adopt in order to encourage men to switch from disposables to system razors? How would buyer decision processes toward new products affect your recommendations?

Source: Portions adapted "The Gillette Company," in Subhash C. Jain, Marketing Strategy & Policy, 3rd ed., Cincinnati, Ohio: Southwestern, 1990. Used with permission.

THE COMEBACK OF CATALOGS

When he came out with the first catalog, *People's Literary Companion*, in 1869, E. C. Allen of Augusta, Maine, stimulated the publication of hundreds of catalogs before Montgomery Ward and Sears initiated theirs in 1872 and 1888, respectively. Early catalogs were successful because they made a variety of merchandise available to rural households, for whom stores were inaccessible. Indeed, there was little reason for these households to patronize local retailers who charged high prices and carried narrow merchandise selections.

Because of low entry and postal costs, the catalog business boomed. In the absence of restrictions on their activities, catalogers aggressively promoted goods of dubious value with outrageous claims, and refused to guarantee or replace merchandise, to accept returned goods, or to refund money. As a result, exit was as easy and frequent as entry.

In the twentieth century, more responsible catalogers, exemplified by Orvis and L. L. Bean, did guarantee their merchandise. Indeed, L. L. Bean is famous for its no-questions-asked return policy, made possible by the quality of the goods. These firms specialized in sturdy, durable goods that were functional, rather than fashionable.

This very lack of fashionability, together with the migration of the population to cities, led to the decline of catalogs in the mid-twentieth century. Their dull black-and-white pages were unappealing to urbanites and suburbanites, who could shop in large, elegant department stores where they could examine and easily return merchandise if it proved unsatisfactory. To such cosmopolitan consumers, catalog buying seemed old-fashioned and undesirable.

Catalogs began a comeback in the 1970s, which mushroomed in the 1980s. Today there are over 8,000 catalogers in the United States, whose combined sales are $38 billion and growing by 15 percent per year. Why have they become so popular? A major reason is the increasing employment of women. Working women have less time for shopping than housewives but more reason to shop—they need working clothes. A solution to this dilemma is to buy through catalogs.

Catalogers responded to this change by greatly improving their offerings. First, they upgraded the catalog's appearance by using color photographs, glossy paper, and slick copy. Second, they instituted toll-free numbers and accepted credit cards to make ordering easier and faster. Third, they used computerized record keeping and sophisticated goods handling to provide faster service. Fourth, they guaranteed their merchandise and offered liberal return policies, which, coupled with credit card acceptance, proved to be a real boon for the consumer. (If you are dissatisfied with merchandise, just don't pay your credit card company. Let them deal with the cataloger!)

But the most important change the catalogers made was to upgrade their merchandise. Plain catalogs that sold your great-grandmother a sewing machine have been replaced by attractive catalogues offering such exciting goods as a robot to answer the door and a fog-free shaving mirror (both available from *Sharper Image*). Anyone who thinks catalogs aren't glamorous or sexy hasn't looked through a Victoria's Secret catalog lately. Where else but through the Neiman Marcus catalog can you buy diamonds that are named for you or purchase a hot-air balloon you have designed yourself?

Many catalogers have specialized. Williams-Sonoma offers gourmet cookware to use with the gourmet foods ordered from Pepperidge Farms and Pfaelzer Bros. If you are going into the hospital, you can order equipment from the Santa Monica Hospital Medical Center. The Nature Company and Seventh Generation sell goods for the environmentally conscious. What a cornucopia of goods—all of them as near as the telephone!

Contrast this with the typical experience in most retail establishments. You drive to the mall; contend with parking; hunt for the right store for what you want to buy; seek out the right item in size, color, and style desired (all the time fighting the crowds); find a sales clerk; and often stand in line to pay. If you can't find what you want, you must endure this process again elsewhere or go without. By restricting your shopping to stores, you limit the assortment of goods you can choose from and depend on the retailer's product selections rather than your own.

Fierce competition among catalogers necessitates more frequent mailings and use of mailing lists purchased from other firms. As a result, American homes receive ever more catalogs, which leads to complaints that they are inundated. However, given the advantages of catalogs, who would really want this to change?

QUESTIONS

1. Are consumers more likely to buy from catalogs in (a) extensive problem-solving situations, (b) limited problem-solving situations, or (c) routine response situations? Explain your answer.

2. How does the use of catalogs affect (a) problem recognition, (b) information search, (c) evaluation of alternatives, and (d) postpurchase behavior?

Sources: Barbara Carlson, "The Grass Is Always Greener on the Socially Conscious Side," *New England Business*, January, 1990, pp. 62ff.; "The Sheer Catalogs," *Forbes*, October 17, 1988, p. 164; "Catalogues for Sale," *Fortune*, July 6, 1987, p. 9; Freeman F. Gosden, "52 Catalog Ideas from My Mailbox in 1985," *Direct Marketing*, March 1986, pp. 108ff.; Freeman F. Gosden, "What I Learned from My Mailbox," *Direct Marketing*, February 1989, pp. 4–7; Gary Levin, "Catalogs Hit Newsstands," *Advertising Age*, August 31, 1987, pp. 3ff.; "Catalogue Cornucopia," *Time*, November 8, 1982, pp. 74–79.

7

Organizational Markets and Organizational Buyer Behavior

Gulfstream Aerospace Corporation sells business jets with price tags as high as $20 million. Locating potential buyers isn't a problem—the organizations that can afford to own and operate multimillion dollar business aircraft are easily identified. Customers include Exxon, American Express, Seagram, Coca-Cola, General Motors, and many others, including King Fahd of Saudi Arabia. Gulfstream's more difficult problems involve reaching key decision makers, understanding their complex motivations and decision processes, analyzing what factors will be important in their decisions, and designing marketing approaches that will convince them to buy.

Gulfstream Aerospace recognizes the importance of *rational* motives and *objective* factors in buyers' decisions. A company buying a jet will evaluate Gulfstream aircraft on quality, performance, prices, operating costs, and service. At times, these may appear to be the only things that drive the buying decision. But having a superior product isn't enough to land the sale; Gulfstream Aerospace must also consider the more subtle *human factors* that affect the choice of a jet.

"The purchase process may be initiated by the chief executive officer (CEO), a board member (wishing to increase efficiency or security), the company's chief pilot, or through vendor efforts like advertising or a sales visit. The CEO will be central in deciding whether to buy the jet, but he or she will be heavily influenced by the company's pilot, financial officer, and perhaps by the board itself.

"Each party in the buying process has subtle roles and needs. The salesperson who tries to impress, for example, both the CEO with depreciation schedules and the chief pilot with minimum runway statistics will almost certainly not sell a plane if he overlooks the psychological and emotional components of the buying decision. 'For the chief executive,' observes one salesperson, 'you need all the numbers for support, but if you can't find the kid inside the CEO and excite him or her with the raw beauty of the new plane, you'll never sell the equipment. If you sell the excitement, you sell the jet.'

"The chief pilot, as an equipment expert, often has veto power over purchase decisions and may be able to stop the purchase of one or another brand of jet by simply expressing a negative opinion about, say, the plane's bad weather capabilities. In this sense, the pilot not only influences the decision but also serves as an information 'gatekeeper' by advising management on the equipment to select. Though the corporate legal staff will handle the purchase agreement and the purchasing department will acquire the jet, these parties may have little to say about whether or how the plane will be obtained, and which type. The users of the jet—middle and upper management of the buying company, important customers, and others—may have at least an indirect role in choosing the equipment.

"The involvement of many people in the purchase decision creates a group dynamic that the selling company must factor into its sales planning. Who makes up the buying group? How will the parties interact? Who will dominate and who submit? What priorities do the individuals have?"

In some ways, selling corporate jets to organizational buyers is like selling cars and kitchen appliances to families. Gulfstream Aerospace asks the same questions as consumer marketers: Who are the buyers and what are their needs? How do buyers make their buying decisions and what factors influence these decisions? What marketing program will be most effective? But the answers to these questions are usually different for the organizational buyer. Thus, Gulfstream Aerospace faces many of the same challenges as consumer marketers—and some additional ones.[1]

In one way or another, most large companies sell to other organizations. Many industrial companies sell *most* of their products to organizations—companies such as Xerox, Du Pont, and countless other large and small firms. Even large consumer products companies do organizational marketing. For example, General Mills makes many familiar products for final consumers—Cheerios, Betty Crocker cake mixes, Gold Medal flour. But to sell these products to final consumers, General Mills must first sell them to the wholesale and retail organizations that serve the consumer market. General Mills also makes products, such as specialty chemicals, that are sold only to other companies.

Organizations make up a vast market. In fact, industrial markets involve many more dollars and items than do consumer markets. Figure 7-1 shows the large number of transactions needed to produce and sell a simple pair of shoes. Hide dealers sell to tanners, who sell leather to shoe manufacturers, who sell shoes to wholesalers, who in turn sell shoes to retailers, who finally sell them to consumers. Each party in the chain buys many other goods and services as well. It is easy to see why there is more organizational buying than consumer buying—many sets of *organizational* purchases were made for only one set of *consumer* purchases.

Organizational buying is "the decision-making process by which formal organizations establish the need for purchased products and services, and identify, evaluate, and choose among alternative brands and suppliers."[2] Companies that sell to other organizations must do their best to understand organizational buyer behavior.

FIGURE 7-1 Organizational transactions involved in producing and distributing a pair of shoes

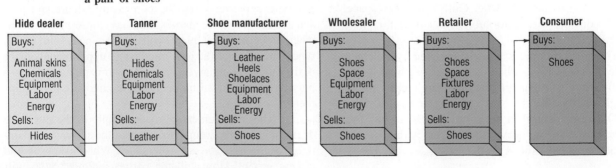

ORGANIZATIONAL MARKETS

Types of Organizational Markets

We examine three types of organizational markets: the *industrial market*, the *reseller market*, and the *government market*. We identify each briefly here and discuss them in more detail later in the chapter.

The Industrial Market

The **industrial market** consists of all the individuals and organizations acquiring goods and services that enter into the production of other products and services that are sold, rented, or supplied to others. The industrial market is *huge*: It consists of more than 13 million organizations which buy more than $3 *trillion* worth of goods and services each year. (That's more money than most of us can imagine—taped end to end, three trillion one-dollar bills would wrap around the earth more than 11,000 times.) Thus, the industrial market is the largest and most diverse organizational market.

The Reseller Market

The **reseller market** consists of all the individuals and organizations that acquire goods for the purpose of reselling or renting them to others at a profit. The reseller market includes more than 466,680 wholesaling firms and 1,503,600 retailing firms that combine to purchase over $4 trillion worth of goods and services a year.[3] Resellers purchase goods for resale and goods and services for conducting their operations. In their role as purchasing agents for their own customers, resellers purchase a vast variety of goods for resale—indeed, almost everything produced passes through some type of reseller.

The Government Market

The **government market** consists of governmental units—federal, state, and local—that purchase or rent goods and services for carrying out their main functions. In 1989, governments purchased more than $1 trillion worth of products and services. The federal government accounts for almost 39 percent of the total spent by governments at all levels, making it the nation's largest single customer.[4] Federal, state, and local government agencies buy an amazing range of products and services. They buy everything from toiletries, clothing, furniture, vehicles, and fuel to sculpture, fire engines, and bombers.

Characteristics of Organizational Markets

In some ways, organizational markets are similar to consumer markets—both involve people who assume buying roles and make purchase decisions to satisfy needs. But in many ways, organizational markets differ from consumer markets.[5] The main differences are in *market structure and demand*, the *nature of the buying unit*, and the types of *decisions and the decision process*.

Market Structure and Demand

The organizational marketer normally deals with *far fewer but far larger buyers* than the consumer marketer. For example, when Goodyear sells replacement tires to final consumers, its potential market includes the owners of 112 million American cars currently in use. But Goodyear's fate in the industrial market depends on getting orders from one of only a few large automakers. Even in large organizational markets, a few buyers normally account for most of the purchasing.

Organizational markets are also more *geographically concentrated*. More than half the nation's industrial buyers are concentrated in seven states: California, New York, Ohio, Illinois, Michigan, Texas, Pennsylvania, and New Jersey. Organizational demand is **derived demand**—it ultimately comes from the demand for consumer goods. General Motors buys steel because consumers buy cars. If consumer demand for cars drops, so will the demand for steel and all the other products used to make cars. Thus, industrial marketers sometimes promote their products directly to final consumers to increase industrial demand (see Marketing Highlight 7–1).[6]

How "NutraSweet" It Is!

About 30 years ago, a G. D. Searle researcher discovered aspartame, a miracle substance that tastes like sugar, contains few calories, and is safe to eat or drink. In 1983 the FDA approved the substance, and Searle looked for the best way to market its miracle to commercial food and beverage producers. It came up with a highly effective "branded ingredient" strategy. Instead of just selling aspartame to commercial customers, Searle gave it a brand name—NutraSweet—and launched the kind of consumer marketing campaign you'd expect to see for a laundry soap or soft drink. Searle marketed NutraSweet directly to consumers, even though consumers couldn't directly buy NutraSweet.

Industrial demand for NutraSweet is *derived demand*—it ultimately comes from consumer demand for products that contain NutraSweet. But before manufacturers bought the new sweetener and put it in their products, they wanted to be certain that their consumers would accept it. Thus, to build commercial demand for NutraSweet, Searle first had to create brand awareness and preference among final consumers. This meant overcoming the public's general mistrust of new sweeteners. People tended to believe the adage that if something tasted too good, it had to be bad for you. Searle needed to prove that, in the case of NutraSweet, this was not true.

Gumballs to the rescue! Searle mailed out thousands of gumballs sweetened with NutraSweet. Letters were included explaining that the new sweetener had few calories, didn't promote tooth decay, and contained nothing artificial. Searle then spent millions on advertising that proclaimed, "Introducing NutraSweet: You can't buy it, but you're going to love it." The ads carried coupons offering free gumballs and other samples.

Mission accomplished. When Coca-Cola, Quaker, Kool-Aid, and other companies began to introduce Nutra-Sweetened products, consumers responded enthusiastically to the new wonder substance. In all sorts of categories—soft drinks, fruit juices, presweetened cereals, frozen desserts, breath mints, and many others—demand increased for products displaying the distinctive red swirl 100 percent Nutra-Sweet logo. NutraSweet became a major selling point for many new brands; it even boosted the sales of entire product categories. For example, within two years of NutraSweet's introduction, following five flat years, sales of powdered soft drinks such as Kool-Aid, Crystal Light, and iced tea mixes had jumped 20 percent. And NutraSweet revolutionized the diet soft drink industry—products containing NutraSweet swept 22 percent of that market.

Monsanto recently acquired Searle and set up a separate subsidiary, NutraSweet Company, to market the successful product. The company now spends more than $30 million a year on consumer advertising for NutraSweet, a product

The distinctive NutraSweet logo now appears on thousands of familiar brands.

consumers can't even buy. But it knows that if it convinces consumers of NutraSweet's merits, they will buy more products that contain the sweetener. If consumers buy more Nutra-Sweetened products, manufacturers will buy more aspartame from NutraSweet Company.

The company's "branded ingredient" strategy has brought sweet success. More than 1200 brands now contain NutraSweet, and the list grows daily. NutraSweet Company rings up more than $600 million worth of sales each year and captures about 65 percent of the total sugar-substitute market. And when Monsanto's patent expires in 1992, competitors can sell aspartame—but they can't use the NutraSweet brand name consumers have learned to look for. How "Nutra-Sweet" it is!

Sources: Based on "How Sweet It Is," *Management Review*, June 1985, p. 8. Also see Judann Dagnoli, "NutraSweet Rivals Stirring," *Advertising Age*, June 26, 1989, p. 7.

Many organizational markets have **inelastic demand.** That is, total demand for many industrial products is not much affected by price changes, especially in the short run. A drop in the price of leather will not cause shoe manufacturers to buy much more leather unless it results in lower shoe prices that, in turn, will increase consumer demand for shoes.

Finally, organizational markets have more *fluctuating demand.* The demand for many industrial goods and services tends to change more—and more quickly—than the demand for consumer goods and services. A small percentage increase in consumer demand can cause large increases in industrial demand. Sometimes a rise of as small as 10 percent in consumer demand can cause as much as a 200 percent rise in industrial demand during the next period.

The Nature of the Buying Unit

As compared with consumer purchases, an organizational purchase usually involves *more buyers* and *more professional purchasing*. Organizational buying is often done by trained purchasing agents who spend their work lives learning how to buy better. The more complex the purchase, the more likely that several people will participate in the decision-making process. Buying committees made up of technical experts and top management are common in the buying of major goods. Organizational marketers must thus have well-trained salespeople to deal with well-trained buyers.

Types of Decisions and the Decision Process

Organizational buyers usually face *more complex* buying decisions than consumer buyers. Purchases often involve large sums of money, complex technical and economic considerations, and interactions among many people at many levels of the buyer's organization. Because the purchases are more complex, organizational buyers may take longer to make their decisions. Thus, the purchase of a large computer system might involve millions of dollars, thousands of technical details, dozens of people ranging from top management to lower-level users, and many months or more than a year of time.

Organizational marketers often roll up their sleeves and work closely with their customers during all stages of the buying process—from helping to define the problem, to finding solutions, to after-sale operation. Here Honeywell tells its customers "Together, we can find the answers."

Ohio University asked Honeywell to help design a communications system that will handle voice, data and video. They got one that transmits everything from...

high-tech to "Hi, Mom."

Ohio University is a leader in high technology. So it was no surprise that they knew exactly what they wanted in an integrated communications system. It would be based on fiber optics and meet their needs well into the next century.

Working together, we developed a system to serve the University's telephones and computer work stations in 110 buildings on the Athens, Ohio, campus. It can handle educational television, an energy control system, plus a security and fire detection system. It also has the growth potential to

link five regional campuses by microwave. Above all, it will give students and faculty unrivaled phone service, both local and long distance.

But Ohio University wanted more than just hardware and software. They wanted team players who knew how to make computer, communications and control systems work together, and who understood the need for continuing and conscientious service. Honeywell was the answer, because working together works. For more information, call 800-328-5111, ext. 1570.

Together, we can find the answers.

Honeywell

The organizational buying process tends to be *more formalized* than the consumer buying process. Large organizational purchases usually call for detailed product specifications, written purchase orders, careful supplier searches, and formal approval. The purchase process may be spelled out in detail in policy manuals.

Finally, in the organizational buying process, buyer and seller are often much *more dependent* on each other. Consumer marketers usually stay at a distance from their customers. But organizational marketers may roll up their sleeves and work closely with their customers during all stages of the buying process—from helping customers define problems, to finding solutions, to supporting after-sale operation. They often customize their offerings to individual customer needs. In the short-run, sales go to suppliers who meet buyers' immediate product and service needs. But organizational marketers must also build close *long-run* relationships with customers. In the long-run, sales are kept by companies that build lasting relationships by meeting current needs *and* thinking ahead to meet the customer's future needs.[7]

Other Characteristics of Organizational Markets

DIRECT PURCHASING. Organizational buyers often buy directly from producers rather than through middlemen, especially for items that are technically complex or expensive. For example, Ryder buys thousands of trucks each year in all shapes and sizes. It rents some of these trucks to move-it-yourself customers (the familiar yellow Ryder trucks), leases some to other companies for their truck fleets, and uses the rest in its own freight-hauling businesses. When Ryder buys GMC trucks, it purchases them directly from General Motors rather than from independent GM truck dealers. Similarly, American Airlines buys airplanes directly from Boeing, Kroger buys package goods directly from Procter & Gamble, and the United States government buys personal computers directly from IBM.

RECIPROCITY. Organizational buyers often select suppliers who also buy from them. An example of reciprocity would be a paper company who buys needed chemicals from a chemical company that in turn buys the company's paper. The Federal Trade Commission and the Justice Department's antitrust division forbid reciprocity if it shuts out competition in an unfair manner. A buyer can still choose a supplier that it also sells something to, but the buyer must be able to show that it is getting competitive prices, quality, and service from that supplier.[8]

LEASING. Organizational buyers are increasingly leasing equipment instead of buying it outright. American companies lease more than $122 billion of equipment each year—everything from printing presses to power plants, helicopters to hay balers, office copiers to off-shore drilling rigs. The lessee gains a number of advantages, such as having more available capital, getting the seller's latest products, receiving better servicing, and gaining some tax advantages. The lessor often ends up with a larger net income and the chance to sell to customers who might not have been able to afford outright purchase.[9]

A MODEL OF ORGANIZATIONAL BUYER BEHAVIOR

In trying to understand organizational buyer behavior, marketers must answer some hard questions. What kinds of buying decisions do organizational buyers make? How do they choose among suppliers? Who makes the decisions? What is the organizational buying-decision process? What factors affect organizational buying decisions?

At the most basic level, marketers want to know how organizational buyers will respond to various marketing stimuli. A simple model of organizational buyer behavior is shown in Figure 7-2.[10] The figure shows that marketing and other stimuli affect the organization and produce certain buyer responses. As with consumer buying, the marketing stimuli for organizational buying consist of the four Ps: product, price, place, and promotion. Other stimuli consist of major forces in the environment: economic, technological, political, cultural, and competitive. All these stimuli enter the organization and

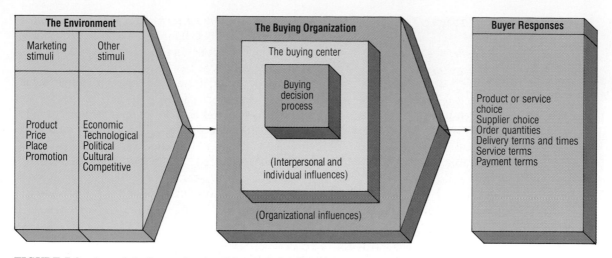

FIGURE 7-2   A model of organizational buyer behavior

are turned into buyer responses: product or service choice, supplier choice, order quantities, and delivery, service, and payment terms. To design good marketing-mix strategies, the marketer must understand what happens within the organization to turn stimuli into purchase responses.

Within the organization, the buying activity consists of two major parts—the buying center (made up of all the people involved in the buying decision) and the buying-decision process. The figure shows that the buying center and the buying-decision process are influenced by internal organizational, interpersonal, and individual factors as well as by external environmental factors.

We now turn to the various elements in this organizational buyer behavior model and how they apply to specific organizational markets. First, we focus on the largest and most important organizational market—the industrial market. Then we consider the special characteristics of organizational buyer behavior in the reseller and government markets.

INDUSTRIAL BUYER BEHAVIOR

The model in Figure 7-2 suggests four questions about industrial buyer behavior: What buying decisions do industrial buyers make? Who participates in the buying process? What are the major influences on buyers? How do industrial buyers make their buying decisions?

What Buying Decisions Do Industrial Buyers Make?

The industrial buyer faces a whole set of decisions in making a purchase. The number of decisions depends on the type of buying situation.

Major Types of Buying Situations

There are three major types of buying situations.[11] At one extreme is the *straight rebuy*, which is a fairly routine decision. At the other extreme is the *new task*, which may call for thorough research. In the middle is the *modified rebuy*, which requires some research. (For examples, see Figure 7-3.)

STRAIGHT REBUY.   In a **straight rebuy,** the buyer reorders something without any modifications. It is usually handled on a routine basis by the purchasing department. Based on past buying satisfaction, the buyer simply chooses from various suppliers on its list. "In" suppliers try to maintain product and service quality. They often propose automatic reordering systems so that the purchasing agent will save reordering time. The "out" suppliers try to offer something new or exploit dissatisfaction so that the buyer will consider them. "Out" suppliers try to get their foot in the door with a small order and then enlarge their purchase share over time.

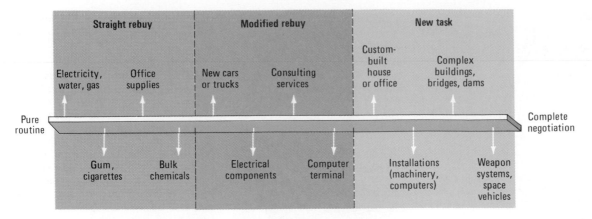

FIGURE 7-3 Three types of industrial buying situations

From Marketing Principles, 3rd ed. by Ben M. Enis. Copyright © 1980 Scott, Foresman and Company. Reprinted by permission.

MODIFIED REBUY. In a **modified rebuy,** the buyer wants to modify product specifications, prices, terms, or suppliers. The modified rebuy usually involves more decision participants. The ''in'' suppliers may become nervous and have to put their best foot forward to protect an account. ''Out'' suppliers see the modified rebuy situation as an opportunity to make a better offer and gain new business.

NEW TASK. The **new task** faces a company buying a product or service for the first time. The greater the cost or risk, the larger the number of decision participants and the greater their information seeking. In the new-task situation, the buyer must obtain a great deal of information about alternative products and suppliers. The buyer must determine product specifications, price limits, delivery terms and times, service terms, payment terms, order quantities, acceptable suppliers, and the selected supplier. Different decision participants influence each decision, and the order in which the decisions are made varies from firm to firm.

The new-task buying situation arises infrequently, but it is very important to marketers because it may later lead to straight or modified rebuys. The new-task situation is the marketer's greatest opportunity and challenge. The marketer not only tries to reach as many people with key buying influences as possible but also provides product information and other related assistance.

Specific Buying Decisions

The buyer makes the fewest decisions in the straight rebuy and the most in the new-task situation. In the new-task situation, the buyer must decide on product specifications, suppliers, price limits, payment terms, order quantities, delivery times, and service terms. The order of these decisions varies with each situation, and different decision participants influence each choice.

The Role of Systems Buying and Selling

Many buyers prefer to buy a packaged solution to a problem rather than making all the separate decisions involved. Called **systems buying,** this practice began with government buying of major weapons and communication systems. Instead of buying and putting all the components together, the government asked for bids from suppliers who would assemble the package or system. The winning supplier is responsible for buying and assembling the components.

Sellers have increasingly recognized that buyers like this method and have adopted the practice of systems selling as a marketing tool.[12] Systems selling is a two-step process. First, the supplier sells a group of interlocking products. For example, the supplier sells not only glue but applicators and dryers as well. Second, the supplier sells a system of production, inventory control, distribution, and other services to meet the buyer's need for a smooth-running operation.

Systems selling is a key industrial marketing strategy for winning and holding accounts. The contract often goes to the firm that provides the most complete system meeting the customer's needs. Consider the following:

The Indonesian government requested bids to build a cement factory near Jakarta. An American firm's proposal included choosing the site, designing the cement factory, hiring the construction crews, assembling the materials and equipment, and turning the finished factory over to the Indonesian government. A Japanese firm's proposal included all of these services, plus hiring and training workers to run the factory, exporting the cement through their trading companies, and using the cement to build some needed roads and new office buildings in Jakarta. Although the Japanese firm's proposal cost more, it won the contract. Clearly the Japanese viewed the problem not as one of just building a cement factory (the narrow view of systems selling) but of running it in a way that would contribute to the country's economy. They took the broadest view of the customer's needs. This is true systems selling.

Who Participates in the Industrial Buying Process?

Who does the buying of the hundreds of billions of dollars worth of goods and services needed by the industrial market? The decision-making unit of a buying organization is called its **buying center,** defined as "all those individuals and groups who participate in the purchasing decision-making process, who share some common goals and the risks arising from the decisions."[13]

The buying center includes all members of the organization who play any of five roles in the purchase decision process.[14]

- USERS: members of the organization who will use the product or service. In many cases, users initiate the buying proposal and help define product specifications.
- INFLUENCERS: people who affect the buying decision. They often help define specifications and also provide information for evaluating alternatives. Technical personnel are particularly important influencers.
- BUYERS: people with formal authority to select the supplier and arrange terms of purchase. Buyers may help shape product specifications, but they play their major role in selecting vendors and negotiating. In more complex purchases, buyers might include high-level officers participating in the negotiations.

This ad recognizes the secretary as a key buying influence.

- DECIDERS: people who have formal or informal power to select or approve the final suppliers. In routine buying, the buyers are often the deciders, or at least the approvers.
- GATEKEEPERS: people who control the flow of information to others. For example, purchasing agents often have authority to prevent salespersons from seeing users or deciders. Other gatekeepers include technical personnel and even personal secretaries.

The buying center is not a fixed and formally identified unit within the buying organization. It is a set of buying roles assumed by different people for different purchases. Within the organization, the size and makeup of the buying center will vary for different products and for different buying situations. For some routine purchases, one person—say, a purchasing agent—may assume all the buying center roles and serve as the only person involved in the buying decision. For more complex purchases, the buying center may include 20 or 30 people from different levels and departments in the organization. One study of organizational buying showed that the typical industrial equipment purchase involved seven people from three management levels representing four different departments.[15]

The buying center concept presents a major marketing challenge. The industrial marketer must learn the following: Who is involved in the decision? What decisions do they affect? What is their relative degree of influence? What evaluation criteria does each decision participant use? Consider the following example:

> The American Hospital Supply Corporation sells disposable surgical gowns to hospitals. It tries to identify the hospital personnel involved in this buying decision. The decision participants turn out to be (1) the vice-president of purchasing, (2) the operating room administrator, and (3) the surgeons. Each party plays a different role. The vice-president of purchasing analyzes whether the hospital should buy disposable gowns or reusable gowns. If analysis favors disposable gowns, then the operating room administrator compares competing products and prices and makes a choice. This administrator considers the gown's absorbency, antiseptic quality, design, and cost and normally buys the brand that meets requirements at the lowest cost. Finally, surgeons affect the decision later by reporting their satisfaction or dissatisfaction with the brand.

The buying center usually includes some obvious participants who are formally involved in the buying decision—as we saw at the beginning of the chapter, the decision to buy a corporate jet will probably involve the company's chief pilot, a purchasing agent, some legal staff, a member of top management, and others formally charged with the buying decision. It may also involve informal, less obvious participants, some of whom may actually make or strongly affect the buying decision. Sometimes even the people in the buying center are not aware of all the buying participants. For example, the decision about which jet to buy may actually be made by a corporate board member who has an interest in flying and knows a lot about airplanes. This board member may work behind the scenes to sway the decision. Thus, many industrial buying decisions result from the complex interactions of ever-changing buying center participants.

What Are the Major Influences on Industrial Buyers?

Industrial buyers are subject to many influences when they make their buying decisions. Some marketers assume that the major influences are economic. They think buyers will favor the supplier who offers the lowest price, or the best product, or the most service. They concentrate on offering strong economic benefits to buyers. But industrial buyers also respond to personal factors:

> It has not been fashionable lately to talk about relationships in business. We're told that it has to be devoid of emotion. We must be cold, calculating, and impersonal. Don't you believe it. Relationships make the world go round. Businesspeople are human and social as well as interested in economics and investments, and salespeople need to appeal to both sides. Purchasers may claim to be motivated by intellect alone, but the professional salesperson knows that they run on both reason and emotion.[16]

Thus, industrial buyers actually respond to both economic and personal factors. When suppliers' offers are very similar, industrial buyers have little basis for strictly rational choice. Because they can meet organizational goals with any supplier, buyers can bring in personal factors. When competing products differ greatly, industrial buyers are more accountable for their choice and pay more attention to economic factors.

Industrial buyers respond to more than just economic factors. In this ad the words stress performance but the illustration suggests a smooth, comfortable ride.

The various groups of influences on industrial buyers—environmental, organizational, interpersonal, and individual—are listed in Figure 7-4 and described below.[17]

Environmental Factors

Industrial buyers are heavily influenced by factors in the current and expected *economic environment*, such as the level of primary demand, the economic outlook, and the cost of money. As economic uncertainty rises, industrial buyers cut back on new investments and attempt to reduce their inventories.

An increasingly important environmental factor is shortages in key materials. Many companies are now more willing to buy and hold larger inventories of scarce materials. Industrial buyers are also affected by technological, political, and competitive develop-

FIGURE 7-4   Major influences on industrial buying behavior

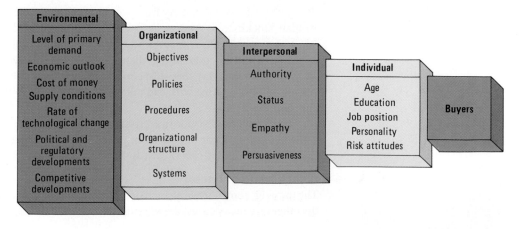

Environmental
- Level of primary demand
- Economic outlook
- Cost of money
- Supply conditions
- Rate of technological change
- Political and regulatory developments
- Competitive developments

Organizational
- Objectives
- Policies
- Procedures
- Organizational structure
- Systems

Interpersonal
- Authority
- Status
- Empathy
- Persuasiveness

Individual
- Age
- Education
- Job position
- Personality
- Risk attitudes

Buyers

ments in the environment. The industrial marketer must watch these factors, determine how they will affect the buyer, and try to turn these problems into opportunities.

Organizational Factors

Each buying organization has its own objectives, policies, procedures, structure, and systems. The industrial marketer must know these *organizational factors* as well as possible. Questions such as these arise: How many people are involved in the buying decision? Who are they? What are their evaluative criteria? What are the company's policies and limits on its buyers? The industrial marketer should be aware of the following organizational trends in the purchasing area.

UPGRADED PURCHASING.   Purchasing departments have often occupied a low position in the management hierarchy, even though they often manage more than half of the company's costs. However, many companies have recently upgraded their purchasing departments. Several large corporations have elevated the heads of purchasing to vice-president. Some companies have combined several functions—such as purchasing, inventory control, production scheduling, and traffic—into a high-level function called *strategic materials management*. Purchasing departments in many multinational companies are responsible for finding sources around the world and for working with strategic partners. "New wave" materials managers are actively building new supply sources. Many companies are looking for top talent, hiring MBAs, and offering higher compensation. This means that industrial marketers must also upgrade their salespeople to match the quality of the new buyers.

CENTRALIZED PURCHASING.   In companies with many divisions, much purchasing is carried out by the separate divisions because of their differing needs. Recently, some companies have recentralized some of the purchasing. Headquarters identifies materials purchased by several divisions and considers buying them centrally. Centralized purchasing gives the company more purchasing clout. The individual plants can buy from another source if they can get a better deal, but in general, centralized purchasing produces substantial savings for the company. For the industrial marketer, this development means dealing with fewer buyers, at a higher level. Instead of the seller's regional sales forces dealing with separate plants, the seller may use a *national account sales force* to deal with the buyer. For example, at Xerox, more than 250 national account managers each handle one to five large national accounts with many scattered locations. The national account managers coordinate the efforts of an entire Xerox team—specialists, analysts, salespeople for individual products—to sell to and service important national customers.[18] National account selling is challenging and demands a high-level salesforce and marketing effort.

LONG-TERM CONTRACTS.   Industrial buyers are increasingly seeking long-term contracts with suppliers. For example, General Motors wants to buy from fewer suppliers who are willing to locate close to their plants and produce high quality components. Another aspect involves companies supplying *electronic order exchange* systems to their customers. The seller places terminals hooked to its own computers in customers' offices. The customer can order instantly by typing orders directly into the computer. Many hospitals order directly from American Hospital Supply using order-taking terminals in their stockrooms. And many bookstores order from Follett's in this way.[19]

PURCHASING PERFORMANCE EVALUATION.   Some companies are setting up incentive systems to reward purchasing managers for especially good purchasing performance, in much the same way that slespeople receive bonuses for especially good selling performance. These systems will lead purchasing managers to increase their pressure on sellers for the best terms.

JUST-IN-TIME PRODUCTION SYSTEMS.   The emergence of just-in-time production systems has had a major impact on organizational purchasing policies. Marketing Highlight 7–2 describes the affects of just-in-time on organizational marketing.

Interpersonal Factors

The buying center usually includes many participants; each affects and is affected by the others. In many cases, the industrial marketer will not know what kinds of *interpersonal*

JUST-IN-TIME PRODUCTION CHANGES ORGANIZATIONAL SELLING

During the past several years, as American businesses have studied the reasons for Japanese success in world markets, they have learned about and adopted several new manufacturing concepts such as just-in-time (JIT) production, early supplier involvement, value analysis, quality circles, total quality control, and flexible manufacturing. The adoption of these practices greatly affects how industrial marketers sell to and service their customers.

JIT, in particular, promises to produce significant changes in industrial marketing. Just-in-time means that production materials arrive at the customer's factory at the exact time they are needed for production, rather than being stored in the customer's inventory until used. The goal of JIT is zero inventory with 100 percent quality. It calls for coordination between the production schedules of supplier and customer so that neither has to carry much inventory. Effective use of JIT reduces inventory and lead times and increases quality, productivity, and adaptability to change. In a 1986 survey of 2,000 purchasing executives, 59 percent indicated that their firm used or planned to use JIT. General Motors, through its JIT programs, reduced inventory-related costs from $8 billion to $2 billion.

Industrial marketers need to be aware of the changes that JIT will cause in organizational purchasing practices, and they must exploit the opportunities that JIT will create. Following are the major features and effects of JIT.

Strict Quality Control
Maximum cost savings from JIT are achieved only if the buyer receives pre-inspected goods. The industrial marketer needs to work closely with the customer and meet the high quality standards that JIT buyers expect.

Frequent and Reliable Delivery
Daily delivery is often the only way to avoid inventory buildup. Increasingly, customers are setting delivery dates with penalties for not meeting them. Apple even penalizes for early delivery while Kasle Steel makes around-the-clock deliveries to the General Motors plant in Buick City. Thus, JIT means that industrial marketers must develop reliable transportation arrangements.

Closer Location
Because JIT involves frequent delivery, many industrial marketers have set up locations closer to their large JIT customers. Closer locations enable them to deliver smaller shipments more efficiently and reliably. Kasle Steel set up a mill within Buick City to serve the General Motors plant there. Thus, JIT means that an industrial marketer may have to make large commitments to major customers.

Telecommunication
New communication technologies let suppliers set up computerized purchasing systems that are hooked up to their customers. One large customer even requires that suppliers put their inventory figures and prices in the system. This allows for online JIT ordering as the computer looks for the lowest prices for available inventory. Such systems reduce transaction costs but put pressure on industrial marketers to keep prices very competitive.

Single Sourcing
JIT requires that the buyer and seller work closely together to reduce costs. Often the industrial customer awards a long-term contract to only one trusted supplier. Single sourcing is increasing rapidly under JIT. Thus, while General Motors still uses more than 3500 suppliers, Toyota—which has totally adopted JIT—uses fewer than 250.

Value Analysis
The major objectives of JIT are to reduce costs and improve quality; value analysis can play a central role in that process. To reduce costs of its product, a customer must not only reduce its own costs but also get its suppliers to reduce their costs. Suppliers with a strong value analysis program have a competitive edge because they can contribute to their customers' value analysis program.

Early Supplier Involvement
Industrial buyers are increasingly bringing industrial marketers into the design process. Thus, industrial marketers must employ qualified people who can work with customers' design teams.

Close Relationship
To make JIT successful, the industrial marketer and customer must work closely together to satisfy the customer's needs. The marketer has to customize offerings for the particular industrial customer. In return, the marketer wins the contract for a specific term. Both parties may invest much time and money to set up the JIT relationship. Because the costs of changing suppliers are high, industrial customers are very selective in choosing suppliers. Thus industrial marketers must improve their skill in *relationship marketing* as compared to *transaction marketing*. The marketer must try to achieve maximum profits over the entire relationship rather than over each transaction.

Sources: See G. H. Manoochehri, "Suppliers and the Just-In-Time Concept," *Journal of Purchasing and Materials Management*, Winter 1984, pp. 16–21; Somerby Dowst, "Buyers Say VA Is More Important Than Ever," *Purchasing*, June 26, 1986, pp. 64–83; Ernest Raia, "Just-in-Time USA," *Purchasing*, February 13, 1986, pp. 48–62; Eric K. Clemons and F. Warren McFarlan, "Telecom: Hook Up or Lose Out," *Harvard Business Review*, July–August 1986, pp. 91–97; Somerby Dowst and Ernest Raia, "Design Team Signals for More Supplier Involvement," *Purchasing*, March 27, 1986, pp. 76–83; and Gary L. Frazier, Robert E. Spekman, and Charles R. O'Neal, "Just-in-Time Exchange Relationships in Industrial Markets," *Journal of Marketing*, October 1988, pp. 52–57.

factors and group dynamics enter into the buying process. As one writer notes: "Managers do not wear tags that say 'decision maker' or 'unimportant person.' The powerful are often invisible, at least to vendor representatives."[20]

Nor does the buying center participant with the highest rank always have the most influence. Participants may have influence in the buying decision because they control rewards and punishments, because they are well liked, because they have special expertise, or because they are related by marriage to the company president.[21] Interpersonal factors are often very subtle. Whenever possible, industrial marketers try to understand these factors and design strategies that take them into account.

Individual Factors

Each participant in the buying-decision process brings in personal motives, perceptions, and preferences. These *individual factors* are affected by age, income, education, professional identification, personality, and attitudes toward risk. Buyers also have different buying styles. Some of the younger, higher-educated buyers may be "computer freaks" who make in-depth analyses of competitive proposals before choosing a supplier. Other buyers may be "tough guys" from the "old school" who are adept at pitting the sellers against one another for the best deal.

How Do Industrial Buyers Make Their Buying Decisions?

The eight stages of the industrial buying process are listed in Table 7-1.[22] The table shows that buyers facing a new task buying situation will usually go through all the stages of the buying process. Buyers making modified or straight rebuys will skip some of the stages. We examine these steps for the typical new task buying situation.

Problem Recognition

The buying process begins when someone in the company recognizes a problem or need that can be met by acquiring a specific good or a service. **Problem recognition** can result from internal or external stimuli. Internally, the company may decide to launch a new product and need new equipment and materials to produce it. Or a machine may break down and need new parts. Some purchased material may turn out to be unsatisfactory and cause the company to search for another supplier. Or a purchasing manager might see a chance to get better prices or quality. Externally, the buyer may get some new ideas at a trade show, see an ad, or receive a call from a salesperson who offers a better product or a lower price.

General Need Description

Having recognized a need, the buyer next prepares a **general need description** that describes the general characteristics and quantity of the needed item. For standard items, this process is not a serious problem. For complex items, however, the buyer will work with others (engineers, users, consultants) to define the item. The team will want to rank the importance of reliability, durability, price, and other attributes desired in the item.

The industrial marketer can help the buying company in this phase. Often, the buyer is not aware of the value of different product characteristics. An alert marketer can help the buyer define the company's needs.

TABLE 7-1 Major Stages of the Industrial Buying Process in Relation to Major Buying Situations	BUYING SITUATIONS		
STAGES OF THE BUYING PROCESS	New Task	Modified Rebuy	Straight Rebuy
1. Problem recognition	Yes	Maybe	No
2. General need description	Yes	Maybe	No
3. Product specification	Yes	Yes	Yes
4. Supplier search	Yes	Maybe	No
5. Proposal solicitation	Yes	Maybe	No
6. Supplier selection	Yes	Maybe	No
7. Order routine specification	Yes	Maybe	No
8. Performance review	Yes	Yes	Yes

Source: Adapted from Patrick J. Robinson, Charles W. Faris, and Yoram Wind, *Industrial Buying and Creative Marketing* (Boston: Allyn & Bacon, 1967), p. 14.

TABLE 7-2
Questions Asked in
Value Analysis

1. Does the use of the item contribute value?
2. Is its cost proportionate to its usefulness?
3. Does it need all its features?
4. Is there anything better for its intended use?
5. Can a usable part be made by a lower-cost method?
6. Can a standard product be found that will be usable?
7. Is the product made on proper tooling, considering the quantities that are used?
8. Do material, labor, overhead, and profit total its cost?
9. Will another dependable supplier provide it for less?
10. Is anyone buying it for less?

Source: Albert W. Frey, *Marketing Handbook*, 2nd ed. (New York: Ronald Press, 1965), Sec. 27, p. 21. Copyright © 1985. Reprinted by permission of John Wiley & Sons, Inc.

Product Specification

The buying organization next develops the item's technical **product specifications.** Often, a value-analysis engineering team will be put to work on the problem. **Value analysis** is an approach to cost reduction in which components are carefully studied to determine if they can be redesigned, standardized, or made by cheaper methods of production. Table 7-2 lists the major questions raised during the value analysis. The team will decide on the best product characteristics and specify them accordingly. Sellers, too, can use value analysis as a tool to help secure a new account. By showing a better way to make an object, outside sellers can turn straight rebuy situations into new-task situations in which their company has a chance for business.

Supplier Search

The buyer now conducts a **supplier search** to find the best vendors. The buyer can look at trade directories, do a computer search, or phone other companies for recommendations. Some vendors will not be considered because they are not large enough to supply the needed quantity or because they have a poor reputation for delivery and service. The buyer will soon compile a small list of qualified suppliers.

The newer the buying task—and the more complex and costly the item—the greater the amount of time spent in searching for suppliers. The supplier's task is to get listed in major directories and build a good reputation in the marketplace. Salespeople should watch for companies in the process of searching for suppliers and make certain that their firm is considered.

Proposal Solicitation

In the **proposal solicitation** stage of the industrial buying process, the buyer invites qualified suppliers to submit proposals. Some suppliers will send only a catalog or a salesperson. When the item is complex or expensive, the buyer will need detailed written proposals from each potential supplier. The buyer will review the suppliers when they make their formal presentations.

Therefore, industrial marketers must be skilled in researching, writing, and presenting proposals. Their proposals should be marketing documents, not just technical documents. Their presentations should inspire confidence. They should make their companies stand out from the competition.

Supplier Selection

The members of the buying center now review the proposals and select a supplier or suppliers. During **supplier selection,** they will consider not only the technical competence of the various suppliers, but also their ability to deliver the item on time and to provide necessary services. The buying center will often draw up a list of the desired supplier attributes and their relative importance. In one survey, purchasing executives listed the following attributes as most important in influencing the relationship between supplier and customer: quality products and services, on-time delivery, ethical corporate behavior, honest communication, and competitive prices.[23] Other important factors include repair

TABLE 7-3
An Example of Vendor Analysis

ATTRIBUTES	RATING SCALE				
	Unacceptable (0)	Poor (1)	Fair (2)	Good (3)	Excellent (4)
Technical and production capabilities					x
Price competitiveness			x		
Product quality					x
Delivery reliability			x		
Service capability					x

4 + 2 + 4 + 2 + 4 = 16

Average score:
16/5 = 3.2

Note: This vendor shows up as strong except on two attributes. The purchasing agent has to decide how important the two weaknesses are. The analysis could be redone using importance weights for the five attributes.
Source: Adapted from Richard Hill, Ralph Alexander, and James Cross, *Industrial Marketing*, 4th ed. (Homewood, IL: Irwin, 1975), pp. 101–4.

and servicing capabilities, technical aid and advice, geographic location, performance history, and reputation.

The members of the buying center will rate the suppliers and identify the most attractive, often using a supplier evaluation method similar to the one shown in Table 7-3.

The importance of various supplier attributes depends on the type of purchase situation the buyer faces.[24] One study of 220 purchasing managers showed that economic criteria were most important in situations involving routine purchases of standard products. Performance criteria became more important in purchases of nonstandard, more complex products. The supplier's ability to adapt to the buyer's changing needs was important for almost all types of purchases.

Buyers may attempt to negotiate with preferred suppliers for better prices and terms before making the final selections. In the end, they may select a single supplier or a few suppliers. Many buyers prefer multiple sources of supply. Then they will not be totally dependent on one supplier in case something goes wrong, and they will be able to compare the prices and performance of several suppliers over time.

Order Routine Specification

The buyer now prepares an **order routine specification.** It includes the final order with the chosen supplier or suppliers, listing the technical specifications, quantity needed, expected time of delivery, return policies, warranties, and so on. In the case of maintenance, repair, and operating items, buyers are increasingly using blanket contracts rather than periodic purchase orders. Writing a new purchase order each time stock is needed is expensive. And the buyer wants to avoid writing fewer and larger purchase orders because doing so results in carrying more inventory.

A *blanket contract* creates a long-term relationship in which the supplier promises to resupply the buyer as needed at agreed prices for a set time period. The stock is held by the seller and the buyer's computer automatically prints out an order to the seller when stock is needed. Blanket contracting leads to more single-source buying and the buying of more items from that source. This practice locks the supplier in tighter with the buyer and makes it difficult for other suppliers to break in unless the buyer becomes dissatisfied with prices or service.

Performance Review

In this stage the buyer reviews supplier performance. The buyer may contact users and ask them to rate their satisfaction. The **performance review** may lead the buyer to continue, modify, or drop the arrangement. The seller's job is to monitor the same factors used by the buyer to make sure that the seller is giving the expected satisfaction.

We have described the buying stages that would operate in a new task buying situation. In the modified rebuy or straight rebuy situation, some of these stages would be compressed or bypassed. The eight-stage model provides a simple view of the industrial buying decision process. The actual process is usually much more complex.[25] Each organization buys in its own way, and each buying situation has unique requirements. Different buying center participants may be involved at different stages of the process. Although certain buying process steps usually occur, buyers do not always follow them in the same order, and they may add other steps. Often, buyers repeat certain stages more than once.

RESELLER BUYER BEHAVIOR

In most ways, reseller buyer behavior is like industrial buyer behavior. Reseller organizations have buying centers whose participants interact to make a variety of buying decisions. They have a buying-decision process that starts with problem recognition and ends with decisions about which products to buy from which suppliers and under what terms. The buyers are affected by a wide range of environmental, organizational, interpersonal, and individual factors. But there are some important differences between industrial and reseller buying behavior. Resellers differ in the types of buying decisions they make, who participates in the buying decision, and how they make their buying decisions.

What Buying Decisions Do Resellers Make? Resellers serve as purchasing agents for *their* customers, so they buy products and brands they think will appeal to their customers. They have to decide what product assortment to carry, what vendors to buy from, and what prices and terms to negotiate. The assortment decision is primary because it positions the reseller in the marketplace. The reseller's assortment strategy will strongly affect the choices of which products to buy and which suppliers to buy from.

Resellers can carry products from only one supplier, several related products or lines from a few suppliers, or a scrambled assortment of unrelated products from many suppliers. Thus, a retail store might carry only Kodak cameras; many brands of cameras; cameras, radios, and stereo equipment; or all these plus stoves and refrigerators. The reseller's assortment will affect its customer mix, marketing mix, and supplier mix.

Who Participates in the Reseller Buying Process? Who does the buying for wholesale and retail organizations? The reseller's buying center may include one or many participants assuming different roles. Some will have formal buying responsibility, and some will be behind-the-scenes influences. In small "mom and pop" firms, the owner usually takes care of buying decisions. In large reseller firms, buying is a specialized function and a full-time job. The buying center and buying process vary for different types of resellers.

Consider supermarkets. In the headquarters of a supermarket chain, specialist buyers have the responsibility for developing brand assortments and listening to new-brand presentations made by salespeople. In some chains these buyers have the authority to accept or reject new items. In many chains, however, they are limited to screening "obvious rejects" and "obvious accepts"; otherwise, they must bring new items to the chain's buying committee for approval. Even when an item is accepted by a buying committee, chain-store managers may not carry it. Altogether, food producers offer the nation's supermarkets more than 10,000 new products each year, and store space does not permit more than 38 percent to be accepted.[26] Thus, the producers face a major challenge in trying to get new items into stores.

How Do Resellers Make Their Buying Decisions? For new items, resellers use roughly the same buying process described for industrial buyers. For standard items, resellers simply reorder goods when the inventory gets low. The orders are placed with the same suppliers as long as their terms, goods, and services are satisfactory. Buyers will try to renegotiate prices if their margins drop due to rising operating costs. In many retail lines, the profit margin is so low (1 to 2

A NEW L'EGGS CUSTOMER IS HATCHED.

Once upon a time little legs had to grow up before they could start wearing L'eggs.
But not anymore.

Introducing Little L'eggs' Tights and Little L'eggs' Knee Highs for ages 2 through 11. This new line, especially designed for stores like yours, has more than the great L'eggs name on it. Little L'eggs has our thinking knit into it. Instead of making our tights out of 100% nylon like others do, we've spun Lycra' Spandex together with a multi-filament nylon.

The result is a tight that fits better and feels softer.

No wonder moms like them five times better than the brand they're currently buying for their daughters. That kind of endorsement translates into a 96% purchase intent. So be prepared for a strong sales performance.

But the good news doesn't stop there.

When you combine Introductory, Bonus and Advertising allowances, you're working with a 57% gross margin! That's very competitive to private label tights. Especially since no private label can match L'eggs 96% brand name awareness.

Little L'eggs is just another example of how we view the importance of discount outlets to L'eggs. And the drawing power of the L'eggs brands to you. When L'eggs brought Underalls' to you, a younger, more fashion conscious woman came into your store. With L'eggs Just My Size', we've attracted large women with fashion needs. While our new Sheer Elegance Silken Mist' brings a more upscale consumer to your door—those seeking department store quality hosiery at discount store prices.

At L'eggs we'll continue to introduce new specialty brands and hardware to increase your margins and open up new markets for you. Call the L'eggs hotline (1-800-423-4714) and we'll help you manage your hosiery section for even greater profits.

As we've learned, sometimes when you satisfy a little need, you hatch a whole new market.

IT PAYS TO SHOW OFF YOUR L'EGGS.

L'eggs

Selling to resellers: In this ad to discount retailers, L'eggs lists plenty of reasons why its new line of Little L'eggs for children will increase the retailer's margins and open up new markets. It offers an innovative design, 5 to 1 consumer preference, 96 percent consumer name recognition, and a 57 percent gross margin.

percent on sales in supermarkets, for example) that a sudden drop in demand or rise in operating costs will drive profits into the red.

Resellers consider many factors besides costs when choosing products and suppliers. For example, a panel of supermarket buyers listed the following as important factors when choosing new products for their stores:[27]

- The product's pricing and profit margins
- The product's uniqueness and the strength of the product category
- The seller's intended positioning and marketing plan for the product
- Test-market evidence of consumer acceptance of the product
- Advertising and sales-promotion support for the product
- The selling company's reputation

Thus, sellers stand the best chance when they can report a promising product, show strong evidence of consumer acceptance, present a well-designed advertising and sales-promotion plan, and provide strong financial incentives to the retailer. Once lucky sellers pass these tests, they still may have to pay substantial charges for shelving the product (called *slotting allowances*) and for removing a failed product (called *exit fees*).

Sellers are facing increasingly advanced buying on the part of resellers. They need to understand the resellers' changing needs and to develop attractive offers that help resellers serve their customers better. Table 7-4 lists several marketing tools used by sellers to make their offer to resellers more attractive.

TABLE 7-4
Vendor Marketing
Tools Used with
Resellers

Cooperative advertising, where the vendor agrees to pay a portion of the reseller's advertising costs for the vendor's product.

Preticketing, where the vendor places a tag on each product listing its price, manufacturer, size, identification number, and color; these tags help the reseller reorder merchandise as it is being sold.

Stockless purchasing, where the vendor carries the inventory and delivers goods to the reseller on short notice.

Automatic reordering systems, where the vendor supplies forms and computer links for automatic reordering of merchandise by the reseller.

Advertising aids, such as glossy photos, broadcast scripts.

Special prices for storewide promotion.

Return and exchange privileges for the reseller.

Allowances for merchandise markdowns by the reseller.

Sponsorship of in-store demonstrations.

GOVERNMENT BUYER BEHAVIOR

The government market offers large opportunities for many companies. Altogether, the federal, state, and local governments contain more than 82,000 buying units. Some companies sell to governments only occasionally or not at all. Others rely on the government market for a large portion of their sales. (See Marketing Highlight 7–3.)

Government buying and industrial buying are similar in many ways. But there are also differences that must be understood by companies that wish to sell products and services to governments.[28] To succeed in the government market, sellers must locate key decision makers, identify the factors that affect buyer behavior, and understand the buying-decision process.

Who Participates in the Government Buying Process?

Who does the buying of the $1 trillion of goods and services each year? Government buying organizations are found at the federal, state, and local levels. The federal level is the largest, and its buying units operate in both the civilian and military sectors.

The federal civilian buying establishment consists of seven categories: departments (such as the Department of Commerce), administrations (General Services Administration), agencies (Environmental Protection Agency), boards (Railroad Retirement Board), commissions (Federal Communications Commission), the executive offices (Office of Management and Budget), and miscellaneous organizations (Tennessee Valley Authority). No single agency buys for all the government's needs, and no single buyer purchases all of any single item of supplies, equipment, or services. Many agencies control a large percentage of their own buying, particularly for industrial products and specialized equipment. At the same time, the *General Services Administration* plays a major role in centralizing the buying of commonly used items in the civilian section (office furniture and equipment, vehicles, fuels) and in standardizing buying procedures for the other agencies.

Federal military buying is carried out by the Defense Department, largely through the *Defense Logistics Agency* and the army, navy, and air force. In an effort to reduce costly duplication, the Defense Logistics Agency buys and distributes supplies used by all military services. It operates six supply centers, which specialize in construction, electronics, fuel, personnel support, industrial products, and general supplies. The trend has been toward "single managers" for major product classifications. Each service branch buys equipment and supplies in line with its own mission. For example, the army has offices that acquire its own material, vehicles, medical supplies and services, and weapons.

State and local buying agencies include school districts, highway departments, hospitals, housing agencies, and many others. Each has its own buying process that sellers must master.

The various government agencies may all be potential targets for sellers who wish to sell to this large market. But sellers should study the purchasing patterns of

ZENITH DATA SYSTEMS TARGETS THE GOVERNMENT MARKET

In 1979, Zenith entered the already overcrowded personal computer market with its Zenith Data Systems (ZDS) division. Like IBM, Tandy, AT&T, and several other competitors, Zenith Data Systems targeted its line of IBM-compatibles at the business and retail markets. But ZDS lacked IBM's marketing muscle; it couldn't sustain the big-budget advertising and marketing campaign needed to challenge big rivals head-on. So in 1981, after limping along for two years, ZDS changed its strategy. It targeted two specialty markets—higher education and the Federal government, markets previously overlooked by IBM and the others. By focusing on these segments, ZDS could avoid expensive advertising and costly direct competition.

Cracking the huge government market, however, required much effort, investment, patience, and positive thinking. ZDS created a government salesforce to handle the special needs of the government market. The new salesforce had to feel its way through the complex, convoluted federal government bidding process, learning how to cut through seemingly endless red tape, bureaucracy, and paperwork along the way. ZDS made its proposals more appealing to cost-conscious government buyers by using the money it saved on advertising to heavily discount its prices. It took ZDS almost two years to land its first government contract, a $29 million order from the air force in 1983 for 6,000 personal computers. Although government business began as a trickle, the trickle soon turned into a flood.

In October 1984, ZDS signed a $100 million contract to supply the navy, air force, and marines with "Tempest-grade" personal computers—machines specially shielded against electronic eavesdropping. In February 1986, ZDS beat out IBM and other large competitors for the government's largest-ever personal computer order, a $242 million contract for more than 200,000 units. That contract eventually grew to bring in more than $500 million worth of business. Also in 1986, ZDS edged out IBM and Data General to win a $27 million contract from the Internal Revenue Service for 15,000 of the company's acclaimed new laptop models. Since then, the company has also won contracts from the U.S. Department of Health and Human Services and several other government agencies. The U.S. Army and Air Force Post Exchange Systems (PXs) carry ZDS products, and the company supplies computers to students and faculty at the military, air force, and naval academies. ZDS has even broken into the state government market, with contracts from the states of Florida, Kansas, and Massachusetts.

Thus, ZDS's strategy to target the government market has met with staggering success. ZDS is now the federal

By focusing on the government market, Zenith Data Systems established itself as a major contender in the microcomputer market.

government's largest personal computer supplier and the world's second-largest producer of IBM-compatibles. From 1982 to 1986, while most of the personal computer industry slid downward and many competitors failed, ZDS's yearly computer sales grew by over 550 percent, to $548 million. When IBM's sales through retail stores slowed under the onslaught of cheap Asian clones, ZDS was having trouble keeping up with orders from government agencies. By 1988, an estimated one-half of all ZDS's computer sales came from the government market.

By focusing on the government market, ZDS quietly established itself as a major contender in the highly competitive personal computer market. ZDS's steady sales to the government made the division particularly attractive to Groupe Bull, the state-owned French computer company, which recently purchased Zenith Data Systems in an attempt to establish a foothold in the U.S. computer market.

Sources: See Thayer C. Taylor, "The PC Fight: Zenith Battles the Heavyweights," *Sales & Marketing Management*, November 1986, pp. 51–55; Kenneth Dreyfack, "Zenith's Side Road to Success in Personal Computers," *Business Week*, December 8, 1986, pp. 100–101; Zenith Is Doing Quite Well, Thank You—In Personal Computers," *Business Week*, July 11, 1988, p. 80; and "Firm Says Dispute on Price Won't Endanger Acquisition," *The Wall Street Journal*, February 22, 1990, p. A11.

different agencies. Agencies differ in quality requirements and the amount of marketing effort needed to make a sale. Some agencies buy standardized products while others buy mostly customized items. Sellers should target agencies and buying centers that match their strengths and objectives.[29]

What Are the Major Influences on Government Buyers?

Like consumer and industrial buyers, government buyers are affected by environmental, organizational, interpersonal, and individual factors. A unique thing about government buying is that it is carefully watched by outside publics. One watchdog is Congress, and certain congressmen have made a career out of exposing government waste. Another

The government market offers many opportunities for companies. Here Southern Bell markets its services to local and county governments.

watchdog is the Office of Management and Budget, which checks on government spending and seeks to improve efficiency. Many private groups also watch government agencies to see how they spend the taxpayers' money.

Because spending decisions are subject to public review, government organizations are buried in paperwork. Elaborate forms must be filled out and signed before purchases are approved. The level of bureaucracy is high, and marketers must cut through the red tape.

Noneconomic criteria are also playing a growing role in government buying. Government buyers are asked to favor depressed business firms and areas, small-business firms, and business firms that avoid race, sex, or age discrimination. Sellers need to keep these factors in mind when deciding to seek government business.

How Do Government Buyers Make Their Buying Decisions?

Government buying practices often seem complex and frustrating to suppliers. Suppliers have voiced many complaints about government purchasing procedures. These include too much paperwork, bureaucracy, needless regulations, emphasis on low bid prices, decision-making delays, frequent shifts in buying personnel, and too many policy changes. Yet the ins and outs of selling to the government can often be mastered in a short time. The government is generally helpful in providing information about its buying needs and procedures. Government is often as eager to attract new suppliers as the suppliers are to find customers.

For example, the Small Business Administration prints a booklet entitled *U.S. Government Purchasing, Specifications, and Sales Directory*, which lists thousands of items most frequently purchased by the government and the specific agencies most frequently buying them. The Government Printing Office issues the *Commerce Business Daily*, which lists major current and planned purchases and recent contract awards, both of which can provide leads to subcontracting markets. The Commerce Department publishes *Business America*, which provides interpretations of government policies and programs and gives concise information on potential worldwide trade opportunities. In several major cities, the General Services Administration operates *Business Service Centers* with staffs to provide a complete education on the way government agencies buy, the steps that suppliers should follow, and the procurement opportunities available. Various trade magazines and associations provide information on how to reach schools, hospitals, highway departments, and other government agencies.

Government buying procedures fall into two types: the *open bid* and the *negotiated contract*. Open-bid buying means that the government office invites bids from qualified suppliers for carefully described items, generally awarding a contract to the lowest bidder. The supplier must consider whether it can meet the specifications and accept the terms. For standard items, such as fuel or school supplies, the specifications are not a hurdle. But specifications may be a hurdle for nonstandard items. The government office is usually required to award the contract to the lowest bidder on a winner-take-all basis. In some cases, allowance is made for the supplier's better product or reputation for completing contracts.

In negotiated contract buying, the agency works with one or more companies and negotiates a contract with one of them covering the project and contract terms. This occurs primarily with complex projects—those involving major research and development costs and risks or those for which there is little competition. The contract can be reviewed and renegotiated if the supplier's profits seem too high.

Many companies that sell to the government have not been marketing oriented—for a number of reasons. Total government spending is determined by elected officials rather than by any marketing effort to develop this market. Government buying has emphasized price, making suppliers invest their effort in technology to bring costs down. When the product's characteristics are carefully specified, product differentiation is not a marketing factor. Nor do advertising or personal selling matter much in winning bids on an open-bid basis.

More companies are now setting up separate marketing departments for government marketing efforts. Rockwell International, Eastman Kodak, and Goodyear are examples. These companies want to coordinate bids and prepare them more scientifically, to propose projects to meet government needs rather than just respond to government requests, to gather competitive intelligence, and to prepare stronger communications to describe the company's competence.[30]

■ SUMMARY

Organizations make up a vast market. There are three major types of organizational markets—the industrial market, the reseller market, and the government market.

In many ways, organizational markets are like consumer markets, but in other ways they are much different. Organizational markets usually have fewer and larger buyers who are more geographically concentrated. Organizational demand is derived, largely inelastic, and more fluctuating. More buyers are usually involved in the organizational buying decision, and organizational buyers are better trained and more professional than consumer buyers. Organizational purchasing decisions are more complex and the buying process is more formal.

The *industrial market* includes firms and individuals that buy goods and services in order to produce other goods and services for sale or rental to others. Industrial buyers make decisions that vary with the three types of buying situations—straight rebuys, modified rebuys, and new tasks. The decision-making unit of a buying organization—the buying center—may consist of many persons playing many roles. The industrial marketer needs to know the following: Who are the major participants? In what decisions do they exercise influence? What is their relative degree of influence? And what evaluation criteria does each decision participant use? The industrial marketer also needs to understand the major environmental, interpersonal, and individual influences on the buying process. The buying process itself consists of eight stages: problem recognition, general need description, product specification, supplier search, proposal solicitation, supplier selection, order routine specification, and performance review. As industrial buyers become more sophisticated, industrial marketers must upgrade their marketing.

The *reseller market* consists of individuals and organizations that acquire and resell goods produced by others. Resellers must decide on their assortment, suppliers, prices, and terms. In small wholesale and retail organizations, buying may be carried on by one or a few individuals; in large organizations, by an entire purchasing department. With new items, the buyers go through a buying process similar to the one described for industrial buyers; with standard items, the buying process consists of routines for reordering and renegotiating contracts.

The *government market* is vast and annually purchases more than a trillion dollars of products and services—for defense, education, public welfare, and other public needs. Government buying practices are highly specialized and specified, with open bidding or negotiated contracts characterizing most of the buying. Government buyers operate under the watchful eye of Congress, the Bureau of the Budget, and many private watchdog groups. Hence they tend to fill out more forms, require more signatures, and respond more slowly in placing orders.

■ QUESTIONS FOR DISCUSSION

1. In what ways can your school be considered an industrial marketer? What are its products and who are its customers?
2. Apple Computer paid top prices for millions of computer memory chips during an industry-wide shortage. Soon afterward, demand for memory dropped, and the chips became cheap and plentiful, leaving Apple with millions of dollars in losses. How would a long-term contract have helped in this situation?
3. Which of the major types of buying situations are represented by the following: (a) Chrysler's purchase of computers that go in cars and adjust engine performance to changing driving conditions, (b) Volkswagen's purchase of spark plugs for its line of Jettas, and (c) Honda's purchase of light bulbs for its new Acura division?
4. If a university decided to introduce polo as a varsity sport, what elements would a systems seller include in a proposal to start a polo program and make it succeed?
5. How could a marketer of office equipment identify the buying center for a law firm's purchase of dictation equipment for each of its partners?
6. Discuss the major environmental factors that would affect the purchase of radar speed detectors by statewide and local police forces.
7. What are the advantages and disadvantages of buying from single suppliers versus multiple suppliers?
8. The NutraSweet Company and other companies have advertised products to the general public that consumers aren't able to buy. How does this strategy help a company sell products to resellers?
9. Assume you are selling a fleet of cars to be used by a company's salesforce. The salespeople need larger cars, which are more profitable for you, but the fleet buyer wants to buy smaller cars. Who might be in the buying center? How might you meet the varying needs of these participants?
10. Compare the major buying influences on industrial, reseller, and government buyers.

■ KEY TERMS

Buying center. All the individuals and units that participate in the organizational buying decision process.

Derived demand. Organizational demand that ultimately comes from (derives from) the demand for consumer goods.

General need description. The stage in the industrial buying process in which the company describes the general characteristics and quantity of a needed item.

Government market. Governmental units—federal, state, and local—that purchase or rent goods and services for carrying out the main functions of government.

Industrial market. All the individuals and organizations acquiring goods and services which enter into the production of other products and services that are sold, rented, or supplied to others.

Inelastic demand. Total demand for a product that is not much affected by price changes, especially in the short run.

Modified rebuy. An industrial buying situation in which the buyer wants to modify product specifications, prices, terms, or suppliers.

New task. An industrial buying situation in which the buyer purchases a product or service for the first time.

Order routine specification. The stage of the industrial buying process in which the buyer writes the final order with the chosen supplier(s), listing the technical specifications, quantity needed, expected time of delivery, return policies, warranties, and so on.

Organizational buying. The decision-making process by which formal organizations establish the need for purchased products and services, and identify, evaluate, and choose among alternative brands and suppliers.

Performance review. The stage of the industrial buying process in which the buyer rates its satisfaction with suppliers, deciding whether to continue, modify, or drop the relationship.

Problem recognition. The stage of the industrial buying process in which someone in the company recognizes a problem or need that can be met by acquiring a good or a service.

Product specification. The stage of the industrial buying process in which the buying organization decides on and specifies the best technical product characteristics for a needed item.

Proposal solicitation. The stage of the industrial buying process in which the buyer invites qualified suppliers to submit proposals.

Reseller market. All the individuals and organizations that acquire goods for the purpose of reselling or renting them to others at a profit.

Straight rebuy. An industrial buying situation in which the buyer routinely reorders something without modification.

Supplier search. The stage of the industrial buying process in which the buyer tries to find the best vendors.

Supplier selection. The stage of the industrial buying process in which the buyer reviews proposals and selects a supplier or suppliers.

Systems buying. Buying a packaged solution to a problem, which avoids making all the separate decisions involved in buying each item or service separately.

Value analysis. An approach to cost reduction in which components are carefully studied to determine if they can be redesigned, standardized, or made by cheaper methods of production.

■ REFERENCES

1. Excerpts from ''Major Sales: Who Really Does the Buying,'' by Thomas V. Bonoma (May–June 1982). Copyright © 1982 by the President and Fellows of Harvard College; all rights reserved. Also see Scott Ticer, ''Why Gulfstream's Rivals are Gazing Up in Envy,'' *Business Week*, February 16, 1987, pp. 66–67; and Sandra D. Atchison, ''The Business Jet Pulls Out of Its Dive,'' *Business Week*, November 21, 1988, pp. 69–72.

2. Frederick E. Webster, Jr., and Yoram Wind, *Organizational Buying Behavior* (Englewood Cliffs, NJ: Prentice Hall, 1972), p. 2.

3. See the *1987 Census of Retail Trade* and the *1987 Census of Wholesale Trade*, U.S. Department of Commerce, Bureau of the Census, August 1989.

4. *Survey of Current Business*, U.S. Department of Commerce, Bureau of Economic Analysis, Vol. 69, No. 12, December 1989.

5. For discussions of similarities and differences in consumer and organizational marketing, see Edward F. Fern and James R. Brown, ''The Industrial/Consumer Marketing Dichotomy: A Case of Insufficient Justification,'' *Journal of Marketing*, Fall, 1984, pp. 68–77; and Ron J. Kornakovich, ''Consumer Methods Work for Business Marketing: Yes; No,'' *Marketing News*, November 21, 1988, pp. 4, 13–14.

6. See William S. Bishop, John L. Graham, and Michael H. Jones, ''Volatility of Derived Demand in Industrial Markets and Its Management Implications,'' *Journal of Marketing*, Spring 1984, pp. 68–77.

7. See Barbara Bund Jackson, ''Build Customer Relationships That Last,'' *Harvard Business Review*, November–December 1985, pp. 120–128.

8. See Louis W. Stern and Thomas L. Eovaldi, *Legal Aspects of Marketing Strategy* (Englewood Cliffs, NJ: Prentice Hall, 1984, pp. 330–331.

9. See Jim Mele, ''Leasing: Preparing for the 1990s,'' *Business Week*, March 19, 1990, pp. 23–32.

10. For a discussion of other organizational buyer behavior models, see Raymond L. Horton, *Buyer Behavior: A Decision-Making Approach* (Columbus, OH: Charles E. Merrill, 1984), Chap. 16.

11. Patrick J. Robinson, Charles W. Faris, and Yoram Wind, *Industrial Buying Behavior and Creative Marketing* (Boston: Allyn & Bacon, 1967). Also see Erin Anderson, Weyien Chu, and Barton Weitz, ''Industrial Purchasing: An Empirical Exploration of the Buyclass Framework,'' *Journal of Marketing*, July 1987, pp. 71–86.

12. For more on systems selling, see Robert R. Reeder, Edward G. Brierty, and Betty H. Reeder, *Industrial Marketing: Analysis, Planning, and Control* (Englewood Cliffs, NJ: Prentice Hall, 1987), pp. 247–50.

13. Webster and Wind, *Organizational Buying Behavior*, p. 6. For more reading on buying centers, see Bonoma, ''Major Sales: Who Really Does the Buying;'' and Donald W. Jackson, Jr., Janet E. Keith, and Richard K. Burdick, ''Purchasing Agents' Perceptions of Industrial Buying Center Influence: A Situational Approach,'' *Journal of Marketing*, Fall 1984, pp. 75–83.

14. Webster and Wind, *Organizational Buying Behavior*, pp. 78–80.

15. Wesley J. Johnson and Thomas V. Bonoma, ''Purchase Process for Capital Equipment and Services,'' *Industrial Marketing Management*, Vol. 10, 1981, pp. 258–59.

16. Clifton J. Reichard, ''Industrial Selling: Beyond Price and Persistence,'' *Harvard Business Review*, March–April 1985, p. 128.

17. Webster and Wind, *Organizational Buying Behavior*, pp. 33–37.

18. Thayer C. Taylor, ''Xerox's Sales Force Learns a New Game,'' *Sales & Marketing Management*, July 1, 1985, pp. 48–51.

19. See Peter Petre, ''How to Keep Customers Happy Captives,'' *Fortune*, September 2, 1985, pp. 42–46.

20. Bonoma, ''Major Sales,'' p. 114.

21. See Ajay Kohli, ''Determinants of Influence in Organizational Buying: A Contingency Approach,'' *Journal of Marketing*, July 1989, pp. 50–65.

22. Robinson, Faris, and Wind, *Industrial Buying*.

23. See ''What Buyers Really Want,'' *Sales & Marketing Management*, October 1989, p. 30.

24. Donald R. Lehmann and John O'Shaughnessy, ''Decision Criteria Used in Buying Different Categories of Products,'' *Journal of Purchasing and Materials Management*, Spring 1982, pp. 9–14.

25. Johnston and Bonoma, ''Purchase Process,'' p. 261.

26. See Ed Fitch, ''Life in the Food Chain Becomes Predatory,'' *Advertising Age*, May 9, 1988, p. S2.

27. ''Retailers Rate New Products,'' *Sales & Marketing Management*, November 1986, pp. 75–77.

28. For more reading on similarities and differences between government and industrial buying, see Jagdish N. Sheth, Robert F. Williams, and Richard M. Hill, ''Government and Business Buying: How Similar Are They?'' *Journal of Purchasing and Materials Management*, Winter 1983, pp. 7–13.

29. See Warren H. Suss, ''How to Sell to Uncle Sam,'' *Harvard Business Review*, November–December 1984, pp. 136–144; and Don Hill, ''Who Says Uncle Sam's a Tough Sell?'' *Sales & Marketing Management*, July 1988, pp. 56–60.

30. For a good summary of U.S. government buying, see John C. Franke, ''Marketing to the Government: Contracts There for Those Who Know Where to Look,'' *Marketing News*, October 9, 1989, pp. 1, 7; and Franke, ''Military Makes Its Own Purchasing Rules,'' *Marketing News*, October 9, 1989, pp. 1, 7.

LOCTITE CORPORATION: NEW MARKETS FOR AN OLD PRODUCT

When studying organizational markets, it is helpful to consider all the goods and services that businesses must buy in order to provide the end users with products they want. For example, did you know that, in one year, dishwasher manufacturers buy 585 miles of rubber hose, 3.7 million water valves, and 734,000 gallons of paint? Manufacturers buy from hundreds of suppliers—most of whom are little-known to the consumers who buy the final product. Loctite Corporation is one such supplier.

Loctite Corporation, a specialty chemical company, manufactures products that bond, seal, and prevent loosening. You may have used a product today that is held together by a Loctite product—in fact, you may now be *wearing* something that contains a Loctite product! Some Loctite adhesives are used in several sectors of the garment industry, including both clothing and shoes. Consumers may also buy Loctite products for their own use. For example, the super glues "Glue Stick" and "Quick Gel," as well as Duro household cements, are Loctite products that may be in your home.

The use of adhesives, however, is relatively new. In 1953, Trinity College Professor Vernon K. Krieble developed the original Loctite "anaerobic" adhesive. This new product competed with the more traditional means of bonding materials, such as screws, nuts and bolts, riveting, and welding. Since that time, industrial designers and engineers have increasingly integrated Loctite products into thousands of production lines to assemble parts more quickly and efficiently. Products assembled with adhesives are lighter, safer, more reliable, and less costly. Maintenance workers also use Loctite products to prevent mechanical parts from loosening, leaking, and wearing. Loctite adhesives and sealants ensure dependability and longer machine life.

Some specific Loctite industrial products and their uses include:

- *Threadlocker adhesives*: to prevent nuts, bolts, and screws from loosening because of shock and vibration.
- *Pipe sealants*: to prevent leakage due to vibration, extreme temperatures, or pressure.
- *Engineering adhesives*: for assembly operations that require strong, durable adhesives that cure quickly at room temperature.
- *Maintenance products*: to maintain, repair, and overhaul machinery and equipment.

Today, adhesives are used to bond many products, including automobiles and airplanes. The Porsche 928, one of the world's fastest production autos, contains seven different Loctite adhesives and sealants with 24 different applications in 90 places. Lockheed now assembles and fastens airplane frames and skin parts using only adhesives, and the revolutionary Lear business jet is also held together by adhesives.

Loctite is the world's major manufacturer of anaerobic and cyanocrylate adhesives and sealants, with annual sales of more than $450 million and a recent growth rate of 18 percent. Its great success can be attributed in part to its sales and distribution network. Loctite management realizes the importance of using the right product for the right application. Well-trained Loctite technical service personnel serve as customer problem solvers. Sixty percent of sales are made through independent distributors, and the remaining 40 percent are made directly to end users. In order to provide technical support for the use of its products, the company maintains close and continued contact with both its distributors and major end users.

Recently, marketing executives at Loctite met to discuss a problem product called RC601—an engineering adhesive. Because the product has shown little or no profit during the past several years, the company performed some marketing research on RC601, hoping to find new uses and new target markets for the product.

The traditional target market for RC601 has been design engineers. RC601 is a thin, liquid-retaining compound supplied in a red bottle. It fills small voids that remain when parts are bonded with cylindrical fasteners (such as bolts). Design engineers typically specify the

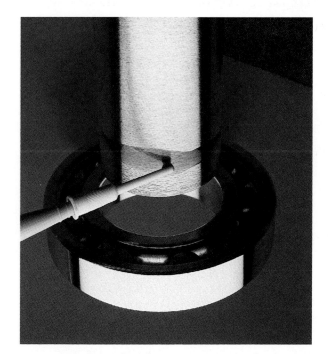

usc of RC601 in the production proccss to allow relaxation of machining tolerance for easier assembly and lower machining costs. In this way, RC601 compensates for the inexact fit of many parts used in numerous production processes.

Inclusion of a particular adhesive in the design of a product is typically a complex decision. Although design engineers actually make the buying decision, other individuals on the new-product development team may be involved—and agreement is often not easy. For example, purchasing agents are concerned with economy, engineers with performance, and production managers with prompt delivery. Furthermore, such factors as the complexity of the production process and the long-term commitment made by specifying the adhesive in a production plan motivate decision makers to evaluate alternatives carefully.

Because design engineers are reluctant to consider new or different products, a sales representative's primary task in selling RC601 is to persuade them to buy the product for the first time. After RC601 is specified in the design of a product and the initial sale is made, almost all product requirements are bought through local distributors. Loctite uses "Product Information Data" sheets as its primary promotion tool in marketing RC601.

Sales and profits of RC601 fell when Loctite introduced newer products (RC609, RC620, and RC680) that appealed more to its target market. The new products have a tolerance to higher temperatures (up to 450 degrees Fahrenheit in some cases).

Marketing research showed that plant maintenance workers need a product that can keep machines with broken parts running until replacement parts arrive. To meet this need, Loctite reformulated RC601 into a gel that can be applied between machinery parts to temporarily repair worn areas and restore correct fits. The new gel has clear advantages in this application. Most importantly, RC601 gets equipment ready to run in one hour—compared with twelve hours for the most commonly used alternative method. A maintenance worker can quickly repair a worn part with the gel and continue operation until a new part can be installed. The product can thus save users as much as $4,000 in time and labor. Because the savings are so great, customers are not price sensitive. Buyers in this situation are more concerned with availability and performance. It is not unusual for maintenance workers to request a particular product by its brand name.

Loctite marketing executives are now trying to develop a marketing mix for the changed product (a gel-like reformulation of RC601) to serve the new target market (maintenance workers). They recognize that the new RC601 will probably need a new name, package, and promotion effort.

QUESTIONS

1. Describe the decision-making process of design engineers and maintenance workers for Loctite products. Be sure to consider the type of buying situation facing each (straight rebuy, modified rebuy, or new task), the stages of the buying process, and the members of the organization who participate in the purchase-decision process.

2. What marketing mix would you recommend to Loctite executives for the new market segment? Your recommendation should include a name for the product, packaging ideas, pricing strategy, and promotional suggestions.

QUALITY CROUTONS

Ray Kroc, the founder of McDonald's, as we know it, believed in sharing his good fortune—not only with his employees, stockholders, and store owners, but also with his suppliers. As McDonald's grew, so too did the company's need for organizations to supply it with food, paper products, and equipment.

It might have been natural for McDonald's to acquire control of their various suppliers to ensure consistency and dependability. As McDonald's expanded horizontally, they could have grown vertically as well. But Ray Kroc did not want it that way. Instead, he chose to use outside suppliers of the needed products and services. McDonald's requires some products to be made to their specifications, but other items they purchase are the same as those available in a local supermarket.

Many of McDonald's suppliers are nationally known companies such as Tyson, Kraft, Hunt's, Gortons, Coca-Cola, Sara Lee, Vlasic, and McCormick. Others are very small operations whose major business—and in some cases, survival—is dependent upon McDonald's. One such firm is Quality Croutons, based in Chicago, Illinois. Quality Croutons supplies approximately 80 percent of the croutons used in McDonald's salads.

George Johnson and David Moore were contacted by the Business Development Group of McDonald's to set up the business. McDonald's was interested in having a minority-owned company supply their croutons. Backed by McDonald's, Johnson and Moore had little trouble arranging the needed financing to start the company, even though neither man had any expertise in the baking business. Although McDonald's is still the company's major customer, Quality Croutons has supplied a variety of other firms since their organization in 1986.

Interestingly, many suppliers conduct business with McDonald's on nothing more than a handshake. Suppliers' products are monitored for consistency through periodic inspection, and if the desired quality is lacking, the agreement can be terminated. But if quality is maintained, so is the relationship. The fact that agreements aren't termi-

nated very often is a testament not only to the careful selection of suppliers by McDonald's but also to their genuine desire to have relationships succeed. If, for example, a supplier is experiencing difficulty providing McDonald's with the proper volume of a high-quality product, McDonald's management will work with the supplier to correct the problem rather than simply drop them.

Obviously the choice of a particular supplier is most critical. Supplier selection involves the senior vice president/chief purchasing officer, the director of purchasing, and other members of management, including representatives from research and development and the business development group. Occasionally, McDonald's chooses suppliers who have sought out a business relationship with them; at other times, McDonald's seeks out existing companies that are in a position to become suppliers. If a suitable existing firm cannot be found, McDonald's will help entrepreneurs establish a business, as they did with Quality Croutons, to provide them with their needed products and services.

Quality Croutons is typical of McDonald's commitment to the minority community. Not only are many of the suppliers and restaurants minority owned or managed, but McDonald's is the nation's largest employer of minority youth. They have also instituted several ethnic programs such as the McDonald's Hispanic Heritage Art Contest, Black History Month, and the McDonald's Hispanic Congressional Internship Program as part of their commitment to society.

QUESTIONS

1. Explain the concept of derived demand as it applies to Quality Croutons and McDonald's.
2. Explain the concept of inelastic demand as it applies to McDonald's buying of croutons.
3. Discuss the buying relationship between McDonald's Corporation and their supplier, Quality Croutons.

Sources: John B. Clark, *Marketing Today, Successes Failures And Turnarounds,* 2nd ed. (Englewood Cliffs, NJ: Prentice Hall, 1991).

CINEPLEX ODEON: BACK TO THE FUTURE

Until very recently, the movie theater industry, run by a collection of aging entrepreneurs and a few powerful public companies, has been fighting for its survival. Competition from videocassettes and cable TV caused a drastic drop in attendance during the 1970s, and movie exhibitors had for decades let their theaters decay. In a typical theater of the 1970s, the lobby carpet, blackened and musty, gave way to the concession stand, hawking watered-down Coke and $1.25 ''buckets'' of popcorn (the small size) covered by an anonymous oily yellow fluid. Inside the movie theater, floors covered with some mysterious glop stuck to your shoes like flypaper.

Musty-smelling seats with sagging springs made you wonder what the place would really look like if the lights were not so dim. Top it off with poor quality projection, and it's no wonder that the industry had fallen on hard times.

The industry's condition in the late 1970s could be explained in part by its fragmentation. The industry was characterized by dozens of regional mom and pop operations. Many theater operators had bought into the business at dirt-cheap prices after 1948—the year an antitrust suit forced the major Hollywood studios to sell their theaters. The new owners got great deals, but as the profits rolled in, many lost touch with their customers and let theaters deteriorate. Moreover, their share of film revenue dropped as network television, cable, and home video ate into profits.

Then, during the late 1970s and early 1980s, many theater owners reacted to appalling industry conditions by converting handsome old movie palaces into tiny ''tenement'' cinemas. To bring theaters into growing suburban neighborhoods, others built ''plexes'' adjacent to malls— new multiscreen theaters that were bigger and more efficient. Although such locations and facilities did save the movie theater industry, they usually lacked pizzazz—most mall complexes have no more charm than a hospital clinic. In these theaters, going to the movies offers little beyond just catching the latest flick. Gone is the moviegoing *experience* that was once a significant part of the attraction— the escape from harsh reality that began when the customer passed through the theater door.

In addition, many theater owners, needing to refurbish, rebuild, and restore their properties, developed multiscreen theaters, creating those cramped screening rooms that moviegoers loathe. But this concept gave owners more flexibility in allocating seats to different screens—moving hits to larger capacity rooms and letting duds pay their way in small ones. Unfortunately, this trend spurred a construction craze among movie operators, and the addition of so many screens created overcapacity. With a shrinking number of moviegoers, the construction boom simply added to the industry's woes.

Since 1979, however, the industry has stabilized. Thanks to such large and aggressive chains as General Cinema, United Artists, and Cineplex Odeon, theater patronage has remained remarkably steady and the number of movie screens has increased each year. Box-office performance still accounts for 60 percent of a film's gross revenues, and success in the television and video-rental markets depends largely on a respectable movie theater run.

In meeting the changing demands of moviegoers, Cineplex Odeon has been the most innovative chain. Its plush theaters feature art-filled lobbies, cafés, and popcorn drenched in real butter—with a price to match. Although many people maintain that showing the right movie is enough to draw patrons, Cineplex Odeon operates under a different philosophy: Moviegoers, like restaurant patrons and department store shoppers, want to be entertained by the *environment* as much as by the *goods*. With such technologies as wide-screen 70-millimeter projection and wraparound Dolby sound, theaters can create a sense of spectacle that no TV set can match.

Garth Drabinsky, a 40-year-old Canadian entertainment lawyer, started the movie chain in 1979. As chairman, president, and chief executive officer, he is the driving force behind Cineplex Odeon—a one-man marching band. His vision is to upgrade moviegoing as much as possible— and then ask customers to pay for it. Customers pay for tuxedo-clad attendants, upscale snacks, and a crisp sound system—all included in the price of their tickets. Drabinsky was thus the man who brought the $7 movie ticket to New York City—a move that aroused both the public and state officials. To encourage exhibitors to keep their prices down, the State Assembly even considered passing a law requiring theater owners to print admission prices in newspaper ads. Drabinsky was unmoved. He believes that the only alternative to the $7 price tag is run-down unkempt theaters and that's not what Cineplex Odeon is about—the desired image is that of a class act. Drabinsky builds the ''Taj Mahals'' of the movie-exhibition business. His theaters are clean, comfortable, and in prime locations.

Rather than appealing to the 18-to-23-year-old ''youth market''—the most active moviegoing population—Cineplex Odeon went with a vengeance after the older, upscale, sophisticated baby-boomer market. When Drabinsky entered the movie business, most theaters had

only one or two screens per location. By contrast, Cineplex clustered as many as 18 small-screen, limited-capacity theaters into single complexes that offered moviegoers a wide variety of films under one roof.

In 1983, Cineplex began re-creating classic movie houses. Cineplex theaters in Clearwater, Florida, Waco, Texas, and Thornhill, Ontario, now resemble the grand old movie palaces of the 1920s and 1930s with contemporary frills added.

Imagine, for example, entering the Cineplex Odeon theater in Toronto's Canada Square office complex. The spacious, circular art-deco lobby boasts a polished granite floor and recessed lighting. A thin band of neon highlights the ceiling dome. Attractive singles and couples sit reading newspapers, sipping espresso, and munching croissant sandwiches and fresh pastries at a charming café with marble tables, dapper red chairs, and thick carpets. Beyond the café is a choice of eight first-run films shown in plush auditoriums. Thus, Cineplex is determined to revive the anticipation, excitement, and fantasy of the great escape that is the essence of the movies.

The Toronto-based company, now the second-largest exhibitor of films in North America, operates more than 500 theaters in 13 of the top 17 markets in the United States and Canada. Its number of "screens" has swollen to more than 1,700; revenues quintupled in five years and profits doubled in one year. Hundreds of additional screens were planned for 1990. Cineplex's success has also forced competitors to raise their standards, resulting in the complete overhaul of an industry that had been allowed to decay.

Cineplex Odeon and other operators have had an enormous impact on the industry. Nineteen eighty-seven saw a post-World War II record year for box-office receipts. Admission revenues were up 12 percent, and attendance was up 6 percent. Of greatest interest is the fact that attendance by the over-40 age group has begun to increase. These results prove that, if they are well treated at their favorite motion picture houses, people can be induced to leave their homes and television sets.

Now pursuing his latest dream, Drabinsky is moving into film and TV production and distribution—he is even running a theme park. Since 1987, Cineplex Odeon has distributed such films as Prince's *Sign o' the Times* and Paul Newman's *The Glass Menagerie*. Its TV production unit made 41 episodes of *Alfred Hitchcock Presents*. The company invested $85 million in the Universal Studio theme park that it is developing jointly with MCA (which owns 49 percent of Cineplex Odeon) near Orlando, Florida. Cineplex Odeon also operates the largest film-processing lab outside of Hollywood.

Thus, entering the decade of the 1990s, the Cineplex Odeon story is still being written. See you at the movies.

QUESTIONS

1. What factors influence a consumer's decision to go to the movies?
2. Describe the buyer-decision process for going to the movies. How does that decision differ from the decision to stay home and watch cable television or rent a video?
3. Consider both demographic trends in the United States and the many factors that influence a consumer's decision to go to the movies. What suggestions would you make to Cineplex Odeon and other theater operators in designing future marketing strategies?

8

Measuring and Forecasting Demand

Qantas, Australia's government-owned international airline is experiencing a demand bonanza. Its market area in the Pacific Basin contains some of the fastest-growing economies in the world, including Japan, Australia, and the four newly industrialized countries of Hong Kong, Singapore, South Korea, and Taiwan. Thus, the area's growth rate for air travel far exceeds world averages. Industry forecasts suggest that Pacific Basin air travel will grow at 10 to 14 percent per year through 1995 and that the area will capture a 40 percent share of all international air passenger traffic by the year 2000.

Such explosive growth presents a huge opportunity for Qantas and the other airlines serving the Pacific Basin. However, it also presents some serious headaches. To take *advantage* of the growing demand, Qantas must first *forecast* it accurately and prepare to *meet* it. Air-travel demand has many dimensions. Qantas must forecast how many and what kinds of people will be traveling, where they will want to go, and when. It must project total demand as well as demand in each specific market it intends to serve. And Qantas must estimate the share of this total demand that it can capture under alternative marketing strategies and in various competitive circumstances. Moreover, it must forecast demand not just for next year, but also for the next two years, five years, and even further into the future.

Forecasting air-travel demand is no easy task. A host of factors affect how much people will travel and where they will go. To make accurate demand forecasts,

Qantas must first anticipate changes in the factors that influence demand—worldwide and country-by-country economic conditions, demographic characteristics, population growth, political developments, technological advances, competitive activity, and many others. Qantas has little control over many of these factors.

Demand can shift quickly and dramatically. For example, relative economic growth and political stability in Japan, Australia, and the other Pacific Basin countries have caused a virtual explosion of demand for air travel there. Ever-increasing numbers of tourists from around the world are visiting these areas. In Australia, for instance, foreign tourism more than doubled between 1984 and 1988, and it is expected to double again by the year 2000. Further, people from the Pacific Basin countries are themselves traveling more. For example, South Korea recently lifted age restrictions on travel, resulting in a 70 percent jump in its outbound passengers. And some 6.8 million Japanese took holidays abroad last year, a 36 percent increase over the previous year. Hong Kong alone experienced a 42 percent increase in Japanese visitors, the equivalent of more than two full Boeing 747s a day. Forecasting demand in the face of such drastic shifts can be difficult.

To make things even more complicated, Qantas must forecast more than just demand. The airline must also anticipate the many factors that can affect its ability to meet that demand. For example, which airport facilities will be available, and how will this affect Qantas? Will enough skilled labor be on hand to staff and maintain its aircraft? In the Pacific Basin, as demand has skyrocketed, the support system has not. A shortage of runways and airport terminal space already limits the number of flights Qantas can schedule, and critical shortages in maintenance and flight crews limit the number of planes the company can operate. As a result, Qantas may decide to purchase fewer, but larger, planes. Fewer planes would require fewer crews. And larger planes can hold more passengers at one time, making infrequent flights more profitable.

Qantas bases many important decisions on its forecasts. Perhaps the most important decision involves aircraft purchases. To meet burgeoning demand, Qantas knows that it will need more planes. But how many more planes? At $44 million for each new Boeing 747, ordering even a few too many planes can be very costly. On the other hand, if Qantas buys too few planes, it has few short-run solutions. Delivery of a new plane takes two years, and almost no second-hand aircraft are available. And because Qantas is already using its fleet to maximum legal capacity, it cannot use its current planes for more flights.

Based on the current optimistic outlook, Qantas plans to increase its number of aircraft by 50 percent during the next four years, at a total investment of $5.4 billion. If it has overestimated demand by even a few percentage points, Qantas will be burdened with costly overcapacity. If it has underestimated demand, it will miss out on profit opportunities and anger customers who are delayed or turned away. For example, in late 1987, Qantas failed to forecast a surprising 40 percent jump in outbound Australian tourism. As a result, newspapers were filled with stories of tourists stranded in Singapore waiting to get flights home and of foreign businesspeople who failed to make important meetings to clinch deals. Qantas lost both sales and goodwill.

But for Qantas, as Australia's flagship airline, the forecasting problem is more than a matter of temporary gains or losses of customer satisfaction and sales—it's a matter of survival. If Qantas cannot meet Australia's travel demands, the government is threatening to take away its primary competitive asset—its license to operate as Australia's sole international carrier. Thus, Qantas has a lot flying on the accuracy of its forecasts.[1]

CHAPTER OBJECTIVES

After reading this chapter, you should be able to:
1. Define a market and identify the important characteristics of people in a market.
2. Discuss the major methods for estimating current market demand.
3. Explain specific techniques that companies use to forecast future demand.

When a company finds an attractive market, it must estimate the market's current size and future potential carefully. The company can lose a lot of profit by overestimating or underestimating the market. This chapter presents the principles and tools for measuring and forecasting market demand. The next chapter looks at the more qualitative aspects of markets and at how companies segment their markets and select the most attractive segments.

Demand can be measured and forecasted on many levels. Figure 8-1 shows *ninety* different types of demand measurement! Demand might be measured for six different

FIGURE 8-1
Ninety types of demand measurement
(6 × 5 × 3)

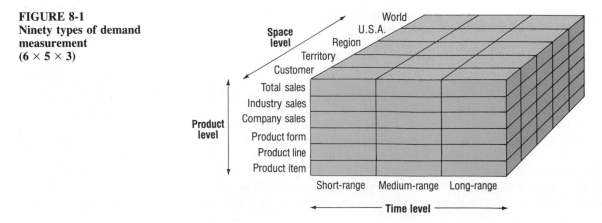

product levels (product item, product line, product form, company sales, industry sales, and total sales), five different *space levels* (customer, territory, region, U.S.A., world), and three different *time levels* (short-range, medium-range, and long-range).

Each type of demand measurement serves a specific purpose. A company might make a short-range forecast of the total demand for a product item to provide a basis for ordering raw materials, planning production, and scheduling short-run financing. Or it might make a long-range forecast of regional demand for its major product line to provide a basis for designing a market expansion strategy.

DEFINING THE MARKET

Market demand measurement calls for a clear understanding of the market involved. The term *market* has acquired many meanings over the years. In its original meaning, a market was a physical place where buyers and sellers gathered to exchange goods and services. Medieval towns had market squares, where sellers brought their goods and buyers shopped for goods. Today's buying and selling occurs all over a city in what are called shopping areas rather than markets.

To an economist, a market describes all the buyers and sellers who transact over some good or service. Thus, the soft drink market consists of sellers such as Coca-Cola, Pepsi-Cola, and Seven-Up, plus all the consumers who buy soft drinks. The economist is interested in the structure, conduct, and performance of each market.

To a marketer, a **market** is the set of all actual and potential buyers of a product. A market is the set of buyers, and an **industry** is the set of sellers. We will adopt this last definition of a market. The size of a market, then, hinges on the number of buyers who might exist for a particular market offer. Those who are in the market for something have three characteristics: *interest*, *income*, and *access*.

Let us apply this to the market for motorcycles. We will leave aside companies that purchase motorcycles and concentrate on the consumer market. Honda, Harley Davidson, and other motorcycle makers must first estimate the number of consumers who have a potential interest in owning a motorcycle. To do this, they could contact a random sample of consumers and ask the following question: "Do you have a strong interest in owning a motorcycle?" If one person out of ten said yes, the makers could assume that 10 percent of the total number of consumers would constitute the potential market for motorcycles. The **potential market** is the set of consumers who profess some level of interest in a particular product or service.

Consumer interest alone is not enough to define the motorcycle market. Potential consumers must have enough income to afford the product. They must be able to answer yes to the following question: "Can you afford to buy a motorcycle?" The higher the price, the fewer the number of people who can answer yes to this question. Thus, market size depends on both interest and income.

Access barriers further reduce motorcycle market size. If motorcycle producers do not distribute their products in certain remote areas because of high shipping costs, potential consumers in those areas are not available as customers. The **available market** is the set of consumers who have interest, income, and access to a particular product or service.

For some market offers, the company might restrict sales to certain groups. A particular state might ban the sale of motorcycles to anyone under 18 years of age. The remaining adults make up the **qualified available market**—the set of consumers who have interest, income, access, and qualifications for the product or service.

The company now has the choice of pursuing the whole qualified available market or concentrating on selected segments. The **served market** (also called the *target market*) is the part of the qualified available market the company decides to pursue. The company, for example, may decide to concentrate its marketing and distribution efforts on the East Coast. The East Coast becomes its served market.

The company and its competitors will end up selling a certain number of motorcycles

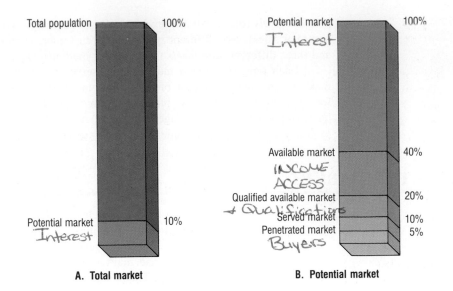

FIGURE 8-2
Levels of market definition

A. Total market

B. Potential market

[handwritten annotations on figure: "Interest" (near Potential market, left bar); "Interest" (near Potential market, right bar top); "INCOME ACCESS" and "+ Qualifications" (near Available market / Qualified available market); "Buyers" (near Penetrated market)]

in its served market. The **penetrated market** is the set of consumers who have already bought motorcycles.

Figure 8-2 brings all these market concepts together with some hypothetical numbers. The bar on the left shows the ratio of the potential market—all interested persons—to the total population. Here, the potential market is 10 percent. The bar on the right shows several breakdowns of the potential market. The available market—those who have interest, income, and access—is 40 percent of the potential market. The qualified available market—those who meet the legal requirements—is 20 percent of the potential market (or 50 percent of the available market). The company concentrates its efforts on 10 percent of the potential market (or 50 percent of the qualified available market). Finally, the company and its competitors have already penetrated 5 percent of the potential market (or 50 percent of the served market).

These definitions of a market are a useful tool for marketing planning. If the company is not satisfied with current sales, it can consider a number of actions. It can try to attract a larger percentage of buyers from its served market. It can lobby for lower qualifications of potential buyers. It can expand to other available markets. It can lower its price to expand the size of the available market. Or it can try to expand the potential market by increasing its advertising to convert noninterested consumers into interested consumers. Honda did this when it ran its successful campaign on the theme "You meet the nicest people on a Honda."

MEASURING CURRENT MARKET DEMAND

We now turn to some practical methods for estimating current market demand. Marketers need to estimate three aspects of current market demand—*total market demand, area market demand,* and *actual sales and market shares.*

Estimating Total Market Demand

The **total market demand** for a product or service is the total volume that would be bought by a defined consumer group in a defined geographic area during a defined time period in a defined marketing environment under a defined level and mix of industry marketing effort.

The most important thing to realize about total market demand is that it is not a fixed number but rather a function of the stated conditions. One of these conditions, for example, is the level and mix of industry marketing effort. Another is the state of the environment. The relationships among total market demand and these conditions is shown in Figure 8-3A. The horizontal axis shows possible levels of industry marketing expenditure during a given time period. The vertical axis shows the resulting demand

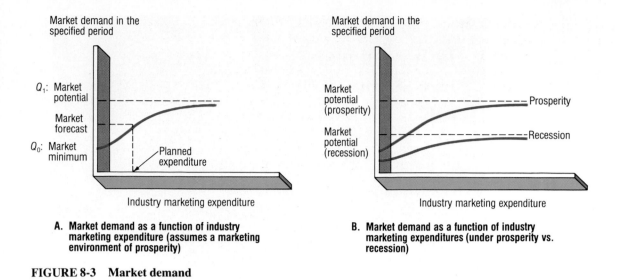

A. **Market demand as a function of industry marketing expenditure (assumes a marketing environment of prosperity)**

B. **Market demand as a function of industry marketing expenditures (under prosperity vs. recession)**

FIGURE 8-3   **Market demand**

level. The curve represents the estimated level of market demand for varying levels of industry marketing expenditure. Some base sales (called the *market minimum*) would take place without any marketing expenditures. Greater marketing expenditures would yield higher levels of demand, first at an increasing rate, and then at a decreasing rate. Marketing expenditures beyond a certain level would not cause much more demand, suggesting an upper limit to market demand called the *market potential*. The industry market forecast shows the level of market demand corresponding to the planned level of industry marketing expenditure in the given environment.

The distance between the market minimum and the market potential shows the overall sensitivity of demand to marketing efforts. We can think of two extreme types of markets, the *expandable* and the *nonexpandable*. The size of an expandable market, such as the market for compact disc players, is strongly affected by the level of industry marketing expenditures. In terms of Figure 8-3A, the distance between Q_0 and Q_1 would be fairly large. The size of a nonexpandable market, such as the market for opera, is not affected to any degree by the level of marketing expenditures; the distance between Q_0 and Q_1 would be fairly small. Organizations selling in a nonexpandable market can take **primary demand**—total demand for all brands of a given product or service—as a given. They concentrate their marketing resources on building **selective demand**, demand for their brand of the product or service.

Given a different marketing environment, we must estimate a new market demand curve. For example, the market for motorcycles is stronger during prosperity than it is during recession. The relationship of market demand to the expenditure is shown in Figure 8-3B. A given level of marketing expenditure will always result in more demand during prosperity than it will during a recession. The point is the marketers should carefully define the situation for which they are estimating market demand.

Companies have developed various practical methods for estimating total market demand. To illustrate one method, suppose that RCA wants to estimate the total annual sales of recorded audiocassette tapes. A common way to estimate total market demand is as follows:

$$Q = n \times q \times p$$

where

Q = total market demand
n = number of buyers in the market
q = quantity purchased by an average buyer per year
p = price of an average unit

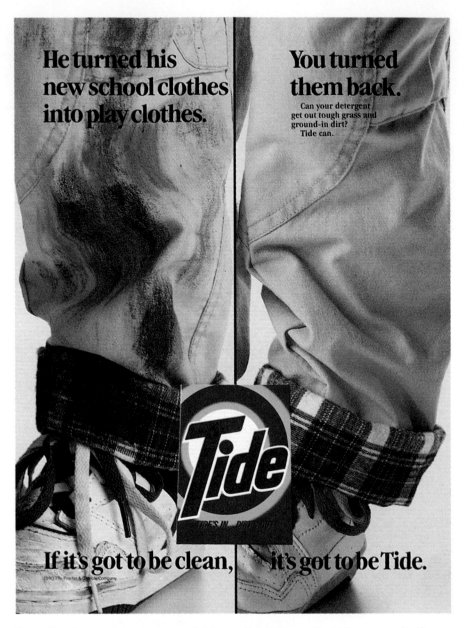

He turned his new school clothes into play clothes.

You turned them back. Can your detergent get out tough grass and ground-in dirt? Tide can.

If it's got to be clean, it's got to be Tide.

Operating in a mature, nonexpandable market, Tide works to increase selective demand: "If it's got to be clean, it's got to be Tide."

Thus, if 100 million people buy cassette tapes each year, and the average buyer buys six tapes per year, and the average price is $10 per tape, then the total market demand for cassette tapes is $6 billion (100,000,000 × 6 × $10).

A variation on the preceding equation is the *chain ratio method*. Using this method, the analyst multiplies a base number by a chain of adjusting percentages. For example, suppose that the U.S. Navy wants to attract 112,000 new male recruits each year from American high schools. The question is whether this is a reasonable target in relation to the market potential. The Navy estimates market potential using the following method:

Total number of male high school graduating students	10,000,000
Percentage who are militarily qualified (no physical, emotional, or mental handicaps)	× .50
Percentage of those qualified who are potentially interested in military service	× .15
Percentage of those qualified and interested in military service who consider the Navy the preferred service	× .30

This chain of numbers shows a market potential of 225,000 recruits. This exceeds the target number of recruits sought, so the U.S. Navy should have little trouble meeting its target if it does a reasonable job of marketing the Navy.[2]

Estimating Area Market Demand

Companies face the problem of selecting the best sales territories and allocating their marketing budget optimally among these territories. To make good selections, they need to estimate the market potential of different territories. Two major methods are available: the *market-buildup method*, used primarily by industrial goods firms, and the *market-factor index method*, used primarily by consumer goods firms.

Market-Buildup Method

The market-buildup method calls for identifying all the potential buyers in each market and estimating their potential purchases. Suppose a manufacturer of mining instruments developed an instrument for assessing the actual proportion of gold content in gold-bearing ores. The portable instrument could be used in the field to assay gold ore. By using it, miners would not waste their time digging deposits of ore containing too little gold to be commercially profitable. The manufacturer wants to price the instrument at $1,000. It sees each mine as buying one or more instruments, depending on the mine's size. The company wants to determine the market potential for this instrument in each mining state and whether to hire a salesperson to cover that state. It would place a salesperson in each state that has a market potential of over $300,000. The company would like to start by finding the market potential in Colorado.

To estimate the market potential in Colorado, the manufacturer can consult the Standard Industrial Classification (SIC) developed by the U.S. Bureau of the Census. The SIC is the government's coding system that classifies industries for purposes of data collection and reporting according to the product produced or operation performed. All industries fall into the ten major divisions shown in column 1 of Table 8-1.[3] Each major industrial group is assigned to a two-digit code. Mining bears the code numbers 10 to 14. Metal mining has the code number 10 (see column 2). Within metal mining are further breakdowns into three-digit SIC numbers (see column 3). The gold and silver ores category has the code number 104. Finally, gold and silver ores are subdivided into further groups, with four-digit code numbers (see column 4). Thus, lode gold has the code number 1042. Our manufacturer is interested in mines that mine lode deposits and placer deposits.

Next, the manufacturer can turn to the Census of Mining to determine the number of gold-mining operations in a state, their locations within the state, the number of

TABLE 8-1
The Standard Industrial Classification (SIC)

(1) MAJOR DIVISIONS IN SIC	(2) GROUP OF INDUSTRIES 2-DIGIT SIC	(3) SUBGROUPS OF INDUSTRIES 3-DIGIT SIC	(4) SPECIFIC INDUSTRIES 4-DIGIT SIC
01–09 Agriculture, forestry, fishing	10 Metal mining	101 Iron ores	
10–14 Mining	11 Anthracite mining	102 Copper ores	
15–19 Contract construction	12 Bituminous coal	103 Lead and zinc ores	
20–39 Manufacturing	13 Crude petroleum and natural gas	104 Gold and silver ores	1042 Lode gold
40–49 Transportation, communications, electric, gas	14 Nonmetallic minerals	105 Bauxite	1043 Placer gold
50–59 Wholesale and retail trade		106 Ferroalloy ores	1044 Silver ores
60–67 Finance, insurance, and real estate		108 Metal mining services	
70–89 Services		109 Miscellaneous metal ores	
90–93 Government			
99 Others			

SIC	(1) NUMBER OF EMPLOYEES	(2) NUMBER OF MINES	(3) POTENTIAL NUMBER OF INSTRUMENT SALES PER EMPLOYEE SIZE CLASS	(4) UNIT MARKET POTENTIAL (2 × 3)	(5) DOLLAR MARKET POTENTIAL (AT $1,000 PER INSTRUMENT)
1042	Under 10	80	1	80	
(lode deposits)	10–50	50	2	100	
	Over 50	20	4	80	
		150		260	$260,000
1043	Under 10	40	1	40	
(placer	10–50	20	2	40	
deposits)	Over 50	10	3	30	
		70		110	110,000
					$370,000

employees, annual sales, and net worth. Using the data on Colorado, the company prepares the market potential estimate shown in Table 8-2. Column 1 classifies mines into three groups based on the number of employees. Column 2 shows the number of mines in each group. Column 3 shows the potential number of instruments that mines in each size class might buy. Column 4 shows the unit market potential (column 2 times column 3). Finally, column 5 shows the dollar market potential, given that each instrument sells for $1,000. Colorado has a dollar market potential of $370,000, and therefore, one salesperson should be hired for Colorado. In the same way, companies in other industries can use the market-buildup method to estimate market potential in specific market areas.

Market-Factor Index Method

Consumer goods companies also have to estimate area market potentials. Consider the following example: A manufacturer of men's dress shirts wishes to evaluate its sales performance relative to market potential in several major market areas, starting with Indianapolis. It estimates total national potential for dress shirts at about $2 billion. The company's current nationwide sales are $140 million, about a 7 percent share of the total potential market. Its sales in the Indianapolis metropolitan area are $1,100,000. It wants to know whether its share of the Indianapolis market is higher or lower than its national 7 percent market share. To find out, the company must first calculate market potential in the Indianapolis area.

A common method of calculating area market potential is to identify market factors that are correlated with potential and combine them into a weighted index. An excellent example of this method is the *buying power index*, which is published each year by *Sales and Marketing Management* magazine in its *Survey of Buying Power*.[4] This survey estimates the buying power for each region, state, and metropolitan area of the nation. The buying power index is based on three factors: the area's share of the nation's *disposable personal income*, *retail sales*, and *population*. The buying power index for a specific area is given by the following formula:

$$B_i = .5y_i + .3r_i + .2p_i$$

where

B_i = percentage of total national buying power in area i
y_1 = percentage of national disposable personal income in area i
r_i = percentage of national retail sales in area i
p_i = percentage of national population in area i

The three coefficients in the formula reflect the relative weights of the three factors.

A NEW TOOL FOR REFINING MARKET DEMAND ESTIMATES
AND CHOOSING THE BEST MARKET TARGETS

In recent years, several new business information services have arisen to help marketing planners link U.S. Census data with life style patterns to better refine their estimates of market potential down to the ZIP code level. Among the leading services are *PRIZM* (by Claritas), *ClusterPlus* (by Donnelley Marketing Information Services), and *Acorn* (C.A.C.I., Inc.). These data services can help marketing planners find the best ZIP code areas in which to concentrate their marketing efforts. We will look at the *PRIZM* system as an example.

Using a host of demographic and socioeconomic factors drawn from the U.S. Census data, the *PRIZM* system has classified every one of the over 500,000 U.S. neighborhood markets into one of forty clusters, such as "blue blood estates," "money and brains," "furs and station wagons," "shotguns and pickups," "tobacco roads," and "grey power." The clusters were formed by manipulating such characteristics as education, income, occupation, family life cycle, housing, ethnicity, urbanization, and others. For example, "blue blood estates" neighborhoods are suburban areas populated mostly by active, college-educated, successful managers and professionals. They include some of America's wealthiest neighborhoods, areas characterized by low household density, highly homogeneous residents, a heavy family orientation, and mostly single-unit housing. On the other hand, the "shotgun and pickups" clusters include the hundreds of small villages and "four-corners" towns that dot America's rural areas. Each of the other 38 clusters has a unique combination of characteristics.

Companies can combine these "geodemographic" *PRIZM* clusters with other data on product and service usage, media usage, and life styles to get a better picture of specific market areas. For example, the "shotguns and pickups" cluster is populated by lower-middle-class, blue-collar consumers who use chain saws and snuff and buy more canning jars, dried soups, and powdered soft drinks. The "Hispanic mix" cluster prefers high-quality dresses, nonfilter cigarettes, and lip gloss. People in this cluster are highly brand conscious, quality conscious, and brand loyal. They have a strong family and home orientation. Such information provides a powerful tool for refining demand estimates, selecting target markets, and shaping promotion messages.

Helene Curtis used *PRIZM* in marketing its Suave shampoo. It found that potential demand is highest in neighborhoods with high concentrations of young working women. These women responded best to advertising messages that Suave is inexpensive, yet will make their hair "look like a million."

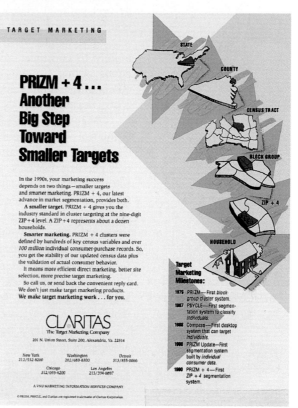

Using services like PRIZM, by Claritas, marketers can refine their estimates of market potential down to the neighborhood level.

An increasing number of manufacturers and retailers are now using geodemographic systems to identify the best clusters and to target their marketing efforts. So are other kinds of organizations. For example, the Seventh Day Adventists recently used clustering techniques to identify the best neighborhoods for recruiting new members.

Sources: "Marketing Firm Slices U.S. into 240,000 Parts to Spur Clients' Sales," *Wall Street Journal*, November 3, 1986, p. 1; Michael J. Weiss, *The Clustering of American* (New York: Harper & Row, 1988); and Leon G. Schiffman and Leslie Lazar Kanuk, *Consumer Behavior*, 4th Ed. (Englewood Cliffs, NJ: Prentice Hall, 1991), Chapter 13.

Using this index, the shirt manufacturer looks up Indianapolis, Indiana, and finds that this market has .4936 percent of the nation's disposable personal income, .5527 percent of the nation's retail sales, and .5015 percent of the nation's population. Thus, it calculates the buying power index for Indianapolis as follows:

$$B = .5(.4936) + .3(.5527) + .2(.5016) = .5129$$

That is, Indianapolis should account for .5129 percent of the nation's total potential demand for dress shirts. Because the total national potential is $2 billion nationally each year, total potential in Indianapolis equals $10,258,000 ($2 billion × .005129). Thus, the company's sales in Indianapolis of $1,100,000 amount to a 10.7 percent share ($1,100,000/$10,258,000) of area market potential. Comparing this with the 7 percent national share, the company appears to be doing better in Indianapolis than it is in other parts of the country.

The weights used in the buying power index are somewhat arbitrary. They apply mainly to consumer goods that are neither low-priced staples nor high-priced luxury goods. Other weights can be used. The manufacturer would also adjust the market potential for additional factors, such as level of competition in the market, local promotion costs, seasonal changes in demand, and unique local market characteristics.

Many companies compute additional area demand measures. Marketers can now refine state-by-state and city-by-city measures down to census tracts or zip code centers. Census tracts are small areas about the size of a neighborhood, and ZIP code centers (designed by the U.S. Postal Service) are larger areas, often the size of small towns. Information on population size, family income, and other characteristics is available for each type of unit. Marketers can use this data for estimating demand in neighborhoods or other smaller geographic units within large cities. Marketing Highlight 8–1 describes some marketing firms that provide ZIP code or census information useful for refining market demand estimates and for improving customer targeting.

Estimating Actual Sales and Market Shares

Besides estimating total and area demand, a company needs to know the actual industry sales taking place in its market. Thus, it must identify its competitors and estimate their sales.

The industry's trade association often collects and publishes total industry sales, although it might not list individual company sales separately. In this way, each company can evaluate its performance against the industry as a whole. Suppose the company's sales are increasing at 5 percent per year and industry sales are increasing at 10 percent. This company is actually losing its relative standing in the industry.

Another way to estimate sales is to buy reports from a marketing research firm that audits total sales and brand sales. For example, Nielsen, IRI, and other marketing research firms use scanner data to audit the retail sales of various product categories in supermarkets and drugstores and then sell this information to interested companies. A company can obtain data on total product category sales as well as on brand sales. It can compare its performance with that of the total industry or any particular competitor to see whether it is gaining or losing in its relative standing.[5]

FORECASTING FUTURE DEMAND

Having looked at ways to estimate current demand, we now examine ways to forecast future market demand. **Forecasting** is the art of estimating future demand by anticipating what buyers are likely to do under a given set of conditions. Very few products or services lend themselves to easy forecasting. Those that do generally involve a product with steady sales or sales growth in a stable, competitive situation. However, most markets do not have stable total and company demand, so good forecasting becomes a key factor in company success. Poor forecasting can lead to overly large inventories, costly price markdowns, or lost sales due to being out of stock. The more unstable the demand, the more the company needs accurate forecasts and elaborate forecasting procedures.

Companies commonly use a three-stage procedure to arrive at a sales forecast. First, they make an *environmental forecast*, followed by an *industry forecast*, finally followed by a *company sales forecast*. The environmental forecast calls for projecting inflation, unemployment, interest rates, consumer spending and saving, business invest-

TABLE 8-3 Some Common Sales Forecasting Techniques	Surveys of buyers' intentions	Time-series analysis
	Composite of salesforce opinions	Leading indicators
	Expert opinion	Statistical demand analysis
	Test market method	

ment, government expenditures, net exports, and other environmental events important to the company. The result is a forecast of gross national product, which is used along with other indicators to forecast industry sales. The company then prepares its sales forecast by assuming that it will win a certain share of industry sales.

Companies use several specific techniques to forecast their sales. Many of these techniques are listed in Table 8-3 and described in the following paragraphs.[6] All forecasts are built on one of three information bases: what people say, what people do, or what people have done. The first basis—*what people say*—involves surveying the opinions of buyers or those close to them, such as salespeople or outside experts. Information is gathered using three methods: surveys of buyer intentions, composites of salesforce opinions, and expert opinion. Building a forecast on *what people do* involves another method, that of putting the product into a test market to assess buyer response. The final basis—*what people have done*—involves analyzing records of past buying behavior or using time-series analysis or statistical demand analysis.

Survey of Buyers' Intentions

One way to forecast what buyers will do is to ask them directly. This suggests that the forecaster should survey buyers. Surveys are especially valuable if the buyers have clearly formed intentions, will carry them out, and can describe them to interviewers.

Several research organizations conduct periodic surveys of consumer buying intentions. These organizations ask questions such as:

Do you intend to buy an automobile within the next six months?										
.00	.10	.20	.30	.40	.50	.60	.70	.80	.90	1.00
No chance		Slight chance		Fair chance		Good chance		Strong chance		For certain

This is called *purchase probability scale*. In addition, the various surveys ask about the consumer's present and future personal finances and expectations about the economy. The various bits of information are combined into a *consumer sentiment measure* (Survey Research Center of the University of Michigan) or a *consumer confidence measure* (Sindlinger and Company). Consumer durable goods companies subscribe to these indexes to help them anticiapte major shifts in consumer buying intentions so that they can adjust their production and marketing plans accordingly.

For *industrial buying*, various agencies carry out intention surveys about plant, equipment, and materials purchases. The two best-known surveys are conducted by the U.S. Department of Commerce and by McGraw-Hill. Most of the estimates have been within 10 percent of the actual outcomes.

Composite of Salesforce Opinions

When buyer interviewing is impractical, the company may base its sales forecasts on information provided by the salesforce. The company typically asks its salespeople to estimate sales, by product, for their individual territories. It then adds up the individual estimates to arrive at an overall sales forecast.

Few companies use their salesforce's estimates without making some adjustments. Salespeople are biased observers. They may be naturally pessimistic or optimistic, or they may go to one extreme or another because of recent sales setbacks or successes. Furthermore, they are often unaware of larger economic developments and do not know how their company's marketing plans will affect future sales in their territories. They may understate demand so that the company will set a low sales quota. They may not have the time to prepare careful estimates or may not consider it worthwhile.

Assuming that these biases can be countered, a number of benefits can be gained by involving the salesforce in forecasting. Salespeople may have better insight into developing trends than does any other group in the company. After participating in the forecasting process, the salespeople may have greater confidence in their quotas and more incentive to achieve them. In addition, "grassroots" forecasting provides estimates broken down by product, territory, customer, and salesperson.[7]

Expert Opinion

Companies can also obtain forecasts by turning to experts. Experts include dealers, distributors, suppliers, marketing consultants, and trade associations. Thus, auto companies survey their dealers periodically for forecasts of short-term demand. Dealer estimates, however, are subject to the same strengths and weaknesses as salesforce estimates.

Many companies buy economic and industry forecasts from well-known firms such as Data Resources, Wharton Econometric, and Chase Econometric. These forecasting specialists are in a better position than the company is to prepare economic forecasts because they have more data available and more forecasting expertise.

Occasionally, companies put together a special group of experts to make a particular kind of forecast. The experts may be asked to exchange views and come up with a group estimate (group discussion method). Or they may be asked to supply their estimates individually, after which the analyst combines them into a single estimate (pooling of individual estimates). Or they may supply individual estimates and assumptions that are reviewed by a company analyst, revised, and followed by further rounds of estimation (Delphi method).[8]

Experts can provide good insights upon which to base forecasts, but they can also be wrong (see Marketing Highlight 8–2). Where possible, the company should back up experts' opinions with estimates obtained using other methods.

Test-Market Method

Where buyers do not plan their purchases carefully or are inconsistent in carrying out their intentions, or where experts are not good guessers, the company may want to conduct a direct test market. A direct test market is especially useful in forecasting sales of a new product or of an established product in a new distribution channel or territory. Test marketing is discussed in Chapter 11.

Companies often forecast sales based on salesforce or expert opinion.

SOMETIMES "EXPERT OPINION" ISN'T ALL IT SHOULD BE

Before you rely too heavily on expert opinion, you might be interested in learning how some past "experts" came out with their predictions:

- "I think there's a world market for about five computers." Thomas J. Watson, IBM Chairman, 1943.
- "With over 50 foreign cars already on sale here, the Japanese auto industry isn't likely to carve out a big slice of the U.S. market for itself." *Business Week*, 1958.
- "TV won't be able to hold on to any market it captures after the first six months. People will soon get tired of staring at a plywood box every night." Daryl F. Zanuck, head of 20th Century Fox, 1946.

- "By 1980, all power (electric, atomic, solar) is likely to be virtually costless." Henry Luce, founder and publisher of *Time*, *Life*, and *Fortune*, 1956.
- "1930 will be a splendid employment year." U.S. Department of Labor, 1929.
- "My imagination refuses to see any sort of submarine doing anything but suffocating its crew and foundering at sea." H. G. Wells, 1902.
- "Airplanes are interesting toys, but of no military value." France's Marshal Foch, 1911.

Source: Adapted from "Sometimes Expert Opinion Isn't All It Should Be," *Go*, September–October 1985, p. 2.

Time-Series Analysis   Many firms base their forecasts on past sales, assuming that the causes of past sales can be uncovered through statistical analysis. The causal relations can then be used to predict future sales. A time series analysis of a product's past sales can be separated into four major components.

The first component, *trend*, is the long-term, underlying pattern of growth or decline in sales resulting from basic changes in population, capital formation, and technology. It is found by fitting a straight or curved line through past sales.

The second component, *cycle*, captures the medium-term, wavelike movement of sales resulting from changes in general economic and competitive activity. The cyclical component can be useful for medium-range forecasting. Cyclical swings, however, are difficult to predict because they do not occur on a regular basis.

The third component, *season*, refers to a consistent pattern of sales movements within the year. The term "season" describes any recurrent hourly, weekly, monthly, or quarterly sales pattern. The seasonal component may be related to weather factors, holidays, and trade customs. The seasonal pattern provides a norm for forecasting short-range sales.

The fourth component, *erratic events*, includes fads, strikes, snowstorms, earthquakes, riots, fires, and other erratic disturbances. These components are by definition unpredictable and should be removed from past data to see the more normal behavior of sales.

Time-series analysis consists of breaking down the original sales into its trend, cycle, season, and erratic components and then recombining these components to produce the sales forecast. For example, suppose an insurance company sold 12,000 new life insurance policies this year. It would like to predict next year's December sales. The long-term trend shows a 5 percent sales growth rate per year. This information alone suggests sales next year of 12,6000 (12,000 × 1.05). However, a business recession is expected next year and will probably result in total sales achieving only 90 percent of the expected trend-adjusted sales. Sales next year will more likely be 11,340 (12,600 × .90). If sales were the same each month, monthly sales would be 945 (11,340/12). However, December is an above-average month for insurance policy sales, with a seasonal index standing at 1.30. Therefore, December sales may be as high as 1,228.5 (945 × 1.3). The company expects no erratic events, such as strikes or new insurance regulations. Thus, it estimates new policy sales next December at 1,228.5 policies.

Leading Indicators   Many companies try to forecast their sales by finding one or more **leading indicators—** other time series that change in the same direction but in advance of company sales.

For example, a plumbing supply company might find that its sales lag the housing starts index by about four months. The housing starts index would then be a useful leading indicator. The National Bureau of Economic Research has identified twelve of the best leading indicators, and their values are published monthly in the *Survey of Current Business.*

Statistical Demand Analysis

Time-series analysis treats past and future sales as a function of time rather than as a function of any real demand factors. But many real factors affect the sales of any product. **Statistical demand analysis** is a set of statistical procedures used to discover the most important real factors affecting sales and their relative influences. The factors most commonly analyzed are prices, income, population, and promotion.

Statistical demand analysis consists of expressing sales (Q) as a dependent variable and trying to explain sales as a function of a number of independent demand variables $X_1, X_2, \ldots, X_n$. That is:

$$Q = f(X_1, X_2, \ldots, X_n)$$

Using a technique called multiple-regression analysis, various equation forms can be statistically fitted to the data in the search for the best predicting factors and equation.[9]

For example, a soft drink company found that the per capita sales of soft drinks by state was well explained by:[10]

$$Q = -145.5 + 6.46X_1 - 2.37X_2$$

where

$$\left(\begin{array}{l} X_1 = \text{mean annual temperature of the state (Fahrenheit)} \\ X_2 = \text{annual per capita income in the state (in hundreds)} \end{array}\right)$$

For example, New Jersey had a mean annual temperature of 54 °F and an annual per capita income of 24 (in hundreds). Using the immediately preceding equation, the company would predict per capita soft drink consumption in New Jersey to be as follows:

$$Q = -145.5 + 6.46(54) - 2.37(24) = 146.6$$

Actual per capita consumption was 143. If the equation predicted this well for other states, it would serve as a useful forecasting tool. Marketing management would predict next year's mean temperature and per capita income for each state and use Equation 8-4 to predict next year's sales.

Statistical demand analysis can be very complex, and the marketer must take care in designing, conducting, and interpreting such analysis. Yet, constantly improving computer technology has made statistical demand analysis an increasingly popular approach to forecasting.

■ SUMMARY

To carry out their responsibilities, marketing managers need measures of current and future market size. We define a market as the set of actual and potential consumers of a market offer. Consumers in the market have interest, income, and access to the market offer. The marketer has to distinguish various levels of the market, such as the potential market, available market, qualified available market, served market, and penetrated market.

One task is to estimate current demand. Marketers can estimate total demand through the chain ratio method, which involves multiplying a base number by successive percentages. Area market demand can be estimated by the market-buildup method or the market-factor index method. Estimating actual industry sales requires identifying competitors and using some method of estimating the sales of each. Finally, companies estimate the market shares of competitors to judge their own relative performance.

For estimating future demand, the company can use one or a combination of seven possible forecasting methods, based on what consumers say (buyers' intentions surveys, composite of salesforce opinions, expert opinion), what consumers do (market tests), or what consumers have done (time-series analysis, leading indicators, and statistical demand analysis). Choosing the best method depends on the purpose of the forecast, the type of product, and the availability and reliability of data.

QUESTIONS FOR DISCUSSION

1. In market measurement and forecasting, what is the more serious problem, to *overestimate* demand or to *underestimate* it?

2. Retailers depend upon the Christmas season for as much as 40% of annual sales. Many analysts forecast the strength of the Christmas retailing season by projecting from the sales level on a *single day*, the Friday after Thanksgiving. What are the issues in using such a forecast? Is it difficult to forecast such highly seasonal demand?

3. Big Brothers and Big Sisters of America is a nonprofit organization with affiliates across the country that help children from single-parent households form long-term relationships with adult volunteers. Describe the potential market, the available market, and the qualified available market for Big Brothers-Big Sisters and its affiliates.

4. List some expandable and nonexpandable markets. Can you think of any markets that have expanded even though they were once considered nonexpandable? What caused the unexpected expansion?

5. Many long-term trends occur because of changes in technology or the environment. What effect have automobile catalytic converters had on the market for leaded and unleaded gasoline? How have higher gasoline prices affected spark plug manufacturers? Were these changes predictable?

6. People are generally less responsive to marketing efforts during a recession than when the economy is booming. Does this imply that marketers should cut back on advertising and other marketing efforts during recessions?

7. Hess's, a chain of department stores, is looking for desirable locations for new stores. Which aspect of market demand would Hess's be interested in measuring—and what measuring methods would they use—in choosing where to locate new stores? What census tract or zip-code information would be relevant?

8. Sales of Izod-Lacoste clothing with the crocodile emblem grew from $15 million in 1969 to $450 million in 1981, but declined so rapidly from their peak that by 1985 parent company General Mills was seeking buyers for the Izod division. How could accurate forecasts of sales be made throughout this period?

9. Assume that you are forecasting the demand for new Kinder Care Learning Centers, which are franchised day care centers for children. What will you predict if you know the birthrate is expected to decline in the 1990's? Will your prediction change if you learn that an increasing number of women with small children are working? How many factors should you consider in making your forecast?

10. As marketing manager for Cat's Pride cat litter, you have seen sales jump 50 percent in the past year, after years of relatively stable sales. How will you forecast sales for the coming year?

11. Identify the trend, cycle, seasonal and erratic components of alcoholic beverage sales. Are these components the same for beer, wine, and distilled spirits? How does your time-series analysis help you predict future sales of alcoholic beverages?

12. What leading indicators might help you predict sales of diapers? Cars? Hamburgers? Can you describe a general procedure for finding leading indicators of product sales?

KEY TERMS

Available market. The set of consumers who have interest, income, and access to a particular product or service.

Forecasting. The art of estimating future demand by anticipating what buyers are likely to do under a given set of conditions.

Industry. The set of all sellers of a product.

Leading indicators. Time series that change in the same direction but in advance of company sales.

Market. The set of all actual and potential buyers of a product.

Penetrated market. The set of consumers who have already bought a particular product or service.

Potential market. The set of consumers who profess some level of interest in a particular product or service.

Primary demand. The level of total demand for all brands of a given product or service—for example, the total demand for motorcycles.

Qualified available market. The set of consumers who have interest, income, access, and qualifications for a particular product or service.

Selective demand. The demand for a given brand of a product or service—for example, the demand for a Honda motorcycle.

Served market (or *target market*). The part of the qualified available market the company decides to pursue.

Statistical demand analysis. A set of statistical procedures used to discover the most important real factors affecting sales and their relative influence; the most commonly analyzed factors are prices, income, population, and promotion.

Time-series analysis. Breaking down past sales of a product or service into its trend, cycle, season, and erratic components, and then recombining these components to produce a sales forecast.

Total market demand. The total volume of a product or service that would be bought by a defined consumer group in a defined geographic area during a defined time period in a defined marketing environment under a defined level and mix of industry marketing effort.

REFERENCES

1. See Hamish McDonald, "Caught on the Hop," *Far Eastern Economic Review*, February 18, 1988, pp. 72–73; "Qantas Embarks on Major Fleet Expansion Plan," *Aviation Week & Space Technology*, June 20, 1988, pp. 39, 42–43; Michael Westlake, "Stand-By Room Only," *Far Eastern Economic Review*, June 2, 1988, pp. 72–75; and Paul Proctor, "Pacific Rim Carriers Struggle to Cope with Impending Traffic Boom," *Aviation Week & Space Technology*, November 20, 1989, pp. 110–111.

2. For more on forecasting total market demand, see F. William

Barnett, "Four Steps to Forecast Total Market Demand," *Harvard Business Review*, July–August 1988, pp. 28–34.

3. For some recent changes within these SIC groups, see Richard Kern, "SIC System on the Mend," *Sales & Marketing Management*, May 1986, p. 20.

4. For more on using this survey, see "A User's Guide to the Survey of Buying Power," *Sales and Marketing Management*, August 7, 1989, pp. A6–A20.

5. For a more comprehensive discussion of measuring market demand, see Philip Kotler, *Marketing Management: Analysis, Planning, Implementation, and Control*, 7th Ed. (Englewood Cliffs, NJ: Prentice Hall, 1991), Chapter 9.

6. For a listing and analysis of these and other forecasting techniques, see David M. Georgoff and Robert G. Murdick, "Manager's Guide to Forecasting," *Harvard Business Review*, January–February 1986, pp. 110–120; and Donald

S. Tull and Del I. Hawkins, *Marketing Research: Measurement and Method*, 4th Ed. (New York: Macmillan, 1987), Chapter 15.

7. For more on the salesforce composite method, see Tull and Hawkins, *Marketing Research: Measurement and Method*, pp. 576–78.

8. See Kip D. Cassino, "Delphi Method: A Practical 'Crystal Ball' for Researchers," *Marketing News*, January 6, 1984, Section 2, pp. 10–11.

9. See Tull and Hawkins, *Marketing Research: Measurement and Method*, pp. 603–606.

10. See "The Du Pont Company," in *Marketing Research: Text and Cases*, 3rd Ed., Harper W. Boyd, Jr., Ralph Westfall, and Stanley Stasch, eds. (Homewood, IL: Irwin, 1977), pp. 498–500.

GENENTECH: FORECASTING EUPHORIA

A year ago, Genentech toasted the regulatory approval of its heart drug TPA with champagne under circus tents, fireworks that closed the local airport, and rock 'n' roll by its biotech band, the Rolling Clones. Today, however, the company's supporters have lost their euphoria. Genentech is a victim of its own success—real success, that is—but success that paled when measured against the fantasy of success that had earlier excited investors, Wall Street, and Genentech itself.

Genentech was founded in 1976 by a biologist and an MBA who had only $500 between them. They dreamed of becoming the first company to prove the potential of reproducing human proteins through biotechnology. Biotechnology companies develop biologically based drugs, as opposed to chemically based drugs, because they believe that these drugs are as effective as chemically based drugs but without the side effects. Genentech had become the first company to commercialize such drugs, and sales grew rapidly (see Table 1 for a sales history). By 1987, it had three products on the market: Humulin, a human insulin; Roferon, an alpha interferon used to treat a variety of leukemia; and Protropin, a human growth hormone.

TABLE 1   Genentech, Inc., Sales and Income

YEAR	SALES (millions)	NET INCOME (millions)	EARNINGS (per share)
1983	$ 42.4	$ 1.1	$.03
1984	65.6	2.7	.05
1985	81.6	5.6	.09
1986	127.3	12.8	.18
1987	218.7	42.2	.50
1988 (est)	380.0	90.0	.50

Source: Copyright © 1990, Value Line Publishing, Inc.; used by permission.

Genentech markets its latest drug, a new thrombolytic drug called TPA, under the name Activase. Heart specialists administer single doses of thrombolytic drugs to patients as soon as possible after a heart attack. These drugs dissolve potentially deadly blood clots often associated with heart attacks. The body produces TPA naturally, but in very small amounts. Before recent advances, scientists had not developed a method to genetically copy the natural TPA substance and to produce enough of it to meet the needs of heart-attack patients.

After spending $200 million over five years to develop TPA, Genentech launched the product in the atmosphere of a crusade against unbelievers in the Food and Drug Administration (FDA) and the medical community. Because a major study, announced in March 1985, indicated that TPA significantly outperformed its predecessor in dissolving deadly blood clots, Genentech management adopted the view that it would be "unethical" for a doctor *not* to use the drug to treat heart attacks. Enthusiastic Wall Street analysts uncritically embraced this view—some even went so far as to predict malpractice suits against doctors who failed to use TPA. Despite this enthusiasm, the FDA refused to approve the drug in May 1987, citing a lack of evidence supporting TPA's effectiveness. However, Genentech submitted further studies confirming that TPA dissolved clots, improved overall heart pumping action, and extended lives. Thus, in November 1987, the FDA approved TPA for sale in the U.S. Within fifteen days, Genentech held a nationwide teleconference to inform 12,000 physicians, hospital pharmacists, and nurses about TPA.

Genentech forecast that it would sell $180 million worth of TPA in 1988 at $2,200 per dose, a price more than 10 times that of rival streptokinase made by Hoechst AG. Analysts, however, began forecasting 1988 sales at $400 million. The firm's stock price soared, rising 47 percent in only two weeks. Despite their own more modest forecasts, the people at Genentech did not argue with the analysts' highly optimistic projections. In fact, Genentech employees *joined* the excitement and invested heavily in the dream. One Genentech chemist recalls, "When the stock was leaping up, it was distracting. People were infatuated. People would ask, 'What's the price this hour?' "

At the end of TPA's first year, Genentech held a 65 percent share of the market for thrombolytic drugs, compared with competitor's streptokinase at 30 percent and urokinase at 5 percent. However, Genentech has captured a large part of a disappointingly small market. Several factors have contributed to this unexpectedly low market growth. Distributors sell 90 percent of TPA to hospitals, which hold it in their pharmacies for use by physicians. Although most hospitals stock TPA, doctors prescribe clot-dissolving drugs for only 120,000 out of the 400,000 patients medically eligible to receive them. Genentech feels that this reluctance is costing lives. Further, hospital pharmacies, under rigid cost controls from Medicare and insurance companies, cannot afford to give up streptokinase, which sells for about $200 per dose. Kirk Raab, president of Genentech, insists that TPA's high price is not to blame, but the market seems to indicate otherwise. Finally, doctors hesitate to use any new product, especially one carrying a small but measurable risk of undesirable side effects. Thus, Genentech appears to have underestimated the complexity of the medical marketplace, its cost regulations, and its innate conservatism. As the president of another biotech firm notes, "It was much too complex [a medical issue] to assume it was going to be zip-dee-do."

If these problems weren't enough, the results emerging from several recent studies show only a modest advantage for TPA—not the huge advantage predicted earlier. For example, in one major study, TPA reduced deaths 27 percent compared with a control group; in another test, streptokinase reduced deaths 21 percent. Another study found that TPA reduced deaths 51 percent in the first two weeks after a heart attack, against 47 percent for Eminase (a streptokinase product made by Beecham) after 30 days. Thus, doctors have been seeing confusing data, and Genentech's marketing team and 194-person salesforce have had a hard sell.

Market confusion will remain until researchers publish the first true head-to-head comparisons of the life-saving abilities of TPA and streptokinase. By the time such comparisons become available, Beecham's Eminase, the next serious contender for TPA's market share, may be on the U.S. market. Still, Mr Raab remains confident. "Eminase is the only product we see on the horizon. And it's a form of streptokinase," he says. "We don't want to underestimate it, but we think TPA is superior." However, some observers believe that Eminase is easier to administer and has fewer side effects. Further, Beecham may price Eminase as much as $500 less than TPA.

Thus, although TPA's first-year sales reached an estimated $180 million, making it the top-selling first-year drug product in history, many analysts saw its performance as disappointing. Genentech's stock fell to one-third its previous levels, leaving many stockholders and employees disgruntled. "To say we oversold is unfair," says Mr. Raab. But he concedes, "We were optimistic as to how fast it would happen. And we undercalled the reluctance of physicians to use a revolutionary therapy."

Genentech now faces the challenge of shifting its marketing strategy and tightening its belt. Some analysts wonder how much profit Genentech can squeeze from TPA before a new generation of drugs enters the fray. Adds a Genentech scientist who saw the value of his stock options plunge, "The transition from dreams to reality is a hard one. The TPA launch was badly handled in that it has made a big success look like something between a disappointment and a failure."

QUESTIONS

1. In what market does Genentech sell TPA? How big are the *potential* market and the *penetrated* market for TPA? Why are the sizes of these two markets so different?

2. Given that a patient receives only one dose of TPA, immediately after a heart attack, what market share would Genentech have needed in order to reach the forecasted $400 million in sales?

3. Given that TPA was a new product in a relatively new market, how might management have attacked the problem of forecasting first-year sales?

4. What marketing mistakes do you think Genentach made?

5. Given Genentech's current position, what marketing strategy changes would you make?

Source: Adapted from M. Chase, "Genentech, Battered by Great Expectations, Is Tightening Its Belt," *The Wall Street Journal*, October 11, 1988.

FORECASTING

The 1974 energy crisis changed American automobile buying behavior and the demand for American automobiles. As lines at gas pumps lengthened and prices rose, fuel efficiency became an increasingly important economic consideration in the purchase of a new car. Unfortunately for American car companies, this newfound desire for fuel economy eliminated many gas-guzzling domestic models from consumers' decision sets; they were replaced by Japanese cars, which had higher fuel efficiency and lower prices.

At the same time, concern over excessive dependence on foreign oil prompted the federal government to pass the corporate average fuel economy (CAFE) law in 1975, giving the Environmental Protection Agency the power to set standard miles-per-gallon ratings that applied to fleet sales of auto manufacturers. By 1978, each fleet had to meet an 18-mpg standard; by 1982, a 24-mpg standard; and by 1985, a 27.5-mpg standard. In Detroit, research on fuel efficiency revved up, and by 1983, Ford and GM had raised their average fuel ratings to 24 mpg, while Chrysler had increased its rating to 27 mpg. By the mid-1980s, the American automakers were catching up with the Europeans and Japanese in providing fuel-efficient autos.

Ironically, after all this effort, demand began to shift back to larger, more luxurious, and expensive cars in the mid-1980s. What had happened to buyers' desire for fuel efficiency? For many Americans, the painful experiences of 1974 were distant memories that had lost their impact. Consumers had adjusted to higher gas prices. In addition, the fuel efficiency of all autos had risen, so a 1980s large car was relatively more economical and fuel-efficient than a 1970s large car had been.

In the meantime, Japanese auto companies, attracted by the higher profit margins on bigger cars, began to produce and promote larger vehicles. As buyers purchased more large cars, this created a problem for domestic producers. They could not meet the CAFE fleet standards because sales of their large cars greatly exceeded sales of their small cars. To increase sales of small cars in order to reduce their fleet mpg, they reduced the price of small cars—in some cases, below cost. Consequently, American car companies were trying to sell small cars in a large-car market—just the reverse of their marketing program of the mid-1970s, when they were pushing large cars in a small-car market.

The energy crisis and its aftermath illustrate the problems of forecasting when sudden shifts in consumer demand occur in an industry with long production lead times and long design cycles. If automotive product offerings are off-cycle with demand, lead times of three to five years render manufacturers unable to defend their market shares by responding to demand changes. To forecast demand, one must correctly anticipate future trends in consumer demand, competitors' actions, and the market environment. Because American companies in the 1970s expected demand for larger autos to continue well into the future, they had neither the designs nor the facilities to quickly shift to production of smaller vehicles when demand changed.

How will consumer demand, competition, and environmental forces affect the demand for autos in the future?

Ecological concerns will encourage governments to push for greater fuel efficiency because of diminishing fuel reserves, and for higher clean air standards because of the "greenhouse effect." To produce greater fuel efficiency, industry is researching alternative engines such as the two-stroke and the gas-turbine engine. To meet clean air standards, it is experimenting with cleaner fuels such as methanol and ethanol. Although this research aims at increasing fuel efficiency, consumer demand for larger autos could result in reduced average fuel efficiency ratings. Thus, in order to produce larger, more fuel-efficient cars, automakers are experimenting with new, lighter-body materials such as polymer-based composites.

But all this research will cost billions of dollars. In Europe and Japan, governmental agencies are willing to underwrite some of this expense, but to date the U.S. government has not shown a similar willingness. So, to recoup their investment, American producers will have to raise prices, which may make it extremely difficult for them to compete with foreign producers.

But in light of the recent threat to oil supplies in the Persian Gulf, there is some hope that the U.S. government will change its stance and decide to underwrite the cost of research. Given the huge runup of oil and gasoline prices due to the war threat in the Gulf in 1990, it is also possible that American consumers will decide to purchase small cars . . . or even to make greater use of mass transit—who knows? At least automakers can console themselves that increased computerization enables them to test new automotive designs and production practices and respond to the market more quickly than they could in the past.

QUESTIONS

1. Suppose that you work for an auto dealer in a city of 150,000 people and wish to forecast demand for automobiles in your town for the next five years. What forecasting techniques would you use?

2. Now suppose you wish to forecast sales of the *brand* of auto that the dealership sells for the next five years. What forecasting techniques would you use?

3. What forecasting techniques would you use to estimate demand for autos over the next 20 years?

Sources: Phil Berg, "A Case of Wizardry That Has Gone Wild," *Advertising Age*, July 25, 1988, pp. S22–S23; "The EPA Gives a Little on Gas Mileage," *Business Week*, July 15, 1985, pp. 38–39; "Eye on the Road," *Car and Driver*, January 1990, p. 7; "Return of the Gas Guzzler," *Forbes*, October 1986, p. 10; "Japan Will Feast at the CAFE," *U.S. News & World Report*, May 29, 1989, p. 11; and Karen Wright, "The Shape of Things to Go," *Scientific American*, May 1990, pp. 92–101.

9

Market Segmentation, Targeting, and Positioning

Procter & Gamble makes ten brands of laundry detergent (Tide, Cheer, Gain, Dash, Bold 3, Dreft, Ivory Snow, Oxydol, Era, and Solo). It also sells seven brands of hand soap (Zest, Coast, Ivory, Safeguard, Camay, Kirk's, and Lava), six shampoos (Prell, Head & Shoulders, Ivory, Pert, Pantene, and Vidal Sassoon), four brands each of liquid dishwashing detergents (Joy, Ivory, Dawn, and Liquid Cascade), toothpaste (Crest, Gleam, Complete, and Denquel), coffee (Folger's, High Point, Butternut, and Maryland Club), and toilet tissue (Charmin, White Cloud, Banner, and Summit), three brands of floor cleaner (Spic & Span, Top Job, and Mr. Clean), and two brands each of deodorant (Secret and Sure), cooking oil (Crisco and Puritan), fabric softener (Downy and Bounce), and disposable diapers (Pampers and Luvs). Moreover, many of the brands are offered in several sizes and forms (for example, you can buy scented or unscented Tide in powder or liquid form). Thus, many P&G brands compete with one another on the same supermarket shelves.

But why would P&G introduce several brands in one category instead of concentrating its resources on a single, leading brand? The answer lies in the fact that different people want different *mixes of benefits* from the products they buy. Take laundry detergents as an example. People use laundry detergents to get their clothes clean. But they also want other things from their detergents, things such as economy, bleaching power, fabric softening, fresh smell, strength or mildness, and lots of suds. We all want *some* of these benefits from our detergent, but

we may have different *priorities* for each benefit. To some people, cleaning and bleaching power are most important; to others, fabric softening is most important; still others want a mild, fresh-scented detergent. Thus, there are groups—or segments—of laundry detergent buyers, and each segment seeks a special combination of benefits.

Procter & Gamble has identified at least ten important laundry detergent segments, and it has developed a different brand designed to meet the special needs of each segment. The ten brands are positioned for different segments as follows:

- *Tide* is the "extra action," all-purpose detergent for extra-tough laundry jobs. It is a family detergent—it "gets out the dirt kids get into. Tide's in, dirt's out."
- *Cheer* is specially formulated for use in hot, warm, or cold water. It's "all tempa-Cheer."
- *Gain* was originally P&G's "enzyme" detergent but was repositioned as the detergent with a lingering fragrance— "for laundry so clean it's bursting with freshness."
- *Dash* is P&G's concentrated-powder detergent with "three powerful dirt dissolvers." It also makes fewer suds, so it won't clog "today's automatic washing machines."
- *Bold 3* originally "powered out dirt." Now, it's the detergent plus fabric softener. It "cleans, softens, and controls static."
- *Ivory Snow* is "Ninety-nine and forty-four one hundredths percent pure." It's the "mild, gentle soap for diapers and baby clothes."
- *Dreft* is also formulated for baby's diapers and clothes, and it contains borax, "nature's natural sweetener."

- *Oxydol* contains bleach. It's for "sparkling whites, a full-power detergent with color-safe bleach."
- *Era* is P&G's concentrated liquid detergent. It contains proteins to clean more stains.
- *Solo* is positioned as a heavy-duty liquid detergent with a fabric softener—"The convenience of a liquid plus a softer wash that doesn't cling."

By segmenting the market and having several detergent brands, Procter & Gamble has an attractive offering for consumers in all important preference groups. All its brands combined hold more than a 50 percent share of the laundry detergent market, much more than any single brand could obtain by itself.

CHAPTER OBJECTIVES

After reading this chapter, you should be able to:

1. Define market segmentation, market targeting, and market positioning.
2. List and discuss the major bases for segmenting consumer and industrial markets.
3. Explain how companies identify attractive market segments and choose a market-coverage strategy.
4. Explain how companies can position their products for maximum advantage in the marketplace.

MARKETS

Organizations that sell to consumer and industrial markets recognize that they cannot appeal to all buyers in those markets—or at least not to all buyers in the same way. Buyers are too numerous, too widely scattered, and too varied in their needs and buying practices. And different companies vary widely in their abilities to serve different segments of the market. Thus, rather than trying to compete in an entire market, sometimes against superior competitors, each company must identify the parts of the market that it can serve best.

Sellers have not always practiced this philosophy. Their thinking passed through three stages:

- *Mass marketing.* In mass marketing, the seller mass-produces, mass-distributes, and mass-promotes one product to all buyers. At one time, Coca-Cola produced only one drink for the whole market, hoping it would appeal to everyone. The argument for mass marketing is that it should lead to the lowest costs and prices and create the largest potential market.
- *Product-variety marketing.* Here, the seller produces two or more products that have different features, styles, quality, sizes, and so on. Later, Coca-Cola produced several soft drinks packaged in different sizes and containers. They were designed to offer variety to buyers rather than to appeal to different market segments. The argument for product-variety marketing is that consumers have different tastes that change over time. Consumers seek variety and change.
- *Target marketing.* Here, the seller identifies market segments, selects one or more of them, and develops products and marketing mixes tailored to each. For example, Coca-Cola now produces several soft drinks for the sugared-cola segment (Coke, Coca-Cola Classic, and Cherry Coke), the diet segment (Diet Coke and Tab), the no-caffeine segment (Caffeine Free Coke), and the noncola segment (Minute Maid sodas).

Today's companies are moving away from mass marketing and product-variety marketing and toward target marketing. Target marketing can better help sellers find their marketing opportunities. Sellers can develop the right product for each target market and adjust their prices, distribution channels, and advertising to reach the target market efficiently. Instead of scattering their marketing efforts (the "shotgun" approach), they can focus on the buyers who have the greater purchase interest (the "rifle" approach).

With the increasing fragmentation of American mass markets into hundreds of micromarkets, each having different needs and life styles, target marketing is increasingly

FIGURE 9-1
Steps in market segmentation, targeting, and positioning

Market segmentation	Market targeting	Market positioning
1. Identify bases for segmenting the market	3. Develop measures of segment attractiveness	5. Develop positioning for each target segment
2. Develop profiles of resulting segments	4. Select the target segment(s)	6. Develop marketing mix for each target segment

taking the form of **micromarketing.** Using micromarketing, companies tailor their marketing programs to the needs and wants of narrowly defined geographic, demographic, psychographic, or benefit segments. The ultimate form of target marketing is *customized marketing*, in which the company adapts its product and marketing program to the needs of a specific customer or buying organization (see Marketing Highlight 9–1 on pages 222, 223).

Target marketing calls for three major steps (Figure 9-1). The first is **market segmentation**—dividing a market into distinct groups of buyers who might call for separate products or marketing mixes. The company identifies different ways to segment the market and develops profiles of the resulting market segments. The second step is **market targeting**—evaluating each segment's attractiveness and selecting one or more of the market segments to enter. The third step is **market positioning**—setting the competitive positioning for the product and a detailed marketing mix. This chapter describes the principles of market segmentation, market targeting, and market positioning.

MARKET SEGMENTATION

Markets consist of buyers, and buyers differ in one or more ways. They may differ in their wants, resources, locations, buying attitudes, and buying practices. Any of these variables can be used to segment a market.

Segmenting a Market   Because buyers have unique needs and wants, each is potentially a separate market. Ideally, then, a seller might design a separate marketing program for each buyer. For example, airplane producers such as Boeing and McDonnell-Douglas face only a few buyers and treat each as a separate market. Using such *complete* market segmentation, they customize their products and marketing programs to satisfy each specific customer.

However, most sellers do not find complete segmentation worthwhile. Instead, they look for broad *classes* of buyers who differ in their product needs or buying responses. For example, General Motors has found that high- and low-income groups differ in their car-buying needs and wants. It also knows that young consumers' needs and wants differ from those of older consumers. Thus, GM has designed specific models for different income and age groups—in fact, it sells models for segments with varied *combinations* of age and income. For example, GM designed its Buick Park Avenue for older, higher-income consumers. Age and income are only two of many bases that companies use for segmenting their markets.

Bases for Segmenting Consumer Markets   There is no single way to segment a market. A marketer has to try different segmentation variables, alone and in combination, to find the best way to view the market structure. Table 9-1 outlines the major variables that might be used in segmenting consumer markets. Here we will look at the major *geographic*, *demographic*, *psychographic*, and *behavioristic variables*.

Geographic Segmentation
Geographic Segmentation calls for dividing the market into different geographical units such as nations, states, regions, counties, cities, or neighborhoods. A company may decide to operate in one or a few geographical areas or to operate in all areas but pay attention to geographical differences in needs and wants. For example, General Foods' Maxwell House ground coffee is sold nationally but is flavored regionally: People in

TABLE 9-1
**Major Segmentation Variables
for Consumer Markets**

VARIABLE	TYPICAL BREAKDOWNS
Geographic	
Region	Pacific, Mountain, West North Central, West South Central, East North Central, East South Central, South Atlantic, Middle Atlantic, New England
County size	A, B, C, D
City size	Under 5,000; 5,000–20,000; 20,000–50,000; 50,000–100,000; 100,000–250,000; 250,000–500,000; 500,000–1,000,000; 1,000,000–4,000,000; 4,000,000 or over
Density	Urban, suburban, rural
Climate	Northern, Southern
Demographic	
Age	Under 6, 6–11, 12–19, 20–34, 35–49, 50–64, 65 +
Sex	Male, female
Family size	1–2, 3–4, 5 +
Family life cycle	Young, single; young, married, no children; young, married, youngest child under 6; young married, youngest child 6 or over; older, married, with children; older, married, no children under 18; older, single; other
Income	Under $10,000; $10,000–$15,000; $15,000–$20,000; $20,000–$30,000; $30,000–$50,000; $50,000 and over
Occupation	Professional and technical; managers, officials, and proprietors; clerical, sales; craftsmen, foremen; operatives; farmers; retired; students; homemakers; unemployed
Education	Grade school or less; some high school; high school graduate; some college; college graduate
Religion	Catholic, Protestant, Jewish, other
Race	White, Black, Asian, Hispanic
Nationality	American, British, French, German, Scandinavian, Italian, Latin American, Middle Eastern, Japanese
Psychographic	
Social class	Lower lowers, upper lowers, working class, middle class, upper middles, lower uppers, upper uppers
Life style	Achievers, believers, strivers
Personality	Compulsive, gregarious, authoritarian, ambitious
Behavioristic	
Purchase occasion	Regular occasion, special occasion
Benefits sought	Quality, service, economy
User status	Nonuser, ex-user, potential user, first-time user, regular user
Usage rate	Light user, medium user, heavy user
Loyalty status	None, medium, strong, absolute
Readiness stage	Unaware, aware, informed, interested, desirous, intending to buy
Attitude toward product	Enthusiastic, positive, indifferent, negative, hostile

the West want stronger coffee than people in the East. Campbell sells Cajun Gumbo Soup in Louisiana and Mississippi, makes its Nacho Cheese soup spicier in Texas and California, and sells its spicy Ranchero Beans only in the South and Southwest.

S. C. Johnson & Son practices geographic segmentation for its arsenal of Raid bug killers by emphasizing the right products in the right geographic areas at the right times:

> Concerned that its dominant share of the household insecticide market had plateaued just above 40 percent, Johnson figured out where and when different bugs were about to start biting, stinging, and otherwise making people's lives miserable. The company promoted cockroach zappers in roach capitals such as Houston and New York and flea sprays in flea-bitten cities like Tampa and Birmingham. Since the program began last year, Raid has increased its market share in 16 of 18 regions and its overall piece of the $450-million-a-year U.S. insecticide market by five percentage points.[1]

Many companies today are "regionalizing" their marketing programs—localizing their products, advertising, promotion, and sales efforts to fit the needs of individual regions, cities, and even neighborhoods.

Demographic Segmentation

Demographic segmentation consists of dividing the market into groups based on such demographic variables as age, sex, family size, family life cycle, income, occupation, education, religion, race, and nationality. Demographic factors are the most popular bases for segmenting customer groups. One reason is that consumer needs, wants, and usage rates often vary closely with demographic variables. Another is that demographic variables are easier to measure than most other types of variables. Even when market segments are first defined using other bases, such as personality or behavior, their demographic characteristics must be known in order to assess the size of the target market and to reach it efficiently. Here, we show how certain demographic factors have been used in market segmentation.

AGE AND LIFE-CYCLE STAGE. Consumer needs and wants change with age. Some companies use **age and life-cycle segmentation,** offering different products or using different marketing approaches for different age and life-cycle segments. For example, Life Stage vitamins come in four versions, each designed for the special needs of specific age segments: chewable Children's Formula for children from 4 to 12 years old; Teen's Formula for teenagers; and two adult versions (Men's Formula and Women's Formula).

Age segmentation: Kid Cuisine frozen dinners are "fun foods kids really like."

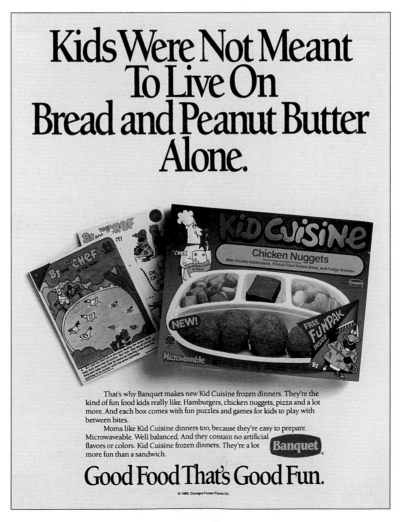

MICROMARKETING—A NEW MARKETING ERA?

For most of this century, major consumer-products companies have held fast to two mass marketing principles, product standardization and national brand identification. They have marketed the same set of products in about the same way to masses of consumers all across the country. But recently, many companies have tried a new approach—*micromarketing*. Instead of marketing in the same way nationally to all customers, they are tailoring their products, advertising, sales promotions, and personal selling efforts to suit the tastes of specific geographic, demographic, psychographic, and benefits segments.

Several factors have fueled the move toward micromarketing. First, the American mass market has slowly broken down into a profusion of smaller micromarkets—the baby boomer segment here, the mature segment there; here the Hispanic market, there the black market; here working women, there single parents; here the Sun Belt, there the Rust Belt. Today, marketers find it very hard to create a single product or program that appeals to all these diverse groups. Second, improved information and marketing research technologies have also spurred regionalization. For example, retail store scanners now allow instant tracking of product sales from store to store, helping companies pinpoint exactly which specific segments are buying what. Third, scanners give retailers mountains of market information, and this information gives them more power over manufacturers. Retailers are often lukewarm about large, national marketing campaigns—instead, they prefer localized promotions targeted toward the characteristics of consumers in their own cities and neighborhoods. Thus, to keep retailers happy, and to get precious retail shelf space for their products, manufacturers must now do more micromarketing.

One of the most common forms of micromarketing is *regionalization*—tailoring brands and promotions to suit individual geographic regions, cities, and even neighborhoods or specific stores. Campbell Soup, a pioneer in regionalization, has created many successful regional brands. For example, it sells spicy Ranchero Beans, Brunswick Stew, and spicy Hot Chili in the Southwest, Cajun Gumbo Soup in the South, and Red Bean Soup in Hispanic areas. In fact, Campbell has reorganized its entire marketing operation to suit its regional strategy. It has divided its market into twenty-two regions. Within each region, sales managers and salespeople now have the authority to work closely with local retailers on displays, coupon offers, price specials, and promotional events geared to local market needs and conditions. For example, one sales manager recently offered Campbell's Pork & Beans at a fifty-year-old price (5 cents) to help a local retailer celebrate its fiftieth anniversary. Campbell has allocated 15 to 20 percent of its total marketing budget to support local marketing, and this allocation may eventually rise to 50 percent.

Beyond regionalization, companies are also targeting specific demographic, psychographic, and benefit micromarkets. For example, for its Crest toothpaste, Procter & Gamble uses six separate advertising campaigns targeting different age and ethnic segments, including children, blacks, and Hispanics. To reach these and other micromarkets, Procter & Gamble has greatly increased its use of highly focused media, such as cable television, direct mail, event sponsorships, electronic point-of-purchase media, and advertising display boards in such locations as doctors' and dentists' waiting rooms or elementary and high school cafeterias. And to satisfy the growing diversity of consumer tastes, P&G has created a shopping basket full of new products and brand extensions in all its categories. For example, where once there was just Tide, now there are Regular Tide, Liquid Tide, Unscented Tide, and Tide with Bleach.

In the extreme, micromarketing becomes customization. Today, customized marketing is coming back in the form of *mass customization*—producing large quantities of custom-designed products to meet individual customers' needs. For example, home buyers in Japan can sit down at a computer with a salesperson and design their own future homes. They create an overall layout, making rooms as large or as small as they want, and then choose their own combinations of specific features from a list of 20,000 standardized parts. Their designs are sent electronically to the factory, where the walls, ceilings, and floors are prepared on an assembly line stretching for one-third of a mile. Prefabricated modules are then delivered to the buyer's property and assembled. Within only thirty days, the family can move into its customized home.

Other marketers are now experimenting with new systems for providing custom-made products, ranging from cars and furniture to clothing. One such system, already installed in eighteen stores across the country, consists of a camera linked to a computer that calculates a customer's measurements and prints a custom-fitted pattern for a bathing suit. The video screen shows the bedazzled and delighted buyer

Johnson & Johnson developed Affinity Shampoo for women over forty to help overcome age-related hair changes. And McDonald's targets children, teens, adults, and seniors with different ads and media. Its ads to teens feature dance-beat music, adventure, and fast-paced cutting from scene to scene; ads to seniors are softer and more sentimental.

Nevertheless, marketers must be careful when using age and life-cycle segmentation. Although you might find some 70-year-olds in wheelchairs, you will find others on the tennis courts. Similarly, whereas some 40-year-old couples are sending their chidren off to college, others are beginning new families. Thus, age is often a poor predictor of a person's life cycle, health, work or family status, needs, and buying power—marketers must guard against age stereotypes.

SEX. **Sex segmentation** has long been used in clothing, hairdressing, cosmetics, and magazines. Recently other marketers have noticed opportunities for sex segmentation.

There's always time for a hot Southern breakfast.

Smooth, creamy Quaker® Instant Grits cook up in seconds, in the bowl or in the microwave. And that makes them right for all those mornings you just can't wait for good Southern taste.

QUAKER INSTANT GRITS

The grits you love. For the way you live.™

Micromarketing: Quaker targets the South with this ad for Quaker Instant Grits, which ran in *Southern Living* magazine.

how the new suit will look from the front, side, and rear. The buyer chooses the fabric from about 150 samples, the custom-made design is sent to the producer's tailors, and the suit is stitched up.

Although micromarketing offers much promise, it also presents some problems. Trying to serve dozens or even hundreds of diverse micromarkets is vastly more complex than mass marketing. And offering many different products and promotion programs results in higher manufacturing and marketing costs. Thus, some marketers view micromarketing as simply a fad—they think companies will quickly find that the extra sales gained will not cover the additional costs.

But others think that micromarketing will revolutionize the way consumer products are marketed. Gone are the days, they say, when a company can effectively market one product to masses of consumers using a single promotion program. To these marketers, micromarketing signals the start of a whole new marketing era.

Sources: See Regis McKenna, ''Marketing in an Age of Diversity,'' *Harvard Business Review*, September–October 1988, pp. 88–95; and Zachary Schiller, ''Stalking the New Consumer,'' *Business Week*, August 18, 1989, pp. 54–62.

For example, most deodorant brands are used by men and women alike. Procter & Gamble, however, developed Secret as the brand specially formulated for a woman's chemistry and then packaged and advertised the product to reinforce the female image. The automobile industry has also begun to use sex segmentation extensively:

With the rapid growth in the number of working women and women car owners, most auto makers are now designing marketing strategies to court women buyers. Last year, women bought 45 percent of all new cars sold in the U.S. and influenced 80 percent of all new-car purchases. Thus women have evolved as a valued target market for the auto companies. Some manufacturers target women directly. For example, Chevrolet devotes 30 percent of its television advertising budget to advertisements for women. It places large advertising spreads designed especially for women consumers in such magazines as *Cosmopolitan* and *Women's Sport and Fitness*. Chevy also sponsored a nationwide series of career conferences for women. Other companies avoid direct appeals, fearing that women will be offended if they see advertising directed toward them. It sometimes comes across as condescending. Instead, companies such as Toyota, Ford, and Pontiac try to include a realistic balance of men and women in their ads without specific reference to gender.[2]

INCOME. **Income segmentation** has long been used by the marketers of such products and services as automobiles, boats, clothing, cosmetics, and travel. Many companies target affluent consumers with luxury goods and convenience services. Stores like Neiman Marcus pitch everything from expensive jewelry, fine fashions, and exotic furs to $4 jars of peanut butter and chocolate at $20 a pound.[3]

But not all companies using income segmentation target the affluent. Many companies, such as Family Dollar stores, profitably target low-income consumers. When Family Dollar real estate experts scout locations for new stores, they look for lower-middle-class neighborhoods where people wear cheap shoes and drive old cars that drip a lot of oil. The income of a typical Family Dollar customer rarely exceeds $17,000 per year, and the average customer spends only about $6 per trip to the store. Yet the store's low-income strategy has made it one of the most profitable discount chains in the country.[4]

At the same time, income does not always predict the customers for a given product. One would think that blue-collar workers would buy Chevrolets and executives would buy Cadillacs, yet many Chevrolets are bought by executives (often as a second car), and some Cadillacs are bought by blue-collar workers (such as high-paid plumbers and carpenters). Blue-collar workers were among the first purchasers of color television sets; it was cheaper for them to buy these sets than to go out to the movies and restaurants.

MULTIVARIATE DEMOGRAPHIC SEGMENTATION. Most companies segment a market using two or more demographic variables. Consider the market for deodorant soaps. The top-selling deodorant soap brands are used by many kinds of consumers, but three demographic variables—sex, age, and geographic region—are the most useful in distinguishing the users of one brand from those of another.[5] Figure 9-2 shows a multivariate segmentation of the deodorant soap market.

Men and women differ in their deodorant soap preferences. Top men's brands include Dial, Safeguard, and Irish Spring. These brands account for over 30 percent of the men's soap market. Women, on the other hand, prefer Dial, Zest, and Coast, which account for 23 percent of the women's soap market. The leading deodorant soaps also appeal differently to different age segments. For example, Dial appeals more to men aged 45 to 68 than to younger men; women aged 35 to 44, however, are more likely than the average woman to use Dial. Coast appeals much more to younger men and women than to older people—men and women aged 18 to 24 are about a third more

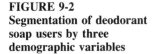

FIGURE 9-2
Segmentation of deodorant soap users by three demographic variables

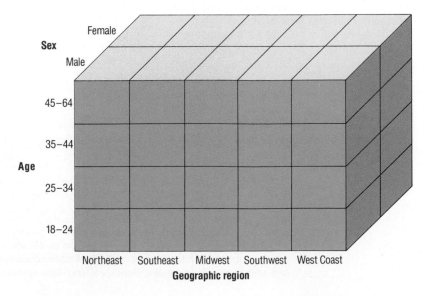

likely than the average to use Coast. Finally, deodorant soap preferences differ by region of the country. Although men in all geographic regions use deodorant soap, New Englanders use more Dial, southerners favor Safeguard, and westerners prefer Irish Spring. Thus, no single demographic variable captures all differences among the needs and preferences of deodorant soap buyers. To better define important market segments, soap marketers must use multivariate demographic segmentation.

Psychographic Segmentation

In **psychographic segmentation,** buyers are divided into different groups based on social class, life style, or personality characteristics. People in the same demographic group can have very different psychographic makeups.

SOCIAL CLASS. We described the seven American social classes in Chapter 5 and showed that social class has a strong affect on preferences in cars, clothes, home furnishings, leisure activities, reading habits, and retailers. Many companies design products or services for specific social classes, building in features that appeal to those classes.

LIFE STYLE. We saw in Chapter 5 that people's interest in various goods is affected by their life styles and that the goods they buy express those life styles. Marketers are increasingly segmenting their markets by consumer life styles. General Foods used life-style analysis to successfully reposition its Sanka decaffeinated coffee. For years, Sanka's market was limited by the product's staid, older image. To turn this situation around, General Foods launched an advertising campaign that positioned Sanka as an ideal beverage for today's healthy, active life styles. The campaign targeted achievers of all ages, using a classic achiever appeal that Sanka "lets you be your best." Advertising showed people leading adventurous life styles, such as kayaking through rapids.[6]

Redbook magazine also targets a specific life-style segment—women it calls *"Redbook* Jugglers." The magazine defines the juggler as a 25- to 44-year-old woman who must juggle husband, family, home, and job. According to *Redbook*, this consumer makes an idea target for marketers of health food and fitness products. She wears out more exercise shoes, swallows more vitamins, drinks more diet soda, and works out more often than do other consumer groups.

PERSONALITY. Marketers have also used personality variables to segment markets, giving their products personalities that correspond to consumer personalities. Successful market segmentation strategies based on personality have been used for such products as women's cosmetics, cigarettes, insurance, and liquor.[7] Honda's marketing campaign for its motor scooters provides another good example of personality segmentation.

> Honda appears to target its Spree, Elite, and Aero motor scooters at the hip and trendy 14- to 22-year-old age group. But the company actually designs ads that appeal to a much broader personality group. One ad, for example, shows a delighted child bouncing up and down on his bed while the announcer says, "You've been trying to get there all your life." The ad reminds viewers of the euphoric feelings they got when they broke away from authority and did things their parents told them not to. And it suggests that they can feel that way again riding a Honda scooter. So while Honda seems to be targeting young consumers, the ads appeal to trend setters and independent personalities in all age groups. In fact, over half of Honda's scooter sales are to young professionals and older buyers—fifteen percent are purchased by the over-50 group. Thus, Honda is appealing to the rebellious, independent kid in all of us.[8]

Behavior Segmentation

In **behavior segmentation,** buyers are divided into groups based on their knowledge, attitude, uses, or responses to a product. Many marketers believe that behavior variables are the best starting point for building market segments.

OCCASIONS. Buyers can be grouped according to occasions when they get the idea, make a purchase, or use a product. **Occasion segmentation** can help firms build up product usage. For example, orange juice is most often consumed at breakfast, but orange growers have promoted drinking orange juice as a cool and refreshing drink at other times of the day. On the other hand, Coca-Cola's "Coke in the Morning" advertising campaign attempts to increase Coke consumption by promoting the beverage as an

Take One Home For The Holidays.

DELTA

© 1989 Delta Air Lines, Inc.

Occasion segmentation: Delta advertises for the holidays.

early morning pick-me-up. Some holidays—Mother's Day and Father's Day, for example—were originally promoted partly to increase the sale of candy, flowers, cards, and other gifts. The Curtis Candy Company promoted the "trick-or-treat" custom at Halloween to encourage every home to have candy ready for eager little callers knocking at the door.

BENEFITS SOUGHT. A powerful form of segmentation is to group buyers according to the different *benefits* that they seek from the product. **Benefit segmentation** requires finding the major benefits people look for in the product class, the kinds of people who look for each benefit, and the major brands that deliver each benefit. One of the best examples of benefit segmentation was conducted in the toothpaste market (see Table 9-2). Research found four benefit segments: those seeking economic, protective, cosmetic, and taste benefits. Each benefit group had special demographic, behavioral, and psychographic characteristics. For example, decay-prevention seekers tended to have large families, were heavy toothpaste users, and were conservative. Each segment also favored certain brands. Most current brands appeal to one of these segments—Crest Tartar Control toothpaste stresses protection and appeals to the family segment; Aim looks and tastes good and appeals to children.

Colgate-Palmolive used benefit segmentation to reposition its Irish Spring soap. Research showed three deodorant soap benefit segments: men who prefer lightly scented deodorant soap; women who want a mildly scented, gentle soap; and a mixed, mostly male segment that wanted a strongly scented, refreshing soap. The original Irish Spring soap did well with the last segment, but Colgate wanted to target the larger middle

TABLE 9-2
Benefit Segmentation of the Toothpaste Market

BENEFIT SEGMENTS	DEMO-GRAPHICS	BEHAVIOR	PSYCHO-GRAPHICS	FAVORED BRANDS
Economy (low price)	Men	Heavy users	High autonomy, value oriented	Brands on sale
Medicinal (decay prevention)	Large families	Heavy users	Hypochondriacal, conservative	Crest
Cosmetic (bright teeth)	Teens, young adults	Smokers	High sociability, active	Aqua-Fresh, Ultra Brite
Taste (good tasting)	Children	Spearmint lovers	High self-involvement, hedonistic	Colgate, Aim

Source: Adapted from Russell J. Haley, ''Benefit Segmentation: A Decision Oriented Research Tool,'' *Journal of Marketing*, July 1968, pp. 30–35.

segment. Thus, it reformulated the soap and changed its advertising to give the product more of a family appeal.[9]

Thus, companies can use benefit segmentation to clarify the benefit segment to which they are appealing, its characteristics, and the major competitive brands. They can also search for new benefits and launch brands that deliver them.[10]

USER STATUS. Many markets can be segmented into nonusers, ex-users, potential users, first-time users, and regular users of a product. High-market-share companies are particularly interested in attracting potential users, while smaller firms will try to attract regular users. Potential users and regular users may require different kinds of marketing appeals. For example, one study found that blood donors are low in self-esteem, low risk takers, and more concerned about their health; nondonors tend to be the opposite on all three dimensions. This suggests that social agencies should use different marketing approaches for keeping current donors and attracting new ones.[11]

USAGE RATE. Markets can also be segmented into light-, medium-, and heavy-user groups. Heavy users are often a small percentage of the market but account for a high percentage of total buying. Figure 9-3 shows usage rates for some popular consumer

FIGURE 9-3
Heavy and light users of common consumer products

Source: See Victor J. Cook and William A. Mindak, ''A Search for Constants: The 'Heavy User' Revisited!'' *Journal of Consumer Marketing*, Vol. 1, No. 4. (Spring 1984), p. 80.

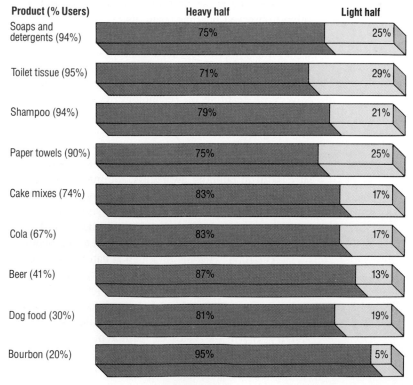

products. Product users were divided into two groups—a light-user half and a heavy-user half—according to their buying rates for the specific products. Using beer as an example, the figure shows that 41 percent of the households studied buy beer. But the heavy-user half accounted for 87 percent of the beer consumed, almost seven times as much as the light-user half. Clearly, a beer company would prefer to attract one heavy user to its brand rather than several light users. Thus, most beer companies target the heavy beer drinkers, using appeals such as Schaefer's "One beer to have when you're having more than one," or Miller Lite's "Tastes great, less filling."

LOYALTY STATUS.   A market can also be segmented by consumer loyalty. Consumers can be loyal to brands (Tide), stores (Sears), and companies (Ford). Buyers can be divided into groups according to their degree of loyalty. Some consumers are completely loyal—they buy one brand all the time. Others are somewhat loyal—they are loyal to two or three brands of a given product or favor one brand while sometimes buying others. Still other buyers show no loyalty to any brand. They either want something different each time they buy or always buy a brand on sale.

Each market is made up of different numbers of each type of buyer. A brand-loyal market is one with a high percentage of buyers showing strong brand loyalty. The toothpaste market and the beer market seem to be fairly high brand-loyal markets. Companies selling in a brand-loyal market have a hard time gaining more market share, and companies trying to enter such a market have a hard time getting in.

A company can learn a lot by analyzing loyalty patterns in its market. It should start by studying its own loyal customers. Colgate finds that its loyal buyers are more middle class, have larger families, and are more health conscious. These characteristics pinpoint the target market for Colgate. By studying its less loyal buyers, the company can detect which brands are most competitive with its own. If many Colgate buyers also buy Crest, Colgate can attempt to improve its positioning against Crest, possibly by using direct-comparison advertising. By looking at customers who are shifting away from its brand, the company can learn about its marketing weaknesses. As for nonloyals, the company may attract them by putting its brand on sale.

Companies must be careful when using brand loyalty in their segmentation strategies. What appear to be brand-loyal purchase patterns might reflect little more than *habit*, *indifference*, a *low price*, or *unavailability* of other brands. Thus, frequent or regular purchasing may not be the same as brand loyalty—marketers must examine the motivations behind observed purchase patterns.

BUYER READINESS STAGE.   At any time, people are in different stages of readiness to buy a product. Some people are unaware of the product; some are aware; some are informed; some are interested; some want the product; and some intend to buy. The relative numbers make a big difference in designing the marketing program. For example, New York Institute of Technology recently began offering self-paced college courses via personal computer. Students can log onto their personal computers at any time and from any location to complete their lessons or "talk" to their teachers.[12] At first, potential students will be unaware of the new program. The initial marketing effort should thus employ high-awareness-building advertising and publicity using a simple message. If successful in building awareness, the marketing program should shift in order to move more people into the next readiness stage—say, interest in the program—by stressing the benefits of the "electronic university." Facilities should be readied for handling the large number of people who may be moved to enroll in the courses. In general, the marketing program must be adjusted to the changing distribution of buyer readiness.

ATTITUDE.   People in a market can be enthusiastic, positive, indifferent, negative, or hostile about a product. Door-to-door workers in a political campaign use a given voter's attitude to determine how much time to spend with that voter. They thank enthusiastic voters and remind them to vote; they spend little or no time trying to change the attitudes of negative and hostile voters. They reinforce those who are positive and try to win the votes of indifferent voters. In such marketing situations, attitudes can be effective segmentation variables.

Bases for Segmenting Industrial Markets

Industrial markets can be segmented using many of the same variables used in consumer market segmentation. Industrial buyers can be segmented geographically or by benefits sought, user status, usage rate, loyalty status, readiness state, and attitudes. Yet, new variables also come into play. As Table 9-3 shows, these include industrial customer demographics, operating characteristics, purchasing approaches, situational factors, and personal characteristics.[13]

The table lists major questions that industrial marketers should ask in determining which customers they want to serve. By going after segments instead of the whole market, a company has a much better chance of delivering value to consumers and of receiving maximum rewards for its close attention to segment consumer needs. Thus, Goodyear and other tire companies should decide which *industries* they want to serve. Manufacturers seeking original-equipment tires vary in their needs. Makers of luxury and high-performance cars want higher-grade tires than do makers of economy models. The tires needed by aircraft manufacturers must meet much higher safety standards than tires needed by farm tractor manufacturers.

Within the chosen industry, a company can further segment by *customer size* or *geographic location*. The company might set up separate systems for dealing with larger or multiple-location customers. For example, Steelcase, a major producer of office furniture, first segments customers into ten industries, including banking, insurance, and electronics. Next, company salespeople work with independent Steelcase dealers to handle smaller, local or regional Steelcase customers in each segment. But many national, multiple-location customers, such as Exxon or IBM, have special needs that may reach beyond the scope of individual dealers. So Steelcase uses national accounts managers to help its dealer networks handle its national accounts.

Within a certain target industry and customer size, the company can segment by *purchase approaches and criteria*. For example, government, university, and industrial laboratories typically differ in their purchase criteria for scientific instruments. Government labs need low prices (because they have difficulty in getting funds to buy instruments) and service contracts (because they can easily get money to maintain instruments). University labs want equipment that needs little regular service because they don't have

---

TABLE 9-3
Major Segmentation Variables for Industrial Markets

Demographic
  Industry: which industries that buy this product should we focus on?
  Company size: what size companies should we focus on?
  Location: what geographical areas should we focus on?

Operating variables
  Technology: what customer technologies should we focus on?
  User/non-user status: should we focus on heavy, medium, or light users or non-users?
  Customer capabilities: should we focus on customers needing many services or few services?

Purchasing approaches
  Purchasing function organization: should we focus on companies with highly centralized or decentralized purchasing organizations?
  Power structure: should we focus on companies that are engineering-dominated, financially-dominated, or marketing-dominated?
  Nature of existing relationships: should we focus on companies with which we already have strong relationships or simply go after the most desirable companies?
  General purchase policies: should we focus on companies that prefer leasing? Service contracts? Systems purchases? Sealed bidding?
  Purchasing criteria: should we focus on companies that are seeking quality? Service? Price?

Situational factors
  Urgency: should we focus on companies that need quick and sudden delivery or service?
  Specific application: should we focus on certain applications of our product rather than all applications?
  Size of order: should we focus on large or small orders?

Personal characteristics
  Buyer-seller similarity: should we focus on companies whose people and values are similar to ours?
  Attitudes toward risk: should we focus on risk-taking or risk-avoiding customers?
  Loyalty: should we focus on companies that show high loyalty to their suppliers?

Source: Adapted from Thomas V. Bonoma and Benson P. Shapiro, *Segmenting the Industrial Market* (Lexington, Ma: Lexington Books, 1983).

Industrial segmentation: Steelcase segments by industry, then has separate systems for dealing with large, geographically dispersed customers.

service people on their payrolls. Industrial labs need highly reliable equipment because they cannot afford downtime.

In general, industrial companies do not focus on one segmentation variable but use a combination of many. One aluminum company used a series of four major variables. It first looked at which *end-use* market to serve: automobile, residential, or beverage containers. Choosing the residential market, it determined the most attractive *product application*: semifinished material, building components, or mobile homes. Deciding to focus on building components, it next considered the best *customer size* to serve and chose large customers. The company further segmented the large-customer, building-components market. It saw customers falling into three *benefit* groups: those who bought for price, those who bought for service, and those who bought for quality. Because the company offered excellent service, it decided to concentrate on the service-seeking segment of the market.

Requirements for Effective Segmentation

Clearly, there are many ways to segment a market—but not all segmentations are effective. For example, buyers of table salt could be divided into blond and brunette customers. But hair color obviously does not affect the purchase of salt. Furthermore, if all salt buyers bought the same amount of salt each month, believed all salt was the same, and wanted to pay the same price, the company would not benefit from segmenting this market.

To be useful, market segments must have the following characteristics:

- **Measurability**—the degree to which the size and purchasing power of the segments can be measured. Certain segmentation variables are difficult to measure. For example, there are 24 million left-handed people in the U.S.—almost equaling the entire population of Canada. Yet few products are targeted toward this left-handed segment. The major problem may be that the segment is hard to identify and measure. There are no data on the demographics of lefties, and the Census Bureau does not keep track of left-handedness in its surveys.

Private data companies keep reams of statistics on other demographic segments, but not on left-handers.[14]

- **Accessibility**—the degree to which the segments can be reached and served. Suppose a perfume company finds that heavy users of its brand are single women who stay out late and socialize a lot. Unless this group lives or shops at certain places and is exposed to certain media, it will be difficult to reach.
- **Substantiality**—the degree to which the segments are large or profitable enough. A segment should be the largest possible homogeneous group worth going after with a tailored marketing program. It would not pay, for example, for an automobile manufacturer to develop cars for persons whose height is less than four feet.
- **Actionability**—the degree to which effective programs can be designed for attracting and serving the segments. For example, although one small airline identified seven market segments, its staff was too small to develop separate marketing programs for each segment.

MARKET TARGETING

Marketing segmentation reveals the market-segment opportunities facing a firm. The firm now has to evaluate the various segments and decide the number of segments to cover and the ones to serve. We now look at how companies evaluate and select target segments.

Evaluating Market Segments

In evaluating different market segments, a firm must look at three factors: segment size and growth, segment structural attractiveness, and company objectives and resources.

Segment Size and Growth

The company must first collect and analyze data on current dollar sales, projected sales-growth rates, and expected profit margins for the various segments. It wants to select segments that have the right size and growth characteristics, but "right size growth" is a relative matter. Some companies will want to target segments with large current sales, a high growth rate, and a high profit margin. However, the largest, fastest-growing segments are not always the most attractive ones for every company. Smaller companies may find that they lack the skills and resources needed to serve the larger segments or that these segments are too competitive. Such companies may select segments that are smaller and less attractive, in an absolute sense, but that are potentially more profitable for them.

Segment Structural Attractiveness

A segment might have desirable size and growth and still not be attractive from a profitability point of view. The company must examine several major structural factors that affect long-run segment attractiveness.[15] For example, the company should appraise the impact of current and potential *competitors*. A segment is less attractive if it already contains many strong and aggressive competitors. Marketers should also consider the threat of *substitute products*. A segment is less attractive if actual or potential substitutes for the product already exist. Substitutes place a limit on the potential prices and profits that can be earned in a segment. The relative *power of buyers* also affects segment attractiveness. If the buyers in a segment possess strong or increasing bargaining power relative to sellers, they will try to force prices down, demand more quality or services, and set competitors against one another, all at the expense of seller profitability. Finally, segment attractiveness depends on the relative *power of suppliers*. A segment is less attractive if the supplier of raw materials, equipment, labor, and services in the segment are powerful enough to raise prices or reduce the quality or quantity of ordered goods and services. Suppliers tend to be powerful when they are large and concentrated, when few substitutes exist, or when the supplied product is an important input.

Company Objectives and Resources

Even if a segment has positive size growth and is structurally attractive, the company must consider its own objectives and resources in relation to that segment. Some attractive segments could be quickly dismissed because they do not mesh with the company's long-run objectives. Although they might be tempting segments in themselves, they might divert the company's attention and energies away from its main goals.

If a segment fits the company's objectives, the company must then decide whether it possesses the skills and resources needed to succeed in that segment. Each segment has certain success requirements. If the company lacks and cannot readily obtain the strengths needed to compete successfully in a segment, it should not enter that segment. But even if the company possesses the *required* strengths, this is not enough. If it is really to win in a market segment, it needs to employ skills and resources *superior* to those of the competition. The company should enter segments only in which it can offer superior value and gain advantages over competitors.

Selecting Market Segments

After evaluating different segments, a company hopes to find one or more market segments worth entering. It must then decide which and how many segments to serve. This is the problem of *target market selection*. A **target market** consists of a set of buyers sharing common needs or characteristics that the company decides to serve. The firm can adopt one of three market-coverage strategies: *undifferentiated marketing*, *differentiated marketing*, or *concentrated marketing*. These strategies are shown in Figure 9-4 and discussed below.

Undifferentiated Marketing

Using an **undifferentiated marketing** strategy, a firm might decide to ignore market segment differences and go after the whole market with one market offer. It focuses on what is *common* in the needs of consumers rather than on what is *different*. The company designs a product and marketing program that appeals to the largest number of buyers. It relies on mass distribution and mass advertising and aims to give the product a superior image in people's minds. An example of undifferentiated marketing is the Hershey Company's marketing some years ago of only one chocolate candy bar for everyone.

FIGURE 9-4
Three alternative market-coverage strategies

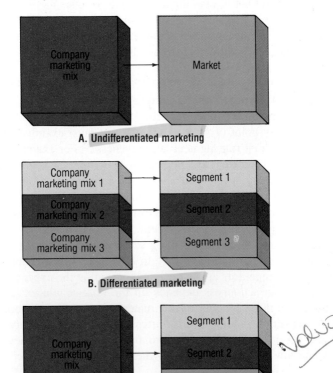

A. Undifferentiated marketing

B. Differentiated marketing

C. Concentrated marketing

Undifferentiated marketing provides cost economies. The narrow product line keeps down production, inventory, and transportation costs. The undifferentiated advertising program keeps down advertising costs. The absence of segment marketing research and planning lowers the costs of marketing research and product management.

But most modern marketers, however, have strong doubts about this strategy. Difficulties arise in developing a product or brand that will satisfy all consumers. Firms using undifferentiated marketing typically develop an offer aimed at the largest segments in the market. When several firms do this, heavy competition develops in the largest segments, and less satisfaction results in the smaller ones. The result is that the larger segments may be less profitable because they attract heavy competition. Recognition of this problem has resulted in firms being more interested in smaller segments of the market.

Differentiated Marketing

Using a **differentiated marketing** strategy, a firm decides to target several market segments and designs separate offers for each. General Motors tries to produce a car for every "purse, purpose, and personality." By offering product and marketing variations, it hopes for higher sales and a stronger position within each market segment. It hopes that a stronger position in several segments will strengthen consumers' overall identification of the company with the product category. And it hopes for greater repeat purchasing because the firm's offer better matches the customer's desire.

A growing number of firms have adopted differentiated marketing. A&P's segmentation strategy is a good example. A&P uses different food store formats to meet the needs of different customer segments:

> A&P's merchandising strategy attempts to provide a supermarket for every kind of shopper: stark black-and-white Futurestores, with the latest in gourmet departments and electronic services, for exclusive neighborhoods; conventional A&P's . . . for middle-class markets; and full-service, warehouse-style Sav-A-Centers, where shoppers have come to expect them.[16]

Differentiated marketing typically creates more total sales than undifferentiated marketing. Procter & Gamble gets a higher total market share with ten brands of laundry detergent than it could with only one. But it also increases the costs of doing business. Modifying a product to meet different market segment requirements usually involves some research and development, engineering, or special tooling costs. A firm usually finds it more expensive to produce, say, ten units of ten different products than one hundred units of one product. Developing separate marketing plans for the separate segments requires extra marketing research, forecasting, sales analysis, promotion planning, and channel management. And trying to reach different market segments with different advertising increases promotion costs. Thus, the company must weigh increased sales against increased costs when deciding on a differentiated marketing strategy.

Concentrated Marketing

A third market-coverage strategy, **concentrated marketing,** is especially appealing when company resources are limited. Instead of going after a small share of a large market, the firm goes after a large share of one or a few submarkets. Many examples of concentrated marketing can be found. In computers, Compaq concentrates on personal computers, Cray focuses on larger, mainframe supercomputers, and Apollo targets the computer work station segment. Oshkosh Truck is the world's largest producer of airport rescue trucks and front-loading concrete mixers. Recycled Paper Products concentrates on the market for alternative greeting cards. And Soho Natural Sodas concentrates on a narrow segment of the soft drink market. Concentrated marketing provides an excellent way for small new businesses to get a foot-hold against larger, more resourceful competitors (see Marketing Highlight 9–2).

Through concentrated marketing, the firm achieves a strong market position in the segments it serves because of its greater knowledge of the segments' needs and the special reputation it acquires. And it enjoys many operating economies because of special-

CONCENTRATED MARKETING: TERRY BIKES FIND A SPECIAL NICHE

Is there room for a budding new competitor alongside Schwinn and the other giants in the bicycle industry? Georgena Terry thinks so. And so do the hundreds of people now riding Terry bikes. Using a concentrated marketing strategy, Terry had developed a small but promising niche in the bicycle market—high performance bikes for women.

There was nothing astonishing about the idea. Three years ago, Terry, then a 34-year-old MBA student, decided to start building bicycles. Oh, sure, she'd specialize in high-priced women's bikes, carving out a niche just as they had taught her at The Wharton Business School. But the $1.3 billion bicycle industry didn't tremble at the thought of diminutive Terry picking up a wrench. True, she might have an interesting twist: Her bikes would have a shorter top tube and a slightly smaller front wheel that would provide a more comfortable ride for women cyclists who put in forty or fifty miles at a clip—but who rides that far? Most folks just use their bikes to pedal down to the Dairy Queen or tool around the neighborhood on Sunday afternoons. Besides, if it turned out she had something, the industry could always wheel out a knockoff.

So when Terry set up shop, no one noticed. But they are noticing now. In 1985, Terry Precision Bicycles for Women Inc. sold twenty bikes. In 1986 it shipped 1,300, and in 1987 it sold 2,500 more. Suddenly, her banker is more friendly, the bicycle magazines are calling to see what she thinks of this or that, and oh, yes, the folks at Schwinn Bicycle Company have suggested that she stop in whenever she's in town.

Terry has succeeded by concentrating on serving the special needs of serious women cyclists. The idea began when Terry herself became interested in biking. She found that she had trouble finding a comfortable riding position. "The standard bicycle—even a woman's bike—is designed for a man. To fit women, who have longer legs and shorter torsos, bike shops shove the seat forward and tilt the handlebars back." That didn't help the five-foot-two, ninety-eight-pound Terry. She began wondering if shortening the frame would improve things. So she picked up a blowtorch—"a friend showed me how to use it so I wouldn't kill myself"—and headed for the basement. She came back up with a bike that had a smaller frame. Friends saw it, borrowed it, and asked if she'd make frames for them. Two years later, she was still turning out frames and making a living—sort of.

In 1985, she got tired of just getting by and started a company. Bicycling was undergoing a miniboom, and 70 percent of all new riders were women, so she'd specialize in women's bikes. In August 1985, she hauled seven or eight of her bikes to the New England Area Rally in Amherst, Massachusetts. "I figured we'd do very well or very badly. Women would either go 'Who cares?' or love it." She sold three bikes that weekend (at $775 each) and took orders for four more. Says Terry, "I have never been more excited in my life."

To her credit, Terry moved deliberately. Her major innovation was the frame, so she concentrated on that and didn't set out to reinvent the (bicycle) wheel. Her marketing plan was equally careful. As word spread, people would call up and ask to buy a bike. "We were thrilled, but always asked the name of their local bicycle shop. We'd then call the shop and say 'Congratulations, you've just sold a Terry bike.'" Retailers, who found themselves making a quick couple of hundred dollars, usually asked for a few more bikes. That's how Terry put together a dealer network.

With almost no money for advertising, Terry concentrated on promotion. She hired a public relations firm that was quick to position her as a female David taking on bicycling's Goliaths. The approach paid off—the bicycle press

ization in production, distribution, and promotion. If the segment is chosen well, the firm can earn a high rate of return on its investment.[17]

At the same time, concentrated marketing involves higher-than-normal risks. The particular market segment can turn sour. For example, when young women suddenly stopped buying sportswear, it caused Bobbie Brooks's earnings to go deeply into the red. Or, larger competitors may decide to enter the same segment. California Cooler's success in the wine cooler segment attracted many large competitors, causing the original owners to sell out to a larger company that had more marketing resources. For these reasons, many companies prefer to diversify in several market segments.

Choosing a Market-Coverage Strategy

Many factors must be considered when choosing a market-coverage strategy. Which strategy is best depends on *company resources*. When the firm's resources are limited, concentrated marketing makes the most sense. The best strategy also depends on the degree of *product variability*. Undifferentiated marketing is more suited for uniform products such a grapefruit or steel. Products that can vary in design, such as cameras and automobiles, are more suited to differentiation or concentration. The *product's stage in the life cycle* must also be considered. When a firm introduces a new product, it is practical to launch only one version, and undifferentiated marketing or concentrated marketing makes the most sense. In the mature stage of the product life cycle, however, differentiated marketing begins to make more sense. Another factor is *market variability*.

discovered Terry and gave her bikes enthusiastic endorsements. That got customers into the stores and bikes out the door. Terry's professional business approach makes her stand out from competitors in a high-end bicycling industry filled with scores of tiny manufacturers that can take months to fill orders and are often unresponsive to both customers and shop owners. Terry, who ships on time, courts retailers, and answers questions from customers, quickly became a favorite.

But even as the marketing plan got her up and pedaling, Terry was moving to forestall competition. Recognizing that her high price would scare off many customers, Terry almost immediately began to segment. She was soon selling her high-end models for $1,200 and, to preempt the foreign competition that she knew would be coming, she signed two Asian companies to build versions of her bike that retail for $450 to $850. The strategy has worked so far. Although six companies, including Fuji America, now market bicycles to women, Terry is holding her own. Competitors' bikes just aren't as good. A recent customer asserts, "Women can tell the difference on a ride around the block. My feet reach the pedals more comfortably, and it is easier to reach the hand brakes. You feel more in control on one of her bikes."

Continued success is far from assured. Over time, her competitors will improve their designs. And the more successful Terry becomes, the more competition she is likely to attract. Yet, she has shown how a company with fewer resources can succeed against larger competitors by concentrating on a small, high-quality segment. At some point, as with many small nichers, Terry may have to think about selling out or joining forces with a bigger company to survive. But that is still a long way off. For now, Terry says, "This is wonderful."

Concentrated marketing: Georgena Terry has shown how a small company can succeed against larger competitors.

Source: Adapted from Paul B. Brown, "Spokeswoman," *Career Futures,* Spring–Summer 1989, pp. 30–32.

If most buyers have the same tastes, buy the same amounts, and react the same way to marketing efforts, undifferentiated marketing is appropriate. Finally, *competitors' marketing strategies* are important. When competitors use segmentation, undifferentiated marketing can be suicidal. Conversely, when competitors use undifferentiated marketing, a firm can gain by using differentiated or concentrated marketing.

MARKET POSITIONING

Once a company has decided which segments of the market it will enter, it must decide which "positions" it wants to occupy in those segments.

What Is Market Positioning?

A product's **position** is the way the product is *defined by consumers* on important attributes—the place the product occupies in consumers' minds relative to competing products. Thus, Tide is positioned as an all-purpose, family detergent; Era is positioned as a concentrated liquid; Cheer is positioned as the detergent for all temperatures. Hyundai and Suburu are positioned on economy; Mercedes and Cadillac are positioned on luxury; Porsche and BMW are positioned on performance.[18]

Consumers are overloaded with information about products and services. They cannot reevaluate products every time they make a buying decision. To simplify buying decision making, they organize products into categories—they "position" products, services, and companies in their minds. A product's position is the complex set of perceptions, impressions, and feelings that consumers hold for the product compared with competing products. Consumers position products with or without the help of marketers, but marketers do not want to leave their products' positions to chance. They *plan* positions that will give their products the greatest advantage in selected target markets, and they *design* marketing mixes to create the planned positions.

Positioning Strategies

Marketers can follow several positioning strategies.[19] They can position their products on specific *product attributes*—Ford Festiva advertises its low price; Saab promotes performance. Products can be positioned on the needs they fill or on the *benefits* they offer—Crest reduces cavities; Aim tastes good. Or products can be positioned according to *usage occasions*—in the summer, Gatorade can be positioned as a beverage for replacing athletes' body fluids; in the winter, it can be positioned as the drink to use when the doctor recommends plenty of liquids. Another approach is to position the product for certain classes of *users*—Johnson & Johnson improved the market share for its baby shampoo from 3 to 14 percent by repositioning the product as one for adults who wash their hair frequently and need a gentle shampoo.

A product can also be positioned directly *against a competitor*. For example, in ads for their personal computers, Compaq and Tandy have directly compared their products with IBM personal computers. In its famous "We're number two, so we try harder" campaign, Avis successfully positioned itself against the larger Hertz. A product may also be positioned *away from competitors*; 7-Up became the number three soft drink when it was positioned as the "un-cola," the fresh and thirst-quenching alternative to Coke and Pepsi. Barbasol television ads position the company's shaving cream and other products as "great toiletries for a lot less money."

Positioning away from competitors: American Express positions itself as a card for special people.

Wilt Chamberlain. Cardmember since 1976.
Willie Shoemaker. Cardmember since 1966.

Membership has its privileges.

Don't leave home without it.
Call 1-800-THE CARD to apply.

Finally, the product can be positioned for different *product classes*. For example, some margarines are positioned against butter, others against cooking oils. Camay hand soap is positioned with bath oils rather than with soap. Marketers often use a *combination* of these positioning strategies. Thus, Johnson & Johnson's Affinity shampoo is positioned as a hair conditioner for women over 40 (product class *and* user). And Arm & Hammer baking soda has been positioned as a deodorizer for refrigerators and garbage disposals (product class *and* usage situation).

Choosing and Implementing a Positioning Strategy

Some firms find it easy to choose their positioning strategy. For example, a firm well known for quality in certain segments will go for this position in a new segment if it sees enough buyers seeking quality. But in many cases, two or more firms will go after the same position. Then, each will have to find other ways to set itself apart, such as promising "high quality for a lower cost" or "high quality with more technical service." That is, each firm must differentiate its offer by building a unique bundle of competitive advantages that appeal to a substantial group within the segment.

The positioning task consists of three steps: identifying a set of possible competitive advantages upon which to build a position, selecting the right competitive advantages, and effectively communicating and delivering the chosen position to the market.

Identifying Possible Competitive Advantages

Consumers typically choose products and services that give them the greatest value. Thus, the key to winning and keeping customers is to understand their needs and buying processes better than competitors do and to deliver more value. To the extent that a company can position itself as providing superior value to selected target markets—either by offering lower prices than competitors or by providing more benefits to justify higher prices—it gains **competitive advantage.**[20] But solid positions cannot be built upon empty promises. If a company positions its product as *offering* the best quality and service, it must then *deliver* the promised quality and service. Thus, positioning begins with actually *differentiating* the company's marketing offer so that it will give consumers more value than competitors offer (see Marketing Highlight 9–3).

Not every company finds many opportunities for differentiating its offer and gaining competitive advantage. Some companies find many minor advantages that are easily copied by competitors and, therefore, highly perishable. The solution for these companies is to keep identifying new potential advantages and introducing them one-by-one to keep competitors off-balance. These companies do not expect to gain a single major permanent advantage, but rather many minor ones that can be introduced to win market share over a period of time.

In what specific ways can a company differentiate its offer from those of competitors? A company or market offer can be differentiated along lines of *product*, *services*, *personnel*, or *image*.

PRODUCT DIFFERENTIATION. A company can differentiate its physical product. At one extreme, some companies offer highly standardized products that allow little variation: chicken, steel, aspirin. Yet even here, some meaningful differentiation is possible. For example, Perdue claims that its branded chickens are better—fresher and tenderer—and gets a 10 percent price premium based on this differentiation.

Other companies offer products that can be highly differentiated, such as automobiles, commercial buildings, and furniture. Here, the company faces an abundance of design parameters.[21] It can offer a variety of standard or optional *features* not provided by competitors. Thus, Volvo provides new and better safety features; Delta Airlines offer wider seating and free in-flight telephone use. Companies can also differentiate their products on *performance*. Whirlpool designs its dishwasher to run more quietly; Procter & Gamble formulates Liquid Tide to get clothes cleaner. *Style* and *design* can also be important differentiating factors. Thus, many car buyers pay a premium for Jaguar automobiles because of their extraordinary look, even though Jaguar may have a poor reliability record. Similarly, companies can differentiate their products on such attributes as *consistency*, *durability*, *reliability*, or *repairability*.

NINTENDO: MORE THAN JUST FUN AND GAMES

In the early 1980s, no home could be without a video game console and a dozen or so cartridges. By 1983, Atari, Coleco, Mattel, and a dozen other companies offered some version of a video-game system and industry sales topped $3.2 billion. But by 1985, in just two short years, home video game sales had plummeted to a meager $100 million. Game consoles gathered dust in closets and cartridges, originally priced as high as $35 each, sold from cardboard cartons in the backs of stores for as low as $5. Industry leader Atari, a subsidiary of Warner-Lambert, was hardest hit when the bottom fell out. Amid soaring losses, Warner fired Atari's president, sacked 4,500 employees, and sold the subsidiary at a fraction of its 1983 worth. Most industry experts simply shrugged their shoulders and blamed the death of the video-game industry on fickle consumer tastes. Video games, they asserted, were just another fad.

But one company, Nintendo, a 100-year-old toy company from Kyoto, Japan, didn't think so. In late 1985, atop the still smoldering ruins of the U.S. video-game business, the company introduced its Nintendo Entertainment System (NES) in the United States. By the end of 1986, just one year later, Nintendo had sold over 1 million NES units. By early 1990, Nintendo and its licensees were reaping annual sales of $2.6 billion in a now revitalized $3.4-billion U.S. video-game industry. Nintendo now captures an astounding 80 percent share of the market, and more than 1 of every 5 American households has a Nintendo system hooked up to one of its television sets.

How did Nintendo manage to single-handedly revive a dying industry? First, it recognized that video-game customers weren't so much fickle as bored. The company sent researchers to visit popular video arcades to find out why alien-

Building competitive advantage: By differentiating itself through superior products and service, Nintendo has built a seemingly invincible quality position in the video game market.

ated home video-game fans still spent hours happily pumping quarters into arcade machines. The researchers found that Nintendo's own Donkey Kong and similar games were still mainstays of the arcades even though home versions were failing. The reason? The arcade games offered better quality, full animation, and challenging plots. Home video games, on the other hand, offered only crude quality and simple plots. Despite their exotic names and introductory hype, each new home game was boringly identical to all the others, featuring slow characters who moved through ugly animated

SERVICES DIFFERENTIATION. In addition to differentiating its physical product, the firm can also differentiate the services that accompany the product. Many possibilities exist. Some companies gain competitive advantage through speedy, reliable, or careful *delivery*. Deluxe, for example, has built an impressive reputation for shipping out replacement checks one day after receiving an order—without being late once in twelve years. Dominoes Pizza promises delivery in less than thirty minutes or takes $3 off the price. *Installation* can also differentiate one buyer from another. IBM, for example, is known for its quality installation service. It delivers all pieces of purchased equipment to the site at one time rather than sending individual components to sit waiting for others to arrive. And when asked to move IBM equipment and install it in another location, IBM often moves competitors' equipment as well. Companies can further distinguish themselves through their *repair* services. Many an automobile buyer would gladly pay a little more and travel a little farther to buy a car from a dealer that provides top-notch repair service.

Some companies differentiate their offers by providing *customer training* service. Thus, General Electric not only sells and installs expensive X-ray equipment in hospitals, it also trains the hospital employees who will use this equipment. Other companies offer free or paid *consulting services*—data, information systems, and advising services that buyers need. For example, McKesson Corporation, a major drug wholesaler, consults with its 12,000 independent pharmacists to help them set up accounting, inventory, and computer ordering systems. By helping its customers compete better, McKesson gains greater customer loyalty and sales.

scenes to the beat of monotonous, synthesized tones. The video kids of the early 1980s had quickly outgrown the elementary challenges of these first-generation home video games.

Nintendo saw the fall of the U.S. video-game industry not as a catastrophe, but as a golden opportunity. It set out to differentiate itself from the ailing competition by offering superior quality—by giving home video-game customers a full measure of quality entertainment value for their money. Nintendo designed a basic game system that sells for under $100 yet boasts near arcade-quality graphics. Equally important, it also developed innovative and high-quality software—"Game Paks" as Nintendo calls them—to accompany the system. The company's Game Pak library features 150 titles—new games are constantly added and mature titles weeded out to keep the selection fresh and interesting. The games contain consistently high-quality graphics, and game plots are varied and challenging. Colorful, cartoon-like characters move fluidly about cleverly animated screens. Amidst a chorus of booings, whistles, and bleeps, players can punch out Mike Tyson or wrestle Hulk Hogan, play ice hockey or golf, solve word and board games. The most popular games, however, involve complex sword-and-sorcery conflicts and the series of Super Mario Brothers fantasy worlds, where young heroes battle to save endangered princesses or to fight the evil ruler, Wart, for peace in the World of Dreams.

Nintendo's quest to deliver superior quality and value, however, goes far beyond selling its home video-game system. The company has also worked to build lasting relationships with its ever-growing customer base. For example, to help young customers having trouble navigating a passage in one of its games, Nintendo set up one of the most extensive telephone hotline systems in the country. Some 100,000 game players telephone each week seeking tips on game strategy from one of 250 Nintendo game counselors. The calls not only help create happy customers, they also provide Nintendo with valuable game-development and marketing information—the company learns first-hand what's hot and what's not. Nintendo also has introduced *Nintendo Power*, a bimonthly magazine that discusses the latest developments in home video-entertainment systems. The magazine became the fastest growing paid-subscription magazine ever—in a little over one year, the magazine's circulation rocketed to more than 1.8 million subscribers. Nintendo further cements its customer relationships by licensing its most popular characters for a variety of uses, not just t-shirts and posters, but also movies, a syndicated TV show, cartoons, and magazines.

Thus, by differentiating itself through superior products and service, and by building strong relationships with its customers, Nintendo has built a seemingly invincible quality position in the video-games market. Still, the company knows that it cannot simply rest on past success. New competitors such as Sega, NEC, INTV, and a revived Atari are already finding market niches as Nintendo junkies become bored and seek the next new video thrill. Hoping to beat Nintendo at its own game—product superiority—they are introducing new systems that offer even richer graphics, more lifelike sound, and more complex plots. Nintendo must find ways to continue to differentiate itself from these aggressive competitors. Nintendo's success in the home video-game market involves more than just fun and games—it involves keeping the fun *in* the games.

Sources: See Rebecca Fannin, "Zap?," *Marketing and Media Decisions*, November 1989, pp. 35–40; Raymond Roel, "The Power of Nintendo," *Direct Marketing*, September 1989, pp. 24–29; Stewart Wolpin, "How Nintendo Revived a Dying Industry," *Marketing Communications*, May 1989, pp. 36–40; Joe Mandese, "Power Plays," *Marketing & Media Decisions*, March 1989, pp. 101–106; and Maria Shao, "The Next Step Up from Nintendo," *Business Week*, May 28, 1990, p. 107.

Companies can find many other ways to add value through differentiated services. In fact, they can choose from a virtually unlimited number of specific services and benefits on which to differentiate themselves from their competitors. Milliken & Company provides one of the best examples of a company that has gained competitive advantage through superior service:

> Milliken sells shop towels to industrial launderers who rent them to factories. These towels are physically similar to competitors' towels. Yet Milliken charges a higher price for its towels and enjoys the leading market share. How can it charge more for essentially a commodity? The answer is that Milliken continuously "decommoditizes" this product through continuous service enhancement for its launderer customers. Milliken trains its customers' salespeople; supplies prospect leads and sales promotional material to them; supplies on-line computer order entry and freight optimization systems; carries on marketing research for customers; sponsors quality improvement workshops; and lends its salespeople to work with customers on Customer Action Teams. Launderers are more than willing to buy Milliken shop towels and pay a price premium because the extra services improve their profitability.[22]

PERSONNEL DIFFERENTIATION. Companies can gain a strong competitive advantage through hiring and training better people than their competitors do. Thus, Singapore Airlines enjoys an excellent reputation largely because of the beauty and grace of its cabin crews. McDonald's people are courteous, IBM people are professional and knowledgeable, and Disney people are friendly and upbeat. The salesforces of such companies as Connecticut General Life and Merck enjoy excellent reputations, which set their companies apart from competitors. Wal-Mart has differentiated its superstores by employing "people greeters" who welcome shoppers, give advice on where to find items, mark merchandise brought back for returns or exchanges, and give children gifts.

Personnel differentiation requires that a company select its customer-contact people carefully and train them well. These personnel must be competent; they must possess the required skills and knowledge. They need to be courteous, friendly, respectful, and considerate. They must perform the service with consistency and accuracy. And they must make an effort to understand customers, to communicate clearly with them, and to respond quickly to customer requests and problems.

IMAGE DIFFERENTIATION. Even when competing companies offer about the same products and accompanying services, buyers may perceive a difference based on company or brand images. Thus, companies work to establish *images* that differentiate them from competitors. A company or brand image should convey a singular and distinctive message that communicates the product's major benefits and positioning. Developing a strong and distinctive image calls for creativity and hard work. A company cannot implant an image in the public's mind overnight using only a few advertisements. If "IBM means service," this image must be supported by everything the company says and does.

Symbols can provide strong company or brand recognition and image differentiation. Companies design signs and logos that provide instant recognition. They associate themselves with objects or characters that symbolize quality or other attributes, such as the Harris Bank lion, the Apple Computer apple, or the Pillsbury doughboy. The company might build a brand around some famous person, as with perfumes such as Passion (Elizabeth Taylor) and Uninhibited (Cher). Some companies even become associated with colors, such as IBM (blue) or Campbell (red and white).

The chosen symbols must be communicated through advertising that conveys the company or brand's personality. The ads attempt to establish a story line, a mood, a performance level—something distinctive about the company or brand. The atmosphere of the physical space in which the organization produces or delivers its products and services can be another powerful image generator. Hyatt hotels have become known for their atrium lobbies and Victoria Station restaurants for their boxcars. Thus, a bank that wants to distinguish itself as the "friendly bank" must choose the right building and interior design, layout, colors, materials, and furnishings.

A company can also create an image through the types of events it sponsors. Perrier, the bottled water company, became known by laying out exercise tracks and sponsoring health sports events. Other organizations, such as AT&T and IBM, have identified themselves with cultural events, such as symphony performances and art exhibits. Still other organizations support popular causes: Heinz gives money to hospitals, and Quaker gives food to the homeless.

Selecting the Right Competitive Advantages

Suppose a company is fortunate enough to discover several potential competitive advantages. It must now choose the ones upon which it will build its positioning strategy. It must decide *how many* differences to promote and *which ones*.

HOW MANY DIFFERENCES TO PROMOTE? Many marketers think that companies should aggressively promote only one benefit to the target market. Rosser Reeves, for example, said a company should develop a *unique selling proposition* (USP) for each brand and stick to it. Each brand should pick an attribute and tout itself as "number one" on that attribute. Buyers tend to better remember "number one," especially in an overcommunicated society. Thus, Crest toothpaste consistently promotes its anti-cavity protection, and Mercedes promotes its great automotive engineering. What are some of the "number one" positions to promote? The major ones are "best quality," "best service," "lowest price," "best value," and "most advanced technology." A company that hammers away at one of these positions and consistently delivers on it will probably become best-known and remembered for it.

Other marketers think that companies should position themselves on more than one differentiating factor. This may be necessary if two or more firms are claiming to be best on the same attribute. Steelcase, an office furniture systems company, differentiates itself from competitors on two benefits: best on-time delivery and best installation support. Volvo positions its automobiles as ''safest'' and ''most durable.'' Fortunately, these two benefits are compatible—a very safe car would also be very durable.

Today, in a time when the mass market is fragmenting into many small segments, companies are trying to broaden their positioning strategies to appeal to more segments. For example, Beecham promotes its Aquafresh toothpaste as offering three benefits: ''anti-cavity protection,'' ''better breath,'' and ''whiter teeth.'' Clearly, many people want all three benefits, and the challenge is to convince them that the brand delivers all three. Beecham's solution was to create a toothpaste that squeezed out of the tube in three colors, thus visually confirming the three benefits. In doing this, Beecham attracted three segments instead of one.

However, as companies increase the number of claims for their brands, they risk disbelief and a loss of clear positioning. In general, a company needs to avoid three major positioning errors. The first is *underpositioning*—failing to ever really position the company at all. Some companies discover that buyers have only a vague idea of the company or that they do not really know anything special about it. The second positioning error is *overpositioning*—giving buyers to narrow a picture of the company. Thus, a consumer might think that the Steuben glass company makes only fine art glass costing $1000 and up, when in fact it makes affordable fine glass starting at around $50. Finally, companies must avoid *confused positioning*—leaving buyers with a confused image of a company. For example, Burger King has struggled without success for years to establish a profitable and consistent position. Since 1986, however, it has fielded five separate advertising campaigns, with themes ranging from ''Herb the nerd doesn't eat here,'' and ''This is a Burger King town,'' to ''The right food for the right times,'' and ''Sometimes you've got to break the rules.'' This barrage of positioning statements has left consumers confused and Burger King with poor sales and profits.[23]

WHICH DIFFERENCES TO PROMOTE? Not all brand differences are meaningful or worthwhile. Not every difference is a differentiator. Each difference has the potential to create company costs as well as customer benefits. Therefore, the company must carefully select the ways in which it will distinguish itself from competitors. A difference is worth establishing to the extent that it satisfies the following criteria:

- *Important*—the difference delivers a highly valued benefit to target buyers.
- *Distinctive*—competitors do not offer the difference, or the company can offer it in a more distinctive way.
- *Superior*—the difference is superior to other ways that customers might obtain the same benefit.
- *Communicable*—the difference is communicable and visible to buyers.
- *Preemptive*—competitors cannot easily copy the difference.
- *Affordable*—buyers can afford to pay for the difference.
- *Profitable*—the company can introduce the difference profitably.

Many companies have introduced differentiations that failed one or more of these tests. The Westin Stamford hotel in Singapore advertises that it is the world's tallest hotel, a distinction that is not important to many tourists—in fact, it turns many off. AT&T's Picturevision phones bombed, partly because the public did not think that seeing the other person was worth the phone's high cost. Polaroid's Polarvision, which produced instantly developed home movies, bombed too. Although Polarvision was distinctive and even preemptive, it was inferior to another way of capturing motion, namely, videocameras.

Some competitive advantages can be quickly ruled out because they are too slight, too costly to develop, or too inconsistent with the company's profile. Suppose that a company is designing its positioning strategy and has narrowed its list of possible competitive advantages to four. The company needs a framework for selecting the one advantage that makes the most sense to develop. Table 9-4 shows a systematic way to evaluate several potential competitive advantages and choose the right one.

TABLE 9-4 Finding Competitive Advantage

COMPETITIVE ADVANTAGE	COMPANY STANDING (1–10)	COMPETITOR STANDING (1–10)	IMPORTANCE OF IMPROVING STANDING (H-M-L)	AFFORD-ABILITY AND SPEED (H-M-L)	COMPETITOR'S ABILITY TO IMPROVE STANDING (H-M-L)	RECOMMENDED ACTION
Technology	8	8	L	L	M	Hold
Cost	6	8	H	M	M	Watch
Quality	8	6	L	L	H	Watch
Service	4	3	H	H	L	Invest

In the table, the company compares its standing on four attributes—technology, cost, quality, and service—to the standing of its major competitor. Let's assume that both companies stand at 8 on technology (1 = low score, 10 = high score), which means they both have good technology. The company questions whether it can gain much by improving its technology further, especially given the high cost of new technology. The competitor has a better standing on cost (8 instead of 6), and this can hurt the company if the market becomes more price-sensitive. The company offers higher quality than its competitors (8 instead of 6). Finally, both companies offer below-average service.

At first glance, it appears that the company should go after cost or service to improve its market appeal relative to the competitor. However, it must consider other factors. First, how important are improvements in each of these attributes to the target customers? The fourth column shows that cost and service improvements would both be highly important to customers. Next, can the company afford to make the improvements? If so, how fast can it complete them? The fifth column shows that the company could improve service quickly and affordably. But if the firm decided to do this, would the competitor be able to improve its service also? The sixth column shows that the competitor's ability to improve service is low, perhaps because the competitor doesn't believe in service or is strapped for funds. The final column then shows the appropriate actions to take on each attribute. It makes the most sense for the company to invest in improving its service. Service is important to customers; the company can afford to improve its service and do it fast; and the competitor probably can't catch up.

Communicating and Delivering the Chosen Position

Once it has chosen a position, the company must take strong steps to deliver and communicate the desired position to target consumers. All the company's marketing-mix efforts must support the positioning strategy. Positioning the company calls for concrete action, not just talk. If the company decides to build a position on better quality and service, it must first *deliver* that position. Designing the marketing mix—product, price, place, and promotion—essentially involves working out the tactical details of the positioning strategy. Thus, a firm that seizes upon a "high-quality position" knows that it must produce high-quality products, charge a high price, distribute through high-class dealers, and advertise in high-quality media. It must hire and train more service people, find retailers who have a good reputation for service, and develop sales and advertising messages that broadcast its superior service. This is the only way to build a consistent and believable high-quality, high-service position.

Companies often find it easier to come up with a good positioning strategy than to implement it. Establishing a position or changing one usually takes a long time. On the other hand, positions that have taken years to build can quickly be lost. Once a company has built the desired position, it must take care to maintain the position through consistent performance and communication. The position must be closley monitored and adapted over time to match changes in consumer needs and competitors' strategies. However, the company should avoid abrupt changes that might confuse consumers. Instead, a product's position should evolve gradually as it adapts to the ever-changing marketing environment.

■ SUMMARY

Sellers can take three approaches to a market. *Mass marketing* is the decision to mass-produce and mass-distribute one product and attempt to attract all kinds of buyers. *Product variety marketing* is the decision to produce two or more market offers differentiated in style, features, quality, or sizes, designed to offer variety to the market and to set the seller's products apart from competitor's products. *Target marketing* is the decision to identify the different groups that make up a market and to develop products and marketing mixes for selected target markets. Sellers today are moving away from mass marketing and product differentiation toward target marketing because this approach is more helpful in spotting market opportunities and developing more effective products and marketing mixes.

The key steps in target marketing are market segmentation, market targeting, and market positioning. *Market segmentation* is the act of dividing a market into distinct groups of buyers who might merit separate products or marketing mixes. The marketer tries different variables to see which give the best segmentation opportunities. For constant marketing, the major segmentation variables are geographic, demographic, psychographic, and behavioral. Industrial markets can be segmented by industrial consumer demographics, operating characteristics, purchasing approaches, and personal characteristics. The effectiveness of segmentation analysis depends on finding segments that are *measurable*, *accessible*, *substantial*, and *actionable*.

Next, the seller has to target the best market segments. The company first evaluates each segment's size and growth characteristics, structural attractiveness, and compatibility with company resources and objectives. It then chooses one of three market-coverage strategies. The seller can ignore segment differences (*undifferentiated marketing*), develop different market offers for several segments (*differentiated marketing*), or go after one or a few market segments (*concentrated marketing*). Much depends on company resources, product variability, product life-cycle stage, and competitive marketing strategies.

Once a company has decided which segments to enter, it must decide on its *market positioning* strategy—on which positions to occupy in its chosen segments. It can position its products on specific product attributes, according to usage occasion, for certain classes of users, or by product class. It can position either against competitors or away from competitors. The positioning task consists of three steps: identifying a set of possible competitive advantages upon which to build a position, selecting the right competitive advantages, and effectively communicating and delivering the chosen position to the market.

■ QUESTIONS FOR DISCUSSION

1. Describe how the Ford Motor Company has moved from mass marketing to product-variety marketing to target marketing. Can you think of other examples of companies whose marketing approaches have evolved over time?

2. What variables are used in segmenting the market for beer? Give examples.

3. Hispanics are now viewed as an attractive, distinct market segment. Can you market the same way to a Puerto Rican seamstress in New York, a Cuban doctor in Miami, and a Mexican laborer in Houston? Discuss the similarities and differences that you see. What does this imply about market segments?

4. Some industrial suppliers make above-average profits by offering service, selection, and reliability—at a premium price. How can these suppliers segment the market to find customers who are willing to pay more for these benefits?

5. An article in *Advertising Age* reported that baseball fans prefer chocolate ice cream if their favorite team in the 1950s was the Dodgers, vanilla ice cream if their team was the Yankees, and strawberry or coffee ice cream if they rooted for the Giants. Does this relationship indicate that team preference can be used as a segmentation variable in marketing ice cream?

6. Are any characteristics of useful market segments more important than the others, or are measurability, accessibility, substantiality, and actionability all equally important? Why?

7. Think about your classmates in this course. Can you segment them into different groups with specific nicknames? What is your major segmentation variable? Could you effectively market products to these segments?

8. What roles do product attributes and perceptions of attributes play in positioning a product? Can an attribute held by several competing brands be used in a successful positioning strategy?

9. A fabric has recently been developed that has the look and feel of cotton but is very stretchable. What segment would you target with casual pants made from this fabric? How would you position these pants?

10. Cadillac diversified with the Cimarron, a smaller, less-expensive Cadillac. Officials said they would consider the car a disaster if it sold only to traditional customers, even if they bought every car produced. The Cadillac merchandising director said, "Our salespersons will tell some buyers, 'This car isn't for you.'" Explain this strategy in terms of market segmentation, targeting, and positioning.

■ KEY TERMS

Accessibility. The degree to which a market segment can be reached and served.

Actionability. The degree to which effective programs can be designed for attracting and serving a given market segment.

Age and life-cycle segmentation. Dividing a market into different age and life-cycle groups.

Behavior segmentation. Dividing a market into groups based on consumers' knowledge, attitude, use, or response to a product.

Benefit segmentation. Dividing the market into groups according to the different benefits that consumers seek from the product.

Competitive advantage. An advantage over competitors gained by offering consumers greater value, either through lower prices or by providing more benefits that justify higher prices.

Concentrated marketing. A market-coverage strategy in which a firm goes after a large share of one or a few submarkets.

Demographic segmentation. Dividing the market into groups based on demographic variables such as age, sex, family size, family life cycle, income, occupation, education, religion, race, and nationality.

Differentiated marketing. A market-coverage strategy in which a firm decides to target several market segments and designs separate offers for each.

Geographic segmentation. Dividing a market into different geographical units such as nations, states, regions, counties, cities, or neighborhoods.

Income segmentation. Dividing a market into different income groups.

Market. The set of all actual and potential buyers of a product.

Market positioning. Formulating competitive positioning for a product and a detailed marketing mix.

Market segmentation. Dividing a market into direct groups of buyers who might require separate products or marketing mixes.

Market targeting. Evalauting each market segment's attractiveness and selecting one or more segments to enter.

Measurability. The degree to which the size and purchasing power of a market segment can be measured.

Micromarketing. A form of target marketing in which companies tailor their marketing programs to the needs and wants of narrowly defined geographic, demographic, psychographic, or benefit segments.

Occasion segmentation. Dividing the market into groups according to occasion when buyers get the idea, make a purchase, or use a product.

Product position. The way the product is defined by consumers on important attributes; the place the product occupies in consumers' minds relative to competing products.

Psychographic segmentation. Dividing a market into different groups based on social class, life style, or personality characteristics.

Sex segmentation. Dividing a market into different groups based on sex.

Substantiality. The degree to which a market segment is large or profitable enough.

Target market. A set of buyers sharing common needs or characteristics that the company decides to serve.

Undifferentiated marketing. A market-coverage strategy in which a firm decides to ignore market segment differences and go after the whole market with one market offer.

■ REFERENCES

1. Thomas Moore, "Different Folks, Different Strokes," *Fortune*, September 16, 1985, p. 65; and Michael Oneal, "Attack of the Bug Killers," *Business Week*, May 16, 1988, p. 81.

2. See Julie Liesse Erickson, "Marketing to Women: It's Tough to Keep Up with Changes," *Advertising Age*, March 7, 1988, p. S1; Raymond Serafin, "Carmakers Step Up Chase for Women," *Advertising Age*, May 16, 1988, p. 76; and Frieda Curtindale, "Marketing Cars to Women," *American Demographics*, November 1988, pp. 29–31. For another example of marketing to women, see Mark Lewyn, "PC Makers, Palms Sweating, Try Talking to Women," *Business Week*, January 15, 1990, p. 48.

3. See Pat Grey Thomas, "Marketing to the Affluent," *Advertising Age*, March 16, 1987, p. S-1.

4. Steve Lawrence, "The Green in Blue-Collar Retailing," *Fortune*, May 27, 1985, pp. 74–77; and Dean Foust, "The Family Feud at Family Dollar Stores," *Business Week*, September 21, 1987, pp. 32–33.

5. Thomas Exter, "Deodorant Demographics," *American Demographics*, December 1987, p. 39.

6. Bickley Townsend, "Psychographic Glitter and Gold," *American Demographics*, November 1985, p. 22.

7. For a detailed discussion of personality and buyer behavior, see Leon G. Schiffman and Leslie Lazar Kanuk, *Consumer Behavior*, 4th Ed. (Englewood Cliffs, NJ: Prentice Hall, 1991), Chapter 4.

8. See Laurie Freeman and Cleveland Horton, "Spree: Honda's Scooters Ride the Cutting Edge," *Advertising Age*, September 5, 1985, pp. 3, 35.

9. See Schiffman and Kanuk, *Consumer Behavior*, p. 48.

10. For more reading on benefit segmentation, see Russell I. Haley, "Benefit Segmentation: Backwards and Forwards," *Journal of Advertising Research*, February–March 1984, pp. 19–25; and Russell I. Haley, "Benefit Segmentation—20 Years Later," *Journal of Consumer Marketing*, Vol. 1, 1984, pp. 5–14.

11. See John J. Burnett, "Psychographic and Demographic Characteristics of Blood Donors," *Journal of Consumer Research*, June 1981, pp. 62–66.

12. See Mark Ivey, "Long-Distance Learning Gets an 'A' at Last," *Business Week*, May 9, 1988, pp. 108–10.

13. See Thomas V. Bonoma and Benson P. Shapiro, *Segmenting the Industrial Market* (Lexington, MA: Lexington Books, 1983). For examples of segmenting business markets, see Kate Bertrand, "Market Segmentation: Divide and Conquer," *Business Marketing*, October 1989, pp. 48–54.

14. See Joe Schwartz, "Southpaw Strategy," *American Demographics*, June 1988, p. 61.

15. See Michael Porter, *Competitive Advantage* (New York: Free Press, 1985), pp. 4–8 and pp. 234–36.

16. Bill Saporito, "Just How Good is the Great A&P?" *Fortune*, March 16, 1987, pp. 92–93.

17. See Stuart Gannes, "The Riches in Market Niches," *Fortune*, April 27, 1987, pp. 227–30.

18. For more reading on positioning, see Yoram Wind, "New Twists for Some Old Tricks," *The Wharton Magazine*, Spring 1980, pp. 34–39; David A. Aaker and J. Gary Shansby, "Positioning Your Product," *Business Horizons*, May–June 1982, pp. 56–62; and Regis McKenna, "Playing for Position," *INC*, April 1985, pp. 92–97.

19. See Wind, "New Twists," p. 36; and Aaker and Shansby, "Positioning Your Product," pp. 57–58.

20. For a good discussion of the concepts of differentiation and competitive advantage and methods for assessing them, see Michael Porter, *Competitive Advantage*, Chapter 2; George S. Day and Robin Wensley, "Assessing Advantage: A Framework for Diagnosing Competitive Superiority," *Journal of Marketing*, April 1988, pp. 1–20; and Philip Kotler, *Marketing Management*, 7th Ed. (Englewood Cliffs, NJ: Prentice Hall, 1991), Chapter 11.

21. See David A. Garvin, "Competing on the Eight Dimensions of Quality," *Harvard Business Review*, November–December 1987, pp. 101–109.

22. See Tom Peters, *Thriving on Chaos* (New York: Alfred A. Knopf, Inc., 1987), pp. 56–57.

23. Mark Landler and Gail DeGeorge, "Tempers Are Sizzling Over Burger King's New Ads," *Business Week*, February 12, 1990, p. 33.

GATORADE: THIRSTING FOR COMPETITIVE POSITIONING

As Quaker Oats Company's Gatorade sports drink enters the 1990s, it holds an estimated 90 percent share of a $600 million worldwide market it created. Invented by a doctor for the University of Florida Gators, Gatorade became a beverage phenomenon. Sales have grown at a 30 percent annual rate over the past five years. "Gatorade is almost generic for the isotonic, or sports, drink category," says Michael Bellas, president of Beverage Marketing Corp., a beverage consulting company in New York. "That's a hard act to follow."

Gatorade's managers used market segmentation techniques to achieve its position; however, the road to dominance was not without its ups and downs. According to Larry Dykstra, manager of marketing research for Quaker Oats, the development of a focused positioning for Gatorade has allowed the company to target core users and identify secondary markets. Before Quaker acquired the beverage in 1983, Gatorade's previous owner had promoted it by portraying users as competitive athletes, adult men, teens, and caricatures of athletes.

"When we acquired Gatorade," recalls Dykstra, "it was a poorly positioned brand, with a lack of consistent focus." This position stood in contrast with the way current users were defined. "There was no message on the uses of this product or under which circumstances and occasions it was supposed to be used."

When Quaker looked at marketing research, Dykstra says the company found that Gatorade's main users were men aged 19 to 44, that they understood the product, had a good perception of what it did, and knew when to drink it and how to use it.

Since Gatorade had been developed and marketed primarily in the South, Quaker wanted to find out if there was an opportunity to market the drink in other areas. A study of attitudes determined that the target could be expanded geographically. "We felt, based on research, that we could take a narrow, solid positioning of the product that was consistent with southern users and market the product in the North," Dykstra says.

"In 1987, we focused in on our primary target, but there have been refinements," Dykstra explains. "We've tried to portray users as accomplished but not professional athletes." Although the drink is perceived as a "serious beverage, the ads have added a fun component by showing people enjoying it together. "We tried to show people who didn't alienate customers, but also people they could aspire to be like."

An effort also was made to portray people's *motivations* for using the product. A computer graphic that portrays thirst quenching was introduced—one which, according to Dykstra, came "across so strong we've started to change the language."

But being well-focused and consistent in developing the product over time can create other problems. "Because Gatorade is narrowly positioned in terms of users and user occasions," explains Dykstra, "growth opportunities are probably limited. So how can we go about identifying new opportunities?"

Competitors' attacks on Gatorade's previously unchallenged position mean that finding new opportunities for the 1990s is even more important. In 1987, Coca-Cola introduced a powdered sports drink, Max; but the drink never made it out of test markets. In 1989, three rookie sports-drink makers tried to muscle in on the thirst-quenching business. PowerBurst Corp. introduced Power-Burst, a drink sweetened with fructose, which it claimed provided sustained energy rather than the short-term energy spike provided by the sweeteners in Gatorade. White Rock Products Corp. introduced Workout Light, a reduced-calorie sports drink. Sports Beverage, Inc., introduced Pro Motion with the claim that it had less sodium and more potassium than Gatorade.

However, Gatorade's most pressing concern centers on Coca-Cola's March 1990, announcement that it would re-enter the sports-drink market and on Pepsi's recent forays. Coca-Cola indicated that it plans to distribute Power-Ade as a fountain product primarily in convenience stores, 95 percent of which have drink fountains. National distribution follows a successful four-month market test in California. Coke's continuing interest in the sports-drink market stems not from the market's size, which is minuscule in comparison to the $40 billion soft-drink market, but from its double-digit volume growth rate, which compares favorably with the soft-drink market's growth rate of 2.5 percent to 3.5 percent.

Although Coke apparently feels the sports-drink market is large enough to warrant its attention, the timing of its entry seems to have been affected by Pepsi's announcement that it will start a second test market for its lightly carbonated sports drink, Mountain Dew Sport. Pepsi indicates that the drink has already been successful in an initial test market, claiming that the drink's sales were 2 to 1 over Gatorade.

Thus, Gatorade faces not only the need to develop new opportunities to spur its growth, but also the need to strengthen its position in order to protect its hold on the sports-drink market.

QUESTIONS

1. What are the major variables that might be used to segment Gatorade's consumer market?
2. Define the core and secondary targets for Gatorade.

3. Describe the position of Gatorade as defined by consumers when the brand was acquired by Quaker Oats in 1983. Trace the changes in positioning strategy until 1987.

4. Evaluate the pros and cons of the current multi-segment targeting strategy.

5. Identify new marketing opportunities that Gatorade should pursue, including new market segments that it should address.

Develop a marketing strategy for addressing one of these opportunities.

Source: Adapted from ''Quaker Looks to Expand Market for Gatorade,'' *Marketing News*, Vol. 22, January 4, 1988, pp. 38–39, published by the American Marketing Association. Also see M. J. McCarthy, ''Coke Fields a Sports Drink to Challenge Gatorade's Hold,'' *Wall Street Journal*, March 6, 1990, and M. Manges, ''Sports-Drink Makers Out to Tackle Gatorade,'' *Wall Street Journal*, August 10, 1989.

THE "OVER-50" MARKET

Ask any marketing executive to identify the next hot market in terms of size and purchasing power and the answer is likely to be the older market—consumers age 50 and older.

Research by such prestigious ad agencies as Grey Advertising, Ogilvy and Mather, and TBWA confirms that today's 50-plus consumers are healthier, wealthier, more active, better educated, and more willing to spend than their age group was in the past. Unlike their parents and grandparents, they aren't sickly, obstinate, and tightfisted. As Grey Research points out, marketers need to see "50-plus consumers as they see themselves—romantic, chic, happy, and joyfully involved with family, friends, and life."

Consider these facts: The over-50 market is expected to grow three times faster than the under-50 market during the next decade. There are 77.2 million baby boomers, the oldest of whom will reach age 50 in the mid-1990s. People over 50 now control 75 percent of the nation's wealth and approximately 50 percent of its discretionary income. By the year 2000, 21 percent of all seniors will have a household income of $50,000 in constant dollars (up from 1985's figure of 12 percent).

Marketers need to realize that older adults tend to see themselves as much younger—10 to 15 years younger—than they really are. Therefore, market segmentation based on age is not as appropriate as segmentation based on life-style or motivation. Other relevant segmenting variables are income and how older adults use their time.

Some marketers who primarily focused on consumer age learned this lesson the hard way. Gerber products, for example, introduced Singles, a line of puréed foods for adults. The product seemed like a natural for denture wearers, but sales did not meet company expectations.

Research indicated that older consumers did not want to be seen buying their meals in what looked like baby food jars. Similarly, Johnson and Johnson found sales of their Affinity shampoo disappointing when it was first marketed as a shampoo for "mature" hair. When the company repositioned the product for the general market, sales improved. Products of other companies such as Coca-Cola, whose ads featured Art Carney with a young boy who plays his grandson, and General Foods, which used the 70+ but still glamorous Lena Horne as a spokesperson for Post Natural Bran Flakes, have been well received. In fact, many companies, including AT&T, Sears, Marriott, Sharp Electronics, Beecham, Travelers, and Whirlpool, have either developed or modified existing products and services for the over-50 market. Their strategy has been to allow customer needs to influence company plans: As customers have changed, so have they. But a good product is not enough; it needs to fit the consumer's life-style. And the marketer should not emphasize the consumer's age. Businesspeople will do well to consider Grey's research, which suggests that marketers show consumers as they see themselves—not as the marketer sees them.

QUESTIONS

1. Identify and discuss the requirements for effective market segmentation for the over-50 market.
2. What is age a poor predictor of consumer life-style for the over-50 market?

Sources: "U.S. Companies Go for the Gray," *Business Week*, April 3, 1989, pp. 64–67; "Tea, Sympathy and Direct Mail," *Forbes*, September 18, 1987, pp. 210–211; "Studies Tell the Story, But Dollars Don't Follow," *Advertising Age*, May 22, 1989, p. 54; and "How to Age Profitability," *American Demographics*, September 1990, pp. 44–45.

COCA-COLA: TARGETING A NEW COKE MACHINE

The world's largest soft drink marketer has a new dream—to put a Coke within easy reach of every office worker. Coca-Cola hopes to realize this dream with BreakMate, a compact fountain dispensing system that may someday make Coke machines as common in the work place as coffee machines. Coca-Cola has been developing the BreakMate for more than 20 years and has tested it in 30 U.S. and foreign cities. Industry observers believe it represents the most expensive soft-drink development project in history.

Beyond its potential impact on Coca-Cola's $8 billion annual soft-drink sales, BreakMate promises to put some fizz in the entire industry. Per capita soft-drink consumption, which now stands at 45 gallons annually, surpassed water consumption in the U.S. in 1986. However, during the past decade, major beverage marketers have assumed that there are few new avenues of distribution to explore. Instead, they have sought growth only through new products, flooding the market with new brands and brand extensions. Retailers have often responded by charging companies fees to put their new brands on store shelves. As a result, the soft-drink manufacturers have seen the market shares of their major brands erode and their costs of doing business rise dramatically.

Coca-Cola's Breakmate signals a new emphasis on distribution and a new battle for the largely untapped office market. Beverage companies consider the office market especially important because of declining coffee consumption and the increasing popularity of carbonated soft drinks. As one industry analyst notes, "Brands have been segmented to death in the soft drink business. The major channels of distribution are full and to get just a small percentage of growth takes tremendous sums of money. The work place would represent a tremendous uncharted market for Coke syrup sales."

Coca-Cola doesn't have the office market all to itself, however. Pepsi introduced a 24 can mini-vending machine in 1988. These small machines, Pepsi claims, have increased its overall vending business by 10 percent. Although Coca-Cola is not positing the BreakMate against canned drinks, it appears to have some advantages. Distributors point out that fountain drinks, at about eight cents per serving, are more economical than cans. The can by itself can cost a dime, and to deliver 10 cases of cans or bottles requires bigger equipment and more storage space. Research also shows that women prefer the 6½ ounce BreakMate fountain drink to a standard 12 ounce can.

Companies have tried to market office fountain systems before. In the early 1970s, Coca-Cola introduced the "Refresh" program for the office, but the program failed because the system consumed too much space and required the use of a bulky carbon-dioxide canister for carbonation. Attempts by other companies to break into the office market have also failed because they required office workers to mix their own syrup and water. Through its competitors' earlier attempts, Coca-Cola learned that a successful fountain system would have to be reliable, easy to use, and small enough to fit almost anywhere.

Bosch-Siemens, the West German appliance maker, has joined forces with Coca-Cola to produce the patented BreakMate. The machine is about the same size as a large microwave oven and weighs only 78 pounds when fully loaded. The customer connects the self-refrigerated BreakMate to a water source or, if no water source is available, uses an option water reservoir attachment. The machine holds three 1-liter syrup cartridges, each of which can produce approximately 30 6½ ounce drinks. Only Coke syrup cartridges work with the BreakMate. The customer also installs a carbon-dioxide cylinder which is good for about 250 drinks. When a user presses one of the three flavor selection buttons, water passes from the refrigerated area into the mixing channel and carbon dioxide is injected to produce carbonated water. Then, a "doser" attached to each syrup cartridge measures the amount of syrup needed to make a perfect soda. Bosch-Siemens has added a light that indicates when the carbon-dioxide container is empty. It has also developed a coin acceptor that accepts nickels, dimes, and quarters for use in offices where users will have to pay. Coca-Cola may also add an ice-crushing mechanism. Ice is not necessary because the machine delivers the drink at 32°F. Depending on the options selected, distributors will be able to buy the machines for $800 to $1,000.

Market tests have convinced Coca-Cola that Break-Mate produces soft drinks of consistent quality. Coca-Cola claims that users find the system as easy to use as a coffee machine.

Coca-Cola has also worked to develop BreakMate's distribution system. Coca-Cola could ship the syrup and carbon-dioxide cylinders needed to replenish the Break-Mate directly to customers by U.P.S. However, the company wants to develop a distributor system to work directly with customers. In Europe, bottler networks service Break-Mate accounts. In the United States, however, most large bottlers aren't providing the required level of service, so coffee distributors, bottled water firms, vending companies, and small independent bottlers will be the primary service providers. These service companies will install the machines and supply the syrup canisters in much the same way they service coffee and vending machines. Coca-Cola promotes BreakMate to coffee distributors who service offices as a system that can help them increase their gross profits. BreakMate allows these distributors to offer a day-long "total refreshment system" that picks up with soft drink sales where coffee consumption leaves off.

Using its experience from the past three years of market testing, Coca-Cola appears to have refined the BreakMate machines and is well along in developing its distribution strategy. However, the company has yet to clarify its end-customer target markets. Coca-Cola's previous research has shown that a standard soft-drink vending machine can be profitable in business locations with 20 or more employees. This means, however, that employees in the more than one million offices in the United States employing fewer than 20 people have limited access to soft drinks. Further, observers estimate that the number of these smaller offices will grow rapidly as the nation moves toward a more service-oriented economy. Therefore, Coca-Cola originally intended to focus on these small-to-medium-sized work locations—offices with 5 to 20 em-

ployees. However, Coca-Cola figures that BreakMate can be profitable in offices with as few as five employees if the office has substantial foot traffic. In addition, distributors could locate the machines in areas of larger offices where employees may have to take a long walk or an elevator ride to get to a larger drink machine.

Given this expanded view of potential BreakMate locations, Coca-Cola faces a real challenge. Coca-Cola and its distributors will not be able to develop and serve the millions of possible locations all at once. Can it segment the market in better ways than just by the number of employees? Will certain types of businesses be more receptive to the BreakMate than others? Will different types of businesses have different buying decision processes?

Coca-Cola believes it has an 18 month lead on rival Pepsi in this new front in the great Cola Wars. But to take advantage of this lead, it must move quickly and effectively to refine its marketing strategy. Moreover, if it succeeds in the office market, Coca-Cola might be able to open still another front—BreakMate might just lead the way to a dispenser that will one day make fountain Coke available in the home.

QUESTIONS

1. What bases can be used to segment the small office market? What market segments can you identify?
2. How would you go about forecasting demand for the BreakMate in each segment? What other criteria would you use to evaluate the segments?
3. Which type of market coverage strategy should Coca-Cola adopt and which specific segment(s) should the company target. Why?
4. How should Coca-Cola position BreakMate to appeal to customers in the target segment(s).

Source: Adapted from Laurie Petersen, "The New Coke Machine," *Adweek's Marketing Week*, September 26, 1988. Used with permission.

10

Designing Products: Products, Brands, Packaging, and Services

Each year, Revlon sells more than $1 billion worth of cosmetics, toiletries, and fragrances to consumers around the world. Its many successful perfume products make Revlon number one in the popular-price segment of the $4 billion fragrance market. In one sense, Revlon's perfumes are no more than careful mixtures of oils and chemicals that have nice scents. But Revlon knows that when it sells perfume, it sells much more than fragrant fluids—it sells what the fragrances will do for the women who use them.

Of course, a perfume's scent contributes to its success or failure. Fragrance marketers agree: "No smell; no sell." Most new aromas are developed by elite "perfumers" at one of fifty or so select "fragrance houses." Perfume is shipped from the fragrance houses in big, ugly oil drums—hardly the stuff of which dreams are made! Although a $180-per-ounce perfume may cost no more than $10 to produce, to perfume consumers the product is much more than a few dollars worth of ingredients and a pleasing smell.

Many things beyond the ingredients and scent add to a perfume's allure. In fact, when Revlon designs a new perfume, the scent may be the *last* element developed. Revlon first researches women's feelings about themselves and their relationships with others. It then develops and tests new perfume concepts that match women's changing values, desires, and life styles. When Revlon finds a promising new concept, it creates a scent to fit it.

Revlon's research in the early 1970s showed that women were feeling more competitive with men and that they were striving to find individual identities. For this new woman of the 1970s, Revlon created Charlie, the first of the "life-style" perfumes. Thousands of women adopted Charlie as a bold statement of independence, and it quickly became the world's best-selling perfume.

In the late 1970s, Revlon research showed a shift in women's attitudes. "Women had made the equality point, which Charlie addressed. Now women were hungering for an expression of feminity." The Charlie girls had grown up; they now wanted perfumes that were subtle rather than shocking. Thus, Revlon subtly shifted Charlie's position: the perfume still makes its "independent life style" statement, but with an added tinge of "feminity and romance." It also launched a perfume for the women of the 1980s—Jontue—which was positioned on a theme of romance.

A perfume's *name* is an important product attribute. Revlon uses such names as Charlie, Fleurs de Jontue, Ciara, and Scoundrel to create images that support each perfume's positioning. Competitors offer perfumes with such names as Obsession, Passion, Uninhibited, Opium, Joy, Exclamation!, White Linen, Youth Dew, and Eternity. These names suggest that the perfumes will do something more than just make you smell better. Oscar de la Renta's Ruffles perfume *began* as a name, one chosen because it created images of whimsy, youth, glamour, and feminity—all well-suited to the target market of young, stylish women. Only later was a scent selected to go with the product's name and positioning.

Revlon must also carefully *package* its perfumes.

To consumers, the bottle and package are the most real symbol of the perfume and its image. Bottles must feel comfortable and be easy to handle, and they must display well in stores. Most importantly, they must support the perfume's concept and image.

So when a woman buys perfume, she buys much, much more than simply fragrant fluids. The perfume's image, its promises, its scent, its name and package, the company that makes it, the stores that sell it—all become a part of the total perfume product. When Revlon sells perfume, it sells more than just the tangible product. It sells life style, self-expression, and exclusivity; achievement, success, and status; femininity, romance, passion, and fantasy; memories, hopes, and dreams.[1]

CHAPTER OBJECTIVES

After reading this chapter, you should be able to:

1. Define *product* and the major classifications of consumer and industrial products.
2. Explain why companies use brands and identify the major branding decisions.
3. Describe the roles of product packaging and labeling.
4. Explain the decisions companies make when developing product lines and mixes.

Clearly, perfume is more than just perfume when Revlon sells it. Revlon's great success in the rough-and-tumble fragrance world comes from developing an innovative product concept. An effective product concept is the first step in marketing-mix planning.

This chapter begins with a deceptively simple question: *What is a product*? We then look at ways to classify products in consumer and industrial markets and look for links between types of products and types of marketing strategies. Next, we see that each product involves several decisions that go beyond basic product design, such as *branding*, *packaging* and *labeling*, and *product-support services*. Finally, we move from decisions about individual products to decisions about building product lines and product mixes.

WHAT IS A PRODUCT?

A Kennex tennis racquet, a Supercuts haircut, a Broadway play, a Hawaiian vacation, a GMC truck, Head skis, and a telephone answering service are all products. We define *product* as follows: A **product** is anything that can be offered to a market for attention, acquisition, use, or consumption that might satisfy a want or need.

Most products are *physical products*, such as automobiles, toasters, shoes, eggs, and books. But *services* such as haircuts, concerts, and vacations are also products. *Persons* can be thought of as products. For example, presidential candidates can be marketed, not in the sense that we "buy" them, but in the sense that we give them attention, vote for them, and support their programs. A *place* like Hawaii can be marketed, in the sense that we might buy land in Hawaii or take a vacation there. An *organization* like the American Red Cross can be marketed, in the sense that we feel positively toward it and support it. Even an *idea* can be marketed, such as healthy eating or safe driving, in the sense that we might adopt the behavior associated with these ideas and promote them to others. Thus, broadly defined, products consist of anything that can be marketed, including physical objects, services, persons, places, organizations, and ideas.

Product planners need to think about the product on three levels. The most basic level is the **core product**, which addresses the question: *What is the buyer really buying*? As illustrated in Figure 10-1, the core product stands at the center of the total product. It consists of the problem-solving services or core benefits that consumers obtain when they buy a product. A woman buying lipstick buys more than lip color. Charles Revson

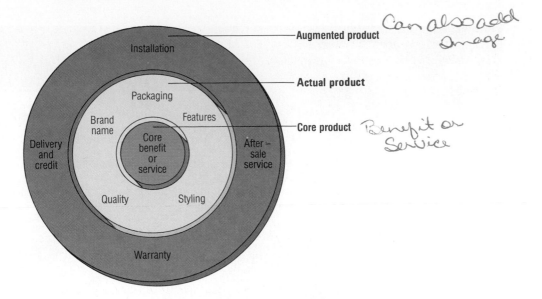

Can also add image

Benefit or Service

FIGURE 10-1
Three levels of product

of Revlon saw this early: "In the factory, we make cosmetics; in the store, we sell hope." Theodore Levitt has pointed out that buyers "do not buy quarter-inch drills; they buy quarter-inch holes." Thus, when designing products, marketers must first define the core of *benefits* the product will provide to consumers.

The product planner must next build an **actual product** around the core product. Actual products may have as many as five characteristics: a *quality level*, *features*, *styling*, a *brand name*, and *packaging*. For example, Sony's Handycam Camcorder is an actual product. Its name, parts, styling, features, packaging, and other attributes have all been carefully combined to deliver the core benefit—a convenient, high-quality way to capture important moments.

Finally, the product planner must build an **augmented product** around the core and actual products by offering additional consumer services and benefits. Sony must offer more than a Camcorder—it must provide consumers with a complete solution to their picture-taking problems. Thus, when consumers buy a Sony Handycam, they receive more than just the camcorder itself. Sony and its dealers might also give buyers a warranty on parts and workmanship, free lessons on how to use the Camcorder, quick repair services when needed, and a toll-free telephone number to call if they have problems or questions. To the consumer, all these augmentations become an important part of the total product.

Thus, a product is more than a simple set of tangible features. In fact, some products (a haircut or a doctor's exam) have no tangible features at all. Consumers tend to see products as complex bundles of benefits that satisfy their needs. When developing products, marketers must first identify the *core* consumer needs the product will satisfy. They must then design the *actual* product and find ways to *augment* it in order to create the bundle of benefits that will best satisfy consumers.

Today, in developed countries, most competition takes place at the product augmentation level. Successful companies add benefits to their offers that will not only *satisfy* the customer but also *delight* the customer. Thus, hotel guests find candy on the pillow, or a bowl of fruit, or a VCR with optional videotapes. The company is saying, "We want to treat you in a special way." However, each augmentation costs the company money. The marketer has to ask whether customers will pay enough to cover the extra cost. Moreover, augmented benefits soon become *expected* benefits. Thus, hotel guests now expect cable television sets, small trays of toiletries, and other amenities in their rooms. This means that competitors must search for still more features and benefits to distinguish their offers. Finally, as companies raise the prices of their augmented products, some competitors can go back to offering a more basic product at a much lower price. Thus, along with the growth of fine hotels such as Four Seasons, Westin, and Hyatt,

The Sony Handycam Pro. So advanced, it even freezes water.

What you see here is something you normally don't see. Something that usually goes by in the blink of an eye. But something thats not too quick for the Sony Handycam Pro™ Video 8® camcorder.

The Sony Handycam™ is designed to capture whatever crosses your path. It comes with a high-speed shutter that goes from 1/60 of a second all the way up to 1/2000 with a succession of steps in between. Add to this its noiseless frame-

by-frame and slow motion advance and not only can you catch everything but you can play it back with amazing accuracy. Whether its your daughter chasing her cat or the cat leaping in the air.

Even in light as low as 5 lux, the Sony CCD image sensor for sharper resolution and low-light sensitivity lets you record each scene with beautifully balanced color.

When you put yourself behind the Handycam, you'll realize its lightweight

construction gives you incredible flexibility no matter what you're shooting. But its size is very deceiving. Because the Handycam is filled with features you'd expect in camcorders twice its size. Like a Flying Erase™ head, which gives you smooth, noise-free transitions between scenes. And an advanced High Fidelity sound system that picks up even the slightest purr.

But, of course, there are those times when even the Handycam Pro isn't enough. Because,

unfortunately, while we usually catch all of the action, we weren't able to catch the vase.

The Sony Handycam Pro. Its everything you want to remember.™

SONY
THE ONE AND ONLY.

Care, tangible, and augmented product: Consumers perceive this Sony Camcorder as a complex bundle of tangible and intangible features and services that deliver a core benefit—a convenient, high-quality way to capture important moments.

we see the emergence of lower-cost hotels and motels like Red Roof Inn, Fairfield Inn, and Motel 6 for clients who want only basic room accommodations.

PRODUCT CLASSIFICATIONS

In seeking marketing strategies for individual products, marketers have developed several product-classification schemes based on product characteristics. We now examine these schemes and characteristics.

Durable Goods, Nondurable Goods, and Services

Products can be classified into three groups according to their *durability* or *tangibility*.[2] **Nondurable goods** are consumer goods that are normally consumed in one or a few uses. Examples include beer, soap, and salt. **Durable goods** are consumer goods that are used over an extended period of time and that normally survive many uses. Examples include refrigerators, automobiles, and furniture. **Services** are activities, benefits, or satisfactions that are offered for sale. Examples include haircuts and repairs. (Because of the growing importance of services in our society, we look at them more closely in Chapter 22).

Consumer Goods

Consumer goods are those bought by final consumers for personal consumption. Marketers usually classify these goods based on *consumer shopping habits*. Consumer goods include *convenience*, *shopping*, *specialty*, and *unsought goods* (see Figure 10-2).[3]

Convenience goods are consumer goods and services that the customer usually buys frequently, immediately, and with a minimum of comparison and buying effort. They are usually low-priced and widely available. Examples include tobacco products,

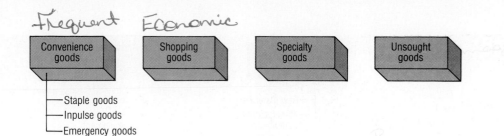

Frequent *Economic*

FIGURE 10-2
Classification of consumer goods

soap, and newspapers. Convenience goods can be further divided into *staples*, *impulse goods*, and *emergency goods*. *Staples* are goods that consumers buy on a regular basis, such as Heinz ketchup, Crest toothpaste, or Ritz crackers. *Impulse goods* are purchased with little planning or search effort. These goods are normally available in many places because consumers seldom seek them out. Thus, candy bars and magazines are placed next to checkout counters because shoppers may not otherwise think of buying them. *Emergency goods* are purchased when a need is urgent—umbrellas during a rainstorm, boots and shovels during the first winter storm. Manufacturers of emergency goods will place them in many outlets to avoid losing a sale when the customer needs these goods.

Shopping goods are consumer goods that the customer, in the process of selection and purchase, usually compares on such bases as suitability, quality, price, and style. When purchasing shopping goods, consumers spend considerable time and effort in gathering information and making comparisons. Examples include furniture, clothing, used cars, and major appliances. Shopping goods can be divided into *uniform* and *nonuniform* goods. The buyer sees uniform shopping goods as similar in quality but different enough in price to justify shopping comparisons. The seller has to "talk price" to the buyer. But in shopping for clothing, furniture, and other nonuniform goods, product features are often more important to the consumer than the price. If the buyer wants a new suit, the cut, fit, and look are likely to be more important than small price differences. The seller of nonuniform shopping goods must, therefore, carry a wide assortment to satisfy individual tastes and must have well-trained salespeople to give information and advice to customers.

Specialty goods are consumer goods that have unique characteristics or brand identification for which a significant group of buyers is willing to make a special purchase effort. Examples include specific brands and types of cars, high-priced photographic equipment, and men's suits. A Jaguar, for example, is a specialty good because buyers are usually willing to travel great distances to buy one. Buyers do not normally compare specialty goods. They invest only the time needed to reach dealers carrying the wanted products. Although dealers do not need convenient locations, they must let buyers know their locations.

Unsought goods are consumer goods that the consumer either does not know about or knows about but does not normally think of buying. New products such as smoke detectors and compact disc players are unsought goods until the consumer is made aware of them through advertising. Classic examples of known but unsought goods are life insurance and encyclopedias. By their very nature, unsought goods require a lot of advertising, personal selling, and other marketing efforts. Some of the most advanced personal-selling methods have developed out of the challenge of selling unsought goods.

Industrial Goods **Industrial goods** are those bought by individuals and organizations for further processing or for use in conducting a business. Thus, the distinction between a consumer good and an industrial good is based on the *purpose* for which the product is purchased. If a consumer buys a lawn mower for use around the home, the lawn mower is a consumer good. If the same consumer buys the same lawn mower for use in a landscaping business, the lawn mower is an industrial good.

Industrial goods can be classified according to how they enter the production

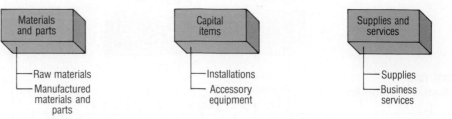

FIGURE 10-3
Classification of industrial goods

process and according to what they cost. The three groups of industrial goods are: *materials and parts*, *capital items*, and *supplies and services* (see Figure 10-3).

Materials and parts are industrial goods that enter the manufacturer's product completely. They fall into two classes: raw materials and manufactured materials and parts.

Raw materials include farm products (wheat, cotton, livestock, fruits, and vegetables) and natural products (fish, lumber, crude petroleum, iron ore). Each is marketed somewhat differently. Farm products are supplied by many small producers, who turn them over to marketing intermediaries, who process and sell them. They are rarely advertised and promoted, but there are some exceptions. From time to time, grower groups will launch campaigns to promote their products—such as potatoes, raisins, oranges, or milk. And some producers even brand their products—such as Sunkist oranges and Chiquita bananas.

Natural products are highly limited in supply. They usually have great bulk and low unit value and require lots of transportation to move them from producer to user. Producers are fewer and larger, and they tend to market natural products directly to industrial users. Because the users depend on these materials, long-term supply contracts are common. The uniformity of natural materials limits demand creation activity. Price and delivery are the major factors affecting the selection of suppliers

Manufactured materials and parts include component materials (iron, yarn, cement, wires) and component parts (small motors, tires, castings). Component materials are usually processed further—for example, pig iron is made into steel, and yarn is woven into cloth. The uniform nature of component materials usually means that price and supplier reliability are the most important purchase factors. Component parts enter the finished product completely with no further change in form, as when small motors are installed in vacuum cleaners and tires are added on automobiles. Most manufactured materials and parts are sold directly to industrial users. Price and service are the major marketing factors, and branding and advertising tend to be less important than price and service.

Capital items are industrial goods that enter the finished product partly. They include two groups: installations and accessory equipment.

Installations consist of buildings (factories, offices) and fixed equipment (generators, drill presses, computers, elevators). Installations are major purchases. They are usually bought directly from the producer after a long decision period. The producers use top-notch salesforces, which often include sales engineers. The producers must be willing to design to specification and to supply postsale services. They use advertising, but much less than personal selling.

Accessory equipment includes portable factory equipment and tools (hand tools, lift trucks) and office equipment (typewriters, desks). These products do not become part of the finished product. They simply aid in the production process. They have a shorter life than installations but a longer life than operating supplies. Most accessory equipment sellers use middlemen because the market is spread out geographically, the buyers are numerous, and the orders are small. Quality, features, price, and service are major factors in supplier selection. The salesforce tends to be more important than advertising, although advertising can be used effectively.

Suppliers and services are industrial goods that do not enter the finished product at all. *Supplies* include operating supplies (lubricants, coal, typing paper, pencils) and maintenance and repair items (paint, nails, brooms). Supplies are the convenience goods of the industrial field because they are usually purchased with a minimum effort or

Component parts: Texas Instruments markets semiconductor chips to manufacturers; price and reliability are important marketing factors.

comparison. They are normally marketed through resellers because of the low unit value of the goods and the great number of customers spread out around the country. Price and service are important factors because suppliers are quite similar and brand preference is not high.

Business services include maintenance and repair services (window cleaning, typewriter repair) and business advisory services (legal, management consulting, advertising). These services are usually supplied under contract. Maintenance services are often provided by small producers, and repair services are often available from the manufacturers of the original equipment. Business advisory services are normally new task buying situations, and the industrial buyer will choose the supplier on the basis of the supplier's reputation and personnel.

Thus, we see that a product's characteristics have a major effect on marketing strategy. At the same time, marketing strategy also depends on such factors as the product's stage in the life cycle, the number of competitors, the degree of market segmentation, and the condition of the economy.

INDIVIDUAL PRODUCT DECISIONS

We now look at decisions relating to the development and marketing of individual products. We discuss decisions about *product attributes*, *branding*, *packaging*, and *labeling*.

Product Attribute Decisions

Developing a product involves defining the benefits that the product will offer. These benefits are communicated and delivered by tangible product attributes, such as *quality*, *features*, and *design*. Decisions about these attributes greatly affect consumer reactions toward a product. Below, we discuss the issues involved in each decision.

Product Quality

In developing a product, the manufacturer has to choose a quality level that will support the product's position in the target market. Quality is one of the marketer's major positioning tools. **Product quality** stands for the ability of a product to perform its

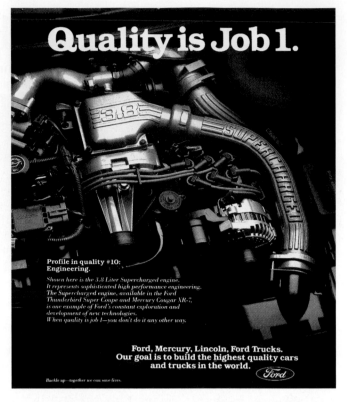

Profile in quality #10:
Engineering.

Shown here is the 3.8 Liter Supercharged engine.
It represents sophisticated high performance engineering.
The Supercharged engine, available in the Ford
Thunderbird Super Coupe and Mercury Cougar XR-7,
is one example of Ford's constant exploration and
development of new technologies.
When quality is job 1—you don't do it any other way.

**Ford, Mercury, Lincoln, Ford Trucks.
Our goal is to build the highest quality cars
and trucks in the world.**

Buckle up—together we can save lives.

**Product quality themes are now attracting stronger interest
among consumers and companies.**

functions. It includes the product's overall durability, reliability, precision, ease of operation and repair, and other valued attributes. Some of these attributes can be measured objectively. From a marketing point of view, however, quality should be measured in terms of buyers' perceptions.

To some companies, improving quality means using better quality control to reduce defects that annoy consumers. But *strategic* quality management means more than this. It means gaining an edge over competitors by offering products that better serve consumers' needs and preferences for quality. As one analyst suggests, "Quality is not simply a problem to be solved; it is a competitive opportunity."[4]

The theme of quality is now attracting stronger interest among consumers and companies. A recent study of 45 fast-growing and profitable companies showed that most of them compete by marketing products that provide more value to consumers rather than ones that cost less.[5] American consumers have been impressed with the product quality in Japanese automobiles and electronics and in European automobiles, clothing, and food. Many consumers are favoring apparel that lasts and stays in style longer instead of trendy clothes. They are more interested in fresh and nutritious foods and gourmet items and less interested in soft drinks, sweets, and TV dinners. A number of companies are catering to this growing interest in quality. Ford, with its "Quality is Job #1" marketing campaign, is an excellent example of a company that mounted a quality drive and is reaping the benefits in increased market share and profitability.[6]

Companies must do more than simply build quality into their products; they must also communicate product quality. The product's look and feel should communicate its quality level. Quality is also communicated through other elements of the marketing mix. A high price usually signals a premium-quality product. The product's brand name, packaging, distribution, and promotion also announce its quality. All these elements must work together to communicate and support the brand's image.[7]

At the same time, we should not leap to the conclusion that the firm should design the highest quality possible. Not all customers want or can afford the high levels of quality offered in such products as a Rolls Royce, or a Sub Zero refrigerator, or a Rolex watch. The manufacturer must choose a quality level that matches target market needs and the quality levels of competing products.

Product Features

A product can be offered with varying features. A "stripped-down" model, one without any extras, is the starting point. The company can create higher-level models by adding more features. Features are a competitive tool for differentiating the company's product from competitors' products. Some companies are very innovative in adding new features. Being the first producer to introduce a needed and valued new feature is one of the most effective ways to compete.

How can a company identify new features and decide which ones to add to its product? The company should periodically survey buyers who have used the product and ask these questions: How do you like the product? Which specific features of the product do you like most? Which features could we add to improve the product? How much would you pay for each feature? The answers provide the company with a rich list of feature ideas. The company can then assess each feature's *customer value* versus its *company cost*. Features that customers value little in relation to costs should be dropped; those that customers value highly in relation to costs should be added.

Product Design

Another way to add product distinctiveness is through **product design.** Some companies have reputations for outstanding design, such as Black & Decker in cordless appliances and tools, Steelcase in office furniture and systems, and Bose in audio equipment. Many companies, however, lack a "design touch." Their product designs function poorly or are dull or common-looking. Yet design can be one of the most powerful competitive weapons in a company's marketing arsenal. Well-designed products win attention and sales:

> They stand out in the material landscape. The sleek, elegant lines of a liquid black automobile as it slips around a curve. A baby bottle carefully crafted to fit the tiny fingers of an infant. The hidden power of trim, triangular speakers as they pulsate with music. The difference is design, that elusive blend of form and function, quality and style, art and engineering.[8]

Design is a larger concept than style. *Style* simply describes the appearance of a product. Styles can be eye-catching or yawn-inspiring. A sensational style may grab attention, but it does not necessarily make the product *perform* better. In some cases, it might even result in worse performance: A chair may look great yet be extremely uncomfortable. Unlike style, *design* is more than skin deep—it goes to the very heart of a product. Good design contributes to a product's usefulness as well as to its looks. A good designer considers appearance but also creates products that are easy, safe, inexpensive to use and service, and simple and economical to produce and distribute.

Several companies are now waking up to the importance of design. The radical new design of the Ford Taurus, with its sleek styling, passenger comforts, engineering advances, and efficient manufacturing, made the car a huge success. Outstanding design was the major factor in the success of Black & Decker's family of cordless power tools. And careful design resulted in Samsonite's successful Oyster molded polypropylene luggage—it is not only light and extremely strong, but also inexpensive to make. All said, good design can attract attention, improve product performance, cut production costs, and give the product a strong competitive advantage in the target market.[9]

Brand Decisions Consumers view a brand as an important part of the product, and branding can add value to the product. For example, most consumers would perceive a bottle of White Linen perfume as a high-quality, expensive product. But the same perfume in an unmarked bottle would likely be viewed as lower in quality, even if the fragrance were identical.

Branding has become a major issue in product strategy. On one hand, developing a branded product requires a great deal of long-term marketing investment, especially for advertising, promotion, and packaging. Manufacturers often find it easier and less expensive to simply make the product and let others do the brand-building. Taiwanese manufacturers took this course: They make a large amount of the world's clothing, consumer electronics, and computers, but these products are sold under non-Taiwanese brand names.

On the other hand, most manufacturers eventually learn that the power lies with the companies that control the brand names. For example, brand-name clothing, electronics, and computer companies can replace their Taiwanese manufacturing sources with cheaper sources in Malaysia and elsewhere. The Taiwanese producers can do little to prevent the loss of sales to less expensive suppliers—consumers are loyal to the brands, not to the producers. Japanese and South Korean companies, however, did not make this mistake. They spent heavily to build up brand names for their products, such as Sony, Panasonic, JVC, Goldstar, and Samsung. Even when these companies can no longer afford to manufacture their products in their homelands, their brand names continue to command customer loyalty.

Powerful brand names have *consumer franchise*—they command strong consumer loyalty. A sufficient number of customers demand these brands and refuse substitutes, even if the substitutes are offered at somewhat lower prices. Companies that develop brands with a strong consumer franchise are insulated from competitors' promotional strategies.

Before going further, we should become familiar with the language of branding. Here are some key definitions.[10] A **brand** is a name, term, sign, symbol, or design, or a combination of these, intended to identify the goods or services of one seller or group of sellers and to differentiate them from those of competitors. A **brand name** is that part of a brand which can be vocalized—the utterable. Examples are Avon, Chevrolet, Tide, Disneyland, American Express, and UCLA. A **brand mark** is that part of a brand which can be recognized but is not utterable, such as a symbol, design, or distinctive coloring or lettering. Examples are the Pillsbury doughboy, the Metro-Goldwyn-Mayer lion, and the red K on a Kodak film box. A **trademark** is a brand or part of a brand that is given legal protection—it protects the seller's exclusive rights to use the brand name or brand mark. Finally, a **copyright** is the exclusive legal right to reproduce, publish, and sell the matter and form of a literary, musical, or artistic work.

Branding poses difficult decisions to the marketer. The key decisions are shown in Figure 10-4 and discussed below.

Branding Decision

The company must first decide whether it should put a brand name on its product. Branding has become so strong that today hardly anything goes unbranded. Salt is packaged in branded containers, oranges are stamped with growers' names, common nuts and bolts are packaged with a distributor's label, and automobile parts—spark plugs, tires, filters—bear brand names that differ from those of the automakers. Even fruits and vegetables are branded. Sunkist oranges, Dole pineapples, and Chiquita bananas command profit margins 10 to 60 percent higher than do unbranded produce. Campbell is even branding mushrooms and has started to test-market premium-priced, branded tomatoes as well as nine vegetable and fruit salads, such as a broccoli and cauliflower mix.[11]

Recently, however, there has also been a return to "nonbranding" certain consumer goods. These "generics" are plainly packaged with no manufacturer identification (see Marketing Highlight 10–1). The intent of generics is to bring down the cost to the consumer by saving on packaging and advertising. Although the popularity of generics peaked in the early 1980s, the issue of whether or not to brand is very much alive today.

This situation highlights some key questions: Why have branding in the first place? Who benefits? How do they benefit? At what cost? Branding helps buyers in many ways. Brand names tell the buyer something about product quality. Buyers who always buy the same brand know that they will get the same quality each time they buy.

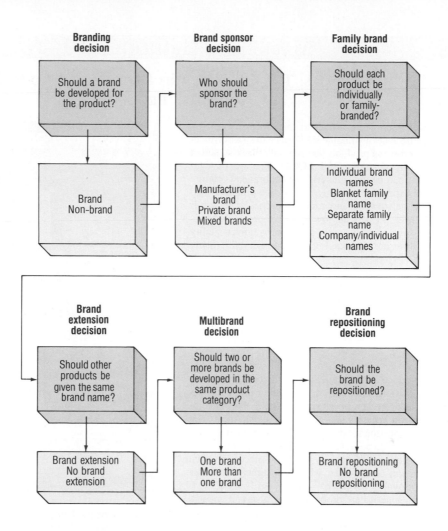

Branding decision	Brand sponsor decision	Family brand decision
Should a brand be developed for the product?	Who should sponsor the brand?	Should each product be individually or family-branded?
Brand Non-brand	Manufacturer's brand Private brand Mixed brands	Individual brand names Blanket family name Separate family name Company/individual names

Brand extension decision	Multibrand decision	Brand repositioning decision
Should other products be given the same brand name?	Should two or more brands be developed in the same product category?	Should the brand be repositioned?
Brand extension No brand extension	One brand More than one brand	Brand repositioning No brand repositioning

FIGURE 10-4
An overview of branding decisions

Familiar brands provide consumer information, recognition, and confidence.

GENERICS: THE GROWTH AND DECLINE OF "NO-BRAND, NO-FRILLS" PRODUCTS

In 1978, Jewel Food Stores shocked the grocery world by devoting an entire aisle of valuable shelf space to an assortment of low-priced, no-name products bearing only black-stenciled labels: TOWELS, SUGAR, CAT FOOD. The age of "generic" products had begun. Generics are unbranded, plainly packaged, less expensive versions of common products such as spaghetti, paper towels, and canned peaches. They offer prices as much as 40 percent lower than those of national brands. The lower price is made possible by lower-quality ingredients, lower-cost packaging, and lower advertising costs.

Generics took brand-name manufacturers by surprise. By the early 1980s, nearly 80 percent of all supermarkets were selling generics, and consumers could buy no-brand products in three of every four product categories. Fueled by inflation and recession, generics captured a 2.4 percent share of the grocery business and $2.8 billion in annual sales in only four years.

The price savings of generics appeal strongly to consumers, but product quality remains an important factor in their buying decisions. Generics sell better in product areas where consumers care less about quality or see little quality difference between generics and national brands. Areas such as paper products, frozen foods, peanut butter, canned vegetables, plastic bags, disposable diapers, and dog food were hardest hit by generics. Generics had less success in such areas as health and beauty aids, where consumers were less willing to trade quality for price.

Although generics are probably here to stay, it appears that their popularity peaked in 1982. Since then, the market share for generics has dropped to 1.5 percent of total grocery volume, or $1.8 billion in annual sales. This decline resulted partly from an improved economy—prices have stabilized, and consumers now have more income than they did when generics exploded in the early 1980s. The decline has also resulted from better marketing strategies by brand-name manufacturers. These marketers responded by emphasizing brand image and quality. For example, when threatened by generic pet foods, Ralston-Purina responded by increasing its quality rather than reducing its price and targeted pet owners who identified strongly with their pets and cared most about quality. Kraft met the generic threat with advertising showing taste tests in which children preferred the taste of Kraft macaroni and cheese to that of the generic brand.

Another strategy is to cut costs and pass the savings along to consumers at lower prices and greater values. Or the brand-name manufacturer can introduce lower-quality, lower-priced products that compete head on with generic products. Union Carbide, for example, produced generic garbage bags to compete with its own Glad line. Procter & Gamble introduced its line of Banner paper products. Al-

Generics peaked in popularity in the early 1980s, but they are probably here to stay.

though this line offered lower quality than other P&G brands, it offered greater quality than generics, and it did so at a competitive price.

Brand-name marketers must continue to convince consumers that their products' higher quality is worth the extra cost. Branded products that offer large quality differences will not be hurt much by generics. Those most threatened are weak national brands and lower-price store brands that offer little additional quality. Why pay 20 to 40 percent more for a branded item when its quality is not very different from that of its generic cousin?

Sources: See Amy Dunkin, "No-Frills Products: 'An Idea Whose Time Has Gone,'" *Business Week*, June 17, 1985, pp. 64–65; Brian F. Harris and Roger A. Strang, "Marketing in an Age of Generics," *Journal of Marketing*, Fall 1985, pp. 70–81; and Julie Franz, "Ten Years May Be Generic Lifetime, *Advertising Age*, March 23, 1987, p. 76.

Brand names also increase the shopper's efficiency. Imagine a buyer going into a supermarket and finding thousands of unlabeled products. Finally, brand names help call consumers' attention to new products that might benefit them—the brand name becomes the basis upon which a whole story can be built about the new product's special qualities.

Branding also gives the seller several advantages. The brand name makes it easier for the seller to process orders and track down problems. Thus, Anheuser-Busch receives an order for a hundred cases of Michelob beer instead of an order for "some of your better beer." The seller's brand name and trademark provide legal protection for unique product features that might otherwise be copied by competitors. Branding lets the seller attract a loyal and profitable set of customers. Branding helps the seller segment markets— Procter & Gamble can offer ten detergent brands, not just one general product for all consumers.

Branding also benefits society as a whole. Those favoring branding suggest that branding leads to higher and more consistent product quality. Branding also increases innovation by giving producers an incentive to look for new features that can be protected against imitating competitors. Thus, branding results in more product variety and choice for consumers. Finally, branding increases shopper efficiency because it provides much more information about products and where to find them. While branding can be overdone in some cases, it clearly adds value to consumers and society.

Brand Sponsor Decision

In deciding to brand a product, the manufacturer has three sponsorship options. The product may be launched as a **manufacturer's brand** (also called a national brand). Or the manufacturer may sell the product to middlemen who give it a **private brand** (also called *middleman brand*, *distributor brand*, or *dealer brand*). Finally, the manufacturer may follow a *mixed-brand* strategy, selling some output under its own brand names and some under private labels. Kellogg's and IBM sell almost all their output under their own manufacturer's brand names. On the other hand, BASF Wyandotte, the world's second-largest antifreeze maker, sells its Alugard antifreeze under about 80 private brands, including K mart, True Value, Pathmark, and Rite Aid. Whirlpool sells output both under its own name and under the Sears Kenmore name.

Manufacturers' brands have dominated the American scene. Consider such well-known brands as Campbell's soup and Heinz ketchup. While most manufacturers create their own brand names, some of them "rent" well-known brand names by paying a royalty for the use of the name (see Marketing Highlight 10–2).

In recent times, however, most large retailers and wholesalers have developed their own brands. The private-label tires of Sears and J. C. Penney are as well known today as the manufacturers' brands of Goodyear and Firestone. Sears has created several names—Diehard batteries, Craftsman tools, Kenmore appliances, Weatherbeater paints— that buyers look for and demand. An increasing number of department stores, supermarkets, service stations, clothiers, drugstores, and appliance dealers are launching private labels.

In the fashion industry, although national brands still dominate, the use of private labels has increased dramatically in recent years. Such manufacturers as Ralph Lauren, Coach, Burberry, Esprit, and Benetton have opened stores that sell only their own labels. Traditional retailers have responded with more private-label goods. For example, Macy's now has more than 50 in-house labels, and in some categories its private labels account for up to 50 percent of sales. The Limited's private labels—including Forenza and Outback Red—represent 70 percent of the chain's sales.[12]

Despite the fact that private brands are often hard to establish and costly to stock and promote, middlemen develop private brands because they can be profitable. Middlemen can often locate manufacturers with excess capacity who will produce the private label at a low cost, resulting in a higher profit margin for the middleman. Private brands also give middlemen exclusive products that cannot be bought from competitors, resulting in greater store traffic and loyalty. For example, if K mart promotes Canon cameras, other stores that sell Canon products will also benefit. Further, if K mart drops the Canon brand, it loses the benefit of its previous promotion for Canon. But if K mart promotes its private brand of Focal cameras, K mart alone benefits from the promotion. And consumer loyalty to the Focal brand becomes loyalty to K mart.

The competition between manufacturers' and middlemen's brands is called *the battle of the brands*. In this battle, middlemen have many advantages. The retailers

LICENSING BRAND NAMES FOR ROYALTIES

Manufacturers or retailers may take years and spend millions to develop consumer preference for their brands. An alternative is to "rent" names that hold magic for consumers. The names or symbols previously created by other manufacturers, the names of well-known celebrities, the characters introduced in popular movies and books—for a fee, any of these can provide a manufacturer's product with an instant and proven brand name. Name and character licensing has become a big business in recent years. Retail sales of licensed products jumped from $4 billion in 1977 to more than $55 billion in 1987, to an estimated $75 billion in 1990.

Apparel and accessories sellers are the largest users, accounting for about 35 percent of all licensing. Producers and retailers pay sizable royalties to adorn their products with the names of such fashion innovators as Bill Blass, Calvin Klein, Pierre Cardin, Gucci, and Halston, all of whom license their names or initials for everything from blouses to ties and linens to luggage. In recent years, designer labels have become so common that many retailers are discarding them in favor of their own store brands in order to regain exclusivity, pricing freedom, and higher margins. Even less fashionable names can bring astounding success. Coca-Cola clothes by Murjani rang up $100 million in retail sales in only two years. Other consumer products companies jumped quickly into corporate fashion licensing—Hershey, Jell-O, Burger King, McDonald's, and others.

Sellers of children's toys, games, food, and other products also make extensive use of name and character licensing. The list of characters attached to children's clothing, toys, school supplies, linens, dolls, lunch boxes, cereals, and other items is almost endless. It ranges from such classics as Disney, Peanuts, Barbie, and Flintstones characters to the Care Bears

and Masters of the Universe—from the venerable Raggedy Ann and Andy to Garfield, Roger Rabbit, and the Teenage Mutant Ninja Turtles.

The newest form of licensing is brand-extension licensing—renting a brand name made famous in one category and using it in a related category. Some currently successful examples include Astroturf sport shoes, Singer sewing supplies, Louisville Slugger baseball uniforms, Old Spice shaving mugs and razors, Fabergé costume jewelry, Winnebago camping equipment, Vidal Sassoon hair-care appliances, and Coppertone swimwear.

Licensed names or characters can add immediate distinction and familiarity to a new product and can set it apart from competitors' products. Customers debating between two similar products will most likely reach for the one with a familiar name on it. In fact, consumers often seek out products that carry their favorite names or characters.

Almost everyone is getting into the licensing act these days, even Harley-Davidson, the motorcycle maker. Over the past eighty years, the Harley-Davidson name has developed a distinct image—some people even tattoo it on their bodies. And Harley-Davidson is now licensing its name for consumer products. One toy manufacturer now markets the Harley-Davidson Big Wheel tricycle, and the company has authorized other products that meet appropriate standards of quality and taste—products ranging from wine coolers, to chocolates, to cologne.

Sources: See Teresa Carson and Amy Dunkin, "What's in a Name? Millions If It's Leased," *Business Week*, April 8, 1985, pp. 97–98; Lori Kessler, "Licensing," *Advertising Age*, June 6, 1988, pp. S1–S3; and Michael Gates, "Creative Licensing," *Incentive*, April 1989, pp. 32–36.

---

control scarce shelf space—many manufacturers, especially the newer and smaller ones, cannot get the shelf space needed to introduce products under their own name. Middlemen give better display space to their own brands and ensure that those brands are better stocked. Middlemen's brands are often priced lower than comparable manufacturers' brands, thus appealing to budget-conscious shoppers. And most shoppers know that the private-label products are often made by one of the larger manufacturers, anyway. Thus, the dominance of manufacturers' brands has weakened somewhat. Some marketers predict that middlemen's brands will eventually knock out all but the strongest manufacturers' brands.

Manufacturers of national brands become very frustrated. They spend a lot on consumer advertising and promotion to build strong brand preference, and so their prices have to be somewhat higher to cover this promotion. At the same time, the large retailers put considerable pressure on the manufacturers to spend more of their promotional money on trade allowances and deals if they want adequate shelf space. Once manufacturers start giving in, they have less to spend on consumer promotion, and their brand leadership starts slipping. This is the national brand manufacturers' dilemma.

Family-Brand Decision

Manufacturers who brand their products face several further choices. At least four brand-name strategies are used:

1. *Individual brand names.* This policy is followed by Procter & Gamble (Tide, Crest, Folger's, Pampers) and General Mills (Bisquick, Gold Medal, Betty Crocker, Nature Valley, Yoplait).

2. *A blanket family name for all products.* This policy is followed by Heinz and General Electric.

3. *Separate family names for all products.* This policy is followed by Sears (Kenmore for appliances, Craftsman for tools, and Homart for major home installations).

4. *Company trade name combined with individual product names.* This policy is followed by Kellogg's (Kellogg's Corn Flakes, Kellogg's Rice Krispies, and Kellogg's Raisin Bran).

What are the advantages of an individual brand-names strategy? A major advantage is that the company does not tie its reputation to the product's acceptance. If the product fails, it does not hurt the company's name.

Using a blanket family name for all products also has some advantages. The cost of introducing the product will be less because there is no need for heavy advertising to create brand recognition and preference. Furthermore, sales will be strong if the manufacturer's name is good. Thus, new soups introduced under the Campbell brand name get instant recognition.

However, when a company produces several types of products, it may not be best to use one blanket family name. Swift & Company uses separate family names for its hams (Premium) and fertilizers (Vigoro). Companies will often invent different family brand names for different quality lines within the same product class.

Finally, some manufacturers want to use their company names along with an individual brand name for each product. The company name adds the firm's reputation to the product, while the individual name sets it apart from other company products. Thus *Quaker Oats* in Quaker Oats Cap'n Crunch taps the company's reputation for breakfast cereal, and *Cap'n Crunch* sets apart and dramatizes the product.

Brand-Extension Decision

A **brand-extension** strategy is any effort to use a successful brand name to launch new or modified products. Procter & Gamble put its Ivory name on dishwashing detergent, liquid hand soap, and shampoo with excellent results, and it used the strength of the Tide name to launch liquid and unscented laundry detergents. Fruit of the Loom took advantage of its 98 percent name recognition to launch new lines of socks, men's fashion underwear, and women's underwear.[13] Honda extended its brand name to power lawn mowers.

Brand extension saves the manufacturer the high cost of promoting new names and creates instant brand recognition of the new product. At the same time, a brand extension strategy involves some risk. Such brand extensions as Bic pantyhose and Life Savers gum met early deaths. If an extension brand fails, it may harm consumer attitudes toward the other products carrying the same brand name. Further, a brand name may not be appropriate to a particular new product, even if it is well made and satisfying—would you consider buying Texaco milk or Alpo chile? And a brand name may lose its special positioning in the consumer's mind through overuse. Some marketing strategies call this the "line-extension" trap.[14] They do not think that the Scott Paper Company benefitted from naming its various paper products ScotTowels, ScotTissues, Scotties, Scotkins, and BabyScott diapers. The Scott name lost meaning, and the products lacked individual personalities compared with such rivals as Charmin, Bounty, Kleenex, and Pampers.

Multibrand Decision

In a **multibrand strategy,** the seller develops two or more brands in the same product category. This marketing practice was pioneered by Procter & Gamble when it introduced Cheer as a competitor for its already successful Tide. Although Tide's sales dropped slightly, the combined sales of Cheer and Tide were higher. Procter & Gamble now produces ten detergent brands.

Manufacturers use multibrand strategies for several reasons. First, they can gain more shelf space, thus increasing the retailer's dependence on their brands. Second, few consumers are so loyal to a brand that they will not try another. The only way to capture the "brand switchers" is to offer several brands. Third, creating new brands develops healthy competition within the manufacturer's organization. Managers of different General Motors brands compete to outperform each other. Finally, a multibrand strategy positions brands on different benefits and appeals, and each brand can attract a separate following.

Companies using a multibrand strategy run the risk of spreading their resources over many marginally profitable brands instead of building a few highly profitable ones. These companies should weed out their weaker brands and carefully screen new ones. Ideally, a company's new brands should take business from competitors' brands, not cannibalize the company's current brands. Or at least the combined profits from the old and new brands should be larger, even if some cannibalization occurs.[15]

Brand-Repositioning Decision

However well a brand is initially positioned in a market, the company may have to reposition it later. A competitor may launch a brand positioned next to the company's brand and cut into its market share, or customer wants may shift, leaving the company's brand with less demand. Marketers should consider repositioning existing brands before introducing new ones. In this way, they can build on existing brand recognition and consumer loyalty.

Repositioning may require changing both the product and its image. P&G repositioned Bold detergent by adding a fabric-softening ingredient; and Arrow added a new line of casual shirts before trying to change its image. Or a brand can be repositioned by changing only the product's image. Ivory soap was repositioned without change from a "baby soap" to an "all natural soap" for adults who want healthy-looking skin. Similarly, Kraft repositioned Velveeta from a "cooking cheese" to a "good tasting, natural, and nutritious" snack cheese. The product remained unchanged, but Kraft used new advertising appeals to change consumer perceptions of Velveeta. When repositioning a brand, the marketer must be careful not to drop or confuse current loyal users. When shifting Velveeta's position, Kraft made certain that the product's new position was compatible with its old one. Thus, it kept loyal customers while attracting new users.[16]

Selecting a Brand Name

The brand name should be carefully chosen. A good name can add greatly to a product's success. Most large marketing companies have developed a formal brand-name selection process. Finding the best brand name is a difficult task. It begins with a careful review of the product and its benefits, the target market, and proposed marketing strategies.

Among the desirable qualities for a brand name are these: (1) It should suggest something about the product's benefits and qualities. Examples: Beautyrest, Craftsman, Sunkist, Spic and Span, Snuggles. (2) It should be easy to pronounce, recognize, and remember. Short names help. Examples: Tide, Aim, Puffs. But longer ones are sometimes effective. Examples: "Love My Carpet" carpet cleaner, "I Can't Believe It's Not Butter" margarine, Better Business Bureau. (3) The brand name should be distinctive. Examples: Taurus, Kodak, Exxon. (4) The name should translate easily into foreign languages. Before spending $100 million to change its name to Exxon, Standard Oil of New Jersey tested the name in fifty-four languages in more than 150 foreign markets. It found that the name Enco referred to a stalled engine when pronounced in Japan.[17] (5) It should be capable of registration and legal protection. A brand name cannot be registered if it infringes on existing brand names, and brand names that are merely descriptive or suggestive may be unprotectable. For example, the Miller Brewing Company registered the name Lite for its low-calorie beer and invested millions to establish the name with consumers. But the courts later ruled that the terms "lite" and "light" are generic or common descriptive terms applied to beer and that Miller could not use the Lite name exclusively.[18]

Once chosen, the brand name must be protected. Many firms try to build a brand name that will eventually become identified with the product category. Such brand names as Frigidaire, Kleenex, Levi's, Jello, Scotch Tape, Formica, and Fiberglas have succeeded in this way. However, their very success may threaten the company's rights

What do you get after spending 75 years making America's favorite dress shirt?

"Members of the University Glee Club of New York City."

Bored.

Arrow

Brand repositioning: Long known for its dress shirts, Arrow repositioned by loosening its collar.

to the name. Many originally protected brand names, such as cellophane, aspirin, nylon, kerosene, linoleum, yo-yo, trampoline, escalator, thermos, and shredded wheat, are now names that any seller can use.[19]

Packaging Decisions

Many products offered to the market have to be packaged. Some marketers have called packaging a fifth *P*, along with price, product, place, and promotion. Most marketers, however, treat packaging as an element of product strategy.

    Packaging includes the activities of designing and producing the container or wrapper for a product. The package may include the product's immediate container (for example, the bottle holding Old Spice After-Shave Lotion); a secondary package that is thrown away when the product is about to be used (the cardboard box containing the bottle of Old Spice); and the shipping package necessary to store, identify, and ship the product (a corrugated box carrying six dozen bottles of Old Spice). Labeling is also part of packaging and consists of printed information appearing on or with the package.

Traditionally, packaging decisions were based primarily on cost and production factors; the primary function of the package was to contain and protect the product. In recent times, however, numerous factors have made packaging an important marketing tool. An increase in self-service means that packages must now perform many sales tasks, from attracting attention, to describing the product, to making the sale. Rising consumer affluence means that consumers are willing to pay a little more for the convenience, appearance, dependability, and prestige of better packages.

Companies are also realizing the power of good packaging to create instant consumer recognition of the company or brand. The Campbell Soup Company estimates that the average shopper sees its familiar red and white can seventy-six times a year, creating the equivalent of $26 million worth of advertising.[20] And innovative packaging can give the company an advantage over competitors. Liquid Tide quickly attained a 10 percent share of the heavy-duty detergent market, partly because of the popularity of its container's innovative drip-proof spout and cap. The first companies to put their fruit drinks in airtight foil and paper cartons (aseptic packages) and toothpastes in pump dispensers attracted many new customers. On the other hand, poorly designed packages can cause headaches for consumers and lost sales for the company (see Marketing Highlight 10–3).

In recent years, product safety has also become a major packaging concern. We have all learned to deal with hard-to-open "child-proof" packages. And after the rash of product tampering scares during the 1980s, most drug producers and food makers are now putting their products in tamper-resistant packages.[21]

Developing a good package for a new product requires making many decisions. The first task is to establish the packaging concept. The **packaging concept** states what the package should *be* or *do* for the product. Should the main functions of the package be to offer product protection, introduce a new dispensing method, suggest certain qualities about the product or the company, or something else? Decisions must then be made on specific elements of the package—size, shape, materials, color, text, and brand mark. These various elements must work together to support the product's position and marketing strategy. The package must be consistent with the product's advertising, pricing, and distribution.

Companies usually consider several different package designs for a new product. To select the best package, they usually test the various designs to find the one that stands up best under normal use, is easiest for dealers to handle, and receives the most favorable consumer response. After selecting and introducing the package, the company should check it regularly in the face of changing consumer preferences and advances in technology. In the past, a package design might last for fifteen years before it needed changes. However, in today's rapidly changing environment, most companies must recheck their packaging every two or three years.[22]

Keeping a package up to date usually requires only minor but regular changes—changes so subtle that they may go unnoticed by most consumers. But some packaging changes involve complex decisions, drastic action, and high cost and risk. For example, Campbell has recently been searching for a new container to replace its venerable old soup can. It has experimented with a variety of containers, such as a sealed plastic bowl that can be popped into a microwave oven to produce hot soup in a hurry, with no can to open and no dishes to wash. Given Campbell's 80 percent share of the canned-soup market, the potential risks and benefits of changing the package are huge. Although the change could cut Campbell's packaging costs by as much as 15 percent, revamping production facilities would cost $100 million or more. And Campbell management estimates that the change would take at least five more years to implement.

Cost remains an important packaging consideration. Developing the packaging for a new product may cost a few hundred thousand dollars and take from a few months to a year. Or, as in the Campbell example, converting to a new package may cost

THOSE FRUSTRATING, NOT-SO-EASY-TO-OPEN PACKAGES

The following letter from an angry consumer to Robert D. Stuart, then chairman of Quaker Oats, expresses beautifully the utter frustration all of us have experienced in dealing with so-called "easy-opening packages."

Dear Mr. Stuart:

I am an 86-year-old widow in fairly good health. (You may think of this as advanced age, but for me that description pertains to the years ahead. Nevertheless, if you decide to reply to this letter I wouldn't dawdle, actuarial tables being what they are.)

As I said, my health is fairly good. Feeble and elderly, as one understands these terms, I am not. My two Doberman Pinschers and I take a brisk 3-mile walk every day. They are two strong and energetic animals and it takes a bit of doing to keep "brisk" closer to a stroll than a mad dash. But I manage because as yet I don't lack the strength. You will shortly see why this fact is relevant.

I am writing to call your attention to the cruel, deceptive and utterly [false] copy on your Aunt Jemima buttermilk complete pancake and waffle mix. The words on your package read, "to open—press here and pull back."

Mr. Stuart, though I push and press and groan and strive and writhe and curse and sweat and jab and push, pose and ram . . . whew!—I have never once been able to do what the package instructs—to "press here and pull back" the [blankety-blank].

It can't be done! Talk about failing strength! Have you ever tried and succeeded?

My late husband was a gun collector who among other lethal weapons kept a Thompson machine gun in a locked cabinet. It was a good thing that the cabinet was locked. Oh, the number of times I was tempted to give your package a few short bursts.

That lock and a sense of ladylike delicacy kept me from pursuing that vengeful fantasy. Instead, I keep a small cleaver in my pantry for those occasions when I need to open a package of your delicious Aunt Jemima pancakes.

For many years that whacking away with my cleaver served a dual purpose. Not only to open the [blankety-blank] package but also to vent my fury at your sadists who willfully and maliciously did design that torture apparatus that passes for a package.

Sometimes just for the [blank] of it I let myself get carried away. I don't stop after I've lopped off the top. I whack away until the package is utterly destroyed in an outburst of rage, frustration, and vindictiveness. I wind up with a floorful of your delicious

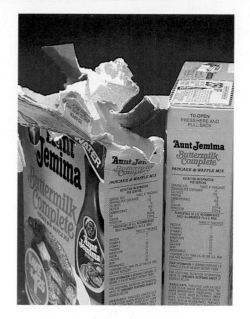

An easy-to-open package?

Aunt Jemima pancake mix. But that's a small price to pay for blessed release. (Anyway, the Pinschers lap up the mess.)

So many ingenious, considerate (even compassionate) innovations in package closures have been designed since Aunt Jemima first donned her red bandana. Wouldn't you consider the introduction of a more humane package to replace the example of marketing malevolence to which you resolutely cling? Don't you care Mr. Stuart?

I'm really writing this to be helpful and in that spirit I am sending a copy to Mr. Tucker, president of Container Corp. I'm sure their clever young designers could be of immeasurable help to you in this matter. At least I feel it's worth a try.

Really, Mr. Stuart, I hope you will not regard me as just another cranky old biddy. I am The Public, the source of your fortunes.

Ms. Roberta Pavloff
Malvern, Pa.

Source: This letter was reprinted in "Some Designs Should Just Be Torn Asunder," *Advertising Age*, January 17, 1983, p. M54.

millions, and implementing a new package design may take several years. Marketers must weigh packaging costs against both consumer perceptions of value added by the packaging and the role of packaging in helping to attain marketing objectives. In making packaging decisions, the company must also heed growing environmental concerns about packaging and make decisions that serve society's interests as well as immediate customer and company objectives (see Marketing Highlight 10–4).

PACKAGING AND PUBLIC POLICY

Packaging is attracting increasing public attention. When making packaging decisions, marketers should heed the following issues.

Fair Packaging and Labeling. The public is concerned about false and potentially misleading packaging and labeling. The Federal Trade Commission Act of 1914 held that false, misleading, or deceptive labels or packages constitute unfair competition. Consumers are also concerned about confusing package sizes and shapes that make price comparisons difficult. The Fair Packaging and Labeling Act, passed by Congress in 1967, set mandatory labeling requirements, encouraged voluntary industry packaging standards, and allowed federal agencies to set packaging regulations in specific industries. The Food and Drug Administration has required processed-food producers to include nutritional labeling that clearly states the amount of protein, fat, carbohydrates, and calories contained in products as well as their vitamin and mineral content as a percentage of the recommended daily allowance. Consumerists have lobbied for additional labeling laws to require *open dating* (to describe product freshness), *unit pricing* (to state the product cost in some standard measurement unit), *grade labeling* (to rate the quality level of certain consumer goods), and *percentage labeling* (to show the percentage of each important ingredient).

Excessive Cost. Critics have claimed that excessive packaging on some products raises prices. They point to secondary "throwaway" packaging and question its value to the consumer. They note that the package sometimes costs more than the contents; for example, Evian moisturizer consists of five ounces of natural spring water packaged as an aerosol spray selling for $5.50. Marketers respond that they also want to keep packaging costs down but that the critics do not understand all the functions of the package.

Scarce Resources. The growing concern over shortages of paper, aluminum, and other materials suggests that industry should try harder to reduce its packaging. For example, the growth of nonreturnable glass containers has resulted in using up to seventeen times as much glass as with returnable containers. Glass and other throwaway bottles also waste energy. Some states have passed laws prohibiting or taxing nonreturnable containers.

Pollution. As much as 40 percent of the total solid waste in this country is made up of packaging material. Many packages end up as broken bottles and bent cans littering the streets and countryside. All this packaging creates a major problem in solid waste disposal, requiring huge amounts of labor and energy.

These packaging questions have mobilized public interest in new packaging laws. Marketers must be equally concerned and try to design fair, economical, and ecological packages for their products.

Labeling Decisions   Sellers may also design labels for their products, ranging from simple tags attached to products to complex graphics that are part of the package. The label might carry only the brand name or a great deal of information. Even if the seller prefers a simple label, the law may require more information.

Labels perform several functions, and the seller has to decide which ones to use. At the very least, the label *identifies* the product or brand, such as the name Sunkist stamped on oranges. The label might also *grade* the product—canned peaches are grade-labeled A, B, and C. The label might *describe* several things about the product—who made it, where it was made, when it was made, its contents, how it is to be used, and how to use it safely. Finally, the label might *promote* the product through attractive graphics.

Labels of well-known brands may seem old-fashioned after a time and need freshening up. For example, the label on Ivory Soap has been revamped eighteen times since the 1890s, but simply, with gradual changes in the lettering. On the other hand, the label on Orange Crush soft drink was substantially changed when its competitors' labels began to picture fresh fruits and pull in more sales. Orange Crush developed a label with new symbols and much stronger, deeper colors to suggest freshness and more orange flavor.

Labels carry with themselves a long history of legal concerns. Labels can mislead customers, fail to describe important ingredients, or fail to include needed safety warnings. As a result, several federal and state laws regulate labeling, the most prominent being the Fair Packaging and Labeling Act of 1966. Labeling has been affected in recent times by *unit pricing* (stating the price per unit of standard measure), *open dating* (stating the expected shelf life of the product), and *nutritional labeling* (stating the nutritional values in the product). Sellers must ensure that their labels contain all the required information.

Product-Support Services Decisions

Customer service is another element of product strategy. A company's offer to the marketplace usually includes some services. Services can be a minor or a major part of the total offer. In fact, the offer can range from a pure good on one hand to a pure service on the other. In Chapter 22, we discuss services as products themselves. Here, we discuss **product-support services**—services that augment actual products. More and more companies are using product-support services as a major tool in gaining competitive advantage.

Good customer service is good for business. It costs less to keep the goodwill of existing customers than it does to attract new customers or woo back lost customers. Firms that provide high-quality service usually outperform their less service-oriented competitors. A recent study by the Strategic Planning Institute compared the performance of businesses that had high customer ratings of service quality with those that had lower ratings. It found that the high-service businesses managed to charge more, grow faster, and make more profits.[23] Clearly, marketers need to think carefully about their service strategies.

Deciding on the Service Mix

A company should design its product and support services to meet the needs of target customers. Thus, the first step in deciding which product-support services to offer is to determine both which services target consumers value and the relative importance of those services. Customers vary in the value they assign to different services. Some stress credit and financing services, fast and reliable delivery, or quick installation. Others put more weight on technical information and advice, training in product use, or after-sale service and repair.

Determining customers' service needs involves more than simply monitoring complaints that come in over toll-free telephone lines or on comment cards. The company should periodically survey its consumers to get ratings of current services as well as ideas for new ones. For example, Cadillac holds regular focus-group interviews with owners and carefully watches complaints that come into its dealerships. It recently found that buyers were most upset by repairs that were not done correctly the first time. As a result, the company set up a system directly linking each dealership with a group of ten engineers who can help walk mechanics through difficult repairs. Such actions helped Cadillac jump in one year from fourteenth to seventh in independent rankings of service.[24]

Products can often be designed to reduce the amount of required servicing. Thus, companies need to coordinate their product-design and service-mix decisions. For example, the Canon home copier uses a disposable toner cartridge that greatly reduces the need for service calls. Kodak and 3M are designing products that can be ''plugged in'' to a central diagnostic facility that performs tests, locates troubles, and fixes equipment over telephone lines. Thus, a key to successful service strategy is to design products that rarely break down, and, if they do, are easily fixable with little service expense.

Delivering Product-Support Services

Finally, companies must decide how they want to deliver product-support services to customers. For example, consider the many ways Maytag might offer repair services on its major appliances. It could hire and train its own service people and locate them across the country. Or it could arrange with distributors and dealers to provide the repair services. Or it could leave it to independent companies to provide these services.

Most equipment companies start out adopting the first alternative, providing their own service. They want to stay close to the equipment and know its problems. They also find that they can make good money running the ''parts and service business.'' As long as they are the only supplier of the needed parts, they can charge a premium price. Indeed, some equipment manufacturers make over half their profits in after-sale service.

Over time, producers shift more of the maintenance and repair service to authorized

Delivering product-support services: GE backs its products with a toll-free customer service center and a fleet of service trucks ("workshops on wheels") that service GE products at customers' homes. It also provides a Quick Fix System, including parts and repair manuals for do-it-yourselfers.

distributors and dealers. These middlemen are closer to customers, have more locations, and can offer quicker, if not better, service. The producer still makes a profit on selling the parts but leaves the servicing cost to middlemen.

Still later, independent service firms emerge. For example, more than 40 percent of all auto service work is now done outside of franchised automobile dealerships, by independent garages and chains such as Midas Muffler, Sears, and K mart. Such independent service firms have emerged in most industries. They typically offer lower cost or faster service than the manufacturer or authorized middlemen.

Ultimately, some large customers start to handle their own maintenance and repair services. Thus, a company with several hundred personal computers, printers, and related equipment might find it cheaper to have its own service people on site.

The Customer-Service Department
Given the importance of customer service as a marketing tool, many companies have set up strong customer-service departments to handle complaints and adjustments, credit service, maintenance service, technical service, and consumer information. For example, Whirlpool, Procter & Gamble, and many other companies have set up hot lines to handle consumer complaints and requests for information. By keeping records on the types of requests and complaints, the customer-service department can press for needed changes in product design, quality control, high-pressure selling, and so on. An active customer-service department coordinates all the company's services, creates consumer satisfaction and loyalty, and helps the company to further set itself apart from competitors.[25]

We have looked at product strategy decisions—branding, packaging, labeling, and services—for individual products. But product strategy also calls for building a product line. A **product line** is a group of products that are closely related either because they function in a similar manner, are sold to the same customer groups, are marketed through the same types of outlets, or fall within given price ranges. Thus, General Motors produces several lines of cars, Revlon produces several lines of cosmetics, and IBM produces several lines of computers. Each product line needs a marketing strategy. Marketers face a number of tough decisions on product-line length and product-line featuring.

Product-Line Length Decision

Product line managers have to decide on product-line length. The line is too short if the manager can increase profits by adding items; the line is too long if the manager can increase profits by dropping items. Product-line length is influenced by company objectives. Companies that want to be positioned as full-line companies or that are seeking high market share and market growth usually carry longer lines. They are less concerned when some items fail to add to profits. Companies that are keen on high profitability generally carry shorter lines consisting of selected items.

Product lines tend to lengthen over time. The product line manager feels pressure to add new products to use up excess manufacturing capacity. The salesforce and distributors will be pressured by the manager for a more complete product line to satisfy customers. The product line manager wants to add items to the product line to increase sales and profits.

However, as the manager adds items, several costs rise: design and engineering costs, inventory carrying costs, manufacturing changeover costs, order processing costs,

Product line: "We design each Olympus for a different kind of photographer."

transportation costs, and promotional costs to introduce new items. Eventually, someone calls a halt to the mushrooming product line. Top management may freeze things because of insufficient funds or manufacturing capacity. Or the controller may question the line's profitability and call for a study. The study will probably show a number of money-losing items, and they will be pruned from the line in a major effort to increase profitability. A pattern of uncontrolled product line growth followed by heavy pruning is typical and may repeat itself many times.

The company must plan product line growth carefully. It can systematically increase the length of its product line in two ways: by *stretching* its line and by *filling* its line.

Product-Line Stretching Decision

Every company's product line covers a certain range of the products offered by the industry as a whole. For example, BMW automobiles are located in the medium-high price range of the automobile market. Toyota focuses on the low to medium price range. **Product-line stretching** occurs when a company lengthens its product line beyond its current range. As shown in Figure 10-5, the company can stretch its line downward, upward, or both ways.

Downward Stretch

Many companies initially locate at the high end of the market and later stretch their lines downward. A company may stretch downward for any number of reasons. It may find faster growth taking place at the low end. Or it may have first entered the high end to establish a quality image and intended to roll downward. The company may add a low-end product to plug a market hole that would otherwise attract a new competitor. Or it may be attacked at the high end and respond by invading the low end. Beech Aircraft has historically produced expensive private aircraft but has recently added less expensive planes to meet a threat from Piper, which began to produce larger planes.

In making a downward stretch, the company faces some risks. The low-end item might provoke competitors to counteract by moving into the higher end. Or the company's dealers may not be willing or able to handle the lower-end products. Or the new low-end item might *cannibalize* higher-end items, leaving the company worse off. Consider the following:

> General Electric's Medical Systems Division is the market leader in CAT scanners, expensive diagnostic machines used in hospitals. GE learned that a Japanese competitor was planning to attack its market. GE executives guessed that the new Japanese model would be smaller, more electronically advanced, and less expensive. GE's best defense would be to introduce a similar lower-priced machine before the Japanese model entered the market. But some

FIGURE 10-5 Product-line stretching decision

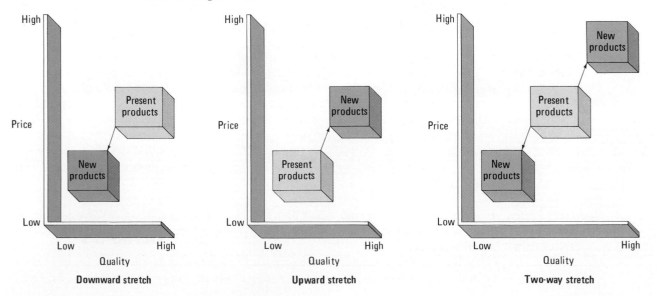

GE executives expressed concern that this lower-priced version would hurt the sales and higher profit margins on their large CAT scanner. One manager finally settled the issue by saying: "Aren't we better off to cannibalize ourselves than to let the Japanese do it?"

A major miscalculation of several American companies has been their failure to plug holes in the lower end of their markets. General Motors resisted building smaller cars, and Xerox resisted building smaller copying machines. Japanese companies found a major opening and moved in quickly and successfully.

Upward Stretch

Companies at the lower end of the market may want to enter the higher end. They may be attracted by a faster growth rate or higher margins at the higher end, or they may simply want to position themselves as full-line manufacturers. For example, General Electric recently added its Monogram line of high-quality, built-in kitchen appliances targeted at the select few households earning more than $100,000 a year and living in homes valued at over $400,000. Sometimes, companies stretch upward in order to add prestige to their current products, as when Chrysler purchased Lamborghini, the maker of exotic, handcrafted sports cars.

An upward-stretch decision can be risky. The higher-end competitors not only are well entrenched but may strike back by entering the lower end of the market. Prospective customers may not believe that the newcomer can produce quality products. Finally, the company's salespeople and distributors may lack the talent and training to serve the higher end of the market.

Two-Way Stretch

Companies in the middle range of the market may decide to stretch their lines in both directions. Sony did this to hold off copycat competitors for its Walkman line of personal tape players. Sony introduced its first Walkman in the middle of the market. As imitative competitors moved in with lower-priced models, Sony stretched downward. At the same time, to add luster to its lower-price models and to attract more affluent consumers, Sony stretched the Walkman line upwards. It now sells more than 100 models, ranging from a plain-vanilla, play-back-only version for $32 to a high-tech, high-quality $450 version that both plays and records. Using this two-way-stretch strategy, Sony now dominates the personal tape player market with a 30 percent share.[26]

The Marriott Hotel group has also performed a two-way stretch of its hotel product line. Alongside regular Marriott hotels, it added the Marriott Marquis line to serve the upper end of the market and the Courtyard and Fairfield Inn lines to serve the lower end. Each branded hotel line is aimed at a different target market. Marriott Marquis aims to attract and please top executives; Marriotts, middle managers; Courtyards, salespeople; and Fairfield Inns, vacationers and others on a low travel budget. The major risk with this strategy is that some travelers will trade down after finding that the lower-price hotels in the Marriott chain give them pretty much everything they want.

Product-Line Filling Decision
A product line can also be lengthened by adding more items within the current range of the line. Among the reasons for **product-line filling** are: reaching for extra profits, trying to satisfy dealers, trying to use excess capacity, trying to be the leading full-line company, and trying to plug holes to keep out competitors. Thus, Sony has added solar-powered and waterproof Walkmans and an ultralight model that attaches to a sweatband for joggers, bicyclers, tennis players, and other exercisers.

However, line filling is overdone if it results in cannibalization and customer confusion. The company should assure that new items are noticeably different from current items.

Product-Line Modernization Decision
In some cases, product line length is adequate, but the line needs to be modernized. For example, a company's machine tools may have a 1950s look and lose out to better-styled competitors' lines.

The issue in product-line modernization is whether to overhaul the line piecemeal or in one fell swoop. A piecemeal approach allows the company to see how customers and dealers like the new styles before changing the whole line. Piecemeal modernization causes less drain on the company's cash flow. A major disadvantage of piecemeal modernization, however, is that it allows competitors to see changes and start redesigning their own lines.

Product-Line Featuring Decision

The product-line manager typically selects one or a few items in the line to feature. This is **product-line featuring.** Sometimes, managers feature promotional models at the low end of the line to serve as "traffic builders." Thus, Sears will announce a special low-priced sewing machine to attract people. And Rolls Royce announced an economy model selling for only $49,000—in contrast to its high-end model selling for $108,000—to bring people into its showrooms. Once the customers arrive, salespeople may try to get them to buy at the high end of the line.

At other times, managers feature a high-end item to give the product line "class." Thus, Audimar Piguet advertises a $25,000 watch, which few people buy but which acts as a "flagship" to enhance the whole line.

PRODUCT-MIX DECISIONS

An organization with several product lines has a product mix. A **product mix** (also called PRODUCT ASSORTMENT) is the set of all product lines and items that a particular seller offers for sale. Avon's product mix consists of four major product lines: cosmetics, jewelry, fashions, and household items. Each product line consists of several sublines. For example, cosmetics breaks down into lipstick, rouge, powder, and so on. Each line and subline has many individual items. Altogether, Avon's product mix includes 1,300 items. A large supermarket handles as many as 14,000 items; a typical K mart stocks 15,000 items; and General Electric manufactures as many as 250,000 items.

A company's product mix can be described as having a certain breadth, length, depth, and consistency. These concepts are illustrated in Table 10-1, which lists selected Procter & Gamble consumer products.

The *breadth* of P&G's product mix refers to the number of different product lines the company carries. Table 10-1 shows a product mix width of six lines. (In fact, P&G produces many more lines, including mouthwashes, paper towels, disposable diapers, and pain relievers.)

The *length* of P&G's product mix refers to the total number of items the company carries. In Table 10-1, the total number is 42. We can also compute the average length of a line at P&G by dividing the total length (here, 42) by the number of lines (here, 6). The average P&G product line as represented in Table 10-1 consists of 7 brands.

TABLE 10-1   Product Mix Breadth and Product Line Length Shown for Selected Procter & Gamble Products

	Detergents	Toothpaste	Bar Soap	Deodorants	Fruit Juices	Lotions
	Ivory Snow	Gleem	Ivory	Secret	Citrus Hill	Wondra
	Dreft	Crest	Camay	Sure	Sunny Delight	Noxema
	Tide	Complete	Lava		Winter Hill	Oil of Olay
	Joy	Denquel	Kirk's		Texsun	Camay
	Cheer		Zest		Lincoln	Raintree
	Oxydol		Safeguard		Speas Farm	Tropic Tan
	Dash		Coast			Bain de Soleil
	Cascade		Oil of Olay			
	Ivory Liquid					
	Gain					
	Dawn					
	Era					
	Bold 3					
	Liquid Tide					
	Solo					

The table is labeled with "PRODUCT MIX BREADTH" spanning across the top (Detergents through Lotions), and "PRODUCT LINE LENGTH" running vertically down the left side.

The *depth* of P&G's product mix refers to the number of versions offered of each product in the line. Thus, if Crest comes in three sizes and two formulations (paste and gel), Crest has a depth of six. By counting the number of versions within each brand, we can calculate the average depth of P&G's product mix.

The *consistency* of the product mix refers to how closely related the various product lines are in end use, production requirements, distribution channels, or some other way. P&G's product lines are consistent insofar as they are consumer goods that go through the same distribution channels. The lines are less consistent insofar as they perform different functions for buyers.

These four dimensions of the product mix provide the handles for defining the company's product strategy. The company can increase its business in four ways. It can add new product lines, thus widening its product mix. In this way, its new lines build on the company's reputation in its other lines. Or the company can lengthen its existing product lines to become a more full-line company. Or the company can add more product versions to each product and thus deepen its product mix. Finally, the company can pursue more product-line consistency—or less—depending upon whether it wants to have a strong reputation in a single field or in several fields.

Thus, product strategy calls for complex decisions on product mix, product line, branding, packaging, and service strategy. These decisions must be made not only with a full understanding of consumer wants and competitors' strategies, but also with increasing attention to the growing public policy affecting product decisions (see Marketing Highlight 10–5).

MARKETING HIGHLIGHT 10–5

PRODUCT DECISIONS AND PUBLIC POLICY

Marketing managers must heed various laws and regulations when making product decisions. The main areas of product concern are as follows.

Product Additions and Deletions. Under the Anti-merger Act, the government can prevent companies from adding products through acquisitions if the effect threatens to lessen competition. Companies dropping products must be aware that they have legal obligations, written or implied, to their suppliers, dealers, and customers who have a stake in the discontinued product.

Patent Protection. A firm must obey the U.S. patent laws when developing new products. A company cannot make its product "illegally similar" to another company's established product. An example is Polaroid's successful suit to prevent Kodak from selling its new instant-picture camera on the grounds that it infringed on Polaroid's instant-camera patents.

Product Quality and Safety. Manufacturers must comply with specific laws regarding product quality and safety. The Federal Food, Drug, and Cosmetic Act protects consumers from unsafe and adulterated food, drugs, and cosmetics. Various acts provide for the inspection of sanitary conditions in the meat- and poultry-processing industries. Safety legislation has been passed to regulate fabrics, chemical substances, automobiles, toys, and drugs and poisons. The Consumer Product Safety Act of 1972 established a Consumer Product Safety Commission, which has the authority to ban or seize potentially hazardous products and set severe penalties for violation of the law. If consumers have been injured by a product that has been defectively designed, they can sue manufacturers or dealers. Product liability suits are now occurring at the rate of more than one million per year, with individual awards often running in the millions of dollars.

This phenomenon has resulted in huge increases in product-liability insurance premiums. For example, until last year, Piper Aircraft's insurance bill averaged $75,000 for every new plane, more than the cost of producing Piper's smaller planes. It recently dropped its insurance and now maintains a staff of five defense attorneys and spends $13 million a year on legal costs. The cost of liability insurance for producers of children's car seats rose from $50,000 in 1984 to more than $750,000 in 1986. Some companies pass these higher rates along to consumers by raising prices. Others are forced to discontinue high-risk product lines.

Product Warranties. Many manufacturers offer written product warranties to convince customers of their product's quality. But these warranties are often limited and written in a language the average consumer does not understand. Too often, consumers learn that they are not entitled to services, repairs, and replacements that seem to be implied. To protect consumers, Congress passed the Magnuson-Moss Warranty Act in 1975. The act requires that full warranties meet certain minimum standards, including repair "within a reasonable time and without charge" or a replacement or full refund if the product does not work "after a reasonable number of attempts" at repair. Otherwise, the company must make clear that it is offering only a limited warranty. The law has led several manufacturers to switch from full to limited warranties and others to drop warranties altogether as a marketing tool.

Sources: See Michael Brody, "When Products Turn," *Fortune*, March 3, 1986, pp. 20–24; "Marketers Feel Product-Liability Pressure," May 12, 1986, pp. 3, 75; Louis W. Stern and Thomas L. Eovaldi, *Legal Aspects of Marketing Strategy* (Englewood Cliffs, NJ: Prentice Hall, 1984), pp. 76–116; and Gail DeGeorge, "Without Cash, Piper May Have Trouble Keeping Its Nose Up," *Business Week*, March 5, 1990, p. 32.

■ SUMMARY

Product is a complex concept that must be carefully defined. Product strategy calls for making coordinated decisions on product items, product lines, and the product mix.

Each product item offered to customers can be viewed on three levels. The *core product* is the essential benefit the buyer is really buying. The *actual product* includes the features, styling, quality, brand name, and packaging of the product offered for sale. The *augmented product* is the actual product plus the various services offered with it, such as warranty, installation, maintenance, and free delivery.

All products can be classified, for example, according to their durability (nondurable goods, durable goods, and services). *Consumer goods* are usually classified according to consumer shopping habits (convenience, shopping, specialty, and unsought goods). *Industrial goods* are classified according to their cost and the way they enter the production process (materials and parts, capital items, and supplies and services).

Companies must develop strategies for the product items in their lines, deciding on product attributes, branding, packaging, labeling, and product-support services. *Product-attribute decisions* involve which product quality, features, and design the company will offer. Regarding *brands*, the company must decide whether to brand at all, whether to choose manufacturing or private branding, whether to use family brand names or individual brand names, whether to extend the brand name to new products, whether to offer several competing brands, and whether to reposition any of its brands.

Products also require *packaging decisions* to create such benefits as protection, economy, convenience, and promotion. Marketers have to develop a packaging concept and test it to be sure that it both achieves desired objectives and is compatible with public policy.

Products also require *labeling* for identification and possible grading, description, and promotion of the product. U.S. laws require sellers to present certain minimum information on the label to inform and protect consumers.

Companies have to develop *product-support services* that are both desired by customers and effective against competitors. The company must decide on the most important services to offer and the best ways to deliver these services. The *service mix* can be coordinated by a customer-service department that handles complaints and adjustments, credit, maintenance, technical service, and customer information. *Customer service* should be used as a marketing tool to create customer satisfaction and competitive advantage.

Most companies produce not a single product, but a product line. A *product line* is a group of products related in function, customer-purchase needs, or distribution channels. Each product line requires a product strategy. *Line stretching* raises the question of whether a line should be extended downward, upward, or in both directions. *Line filling* raises the question of whether additional items should be added within the present range of the line. *Line featuring* raises the question of which items to feature in promoting the line.

Product mix describes the set of product lines and items offered to customers by a particular seller. The product mix can be described by its length, width, depth, and consistency. The four dimensions of the product mix are the tools for developing the company's product strategy.

■ QUESTIONS FOR DISCUSSION

1. What are the core, tangible, and augmented products of the educational experience that universities offer?

2. How would you classify the product offered by restaurants: as nondurable goods or as services? Why?

3. Compare the number of retail outlets for each type of consumer good (convenience, shopping, specialty, or unsought) in a particular geographic area. Give examples.

4. In recent years, U.S. automakers have tried to reposition many of their brands to the high-quality end of the market. How well have they succeeded? What else could they do to change consumer's perceptions of their cars?

5. Why are many people willing to pay more for branded products than for unbranded products? What does this tell you about the value of branding?

6. Changing an established brand name is expensive and time consuming. What were the benefits and drawbacks of changing such established company names as ESSO (ENCO), Bank Americard, and Datsun, to new names—EXXON, VISA, and Nissan?

7. Think of several products you buy regularly and describe how their packaging or labels could be improved. If you think the packaging change would add to the cost of the product, how much more would you be willing to pay for the improved design?

8. For many years there was one type of Coca-Cola, one type of Tide, and one type of Crest (in mint and regular flavors). Now we find Coke in 6 or more varieties, Regular, Liquid, and Unscented Tide, and Crest Gel with sparkles for kids. What issues do these brand extensions raise for manufacturers, retailers, and consumers?

9. Compare the product mix of McDonald's to Kentucky Fried Chicken. Are there differences in width or depth? How could they stretch their lines upward or downward?

10. Compare brand extension by the brand owner with licensing a brand name for use by another company. What are the opportunities and risks of each approach?

■ KEY TERMS

Actual product. A product's parts, styling, features, brand name, packaging, and other attributes that combine to deliver core product benefits.

Augmented product. Additional consumer services and benefits built around the core and actual products.

Brand. A name, term, sign, symbol, or design, or a combination of these, intended to identify the goods or services of one seller or group of sellers and to differentiate them from those of competitors.

Brand-extension. A new or modified product launched under an already successful brand name.

Brand mark. That part of a brand that can be recognized but that is not utterable, such as a symbol, design, or distinctive coloring or lettering. Examples are the Pillsbury doughboy, the Metro-Goldwyn-Mayer lion, and the red K on the Kodak film box.

Brand name. That part of a brand that can be vocalized—the utterable, such as Avon, Chevrolet, Tide, Disneyland, American Express, and UCLA.

Capital items. Industrial goods that enter the finished product partly, including installations and accessory equipment.

Consumer goods. Those bought by final consumers for personal consumption.

Convenience goods. Consumer goods that the customer usually buys frequently, immediately, and with the minimum of comparison and buying effort.

Copyright. The exclusive legal right to reproduce, publish, and sell the matter and form of a literary, musical, or artistic work.

Core product. The problem-solving services or core benefits that consumers are really buying when they obtain a product.

Durable goods. Consumer goods that are usually used over an extended period of time and that normally survive many uses.

Industrial goods. Goods bought by individuals and organizations for further processing or for use in conducting a business.

Manufacturer's brand (or national brand). A brand created and owned by the producer of a product or service.

Materials and parts. Industrial goods that enter the manufacturer's product completely, including raw materials and manufactured materials and parts.

Multibrand strategy. A strategy under which one seller develops two or more brands in the same product category.

Nondurable goods. Consumer goods that are normally consumed in one or a few uses.

Packaging. The activities of designing and producing the container or wrapper for a product.

Packaging concept. What the package should *be* or *do* for the product.

Private brand (or middleman, distributor, or dealer brand). A brand created and owned by a reseller of a product or service.

Product. Anything that can be offered to a market for attention, acquisition, use, or consumption that might satisfy a want or need. It includes physical objects, services, persons, places, organizations, and ideas.

Product design. The process of designing a product's style and function: creating a product that is attractive; easy, safe, and inexpensive to use and service; and simple and economical to produce and distribute.

Product line. A group of products that are closely related either because they function in a similar manner, are sold to the same customer groups, are marketed through the same types of outlets, or fall within given price ranges.

Product-line featuring. Selecting one or a few items in a product line to feature.

Product-line filling. Increasing the product line by adding more items within the present range of the line.

Product-line stretching. Increasing the product line by lengthening it beyond its current range.

Product mix (or **product assortment**). The set of all product lines and items that a particular seller offers for sale to buyers.

Product quality. The ability of a product to perform its functions; it includes the product's overall durability, reliability, precision, ease of operation and repair, and other valued attributes.

Product-support services. Services that augment actual products.

Services. Activities, benefits, or satisfactions that are offered for sale.

Shopping goods. Consumer goods that the customer, in the process of selection and purchase, characteristically compares on such bases as suitability, quality, price, and style.

Specialty goods. Consumer goods with unique characteristics or brand identification for which a significant group of buyers is willing to make a special purchase effort.

Supplies and services. Industrial goods that do not enter the finished product at all.

Trademark. A brand or part of a brand that is given legal protection—the trademark protects the seller's exclusive rights to use the brand name or brand mark.

Unsought goods. Consumer goods that the consumer either does not know about or knows about but does not normally think of buying.

◼ REFERENCES

1. See Bess Gallanis, "New Strategies Revive the Rose's Fading Bloom," *Advertising Age*, February 27, 1984, pp. M9–M11; "What Lies Behind the Sweet Smell of Success," *Business Week*, February 27, 1984, pp. 139–143; S. J. Diamond, "Perfume Equals Part Mystery, Part Marketing," *Los Angeles Times*, April 22, 1988, Section 4, p. 1; and Adrienne Ward, "Passion Inflames Celebrity Fragrances," *Advertising Age*, February 27, 1989, pp. S8–9.

2. See Peter D. Bennett, *Dictionary of Marketing Terms* (Chicago: American Marketing Association, 1988).

3. See Bennett, *Dictionary of Marketing Terms*. For more information on product classifications, see Patrick E. Murphy and Ben M. Enis, "Classifying Products Strategically," *Journal of Marketing*, July 1986, pp. 24–42.

4. David A. Garvin, "Competing on Eight Dimensions of Quality," *Harvard Business Review*, November–December 1987, p. 109. Also see Robert Jacobson and David A.

Aaker, "The Strategic Role of Product Quality," *Journal of Marketing*, October 1987, pp. 31–44.

5. Tom Peters and Perry Pascarella, "Searching for Excellence: The Winners Deliver on Value," *Industry Week*, April 16, 1984, pp. 61–62.

6. For more examples, see Joel Dreyfuss, "Victories in the Quality Crusade," *Fortune*, October 10, 1988, pp. 80–88.

7. For a discussion of consumer perceptions of quality, see Valerie A. Zeithaml, "Consumer Perceptions of Price, Quality, and Value: A Means–End Model and Synthesis of Evidence," *Journal of Marketing*, July 1988, pp. 2–22.

8. Bruce Nussbaum, "Smart Design: Quality Is the New Style," *Business Week*, April 11, 1988, pp. 102–08.

9. For more on design, see Philip Kotler, "Design: A Powerful but Neglected Stragetic Tool," *Journal of Business Strategy*, Fall 1984, pp. 16–21; Robert A. Abler, "The Value-Added

of Design,'' *Business Marketing*, September 1986, pp. 96–103; and Bruce Nussbaum, ''Designed in America,'' *Business Week*, special issue on innovation, June 1989, p. 138.

10. See Bennett, *Dictionary of Marketing Terms*.

11. See Eleanor Johnson Tracy, ''Here Come Brand-Name Fruit and Veggies,'' *Fortune*, February 18, 1985, p. 105; and Alice Z. Cuneo, ''Companies Find Brands Bear Fruit at the Farm Stand, *Advertising Age*, May 9, 1988, p. S8.

12. Walter J. Salmon and Karen A. Cmar, ''Private Labels are Back in Fashion,'' *Harvard Business Review*, May–June 1987, pp. 99–106.

13. See Michael Oneal, ''Fruit of the Loom Escalates the Underwars,'' *Business Week*, February 22, 1988, pp. 114–118.

14. See Al Ries and Jack Trout, *Positioning: The Battle for Your Mind* (New York: McGraw-Hill, 1981). For more on consumer attitudes toward brand extensions, see David A. Aaker and Kevin L. Keller, ''Consumer Evaluations of Brand Extensions,'' *Journal of Marketing*, January 1990, pp. 27–41.

15. See Mark B. Taylor, ''Cannibalism in Multibrand Firms,'' *Journal of Business Strategy*, Spring 1986, pp. 69–75.

16. See Bess Gallanis, ''Positioning Old Products in New Niches,'' *Advertising Age*, May 3, 1984, p. M50; and ''Marketers Should Consider Restaging Old Brands Before Launching New Ones,'' *Advertising Age*, December 10, 1982, p. 5.

17. Walter Stern, ''A Good Name Can Mean a Brand of Fame,'' *Advertising Age*, January 17, 1983, p. M53.

18. Thomas M. S. Hemnes, ''How Can You Find a Safe Trademark?'' *Harvard Business Review*, March–April 1985, p. 44.

19. For a discussion of legal issues surrounding the use of brand names, see Dorothy Cohen, ''Trademark Strategy,'' *Journal of Marketing*, January 1986, pp. 61–74; ''Trademark Woes: Help Is Coming,'' *Sales & Marketing Management*, January 1988, p. 84; and Jack Alexander, ''What's in a Name? Too Much, Said the FCC,'' *Sales & Marketing Management*, January 1989, pp. 75–78.

20. Bill Abrams, ''Marketing,'' *The Wall Street Journal*, May 20, 1982, p. 33.

21. See Fred W. Morgan, ''Tampered Goods: Legal Developments and Marketing Guidelines,'' *Journal of Marketing*, April 1988, pp. 86–96.

22. See Alicia Swasy, ''Sales Lost Their Vim? Try Repackaging,'' *Wall Street Journal*, October 11, 1989, p. B1.

23. Bro Uttal, ''Companies That Serve You Best,'' *Fortune*, December 7, 1987, pp. 98–116. See also ''Customer Service: Up the Bottom Line,'' *Sales & Marketing Management*, January 1989, pp. 1–2; and William H. Davidow, ''Customer Service: The Ultimate Marketing Weapon,'' *Business Marketing*, October 1989, pp. 56–64.

24. Bro Uttal, ''Companies That Serve You Best,'' p. 116.

25. For more examples of how companies have used customer service as a marketing tool, see ''Making Service a Potent Marketing Tool,'' *Business Week*, June 11, 1984, pp. 164–70; Bill Kelley, ''Five Companies That Do It Right—And Make It Pay,'' *Sales & Marketing Management*, April 1988, pp. 57–64; and Patricia Sellers, ''How to Handle Customers' Gripes, *Fortune*, October 24, 1988, pp. 88–100.

26. See Amy Borrus, ''How Sony Keeps the Copycats Scampering,'' *Business Week*, June 1, 1987, p. 69.

COLGATE: SQUEEZING MORE FROM A BRAND NAME

You probably know about Colgate toothpaste—perhaps you've even used it. But what would you think of Colgate aspirin or Colgate antacid? How about Colgate laxative or Colgate dandruff shampoo?

That's exactly what Colgate-Palmolive wants to know. To find out how consumers would react to such products sold under the Colgate brand, the massive packaged-goods company has quietly established a test market in Peoria, Illinois, to test a line of ten over-the-counter (OTC) health-care products, all using the Colgate name. The line includes Colgate aspirin-free pain reliever, to compete with Tylenol; Colgate ibuprofen, to compete with Advil; Colgate cold tablets, to compete with Contac; Colgate night-time cold medicine, to compete with Nyquil; Colgate antacid, to compete with Rolaids; Colgate natural laxative, to compete with Metamucil; and Colgate dandruff shampoo, to compete with Head & Shoulders.

Colgate's new line represents a significant departure from the higher-margin, high-visibility household goods that Colgate traditionally markets. Colgate chairman Reuben Marks indicates that "The Colgate name is already strong in oral hygiene, now we want to learn whether it can represent health care across the board. We need to expand into more profitable categories."

Colgate won't talk specifically about its new line, but Peoria drugstore operators say the company began the test marketing last fall. Since then, Colgate has blitzed the town with coupons and ads. Representatives have given away free tubes of toothpaste with other Colgate purchases and handed out coupons worth virtually the full price of the new products. One store owner notes, "They're spending major money out here."

If all that promotional support weren't enough, the manager of one Walgreen store points out that Colgate has priced its line well below competing brands, as much as 20 percent below. The same manager reports that the new products' sales are strong but also adds, "With all the promotion they've done, they should be. They're cheaper, and they've got Colgate's name on them."

Yet, even if Colgate's test is a resounding success, marketing consultants say expanding the new line could prove dangerous and ultimately more expensive than Colgate can imagine. "If you put the Colgate brand name on a bunch of different products, if you do it willy-nilly at the lowest end, you're going to dilute what it stands for—and if you stand for nothing, you're worthless," observes Clive Chajet, chairman of Lippincott & Margulies, a firm that handles corporate identity projects.

Mr. Chajet suggests that Colgate also might end up alienating customers by slapping its name on so many products. If consumers are "dissatisfied with one product, they might be dissatisfied with everything across the board.

I wouldn't risk it," he says. What would have happened to Johnson & Johnson during the Tylenol poison scare, he asks, if the Tylenol name were plastered across everything from baby shampoo to birth control pills?

Colgate's test is one of the bolder forays into line extensions by consumer products companies. Companies saddled with "mature" brands—brands that can't grow much more—often try to use those brands' solid gold names to make a new fortune, generally with a related product. Thus, Procter & Gamble's Ivory soap came up with a shampoo and conditioner. Coca-Cola concocted Diet Coke. Arm & Hammer baking soda expanded into carpet deodorizer.

Unlike those products, however, Colgate's new line moves far afield from its familiar turf. And although its new line is selling well, sales might not stay so strong without budget prices and a barrage of advertising and promotion. "People are looking at it right now as a generic-style product," observes one store manager. "People are really price conscious, and as long as the price is cheaper, along with a name that you can trust, people are going to buy that over others."

Al Ries, chairman of Trout & Ries, a Greenwich, Connecticut, marketing consultant, questions whether any line extensions make sense—not only for Colgate, but for other strong brand names. He says the reason Colgate has been able to break into the over-the-counter drug market in the first place is because other drugs have expanded and lost their niches; Tylenol and Alka-Seltzer both now make cold medicines, for example, and "that allows an opportunity for the outsiders, the Colgates, to come in and say there's no perception that anybody is any different. The consumer will look for any acceptable brand name."

Mr. Ries argues that Colgate and the traditional over-the-counter medicine companies are basically turning their products into generic drugs instead of brands. They're losing "the power of a narrow focus," he says, adding, "It reflects stupidity on the part of the traditional over-the-counter marketers. . . . If the traditional medicines maintained their narrow focus, they wouldn't leave room for an outsider such as Colgate."

If Colgate is too successful, meanwhile, it also risks cannibalizing its flagship product. Consultants note that almost all successful line extensions, and a lot of not-so-successful ones, hurt the product from which they took their name. They cite Miller High Life, whose share of the beer market has dwindled since the introduction of Miller Lite. "If Colgate made themselves to mean over-the-counter medicine, nobody would want to buy Colgate toothpaste," contends Mr. Ries.

Mr. Chajet agrees. Colgate could "save tens of millions of dollars by not having to introduce a new brand name'' for its new products, he says. But in doing so, it might also ''kill the goose that laid the golden egg.'' Other marketing consultants believe that Colgate may be able to break into the market but that it will take a lot of time and money. ''They just don't bring a lot to the OTC party,'' one consultant indicates.

Although chairman Marks admits that Colgate will continue to try to build share in its traditional cleanser and detergent markets, the company seems to consider personal care as a stronger area. But leveraging a name into new categories can be tricky, requiring patience from skeptical retailers and fickle consumers. ''It isn't so much a question of where you can put the brand name,'' says one marketing consultant. ''It's what products the consumer will let you put the brand name on.''

QUESTIONS

1. What core product is Colgate selling when it sells toothpaste or the other products in its new line?
2. How would you classify these new products? What implications does this classification have for marketing the new line?
3. What brand decisions has Colgate made? What kinds of product-line decisions? Are these decisions consistent?
4. If you were the marketing manager for the extended Colgate line, how would you package the new products? What risks do you see in these packaging decisions?

Source: Adapted from Joanne Lipman, ''Colgate Tests Putting Its Name on Over-the-Counter Drug Line,'' *The Wall Street Journal*, July 19, 1989. Used with permission. Also see Dan Koeppel, ''Now Playing in Peoria: Colgate Generics,'' *Adweek's Marketing Week*, September 18, 1989, p. 5.

NEOGENERICS: A GENERIC WITH A NEW NAME

In the late 1970s, Americans were faced with high inflation. To help consumers reduce their grocery bills, Jewel Foods introduced generic grocery items. These goods were packaged in plain black-and-white containers and were identified by product—for example, green beans—rather than by brand name. Lower costs were made possible by eliminating advertising, using standard-grade goods, lowering the quality of nonfood items, and omitting packaging features such as pouring spouts.

By introducing generics, Jewel Foods created a major controversy. Industry critics denounced them low in quality and a poor value for the dollar, and contended that American consumers would not buy these watered-down imitations of brands that manufacturers had spent many years and dollars promoting. Predictions that generics wouldn't last two years were changed to five years, then eight years, then ten years. Yet some generics are still on the market.

On the other side, proponents of generics hailed them as "a return to the basics," "an elimination of frills," and a "celebration of austerity" that expressed "reverse snobbishness." They contended that Americans did not want trivial product and packaging improvements that added unnecessary expense to products, and that the elimination of branding would do away with the need for advertising. They pointed out that the nutritional value of generics was just as high as that of national brands; that blind taste tests demonstrated that consumers sometimes preferred the taste of generics; that generics were easy to find in the store because consumers only had to look for plain black-and-white labels; and that they cost 10 to 40 percent less than brands.

Either because they desired to reduce their grocery bills or because they were curious about the generics, many Americans bought them. At their sales peak in the early 1980s, generics were available in most U.S. cities and could be purchased in over 300 product categories. But when sales declined in the mid-1980s, retailers dropped them from many product categories.

What happened to those generic grocery items that weren't withdrawn from the market? Consumers can still find some of the original generics among the basic foodstuffs such as rice and sugar and the nonfood basics such as plastic bags and paper towels. But they must hunt carefully for them because they aren't available in many stores.

Most of today's generics do not resemble the original generic products. The plain black-and-white labels have been replaced with colored labels, and these new generics have names such as Kroger's Cost Cutters and Proctor & Gamble's Banner. But they still retain some of the features of the original generics—lower quality, fewer packaging features, and lower prices. Because of these changes, the new generics have been dubbed "neogenerics."

Before the advent of generics, there were manufacturers' and distributors' brands in grocery stores. Manufacturers' brands are well-known national brands, such as Nabisco, as well as such lesser-known packers' labels as Lady Lee. Distributors' brands consist of private or retailer's brands such as A & P's Jane Parker brand and Safeway's own brand.

Generics or neogenerics constitute a third type of "brand"—the effect of which is to increase the consumer's choice of brands and price levels. Now consumers have more latitude in matching product quality to intended use: They can use generic rice in a casserole and serve Comet rice as a separate dish, or buy Glad trash bags for heavy loads and Cost Cutter bags for lighter-weight uses.

Because most neogenerics are distributors' brands, they offer retailers the opportunity to increase their percentage of sales—frequently at the expense of manufacturers' brands. In the battle for retail shelf space and sales, neogenerics could tip the balance of power to retailers. Even if manufacturers respond with lower-cost products, this would still benefit consumers.

However, this increase in sales could reduce retailers' profits because generics and neogenerics are lower-margin items. Since the grocery industry has very narrow margins, reduced profit margins are highly undesirable. To survive will require retailers to become more skillful product managers. They will have to manage more types of brands and successfully promote other higher-margin items to offset the reduced profit impact of neogenerics.

QUESTIONS

1. In which goods classification (convenience, shopping, specialty) are generic grocery products found today?

2. How does the introduction of generics/neogenerics affect the retailer's product lines? What kinds of brand decisions must the retailer make?

3. Purchases of generics involve a risk that the product will not work or could even be harmful. Why, then, do consumers buy generic prescription drugs?

Sources: Suzanne F. Bauschard, "The Generic Metamorphosis: Now They're Third-Tier Brands with Names, Colorful Labels," *Marketing News*, 15 (April 30, 1982): 1, 7; Charles Burck, "Plain Labels Challenge the Supermarket Establishment," *Fortune*, 99 (March 26, 1979); 70–76; Martha R. McEnally and Jon M. Hawes, "The Market for Generic Brand Grocery Products: A Review and Extension," *Journal of Marketing*, 48 (Winter 1984): 75–83.

11

Designing Products: New-Product Development and Product Life-Cycle Strategies

The 3M Company markets more than 60,000 products, ranging from sandpaper, adhesives, and floppy disks to contact lenses, laser optical disks, translucent braces, and heart–lung machines; from coatings that sleeken boat hulls to hundreds of sticky tapes—Scotch Tape, masking tape, super-bonding tape, and even refastening disposable diaper tape. 3M views *innovation* as its path to growth and new products as its lifeblood. The company's long-standing goal is to derive an astonishing 25 percent of each year's sales from products introduced within the previous five years. More astonishing, it usually succeeds! Each year 3M launches more than 200 new products. And last year, 32 percent of its almost $11 billion in sales came from products introduced within the past five years. Its legendary emphasis on innovation has consistently made it one of America's most admired companies.

New products don't just happen. 3M works hard to create an environment that supports innovation. It invests 6.5 percent of its annual sales in research and development—twice as much as the average company. Its "Innovation Task Force" seeks out and destroys corporate bureaucracy that might interfere with new-product progress. Hired consultants help 3M find ways to make employees more inventive.

3M encourages everyone to look for new products. The company's renowned "15 percent rule" allows all employees to spend up to 15 percent of their time "bootlegging"—working on projects of personal interest whether those projects directly benefit the company or not. When

a promising idea comes along, 3M forms a venture team made up of the researcher who developed the idea and volunteers from manufacturing, sales, marketing, and legal. The team nurtures the product and protects it from company bureaucracy. Team members stay with the product until it succceds or fails and then return to their previous jobs. Some teams have tried three or four times before finally making a success of an idea. Each year, 3M hands out "Golden Step Awards" to venture teams whose new products earned more than $2 million in U.S. sales or $4 million in worldwide sales within three years of introduction.

3M knows that it must try thousands of new-product ideas to hit one big jackpot. One well-worn slogan at 3M is, "You have to kiss a lot of frogs to find a prince." "Kissing frogs" often means making mistakes, but 3M accepts blunders and dead ends as a normal part of creativity and innovation. In fact, its philosophy seems to be, "If you aren't making mistakes, you probably aren't doing anything." But as it turns out, "blunders" have turned into some of 3M's most successful products. Old-timers at 3M love to tell the story about the chemist who accidentally spilled a new chemical on her tennis shoes. Some days later, she noticed that the spots hit by the chemical had not gotten dirty. Eureka! The chemical eventually became Scotchgard fabric protector.

And then there's the one about 3M scientist Spencer Silver. Silver started out to develop a super-strong adhesive; instead, he came up with one that didn't stick very well at all. He sent the apparently useless substance on to other 3M researchers to see whether they could find something to do with it. Nothing happened for several years. Then Arthur Fry, another 3M scientist, had a problem—and an idea. As a choir member in a local church, Mr. Fry was having trouble marking places in his hymnal— the little scraps of paper he used kept falling out. He tried dabbing some of Mr. Silver's weak glue on one of the scraps. It stuck nicely and later peeled off without damaging the hymnal. Thus was born 3M's Post-It Notes, a product that now sells almost $100 million a year![1]

CHAPTER OBJECTIVES

After reading this chapter, you should be able to:

1. List and define the steps in new-product development.
2. Explain how companies find and develop new-product ideas.
3. Describe the stages of the product life cycle.
4. Explain how marketing strategy changes during a product's life cycle.

A company has to be good at developing new products. It also must manage them in the face of changing tastes, technologies, and competition. Every product seems to go through a life cycle—it is born, goes through several phases, and eventually dies as newer products come along that better serve consumer needs.

This product life cycle presents two major challenges. First, because all products eventually decline, the firm must find new products to replace aging ones (the problem of *new-product development*). Second, the firm must understand how its products age and adapt its marketing strategies as products pass through life-cycle stages (the problem of *product life-cycle strategies*). We first look at the problem of finding and developing new products and then at the problem of managing them successfully over their life cycles.

NEW-PRODUCT DEVELOPMENT STRATEGY

Given the rapid changes in tastes, technology, and competition, a company cannot rely solely on its existing products. Customers want and expect the new and improved products that competition will do its best to provide. Every company needs a new-product development program. One expert estimates that half of the profits of all U.S. companies come from products that didn't exist ten years ago.[2]

A company can obtain new products in two ways. One is through *acquisition*—buying a whole company, a patent, or a license to produce someone else's product. The other is through **new-product development** in the company's own research and development department. As the costs of developing and introducing major new products have climbed, many large companies have decided to acquire existing brands rather than create new ones. Others have saved money by copying competitors' brands or by reviving old brands (see Marketing Highlight 11–1).

By *new products* we mean original products, product improvements, product modifications, and new brands that the firm develops through its own research and development efforts. In this chapter, we concentrate on new-product development.

Innovation can be very risky. Ford lost $350 million on its Edsel automobile; RCA lost $580 million on its SelectaVision videodisc player; Texas Instruments lost a staggering $660 million before withdrawing from the home computer business; and the Concorde aircraft will never pay back its investment. Following are several other consumer products, each launched by sophisticated companies, that failed:

- Juice Works fruit juice for children (Campbell)
- Cue toothpaste (Colgate)

GETTING AROUND THE HIGH COSTS AND RISKS OF NEW-PRODUCT DEVELOPMENT

The average cost of developing and introducing a major new product from scratch has jumped to well over $100 million. What's worse, many of these costly new products fail. So companies are now pursuing new product strategies that are less costly and risky than developing completely new brands. We discuss two of these strategies—*licensing* and *brand extensions*—in Chapter 9. Here we describe three other new product strategies, *acquiring new brands*, *developing "me-too" products*, and *reviving old brands*.

Acquiring New Products

Instead of building its own new products, a company can buy another company and its established brands. During the 1980s, big consumer companies gobbled one another in a dramatic flurry: Procter & Gamble acquired Richardson-Vicks and Noxell; R. J. Reynolds bought Nabisco; Philip Morris obtained General Foods and Kraft; Nestlé absorbed Carnation; General Electric bought RCA; Bristol-Myers merged with Squibb; and Unilever picked up Chesebrough-Ponds.

Such acquisitions can be tricky. The company must be certain that the acquired products blend well with its own current products and that the firm has the skills and resources needed to continue to run the acquired products profitably. Acquisitions can also run into snags with government regulators. For example, even under the Reagan Administration's loose antitrust policy, regulators did not allow Pepsi to acquire 7-Up or Coke to buy Dr Pepper. Finally, such acquisitions have high price tags. Nestlé paid $3 billion for Carnation, RJR paid $4.9 billion for Nabisco, GE forked over $6.1 billion for RCA, and Philip Morris coughed up $12.6 billion for Kraft. Not many companies can afford to buy up market-winning brands.

But despite high initial outlays, buying established brands may be cheaper in the long run than paying the enormous costs of trying to create well-known brand names from scratch. And acquiring proven winners eliminates almost all the risks of new-product failure. Acquisition also provides a quick and easy way to gain access to new markets or strengthen positions in current markets. For example, by acquiring Richardson-Vicks, P&G moved immediately into the health and beauty aids market. It also strengthened its hold in the home remedies segment by getting a medicine cabinet full of such top brands as Vicks VapoRub, Formula 44D Cough Syrup, Sinex, Nyquil, and Clearasil to add to its own Pepto-Bismol and Chloraseptic brands.

Developing "Me-Too" products

In recent years, many companies have used "me-too" product strategies—introducing imitations of successful competitors' products. Thus, Tandy, AT&T, Compaq, and many others produce IBM-compatible personal computers. Moreover, these "clones" sometimes sell for less than half the price of the IBM models they emulate. Me-too products have also hit the fragrance industry. Several companies now offer smell-alike "knock-offs" of popular, high-priced perfumes such as Obsession, Opium, and Georgio at 20 percent of the originals' prices. The success of knock-off fragrances has also

inspired a wave of look-alike designer fashions and imitative versions of prestige cosmetics and hair-care brands. Imitation is now fair play for products ranging from soft drinks and food to mousses and minivans.

Me-too products are often quicker and less expensive to develop. The market leader pioneers the technology and bears most of the product-development costs. The imitative products sometimes give consumers even more value than the market-leading originals: The copycat company can build on the leader's design and technology to create an equivalent product at a lower price, or an even better product at the same or a higher price. Me-too products are also less costly and risky to introduce—they enter a proven market already developed by the market leader. Thus, IBM invested millions to develop its personal computers and cultivate a market; the clone makers simply rode IBM's generous coattails.

However, a me-too strategy also has some drawbacks. The imitating company enters the market late and must battle a successful, firmly entrenched competitor. Some me-too products never take much business from the leader. Others succeed broadly and end up challenging for market leadership. Still others settle into small but profitable niches in the market created by the leader.

Reviving Old Products

Many companies have found "new gold in the old" by reviving once successful brands that are now dead or dying. Many old and tarnished brand names still hold magic for consumers. Often, simply reviving, reformulating, and repositioning an old brand can give the company a successful "new" product at a fraction of the cost of building new brands.

There are some classic examples of brand revivals— Arm & Hammer Baking Soda sales spurted after it was promoted as deodorizer for refrigerators, garbage disposals, cars, and kitty litter boxes. Ivory Soap reversed its sales decline in the early 1970s when it was promoted for adult use rather than just for babies. Danon Yogurt sales rocketed when it was linked to healthy living. In recent years, Warner-Lambert revived Black Jack gum, playing on the nostalgia of its 110-year-old name; Coca-Cola rejuvenated Fresca by adding NutraSweet and real fruit juice; and Campbell expanded the appeal of V8 Juice by tying it to today's fitness craze.

Sometimes, a dead product rises again with a new name, as happened with Nestlé's New Cookery brand of low-fat, low-sugar, low-salt entrees. Some years ago, Nestlé withdrew the product when it failed in test market—the company faulted the times, the product's name, and ordinary packaging. But New Cookery was well-suited to today's health-conscious consumers, and Stouffer, a Nestlé company, revived the line under the Lean Cuisine brand. Lean Cuisine proved a resounding success.

Sources: See Pat Sloan, "Knock-Offs Deliver Blows to Fragrance Market," *Advertising Age*, March 2, 1987, p. S14; Arthur Bragg, "Back to the Future," *Sales and Marketing Management*, November 1986, pp. 61–62; and Michael Oneal, "The Best and Worst Deals of the '80s," *Business Week*, January 15, 1990, pp. 52–58.

- Vim tablet detergent (Lever)
- LA low alcohol beer (Anheuser-Busch)
- PCjr personal computer (IBM)
- Zap Mail electronic mail (Federal Express)
- Polarvision instant movies (Polaroid)
- Premier ''smokeless'' cigarettes (R. J. Reynolds)

One study found that the new-product failure rate was 40 percent for consumer products, 20 percent for industrial products, and 18 percent for services. A recent study of 700 consumer and industrial firms found an overall success rate for new products of only 65 percent. Still another source estimates that of the 2,500 new products introduced each year, some 90 percent survived fewer than three years![3]

Why do so many new products fail? There are several reasons. A high-level executive might push a favorite idea in spite of poor marketing research findings. Or although an idea may be good, the market size may have been overestimated. Perhaps the actual product was not designed as well as it should have been. Or maybe it was incorrectly positioned in the market, priced too high, or advertised poorly. Sometimes the costs of product development are higher than expected, and sometimes competitors fight back harder than expected.

Successful new-product development may be even more difficult in the future. Keen competition has lead to increasing market fragmentation—companies must now aim at smaller market segments rather than at the mass market, with the likely results of smaller sales and profits for each product. New products must meet growing social and governmental constraints, such as consumer safety and ecological standards. The costs of finding, developing, and launching new products will rise steadily because of rising manufacturing, media, and distribution costs. Many companies cannot afford or cannot raise the funds needed for new-product development—they emphasize product modification and imitation rather than true innovation. Even when a new product is successful, rivals are so quick to follow suit that the new product is typically fated for only a happy but short life. Thus, IBM finds dozens of imitators offering IBM-compatible computers, and Apple finds foreign ''knockoffs'' (copies) of its computers being sold in the Far East.

So companies face a problem—they must develop new products, but the odds weigh heavily against success. The solution lies in strong new-product planning. Top management is ultimately accountable for the new-product success record. It cannot simply ask the new-product manager to come up with great ideas. Top management must define the business domains and product categories that the company wants to emphasize. In one food company, the new-product manager spent thousands of dollars researching a new snack idea only to hear the president say, ''Drop it. We don't want to be in the snack business.''

Top management must establish specific criteria for new-product idea acceptance, especially in large multidivisional companies in which all kinds of projects bubble up as favorites of various managers. These criteria vary with the specific *strategic role* the product is expected to play. The product's role might be to help the company maintain its industry position as an innovator, to defend a market-share position, or to get a foothold in a future new market. Or the new product might help the company take advantage of its special strengths or exploit technology in a new way. For example, the Gould Corporation set the following acceptance criteria for new products aimed at exploiting a technology in a new way: (1) the product can be introduced within five years; (2) the product has a market potential of at least $50 million and a 15 percent growth rate; (3) the product will provide at least 30 percent return on sales and 40 percent on investment; and (4) the product will achieve technical or market leadership.

Another major decision facing top management is how much to budget for new-product development. New-product outcomes are so uncertain that using normal investment criteria for budgeting is difficult. Some companies solve this problem by encouraging and financing as many projects as possible, hoping to achieve a few winners. Other companies set their research and development (R&D) budgets by applying a conventional

TABLE 11-1 Ways Companies Organize for New Product Development	**Product managers**
	Many companies assign responsibility for new-product ideas to their product managers. Because these managers are close to the market and competition, they are ideally situated to find and develop new-product opportunities. In practice, however, this system has several faults. Product managers are usually so busy managing their product lines that they give little thought to new products other than brand modifications or extensions. They also lack the specific skills and knowledge needed to critique and develop new products.
	New-product managers
	General Foods and Johnson & Johnson have new-product managers who report to group product managers. This position ''professionalizes'' the new-product function. On the other hand, new-product managers tend to think in terms of product modifications and line extensions limited to their current product and markets.
	New-product committees
	Most companies have a high-level management committee charged with reviewing and approving new-product proposals. It usually consists of representatives from marketing, manufacturing, finance, engineering, and other departments. Its function is not developing or coordinating new products so much as reviewing and approving new-product plans.
	New-product departments
	Large companies often establish a new-product department headed by a manager who has substantial authority and access to top management. The department's major responsibilities include generating and screening new ideas, working with the R&D department, and carrying out field testing and commercialization.
	New-product venture teams
	The 3M Company, Dow, Westinghouse, and General Mills often assign major new-product development work to venture teams. A venture team is a group brought together from various operating departments and charged with developing a specific product or business. Team members are relieved of their other duties, and given a budget and a time frame. In some cases, this team stays with the product long after it is successfully introduced.

percentage-to-sales figure or by spending as much as the competition spends. Still other companies decide how many successful new products they need and work backward to estimate the required R&D investment.

Another important factor in new-product-development work is to set up effective organizational structures for nurturing and handling new products. Table 11-1 discusses the most common organizational arrangement—product managers, new-product managers, new-product committees, and venture teams.

Thus, successful new-product development requires a total company effort. The most successful innovating companies make a consistent commitment of resources to new-product development, design a new-product strategy that is linked to their strategic planning process, and set up formal and sophisticated organizational arrangements for managing the new-product development process.

The *new-product development process* for finding and growing new products consists of eight major steps. These steps are shown in Figure 11-1 and described below.

Idea Generation New-product development starts with **idea generation,** the systematic search for new-product ideas. A company typically must generate many ideas in order to find a few good ones. Figure 11.2 shows the number of ideas that typically survive at each stage of the development process. In 1968, fifty-eight new-product ideas yielded only one good one. In 1981, companies were able to turn one out of seven ideas into a successful new product. The improvement shows that many companies are prescreening and planning more effectively and investing money only in the best ideas, rather than using a shotgun approach.

FIGURE 11-1 Major stages in new product development

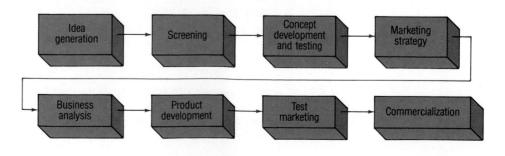

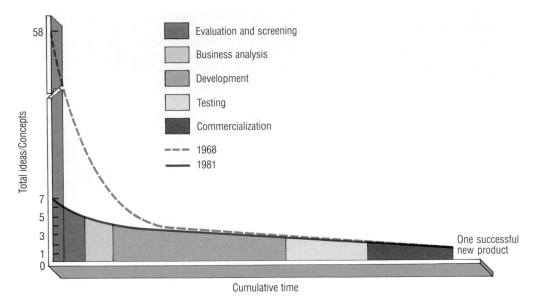

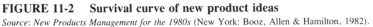

FIGURE 11-2   Survival curve of new product ideas

Source: *New Products Management for the 1980s* (New York: Booz, Allen & Hamilton, 1982).

The search for new product ideas should be systematic rather than haphazard. Top management needs to carefully define its new-product development strategy. It should state which products and markets to emphasize. It should state what the company wants from its new products, whether it be high cash flow, market share, or some other objective. It should state the effort to be devoted to developing original products, changing existing products, and imitating competitors' products. Otherwise, the company might find many ideas, but most will not be good ones for its type of business.

To obtain a flow of new-product ideas, the company can tap many idea sources. Major sources of new-product ideas include the following:

- *Internal sources.* One study found that more than 55 percent of all new-product ideas come from within the company.[4] The company can find new ideas through formal research and development. It can pick the brains of its scientists, engineers, and manufacturing people. Or company executives can brainstorm new-product ideas. The company's salespeople are another good source because they are in daily contact with customers. Toyota claims that employees submit two million ideas annually—about 35 suggestions per employee—and that more than 85 percent of them are implemented.

- *Customers.* Almost 28 percent of all new-product ideas come from watching and listening to customers. Consumer needs and wants can be obtained from consumer surveys. The company can analyze customer questions and complaints to find new products to better solve consumer problems. Company engineers or salespeople can meet with customers to get suggestions. General Electric's Video Products Division has its design engineers talk with final consumers to get ideas for new home electronics products. National Steel has a product application center where company engineers work with automotive customers to discover customer needs that might require new products.[5] Finally, consumers often create new products on their own, and companies can benefit by finding these products and putting them on the market. Pillsbury gets promising new recipes through its annual Bake-Off—one of Pillsbury's four cake-mix lines and several variations of another came directly from Bake-Off winners' recipes. About one-third of all the software IBM leases for its computers is developed by outside users.[6]

- *Competitors.* About 27 percent of new-product ideas come from analyzing competitors' products. The company can watch competitors' ads and other communications to get clues about their new products. Companies buy competing new products, take them apart to see how they work, analyze their sales, and decide whether the company should bring out a new product of its own. For example, when designing its highly successful Taurus, Ford tore down more than 50 competing models, layer by layer, looking for things to copy or improve upon. It copied the Audi's accelerator-pedal "feel," the Toyota Supra fuel gauge, the BMW 528e tire and jack storage system, and 400 other such outstanding features.[7]

Pillsbury's BAKEOFF promotes consumer goodwill and sometimes produces new-product ideas.

- *Distributors and Suppliers.* Resellers are close to the market and can pass along information about consumer problems and new-product possibilities. Suppliers can tell the company about new concepts, techniques, and materials that can be used to develop new products.
- *Other sources.* Other idea sources include trade magazines, shows, and seminars; government agencies; new-product consultants; advertising agencies; marketing-research firms; university and commercial laboratories; and inventories.

Idea Screening　The purpose of idea generation is to create a large number of ideas. The purpose of the succeeding stages is to *reduce* that number. The first idea-reducing stage is **idea screening.** The purpose of screening is to spot good ideas and drop poor ones as soon as possible. Product-development costs rise greatly in later stages. The company wants to go ahead only with the product ideas that will turn into profitable products.

Most companies require their executives to write up new-product ideas on a standard form that can be reviewed by a new-product committee. The write-up describes the product, the target market, and the competition and makes some rough estimates of market size, product price, development time and costs, manufacturing costs, and rate of return. The committee than evaluates the idea against a set of general criteria. At Kao Company of Japan, for example, the committee asks questions such as these: Is the product truly useful to consumers and society? Is this product good for our particular company? Does it mesh well with the company's objectives and strategies? Do we have the people, skills, and resources to make it succeed? Is its cost performance superior to competitive products? Is it easy to advertise and distribute?

Surviving ideas can be further screened using a simple rating process such as the one shown in Table 11-2. The first column lists factors required for the successful launching of the product in the marketplace. In the next column, management rates these factors on their relative importance. Thus, management believes that marketing skills and experience are very important (.20) and purchasing and supplies competence is of minor importance (.05). Next, on a scale of .0 to 1.0, management rates how well the new product idea fits the company's profile on each factor. Here management feels that the product idea fits very well with the company's marketing skills and experience (.9) but not too well with its purchasing and supplies capabilities (.5). Finally, management multiplies the importance of each success factor by the rating of fit to obtain an overall rating of the company's ability to launch the product successfully. Thus, if marketing is an important success factor and this product fits the company's marketing skills, this

TABLE 11-2
Product Idea Rating Process

NEW PRODUCT SUCCESS FACTORS	(A) RELATIVE IMPOR- TANCE	(B) FIT BETWEEN PRODUCT IDEA AND COMPANY CAPABILITIES .0 .1 .2 .3 .4 .5 .6 .7 .8 .9 1.0	IDEA RATING (A × B)
Company strategy and objectives	.20	X (.8)	.160
Marketing skills and experience	.20	X (.9)	.180
Financial resources	.15	X (.7)	.105
Channels of distribution	.15	X (.8)	.120
Production capabilities	.10	X (.8)	.080
Research and development	.10	X (.7)	.070
Purchasing and supplies	.05	X (.5)	.025
Total	1.00		.740*

* Rating scale: .00–.40, poor; .50–.75, fair; .76–1.00 good. Minimum acceptance level: .70

will increase the overall rating of the product idea. In the example, the product idea scored .74, which places it at the high end of the "fair idea" level.

The checklist promotes a more systematic product idea evaluation and basis for discussion—however, it is not designed to make the decision for management.[8]

Concept Development and Testing

Attractive ideas must now be developed into product concepts. It is important to distinguish between a *product idea*, a *product concept*, and a *product image*. A **product idea** is an idea for a possible product that the company can see itself offering to the market. A **product concept** is a detailed version of the idea stated in meaningful consumer terms. A **product image** is the way consumers perceive an actual or potential product.

Concept Development

Suppose a car manufacturer figures out how to design an electric car that can go as fast as 60 miles an hour and as far as 80 miles before needing to be recharged. The manufacturer estimates that the electric car's operating costs will be about half of those of a regular car.

This is a product idea. Customers, however, do not buy a product idea; they buy a product *concept*. The marketer's task is to develop this idea into some alternative product concept, find out how attractive each concept is to customers, and choose the best one.

The following product concepts might be created for the electric car:

- *Concept 1.* An inexpensive subcompact designed as a second family car to be used around town. The car is ideal for loading groceries and hauling children, and it is easy to enter.
- *Concept 2.* A medium-cost, medium-size car designed as an all-purpose family car.
- *Concept 3.* A medium-cost sporty compact appealing to young people.
- *Concept 4.* An inexpensive subcompact appealing to conscientious people who want basic transportation, low fuel cost, and low pollution.

Concept Testing

Concept testing calls for testing these concepts with a group of target consumers. The concepts may be presented through word or picture descriptions. Here is concept 1:

> An efficient, fun-to-drive, electric-powered subcompact car that seats four. Great for shopping trips and visits to friends. Costs half as much to operate as similar gasoline-driven cars. Goes up to 60 miles an hour and does not need to be recharged for 80 miles. Priced at $8,000.

Consumers may then be asked to react to this concept by answering the questions in Table 11-3. The answers will help the company decide which concept has the strongest

A prototype of an electric car. This one has a top speed of 60 miles per hour and an in-city driving range of 80 miles.

TABLE 11-3
Questions for Electric Car
Concept Test

1. Do you understand the concept of an electric car?
2. What do you see as the benefits of an electric car compared with a conventional car?
3. Do you believe the claims about the electric car's performance?
4. Would the electric car meet all your automobile needs?
5. What improvements can you suggest in the car's various features?
6. Would you prefer an electric car to a conventional car? For what uses?
7. What do you think the price of the electric car should be?
8. Who would be involved in your purchase decision for such a car? Who would drive it?
9. Would you buy an electric car? (Definitely, probably, probably not, definitely not)

appeal. For example, the last question asks about the consumer's intention-to-buy. Suppose 10 percent of the consumers said they "definitely" would buy and another 5 percent said "probably." The company could project these figures to the population size of this target group to estimate sales volume. Even then, the estimate is uncertain because people do not always carry out their stated intentions.[9]

Marketing Strategy Development

Suppose concept 1 for the electric car tests out best. The next step is **marketing-strategy development,** designing an initial marketing strategy for introducing this car into the market.

The **marketing strategy statement** consists of three parts. The first part describes the target market, the planned product positioning, and the sales, market share, and profit goals for the first few years. Thus:

> The target market is households that need a second car for shopping trips, running errands, and visits to friends. The car will be positioned as more economical to buy and operate, and more fun to drive, than cars now available to this market. The company will aim to sell 200,000 cars in the first year, at a loss of not more than $3 million. The second year will aim for sales of 220,000 cars and a profit of $5 million.

The second part of the marketing strategy statement outlines the product's planned price, distribution, and marketing budget for the first year:

> The electric car will be offered in three colors and will have optional air-conditioning and power-drive features. It will sell at a retail price of $8,000, with 15 percent off the list price to dealers. Dealers who sell more than ten cars per month will get an additional discount of 5 percent on each car sold that month. An advertising budget of $10 million will be split 50-50 between national and local advertising. Advertising will emphasize the car's economy and fun. During the first year, $100,000 will be spent on marketing research to find out who is buying the car and to determine their satisfaction levels.

The third part of the marketing strategy statement describes the planned long-run sales, profit goals, and marketing-mix strategy:

> The company intends to capture a 3 percent long-run share of the total auto market and realize an after-tax return on investment of 15 percent. To achieve this, product quality will start high and be improved over time. Price will be raised in the second and third years if competition permits. The total advertising budget will be raised each year by about 10 percent. Marketing research will be reduced to $60,000 per year after the first year.

Business Analysis

Once management has decided on its product concept and marketing strategy, it can evaluate the business attractiveness of the proposal. **Business analysis** involves a review of the sales, costs, and profit projections to find out whether they satisfy the company's objectives. If they do, the product can move to the product development stage.

To estimate sales, the company should look at the sales history of similar products and should survey market opinion. It should estimate minimum and maximum sales to learn the range of risk. After preparing the sales forecast, management can estimate the expected costs and profits for the product. The costs are estimated by the R&D, manufacturing, accounting, and finance departments. The planned marketing costs are included in the analysis. The company then uses the sales and costs figures to analyze the new peoduct's financial attractiveness.

Product Development

If the product concept passes the business test, it moves into **product development.** Here, R&D or engineering develop the product concept into a physical product. So far, the product has existed only as a word description, a drawing, or perhaps a crude mockup. The product-development step, however, now calls for a large jump in investment. It will show whether the product idea can be turned into a workable product.

The R&D department will develop one or more physical versions of the product concept. It hopes to design a prototype that will not only satisfy and excite consumers, but also one that can be produced quickly and at budgeted costs.

Developing a successful prototype can take days, weeks, months, or even years. The prototype must have the required functional features and also convey the intended psychological characteristics. The electric car, for example, should strike consumers as being well built and safe. Management must learn how consumers decide how well built a car is. Some consumers slam the door to hear its "sound." If the car does not have "solid-sounding" doors, consumers will think it is poorly built.

When the prototypes are ready, they must be tested. Functional tests are then conducted under laboratory and field conditions to make sure that the product performs safely and effectively. The new car must start well; it must be comfortable; it must be able to go around corners without overturning. Consumer tests are conducted in which consumers test-drive the car and rate its attributes.

When designing products, the company should look beyond simply creating products that satisfy consumer needs and wants. Too often, companies design their new products without enough concern about how the designs will be produced—their main goal is to create customer-satisfying products. The designs are then passed along to manufacturing, where engineers must try to find the best ways to produce the product. Recently, however, many companies have adopted a new approach toward product development called *design for manufacturability and assembly* (DFMA). Using this approach, companies work to fashion products that are *both* satisfying to consumers *and* easy to manufacture. This often results not only in lower costs, but also in higher quality and more reliable products. For example, using DFMA analysis, Texas Instruments recently redesigned an infrared gun-sighting mechanism that it supplies to the Pentagon: the redesigned product required 75 fewer parts, 78 percent fewer assembly steps, and 85 percent less assembly time. The new design not only reduced production time and costs, it also worked better than the previous, more complex version. Thus, DFMA can be a potent weapon in helping companies to get products to market sooner and offer higher quality at lower prices.[10]

Test Marketing   If the product passes functional and consumer tests, the next step is test marketing. **Test marketing** is the stage at which the product and marketing program are introduced into more realistic market settings.

Test marketing lets the marketer get experience with marketing the product, find potential problems, and learn where more information is needed before going to the great expense of full introduction. The basic purpose of test marketing is to test the product itself in real market situations. But test marketing also allows the company to test its entire marketing program for the product—its positioning strategy, advertising, distribution, pricing, branding and packaging, and budget levels. The company uses test marketing to learn how consumers and dealers will react to handling, using, and repurchasing the product. Test marketing results can be used to make better sales and profit forecasts. Thus, a good test market can provide a wealth of information about the potential success of the product and marketing program (see Marketing Highlight 11–2).

The amount of test marketing needed varies with each new product. Test marketing costs can be enormous, and test marketing takes time during which competitors may gain advantages. When the costs of developing and introducing the product are low or when management is already confident that the new product will succeed, the company may do little or no test marketing. Minor modifications of current products or copies of successful competitor products might not need testing. For example, Procter & Gamble introduced its Folger's decaffeinated coffee crystals without test marketing, and Pillsbury rolled out Chewy granola bars and chocolate-covered Granola Dipps with no standard test market. But when introducing the new product requires a large investment, or when management is not sure of the product or marketing program, the company may do a lot of test marketing. In fact, some products and marketing programs are tested, withdrawn, changed, and retested many times during a period of several years before they are finally introduced. The costs of such test markets are high, but they are often small compared with the costs of making a major mistake.

Thus, whether a company test markets, and the amount of testing it does, depends on the investment cost and risk of introducing the product on the one hand, and on the testing costs and time pressures on the other. Test marketing methods vary with the type of product and market situation, and each method has advantages and disadvantages.

When they do use test marketing, consumer-products companies usually choose one of three approaches—standard test markets, controlled test markets, or simulated test markets.

Standard Test Markets

Standard test markets test the new consumer product in situations like those it would face in a full-scale launch. The company finds a small number of representative test cities where the company's salesforce tries to persuade resellers to carry the product and give it good shelf space and promotional support. The company puts on a full advertising and promotion campaign in these markets and uses store audits, consumer and distributor surveys, and other measures to gauge product performance. The results are used to forecast national sales and profits, to discover potential product problems, and to fine-tune the marketing program (see Marketing Highlight 11–2).

Standard market tests have some drawbacks. First, they take a long time to complete—sometimes from one to three years. If it turns out that the testing was unnecessary, the company will have lost many months of sales and profits. Second, extensive standard test markets may be very costly—the average standard test market costs more than $3 million, and costs can go much higher. Procter & Gamble spent $15 million developing Duncan Hines ready-to-eat cookies in test market.[11] Finally, standard test markets give competitors a look at the company's new product well before it is introduced nationally. Many competitors will analyze the product and monitor the company's test market results. If the testing goes on too long, competitors will have time to develop defensive strategies and may even beat the company's product to the market. Furthermore,

A TEST MARKET THAT REALLY MADE A DIFFERENCE

Some test markets do little more than confirm what management already knew. Others prune the new-product losers—half of all test-marketed consumer products are killed before they reach national distribution. Still other test markets provide highly useful information that can save a promising product or turn an otherwise average product into a blockbuster. Here's a story about a test market that really made a difference.

After its stunning success several years ago with Dole Fruit 'n Juice Bars, Dole Foods worked feverishly to find a follow-up product with the same consumer appeal. It soon came up with Fruit and Cream Bars. Before investing in a costly national rollout, Dole decided to run a test market. The company began the test market with high expectations—the Fruit and Cream brand manager predicted high sales and market share.

In the test market, Dole offered Fruit and Cream in three flavors—strawberry, blueberry, and peach—packed four to a box. Packaging modestly mentioned "100% natural" ingredients and showed a bowl of fruit and cream. Dole supported the test market with standard advertising and promotion, including television, newspaper, direct-mail, point-of-purchase, and coupon campaigns to stimulate trial and repeat purchasing. Fruit and Cream ads targeted upscale consumers aged 25 to 54 with kids, centering on the product and its taste and health appeal.

The test market quickly yielded some surprises. It showed that Fruit and Cream had much broader appeal than Dole had expected. By the end of the third month, it had become the number one brand in the test market area. Focus groups showed that Fruit and Cream buyers saw the product as a real treat and felt they could eat it without feeling too much caloric guilt. Consumers said that Fruit and Cream's natural ingredients and natural taste made it superior to the competition. Despite dazzling sales performance, however, Dole discovered that its television advertising performed poorly—sales didn't jump when the television campaign began.

Based on the test-market results, Dole made several changes in the Fruit and Cream marketing mix. It redesigned the packaging to greatly increase the size of the "100% natural" claim. And a new package picture showed cream being poured over the fruit, a subtle difference that emphasized Fruit and Cream's appetite appeal. Dole created a new advertising campaign that created a mellow feeling and focused more heavily on natural taste. The new ads used a Golden Oldie song, *You're Sweet 16, Peaches and Cream*, and stressed the luxury in the product. Dole also shortened the

Dole Fruit and Cream Bars: Test marketing really made a difference.

test market from one year to six months, raised its forecast of Fruit and Cream sales, and rushed to get two more flavors (banana and raspberry) ready.

With all the marketing changes, Dole was convinced that Fruit and Cream would take off like a rocket when it went national. But test markets can't predict future market events. Four new competing fruit-based novelty ice cream products came out at the same time as Fruit and Cream—two from Chiquita, one from Jell-O, and one from Minute Maid. The result was a marketer's nightmare. Fruit and Cream missed all its sales projections. But so did all the competitors, and Fruit and Cream held on, achieving a 3 percent market share instead of the expected 4 percent. The dust finally settled, and Dole hit its original projections the following year.

No test market can predict future competitor actions and reactions, economic conditions, changing consumer tastes, or other factors that can affect a new product's success. It can only show how consumers in a selected market area react to a new product and its marketing program. But the people at Dole are still strong believers. According to the Fruit and Cream brand manager, "Without the changes we made as a result of the test market, we would have been hurt much more than we were."

Source: Adapted from Leslie Brennan, "Test Marketing Put to the Test," *Sales and Marketing Management*, March 1987, pp. 65–68.

competitors often try to distort test market results by cutting their prices in test cities, increasing their promotion, or even buying up the product being tested. Despite these disadvantages, standard test markets are still the most widely used approach for major testing. But many companies today are shifting toward quicker and cheaper controlled and simulated test marketing methods.

Controlled Test Markets

Several research firms keep controlled panels of stores which have agreed to carry new products for a fee. The company with the new product specifies the number of stores and geographical locations it wants. The research firm delivers the product to the participating stores and controls shelf location, amount of shelf space, displays and point-of-purchase promotions, and pricing according to specified plans. Sales results are tracked to determine the impact of these factors on demand.

Controlled test marketing systems like Nielsen's ERIM TESTSIGHT and Information Resources Inc.'s (IRI) BehaviorScan track individual behavior from the television set to the checkout counter. IRI, for example, keeps a panel of about 3,000 shoppers in eight carefully selected small cities. It uses microcomputers to measure TV viewing in each panel household and can send special commercials to panel-member television sets. Panel consumers buy from cooperating stores and show identification cards when making purchases. Detailed electronic scanner information on each consumer's purchases is fed into a central computer, where it is combined with the consumer's demographic and TV viewing information and reported daily. Thus, BehaviorScan can provide store-by-store, week-by-week reports on the sales of new products being tested. And because the scanners record the specific purchases of individual consumers, the system can also provide information on repeat purchases and how different types of consumers are reacting to the new product, its advertising, and various other elements of the marketing program.

Controlled test markets take less time than standard test markets (six months to a year) and usually cost less (a year-long BehaviorScan test might cost from $200,000 to $2,000,000). However, some companies are concerned that the limited number of small cities and panel consumers used by the research services may not be representative of their products' markets or target consumers. And, as in standard test markets, controlled test markets allow competitors to get a look at the company's new product.[12]

Simulated Test Markets

Companies also can test new products in a simulated shopping environment. The company or research firm shows a sample of consumers ads and promotions for a variety of products, including the new product being tested. The consumers are given a small amount of money and are invited into a real or laboratory store where they may keep the money or use it to buy items. The company notes how many consumers buy the new product and competing brands. This simulation provides a measure of trial purchase and assesses the commercial's effectiveness against competing commercials. Consumers are then asked the reasons for their purchase or nonpurchase. Some weeks later they are interviewed by phone to determine product attitudes, usage, satisfaction, and repurchase intentions. Sophisticated computer models are used to project national sales from results of the simulated test market.

Simulated test markets overcome some of the disadvantages of standard and controlled test markets. They usually cost much less ($35,000 to $75,000) and can be run in eight weeks. And the new product is kept out of competitors' view. Yet, because of their small samples and simulated shopping environments, many marketers do not think that simulated test markets are as accurate or reliable as larger, real-world tests. Still, simulated test markets are widely used, often as "pre-test" markets. Because they are fast and inexpensive, one or more simulated tests can be run to quickly assess a new product or its marketing program. If the pretest results are strongly positive, the product might be introduced without further testing. If the results are very poor, the product might be dropped or substantially redesigned and retested. If the results are promising but indefinite, the product and marketing program can be tested further in controlled or standard test markets.[13]

Test Marketing Industrial Goods

Industrial marketers use different methods for test marketing their new products. For example, they may conduct *product-use tests*. Here the industrial marketer selects a small group of potential customers who agree to use the new product for a limited time. The manufacturer's technical people watch how these customers use the product. From this test the manufacturer learns about customer training and servicing requirements. After the test, the marketer asks the customer about purchase intent and other reactions.

New industrial products can also be tested at *trade shows*. These shows draw a large number of buyers who view new products in a few concentrated days. The manufacturer sees how buyers react to various product features and terms and can assess buyer interest and purchase intentions. The industrial marketer can also test new industrial products in *distributor and dealer display rooms*, where they may stand next to other company products and possibly competitors' products. This method yields preference and pricing information in the normal selling atmosphere for the product.

Finally, some industrial marketers use *standard or controlled test markets* to measure the potential of their new products. They produce a limited supply of the product and give it to the salesforce to sell in a limited number of geographical areas. The company gives the product full advertising, sales promotion, and other marketing support. Such test markets let the company test the product and its marketing program in real market situations.

Commercialization

Test marketing gives management the information needed to make a final decision about whether to launch the new product. If the company goes ahead with **commercialization**—introducing the new product into the market—it will face high costs. The company will have to build or rent a manufacturing facility. And it may have to spend, in the case of a new consumer packaged good, $10 million to $100 million for advertising and sales promotion alone in the first year. For example, McDonald's spent more than $5 million dollars *per week* advertising the introduction of its McDLT sandwich.

The company launching a new product must make four decisions.

When?

The first decision is whether the time is right to introduce the new product. If the electric car will eat into the sales of the company's other cars, its introduction may be delayed. Or if the electric car can be improved further, or if the economy is down, the company may wait to launch it the following year.[14]

Where?

The company must decide whether to launch the new product in a single location, a region, several regions, the national market, or the international market. Few companies have the confidence, capital, and capacity to launch new products into full national distribution. They will develop a planned *market rollout* over time. In particular, small companies may select an attractive city and conduct a blitz campaign to enter the market. They may then enter other cities one at a time. Larger companies can introduce their products into a whole region then move to the next. Companies with national distribution networks, such as auto companies, often launch their new models in the national market.

To Whom?

Within the rollout markets, the company must target its distribution and promotion to the best prospect groups. The company has already profiled the prime prospects in earlier test marketing. It must now fine-tune its market identification, looking especially for early adopters, heavy users, and opinion leaders.

How?

The company must also develop an action plan for introducing the new product into the selected markets. It must spend the marketing budget on the marketing mix and various other activities. Thus, the electric car's launch may be supported by a publicity campaign and then by offers of gifts to draw more people to the showrooms. The company needs to prepare a separate marketing plan for each new market.

Speeding Up New-Product Development

Many companies organize their new-product development process into an orderly sequence of steps, starting with idea generation and ending with commercialization. Under this **sequential product development** approach, one company department works individually to complete its stage of the process before passing the new product along to the next department and stage. This orderly, step-by-step process can help bring control to complex and risky projects. But it can also be dangerously slow. In fast-changing, highly competitive markets, such slow-but-sure product development can cost the company potential sales and profits at the hands of more nimble competitors. Today, in order to get their new products to market more quickly, many companies are dropping the *sequential product development* approach in favor of the faster, more flexible **simultaneous product development** approach. Under the new approach, various company departments work closely together, overlapping the steps in the product-development process to save time and increase effectiveness (see Marketing Highlight 11–3).

PRODUCT LIFE-CYCLE STRATEGIES

After launching the new product, management wants the product to enjoy a long and happy life. Although it does not expect the product to sell forever, management wants to earn a decent profit to cover all the effort and risk that went into it. Management is aware that each product will have a life cycle, although the exact shape and length is not known in advance.

The sales and profit patterns in a typical **product life cycle (PLC)** are shown in Figure 11-3. The product life cycle is marked by five distinct stages:

1. *Product development* begins when the company finds and develops a new-product idea. During product development, sales are zero and the company's investment costs add up.
2. *Introduction* is a period of slow sales growth as the product is being introduced in the market. Profits are nonexistent in this stage because of the heavy expenses of product introduction.
3. *Growth* is a period of rapid market acceptance and increasing profits.
4. *Maturity* is a period of slowdown in sales growth because the product has achieved acceptance by most potential buyers. Profits level off or decline because of increased marketing outlays to defend the product against competition.
5. *Decline* is the period when sales fall off and profits drop.

Not all products follow this S-shaped product life cycle. Some products are introduced and die quickly. Others stay in the mature stage for a long, long time. Some

FIGURE 11-3
Sales and profits over the product's life from inception to demise

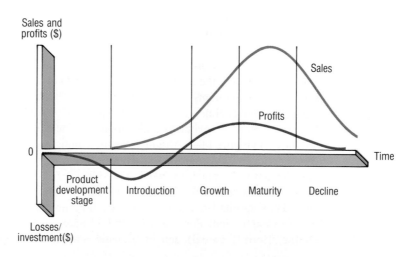

SIMULTANEOUS PRODUCT DEVELOPMENT: SPEEDING NEW PRODUCTS TO MARKET

Philips, the giant Dutch consumer electronics company, marketed the first practical videocassette recorder in 1972, gaining a three-year lead on its Japanese competitors. But in the seven years that it took Philips to develop its second generation of VCR models, Japanese manufacturers had launched at least three generations of new products. A victim of its own creaky product-development process, Philips never recovered from the Japanese onslaught. Today, the company is an also-ran with only a two percent market share; it still loses money on VCRs. The Philips story is typical: During the past few decades, dozens of large companies have fallen victim to competitors with faster, more flexible new-product development programs. In today's fast-changing, fiercely competitive world, turning out new products too slowly can result in product failures, lost sales and profits, and crumbling market positions.

Large companies have traditionally used a "sequential product development" approach in which new products are developed in an orderly series of steps. In a kind of relay race, each company department completes its phase of the development process before passing the new product on. The sequential process has merits—it helps bring order to risky and complex new-product development projects. But the approach can also be fatally slow.

To speed up their product-development cycles, many companies are now adopting a faster, more agile, team-oriented approach called "simultaneous product development." Instead of passing the new product from department to department, the company assembles a team of people from various departments that stays with the new product from start to finish. Such teams usually include representatives from marketing, finance, design, manufacturing, and legal departments, and even supplier companies. Simultaneous development is more like a rugby match than a relay race—team members pass the new product back and forth as they move downfield toward the common goal of a speedy and successful new-product launch.

Top management gives the product development team general strategic direction but no clear-cut product idea or work plan. It challenges the team with stiff and seemingly contradictory goals—"turn out carefully planned and superior new products, but do it quickly"—then gives the team whatever freedom and resources it needs to meet the challenge. The team becomes a driving force that pushes the product forward. In the sequential process, a bottleneck at one phase can seriously slow or even halt the entire project. In the simultaneous approach, if one functional area hits snags, it works to resolve them while the team moves on.

The Allen-Bradley Company, a maker of industrial controls, provides an example of the tremendous benefits gained by using simultaneous development. Under the old sequential approach, the company's marketing department handed off a new product idea to designers. The designers, working in isolation, prepared concepts and passed them along to product engineers. The engineers, also working by themselves, developed expensive prototypes and handed them off to manufacturing, which tried to find a way to build the new product. Finally, after many years and dozens of costly design compromises and delays, marketing was asked to sell the new product—which it often found to be too high-priced or sadly out-of-date. Now, Allen-Bradley has adopted the simultaneous product-development approach. All of the company's departments work together—from beginning to end—to design and develop new products that meet customer needs and company capabilities. The results have been astonishing. For example, the company recently developed a new electrical control in just two years; under the old system, it would have taken six years.

---

enter the decline stage, and are then cycled back into the growth stage through strong promotion or repositioning.

The PLC concept can describe a *product class* (gasoline-powered automobiles), a *product-form* (station wagons), or a *brand* (the Ford Taurus). The PLC concept applies differently in each case. Product classes have the longest life cycles. The sales of many product classes stay in the mature stage for a long time. Product forms, on the other hand, tend to have the standard PLC shape. Product forms such as the "dial telephone" and "cream deodorants" passed through a regular history of introduction, rapid growth, maturity, and decline. A specific brand's life cycle can change quickly because of changing competitive attacks and responses. The life cycles of several toothpaste brands are shown in Figure 11-4. Although teeth-cleaning products (product class) and toothpastes (product form) have enjoyed fairly long life cycles, the life styles of specific brands have tended to be much shorter.

The PLC concept can also be applied to what are known as styles, fashions, and fads. Their special life cycles are shown in Figure 11-5. A **style** is a basic and distinctive mode of expression. For example, styles appear in homes (colonial, ranch, Cape Cod), clothing (formal, casual), and art (realistic, surrealistic, abstract). Once a style is invented,

Ford's successful Taurus was the first American car developed using parallel product development.

The auto industry has also discovered the benefits of simultaneous product development. The approach is called "simultaneous engineering" at GM, the "team concept" at Ford, and "process-driven design" at Chrysler. The first American cars built using this process, the Ford Taurus and Mercury Sable, have been major marketing successes. Ford squeezed 14 weeks from its product-development cycle by simply getting the engineering and finance departments to review designs at the same time instead of sequentially. It claims that such actions have helped cut average engineering costs for a project by 35 percent. In an industry which has typically taken five or six years to turn out a new model, Mazda now brags about two- to three-year product-development cycles—a feat that would be impossible without simultaneous development.

However, the parallel approach has some limitations. Super-fast product development can be riskier and more costly than the slower, more orderly sequential approach. And it often creates increased organizational tension and confusion. But in rapidly changing industries facing increasingly shorter product life cycles, the rewards of fast and flexible product development far exceed the risks. Companies that get new and improved products to the market faster than competitors gain a dramatic competitive edge. They can respond more quickly to emerging consumer tastes and charge higher prices for more advanced designs. As one auto industry executive states, "What we want to do is get the new car approved, built, and in the consumer's hands in the shortest time possible . . . Whoever gets there first gets all the marbles."

Sources: Hirotaka Takeuchi and Ikujiro Nonaka, "The New New Product Development Game," *Harvard Business Review*, January–February 1986, pp. 137–146; Bro Uttal, "Speeding New Ideas to Market," *Fortune*, March 2, 1987, pp. 62–65, William Jeanes, "The Idea that Saved Detroit," *Northwest*, September 1987, pp. 15–19; and John Bussey and Douglas R. Sease, "Speeding Up: Manufacturers Strive to Slice Time Needed to Develop New Products," *The Wall Street Journal*, February 23, 1988, pp. 1, 24.

FIGURE 11-4
Product life cycles for selected toothpaste brands from 1936 to 1982
Source: "Life Beyond the Life Cycle," *The Nielsen Researcher*, Number 1, 1984, p. 3.

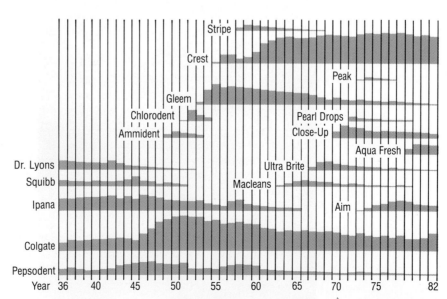

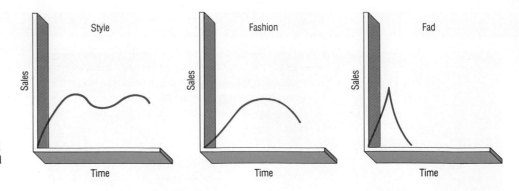

FIGURE 11-5
Marketers need to understand and predict style, fashion, and fad.

it may last for generations, coming in and out of vogue. A style has a cycle showing several periods of renewed interest.

A **fashion** is a currently accepted or popular style in a given field. For example, the "preppie look" in the clothing of the late 1970s gave way to the "loose and layered look" of the mid- to late-1980s. Fashions pass through many stages. First, a small number of consumers typically take an interest in something new to set themselves apart. Then, other consumers take an interest out of a desire to copy the fashion leaders. Next, the fashion becomes popular and is adopted by the mass market. Finally, the fashion fades away as consumers start moving toward other fashions that are beginning to catch their eye. Thus, fashions tend to grow slowly, remain popular for a while, then decline slowly.

Fads are fashions that enter quickly, are adopted with great zeal, peak early, and decline very fast. They last only a short time and tend to attract only a limited following. Fads often have a novel or quirky nature, as when people started buying Rubik's Cubes, Trivial Pursuit games, "pet rocks," Cabbage Patch dolls, or yo-yos. Fads appeal to people looking for excitement, a way to set themselves apart, or something to talk

Some products stay in the maturity stage of the product life cycle for a long, long time: Kikkoman is 358 years old!

about to others. Fads do not survive for long because they do not normally satisfy a strong need or satisfy it well.

The PLC concept can be applied by marketers as a useful framework for describing how products and markets work. But using the PLC concept for forecasting product performance or for developing marketing strategies presents some practical problems.[15] For example, managers may have trouble identifying which stage of the PLC the product is in, pinpointing when the product moves into the next stage, and determining the factors that affect the product's movement through the stages. In practice, it is difficult to forecast the sales level at each PLC stage, the length of each stage, and the shape of the PLC curve.

Using the PLC concept to develop marketing strategy can also be difficult because strategy is both a cause and result of the product's life cycle. The product's current PLC position suggests the best marketing strategies, and the resulting marketing strategies affect product performance in later life-cycle stages. Yet, when used carefully, the PLC concept can help in developing good marketing strategies for different stages of the product life cycle.

We looked at the product-development stage of the product life cycle in the first part of the chapter. We now look at strategies for each of the other life-cycle stages.

Introduction Stage

The **introduction stage** starts when the new product is first launched. Introduction takes time, and sales growth is apt to be slow. Such well-known products as instant coffee, frozen orange juice, and powdered coffee creamers lingered for many years before they entered a stage of rapid growth.

In this stage, as compared to other stages, profits are negative or low because of the low sales and high distribution and promotion expenses. Much money is needed to attract distributors and build their inventories. Promotion spending is relatively high. The goals now are to inform consumers of the new product and to get them to try it. Because the market is not generally ready for product refinements at this stage, the company and its few competitors produce basic versions of the product. These firms focus their selling on those buyers who are the readiest to buy—usually the higher-income groups.

A company might adopt one of several marketing strategies for introducing a new product. It can set a high or low level for each marketing variable, such as price, promotion, distribution, and product quality. Considering only price and promotion, for example, management might launch the new product with a high price and low promotion spending. The high price helps recover as much gross profit per unit as possible while the low promotion spending keeps marketing spending down. Such a strategy makes sense when the market is limited in size, most consumers in the market know about the product and are willing to pay a high price, and there is little immediate potential competition.

On the other hand, a company might introduce its new product with a low price and heavy promotion spending. This strategy promises to bring the fastest market penetration and the largest market share—it makes sense under these conditions: the market is large; potential buyers are price sensitive and unaware of the product; potential competition is strong; and the company's unit manufacturing costs fall with the scale of production and accumulated manufacturing experience.

A company, especially the *market pioneer*, must choose its launch strategy carefully. It should realize that the initial strategy is just the first step in a grander marketing plan for the product's entire life-cycle. If the pioneer chooses its launch strategy to make a "killing," it will be sacrificing long-run revenue for the sake of short-run gain. As the pioneer moves through later stages of the life cycle, it will have to continuously formulate new pricing, promotion, and other marketing strategies. It has the best chance of building and retaining market leadership if it plays its cards correctly from the start.

Growth Stage

If the new product satisfies the market, it will enter a **growth stage,** in which sales will start climbing quickly. The early adopters will continue to buy, and later buyers

To sustain growth, Sony keeps adding new features to its Walkman line.

will start following their lead, especially if they hear favorable word of mouth. Attracted by the opportunities for profit, new competitors will enter the market. They will introduce new product features, and the market will expand. The increase in competitors leads to an increase in the number of distribution outlets, and sales jump just to build reseller inventories. Prices remain where they are or fall only slightly. Companies keep their promotion spending at the same or a slightly higher level: Educating the market remains a goal, but now the company must also meet the competition.

Profits increase during this growth stage, as promotion costs are spread over a large volume and unit-manufacturing costs fall. The firm uses several strategies to sustain rapid market growth as long as possible. It improves product quality and adds new-product features and models. It enters new market segments and new distribution channels. It shifts some advertising from building product awareness to building product conviction and purchase, and it lowers prices at the right time to attract more buyers.

The firm in the growth stage faces a tradeoff between high market share and high current profit. By spending a lot of money on product improvement, promotion, and distribution, it can capture a dominant position. But it gives up maximum current profit in the hope of making this up in the next stage.

Maturity Stage   At some point, a product's sales growth will slow down, and the product will enter a **maturity stage.** This maturity stage normally lasts longer than the previous stages, and it poses strong challenges to marketing management. Most products are in the maturity stage of the life cycle, and therefore most of marketing management deals with the mature product.

The slowdown in sales growth results in many producers with many products to sell. In turn, this overcapacity leads to greater competition. Competitors begin marking down prices, increasing their advertising and sales promotions, and upping their R&D budgets to find better versions of the product. These steps mean a drop in profit. Some of the weaker competitors start dropping out, and the industry eventually contains only well-established competitors.

Product managers should not simply defend the product. A good offense is the best defense. They should consider modifying the market, product, and marketing mix.

Market Modification

During this stage, the company tries to increase the consumption of the current product. It looks for new users and market segments, as when Johnson & Johnson targeted the adult market with its baby powder and shampoo. The manager also looks for ways to increase usage among present customers. Campbell does this by offering recipes and convincing consumers that ''soup is good food.'' Or the company may want to reposition the brand to appeal to a larger or faster-growing segment, as Arrow did when it introduced its new line of casual shirts and announced, "We're loosening our collars."

Product Modification

The product manager can also change product characteristics—such as product quality, features, or style—to attract new users and more usage.

A strategy of *quality improvement* aims at increasing product performance: durability, reliability, speed, taste. This strategy is effective when the quality can be improved, when buyers believe the claim of improved quality, and when enough buyers want higher quality.

A strategy of *feature improvement* adds new features that expand the product's usefulness, safety, or convenience. Feature improvement has been successfully used by Japanese makers of watches, calculators, and copying machines. For example, Seiko keeps adding new styles and features to its line of watches.

A strategy of *style improvement* aims to increase the attractiveness of the product. Thus, car manufacturers restyle their cars to attract buyers who want a new look. The makers of consumer food and household products introduce new flavors, colors, ingredients, or packages to revitalize consumer buying.

Marketing-Mix Modification

The product manager can also try to improve sales by changing one or more marketing-mix elements. Prices can be cut to attract new users and competitors' customers. A better advertising campaign can be launched. Aggressive sales promotion (trade deals, cents-off, premiums, contests) can be used. The company can also move into larger market channels, using mass merchandisers, if these channels are growing. Finally, the company can offer new or improved services to the buyers.

Decline Stage

The sales of most product forms and brands eventually dip. The decline may be slow, as in the case of oatmeal cereal; or rapid, as for video games. Sales may plunge to zero, or they may drop to a low level where they continue for many years. This is the **decline stage.**

Sales decline for many reasons, including technological advances, shifts in consumer tastes, and increased competition. As sales and profits decline, some firms withdraw from the market. Those remaining may reduce the number of their product offerings. They may drop smaller market segments and marginal trade channels. They may cut the promotion budget and reduce their prices further.

Carrying a weak product can be very costly to a firm, and not just in profit terms. There are many hidden costs—the weak product may take up too much of management's time. It often requires frequent price and inventory adjustments. It requires advertising and salesforce attention that might better be used to make "healthy" products more profitable. Its failing reputation can cause customer concerns about the company and its other products. The biggest cost may well lie in the future. Keeping weak products delays the search for replacements, creates a lopsided product mix, hurts current profits, and weakens the company's foothold on the future.

For these reasons, companies need to pay more attention to their aging products. The first task is to identify those products in the decline stage by regularly reviewing the sales, market shares, cost, and profit trends; then, for each declining product, management must decide whether to maintain, harvest, or drop.

Management may decide to *maintain* its brand without change in the hope that competitors will leave the industry. For example, Procter & Gamble made good profits by remaining in the declining liquid-soap business as others withdrew. Or management may decide to reposition the brand in hopes of moving it back into the growth stage of the product life cycle. Miller did this with its Miller High Life brand in the 1970s: Sales grew rapidly when Miller moved from an upper-income, "champagne of bottled beers" position to a more middle-American one.

TABLE 11-4
Product Life Cycle:
Characteristics and Responses

	INTRODUCTION	GROWTH	MATURITY	DECLINE
Characteristics				
Sales	Low	Fast growth	Slow growth	Decline
Profits	Negligible	Peak levels	Declining	Low or zero
Cash flow	Negative	Moderate	High	Low
Customers	Innovative	Mass market	Mass market	Laggards
Competitors	Few	Growing	Many rivals	Declining number
Responses				
Strategic focus	Expand market	Market penetration	Defend share	Productivity
Marketing expenditures	High	High (declining %)	Falling	Low
Marketing emphasis	Product awareness	Brand preference	Brand loyalty	Selective
Distribution	Patchy	Intensive	Intensive	Selective
Price	High	Lower	Lowest	Rising
Product	Basic	Improved	Differentiated	Unchanged

Source: Peter Doyle, "The Realities of the Product Life Cycle," *Quarterly Review of Marketing*, Summer 1976, p. 5.

Management may decide to *harvest* the product, which means reducing various costs (plant and equipment, maintenance, R&D, advertising, salesforce) and hoping that sales hold up. If successful, harvesting will increase the company's profits in the short run. Or management may decide to *drop* the product from the line. It can sell it to another firm or simply liquidate it at salvage value. If the company plans to find a buyer, it will not want to run down the product through harvesting.[16]

The key characteristics of each stage of the product life cycle are summarized in Table 11-4. The table also lists the marketing responses made by companies in each stage.[17]

■ SUMMARY

Organizations must develop new products and services. Their current products face limited life spans and must be replaced by newer products. But new products can fail—the risks of innovation are as great as the rewards. The key to successful innovation lies in a total-company effort, strong planning, and a systematic *new-product development process*.

The new-product development process consists of eight stages: *idea generation, idea screening, concept development and testing, marketing strategy development, business analysis, product development, test marketing,* and *commercialization*. The purpose of each stage is to decide whether the idea should be further developed or dropped. The company wants to minimize the chances of poor ideas moving forward and good ideas being rejected.

Each product has a *life cycle* marked by a changing set of problems and opportunities. The sales of the typical product follow an S-shaped curve made up of five stages. The cycle begins with the *product development stage* when the company finds and develops a new-product idea. The *introduction stage* is marked by slow growth and low profits as the product is being pushed into distribution. If successful, the product enters a *growth stage* marked by rapid sales growth and increasing profits. During this stage, the company tries to improve the product, enter new market segments and distribution channels, and reduce its prices slightly. Then comes a *maturity stage* in which sales growth slows down and profits stabilize. The company seeks strategies to renew sales growth, including market, product, and marketing mix modification. Finally, the product enters a *decline stage* in which sales and profits dwindle. The company's task during this stage is to identify the declining product and decide whether it should be maintained, harvested, or dropped. If dropped, the product can be sold to another firm or liquidated for salvage value.

■ QUESTIONS FOR DISCUSSION

1. Before videotape cameras were available for home use, Polaroid introduced Polavision, a system for making home movies that did not require laboratory processing. Like most other home movie systems, Polavision film cassettes lasted only a few minutes and did not record sound. Despite the advantage of "instant developing" and heavy promotional expenditures by Polaroid, Polavision never gained wide acceptance. Why do you think Polavision flopped, given Polaroid's previous record of new product successes?

2. List all the new product ideas for your favorite fast-food chain you can think of. Of these ideas, which do you think would have a chance of succeeding?

3. Less than one third of new product ideas come from the customer. Does this low percentage conflict with the marketing concept's philosophy of "find a need and fill it"? Why or why not?

4. Many companies have formal new-product development systems and committees. Yet one recent study found that most successful new products were those that had been kept away from the formal system. Why might this be true?

5. What factors would you consider in choosing cities for test marketing a new snack? Would where you live be a good test market? Why or why not?

6. NutraSweet, the NutraSweet Company's brand name for aspartame, was approved for use in foods in 1981. In 1992, the company's patent expires, and other companies will be able to sell their own brands of aspartame. Describe

NutraSweet's probable life cycle from 1980 to 1999.

8. How can a company distinguish products with long life cycles from current fads and fashions? What products on the market now do you think are fads or fashions that will soon disappear?

9. Test market results for a new product are usually better than the business results the same brand achieves after it is launched. Name some reasons for this phenomenon.

10. Recent evidence suggests that consuming oatmeal, and especially oat bran, may be helpful in reducing people's levels of cholesterol. What impact could this health benefit have on the life cycle of oatmeal and oat-based products?

11. Think of some new products you have seen. How truly new and innovative are they? Are companies being risk averse because "pioneers are the ones who get shot?"

■ KEY TERMS

Business analysis. A review of the sales, costs, and profit projections for a new product to find out whether these factors satisfy the company's objectives.

Commercialization. Introducing a new product into the market.

Concept testing. Testing new product concepts with a group of target consumers to find out if the concepts have strong consumer appeal.

Decline stage. The product life cycle stage at which a product's sales decline.

Fads. Fashions that enter quickly, are adopted with great zeal, peak early, and decline fast.

Fashion. A currently accepted or popular style in a given field.

Growth stage. The product life cycle stage at which a product's sales start climbing quickly.

Idea generation. The systematic search for new-product ideas.

Idea screening. Screening new product ideas in order to spot good ideas and drop poor ones as soon as possible.

Introduction stage. The product life cycle stage when the new product is first distributed and made available for purchase.

Marketing strategy development. Designing an initial marketing strategy for a new product based on the product concept.

Marketing strategy statement. A statement of the planned strategy for a new product that outlines the intended target market, the planned product positioning, plus the sales, market share, and profit goals for the first few years.

Maturity stage. The stage in the product life cycle in which sales growth slows or levels off.

New-product development. The development of original products, product improvements, product modifications, and new brands through the firm's own R&D efforts.

Product concept. A detailed version of the new-product idea stated in meaningful consumer terms.

Product development. Developing the product concept into a physical product in order to assure that the product idea can be turned into a workable product.

Product idea. An idea for a possible product that the company can envision offering to the market.

Product image. The way consumers perceive an actual or potential product.

Product life cycle (PLC). The course of a product's sales and profits during its lifetime. It involves five distinct stages: product development, introduction, growth, maturity, and decline.

Sequential product development. A new-product development approach in which one company department works individually to complete its stage of the process before passing the new product along to the next department and stage.

Simultaneous product development. An approach to developing new products in which various company departments work closely together, overlapping the steps in the product-development process to save time and increase effectiveness.

Style. A basic and distinctive mode of expression.

Test marketing. The stage of new-product development in which the product and marketing program are tested in more realistic market settings.

■ REFERENCES

1. See Steven Greenhouse, "An Innovator Gets Down to Business," *The New York Times*, October 12, 1986, Section 3, pp. 1, 8; Russell Mitchell, "Masters of Innovation: How 3M Keeps Its New Products Coming," *Business Week*, April 10, 1989, pp. 58–64; and Brain Dumaine, "Leaders of America's Most Admired: Ability to Innovate," *Fortune*, January 29, 1990, pp. 43–44.

2. See "Products of the Year," *Fortune*, December 9, 1985, pp. 106–12.

3. See *New Product Management for the 1980s* (New York: Booz, Allen & Hamilton, 1982); C. Merle Crawford, "New

Product Failure Rates: A Reprise," *Research Management*, July–August 1987, pp. 20–24; and Lois Therrien, "Want Shelf Space at the Supermarket? Ante Up," *Business Week*, August 7, 1989, pp. 60–61.

4. See Leigh Lawton and A. Parasuraman, "So You Want Your New Product Planning to Be Productive," *Business Horizons*, December 1980, pp. 29–34.

5. See "Listening to the Voice of the Marketplace," *Business Week*, February 21, 1983, p. 90ff.

6. See Eric vonHipple, "Get New Products from Consumers," *Harvard Business Review*, March–April 1982, pp. 117–22.

7. Russell Mitchell, "How Ford Hit the Bullseye with Taurus," *Business Week*, June 30, 1986, pp. 69–70; and "Copycat Stuff? Hardly!" *Business Week*, September 14, 1987, p. 112.

8. For more on idea screening, see Tom W. White, "Use Variety of Internal, External Sources to Gather and Screen New Product Ideas," *Marketing News*, September 16, 1983, Sec. 2, p. 12.

9. For more on product concept testing, see William L. Moore, "Concept Testing," *Journal of Business Research*, Vol. 10, 1982, pp. 279–94; and David A. Schwartz, "Concept Testing Can Be Improved—and Here's How," *Marketing News*, January 6, 1984, pp. 22–23.

10. See Otis Port, "Pssst! Want a Secret for Making Superproducts?" *Business Week*, October 2, 1989, pp. 106–110.

11. Julie Franz, "Test Marketing: Traveling Through a Maze of Choices," *Advertising Age*, February 13, 1986, pp. 11+.

12. For more on controlled test markets, see Felix Kessler, "High-Tech Shocks in Ad Research," *Fortune*, July 7, 1986, pp. 58–62.

13. For more on simulated test markets, see Kevin Higgins, "Simulated Test Marketing Winning Acceptance," *Marketing News*, March 1, 1985, pp. 15, 19; and Howard Schlossberg, "Simulated vs. Traditional Test Marketing," *Marketing News*, October 23, 1989, pp. 1–2.

14. See Robert J. Thomas, "Timing—The Key to Market Entry," *The Journal of Consumer Marketing*, Summer 1985, pp. 77–87.

15. See George S. Day, "The Product Life Cycle: Analysis and Applications Issues," *Journal of Marketing*, Fall 1981, pp. 60–67; John E. Swan and David R. Rink, "Fitting Marketing Strategy to Varying Life Cycles," *Business Horizons*, January–February 1982, pp. 72–76; and Sak Onkvisit and John J. Shaw, "Competition and Product Management: Can the Product Life Cycle Help?" *Business Horizons*, July–August 1986, pp. 51–62.

16. See Laurence P. Feldman and Albert L. Page, "Harvesting: The Misunderstood Market Exit Strategy," *Journal of Business Strategy*, Spring 1985, pp. 79–85.

17. For a more comprehensive discussion of marketing strategies over the course of the product life cycle, see Philip Kotler, *Marketing Management*, 7th ed. (Englewood Cliffs, NJ: Prentice Hall, 1991), Chapter 13.

HOLLY FARMS: THE CHICKEN THAT LAID AN EGG

Holly Farms Corporation thought it had created the Cadillac of poultry with its roasted chicken.

The fully cooked bird seemed just the ticket for today's busy consumers: a modern, more convenient alternative to raw chicken. It scored big in a year of test marketing.

The company began phasing in national distribution of the product last fall. But it fared so dismally that the planned expansion into more markets was halted so Holly Farms could reconsider its marketing strategy.

One analyst, Bonnie Rivers of Salomon Brothers, Inc., cites the blunder as a major reason she recently slashed her estimate for Holly Farms' profit for the year ending May 31 by 22%, to $2.25 a share from $2.90. Higher feed and persistently low chicken prices also contributed to the lower profit projection, she says. In fiscal 1987, the Memphis, Tennessee-based poultry and food concern earned $71.7 million, or $4.31 a share, on revenue of $1.42 billion.

Losing a Lot of Business

Company executives acknowledge that the roasted-chicken product will hurt fiscal 1988 earnings, but they won't make any projections. "We're just losing a lot of business," says John Creel, Holly Farms' senior director of sales and marketing. Grocers are buying far less of the product than Holly Farms had hoped, he says, because they believe it doesn't last long enough on the shelf. Until this problem is solved, Holly Farms decided not to expand distribution of its roasted chicken, now available in about 50% of the nationwide market.

Holly Farms' experience is a classic example of how a food company can stumble in launching a product. Although the extensive test marketing identified strong consumer support for the product—22% of Atlanta women surveyed said they had tried it, and of those, 90% said they would buy it again—the company failed to detect the concerns and resistance of its front-line customer, the grocer.

Several grocers concur that the problem isn't with the roasted chicken itself. Ray Heatherington, meat merchandising manager for Safeway Stores, Inc.'s Northern California division, calls the product—which comes in Cajun, barbecue, and original flavors—"outstanding." But his stores dropped it after several weeks, because of the short shelf life.

Holly Farms says the quality lasts at least 18 days. So to be safe, it marks the last sale date as 14 days after the chicken is roasted. But it can take as long as nine days to get the chicken to stores from the North Carolina plant, on which Holly Farms spent $20 million just for

handling the roasted-chicken product. That doesn't give grocers much lead time. To avoid being stuck with an outdated backlog, many are waiting until they run out before reordering.

In the case of raw chicken, shelf life isn't a factor because the product's high volume means it is sold in the first few days after delivery and grocers know from experience how much to stock.

A Hard Sell

A general suspicion of new products also has probably hurt the effort. "It's a hard sell to get into the supermarket, particularly if you've got a new product that the consumers and retailers haven't seen before," says Joe Scheringer, an editor at *Grocery Marketing* magazine. The meat department is probably the most resistant to change, he adds.

Some competitors believe Holly Farms didn't do enough preliminary groundwork with retailers. Holly Farms acknowledges it probably didn't go far enough to tailor its marketing program to each supermarket chain or spend sufficient time educating meat managers.

But it plans to mend fences soon. Hoping to lengthen the shelf life by 5 to 10 days, Holly Farms is developing a new system to pack chickens. To shorten delivery time, the company is considering giving the product its own distribution system, instead of delivering it along with raw poultry.

Holly Farms also plans to shift a hefty portion of its marketing budget out of television and radio and into

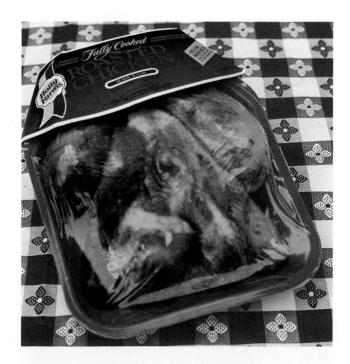

the grocery store in the form of promotions, coupons, consumer demonstrations, and contests for meat managers. Nearly two-thirds of Holly Farms' roughly $14 million in a half year's marketing expenditures for the product went to media advertising; that proportion is being lowered to about one-half, the company said.

High Hopes for a Blockbuster

Holly Farms still believes the roasted-chicken product will be a blockbuster. So does Salomon Brothers' Ms. Rivers, who says, "I definitely agree with what they're doing and why they're doing it."

At least one competitor is reserving judgment: Tyson Foods, Inc., of Springdale, Arkansas, which is test marketing a similar chicken product in Indianapolis, says it has no immediate plans to broaden distribution, in part because of Holly Farms' experience.

QUESTIONS

1. Identify and briefly discuss the changes needed in Holly Farms' marketing strategy for roasted chicken.
2. What could Holly Farms have done prior to introducing roasted chicken to avoid its marketing blunder?
3. What lesson can we learn from Holly Farms about the relationship between test market results and marketing success or failure?

DOES OAT BRAN WORK?

Everyone seems to be selling it, and we've all heard it over and over again that oat bran can lower cholesterol levels. But a study detailed in the *New England Journal of Medicine* says it's not necessarily so. This prompts the question: Is oat bran good for your health or not?

Judging by the number of new oat bran cereals introduced in the last few years, cereal manufacturers suggest the answer is yes. Kellogg, the nation's leader with 40 percent of the ready-to-eat cereal market, recently introduced Heartwise, Common Sense Oatbran, S. W. Graham, Nut and Honey, Crunch Biscuits, Oatbake, and Golden Crunch Mueslix for health-conscious consumers. General Mills, holding a 27 percent share of the market, has introduced Benefit; Ralson Purina with 5 percent of the market, has put out Oatbran Options; Nabisco, with 6 percent of the market, has introduced Wholesome and Harty, a hot breakfast cereal; and Quaker Oats Company, with 8 percent of the market, has brought out a new ready-to-eat version of its Quaker Oatbran. (It should be noted that Heartwise and Benefit also contain an exotic grain called psyllium, which like oat bran, is being hailed as a cholesterol reducer, and that S. W. Graham is made from whole-wheat flour. Both ingredients are aimed at health-conscious consumers.)

Consider the impact the oat bran mania has had on one cereal alone. General Mills' Cheerios is now the most popular cereal in the United States, having replaced Kellogg's Frosted Flakes. Cheerios gained a startling 3.1 percentage points in market share (from 6.2 to 9.9 percent in just 12 months—with each percentage point worth $66 million in revenues. General Mills has benefited enormously from the oat bran craze—more so than Kellogg, because while 20 percent of Kellogg's cereals are made with oats, 40 percent of General Mills cereals are.

Oat bran was a manufacturer's dream come true. Consumers loved it—not for the taste, but because research suggested you could eat it and reduce your cholesterol level and the chance you would get heart disease. Cereal makers loved it for the profits to be made, and farmers loved it because it increased the demand for their grain. The demand for oat bran increased by 800 percent in 1988 alone, and the growth has been sustained. In 1989,

sales of all oat bran products totaled over $1 billion. It seems that high-fiber food is the hottest craze to hit supermarket shelves in years.

There is now some evidence that rice bran and corn bran also have cholesterol-reducing properties. Although this evidence is preliminary and far from conclusive, it might stimulate the market for these grains as well.

But what of the oat bran study reported in the *New England Journal of Medicine*, which concluded that "Oatbran has little cholesterol-lowering effect and that high-fiber and low-fiber dietary grain supplements reduce serum cholesterol levels about equally, probably because they replace dietary fats." Dr. Timothy Johnson of *ABC News* makes these points: (1) A low-fat diet is extremely important in lowering cholesterol, and the extent to which oat bran contributes to this is debatable; (2) despite the criticism raised by the *New England Journal of Medicine* study of some of the hype about oat bran, it is a nutritious food worth eating in moderation; (3) the benefit of grain fiber, both soluble and insoluble, on the gastrointestinal tract is considerable—perhaps decreasing the risk of several ailments, including colon cancer.

So the answer to the question posed appears to be: If consumers substitute oat and oat bran products for cheese and eggs and other foods that are high in cholesterol, they will succeed in lowering their cholesterol level— but through the substitution effect rather than through any independent cholesterol-lowering benefit from oat bran.

QUESTIONS

1. Explain how cereal manufacturers, upon finding their products in the market maturity stage of the product life cycle, can rejuvenate sales.

2. If oat bran is found to have no unique ability to lower cholesterol levels, what is likely to happen to those products whose main attribute is oat bran?

Sources: "Big G Is Growing Fat on Oat Cuisine," *Business Week*, September 18, 1989, p. 29; "Kellogg Pours It On," *Advertising Age*, August 28, 1989, pp. 1, 52; "Cereal Makers Roll More Oats," *Advertising Age*, March 6, 1989, p. 34; "Comparison of the Effects of Oat Bran and Low-Fiber Wheat on Serum Lipoprotein Levels and Blood Pressure," *The New England Journal of Medicine*, January 18, 1990, pp. 147–152; "Kellogg Pours Out More New Cereals," *Advertising Age*, July 25, 1988, pp. 2, 66; and "The Next Wave of High Fiber Grains," *U.S. News & World Report*, May 22, 1989, p. 73.

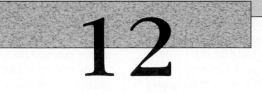

12

Pricing Products:
Pricing Considerations
and Approaches

A consumer buying a videocassette recorder from Sears faces a bewildering array of models and prices. The recent Sears catalog features 14 different VCR models at 12 different prices, ranging from $219.99 to $629.99. However, although consumers may have trouble choosing among the different prices, Sears probably has more trouble *setting* them. Sears must consider numerous factors in its complex price-setting process.

In setting prices, Sears must first consider its overall *marketing objectives* and the role of price in the marketing mix. Should Sears price to maximize current profits on VCRs or to maximize long-run market share? Should it use a high-price/low-volume strategy or a low-price/high-volume strategy? The giant retailer must also consider its *costs*—the costs of making VCRs or buying them from suppliers, the costs of shipping, storing, stocking, and selling inventory, and the costs of providing customer services. Sears must price its VCRs to cover these costs plus a target profit.

However, if Sears considered only costs when setting prices it would ignore other important factors. Beyond costs, Sears must also understand the relationship between price and *demand* for its VCRs and must set prices that match consumer value perceptions. If Sears charges more than buyers' perceived value, its VCRs will sell poorly. If it charges less, its VCRs may sell very well but will provide less overall revenue. Finally, Sears must consider *competitors'* VCR quality and prices. If Sears charges more for VCRs that are similar to those of its major competitors, it risks losing sales. If it sets prices much lower

than those of comparable products, it will lose profit opportunities even though winning sales from competitors.

Thus, Sears sets its VCR prices on the basis of numerous factors—overall marketing objectives, costs, competitors' prices, and consumer value perceptions and demand. But setting basic prices is just the beginning. Sears must now adjust these prices to account for different buyers and different market situations. For example, because consumers vary in how they value different VCR features, Sears offers many models for different price segments. The basic VHS 117-channel, two-head model with no extras sells for $294.97. At the other extreme, Sears' best model—a 120-channel, four-head, stereo VCR with 35 function remote control, on-screen programming, picture-in-picture capability, and multi-channel scan and freeze features—goes for $629.99. Thus, Sears offers a model to fit any consumer preference and pocketbook.

Sears also adjusts its prices for psychological impact. For example, instead of charging $300 for its basic model, Sears charges $294.97. This price suggests a bargain, and consumers will perceive the model as belonging to the under-$300 rather than the $300-and-over price range. Sears also adjusts prices to meet market conditions and competitor actions. After Christmas, for example, Sears might knock $100 off the price of its best model, both to clear inventories and to boost demand. Thus Sears must constantly adjust prices to account for buyer differences and changing market conditions. And it must do this for each of the thousands of products it sells.

Sears' pricing strategies have played a major role

in the company's ups and downs over the course of ten decades. Sears originally became America's largest retailer by offering quality merchandise at affordable prices. In the late 1960s, however, the company decided to upgrade its merchandise and raise prices. When higher prices caused many loyal shoppers to switch to lower-priced competitors, Sears began using weekly price-off sales to make its prices more competitive. Despite this strategy of continuous sales, however, Sears continued to lose customers to K mart, Wal-Mart, and other discounters. Its market share slid 33 percent during the 1980s, and America's largest retailer found itself in big trouble.

In the spring of 1989, in what it called the biggest change in its 102-year history, Sears launched a bold new pricing strategy. Scrapping its decades-old weekly-sales approach, it adopted a no-sales, *everyday low-price* strategy. Sears closed all of its 824 stores for 42 hours and retagged every piece of merchandise, slashing prices by as much as 50 percent! In its biggest-ever advertising campaign, the huge retailer proclaimed, "We've lowered our prices on over 50,000 items! Sears: your money's worth and a whole lot more."

Sears bet that its new everyday low-price strategy would pull consumers back into its stores and revive sagging profits. And at first, sales did surge under the new pricing policy. But the ploy involved many risks, and after the initial fanfare died down, Sears' sales and profits began once more to decline. To be successful with everyday low *prices*, Sears first had to achieve everyday low *costs*. However, its costs have traditionally run much higher than those of its competitors. With its bloated cost structure, the price slashing left Sears with paper-thin margins, causing profits to fall. Beyond cost problems, Sears faced the even tougher problem in trying to change consumer perceptions of its prices and practices. For decades, Sears had conditioned customers to "hold out" for its traditional price-off sales. The rapid switch to a one-price policy and everyday low-price position confused consumers. Moreover, consumers who were being assaulted by everyday low-price claims from many retailers weren't paying much attention to such claims anymore. Worse yet, surveys showed that consumers simply did not believe that Sears' new prices *were* the lowest in the marketplace.

By early 1990, after only ten months, Sears' everyday low-price strategy appeared to be on the way out. The company began to phase in a new strategy which put less emphasis on price and more on "value," returning to its traditional strengths—reliability, merchandise return, and "satisfaction guaranteed" policies. And it began again to feature major sales events to stimulate consumer excitement and buying. Thus, Sears continues to have difficult pricing strategy problems. How well the huge retailer handles these problems will dramatically affect its sales and profits—perhaps even its survival.[1]

CHAPTER OBJECTIVES

After reading this chapter, you should be able to:

1. Explain how marketing objectives and marketing mix strategy, costs, and other internal company factors affect pricing decisions.
2. List and discuss factors outside the company that affect pricing decisions.
3. Explain how price setting depends on consumer perceptions of price and on the price-demand relationship.
4. Compare the three general pricing approaches.

All profit organizations and many nonprofit organizations must set prices on their products or services. *Price* goes by many names:

> Price is all around us. You pay *rent* for your apartment, *tuition* for your education, and a *fee* to your physician or dentist. The airline, railway, taxi, and bus companies charge you a *fare*; the local utilities call their price a *rate*; and the local bank charges you *interest* for the money you borrow. The price for driving your car on Florida's Sunshine Parkway is a *toll*, and the company that insures your car charges you a *premium*. The guest lecturer charges an *honorarium* to tell you about a government official who took a *bribe* to help a shady character steal *dues* collected by a trade association. Clubs or societies to which you belong may make a special *assessment* to pay unusual expenses. Your regular lawyer may ask for a *retainer* to cover her services. The "price" of an executive is a *salary*, the price of a salesperson may be a *commission*, and the price of a worker is a *wage*. Finally, although economists would disagree, many of us feel that *income taxes* are the price we pay for the privilege of making money.[2]

Simply defined, **price** is the amount of money charged for a product or service. More broadly, price is the sum of the values consumers exchange for the benefits of having or using the product or service.

How are prices set? Historically, prices were usually set by buyers and sellers bargaining with each other. Sellers would ask for a higher price than they expected to get, and buyers would offer less than they expected to pay. Through bargaining, they would arrive at an acceptable price. Individual buyers paid different prices for the same products, depending on their needs and bargaining skills.

Today, most sellers set *one* price to *all* buyers. This idea was helped along by the development of large-scale retailing at the end of the 19th century. F. W. Woolworth, Tiffany and Co., John Wanamaker, J. L. Hudson, and others advertised a "strictly one-price policy" because they carried so many items and had so many employees.

Historically, price has been the major factor affecting buyer choice. This is still true in poorer nations, among poorer groups, and with commodity products. However, nonprice factors have become more important in buyer-choice behavior in recent decades.

Price is the only element in the marketing mix that produces revenue; all other elements represent costs. Furthermore, pricing and price competition have been rated as the number one problem facing marketing executives.[3] Yet many companies do not handle pricing well. The most common mistakes are: pricing that is too cost-oriented; prices that are not revised often enough to reflect market changes; pricing that does not take the rest of the marketing mix into account; and prices that are not varied enough for different product items and market segments.

In this and the next chapter, we focus on the problem of setting prices. This chapter looks at the factors marketers must consider when setting prices and at general pricing approaches. In the next chapter, we examine pricing strategies for new-product pricing, product-mix pricing, initiating and responding to price changes, and adjusting prices for buyer and situational factors.

FACTORS TO CONSIDER WHEN SETTING PRICES

A company's pricing decisions are affected by many internal company factors and external environmental factors. These factors are shown in Figure 12-1. *Internal factors* include the company's marketing objectives, marketing mix strategy, costs, and organization. *External factors* include the nature of the market and demand, competition, and other environmental factors.

Internal Factors Affecting Pricing Decisions

Marketing Objectives

Before setting price, the company must decide on its strategy for the product. If the company has selected its target market and positioning carefully, then its marketing mix strategy, including price, will be fairly straightforward. For example, if General Motors decides to produce a new sports car to compete with European sports cars in the high-income segment, this suggests charging a high price. Motel 6, Econo Lodges, and Red Roof Inns have positioned themselves as motels that provide economical rooms for budget-minded travelers; this position requires charging a low price. Thus, pricing strategy is largely determined by past decisions on market positioning.

FIGURE 12-1
Factors affecting price decisions

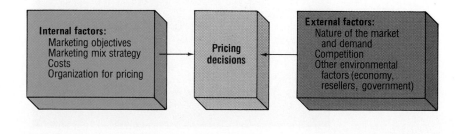

At the same time, the company may seek additional objectives. The clearer a firm is about its objectives, the easier it is to set price. Examples of common objectives are *survival*, *current profit maximization*, *market-share maximization*, and *product quality leadership*.

SURVIVAL. Companies set *survival* as their major objective if they are troubled by too much capacity, heavy competition, or changing consumer wants. To keep a plant going, a company may set a low price, hoping to increase demand. In this case, profits are less important than survival. In recent years, many automobile dealers have resorted to pricing below cost or offering large price rebate programs in order to survive. As long as their prices cover variable costs and some fixed costs, they can stay in business until conditions change or other problems are corrected.

CURRENT PROFIT MAXIMIZATION. Many companies want to set a price that will maximize current profits. They estimate what demand and costs will be at different prices and choose the price that will produce the maximum current profit, cash flow, or return on investment. In all cases, the company wants current financial outcomes rather than long-run performance.

MARKET-SHARE LEADERSHIP. Other companies want to obtain the dominant market share. They believe that the company with the largest market share will enjoy the lowest costs and highest long-run profit. To become the market-share leader, they set prices as low as possible. A variation of this objective is to pursue a specific market-share gain. Say the company wants to increase its market share from 10 percent to 15 percent in one year. It will search for the price and marketing program that will achieve this goal.

PRODUCT-QUALITY LEADERSHIP. A company might decide it wants to have the highest quality product on the market. This normally calls for charging a high price to cover the high product quality and high cost of R&D. For example, the Sub-Zero Freezer Company seeks product-quality leadership. Sub-Zero makes the Rolls-Royce of refrigerators—custom-made, built-in units that look more like hardwood cabinets or pieces of furniture than refrigerators. By offering the highest-quality, Sub-Zero sells more than $50 million worth of fancy refrigerators a year, priced at up to $3000 each.[4]

Sub-Zero charges a premium price for its custom-made refrigerators to attain product-quality leadership.

OTHER OBJECTIVES. A company might also use price to attain other more specific objectives. It can set prices low to prevent competition from entering the market or set prices at competitors' levels to stabilize the market. Prices can be set to keep the loyalty and support of resellers or to avoid government intervention. Prices can be temporarily reduced to create excitement for a product or to draw more customers into a retail store. One product may be priced to help the sales of other products in the company's line. Thus, pricing may play an important role in helping to accomplish the company's objectives at many levels.

Marketing-Mix Strategy

Price is only one of the marketing-mix tools that the company uses to achieve its marketing objectives. Price decisions must be coordinated with product design, distribution, and promotion decisions to form a consistent and effective marketing program. Decisions made for other marketing-mix variables may affect pricing decisions. For example, producers who use many resellers expected to support and promote their products may have to build larger reseller margins into their prices. The decision to develop a high-quality position will mean that the seller must charge a higher price to cover higher costs.

The company often makes its pricing decision first and then bases other marketing-mix decisions on the price it wants to charge. For example, Hyundai, Honda, and other makers of low-budget cars discovered a market segment for affordable cars and

Jaguar positions on quality and other nonprice factors—its price adds prestige.

designed models to sell within the price range that this segment was willing to pay. Here, price was a crucial product positioning factor that defined the product's market, competition, and design. The intended price determined what product features could be offered and what production costs could be incurred.

Thus, the marketer must consider the total marketing mix when setting prices. If the product is positioned on nonprice factors, then decisions about quality, promotion, and distribution will strongly affect price. If price is a critical positioning factor, then price will strongly affect decisions on the other marketing mix elements. In most cases, the company will consider all the marketing-mix decisions together when developing the marketing program.

Costs

Costs set the floor for the price that the company can charge for its product. The company wants to charge a price that both covers all its costs for producing, distributing, and selling the product and delivers a fair rate of return for its effort and risk. A company's costs may be an important element in its pricing strategy. Many companies work to become the "low-cost producers" in their industries. Companies with lower costs can set lower prices that result in greater sales and profits (see Marketing Highlight 12–1).

TYPES OF COSTS. A company's costs take two forms, fixed and variable. FIXED COSTS (also known as overhead) are costs that do not vary with production or sales level. Thus, a company must pay bills each month for rent, heat, interest, and executive salaries, whatever the company's output. Fixed costs go on no matter what the production level.

Variable costs vary directly with the level of production. Each hand calculator produced by Texas Instuments involves a cost of plastic, wires, packaging, and other inputs. These costs tend to be the same for each unit produced. They are called variable because their total varies with the number of units produced.

Total costs are the sum of the fixed and variable costs for any given level of production. Management wants to charge a price that will at least cover the total production costs at a given level of production. The company must watch its costs carefully. If it costs the company more than its competitors to produce and sell its product, the company will have to charge a higher price or make less profit, putting it at a competitive disadvantage.

COSTS AT DIFFEERENT LEVELS OF PRODUCTION. To price wisely, management needs to know how its costs vary with different levels of production. For example, suppose Texas Instruments (TI) has built a plant to produce 1,000 hand calculators per day. Figure 12-2A shows the typical short-run average cost curve (SRAC). It shows that the cost per calculator is high if TI's factory produces only a few per day. But as production approaches 1,000 calculators per day, average cost falls. This is because fixed costs are spread over more units, with each unit bearing a smaller fixed cost. TI

FIGURE 12-2
Cost per unit at different levels of production per period

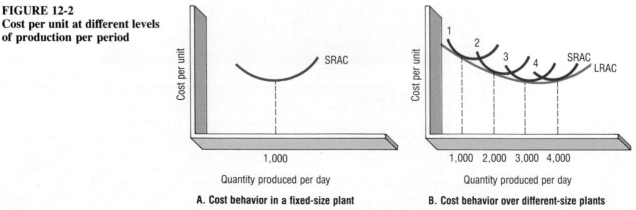

A. Cost behavior in a fixed-size plant

B. Cost behavior over different-size plants

can try to produce more than 1,000 calculators per day, but average costs will increase because the plant becomes inefficient. Workers have to wait for machines, the machines break down more often, and workers get in each other's way.

If TI believed it could sell 2,000 calculators a day, it should consider building a larger plant. The plant would use more efficient machinery and work arrangements, and the unit cost of producing 2,000 units per day would be less than that of 1,000 units per day as shown in the long-run average cost (LRAC) curve (Figure 12-2B). In fact, a 3,000-capacity plant would even be more efficient, according to Figure 12-2B. But a 4,000 daily production plant would be less efficient because of increasing diseconomies of scale—too many workers to manage, increased paperwork slowing things down, and so on. Figure 12-2B shows that a 3,000 daily production plant is the best size to build if demand is strong enough to support this level of production.

COSTS AS A FUNCTION OF PRODUCTION EXPERIENCE. Suppose TI runs a plant that produces 3,000 calculators per day. As TI gains experience in producing hand calculators, it learns how to do it better. Workers learn shortcuts and become more familiar with their equipment. With practice, the work becomes better organized, and TI finds better equipment and production processes. With higher volume, TI becomes more efficient and gains economies of scale. As a result, average cost tends to fall with accumulated

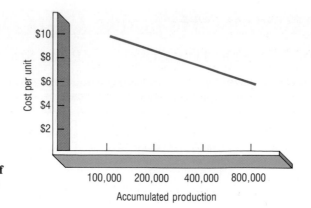

FIGURE 12-3
Cost per unit as a function of accumulated production: the experience curve

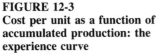

production experience. This is shown in Figure 12-3.[5] Thus the average cost of producing the first 100,000 calculators is $10 per calculator. When the company has produced the first 200,000 calculators, the average cost has fallen to $9. After its accumulated production experience doubles again to 400,000, the average cost is $8. This drop in the average cost with accumulated production experience is called the **experience curve** (or the *learning curve*).

If a downward-sloping experience curve exists, this is highly significant for the company. Not only will the company's unit production cost fall, it will fall faster if the company makes and sells more during a given period. But the market has to stand ready to buy the higher output. And to take advantage of the experience curve, TI must get a large market share early in the product's life cycle. This suggests the following pricing strategy. TI should price its calculators low; its sales will then increase, and its costs will decrease through gaining more experience, and then it can lower its prices further.

Some companies have built successful strategies around the experience curve. For example, during the 1980s, Bausch & Lomb solidified its position in the soft contact lens market by using computerized lens design and steadily expanding its one Soflens plant. As a result, its market share climbed steadily to 65 percent. Yet a single-minded focus on reducing costs and exploiting the experience curve does not always work. Experiences curves became somewhat of a fad during the 1970s, and like many fads, the strategy was sometimes misused. Experience curve pricing carries some major risks. The aggressive pricing might give the product a cheap image, as happened when Texas Instruments ran the price of its personal computers down to just $99 compared to competitors' machines selling for more than $300. The strategy also assumes that competitors are weak and not willing to fight it out by meeting the company's price cuts. Finally, while the company is building volume under one technology, a competitor may find a lower-cost technology which lets it start at lower prices than the market leader, who still operates on the old experience curve.[6]

Organizational Considerations

Management must decide who within the organization should set prices. Companies handle pricing in a variety of ways. In small companies, prices are often set by top management rather than by the marketing or sales department. In large companies, pricing is typically handled by divisional or product-line managers. In industrial markets, salespeople may be allowed to negotiate with customers within certain price ranges—even so, top management sets the pricing objectives and policies and often approves the prices proposed by lower-level management or salespeople.[7] In industries in which pricing is a key factor (aerospace, railroads, oil companies), companies will often have a pricing department to set the best prices or help others in setting them. This department reports to the marketing department or top management. Others who have an influence on pricing include sales managers, production managers, finance managers, and accountants.

External Factors Affecting Pricing Decisions

The Market and Demand

Costs set the lower limits of prices, while the market and demand set the upper limit. Both consumer and industiral buyers balance the price of a product or service against the benefits of owning it. Thus, before setting prices, the marketer must understand the relationship between price and demand for its product.

In this section, we explain at how the price-demand relationship varies for different types of markets and at how buyer perceptions of price affect the pricing decision. Then we discuss methods for measuring the price-demand relationship.

PRICING IN DIFFERENT TYPES OF MARKETS. The seller's pricing freedom varies with different types of markets. Economists recognize four types of markets, each presenting a different pricing challenge.

Under **pure competition,** the market consists of many buyers and sellers trading in a uniform commodity such as wheat, copper, or financial securities. No single buyer or seller has much affect on the going market price. A seller cannot charge more than the going price because buyers can obtain as much as they need at this price. Nor would sellers charge less than the market price because they can sell all they want at that price. If price and profits rise, new sellers can easily enter the market. In a purely competitive market, marketing research, product development, pricing, advertising, and sales promotion play little or no role. Thus, sellers in these markets do not spend much time on marketing strategy.

Under **monopolistic competition,** the market consists of many buyers and sellers who trade over a range of prices rather than a single market price. A range of prices occurs because sellers can differentiate their offers to the buyers. Either the physical product can be varied in quality, features, or style, or the accompanying services can be varied. Buyers see differences in sellers' products and will pay different prices. Sellers try to develop differentiated offers for different customer segments and, in addition to price, freely use branding, advertising, and personal selling to set their offers apart.

Monopolistic competition: In the industrial market, Stanley sets its hinges apart from dozens of other brands using both price and nonprice factors.

Because there are many competitors, each firm is less affected by competitors' marketing strategies than in oligopolistic markets. For example, H.J. Heinz, Vlasic, and several other national brands of pickles compete with dozens of regional and local brands, all differentiated by price and non-price factors.

Under **oligopolistic competition,** the market consists of a few sellers who are highly sensitive to each other's pricing and marketing strategies. The product can be uniform (steel, aluminum) or non-uniform (cars, computers). The sellers are few because it is difficult for new sellers to enter the market. Each seller is alert to competitors' strategies and moves. If a steel company slashes its price by 10 percent, buyers will quickly switch to this supplier. The other steelmakers must respond by lowering their prices or increasing their services. An oligopolist is never sure that it will gain anything permanent through a price cut. On the other hand, if an oligopolist raises its price, its competitors might not follow this lead. The oligopolist would then have to retract its price increase or risk losing customers to competitors.

A **pure monopoly** consists of one seller. The seller may be a government monopoly (the U.S. Postal Service), a private regulated monopoly (a power company), or a private nonregulated monopoly (Du Pont when it introduced nylon). Pricing is handled differently in each case. A government monopoly can pursue a variety of pricing objectives. It might set a price below cost because the product is important to buyers who cannot afford to pay full cost. Or the price might be set either to cover costs or to produce good revenue. Or it might be set quite high to slow down consumption. In a regulated monopoly, the government permits the company to set rates that will yield a "fair return," one that will let the company maintain and expand its operations as needed. Non-regulated monopolies are free to price at what the market will bear. However, they do not always charge the full price for a number of reasons: desire not to attract competition, desire to penetrate the market faster with a low price, fear of government regulation.

CONSUMER PERCEPTIONS OF PRICE AND VALUE.   In the end, the consumer will decide whether a product's price is right. When setting prices, the company must consider consumer perceptions of price and how these perceptions affect consumers' buying decisions. Pricing decisions, like other marketing mix decisions, must be buyer-oriented:

> Pricing requires more than technical expertise. It requires creative judgment and awareness of buyers' motivations. . . . The key to effective pricing is the same one that opens doors . . . in other marketing functions: a creative awareness of who buyers are, why they buy and how they make their buying decisions. The recognition that buyers differ in these dimensions is as important for effective pricing as it is for effective promotion, distribution, or product development.[8]

When consumers buy a product, they exchange something of value (the price) to get something of value (the benefits of having or using the product). Effective, buyer-oriented pricing involves understanding how much value consumers place on the benefits they receive from the product and then setting a price that fits this value. Such benefits include both actual and perceived benefits. For example, calculating the cost of ingredients in a meal at a fancy restaurant is relatively easy. But assigning a value to other satisfactions such as taste, environment, relaxation, conversation, and status is very hard. And these values will vary both for different consumers and for different situations. Thus, a company will often find it hard to measure the values customers will attach to its product. But the consumer does use these values to evaluate a product's price. If consumers perceive that the price is greater than the product's value, they will not buy the product. If consumers perceive that the price is below the product's value, they will buy it, but the seller loses profit opportunities (see Marketing Highlight 12–2).

Marketers must therefore try to understand the consumer's reasons for buying the product then set price according to consumer perceptions of the product's value. Because consumers vary in the values they assign to different product features, marketers often vary their pricing strategies for different price segments. They offer different sets of product features at different prices. For example, television manufacturers offer small,

DEMAND DRIVES MIATA'S PRICES

How much would you pay for a curvaceous new two-seat convertible which has the reliability of modern engineering yet the look, feel, and sound of such classic roadsters as the 1959 Triumph TR3, the 1958 MGA, the 1962 Lotus Elan, or the Austin-Healy Sprite? The car is the Mazda MX-5 Miata, *the* hot new car of 1990. Not only have consumers raved about its looks, car critics have passionately praised its performance. According to *Car and Driver*, if the Miata "were any more talented or tempting, driving one would be illegal." And judging on design, performance, durability and reliability, entertainment, and value, *Road & Track* named it one of the five best cars in the world. Other cars in the rankings along with the Miata included the Porsche 911 Carrera, the Corvette ZR-1, the Mercedes-Benz 300 E, and the $140,000 Ferrari Testarossa. Not bad company for a car with a base sticker price of just $13,800 that was designed "just to be fun." Besides its good looks, performance, and price, the Miata has rocketed to success in the marketplace because it has no substitutes. Its closest competitors are the Honda CRX Si and the Toyota MR2, but they lack its singular looks and neither comes as a convertible. Thus, the Miata has driven rivals to despair and customers into a covetous swoon.

Mazda had a hard time with the question of how to price its classy little car. The Japanese producer carefully controlled costs to keep the Miata's base price below $15,000. But it seems that consumers cared little about Mazda's costs, or about its intended price. When the Miata debuted, sales soared—and so did its prices. The first few thousand Miatas to arrive at Mazda dealerships sold out instantly. To make things even more interesting, Mazda planned to ship only 20,000 Miatas (in three colors—red, white, and blue) to its 844 dealers in 1989, and only 40,000 more during 1990. Thus, demand exceeded the limited supply by a reported ratio of ten to one.

Miata was in so much demand that dealers jacked up the price way beyond the sticker and still had barely enough cars to sell. Because of the car's popularity, customers were more than willing to pay the higher price. In fact, some were almost eager! As one dealer noted, "People are offering more than what we're asking just to get [the car]." On average,

Many consumers paid more than the sticker price to own a Miata. To them, the value of the classy little car added up to more than the costs of its mechanical parts.

dealers across the U.S. marked prices up $4,000—in California, they added as much as $8,000. Some enterprising owners even offered to sell their Miatas for prices ranging up to $45,000. Ads appear daily in the *Los Angeles Times* from owners in Kansas, Nebraska, or Michigan proffering their Miatas for $32,000 plus delivery fees.

Thus, although companies often focus on costs as a key to setting prices, consumers rarely know of or care about the seller's costs. What really counts is what consumers are willing to pay for the benefits of owning the product. To some consumers, the sharp little Miata adds up to much more than the costs of its mechanical parts. To them, it delivers the same pleasures and prestige as cars selling at much higher prices. Thus, even at above-sticker prices, most Miata buyers got a good deal. Mazda, on the other hand, left a lot of money on the table.

Sources: Rebecca Fannin, "Mazda's Sporting Chance," *Marketing & Media Decisions*, October 1989, pp. 24–30; S. C. Gwynne, "Romancing the Roadster," *Time*, July 24, 1989, p. 39; and "The Roadster Returns," *Consumer Reports*, April 1990, pp. 232–234.

---

inexpensive models for consumers who want basic sets and larger, higher-priced models loaded with features for consumers who want the extras.

Buyer-oriented pricing means that the marketer cannot design a product and marketing program and then set the price. Good pricing begins with analyzing consumer needs and price perceptions. Price must be considered along with the other marketing-mix variables *before* the marketing program is set.[9]

ANALYZING THE PRICE-DEMAND RELATIONSHIP. Each price the company might charge will lead to a different level of demand. The relation between the price charged and the resulting demand level is shown in the familiar **demand curve** in Figure 12-4A. The demand curve shows the number of units the market will buy in a given time period at different prices that might be charged. In the normal case, demand and price are inversely related: That is, the higher the price, the lower the demand. Thus, the company would sell less if it raised its price from P_1 to P_2. In short, consumers with limited budgets will probably buy less of something if its price is too high.

Most demand curves slope downward in either a straight or a curved line, as in

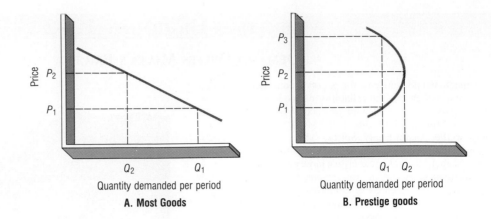

FIGURE 12-4
Two hypothetical demand schedules

Price

P_2
P_1

Q_2 Q_1
Quantity demanded per period
A. Most Goods

Price

P_3
P_2
P_1

Q_1 Q_2
Quantity demanded per period
B. Prestige goods

Figure 12-4A. But for prestige goods, the demand curve sometimes slopes upward, as in Figure 12-4B. For example, one perfume company found that by raising its price from P_1 to P_2, it sold more perfume rather than less; consumers thought the higher price meant a better or more desirable perfume. However, if the company charges too high a price (P_3), the level of demand will be lower than at P_2.

Most companies try to measure their demand curves. The type of market makes a difference. In a monopoly, the demand curve shows the total market demand resulting from different prices. If the company faces competition, its demand at different prices will depend on whether competitor's prices stay constant or change with the company's own prices. Here, we assume that competitor's prices remain constant. Later in this chapter, we discuss what happens when competitor's prices change. To measure a demand curve requires estimating demand at different prices. Figure 12-5 shows the estimated demand curve for Quaker State motor oil. Demand rises as the price is lowered from 73 cents to 38 cents, then drops between 38 cents and 32 cents, possibly due to people thinking that the oil is too cheap and may damage the car.

In measuring the price-demand relationship, the market researcher must not allow other factors affecting demand to vary. For example, if Quaker State also raised its advertising budget at the same time that it lowered its price, we would not know how much of the increased demand was due to the lower price and how much to the increased advertising. The same problem arises if a holiday weekend occurs when the lower price is set—more travel over the holidays causes people to buy more oil.

Economists show the impact of nonprice factors on demand through shifts in the demand curve rather than movements along it. Suppose the initial demand curve is D_1 in Figure 12-6. The seller is charging P and selling Q_1 units. Now suppose the economy suddenly improves or the seller doubles its advertising budget. The higher demand is reflected through an upward shift of the demand curve from D_1 to D_2. Without changing the price P, the seller's demand is now Q_2.

FIGURE 12-5
Demand schedule for Quaker State motor oil

Reprinted by permission of the publisher from "Price-Quality Relationships and Price Elasticity Under In-Store Experimentation," by Sidney Bennett and J. B. Wilkinson. Journal of Business Research, *January 1974, pp. 30–34. Copyright 1974 by Elsevier Science Publishing Co.*

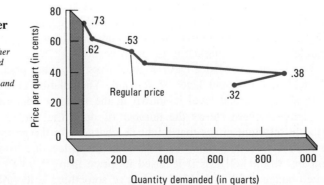

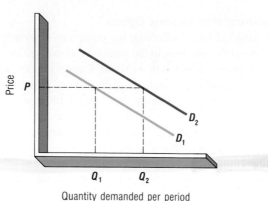

FIGURE 12-6
Effects of promotion and other nonprice variables on demand shown through shifts of the demand curve

Price

P

D_2

D_1

Q_1 Q_2

Quantity demanded per period

PRICE ELASTICITY OF DEMAND.   Marketers also need to know **price elasticity**—how responsive demand will be to a change in price. Consider the two demand curves in Figure 12-7. In Figure 12-7A, a price increase from P_1 to P_2 leads to a relatively small drop in demand from Q_1 to Q_2. In Figure 12-7B, the same price increase leads to a large drop in demand from Q_1^1 to Q_2^1. If demand hardly changes with a small change in price, we say the demand is *inelastic*. If demand changes greatly, we say the demand is *elastic*. The price elasticity of demand is given by the following formula:

$$\text{price elasticity of demand} = \frac{\%\ \text{change in quantity demanded}}{\%\ \text{change in price}}$$

Suppose demand falls by 10 percent when a seller raises its price by 2 percent. Price elasticity of demand is therefore −5 (the negative sign confirms the inverse relation between price and demand) and demand is elastic. If demand falls by 2 percent with a 2 percent increase in price, then elasticity is −1. In this case, the seller's total revenue stays the same: The seller sells fewer items but at a higher price that preserves the same total revenue. If demand falls by 1 percent when price is increased by 2 percent, then elasticity is −½ and demand is inelastic. The less elastic the demand, the more it pays for the seller to raise the price.

What determines the price elasticity of demand? Buyers are less price sensitive when the product they are buying is unique or when it is high in quality, prestige, or exclusiveness. They are also less price sensitive when substitute products are hard to find or when they cannot easily compare the quality of substitutes. Finally, buyers are less price sensitive when the total expenditure for a product is low relative to their income or when the cost is shared by another party.[10]

If demand is elastic rather than inelastic, sellers will consider lowering their price. A lower price will produce more total revenue. This makes sense as long as the extra costs of producing and selling more do not exceed the extra revenue.

Figure 12-7
Inelastic and elastic demand

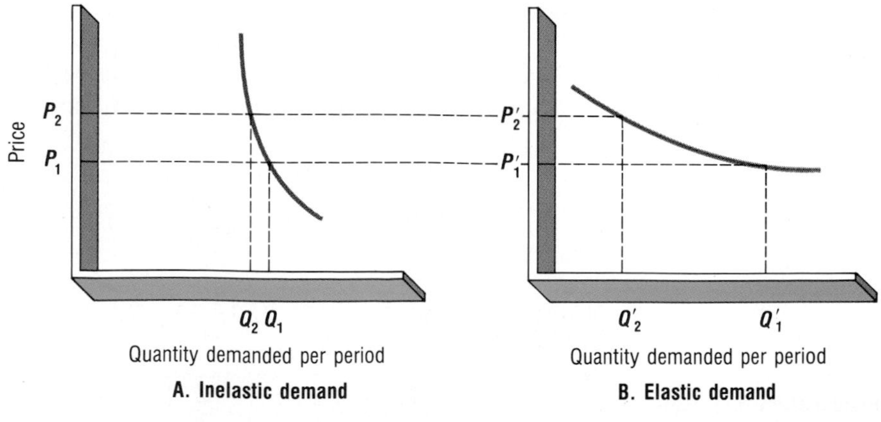

Price

P_2

P_1

Q_2 Q_1

Quantity demanded per period

A. Inelastic demand

P_2'

P_1'

Q_2' Q_1'

Quantity demanded per period

B. Elastic demand

Competitors' Prices and Offers

Another external factor affecting the company's pricing decisions is competitors' prices and their possible reactions to the company's own pricing moves. A consumer considering buying a Canon camera will evaluate Canon's price and value against the prices and values of comparable products made by Nikon, Minolta, Pentax, and others. In addition, the company's pricing strategy may affect the nature of the competition it faces. If Canon follows a high-price, high-margin strategy, it may attract competition. A low-price, low-margin strategy, however, may stop competitors or drive them out of the market.

The company needs to learn the price and quality of each competitor's offer. Canon might do this in several ways. It can send out comparison shoppers to price and compare Nikon, Minolta, and other competitors' products. It can get competitors' price lists and buy competitors' equipment and take it apart. It can ask buyers how they view the price and quality of each competitor's camera.

Once Canon is aware of competitors' prices and offers, it can use them as a starting point for its own pricing. If Canon's cameras are similar to Nikon's, it will have to price close to Nikon or lose sales. If Canon's cameras are not as good as Nikon's, the firm will not be able to charge as much. If Canon's products are better than Nikon's, it can charge more. Basically, Canon will use price to position its offer relative to competitors.

Other External Factors

When setting prices, the company must also consider other factors in its external environment. For example, *economic conditions* can have a strong impact on the outcomes of the firm's pricing strategies. Economic factors such as inflation, boom or recession, and interest rates affect pricing decisions because they affect both the costs of producing a product and consumer perceptions of the product's price and value.

The company must consider what impact its prices will have on other parties in its environment. How will *resellers* react to various prices? The company should set prices that give resellers a fair profit, encourage their support, and help them to sell the product effectively. The *government* is another important external influence on pricing decisions. Marketers need to know the laws affecting price and make sure their pricing policies are legal. The major laws affecting price are summarized in Marketing Highlight 12–3.

GENERAL PRICING APPROACHES

The price the company charges will be between one that is too low to produce a profit and one that is too high to produce any demand. Figure 12-8 summarizes the major considerations in setting price. Product costs set a floor to the price; consumer perceptions of the product's value set the ceiling. The company must consider competitors' prices and other external and internal factors to find the best price between these two extremes.

Companies set prices by selecting a general pricing approach that includes one or more of these three sets of factors. We describe the following approaches: the *cost-based approach* (cost-plus pricing, breakeven analysis, and target profit pricing), the

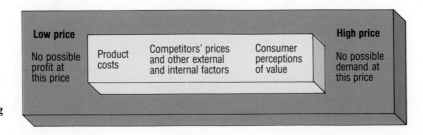

FIGURE 12-8
Major considerations in setting price

PRICE DECISIONS AND PUBLIC POLICY

Sellers must understand the law in pricing their products. In particular, they must avoid the following practices.

Price Fixing. Sellers must set prices without talking to competitors. Otherwise, price collusion is suspected. Price fixing is illegal per se—that is, the government does not accept any excuses for price fixing. The only exception is where price agreements are carried out under the supervision of a government agency, as in many local milk industry agreements, in the regulated transportation industries, and in fruit and vegetable cooperatives.

Resale Price Maintenance. A manufacturer cannot require dealers to charge a specified retail price for its product. However, the seller can propose a manufacturer's *suggested* retail price to the dealers. The manufacturer cannot refuse to sell to a dealer who takes independent pricing action, nor punish the dealer by shipping late or denying advertising allowances. However, the manufacturer can refuse to sell to a dealer on other grounds presumably not related to the dealer's pricing.

Price Discrimination. The Robinson-Patman Act seeks to ensure that sellers offer the same price terms to a given level of trade. For example, every retailer is entitled to the same price terms whether the retailer is Sears or the local bicycle shop. However, price discrimination is allowed if the seller can prove its costs are different when selling to different retailers—for example, that it costs less per unit to sell a large volume of bicycles to Sears than to sell a few bicycles to a local dealer. Or the seller can discriminate in its pricing if the seller manufactures different qualities of the same product for different retailers. The seller has to prove that these differences are proportional. Price differentials may also be used to "meet competition" in "good faith," providing the firm is trying to meet competitors at

its own level of competition and that the price discrimination is temporary, localized, and defensive rather than offensive.

Minimum Pricing. A seller is not allowed to sell below cost with the intention of destroying competition. Wholesalers and retailers in more than half the states face laws requiring a minimum percentage markup over their cost of merchandise plus transportation. Designed to stop unfair-trade practices, these laws attempt to protect small merchants from larger merchants who might sell items below cost to attract customers.

Price Increases. Companies are free to increase their prices to any level except in times of price controls. The major exception to the freedom of pricing is regulated public utilities. Because utilities have monopoly power, their rates are regulated in the public interest. The government has also used its influence from time to time to discourage major industry price hikes during periods of shortages or inflation.

Deceptive Pricing. Deceptive pricing is more common in the sale of consumer goods than industrial goods, because consumers typically possess less information and buying skill. In 1958, the Automobile Information Disclosure Act required auto manufacturers to affix on auto windshields a statement of the manufacturer's suggested retail price, the prices of optional equipment, and the dealer's transportation charges. In the same year, the FTC issued its Guides Against Deceptive Pricing, warning sellers not to advertise a price reduction unless it was a saving from the usual retail price, not to advertise "factory" or "wholesale" prices unless such prices were what they claimed to be, not to advertise comparable value prices on imperfect goods, and so forth.

Source: See Thomas T. Nagle, *The Strategy and Tactics of Pricing* (Englewood Cliffs, NJ: Prentice Hall, 1987), pp. 321–37

---

buyer-based approach (perceived-value pricing), and the *competition-based approach* (going-rate and sealed-bid pricing).

Cost-Based Pricing

Cost-Plus Pricing

The simplest pricing method is **cost-plus-pricing**—adding a standard markup to the cost of the product. Construction companies, for example, submit job bids by estimating the total project cost and adding a standard markup for profit. Lawyers, accountants, and other professionals typically price by adding a standard markup to their costs. Some seller tell their customers they will charge cost plus a specified markup; for example, aerospace companies price this way to the government.

To illustrate markup pricing, suppose a toaster manufacturer had the following costs and expected sales:

Variable cost	$10
Fixed cost	$300,000
Expected unit sales	50,000

Then the manufacturer's cost per toaster is given by:

$$\text{Unit cost} = \text{Variable cost} + \frac{\text{fixed costs}}{\text{unit sales}} = \$10 + \frac{\$300,000}{50,000} = \$16$$

Now suppose the manufacturer wants to earn a 20 percent markup on sales. The manufacturer's markup price is given by:[11]

$$\text{Markup price} = \frac{\text{unit cost}}{(1 - \text{desired return on sales})} = \frac{\$16}{1 - .2} = \$20$$

The manufacturer would charge dealers $20 per toaster and make a profit of $4 a unit. The dealers in turn will mark up the toaster's price. If dealers want to earn 50 percent on sales price, they will mark up the toaster to $40 ($20 + 50% of $40). This number is equivalent to a *markup on cost* of 100 percent ($20/$20).

Markups vary considerably among different goods. Some common markups (on price, not cost) in supermakets are 9 percent on baby foods, 14 percent on tobacco products, 20 percent on bakery products, 27 percent on dried foods and vegetables, 37 percent on spices and extracts, and 50 percent on greeting cards.[12] But these markups vary widely from the averages. In the spices and extracts category, for example, markups on retail price range from a low of 19 percent to a high of 56 percent. Markups are generally higher on seasonal items (to cover the risk of not selling), specialty items, slower moving items, items with high storage and handling costs, and items with inelastic demand.

Does using standard markups to set prices make logical sense? Generally, no. Any pricing method that ignores current demand and competition is not likely to lead to the best price. Suppose the toaster manufacturer charges $20 but only sells 30,000 toasters instead of 50,000. Then the unit cost is higher because the fixed costs are spread over fewer units, and the realized percentage markup on sales is lower. Markup pricing only works if that price actually brings in the expected level of sales.

Still, markup pricing remains popular for many reasons. First, sellers are more certain about costs than about demand. By tying the price to cost, sellers simplify pricing—they do not have to make frequent adjustments as demand changes. Second, when all firms in the industry use this pricing method, prices tend to be similar and price competition is thus minimized. Third, many people believe that cost-plus pricing is fairer to both buyers and sellers. Sellers earn a fair return on their investment but do not take advantage of buyers when buyers' demand becomes great.

Breakeven Analysis and Target Profit Pricing

Another cost-oriented pricing approach is **breakeven pricing** or a variation called **target profit pricing.** The firm tries to determine the price at which it will break even or make the target profit it is seeking. Target pricing is used by General Motors, which prices its automobiles to achieve a 15 to 20 percent profit on its investment. This pricing method is also used by public utilities, which are constrained to make a fair return on their investment.

Target pricing uses the concept of a *breakeven chart*. A breakeven chart shows the total cost and total revenue expected at different sales volume levels. Figure 12-9 shows a breakeven chart for the toaster manufacturer previously discussed. Fixed costs are $300,000 regardless of sales volume. Variable costs are added to fixed costs to form total costs, which rise with volume. The total revenue curve starts at zero and rises with each unit sold. The slope of the total revenue curve reflects the price of $20 per unit.

The total revenue and total cost curves cross at 30,000 units. This is the *breakeven volume*. At $20, the company must sell at least 30,000 units to break even; that is, for total revenue to cover total cost. Breakeven can be calculated using the following formula:

$$\text{Breakeven volume} = \frac{\text{fixed cost}}{\text{price} - \text{variable cost}} = \frac{\$300,000}{\$20 - \$10} = \$30,000$$

If the company wants to make a target profit, it must sell more units at $20 each. Suppose the toaster manufacturer has invested $1 million in the business and wants to set price to earn a 20 percent return, or $200,000. It must sell at least 50,000 units at $20 each. If the company charges a higher price, it will not need to sell as many toasters to achieve its target return. But the market may not buy even this lower volume at the higher price. Much depends on the price elasticity and competitors' prices.

The manufacturer should consider different prices and estimate breakeven volumes,

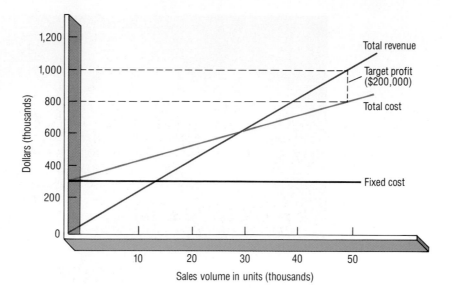

FIGURE 12-9
Breakeven chart for determining target price

probable demand, and profits for each. This is shown in Table 12-1. The table shows that as price increases, breakeven volume drops (column 2). But as price increases, demand for the toasters also falls off (column 3). At the $14 price, because the manufacturer clears only $4 per toaster ($14 less $10 in variable costs), it must sell a very high volume to break even. Even though the low price attracts many buyers, demand still falls below the high breakeven point, and the manufacturer loses money. At the other extreme, with a $22 price the manufacturer clears $12 per toaster and must sell only 25,000 units to break even. But at this high price, consumers buy too few toasters, and profits are negative. The table shows that a price of $18 yields the highest profits. Note that none of the prices produce the manufacturer's target profit of $200,000. To achieve this target return, the manufacturer will have to search for ways to lower fixed or variable costs, thus lowering the breakeven.

Buyer-Based Pricing

An increasing number of companies are basing their prices on the product's perceived value. **Perceived-value pricing** uses buyers' perceptions of value, not the seller's cost, as the key to pricing. The company uses the nonprice variables in the marketing mix to build up perceived value in the buyers' minds. Price is set to match the perceived value.

Consider the various prices different restaurants charge for the same items. A consumer who wants a cup of coffee and a slice of apple pie may pay $1.25 at a drugstore counter, $2.00 at a family restaurant, $3.50 at a hotel coffee shop, $5.00 for hotel room service, and $7.00 at an elegant restaurant. Each succeeding restaurant can charge more because of the value added by the atmosphere.

The company using perceived-value pricing must find out the value in the buyer's minds for different competitive offers. In the preceding example, consumers could be asked how much they would pay for the same coffee and pie in the different surroundings.

TABLE 12-1
Breakeven Volume and Profits at Different Prices

(1) PRICE	(2) UNIT DEMAND NEEDED TO BREAK EVEN	(3) EXPECTED UNIT DEMAND AT GIVEN PRICE	(4) TOTAL REVENUES (1) × (3)	(5) TOTAL COSTS*	(6) PROFIT (4) − (5)
$14	75,000	71,000	$ 994,000	$1,100,000	−$32,000
16	50,000	67,000	1,072,000	970,000	102,000
18	37,500	60,000	1,080,000	900,000	180,000
20	30,000	42,000	840,000	720,000	120,000
22	25,000	23,000	506,000	530,000	−24,000

* Assumes fixed costs of $300,000 and constant unit variable costs of $10.

In a disposable world, is there a place for a vase designed to last centuries?

Some Waterford® patterns available today were designed over 200 years ago. To many, this ability to transcend time may seem remarkable. To us, it's simply the criterion that determines whether or not a design is worthy of the designation "Waterford."

WATERFORD
Steadfast in a world of wavering standards.

Perceived value: A less expensive vase would hold flowers, but some consumers will pay much more for the intangibles.

Sometimes consumers could be asked how much they would pay for each benefit added to the offer. If the seller charges more than the buyers' perceived value, the company's sales will suffer. Many companies overprice their products, and their products sell poorly. Other companies underprice. Underpriced products sell very well, but they produce less revenue than they would if price were raised to the perceived-value level.[13]

Competition-Based Pricing

Going-Rate Pricing

In **going-rate pricing**, the firm bases its price largely on *competitors'* prices, with less attention paid to its *own* costs or demand. The firm might charge the same, more, or less than its major competitors. In oligopolistic industries that sell a commodity such as steel, paper, or fertilizer, firms normally charge the same price. The smaller firms follow the leader: They change their prices when the market leader's prices change, rather than when their own demand or cost changes. Some firms may charge a bit more or less, but they hold the amount of difference constant. Thus minor gasoline retailers usually charge a few cents less than the major oil companies, without letting the difference increase or decrease.

Going-rate pricing is quite popular. When demand elasticity is hard to measure, firms feel that the going price represents the collective wisdom of the industry concerning

TABLE 12-2
Effect of Different Bids
on Expected Profit

COMPANY'S BID	COMPANY'S PROFIT (1)	PROBABILITY OF WINNING WITH THIS BID (ASSUMED) (2)	EXPECTED PROFIT [(1) × (2)]
$ 9,500	$ 100	.81	$ 81
10,000	600	.36	216
10,500	1,100	.09	99
11,000	1,600	.01	16

the price that will yield a fair return. They also feel that holding to the going price will avoid harmful price wars.

Sealed-Bid Pricing

Competition-based pricing is also used when firms *bid* for jobs. Using **sealed-bid pricing,** a firm bases its price on how it thinks competitors will price rather than on its own costs or demand. The firm wants to win a contract, and winning the contract requires pricing lower than other firms.

Yet the firm cannot set its price below a certain level. It cannot price below cost without harming its position. On the other hand, the higher it sets its price above its costs, the lower its chance of getting the contract.

The net effect of the two opposite pulls can be described in terms of the *expected profit* of the particular bid (see Table 12-2). Suppose a bid of $9,500 would yield a high chance (say .81) of getting the contract, but only a low profit (say $100). The expected profit with this bid is therefore $81. If the firm bid $11,000, its profit would be $1,600, but its chance of getting the contract might be reduced to .01. The expected profit would be only $16. Thus, the company might bid the price that would maximize the expected profit. According to Table 12-2, the best bid would be $10,000, for which the expected profit is $216.

Using expected profit as a basis for setting price makes sense for the large firm that makes many bids. By playing the odds, the firm will make maximum profits in the long run. But a firm that bids only occasionally or needs a particular contract badly will not find the expected-profit approach useful. The approach, for example, does not distinguish between a $100,000 profit with a .10 probability and a $12,500 profit with an .80 probability. Yet the firm that wants to keep production going would prefer the second contract to the first.

■ SUMMARY

Despite the increased role of nonprice factors in the modern marketing process, *price* remains an important element in the marketing mix. Many internal and external factors influence the company's pricing decisions. *Internal factors* include the firm's *marketing objectives*, *marketing mix strategy*, *costs*, and *organization for pricing*.

The pricing strategy is largely determined by the company's *target market and positioning objectives*. Common pricing objectives include survival, current profit maximization, market-share leadership, and product quality leadership.

Price is only one of the marketing mix tools the company uses to accomplish its objectives, and pricing decisions affect and are affected by product design, distribution, and promotion decisions. Price decisions must be carefully coordinated with the other marketing mix decisions when designing the marketing program.

Costs set the floor for the company's price—the price must cover all the costs of making and selling the product,

plus a fair rate of return. Management must decide who within the organization is responsible for setting price. In large companies, some pricing authority may be delegated to lower-level managers and salespeople, but top management usually sets pricing policies and approves proposed prices. Production, finance, and accounting managers also influence pricing.

External factors that influence pricing decisions include the nature of the market and demand, competitors' prices and offers, and other external factors such as the economy, reseller needs, and government actions. The seller's pricing freedom varies with different types of markets. Pricing is especially challenging in markets characterized by monopolistic competition or oligopoly.

In the end, the consumer decides whether the company has set the right price. The consumer weighs the price against the perceived values of using the product—if the price exceeds the sum of the values, consumers will not buy the product. Consumers differ in the values they assign to different product features, and marketers often vary their pricing strategies for different price segments. When assessing the market and demand, the company estimates the demand schedule, which shows the probable quantity purchased per period at alternative price levels. The more *inelastic* the demand, the higher the company can set its price. *Demand* and *consumer value perceptions* set the ceiling for prices.

Consumers compare a product's price to the prices of competitors' products. A company must learn the price and quality of competitors' offers and use them as a starting point for its own pricing.

The company can select one or a combination of three general pricing approaches: the *cost-based approach* (cost-plus or breakeven analysis and target profit pricing), the *buyer-based* (perceived-value) *approach*, and the *competition-base* (going-rate or sealed-bid pricing) *approach*.

■ QUESTIONS FOR DISCUSSION

1. Certain ''inexpensive'' products that waste energy, provide few servings per container, or require frequent maintenance may *cost* much more to own and use than products selling for a higher *price*. How can marketers use this information on ''true cost'' to gain a competitive edge in pricing and promoting their products?

2. Armco, a major sheet metal producer, has developed a process for galvanizing steel sheets so that they can be painted—something not previously possible. These sheets could be used in car-body parts to prevent rust. What factors should Armco consider in setting a price for this new product?

3. Many supermarkets put unit pricing labels on their shelves, which tell consumers the actual cost per ounce or item. Would these make the customer focus more on price? What changes in buying behavior would you expect?

4. Which type of cost is more relevant in setting the price of a product—fixed costs or variable costs? Why?

5. Detergent A is priced at $2.19 for 32 ounces, while detergent B is priced at $1.99 for 26 ounces. Which appears most attractive? Which is the better value, assuming equal quality? Is there a psychological reason to price in this way?

6. Genentech, a high technology pharmaceutical company, has developed a clot-dissolving drug called TPA that will halt a heart attack in progress. TPA saves lives, minimizes hospital stays, and reduces damage to the heart itself. It is priced at $2,200 per dose. What pricing approach does Genentech appear to be using? Is demand for this drug likely to be elastic with price?

7. In a supermarket, will hamburger or steak have the higher price elasticity of demand? If the demand for steak is elastic, what effect would raising the price of steak have on the profits of the meat department?

8. In test markets, Procter & Gamble replaced 16-ounce packages of regular Folgers coffee with 13-ounce ''fast roast'' packages. Fast-roast processing allows Procter & Gamble to use fewer green coffee beans per pack with no impact on flavor or the number of servings per package. What pricing approach was appropriate for setting the price for the fast roast coffee—cost-based, buyer-based, or competition-based?

9. You have inherited an automatic car wash with annual fixed costs of $50,000 and variable costs of 50 cents per car. You think people would be willing to pay $1 to have their car washed. What would be the break-even volume at that price?

10. Sales of Fleischmann's gin *increased* when prices were raised 22 percent during a two-year period. What does this tell you about the demand curve and the elasticity of demand for Fleischmann's gin? What does this suggest about using perceived-value pricing in marketing alcoholic beverages?

11. Columnist Dave Barry jokes that federal law requires this message under the sticker price of new cars: ''WARNING· TO STUPID PEOPLE: DO NOT PAY THIS AMOUNT.'' Why is the sticker price generally higher than the actual selling price of a car? How do car dealers set the actual prices of the cars they sell?

■ KEY TERMS

Breakeven pricing (target profit pricing). Setting price to break even on the costs of making and marketing a product, or to make the desired profit.

Cost-plus pricing. Adding a standard markup to the cost of the product.

Demand curve. A curve that shows the number of units the market will buy in a given time period, at different prices that might be charged.

Experience curve (learning curve). The drop in the average per-unit production cost that comes with accumulated production experience.

Fixed costs. Costs that do not vary with production or sales level.

Going-rate pricing. Setting price based largely on following competitors' prices rather than on company costs or demand.

Monopolistic competition. A market in which many buyers and sellers trade over a range of prices rather than a single market price.

Oligopolistic competition. A market in which there are a few sellers who are highly sensitive to each other's pricing and marketing strategies.

Perceived-value pricing. Setting price based on buyers' perceptions of value rather than on the seller's cost.

Price. The amount of money charged for a product or service, or the sum of the values consumers exchange for the benefits of having or using the product or service.

Price elasticity. A measure of the sensitivity of demand to changes in price.

Pure competition. A market in which many buyers and sellers trade in a uniform commodity—no single buyer or seller has much effect on the going market price.

Pure monopoly. A market in which there is a single seller—it may be a government monopoly, a private regulated monopoly, or a private nonregulated monopoly.

Sealed-bid pricing. Setting price based on how the firm thinks competitors will price rather than on its own costs or demand—used when a company bids for jobs.

Total costs. The sum of the fixed and variable costs for any given level of production.

Variable costs. Costs that vary directly with the level of production.

■ REFERENCES

1. See James E. Ellis and Brian Bremner, "Will the Big Markdown Get the Big Store Moving Again?" *Business Week*, March 13, 1989, pp. 110–14; Bremner, "Now Sears Has Everyday Low Profits, Too," *Business Week*, August 21, 1989; and Kate Fitzgerald, "Sears' Plan on the Ropes," January 8, 1990, pp. 1, 42.

2. See David J. Schwartz, *Marketing Today: A Basic Approach*, 3rd ed. (New York: Harcourt Brace Jovanovich, 1981), pp. 270–73.

3. See "Segmentation Strategies Create New Pressure among Marketers," *Marketing News*, March 28, 1986, p. 1.

4. Kathleen Deveny, "Sub-Zero Isn't Trembling Over a Little Competition," Business Week, March 3, 1986, p. 118.

5. Here accumulated production is drawn on a semi-log scale so that equal distances represent the same percentage increase in output.

6. For more on experience curve strategies, see Pankaj Ghemawat, "Building Strategy on the Experience Curve," *Harvard Business Review*, March–April 1985, pp. 143–149; George S. Day and David B. Montgomery, "Diagnosing the Experience Curve," *Journal of Marketing*, Spring 1983, pp. 44–58; and William W. Alberts, "The Experience Curve Doctrine Reconsidered," *Journal of Marketing*, July 1989, pp. 36–49.

7. See P. Ronald Stephenson, William L. Cron, and Gary L. Frazier, "Delegating Pricing Authority to the Sales Force: The Effects on Sales and Profit Performance," *Journal of Marketing*, Spring 1979, pp. 21–28.

8. Thomas T. Nagle, "Pricing as Creative Marketing," *Business Horizons*, July–August 1983, p. 19.

9. See Thomas T. Nagle, *The Strategy and Tactics of Pricing* (Englewood Cliffs, NJ: Prentice Hall, 1987), pp. 1–9.

10. Ibid., Ch. 3.

11. The arithmetic of markups and margins is discussed in Appendix 1, "Marketing Arithmetic."

12. "Supermarket 1984 Sales Manual," *Progressive Grocer*, July, 1984.

13. For more on value-based pricing, see John L. Forbis and Nitin T. Mehta, "Value-Based Strategies for Industrial Products," *Business Horizons*, May–June 1981, pp. 32–42; and Ely S. Lurin, "Make Sure Product's Price Reflects Its True Value," *Marketing News*, May 8, 1987, p. 8.

SILVERADO JEWELRY: A PRICING PARADOX

Silverado Jewlery Store, located in downtown Tempe, Arizona, specializes in hand-crafted jewelry made by local Native Americans. Sheila Becker, the owner of Silverado, has just returned from a buying trip and is discussing an interesting pricing phenomenon with assistant store manager Mary Meindl.

Several months ago, the store had received a selection of mother-of-pearl stone and silver bracelets, earrings, and necklaces. Unlike the blue-green tones in typical turquoise jewlery designs, mother-of-pearl stone is pink with white marbling. In terms of size and style, the selection included a wide range of items. While some were small, round, rather simple designs, others were larger, bolder designs that were quite intricate. In addition, the collection included an assortment of traditionally styled men's studded string ties.

Sheila had purchased the mother-of-pearl selection at a very reasonable cost and was quite pleased with the distinctive product assortment. She thought the jewelry would appeal particularly to the general buyer seeking an alternative to the turquoise jewelry usually offered in shops all around Tempe. She priced the new jewelry so that shoppers would receive a good value for their money but also included a markup sufficient to cover the costs of doing business plus an average profit margin.

After the items had been displayed in the store for about a month, Sheila was disappointed in their sales. She decided to try several merchandising tactics that she had learned as a student at the University of Nevada. For example, realizing that the location of an item in the store will often influence whether or not patrons will examine merchandise, she moved the mother-of-pearl jewelry to a glass display case just to the right of the store entrance.

When sales of the mother-of-pearl merchandise still remained sluggish after the relocation, she decided to talk to store clerks about the jewelry during their weekly meeting. Suggesting that they put more effort into "pushing" this particular line, she provided them with a detailed description of the mother-of-pearl stone and supplied a short, scripted talk that they could memorize and recite for customers.

Unfortunately, this approach also failed. At this point, Sheila was preparing to leave on a buying trip. Frustrated over the sagging sales of the mother-of-pearl jewelry and anxious to reduce current inventory in order to make room for the newer selections that she would be buying, she decided to take drastic action: She would cut the mother-of-pearl prices in half. On her way out of the store, she hastily left a note for Mary Meindl. The note read:

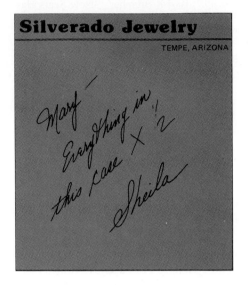

Upon her return, Sheila was pleasantly surprised to find that the entire selection of mother-of-pearl jewelry had been sold. "I really can't understand why," she commented to Mary Meindl, "but that mother-of-pearl stuff just didn't appeal to our customers. I'll have to be more careful the next time I try to increase our variety of stones." Mary responded that although she couldn't quite understand why Sheila wanted to raise the price of slow-moving merchandise, she was surprised at how quickly it had sold at higher price. Sheila was puzzled. "What higher price?" she asked. "My note said to cut the prices in half." "In *half*?" replied a startled Mary. "I thought your note said, 'Everything in this case *times two*!'" As a result, Mary had *doubled* rather than halved the prices.

QUESTIONS

1. Explain what happened in this situation. Why did the jewelry sell so quickly at twice its normal price?

2. What assumption had Sheila Becker made about the demand curve for the mother-of-pearl jewelry? What did the demand curve for this particular product actually look like?

3. In what type of market is Silverado Jewelry operating (pure competition, monopolistic competition, oligopolistic competition, or pure monopoly)? What leads you to this conclusion?

4. How would the concept of psychological pricing be useful to Sheila Becker? How would you advise her about future pricing decisions?

PERFUME

It seems $180 or so an ounce isn't too high a price to pay to feel good about yourself—or so the marketers of perfumes hope.

There are over 700 different brands of perfume on the market, with new brands introduced each year. Celebrities such as Cher, Sophia Loren, Jane Seymour, Elizabeth Taylor, and Linda Evans are spokespersons for brands they hope women will enjoy. Even designers and high-profile stores have been getting in on the act.

Marketers hope that when a consumer buys a perfume, she will adopt it as her own. The right perfume can help a woman feel feminine and attractive, independent and confident, special and with a more positive outlook. So, is $180 too much to spend to feel good about yourself? Many consumers believe the benefits are well worth the price.

But consumers might be surprised to learn that the cost of producing many perfumes is actually quite low. The ingredients might cost $5, with a similar amount going for the bottle and package. The sales representative might receive an additional $5, with the balance of the sales price split between the retailer and the producer of the brand.

The makers of Obsession spent $17 million to launch their perfume, while it cost an estimated $10 million to promote Poison. The high profile of glamorous celebrities and organizations such as Giorgio's helps promote an image of prestige. The high price enhances the image.

Bic, the company famous for its disposable pens, razors, and lighters, decided to challenge conventional wisdom by introducing its own potion with a suggested retail price of $5. There were actually four perfumes—two for women (Parfum Bic Jour and Parfum Bic Noir) and two for men (Parfum Bic for Men and Parfum Bic Sport).

Société Bic, the French parent concern, decided to launch the four perfumes in the U.S. market despite mixed sales results in the French, Italian, and British markets, where the perfumes were introduced in 1988. BIC Corpora-tion, a Milford, Connecticut unit, expected to sell the perfumes through traditional BIC distribution channels such as drugstores, supermarkets, and mass merchandisers. Their strategy was to maintain the BIC heritage of offering high quality at affordable prices and products that are convenient to purchase and convenient to use. BIC was out to serve the customer who was interested in a fine-quality product that was affordable enough to use every day. While the scent was subtle and the price modest, the message wasn't. BIC spent $22 million on advertising and promotion in the first year alone.

The ads, with the tag line ''Paris in Your Pocket,'' featured a stylized yet playful look at Paris. The theme, written in impressionistic watercolors, was augmented by depictions of a 10-franc coin, a gendarme's cap, and a miniature Eiffel Tower. Of the $22 million budget, $15 million was devoted to a media/print campaign and $7 million was spent on promotions such as scent strips in stores and $35 French scarfs available for $5 with any $5 purchase of the perfume.

Clearly BIC hoped to succeed where Bristol-Myers hadn't. Bristol-Myers had introduced a $5 fragrance called Savvy in the 1970s, but later withdrew it because sales did not meet company expectations.

QUESTIONS

1. Explain the nature of the demand curve for a prestige product as it applies to more expensive perfumes.
2. Assuming perfume marketers are in monopolistic competition, discuss the relative freedom they have in pricing.
3. Discuss the elasticity of demand facing marketers of more expensive perfumes.
4. What factors are likely to influence the price elasticity of demand for perfume?

Sources: ''France's BIC Bets U.S. Consumers Will Go for Perfume on the Cheap,'' *The Wall Street Journal*, January 12, 1989, p. B 4; ''$22 Million Campaign Urges: Spritz Your BIC,'' *Advertising Age*, February 20, 1989, pp. 3–69; ''Will $4 Perfume Do the Trick for BIC?'', *Business Week*, June 20, 1988, pp. 89–92; ''BIC Begins Campaign for New Perfume Line,'' *The New York Times*, March 20, 1989, p. 9; and ''Of Flicks and Flickers,'' *Financial World*, January 10, 1989, pp. 60–61.

13

Pricing Products: Pricing Strategies

Caterpillar Tractor Company, the world's leading maker of heavy construction and mining equipment, has been locked in a long price war with Japanese challenger Komatsu Ltd. In this bloody battle, both companies are using price to buy long-run market share, even if it means lower profits or losses in the short-run.

For more than 50 years, Caterpillar has dominated the U.S. and world markets for giant construction equipment. It built its 40 percent market share by emphasizing high product quality, dependable after-sale service, and a strong dealer body. It used a premium pricing strategy—making high profit margins by convincing buyers that Cat's higher quality and trouble-free operation provided greater value and justified a higher price.

But all this began to change during the early 1980s when Komatsu entered the U.S. market. The Japanese firm started cautiously in the United States, offering only a few products. It realized the importance of nonprice factors in the buyer's purchase decision. Like Caterpillar, Komatsu stressed high quality, and it expanded slowly to allow its parts and service capacity to keep up with sales. But Komatsu's major weapon for taking share from Caterpillar was price. A strong dollar and lower manufacturing costs allowed Komatsu to cut prices ruthlessly—its initial prices were as much as 40% lower than Caterpillar's. On a giant dump truck sold by Cat for $500,000, that could mean a savings of as much as $200,000! Riding its strong price advantage, Komatsu targeted a 15 percent market share.

Caterpillar fought back to protect its number one market position, and the price war was on. To support lower prices, Cat reduced its workforce by a third and slashed costs by 27 percent. It vowed to meet Komatsu's prices and in some cases even initiated price cutting. With heavy discounting by both companies, manufacturer's list prices soon became meaningless. For example, a bulldozer which lists for $140,000 might regularly sell for $110,000. In the battle for market share, all competitors lost profits. Lesser companies such as International Harvester (Navistar) and Clark Equipment were driven to the brink of ruin. Caterpillar and Komatsu also suffered. Starting in 1982, after 50 straight years of profits, Caterpillar lost $1 billion in less than three years. And Komatsu, even with its cost advantages, saw its profits decline by 30 percent.

Despite its losses, Caterpillar continued its relentless drive to cut costs and hold the line on prices. This strategy has recently begun to pay off. Thanks to an effective cost-cutting program and a falling dollar, Caterpillar has raised its prices just 5 percent a year since 1986. At the same time, it has actually improved its already vaunted quality. As a result, the company has rebounded strongly, winning back share and profits in its world markets. By contrast, facing a sharply rising yen, Komatsu has had to raise its prices seven times during the last three years. Its market share, which peaked in 1986 at 12 percent, has now dropped to 9 percent.

Thus, the long and damaging price war appears to be coming to an end. Although fierce price competition continues, Komatsu's recent round of price increases may be a signal that it wants to end the fighting and return to peaceful coexistence and better profits for both companies. It hopes that Caterpillar will respond with equivalent price increases. Says the president of Komatsu America, "If they don't meet our price increase, I'll have to think of some kind of countermeasure to ensure the survival of Komatsu and our distributors. It all depends on how much our market share declines."[1]

In this chapter, we focus on pricing dynamics. A company sets not a single price, but rather a *pricing structure* that covers different items in its line. This pricing structure changes as products move through their life cycles. The company adjusts product prices to reflect changing costs and demand and to account for variations in buyers and situations. As the competitive environment changes, the company considers initiating price changes at times and responding to them at others. This chapter examines the major dynamic pricing strategies available to management. In turn, we look at *new-product pricing strategies* for products in the introductory stage of the product life cycle, *product-mix pricing strategies* for related products in the product mix, *price-adjustment strategies* that account for customer differences and changing situations, and *strategies for initiating and responding to price changes.*[2]

NEW-PRODUCT PRICING STRATEGIES

Pricing strategies usually change as the product passes through its life cycle. The introductory stage is especially challenging. We can distinguish between pricing a real product innovation that is patent-protected and pricing a product that imitates existing products.

Pricing an Innovative Product

Companies bringing out an innovative, patent-protected product can choose between *market-skimming pricing* and *market-penetration pricing*.

Market-Skimming Pricing

Many companies that invent new products set high prices initially to "skim" revenues layer by layer from the market. Polaroid is a prime user of **marker-skimming pricing.** On its original instant camera, it charged the highest price it could, given the benefits of its new product over other products customers might buy. Polaroid set a price that made it just worthwhile for some segments of the market to adopt the new camera. After an initial sales slowdown, it then lowered the price to draw in the next price-sensitive layer of customers. Polaroid also used the same approach with its new Spectra camera. It introduced the Spectra at about twice the price of its previous entry in the field. After about a year, it began bringing out simpler, lower-priced versions to draw in new segments. In this way, Polaroid skimmed a maximum amount of revenue from the various segments of the market.[3]

Market skimming makes sense only under certain conditions. First the product's quality and image must support its higher price, and enough buyers must want the

Market skimming: Polaroid introduced its Spectra at a high price, then brought out lower-priced versions to draw in new segments.

product at that price. Second, the costs of producing a small volume cannot be so high that they cancel the advantage of charging more. Finally, competitors should not be able to enter the market easily and undercut the high price.

Market-Penetration Pricing

Rather than setting a high initial price to *skim* small but profitable market segments, other companies set a low initial price in order to *penetrate* the market quickly and deeply—to quickly attract a large number of buyers and win a large market share. Texas Instruments (TI) is a prime user of **market-penetration pricing.** TI will build a large plant, set its price as low as possible, win a large market share, realize falling costs, and then cut its price further as costs fall. Warehouse stores and discount retailers also use penetration pricing. They charge low prices to attract high volume; the high volume results in lower costs which, in turn, let the discounter keep prices low.

Several conditions favor setting a low price. The market must be highly price-sensitive so that a low price produces more market growth. Production and distribution costs must fall as sales volume increases. And the low price must help to keep out the competition.

Pricing an Imitative New Product

A company that plans to develop an imitative new product faces a product-positioning problem. It must decide where to position the product on quality and price. Figure 13-1 shows nine possible price-quality strategies. If the existing market leader has taken Box 1 by producing the premium product and charging the highest price, then the newcomer might prefer to use one of the other strategies. It could design a high-quality product and charge a medium price (Box 2), design a medium-quality product and charge a medium price (Box 5), and so on. The newcomer must consider the size and growth rate of the market in each box and the competitors it would face.

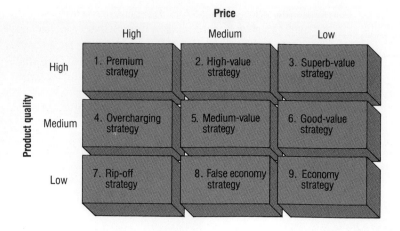

FIGURE 13-1
Nine price/quality strategies

PRODUCT-MIX PRICING STRATEGIES

The strategy for setting a price on a product often has to be changed when the product is part of a product mix. In this case, the firm looks for a set of prices that maximize the profits on the total product mix. Pricing is difficult because the various products have related demand and costs and face different degrees of competition. We present five *product-mix pricing* situations.

Product-Line Pricing
Companies usually develop product lines rather than single products. For example, Snapper makes many different lawn mowers, ranging from simple walk-behind versions priced at $259.95, $299.95, and $399.95 to elaborate riding mowers priced at $1000 or more. Each successive lawn mower in the line offers more features. In **product-line pricing**, management must determine the price steps to set between the various mowers.

Product-line pricing: Snapper sells a lawn mower for every pocketbook.

The price steps should take into account cost differences between the mowers, customer evaluations of their different features, and competitors' prices. If the price difference between two successive lawn mowers is small, buyers will usually buy the more advanced mower, which increases company profits if the cost difference is smaller than the price difference. If the price difference is large, customers will generally buy the less advanced mowers.

In many industries, sellers use well-established *price points* for the products in their line. Thus men's clothing stores might carry men's suits at three price levels: $185, $285, and $385. The customer will likely associate low-, average-, and high-quality suits with the three ''price points.'' Even if the three prices are raised a little, men will normally buy suits at their own preferred price points. The seller's task is to establish perceived quality differences that support the price differences.

Optimal-Product Pricing

Many companies use **optional-product pricing**—offering to sell optional or accessory products along with their main product. A car buyer can order electric windows, defoggers, and cruise control. Pricing these options is a sticky problem. Automobile companies must decide which items to build into the base price and which to offer as options. General Motors' normal pricing strategy is to advertise a stripped-down model for $9,000 in order to pull people into showrooms and then devote most of the showroom space to option-loaded cars priced at $11,000 or $12,000. The economy model is stripped of so many comforts and conveniences that most buyers reject it. When GM launched its new front-wheel drive J-cars in the early 1980s, it took a clue from the Japanese automakers and included in the sticker price many useful items previously sold only as options. The advertised price then represented a well-equipped car.

Captive-Product Pricing

Companies that make products which must be used along with a main product use **captive-product pricing.** Examples of captive products are razor blades, camera film, and computer software. Producers of the main products (razors, cameras, and computers) often price them low and set high markups on the supplies. Thus, Polaroid prices its cameras low because it makes its money on selling film. Those camera makers who do not sell film must price their cameras higher in order to make the same overall profit.

In the case of services, this strategy is called **two-part pricing.** The price of the service is broken into a *fixed fee* plus *variable usage rate*. A telephone company charges a monthly rate plus charges for calls beyond some minimum number. Amusement parks charge admission plus fees for food, midway attractions, and rides over a minimum. The service firm must decide how much to charge for the basic service and how much for the variable usage. The fixed amount should be low enough to induce usage of the service. Profit can be made on the variable usage fees.

By-Product Pricing

In producing processed meats, petroleum products, chemicals, and other products, there are often by-products. If the by-products have no value and getting rid of them is costly, this will affect the pricing of the main product. Using **by-product pricing,** the manufacturer will seek a market for these by-products and should accept any price that covers more than the cost of storing and delivering them. This practice allows the seller to reduce the main product's price to make it more competitive.

Product-Bundle Pricing

Using **product-bundle pricing,** sellers often combine several of their products and offer the bundle at a reduced price. Thus theaters and sports teams sell season tickets at less than the cost of single tickets; hotels sell specially priced packages that include room, meals, and entertainment; automobile companies sell attractively priced options packages. Price bundling can promote the sales of products consumers might not otherwise buy, but the combined price must be low enough to get them to buy the bundle.[4]

Product-bundle pricing: Hyatt offers a specially priced package.

PRICE-ADJUSTMENT STRATEGIES

Companies usually adjust their basic prices to account for various customer differences and changing situations. We discuss the following adjustment strategies: *discount pricing and allowances*, *discriminatory pricing*, *psychological pricing*, *promotional pricing*, and *geographical pricing*.

Discount Pricing and Allowances

Most companies adjust their basic price to reward customers for certain responses, such as early payment of bills, volume purchases, and buying off-season. These price adjustments are called *discounts* and *allowances*.

Cash Discounts

A **cash discount** is a price reduction to buyers who pay their bills promptly. A typical example is "2/10, net 30," which means that although payment is due within 30 days, the buyer can deduct 2 percent if the bill is paid within ten. The discount cannot be reserved for favored customers; it must be granted to all buyers meeting these terms. Such discounts are customary in many industries; they help improve the sellers' cash situation, reduce bad debts, and lower credit-collection costs.

Quantity Discounts

A **quantity discount** is a price reduction to buyers who buy large volumes. A typical example might be "$10 per unit for less than 100 units, $9 per unit for 100 or more units." Like cash discounts, quantity discounts must be offered to all customers and they must not exceed the seller's cost savings associated with selling large quantities. These savings include lower selling, inventory, and transportation expenses. Discounts provide an incentive to the customer to buy more from a given seller rather than buying from many sources.

Functional Discounts

A **functional discount** (also called a *trade discount*) is offered by the seller to trade channel members—retailers and wholesalers—who perform certain functions such as selling, storing, and record-keeping. Manufacturers may offer different functional discounts to different trade channels because of the varying services they perform, but manufacturers must offer the same functional discounts within each trade channel.

Seasonal Discounts

A **seasonal discount** is a price reduction to buyers who buy merchandise or services out-of-season. Seasonal discounts allow the seller to keep production steady during an entire year. Ski manufacturers offer seasonal discounts to retailers in the spring and summer to encourage early ordering. Hotels, motels, and airlines offer seasonal discounts in their slow periods.

Allowances

Allowances are other types of reductions from the list price. For example, **trade-in allowances** are price reductions given for turning in an old item when buying a new one. Trade-in allowances are most common in the automobile industry and are also given for some other durable goods. **Promotional allowances** are payments or price reductions to reward dealers for participating in advertising and sales-support programs.

Discriminatory Pricing

Companies often adjust their basic prices to allow for differences in customers, products, and locations. In **discriminatory pricing,** the company sells a product or service at two or more prices, even though the difference in prices is not based on differences in costs. Discriminatory pricing takes several forms:

- *Customer-segment pricing*—different customers pay different prices for the same product or service. Museums, for example, often charge a lower admission for students and senior citizens.
- *Product-form pricing*—different versions of the product are priced differently but not according to differences in their costs. Black & Decker prices its most expensive iron at $54.98, which is twelve dollars more than its next most expensive iron. The top model has a self-cleaning feature, yet this extra feature costs only a few more dollars to make.
- *Location pricing*—different locations are priced differently even though the cost of offering each location is the same. For instance, a theatre varies its seat prices because of audience preferences for certain locations. State universities charge higher tuition for out-of-state students.
- *Time pricing*—prices are varied seasonally, by the month, by the day, and even by the hour. Public utilities vary their prices to commercial users by time of day and weekend versus weekday. The telephone company offers lower "off-peak" charges, and resorts give seasonal discounts.

For discriminatory pricing to be an effective strategy for the company, certain conditions must exist. The market must be segmentable and the segments must show different degrees of demand. Members of the segment paying the lower price should not be able to turn around and resell the product to the segment paying the higher price. Competitors should not be able to undersell the firm in the segment being charged the higher price. Nor should the costs of segmenting and watching the market exceed the extra revenue obtained from the price difference. The practice should not lead to customer resentment and ill will. Finally, the discriminatory pricing must be legal.

With the deregulation of certain industries, such as airlines and trucking, companies in these industries have used more discriminatory pricing. Consider the pricing used by airlines. The passengers on a plane bound from Raleigh to Los Angeles may pay as many as ten different round-trip fares for the same flight—first class; first class-night; first class-night, child; first class-youth; coach; coach-night; coach-night, child; Super-Saver, nonrefundable fare; Super-Saver, 25 percent cancellation penalty; and military

Discriminatory pricing: AT&T offers lower prices to those who make calls at "offpeak" hours.

personnel. These fares vary from $238 to $1512! Travelers who check carefully benefit from the intense competition among different carriers flying this route.

Psychological Pricing
Price indicates something about the product. For example, many consumers use price to judge quality. A $100 bottle of perfume may contain only $3 worth of scent, but some people are willing to pay $100 because this price indicates something special.

In using **psychological pricing,** sellers consider the psychology of prices and not simply the economics. For example, one study of the relationship between price and quality perceptions of cars found that consumers perceive higher-priced cars as having higher quality.[5] By the same token, higher quality cars are perceived to be even higher priced than they actually are! When consumers can judge the quality of a product by examining it or by calling upon past experience with it, they use price less to judge quality. But when consumers cannot judge quality because they lack the information or skill, price becomes an important quality signal (see Marketing Highlight 13–1).[6]

Another aspect of psychological pricing is **reference prices.** These are prices that buyers carry in their minds and refer to when they look at a given product. The reference price might be formed by noting current prices, remembering past prices, or assessing the buying situation. Sellers can influence or use these consumers' reference prices when setting price. For example, a company could display its product next to more expensive ones in order to imply that it belongs in the same class. Department stores often sell women's clothing in separate departments differentiated by price: Clothing found in the more expensive department is assumed to be of better quality. Companies can also influence consumers' reference prices by stating high manufacturer's suggested prices, or by indicating that the product was originally priced much higher, or by pointing to a competitor's higher price.

Even small differences in price can suggest product differences. Consider a stereo

344   PART IV   ■   DEVELOPING THE MARKETING MIX

priced at $300 compared to one priced at $299.95. The actual price difference is only 5 cents, but the psychological difference can be much greater. For example, some consumers will see the $299.95 as a price in the $200 range rather than the $300 range. Although the $299.95 will more likely be seen as a bargain price, the $300 price suggests more quality. Some psychologists argue that each digit has symbolic and visual qualities that should be considered in pricing. Thus, 8 is round and even and creates a soothing effect, and 7 is angular and creates a jarring effect.

Promotional Pricing

With **promotional pricing,** companies temporarily price their products below list price, and sometimes even below cost. Promotional pricing takes several forms. Supermarkets and department stores often price a few products as *loss leaders* to attract customers to the store in the hope that they will buy other items at normal markups. Sellers also use *special-event pricing* in certain seasons to draw more customers. Thus, linens are promotionally priced every January to attract weary Christmas shoppers back into stores. Manufacturers sometimes offer *cash rebates* to consumers who buy the product from dealers within a specified time. The manufacturer sends the rebate directly to the customer. Rebates have recently been popular with autos, durable goods, and small appliance producers. Some manufacturers offer *low-interest financing*, *longer warranties*, or *free maintenance* to reduce the consumer's "price." This practice has recently become a favorite of the auto industry. Or, the seller may simply offer *discounts* from normal prices to increase sales and reduce inventories.

Geographical Pricing

A company must also decide how to price its products to customers in different parts of the country. Should the company risk losing the business of more distant customers by charging them higher prices to cover the higher shipping costs? Or should the company charge the same to all customers regardless of location? Following are five geographical pricing strategies for this hypothetical situation:

> The Peerless Paper Company is located in Atlanta, Georgia, and sells paper products to customers across the United States. The cost of freight is high and affects the companies from whom customers buy their paper. Peerless wants to establish a geographical pricing policy. It is trying to determine how to price a $100 order to three specific customers: Customer A (Atlanta), Customer B (Bloomington, Indiana), and Customer C (Compton, California).

FOB-Origin Pricing

On one hand, Peerless can ask each customer to pay the shipping cost from Atlanta factory to the customer's location. All three customers would pay the same factory price of $100, with Customer A paying, say, $10 for shipping, Customer B $15, and Customer C $25. Called **fob-origin pricing,** this practice means that the goods are

Promotion pricing: Companies often reduce their prices temporarily to produce sales.

placed *free on board* (hence, *FOB*) a carrier, at which point the title and responsibility pass to the customer, who pays the freight from the factory to the destination.

Because each customer picks up its own cost, supporters of FOB pricing feel that this is the fairest way to assess freight charges. The disadvantage, however, is that Peerless will be a high-cost firm to distant customers. If Peerless's main competitor happens to be in California, this competitor will no doubt outsell Peerless in California. In fact, the competitor would outsell Peerless in most of the West, while Peerless would dominate the East. A vertical line could actually be drawn on a map connecting the cities where the two companies' prices plus freight would be roughly equal. Peerless would have the price advantage east of this line, and its competitor would have the price advantage west of this line.

Uniform Delivered Pricing
By contrast, **uniform delivered pricing** is the exact opposite of FOB pricing. The company charges the same price plus freight to all customers regardless of their location.

The freight charge is set at the average freight cost. Suppose this is $15. Uniform delivered pricing therefore results in a high charge to the Atlanta customer (who pays $15 freight instead of $10) and a lower charge to the Compton customer (who pays $15 instead of $25). The Atlanta customer would prefer to buy paper from another local paper company that uses FOB-origin pricing. On the other hand, Peerless has a better chance to win the California customer. Other advantages are that uniform delivered pricing is fairly easy to administer and lets the firm advertise its price nationally.

Zone Pricing

Zone pricing falls between FOB-origin pricing and uniform delivered pricing. The company sets up two or more zones. All customers within a given zone pay a single total price, and this price is higher in the more distant zones. For example, Peerless might set up an East Zone and charge $10 freight to all customers in this zone, a Midwest Zone in which it charges $15, and a West Zone where it charges $25. In this way, the customers within a given price zone receive no price advantage from the company. Customers in Atlanta and Boston pay the same total price to Peerless. The complaint, however, is that the Atlanta customer is paying part of the Boston customer's freight cost. In addition, even though they may be within a few miles of each other, a customer just barely on the west side of the line dividing the East and Midwest pays more than one just barely on the east side of the line.

Basing-Point Pricing

Using **basing-point pricing,** the seller selects a given city as a "basing point" and charges all customers the freight cost from that city to the customer location regardless of the city from which the goods are actually shipped. For example, Peerless might set Chicago as the basing point and charge all customers $100 plus the freight from Chicago to their locations. This means that an Atlanta customer pays the freight cost from Chicago to Atlanta even though the goods may be shipped from Atlanta. Using a basing-point location other than the factory raises the total price to customers near the factory and lowers the total price to customers far from the factory.

If all sellers used the same basing-point city, delivered prices would be the same for all customers and price competition would be eliminated. Such industries as sugar, cement, steel, and automobiles used basing-point pricing for years, but this method is less popular today. Some companies set up multiple basing points to create more flexibility: They quote freight charges from the basing-point city nearest to the customer.

Freight Absorption Pricing

Finally, the seller who is eager to do business with a certain customer or geographical area might use **freight-absorption pricing.** This involves absorbing all or part of the actual freight charges in order to get the business. The seller might reason that if it can get more business, its average costs will fall and more than compensate for its extra freight cost. Freight-absorption pricing is used for market penetration and also to hold on to increasingly competitive markets.

PRICE CHANGES

Initiating Price Changes

After developing their price structures and strategies, companies may face occasions when they will want either to cut or to raise prices.

Initiating Price Cuts

Several situations may lead a firm to consider cutting its price. One is excess capacity. The firm needs more business and cannot get it through increased sales effort, product improvement, or other measures. In the late 1970s, many companies dropped "follow-the-leader pricing"—that is, charging about the same price as their leading competitor—and aggressively cut prices to boost their sales. But as the airline, construction equipment, and other industries have learned in recent years, cutting prices in an industry loaded with excess capacity may lead to price wars as competitors try to retain market share.

Another situation is falling market share in the face of strong price competition. Several American industries—automobiles, consumer electronics, cameras, watches, and steel—have been losing market share to Japanese competitors whose high-quality products carry lower prices than their American counterparts. Zenith, General Motors, and other American companies have resorted to more aggressive pricing action. General Motors, for example, cut its sub-compact car prices by 10 percent on the West Coast, where Japanese competition is strongest.

Companies may also cut prices in a drive to dominate the market through lower costs. Either the company starts with lower costs than its competitors or it cuts prices in the hope of gaining market share that will cut costs through larger volume. Bausch and Lomb used an aggressive low-cost, low-price strategy to become the leader in the competitive soft contact lens market (see Marketing Highlight 13–2).

Initiating Price Increases

On the other hand, many companies have had to *raise* prices in recent years. They do this knowing that the price increases may be resented by customers, dealers, and their own salesforce. Yet a successful price increase can greatly increase profits. For example, if the company's profit margin is 3 percent of sales, a 1 percent price increase will increase profits by 33 percent if sales volume is unaffected.

A major factor in price increases is cost inflation. Rising costs squeeze profit margins and lead companies to regular rounds of price increases. Companies often raise their prices by more than the cost increase in anticipation of further inflation. Companies do not want to make long-run price agreements with customers—they fear that cost inflation will eat into profit margins. Another factor leading to price increases

---

MARKETING HIGHLIGHT 13–2

BAUSCH AND LOMB'S HARDBALL PRICING

Bausch & Lomb was the first company to develop and sell soft contact lenses. For many years after introducing these lenses in the early 1970s, B&L held 100 percent of the market. But in the late 1970s, as a dozen competitors entered the soft lens market, Bausch & Lomb quickly lost its market-share dominance. To make matters worse, the company was late in developing extended-wear lenses—thinner soft lenses that can be worn for up to a month at a time without taking them out. By the early 1980s, B&L's overall share had dropped to less than 50 percent, largely because it had no share of the fast-growing extended-wear lens segment.

Bausch finally brought out its own brand of extended-wear lenses in 1983—two years after competitors' entries. To overcome its late start, B&L used all of its considerable marketing strength and a tough marketing strategy. At the heart of this strategy was aggressive low pricing. *Business Week* describes Bausch's "hardball pricing" and competitors' reactions:

> [Bausch & Lomb's] entry price of $20 was 50% or more below the industry norm for extended-wear lenses. . . . [Competitor] CooperVision hit back in March with a new, top-quality lens it offered for about $15 wholesale. Bausch retaliated in April by lowering all its prices even further. Now its high-water model wholesales for $10 to $15, while its basic low-water lens lists at $8 to $13 depending on volume, and a

new daily-wear lens has been introduced at a low price of $7 to $12.

> Thus, shortly after entering the market, Bausch was selling its high-quality lenses for only 20 to 30 percent of competitors' previous prices. The company's aggressive initial pricing—and its quick reactions to competitors' price thrusts—paid off well:

> Within a month, B&L's sales staff had supplies of the new lenses in more than 90% of the 12,000 professional eye-care outlets in the U.S. that sell contact lenses. Within four months, Bausch captured 37% of the [extended-wear lens] market and was the No. 1 marketer.

> Bausch & Lomb's low price resulted in large volume, which in turn lowered unit-production costs, allowing still lower prices. Bausch is now firmly positioned as the industry's lost-cost, low-price producer, and its competitors face some tough decisions. Bausch's low prices have sent competitors scrambling in a race to figure out how to respond. Those that cannot find a good answer will have to drop out of the running.

Sources: Excerpts from "Bausch and Lomb: Hardball Pricing Helps It To Regain Its Grip in Contact Lenses," *Business Week*, July 16, 1984, pp. 78–80. Also see Lois Therrien, "Bausch & Lomb is Correcting Its Vision of Research," *Business Week*, March 30, 1987, p. 91.

---

is overdemand: When a company cannot supply all its customers' needs, it can raise its prices, ration products to customers, or both.

Companies can increase their prices in a number of ways to keep up with rising costs.[7] Prices can be raised almost invisibly by dropping discounts and adding higher-priced units to the line. Or prices can be pushed up openly. In passing on price increases to customers, the company needs to avoid the image of price gouger. The price increases should be supported with a company communication program telling customers why prices are being increased. The company salesforce should help customers find ways to economize.

When possible, the company considers ways to meet higher costs or demand without raising prices. For example, it can shrink the product instead of raising the price, as candy bar manufacturers often do. Or it can substitute less expensive ingredients, or remove certain product features, packaging, or services. Or it can "unbundle" its products and services, removing and separately pricing elements that were formerly part of the offer. IBM, for example, now offers training as a separately priced service. Many restaurants have shifted from dinner pricing to a la carte pricing.

Buyer Reactions to Price Changes

Whether the price is raised or lowered, the action will affect buyers, competitors, distributors, and suppliers and may interest government as well. Customers do not always put a straightforward interpretation on price changes. They may view a price *cut* in several ways. For example, what would you think if IBM were to suddenly cut its personal computer prices in half? You might think that these computers are about to be replaced by newer models, or that they have some fault and are not selling well. You might think that IBM is in financial trouble and may not stay in the business long enough to

Buyer reactions to price changes? What would you think if the price of Joy was suddenly cut in half?

supply future parts. You might believe that quality has been reduced. Or you might think that the price will come down even further and that it will pay to wait and see.

Similarly, a price *increase*, which would normally lower sales, may have some positive meanings for buyers. What would you think if IBM *raised* the price of its latest personal computer model? You might think that the item is very "hot" and may be unobtainable unless you buy it soon. You might think that the computer is an unusually good value or that IBM is greedy and charging what the traffic will bear.

Competitor Reactions to Price Changes

A firm considering a price change has to worry about competitors' as well as customers' reactions. Competitors are most likely to react when the number of firms involved is small, when the product is uniform, and when the buyers are well informed.

How can the firm figure out the likely reactions of its competitors? Assume that the firm faces one large competitor. If the competitor tends to react in a set way to price changes, that reaction can be anticipated. But if the competitor treats each price change as a fresh challenge and reacts according to its self-interest, the company must analyze the competitor's self-interest each time.

The problem is complex because the competitor can interpret a company price cut in many ways. It might think that the company is trying to grab a larger market share, that the company is doing poorly and trying to boost its sales, or that the company wants the whole industry to cut prices to increase total demand.

When there are *several* competitors, the company must guess *each* competitor's likely reaction. If all competitors behave alike, this amounts to analyzing only a typical competitor. However, if the competitors do not behave alike—perhaps because of differences in size, market shares, or policies—then separate analyses are necessary. On the other hand, if some competitors will match the price change, there is good reason to expect that the rest will also match it.

Responding to Price Changes

Now let's reverse the question and ask how a firm should respond to a price change by a competitor. The firm needs to consider several issues. Why did the competitor change the price? Was it to take more market share, to use excess capacity, to meet changing cost conditions, or to lead an industry-wide price change? Does the competitor plan to make the price change temporary or permanent? What will happen to the company's market share and profits if it doesn't respond? Are other companies going to respond? And what are the competitor's and other firms' responses likely to be to each possible reaction?

FIGURE 13-2
Price reaction program for meeting a competitor's price cut

Source: Redrawn with permission from a working paper by Raymond J. Trapp, Northwestern University, 1964.

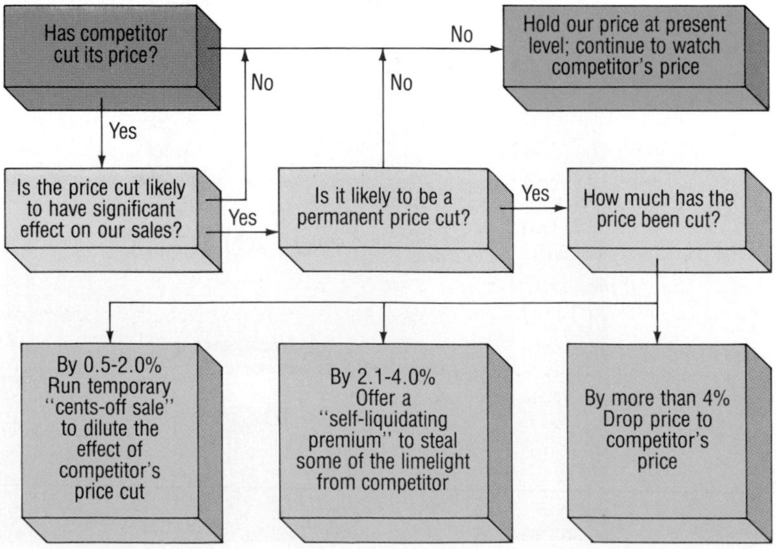

Besides these issues, the company must make a broader analysis. It must consider its own product's stage in the life cycle, its importance in the company's product mix, the intentions and resources of the competitor, and possible consumer reactions to price changes.

The company cannot always make an extended analysis of its alternatives at the time of a price change. The competitor may have spent much time preparing this decision, but the company may have to react within hours or days. About the only way to cut down reaction time is to plan ahead for both possible competitor's price changes and possible responses. Figure 13-2 shows one company's price reaction program for meeting a competitor's possible price cut. Reaction programs for meeting price changes are most often used in industries in which price changes occur often and quick reactions are important. Examples can be found in the meatpacking, lumber, and oil industries.

■ SUMMARY

Pricing is a dynamic process. Companies design a *pricing structure* that covers all their products, change it over time, and adjust it to account for different customers and situations.

Pricing strategies usually change as a product passes through its life cycle. In pricing innovative new products, the company can follow a *skimming policy* by setting prices high initially to "skim" the maximum amount of revenue from various segments of the market. Or it can use *penetration pricing* by setting a low initial price to win a large market share. The company can decide on one of nine price-quality strategies for introducing an imitative product.

When the product is part of a product mix, the firm searches for a set of prices that will maximize the profits from the total mix. The company decides on *price zones* for items in its product line and on the pricing of *optional products*, *captive products*, and *by-products*.

Companies apply a variety of *price-adjustment strategies* to account for differences in consumer segments and situations. One is *geographical pricing*, whereby the company decides how to price to distant customers, choosing from such alternatives as FOB pricing, uniform delivered pricing, zone pricing, basing-point pricing, and freight absorption pricing. A second is *discount*

pricing and allowances—the company establishes cash discounts, quantity discounts, functional discounts, seasonal discounts, and allowances. A third is *discriminatory pricing*—the company sets different prices for different customers, product forms, places, or times. A fourth is *psychological pricing*—the company adjusts the price to better communicate a product's intended position. A fifth is *promotional pricing*—the company decides on loss-leader pricing, special-event pricing, and psychological discounting.

When a firm considers initiating a *price change*, it must consider customers' and competitors' reactions. Customers' reactions are influenced by the meaning customers see in the price change. Competitors' reactions flow from a set reaction policy or a fresh analysis of each situation. The firm initiating the price change must also anticipate the probable reactions of suppliers, middlemen, and government.

The firm that faces a price change initiated by a competitor must try to understand the competitor's intent and both the likely duration and impact of the change. If swiftness of reaction is desirable, the firm should preplan its reactions to different possible price actions by competitors.

■ QUESTIONS FOR DISCUSSION

1. Describe which strategy—market skimming or market penetration—these companies use in pricing their products: (a) McDonald's, (b) Curtis Mathes (television and other home electronics), (c) Bic Corporation (pens, lighters, shavers, and related products), and (d) IBM. Are these the right strategies for these companies? Why or why not?

2. A by-product of manufacturing tennis balls is "dead" balls—those that do not bounce high enough to meet standards (that is, they bounce less than 53 inches when dropped from 100 inches onto a concrete surface). What strategy should be used for pricing these balls?

3. What types of discount pricing tactics might a snow-ski manufacturer use in dealing with the retail outlets that carry its products?

4. The formula for chlorine bleach is virtually identical for all brands. Clorox charges a premium price for this same product, yet remains the unchallenged market leader. Discuss what this implies about the value of a brand name. Are there ethical issues involved in this type of pricing?

5. A clothing store sells men's suits at three price levels—$180, $250, and $340. If shoppers use these price points

as reference prices in comparing different suits, what would be the effect of adding a new line of suits at a cost of $280? Would you expect sales of the $250 suit to increase, decrease, or stay the same?

6. Carpet Fresh was the leading carpet deodorizer, priced at $2.49 for 13 ounces. Arm & Hammer launched a competitor priced at $1.99 for 26 ounces, and quickly became the number-one brand. Discuss the psychological aspects of this pricing. Does this superb-value strategy fit with Arm & Hammer's image?

7. When the dollar is weak, import prices rise and Mercedes and Porsche prices rise with them. Yet when the dollar strengthens, the prices for these cars are kept high, yielding unusually large profits. Discuss whether Mercedes and Porsche should drop prices when their costs drop. What effect would this have on used car prices and trade-in values?

8. If McDonald's cut the price of Big Macs to 99 cents, how would you expect competing hamburger chains to react? Would they react the same way if the price decrease were for Chicken McNuggets rather than Big Macs? Why or why not?

9. Product-bundle pricing is popular in the computer industry. The Osborne computer succeeded because it included free software worth more than the computer itself. Is bundled software perceived as a good value by consumers? What is the variable cost of making an additional copy of a computer program? Does this appear to be a profitable strategy?

■ KEY TERMS

Basing-point pricing. A geographic pricing strategy in which the seller designates a city as a basing point and charges all customers the freight cost from that city to the customer location, regardless of the city from which the goods are actually shipped.

By-product pricing. Setting a price for by-products in order to make the main product's price more competitive.

Captive-product pricing. The pricing of products that must be used along with a main product, such as blades for a razor and film for cameras.

Cash discount. A price reduction to buyers who pay their bills promptly.

Discriminatory pricing. Selling a product or service at two or more prices and the difference in prices is not based on differences in costs.

FOB-origin pricing. A geographic pricing strategy in which goods are placed free on board a carrier, and the customer pays the freight from the factory to the destination.

Freight absorption pricing. A geographic pricing strategy in which the company absorbs all or part of the actual freight charges in order to get the business.

Functional discount. A price reduction offered by the seller to trade channel members who perform certain functions such as selling, storing, and recordkeeping.

Market-penetration pricing. Setting a low price for a new product in order to attract a large number of buyers and a large market share.

Market-skimming pricing. Setting a high price for a new product to skim maximum revenue from the segments willing to pay the high price; the company makes fewer but more profitable sales.

Optional-product pricing. The pricing of optional or accessory products along with a main product.

Product-bundle pricing. Combining several products and offering the bundle at a reduced price.

Product-line pricing. Setting the price steps between various products in a product line based on cost differences between the products, customer evaluations of different features, and competitors' prices.

Promotional allowance. A payment or price reduction to reward dealers for participating in advertising and sales-support programs.

Promotional pricing. Temporarily pricing products below the list price, and sometimes even below cost, to increase short-run sales.

Psychological pricing. A pricing approach which considers the psychology of prices and not simply the economics—the price is used to say something about the product.

Quantity discount. A price reduction to buyers who buy large volumes.

Reference prices. Prices that buyers carry in their minds and refer to when they look at a given product.

Seasonal discount. A price reduction to buyers who buy merchandise or services out of season.

Trade-in allowance. A price reduction given for turning in an old item when buying a new one.

Two-part pricing. A strategy for pricing services in which price is broken into a fixed fee plus a variable usage rate.

Uniform delivered pricing. A geographic pricing strategy in which the company charges the same price plus freight to all customers regardless of their location.

Zone pricing. A geographic pricing strategy in which the company sets up two or more zones—all customers within a zone pay the same total price, and this price is higher in the more distant zones.

■ REFERENCES

1. See Bill Kelley, "Komatsu in Cat Fight," *Sales and Marketing Management*, April 1986, pp. 50–53; Jack Willoughby, "Decision Time in Peoria," *Forbes*, January 27, 1986, p. 36; Dexter Hutchins, "Caterpillar's Triple Whammy," *Fortune*, October 27, 1986; and Brian Bremner, "Can Caterpillar Inch Its Way Back to Heftier Profits?" *Business Week*, September 25, 1989, pp. 75–78.

2. For a comprehensive description and comparison of various pricing strategies, see Gerald J. Tellis, "Beyond the Many Faces of Price: An Integration of Pricing Strategies," *Journal of Marketing*, October 1986, pp. 146–60.

3. See James E. Ellis, "Spectra's Instant Success Gives Polaroid a Shot in the Arm," *Business Week*, November 3, 1986, pp. 32–34; and Thomas T. Nagle, *The Strategy and Tactics of Pricing* (Englewood Cliffs, NJ: Prentice Hall, 1987), pp. 116–117.

4. See Tellis, "Beyond the Many Faces of Price," p. 155; and Nagle, *The Strategy and Tactics of Pricing*, pp. 170–172.

5. Gary M. Erickson and Johny K. Johansson, "The Role of Price in Multi-Attribute Product Evaluations," *Journal of Consumer Research*, September 1985, pp. 195–199.

6. See Nagle, *The Strategy and Tactics of Pricing*, pp. 66–68; and Tellis, "The Many Faces of Price," pp. 152–53.

7. Norman H. Fuss, Jr., "How to Raise Prices—Judiciously—to Meet Today's Conditions," *Harvard Business Review*, May–June 1975, p. 10; and Mary Louise Hatten, "Don't Get Caught with Your Prices Down," *Business Horizons*, March–April 1982, pp. 23–28.

EAST LINE RAILWAY: THE WISCONSIN CANNED GOODS PROJECT

Sitting in his office at the headquarters of East Line Railway, Carl Meyers is hard at work. As marketing analyst for the Food Products Transportation Group, Meyers develops strategy and sets prices for the transportation of canned goods in boxcars. In the coming year, East Line wants to increase the volume of canned goods shipped in boxcars from the Midwest to the East Coast. For starters, Meyers will target the market for shipments of Wisconsin canned goods to the New York City/Northern New Jersey metropolitan area—one of the biggest food-consuming areas within the East Line system.

Wisconsin canned goods consist mostly of beans, peas, and fruit. Wisconsin canners ship almost 1½-million tons of canned goods annually to the East Coast, much of it to the NY/NJ metropolitan area. In addition, a majority of Wisconsin canners are located along rail lines and have facilities for loading boxcars. Despite this fact, East Line Railway handled only 327 carloads (about 20,600 tons) from Wisconsin to the NY/NJ area in 1988. The remainder of the goods was moved by truck. Thus, Meyers sees significant potential for increasing market share.

Because a boxcar holds 126,000 pounds of canned goods (a truck holds only 42,000), East Line Railway can profitably offer the customer a significantly lower per-unit shipping price than can a trucking firm. Also,

the average length of haul from Wisconsin to NY/NJ is 975 miles—well above the theoretical 300 to 400-mile point below which it is harder for rail shipping to compete with truck hauling.

Trucks do in fact offer advantages over boxcars in certain situations—for example, when the shipment size is too small to fill an entire boxcar or when perishability makes speed of transit a priority. On the other hand, not only do canned goods have a relatively long shelf life, but they can be purchased in bulk and stored in large regional warehouses for shipment to stores as needed. Moreover, a properly loaded railcar often creates less damage than shipping by truck. Finally, shipping by train is often more convenient: Although they may have only 25 minutes to unload a truck (a job that must be done by appointment), customers can take up to three days to unload a boxcar placed at a loading dock.

Taking all these factors into account, Meyers thinks that to be competitive the rail price must be 15 percent lower than the equivalent truck price. This price differential covers both the cost of the longer time the product spends enroute and increased unloading costs. In 1988, the average rail rate for the 327 carloads of canned goods handled by East Line Railway from various origins in Wisconsin to the NY/NJ metropolitan area was $2.78 per hundred

FIGURE 1 Major Truckload Carrier Pricing Regions

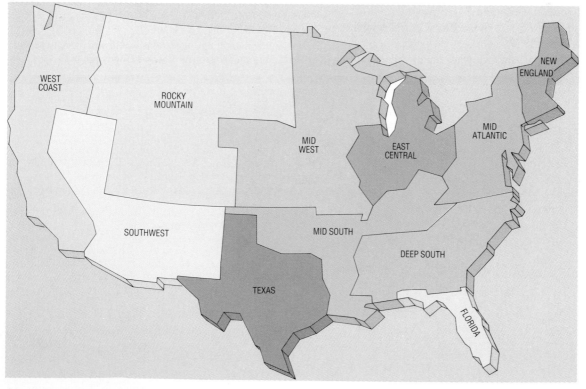

TABLE 1 Representative Over-the-Road Truck Price Levels (cents per mile)

FROM:	Deep South	East Central	Florida	Mid Atl	Mid South	Mid West	New England	Rocky Mt	South West	Texas	West Coast
Deep South	135	95	155	110	115	95	110	110	115	110	93
E. Central	110	150	125	130	120	115	135	118	118	115	95
Florida	85	80	100	95	85	85	95	100	95	95	92
Mid Atlantic	82	80	115	140	82	80	150	100	98	95	94
Mid South	115	105	130	125	140	105	128	114	120	125	95
Mid West	112	110	130	132	118	130	135	125	125	122	100
New England	82	80	115	130	80	80	150	97	95	95	94
Rocky Mt.	88	80	108	97	90	83	97	100	115	95	95
South West	94	85	105	95	90	84	96	105	125	95	94
Texas	90	85	115	95	95	82	95	100	120	105	92
West Coast	95	90	105	98	95	90	99	120	125	92	110

weight (cwt.): For example, 126,000 lbs. of canned goods divided by 100 equals 1260 cwt. times $2.78 per cwt. equals $3,503 revenue per carload. East Line Railway's variable cost per carload ranges from $1,350 to $1,450 per carload.

Meyers uses this data—plus the information contained in Figure 1 and Table 1—to make his pricing decision. Figure 1 shows the pricing regions for the trucking industry. All customers within a given zone pay the same price per mile of truck transportation. Table 1 provides the cents-per-mile figures for a truckload of goods shipped form one price zone to another. For example, looking across the first row of Table 1, you will see that shipments within the Deep South are charged $1.35 per mile, while shipments from the Deep South to the East Central region are charged $.95 per mile.

For ease of comparison, Meyers usually made all the calculations "per carload." Meyers must first decide whether to revise last year's rates.

QUESTIONS

1. What factors influence East Line Railway's share of canned goods shipments form Wisconsin to the New York/New Jersey metropolitan area?
2. What were East Line Railway's total revenues and profits from the 327 boxcars of canned goods hauled from Wisconsin to NY/NJ in 1988?
3. How does the price of shipping by truck (see Figure 1 and Table 1) compare to the current boxcar rate?
4. Taking into account costs, competition, and demand factors, what price should Meyers charge for shipments of Wisconsin canned goods to the NY/NJ area?
5. What other marketing suggestions would you make to Meyers concerning the Wisconsin Canned Goods project?

UPJOHN PRICES MINOXIDIL

Sometimes companies accidentally discover a product idea that looks like a winner and management becomes so enthusiastic that it is blinded to problems either with the product itself or with elements of its market mix such as price. Consider the Upjohn Company's experience with Rogaine—a product that restores hair growth on some balding people.

While researching the usefulness of a white crystalline solid called minoxidil to treat hypertension, Upjohn's scientists discovered that some patients began to grow hair on various parts of their bodies—their chests, arms, legs, cheeks, and even the crown of their heads. Initially, the scientists ignored this side effect, but eventually they wondered what would happen if they mixed minoxidil into a topical solution for men to rub onto their scalps. The results were encouraging, so they began nationwide tests with more than 2,300 men.

During the testing period, rumors of minoxidil's efficacy in promoting hair growth spread wildly. Some dermatologists, doctors, and pharmacists prepared hair-restoring treatments for their patients by crushing tablets of minoxidil and combining the powder with water, alcohol, or cold cream. Consumers bombarded the company with letters and telephone calls demanding to know more about the drug and when it would be available. Wall Street security analysts estimated that sales would reach $125 million in 1989 if only 8.5 percent of the 35 million bald men in the United States used Upjohn's product, and that worldwide sales could reach $1 billion per year in the 1990s.

In 1985, Upjohn applied to the FDA for approval of a minoxidil-based ointment, it called Regaine for use as a hair restorer. FDA personnel spent two and one-half years studying Upjohn's 70,000-page report regarding Regaine's effectiveness. What did they learn? Among men using a 2 percent minoxidil solution, 8 percent experienced dense new hair growth, 31 percent had moderate new hair growth, and 61 percent experienced little or no hair growth. The product works best for men under 30; its efficacy declines with age; it is most effective on the crown of the head, and is relatively ineffective in preventing hair loss at the temples. The new hair tends to be thinner than the individual's original hair, and much of it consists of vellus hairs (commonly referred to as "peach fuzz"). To maintain the new hair growth, people must continue to use the product indefinitely. In August 1988, the FDA approved the product for sale on a prescription-only basis. Because one FDA official objected that the name Regaine implied total efficacy, Upjohn renamed the product Rogaine.

While approval of Rogaine was pending, the FDA banned all nonprescription products that claim, but cannot prove, that they restore hair on balding heads. Thus, in a few strokes of the regulatory pen, the agency eliminated Upjohn's competition. Rogaine's future looked very rosy indeed when it was launched in October 1988.

By early 1989, however, it was clear that sales of Rogaine were far below expectations. Upjohn management tried a more aggressive marketing campaign: It increased television and print advertising to consumers, used ads containing stronger sales appeals, and ordered company salespeople to redouble their promotion to doctors. All these efforts failed to stimulate sales.

In reassessing the product and its marketing mix, Upjohn has decided that price is the problem: Rogaine costs between $55 and $65 per month to use, and must be applied twice daily for at least six months before the consumer can tell if it will be effective. In addition, using Rogaine requires making visits to the doctor to obtain a prescription and to monitor progress—another expense.

The product's sales manager suggested lowering the price, but other managers rejected this idea because they feared that a low price would suggest a "snake oil" product. They believed that a high-quality, proven-effective product should have a high price. Still, management realizes, that it must find a way to reduce price, so it is contemplating using one of two price promotions. The first is a $10 reduction in the price of the first month's supply of Rogaine, the second is a $20 rebate obtainable by sending in four Rogaine box tops. Although Rogaine's sales manager has argued that these promotions will not reduce the price enough to be effective, the rest of Upjohn's management team likes the promotions because they are temporary, and thus should not damage Rogaine's high-price image.

QUESTIONS

1. Is Upjohn using a market-penetration or a market-skimming strategy? Is this strategy suitable for Rogaine? Should management reduce the price of Rogaine?

2. Suppose you were losing your hair. How much would it cost you to use Rogaine before you would know whether it was working for you? Do you think it would be worth the cost?

3. Are the two price promotions under consideration appropriate for a product such as Rogaine? If you had to decide between them, which one would you choose?

Sources: "Baldness: Is There Hope?", Consumer Reports, September 1988, pp. 543–547; "A Hairy Gamble?", Forbes, August 27, 1984, pp. 150–151; Stephen W. Quickel, "Bald Spot," Business Month, November 1989, pp. 36–43; and Adam Smith, "Upjohn's Bald Ambitions," Esquire, October 1986, pp. 73–74.

14

Placing Products: Distribution Channels and Physical Distribution

Winn-Dixie Stores, the nation's fifth largest supermarket with more than $9 billion in yearly sales in the southeastern United States, is part of a complex food-industry distribution channel consisting of consumer package-goods companies, wholesale food distributors, and grocery retailers. Usually, the members of this channel work closely together toward a common goal of profitably marketing food products to consumers. But too often distribution channels don't operate as smoothly as they should—conflicts and power struggles sometimes flare up. This fact is highlighted by a recent incident that pitted Winn-Dixie against Procter & Gamble, Pillsbury, and several of its other major suppliers.

In late 1988, Winn-Dixie stunned food producers when it announced that it would no longer accept promotional allowances on a market-by-market basis. Instead, it would expect its suppliers to adopt a uniform-pricing policy in which promotional allowances offered to any *one* of Winn-Dixie's 1260 stores would be made to *all* of its stores. In the future, the company would place chain-wide orders at the lowest available prices, even if those prices were offered in only one of its markets.

To Winn-Dixie, this new policy made good business sense. The supermarket chain claimed that most of its competitors were already attaining the lowest prices for all their stores through "diverting"—a legally questionable practice through which a retailer buys larger-than-needed quantities of a product in areas where it is on sale and then ships the excess to its stores in other areas. Many retailers routinely scour the country looking for the best prices on various grocery products. About 5 percent of the goods on grocery store shelves get there via diverting. Winn-Dixie argued that a uniform-pricing policy would help make this time-consuming and inefficient diverting process unnecessary.

Winn-Dixie's new policy caused a furor among major package-goods marketers, most of whom are strongly wedded to regional marketing strategies (see Marketing Highlight 9–1). If they complied with Winn-Dixie's demands for uniform price allowances, they would be compelled under the law to provide the same price breaks to all of their retail customers across Winn-Dixie's 13-state trading area. This action would greatly reduce their ability to use regional marketing strategies in which prices and promotions are tailored to local competitors and conditions.

For these reasons, several of Winn-Dixie's largest and most powerful suppliers refused to go along with its demands, and the battle was joined. Procter & Gamble, Pillsbury, Campbell, Quaker, and General Foods announced that they would continue their nonstandard, regional-pricing policies. Despite huge potential losses of sales and customer goodwill, Winn-Dixie began to drop selected products of these major suppliers from its shelves. In response, some of the food producers threatened retaliatory coupon blitzes in Winn-Dixie's market to boost demand for the discontinued products and to lure Winn-Dixie consumers to competing stores.

The standoff lasted for many months. But in the face of heavy pressure from some of the nation's most powerful marketers, Winn-Dixie couldn't make its new uniform-pricing policy stick. After obtaining only modest concessions from suppliers, it gracefully backed away from forcing the issue and began restoring discontinued products to its shelves.

The Winn-Dixie incident demonstrates the dynamic forces of cooperation, power, and conflict found in distribution channels. Clearly, for the good of all parties, Winn-Dixie and its suppliers must work as partners to market products to consumers. For decades, the giant food marketers have served as "senior partners" in this relationship

largely controlling marketing practices in their distribution channels. But as more and more products compete for limited supermarket shelf space, and as scanners give retailers ever-greater leverage through market information, the balance of channel power is shifting toward grocery retailers. Increasingly, supermarket chains are taking control of the marketing process. Thus, although Winn-Dixie may not have won a clear victory in this battle, it made its point. Gone are the days when the giant package-goods marketers can simply dictate channel terms and policies.[1]

CHAPTER OBJECTIVES

After reading this chapter you should be able to:

1. Explain why companies use distribution channels and the functions these channels perform.
2. Discuss how channel members interact, and how they organize to do the work of the channel.
3. Identify the major distribution channel alternatives open to a company.
4. Explain how companies select, motivate, and evaluate channel members.
5. Discuss the issues firms face when setting up physical distribution systems.

Marketing-channel decisions are among the most important facing management. A company's channel decisions directly affect every other marketing decision. The company's pricing depends on whether it uses mass merchandisers or high quality specialty stores. The firm's salesforce and advertising decisions depend upon how much persuasion, training, and motivation the dealers need. Whether a company develops or acquires certain new products may depend on how well those products fit the abilities of its channel members.

However, companies often pay too little attention to their distribution channels, sometimes with damaging results. For example, automobile manufacturers have lost large shares of their parts and service business to companies like NAPA, Midas, Goodyear, and others because they have resisted making needed changes in their dealer franchise networks. On the other hand, many companies have used imaginative distribution systems to gain a competitive advantage. Federal Express's creative and imposing distribution system made it the leader in small-package delivery industry. And American Hospital Supply gained a strong advantage over its competition by linking its distribution system directly to hospitals through a sophisticated data-processing system.[2]

Distribution-channel decisions often involve long-term commitments to other firms. A furniture manufacturer can easily change its advertising, prices, or promotion programs. It can scrap old product designs and introduce new ones as market tastes demand. But when it sets up a distribution channel through contracts with independent dealers, it cannot readily replace this channel with company-owned branches if conditions change. Therefore, management must design its channels carefully, with an eye on tomorrow's likely selling environment as well as today's.

In this chapter, we examine four major distribution channel questions: *What is the nature of distribution channels? How do channel firms interact and organize to do the work of the channel? What problems do companies face in designing and managing their channels? What role does physical distribution play in attracting and satisfying customers?* In the next chapter, we look at distribution channel issues from the viewpoint of retailers and wholesalers.

THE NATURE OF DISTRIBUTION CHANNELS

Most producers use middlemen to bring their products to market. They try to forge a distribution channel. A **distribution channel** is a set of interdependent organizations involved in the process of making a product or service available for use or consumption by the consumer or industrial user.[3]

Why Are Middlemen Used?

Why do producers give some of the selling job to middlemen? Doing so means giving up some control over how and to whom the products are sold. But producers gain certain advantages from using middlemen. These advantages are described below.

Many producers lack the financial resources to carry out direct marketing. For example, General Motors sells its automobiles through thousands of independent franchise dealers. Even General Motors would be hard pressed to raise the cash to buy out its dealers.

Direct marketing would require many producers to become middlemen for the products of other producers in order to achieve mass-distribution economies. For example, the Wrigley Company would not find it practical to set up small retail gum shops around the country or to sell gum door to door or by mail order. It would have to sell gum along with many other small products and would end up in the drugstore and foodstore business. Wrigley finds it easier to work through a network of privately owned distributors.

Even producers who can afford to set up their own channels can often earn a greater return by increasing their investment in their main business. If a company earns a 20 percent rate of return on manufacturing and foresees only a 10 percent return on retailing, it will not want to do its own retailing.

From the Coca-Cola Company, to the bottler, to the retailer, to the consumer—channel members must all work together to make Coke successful.

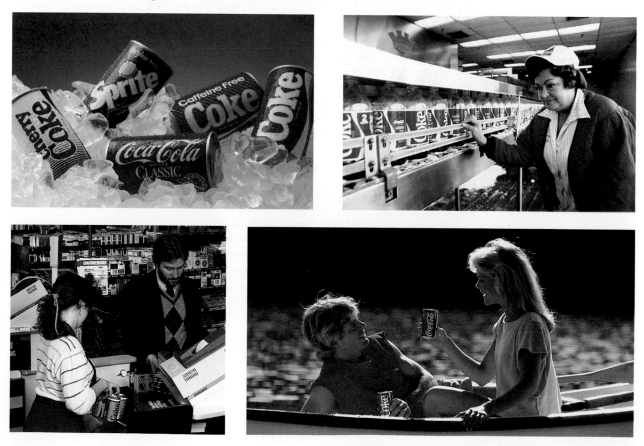

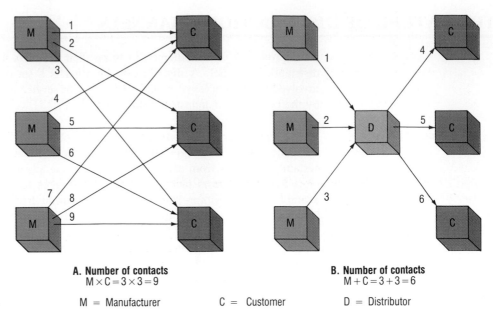

FIGURE 14-1
How a distributor reduces the
number of channel transactions

A. Number of contacts
$M \times C = 3 \times 3 = 9$

M = Manufacturer   C = Customer

B. Number of contacts
$M + C = 3 + 3 = 6$

D = Distributor

The use of middlemen largely boils down to their greater efficiency in making goods available to target markets. Through their contacts, experience, specialization, and scale of operation, middlemen usually offer the firm more than it can achieve on its own.

Figure 14-1 shows one way that using middlemen can provide economies. Part A shows three producers each using direct marketing to reach three customers. This system requires nine different contacts. Part B shows the three producers working through one distributor, who contacts the three customers. This system requires only six contacts. In this way, middlemen reduce the amount of work that must be done by both producers and consumers.

From the economic system's point of view, the role of middlemen is to transform the assortment of products made by producers into the assortments wanted by consumers. Producers make narrow assortments of products in large quantities. But consumers want broad assortments of products in small quantities. In the distribution channels, middlemen buy the large quantities of many producers and break them down into the smaller quantities and broader assortments wanted by consumers. Thus, middlemen play an important role in matching supply and demand.

Distribution Channel
Functions

A distribution channel moves goods from producers to consumers. It overcomes the major time, place, and possession gaps that separate goods and services from those who would use them. Members of the marketing channel perform many key functions:

- *Information*—gathering and distributing marketing research and intelligence information about actors and forces in the marketing environment needed for planning and aiding exchange.
- *Promotion*—developing and spreading persuasive communications about an offer.
- *Contact*—finding and communicating with prospective buyers.
- *Matching*—shaping and fitting the offer to the buyer's needs, including such activities as manufacturing, grading, assembling, and packaging.
- *Negotiation*—reaching an agreement on price and other terms of the offer so that ownership or possession can be transferred.
- *Physical distribution*—transporting and storing goods.
- *Financing*—acquiring and using funds to cover the costs of the channel work.
- *Risk taking*—assuming the risks of carrying out the channel work.

The first five functions help to complete transactions; the last three help fulfill the completed transactions.

The question is not *whether* these functions need to be performed—they must be—but rather *who* is to perform them. All the functions have three things in common—they use up scarce resources, they can often be performed better through specialization, and they can be shifted among channel members. To the extent that the manufacturer performs them, its costs go up and its prices have to be higher. At the same time, when some functions are shifted to middlemen, the producer's costs and prices are lower, but the middlemen must add a charge to cover their work. In dividing the work of the channel, the various functions should be assigned to the channel members who can perform them most efficiently and effectively to provide satisfactory assortments of goods to target consumers.

Number of Channel Levels

Distribution channels can be described by the number of channel levels. Each layer of middlemen that perform some work in bringing the product and its ownership closer to the final buyer is a **channel level.** Because the producer and the final consumer both perform some work, they are part of every channel. We use the *number of intermediary levels* to indicate the *length* of a channel. Figure 14-2A shows several consumer distribution channels of different lengths.

Channel 1, called a **direct-marketing channel,** has no intermediary levels. It consists of a manufacturer selling directly to consumers. For example, Avon and World Book Encyclopedia sell their products door-to-door; Franklin Mint sells collectibles through mail order; Singer sells its sewing machines through its own stores. Channel 2 contains one middleman level. In consumer markets, this level is typically a retailer. For example, large retailers such as Sears and K mart sell televisions, cameras, tires, furniture, major appliances, and many other products that they buy directly from manufacturers. Channel 3 contains two middleman levels. In consumer markets, these levels

FIGURE 14-2
Consumer and industrial marketing channels

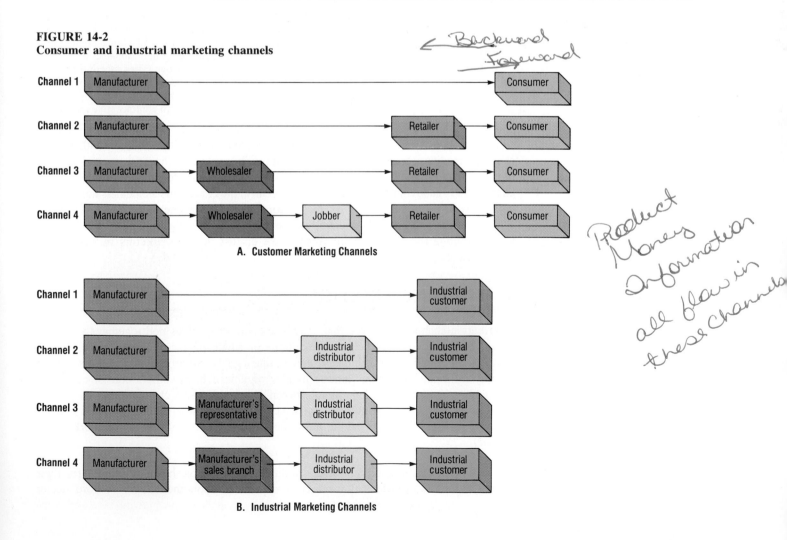

A. Customer Marketing Channels

B. Industrial Marketing Channels

are typically a wholesaler and a retailer. This channel is often used by small manufacturers of food, drug, hardware, and other products. Channel 4 contains three middleman levels. In the meatpacking industry for example, jobbers usually come between wholesalers and retailers. The jobber buys from wholesalers and sells to smaller retailers who are not generally served by larger wholesalers. Distribution channels with more levels are sometimes found, but less often. From the producer's point of view, a greater the number of levels means less control. And, of course, the more levels, the greater the channel's complexity.

Figure 14-2B shows some common industrial distribution channels. The industrial-goods producer can use its own salesforce to sell directly to industrial customers. It can also sell to industrial distributors who in turn sell to industrial customers. It can sell through manufacturer's representatives or its own sales branches to industrial customers, or use them to sell through industrial distributors. Thus zero-, one-, and two-level distribution channels are common in industrial goods markets.

All of the institutions in the channel are connected by several types of *flows*. These include the *physical flow* of products, the *flow of ownership*, *payment flow*, *information flow*, and *promotion flow*. These flows can make even channels with only one or a few levels very complex.

Channels in the Service Sector

The concept of distribution channels is not limited to the distribution of physical goods. Producers of services and ideas also face the problem of making their output *available* to target populations. They develop ''educational distribution systems'' and ''health delivery systems.'' They must determine agencies and locations for reaching a widely spread population:

> Hospitals must be located in geographic space to serve the people with complete medical care, and we must build schools close to the children who have to learn. Fire stations must be located to give rapid access to potential conflagrations, and voting booths must be placed so that people can cast their ballots without expending unreasonable amounts of time, effort, or money to reach the polling stations. Many of our states face the problem of locating branch campuses to serve a burgeoning and increasingly well-educated population. In the cities we must create and locate playgrounds for the children. Many overpopulated countries must assign birth control clinics to reach the people with contraceptive and family planning information.[4]

Distribution channels also are used in ''person'' marketing. Before 1940, professional comedians could reach audiences through vaudeville houses, special events, nightclubs, radio, movies, carnivals, and theaters. In the 1950s television became a strong channel and vaudeville disappeared. More recently, the comedians's channels have grown to include promotional events, product endorsements, cable television, and videotapes. Politicians must also find cost-effective channels—mass media, rallies, coffee hours—for distributing their messages to voters.[5] We discuss person marketing in more depth in Chapter 22.

CHANNEL BEHAVIOR AND ORGANIZATION

Distribution channels are more than simple collections of firms tied together by various flows. They are complex behavioral systems in which people and companies interact to accomplish individual, company, and channel goals. Some channel systems consist of only informal interactions among loosely organized firms; others consist of formal interactions guided by strong organizational structures. And channel systems do not stand still—new types of middlemen surface and whole new channel systems evolve. Here we look at channel behavior and at how members organize to do the work of the channel.

Channel Behavior

A distribution channel consists of dissimilar firms that have banded together for their common good. Each channel member is dependent upon the others. A Ford dealer depends on the Ford Motor Company to design cars that meet consumer needs. In turn, Ford depends on the dealer to attract consumers, to persuade them to buy Ford cars, and to service cars after the sale. The Ford dealer also depends on other dealers to provide good sales and service that will uphold the reputation of Ford and its dealer body. In fact, the success of individual Ford dealers depends on how well the entire Ford distribution channel competes with the channels of other auto manufacturers.

Each channel member plays a role in the channel and specializes in performing one or more functions. For example, IBM's role is to produce personal computers that consumers will like and to create demand through national advertising. Computerland's role is to display these computers in convenient locations, to answer buyers' questions, to close sales, and to provide service. The channel will be most effective when each member is assigned the tasks it can do best.

Ideally, because the success of individual channel members depends on overall channel success, all channel firms should work together smoothly. They should understand and accept their roles, coordinate their goals and activities, and cooperate to attain overall channel goals. By cooperating, they can more effectively sense, serve, and satisfy the target market.

But individual channel members rarely take such a broad view. They are usually more concerned with their own short-run goals and their dealings with those firms closest to them in the channel. Cooperating to achieve overall channel goals sometimes means giving up individual company goals. Although channel members are dependent upon one another, they often act alone in their own short-run best interests. They often disagree on the roles each should play—on who should do what and for what rewards. Such disagreements over goals and roles generate **channel conflict.**

Horizontal conflict is conflict between firms at the same level of the channel. Some Ford dealers in Chicago complain about other dealers in the city stealing sales from them by being too aggressive in their pricing and advertising or by selling outside their assigned territories. Some Pizza Inn franchisees complaining about other Pizza Inn franchisees cheating on ingredients, giving poor service, and hurting the overall Pizza Inn image.

Vertical conflict is even more common and refers to conflicts between different levels of the same channel. For example, General Motors came into conflict with its dealers some years ago by trying to enforce policies on service, pricing, and advertising. And Coca-Cola came into conflict with some of its bottlers who agreed to bottle competitor Dr Pepper. A large chain saw company caused conflict when it decided to bypass its wholesale distributors and sell directly to large retailers such as J. C. Penney and K mart, which then competed directly with its smaller retailers.

Some conflict in the channel takes the form of healthy competition. This competition can be good for the channel—without it, the channel could become passive and noninnovative. But sometimes conflict can damage the channel. For the channel as a whole to perform well, each channel member's role must be specified and channel conflict must be managed. Cooperation, assigning roles, and conflict management in the channel are attained through strong channel leadership. The channel will perform better if it contains a firm, agency, or mechanism that has the power to assign roles and manage conflict.

In a large company, the formal organization structure assigns roles and provides needed leadership. But in a distribution channel made up of independent firms, leadership and power are not formally set. Traditionally, distribution channels have lacked the leadership needed to assign roles and manage conflict. In recent years, however, new types of channel organizations have appeared that provide stronger leadership and improved performance.[6]

Channel Organization   Historically, distribution channels have been loose collections of independent companies, each showing little concern for overall channel performance. These *conventional distribution channels* have lacked strong leadership and have been troubled by damaging conflict and poor performance.

Growth of Vertical Marketing Systems

One of the biggest recent channel developments has been the *vertical marketing systems* that have emerged to challenge conventional marketing channels. Figure 14-3 contrasts the two types of channel arrangements.

A **conventional distribution channel** consists of one or more independent producers, wholesalers, and retailers. Each is a separate business seeking to maximize its own profits, even at the expense of profits for the system as a whole. No channel member has much control over the other members, and no formal means exist for assigning roles and resolving channel conflict. By contrast, a **vertical marketing system** (VMS) consists of producers, wholesalers, and retailers acting as a unified system. Either one channel member owns the others, has contracts with them, or wields so much power that they all cooperate.[7] The vertical marketing system can be dominated by the producer, wholesaler, or retailer. VMS's came into being to control channel behavior and manage channel conflict. They achieve economies through size, bargaining power, and elimination of duplicated services. VMS's have become dominant in consumer marketing, serving as much as 64 percent of the total market.

We look now at the three major types of VMS's shown in Figure 14-4. Each type uses a different means for setting up leadership and power in the channel. In a *corporate VMS*, coordination and conflict management are attained through common ownership at different levels of the channel. In a *contractual VMS*, they are attained through contractual agreements among channel members. In an *administered VMS*, leadership is assumed by one or a few dominant channel members.

CORPORATE VMS. A **corporate VMS** combines successive stages of production and distribution under single ownership. For example, Sears obtains more than 50 percent of its goods from companies that it partly or wholly owns. Sherwin-Williams makes paint but also owns and operates 2000 retail outlets. Giant Food Stores operates an ice-making facility, a soft-drink bottling operation, an ice-cream making plant, and a bakery that supplies Giant stores with everything from bagels to birthday cakes.[8] And Gallo, the world's largest wine maker, does much more than simply turn grapes into wine:

> The [Gallo] brothers own Fairbanks Trucking Company, one of the largest intrastate truckers in California. Its 200 semis and 500 trailers are constantly hauling wine out of Modesto and raw materials back in—including . . . lime from Gallo's quarry east of Sacramento. Alone among wine producers, Gallo makes bottles—two million a day—and its Midcal Aluminum Co. spews out screw tops as fast as the bottles are filled. Most of the country's 1,300 or so wineries concentrate on production to the neglect of marketing. Gallo, by contrast, participates in every aspect of selling short of whispering in the ear of each imbiber. The company owns its distributors in about a dozen markets and probably would buy many . . . more . . . if the laws in most states did not prohibit doing so.[9]

In such corporate systems, cooperation and conflict management are handled through regular organizational channels.

CONTRACTUAL VMS. A **contractual VMS** consists of independent firms at different levels of production and distribution who join together through contracts to obtain more

FIGURE 14-3
Comparison of conventional marketing channel with vertical marketing system

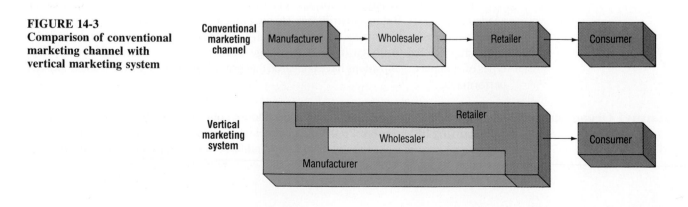

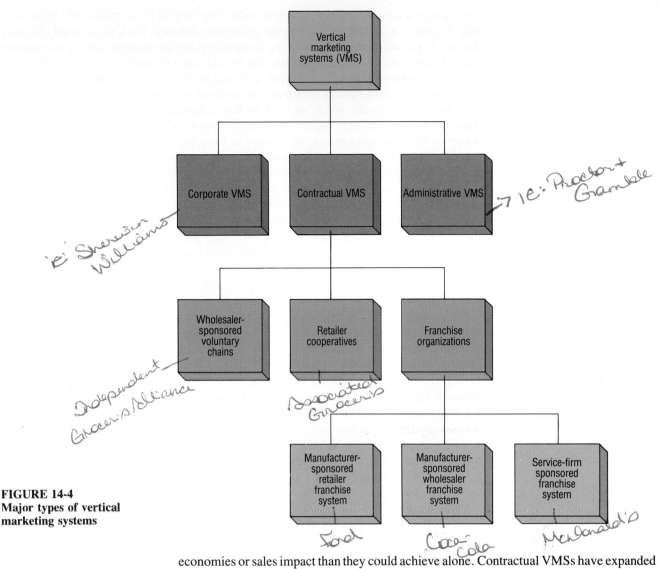

FIGURE 14-4
Major types of vertical marketing systems

[Handwritten annotations on figure: "ie: Sherwin Williams" (Corporate VMS); "ie: Procter + Gamble" (Administrative VMS); "Independent Grocer's Alliance" (Wholesaler-sponsored voluntary chains); "Associated Grocer's" (Retailer cooperatives); "Ford" (Manufacturer-sponsored retailer franchise system); "Coca Cola" (Manufacturer-sponsored wholesaler franchise system); "McDonald's" (Service-firm sponsored franchise system)]

economies or sales impact than they could achieve alone. Contractual VMSs have expanded rapidly in recent years. There are three types of contractual VMS's.

Wholesaler-sponsored voluntary chains are systems in which wholesalers organize voluntary chains of independent retailers to help them compete with large chain organizations. The wholesaler develops a program in which independent retailers standardize their selling practices and achieve buying economies that let the group compete effectively with chain organizations. Examples include the Independent Grocers Alliance (IGA), Western Auto, and Sentry Hardwares.

Retailer cooperatives are systems in which retailers organize a new, jointly-owned business to carry on wholesaling and possibly production. Members buy most of their goods through the retailer co-op and plan their advertising jointly. Profits are passed back to members in proportion to their purchases. Nonmember retailers may also buy through the co-op but do not share in the profits. Examples include Certified Grocers, Associated Grocers, and True Value Hardware.

In **franchise organizations,** a channel member called a *franchiser* links several stages in the production-distribution process. Franchising has been the fastest-growing retailing form in recent years. The more than 500,000 franchise operations in the U.S now account for about one-third of all retail sales and may account for one-half by the year 2000.[10] Almost every kind of business has been franchised—from motels and fast-food restaurants to dentists and dating services, from wedding consultants and maid services to funeral homes and tub and tile refinishers. Although the basic idea is an old one, some forms of franchising are quite new.

There are three forms of franchises. The first form is the *manufacturer-sponsored retailer franchise system*, as found in the automobile industry. Ford, for example, licenses dealers to sell its cars; the dealers are independent businesspeople who agree to meet various conditions of sales and service. The second type of franchise is the *manufacturer-sponsored wholesaler franchise system*, as found in the soft-drink industry. Coca-Cola, for example, licenses bottlers (wholesalers) in various markets who buy its syrup concentrate and then carbonate, bottle, and sell the finished product to retailers in local markets. The third franchise form is the *service-firm-sponsored retailer franchise system*, in which a service firm licesnes a system of retailers to bring its service to consumers. Examples are found in the auto rental business (Hertz, Avis), the fast-food service business (McDonald's, Burger King), and the motel business (Holiday Inn, Ramada Inn).

The fact that most consumers cannot tell the difference between contractual and corporate VMS's shows how successfully the contractual organizations compete with corporate chains. The various contractual VMS's are discussed more fully in chapter 15.

ADMINISTERED VMS. An **administered VMS** coordinates successive stages of production and distribution—not through common ownership or contractual ties but through the size and power of one of the parties. Manufacturers of a top brand can obtain strong trade cooperation and support from resellers. Thus, General Electric, Procter & Gamble, Kraft, and Campbell Soup can command unusual cooperation from resellers regarding displays, shelf space, promotions, and price policies. And large retailers like Sears and Toys 'R' Us can exert strong influence on manufacturers that supply the product they sell (see Marketing Highlight 14–1).

Growth of Horizontal Marketing Systems

Another channel development is **horizontal marketing systems,** in which two or more companies at one level join together to follow a new marketing opportunity.[11] By working together, companies can combine their capital, production capabilities, or marketing resources to accomplish more than any one company working alone. Companies might join forces with competitors or non-competitors.[12] They might work with each other on a temporary or permanent basis, or they may create a separate company. Here are some examples:

- Pillsbury lacked the resources to market its new line of refrigerated dough products because they required special refrigerated display cases. So it set up an arrangement with Kraft in which Pillsbury makes and advertises its refrigerated dough products while Kraft uses its expertise to sell and distribute these products to the stores.
- The Lamar Savings Bank of Texas arranged to locate its savings offices and automated teller machines in Safeway stores. Lamar gained quick market entry at a low cost and Safeway was able to offer in-store banking convenience to its customers.
- H&R Block and Hyatt Legal Services formed a joint venture in which Hyatt houses its legal clinics in H&R Block's tax preparation offices. Hyatt pays a fee for office space, secretarial assistance, and office equipment usage. By locating in H&R Block's nationwide office network, Hyatt gains quick market penetration. In turn, H&R Block benefits from renting its facilities, which otherwise have a highly seasonal pattern.
- General Motors and Procter & Gamble teamed up for a car-giveaway contest—consumers finding special plastic keys in Crest, Tide, and other P&G products could win a new Chevrolet Beretta, Corsica, or pickup truck.
- Sears and McDonald's joined forces to market the McKids line of "Fun clothes for small fries." McDonald's franchisees and Sears stores work together to develop local promotion programs.

Such symbiotic marketing arrangements have increased dramatically in recent years and the end is nowhere in sight.

Growth of Multichannel Marketing Systems

In the past, many companies used a single channel to sell to a single market or market segment. Today, with the proliferation of customer segments and channel possibilities, more and more companies have adopted multichannel distribution. Such **multichannel**

Toys 'Я' Us Administers Its Channel

Toys 'Я' Us operates 411 toy supermarkets that pull in $4 billion in annual sales and capture almost 25 percent of the huge U.S. toy market. And the giant retailer is growing explosively—some experts predict that its market share will double during the next decade. Because of its size and massive market power, Toys 'Я' Us exerts strong influence on toy manufacturers, on their product, pricing, and promotion strategies—and almost everything else they do.

Critics worry that Toys 'Я' Us is *too* big and influential and that it takes unfair advantage of toy producers. The reactions of Toys 'Я' Us buyers can make or break a new toy. For example, Hasbro invested about $20 million to develop Nemo—a home video game system to compete with the hugely successful Nintendo system—but then quickly cancelled the project when Toys 'Я' Us executives reacted negatively. Toys 'Я' Us sells their toys at everyday low prices. This sometimes frustrates toy manufacturers because Toys 'Я' Us is selling toys at far below recommended retail prices, forcing producers to settle for lower margins and profits. And some analysts have accused Toys 'Я' Us of placing an unfair burden on smaller toy makers by requiring all of its suppliers to pay a fee if they want their toys to be included in Toys 'Я' Us newspaper advertisements.

But other industry experts think that Toys 'Я' Us helps the toy industry more than hurts it. For example, whereas other retailers feature toys only at Christmas, Toys 'Я' Us has created a year-round market for toys. Moreover, its low prices cause greater overall industry sales and force producers to operate more efficiently. And Toys 'Я' Us shares its extensive market data with toy producers, giving them immediate feedback on which products and marketing programs are working and which are not.

Clearly, Toys 'Я' Us and the toy manufacturers need each other—the toy makers need Toys 'Я' Us to market their products aggressively, and the giant retailer needs a corps of healthy producers to provide a constant stream of popular new products to fill its shelves. Through the years, both sides have recognized this interdependence. For example, in the mid-1970s, when Toys 'Я' Us was threatened by bankruptcy because of the financial problems of its parent company, the Toy Manufacturers Association worked directly with banks to save the troubled retailer. The banks granted credit to Toys 'Я' Us largely because several major toy manufacturers were willing to grant such credit on their own. By taking such action, the association demonstrated a clear recognition that the entire toy industry benefited by keeping Toys 'Я' Us healthy.

Similarly, Toys 'Я' Us has recognized its stake in seeing that toy manufacturers succeed. In recent years, as flat toy sales have plunged many large manufacturers into deep financial trouble, Toys 'Я' Us has provided a strong helping hand. For example, Toys 'Я' Us often helps toy manufacturers through cash shortages and other financial difficulties by granting credit and prepaying bills. Also, its savvy buyers preview new products for toy makers, making early and valuable suggestions on possible design and marketing improvements. Such advice helped Galoob Toys convert its Army Gear line—toys that change into different weapons—from a potential flop into a top 20 seller. And on advice from Toys 'Я' Us, Ohio Arts altered the advertising strategy for its Zaks plastic building toys, increasing sales by 30 percent. The president of Tyco Toys concludes, "Toys 'Я' Us gets a lot of flak for being large and taking advantage of manufacturers, but I would like to have more customers who help us as much as they do."

Sources: Amy Dunkin, "How Toys 'Я' Us Controls the Game Board," *Business Week*, December 19, 1988, pp. 58–60; Louis W. Stern and Adel I. El-Ansary, *Marketing Channels*, (Englewood Cliffs, NJ: Prentice Hall, 1988), pp. 14–15; and Faye Rice, "Superelf Plans for Xma$," *Fortune*, September 11, 1989, pp. 151–52.

Administered channels: Large retailers like Toys Я Us can exert strong influence on other members of the marketing channel.

Just where did we get the idea kids' clothes could be more fun?

Horizontal marketing systems: Sears and McDonald's team up to sell McKids, "Fun clothes for small fries."

marketing occurs when a single firm sets up two or more marketing channels to reach one or more customer segments.[13] For example, General Electric sells large home appliances both through independent retailers (department stores, discount houses, catalog houses) and directly to large housing-tract builders, thus competing to some extent with its own retailers. McDonald's sells through a network of independent franchisees but owns more than one-fourth of its outlets. Thus, the wholly owned restaurants compete to some extent with those owned by McDonald's franchisees.

The multichannel marketer gains sales with each new channel but also risks offending existing channels. Existing channels can cry "unfair competition" and threaten to drop the marketer unless it limits the competition or repays them in some way, perhaps by offering them exclusive models or special allowances.

In some cases, the multichannel marketer's channels are all under its own ownership and control. For example, J.C. Penney operates department stores, mass-merchandising stores, and specialty stores, each offering different product assortments to different market segments; in such cases there is no conflict with outside channels, but the marketer might face internal conflict over how much financial support each channel deserves.

CHANNEL DESIGN DECISIONS

We now look at several channel decision problems facing manufacturers. In designing marketing channels, manufacturers struggle between what is ideal and what is practical. A new firm usually starts by selling in a limited market area. Because it has limited capital, it typically uses only a few existing middlemen in each market—a few manufacturers' sales agents, a few wholesalers, some existing retailers, a few trucking companies, and a few warehouses. Deciding on the best channels might not be a problem: The problem might be to convince one or a few good middlemen to handle the line.

If the new firm is successful, it might branch out to new markets. Again, the manufacturer will tend to work through the existing middlemen, although this strategy might mean using different *types* of marketing channels in different areas. In smaller markets, the firm might sell directly to retailers; in larger markets, it might sell through distributors. In one part of the country, it might grant exclusive franchises because the merchants normally work this way; in another, it might sell through all outlets willing to handle the merchandise. The manufacturer's channel system thus evolves to meet local opportunities and conditions.

Designing a channel system calls for analyzing consumer service needs, setting the channel objectives and constraints, identifying the major channel alternatives, and evaluating them.

Analyzing Consumer Service Needs

Designing the distribution channel starts with determining which services consumers in various target segments want from the channel. Channel services fall into five categories:[14]

- *Lot size*—Do consumers want to buy one unit or many? The smaller the lot size, the greater the level of service provided by the channel.
- *Market decentralization*—Do consumers want to buy from nearby locations, or will they buy from more distant centralized locations by traveling, phoning, or buying through the mail? The more decentralized the channel, the greater the service it provides.
- *Waiting time*—Do consumers want immediate delivery, or are they willing to wait? Faster delivery means greater service from the channel.
- *Product variety*—Do consumers value breadth of assortment or do they prefer specialization? The greater the assortment provided by the channel, the higher the service level.
- *Service backup*—Do consumers want many add-on services (delivery, credit, repairs, installation), or will they obtain these services elsewhere? More add-on services mean a higher level of channel service.

Consider the distribution channel service needs of personal computer buyers:

The delivery of service might include such things as demonstration of the product before the sale or provision of long-term warranties and flexible financing. After the sale, there might be training programs for using the equipment and a program to install and repair it. Customers might appreciate "loaners" while their equipment is being repaired or technical advice over a telephone hot line.[15]

Thus, to design an effective channel, the designer must know the service levels desired by consumers. But providing all the desired services may not be possible or practical. The company and its channel members may not have the resources or skills needed to provide all the desired services. And providing higher levels of service results in higher costs for the channel and higher prices for consumers. The company must balance consumer service needs against not only the feasibility and costs of meeting these needs but against customer price preferences. The success of discount retailing shows that consumers are often willing to accept lower service levels if lower service level means lower prices.

Setting the Channel Objectives and Constraints

Channel objectives should be stated in terms of the desired service level of target consumers. Usually, a company can identify several segments wanting different levels of channel service. The company should decide which segments to serve and the best channels to use in each case. In each segment, the company wants to minimize the total channel cost of delivering the desired service level.

The company's channel objectives are also influenced by the nature of its products, company policies, middlemen, competitors, and the environment. *Product characteristics* greatly affect channel design. For example, perishable products require more direct marketing to avoid delays and too much handling. Bulky products, such as building materials or soft drinks, require channels that minimize shipping distance and amount of handling.

Company characteristics also play an important role. For example, the company's size and financial situation determine which marketing functions it can handle itself and which it gives to middlemen. And a company marketing strategy based on speedy customer delivery affects the functions that the company wants its middlemen to perform, the number of its outlets, and the choice of its transportation methods.

Middlemen characteristics influence channel design. The company must find middlemen who are willing and able to perform the needed tasks. In general, middlemen differ in their abilities to handle promotion, customer contact, storage, and credit. For

Product characteristics affect channel decisions: Fresh flowers must be delivered quickly with a minimum of handling.

example, manufacturer's representatives who are hired by several different firms can contact customers at a low cost per customer because several clients share the total cost. But the selling effort behind the product is less intense than if the company's own salesforce did the selling.

When designing its channels, a company needs to consider *competitors' channels*. It may want to compete in or near the same outlets that carry competitors' products. Thus, food companies want their brands to be displayed next to competing brands; Burger King wants to locate near McDonald's. In other industries, producers may avoid the channels used by competitors. Avon decided not to compete with other cosmetics makers for scarce positions in retail stores and instead created a profitable door-to-door selling operation.

Finally, *environmental factors* such as economic conditions and legal constraints affect channel design decisions. For example, in a depressed economy, producers want to distribute their goods in the most economical way, using shorter channels and dropping unneeded services that add to the final price of the goods. Legal regulations prevent channel arrangements that "may tend to substantially lessen competition or tend to create a monopoly."

Identifying the Major Alternatives

When the company has defined its channel objectives, it should next identify its major channel alternatives in terms of *types* of middlemen, *number* of middlemen, and the *responsibilities* of each channel member.

Types of Middlemen

A firm should identify the types of middlemen available to carry on its channel work. For example, suppose a manufacturer of test equipment has developed an audio device that detects poor mechanical connections in any machine with moving parts. Company executives think that this product would have a market in all industries where electric, combustion, or steam engines are made or used. This market includes such industries as aviation, automobile, railroad, food canning, construction, and oil. The company's current salesforce is small, and the problem is how best to reach these different industries. The following channel alternatives might emerge from management discussion:

- *Company salesforce*—Expand the company's direct salesforce. Assign salespeople to territories and have them contact all prospects in the area, or develop separate company salesforces for different industries.
- *Manufacturer's agency*—Hire manufacturer's agencies—independent firms whose salesforces handle related products from many companies—in different regions or industries to sell the new test equipment.

■ *Industrial distributors*—Find distributors in the different regions or industries who will buy and carry the new line. Give them exclusive distribution, good margins, product training, and promotional support.

Sometimes, a company must develop a channel other than the one it prefers because of the difficulty or cost of using the preferred channel. Still, the decision sometimes turns out extremely well. For example, the U.S. Time Company first tried to sell its inexpensive Timex watches through regular jewelry stores. But most jewelry stores refused to carry them. The company then managed to get its watches into mass-merchandise outlets. This turned out to be a wise decision because of the rapid growth of mass merchandising.

Number of Middlemen

Companies also must determine the number of middlemen to use at each level. Three strategies are available.

INTENSIVE DISTRIBUTION   Producers of convenience goods and common raw materials typically seek **intensive distribution**—stocking their product in as many outlets as possible. These goods must be available where and when consumers want them. For example, toothpaste, candy, and other similar items are sold in millions of outlets to provide maximum brand exposure and consumer convenience.

EXCLUSIVE DISTRIBUTION   By contrast, some producers purposely limit the number of middlemen handling their products. The extreme form of this practice is **exclusive distribution,** whereby a limited number of dealers are given the exclusive right to distribute the company's products in their territories. Exclusive distribution is often found in the distribution of new automobiles and prestige women's clothing. By granting exclusive distribution, the manufacturer hopes for stronger distributor selling support and more control over middlemen's prices, promotion, credit, and services. Exclusive distribution often enhances the product's image and allows higher markups.

SELECTIVE DISTRIBUTION   Between intensive and exclusive distribution lies **selective distribution**—the use of more than one but less than all the middlemen who are willing to carry a company's products. The company does not have to spread its efforts over many outlets, including many marginal ones. It can develop a good working relationship with selected middlemen and expect a better-than-average selling effort. Selective distribution lets the producer gain good market coverage with more control and less cost than intensive distribution. Most television, furniture, and small appliance brands are distributed selectively.

Responsibilities of Channel Members

The producer and middlemen need to agree on the terms and responsibilities of each channel member. They should agree on price policies, conditions of sale, territorial

Convenience goods, such as cleaning products, are sold through every available outlet. Prestige goods, such as furs, are sold exclusively through a limited number of stores.

rights, and specific services to be performed by each party. The producer should establish a list price and a fair set of discounts for middlemen. It must define each middleman's territory and be careful where it places new resellers. Mutual services and duties need to be carefully spelled out, especially in franchise and exclusive distribution channels. For example, McDonald's provides franchisees with promotional support, a record-keeping system, training, and general management assistance. In turn, franchisees must meet company standards for physical facilities, cooperate with new promotion programs, provide requested information, and buy specified food products.

Evaluating the Major Channel Alternatives

Suppose a company has identified several channel alternatives and wants to select the one that will best satisfy its long-run objectives. The firm must evaluate each alternative against economic, control, and adaptive criteria. Consider the following situation:

> A Memphis furniture manufacturer wants to sell its line through retailers on the West Coast. The manufacturer is trying to decide between two alternatives.
>
> **1.** It could hire ten new sales representatives who would operate out of a sales office in San Francisco. They would receive a base salary plus a commission on their sales.
> **2.** It could use a San Francisco manufacturer's sales agency that has extensive contacts with retailers. The agency has thirty salespeople who would receive a commission based on their sales.

Economic Criteria

Each channel alternative will produce a different level of sales and costs. The first step is to determine the sales levels that would be produced by a company salesforce compared to a sales agency. Most marketing managers believe that a company salesforce will sell more. Company salespeople sell only the company's products and are better trained to handle them. They sell more aggressively because their future depends on the company. And they are more successful because customers prefer to deal directly with the company.

On the other hand, the sales agency could possibly sell more than a company salesforce. First, the sales agency has thirty salespeople, not just ten. Second, the agency salesforce may be just as aggressive as a direct salesforce, depending on how much commission the line offers in relation to other lines carried. Third, some customers prefer dealing with agents who represent several manufacturers rather than with salespeople from one company. Fourth, agency has many existing contacts, whereas a company salesforce would have to build them from scratch.

The next step is to estimate the costs of selling different volumes through each channel. The costs are shown in Figure 14-5. The fixed costs of using a sales agency are lower than those of setting up a company sales office. But costs rise faster through a sales agency because sales agents get a larger commission than company salespeople. There is one sales level (S_B) at which selling costs are the same for the two channels. The company would prefer to use the sales agency at any sales volume below S_B, and the company sales branch at any volume higher than S_B. In general, sales agents tend to be used by smaller firms, or by larger firms in smaller territories where the sales volume is too low to warrant a company salesforce.

FIGURE 14-5
Breakeven cost chart for the choice between a company salesforce and a manufacturer's sales agency

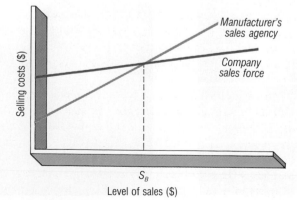

Control Criteria

Next, evaluation must be broadened to consider control issues with the two channels. Using a sales agency poses more of a control problem. A sales agency is an independent business firm interested in maximizing its profits. The agent may concentrate on the customers who buy the largest volume of goods from their entire mix of client companies rather than those most interested in a particular company's goods. And the agency's salesforce may not master the technical details of the company's products or handle its promotion materials effectively.

Adaptive Criteria

Each channel involves some long-term commitment and loss of flexibility. A company using a sales agency may have to offer a five-year contract. During this period, other means of selling, such as a company salesforce, may become more effective, but the company cannot drop the sales agency. To be worthy of consideration, a channel involving a long commitment should be greatly superior on economic or control grounds.

CHANNEL MANAGEMENT DECISIONS

Once the company has reviewed its channel alternatives and decided on the best channel design, it must implement and manage the chosen channel. Channel management calls for selecting and motivating individual middlemen and evaluating their performance over time.

Selecting Channel Members

Producers vary in their ability to attract qualified middlemen. Some producers have no trouble signing up middlemen. For example, IBM has no trouble attracting retailers to sell its personal computers. In fact, it has to turn down many would-be resellers. In some cases, the promise of exclusive or selective distribution for a desirable product will draw enough applicants.

At the other extreme are producers who have to work hard to line up enough qualified middlemen. When Polaroid started, it could not get photography stores to carry its new cameras and had to go to mass-merchandising outlets. Similarly, small food producers often have difficulty getting grocery stores to carry their products.

When selecting middlemen, the company should determine which characteristics distinguish the better middlemen. It will want to evaluate the middlemen's years in business, other lines carried, growth and profit record, profitability, cooperativeness, and reputation. If the middlemen are sales agents, the company will want to evaluate the number and character of other lines carried and the size and quality of the salesforce. If the middleman is a retail store that wants exclusive or selective distribution, the company will want to evaluate the store's customers, location, and future growth potential.

Motivating Channel Members

Once selected, middlemen must be continuously motivated to do their best. The company must sell not only *through* the middlemen, but *to* them. Most producers see the problem as finding ways to gain middlemen's cooperation.[16] They use the carrot-and-stick approach. They offer such *positive* motivators as higher margins, special deals, premiums, cooperative advertising allowances, display allowances, and sales contests. At times they will use *negative* motivators such as threatening to reduce margins, to slow down delivery, or to end the relationship altogether. A producer using this approach usually has not done a good job of studying the needs, problems, strengths, and weaknesses of its distributors.

More advanced companies try to forge long-term partnerships with their distributors through **distribution programming.** This involves building a planned, professionally managed, vertical marketing system that meets the needs of both the manufacturer *and* the distributors.[17] The manufacturer sets up a department in the marketing area called *distributor relations planning.* Its job is to identify the distributors' needs and build programs to help each distributor market the company's product. This department and the distributors jointly plan the merchandising goals, inventory levels, merchandising

DISTRIBUTION DECISIONS AND PUBLIC POLICY

For the most part, companies are free under the law to develop whatever channel arrangements suit them. In fact, the laws affecting channels seek to prevent exclusionary tactics of others that might keep the company from using a desired channel. Of course, this means that the company must itself avoid using such exclusionary tactics. Most channel law deals with the mutual rights and duties of the channel members once they have formed a relationship.

Exclusive Dealing

Many producers and wholesalers like to develop exclusive channels for their products. When the seller allows only certain outlets to carry its products, this strategy is called *exclusive distribution*. When the seller requires these dealers not to handle competitors' products, its strategy is called *exclusive dealing*. Both parties benefit from exclusive arrangements. The seller obtains more loyal and dependable outlets. The dealers obtain a steady source of supply and stronger seller support. But exclusive arrangements exclude other producers from selling to these dealers. This situation brings exclusive dealing contracts under the scope of the Clayton Act of 1914. They are legal as long as they do not substantially lessen competition or tend to create a monopoly, and as long as both parties enter into the agreement voluntarily.

Exclusive Territories

Exclusive dealing often includes exclusive territorial agreements. The producer may agree not to sell to other dealers in a given area, or the buyer may agree to sell only in its own territory. The first practice is normal under franchise systems as a way to increase dealer enthusiasm and commitment. And it is perfectly legal—a seller has no legal obligation to sell through more outlets than it wishes. The second practice, whereby the producer tries to keep a dealer from selling outside its territory, has become a major legal issue.

Tying Agreements

Producers of a strong brand sometimes sell it to dealers only if the dealers will take some or all of the rest of the line. This is called *full-line forcing*. Such tying agreements are not necessarily illegal, but they do violate the Clayton Act if they tend to lessen competition substantially. The practice may prevent consumers from freely choosing among competing suppliers of these other brands.

Dealers' Rights

Producers are free to select their dealers, but their right to terminate dealers is somewhat restricted. In general, sellers can drop dealers "for cause." But they cannot drop dealers, for example, if the dealers refuse to cooperate in a doubtful legal arrangement, such as exclusive dealing or tying agreements.

---

strategies, sales-training, and advertising and promotion plans. The aim is to convince distributors that they can make their money by being part of an advanced vertical marketing system.

Evaluating Channel Members

The producer must regularly check middlemen's performance against such standards as sales quotas, average inventory levels, customer delivery time, treatment of damaged and lost goods, cooperation in company promotion and training programs, and services to the customer. The company should recognize and reward middlemen who are performing well. Middlemen who are performing poorly should be helped or, as a last resort, replaced.

A company may periodically "requalify" its middlemen and prune the weaker ones. For example, when IBM first introduced its PS/2 personal computers, it reevaluated its dealers and allowed only the best ones to carry the new models. Each IBM dealer had to submit a business plan, send a sales and service employee to IBM training classes, and meet new sales quotas. Only about two-thirds of IBM's 2,200 dealers qualified to carry the PS/2 models.[18]

Manufacturers need to be sensitive to their dealers. Those who treat their dealers lightly risk not only losing their support but also causing some legal problems. Marketing Highlight 14–2 describes various rights and duties pertaining to manufacturers and their channel members.

PHYSICAL DISTRIBUTION DECISIONS

We are now ready to look at *physical distribution*—how companies store, handle, and move goods for availability to customers at the right time and place. Here we consider the *nature*, *objectives*, *systems*, and *organizational aspects* of physical distribution.

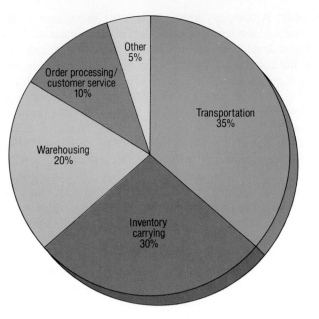

FIGURE 14-6
Costs of physical distribution elements as a percent of total physical distribution costs
Source: See Cynthia R. Milsap, "Distribution Costs Fall—Rules Off," *Business Marketing*, February 1985, p. 9.

Nature of Physical Distribution

The main elements of the physical distribution mix are shown in Figure 14-6. **Physical distribution** involves planning, implementing, and controlling the physical flow of materials and final goods from points of origin to points of use to meet the needs of customers at a profit. The major physical distribution cost is transportation, followed by inventory carrying, warehousing, order processing, and customer service.

Management in most companies has become concerned about the total cost of physical distribution, and experts believe that large savings can be gained in the physical distribution area. Poor physical-distribution decisions result in high costs. Even large companies sometimes make too little use of modern decision tools for coordinating inventory levels, transportation modes, and plant, warehouse, and store locations. For example, at least partly to blame for Sears' slow sales growth and sinking earnings during the past several years is its antiquated and costly distribution system. Outmoded multistory warehouses and non-automated equipment have made Sears much less efficient than its competitors. Distribution costs amount to 8 percent of sales at Sears compared to less than 3 percent at close competitors K mart and Wal-Mart.[19]

Moreover, physical distribution is more than a cost—it is a potent tool in demand creation. Companies can attract more customers by giving better service or lower prices through better physical distribution. On the other hand, companies lose customers when they fail to supply goods on time.

The Physical Distribution Objective

Many companies state their objective as getting the right goods to the right places at the right time for the least cost. Unfortunately, no physical distribution system can *both* maximize customer service *and* minimize distribution costs. Maximum customer service implies large inventories, the best transportation, and many warehouses—all of which raise distribution costs. Minimum distribution cost implies cheap transportation, low inventories, and few warehouses.

The company cannot simply let each physical distribution manager keep down costs. Transportation, warehousing, and order-processing costs interact, often in an inverse way. For example, low inventory levels reduce inventory carrying costs. But they also increase costs from stockouts, back orders, paperwork, special production runs, and high-cost, fast-freight shipments. Because physical distribution costs and activities involve strong tradeoffs, decisions must be made on a total system basis.

The starting point for designing the system is to study what customers want and what competitors are offering. Customers want several things from suppliers: on-time delivery, sufficiently large inventories, ability to meet emergency needs, careful handling of merchandise, good after-sale service, and willingness to take back or replace defective goods. A company must research the importance of these services to customers. For example, service-repair time is very important to buyers of copying equipment. So Xerox developed a service-delivery standard that can "put a disabled machine anywhere in the continental United States back into operation within three hours after receiving the service request." Xerox runs a service division with 12,000 service and parts personnel.

The company will normally want to offer at least the same level of service as competitors. But the objective is to maximize profits, not sales. The company must consider the costs of providing higher levels of service. Some companies offer less service and charge a lower price. Other companies offer more service than competitors and charge higher prices to cover higher costs.

The company ultimately must set physical distribution objectives to guide its planning. For example, Coca-Cola wants "to put Coke within an arm's length of desire." Companies go further and define standards for each service factor. One appliance manufacturer has set the following service standards: to deliver at least 95 percent of the dealer's orders within seven days of order receipt, to fill the dealer's order with 99 percent accuracy, to answer dealer questions on order status within three hours, and to ensure that damage to merchandise in transit does not exceed 1 percent.

Given a set of objectives, the company is ready to design a physical distribution system that will minimize the cost of attaining these objectives. The major decision issues are: How should orders be handled (*order processing*)? Where should stocks be located (*warehousing*)? How much stock should be kept on hand (*inventory*)? And how should goods be shipped (*transportation*)?

Order Processing

Physical distribution begins with a customer order. The order department prepares invoices and sends them to various departments. Items out of stock are back ordered. Shipped items are accompanied by shipping and billing documents with copies going to various departments.

The company and customers benefit when the order processing steps are carried out quickly and accurately. Ideally, salespeople send in their orders daily, often using online computers. The order department quickly processes these orders and the warehouse sends the goods out on time. Bills go out as soon as possible. The computer is often used to speed up the order-shipping-billing cycle. For example, General Electric operates a computer-based system that, upon receipt of a customer's order, checks the customer's credit standing and whether and where the items are in stock. The computer then issues an order to ship, bills the customer, updates the inventory records, sends a production order for new stock, and relays the message back to the salesperson that the customer's order is on its way—all in less than fifteen seconds.

Warehousing

Every company must store its goods while they wait to be sold. A storage function is needed because production and consumption cycles rarely match. For example, Snapper, Toro, and other lawn mower makers must produce all year long and store up their product for the heavy spring and summer buying season. The storage function overcomes differences in needed quantities and timing.

The company must decide on the best number of stocking locations. The more stocking locations, the more quickly goods can be delivered to customers. However, warehousing costs go up. The company must balance the level of customer service against distribution costs.

Some company stock is kept at or near the plant with the rest in warehouses around the country. The company might own private warehouses, rent space in public warehouses, or both. Companies have more control by owning warehouses, but that ties up capital and is less flexible if desired locations change. Public warehouses, on the other hand, charge for the rented space and provide additional services (at a cost) for inspecting goods, packaging them, shipping them, and invoicing them. By using public warehouses companies also have a wide choice of locations and warehouse types.

Companies may use either *storage warehouses* or *distribution centers*. Storage warehouses store goods for moderate to long periods. **Distribution centers** are designed

This Xerox automated warehouse is a high-rise storage facility which uses robots for automatic storage and retrieval.

to move goods rather than just store them. They are large and highly automated warehouses designed to receive goods from various plants and suppliers, take orders, fill them efficiently, and deliver goods to customers as quickly as possible. For example, Wal-Mart Stores, a regional discount chain, operates four distribution centers. One center, which serves the daily needs of 165 Wal-Mart stores, contains about 28 acres of space under a single roof. Laser scanners route as many as 190,000 cases of goods per day along 11 miles of conveyer belts, and the center's 1,000 workers load or unload 310 trucks daily.[20]

Warehousing facilities and equipment technology have improved greatly in recent years. Older multistoried warehouses with slow elevators and outdated materials-handling methods are facing competition from newer single-stored *automated warehouses* with advanced materials-handling systems under the control of a central computer. In these warehouses, only a few employees are necessary. The computer reads orders and directs lift trucks, electric hoists, or robots to gather goods, move them to loading docks, and issue invoices. These warehouses have reduced worker injuries, labor costs, theft, and breakage and have improved inventory control.

Inventory　Inventory levels also affect customer satisfaction. Marketers would like their companies to carry enough stock to fill all customer orders right away. However, it costs too much for a company to carry that much inventory. Inventory costs rise at an increasing rate as the customer service level approaches 100 percent. To justify larger inventories, management needs to know whether sales and profits will increase accordingly.

Inventory decisions involve knowing *when* to order and *how much* to order. In deciding when to order, the company balances the risks of running out of stock against the costs of carrying too much. In deciding how much to order, the company needs to balance order-processing costs against inventory-carrying costs. Larger average-order size means fewer orders and lower order-processing costs, but it also means larger inventory-carrying costs.

Transportation　Marketers need to take an interest in their company's *transportation* decisions. The choice of transportation carriers affects the pricing of the products, delivery performance, and condition of the goods when they arrive—all of which affects customer satisfaction.

In shipping goods to its warehouses, dealers, and customers, the company can choose among five transportation modes: rail, water, truck, pipeline, and air. The characteristics of each transportation mode characteristics are summarized in Table 14-1 and discussed in the following paragraphs.

TABLE 14-1
Characteristcs of Major
Transportation Modes

TRANSPORTATION MODE	INTERCITY CARGO VOLUME* (%)			TYPICAL PRODUCTS SHIPPED
	1970	1980	1987	
Rail	771 (39.8%)	932 (37.5%)	976 (36.5%)	Farm products, minerals, sand, chemicals, automobiles
Truck	412 (21.3)	555 (22.3)	666 (24.9)	Clothing, food, books, computers, paper goods.
Water	319 (16.5)	407 (16.4)	435 (16.3)	Oil, grain, sand, gravel, metallic ores, coal
Pipeline	431 (22.3)	588 (23.6)	587 (22.0)	Oil, coal, chemicals
Air	3.3 (0.17)	4.8 (0.19)	8.7 (0.34)	Technical instruments, perishable products, documents

* In billions of cargo ton-miles
Source: Statistical Abstract of the United States, 1989.

Rail

Although railroads lost share until the mid-1970s, they remain the nation's largest carrier, accounting for 37 percent of total cargo moved. Railroads are one of the most cost-effective modes for shipping large amounts of bulk products—coal, sand, minerals, farm and forest products—over long distances. In addition, railroads have recently begun to increase their customer services. They have designed new equipment to handle special categories of goods, provided flatcars for carrying truck trailers by rail (piggyback), and provided such in-transit services as the diversion of shipped goods to other destinations enroute and the processing of goods en route.

Truck

Trucks have steadily increased their share of transportation and now account for 25 percent of total cargo. They account for the largest portion of transportation *within* cities as opposed to *between* cities. Each year in the United States, trucks travel more than 140 billion miles—equal to nearly 300,000 round trips to the moon.[21] Trucks are highly flexible in their routing and time schedules. They can move goods door to door, saving shippers the need to transfer goods from truck to rail and back again at a loss of time and risk of theft or damage. Trucks are efficient for short hauls of high-value merchandise. In many cases, their rates are competitive with railway rates, and trucks can usually offer faster service.

Water

A large amount of goods moves by ships and barges on U.S. coastal and inland waterways. By themselves, Mississippi River barges account for 15 percent of the freight shipped in the United States. The cost of water transportation is very low for shipping bulky, low-value, nonperishable products such as sand, coal, grain, oil, and metallic ores. On the other hand, water transportation is the slowest mode and is sometimes affected by the weather.

Pipeline

Pipelines are a specialized means of shipping petroleum, natural gas, and chemicals from sources to markets. Pipeline shipment of petroleum products costs less than rail shipment but more than water shipment. Most pipelines are used by their owners to ship their own products.

Air

Although air carriers transport less than 1 percent of the nation's goods, they are becoming more important as a transportation mode. Air freight rates are much higher than rail or truck rates, but air freight is ideal when speed is needed or distant markets have to be reached. Among the most frequently air-freighted products are perishables (fresh fish, cut flowers) and high-value, low-bulk items (technical instruments, jewelry). Companies find that air freight reduces inventory levels, warehouse numbers, and packaging costs.

Choosing Transportation Modes

Until the late 1970s, routes, rates, and service in the transportation industry were heavily regulated by the federal government. Today, most of these regulations have been eased. Deregulation has caused rapid and substantial changes. Railroads, ships and barges, trucks, airlines, and pipeline companies are now much more competitive, flexible, and responsive to the needs of their customers. These changes have resulted in better services and lower prices for shippers. But such changes also mean that marketers must do better transportation planning if they want to take full advantage of new opportunities in the changing transportation environment.[22]

In choosing a transportation mode for a product, shippers consider as many as five criteria, as shown in Table 14-2. Thus, if a shipper needs speed, air and truck are the prime choices. If the goal is low cost, then water and pipeline might be best. Trucks appear to offer the most advantages—a fact that explains their growing share of the transportation market.

Thanks to *containerization*, shippers are increasingly combining two or more modes of transportation. **Containerization** consists of putting goods in boxes or trailers that are easy to transfer between two transportation modes.[23] *Piggyback* describes the use of rail and trucks; *fishyback*, water and trucks; *trainship*, water and rail; and *airtruck*, air and trucks. Each combination offers advantages to the shipper. For example, piggyback not only is cheaper than trucking alone but also provides flexibility and convenience.

Organizational Responsibility for Physical Distribution

Decisions on warehousing, inventory, and transportation require much coordination. many companies have created permanent committees made up of managers responsible for different physical distribution activities. These committees meet often to set policies for improving overall distribution efficiency. Some companies even have a vice-president of physical distribution who reports to the marketing vice-president, the manufacturing

Combining modes of transportation through containerization (clockwise): piggyback, fishyback, airtruck, and trainship.

TABLE 14-2
Rankings of Transportation Modes (1 = Highest Rank)

	SPEED (door-to-door delivery time)	DEPENDABILITY (meeting schedules on time)	CAPABILITY (ability to handle various products)	AVAILABILITY (no. of geographic points served)	COST (per ton-mile)
Rail	3	4	2	2	3
Water	4	5	1	4	1
Truck	2	2	3	1	4
Pipeline	5	1	5	5	2
Air	1	3	4	3	5

Source: See Carl M. Guelzo, *Introduction to Logistics Management* (Englewood Cliffs, NJ: Prentice Hall, 1986), p. 46.

vice-president, or even the president. The location of the physical-distribution department within the company is a secondary concern. The important thing is that the company coordinate its physical distribution and marketing activities in order to create high market satisfaction at a reasonable cost.

■ SUMMARY

Distribution channel decisions are among the most complex and challenging decisions facing the firm. Each channel system creates a different level of sales and costs. Once a distribution channel has been chosen, the firm must usually stick with it for a long time. The chosen channel strongly affects, and is affected by, the other elements in the marketing mix.

Each firm needs to identify alternative ways to reach its market. Available means vary from direct selling to using one, two, three, or more intermediary *channel levels*. The organizations making up the marketing channel are connected by product, title, payment, information, and promotion flows. Marketing channels face continuous and sometimes dramatic change. Three of the most important trends are the growth of *vertical*, *horizontal*, and *multichannel marketing systems*. These trends affect channel cooperation, conflict, and competition.

Channel design begins with assessing customer channel service needs and company channel objectives and constraints. The company then identifies the major channel alternatives in terms of the *types* of intermediaries, the *number* of intermediaries, and the *channel responsibilities* of each. Each channel alternative has to be evaluated according to economic, control, and adaptive criteria. Channel management calls for selecting qualified middlemen and motivating them. Individual channel members must be evaluated regularly.

Just as the marketing concept is receiving increased recognition, more business firms are paying attention to the physical distribution concept. *Physical distribution* is an area of potentially high cost savings and improved customer satisfaction. When order processors, warehouse planners, inventory managers, and transportation managers make decisions, they affect each other's costs and ability to handle demand. The physical distribution concept calls for treating all these decisions within a unified framework. The task is to design physical distribution systems that minimize the total cost of providing a desired level of customer services.

■ QUESTIONS FOR DISCUSSION

1. The Book-of-the-Month Club has been successfully marketing books by mail for more than 50 years. Why do so few publishers sell books by mail? How has the BOMC survived competition from B. Dalton, Waldenbooks, and other large booksellers in recent years?

2. Discount malls, so-called "factory outlet centers," are increasing in popularity. Many of their stores are operated by manufacturers who normally sell only through middlemen. What sort of merchandise is sold in these stores? Do these stores compete with the manufacturer's normal retailers? What are the pros and cons of operating these stores?

3. What organizations are needed to conduct the flows of products, ownership, payment, information, and promotion from the manufacturer to the customer? Are these organizations considered to be part of the distribution channel?

4. Chrysler owns rental car companies which operate fleets of Chrysler cars. How does Chrysler benefit from owning this distribution channel? Does this create any channel conflicts with Chrysler's existing dealers?

5. Why is franchising such a fast-growing form of retail organization?

6. Why have horizontal marketing arrangements become more common in recent years? Suggest several pairs of companies that you think could have successful horizontal marketing programs.

7. Describe the channel service needs of (a) consumers buying a computer for home use, (b) retailers buying computers to resell to individual consumers, and (c) purchasing agents buying computers for company use. What channels would a computer manufacturer design to satisfy these different service needs?

8. Which distribution strategies—intensive, selective, or exclusive—are used for the following products: (a) Piaget watches, (b) Acura automobiles, (c) Snickers candy bars. Why?

9. How do physical distribution decisions differ from channel decisions?

10. When planning desired inventory levels, what consequences of running out of stock need to be considered?

■ KEY TERMS

Administered VMS. A vertical marketing system that coordinates successive stages of production and distribution, not through common ownership or contractual ties but through the size and power of one of the parties.

Channel conflict. Disagreement among marketing channel members on goals and roles—on who should do what and for what rewards.

Channel level. A layer of middlemen that perform some work in bringing the product and its ownership closer to the final buyer.

Containerization. Putting the goods in boxes or trailers that are easy to transfer between two transportation modes. They are used in "multimode" systems commonly referred to as piggyback, fishyback, trainship, and airtruck.

Contractual VMS. A vertical marketing system in which independent firms at different levels of production and distribution join together through contracts to obtain more economies or sales impact than they could achieve alone.

Conventional distribution channel. A channel consisting of one or more independent producers, wholesalers, and retailers, each a separate business seeking to maximize its own profits even at the expense of profits for the system as a whole.

Corporate VMS. A vertical marketing system which combines successive stages of production and distribution under single ownership—channel leadership is established through common ownership.

Direct-marketing channel. A marketing channel that has no intermediary levels.

Distribution center. A large and highly automated warehouse designed to receive goods from various plants and suppliers, take orders, fill them efficiently, and deliver goods to customers as quickly as possible.

Distribution channel (marketing channel). A set of interdependent organizations involved in the process of making a product or service available for use or consumption by the consumer or industrial user.

Distribution programming. Building a planned, professionally managed, vertical market system that meets the needs of both the manufacturer *and* the distributors.

Exclusive distribution. Giving a limited number of dealers the exclusive right to distribute the company's products in their territories.

Franchise organization. A contractual vertical marketing system in which a channel member called a franchiser links several stages in the production-distribution process.

Horizontal marketing systems. A channel arrangement in which two or more companies at one level join together to follow a new marketing opportunity.

Intensive distribution. Stocking the product in as many outlets as possible.

Multichannel marketing. Multichannel distribution, as when a single firm sets up two or more marketing channels to reach one or more customer segments.

Physical distribution. The tasks involved in planning, implementing, and controlling the physical flow of materials and final goods from points of origin to points of use to meet the needs of customers at a profit.

Retailer cooperatives. Contractual vertical marketing systems in which retailers organize a new, jointly owned business to carry on wholesaling and possibly production.

Selective distribution. The use of more than one but less than all the middlemen who are willing to carry the company's products.

Vertical marketing system (VMS). A distribution channel structure in which producers, wholesalers, and retailers act as a unified system—either one channel member owns the others, or has contracts with them, or has so much power that they all cooperate.

Wholesaler-sponsored voluntary chains. Contractual vertical marketing systems in which wholesalers organize voluntary chains of independent retailers to help them compete with large corporate chain organizations.

■ REFERENCES

1. Julie Liesse Erickson and Judann Dagnoli, "Winn-Dixie, Food Giants Mend Fences," *Advertising Age*, January 9, 1989, pp. 1, 45; Judann Dagnoli and Laurie Freeman, "P&G, Pillsbury Just Say No to Big Retail Chain," *Advertising Age*, October 3, 1988, pp. 2, 68; Julie Liesse Erickson, "Grocery Chain Dumps Major Package Goods," *Advertising Age*, October 10, 1988, pp. 1, 75; Laurie Freeman and Julie Liesse Erickson, "Grocers Join Winn-Dixie," *Advertising Age*, November 7, 1988, pp. 3, 78; and "Some Deals Are Positively Diverting," *Sales & Marketing Management*, October 1988, p. 42.

2. See Louis W. Stern and Frederick D. Sturdivant, "Customer-Driven Distribution Systems," *Harvard Business Review*, July–August 1987, p. 34.

3. Louis Stern and Adel I. El-Ansary, *Marketing Channels*, 3d. ed. (Englewood Cliffs, NJ: Prentice Hall, 1988), p. 3.

4. Ronald Abler, John S. Adams, and Peter Gould, *Spatial Organizations: The Geographer's View of the World* (Englewood Cliffs, NJ: Prentice-Hall, 1971), pp. 531–32.

5. See Irving Rein, Philip Kotler, and Martin Stoller, *High Visibility* (New York: Dodd, Mead, Inc., 1987).

6. For an excellent summary of channel conflict and power, see Stern and El-Ansary, *Marketing Channels*, chapters 6 and 7.

7. See Bert C. McCammon, Jr., "Perspectives for Distribution Programming," in *Vertical Marketing Systems*, Louis P. Bucklin, ed. (Glenview, IL: Scott Foresman, 1970), pp. 32–51.

8. Janet Myers, "Giant Stocks Up on Service, Vertical Integration," *Advertising Age*, April 28, 1986, p. S4.

9. Jaclyn Fierman, "How Gallo Crushes the Competition," *Fortune*, September 1, 1986, p. 27.

10. See Laura Zinn, "Want to Buy a Franchise? Look Before You Leap," *Business Week*, May 23, 1988, pp. 186–187; and "Why Franchising Is Taking Off," *Fortune*, February 12, 1990, p. 124.

11. This has been called "symbiotic marketing." For more reading, see Lee Adler, "Symbiotic Marketing," *Harvard*

Business Review, November–December 1966, pp. 59–71; and P. "Rajan" Varadarajan and Daniel Rajaratnam, "Symbiotic Marketing Revisited," *Journal of Marketing*, January 1986, pp. 7–17.

12. See Gary Hamel, Yves L. Doz, and C. K. Prahalad, "Collaborate with Your Competitors—and Win," *Harvard Business Review*, January–February 1989, pp. 133–139.

13. See Robert E. Weigand, "Fit Products and Channels to Your Markets," *Harvard Business Review*, January–February 1977, pp. 95–105.

14. See Stern and Sturdivant, "Customer-Driven Distribution Systems," p. 35.

15. Ibid., p. 35.

16. See Bert Rosenbloom, *Marketing Channels: A Management View* (Hinsdale, IL: Dryden Press, 1978), pp. 192–203.

17. See McCammon, "Perspectives for Distribution Programming," p. 43; and James A. Narus and James C. Anderson, "Turn Your Industrial Distributors into Partners," *Harvard Business Review*, March–April 1986, pp. 66–71.

18. See Katherine M. Hafner, "Computer Retailers: Things Have Gone from Worse to Bad," *Business Week*, June 8, 1987, p. 104.

19. Patricia Sellers, "Why Bigger Is Badder at Sears," *Fortune*, December 5, 1988, p. 82.

20. John Huey, "Wal-Mart: Will It Take Over the World?" *Fortune*, January 30, 1989, pp. 52–64.

21. See "Trucking," *Fortune*, November 22, 1987, p. 148.

22. See Lewis M. Schneider, "New Era in Transportation Strategy," *Harvard Business Review*, March–April 1985, pp. 118–126.

23. For more discussion, see Norman E. Hutchinson, *An Integrated Approach to Logistics Management* (Englewood Cliffs, NJ: Prentice Hall, 1987), p. 69.

COMPAQ COMPUTER: A COSTLY CHANNEL CONFLICT

In February 1989, Compaq Computer abruptly ended a seven-year relationship with Businessland, the nation's largest publicly held computer store chain. With this startling decision, Compaq lost distribution in stores that accounted for 7 percent of its revenues and provided a key link to its corporate customer segment. The break ended a three-year history of disagreements between the two firms over Businessland's reported demands for preferential pricing and promotion treatment from Compaq. Instead of knuckling under to the pressure, Compaq severed the relationship.

Compaq's major competitor, IBM, which accounts for a whopping 31 percent of all Businessland sales, played a major role in the conflict. IBM had been aggressively wooing Businessland with sweetheart deals and bigger discounts than those that it offered to other IBM dealers. Using a much disputed promotion program, IBM allowed Businessland to use IBM market-development funds to encourage sales of IBM machines over other brands. Amidst an ongoing debate over pricing discounts, IBM also began to sell PCs to Businessland and Computerland, the two largest chains, at about 4 percent less than it sold them to its other dealers. The two dealers then used the extra revenue to boost commissions and run advertising.

IBM also started giving money, known as "flexfunds," to computer dealers who pledged to increase sales of IBM products. Use of such funds had previously been limited to such activities as advertising and sales-training programs, but when IBM loosened its restrictions, Businessland, breaking with industry tradition, began to use these funds to supplement the commissions that it paid its 700 salespeople for selling IBM products. Finally, whereas other vendors' programs feed money back to dealers only *after* they've met sales quotas, IBM gave dealers up-front cash for the mere *promise* of increased sales. In return, Businessland pledged to boost IBM sales by as much as 50 percent. As a result, some Businessland salespeople were being paid five to ten times more commission for selling IBM than for selling Compaq.

Businessland then tried to exact special treatment from Compaq similar to that which it was getting from IBM. The chain attempted to use the IBM deal to exert pressure on Compaq to ease restrictions on its funding programs and permit similar salesforce incentives. Businessland repeatedly stressed that for Compaq to become one of its "strategic partners," the manufacturer would have to give the store chain preferential treatment. But unlike IBM, which negotiates terms on a dealer-by-dealer basis, Compaq has always had a two-tier pricing structure that it applied to all dealers and has long prided itself on its scrupulously even-handed policy toward all of its deal-

ers. Favoring one dealer over another with special agreements simply was not consistent with the straightforward dealer strategy that had helped make Compaq so successful. Thus, when pressured by Businessland for special treatment, Compaq held fiercely to its philosophy that all dealers be treated fairly and equitably. Rather than yield to the dealer's demands, Compaq turned Businessland loose. However, conflicts between dealers and computer manufacturers are far from over. For example, Compaq expects that by publicizing IBM's discount arrangement with Businessland, it may stir other dealers into demanding the same arrangement from IBM. And what appears to be a successful coup may come back to haunt IBM. If IBM must give the same discounts to other dealers, its profits may suffer.

Although squabbles over discounts and salesforce incentive programs are the most obvious cause of the dramatic divorce of Compaq and Businessland, there appears to be another deeper reason. Compaq's decision to separate came just weeks after Businessland publicly endorsed IBM's new Micro Channel Architecture (MCA) instead of the Extended Industry Standard Architecture (EISA) used by Compaq. A computer's architecture dictates how the computer interfaces with its peripherals, such as its printer or modem. In an effort to gain a tighter proprietary grip on new technology, IBM is trying to set a new standard for the industry—one that cannot be cloned. IBM's new MCA is much faster at transferring information between the computer and its peripherals but is not compatible with previous standards. On the other hand, the competing EISA, which has the speed of MCA, is compatible with earlier equipment.

Many analysts have speculated that the real reason for the Compaq-Businessland split was the battle over which PC-design standard would dominate. IBM has worked hard to establish the micro channel as the industry standard. It has wooed dealers by eliminating unpopular sales quotas and by hiking allowances for training and technical support. IBM reps even make joint sales calls with dealers.

However, IBM's Micro Channel design, first featured in its Personal System/2 Computers in 1987, got off to a slow start that gave Compaq—backed by eight other producers—time to propose the alternative EISA design. By jointly developing EISA, the nine computer companies hoped to challenge IBM's hold on PC-design standards. As the struggle between Compaq and IBM intensified, however, Businessland complained that EISA's challenge to MCA created confusion at the customer level, where users would have to sort out which architecture would ultimately prevail. Finally, two years after the MCA/EISA debate began, Businessland officials announced that they would emphasize the IBM standard and support EISA only when requested by customers. This decision came as a harsh blow to Compaq. Thus, the break between Compaq and Businessland may be the first indication that the success or failure of MCA versus EISA will depend on which camp musters the broadest support at the retail level.

Most industry analysts contend that Compaq will recover from the breakup faster than Businessland: Businessland accounted for 7 percent of Compaq's sales in 1988 but garnered 15 percent of its own revenues from sales of Compaq computers. Moreover, other Compaq dealers will be more than delighted to pick up Businessland's share of Compaq sales—they are already aggressively courting Businessland's former Compaq customers. Finally, buyers who prefer Compaq aren't likely to switch to IBM merely to buy from Businessland.

Others argue, however, that the divorce will hurt Compaq more. With the split, Compaq has lost a prime channel to the corporate market. However, still others point out that corporate buyers often do not feel much loyalty to dealers. Many buyers chose Compaq as their *computer* instead of Businessland as their *vendor*—they will now seek a different dealer, not a different manufacturer.

Compaq is a savvy computer marketer. It now holds about 8 percent of the $23.2 billion U.S. personal computer market, mostly obtained by taking advantage of IBM's missteps—often churning out sleek, high-performance computers that are better and faster than Big Blue's. Moreover, while Compaq's share has grown in recent years, IBM's share has dwindled to 21 percent, down from about 31 percent in 1987. Compaq's revenues have more than tripled since 1986, and earnings have risen sixfold. So, although some analysts see Compaq's move to cut off Businessland as an uncharacteristically emotional reaction, others see it as a boldly calculated strategic move.

QUESTIONS

1. What functions do dealers perform in the PC market? Why are they needed?
2. What kind of channel organization does IBM have in the PC market? What kind does Compaq have?
3. How do the goals of different channel members fuel the channel conflicts discussed in the case? Who is helped or harmed by these conflicts?
4. What recommendations would you make to Compaq regarding its channel design?

PRO IMAGE

The marketing of professional and college team sportswear and novelty items is a $3 billion-a-year industry. Since 1985, approximately 300 sports fan shops have opened. Most are independent operations, but franchisors are an increasingly important part of the retailing scene. Pro Image wasn't the first franchisor of the one-stop sports fan shop, but they are battling to lead the pack. In the franchise field, Pro Image competes with such firms as SpectAthlete, Sports Fantasy, Fan Fair, and Sports Arena Ltd.

Fan shops seems to sell just about anything from T-shirts, sweatshirts, sweaters, and caps to coffee mugs, key chains, pennants, bedspreads, and football helmet telephones. While many items are licensed from teams and emblazoned with team logos, most shops also sell authentic merchandise like team jackets and jerseys.

Pro Image was founded in 1985 by Chad and Kevin Olson. Three years later they controlled over 130 stores, with an additional 100 franchised. Each franchise store costs roughly $100,000: approximately $16,000 for the franchise fee and the rest for inventory and store improvements.

Since Pro Image recognizes the importance of a good location, it requires franchisees to locate in high-traffic regional malls. Pro Image assists franchisees in site selection, lease negotiation, and advertising. Store owners must create an upscale image with glass store fronts and wood-slat wall displays. Pro Image requires new owners to attend a four-day training session. They also sponsor an annual convention. Other assistance includes a business hotline and a computerized inventory and sales system. As an added service, they stock hard-to-get items in a 4,500-square-foot warehouse, making them more readily available to franchisees.

Pro Image recognizes that consumers want to wear what their sports heroes wear on the field. Therefore, they stock authentic merchandise that comes directly from the same manufacturers that supply leagues and teams. But authentic merchandise carries a relatively high price. Replica merchandise is available for the more price-conscious. Though it's very similar to the authentic merchandise, it's not exactly the same product worn by the pro players.

The main customer base for Pro Image is men between 18 and 40, although women are becoming increasingly important customers. They purchase the product for themselves, their spouses, or their children.

Competition for the sports fan market is intense. Pro Image must battle not only other franchise operations but also independents, department stores, general retailers, and athletic stores that sell similar merchandise. The latter three constitute the major competition for Pro Image since they control approximately 90 percent of the total licensed merchandise market.

Retailers and their customers aren't the only ones benefiting from the boom in sportswear and novelty item merchandising. Consider NFL Properties, the licensing arm of the National Football League. Since 1980, NFL Properties has seen its souvenir revenues increase by nearly 400 percent to approximately $1.5 billion. The licensing division of NFL Properties oversees the authorization and sale of more than 700 items.

Team owners love NFL Properties. In the past decade, with two player strikes, relatively stagnant television income, and escalating player salaries, team owners have come to appreciate the approximately $1.5 million they receive each year from Properties' activities.

Also benefiting are a variety of charities. Each year NFL Properties raises and distributes nearly $700,000 to deserving organizations.

QUESTIONS

1. Explain why an organization such as NFL Properties might choose to have independent retailers, franchise operations, department stores, mass merchandisers, and athletic stores sell NFL-authorized merchandise to consumers rather than sell the merchandise directly to consumers through their own chain of retail outlets.

2. Discuss the nature of the vertical marketing system employed by Pro Image.

3. Suppose you are interested in opening a sports fan shop. What do you see as the advantages and disadvantages of becoming part of a franchise operation?

Sources: "NFL Properties' Values Booming," *The Sporting News*, October 30, 1989, p. 64; "Franchising Jockeying for Position," *Venture*, September 1988, pp. 76–80; and "Unlicensed Comic Books Have NFL in Poor Humor," *Advertising Age*, December 19, 1988, p. 36.

Placing Products:
Retailing and Wholesaling

When Scandinavian furniture giant IKEA (pronounced *eye-KEY-ah*) opened its first U.S. store in 1985, it caused quite a stir. On opening day, people flocked to the suburban Philadelphia store from as far away as Washington, D.C. Traffic on the nearby turnpike backed up for six miles, and at one point the store was so tightly jammed with customers that management ordered the doors closed until the crowds thinned out. In the first week, the IKEA store packed in 150,000 people who bought more than $1 million worth of furniture. And when the dust had settled, the store was still averaging 50,000 customers a week.

IKEA is one of a new breed of retailers called "category killers." They get their name from their marketing strategy: carry a huge selection of merchandise in a single product category at such good prices that you destroy the competition. Category killers are now striking in a wide range of industries, including furniture, toys, records, sporting goods, housewares, and consumer electronics.

An IKEA store is about three football fields in size. Each store stocks more than 6,000 items—all furnishings and housewares, ranging from coffee mugs to leather sofas to kitchen cabinets. IKEA sells Scandinavian design "knock-down" furniture; each item reduces to a flat-pack kit for assembly at home. Consumers browse through the store's comfortable display area, where signs and stickers on each item note its price, details of its construction, assembly instructions, its location in the adjacent warehouse—even which other pieces complement the item.

Customers wrestle desired items from warehouse stacks, haul their choices away on large trollies, and pay at giant-size checkout counters. The store provides a reasonably-priced restaurant for hungry shoppers and a supervised children's play area for weary parents. But best of all, IKEA has low prices. The store operates on the philosophy of providing a wide variety of well-designed home furnishing at prices that the majority of people can afford.

Although the first category killer, Toys 'Я' Us, appeared during the late 1950s, other retailers have only recently adopted the idea. Unlike warehouse clubs and other "off-price" retailers, which offer the lowest prices but few choices within any given category, category killers offer an exhaustive selection in one line. Toys 'Я' Us stocks 18,000 different toy items in football-field-size stores. Huge Sportmart stores stock 100,000 sports goods items including 70 types of sleeping bags, 265 styles of athletic socks, 12,000 pairs of shoes, and 15,000 fishing lures. Tower Records stores carry as many as 75,000 titles—25 times more than the average competitor. And Branden's, the housewares and home furnishings category killer, offers a choice of 30 different coffee pots, 25 irons, 100 patterns of bed sheets, and 800 kitchen gadgets. With such large assortments, category killers generate big sales that often allow them to charge prices as low as those of their discount competitors.

However, the category killers face a few problems. IKEA has encountered occasional difficulty managing its huge inventory, sometimes overpromising or inconveniencing customers. The company's expansive stores also require large investments and huge markets. And some consumers find that they want more personal service than IKEA gives or that the savings aren't worth the work required to find products in the huge store, haul them out, and assemble them at home. Despite such problems, IKEA has prospered beyond its founders' dreams. It now has 89 stores in 19 countries racking up annual sales of more than $3 billion. It recently opened stores in Washington, D.C., Baltimore, and Pittsburgh with plans for more in New Jersey, Long Island, and Burbank. In all, IKEA plans to open 60 stores around the country during the next 25 years.

Most retailing experts predict great success for stores like IKEA. One retailing analyst, Wallace Epperson, Jr., "estimates IKEA will win at least a 15 percent share of any market it enters and will expand the market as it does so. If Mr. Epperson is any indication, IKEA's prospects are good. Touring IKEA in his professional capacity, Mr. Epperson couldn't resist the store. 'I spent $400,' he said. 'It's incredible.' "[1]

CHAPTER OBJECTIVES

After reading this chapter, you should be able to:
1. Explain the roles of retailers and wholesalers in the distribution channel.
2. Describe the major types of retailers and give examples of each.
3. Identify the major types of wholesalers and give examples of each.
4. Explain the marketing decisions facing retailers and wholesalers.

This chapter looks at *retailing* and *wholesaling*. In the first section, we look at retailing's nature and importance, major types of store and non-store retailers, decisions retailers make, and the future of retailing. In the second section, we discuss the same topics for wholesalers.

RETAILING

What is retailing? We all know that Sears and K mart are retailers, but so are Avon representatives, the local Holiday Inn, and a doctor seeing patients. We define **retailing** as all the activities involved in selling goods or services directly to final consumers for their personal, nonbusiness use. Many institutions—manufacturers, wholesalers, retailers—do retailing. But most retailing is done by **retailers**—businesses whose sales come *primarily* from retailing. And although most retailing is done in retail stores, in recent years nonstore retailing—selling by mail, by telephone, by door-to-door contact, by vending machines, by numerous electronic means—has grown explosively. Because store retailing accounts for most of the retail business, we discuss it first. Then we look at nonstore retailing.

STORE RETAILING

Retail stores come in all shapes and sizes, and new retail types keep emerging. They can be classified by one or more of several characteristics: *amount of service, product line sold, relative prices, control of outlets,* and *type of store cluster.* These classifications and the corresponding retailer types are shown in Table 15-1.

Amount of Service   Different products need different amounts of service, and customer-service preferences vary. We discuss three levels of service—self service, limited service, and full service—and the types of retailers that use them.

Self-service retailing in this country grew rapidly during the Great Depression of the 1930s. Customers were willing to perform their own "locate-compare-select"

TABLE 15-1
Different Ways to Classify Retail Outlets

AMOUNT SERVICE	PRODUCT LINE SOLD	RELATIVE PRICE EMPHASIS	CONTROL OF OUTLETS	TYPE OF STORE CLUSTER
Self-service	Specialty store	Discount store	Corporate chain	Central business district
Limited service	Department store	Off-price retailers	Voluntary chain and retailer cooperative	Regional shopping center
Full service	Supermarket	Catalog show-room	Consumer cooperative	Community shopping center
	Convenience store		Franchise organization	Neighborhood shopping center
	Combination store, superstore, and hypermarket		Merchandising conglomerate	
	Service business			

process to save money. Today, self-service is the basis of all discount operations and is typically used by sellers by convenience goods (for example, supermarkets) and nationally branded, fast-moving shopping goods (for example, catalog showrooms such as Best Products or Service Merchandise).

Limited-service retailers such as Sears or J. C. Penney provide more sales assistance because they carry more shopping goods about which customers need more information. They also offer additional services such as credit and merchandise return not usually offered by low-service stores. Their increased operating costs result in higher prices.

In **full-service retailers,** such as specialty stores and first-class department stores, salespeople assist customers in every phase of the shopping process. Full-service stores usually carry more specialty goods and slower moving items such as cameras, jewelry, and fashions, for which customers like to be "waited on." They provide more liberal return policies, various credit plans, free delivery, home servicing, and extras such as lounges and restaurants. More services result in much higher operating costs, costs which are passed along to customers as higher prices.

Product Line Sold

Retailers can also be classified by the length and breadth of their product assortments. Among the most important types are the *specialty store*, the *department store*, the *supermarket*, the *convenience store*, and the *superstore*.

Specialty Store

A **specialty store** carries a narrow product line with a deep assortment within that line. Examples include stores selling sporting goods, furniture, books, electronics, flowers, or toys. Specialty stores can be further classified by the narrowness of their product lines. A clothing store is a *single-line store*, a men's clothing store is a *limited-line store*, and a men's custom shirt store is a *superspecialty store*.

Today, specialty stores are flourishing for several reasons. The increasing use of market segmentation, market targeting, and product specialization has resulted in a greater need for stores that focus on specific products and segments. And because of changing consumer life styles and the increasing number of two-income households, many consumers have greater incomes but less time to spend shopping. They are attracted to specialty stores that provide high quality products, convenient locations, good hours, excellent service, and quick entry and exit.

Department Store

A **department store** carries a wide variety of product lines—typically clothing, home furnishings, and household goods. Each line is operated as a separate department managed by specialist buyers or merchandisers. Examples of well-known department stores include Bloomingdale's (New York), Marshall Field (Chicago), and Filene's (Boston). *Specialty department stores*, which carry only clothing, shoes, cosmetics, luggage, and gift items, can also be found. Examples are Saks Fifth Avenue and I. Magnin.

Department stores grew rapidly through the first half of the century. But after World War II, they began to lose ground to other types of retailers, including discount

Specialty stores focus on specific products and segments.

stores, specialty store chains, and "off-price" retailers. The heavy traffic, poor parking, and general decaying of central cities, where many department stores had made their biggest investments, made downtown shopping less appealing. As a result, many department stores closed or merged with others.

Nonetheless, department stores are today waging a "comeback war." Most have opened suburban stores and many have added "bargain basements" to meet the discount threat. Still others have remodeled their stores or set up "boutiques" that compete with specialty stores. Many are trying mail-order and telephone selling. In recent years, many large department stores have been joining rather than fighting the competition by diversifying into discount and specialty stores. Dayton-Hudson, for example, operates Target (discount stores), Mervyn's (lower-price clothing), B. Dalton (books), and many other discount and specialty chains in addition to its Dayton's, Hudson's, and other department stores. These discount and specialty operations now account for more than 80 percent of total corporate sales.[2]

Supermarket

Supermarkets are large, low-cost, low-margin, high-volume, self-service stores that carry a wide variety of food, laundry, and household products. Most U.S. supermarket stores are owned by supermarket chains such as Safeway, Kroger, A&P, Winn-Dixie, Publix, Food Lion, and Jewel. Chains account for almost 70 percent of all supermarket sales.

The first supermarkets introduced the concepts of self-service, customer turnstiles, and checkout counters. Supermarket growth took off in the 1930s for several reasons. The Great Depression made consumers more price conscious, and mass automobile ownership reduced the need for small neighborhood stores. An increase in brand preselling through advertising reduced the need for salesclerks. Finally, stores selling grocery, meat, produce, and household goods in a single location allowed one-stop shopping and lured consumers from greater distances, giving supermarkets the volume needed to offset their lower margins.

However, most supermarkets today are facing slow sales growth because of slower population growth and an increase in competition from convenience stores, discount food stores, and superstores. They have also been hit hard by the rapid growth of out-of-home eating. Thus, supermarkets are looking for new ways to build their sales. Most chains now operate fewer but larger stores. They practice "scrambled merchandising," carrying many non-food items—beauty aids, housewares, toys, prescriptions, appliances, videocassettes, sporting goods, garden supplies—hoping to find high-margin lines to improve profits.

Supermarkets are also improving their facilities and services to attract more customers. Typical improvements are better locations, improved decor, longer store hours, check-cashing, delivery, and even childcare centers. Although consumers have always expected supermarkets to offer good prices, convenient locations, and speedy checkout, today's more affluent and sophisticated food buyer wants more. Many supermarkets, therefore, are "moving upscale" with the market, providing "from-scratch" bakeries, gourmet deli counters, and seafood departments.[3] Finally, to attract more customers, large supermarket chains are starting to customize their stores for individual neighborhoods. They are tailoring store size, product assortments, prices, and promotions to the economic and ethnic needs of local markets.

Convenience Store

Convenience stores are small stores which carry a limited line of high-turnover convenience goods. Examples include 7-Eleven, Circle K, and Stop-N-Go Stores. These stores locate near residential areas and remain open long hours, seven days a week. Convenience stores must charge high prices to make up for higher operating costs and lower sales volume. But they satisfy an important consumer need. Consumers use convenience stores for "fill-in" purchases at off hours or when time is short, and they are willing to pay for the convenience. The number of convenience stores increased from about 2,000 in 1957 to more than 80,000 in 1989.

However, the convenience store industry has lately suffered from overcapacity as its primary market of young blue-collar men has shrunk. As a result, many convenience store operators are redesigning their stores with female customers in mind. They are upgrading colors, dropping video games, improving parking and lighting, and pricing more competitively. The major convenience chains are also experimenting with micromarketing—tailoring each store's merchandise to the specific needs of its surrounding neighborhood. For example, a Stop-N-Go in an affluent neighborhood carries fresh produce, gourmet pasta sauces, chilled Evian water, and expensive wines, while a store in an Hispanic neighborhood carries Spanish-language magazines. Through such moves, convenience stores hope to remain strongly differentiated from other types of food stores while adapting to today's fast-paced consumer life styles.[4]

Superstore, Combination Store, and Hypermarket

These three types of stores are larger than the conventional supermarket. **Superstores** are almost twice the size of regular supermarkets and carry a large assortment of routinely purchased food and nonfood items. They offer such services as dry cleaning, post offices, photo finishing, check cashing, bill paying, lunch counters, car care, and pet care. Because of their wider assortment, superstore prices are 5 to 6 percent higher than those of conventional supermarkets. Many leading chains are moving toward superstores. Examples include Safeway's Pak 'N Pay and Pathmark Super Centers. Almost 80 percent of Safeway's new stores during the past several years have been superstores. In 1975, superstores accounted for only about 3 percent of total food store sales, but by 1986 they took in more than 26 percent of the business. In 1986, 39 percent of all new grocery stores opened were superstores.[5]

Combination stores are combined food and drug stores. They average about one and one-half football fields in size—about twice the size of superstores. Examples are A&P's Family Mart and Kroger-Sav-On. Combination stores take in less than 5 percent of the business done by food stores but account for 21 percent of new grocery store openings.

Hypermarkets are even bigger than combination stores, perhaps as large as *six* football fields. They combine supermarket, discount, and warehouse retailing. A typical hypermarket may have 50 check-out counters. They carry more than routinely purchased goods, also selling furniture, appliances, clothing, and many other things. The hypermarket operates like a warehouse. Products in wire "baskets" are stacked high on metal racks;

Hypermarkets: Huge stores that combine supermarket, discount, and warehouse retailing.

forklifts move through aisles during selling hours to restock shelves. The store gives discounts to customers who carry their own heavy appliances and furniture out of the store. Examples include Bigg's in Cincinnati, Ralph's Giant Stores in Southern California, and Carrefour in Philadelphia. Hypermarkets have grown quickly in Europe and now appear to be catching on in the United States, with major retailers such as K mart and Wal-Mart now opening such giant stores. Industry experts estimate that 150 hypermarkets were operating in the U.S. in 1990.

However, the major advantage of hypermarkets—their size—can also be a major drawback for some consumers. Many people, especially older shoppers, balk at the serious walking. And despite their size and volume of sales, most hypermarkets have only limited product variety. Surveys indicate 25 percent lower customer satisfaction with hypermarkets than conventional supermarkets, leaving some experts skeptical about the future of these giant stores.[6]

Service Business

For some businesses, the "product line" is actually a service. Service retailers include hotels and motels, banks, airlines, colleges, hospitals, movie theaters, tennis clubs, bowling alleys, restaurants, repair services, hair care shops, and dry cleaners. Service retailers in the United States are growing faster than product retailers, and each service industry has its own retailing drama. Banks look for new ways to distribute their services, including automatic tellers, direct deposit, and telephone banking. Health organizations are changing the ways consumers get and pay for health services. The amusement industry has spawned Disney World and other theme parks. H&R Block has built a franchise network to help consumers pay as little as possible to Uncle Sam.

Relative Prices

Retailers can also be classified according to their prices. Most retailers charge regular prices and offer normal quality goods and customer service. Some offer higher quality goods and service at higher prices. The retailers that feature low prices are discount stores, "off-price" retailers, and catalog showrooms.

Discount Store

A **discount store** sells standard merchandise at lower prices by accepting lower margins and selling higher volume. The use of occasional discounts or specials does not make a discount store. A true discount store *regularly* sells its merchandise at lower prices, offering mostly national brands, not inferior goods. The early discount stores cut expenses by operating in warehouse-like facilities in low-rent but heavily traveled districts. They slashed prices, advertised widely, and carried a reasonable width and depth of products.

In recent years, facing intense competition from other discounters and department stores, many discount retailers have "traded up." They have improved decor, added new lines and services, and opened suburban branches, which has led to higher costs and prices. And as some department stores have cut their prices to compete with discounters, the distinction between many discount and department stores has become blurred. As a result, several major discount stores folded during the 1970s because they lost their price advantage. And many department store retailers have upgraded their stores and services, once again setting themselves apart from the improved discounters.

Off-Price Retailers

When the major discount stores traded up, a new wave of **off-price retailers** moved in to fill the low-price, high-volume gap. Ordinary discounters buy at regular wholesale prices and accept lower margins to keep prices down. Off-price retailers, on the other hand, buy at less than regular wholesale prices and charge consumers less than retail. They tend to carry a changing and unstable collection of higher-quality merchandise, often leftover goods, overruns, and irregulars obtained at reduced prices from manufacturers or other retailers. Off-price retailers have made the biggest inroads in clothing, accessories, and footwear. But they can be found in all areas, from no-frills banking and discount brokerages to food stores and electronics (see Marketing Highlight 15–1).

The three main types of off-price retailers are *factory outlets*, *independents*, and *warehouse clubs*. **Factory outlets** are owned and operated by manufacturers and normally carry the manufacturer's surplus, discontinued, or irregular goods. Examples are The Burlington Coat Factory Warehouse, Manhattan's Brand Name Fashion Outlet, and the other well-known factory outlets of Levi Strauss, Carter's, and Ship 'n Shore. Such outlets sometimes group together in *factory outlet malls*, where dozens of outlet stores offer prices as low as 50 percent below retail on a wide range of items. The number of factory outlet malls grew from less than 60 in 1980 to over 370 in 1986.[7]

Independent off-price retailers either are owned and run by entrepreneurs or are divisions of larger retail corporations. Although many off-price operations are run by smaller independents, most large off-price retailer operations are owned by bigger retail chains. Examples include Loehmann's (operated by Associated Dry Goods, owner of Lord & Taylor), Designer Depot (K mart), Filene's Basement (Federated Department Stores), and T. J. Maxx (Zayre).

Warehouse clubs (or *wholesale clubs*) sell a limited selection of brand-name grocery items, appliances, clothing, and a hodgepodge of other goods at deep discounts to members who pay $25 to $50 annual membership fees. Examples are the Price Club, Sam's Wholesale Club, BJ's Wholesale Club, and Pace Membership Warehouse. These wholesale clubs operate in huge, low-overhead, warehouse-like facilities and offer few frills. Often, stores are drafty in the winter and stuffy in the summer. Customers themselves must wrestle furniture, heavy appliances, and other large items into the checkout line. Such clubs make no home deliveries and accept no credit cards. But they do offer rock-bottom prices—typically 20 percent to 40 percent below supermarket and discount-store prices.[8]

Off-price retailing blossomed during the early 1980s, but competition has stiffened as more and more off-price retailers have entered the market. The growth of off-price retailing slowed a bit because of an upswing in the economy and more effective counterstrategies by department stores and regular discounters. Still, off-price retailing remains a vital and growing force in modern retailing.[9]

Catalog Showroom

A **catalog showroom** sells a wide selection of high-markup, fast-moving, brand-name goods at discount prices. These include jewelry, power tools, cameras, luggage, small appliances, toys, and sporting goods. Catalog showrooms make their money by cutting costs and margins to provide low prices that will attract a higher volume of sales. The catalog showroom industry is led by companies such as Best Products and Service Merchandise.

Emerging in the late 1960s, catalog showrooms became one of retailing's hottest new forms. But catalog showrooms have been struggling in recent years to hold their share of the retail market. For one thing, department stores and discount retailers now

OFF-PRICE RETAILING AT 47TH STREET PHOTO

On the surface, 47th Street Photo doesn't look like much of a retailing operation. Its main store is a small, dingy affair located above Kaplan's Delicatessen on New York's West 47th Street. Its second store, a small computer outlet located a few blocks away, is only slightly more attractive. But beneath the surface, 47th Street Photo represents the state of the art in off-price retailing—selling quality branded merchandise at large discounts. In business for only fifteen years, 47th Street's two tiny stores annually sell more than $100 million worth of electronics products, and its sales are growing at 25 percent a year.

47th Street Photo is typical of the new discounters that emerged at retailing's low end to fill the gap created when more mature discount institutions began to trade up their merchandise, services, and prices. 47th Street maintains a low-cost, low-margin, high-volume philosophy. It carries a huge inventory of more than 25,000 fast-moving branded electronics products, including such items as cameras and camera equipment (only 30 percent of its business), personal computers, calculators, typewriters, telephones, answering machines, and videotape machines. It keeps its cost down through low-cost, no-frills facilities, efficient operations, and smart buying. Then it offers customers the lowest prices and turns its inventory quickly.

47th Street Photo's customers endure more abrupt treatment and enjoy fewer services than they would at plusher specialty stores. Like a well-run restaurant, 47th Street "gets 'em in, feeds 'em, and gets 'em out." Customers lineup at the sales counter to be waited on by efficient but curt salespeople who prefer that customers know what they want before coming in. In-store product inspections and comparisons are discouraged and salespeople offer little information or assistance.

But the price is right! 47th Street Photo regularly monitors competitor prices to be certain that its own prices support its "lowest-price" position. Price examples: suggested retail price of the Canon PC-20 copier, $1,295; at 47th Street Photo, it's $880. Macy's offers a Brother typewriter for $400, and on a recent Sunday it's out of stock. At 47th Street the same model is $289 and, of course, in stock.

Half of 47th Street Photo's sales comes from mail-order and telephone customers. Its 224-page catalog, toll-free telephone numbers, and packed ads in the *New York Times*, *The Wall Street Journal*, and several other business and special interest magazines make New York's "only dopes pay retail" shopping style available to the rest of the country. Over the years, 47th Street has built a solid reputation for trustworthiness. A price is a price—no bait-and-switch, no haggling or hidden prices.

So on the surface, 47th Street Photo doesn't look like much of a retailing operation. But behind its low-overhead exterior is a gutsy, finely tuned merchandising machine.

Source: Adapted from John Merwin, "The Source," *Forbes*, April 9, 1984, pp. 74–78.

47th Street Photo doesn't look like much, but it's a finely tuned merchandising machine.

run regular sales that match showroom prices. In addition, off-price retailers consistently beat catalog prices. As a result, many showroom chains are broadening their lines, doing more advertising, renovating their stores, and adding services in order to attract more business.

Control of Outlets About 80 percent of all retail stores are independents, and they account for two-thirds of all retail sales. Other forms of ownership include the *corporate chain*, the *voluntary chain and retailer cooperative*, the *franchise organization*, and the *merchandising conglomerate*.

Corporate Chain

The chain store is one of the most important retail developments of this century. **Chain stores** are two or more outlets that are commonly owned and controlled, employ central buying and merchandising, and sell similar lines of merchandise. Corporate chains appear in all types of retailing, but they are strongest in department stores, variety stores, food stores, drug stores, shoe stores, and women's clothing stores. Corporate chains gain many advantages over independents. Their size allows them to buy in large quantities at lower prices. They can afford to hire corporate-level specialists to deal with such areas as pricing, promotion, merchandising, inventory control, and sales forecasting. And chains gain promotional economies because their advertising costs are spread over many stores and a large sales volume.

Voluntary Chain and Retailer Cooperative

The great success of corporate chains caused many independents to band together in one of two forms of contractual associations. One is the *voluntary chain*—a wholesaler-sponsored group of independent retailers that engages in group buying and common merchandising. Examples include the Independent Grocers Alliance (IGA), Sentry Hardwares, and Western Auto. The other form of contractual association is the *retailer cooperative*—a group of independent retailers that band together to set up a jointly owned central wholesale operation and conduct joint merchandising and promotion efforts. Examples include Associated Grocers and True Value Hardware. These organizations give independents the buying and promotion economies they need to meet the prices of corporate chains.

Consumer Cooperative

A **consumer cooperative** is a retail firm owned by its customers. Residents of a community may start a consumer co-op when they feel local retailers are charging too much or providing poor product assortment or quality. The members contribute money to open their own store and they vote on its policies and elect managers. The store may set low prices or give members dividends based on their purchase levels. Although there are a few thousand cooperatives in the United States, they have never become an important retailing force.

Franchise Organization

A **franchise** is a contractual association between a manufacturer, wholesaler, or service organization (the franchiser) and independent businesspeople (franchisees) who buy the right to own and operate one or more units in the franchise system. The main difference between a franchise and other contractual systems (voluntary chains and retail cooperatives) is that franchise systems are normally based either on some unique product or service, on a method of doing business, or on the trade name, goodwill, or patent that the franchiser has developed. Franchising has been prominent in fast foods, motels, gas stations, video stores, health and fitness centers, auto rentals, hair cutting, real estate, travel agencies, and dozens of other product and service areas.

The compensation received by the franchiser may include an initial fee, a royalty on sales, lease fees for equipment, and a share of the profits. McDonald's franchisees may invest as much as $600,000 in initial start-up costs for a franchise. Then McDonald's charges a 3.5 percent service fee and a rental charge of 8.5 percent of the franchisee's volume. It also requires franchisees to go to Hamburger University for three weeks to learn how to manage the business.[10]

Merchandising Conglomerate

Merchandising conglomerates are corporations that combine several different retailing forms under central ownership and that share some distribution and management functions. Examples include Dayton-Hudson, Campeau Corporation (Federated Department Stores and Allied Stores), J. C. Penney, and F. W. Woolworth. For example, F. W. Woolworth, in addition to its variety stores, operates 28 specialty chains, including Kinney Shoe

Stores, Afterthoughts (costume jewelry and handbags), Face Fantasies (budget cosmetics), Herald Square Stationers, Frame Scene, Foot Locker (sports shoes), and Kids Mart. Diversified retailing, which provides superior management systems and economics that benefit all the separate retail operations, is likely to increase during the 1990s.

Type of Store Cluster

Most stores today cluster together to increase their customer pulling power and to give consumers the convenience of one-stop shopping. The main types of store clusters are the *central business district* and the *shopping center*.

Central Business District

Central business districts were the main form of retail cluster until the 1950s. Every large city and town had a central business district with department stores, specialty stores, banks, and movie theaters. However, when people began to move to the suburbs, these central business districts, with their traffic, parking, and crime problems, began to lose business. Downtown merchants opened branches in suburban shopping centers, and the decline of the central business districts continued. In recent years, many cities joined have with merchants to try to revive downtown shopping areas by building malls and providing underground parking. Some central business districts have made a comeback; others remain in a slow and possibly irreversible decline.

Shopping Center

A **shopping center** is a group of retail businesses planned, developed, owned, and managed as a unit. A *regional shopping center*, the largest and most dramatic shopping center, is like a mini-downtown. It contains 40 to 100 stores and pulls customers from a wide area. Larger regional malls often have several department stores and a wide variety of specialty stores on several shopping levels. Many have added new types of retailers—dentists, health clubs, and even branch libraries.

A *community shopping center* contains 15 to 50 retail stores. It normally contains a branch of a department or variety store, a supermarket, specialty stores, professional offices, and sometimes a bank. Most shopping centers are *neighborhood shopping centers* that generally contain 5 to 15 stores. They are close and convenient for consumers. They usually contain a supermarket and several service stores—a dry cleaner, self-service laundry, drugstore, barber or beauty shop, a hardware, or other stores.

A regional shopping center is like a mini-downtown.

Combined, all shopping centers now account for about one-third of all retail sales, but they may be reaching their saturation point. Many areas contain too many malls, and as sales-per-square-foot are dropping, vacancy rates are climbing. Some experts predict a shopping mall "shakeout," with as many as 20 percent of the regional shopping malls now operating in the U.S. closing by the year 2000. The current trend is toward smaller malls located in medium-size and smaller cities in fast-growing areas such as the Southwest.[11]

NON-STORE RETAILING

Although most goods and services are sold through stores, non-store retailing has been growing much faster than store retailing. Non-store retailing now accounts for more than 14 percent of all consumer purchases, and it may account for a third of all sales by the end of the century. Nonstore retailing: includes *direct marketing*, *direct selling*, and *automatic vending*.

Direct Marketing   **Direct marketing** uses various advertising media to interact directly with consumers, generally calling for the consumer to make a direct response. Mass advertising typically reaches an unspecified number of people, most of whom are not in the market for a product or will not buy it until some future date. Direct advertising vehicles are used to obtain immediate orders directly from targeted consumers. Although direct marketing initially consisted mostly of direct mail and mail-order catalogs, it has taken on several additional forms in recent years, including telemarketing, direct radio and television marketing, and electronic marketing.

Growth and Advantages of Direct Marketing

Direct marketing has boomed in recent years. All kinds of organizations use direct marketing: manufacturers, retailers, services companies, catalog merchants, nonprofit organizations. Its growing use in consumer marketing is largely a response to the "demassification" of mass markets, which has resulted in an ever-greater number of fragmented market segments with highly individualized needs and wants. Direct marketing allows sellers to focus efficiently on these mini-markets with offers that better match specific consumer needs.

Other trends have also fueled the growth of direct marketing. Because of the substantial number of women who have entered the workforce, households have less time to shop. The higher costs of driving, traffic congestion and parking headaches, the shortage of retail sales help, and longer lines at checkout counters, all have promoted in-home shopping. The development of toll-free telephone numbers and the increased use of credit cards have helped sellers to more easily reach and transact with consumers outside of stores. Finally, the growth of computer power has allowed marketers to build better customer databases from which they can select the best prospects for specific products they wish to advertise.

Direct marketing has also grown rapidly in business-to-business marketing. It can help to reduce the high costs of reaching business markets through the salesforce. Lower-cost media such as telemarketing and direct mail can be used to identify the best prospects and prime them before making an expensive sales call.

Direct marketing provides many benefits to consumers. People who buy through direct mail or by telephone say that such shopping is convenient, hassle-free, and fun. It saves them time. And it introduces them to new life styles and a larger selection of merchandise. Consumers can compare products and prices from their armchairs by browsing through catalogs. They can order and receive products without having to leave their homes. Industrial customers can learn about and order products and services without tying up time by meeting and listening to salespeople.

Direct marketing also provides benefits to sellers. It allows greater *selectivity*. A direct marketer can buy a mailing list containing the names of almost any group—millionaires, parents of new-born babies, left-handed people, or recent college graduates.

The direct-marketing message can be *personalized* and *customized*. Eventually, according to one expert, "We will store hundreds . . . of messages in memory. We will select ten thousand families with twelve or twenty or fifty specific characteristics and send them very individualized laser-printed letters."[12] With direct marketing, the seller can build a *continuous relationship* with each customer. New parents will receive regular mailings describing new clothes, toys, and other products that their growing baby will need. Direct marketing can be *timed* to reach prospects at just the right moment. Moreover, because it reaches more interested prospects at the best times, direct marketing materials receive *higher readership and response*. Direct marketing also permits easy *testing* of specific messages and media. And because results are direct and immediate, direct marketing lends itself more readily to *response measurement*. Finally, direct marketing provides *privacy*—the direct marketer's offer and strategy are not visible to competitors.

Forms of Direct Marketing

The four major forms of direct marketing are *direct mail and catalog marketing*, *telemarketing*, *television marketing*, and *electronic shopping*.

DIRECT MAIL AND CATALOG MARKETING. **Direct-mail marketing** involves single mailings that include letters, ads, samples, foldouts, and other "salespeople on wings" sent to prospects on mailing lists. The mailing lists are developed from customer lists, or obtained from mailing-list houses that provide names of people fitting almost any description—the superwealthy, mobile home owners, veterinarians, pet owners, or about anything else.

A recent study showed that direct mail and catalogs accounted for 48 percent of all direct-response offers leading to eventual orders (compared with telephone at 7 percent, circulars at 7 percent, and magazines and newspapers, each at 6 percent.[13] Direct mail is increasingly popular because it permits high target-market selectivity, can be personalized, is flexible, and allows easy measurement of results. While the cost-per-thousand-people-reached is higher than with such mass media as television or magazines, the people who are reached are much better prospects. More than 35 percent of Americans have responded to direct-mail ads, and the number is growing. Direct mail has proved very successful in promoting books, magazine subscriptions, and insurance and is increasingly being used to sell novelty and gift items, clothing, gourmet foods, and industrial products. Direct mail is also used heavily by charities, which raised over $35 billion in 1986 and accounted for about 25 percent of all direct-mail revenues.[14]

Catalog marketing involves selling through catalogs mailed to a select list of customers or made available in stores. This approach is used by huge general merchandise retailers, such as Sears, J. C. Penney, and Spiegel, that carry a full line of merchandise. But recently, the giants have been challenged by thousands of specialty catalogs with more sharply focused audiences. These smaller catalog retailers have successfully filled highly specialized market niches.

Consumers can buy just about anything from a catalog. Over 12.4 billion copies of more than 8,500 different catalogs are mailed out annually, and the average household receives at least 50 catalogs a year.[15] Hanover House sends out 22 different catalogs selling everything from shoes to decorative lawn birds. Sharper Image sells $2,400 jet-propelled surf boards. The Banana Republic Travel and Safari Clothing Company features everything you would need to go hiking in the Sahara or the rain forest. The list of specialty catalogers is almost endless. Recently, specialty department stores such as Neiman-Marcus, Bloomingdale's and Saks Fifth Avenue have begun sending catalogs to cultivate upper-middle-class markets for high-priced, often exotic, merchandise. Several major corporations have also developed or acquired mail-order divisions. For example, Avon now issues ten women's fashion catalogs along with catalogs for children's and men's clothes. Hershey and other food companies are investigating catalog opportunities. Even Walt Disney Company is getting into cataloging; it mails out more than 6 million catalogs each year featuring videos, stuffed animals, and other Disney items.

Most consumers enjoy receiving catalogs and will sometimes even pay to get them. Many catalog marketers are now even selling their catalogs at book stores and

Almost 12 billion catalogs are mailed out each year; the average household receives 50 catalogs annually.

magazine stands. Some companies, such as Royal Silk, Neiman-Marcus, Sears, and Spiegel, are also experimenting with videotape catalogs, or "videologs." Royal Silk sells a 35-minute video catalog to its customers for $5.95 and plans to market them to video stores. The tape contains a polished presentation of Royal Silk products, tells customers how to care for silk, and provides ordering information.[16]

TELEMARKETING. **Telemarketing,** using the telephone to sell directly to consumers, has become the major direct marketing tool. Marketers spend an estimated $41 billion each year in telephone charges to help sell their products and services.[17] Telemarketing blossomed in the late 1960s with the introduction of inward and outward Wide Area Telephone Service (WATS). With IN WATS, marketers can use toll-free 800 numbers to receive orders from television and radio ads, direct mail, or catalogs. With OUT WATS, they can use the phone to sell directly to consumers and businesses.

During January 1982 more than 700 people dialed an 800 number every minute in response to television commercials. The average household receives 19 telephone sales calls each year and makes 16 calls to place orders. Some telemarketing systems are fully auotmated. For example, automatic dialing and recorded message players (ADRMPs) self-dial numbers, play a voice-activated advertising message, and take orders from interested customers on an answering-machine device or by forwarding the call to an operator. Telemarketing is used in business marketing as well as consumer marketing. In fact, more than $115 billion worth of industrial products were marketed by phone last year. For example, General Electric uses telemarketing to generate and qualify sales leads and to manage small accounts. Raleigh Bicycles used telemarketing to reduce the amount of personal selling needed for contacting its dealers; in the first year, salesforce travel costs were reduced 50 percent, and sales in a single quarter increased 34 percent.[18]

TELEVISION MARKETING. **Television marketing** takes one of two major forms. The first is *direct-response advertising.* Direct marketers air television spots, often 60 or 120 seconds long, that persuasively describe a product and give customers a toll-free number for ordering. Late-night television viewers might even encounter a one-half hour long advertising program for a single product. Direct-response advertising works well for magazines, books, small appliances, tapes and CDs, collectibles, and many other products. Some successful direct-response ads run for years and become classics. Dial Media's ads for Ginsu knives ran for seven years and sold almost three million sets of knives worth more than $40 million in sales; its Armourcote cookware ads generated more than twice that much.[19]

Home shopping channels, another form of television direct marketing, are television programs or entire channels dedicated to selling goods and services. The largest is the Home Shopping Network (HSN). With HSN, viewers tune in the Home Shopping Club, which broadcasts 24 hours a day. The program's hosts offer bargain prices on products ranging from jewelry, lamps, collectibles dolls, and clothing to power tools and consumer electronics—usually obtained by HSN at closeout prices. The show is upbeat, with the hosts honking horns, blowing whistles, and praising viewers for their good taste. Viewers call an 800 number to order goods. At the other end, 400 operators handle more than 1,200 incoming lines, entering orders directly into computer terminals. Orders are shipped within 48 hours.

Sales through home shopping channels will grow from $450 million in 1986 to an estimated $2 billion in 1991. More than half of all U.S. homes have access to HSN or other home shopping channels, such as Cable Value Network, Value Club of America, Home Shopping Mall, or TelShop. Sears, K mart, J. C. Penney, Spiegel, and other major retailers are now looking into the home shopping industry. Some experts contend that TV home shopping is just a fad, but most think it is here to stay.[20]

ELECTRONIC SHOPPING.   The major form of **electronic shopping is** *videotex*. Videotex is a two-way system that links consumers with the seller's computer data banks by cable or telephone lines. The videotex service makes up a computerized catalog of products offered by producers, retailers, banks, travel organizations, and others. Consumers use an ordinary television set with a special keyboard device connected to the system by two-way cable. Or they hook into the system by telephone using a home computer. For example, a consumer wanting to buy a new compact-disk player could request a list of all CD brands in the computerized catalog, compare the brands, then order using a charge card—all without leaving home.

Videotex is still a fairly new idea. In recent years, several large videotex systems have failed because of too few subscribers or too little use. Two currently successful systems in the United States, however, are Compuserve and Prodigy. Prodigy, developed through a partnership by IBM and Sears, offers in-home shopping services and much more. Through Prodigy, subscribers can order thousands of products and services electronically from dozens of major stores and catalogs; do their banking with local banks; book airline, hotel, and car rental reservations; play games, quizzes, and contests; check *Consumer Reports* ratings of various products; receive the latest sports scores and stats; obtain weather forecasts; and exchange messages with other subscribers around the country. Although relatively few consumers now subscribe to such electronic systems, the number will grow in future years as more consumers acquire cable television and personal computers and as consumers discover the wonders of electronic shopping.[21]

Integrated Direct Marketing and Direct Marketing Databases

Most direct marketers use only a single advertising vehicle and a "one-shot" effort to reach and sell a prospect. Or, they might use a single vehicle but multiple stages in a campaign to trigger purchases. For example, a magazine publisher might send a series of four direct mail notices to a household to get a subscriber to renew before giving up. A more powerful approach is **integrated direct marketing**, which involves using multiple vehicle, multiple stage campaigns. Such campaigns can greatly improve response:

> When a mailing piece which might generate a 2 percent response on its own is supplemented by a toll-free 800-number ordering channel, we regularly see response rates rise by 50 percent. A skillfully integrated outbound telemarketing effort can add another 500 percent lift in response. Suddenly our 2 percent response has grown to 13 percent or more by adding interactive marketing channels to a "business as usual" mailing. The dollars and cents involved in adding media to the integrated media mix are normally marginal on a cost-per-order basis because of the high level of responses generated. . . . Adding media to a marketing program will raise total response . . . because people are inclined to respond to different stimuli.[22]

More elaborate integrated marketing campaigns can be used. Consider the following multi-media, multi-stage campaign:

Paid ad with a → Direct → Outbound → Face-to-face
response channel   mail   telemarketing   sales call

Here, the paid ad creates product awareness and stimulates inquiries. The company immediately sends direct mail to those who inquire. Within a few days, the company follows up with a phone call seeking an order. Some prospects will order by phone; others might request a face-to-face sales call. In such a campaign, the marketer seeks to improve response rates and profits by adding media and stages that contribute more to additional sales than to additional costs.

In order to successfully employ integrated direct marketing, companies must develop effective marketing database systems. A **marketing database** is an organized set of data about individual customers or prospects that can be used to generate and qualify customer leads, sell products and services, and maintain customer relationships.

Most database companies have not yet built effective marketing database systems. Mass marketers generally know little about individual customers. Retailers may know a lot about their charge account customers but almost nothing about their cash or credit card customers. Banks may develop customer database for each separate product or service but fail to tie this information together into complete customer profiles that could be used for cross-selling products and services.

Building a marketing database takes time and involves much cost, but when it works properly, such a database can pay handsome dividends. For example, a General Electric customer database contains each customer's geographic, demographic, psychographic characteristics, and appliance purchasing history. GE direct marketers can use this database to assess how long specific customers have owned their current appliances and which past customers might be ready to purchase again. They can determine which customers need a new GE videorecorder, or compact disk player, or stereo receiver, or something else to go with other recently purchased electronics products. Or they can identify the best past GE purchasers and send them gift certificates or other promotions to apply against their next purchases of GE appliances. Clearly, a rich customer database allows GE to build profitable new business by locating good prospects, anticipating customer needs, cross-selling products and services, and rewarding loyal customers.[23] (See Marketing Highlight 15–2 for another example.)

Direct Selling

Door-to-door retailing, which started centuries ago with roving peddlers, has grown into a huge industry. More than 600 companies sell either via door-to-door, office-to-office, or at home sales parties. The pioneers in door-to-door selling are the Fuller Brush Company, vacuum cleaner companies such as Electrolux, and book-selling companies such as World Book and Southwestern. The image of door-to-door selling improved greatly when Avon entered the industry with its Avon representative—the homemaker's friend and beauty consultant. Tupperware and Mary Kay Cosmetics helped to popularize home-sales parties, in which several friends neighbors attend a party at a private home where products are demonstrated and sold.

The advantages of door-to-door selling are consumer convenience and personal attention. But the high costs of hiring, training, paying, and motivating the salesforce result in higher prices. Although some door-to-door companies are still thriving, door-to-door selling has a somewhat uncertain future. The increase in the number of single-person and working-couple households decreases the chances of finding a buyer at home. Home-party companies are having trouble finding nonworking women who want to sell products part-time. And with recent advances in interactive direct marketing technology, the door-to-door salesperson may well be replaced in the future by the household telephone, television, or home computer.

Automatic Vending

Automatic vending is not new. In 215 B.C. Egyptians could buy sacrificial water from coin-operated devices. But this method of selling soared after World War II. Today's automatic vending uses space-age and computer technology to sell a wide variety of convenience and impulse goods—cigarettes, beverages, candy, newspapers, foods and

DATABASE MARKETING: FINGERHUT BUILDS STRONG CUSTOMER RELATIONSHIPS

The envelope in the mailbox is a screamer. Exclamation points abound and big type yells "Free merchandise enclosed!" and "Do not destroy!" Inside is a spoon engraved with the customer's initial, a sample of a 50-piece set of monogrammed flatware available for just $19.95 or on credit, with no money down and just six easy payments of $4.41 each, including a no-risk, 30-day home trial.

This mouthful of an offer is from Fingerhut, the huge direct mail marketer. Fingerhut hopes that it will be the start of a long direct mail relationship. If customers respond to the flatware offer, Fingerhut asks them to fill out two questionnaires. One questionnaire asks customers about the kinds of products that interest them. The other, for Fingerhut's "Birthday Club," asks them about their families—number of children, ages, and birthdays. Using information from these two questionnaires, along with information about later customer purchases, Fingerhut has built an impressive marketing database that allows it to target the most likely buyers with products that interest them most. Instead of sending out the same catalogs and direct mail letters to all of its customers, Fingerhut tailors its offers based on what each customer is likely to buy. Moreover, promotions such as the Birthday Club provide opportunities to create special offers that sell more products and help Fingerhut to further refine its customer database. A month before a child's birthday, Birthday Club customers receive a free birthday gift for their child if they agree to try any one of the products Fingerhut offers in an accompanying mailing. Customers who respond to these and other offers might become one of 12 million "promotable" customers, who receive at least one mailing a week from the direct mail company.

The Fingerhut catalog offers 500 to 700 products, mostly domestics and household electronics, with prices ranging from $15 to $600. Fingerhut operates on a *huge* scale. Each year, it sends out about 400 million mailings—that's more than 1 million mailings per day to a portion of the 20 million households detailed in the company's database.

The key to Fingerhut's success is the long-term relationships that it builds with its customers. Fingerhut carefully matches its direct-mail offers to individual customer needs, characteristics, and purchasing histories, and then makes it as easy as possible for targeted customers to buy. Fingerhut tries to establish a strong relationship that goes beyond its merchandise. Credit is an important cornerstone of that relationship. The average Fingerhut customer, typically an "empty-nester" or someone just starting a family, has a household income of $18,000. The customer's median age is 38 and 90 percent are female. Despite selling to lower-income consumers, Fingerhut controls its credit risks by what it offers to whom. It avoids zip codes with high bad-debt levels. And when a new customer makes a first order, the item is limited to $20 to $30. If the customer pays promptly, the next mailing offers higher-ticket items. Customers who don't pay on time are cut off. Good customers, who pay their bills regularly, get cards and rewards to reinforce this behavior. For example, the typical award envelope cheers

snacks, hosiery, cosmetics, paperback books, T-shirts, insurance policies, pizza, audio tapes and videocassettes, and even shoeshines and fishing worms. Vending machines are found everywhere, in factories, offices, lobbies, retail stores, gasoline stations, airports, and train and bus terminals. Automatic teller machines provide bank customers with checking, savings, withdrawals, and funds-transfer services. As compared with store retailing, vending machines offer consumers greater convenience (24 hours, self-service) and fewer damaged goods. But the expensive equipment and labor required for automatic vending make it a costly channel, and prices of vended goods are often 15 to 20 percent higher than those in retail stores. Customers must also put up with aggravating machine breakdowns, out-of-stock items, and the fact that merchandise cannot be returned.

RETAILER MARKETING DECISIONS

Retailers are searching for new marketing strategies to attract and hold customers. In the past, they attracted customers with unique products, more or better services than competitors, or credit cards. Today, national brand manufacturers, in their drive for volume, have placed their branded goods everywhere. Thus, stores offer more similar assortments—national brands are found not only in department stores, but also in mass-merchandise and off-price discount stores. As a result, stores are looking more and more alike; they have become "commoditized." In any city, a shopper can find many stores but few assortments.

Service differentiation among retailers has also eroded. Many department stores have trimmed their services while discounters have increased theirs. Customers have

Fingerhut finds out what consumers want then creates "loud" promotions so they will shop Fingerhut again and again.

"Congratulations! You've been selected to receive our 'exceptional customer award!' " and contains a certificate suitable for framing.

Fingerhut stays in continuous touch with its preferred customers through regular special promotions—an annual sweepstakes, free gifts, a deferred billing promotion, and others. These special offers are all designed with one goal in mind: to create a reason for Fingerhut to be in the customer's mailbox. Once in the mailbox, the screaming mailers get attention. As one Fingerhut executive comments, "In the direct mail business, you have to create promotions to get the mail opened. We test every variable before we mail out, so we generally get a high response." In these tests, the company has found that "loud" mailings consistently work better than "quiet" ones.

The skillful development and use of a comprehensive marketing database have made Fingerhut one of the nation's largest direct mail marketers. It is currently tied for third largest with Spiegel—only giants Sears and J.C. Penney do more direct mail business. Fingerhut receives 10 million orders a year, with an average order size of $80 to $100. In fact, one in every six U.S. households has bought something from the company. Fingerhut's success is no accident. "Most of our competitors use a full catalog; they could care less about what the individuals want," notes the Fingerhut executive. "Fingerhut finds out what each customer wants and builds an event around each promotion."

Sources: Adapted from Eileen Norris, "Fingerhut Gives Customers Credit," *Advertising Age*, March 6, 1986, p. 19. Also see Janet Meyers, "Sidestepping the System, Time Finds the Going Slow," *Advertising Age*, September 25, 1989, pp. S2, S8–S9.

become smarter and more price sensitive. They see no reason for paying more for identical brands, especially when service differences are shrinking. And because bank credit cards are now accepted at most stores, consumers no longer need credit from a particular store. For all these reasons, many retailers today are rethinking their marketing strategies.[24]

Retailers face major marketing decisions about their *target markets*, *product assortment and services*, *price*, *promotion*, and *place*.

Target Market Decision   Retailers must first define their target markets and then decide how they will position themselves in these markets. Should the store focus on upscale, midscale, or downscale shoppers? Do target shoppers want variety, depth of assortment, convenience, or low prices? Until they define and profile their markets, retailers cannot make consistent decisions about product assortment, services, pricing, advertising, store decor, or any of the other decisions that must support their positions.

Too many retailers fail to define their target markets and positions clearly. They try to have "something for everyone" and end up satisfying no market well. Even large department stores such as Sears must define their major target markets in order to design effective marketing strategies.

Some retailers define their target markets quite well. Here are two examples whose founders are now among the richest men in America:

- Leslie H. Wexner borrowed $5,000 in 1963 to create *The Limited*, which started as a single store targeted to young, fashion conscious women. All aspects of the store—clothing assortment, fixtures, music, colors, personnel—were orchestrated to match the target con-

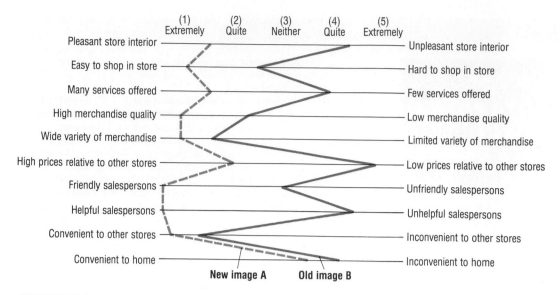

	(1) Extremely	(2) Quite	(3) Neither	(4) Quite	(5) Extremely	

Pleasant store interior — Unpleasant store interior
Easy to shop in store — Hard to shop in store
Many services offered — Few services offered
High merchandise quality — Low merchandise quality
Wide variety of merchandise — Limited variety of merchandise
High prices relative to other stores — Low prices relative to other stores
Friendly salespersons — Unfriendly salespersons
Helpful salespersons — Unhelpful salespersons
Convenient to other stores — Inconvenient to other stores
Convenient to home — Inconvenient to home

New image A   Old image B

FIGURE 15-1
A comparison between the old and the new image of a store seeking to appeal to a class market
Source: Adapted from David W. Cravens, Gerald E. Hills, and Robert B. Woodruff, *Marketing Decision Making: Concepts and Strategy* (Homewood, Il.: Irwin, 1976), p. 234.

sumer. He continued to open more stores, but a decade later his original customers were no longer in the "young" group. To catch the new "youngs," he started the Limited Express. Over the years, he started or acquired other highly targeted store chains, including Lane Bryant, Victoria's Secrets, Lerner, and others to reach new segments. Today The Limited operates over 3,400 stores in seven different segments of the market with sales of more than $4.5 billion.

- Sam Walton and his brother opened the first *Wal-Mart* discount store in Rogers, Arkansas in 1962. It was a big, flat, warehouse-type store that sold everything from apparel to automotive supplies to small appliances at the lowest possible prices to small-town America. Today, Wal-Mart operates 1,300 stores, 80 percent located in towns of 15,000 or less, selling $20 million worth of merchandise annually. Wal-Mart spends considerably less than Sears and K Mart on advertising, yet its sales are growing at the rate of 30 percent a year. Sam Walton's secret: target small town America, listen to the customers, treat the employees as partners, and keep a tight rein on expenses. A sign reading "Satisfaction Guaranteed" hangs prominently at each store's entrance and customers are often welcomed by a "people greeter" eager to lend a helping hand. Sam Walton recently launched a successful new set of stores called Sam's Wholesale Club which provides members (small businesses, government employees, and others) with superdiscounts on furniture, appliances, supplies, and food products.

A retailer should do periodic marketing research to check that it is satisfying its target customers. Consider a store that wants to attract wealthy consumers, but whose *store image* is shown by the red line in Figure 15-1. This store does not currently appeal to its target market—it must change its target market or redesign itself as a "classier" store. Suppose the store then upgrades its products, services, and salespeople and raises its prices. Some time later, a second customer survey may reveal the image shown by the blue line in Figure 15-1. The store has established a position that matches its target market choice.

Product Assortment and Services Decision

Retailers must decide on three major product variables: *product assortment, services mix*, and *store atmosphere*.

The retailer's *product assortment* must match target shoppers' expectations. The retailer must determine both the product assortment's *width* and its *depth*. Thus, a restaurant can offer a narrow and shallow assortment (small lunch counter), a narrow and deep assortment (delicatessen), a wide and shallow assortment (cafeteria), or a wide and deep assortment (large restaurant). Another product assortment element is the *quality* of the goods: The customer is interested not only in the range of choice but also in the quality of the products available.

However, no matter what the store's product assortment and quality level, there will always be competitors with similar assortments and quality. Therefore, the retailer must search for other ways to *differentiate* itself from similar competitors. It can use any of several product differentiation strategies. For one, it can offer merchandise that no other competitor carries—its own private brands or national brands on which it holds exclusives. Thus, The Limited designs most of the clothes carried by its store and Saks gets exclusive rights to carry a well known designer's labels. Second, the retailer can feature blockbuster merchandising events. Bloomingdale's is known for running spectacular shows featuring goods from a certain country, such as India or China. Or the retailer can offer surprise merchandise, as when Loehmann's offers surprise assortments of seconds, overstocks, and closeouts. Finally, the retailer can differentiate itself by offering a highly targeted product assortment—Lane Bryant carries goods for larger women; Brookstone offers an unusual assortment of gadgets in what amounts to an adult toy store.

Retailers also must decide on a *services mix* to offer customers. The old "mom and pop" grocery stores offered home delivery, credit, and conversation—services that today's supermarkets ignore. The services mix is one of the key tools of nonprice competition for setting one store apart from another. Table 15-2 lists some of the major services that full-service retailers can offer.

The *store's atmosphere* is another element in its product arsenal. Every store has a physical layout that makes moving around in it either hard or easy. Every store has a "feel"; one store is cluttered, another charming, a third plush, a fourth somber. The store must have a planned atmosphere that suits the target market and moves customers to buy. A bank should be quiet, solid, and peaceful; a nightclub should be flashy, loud, and vibrating. Increasingly, retailers are working to create shopping environments that match their target markets. Chains such as the Banana Republic and Laura Ashley are turning their stores into theaters that transport customers into unusual, exciting shopping environments. Even conservative Sears divides the clothing areas within each store into six distinct "shops," each with its own selling environment designed to meet the tastes of individual segments.

Price Decision

A retailer's price policy is a crucial positioning factor and must be decided in relation to its target market, its product and service assortment, and its competition. All retailers would like to charge high markups and achieve high volume, but the two seldom go together. Most retailers seek *either* high markups on lower volume (most specialty stores) *or* low markups on higher volume (mass merchandisers and discount stores).

TABLE 15-2
Typical Retail Services

PRIMARY SERVICES	SUPPLEMENTAL SERVICES	
Alterations	Baby strollers	Packaging and gift wrapping
Complaint handling	Bill payment	
Convenient store hours	Bridal registries	Product locator
Credit	Check cashing	Restaurants or snack counters
Delivery	Children's play rooms	
Fitting rooms	Demonstrations	Shopping consultants
Installation and assembly	Layaway	Shopping information
Merchandise returns and adjustments	Lost and found	Shows, displays, and exhibits
Parking	Personal shopping	Speical ordering
Rest rooms	Package checkrooms	Wheelchairs
Service and repair		
Telephone ordering		

Store atmospheres: Chanel (left) and Bergdorf Goodman (right) create very different store atmospheres to match their different target markets.

Thus, Bijan's on Rodeo Drive in Beverly Hills prices men's suits starting at $1,000 and shoes at $400—it sells a low volume but makes a hefty profit on each sale. At the other extreme, T. J. Maxx sells brand-name clothing at discount prices, settling for a lower margin on each sale but selling at a much higher volume.

Retailers must also pay attention to pricing tactics. Most retailers will put low prices on some items to serve as "traffic builders" or "loss leaders." On some occasions, they run store-wide sales. On others, they plan markdowns on slower-moving merchandise. For example, shoe retailers expect to sell 50 percent of their shoes at the normal markup, 25 percent at a 40 percent markup, and the remaining 25 percent at cost.

Promotion Decision Retailers use the normal promotion tools—advertising, personal selling, sales promotion, and public relations—to reach consumers. Retailers advertise in newspapers, magazines, radio, and television. Advertising may be supported by circulars and direct mail pieces. Personal selling requires careful training of salespeople in how to greet customers, meet their needs, and handle their complaints. Sales promotions may include in-store demonstrations, displays, contests, and visiting celebrities. Public relations activities such as press conferences and speeches, store openings, special events, newsletters, magazines, and public service activities are always available to retailers.

Place Decision Retailers often cite three critical factors in retailing success: *location*, *location*, and *location*. A retailer's location is key to its ability to attract customers. And the costs of building or leasing facilities have a major impact on the retailer's profits. Thus, site location decisions are among the most important the retailer makes. Small retailers may have to settle for whatever locations they can find or afford. Large retailers usually employ specialists who select locations using advanced methods.[25]

THE FUTURE OF RETAILING

Several trends will affect the future of retailing. First, the slowdown in population and economic growth means that retailers will no longer enjoy sales and profit growth through natural expansion in current and new markets. Growth will have to come from increasing shares of current markets. But greater competition and new types of retailers will make it harder to improve market shares. Consumer demographics, life styles, and shopping patterns are changing rapidly. To be successful, then, retailers will have to choose target segments carefully and position themselves strongly.

Moreover, quickly rising costs will make more efficient operation and smarter buying essential to successful retailing. Thus, retail technologies are growing in importance as competitive tools. Progressive retailers are using computers to produce better forecasts, control inventory costs, order electronically from suppliers, communicate between stores, and even sell to consumers within stores. They are adopting checkout-scanning systems, in-store television, online transaction processing, and electronic funds transfer.

Many retailing innovations are partially explained by the **wheel of retailing** concept.[26] According to this concept, many new types of retailing forms begin as low-margin, low-price, low-status operations. They challenge established retailers that have become ''fat'' by letting their costs and margins increase. The new retailers' success leads them to upgrade their facilities and offer more services. In turn, their costs increase, forcing them to increase their prices. Eventually, the new retailers become like the conventional retailers they replaced. The cycle begins again when still newer types of retailers evolve with lower costs and prices (see Marketing Highlight 15–3). The wheel of retailing concept seems to explain the initial success and later troubles of department stores, supermarkets, and discount stores and the recent success of off-price retailers.

New retail forms will continue to emerge to meet new consumer needs and new situations. But the life cycle of new retail forms is getting shorter. Department stores took about 100 years to reach the mature stage of the life cycle; more recent forms, such as catalog showrooms and furniture warehouse stores, reached maturity in about

---

MARKETING HIGHLIGHT 15–3

THE WHEEL OF RETAILING TURNS AT K MART

Until recently, K mart has been the model for discount department stores and has held unswervingly to the principles of discount merchandising. But like many other discount retailers in recent years, facing stiffer competition from both department stores and new forms of low-price retailers, K mart has moved away from the formula that made it the number-two retailer in the country (behind Sears). To better position itself for the highly competitive 1990s, K mart is attempting to trade up and away from its no-frills, low-price strategy toward a more upscale philosophy emphasizing brand name products, quality, and value rather than low prices. With this new strategy, K mart hopes to get more business from the increasing numbers of more affluent consumers—consumers who previously shopped at K mart only to ''cherry-pick'' sales items.

To establish its new image, K mart has been making gradual but sweeping changes in its merchandise assortment and store facilities. Its broadened and upgraded product assortment now includes more well-known national brands and higher-quality store brands. More store space is being devoted to fashions, sporting goods, electronics, and other higher-margin goods. Although K mart still has its famous in-store bluelight specials (''Attention K mart shoppers!''), its advertising now features fewer sales, more branded products, celebrity spokespeople, and more ''life style'' appeals.

K mart will spend a whopping $2.3 billion during the next five years to modernize and upgrade its more than 2,200 stores. New stores will be larger and fresher looking. The retailer is replacing the plain fixtures and long rows of racks with wider, taller display shelves, widening the aisles, and installing track lighting. Store space is being modularized into special departments—a ''Kitchen Korner,'' home electronics center, nutrition center, hardcover-books section, and others—to provide a more pleasing shopping environment for more discriminating shoppers.

Thus, the wheel of retailing is turning at K mart. The new, upgraded K mart stores will more closely resemble Sears' or Penney's stores than discount stores. K mart wants to position itself on the cutting edge of consumer tastes. It hopes to convince consumers that K mart now makes it easy and affordable to dress, or decorate, or do just about anything else in a classy way. But the new strategy could be risky. While K mart attempts to woo more upscale consumers, other discounters will emerge and try to lure away the core of price-conscious, lower-scale consumers that made K mart so successful.

However, K mart is taking steps to assure that it won't be displaced at the bottom of the retailing ladder. At the same time that it is upgrading its K mart stores, the company is also moving into ''off-price'' and other new forms of discount retailing to pick up the low-end business that might be lost under the new upscale strategy. In recent years, for example, K mart has developed or acquired a number of discount specialty chains—Designer Depot (designer label clothing at large discounts), Garment Rack (lower-quality clothing), Accent (quality gifts and housewares at discount prices), Bishop Buffets and Furr's Cafeterias (inexpensive food), Builders Square (do-it-yourself hardware), Sports Giant (sporting goods), American Fare (hypermarkets), Pay Less Drug Stores, and other businesses that combine for about 25 percent of total company sales. And the company is considering additional discount operations in such areas as toys, jewelry, and books. Thus, rather than falling victim to the wheel of retailing, K mart hopes to use it to advantage.

Sources: See Patricia Strnad, ''K mart's Antonini Moves Far Beyond Retail ''Junk'' Image,'' *Advertising Age*,'' July 25, 1988, pp. 1, 67; Patricia Strnad and Judith Graham, ''K mart's Hyperactive,'' *Advertising Age*, January 23, 1989, pp. 1, 54; and Faye Rice, ''Why K mart Has Stalled,'' *Fortune*, October 9, 1989, p. 79.

10 years. Retailers can no longer sit back with a successful formula. To remain successful, they must keep adapting.[27]

WHOLESALING

Wholesaling includes all activities involved in selling goods and services to those buying for resale or business use. A retail bakery does wholesaling when it sells pastry to the local hotel. But we call **wholesalers** those firms engaged *primarily* in wholesaling activity.

Wholesalers differ from retailers in several ways. First, because they deal mostly with business customers rather than final consumers, wholesalers pay less attention to promotion, atmosphere, and location. Second, wholesalers usually cover larger trade areas and have larger transactions than retailers. Third, wholesalers face different legal regulations and taxes.

Wholesalers buy mostly from producers and sell mostly to retailers, industrial consumers, and other wholesalers. But why are wholesalers used at all? For example, why would a producer use wholesalers rather than selling directly to retailers or consumers? Quite simply, wholesalers are often better at performing one or more of the following channel functions:

- *Selling and promoting*—Wholesalers' salesforces help manufacturers reach many small customers at a low cost. The wholesaler has more contacts and is often more trusted by the buyer than the distant manufacturer.
- *Buying and assortment building*—Wholesalers can select items and build assortments needed by their customers, thereby saving the consumers much work.
- *Bulk-breaking*—Wholesalers save their customers money by buying in carload lots and breaking bulk (breaking large lots into small quantities).
- *Warehousing*—Wholesalers hold inventories, thereby reducing the inventory costs and risks of suppliers and customers.
- *Transportation*—Wholesalers can provide quicker delivery to buyers because they are closer than the producers.
- *Financing*—Wholesalers finance their customers by giving credit, and they finance their suppliers by ordering early and paying bills on time.
- *Risk bearing*—Wholesalers absorb risk by taking title and bearing the cost of theft, damage, spoilage, and obsolescence.
- *Market information*—Wholesalers give information to suppliers and customers about competitors, new products, and price developments.
- *Management services and advice*—Wholesalers often help retailers to train their salesclerks, improve store layouts and displays, and set up accounting and inventory control systems.

TYPES OF WHOLESALERS

Wholesalers fall into three major groups (see Table 15-3): *merchant wholesalers, brokers and agents*, and *manufacturers' sales branches and offices*.

TABLE 15-3
Classification of Wholesalers

MERCHANT WHOLESALERS	BROKERS AND AGENTS	MANUFACTURERS' AND RETAILERS' BRANCHES AND OFFICES
Full-service wholesalers	Brokers	Sales branches and offices
Wholesale merchants	Agents	Purchasing offices
Industrial distributors		
Limited-service wholesalers		
Cash-and-carry wholesalers		
Truck wholesalers		
Drop shippers		
Rack jobbers		
Producers' cooperatives		
Mail order wholesalers		

Merchant Wholesalers

Merchant wholesalers are independently owned businesses that take title to the merchandise they handle. They are the largest single group of wholesalers, accounting for roughly 50 percent of all wholesaling. Merchant wholesalers include two broad types: *full-service wholesalers* and *limited-service wholesalers*.

Full-Service Wholesalers

Full-service wholesalers provide a full set of services such as carrying stock, using a salesforce, offering credit, making deliveries, and providing management assistance. They are either *wholesale merchants* or *industrial distributors*.

Wholesale merchants sell mostly to retailers and provide a full range of services. They vary in the width of their product line. Some carry several lines of goods to meet the needs of both general merchandise retailers and single-line retailers. Others carry one or two lines of goods in a greater depth of assortment. Examples are hardware wholesalers, drug wholesalers, and clothing wholesalers. Some specialty wholesalers carry only part of a line in great depth. Examples are health food wholesalers, seafood wholesalers, and automotive parts wholesalers. They offer customers deeper choice and greater product knowledge.

Industrial distributors are merchant wholesalers who sell to producers rather than to retailers. They provide inventory, credit, delivery, and other services. They may carry a broad range of merchandise, a general line, or a specialty line. Industrial distributors may concentrate on such lines as maintenance and operating supplies, original equipment goods (such as ball bearings and motors), or equipment (such as power tools and fork-lift trucks).

Limited-Service Wholesalers

Limited-service wholesalers offer fewer services to their suppliers and customers.

Cash-and-carry wholesalers carry a limited line of fast-moving goods, sell to small retailers for cash, and normally do not deliver. A small fish store retailer, for example, normally drives at dawn to a cash-and-carry fish wholesaler and buys several crates of fish, pays on the spot, drives the merchandise back to the store, and unloads it.

Truck wholesalers (also called truck jobbers) perform a selling and delivery fashion. They carry a limited line of goods (such as milk, bread, or snack foods) that they sell for cash as they make their rounds of supermarkets, small groceries, hospitals, restaurants, factory cafeterias, and hotels.

A typical Fleming Companies, Inc. wholesale food distribution center. The average Fleming warehouse contains 500,000 square feet of floor space (with 30-foot high ceiling,) carries 16,000 different food items, and serves 150 to 200 retailers within a 500-mile radius.

Drop shippers operate in bulk industries such as coal, lumber, and heavy equipment. They do not carry inventory or handle the product. Once an order is received, they find a producer who ships the goods directly to the customer. The drop shipper takes title and risk from the time the order is accepted to the time it is delivered to the customer. Because drop shippers do not carry inventory, their costs are lower and they can pass on some savings to customers.

Rack jobbers serve grocery and drug retailers, mostly in the area of nonfood items. These retailers do not want to order and maintain displays of hundreds of nonfood items. Rack jobbers send delivery trucks to stores, and the delivery person sets up racks of toys, paperbacks, hardware items, health and beauty aids, or other items. They price the goods, keep them fresh, and keep inventory records. Rack jobbers sell on consignment; they retain title to the goods and bill the retailers only for the goods sold to consumers. Thus, they provide such services as delivery, shelving, inventory, and financing. They do little promotion because they carry many branded items that are already highly advertised.

Producers' cooperatives, owned by farmer-members, assemble farm produce to sell in local markets. Their profits are divided among members at the end of the year. They often try to improve product quality and promote a co-op brand name, such as Sun Maid raisins, Sunkist oranges, or Diamond walnuts.

Mail-order wholesalers send catalogs to retail, industrial, and institutional customers offering jewelry, cosmetics, special foods, and other small items. Their main customers are businesses in small outlying areas. They have no salesforces to call on customers. The orders are filled and sent by mail, truck, or other means.

Brokers and Agents

Brokers and *agents* differ from merchant wholesalers in two ways: They do not take title to goods, and they perform only a few functions. Their main function is to aid in buying and selling, and for these services they earn a commission on the selling price. Like merchant wholesalers, they generally specialize by product line or customer type. They account for 11 percent of the total wholesale volume.

Brokers

A **broker** brings buyers and sellers together and assists in negotiation. Brokers are paid by the parties hiring them. They do not carry inventory, get involved in financing, or assume risk. The most familiar examples are food brokers, real estate brokers, insurance brokers, and security brokers.

Agents

Agents represent buyers or sellers on a more permanent basis. There are several types. *Manufacturers' agents* (also called manufacturers' representatives) are the most numerous type of agent wholesaler. They represent two or more manufacturers of related lines. They have a formal agreement with each manufacturer covering prices, territories, order-handling procedures, delivery and warranties, and commission rates. They know each manufacturer's product line and use their wide contacts to sell the products. Manufacturers' agents are used in such lines as apparel, furniture, and electrical goods. Most manufacturers' agents are small businesses, with only a few employees who are skilled salespeople. They are hired by small producers who cannot afford to maintain their own field salesforces and by large producers who want to open new territories or sell in areas that cannot support a full-time salesperson.

Selling agents contract to sell a producer's entire output—either the manufacturer is not interested in doing the selling or feels unqualified. The selling agent serves as a sales department and has much influence over prices, terms, and conditions of sale. The selling agent normally has no territory limits. Selling agents are found in such product areas as textiles, industrial machinery and equipment, coal and coke, chemicals, and metals.

Purchasing agents generally have a long-term relationship with buyers. They make purchases for buyers and often receive, inspect, warehouse, and ship goods to the buyers.

One type consists of *resident buyers* in major apparel markets, purchasing specialists who look for apparel lines that can be carried by small retailers located in small cities. They know a great deal about their product lines and provide helpful market information to clients but can obtain the best goods and prices available.

Commission merchants (or houses) are agents that take physical possession of products and negotiate sales. They are not normally used on a long-term basis. They are used most often in agricultural marketing by farmers who do not want to sell their own output and who do not belong to cooperatives. Typically, the commission merchant will take a truckload of farm products to a central market, sell it for the best price, deduct a commission and expenses, and pay the balance to the farmer.

Manufacturers' Sales Branches and Offices

The third major type of wholesaling is that done in **manufacturers' sales branches and offices** by sellers or buyers themselves rather than through independent wholesalers. Manufacturers' offices and sales branches account for about 31 percent of all wholesale volume. Manufacturers often set up their own sales branches and offices to improve inventory control, selling, and promotion. *Sales branches* carry inventory and are found in such industries as lumber and automotive equipment and parts. *Sales offices* do not carry inventory and are most often found in dry goods and notion industries. Many retailers set up *purchasing offices* in major market centers such as New York and Chicago. These purchasing offices perform a role similar to that of brokers or agents but are part of the buyer's organization.

WHOLESALER MARKETING DECISIONS

Wholesalers have experienced mounting competitive pressures in recent years. They have faced new sources of competition, more demanding customers, new technologies, and more direct buying programs by large industrial, institutional, and retail buyers. As a result they have had to improve their strategic decisions on target markets, product assortments and services, price, promotion, and place.

Target Market Decision

Wholesalers, like retailers, must define their target markets—they cannot serve everyone. They can choose a target group by size of customer (only large retailers), type of customer (convenience food stores only), need for service (customers who need credit), or other factors. Within the target group, they can identify the more profitable customers, design stronger offers, and build better relationships with them. They can propose automatic reordering systems, set up management-training and advising systems, or even sponsor a voluntary chain. They can discourage less profitable customers by requiring larger orders or adding service charges to smaller ones.

Product Assortment and Services Decision

The wholesaler's ''product'' is its assortment. Wholesalers are under great pressure to carry a full line and stock enough for immediate delivery. But this practice can damage profits. Wholesalers today are cutting down on the number of lines they carry, choosing to carry only the more profitable ones. Wholesalers are also rethinking which services count most in building strong customer relationships and which should be dropped or charged for. The key is to find the mix of services most valued by their target customers.

Price Decision

Wholesalers usually mark up the cost of goods by a standard percentage—say, 20 percent. Expenses may run 17 percent of the gross margin, leaving a profit margin of 3 percent. In grocery wholesaling, the average profit margin is often less than 2 percent. Wholesalers are trying new pricing approaches. They may cut their margin on some lines in order to win important new customers. They may ask suppliers for special price breaks when they can turn them into an increase in the supplier's sales.

Promotion Decision

Most wholesalers are not promotion-minded. Their use of trade advertising, sales promotion, personal selling, and public relations is largely scattered and unplanned. Many are behind the times in personal selling. They still see selling as a single salesperson talking to a single customer instead of a team effort to sell, build, and service major accounts. And wholesalers also need to adopt some of the nonpersonal promotion techniques used by retailers. They need to develop an overall promotion strategy and to make greater use of supplier promotion materials and programs.

Place Decision Wholesalers typically locate in low-rent, low-tax areas and have tended to invest little money in their buildings, equipment, and systems. As a result, their materials-handling and order-processing systems are often out of date. In recent years, however, large and progressive wholesalers are reacting to rising costs by investing in automated warehouses and online ordering systems. Orders are fed from the retailer's system directly into the wholesaler's computer, and the items are picked up by mechanical devices and automatically taken to a shipping platform where they are assembled. Many wholesalers are turning to computers to carry out accounting, billing, inventory control, and forecasting. Progressive wholesalers are adapting their services to the needs of target customers and finding cost-reducing methods of doing business.

TRENDS IN WHOLESALING

Progressive wholesalers constantly watch for better ways to meet the changing needs of their suppliers and target customers. They recongize that, in the long run, their only reason for existence comes from increasing the efficiency and effectiveness of the entire marketing channel. To achieve this aim, they must constantly improve their services and reduce their costs.[28]

Foremost-McKesson, a large drug wholesaler, provides an example of progressive wholesaling. To survive, it had to remain more cost-effective than manufacturers' sales

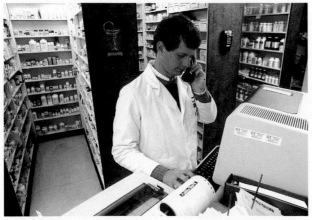

Drug wholesaler Foremost-McKesson improved efficiency by setting up direct computer links with manufacturers and retail pharmacies.

branches. Thus, the company automated 72 of its warehouses, established direct computer links with 32 drugs manufacturers, designed a computerized accounts-receivable program for pharmacists, and provided drugstores with computer terminals for ordering inventories. Retailers can even use the McKesson computer system to maintain medical profiles on their customers. Thus, Foremost-McKesson has delivered better value to both manufacturers and retail customers.

One study projects several developments in the wholesaling industry.[29] Consolidation will significantly reduce the number of firms in the industry. The remaining wholesaling companies will grow larger, primarily through acquisition, merger, and geographic expansion. Geographic expansion will require distributors to learn how to compete effectively over wider and more diverse areas. Wholesalers will be helped in this by the increased use of computerized and automated systems; by 1990, more than three-fourths of all wholesalers will be using online order systems.

The distinction between large retailers and large wholesalers continues to blur. Many retailers now operate formats such as wholesale clubs and hypermarkets that perform many wholesale functions. In return, many large wholesalers are creating their own retailing operations. Super Valu, Fleming, and Wetterau, all leading wholesalers, now operate their own retail outlets.

Wholesalers will continue to increase the services they provide to retailers—retail pricing, cooperative advertising, marketing- and management-information reports, accounting services, and others. Rising costs on the one hand, and the demand for increased services on the other, will put the squeeze on wholesaler profits. Wholesalers who do not find efficient ways to deliver value to their customers will soon drop by the wayside.

■ SUMMARY

Retailing and wholesaling consist of many organizations bringing goods and services from the point of production to the point of use. *Retailing* includes all activities involved in selling goods or services directly to final consumers for their personal, nonbusiness use. Retailers can be classified as store retailers and nonstore retailers. *Store retailers* can be further classified by the *amount of service* they provide (self-service, limited service, or full service); *product line sold* (specialty stores, department stores, supermarkets, convenience stores, combination stores, superstores, hypermarkets, and service businesses); *relative prices* (discount stores, off-price retailers, and catalog showrooms); *control of outlets* (corporate chains, voluntary chains and retailer cooperatives, consumer cooperatives, franchise organizations, and merchandising conglomerates); and *type of store cluster* (central business districts and shopping centers).

Although most goods and services are sold through stores, nonstore retailing has been growing much faster than store retailing. *Nonstore retailers* now account for more than 14 percent of all consumer purchases, and they may account for a third of all sales by the end of the century. Nonstore retailing consists of *direct marketing* (direct mail and catalog retailing, telemarketing, television marketing, and electronic shopping), *door-to-door selling*, and *automatic vending*. Integrated direct marketing, using multiple vehicle, multiple stage campaigns, can greatly improve direct marketing response. In order to employ integrated direct marketing, companies must develop effective marketing database systems.

Each retailer must make decisions about its target markets, product assortment and services, price, promotion, and place. Retailers need to choose target markets carefully and position themselves strongly.

Wholesaling includes all the activities involved in selling goods or services to those who are buying for the purpose of resale or for business use. Wholesalers perform many functions, including selling and promoting, buying and assortment building, bulk-breaking, warehousing, transporting, financing, risk bearing, supplying market information, and providing management services and advice. Wholesalers fall into three groups. *Merchant wholesalers* take possession of the goods. They include *full-service wholesalers* (wholesale merchants, industrial distributors) and *limited-service wholesalers* (cash-and-carry wholesalers, truck wholesalers, drop shippers, rack jobbers, producers' cooperatives, and mail-order wholesalers). *Agents* and *brokers* do not take possession of the goods but are paid a commission for aiding buying and selling. *Manufacturers' sales branches and offices* are wholesaling operations conducted by nonwholesalers to bypass the wholesalers. Wholesaling is holding its own in the economy. Progressive wholesalers are adapting their services to the needs of target customers and are seeking cost-reducing methods of doing business.

■ QUESTIONS FOR DISCUSSION

1. In deciding where to shop, many consumers are coming to value quality of service more than such factors as price or convenience. If this trend continues, what impact will it have on full-service retailers? Will it have the same impact on self-service and limited-service retailers?

2. Which would do more to increase a convenience store's sales, an increase in the length or in the breadth of its product assortment? Why?

3. Off-price retailers provide tough price competition to other retailers. Will large retailers' growing power in channels

of distribution affect manufacturers' willingness to sell to off-price retailers at below regular wholesale rates? What policy should Sony have toward selling to off-price retailers?

4. Postal rate hikes make direct mail, catalogs, and product delivery more expensive. How would you expect direct mail and catalog marketers to respond to an increase in postage rates?

5. Warehouse clubs that are restricted to members only, such as Costco and Sam's Wholesale, are growing rapidly. They offer a very broad but shallow line of products, often in institutional packaging, at very low prices. Some members buy for resale, others to supply a business, and still others buy for personal use. Are these stores wholesalers or retailers? How can you make a distinction?

6. A typical "country store" in a farming community sells a variety of food and nonfood items—snacks, staples, hardware, and many other types of goods. What kinds of wholesalers do the owners of such stores use to obtain the items they sell? Are these the same suppliers that a supermarket uses?

7. How would a small producer of lawn and garden tools prefer to sell its output: through a manufacturers' agent or through a selling agent? Why?

8. Are there any fundamental differences between retailers, wholesalers, and manufacturers in the types of marketing decisions they make? Give examples of the marketing decisions made by the three groups that show their similarities and differences.

9. Why has the promotion area of marketing strategy traditionally been weak for wholesalers? How can wholesalers use promotion to improve their competitive positions?

10. As the distinction between large retailers and large wholesalers gets more and more blurred, which strategy do you think will be more common: retailers dealing directly with manufacturers rather than through wholesalers, or wholesalers setting up their own retailing operations to sell to consumers? Why?

11. Sears has suffered serious erosion of its Kenmore appliance and home electronics business from discounters such as Circuit City and Best Buy. To compete, Sears has launched "Sears Brand Central" to sell national brands at everyday low prices—even though Sears' fixed costs are much higher than their competitors. Do you think Sears can reverse the wheel of retailing? Make a specific recommendation to the Sears board of directors on what to do next.

■ KEY TERMS

Agent. A wholesaler who represents buyers or sellers on a more permanent basis, performs only a few functions, and does not take title to goods.

Automatic vending. Selling through vending machines.

Broker. A wholesaler who does not take title to goods and whose function is to bring buyers and sellers together and assist in negotiation.

Catalog showroom. A retail operation that sells a wide selection of high-markup, fast-moving brand-name goods at discount prices.

Catalog marketing. Direct marketing through catalogs mailed to a select list of customers or made available in stores.

Chain stores. Two or more outlets that are commonly owned and controlled, have central buying and merchandising, and sell similar lines of merchandise.

Combination stores. Combined food and drug stores.

Consumer cooperative. A retail firm that is owned by its customers.

Convenience store. A small store, located near a residential area, open long hours seven days a week, and carrying a limited line of high-turnover convenience goods.

Department store. A retail organization that carries a wide variety of product lines—typically clothing, home furnishings, and household goods; each line is operated as a separate department managed by specialist buyers or merchandisers.

Direct marketing. Marketing through various advertising media that interact directly with consumers, generally calling for the consumer to make a direct response.

Direct-mail marketing. Direct marketing through single mailings that include letters, ads, samples, foldouts, and other "salespeople on wings" sent to prospects on mailing lists.

Discount store. A retail institution that sells standard merchandise at lower prices by accepting lower margins and selling at higher volume.

Door-to-door retailing. Selling via door-to-door, office-to-office, or at home sales parties.

Electronic shopping. Direct marketing through a two-way system that links consumers with the seller's computerized catalog by cable or telephone lines.

Factory outlets. Off-price retailing operations that are owned and operated by manufacturers and that normally carry the manufacturer's surplus, discontinued, or irregular goods.

Franchise. A contractual association between a manufacturer, wholesaler, or service organization (a franchiser) and independent business people (franchisees) who buy the right to own and operate one or more units in the franchise system.

Full-service retailer. Retailers that provide a full range of services to shoppers.

Full-service wholesalers. Wholesalers that provide a full set of services such as carrying stock, using a salesforce, offering credit, making deliveries, and providing management assistance.

Hypermarkets. Huge stores that combine supermarket, discount, and warehouse retailing; in addition to food, they carry furniture, appliances, clothing, and many other things.

Independent off-price retailers. Off-price retailers that are either owned and run by entrepreneurs or are divisions of larger retail corporations.

Integrated direct marketing. Direct marketing campaigns which use multiple vehicles, and multiple stages to improve response rates and profits.

Limited-service retailers. Retailers that provide only a limited number of services to shoppers.

Limited-service wholesalers. Wholesalers that offer only limited services to their suppliers and customers.

Manufacturers' sales branches and offices. Wholesaling by sellers or buyers themselves rather than through independent wholesalers.

Marketing database. An organized set of data about individual customers or prospects that can be used to generate and qualify customer leads, sell products and services, and maintain customer relationships.

Merchandising conglomerates. Corporations that combine several different retailing forms under central ownership and that share some distribution and management functions.

Merchant wholesaler. An independently owned business that takes title to the merchandise it handles.

Off-price retailers. Retailers that buy at less than regular wholesale prices and sell at less than retail, usually carrying a changing and unstable collection of higher-quality merchandise, often leftover goods, overruns, and irregulars obtained from manufacturers at reduced prices. They include factory outlets, independents, and warehouse clubs.

Retailers. Businesses whose sales come *primarily* from retailing.

Retailing. All activities involved in selling goods or services directly to final consumers for their personal, non-business use.

Self-service retailers. Retailers that provide few or no services to shoppers; shoppers perform their own locate-compare-select process.

Shopping center. A group of retail businesses planned, developed, owned, and managed as a unit.

Specialty store. A retail store that carries a narrow product line with a deep assortment within that line.

Supermarkets. Large, low-cost, low-margin, high-volume, self-service stores that carry a wide variety of food, laundry, and household products.

Superstore. A store almost twice the size of a regular supermarket carrying a large assortment of routinely purchased food and nonfood items, and offering such services as dry cleaning, post offices, photo finishing, check cashing, bill paying, lunch counters, car care, and pet care.

Telemarketing. Using the telephone to sell directly to consumers.

Television marketing. Direct marketing via television using direct-response advertising or home shopping channels.

Warehouse clubs (or **wholesale clubs**). Off-price retailers that sell a limited selection of brand-name grocery items, appliances, clothing, and a hodgepodge of other goods at deep discounts to members who pay annual membership fees.

Wheel of retailing concept. A concept of retailing which states that new types of retailers usually being as low-margin, low-price, low-status operations but later evolve into higher-priced, higher-service operations, eventually becoming like the conventional retailers they replaced.

Wholesalers. Firms engaged *primarily* in wholesaling activity.

Wholesaling. All activities involved in selling goods and services to those buying for resale or business use.

■ REFERENCES

1. The quote is from Steven Weiner, "With Big Selection and Low Prices, 'Category Killer' Stores Are a Hit," *The Wall Street Journal*, June 17, 1986, p. 33. Also see Bill Kelley, "The New Wave from Europe," *Sales & Marketing Management*, November 1987, pp. 45–50; Ivan S. Cutler, "IKEA Steps Up Assault on U.S. Furniture," *Furniture Today*, August 21, 1989, pp. 8–9; and Seth Chandler, "Swedish Marketers Going Global," *Advertising Age*, April 16, 1990, p. 38.

2. For more on department stores, see Arthur Bragg, "Will Department Stores Survive?" *Sales and Marketing Management*, April 1986, pp. 60–64; and Anthony Ramirez, "Department Stores Shape Up," *Fortune*, September 1, 1986, pp. 50–52.

3. See John Schwartz, "Super-Duper Supermarkets," *Newsweek*, June 27, 1988, pp. 40–41; and Belinda Hulin-Salkin, "Food Stores Turn Shopping into a Carefully Catered Affair," *Advertising Age*, October 3, 1988, pp, S1, S16.

4. See Toni Mack, "A Six-Pack of Cabernet, Please," *Forbes*, September 18, 1989, pp. 168–69; "Stop-N-Go Micromarkets New Upscale Mix," *Chain Store Age Executive*, January 1990, p. 145; and Christy Fisher, "Convenience Chains Pump for New Life," *Advertising Age*, April 23, 1990, p. 80.

5. See Ruth Hamel, "Food Fight," *American Demographics*, March 1989, p. 38.

6. See "How Much Hype in Hypermarkets?" *Sales & Marketing Management*, April 1988, pp. 56–63; Todd Mason, "The Return of the Amazing Colossal Store," *Business Week*, August 22, 1988, pp. 59–61; Bob Geiger, "Going 'Hyper' in a Hypermarket," *Advertising Age*, May 8, 1989, pp. S21–S22; and Kevin Kelly, "Wal-Mart Gets Lost in the Vegetable Aisle," *Business Week*, May 26, 1990, p. 48.

7. See Lois Therrien and Amy Dunkin, "The Wholesale Success of Factory Outlet Malls," *Business Week*, February 3, 1986, pp. 92–94; and Jay A. Wedeven, "Factory-Outlet Retailers Find There's Strength in Numbers," *Marketing News*, April 25, 1988, pp. 7, 26.

8. See Janice Steinberg, "Wholesale Clubs Add Some Bulk," *Advertising-Age*, May 9, 1988, p. S24; and Andrew Kupfer, "The Final Word in No Frills Shopping," *Fortune*, March 13, 1989, p. 30.

9. See Jack G. Kaikati, "Don't Discount Off-Price Retailers," *Harvard Business Review*, May–June 1985, pp. 85–92; and "Off-Pricers Grab Growing Retail Market Share," *Marketing News*, March 13, 1987, pp. 9, 14.

10. See "Why Franchising Is Taking Off," *Fortune*, February 12, 1990, p. 124.

11. See Francesca Turchiano, "The Unmalling of America," *American Demographics*, April 1990, pp. 36–42.

12. See Mary Lou Roberts and Paul D. Berger, *Direct Marketing Management* (Englewood Cliffs, NJ: Prentice Hall, 1989), pp. 11–15.

13. See Eileen Norris, "Alternative Media Try to Get Their Feet in the Door," *Advertising Age*, October 17, 1985, p. 15.

14. Arnold Fishman, "The 1986 Mail Order Guide," *Direct Marketing*, July 1987, p. 40.

15. Janice Steinberg, "Cacophony of Catalogs Fill All Niches," *Advertising Age*, October 26, 1987, pp. S1–2; and Annetta Miller, "Up to the Chin in Catalogs," *Newsweek*, November 20, 1989, pp. 57–58.

16. Elaine Santoro, "Royal Silk Shines," *Direct Marketing*, April 1987, p. 53. Also see Carol Boyd Leon, "Selling Through VCR," *American Demographics*, December 1987, pp. 40–47; and Judith Graham, "Neiman-Marcus Tries Video Catalog," *Advertising Age*, March 21, 1988, p. 68.

17. Rudy Oetting, "Telephone Marketing: Where We've Been and Where We Should Be Going," *Direct Marketing*, February 1987, p. 98.

18. Bill Kelley, "Is There Anything that Can't Be Sold by

Phone?'' *Sales & Marketing Management*, April 1989, pp. 60–64.

19. Jim Auchmute, "But Wait There's More!" *Advertising Age*, October 17, 1985, p. 18.

20. See Mary J. Pitzer, "A Bargain Basement Where the TV Reception Is Great," *Business Week*, May 30, 1988, p. 79; and Howard Schlossberg, "Picture Still Looks Bright for TV Shopping Networks," *Marketing News*, October 23, 1989, p. 8.

21. See Bill Saporito, "Are IBM and Sears Crazy? Or Canny?" *Fortune*, September 28, 1987, pp. 74–80; Alison Fahey, "Prodigy Videotex Expands Its Reach," *Advertising Age*, April 24, 1989, p. 75.

22. Ernin Roman, *Integrated Direct Marketing* (New York: McGraw-Hill, 1988), p. 108.

23. See Joe Schwartz, "Databases Deliver the Goods," *American Demographics*, September 1989, pp. 23–25.

24. For a fuller discussion, see Lawrence H. Wortzel, "Retailing Strategies for Today's Mature Marketplace," *The Journal of Business Strategy*, Spring 1987, pp. 45–56.

25. For more on retail site location, see R. L. Davies and D. S. Rogers, eds., *Store Location and Store Assessment Research* (New York: John Wiley & Sons, 1984); and Avijit Ghosh and C. Samual Craig, "An Approach to Determining Optimal Locations for New Services," *Journal of Marketing Research*, November 1986, pp. 354–362.

26. See Malcolm P. McNair and Eleanor G. May, "The Next Revolution of the Retailing Wheel, *Harvard Business Review*, September–October 1978, pp. 81–91; and May, "A Retail Odyssey," *Journal of Retailing*, Fall 1989, pp. 356–367.

27. For more on retailing trends, see Eleanor G. May, C. William Ress, and Walter J. Salmon, *Future Trends in Retailing* (Cambridge, Mass.: Marketing Science Institute, February 1985); Louis W. Stern and Adel I. El-Ansary, *Marketing Channels* (Englewood Cliffs, NJ: Prentice Hall, 1988); and Daniel Sweeney, "Toward 2000," *Chain Store Age Executive*, January 1990, pp. 27–39.

28. See James A. Narus and James C. Anderson, "Contributing as a Distributor to Partnerships with Manufacturers," *Business Horizons*, September–October, 1987.

29. See Arthur Andersen & Co., *Facing the Forces of Change: Beyond Future Trend in Wholesale Distribution* (Washington, D.C.: Distribution Research and Education Foundation, 1987), p. 7. Also see Joseph Weber, "Mom and Pop Move Out of Wholesaling," *Business Week*, January 9, 1989, p. 91.

SEARS: SEEKING A MORE FASHIONABLE IMAGE

Suppose your local hardware store suddenly decided to open a women's fashion department, installing racks of lace dresses and floral print blouses next to the nails, socket wrenches, and paint cans. A questionable plan? Then consider the plight of Sears, Roebuck & Company. Sears became the nation's largest retailer by making household names out of "hard goods" brands such as Craftsman tools, Kenmore appliances, Weatherbeater paints, Road-Handler tires, and DieHard batteries. However, Sears' preoccupation with hard goods has also hurt the retailer. Sears' merchandise operations lost market share steadily throughout the 1980s. In 1989, its U.S. stores and catalogs contributed just 16.6 percent of total profit from the company's operating groups, as compared with a 41 percent contribution just five years ago.

Further, consider the plight of Ms. Lee Hogan Cass. Sears just hired Ms. Cass to be its women's fashion director. You might ask: What's so unusual about that? For starters, the position has been vacant for nine years! Sears decided to refill the fashion director's position as part of a sweeping strategy designed to restore its stores to prominence. In earlier moves, it had switched to a radical "everyday low pricing" strategy, added national brands such as Panasonic and Whirlpool, and revamped displays into what it calls "power formats." Yet, in the first three months of 1990, U.S. retail operations recorded a net loss of $134 million—one of Sears' worst quarters ever.

Why would Sears, known for its hard goods, turn to women's fashions as the latest vehicle in its attempted rescue operation? The major reason is that, over the years, Sears has located more than two-thirds of its 850 stores in shopping malls. Today, most shoppers at these retail mini-cities are on a mission to do one thing: buy clothes. Apparel accounts for more than 70 percent of nonfood sales in malls, and women today stock more than three-quarters of their wardrobes with clothes bought in malls. Because Sears cannot relocate two-thirds of its stores, it must join the trend toward soft goods. Although Sears also sells men's and children's clothing, selling women's apparel causes the most problems. As one market researcher notes, "It's going to be enormously hard, . . . but Sears has to figure out how to get women to come into the store." Unless Sears can attract more women, its growth prospects will remain dim.

Enter Ms. Cass, the new women's fashion director. A retailing veteran who held a similar position with the Broadway department store chain in Southern California, Ms. Cass notes that Sears "should be the best moderate department store in America." But, she adds, "I don't think we are now." Ms. Cass may have a tough job in attempting to revitalize women's fashions sales at hard-ware-oriented Sears. The company has always sold women's apparel; executives at the first Sears store insisted that "monkey wrenches, paint, hardware, and tires be amply displayed along with the women's soft goods, making shopping a family affair." But Sears' management clearly puts fashion in the back seat. Executives like to refer to clothing as "wearing apparel" and have typically promoted fashion items the way they might promote new tires. For example, one 1930s Sears ad boasted, "Rain-spots won't show on these ALL-WEATHER pure silk stockings." The company has also been slow to pounce on trends. In the past, it often stuck with the same merchandise for what seemed an eternity. In the early 1980s, however, Sears picked up on an earlier fashion initiative and added fashion model Cheryl Tiegs' name to a new line of low-priced sportswear. The line became a big hit, but the clothes soon began to look alike, year after year, and quality slipped. Sears waited nine years, then dropped the line.

With this background, Sears' women's department became the "bag lady" of retailing. In most stores, the shabby and cluttered women's fashion areas have too few mirrors and fitting rooms. Skirts, blouses, and jackets are jumbled onto cheap racks and sold primarily on the basis of price. Signs trumpet $19.99 outfits and two-for-one bra sales. The Craftsman mentality even extends to something called the Zip & Dash housedress. Sears has promoted the shapeless polyester dress as one of its top offerings because it is durable and doesn't need ironing. Sears' buyers have also traditionally chosen apparel colors the way customers buy the company's paint, from something called a "color card." Divided into palettes, such as pastels and brights, the color-card approach often leads to a mind-numbing array of hues on the sales floor.

The upshot: Store sales of women's clothing never amounted to much. Today, they account for less than 10 percent of the merchandise group's $32 billion in annual revenue, even though the women's department takes up a far greater percentage of selling space in the store. Moreover, while the typical Sears store still attracts a broad spectrum of customers, shoppers in its women's department tend to be females over 40 with household incomes of less than $30,000.

Sears knows that it has been slow to get started on its makeover. Big rivals, such as J. C. Penny, are already well along with their own fashion overhauls. Sensing the trend in shopping malls almost a decade ago, Penney dumped most of its hard goods and made itself over to look more like a department store, a strategy that made it one of the hottest companies in retailing. Sears doesn't need to go that far—and doesn't intend to. With J. C.

Penny's exit from hard goods, Sears now enjoys the advantage of being the lone hard-goods supplier in many shopping centers.

As Sears and Ms. Cass kick off their own efforts to revamp Sears' fashion business, they know they face many problems. Sears' efforts to convince major apparel houses that it is truly serious about clothes have sometimes fallen on deaf ears. Ms. Cass called a long-time friend, Bernard Claus, hoping to add his large and influential apparel company to Sears' roster of suppliers. He turned her down flat. Mr. Claus, whose clothes range up to $200 in price and are widely sold in department stores, says: "I think of us as being upper-moderate. That range is too high for the kind of mix and environment at Sears."

While Sears has been trying to change, few people in the company have any illusions about how far it still has to go. Its store in Niles, Illinois, though far from the worst example, illustrates the problem. Fresh labels have been added, such as Personal and Middlebrook Park, but they are mixed with staler lines, such as the Stefanie Powers collection and Goolagong sportswear. And garish red signs plastered on the racks announce "As Advertised"

prices. None of the customers in the aisles appear to be younger than 50 and, for some unknown reason, a mound of Rubbermaid picnic coolers lurks in the middle of the department waiting for buyers.

A lot more work lies ahead, acknowledges Ms. Cass. "There's only one way to go," she says, "which is up."

QUESTIONS

1. How would you characterize Sears' overall retail store strategy in terms of amount of service, product line sold, relative prices, control of outlets, and type of store cluster?

2. Why has Sears' experienced problems in recent years? How have its positioning and other marketing decisions contributed to these problems? What changes in retailing have caused problems?

3. Evaluate Sears' past marketing efforts with respect to its women's fashions operations.

4. Assume the role of Ms. Cass. Develop a marketing plan for turning Sears' women's fashion business around? Be specific. How would you implement your plan?

Source: Adapted from Francine Schwadel, "Its Earnings Sagging, Sears Upgrades Line of Women's Apparel," *The Wall Street Journal*, May 9, 1990. Used with permission.

HOME SHOPPING

It's a video flea market. It's cubic zirconium city. It has glamour and glitz, hard selling, corny antics, and the fervor of a televangelist or a telethon host. It's—Home Shopping Network (HSN), bringing you the best of close-out and liquidation merchandise at prices you're not gonna believe! Variously described as schlocky, vulgar, tacky, boring, and ghastly video wallpaper, HSN has nevertheless demonstrated the power of television as a selling medium. Although it may be far from high-tech, sophisticated programming with two-way interactive cable TV shopping, it works.

In its first two years, HSN indeed did very well. Initially, HSN's developers relied on discontinued and remainder merchandise. However, their horn-tooting, perpetually smiling hosts proved so proficient at moving merchandise that HSN could no longer depend on leftovers, so it signed up a fleet of worldwide suppliers to produce merchandise under the Home Shopping Club brand. The telephones continued to ring, and sales jumped from $17 million in 1986 to over $455 million in the first half of 1987.

HSN's phenomenal success generated the speedy entrance of competition. A Pennsylvania firm, QVC, signed an agreement to sell Sears merchandise. *Close Out Merchandise Buyers* (COMB) in Minneapolis developed Cable Value Network (CVN). Financial News Network started TelShop; Fox Television, Lorimar-Telepictures, and Horn & Hardart started ValueTelevision; and Crazy Eddie in New York inaugurated his own Home Entertainment Shopping Network. Catalog companies produced videotapes of their merchandise to show on American Catalog Shopper Network (ACSM). HSN expanded to Canada. Entry costs were low—one studio, one bank of telephones, and one warehouse. At 10 to 15 percent, margins were high compared to those for traditional retailers, and the potential market in the United States was more than 40 million homes with cable television.

The airwaves were flooded with salespeople. Channels tried more tasteful, informative formats designed to appeal to upscale consumers. Celebrity hosts such as Pat Boone, Meredith MacRae, and Richard Simmons touted the virtues of upmarket goods, *and* demonstrated the goods as well. Networks such as QVC divided their shows into hour-long segments devoted to one type of merchandise such as toys or home furnishings. HSN started HSN2 to sell more trendy merchandise, and produced a game show on which contestants vied for HSN merchandise.

Inevitably, all this competition resulted in a shakeout. QVC and CVN merged. TelShop and ValueTelevision, among others, failed. HSN's stock price declined from a high of $133 per share to a low of $5 in the first half of 1988.

Other problems surfaced. When HSN's telephone lines clogged, causing many customers to be cut off, it may have lost 50 percent of its sales and alienated many of its consumers. To broaden their appeal, HSN and other cable sellers offered more expensive merchandise such as tour packages, luxury cruises, insurance, furs, high-priced electronics, and a prescription service—many of which failed. With all these problems, HSN's sales declined in 1988 and have not fully recovered. Returned merchandise increased from less than 8 percent to nearly 15 percent of sales. And HSN's game show flopped because it couldn't compete with the Iran-Contra congressional hearings.

Yet for all its defects, HSN has made electronic mass marketing a reality. Before HSN, the sales possibilities inherent in cable hookups, telephone lines, and home computers were unexplored. Since HSN, distributors and retailers have responded with other electronic devices. They are using videologs (catalogs on videotape) to sell goods at the wholesale and retail levels. Video kiosks set up in many locations disseminate shopping and product information and dispense goods. Closed-circuit TV and videotaped ads are used in-store to promote merchandise. Some grocery stores use video carts (called "ads on wheels") and talking shelf facings activated by movement in the aisles.

Nor are computers being overlooked. By including more retailers and offering a better selection of merchandise, CompuServe has upgraded and expanded its computer shopping program, Electronic Mall. Computers are used in-store as electronic catalogs customers can look through to select merchandise. Elizabeth Arden and Shiseido Cosmetics use computers for in-store makeovers: The computer scans the customer's skin to define its color and tone, and then electronically experiments with different makeups and hair colors. The results are shown as before and after pictures on the monitor. Guerlain uses computers to select appropriate scents for customers. These in-store promotions increase sales 300 percent during the promotion period, and usually produce year-long increases of 25 to 37 percent.

All of these changes promise that retailing in the 1990s will look and sound very different from what we have known.

QUESTIONS

1. How does HSN affect consumer decision processes?
2. Why has nonstore retailing grown in popularity in recent years?
3. What factors are likely to inhibit electronic marketing systems?

Sources: Sandra Lee Breisch, "Cosmetic Beauty Is in the Eye of the Computer," *Advertising Age*, March 2, 1987, p. S12; "Blame the Phone Company: A Strategy Goes on Trial," *Business Week*, June 12, 1989, p. 30; "Home Shopping: Is It a Revolution in Retailing—or Just a Fad?" *Business Week*, December 15, 1986, pp. 62–69; Judann Dagnoli; "Home Shopping Net Expands Its Game Plan," *Advertising Age*, June 22, 1987, p. 44; "Can You Believe This Price?" *Time*, October 20, 1986, p. 68; and John F. Wasik, "Shopping on 'The Tube,'" *Consumer Digest*, November/December, 1986, pp. 12–15.

16

Promoting Products: Communication and Promotion Strategy

M ost Quaker Oats brands have become staples in American pantries. With a 68-percent share, Quaker dominates the hot cereal market, and its Aunt Jemima brand is tops in frozen breakfast products and pancake mixes. Quaker captures 25 percent of the huge pet food market (Gravy Train, Gainesburgers, Cycle, Ken-L Ration, Kibbles 'n Bits). Moreover, it's the number four ready-to-eat cereal producer (Cap'n Crunch, Life, Oh!s, 100% Natural). Other leading Quaker brands include Gatorade, Van Camp's Pork and Beans, Granola Bars, and Rice-A-Roni. In all, brands with leading market shares account for more than 60 percent of Quaker's nearly $5.6 billion in yearly sales.

A company the size of Quaker has much to say to its many publics and has several promotion tools to say it with. Hundreds of Quaker employees work in advertising, personal selling, sales promotion, and public relations units around the company. A half dozen large advertising and public relations agencies aim carefully planned communications to consumers, retailers, the media, stockholders, employees, and other publics.

As consumers, we know a good deal about Quaker's advertising: Each year Quaker bombards us with about $250 million worth of advertising telling us about its brands and persuading us to buy them. Quaker also spends heavily on consumer sales promotions such as coupons, premiums, and sweepstakes to coax us further. You may remember the "Treasure Hunt" promotion in which Quaker gave away $5 million in silver and gold coins randomly inserted in Ken-L Ration packages. Then there was the "Where's

the Cap'n?" promotion: Quaker removed the picture of Cap'n Horatio Crunch from the front of its cereal boxes and then provided clues to his location on the back. Consumers who used the clues to find the Cap'n could win cash prizes. The 14-week promotion cost Quaker $18 million but increased sales by 50 percent. Consumer advertising and sales promotions work directly to create consumer demand, and this demand "pulls" Quaker products through its channel.

But consumer advertising and sales promotions account for only a small portion of Quaker's total promotion mix. The company spends many times as much on behind-the-scenes promotion activities that "push" its products toward consumers. Personal selling and trade promotions are major weapons in Quaker's battle for retailer support. The company's main objective is shelf space in more than 300,000 supermarkets, convenience stores, and corner groceries across the country. Quaker's army of salespeople court retailers with strong service, trade allowances, attractive displays, and other trade promotions. They urge retailers to give Quaker products more and better shelf space and to run ads featuring Quaker brands. These push-promotion activities work closely with pull-promotion efforts to build sales and market share. The pull activities persuade consumers to look for Quaker brands; the push activities ensure that Quaker products are available, easy to find, and effectively merchandised when consumers start looking.

In addition to advertising, sales promotion, and personal selling, Quaker communicates through publicity and public relations. The company's publicity department and public relations agency place newsworthy information about Quaker and its products in the news media. They prepare annual reports to communicate with investor and financial publics and hold press conferences to communicate with the media publics. Quaker sponsors many public relations activities to promote the company as a good citizen. For example, the Quaker Oats Foundation donates millions of dollars in cash and products each year to worthy causes, matches employee donations to non-profit organizations, donates food to needy people, and supports a network of centers providing therapy for families with handicapped children.

Quaker owes much of its success to quality products that appeal strongly to millions of consumers around the world. But success also depends on Quaker's skill in telling its publics about the company and its products. All of Quaker's promotion tools—advertising, personal selling, sales promotion, and public relations—must blend harmoniously into an effective communication program to tell the Quaker story.[1]

CHAPTER OBJECTIVES

After reading this chapter, you should be able to:

1. Name and define the four tools of the promotion mix.
2. Discuss the elements of the marketing communication process.
3. Explain the methods for setting the promotion budget.
4. Discuss the factors that affect the design of the promotion mix.

Modern marketing calls for more than developing a good product, pricing it attractively, and making it available to target customers. Companies must also *communicate* with their customers. And what is communicated should not be left to chance.

To communicate well, companies often hire advertising agencies to develop effective ads, sales-promotion specialists to design sales incentive programs, and public relations firms to develop corporate images. They train their salespeople to be friendly, helpful, and persuasive. For most companies the question is not *whether* to communicate, but *how much to spend* and *in what ways*.

A modern company manages a complex marketing-communications system (see Figure 16-1). The company communicates with its middlemen, consumers, and various publics. Its middlemen communicate with their consumers and publics. Consumers have word-of-mouth communication with each other and with other publics. Meanwhile, each group provides feedback to every other group.

A company's total marketing communications program—called its **promotion mix**—consists of the specific blend of advertising, sales promotion, public relations

FIGURE 16-1   The marketing communications system

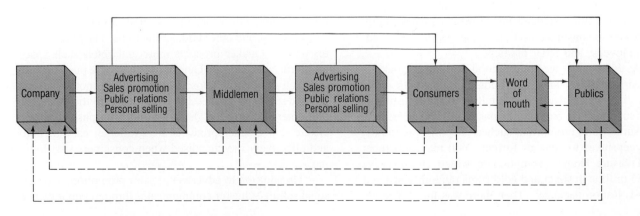

and personal selling that the company uses to pursue its advertising and marketing objectives. The four major promotion tools are defined below:

Advertising: Any paid form of nonpersonal presentation and promotion of ideas, goods, or services by an identified sponsor.

Sales promotion: Short-term incentives to encourage purchase or sales of a product of service.

Public relations: Building good relations with the company's various publics by obtaining favorable publicity, building up a good ''corporate image,'' and handling or heading off unfavorable rumors, stories, and events.

Personal selling: Oral presentation in a conversation with one or more prospective purchasers for the purpose of making sales.[2]

Within these categories are specific tools such as sales presentations, point-of-purchase displays, specialty advertising, trade shows, fairs, demonstrations, catalogs, literature, press kits, posters, contests, premiums, coupons, and trading stamps. At the same time, communication goes beyond these specific promotion tools. The product's design, its price, the shape and color of its package, and the stores that sell it *all* communicate something to buyers. Therefore, although the promotion mix is the company's primary communication activity, the entire marketing mix—promotion *and* product, price, and place—must be coordinated for greatest communication impact.

This chapter looks at two questions: *What are the major steps in developing effective marketing communication? How should the promotion budget and mix be determined?* Chapter 17 focuses on mass-communication tools—advertising, sales promotion, and public relations. Chapter 18 examines the salesforce as a communication and promotion tool.

STEPS IN DEVELOPING EFFECTIVE COMMUNICATION

Marketers need to understand how communication works. Communication involves the nine elements shown in Figure 16-2. Two elements are the major parties in a communication—*sender* and *receiver*. Another two are the major communication tools—*message* and *media*. Four are major communication functions—*encoding, decoding, response,* and *feedback*. The last element is *noise* in the system. These elements are defined below and applied to a McDonald's television ad:

- *Sender*: The *party sending the message* to another party—McDonald's.
- *Encoding*: The process of *putting thought into symbolic form*—McDonald's advertising agency assembles words and illustrations into an advertisement that will convey the intended message.

FIGURE 16-2   Elements in the communication process

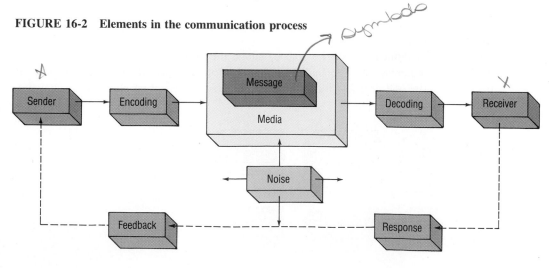

- *Message*: The *set of symbols* that the sender transmits—the actual McDonald's advertisement.
- *Media*: The *communication channels* through which the message moves from sender to receiver—in this case, television and the specific television programs McDonald's selects.
- *Decoding*: The process by which the receiver *assigns meaning to the symbols* encoded by the sender—a consumer watches the ad and interprets the words and illustrations it contains.
- *Receiver*: The *party receiving the message* sent by another party—the consumer who watches the McDonald's ad.
- *Response*: The *reactions of the receiver* after being exposed to the message—any of hundreds of possible responses such as the consumer likes McDonald's better, is more likely to eat at McDonald's next time, or . . . nothing.
- *Feedback*: That part of the *receiver's response communicated back to the sender*—McDonald's research shows that consumers like and remember the ad, or consumers write or call McDonald's praising or criticizing the ad or McDonald's products.
- *Noise*: The *unplanned static or distortion* during the communication process that results in the receiver's getting a different message than the sender sent—the consumer has poor TV reception or is distracted by family members while watching the ad.

This model points out the key factors in good communication. Senders need to know what audiences they want to reach and what responses they want. They must be good at encoding messages that take into account how the target audience decodes them. They must send the message through media that reach target audiences. And they must develop feedback channels so that they can assess the audience's response to the message.

Thus, the marketing communicator must make the following decisions: (1) identify the target audience, (2) determine the response sought, (3) choose a message, (4) choose the media through which to send the message, (5) select the message source, and (6) collect feedback.

Identifying the Target Audience

A marketing communicator starts with a clear target audience in mind. The audience may be potential buyers or current users, those who make the buying decision or those who influence it. The audience may be individuals, groups, special publics, or the general public. The target audience will heavily affect the communicator's decisions on *what* will be said, *how* it will be said, *when* it will be said, *where* it will be said, and *who* will say it.

Determining the Response Sought

Once the target audience has been defined, the marketing communicator must decide what response is sought. Of course, in most cases, the final response is *purchase*. But purchase is the result of a long process of consumer decision making. The marketing communicator needs to know where the target audience now stands and to what state it needs to be moved.

The target audience may be in any of six **buyer readiness states**—*awareness*, *knowledge*, *liking*, *preference*, *conviction*, or *purchase*, which are shown in Figure 16-3.

Awareness

First, the communicator must be able to gauge the target audience's awareness of the product or organization. The audience may be totally unaware of it, know only its name, or know one or a few things about it. If most of the target audience is unaware,

FIGURE 16-3
Buyer readiness states

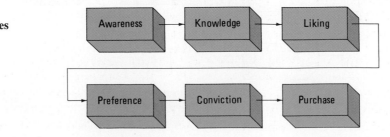

the communicator tries to build awareness—perhaps starting with simple name recognition. This process can begin with simple messages repeating the name. Even then, building awareness takes time. Suppose a small Iowa college called Pottsville seeks applicants from Nebraska but has no name recognition in Nebraska. And suppose there are 30,000 high school seniors in Nebraska who may be interested in Pottsville College. The college might set the objective of making 70 percent of these students aware of Pottsville's name within one year.

Knowledge

The target audience might be aware of the company or product but know little else. Pottsville may want its target audience to know that it is a private four-year college with excellent programs in English and the language arts. Pottsville College therefore needs to learn how many people in its target audience have little, some, or much knowledge about Pottsville. The college may then decide to select product knowledge as its first communication objective.

Liking

If target audience members *know* the product, how do they *feel* about it? We can develop a scale covering degrees of liking, for example, "dislike very much," "dislike somewhat," "indifferent," "like somewhat," and "like very much." If the audience looks unfavorably on Pottsville College, the communicator must learn why and then develop a communications campaign to create favorable feelings. If the unfavorable view is based on real problems of the college, then communications alone cannot do the job. Pottsville will have to fix its problems and then communicate its renewed quality. Good public relations call for "good deeds followed by good words."

Preference

The target audience might *like* the product but not *prefer* it to others. In this case, the communicator must try to build consumer preference. The communicator will promote the product's quality, value, performance, and other features. The communicator can check on the campaign's success by measuring the audience's preferences again after the campaign. If Pottsville College finds that many high school seniors like Pottsville but choose to attend other colleges, it will have to identify those areas where its offerings are better than those of competing colleges. It must then promote its advantages to build preference among prospective students.

Conviction

A target audience might *prefer* the product but not develop a *conviction* about buying it. Thus, some high school seniors may prefer Pottsville but may not be sure they want to go to college. The communicator's job is to build conviction that going to college is the right thing to do.

Purchase

Finally, some members of the target audience might have *conviction* but not quite get around to making the *purchase*. They may wait for more information or plan to act later. The communicator must lead these consumers to take the final step. Actions might include offering the product at a low price, offering a premium, or letting consumers try it on a limited basis. Thus, Pottsville might invite selected high school students to visit the campus and attend some classes. Or it might offer scholarships to deserving students.

In discussing buyer readiness states, we have assumed that buyers pass through cognitive (awareness, knowledge), affective (liking, preference, conviction), and behavioral (purchase) stages, in that order. This "learn-feel-do" sequence is appropriate when buyers have high involvement with a product category and perceive brands in the category to be highly differentiated, as is the case when they purchase a product such as an automobile. But consumers often follow other sequences. For example, they might follow a "do-feel-learn" sequence for high involvement products with little perceived differentiation, as when they buy aluminum siding. Still a third sequence is the "learn-do-feel" sequence, where consumers have low involvement and perceive little differentiation, as is the case when they buy a product such as salt. By understanding consumers' buying stages and the appropriate sequence, the marketer can do a better job of planning communications.

Choosing a Message

Having defined the desired audience response, the communicator turns to developing an effective message. Ideally, the message should get *Attention*, hold *Interest*, arouse *Desire*, and obtain *Action* (a framework known as the *AIDA model*). In practice, few messages take the consumer all the way from awareness to purchase, but the AIDA framework does suggest the desirable qualities of a good message.

In putting the message together, the marketing communicator must solve three problems: what to say (*message content*), how to say it logically (*message structure*), and how to say it symbolically (*message format*).

Message Content

The communicator has to figure out an appeal or theme that will produce the desired response. There are three types of appeals. **Rational appeals** relate to the audience's self-interest. They show that the product will produce the desired benefits. Examples are messages showing a product's quality, economy, value, or performance. Thus, in ads for its Excel car, Hyundai offers "cars that make sense," stressing low price, operating economy, and sensible features. When pitching computer systems to business users, IBM salespeople talk about quality, performance, reliability, and improved productivity.

Emotional appeals attempt to stir up either negative or positive emotions that can motivate purchase. These include fear, guilt, and shame appeals that get people to do things they should (brush their teeth, buy new tires) or stop doing things they shouldn't (smoke, drink too much, overeat). For example, a recent Crest ad invoked mild fear when it claimed, "There are some things you just can't afford to gamble with" (cavities). So did Michelin tire ads that featured cute babies and suggested, "Because so much is

A mild fear appeal: "When you get a cavity, there's no second chance."

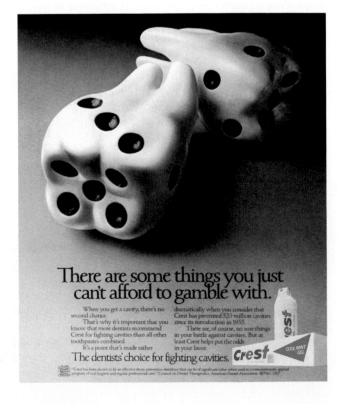

There are some things you just can't afford to gamble with.

When you get a cavity, there's no second chance.
That's why it's important that you know that more dentists recommend Crest for fighting cavities than all other toothpastes combined.
It's a point that's made rather

dramatically when you consider that Crest has prevented 523 million cavities since its introduction in 1955.
There are, of course, no sure things in your battle against cavities. But at least Crest helps put the odds in your favor.

The dentists' choice for fighting cavities. **Crest**

riding on your tires." Communicators also use positive emotional appeals such as love, humor, pride, and joy. Thus AT&T's long-running ad theme, "Reach out and touch someone," stirs a bundle of strong emotions.

Moral appeals are directed to the audience's sense of what is right and proper. They are often used to urge people to support such social causes as a cleaner environment, better race relations, equal rights for women, and aid to the needy. An example is the March of Dimes appeal: "God made you whole. Give to help those He didn't."

Message Structure

The communicator also has to decide how to handle three message structure issues. The first is whether to draw a conclusion or leave it to the audience. Early research showed that drawing a conclusion was usually more effective. More recent research, however, suggests that in many cases the advertiser is better off asking questions and letting buyers come to their own conclusions. The second message structure issue is whether to present a one-sided or two-sided argument. Usually, a one-sided argument is more effective in sales presentations—except when audiences are highly educated and negatively disposed. The third message structure issue is whether to present the strongest arguments first or last. Presenting them first gets strong attention but may lead to an anticlimactic ending.[3]

Message Format

The communicator also needs a strong *format* for the message. In a print ad, the communicator has to decide on the headline, copy, illustration, and color. To attract attention, advertisers can use novelty and contrast, eye-catching pictures and headlines, distinctive formats, message size and position, and color, shape, and movement. If the message is to be carried over the radio, the communicator has to choose words, sounds, and voices. The "sound" of an announcer promoting a used car should be different from one promoting quality furniture.

If the message is to be carried on television or in person, then all these elements plus body language have to be planned. Presenters plan their facial expressions, gestures, dress, posture, and hair style. If the message is carried on the product or its package, the communicator has to watch texture, scent, color, size, and shape. For example, color plays a major communication role in food preferences. When consumers sampled four cups of coffee that had been placed next to brown, blue, red, and yellow containers (all the coffee was identical, but the consumers did not know this), 75 percent felt that the coffee next to the brown container tasted too strong; nearly 85 percent judged the coffee next to the red container to be the richest; nearly everyone felt that the coffee next to the blue container was mild; and the coffee next to the yellow container was seen as weak. Thus, if a coffee company wants to communicate that its coffee is rich, it should probably use a red container along with label copy boasting the coffee's rich taste.

Choosing Media The communicator must now select *channels of communication*. There are two broad types of communication channels—*personal* and *nonpersonal*.

Personal Communication Channels

In **personal communication channels,** two or more people communicate directly with each other. They might communicate face-to-face, person-to-audience, over the telephone, or even through the mail. Personal communication channels are effective because they allow for personal addressing and feedback.

Some personal-communication channels are directly controlled by the communicator. For example, company salespeople contact buyers in the target market. But other personal communications about the product may reach buyers through channels not directly controlled by the company. These might include independent experts making statements to target buyers—consumer advocates, consumer buying guides, and others. Or they might be neighbors, friends, family members, and associates talking to target buyers. This last channel, known as **word-of-mouth influence,** has considerable effect in many product areas.

Personal influence carries great weight for products that are expensive, risky, or highly visible. For example, buyers of automobiles and major appliances often go beyond mass-media sources to seek the opinions of knowledgeable people.

Companies can take several steps to put personal-communication channels to work. They can devote extra effort to selling their products to well-known people or companies, who may in turn influence others to buy. They can create *opinion leaders*—people whose opinions are sought by others—by supplying certain people with the product on attractive terms. For example, companies can work through community members such as disc jockeys, class presidents, and presidents of local organizations. And they can use influential people in their advertisements or develop advertising that has high "conversation value." Finally, the firm can work to manage word-of-mouth communications by finding out what consumers are saying to others, taking appropriate actions to satisfy consumers and correct problems, and helping consumers seek information about the firm and its products.[4]

Nonpersonal Communication Channels

Nonpersonal communication channels are media that carry messages without personal contact or feedback. They include media, atmospheres, and events. Major **media** consist of print media (newspapers, magazines, direct mail), broadcast media (radio, television), and display media (billboards, signs, posters). **Atmospheres** are designed environments that create or reinforce the buyer's leanings toward buying a product. Thus, lawyers' offices and banks are designed to communicate confidence and other things that might be valued by the clients. **Events** are occurrences staged to communicate messages to target audiences. Public relations departments arrange press conferences, grand openings, public tours, and other events to communicate with specific audiences.

Nonpersonal communication affects buyers directly. In addition, using mass media often affects buyers indirectly by causing more personal communication. Mass communications affect attitudes and behavior through a *two-step flow-of-communication process.* In this process, communications first flow from television, magazines, and other mass media to opinion leaders and then from these to the less active sections of the population.[5] This two-step flow process means the effect of mass media is not as direct, powerful, and automatic as once supposed. Rather, opinion leaders step between the mass media and their audiences. Opinion leaders are more exposed to mass media, and they carry messages to people who are less exposed to media.

The two-step flow concept challenges the notion that people's buying is affected by a "trickle-down" of opinions and information from higher social classes. Because people mostly interact with others in their own social class, they pick up their fashion and other ideas from people *like themselves* who are opinion leaders. The two-step-flow concept also suggests that mass communicators should aim their messages directly at opinion leaders, letting them carry the message to others.

Selecting the Message Source

The message's impact on the audience is also affected by how the audience views the sender. Messages delivered by highly credible sources are more persuasive. For example, pharmaceutical companies want doctors to tell about their products' benefits because doctors are very credible figures. Many food companies are now promoting to doctors, dentists, and other healthcare providers in an effort to motivate these professionals to recommend their products to patients (see Marketing Highlight 16–1). Marketers also hire well-known actors and athletes to deliver their messages. Bill Cosby speaks for Jell-O, Michael J. Fox tells us about Pepsi, and basketball star Michael Jordan soars for Nike.[6]

But what factors make a source credible? The three factors most often found are expertise, trustworthiness, and likability. *Expertise* is the degree to which the communicator appears to have the authority needed to back the claim. Doctors, scientists, and professors rank high on expertise in their fields. *Trustworthiness* is related to how objective

PROMOTING PRODUCTS THROUGH DOCTORS AND OTHER PROFESSIONALS

Food marketers are discovering that the best way to a consumer's stomach may be through a doctor's recommendation. Facing a deluge of health claims being made for different food products, today's more nutrition-conscious consumers often seek advice from doctors and other healthcare professionals about which products are best for them. Kellogg, Procter & Gamble, Quaker, and other large food companies are increasingly recognizing what pharmaceutical companies have known for years—professional recommendations can strongly influence consumer-buying decisions. So they are stepping up promotion to doctors, dentists, and others, hoping to inform them about product benefits and motivate them to recommend the promoted brands to their patients.

Doctors receive the most attention from food marketers. For example, Cumberland Packing runs ads in medical journals for its Sweet 'N Low sugar substitute, saying, "It's one thing you can do to make your patient's diet a little easier to swallow." And Kellogg launched its "Project Nutrition" promotion to sell doctors on the merits of eating high-fiber cereal breakfasts. The promotion consists of cholesterol screenings of 100,000 Americans across the country, ads targeting doctors in the *Journal of the American Medical Association* and the *New England Journal of Medicine*, and a new quarterly newsletter called *Health Vantage* mailed to 50,000 U.S. medical professionals. Similarly, Quaker sends a quarterly newsletter, *Fiber Report*, to doctors nationwide; it includes articles, research reports, and feature stories about the importance of fiber in diets.

Procter & Gamble provides literature about several of its products that doctors can pass along to patients. One booklet for Citrus Hill Calcium Plus orange juice even contains a 20-cents-off coupon. And P&G actively seeks medical endorsements. Years ago, a heavily promoted American Dental Association endorsement helped make P&G's Crest the lead-

ing toothpaste brand. The company hopes that an endorsement obtained from the American Medical Women's Association will give a similar boost to its Citrus Hill calcium-fortified fruit juices.

Other professionals targeted by food companies include dentists, veterinarians, teachers, and even high school coaches. The makers of Trident gum, Equal sugar substitute, Plax mouth rinse, and dozens of other products reach dentists through colorful brochures, samples, and ads in dental journals. Quaker does extensive product sampling of its Gaines and Ken-L Ration pet foods through veterinarians. Quaker also runs ads for Gatorade in magazines read by high school sports trainers and coaches; it sponsors a fleet of vans that comb the country, offering Gatorade information and samples in key markets. Thus, food companies actively court as spokespeople any professionals who provide health or nutrition advice to their customers.

Many doctors and other healthcare providers welcome the promotions as good sources of information about healthy foods and nutrition that can help them give better advice to their patients. Others, however, do not feel comfortable recommending specific food brands; some even resent attempts to influence them through promotion. It will take a lot of time and investment to get these professionals to change their habits. But the results will be worth the effort and expense. If a company can convince key healthcare providers that the product is worthy of endorsement, it will gain powerful marketing allies. As one marketer puts it, "If a doctor hands you a product to use, that recommendation carries a lot of weight."

Sources: See Laurie Freeman and Liesse Erickson, "Doctored Strategy: Food Marketers Push Products through Physicians," *Advertising Age*, March 28, 1988, p. 12.

Celebrities impart some of their own likability and trustworthiness to the products they endorse.

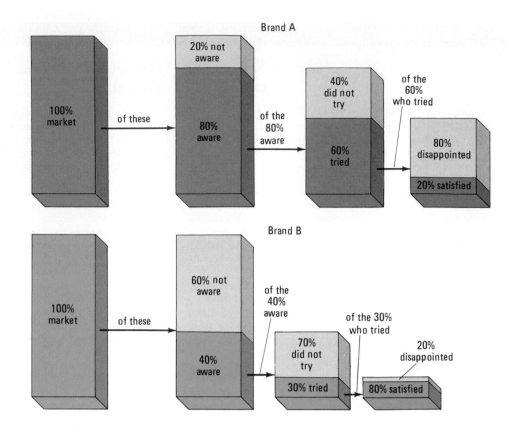

FIGURE 16-4
Current consumer states for two brands

and honest the source appears to be. Friends, for example, are trusted more than salespeople. *Likability* is how attractive the source is to the audience; people like sources who are open, humorous, and natural. Not surprisingly, the most highly credible source is a person scoring high on all three factors—expertise, trustworthiness, and likability.

Collecting Feedback After sending the message, the communicator must reach its effect on the target audience. This involves asking the target audience whether they remember the message, how many times they saw it, what points they recall, how they felt about the message, and their past and present attitudes toward the product and company. The communicator would also like to measure behavior resulting from the message—how many people bought a product, talked to others about it, or visited the store.

Figure 16-4 shows an example of feedback measurement. Looking at Brand A, we find that 80 percent of the total market is aware of it, that 60 percent of those aware of it have tried it, but that only 20 percent of those who tried it were satisfied. These results suggest that although the communication program is creating *awareness*, the product fails to give consumers the *satisfaction* they expect. The company should therefore try to improve the product while staying with the successful communication program. On the other hand, only 40 percent of the total market is aware of Brand B, that only 30 percent of those have tried it, but that 80 percent of those who have tried it are satisfied. In this case, the communication program needs to be stronger to take advantage of the brand's power to obtain satisfaction.

SETTING THE TOTAL PROMOTION BUDGET AND MIX

We have looked at the steps in planning and sending communications to a target audience. But how does the company decide on the total *promotion budget* and its division among the major promotional tools to create the *promotion mix*?

**Setting the Total
Promotion Budget**

One of the hardest marketing decisions facing companies is how much to spend on promotion. John Wanamaker, the department store magnate, once said: "I know that half of my advertising is wasted, but I don't know which half. I spent $2 million for advertising, and I don't know if that is half enough or twice too much." Thus, it is not surprising that industries and companies vary widely in how much they spend on promotion. Promotion spending may be 20 to 30 percent of sales in the cosmetics industry and only 5 to 10 percent in the industrial machinery industry. Within a given industry, both low- and high-spending companies can be found.

How do companies determine their promotion budget? Four common methods used to set the total budget for advertising are: the *affordable method*, the *percentage-of-sales method*, the *competitive-parity method*, and the *objective-and-task method*.[7]

Affordable Method

Many companies use the **affordable method:** They set the promotion budget at what they they think the company can afford. One executive has explained this method as follows: "Why it's simple. First, I go upstairs to the controller and ask how much they can afford to give this year. He says a million and a half. Later, the boss comes to me and asks how much we should spend and I say 'Oh, about a million and a half.' "[8]

Unfortunately, this method of setting budgets completely ignores the effect of promotion on sales volume. It leads to an uncertain annual promotion budget, which makes long-range market planning difficult. Although the affordable method can result in overspending on advertising, it more often results in underspending.

Percentage-of-Sales Method

Many companies use the **percentage-of-sales method,** setting their promotion budget at a certain percentage of current or forecasted sales. Or they budget a percentage of the sales price. Automobile companies usually budget a fixed percentage for promotion based on the planned car price. Oil companies set the budget at some fraction of a cent for each gallon of gasoline sold under their labels.

A number of advantages are claimed for the percentage-of-sales method. First, using this method means that promotion spending is likely to vary with what the company can "afford." It also helps management to think about the relationship between promotion spending, selling price, and profit-per-unit. Finally, it supposedly creates competitive stability because competing firms tend to spend about the same percent of their sales on promotion.

However, in spite of these claimed advantages, the percentage-of-sales method has little to justify it. It wrongly views sales as the *cause* of promotion rather than as the *result*. The budget is based on availability of funds rather than on opportunities. It may prevent the increased spending sometimes needed to turn around falling sales. Because the budget varies with year-to-year sales, long-range planning is difficult. Finally, the method does not provide any basis for choosing a *specific* percentage, except what has been done in the past or what competitors are doing.

Competitive-Parity Method

Other companies use the **competitive-parity method,** setting their promotion budgets to match competitors' outlays. They watch competitors' advertising or get industry promotion-spending estimates from publications or trade associations, and then set their budgets based on the industry average.

Two arguments support this method. First, competitors' budgets represent the collective wisdom of the industry. Second, spending what competitors spend helps prevent promotion wars. Unfortunately, neither argument is valid. There are no grounds for believing that the competition has a better idea of what a company should be spending on promotion than the company itself does. Companies differ greatly, and each has its own special promotion needs. Furthermore, no evidence indicates budgets based on competitive parity prevent promotion wars.

Objective-and-Task Method

The most logical budget setting method is the **objective-and-task method.** Using it, marketers develop their promotion budgets by (1) defining specific objectives, (2) determining the tasks that must be performed to achieve these objectives, and (3) estimating the costs of performing these tasks. The sum of these costs is the proposed promotion budget.

The objective-and-task method makes management spell out its assumptions about the relationship between dollars spent and promotion results. But it is also the most difficult method to use. It is often hard to figure out which specific tasks will achieve specific objectives. For example, suppose Sony wants 95 percent awareness for its new Watchman personal videocassette player during the six-month introductory period. What specific advertising messages and media schedules would Sony need in order to attain this objective? How much would these messages and media schedules cost? Sony management must consider such questions even though they are hard to answer. With the objective-and-task method, the company sets its promotion budget based on what it wants to accomplish with promotion.

Setting the Promotion Mix

The company must now divide the total promotion budget among the major promotion tools—advertising, personal selling, sales promotion, and public relations. It must carefully blend the promotion tools into a coordinated *promotion mix* that will achieve its advertising and marketing objectives. Companies within the same industry differ greatly in how they design their promotion mixes. Avon spends most of its promotion funds on personal selling and catalog marketing (its advertising is only 1.5 percent of sales), whereas Revlon spends heavily on consumer advertising (about 8 percent of sales). Electrolux sells 75 percent of its vacuum cleaners door-to-door, whereas Hoover relies more on advertising. Thus, a company can achieve a given sales level with various mixes of advertising, personal selling, sales promotion, and public relations.

Companies are always looking for ways to improve promotion by replacing one promotion tool with another that will do the same job more economically. Many companies have replaced a portion of their field-sales activities with telephone sales and direct mail. Other companies have increased their sales-promotion spending in relation to advertising to gain quicker sales.

Designing the promotion mix is even more complex when one tool must be used to promote another. Thus, when McDonald's decides to run Million Dollar Sweepstakes in its fast-food outlets (a sales promotion), it has to run ads to inform the public. When General Mills uses a consumer advertising/sales promotion campaign to back a new cake mix, it has to set aside money to promote this campaign to the resellers to win their support.

Many factors influence the marketer's choice of promotion tools.

The Nature of Each Promotion Tool

Each promotion—*advertising*, *personal selling*, *sales promotion*, and *public relations*—has unique characteristics and costs. Marketers must understand these characteristics in order to correctly select their tools.

ADVERTISING. Because of the many forms and uses of advertising, generalizing about its unique qualities as a part of the promotion mix is difficult. Yet several qualities can be noted. Advertising's public nature suggests that the advertised product is standard and legitimate. Because many people see ads for the product, buyers know that purchasing the product will be publicly understood and accepted. Advertising also lets the seller repeat a message many times, and it lets the buyer receive and compare the messages of various competitors. Large-scale advertising by a seller says something positive about the seller's size, popularity, and success.

Advertising is also very expressive, letting the company dramatize its products through the artful use of print, sound, and color. On the one hand, advertising can be used to build up a long-term image for a product (such as Coca-Cola ads) and, on the other, to trigger quick sales (as when Sears advertises a weekend sale). Advertising can reach masses of geographically spread out buyers at a low cost per exposure.

Advertising also has some shortcomings. Although it reaches many people quickly, advertising is impersonal and cannot be as persuasive as a company salesperson. Advertising is able to carry on only a one-way communication with the audience and the audience does not feel that it has to pay attention or respond. In addition, advertising can be very costly. Although some forms, such as newspaper and radio advertising, can be done on small budget, other forms, such as network TV advertising, require very large budgets.

PERSONAL SELLING.   Personal selling is the most effective tool at certain stages of the buying process, particularly in building up buyers' preferences, convictions, and actions. As compared with advertising, personal selling has several unique qualities. It involves personal interaction between two or more people, so each person can observe the other's needs and characteristics and make quick adjustments. Personal selling also lets all kinds of relationships spring up, ranging from a matter-of-fact selling relationship to a deep personal friendship. The effective salesperson keeps the customer's interests at heart in order to build a long-run relationship. Finally, with personal selling the buyer usually feels a greater need to listen and respond, even if the response is a polite "no thank you."

These unique qualities come at a cost. A salesforce requires a longer-term commitment than advertising—advertising can be turned on and off, but salesforce size is harder to change. And personal selling is the company's most expensive promotion tool, costing industrial companies an average of $225 per sales call.[9] American firms spend up to three times as much on personal selling as they do on advertising.

SALES PROMOTION.   Sales promotion includes a wide assortment of tools—coupons, contests, cents-off deals, premiums, and others—and these tools have many unique qualities. They attract consumer attention and provide information that may lead the consumer to buy the product. They offer strong incentives to purchase by providing inducements or contributions that give additional value to consumers. And sales promotions invite and reward quick response. Advertising says "buy our product." Sales promotion says "buy it now."

Companies use sales-promotion tools to create a stronger and quicker response.

With personal selling, the customer feels a greater need to listen and respond, even if the response is a polite "No thank you."

Sales promotion can be used to dramatize product offers and to boost sagging sales. Sales promotion effects are usually short-lived, however, and are not effective in building long-run brand preference.

PUBLIC RELATIONS. Public relations offers several advantages. One is believability—news stories, features, and events seem more real and believable to readers than do ads. Public relations can reach many prospects who avoid salespeople and advertisements; the message gets to the buyers as "news" rather than as a sales-directed communication. And like advertising, public relations can dramatize a company or product.

Marketers tend to underuse public relations or use it as an afterthought. Yet a well-thought-out public relations campaign used with other promotion mix elements can be very effective and economical.

Factors in Setting the Promotion Mix

Companies consider many factors when developing their promotion mixes, including the following: type of product and market; "push versus pull" strategy; buyer readiness state; and product life cycle stage.

TYPE OF PRODUCT AND MARKET. The importance of different promotion tools varies between consumer and industrial markets. The differences are shown in Figure 16-5. Consumer goods companies usually spend more on advertising, less on sales promotion, followed by personal selling, and then public relations. Industrial goods companies spend more on personal selling, followed by sales promotion, advertising, and public relations. In general, personal selling is more heavily used with expensive and risky goods and in markets with fewer and larger sellers.

Although advertising is less important than sales calls in industrial markets, it still plays an important role. Advertising can build product awareness and knowledge, develop sales leads, and reassure buyers. Similarly, personal selling can add greatly to consumer-goods marketing efforts. It is simply not the case that "salespeople put products on shelves and advertising takes them off." Well-trained consumer-goods salespeople can sign up more dealers to carry a particular brand, convince them to give the brand more shelf space, and urge them to use special displays and promotions.

PUSH VERSUS PULL STRATEGY The promotional mix is heavily affected by whether the company chooses a *push* or *pull* strategy. The two strategies are contrasted in Figure 16-6. A **push-strategy** involves "pushing" the product through distribution channels to final consumers. The manufacturer directs its marketing activities (primarily personal selling and trade promotion) at channel members to induce them to order and carry the product and to promote it to final consumers. Using a **pull strategy,** the manufacturer directs its marketing activities (primarily advertising and consumer promotion) toward

FIGURE 16-5   Relative importance of promotion tools in consumer versus industrial markets

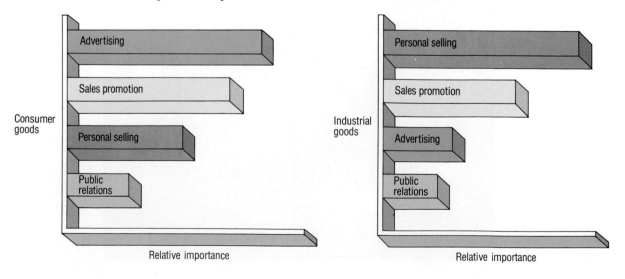

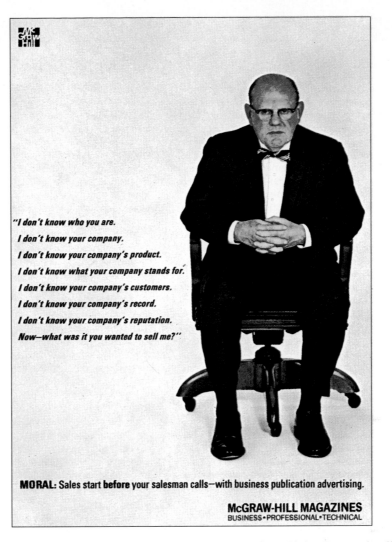

"*I don't know who you are.*

I don't know your company.

I don't know your company's product.

I don't know what your company stands for.

I don't know your company's customers.

I don't know your company's record.

I don't know your company's reputation.

Now—what was it you wanted to sell me?"

MORAL: Sales start **before** your salesman calls—with business publication advertising.

McGRAW-HILL MAGAZINES
BUSINESS·PROFESSIONAL·TECHNICAL

Advertising can play a dramatic role in industrial marketing as shown in this classic McGraw-Hill ad.

final consumers to induce them to buy the product. If the strategy is effective, consumers will then demand the product from channel members, who will in turn demand it from producers. Thus, under a pull strategy, consumer demand "pulls" the product through the channels.

Some small industrial-goods companies use only push strategies; some direct market-

FIGURE 16-6
Push versus pull strategy

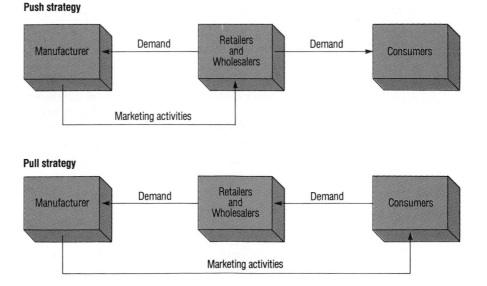

Push strategy

Manufacturer — Demand → Retailers and Wholesalers — Demand → Consumers

Marketing activities

Pull strategy

Manufacturer ← Demand — Retailers and Wholesalers ← Demand — Consumers

Marketing activities

ARE CONSUMER GOODS COMPANIES GETTING TOO "PUSHY"

Consumer-package goods companies such as Procter & Gamble, General Goods, Quaker, Campbell, and Gillette grew into giants by using mostly pull promotion strategies. They used massive doses of national advertising to differentiate their products, build market share, and maintain customer loyalty. But during the past two decades, these companies have gotten more "pushy," deemphasizing national advertising and putting more of their promotion budgets into personal selling and sales promotions. Trade promotions (trade allowances, displays, cooperative advertising) now account for 39 percent of total consumer product company marketing spending; consumer promotions (coupons, cents-off deals, premiums) account for another 27 percent. That leaves only 34 percent of total marketing spending for media advertising, down from 42 percent just ten years ago.

Why have these companies shifted so heavily toward push strategies? One reason is that mass media campaigns have become more expensive and less effective these days. Network television costs have risen sharply while audiences have fallen off, making national advertising less cost-effective. Companies have also increased their market segmentation efforts and are tailoring their marketing programs more narrowly, making national advertising less suitable than localized retailer promotions. And in these days of brand extensions and me-too products, companies have sometimes had trouble finding meaningful product differences to feature in advertising. So they have differentiated their products through price reductions, premium offers, coupons, and other push techniques.

Another factor speeding the shift from pull to push has been the greater strength of retailers. Today's retailers are larger and have more access to product sales and profit information. They now have the power to demand and get what they want—and what they want is more push. While national advertising bypasses them on its way to the masses, push promotion benefits them directly. Consumer promotions give retailers an immediate sales boost, and cash from trade allowances pads retailer profits. Thus, producers must often use push just to obtain good shelf space and advertising support from important retailers.

However, many marketers are concerned that the reckless use of push will lead to fierce price competition and a never-ending spiral of price slashing and deal making. This situation would result in lower margins, and companies would have less to invest in the research and development, packaging, and advertising needed to improve products and maintain long-run consumer preference and loyalty. If used improperly, push promotion can mortgage a brand's future for short-term gains. Sales promotion buys short-run reseller support and consumer sales, but advertising builds long-run brand value and consumer preference. By robbing the advertising budget to pay for more sales promotion, companies might win the battle for short-run earnings but lose the war for long-run consumer loyalty and market share.

Thus, many consumer companies are now rethinking their promotion strategies and reversing the trend by shifting their promotion budgets back slightly toward advertising. Push strategies remain very important—in package-goods marketing, short-run success often depends more on retailer support than on the producer's advertising. But many companies have realized that it's not a question of sales promotion versus advertising, or of push versus pull. Success lies in finding the best mix of the two: consistent advertising to build long-run brand value and consumer preference, and sales promotion to create short-run trade support and consumer excitement. The company needs to blend both push and pull elements into an integrated promotion program that meets immediate consumer and retailer needs as well as long-run strategic needs.

Sources: Thomas Exter, "Advertising and Promotion: The One-Two Punch," *American Demographics*, March 1990, pp. 18–22; James C. Schroer, "Ad Spending: Growing Marketing Share," *Harvard Business Review*, January–February 1990, pp. 44–48; Laurie Freeman and Jennifer Lawrence, "Brand Building Gets New Life," *Advertising Age*, September 4, 1989, pp. 3, 34; and Robert D. Buzzell, John A. Quelch, and Walter J. Salmon, "The Costly Bargain of Trade Promotion," *Harvard Business Review*, March–April 1990, pp. 141–49.

ing companies use only pull. Most large companies use some combination of both. For example, Procter & Gamble uses mass media advertising to pull its products and a large salesforce and trade promotions to push its products through the channels. In recent years, consumer goods companies have been decreasing the pull portions of their promotion mixes in favor of more push (see Marketing Highlight 16–2).

BUYER READINESS STATE. Promotional tools vary in their effects at the different stages of buyer readiness discussed earlier in the chapter. Advertising, along with public relations, plays the major role in the awareness and knowledge stages, more important than that played by "cold calls" from salespeople. Customer liking, preference, and conviction are more affected by personal selling, which is closely followed by advertising. Finally, closing the sale is mostly done with sales calls and sales promotion. Clearly, personal selling, given its high costs, should focus on the later stages of the customer buying process.

PRODUCT LIFE CYCLE STAGE. The effects of different promotion tools also vary with stages of the product life cycle. In the introduction stage, advertising and public relations are good for producing high awareness, and sales promotion is useful in promoting early trial. Personal selling must be used to get the trade to carry the product. In the growth stage, advertising and public relations continue to be powerful, while sales promotion can be reduced because fewer incentives are needed. In the mature stage, sales promotion again becomes important relative to advertising. Buyers know the brands, and advertising is needed only to remind them of the product. In the decline stage, advertising is kept at a reminder level, public relations is dropped, and salespeople give the product only a little attention. Sales promotion, however, might continue strong.[10]

Responsibility for Marketing Communications Planning

Members of the marketing department often have different views on how to split the promotion budget. The sales manager would rather hire two more salespeople than spend $100,000 on a single television commercial. The public relations manager feels that he or she can do wonders with some money shifted from advertising to public relations.

In the past, companies left these decisions to different people. No one person was responsible for thinking through the roles of the various promotion tools and coordinating the promotion mix. Today, some companies have appointed marketing communications directors who are responsible for all of the company's marketing communications. This director develops policies for using the different promotion tools, keeps track of all promotion spending by product, tool, and results, and coordinates the promotion mix activities when major campaigns take place.

■ SUMMARY

Promotion is one of the four major elements of the company's marketing mix. The main promotion tools—*advertising, sales promotion, public relations*, and *personal selling*—work together to achieve the company's communication objectives.

In preparing marketing communications, the communicator must understand the nine elements of any communication process: *sender, receiver, encoding, decoding, message, media, response, feedback*, and *noise*. The communicator's first task is to identify the target audience and its characteristics. Next, the communicator has to define the response sought, whether it be *awareness, knowledge, liking, preference, conviction*, or *purchase*. Then a message should be constructed with an effective content, structure, and format. Media must be selected, both for personal communication and nonpersonal communication. The message must be delivered by a credible *source*—someone

who is an expert, trustworthy, and likable. Finally, the communicator must collect *feedback* by watching how much of the market becomes aware, tries the product, and is satisfied in the process.

The company has to decide how much to spend for promotion. The most popular approaches are to spend what the company can afford, use a percentage of sales, base promotion on competitors' spending, or base it on an analysis and costing of the communication objectives and tasks.

The company splits the *promotion budget* among the major tools, which creates the *promotion mix*. Companies are guided by the characteristics of each promotion tool, the type of product/market, the desirability of a *push* or a *pull* strategy, the *buyer's readiness state*, and the *product life-cycle stage*. The different promotion activities require strong coordination for maximum impact.

■ QUESTIONS FOR DISCUSSION

1. Which form of marketing communications does each of the following represent? (a) a U2 tee shirt sold at a concert, (b) a *Rolling Stone* interview with George Michael arranged by his manager, (c) a scalper auctioning tickets at a Michael Jackson concert, and (d) a record store selling Prince albums for $2-off during the week his latest movie opens.

2. The Department of Defense spends two-thirds of the U.S. government's advertising budget. How does the U.S. Army coordinate its promotion and marketing mixes in its efforts to obtain recruits?

3. Companies spend billions of dollars on advertising to build a quality image for their products. At the same time they spend billions more on discount-oriented sales promotions, offering lower price as a main reason to purchase. Discuss whether promotion is enhancing or reducing the effect of advertising. Can you find an example where they enhance one another?

4. Long-distance telephone services have tried to attract customers with emotional appeals ("AT&T. Reach out and touch someone") and with rational appeals ("If your long distance bills are too much, call MCI"). Which approach do you think is more effective? Why?

5. Bill Cosby has appeared in ads for such products and companies as Jell-O, Coke, Texas Instruments, and E.F. Hutton. Is he a credible source for *all* these companies, or does his credibility vary? Is he chosen for his credibility as a spokesperson or for some other characteristic?

6. How can an organization get feedback on the effects of its communication efforts? Describe how (a) the March of Dimes and (b) Procter & Gamble can get feedback on the results of their communications.

7. When a decline in oil prices caused economic troubles in Texas and nearby states, Houston-based National Convenience Stores stopped advertising to cut costs. Which budgeting approach were they following? What approach would you have recommended?

8. Why do some industrial marketers advertise on national television, when their target audience is only a fraction of the people they have paid to reach with their message? List some nonconsumer-oriented commercials you have seen on TV and describe what the marketers were trying to accomplish.

9. How does the number of levels in the channel of distribution influence the decision to use a push or a pull strategy? What other factors are involved in this decision?

10. Recently pharmaceutical companies have begun to communicate directly with consumers via the mass media, even though they cannot mention prescription products by name. Ads promise that there is help available for baldness or cigarette addiction ("Ask your doctor"). Is this advertising or public relations? Do you think it is effective?

■ KEY TERMS

Advertising. Any paid form of nonpersonal presentation and promotion of ideas, goods, or services by an identified sponsor.

Affordable method. Setting the promotion budget at what management thinks the company can afford.

Atmospheres. Designed environments that create or reinforce the buyer's leanings toward consumption of a product.

Buyer-readiness states. The stages consumers normally pass through on their way to purchase, including awareness, knowledge, liking, preference, conviction, or purchase.

Competitive-parity method. Setting the promotion budget to match competitors' outlays.

Emotional appeals. Message appeals that attempt to stir negative or positive emotions that will motivate purchase; examples include fear, guilt, shame, love, humor, pride, and joy appeals.

Events. Occurrences staged to communicate messages to target audiences, such as news conferences, grand openings, or others.

Media. Nonpersonal communications channels including print media (newspapers, magazines, direct mail), broadcast media (radio, television), and display media (billboards, signs, posters).

Moral appeals. Message appeals that are directed to the audience's sense of what is right and proper.

Nonpersonal communication channels. Media that carry messages without personal contact or feedback, including media, atmosphere, and events.

Objective-and-task-method. Developing the promotion budget by (1) defining specific objectives, (2) determining the tasks that must be performed to achieve these objectives, and (3) estimating the costs of performing these tasks; the sum of these costs is the proposed promotion budget.

Percentage-of-sales method. Setting the promotion budget at a certain percentage of current or forecasted sales or as a percentage of the sales price.

Personal communication channels. Channels through which two or more people communicate directly with each other, including face-to-face, person-to-audience, over the telephone, or through the mail.

Personal selling. Oral presentation in a conversation with one or more prospective purchasers for the purpose of making sales.

Promotion mix. The specific mix of advertising, personal selling, sales promotion, and public relations a company uses to pursue its advertising and marketing objectives.

Public relations. Building good relations with the company's various publics by obtaining favorable publicity, building up a good "corporate image," and handling or heading off unfavorable rumors, stories, and events.

Pull strategy. A promotion strategy that calls for spending a lot on advertising and consumer promotion to build up consumer demand; if successful, consumers will ask their retailers for the product, the retailers will ask the wholesalers, and the wholesalers will ask the producers.

Push strategy. A promotion strategy that calls for using the salesforce and trade promotion to push the product through channels; the producer promotes the product to wholesalers, the wholesalers promote to retailers, and the retailers promote to consumers.

Rational appeals. Message appeals that relate to the audience's self-interest and show that the product will produce the claimed benefits; examples include appeals of product quality, economy, value, or performance.

Sales promotion. Short-term incentives to encourage purchase or sales of a product or service.

Word-of-mouth influence. Personal communication about a product between target buyers and neighbors, friends, family members, and associates.

■ REFERENCES

1. See Richard Edel, "No End in Site for Promotion's Upward Spiral," *Advertising Age*, March 23, 1987, p. S2; and Julie Liessee Erickson, "Quaker Fortifies Oatmeal Position," *Advertising Age*, January 11, 1988, p. 54; Lois Therrien, "Quaker Oats' Pet Peeve," *Business Week*, July 31, 1989, pp. 32–33; and Joshua Levine, "Locking Up the Weekend Warriors," *Forbes*, October 2, 1989, pp. 234–35.

2. These definitions, except for *sales promotion*, are from *Marketing Definitions: A Glossary of Marketing Terms* (Chicago: American Marketing Association, 1960). Also see Peter D. Bennett, *Dictionary of Marketing Terms* (Chicago: American Marketing Association, 1988).

3. For more on message content and structure, see Leon G. Schiffman and Leslie Lazar Kanuk, *Consumer Behavior*, 4th ed. (Englewood Cliffs, NJ: Prentice Hall, 1991), Ch. 10; and Frank R. Kardes, "Spontaneous Inference Processes in Advertising: The Effects of Conclusion Omission and Involvement on Persuasion." *Journal of Consumer Research*, September 1988, pp. 225–33.

4. See K. Michael Haywood, "Managing Word of Mouth Communications," *Journal of Services Marketing*, Spring 1989, pp. 55–67.

5. See P. F. Lazarsfeld, B. Berelson, and H. Gaudet, *The People's Choice*, 2nd ed. (New York: Columbia University Press, 1948). p. 151; and Schiffman and Kanuk, *Consumer Behavior*, pp. 571–72.

6. See Michael Oneal and Peter Finch, "Nothing Sells Like Sports," *Business Week*, August 31, 1987; and Pat Sloan and Laurie Freeman, "Advertisers Willing to Share Their Stars," *Advertising Age*, March 21, 1988, pp. 4, 81.

7. For a more comprehensive discussion on setting promotion budgets, see Michael L. Rothschild, *Advertising* (Lexington, Mass.: D. C. Heath, 1987), Chap. 20.

8. Quoted in Daniel Seligman, "How Much for Advertising?" *Fortune*, December 1956, p. 123.

9. See "The Rise (and Fall) of Cost Per Call," *Sales & Marketing Management*, April 1990, p. 26.

10. For more on advertising and the product life cycle, see John E. Swan and David R. Rink, "Fitting Market Strategy to Product Life Cycles," *Business Horizons*, January–February 1982, pp. 60–67.

THE PEPSI *and* COCA-COLA CHALLENGE: A COLA WITH BREAKFAST

Ron Watson wrestled his 18-wheeler onto an exit ramp on Interstate 85 just south of the Virginia-North Carolina border. Although it was only 7 A.M., Ron had already been driving almost four hours since leaving his trucking company's main terminal in Charlotte, North Carolina, and the 26-year-old driver's stomach felt empty. Ron pulled into a truck stop and parked. He picked up the morning paper as he entered the restaurant, then sauntered over to the counter. A waitress who appeared to be still half asleep handed Ron a menu and asked if he was ready to order.

"Sure," he nodded, "I'd like two eggs, sunny-side up, a side order of pancakes, and a Pepsi." The waitress, who had been busy scribbling his order, stopped writing and eyed Ron suspiciously. Another customer seated nearby looked up from his paper.

"Did you say Pepsi?" the waitress asked as if her sleepiness had affected her hearing.

"That's right," Ron replied, a smile brightening his face. "Been drinking Pepsi with breakfast for years. You ought to give it a try."

"No thanks!" the waitress replied as she scratched "Pepsi" on the order pad and turned towards the kitchen. As she walked away, she mumbled, "Takes all kinds."

Ron Watson has gotten used to funny looks when he orders breakfast, but he's not alone. Thousands of other customers have joined the ranks of those who like a cold cola drink with breakfast instead of the traditional hot coffee. In fact, the Coffee Development Group, an industry trade association, estimates that per capita daily coffee consumption peaked in 1962 at 3.12 cups and has been steadily declining ever since to the present level of 1.76 cups. At the same time, the soft drink industry calculates that morning soft drink consumption accounts for 12 percent of total soft drink sales, up from 9 percent 10 years ago.

Soft drink manufacturers have paid close attention to this 3 percentage-point gain in a market where 1 percent of market share represents more than $400 million in retail sales. Although the change has been gradual, industry analysis argue that the trend testifies to the power of sophisticated advertising. In recent decades, they note, soft-drink manufacturers have outspent almost all other producers of nonalcoholic beverages. And they have poured money into advertising designed to persuade young people to drink more soda. These young people have grown up with soft drinks and are now a major buying force. Further, the rapid growth in fast food merchandising, the explosive growth of the vending industry, and the proliferation of convenience stores have made soft drinks available almost everywhere at almost any time. As a result, the *Beverage Industry Digest* reports that people between the ages of

24 and 44 represent the largest group of soft drink consumers, accounting for 27 percent of total market sales.

Citing what it calls a "watershed movement," Coca-Cola became the first company to take direct action to take advantage of the growth in morning consumption of soft drinks. In 1987, the company tested a promotional campaign dubbed "Coke in the Morning" in cities across the U.S. Early in 1988, Coca-Cola made the program available to its bottlers across the country. But the campaign does not directly attack coffee, which still accounts for 47 percent of morning beverages sold, compared with 21 percent for juices, 17 percent for milk, 7 percent for tea, and only 4 percent for soft drinks. Rather, the campaign, designed by Coca-Cola's advertising agency McCann-Erickson, focuses on the time after the consumer leaves home in the morning and on the mid-morning coffee break.

At first, Pepsi-Cola Company, like the rest of the industry, stood by to see what would result from Coca-Cola's efforts. Now, however, Pepsi-Cola appears to be charging in with an even more aggressive strategy than Coca-Cola's. In late 1989, Pepsi-Cola announced that it was launching its new strategy in test markets in the

Midwest. Pepsi-Cola's test markets revealed just how aggressive the new strategy will be. First, rather than just positioning its regular product for morning consumption, Pepsi-Cola has developed a new brand, Pepsi A.M., designed specifically for the morning segment. Pepsi A.M. comes in both diet and regular forms. Whereas regular Pepsi contains 3.2 milligrams of caffeine per fluid ounce and Coca-Cola Classic contains 3.8 milligrams, Pepsi A.M. has 4 milligrams. Still, Pepsi A.M.'s caffeine level contains only about one-quarter the level of caffeine found in a cup of regular coffee. Pepsi-Cola also lowered the level of carbonation in the new drink.

Pepsi-Cola's promotional strategy for Pepsi A.M. is as important to the marketing effort as the product change. The ads attack coffee head on. For example, one print ad shows a series of cups of coffee and one Pepsi A.M. can. Printed under the Pepsi A.M. can is the message, "A refreshing break from the daily grind."

Both Coca-Cola, with its subtle approach, and Pepsi-Cola, with its aggressive campaign, face a real challenge in attempting to pry open the morning beverage market. Coffee drinkers are known for their loyalty. Further, both companies must overcome the "yuck factor"—like Ron Watson's waitress, many consumers find drinking cola in the morning disgusting. Finally, as you might guess, the coffee industry is not likely to sit quietly by and watch Pepsi and Coke steal its market.

Thus, Pepsi and Coke may one day challenge one another for shares of a growing morning-cola market. But before they can battle each other in this segment, as they do in other segments, they must first win the battle with tradition to obtain a place for colas at the breakfast table and in the coffee break.

QUESTIONS

1. What is the target audience for Coca-Cola's "Coke in the Morning" campaign? What is the target for Pepsi A.M.? Are these audiences the same?
2. What buyer responses are Coca-Cola and Pepsi-Cola trying to generate from their target customers?
3. What general message content and message structure decisions should the two companies make in setting their message strategies?
4. What promotion mixes should the companies use? Should the two companies use the same or different mixes? Why?
5. Given the promotion mixes you recommend, what specific ads and other promotion ideas would you recommend to Pepsi-Cola and Coca-Cola to help them win over the morning cola market?

A 30-SECOND SPOT

The AIDA concept suggests that effective advertisements are supposed to get *Attention*, hold *Interest*, arouse *Desire*, and obtain *Action*—ideally, the purchase of the advertised product or service. But the average person is exposed to approximately 1,500 advertisements per day. In this cluttered environment, how does one company promote its product so that it stands out from the rest?

Phyllis George, the former Miss America, TV personality, and First Lady of Kentucky, faced such a formidable task when she introduced her new product—Chicken by George. Chicken by George is a line of fresh chicken breasts marinated in one of eight sauces. The boneless entrees, found in the fresh poultry case in the supermarket, were designed for consumers who desired a quality product with ease of preparation.

The market for fresh chicken is dominated by regional and store brands, with a few exceptions such as Perdue and Holly Farms, which are national brands. Frozen prepared chicken is more competitive, with brands like Swanson, Banquet, and Tyson competing with local brands. Both markets, of course, compete against restaurants that prominently feature chicken, such as Kentucky Fried Chicken, Popeye's, and Church's.

To stand out against the competition, Ms. George positioned herself as the First Lady of Chicken. This play on words could be interpreted not only to mean she is a woman challenging a male-dominated market (most companies featuring chicken such as Perdue, Tyson, and Kentucky Fried Chicken were started by men), but also that she is the wife of a former governor.

The chicken was first introduced in George's home state of Kentucky, but was taken national when Hormel bought the firm in 1989. A $10 million ad campaign supported the national rollout. Local exposure during the Super Bowl telecast substantially increased consumer awareness. Phyllis George continues as chair of the company and chief spokesperson. Hormel views her involvement with the product's conception as well as her credibility and recognition as tremendous assets as the product moves to markets beyond Kentucky.

Hormel's purchase of Chicken by George is contributing to the company's goal of becoming a consumer-driven, value-added food marketer. While its Chili, Dinty Moore Beef Stew, and Spam remain the company's standards, Hormel's lineup now includes Top Shelf, Shelf-Stable Entrees, and New Traditions Microwave Convenience foods. Also slated for introduction is Kids Kitchen, a line of microwaveable entrees for children. If Chicken by George is a success, Hormel hopes to apply the same process to beef, pork, fish, and turkey.

QUESTIONS

1. Identify the nine major elements in the communication process and discuss them relative to the advertisement shown in the video for Chicken by George.

2. Phyllis George sold her company to the George A. Hormel Company in August 1988, yet she was kept on as chief spokesperson for Chicken by George because Hormel believed she would enhance the sales of the product as it moved into national distribution. What factors make a spokesperson or source credible? Apply these factors to Phyllis George.

Sources: "The Comeback of Phyllis George," *McCall's*, September 1989, pp. 12–14; "Meatpacker's Makeover," *Advertising Age*, November 21, 1988, p. 53; and "Hormel Rolls Out Branded Poultry," *Advertising Age*, January 30, 1989.

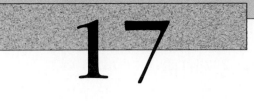

Promoting Products: Advertising, Sales Promotion, and Public Relations

Moving into the 1990s, Eveready set out to re-charge its image. It focused on its Energizer brand, which was locked in a head-to-head battle with Duracell for the top spot in the huge alkaline battery segment. The key would be to create a distinctive image for Energizer and to generate consumer excitement, a difficult task in the battery industry, which has traditionally been dominated by a few, largely undifferentiated brands. The solution? Perhaps the most innovative new advertising campaign of the year, featuring an improbable pink, drum-thumping bunny!

Imagine this hare-raising scene: You're sitting in front of the television staring blankly at the screen, watching a seemingly endless stream of the same old TV commercials. On comes an Energizer ad featuring a haughty pink mechanical bunny, drumming harder and longer than a throng of other bunnies. Suddenly, the rabbit marches out of its commercial, off the TV set, and out of the studio. Off-camera voices shout "stop that bunny!" But, of course, there's no slowing him down. He proceeds to march through a series of 15 second parodies of commercials for other products—coffee, decongestant, and wine—totally disrupting all of them. In later ads, this pink marauder goes on to disrupt cleverly designed spoofs of ads for "Alarm!" bath soap, "Pigskins" snack chips, and a greatest-hits record, "The Best of Olga Montiera," a fictional harpist. Eventually, he is even found bursting into ads for Purina Cat Chow and other real products from Ralston-Purina, Eveready Battery's parent company.

What makes the Energizer Bunny campaign so spe-cial? It's not so much the pink bunny—he appeared in the previous year's campaign without raising much of a stir. It's more the campaign's breakthrough execution, the element of surprise that leaves consumers wondering where the renegade rabbit will turn up next. Consumers also appear to enjoy the campaign's tongue-in-cheek poke at the advertising industry. Many consumers resent the seemingly constant interruptions of their favorite television programs by unimaginative commercials. In the Energizer ad, however, the tireless bunny interrupts the *commercials*. And the clever parodies give voice to many consumers' feelings about the mediocrity of some of today's television advertising.

The Energizer Bunny has been good for Eveready's business. Awareness among consumers has risen 50 per-cent since the campaign began, and Energizer sales showed double-digit gains during the critical Christmas season. The company has received an overwhelming quantity of consumer mail, most of it extremely positive. Although Eveready took a chance in lampooning commercials, the public seems to like it. The campaign has also won awards and generated much publicity. *Advertising Age* selected the first Energizer Bunny ad as the best advertising spot of 1989. And the pink bunny has become a regular topic for stand-up comics and talk-show hosts. It recently made an unscheduled appearance on the "Late Night With David Letterman Show." Letterman knocked off the bunny's head with a baseball bat, but the body kept on going.

Eveready is now trying to expand the campaign's

impact by putting the bunny's image on packages and creating bunny promotions. However, Eveready will probably move cautiously—it won't let its popular bunny march through just anybody's commercial. It doesn't want to risk burning out its fresh and innovative advertising idea by letting it get too hot, too quickly. But the company's ad agency has lots of ideas for new Energizer Bunny advertisements. As one advertising agency executive puts it, "there's plenty of bad advertising they can parody."[1]

CHAPTER OBJECTIVES

After reading this chapter, you should be able to:

1. Define the roles of advertising, sales promotion, and public relations in the promotion mix.
2. Describe the major decisions in developing an advertising program.
3. Explain how sales promotion campaigns are developed and implemented.
4. Explain how companies use public relations to communicate with their publics.

Companies must do more than make good products—they must inform consumers about product benefits and carefully position products in consumers' minds. To do this, they must skillfully use the mass-promotion tools of *advertising*, *sales promotion*, and *public relations*. We examine these tools in this chapter.

ADVERTISING

We define **advertising** as any paid form of nonpersonal presentation and promotion of ideas, goods, or services by an identified sponsor. In 1989, advertising ran up a bill of almost $125 billion. The spenders included not only business firms, but museums, professionals, and social organizations that advertise their causes to various target publics. In fact, the thirty-sixth largest advertising spender is a nonprofit organization—the U.S. government.

The top 100 national advertisers account for about one-fourth of all advertising.[2] Table 17-1 lists the top ten advertisers in 1989. Philip Morris is the leader with more than $2 billion, or 9.9 percent of its total U.S. sales. The other major spenders are found in the auto, food, retailing, and tobacco industries. Advertising as a percentage of sales is low in the auto industry and high in food, drugs, toiletries, and cosmetics,

TABLE 17-1
Top 10 National Advertisers

RANK	COMPANY	TOTAL U.S. ADVERTISING (Millions)	TOTAL U.S. SALES (Millions)	ADVERTISING AS A PERCENT OF SALES
1	Philip Morris	$2,058	$20,866	9.9%
2	Procter & Gamble	1,507	11,805	12.8
3	General Motors	1,294	91,260	1.4
4	Sears	1,045	50,251*	2.1
5	RJR Nabisco	815	12,635	6.4
6	Grand Metropolitan	774	3,211	24.1
7	Eastman Kodak	736	10,024	7.3
8	McDonald's	728	11,380	6.4
9	PepsiCo	712	10,551	6.7
10	Kellogg	683	2,766	24.7

* Worldwide sales—U.S. sales not available
Source: Reprinted with permission from the September 27, 1989 issue of *Advertising Age*, Copyright 1989, Crain Communications, Inc.

HISTORICAL MILESTONES IN ADVERTISING

Advertising goes back to the very beginnings of recorded history. Archaeologists working in the countries around the Mediterranean Sea have dug up signs announcing various events and offers. The Romans painted walls to announce gladiator fights, and the Phoenicians painted pictures promoting their wares on large rocks along parade routes. A Pompeii wall painting praised a politician and asked for the people's votes.

Another early form of advertising was the town crier. During the Golden Age in Greece, town criers announced the sale of slaves, cattle, and other goods. An early "singing commercial" went as follows: "For eyes that are shining, for cheeks like the dawn/For beauty that lasts after girlhood is gone/For prices in reason, the woman who knows/Will buy her cosmetics of Aesclyptos."

Another early advertising form was the mark that tradespeople placed on their goods, such as pottery. As the person's reputation spread by word of mouth, buyers began to look for his special mark, just as trademarks and brand names are used today. More than 1,000 years ago in Europe, Osnabruck linen was carefully controlled for quality and commanded a price 20 percent higher than unbranded Westphalian linens. As production became more centralized and markets became more distant, the mark became more important.

The turning point in the history of advertising came in the year 1450 when Johann Gutenberg invented the printing press. Advertisers no longer had to produce extra copies of a sign by hand. The first printed advertisement in the English language appeared in 1478.

In 1622, advertising got a big boost with the launching of the first English newspaper, *The Weekly Newes*. Later, Joseph Addison and Richard Steele published the *Tatler* and became supporters of advertising. Addison gave this advice to copy writers: "The great art in writing advertising is the finding out the proper method to catch the reader, without which a good thing may pass unobserved, or be lost among commissions of bankrupts." The September 14, 1710, issue of the *Tatler* contained ads for razor strops, patent medicine, and other consumer products.

Advertising had its greatest growth in the United States. Ben Franklin has been called the father of American advertising because his *Gazette*, first published in 1729, had the largest circulation and advertising volume of any paper in colonial America. Several factors led to America's becoming the cradle of advertising. First, American industry led in mass production, which created surpluses and the need to convince consumers to buy more. Second, the development of a fine network of waterways, highways, and roads allowed the transportation of goods and advertising media to the countryside. Third, the establishment in 1813 of compulsory public education increased literacy and the growth of newspapers and magazines. The invention of radio and, later, television created two more amazing media for the spread of advertising.

followed by gum, candy, and soaps. Companies spending the largest percentages of their sales on advertising were Noxell (33 percent) and Warner-Lambert (30 percent).

The roots of advertising can be traced to early history (see Marketing Highlight 17–1). Although advertising is mostly used by private enterprise, it is employed in all the countries of the world, including socialist countries. Advertising is a good way to inform and persuade, whether the purpose is to sell Coca-Cola worldwide or to get consumers in a developing nation to drink milk or use birth control.

Organizations handle advertising in different ways. In small companies, advertising might be handled by someone in the sales department. Large companies set up advertising departments whose job is to set the advertising budget, work with the ad agency, and handle direct-mail advertising, dealer displays, and other advertising not done by the agency. Most large companies use outside advertising agencies because they offer several advantages (see Marketing Highlight 17–2).

MAJOR DECISIONS IN ADVERTISING

Marketing management must make five important decisions when developing an advertising program. These decisions are listed in Figure 17-1.

Setting Objectives   The first step in developing an advertising program is to set *advertising objectives*. These objectives should be based on past decisions about the target market, positioning, and marketing mix. The marketing positioning and mix strategy defines the job that advertising must do in the total marketing program.

Many communication and sales objectives can be set for advertising. Colley lists fifty-two possible advertising objectives in his well-known *Defining Advertising Goals*

HOW DOES AN ADVERTISING AGENCY WORK?

Madison Avenue is a familiar name to most Americans. It's a street in New York City where some major advertising agency headquarters are located. But most of the nation's 10,000 agencies are found outside New York, and almost every city has at least one agency, even it it's a one-person shop. Some ad agencies are huge—the largest U.S. agency, Young & Rubicam, has annual worldwide billings (the dollar amount of advertising placed for clients) of more than $6 billion. Dentsu, a Japanese agency, is the world's largest agency with billings of more than $10 billion.

Advertising agencies were started in the mid-to-late 1800s by salespeople and brokers who worked for the media and received a commission for selling advertising space to various companies. As time passed, the salespeople began to help customers prepare their ads. Eventually, they formed agencies and grew closer to the advertisers than to the media. Agencies offered both more advertising and more marketing services to their clients.

Even companies with strong advertising departments use advertising agencies. Agencies employ specialists who can often perform advertising tasks better than the company's own staff. Agencies also bring an outside point of view to solving the company's problems, along with the experience of working with different clients and situations. Agencies are paid partly from media discounts and often cost the firm very little. And because the firm can drop its agency at any time, an agency works hard to do a good job.

Advertising agencies usually have four departments: *creative*, which develops and produces ads; *media*, which selects media and places ads; *research*, which studies audience characteristics and wants; and *business*, which handles the agency's business activities. Each account is supervised by an account executive, and people in each department are usually assigned to work on one or more accounts.

Agencies often attract new business through their reputation or size. Generally, however, a client invites a few agencies to make a presentation for its business and then selects one of them.

Ad agencies have traditionally been paid through commissions and some fees. Under this system, the agency usually receives 15 percent of the media cost as a rebate. Suppose the agency buys $60,000 of magazine space for a client. The magazine bills the advertising agency for $51,000 ($60,000 less 15 percent), and the agency bills the client for $60,000, keeping the $9,000 commission. If the client bought space directly from the magazine, it would have paid $60,000 because commissions are only paid to recognized advertising agencies.

However, both advertisers and agencies have become more and more unhappy with the commission system. Larger advertisers complain that they pay more for the same services received by smaller ones simply because they place more advertising. Advertisers also believe that the commission system drives agencies away from low-cost media and short advertising campaigns. Agencies are unhappy because they perform extra services for an account without getting any more pay. As a result, the trend is now toward paying either a straight fee or a combination commission and fee. And some large advertisers are tying agency compensation to the performance of the agency's advertising campaigns. Today, only about 35 percent of companies still pay their agencies on a commission-only basis.

Another trend is also hitting the advertising agency business: In recent years, as growth in advertising spending has slowed, many agencies have tried to keep growing by gobbling up other agencies, thus creating huge agency holding companies. One of the largest of these agency "megagroups," Saatchi & Saatchi PLC, includes several large agencies—Saatchi & Saatchi Compton, Ted Bates Worldwide, DFS Dorland Worldwide, and others—with combined billings exceeding $15 billion. Many agencies have also sought growth by diversifying into related marketing services. These new "mega-group" agencies offer a complete list of integrated marketing and promotion services under one roof, including advertising, sales promotion, public relations, direct marketing, and marketing research.

Sources: See Walecia Konrad, "A Word from the Sponsor: Get Results—Or Else," *Business Week*, July 4, 1988, p. 66; "Saatchi Leads Top 11 Mega-Groups," *Advertising Age*, March 29, 1989; and R. Craig Endicott, "Ad Age 500 Grows 9.7%," *Advertising Age*, March 26, 1990, pp. S1–S2.

FIGURE 17-1 Major decisions in advertising

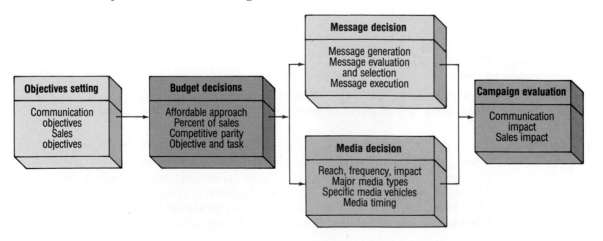

TABLE 17-2
Possible Advertising Objectives

Informative advertising:	
Telling the market about a new product	Describing available services
Suggesting new uses for a product	Correcting false impressions
Informing the market of a price change	Reducing consumers' fears
Explaining how the product works	Building a company image

Persuasive advertising:	
Building brand preference	Persuading customer to purchase now
Encouraging switching to your brand	Persuading customer to receive a sales call
Changing customer's perception of product attributes	

Reminder advertising:	
Reminding consumers that the product may be needed in the near future	Keeping it in their minds during off-seasons
	Maintaining its top-of-mind awareness
Reminding them where to buy it	

for Measured Advertising Results.[3] He outlines a method called DAGMAR (after the book's title) for turning advertising objectives into specific measurable goals.

An **advertising objective** is a specific communication *task* to be accomplished with a specific *target* audience during a specific period of *time*. Advertising objectives can be classified by purpose, whether their aim is to *inform*, *persuade*, or *remind*. Table 17-2 lists examples of these objectives. **Informative advertising** is used heavily when introducing a new product category, when the objective is to build primary demand. Thus, producers of compact disk players first informed consumers of the sound and convenience benefits of CDs. **Persuasive advertising** becomes more important as competition increases and a company's objective is to build selective demand. For example, when compact disk players became established and accepted, Sony began trying to persuade consumers that its brand offers the best quality for their money.

Some persuasive advertising has become **comparison advertising,** which compares one brand directly or indirectly with one or more other brands. For example, in its classic comparison campaign, Avis positioned itself against market-leading Hertz by claiming, "We're number two, so we try harder." Procter & Gamble positioned Scope against Listerine, claiming that minty-fresh Scope "fights bad breath and doesn't give medicine breath." Comparison advertising has also been used for such products as soft drinks, computers, deodorants, toothpastes, automobiles, wines, and pain relievers.

Reminder advertising is important for mature products—it keeps consumers thinking about the product. Expensive Coca-Cola ads on television are designed to remind people about Coca-Cola, not to inform or persuade them.

Setting the Advertising Budget

After determining its advertising objectives, the company can next set its *advertising budget* for each product. The role of advertising is to affect demand for a product. The company wants to spend the amount needed to achieve the sales goal. Four commonly used methods for setting the advertising budget are discussed in Chapter 16. Here we describe some specific factors that should be considered when setting the advertising budget:

- *Stage in the product life cycle*—New products typically need large advertising budgets to build awareness and to gain consumer trial. Mature brands usually require lower budgets as a ratio to sales.
- *Market share*—High market-share brands usually need more advertising spending as a percent of sales than low-share brands. Building market or taking share from competitors requires larger advertising spending than simply maintaining current share.
- *Competition and clutter*—In a market with many competitors and high advertising spending, a brand must advertise more heavily to be heard above the noise in the market.
- *Advertising frequency*—When many repetitions are needed to put across the brand's message to consumers, the advertising budget must be larger.

Comparison advertising: Here Budget Gourmet compares itself directly to competitor Lean Cuisine.

- *Product differentiation*—A brand that closely resembles other brands in its product class (cigarettes, beer, soft drinks) requires heavy advertising to set it apart. When the product differs greatly from competitors, advertising can be used to point out the differences to consumers.[4]

Companies such as Du Pont and Anheuser-Busch often run experiments as part of their advertising budgeting process. For example, Anheuser-Busch recently began testing a new ultrapremium beer, named "Anheuser," with no advertising at all. No major beer is likely to survive without advertising, but in this case the company wants to see if this specialty beer can make it on word-of-mouth alone. In fact, the lack of advertising might even add to the beer's allure. If the new brand succeeds without advertising, Anheuser-Busch will probably take a careful look at the more than $500 million it spends each year advertising its other products.[5]

Setting the advertising budget is no easy task. How does a company know if it is spending the right amount? Some critics charge that large consumer packaged goods firms tend to spend too much on advertising, and industrial companies generally underspend on advertising.[6] They claim that the large consumer companies use image advertising extensively without really knowing its effects. They overspend as a form of "insurance" against not spending enough. On the other hand, industrial advertisers rely too heavily on their salesforces to bring in orders. They underestimate the power of company and product image in preselling industrial customers. Thus, they do not spend enough on advertising to build customer awareness and knowledge.

How much impact does advertising really have on consumer buying and brand loyalty? A recent research study analysing household purchases of frequently bought consumer products came up with the following surprising conclusion:

> Advertising appears effective in increasing the volume purchased by loyal buyers but less effective in winning new buyers. For loyal buyers, high levels of exposure per week may be unproductive because of a leveling off of ad effectiveness . . . Advertising appears unlikely to have some cumulative effect that leads to loyalty. . . . Features, displays, and especially price have a stronger impact on response than does advertising.[7]

These findings did not sit well with the advertising community, and several people attacked the study's data and methodology. They claimed that the study measured mostly short-run sales effects. Thus, it favored pricing and sales promotion activities which tend to have more immediate impact. Most advertising, on the other hand, takes many months or even years to build strong brand positions and consumer loyalty. These long-run effects are difficult to measure. This debate underscores the fact that the subject of measuring the results of advertising spending remains poorly understood.

Creating the Advertising Message

A large advertising budget does not guarantee a successful advertising campaign. Two advertisers can spend the same amount on advertising yet have very different results. Studies have shown that creative advertising messages can be more important to advertising success than the number of dollars spent. No matter how big the budget, advertising can succeed only if commercials gain attention and communicate well. The budget must be invested in effective advertising messages.

Good advertising messages are especially important in today's costly and cluttered advertising environment. The average consumer has 22 television stations to choose from, plus about 11,500 magazines. Add the countless radio stations and a continuous barrage of catalogs, direct-mail ads, and out-of-home media, and consumers are bombarded with ads at home, at work, and at all points in between.[8]

While all this advertising clutter might bother some consumers, it also causes big problems for advertisers. Take the situation facing network television advertisers. They typically pay $100,000 to $200,000 for 30 seconds of advertising time during a popular prime-time TV program—even more if it's an especially popular program such as "The Cosby Show" ($380,000 per spot) or an event like the Super Bowl ($725,000!). In such cases, their ads are sandwiched in with a clutter of some 60 other commercials, announcements, and network promotions per hour. But wait—if you're an advertiser, things get even worse! Until recently, television viewers were pretty much a captive audience for advertisers. Viewers had only a few channels to choose from. Those who found the energy to get up and change channels during boring commercial breaks usually found only more of the same on the other channels. But with the growth in cable TV, VCRs, and remote-control units, today's viewers have many more options. They can actually avoid ads by watching commercial-free cable channels. They can "zap" commercials by pushing the fast-forward button during taped programs. With remote control, they can instantly turn off the sound during a commercial or "zip" around the channel to see what else is on. Advertisers take such "zipping" and "zapping" seriously. One expert predicts that by the year 2000, 60 percent of all TV viewers may be regularly tuning out commercials.[9]

Thus, just to gain and hold attention, today's advertising messages must be better planned, more imaginative, more entertaining, and more rewarding to consumers. Creative strategy will therefore play an increasingly important role in advertising success. Advertisers go through three steps to develop a creative strategy: *message generation*, *message evaluation and selection*, and *message execution*.

Message Generation

Creative people have different ways to find advertising message ideas. Many creative people start by talking to consumers, dealers, experts, and competitors. Others try to imagine consumers using the product and figure out the benefits consumers seek when buying and using it. Generally, although advertisers create many possible messages, only a few will ultimately be used.

Message Evaluation and Selection

The advertiser must evaluate the possible messages. The appeals used in messages should have three characteristics. First, they should be *meaningful*, pointing out benefits that make the product more desirable or interesting to consumers. Second, appeals should be *distinctive*—they should tell how the product is better than competing brands. Finally, they must be *believable*. It may be hard to make message appeals believable because many consumers doubt the truth of advertising in general. One study found that, on average, consumers rate advertising messages as "somewhat unbelievable."[10]

Thus, advertisers should evaluate their advertising messages on the above factors. For example, The March of Dimes searched for an advertising theme to raise money for its fight against birth defects.[11] Twenty possible messages came out of a brainstorming session. A group of young parents were asked to rate each message for interest, distinctiveness, and believability, giving up to 100 points for each. For example, the message "Five hundred thousand unborn babies die each year from birth defects" scored 70, 60, and 80 on interest, distinctiveness, and believability, while the message "Your next baby could be born with a birth defect" scored 58, 50, and 70. The first message was thus rated higher than the second and was used in advertising.

Message Execution

The impact of the message depends not only on *what* is said, but also on *how* it is said—its message execution. The advertiser has to put the message across in a way that wins the target market's attention and interest.

The advertiser usually begins with a statement of the objective and approach of the desired ad. Here is such a statement for a Pillsbury product called 1869 Brand Biscuits:

> The objective of the advertising is to convince biscuit users that now they can buy a canned biscuit that's as good as homemade—Pillsbury's 1869 Brand Biscuits. The content of the advertising will emphasize that the biscuits look like homemade biscuits, have the same texture as homemade, and taste like homemade biscuits. Support for the "good as homemade" promise will be twofold: (1) 1869 Brand Biscuits are made from a special kind of flour (soft wheat flour) used to make homemade biscuits but never before used in making canned biscuits, and (2) the use of traditional American biscuit recipes. The tone of the advertising will be a news announcement, tempered by a warm, reflective mood coming from a look back at traditional American baking quality.

The creative people must find a style, tone, words, and format for executing the message. Any message can be presented in different *execution styles*, such as:

- *Slice-of-life*—This style shows one or more people using the product in a normal setting. A family seated at the dinner table might talk about a new biscuit brand.
- *Life style*—This style shows how a product fits in with a life style. For example, a National Diary Board ad shows women exercising and talks about how milk adds to a healthy, active life style.
- *Fantasy*—This style creates a fantasy around the product or its use. For instance, Revlon's first ad for Jontue showed a barefoot woman wearing a chiffon dress and coming out of an old French barn, crossing a meadow, meeting a handsome young man on a white horse, and riding away with him.
- *Mood or image*—This style builds a mood or image around the product, such as beauty, love, or serenity. No claim is made about the product except through suggestion. Many coffee ads create moods.
- *Musical*—This style shows one or more people or cartoon characters singing a song about the product. Many soft drink ads have used this format.
- *Personality symbol*—This style creates a character that represents the product. The character might be *animated* (the Jolly Green Giant, Cap'n Crunch, Garfield the Cat) or *real* (the Marlboro man, Betty Crocker, Morris the 9-Lives Cat).
- *Technical expertise*—This style shows the company's expertise in making the product. Thus, Hills Brothers shows one of its buyers carefully selecting the coffee beans, and Gallo tells about its many years of winemaking.
- *Scientific evidence*—This style presents survey or scientific evidence that the brand is better or better liked than one or more other brands. For years, Crest toothpaste has used scientific evidence to convince buyers that Crest is better than other brands at fighting cavities.
- *Testimonial evidence*—This style features a highly believable or likable source endorsing the product. It could be a celebrity like Bill Cosby (Jell-o Pudding or Kodak film) or ordinary people saying how much they like a given product.

The advertiser must also choose a *tone* for the ad. Procter & Gamble always uses a positive tone: Its ads say something very positive about its products. P&G also

**Message execution styles: Cunard builds a fantasy around its cruise vacations;
9-Lives created Morris the 9-Lives cat as a personality symbol.**

avoids humor that might take attention away from the message. By contrast, ads for Bud Light beer use humor and poke fun at people who order "just any light."

Memorable and attention-getting *words* must be found. For example, the themes listed below on the left would have had much less impact without the creative phrasing on the right:

Theme	Creative Copy
▪ 7-Up is not a cola	▪ "The Uncola"
▪ Ride in our bus instead of driving your car.	▪ "Take the bus, and leave the driving to us." (Greyhound)
▪ If you drink much beer, Schaefer is a good beer to drink.	▪ "The one to have when you're having more than one."
▪ We don't rent as many cars, so we have to do more for our customers.	▪ "We're number two, so we try harder." (Avis)
▪ Hanes socks last longer than less expensive ones.	▪ "Buy cheap socks and you'll pay through the toes."
▪ Nike shoes will help you jump higher and play better basketball	▪ "Parachute not included."

Finally, *format* elements will make a difference in an ad's impact as well as its cost. A small change in the way an ad is designed can make a big difference in its effect. The *illustration* is the first thing the reader notices, and that illustration must be strong enough to draw attention. Then the *headline* must effectively entice the right people to read the copy. The *copy*—the main block of text in the ad—must be simple but strong and convincing. Moreover, these three elements must also work effectively *together*. Even then, a truly outstanding ad will be noted by less than 50 percent of the exposed audience; about 30 percent of the exposed audience will recall the main point of the headline; about 25 percent will remember the advertiser's name; and less than 10 percent will have read most of the body copy. Less than outstanding ads, unfortunately, will not achieve even these results.

**Guess who didn't send it
by Federal Express.**

Federal Express deliver over 1.2 million parcels daily in 360 aeroplanes and 25,400 vehicles, to 111 countries worldwide. And we don't just promise to get there, we get there on time. In fact, our unequalled track record has made us the No. 1 air package carrier in America. Because we understand that if we don't meet our deadlines, you won't meet yours. See Yellow Pages for your nearest Federal Express Office.

Federal Express. When it absolutely, positively has to be there on time.

In this ad, the illustration, the headline, and the copy work closely together to deliver the company's message.

Selecting Advertising Media

The advertiser next chooses advertising media to carry the message. The major steps in media selection are (1) deciding on *reach*, *frequency*, and *impact*; (2) choosing among major *media types*; (3) selecting specific *media vehicles*; and (4) deciding on *media timing*.

Deciding on Reach, Frequency, and Impact

To select media, the advertiser must determine the reach and frequency necessary to achieve advertising objectives. **Reach** is a measure of the *percentage* of people in the target market who are exposed to the ad campaign during a given period of time. For example, the advertiser might try to reach 70 percent of the target market during the first three months. **Frequency** is a measure of how many *times* the average person in the target market is exposed to the message. For example, the advertiser might want an average exposure frequency of three. The advertiser must also decide on **media impact**—the *qualitative value* of a message exposure through a given medium. For example, for products that need to be demonstrated, messages on television may have more impact than messages on radio because television uses sight *and* sound. The same message in one magazine (say, *Newsweek*) may be more believable than in another (say, *The National Enquirer*).

Suppose the advertiser's product might appeal to a market of one million consumers.

The goal is to reach 700,000 consumers (70 percent of 1,000,000). Because the average consumer will receive three exposures, 2,100,000 exposures (700,000 × 3) must be bought. If the advertiser wants exposures of 1.5 impact (assuming 1.0 impact is the average), a rated number of exposures of 3,150,000 (2,100,000 × 1.5) must be bought. If a thousand exposures with this impact cost $10, the advertising budget will have to be $31,500 (3,150 × $10). In general, the more reach, frequency, and impact the advertiser seeks, the higher the advertising budget will have to be.

Choosing among Major Media Types

The media planner has to know the reach, frequency, and impact of each of the major media types. The major advertising media are summarized in Table 17-3. The major media types, in order of their advertising volume, are newspapers, television, direct mail, radio, magazines, and outdoor. Each medium has advantages and limitations.

Media planners consider many factors when making their media choices. The *media habits of target consumers* will affect media choice—for example, radio and television are the best media for reaching teenagers. So will the *nature of the product*—dresses are best shown in color magazines, and Polaroid cameras are best demonstrated on television. Different *types of messages* may require different media. A message announcing a major sale tomorrow will require radio or newspapers; a message with a lot of technical data might require magazines or direct mailings. *Cost* is also a major factor in media choice. While television is very expensive, newspaper advertising costs much less. The media planner looks at both total cost of using a medium and at the cost per thousand exposures—the cost of reaching 1000 people using the medium.

Ideas about media impact and cost must be reexamined regularly. For a long time, television and magazines dominated in the media mixes of national advertisers, with other media often neglected. Recently, however, the costs and clutter of these media have gone up, audiences have dropped, and marketers are adopting strategies

TABLE 17-3 Profiles of Major Media Types

MEDIUM	VOLUME IN BILLIONS	PERCENTAGE	EXAMPLE OF COST	ADVANTAGES	LIMITATIONS
Newspapers	$ 31.2	26.4%	$33,615 for one page, weekday *Chicago Tribune*	Flexibility; timeliness; good local market coverage; broad acceptance; high believability	Short life; poor reproduction quality; small "pass along" audience
Television	25.7	21.8%	$1,500 for thirty seconds of prime time in Chicago	Combines sight, sound, and motion; appealing to the senses; high attention; high reach	High absolute cost; high clutter; fleeting exposure; less audience selectivity
Direct mail	21.1	17.9%	$1,800 for the names and addresses of 40,000 veterinarians	Audience selectivity; flexibility; no ad competition within the same medium; personalization	Relatively high cost; "junk mail" image
Radio	7.8	6.6%	$700 for one minute of drive time (during commuting hours, A.M. and P.M.) in Chicago	Mass use; high geographic and demographic selectivity; low cost	Audio presentation only; lower attention than television; nonstandardized rate structures; fleeting exposure
Magazines	6.1	5.2%	$100,980 for one page, four-color, in *Newsweek*	High geographic and demographic selectivity; credibility and prestige; high-quality reproduction; long life; good pass-along readership	Long ad purchase lead time; some waste circulation; no guarantee of position
Outdoor	1.1	0.9%	$25,500 per month for seventy-one billboards in metropolitan Chicago	Flexibility; high repeat exposure; low cost; low competition	No audience selectivity; creative limitations
Other	25.0	21.2%			
Total	118.0	100.0%			

Source: Columns 2 and 3 are from *Advertising Age*, May 14, 1990, p. 12, Printed with permission. Copyright © 1990. Crain Communications, Inc.

ADVERTISERS SEEK ALTERNATIVE MEDIA

As network television costs soar and audiences shrink, many advertisers are looking for new ways to reach consumers. And the move toward micromarketing strategies, focused more narrowly on specific consumer groups, has also fueled the search for alternative media to replace or supplement network television. Advertisers are shifting larger portions of their budgets to media that cost less and target more effectively.

Two media benefiting most from the shift are outdoor advertising and cable television. Billboards have undergone a resurgence in recent years. Advertisers now spend more than $1.5 billion annually on outdoor media, a 25 percent increase from four years ago. Gone are the ugly eyesores of the past; in their place we now see cleverly designed, colorful, attention-grabbers. Outdoor advertising provides an excellent way to reach important local consumer segments.

beamed at narrower segments. As a result, TV and magazine advertising revenues have leveled off or declined. Advertisers are increasingly turning to alternative media, ranging from cable TV and outdoor advertising to parking meters and shopping carts (see Marketing Highlight 17–3).

Given these and other media characteristics, the media planner must decide how much of each media type to buy. For example, in launching its new biscuit, Pillsbury might decide to spend $3 million on daytime network television, $2 million on women's magazines, and $1 million on daily newspapers in 20 major markets.

Selecting Specific Media Vehicles

The media planner must now choose the best **media vehicles**—specific media within each general media type. For example, television vehicles include ''Roseanne,'' ''The

Marketers have discovered a dazzling array of "alternative media."

Cable television is also booming. Today, more than 57 percent of all U.S. households subscribe to cable, up from just 20 percent in 1980, And cable TV advertising revenues now exceed $2 billion a year, compared with a mere $58 million in 1980. Industry experts expect that cable television advertising will continue to grow explosively through the 1990s. Cable systems allow narrow programming formats such as all sports, all news, nutrition programs, arts programs, and others that target select groups. Advertisers can take advantage of such "narrowcasting" to "rifle in" on special market segments rather than use the "shotgun" approach offered by network broadcasting.

Cable TV and outdoor advertising seem to make good sense. But increasingly, ads are popping up in far less likely places. In their efforts to find less costly and more highly targeted ways to reach consumers, advertisers have discovered a dazzling collection of "alternative media." As consumers, we're used to ads on television, in magazines and newspapers, on the radio, and along the roadways. But these days, no matter where you go or what you do, you will probably run into some new form of advertising.

Tiny video screens attached to shopping carts, triggered by the aisle in which the consumer is shopping, show ads from national advertisers and flash messages about store specials. Signs atop parking meters hawk everything from Jeeps to Minolta cameras to Recipe dog food. You escape to the ballpark, only to find billboard-size video screens running

Budweiser ads while a blimp with an electronic message board circles lazily overhead. You pay to see a movie at your local theater, but first you see a two-minute science fiction fantasy that turns out to be an ad for General Electric portable stereo boxes. Then the movie itself is full of not-so-subtle promotional plugs for Pepsi, Dominoes Pizza, Alka-Seltzer, MasterCard, Fritos, or one of a dozen other products. Boats cruise along public beaches flashing advertising messages for Sundown Sunscreen or Gatorade to sunbathers. Even your church bulletin carries ads for Campbell's Soup.

Some of these alternative media seem a bit far-fetched, and they sometimes irritate consumers. But for many marketers, these media can save money and provide a way to hit selected consumers where they live, shop, work, and play. Of course, this may leave you wondering if there are any commercial-free havens remaining for ad-weary consumers. The back seat of a taxi, perhaps, or stalls in a public restroom? Forget it! Both have already been invaded by innovative marketers.

Sources: See Alison Leigh Cowan, "Marketers Worry as Ads Crop Up in Unlikely Places," *Raleigh News and Observer*, February 21, 1988, p. 11; Alan Radding, "Outdoor Faces Its Flaws," *Advertising Age*, October 9, 1989; "Freedom of Choice Drive's Cable's Growth," *Advertising Age*, February 19, 1990, pp. 16–17; Ira Teinowitz, "VideOcart Starts to Roll for IRI," *Advertising Age*, January 8, 1990, p. 30; and John McManus, "Growing Pains," *Adweek*, April 2, 1990, pp. 24–26.

Bill Cosby Show," "Sixty Minutes," and the "CBS Evening News." Magazine vehicles include *Newsweek*, *People*, *Sports Illustrated*, and *Reader's Digest*. If advertising is placed in magazines, the media planner must look up circulation figures and the costs of different ad sizes, color options, ad positions, and frequencies for various specific magazines. The planner then evaluates each magazine on such factors as credibility, status, reproduction quality, editorial focus, and advertising submission deadlines. The media planner decides which vehicles give the best reach, frequency, and impact for the money.

Media planners also compute the cost per thousand persons reached by a vehicle. If a full-page, four-color advertisement in *Newsweek* costs $100,000 and *Newsweek's* readership is 3.3 million people, the cost of reaching each one thousand persons is about $30. The same advertisement in *Business Week* may cost only $57,000 but reach only 775,000 persons, at a cost per thousand of about $74. The media planner would rank each magazine by cost per thousand and favor those magazines with the lower cost per thousand for reaching target consumers.

The media planner must also consider the costs of producing ads for different media. While newspaper ads may cost very little to produce, flashy television ads may cost millions. On average, advertisers must pay $118,000 to produce a single 30-second television commercial. Timex paid a cool million to make one 30-second ad for its Atlantis 100 sports watch, and Apple Computer recently spent $6 million to produce 11 spots.[12]

The media planner must thus balance media cost measures against several media impact factors. First, costs should be balanced against the media vehicle's *audience quality*. For a baby lotion advertisement, *New Parents* magazine would have a high-exposure value; *Gentlemen's Quarterly* would have a low-exposure value. Second, the media planner should consider *audience attention*. Readers of *Vogue*, for example, typically pay more attention to ads than do readers of *Newsweek*. Third, the planner should assess the vehicle's *editorial quality*—*Time* and *The Wall Street Journal* are more believable and prestigious than *The National Enquirer*.

Media planners are increasingly developing more sophisticated measures of media effectiveness and using them in mathematical models to arrive at the best media mix. Many advertising agencies use computer programs to select the initial media and then make further media schedule improvements based on subjective factors not considered by the media selection model.[13]

Deciding on Media Timing

The advertiser must also decide how to schedule the advertising over the course of a year. Suppose sales of a product peak in December and drop in March. The firm can vary its advertising to follow the seasonal pattern, to oppose the seasonal pattern, or to be the same all year. Most firms do some seasonal advertising. Some do *only* seasonal advertising: For example, Hallmark advertises its greeting cards only before major holidays.

Finally, the advertiser has to choose the pattern of the ads. **Continuity** means scheduling ads evenly within a given period. **Pulsing** means scheduling ads unevenly during a given time period. Thus, 52 ads could either be scheduled at one per week during the year or pulsed in several bursts. Those who favor pulsing feel that the audience will learn the message more completely and that money can be saved. For example, Anheuser-Busch found that Budweiser could drop advertising in a given market with no harm to sales for at least a year and a half. Then the company could use a six-month burst of advertising and regain the past sales growth rate. This finding led Budweiser to adopt a pulsing strategy.[14]

Advertising Evaluation

The advertising program should regularly evaluate the *communication effects* and *sales effects* of advertising.

Measuring the Communication Effect

Measuring the communication effect tells whether an ad is communicating well. Called **copy testing,** it can be done before or after an ad is printed or broadcast. There are three major methods of advertising *pretesting*. The first is through *direct rating*, in which the advertiser exposes a consumer panel to alternative ads and asks them to rate the ads. These direct ratings indicate how well the ads get attention and how they affect consumers. Although an imperfect measure of an ad's actual impact, a high rating indicates a potentially more effective ad. In *portfolio tests*, consumers view or listen to a portfolio of advertisements, taking as much time as they need. They then are asked to recall all the ads and their content, aided or unaided by the interviewer. Their recall level indicates the ability of an ad to stand out and its message to be understood and remembered. *Laboratory tests* use equipment to measure consumers'

ADVERTISING DECISIONS AND PUBLIC POLICY

By law, companies must avoid deception or discrimination in their use of advertising. Here are the major issues:

False Advertising. Advertisers must not make false claims, such as stating that a product cures something that it does not. Advertisers must avoid false demonstrations, such as using sand-covered plexiglass instead of sandpaper in a commercial to demonstrate that a razor blade can shave sandpaper.

Deceptive Advertising. Advertisers must not create ads that have the capacity to deceive, even though no one may be deceived. A floor wax cannot be advertised as giving six months' protection unless it does so under typical conditions, and a diet bread cannot be advertised as having fewer calories simply because its slices are thinner. The problem is to tell the difference between deception and "puffery," simple acceptable exaggerations not intended to be believed.

Bait-and-Switch Advertising. The seller should not attract buyers on false pretenses. For example, let's say a seller advertises a $79 sewing machine. When consumers try to buy the advertised machine, the seller refuses to sell it, downplays its features, shows a faulty one, or promises unreasonable delivery dates, trying to switch the buyer to a more expensive machine.

Promotional Allowances and Services. The company must make promotional allowances and services available to all customers on proportionately equal terms.

---

physiological reactions to an ad—heartbeat, blood pressure, pupil dilation, perspiration. These tests measure an ad's attention-getting power but reveal little about its impact on beliefs, attitudes, or intentions.

There are two popular methods of *posttesting* ads. Using *recall tests*, the advertiser asks people who have been exposed to magazines or television programs to recall everything they can about the advertisers and products they saw. Recall scores indicate the ad's power to be noticed and retained. In *recognition tests*, the researcher asks readers of a given issue of, say, a magazine to point out what they recognize as having seen before. Recognition scores can be used to assess the ad's impact in different market segments and to compare the company's ads with competitors' ads.

Measuring the Sales Effect

What sales are caused by an ad that increases brand awareness by 20 percent and brand preference by 10 percent? The sales effect of advertising is often harder to measure than the communication effect. Sales are affected by many factors besides advertising—such as product features, price, and availability.

One way to measure the sales effect of advertising is to compare past sales with past advertising expenditures. Another way is through experiments. Du Pont was one of the first companies to use advertising experiments.[15] Du Pont's paint department divided 56 sales territories into high, average, and low market-share territories. In one-third of the group, Du Pont spent the normal amount for advertising; in another third, the company spent two and one-half times the normal amount; and in the remaining third, it allotted four times the normal amount. At the end of the experiment, Du Pont estimated how many extra sales had been created by higher levels of advertising expenditure. It found that higher advertising spending increased sales at a diminishing rate and that the sales increase was weaker in its high market share territories.

To spend a large advertising budget wisely, advertisers must define their advertising objectives, make careful budget, message, and media decisions, and evaluate the results. Advertising also draws much public attention, because of its power to affect life styles and opinions. Advertising faces increased regulation to ensure that it performs responsibly (see Marketing Highlight 17–4).[16]

SALES PROMOTION

Advertising is joined by two other mass promotion tools—*sales promotion* and *public relations*. **Sales promotion** consists of short-term incentives to encourage purchase or sales of a product or service. Whereas advertising offers reasons to buy a product or service, sales promotion offers reasons to buy *now*. Examples are found everywhere:

A coupon in the Sunday newspaper clearly indicates a 40 cent savings on brand X coffee. The end-of-the-aisle display confronts an impulse buyer with a wall of snackfood. A family buys a camcorder and gets a free traveling case, or buys a car and gets a check for a $500 rebate. An appliance retailer is given a 10 percent manufacturer discount on January's orders if the retailer advertises the product in the local newspaper.[17]

Sales promotion includes a wide variety of promotion tools designed to stimulate earlier or stronger market response. It includes **consumer promotion**—samples, coupons, rebates, prices-off, premiums, contests, trading stamps, demonstrations; **trade promotion**—buying allowances, free goods, merchandise allowances, cooperative advertising, push money, dealer sales contests; and **salesforce promotion**—bonuses, contests, sales rallies.

Rapid Growth of Sales Promotion

Sales promotion tools are used by most organizations, including manufacturers, distributors, retailers, trade associations, and nonprofit institutions. Estimates of annual sales promotion spending run as high as $125 billion, and this spending has increased rapidly in recent years.[18] A few decades ago, the advertising-to-sales promotion ratio was about 60/40. Today, in many consumer packaged goods companies, the picture is reversed, with sales promotion accounting for 60 to 70 percent of all the marketing expenditures. Sales promotion expenditures have been increasing 12 percent annually compared with advertising's increase of 7.6 percent.

Several factors have contributed to the rapid growth of sales promotion, particularly in consumer markets. Inside the company, promotion is now more accepted by top management as an effective sales tool and more product managers are qualified to use sales promotion tools. Furthermore product managers face greater pressures to increase their current sales. Externally, the company faces more competition, and competing brands are less differentiated. Competitors are using more and more promotions, and consumers have become more deal oriented. Advertising efficiency has declined because of rising costs, media clutter, and legal restraints. Finally, retailers are demanding more deals from manufacturers.

The growing use of sales promotion has resulted in *promotion clutter*, similar to advertising clutter. The danger is that consumers will start tuning out promotions, weakening the ability to trigger immediate purchase. Manufacturers are now searching for ways to rise above the clutter, such as offering larger coupon values or creating more dramatic point-of-purchase displays.

Purpose of Sales Promotion

Sales promotion tools vary in their specific objectives. A free sample stimulates consumer trial; a free management advisory service cements a long-term relationship with a retailer.

Sellers use sales promotions to attract new tryers, to reward loyal customers, and to increase the repurchase rates of occasional users. New tryers are of three types—nonusers of the product category, loyal users of another brand, and users who frequently switch brands. Sales promotions often attract the brand switchers because nonusers and users of other brands do not always notice or act on a promotion. Brand switchers are mostly looking for low price or good value. Sales promotions are unlikely to turn them into loyal brand users. Thus, sales promotions used in markets where brands are very similar usually produce high short-run sales response but little permanent market share gain. In markets where brands differ greatly, however, sales promotions can alter market shares more permanently.

Many sellers think of sales promotion as a tool for breaking down brand loyalty and advertising as a tool for building up brand loyalty. Thus, an important issue for marketing managers is how to divide the budget between sales promotion and advertising. Ten years ago, marketing managers would first decide how much they needed to spend on advertising, and then put the rest into sales promotion. Today, more and more marketing managers first decide how much they need to spend on trade promotion, then decide what they will spend on consumer promotion, and then budget whatever is left over for advertising.

There is a danger, however, in letting advertising take a back seat to sales promotion. When a company price-promotes a brand too much of the time, consumers begin to think of it as a cheap brand. Soon many consumers will buy the brand only when it is a deal. No one knows the exact parameters, but the risk increases greatly if a company puts a well-known, leading brand on promotion more than 30 percent of the time.[19] Marketers rarely use sales promotion for dominant brands because the promotions would do little more than subsidize current users.

Most analysts believe that sales promotion activities do not build long-term consumer preference and loyalty, as does advertising. Instead, promotion usually produces only short-term sales that cannot be maintained. Small-share competitors find it advantageous to use sales promotion because they cannot afford to match the large advertising budgets of the market leaders. Nor can they obtain shelf space without offering trade allowances, or stimulate consumer trial without offering consumer incentives. Thus, price competition is often used for small brands seeking to enlarge their shares, but it is usually less effective for a market leader whose growth lies in expanding the entire product category.[20]

The upshot is that many consumer packaged goods companies believe they are forced to use more sales promotion than they would like. Recently, Kellogg, Kraft, Procter & Gamble, and several other market leaders have announced that they will put growing emphasis on pull promotion and increase their advertising budgets. They blame the heavy use of sales promotion for causing decreasing brand loyalty, increasing consumer price sensitivity, a focus on short-run marketing planning, and an erosion of brand-quality image.

Some marketers, however, dispute this.[21] They argue that the heavy use of sales promotion is a symptom of these problems, not a cause. They point to more basic causes, such as slower population growth, more educated consumers, industry overcapacity, the decreasing effectiveness of advertising, the growth of reseller power, and the emphasis in U.S. businesses on short-run profits.

These marketers assert that sales promotion provides many important benefits to manufacturers as well as consumers. Sales promotions let manufacturers adjust to short term changes in supply and demand and to differences in customer segments. They let manufacturers charge a higher list price to test "how high is high." Sales promotions encourage consumers to try new products instead of always staying with their current ones. They lead to more varied retail formats, such as the everyday-low-price store or the promotional-pricing store; this gives consumers more choice. Finally, sales promotions lead to greater consumer awareness of prices, and consumers themselves enjoy some satisfaction from being smart shoppers when they take advantage of price specials.

Sales promotions are usually used together with advertising or personal selling. Consumer promotions must usually be advertised and can add excitement and pulling power to ads. Trade and salesforce promotions support the firm's personal selling process. In using sales promotion, a company must set objectives, select the right tools, develop the best program; pretest and implement it, and evaluate the results.

Setting Sales
Promotion Objectives

Sales promotion objectives vary widely. Sellers may use *consumer promotions* to increase short-term sales or to help build long-term market share. The objective may be to entice consumers to try a new product, lure consumers away from competitors' products, get consumers to "load up" on a mature product, or hold and reward loyal customers. Objectives for *trade promotions* include getting retailers to carry new items and more inventory, getting them to advertise the product and give it more shelf space, and getting them to buy ahead. For the *salesforce*, objectives include getting more salesforce support for current or new products or getting salespeople to sign up new accounts.

In general, sales promotions should be **consumer franchise building**—they should promote the product's positioning and include a selling message along with the deal. Ideally, the objective is to build long-run consumer demand rather than to prompt temporary brand switching. If properly designed, every sales promotion tool has consumer franchise building potential.[22]

Selecting Sales Promotion Tools

Many tools can be used to accomplish sales promotion objectives. The promotion planner should consider the type of market, the sales promotion objectives, the competition, and the costs and effectiveness of each tool. The main consumer and trade promotion tools are described below.

Consumer Promotion Tools

The main consumer promotion tools include samples, coupons, cash refunds, price packs, premiums, advertising specialties, patronage rewards, point-of-purchase displays and demonstrations, and contests, sweepstakes, and games.

Samples are offers of a trial amount of a product. Some samples are free; for others, the company charges a small amount to offset its cost. The sample might be delivered door to door, sent in the mail, handed out in a store, attached to another product, or featured in an ad. Sampling is the most effective—but most expensive—way to introduce a new product. For example, Lever Brothers had so much confidence in its new Surf detergent that it spent $43 million to distribute free samples to four of every five American households.

Coupons are certificates that give buyers a saving when they purchase specified products. More than 263 billion coupons are distributed in the U.S. each year, with a total face value of more than $65 billion. Consumers redeem about 10.5 billion of these coupons, saving almost $4.5 billion on their shopping bills.[23] Coupons can be mailed, included with other products, or placed in ads. Several package goods companies are experimenting with point-of-sale coupon dispensing machines and computerized printers that automatically print coupons at the cash register when certain products pass over the scanner.[24] Coupons can stimulate sales of a mature brand and promote early trial of a new brand.

Companies send out over 200 billion coupons each year and spend hundreds of millions of dollars on samples.

Cash refund offers (or **rebates**) are like coupons except that the price reduction occurs after the purchase rather than at the retail outlet. The consumer sends a "proof of purchase" to the manufacturer who then "refunds" part of the purchase price by mail. Toro ran a clever preseason promotion on certain of its snowblower models, offering a rebate if the snowfall in the buyer's market area turned out below average. Competitors were not able to match this offer on such short notice, and the promotion was very successful. On the other hand, automobile rebates have become so common in the automotive industry that many car buyers postpone purchasing until a rebate is announced. Because most auto companies match each other's rebates, each company gains little. The money could be better spent on advertising to build stronger brand images.

Price packs (also called **cents-off deals**) offer consumers savings off the regular price of a product. The reduced prices are marked by the producer directly on label or package. Price packs can be single packages sold at a reduced price (such as two for the price of one), or two related products banded together (such as a toothbrush and toothpaste). Price packs are very effective—even more so than coupons—in stimulating short-term sales.

Premiums are goods offered either free or at low cost as an incentive to buy a product. In its "Treasure Hunt" promotion, for example, Quaker Oats inserted $5 million of gold and silver coins in Ken-L Ration dog food packages. In its recent premium promotion, Cutty Sark scotch offered a brass tray with the purchase of one bottle of Cutty and a desk lamp with the purchase or two. A premium may come inside (in-pack) or outside (on-pack) the package. The package itself, if reusable (such as a decorative tin), may serve as a premium. Premiums are sometimes mailed to consumers who have sent in a proof of purchase, such as a box top. A *self-liquidating premium* is a premium sold below its normal retail price to consumers who request it. For example, manufacturers now offer consumers all kinds of premiums bearing the company's name: Budweiser fans can order T-shirts, hot-air balloons, and hundreds of other items with Bud's name on them at unusually low prices.

Advertising specialties are useful articles imprinted with an advertiser's name given as gifts to consumers. Typical items include pens, calendars, key rings, matches, shopping bags, t-shirts, caps, and coffee mugs. U.S. companies spend more than $4 billion each year on advertising specialties. Such items can be very effective. In a recent study, 63 percent of all consumers surveyed were either carrying or wearing an ad specialty item. More than three-quarters of those who had an item could recall the advertiser's name or message before showing the item to the interviewer.[25]

Patronage rewards are cash or other awards for the regular use of a certain company's products or services. For example, airlines offer "frequent flyer plans," awarding points for miles traveled that can be turned in for free airline trips. Marriott Hotels has adopted an "honored guest" plan that awards points for users of their hotels. Baskin-Robbins offers frequent-purchase awards—for every ten purchases, customers receive a free quart of ice cream. Polaroid and Pan Am jointly offer a "Frequent Smileage Program." When members buy eligible Polaroid products, they earn points which can be used to earn free tickets on Pan Am. Trading stamps are also patronage rewards in that customers receive stamps when buying from certain merchants and can redeem them for either goods at redemption centers or through mail order catalogs.[26]

Point-of-purchase (POP) promotions include displays and demonstrations that take place at the point of purchase or sale. An example is a five-foot-high cardboard display of Cap'n Crunch next to Cap'n Crunch cereal boxes. Unfortunately, many retailers do not like to handle the hundreds of displays, signs, and posters they receive from manufacturers each year. Manufacturers have thus responded by offering better POP materials, tying them in with television or print messages and offering to set them up. A good example is the award-winning Pepsi "tipping can" display. From an ordinary display of Pepsi six-packs along a supermarket aisle, a mechanically rigged six-pack begins to tip forward, grabbing the attention of passing shoppers who think the six-pack is falling. A sign reminds shoppers, "Don't forget the Pepsi!" In test market stores, the display helped get more trade support and greatly increased Pepsi sales.

Pepsi's tipping can and tipping bottle displays grab shopper attention.

Contests, sweepstakes, and games give consumers the chance to win something—cash, trips, or goods—by luck or through extra effort. A *contest* calls for consumers to submit an entry—a jingle, guess, suggestion—to be judged by a panel that will select the best entries. A *sweepstakes* calls for consumers to submit their names for a drawing. A *game* presents consumers with something every time they buy—bingo numbers, missing letters—that may or may not help them win a prize. A sales contest urges dealers or the salesforce to increase their efforts, with prizes going to the top performers.

Trade Promotion Tools

More sales promotion dollars are directed to retailers and wholesalers (55 percent) than to consumers (45 percent)![27] Trade promotion can persuade retailers or wholesalers to carry a brand, give it shelf space, promote it in advertising, and push it to consumers. Shelf space is so scarce these days that manufacturers often have to offer price-offs, allowances, buy-back guarantees, or free goods to get on the shelf and, once there, to stay on it.

Manufacturers use several trade-promotion tools. Many of the tools used for consumer promotions—contests, premiums, displays—can also be used as trade promotions. Or the manufacturer may offer a straight **discount** off the list price on each case purchased during a stated period of time (also called a *price-off*, *off-invoice*, or *off-list*). The offer encourages dealers to buy in quantity or carry a new item. Dealers can use the discount for immediate profit, for advertising, or for price reductions to their customers.

Manufacturers may also offer an **allowance** (usually so much off per case) in return for the retailer's agreement to feature the manufacturer's products in some way. An *advertising allowance* compensates retailers for advertising the product. A *display allowance* compensates them for using special displays.

Manufacturers may offer *free goods*, which are extra cases of merchandise, to middlemen who buy a certain quantity or who feature a certain flavor or size. They may offer *push money*—cash or gifts to dealers or their salesforce to "push" the manufacturer's goods. Manufacturers may give retailers free *specialty advertising items* that carry the company's name, such as pens, pencils, calendars, paperweights, matchbooks, memo pads, ashtrays, and yardsticks.

Business Promotion Tools

Companies spend billions of dollars each year on promotion to industrial customers. These promotions are used for such purposes as generating business leads, stimulating purchases, rewarding customers, and motivating salespeople. Business promotion includes many of the same tools used for consumer or trade promotions. We focus on two major business promotion tools—conventions and trade shows, and sales contests.

Many companies and trade associations organize *conventions and trade shows* to promote their products. Firms selling to the industry show their products at the trade show. More than 5,600 trade shows take place every year, drawing approximately 80 million people. Vendors get many benefits, such as finding new sales leads, contacting customers, introducing new products, meeting new customers, selling more to present customers, and educating customers with publications and audio-visual materials.

Trade shows help companies reach many prospects not reached through their salesforces. About 90 percent of a trade show's visitors see a company's salespeople for the first time. The average attendee spends almost 8 hours viewing exhibits during a two-day period and spends an average of 22 minutes at each exhibit. About 85 percent of the attendees make a final purchase decision for one or more products displayed. The average costs per visitor reached (including exhibits, personnel travel, living and salary expenses, and preshow promotion costs) is $87, less than the average cost of an industrial sales call.

Business marketers may spend as much as 35 percent of their annual promotion budgets on trade shows. They face several decisions, including which trade shows to participate in, how much to spend on each trade show, how to build dramatic exhibits that attract attention, and how to effectively follow up sales leads.[28]

A *sales contest* is a contest involving salespeople or dealers to motivate them to increase their sales performance during a given period, with prizes going to those who best succeed. Most companies sponsor annual or more frequent sales contests for their salesforce. Called "incentive programs," they motivate and give recognition to good company performers. The good performers may receive trips, cash prizes, or gifts. Some companies award points for performance which the receiver can turn in for any of a variety of prizes. Sales contests work best when tied to measurable and achievable sales objectives (such as finding new accounts, reviving old accounts, or increasing account profitability) and when employees believe they have an equal chance. Otherwise, employees who do not think the contest's goals are reasonable or equitable will not take the challenge.[29]

Developing the Sales Promotion Program

The marketer must make some other decisions in order to define the full sales promotion program. First, the marketer must determine the *size of the incentive*. A certain minimum incentive is necessary if the promotion is to succeed. A larger incentive will produce more sales response. Some of the large firms who sell consumer package goods have a sales promotion manager who studies past promotions and recommends incentive levels to brand managers.

The marketer must also set *conditions for participation*. Incentives might be offered to everyone or only to select groups. A premium might be offered only to those who turn in boxtops. Sweepstakes might not be offered in certain states, or to families of company personnel, or to persons under a certain age.

The marketer must then decide how to *promote and distribute the promotion* program itself. A fifty cents-off coupon could be given out in a package, at the store, by mail, or in an advertisement. Each distribution method involves a different level of reach and cost. The *length of the promotion* is also important. If the sales promotion period is too short, many prospects (who may not be buying during that time) will miss it. If the promotion runs too long, the deal will lose some of its "act now" force. Brand managers need to set calendar dates for the promotions. The dates will be used by production, sales, and distribution. Some unplanned promotions may also be needed, requiring cooperation on short notice.

Finally, the marketer must determine the *sales promotion budget*. It can be developed in two ways. The marketer can choose the promotions and estimate their total cost. However, the more common way is to use a percentage of the total budget for sales promotion. One study found three major problems in how companies budget for sales promotion. First, they do not consider cost effectiveness. Second, instead of spending to achieve objectives, they simply extend the previous year's spending, take a percentage of expected sales, or use the "affordable approach." Finally, advertising and sales promotion budgets are too often prepared separately.[30]

Pretesting and Implementing

Whenever possible, sales promotion tools should be *pretested* to find out if they are appropriate and of the right incentive size. Yet few promotions are ever tested ahead of time—70 percent of companies do not test sales promotions before starting them.[31] Nevertheless, consumer sales promotions can be quickly and inexpensively pretested. For example, consumers can be asked to rate or rank different possible promotions or promotions can be tried on a limited basis in selected geographic areas.

Companies should prepare implementation plans for each promotion, covering lead time and sell-off time. *Lead time* is the time necessary to prepare the program before launching it. *Sell-off* time begins with the launch and ends when the promotion ends.

Evaluating the Results

Evaluation is also very important. Yet many companies fail to evaluate their sales promotion programs and other evaluate them only superficially. Manufacturers can use one of many evaluation methods. The most common method is to compare sales before, during, and after a promotion. Suppose a company has a 6 percent market share before the promotion, which jumps to 10 percent during the promotion, falls to 5 percent right after, and rises to 7 percent later on. The promotion seems to have attracted new tryers and more buying from current customers. After the promotion, sales fell as consumers used up their inventories. The long-run rise to 7 percent means that the company gained some new users. If the brand's share returned to the old level, then the promotion had changed only the *timing* of demand rather than the *total* demand.

Consumer research would show the kinds of people who responded to the promotion and what they did after it. *Surveys* can provide information on how many consumers recall the promotion, what they thought of it, how many took advantage of it, and how it affected their buying. Sales promotions can also be evaluated through *experiments* that vary such factors as incentive value, length, and distribution method.

Clearly, sales promotion plays an important role in the total promotion mix. To use it well, the marketer must define the sales promotion objectives, select the best tools, design the sales promotion program, pretest and implement it, and evaluate the results. Marketing Highlight 17–5 describes some award-winning sales promotion campaigns.

PUBLIC RELATIONS

Another major mass promotion tool is **public relations**—building good relations with the company's various publics by obtaining favorable publicity, building up a good "corporate image," and handling or heading off unfavorable rumors, stories, and events.

AWARD-WINNING SALES PROMOTIONS

Each year American companies bombard consumers with thousands upon thousands of assorted sales promotions. Some fizzle badly, never meeting their objectives; other yield blockbuster returns. Here are examples of some award-winning sales promotions.

Quaker's "Where's the Cap'n" Contest

In this contest for kids, Quaker removed the likeness of Cap'n Crunch from the front of its cereal boxes and offered cash rewards totaling a million dollars to children who could find him. Clues to the Cap'n's whereabouts were provided inside the box, along with a free detective kit. Quaker supported the contest with large amounts of advertising during children's network television programming and in children's magazines. Coupons offering discounts on boxes of Cap'n Crunch cereal were distributed to parents. The promotion's objective: to turn around the brand's declining sales and market share. It accomplished this objective—and more. The contest became a major media event. Although it cost Quaker $18 million, brand awareness rose quickly, and Cap'n Crunch sales increased by a dramatic 50 percent!

9-Lives "Free Health Exam for Your Cat" Offer

In this unusual premium promotion, Star-Kist Foods teamed with the American Animal Hospital Association to offer cat owners a free $15 cat physical in exchange for proofs of purchase from 9-Lives cat food products. The 1,500 AAHA members donated their services to get cat owners into the habit of regular pet checkups. Star-Kist supported the premium offer with 63 million coupons and trade discounts to boost retailer support. The promotion cost about $600,000 (excluding media). Consumers redeemed coupons at a rate 40 percent higher than normal, and Star-Kist gave out more than 50,000 free exam certificates. During the promotion, 9-Lives canned products achieved their highest share of the market in two years.

The "Red Baron Fly-In" Promotion

Red Baron Pizza Service used an imaginative combination of special events, couponing, and charitable activities to boost sales of its frozen pizza. The company re-created World War I flying ace Baron Manfred von Richtofen—complete with traditional flying gear and open-cockpit Stearman biplanes—as its company spokesperson. Red Baron pilots barnstormed 13 markets, showed the plane, performed stunts, gave out coupons, and invited consumers to "come fly with the Red Baron." The company donated $500 to a local youth organization in each market and urged consumers to match the gift. Trade promotions and local tie-in promotions boosted retailer support. The total budget: about $1 million. The results: For the four-week period during and after the fly-ins, unit sales in the 13 markets jumped an average of 100 percent. In the 90 days following the fly-in, sales in some markets increased as much as 400 percent.

Georgia-Pacific's "World's Fastest Roofer" Contest

Georgia-Pacific developed this creative business promotion to acquaint its roofing contractor target market with the full range of G-P's products and to celebrate the industry's "unsung heroes"—roofers. Most important, the contest would give roofers hands-on experience with Summit, a new high-quality shingle whose key feature was its ease of installation. Contestants installed 100 square feet of shingles. Judges chose the winner based on a combination of roofing speed and job quality. First prize was an all-expenses-paid trip to Hawaii for two. The contest began with eight regional eliminations held at G-P distribution centers around the country. Months in advance, each distribution center promoted the contest to area roofers using direct mail promotional materials furnished by the G-P public relations department. In all, more than 150 roofers competed in the local contests. The eight regional winners were flown to Atlanta to compete in the national contest, timed to coincide with National Roofing Week. Tic-ins with a home-oriented Atlanta radio station resulted in widespread on-air promotion and raised several thousand dollars for an Atlanta children's hospital. The mayor of Atlanta issued a proclamation recognizing roofers, National Roofing Week, and Georgia-Pacific. Caps, T-shirts, and posters were used to merchandise the event both locally and nationally. After the contest, G-P sent a print and video media kit to key national media, Atlanta media, and media in the home towns of contest participants. The budget: only $50,000 to $75,000. The results: the promotion generated more than 2.5 million media impressions and increased sales in Georgia-Pacific's targeted markets by 90 percent.

Sources: See William A. Robinson, "The Best Promotions of 1983," *Advertising Age,* May 31, 1984, pp. 10–12; Robinson, "1985 Best Promotions of the Year," *Advertising Age,* May 5, 1986, pp. S10–11; and Robinson, "Event Marketing at the Crossroads," *Promote,* November 14, 1988, pp. P.11–P.23. For other examples, see Alison Fahey, "CBS, K mart lead Reggie Winners," *Advertising Age,* March 19, 1990, p. 47.

The old name for marketing public relations was **publicity**, which was seen simply as activities to promote a company or its products by planting news about it in media not paid for by the sponsor. Public relations is a much broader concept that includes publicity and many other activities. Public relations departments use many different tools:

- *Press relations*: Placing newsworthy information into the news media to attract attention to a person, product, or service.
- *Product publicity*: Publicizing specific products.
- *Corporate communications*: Creating internal and external communications to promote understanding of the firm or institution.
- *Lobbying*: Dealing with legislators and government officials to promote or defeat legislation and regulation.

• *Counseling*: Advising management about public issues and company positions and image.[32]

Public relations is used to promote products, people, places, ideas, activities, organizations, and even nations. Trade associations have used public relations to rebuild interest in declining commodities such as eggs, apples, milk, and potatoes. New York City's image turned around when its "I Love New York" compaign took root, bringing millions more tourists to the city. Johnson & Johnson's masterly use of public relations played a major role in saving Tylenol from extinction after its product tampering scare. Lee Iaccoca's speeches and autobiography helped create a new winning image for Chrysler. Nations have used public relations to attract more tourists, foreign investment, and international support.

Public relations can have a strong impact on public awareness at a much lower cost than advertising. The company does not pay for the space or time in the media. It pays for a staff to develop and circulate information and manage events. If the company develops an interesting story, it could be picked up by several different media, having the same effect as advertising that would cost millions of dollars. And it would have more credibility than advertising. Public relations results can sometimes be spectacular. Consider the case of Cabbage Patch dolls:

> Public relations played a major role in making Coleco's Cabbage Patch dolls an overnight sensation. The dolls were formally introduced at a Boston press conference where local school children performed a mass adoption ceremony for the press. Thanks to Coleco's public relations machine, child psychologists publicly endorsed the Cabbage Patch Kids, and Dr. Joyce Brothers and other newspaper columnists proclaimed that the Kids were healthy playthings. Major women's magazines featured the dolls as ideal Christmas gifts, and after a five minute feature on the "Today" show, the Kids made the complete talk-show circuit. Marketers of other products used the hard-to-get Cabbage Patch dolls as premiums, and retailers used them to lure customers into their stores. The word spread, and every child just *had* to have one. The dolls were quickly sold out, and the great "Cabbage Patch Panic" began.

Despite its potential strengths, public relations is often described as a marketing stepchild because of its limited and scattered use. The public relations department is usually located at corporate headquarters. Its staff is so busy dealing with various publics—

The great "Cabbage Patch Panic."

stockholders, employees, legislators, city officials—that public relations programs in support of product marketing objectives may be ignored. And marketing managers and public relations practitioners do not always talk the same language. Many public relations practitioners see their job as simply communicating. Marketing managers, on the other hand, tend to be much more interested in how advertising and public relations affect sales and profits.

However, this situation is changing. Many companies now want their public relations departments to manage all of their activities with a view toward marketing the company and improving the bottom line. Some companies are setting up special units called *marketing public relations* to support corporate and product promotion and image making directly. Many companies hire marketing public relations firms to handle their PR programs or to assist the company public relation team. In a recent survey of marketing managers, three-fourths reported that their companies use marketing public relations. They found it particularly effective in building brand awareness and knowledge for both new and established products. In several cases, it proved more cost-effective than advertising.[33]

Major Public Relations Tools

Public relations professionals use several tools. One of the major tools is *news*. PR professionals find or create favorable news about the company and its products or people. Sometimes news stories occur naturally, and sometimes the PR person can suggest events or activities that would create news. *Speeches* can also create product and company publicity. Lee Iaccoca's charismatic talks to large audiences helped to sell Chrysler cars to consumers and stock to investors. Increasingly, company executives must field questions from the media or give talks at trade associations or sales meetings, and these events can build or hurt the company's image. Another common PR tool is *special events*, ranging from news conferences, press tours, grand openings, and fireworks displays to laser shows, hot-air balloon releases, multimedia presentations, and star-studded spectaculars that will reach and interest target publics.

Public relations people also prepare *written materials* to reach and influence their target markets. These materials include annual reports, brochures, articles, and company newsletters and magazines. *Audio-visual materials* such as films, slide-and-sound programs, and video and audio cassettes are increasingly being used as communication tools. *Corporate identity materials* can also help to create a corporate identity that the public immediately recognizes. Logos, stationery, brochures, signs, business forms, business cards, buildings, uniforms, and company cars and trucks—all become marketing tools when they are attractive, distinctive, and memorable.

Companies can also improve public goodwill by contributing money and time to *public service activities*. For example, Procter & Gamble and Publishers' Clearing House held a joint promotion to aid the Special Olympics. The Publishers' Clearing House mailing included product coupons, and Procter & Gamble donated ten cents per redeemed coupon to the Special Olympics. Another example is B. Dalton Booksellers' earmarking $3 million during a four-year period for the fight against illiteracy.[34]

Major Public Relations Decisions

In considering when and how to use product public relations, management should set PR objectives, choose the PR messages and vehicles, implement the PR plan, and evaluate the results.

Setting Public Relations Objectives

The first task is to set *objectives* for public relations. Some years ago, the Wine Growers of California hired a public relations firm to develop a program to support two major marketing objectives: to convince Americans that wine drinking is a pleasant part of good living and to improve the image and market share of California wines among all wines. The following public relations objectives were set: develop magazine stories about wine and get them placed in top magazines (such as *Time* and *House Beautiful*) and in newspapers (food columns and feature sections); develop stories about the many health values of wine and direct them to the medical profession; and develop specific publicity for the young adult market, the college market, governmental bodies, and

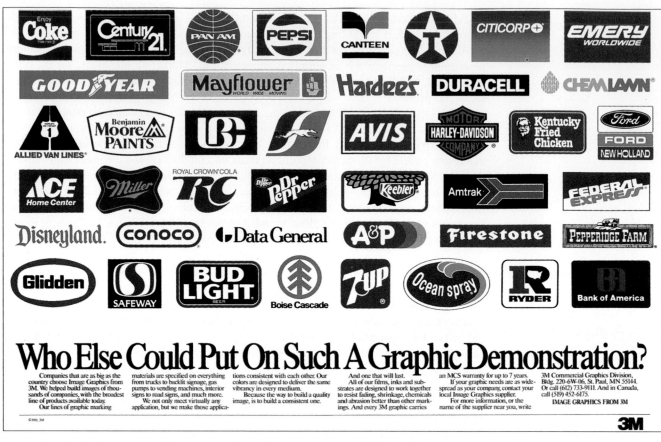

Attractive, distinctive, memorable company logos become strong marketing tools.

various ethnic communities. These objectives were turned into specific goals so that final results could be evaluated.

Choosing Public Relations Messages and Vehicles

The organization next finds interesting stories to tell about the product. Suppose a little-known college wants more public recognition. It will search for possible stories. Do any faculty members have unusual backgrounds, or are any working on unusual projects? Are any interesting new courses being taught or any interesting events taking place on campus? Usually, this search will uncover hundreds of stories that can be fed to the press. The chosen stories should reflect the image sought by this college.

If there are not enough stories, the college could sponsor newsworthy events. In this manner, the organization creates news rather than finds it. Ideas might include hosting major academic conventions, inviting well-known speakers, and holding news conferences. Each event creates many stories for many different audiences.

Event creation is especially important in publicizing fundraising drives for nonprofit organizations. Fundraisers have developed a large set of special events such as art exhibits, auctions, benefit evenings, book sales, contests, dances, dinners, fairs, fashion shows, phonothons, rummage sales, tours, and walkathons. No sooner is one type of event created, such as a walkathon, then competitors create new versions, such as readathons, bikeathons, and jogathons.

Implementing the Public Relations Plan

Implementing public relations requires care. Take the matter of placing stories in the media. A *great* story is easy to place—but most stories are not great and may not get past busy editors. Therefore, one of the main assets of public relations people is their personal relationships with media editors. In fact, PR professionals are often former journalists who know many media editors and know what they want. They view media editors as a market to be satisfied so that editors will continue to use their stories.

Evaluating Public Relations Results

Public relations results are difficult to measure because PR is used with other promotion tools and its impact is often indirect. If PR is used before other tools come into play, its contribution is easier to evalute.

The easiest measure of publicity effectiveness is the number of exposures in the media. Public relations people give the client a ''clippings book'' showing all the media that carried news about the product and a summary such as the following:

> Media coverage included 3,500 column inches of news and photographs in 350 publications with a combined circulation of 79.4 million; 2,500 minutes of air time on 290 radio stations and an estimated audience of 65 million; and 660 minutes of air time on 160 television stations with an estimated audience of 91 million. If this time and space had been purchased at advertising rates, it would have amounted to $1,047,000.[35]

However, this exposure measure is not very satisfying. It does not tell how many people actually read or heard the message, nor what they thought afterward. In addition, because the media overlap in readership and viewership, it does not give information on the *net* audience reached.

A better measure is the change in product awareness, knowledge, and attitude resulting from the publicity campaign. Assessing the change requires measuring the before-and-after levels of these measures. The Potato Board learned, for example, that the number of people who agreed with the statement ''Potatoes are rich in vitamins and minerals'' went from 36 percent before its public relations campaign to 67 percent after the campaign. That change represented a large increase in product knowledge.

Sales and profit impact, if obtainable, is the best measure of public relations effort. For example, 9-Lives sales increased 43 percent at the end of a major ''Morris the Cat'' publicity campaign. However, advertising and sales promotion had also been stepped up, and their contribution has to be considered.

■ SUMMARY

Three major tools of mass-promotion are advertising, sales promotion, and public relations. They are mass-marketing tools as opposed to personal selling, which targets specific buyers.

Advertising—the use of paid media by a seller to inform, persuade, and remind about its products or organization—is a strong promotion tool. American marketers spend more than $125 billion each year on advertising, and it takes many forms and has many uses. *Advertising decision making* is a five-step process consisting of setting objectives, budget decision, message decision, media decision, and evaluation. Advertisers should set clear *objectives* as to whether the advertising is supposed to inform, persuade, or remind buyers. The advertising *budget* can be based on what is affordable, a percentage of sales, competitors' spending, or objectives and tasks. The *message decision* calls for designing messages, evaluating them, and executing them effectively. The *media decision* calls for defining reach, frequency, and impact goals; choosing major media types; select-

ing media vehicles; and scheduling the media. Finally, *evaluation* calls for evaluating the communication and sales effects of advertising before, during, and after the advertising is placed.

Sales promotion covers a wide variety of short-term incentive tools—coupons, premiums, contests, buying allowances—designed to stimulate consumers, the trade, and the company's own salesforce. Sales promotion spending has been growing faster than advertising spending in recent years. Sales promotion calls for setting sales promotion objectives; selecting tools; developing, pretesting, and implementing the sales promotion program; and evaluating results.

Public-relations—which involves gaining favorable publicity and creating a favorable company image—is the least used of the major promotion tools, although it has great potential for building awareness and preference. Public relations involves setting PR objectives; choosing PR messages and vehicles; implementing the PR plan; and evaluating PR results.

■ QUESTIONS FOR DISCUSSION

1. Is it feasible for an advertising agency to work for two competing clients at the same time? How much competition

between accounts handled by an agency is ''too much'' competition?

2. According to advertising expert Steuart Henderson Britt, good advertising objectives explain in detail the intended audience, the advertising message, the desired effects, and the criteria for determining effectiveness (for example, not just "increase awareness," but "increase awareness 20 percent"). Why should these components be part of the advertising objective? What are some effects, or tasks, an advertiser might want a campaign to achieve?

3. What are some benefits and drawbacks of comparison advertising? Which has more to gain from using comparison advertising, the leading brand in a market or a lesser brand? Why?

4. Surveys show that many Americans are skeptical of advertising claims. Do you mistrust advertising? Discuss the reasons for this. What should advertisers do to increase credibility?

5. Manufacturers distribute coupons nearly every week in some product categories such as coffee, breakfast cereal, and snack foods. Does this affect brand loyalty? In what ways?

6. What factors call for more *frequency* in an advertising media schedule? What factors call for more *reach*? How can you increase one without sacrificing the other or increasing the advertising budget?

7. An ad states that Almost Home cookies are the "moistest, chewiest, most perfectly baked cookies the world has ever tasted" except for homemade cookies. If you think some other brand of cookies is moister or chewier, is the Almost Home claim false? Should this type of claim be regulated?

8. Which forms of sales promotion are most effective in getting consumers to try a product? Which are most effective in building loyalty to a product?

9. Why are many companies spending more on trade promotions and consumer promotions than on advertising? Is heavy spending on sales promotion a good strategy for long-term profits?

10. Companies often run advertising, sales promotion, and public relations efforts at the same time. Can their effects be separated? Discuss how a company might evaluate the effectiveness of each element in this mix.

11. Describe several ads that you think are particularly effective and compare them with other ads that you think are ineffective. How would you improve the less effective ads?

■ KEY TERMS

Advertising. Any paid form of nonpersonal presentation and promotion of ideas, goods, or services by an identified sponsor.

Advertising objective. A specific communication *task* to be accomplished with a specific *target* audience during a specific period of *time*.

Advertising specialties. Useful articles imprinted with an advertiser's name given as gifts to consumers.

Allowance. Promotional money paid by manufacturers to retailers in return for an agreement to feature the manufacturer's products in some way.

Cash refund offers (rebates). Offers to refund part of the purchase price of a product after the purchase to consumers who send a "proof of purchase" to the manufacturer.

Comparison advertising. Advertising that compares one brand directly or indirectly to one or more other brands.

Consumer franchise building promotions. Sales promotions that promote the product's positioning and include a selling message along with the deal.

Consumer promotion. Sales promotion designed to stimulate consumer purchasing, including samples, coupons, rebates, prices-off, premiums, patronage rewards, displays, and contests and sweepstakes.

Contests, sweepstakes, and **games.** Promotional events that give consumers the chance to win something—such as cash, trips, or goods—by luck or through extra effort.

Continuity. Scheduling ads evenly within a given period.

Copy testing. Measuring the communication effect of an advertisement before or after it is printed or broadcast.

Coupons. Certificates that give buyers a saving when they purchase a product.

Discount. A straight reduction in price on purchases during a stated period of time.

Frequency. The number of times the average person in the target market is exposed to an advertising message during a given period.

Media impact. The qualitative value of an exposure through a given medium.

Informative advertising. Advertising used to inform consumers about a new product or feature and to build primary demand.

Media vehicles. Specific media within each general media type, such as specific magazines, television shows, or radio programs.

Patronage rewards. Cash or other awards for the regular use of a certain company's products or services.

Persuasive advertising. Advertising used to build selective demand for a brand by persuading consumers that it offers the best quality for their money.

Point-of-purchase promotions (POP). Displays and demonstrations that take place at the point of purchase or sale.

Premiums. Goods offered either free or at low cost as an incentive to buy a product.

Price packs (cents-off deals). Reduced prices that are marked by the producer directly on label or package.

Public relations. Building good relations with the company's various publics by obtaining favorable publicity, building up a good "corporate image," and handling or heading off unfavorable rumors, stories, and events. Major PR tools include press relations, product publicity, corporate communications, lobbying, and counseling.

Publicity. Activities to promote a company or its products by planting news about it in media not paid for by the sponsor.

Pulsing. Scheduling ads unevenly in bursts during a time period.

Reach. The percentage of people in the target market exposed to an ad campaign during a given period.

Reminder advertising. Advertising used to keep consumers thinking about a product.

Sales promotion. Short-term incentives to encourage purchase or sales of a product or service.

Salesforce promotion. Sales promotion designed to motivate the salesforce and make salesforce selling efforts more effective, including bonuses, contests, and sales rallies.

Samples. Offers of a trial amount of a product to consumers.

Trade promotion. Sales promotion designed to gain reseller support and to improve reseller selling efforts, including discounts, allowances, free goods, cooperative advertising, push money, and conventions and trade shows.

■ REFERENCES

1. See "Advertising Age Best Advertising of 1989: Pink Bunny Romps Through 'Best' TV Spot," *Advertising Age*, April 30, 1990, p. 29; "Creatives Charge Up Bunny Ideas," *Advertising Age*, November 27, 1989, pp. 3, 114; Julie Liesse Erickson, "Ralston Lesson: Batteries Aren't Groceries," *Advertising Age*, November 27, 1989; and Vera Vaughan, "That Cute Pink Bunny," *Business Today*, Winter 1990, p. 78.

2. Statistical information in this section on advertising's size and composition draws on the September 27, 1989 special issue of *Advertising Age* on the hundred leading national advertisers. Also see Robert J. Coen, "Tough Times for Ad Spending," *Advertising Age*, May 14, 1990, pp. 12, 59.

3. Russell H. Colley, *Defining Advertising Goals for Measured Advertising Results* (New York: Association for National Advertisers, 1961). For a more complete discussion of DAG-MAR, see Michael L. Rothschild, *Advertising* (Lexington, Mass.: D. C. Heath, 1987), pp. 142–55.

4. See Donald E. Schultz, Dennis Martin, and William P. Brown, *Strategic Advertising Campaigns* (Chicago: Crain Books, 1984), pp. 192–97.

5. See Scott Hume, "Anheuser Beer Arrives without Ads," *Advertising Age*, July 6, 1987, p. 2.

6. For example, see David A. Aaker and James Carman, "Are You Overspending?" *Journal of Advertising Research*, August/September 1982, pp. 57–70.

7. Gerald J. Tellis, "Advertising Exposure, Loyalty, and Brand Purchase: A Two-Stage Model of Choice," *Journal of Marketing Research*, May 1988, pp. 134–35.

8. See Bickley Townsend, "The Media Jungle," *American Demographics*, December 1988, p. 8.

9. Christine Dugas, "And Now, A Wittier Word from Our Sponsors," *Business Week*, March 24, 1986, p. 90. Also see Felix Kessler, "In Search of Zap-Proof Commercials," *Fortune*, January 21, 1985, pp. 68–70; and Dennis Kneale, " 'Zapping' of TV Ads Appears Pervasive," *The Wall Street Journal*, April 25, 1988, p. 29.

10. See "Ad Quality Good, Believability Low," *Advertising Age*, May 31, 1984, p. 3.

11. See William A. Mindak and H. Malcolm Bybee, "Marketing's Application to Fund Raising," *Journal of Marketing*, July 1971, pp. 13–18.

12. Janet Meyers and Laurie Freeman, "Marketers Police TV Commercial Costs, *Advertising Age*, April 3, 1989, p. 51.

13. See Roland T. Rust, *Advertising Media Models: A Practical Guide* (Lexington, MA: Lexington Books, 1986).

14. Philip H. Dougherty, "Bud 'Pulses' the Market," *New York Times*, February 18, 1975, p. 40.

15. See Robert D. Buzzell, "E. I. Du Pont de Nemours & Co.: Measurement of Effects of Advertising," in his *Mathematical Models and Marketing Management* (Boston: Division of Research, Graduate School of Business Administration, Harvard University, 1964), pp. 157–79.

16. For more on the legal aspects of advertising and sales promotion, see Louis W. Stern and Thomas L. Eovaldi, *Legal Aspects of Marketing Strategy* (Englewood Cliffs, NJ: Prentice Hall, 1984), Chaps. 7 and 8.

17. From Robert C. Blattberg and Scott A. Neslin, *Sales Promotion: Concepts, Methods, and Strategies* (Englewood Cliffs, NJ: Prentice Hall, 1990). This text provides an excellent summary of sales promotion concepts and strategies.

18. Alison Fahey, "Shops See Surge in Promotion Revenues," *Advertising Age*, February 20, 1989, p. 20.

19. For a good summary of the research on whether promotion erodes consumer preference and loyalty for leading brands, see Blattberg and Neslin, *Sales Promotion: Concepts, Methods, and Strategies*, pp. 471–75.

20. See F. Kent Mitchel, "Advertising/Promotion Budgets: How Did We Get Here, and What Do We Do Now?" *The Journal of Consumer Marketing*, Fall 1985, pp. 405–47.

21. See Paul W. Farris and John A. Quelch, "In Defense of Price Promotion," *Sloan Management Review*, Fall 1987.

22. See Roger Strang, Robert M. Prentice, and Alden G. Clayton, *The Relationship between Advertising and Promotion in Brand Strategy* (Cambridge, MA: Marketing Science Institute, 1975), chap. 5; and P. Rajan Varadarajan, "Cooperative Sales Promotion: An Idea Whose Time Has Come," *Journal of Consumer Marketing*, Winter 1986, pp. 15–33.

23. See "Coupons," *Progressive Grocer 1987 Nielsen Review*, September 1987 pp. 16–18; Alison Fahey, "Red Letter Cut from Coupon War," *Advertising Age*, April 3, 1989, p. 38; and Scott Hume, "Coupons Go In-Store," *Advertising Age*, May 21, 1990, p. 45.

24. See Jan Larson, "Farewell to Coupons?" *American Demographics*, February 1990, pp. 14–18.

25. See J. Thomas Russell and Ronald Lane, *Kleppner's Advertising Procedure*, 11th ed. (Englewood Cliffs, NJ: Prentice Hall, 1990), pp. 383–86; and "Power to the Key Ring and T-Shirt," *Sales & Marketing Management*, December 1989, p. 14.

26. See Tammi Wright, "Frequent Flier Programs Spawn Host of Imitators, *Marketing News*, May 8, 1989, pp. 2, 8.

27. See Felix Kessler, "The Costly Coupon Craze," *Fortune*, June 9, 1986, p. 83.

28. See Thomas V. Bonoma, "Get More Out of Your Trade Shows," *Harvard Business Review*, January–February 1983, pp. 75–83; and Jonathan M. Cox, Ian K. Sequeira, and Alissa Eckstein, "1988 Trade Show Trends: Shows Grow in Size; Audience Quality Remains High," *Business Marketing*, June 1989, pp. 57–60.

29. For more on sales contests, see C. Robert Patty and Robert Hite, *Managing Sales People*, 3d ed. (Englewood Cliffs, NJ: Prentice Hall, 1988), pp. 313–27.

30. Roger A. Strang, "Sales Promotion—Fast Growth, Faulty Management," *Harvard Business Review*, July–August 1976, p. 119.

31. "Pretesting Phase of Promotions Is Often Overlooked," *Marketing News*, February 29, 1988, p. 10.

32. Adapted from Scott M. Cutlip, Allen H. Center, and Glen M. Brown, *Effective Public Relations*, 6th ed. (Englewood Cliffs, NJ: Prentice Hall, 1985), pp. 7–17.

33. Tom Duncan, *A Study of How Manufacturers and Service Companies Perceive and Use Marketing Public Relations* (Muncie, Ind.: Ball State University, December, 1985).

34. For more examples, see Laurie Freeman and Wayne Walley, "Marketing with a Cause Takes Hold," *Advertising Age*, May 16, 1988, p. 34; and P. Rajan Varadarajan and Anil Menon, "Cause-Related Marketing: A Coalignment of Mar-

keting Strategy and Corporate Philanthropy, *Journal of Marketing*, July 1988, pp. 58–74.

35. Arthur M. Merims, "Marketing's Stepchild: Product Publicity," *Harvard Business Review*, November–December 1972, pp. 111–12. Also see Katharine D. Paine, "There *Is* a Method for Measuring PR," *Marketing News*, November 6, 1987, p. 5.

PILLSBURY CO.: THE "BIG CHEESE" IN THE PIZZA WARS

For generations of American consumers, the Pillsbury Doughboy has been a cute and cuddly symbol of outstanding food products. But to competitors, confronted with Pillsbury's increasingly aggressive marketing stance, the Doughboy must seem more like the monstrous marshmallow creature from *Ghostbusters*. Nearing its 120th birthday, Pillsbury has lessened its dependence on baking products and increased its emphasis on ready-to-eat convenience products. One such product is frozen pizza. Pillsbury first introduced microwavable frozen pizza under its own brand name and then acquired several large competitors, including Totino's in 1975 and Jeno's in 1985. With more than 50 percent of the market, it was certainly the "Big Cheese" of frozen pizza. However, bringing the Pillsbury, Totino's, and Jeno's brands under a single corporate umbrella has been challenging, and Pillsbury's pizza sales have recently sagged: In effect, Pillsbury has been marketing against itself. Future success will depend on the company's ability both to position its various brands relative to one another and to communicate these positions to consumers.

Frozen pizza accounts for more than $1 billion in sales annually. However, the market is growing rather slowly—at only about 1.5 percent per year. Thus, the industry has become fiercely competitive. In the battle for market share, large national competitors must increase sales by attracting buyers from each other, from small regional processors, and even from local pizzerias. Regional competitors, fighting for their existence, are increasingly cutting prices, and other heavyweights are entering the frozen pizza field. For example, Kraft acquired its first pizza brand, Tombstone Pizza, in 1986.

Lifestyle changes also continue to influence the industry. Americans eat one billion tons of pizza annually—nearly 22.5 pounds per person. Ninety-six percent of all U.S. households now eat pizza about 30 times yearly. Although frozen pizza represents only about 30 percent of all pizza purchases, consumers eat over 70 percent of all pizza, including pizzeria pizza, at home.

Moreover, regional pizza tastes vary widely, and such variety makes it difficult for national brands to customize—a fact that makes it easier for small regional brands to survive. Regional taste differences also explain why, until recently, the frozen pizza industry was highly fragmented—that is, why there were no particularly strong national brands. At this time, the market has segmented into two distinct niches: popularly-priced and premium. The popularly-priced segment showed no growth from 1983 to 1988. The premium segment, on the other hand, grew 13 percent during the same period.

Advertising and sales-promotion trends have further influenced the competitive environment. Advertising expenditures for the industry amount to 2 percent of sales—among the lowest for food products of any kind. On the other hand, frozen pizza marketers spend a considerable amount of money at the retail level in the form of display allowances, advertising allowances, and deals to the trade. They also offer numerous consumer incentives, usually promotional price specials and coupons. Almost one-third of all frozen pizza sold uses some sort of price reduction to woo consumers. Hardly a week goes by without some special promotion for various items in the frozen pizza case.

Naturally, retailers prefer profit-producing brands. With limited freezer cabinet space, they favor sellers who spend the most on advertising and promotion, especially trade allowances, which improve profitability directly. On the other hand, Pillsbury and other manufacturers recognize that such allowances and most other types of sales promotion only stimulate *short-term* sales and build little long-term consumer loyalty. Nevertheless, some competitors, especially marginal manufacturers, prefer to spend to spur immediate sales.

As if heated competition within their own ranks weren't enough of a headache, frozen pizza marketers continue to face stiff challenges on a number of other fronts. Most formidable, perhaps, is the continued growth of home-delivery services, which expanded at a 20-percent rate for the second year in a row. Also disturbing is the fact that the consumption of "fresh" or "deli" pizzas—those made and baked at a growing number of supermarkets—soared 47 percent from 1986 to 1987. Meanwhile, 40 percent of all U.S. supermarkets now offer fresh pizza. And much of the movement to fresh pizza has been prompted by consumers' perceptions of a decline in the quality of frozen pizzas.

To understand Pillsbury's standing in the intensely competitive frozen pizza market, one need only trace its recent pattern of acquisitions. In 1975, Pillsbury acquired Totino's, a frozen pizza company with an annual sales-growth rate of 20 percent. Within two years, Pillsbury had developed Totino's revolutionary crisp-crust technology, and the company put into action an aggressive marketing plan that made it the leader in frozen pizzas. The key aspects of the plan were product improvement, aggressive promotion, and coverage of both the high- and popularly-priced market segments. Within three years, despite both new competitive entries sponsored by General Mills (Saluto), H.J. Heinz (La Pizzeria), Nestlé (Stouffer's), and Quaker Oats (Celeste) and more vigorous competition from more than 100 smaller regional firms, Totino's was the leading brand of frozen pizza in the United States.

In 1984, Pillsbury introduced a frozen pizza designed exclusively for microwave ovens. This product was introduced under the Pillsbury Microwave brand name, which includes other microwavable products such as pancakes and popcorn. The new Pillsbury Microwave Pizza represented a major breakthrough in microwave technology. Because microwaves are, in effect, steamers, they usually turn bread soggy. But through a patented process called "susceptor technology," Pillsbury achieved the long-sought crisp crust. Basically, the pizza is packed in an aluminum foil tray that provides heat while preventing microwave electrons from penetrating to the product itself. In essence, the package becomes its own disposable oven. Pillsbury used the same technology to create another line of frozen pizza—Pillsbury's French Bread Pizza.

Meanwhile, Jeno's, the former leader in the frozen pizza market, sought to regain leadership by introducing its own "Crisp and Tasty Crust" pizza. But Jeno's lagged Totino's by two years in product and packaging innovations. Thus, by the early 1980s, although it had increased its market share by acquiring Chef Saluto from General Mills and two regional brands, John's and Gino's, Jeno's still remained in second place.

Pillsbury then acquired archrival Jeno's in 1985. This acquisition added important market depth to Pillsbury's pizza business and provided opportunities for brand differentiation, product-quality improvements, and operating efficiencies. With such brands as Totino's, Jeno's, Pillsbury Microwave, My Classic, Mr. P's, Fox DeLuxe, and Chef Saluto, pizza became one of the highest volume products in Pillsbury's Consumer Foods portfolio.

Although linking Jeno's with Totino's obviously made Pillsbury a powerful force in the frozen pizza industry, it also caused problems for the company. How do you market one-time competing brands to retailers who are concerned that the absence of competition between the two will make wheeling and dealing for sales-promotion dollars more difficult? Gone, it would seem, were the days when Totino's and Jeno's, each looking for a competitive edge, bashed each other with discounts and deals to retailers. Retailers wanted to know what this situation meant for them in the long run.

One thing seemed certain: Pillsbury wanted to position its two major pizza brands so that one complemented the other. Thus, it made a number of product and pricing changes to reposition Totino's as a premium brand while retaining its popular-price position for Jeno's. Pillsbury reformulated Jeno's Crisp 'n Tasty brand—the number-two national frozen pizza line—so that it boasted a better-tasting crust and improved sauce. As for Totino's, what had been Totino's Party Pizza line in 1987—often on sale for 89 cents or even less—became Totino's Temptin' Toppings Pizza. To justify a price boost, Pillsbury reformulated the line to provide 35 percent more toppings, bigger pieces of meat, and a thicker sauce with more tomato flavor. Next, the company expanded Totino's Microwave Pizza line by adding a new full-sized (11.9-ounce to 14-ounce) product in five flavors, featuring "50 percent more pizza by weight than most other microwave pizzas." Finally, Pillsbury rolled out the premium, family-sized Totino's Pan Pizza, with nearly one pound of toppings, a thick and chewy crust, and its own bake-and-serve pan that has an authentic pizzeria look. The line included four types of pizza available at a hefty $4.79–$5.19 each—still less than most family-sized pizzeria versions. With this product—and ads claiming "Pizza worth coming home to"—Pillsbury openly challenged eat-in and take-out pizzerias, where pan pizza had proved far more than a flash in the pan.

Nevertheless, the new positioning strategy for its long line of frozen pizza brands failed to take hold: Pillsbury was unable to convince retailers and consumers that Totino's and Jeno's were unmistakably different—and thus damaged both. Surprisingly, the company's frozen pizza sales declined 7 percent in unit sales from 1987 to 1988. In view of the new competitive situation and changing consumer lifestyles, Pillsbury's management must now reconsider its marketing objectives and activities, especially with regard to advertising and promotion.

QUESTIONS

1. Describe the consumer's buying-decision process for frozen pizza.
2. Describe the factors that influence a retailer's decision about which frozen pizza brands to stock and support.
3. What are the advantages and disadvantages of each type of promotional tool (advertising, consumer promotion, and trade promotion)? What role should each play in promoting Pillsbury's frozen pizza brands?

SKIN SO SOFT

Is Skin So Soft a bath oil or an insect repellent? Avon, the makers of Skin So Soft (SSS), insists it is a bath oil. But while the company appreciates the revenue from sales to sports enthusiasts, pet owners, outdoorsmen, and even the military, Avon knows that those customers are purchasing Skin So Soft for a reason other than to smell nice. It seems that the product, when mixed with equal parts of water and applied to the skin, is an effective insect repellent.

Avon officials claim to be baffled about why mosquitoes, fleas, and other bugs don't like their product. Scientists say there is no ingredient in SSS that should make it act like a repellent, but speculate that the fragrance, a proven people pleaser, is offensive to the keen sense of smell of some insects. SSS clearly doesn't ward off all bugs, and some research suggests that it is effective on only one strain of mosquito. The research also suggests that its effectiveness is short-lived. But that hasn't slowed the sales of SSS. Even pet owners are getting in on the act. According to one study, the flea count on dogs can be cut by one-third in just two days after a sponge bath with a mixture of SSS and water, and fleas seem to stay off longer than when regular flea dips are used alone. An added benefit is that the mixture leaves the dog's coat shinier and more pleasant-smelling. Unfortunately, the treatment doesn't work for cats; it seems their skin is too sensitive for the chemicals in the mixture. Horses, however, benefit from the treatment.

Avon is prohibited by law from touting SSS as an insect repellent. But advertisements such as "Millions of People Know the Secret of Skin So Soft, Do You?" are beginning to bug Avon's competitors, the makers of traditional insect repellents. They believe that Avon should register the product with the EPA and subject it to the safety and effectiveness testing required by law. Avon professes innocence and maintains any benefits from secondary usage are spread by word of mouth among its devotees.

Recent findings that some traditional insect repellents contain chemicals suspected of being hazardous to health have enhanced the sales of Skin So Soft, currently in the tens of millions of dollars—prompting one to wonder if SSS should really be translated as Sweet Smell of Success.

QUESTIONS

1. Explain how Avon could use the various consumer promotion tools to increase the short-term sales of Skin So Soft and to help build the product's long-term market share.

2. Avon is prohibited by law from advertising Skin So Soft as an insect repellent, so word of its effectiveness as a repellent is primarily spread by devotees. What are the relative advantages and disadvantages of this word-of-mouth "advertising"?

Sources: "Offbeat Bite-Fighter for Flea High Season," Self, May 1988, p. 36; "A Rumor That Keeps Buzzing," Time, September 5, 1988, p. 53; and "Deet Is Still the Buzz Word," Boston Globe, July 12, 1989, p. 25.

18

Promoting Products: Personal Selling and Sales Management

November 7:	United Airlines announces it will buy 110 Boeing 737s and six 747s. Price: $3.1 billion
October 22:	Northwest Airlines announces it will buy 10 Boeing 747s and 10 Boeing 757s. Price: $2 billion
October 9:	International Lease Finance announces it will buy two Boeing 737s. Price: $50 million.
October 8:	USAir announces it will buy two Boeing 737s. Price: $50 million.
October 2:	Western Airlines announces it will buy 12 Boeing 737s. Price: $250 million.
October 1:	Republic Airlines announces it will buy six Boeing 757s. Price: $240 million.

Not a bad couple of weeks' work! But you might expect such success from a company with a 60 percent share of the commercial airplane market, a company whose average order size is $34.9 million, and a company whose dedication to making a sale has been called obsessive. The company, of course, is Boeing, the $16.9 billion aerospace giant. In a field where big sales are seldom big news, Boeing got everyone's attention when it received orders worth $6.23 billion (the sales listed, plus others) in one six-week period.

Most of the responsibility for marketing Boeing's commercial aircraft falls on the shoulders of the company's salesforce. In some ways, selling airplanes differs from selling other industrial products. Nationwide, there are only 55 potential customers; there are only three major competitors (Boeing, McDonnell-Douglas, and Airbus); and the high-tech product is especially complex and challenging. But in many other ways, selling commercial aircraft is like selling any other industrial product. The salespeople determine needs, demonstrate how their product fulfills needs, try to close the sale, and follow up after the sale.

To determine needs, Boeing salespeople become experts on the airlines for which they are responsible, much like Wall Street analysts would. They find out where each airline wants to grow, when it wants to replace planes, and details of its financial situation. Then they find ways to fulfill customer needs. They run Boeing and competing planes through computer systems, simulating the airline's routes, cost per seat, and other factors to show that their planes are most efficient. And, more than likely, they'll bring in financial planning, and technical people to answer any questions.

Then the negotiations begin. Deals are cut, discounts made, training programs offered; sometimes top executives from both the airline and Boeing are brought in to close the deal. The selling process is nerve-rackingly slow—it can take two or three years from the day the salesperson makes the first presentation to the day the sale is announced. After getting the order, salespeople must then keep in almost constant touch to keep track of the account's equipment needs and to make certain the customer stays satisfied. Success depends on building solid, long-term relationships with customers based on performance and trust. According to one analyst, Boeing's salespeople "are the vehicle by which information is collected and contacts are made so all other things can take place."

The Boeing salesforce consists of experienced salespeople who use a conservative, straightforward sales approach. They are smooth and knowledgeable, and they like to sell on facts and logic rather than hype and promises. In fact, they tend to understate rather than overstate product benefits. For example, one writer notes that "they'll always underestimate fuel efficiency. They'll say it's a five percent savings, and it'll be eight." Thus, a customer thinking about making a $2 billion purchase can be certain that after the sale, Boeing products will live up to expectations.

Boeing salespeople have a head start on the competition. They have a broad mix of excellent products to sell, and Boeing's size and reputation help them get orders. Its salespeople are proud to be selling Boeing aircraft, and their pride creates an attitude of success that is perhaps best summed up by the company's director of marketing communications. "The popular saying is that Boeing is the Mercedes of the airline industry. We think that's backward. We like to think that Mercedes is the Boeing of the auto industry."[1]

CHAPTER OBJECTIVES

After reading this chapter, you should be able to:

1. Discuss the role of a company's salespeople.
2. Identify the six major salesforce management decisions.
3. Explain how companies set salesforce objectives and strategy.
4. Explain how companies recruit, select, and train salespeople.
5. Describe how companies supervise salespeople and evaluate their effectiveness.

Robert Louis Stevenson once noted that "everyone lives by selling something." Salesforces are found in nonprofit as well as profit organizations. Recruiters are a college's salesforce for attracting students. Churches use membership committees to attract new members. The U.S. Agricultural Extension Service sends agricultural specialists to sell farmers on new farming methods. Hospitals and museums use fundraisers to contact donors and raise money.

The people who do the selling go by many names: *salespeople*, *sales representatives*, *account executives*, *sales consultants*, *sales engineers*, *field representatives*, *agents*, *district managers*, and *marketing representatives*. Selling is one of the oldest professions in the world (see Marketing Highlight 18–1).

There are many stereotypes of salespeople. "Salesman" may bring to mind the image of Arthur Miller's pitiable Willy Loman in *Death of a Salesman* or Meredith Willson's cigar-smoking, back-slapping, joke-telling Harold Hill in *The Music Man*. Salespeople are typically pictured as outgoing and sociable—although many salespeople actually dislike unnecessary socializing. They are blamed for forcing goods on people—although buyers often search out salespeople.

Actually the term **salesperson** covers a wide range of positions whose differences are often greater than their similarities. Here is one popular classification of sales positions:

- Positions in which the salesperson's job is largely to *deliver* the product, such as milk, bread, fuel, oil.
- Positions in which the salesperson is largely an inside *order taker*, such as the department store salesperson standing behind the counter, or an outside order taker, such as the packing-house, soap, or spice salesperson.
- Positions in which the salesperson is not expected or permitted to take an order but only *builds goodwill or educates buyers* (called "missionary" selling)—the "detailer" for a pharmaceutical company who calls on doctors to educate them about the company's drug products and to urge them to prescribe these products to their patients.
- Positions in which the major emphasis is on *techncial knowledge*—the engineering salesperson who is mostly a consultant to client companies.

MILESTONES IN THE HISTORY OF SELLING AND SALESMANSHIP

Selling goes back to the dawn of history. Paul Hermann described a Bronze Age traveling salesman's sample case: ". . . a solid wooden box, 26 inches in length, containing in specially hollowed compartments various types of axes, sword blades, buttons, etc." Early sellers and traders were not held in high esteem. The Roman word for salesman meant "cheater," and Mercury, the god of cunning and barter, was regarded as the patron deity of merchants and traders.

The buying and selling of commodities flourished through the centuries and centered in market towns. Traveling peddlers carried goods to the homes of prospective customers who were unable to get to the market towns.

The first salesmen in the United States were Yankee peddlers (pack peddlers), who carried clothing, spices, household wares, and notions in backpacks from East Coast manufacturing centers to settlers in the western frontier regions. The pack peddlers also traded with the Indians, exchanging knives, beads, and ornaments for furs. Many traders came to be viewed as shrewd, unprincipled tricksters who would not think twice about putting sand in the sugar, dust in the pepper, and chicory in the coffee. They often sold colored sugar water as "medicine" guaranteed to cure all possible ills.

In the early 1800s, some peddlers began to use horse-drawn wagons and to stock heavier goods, such as furniture, clocks, dishes, weapons, and ammunition. Some of these wagon peddlers settled in frontier villages and opened the first general stores and trading posts.

The larger retailers traveled once or twice a year to the nearest major city to replenish their stock. Eventually, wholesalers and manufacturers hired greeters, or drummers, who would seek out and invite retailers to visit the displays of their employers. The drummers would meet incoming trains and ships to beat their competitors. In time, the drummers traveled to their customers' places of business. Before 1860, there were fewer than 1,000 traveling salesmen, many of whom were credit investigators who also took orders for goods. By 1870, there were 7,000; by 1880, 28,000; and by 1900, 93,000 traveling salesmen.

Modern selling and sales management techniques were refined by John Henry Patterson (1844–1922), widely regarded as the father of modern salesmanship. Patterson ran the National Cash Register Company (NCR). He asked his best salesmen to demonstrate their sales approaches to the other salesmen. The best sales approach was printed in a "Sales Primer" and distributed to all NCR salesmen to be followed to the letter. This was the beginning of the canned sales approach. In addition, Patterson assigned his salesmen exclusive territories and sales quotas to stretch their effort. He held frequent sales meetings that served as both sales training sessions and social gatherings. He sent his salesmen regular communications on how to sell. One of the young men trained by Patterson was Thomas J. Watson, who later founded IBM. Patterson showed other companies the way to turn a salesforce into an effective tool for building sales and profits.

The term "salesperson" covers a wide range of positions, from selling in a retail store to the engineering salesperson who consults with client companies.

FIGURE 18–1
Major steps in salesforce management

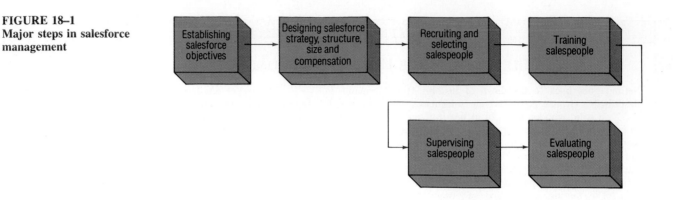

- Positions that demand the *creative selling* of tangible products, like appliances, houses, or industrial equipment, or of intangibles such as insurance, advertising services, or education.[2]

This list ranges from the least to the most creative types of selling. For example, the jobs at the top of the list call for servicing accounts and taking orders, while others call simply for hunting down buyers and getting them to buy. We focus on the more creative types of selling and on the process of building and managing an effective salesforce. We define **salesforce management** as the analysis, planning, implementation, and control of salesforce activities. It includes setting salesforce objectives, designing salesforce strategy, and recruiting, selecting, training, supervising, and evaluating the firm's salespeople. The major salesforce management decisions are shown in Figure 18-1.

SETTING SALESFORCE OBJECTIVES

Companies set different objectives for their salesforces. IBM's salespeople are to "sell, install, and upgrade" customer computer equipment; AT&T salespeople should "develop, sell, and protect" accounts. Salespeople usually perform one or more of many tasks. They find and develop new customers and communicate information about the company's products and services. They sell products by approaching customers, presenting their products, answering objections, and closing sales with customers. In addition, salespeople provide services to customers, carry out market research and intelligence work, and fill out sales call reports.

Some companies are very specific about their salesforce objectives and activities. One company advises its salespeople to spend 80 percent of their time with current customers and 20 percent with prospects, and 85 percent of their time on current products and 15 percent on new products. This company believes that if such norms are not set, salespeople tend to spend almost all of their time selling current products to current accounts and neglect new products and new prospects.

As companies move toward a stronger market orientation, their salesforces need to become more market-focused and customer-oriented. The old view is that salespeople should worry about sales and the company should worry about profit. However, the newer view holds that salespeople should be concerned with more than just producing *sales*—they must also know how to produce *customer satisfaction* and *company profit*. They should know how to look at sales data, measure market potential, gather market intelligence, and develop marketing strategies and plans. Salespeople need marketing-analysis skills, especially at higher levels of sales management. A market-oriented rather than a sales-oriented salesforce will be more effective in the long run.

DESIGNING SALESFORCE STRATEGY

Once the company has set its salesforce objectives, it is ready to face questions of salesforce strategy, structure, size, and compensation.

Salesforce Strategy
Every company competes with other firms to get orders from customers. Thus, it must base its strategy on an understanding of the customer buying process. A company can use one or more of several sales approaches to contact customers. An individual salesperson can talk to a prospect or customer in person or over the phone. Or a salesperson can make a sales presentation to a buying group. A sales *team* (such as a company executive, a salesperson, and a sales engineer) can make a sales presentation to a buying group. In *conference selling*, a salesperson brings resource people from the company to meet with one or more buyers to discuss problems and opportunities. In *seminar selling*, a company team conducts an educational seminar for technical people in a customer company about state-of-the-art developments.

Thus, the salesperson often acts as an "account manager" who arranges contacts between people in the buying and selling companies. Because salespeople need help from others in the company, selling calls for teamwork. Others who might assist salespeople include top management, especially when major sales are at stake; technical people who provide technical information to customers; customer-service representatives who provide installation, maintenance, and other services to customers; and office staff such as sales analysts, order processors, and secretaries.

Once the company decides on a desirable selling approach, it can use either a direct or a contractual salesforce. A *direct (or company) salesforce* consists of full- or part-time employees who work exclusively for the company. This salesforce includes *inside salespeople*, who conduct business from their offices using the telephone or receive visits from prospective buyers, and *field salespeople*, who travel to call on customers. A *contractual sales force* consists of manufacturers' reps, sales agents, or brokers, who are paid a commission based on their sales.

Salesforce Structure
Salesforce strategy influences the structure of the salesforce. The salesforce structure decision is simple if the company sells one product line to one industry with customers in many locations. In that case the company would use a *territorial salesforce structure*. If the company sells many products to many types of customers, it might need a *product salesforce structure* or a *customer salesforce structure*.

Territorial Salesforce Structure
In the **territorial salesforce structure**, each salesperson is assigned to an exclusive territory in which to sell the company's full line. This salesforce structure is the simplest sales organization and has many advantages. It clearly defines the salesperson's job, and because only one salesperson works the territory, he or she gets all the credit or blame for territory sales. The territorial structure also increases the salesperson's desire to build local business ties that, in turn, improve the salesperson's selling effectiveness. Finally, because each salesperson travels within a small geographic area, travel expenses are relatively small.

Territorial sales organization is often supported by many levels of sales management positions. For example, Campbell Soup recently changed from a product salesforce structure to a territorial one, in which each salesperson is responsible for selling all Campbell Soup products. Starting at the bottom of the organizations, *sales merchandisers* report to *sales representatives*, who report to *retail supervisors*, who report to *directors of retail sales operations*, who report to one of 22 *regional sales managers*. Regional sales managers report to one of four *general sales managers* (West, Central, South, and East), who report to a *vice president and general sales manager*.[3]

Product Salesforce Structure
Salespeople must know their products—especially when the products are numerous, unrelated, and complex. This need, together with the trend toward product management, has led many companies to the **product salesforce structure**, in which the salesforce sells along product lines. For example, Kodak uses different sales forces for its film products and its industrial products. The film products salesforce deals with simple

products that are intensively distributed, while the industrial products salesforce deals with complex products that require technical understanding.

The product structure, however, can lead to problems if many of the company's products are bought by the same customers. For example, the American Hospital Supply Corporation (AHS) has several product divisions, each with a separate salesforce. Several AHS salespeople might end up calling on the same hospital on the same day. This means that they travel the same routes and that each waits to see the same customer's purchasing agents. These extra costs must be compared with the benefits of better product knowledge and attention to individual products.

Customer Salesforce Structures

Companies often use a **customer salesforce structure,** in which they organize the salesforce along customer or industry lines. Separate salesforces may be set up for different industries, for serving current customers versus finding new ones, and for major versus regular accounts. Xerox, for example, classifies its customers into four major groups, each served by a different salesforce. The top group consists of large national accounts with multiple and scattered locations; these customers are handled by 250 to 300 *national account managers*. Next are major accounts that, although not national in scope, may have several locations within a region; these are handled by one of Xerox's 1,000 or so *major account managers*. The third customer group consists of standard commercial accounts with annual sales potential of $5,000 to $10,000; they are served by *account representatives*. All other customers are handled by *marketing representatives*.[4]

The biggest advantage of customer specialization is that each salesforce can know more about specific customer needs. It can also reduce total salesforce costs. At one time a pump manufacturer used highly trained sales engineers to sell to all its customers— to manufacturers who needed highly technical assistance and to wholesalers who did not. Later the company split its salesforce and used lower-paid, less technical salespeople to deal with the wholesalers. This change reduced salesforce costs without reducing customer service.

The major disadvantage of a customer structure arises when customers are scattered across the country. Such geographical disbursement means a great deal of travel by each of the company's salesforces.

Complex Salesforce Structures

When a company sells a wide variety of products to many types of customers over a broad geographical area, it often combines several types of salesforce structures. Salespeople can be specialized by territory and product, by territory and market, by product and market, or by territory, product, and market. A salesperson might then report to one or more line and staff managers.[5]

Salesforce Size   Once the company has set its strategy and structure, it is ready to consider *salesforce size*. Salespeople constitute one of the company's most productive—and most expensive— assets. Therefore, increasing their number will increase both sales and costs.

Many companies use some form of **workload approach** to set salesforce size. Under this approach, a company groups accounts into different size classes and then determines how many salespeople are needed to call on them the desired number of times. The company might think as follows: Suppose we have 1000 Type-A accounts and 2000 Type-B accounts. Type-A accounts require 36 calls a year and Type-B accounts 12 calls a year. In this case, the salesforce's *workload*—the number of calls it must make per year—is 60,000 calls $[(1,000 \times 36) + (2,000 \times 12) = 36,000 + 24,000 = 60,000]$. Suppose our average salesperson can make 1,000 calls a year. The company thus needs 60 salespeople (60,000/1,000).

Salesforce Compensation   To attract needed salespeople, a company must have an attractive compensation plan. These plans vary greatly both by industry and by companies within the same industry.

The level of compensation must be close to the "going rate" for the type of sales job and needed skills. For example, the average earnings of an experienced, middle-level industrial salesperson in 1990 amounted to about $41,000.[6] To pay less than the going rate would attract too few quality salespeople; to pay more would be unnecessary.

Compensation is made up of several elements—a fixed amount, a variable amount, expenses, and fringe benefits. The fixed amount, usually a salary, gives the salesperson some stable income. The variable amount, which might be commissions or bonuses based on sales performance, rewards the salesperson for greater effort. Expense allowances, which repay salespeople for job-related expenses, let salespeople undertake needed and desirable selling efforts. Fringe benefits, such as paid vacations, sickness or accident benefits, pensions, and life insurance, provide job security and satisfaction.

Management must decide what *mix* of these compensation elements makes the most sense for each sales job. Different combinations of fixed and variable compensation give rise to four basic types of compensation plans—straight salary, straight commission, salary plus bonus, and salary plus commissions. A recent study of salesforce compensation plans showed that about 14 percent paid straight salary, 19 percent paid straight commission, 26 percent paid salary plus bonus, and 37 percent paid salary plus commission, and 10 percent paid salary plus commission plus bonus.[7]

RECRUITING AND SELECTING SALESPEOPLE

Having set the strategy, structure, size, and compensation for the salesforce, the company now must set up systems for *recruiting and selecting*, *training*, *supervising*, and *evaluating salespeople*.

Importance of Careful Selection

At the heart of successful salesforce operation is the selection of good salespeople. The performance levels of an average and a top salesperson can be quite different. In a typical salesforce, the top 30 percent of the salespeople might bring in 60 percent of the sales. Careful salesperson selection can thus greatly increase overall salesforce performance.

Beyond the differences in sales performance, poor selection results in costly turnover. One study found an average annual salesforce turnover rate for all industries of 27 percent. The costs of high turnover can be considerable. When a salesperson quits, the costs of finding and training a new salesperson—plus the costs of lost sales—can run as high as $50,000 to $75,000. And a salesforce with many new people is less productive.[8]

What Makes a Good Salesperson?

Selecting salespeople would not be a problem if the company knew what traits to look for. If it knew that good salespeople were outgoing, aggressive, and energetic, these characteristics could simply be checked among applicants. But many successful salespeople are also bashful, mild-mannered, and very relaxed. Successful salespeople include some men and women who are tall and short, some who speak well and some who speak poorly, some who dress well and some who dress shabbily.

Still, the search continues for the magic list of traits that spells sure-fire sales ability. Many such lists have been drawn up. One survey suggests that good salespeople have lots of enthusiasm, persistence, initiative, self-confidence, and job commitment. They are committed to sales as a way of life and have a strong customer orientation. Another study suggests that good salespeople are independent, self-motivated, and excellent listeners. Still another study advises that salespeople should be persistent, enthusiastic, a friend to the customer, attentive, and—above all—honest.[9] Charles Garfield found that good salespeople are goal-directed risk takers who identify strongly with their customers (see Marketing Highlight 18–2).

How can a company find out what traits salespeople in its industry should have? Job *duties* suggest some of the traits to look for. Is there a lot of paper work? Does the job call for much travel? Will the salesperson face a lot of rejections? The successful salesperson should be suited to these duties. The company should also look at the characteristics of its most successful salespeople for clues to needed traits.

WHAT MAKES A SUPERSALESPERSON?

Charles Garfield, clinical professor of psychology at the University of California, San Francisco School of Medicine, claims that his twenty-year analysis of more than 1,500 super-achievers in every field of endeavor is the longest-running to date. *Peak Performance–Mental Training Techniques of the World's Greatest Athletes* is the first book Garfield wrote about his findings. Although he says it will be followed shortly by a book on business that will cover supersalespeople, many companies (such as IBM, which took 3,000) have ordered the current book for their salesforces. Garfield says that the complexity and speed of change in today's business world requires a peak performer in sales to possess greater mastery of different fields than to be one in science, sports, or the arts. The following are the most common characteristics he has found in peak sales performance:

- Supersalespeople are always taking risks and making innovations. Unlike most people, they stay out of the "comfort zone" and try to surpass their previous levels of performance.

- Supersalespeople have a powerful sense of mission and set the short-, intermediate-, and long-term goals necessary to fulfill that mission. Their personal goals are always higher than sales quotas set by their managers. Supersalespeople also work well with managers, especially if managers are also interested in peak performance.

- Supersalespeople are more interested in solving problems than in placing blame or bluffing their way out of situations. Because they view themselves as professionals in training, they are always upgrading their skills.

- Supersalespeople see themselves as partners with their customers and as team players rather than adversaries. While peak performers believe their task is to communicate with people, mediocre salespeople psychologically change their customers into objects and talk about the number of calls and closes they made as if it had nothing to do with human beings.

- Whereas supersalespeople take each rejection as information they can learn from, mediocre salespeople personalize rejection.

- The most surprising finding is that, like peak performers in sports and the arts, supersalespeople use mental rehearsal. Before every sale, they review it in their mind's eye, from shaking the customer's hand when they walk in to discussing the customer's problems and asking for the order.

Source: "What Makes a Supersalesperson?" *Sales & Marketing Management*, August 13, 1984, p. 86. Also see "What Makes a Top Performer?" *Sales & Marketing Management*, May 1989, pp. 23–24; and Timothy J. Trow, "The Secret of a Good Hire: Profiling," *Sales & Marketing Management*, May 1990, pp. 44–55.

Recruiting Procedures

After management had decided on needed traits, it must *recruit*. The personnel department looks for applicants by getting names from current salespeople, using employment agencies, placing job ads, and contacting college students. Companies have sometimes found it hard to sell college students on selling. Many students think that selling is a job and not a profession, that salespeople must be deceitful to be effective, and that selling involves too much insecurity and travel. In addition, some women believe that selling is a man's career. To counter such objections, recruiters talk about high starting salaries, income growth, and the fact that more than one-fourth of the presidents of large U.S. corporations started out in marketing and sales. They point out that 28 percent of the people now selling industrial products are women; in some industries, such as textiles and apparel, and banking and financial services, the proportion of women in the salesforces is about 60 percent (see Marketing Highlight 18-3).[10]

Selecting Salespeople

Recruiting will attract many applicants, from which the company must select the best. The selection procedure can vary from a single informal interview to lengthy testing and interviewing. Many companies give formal tests to sales applicants. Tests typically measure sales aptitude, analytical and organizational skills, personality traits, and other characteristics.[11] Test results count heavily in such companies as IBM, Prudential, Procter & Gamble, and Gillette. Gillette claims that tests have reduced turnover by 42 percent and have correlated well with the later performance of new salespeople. But test scores provide only one piece of information in a set that includes personal characteristics, references, past employment history, and interviewer reactions.

TRAINING SALESPEOPLE

Many companies used to send their new salespeople into the field almost immediately after hiring them. They would be given samples, order books, and general instructions ("sell west of the Mississippi"). Training programs were luxuries. To many companies,

Companies spend hundreds of millions of dollars to train their salespeople in the art of selling.

a training program translated into much expense for instructors, materials, space, and salary for a person who was not yet selling, plus lost sales opportunities because the person was not in the field.

Today's new salespeople, however, may spend from a few weeks to many months in training. The average training period is 3.8 months. IBM spends $1 billion a year educating its work force and customers. Initial sales training lasts 13 months, and new salespeople are not on their own for two years! And IBM expects its salespeople to spend 15 percent of their time each year in additional training.[12]

Training programs have several goals. Salespeople need to know and identify with the company, so most companies spend the first part of the training program describing the company's history and objectives, its organization, its financial structure and facilities, and its chief products and markets. Because salespeople also need to know the company's products, sales trainees are shown how products are produced and how they work in various uses. Because salespeople need to know customers' and competitors' characteristics, the training program teaches them about competitors' strategies and about different types of customers and their needs, buying motives, and buying habits. Salespeople need to know how to make effective presentations, so they get training in the principles of selling, and the company outlines the major sales arguments for each product. Finally, salespeople need to understand field procedures and responsibilities. They learn how to divide time between active and potential accounts and how to use an expense account, prepare reports, and route communications effectively.

SUPERVISING SALESPEOPLE

New salespeople need more than a territory, compensation, and training—they need *supervision*. Through supervision, the company *directs* and *motivates* the salesforce to do a better job.

Directing Salespeople　　How much sales management should be involved in helping salespeople manage their territories? It depends on everything from the company's size to the experience of its salesforce. Thus, companies vary widely in how closely they supervise their salespeople. And what works for one company may not work for another.[13]

Developing Customer Targets and Call Norms
Most companies classify customers into A, B, and C accounts, based on the account's sales volume, its profit potential, and its growth potential. They set the desired number of calls per period on each account class. Thus, A accounts may receive nine calls a year, B accounts six calls, and C accounts three calls. Such call norms depend upon competitive call norms and profits expected from the account.

ON THE JOB WITH TWO SUCCESSFUL SALESWOMEN

The word "salesman" now has an archaic ring. The entry of women into what was once the male bastion of professional selling has been swift and dramatic. More than 28 percent of people selling industrial products are women, versus just 7 percent in 1975. In some industries this percentage reaches as high as 60 percent. Here are two examples of highly successful technical saleswomen.

Catherine Hogan, Account Manager, Bell Atlantic Network Services

As an undergraduate student, Catherine Hogan had few thoughts about a career in sales, especially *technical* sales. "I was a warm, fuzzy person," she says, "artsy craftsy." Now, just six years later, she's in the thick of it, successfully handling a complex line of technical products in what was once a male-dominated world. Why the change? "I needed to get out there and feel the heat—take risks, handle customers, and be responsible for their complaints," says Hogan. Still far from being a technical person, she has quickly acquired a working knowledge of modern communications services and how they can be delivered to businesses through Bell Atlantic's phone network.

So rapidly is the company diversifying that, artsy-craftsy or no, Hogan finds herself studying new hardware, software, and leasing programs so she can explain them to both business customers and Bell's own account executives, who have ongoing responsibilities for those customers. The account executives can handle their customers' local applications by themselves but team up with Hogan when customers want long-distance voice or data services. This sort of cooperative selling requires empathy and skill. On joint calls, Hogan is careful not to interfere when the account executive is negotiating with a customer.

On a more personal level, Hogan has worked through the pros and cons of being something of a novelty in an industry undergoing wrenching change. "People are used to seeing middle-age white males with a technical background in this industry," she says. "It's challenging being young, female, and ethnic." Her advice to others in similar situations? "Go beyond what the world prescribes for you. Be strong enough to lance the dragon but soft enough to wear silk."

Joyce Nardone, Sales Manager, Facsimile Division, Amfax America

For a vivid picture of what it takes to succeed in sales, listen to Joyce Nardone exclaim about the terrors and triumphs of selling to strangers who've never heard your name before you walk in the door. "I'm good at cold-calling, but it takes a long time to learn to take rejection," she says. "Sometimes just getting out of the car is a feat in itself."

So resilient is the 24-year-old Joyce, however, that prior to her recent promotion to management, she compiled an impressive record knocking on doors for Amfax America, an office equipment dealer whose main line is Sharp facsimile machines and copiers. "You have to be friendly and upbeat," she says. "If you look like a winner, they'll buy from you."

As good as she is at cold-calling, Nardone adds a special ingredient in a business that traditionally has been built around the one-time sale: She keeps up with her customers and makes sure they're satisfied with the product. "I have over 100 clients, and I consider them my friends," she says. "Most people don't bother to go back, but I'll bring them a free roll of paper or fax them a Hanukkah or Christmas card." As a result, customers often refer other companies to Nardone, so she has a steady stream of new business.

Developing Prospect Targets and Call Norms

Companies often specify how much time their salesforces should spend prospecting for new accounts. For example, Spector Freight wants its salespeople to spend 25 percent of their time prospecting and to stop calling on a prospect after three unsuccessful calls. Companies set prospecting standards for several reasons. If left alone, many salespeople will spend most of their time with current customers. Current customers are better known quantities. Whereas a prospect may never deliver any business, salespeople can depend upon current accounts for some business. Unless salespeople are rewarded for opening new accounts, they may avoid new account development. Some companies thus rely on a special salesforce to open new accounts.

Using Sales Time Efficiency

Salespeople need to know how to use their time efficiently. One tool is the *annual call schedule* showing which customers and prospects to call on in which months, and which activities to carry out. Activities include taking part in trade shows, attending sales meetings, and carrying out marketing research. Another tool is *time and duty analysis*. In addition to time spent selling, the salesperson spends time traveling, waiting, eating and taking breaks, and doing administrative chores.

Figure 18-2 shows how salespeople spend their time. On average, actual face-to-face selling time accounts for only 32 percent of total working time! If selling time could be raised from 32 to 40 percent, this would be a 25 percent increase in the time

Successful saleswomen Catherine Hogan and Joyce Nardone—the word "salesman" now has an archaic ring.

Fortunately, management recognizes her talents, too. Nardone is now in charge of the salesforce for Amfax's Facsimile Division. As manager, she is responsible for training, motivation, and overall performance of eight direct salespeople. She also coordinates advertising and trade show exhib-its. Her advice to new salespeople? "To discover a customer's needs, *listen* to him!"

Source: Adapted from portions of Martin Everett, "Selling's New Breed: Smart and Feisty," *Sales & Marketing Management*, October 1989, pp. 52–64.

spent selling. Companies are always looking for ways to save time—using phones instead of traveling, simplifying recordkeeping forms, finding better call and routing plans, and supplying more and better customer information.

Advances in technological equipment—desktop and laptop computers, videocassette

FIGURE 18–2
How salespeople spend their time
Source: Dartnell Corporation; 26th Survey of Sales Force Compensation. © 1990; Dartnell Corporation

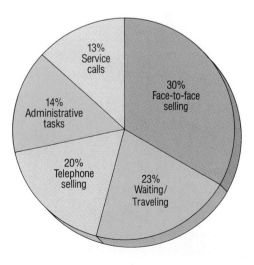

recorders, videodiscs, automatic dialers, teleconferencing—have allowed dramatic breakthroughs in improving salesforce productivity. Salespeople have truly gone "electronic." One expert predicts that by 1991, 28 percent of all salespeople will use personal computers on the job. Salespeople use computers to profile customers and prospects, analyze and forecast sales, schedule sales calls, enter orders, check inventories and order status, prepare sales and expense reports, process correspondence, and carry out many other activities. A recent survey showed a 43 percent productivity gain for salesforces using personal computers. Here are some examples of companies that have successfully introduced the machines into their salesforce operations:

> Shell Chemical Company developed a laptop computer package consisting of several applications. Although many salespeople initially resisted the computer—they couldn't type, or they didn't have time to learn the software, or whatever—some applications had great appeal. Salespeople responded first to the *automatic expense statement* program, which made it easier for them to record expenses and get reimbursed quickly. Soon, they discovered the *sales inquiry function*, which gave them immediate access to the latest account information, including phone numbers, addresses, recent developments, and prices. They no longer had to wait for clerical staff to give them out-of-date information. Before long, salespeople were using the entire package. *Electronic mail* allowed them to quickly receive and send messages to others. Various *corporate forms*, such as territory work plans and sales call reports, could be filled out faster and sent electronically. Other useful applications included an *appointment calendar*, a *"to-do list" function*, a *spreadsheet program*, and a *graphics package* which helped salespeople prepare charts and graphs for customer presentations. Today, even salespeople who initially resisted computer package wonder how they ever got along without it.[14]

> At the end of each workday, 10,000 Frito-Lay salespeople plug their hand-help computers into minicomputers at their local sales offices or into modems at home. Then they sit back and relax while report's of their day's efforts are zapped to Frito-Lay headquarters in Dallas. Twenty-four hours later, Frito-Lay's marketing managers have a complete report

Many companies are computerizing their salesforces to make salespeople more efficient and effective.

TELEMARKETING: A PHONE CAN BE BETTER THAN A FACE

Selling face-to-face is by far the best way to achieve personal rapport with a prospect, right? Wrong, says LeRoy Benham, president of Climax Portable Machine Tools. By combining telemarketing and computers, a small company can save money and lavish the kind of attention on buyers that will amaze them.

True, such a strategy depends on both the nature of your market and your stake in it, but few would argue with Benham's track record. At a time when most U.S. machine tool manufacturers have been in a deep depression, Benham has carved out a niche for his portable cutting tools. This year, sales will rise 20 percent to $5 million. Company profits will climb more than 20 percent for the third year in a row since Climax began phasing out its distributor network and switched to telephone selling.

Under the old system, sales engineers spent one-third of their time on the road, training distributor salespeople and accompanying them on calls. "They'd make about four contacts a day," says Benham. "They found they actually got more information from the prospects when they were back here setting up travel appointments by phone." Now, each of the five sales engineers on Benham's telemarketing team calls about 30 prospects a day, following up on leads generated by ads and direct mail. Because it takes about five calls to close a sale, the sales engineers update a computer file on prospects each time they speak to them, noting their degree of commitment, requirements, next-call date, and personal comments. "If anyone mentions he's going on a fishing trip, our sales engineer enters that in the computer and uses it to personalize the next phone call," says Benham, noting that's just one way to build good relations. Another: The first mailing to a prospect includes the sales engineer's business card with his picture on it.

Telemarketers use the phone to find new prospects and sell to them.

Of course, it takes more than friendliness to sell $15,000 machine tools (special orders may run $200,000) over the phone, but Benham has proof that personality pays. When Climax customers were asked, "Do you see the sales engineer often enough?" the response was overwhelmingly positive. Obviously, many people didn't realize that the only contact they'd had with Climax had been on the phone.

Source: Adapted from "A Phone Is Better Than a Face," *Sales and Marketing Management*, October 1987, p. 29.

---

analyzing the sales performance Fritos, Doritos, and the company's other brands the day before—by total, brand, and location. The system not only helps Frito-Lay's marketing managers make better decisions, it makes the salespeople more efficient and effective. Now, instead of spending hours filling out reports, Frito-Lay salespeople let the computers do the grunt work and spend the extra time selling. As a result of the system, sales are going up 10 to 12 percent a year without the addition of a single salesperson.[15]

To reduce time demands on their *outside salesforces*, many companies have increased the size of their *inside salesforces*. Inside salespeople include three types. *Technical support people* provide technical information and answers to customers' questions. *Sales assistants* provide clerical backup for outside salespeople. They call ahead and confirm appointments, conduct credit checks, follow up on deliveries, and answer customers' questions when outside salespeople cannot be reached. *Telemarketers* use the phone to find new leads, qualify prospects, and sell to them (see Marketing Highlight 18–4). A telemarketer can call as many as 50 customers a day, compared to the average 4 that an outside salesperson can see. The inside salesforce frees outside salespeople to spend more time selling to major accounts and finding major new prospects.[16]

Motivating Salespeople

Some salespeople will do their best without any special urging from management. To them, selling may be the most fascinating job in the world. But selling often involves frustration. Salespeople usually work alone, and they must sometimes travel away from home. They may face aggressive, competing salespeople and difficult customers. They sometimes lack the authority to do what is needed to win a sale and may thus lose large orders they have worked hard to obtain. Therefore, salespeople often need special encouragement to work at their best level. Management can boost salesforce morale and performance through its *organizational climate*, *sales quotas*, and *positive incentives*.

Organizational Climate

Organizational climate describes the feeling that salespeople have about their opportunities, value, and rewards for a good performance within the company. Some companies treat salespeople as if they are not very important. Other companies treat their salespeople as their prime movers and allow virtually unlimited opportunity for income and promotion. Not surprisingly, a company's attitude toward its salespeople affects their behavior. If they are held in low esteem, there is high turnover and poor performance. If they are held in high esteem, there is less turnover and higher performance.

Treatment from the salesperson's immediate superior is especially important. A good sales manager keeps in touch with the salesforce through letters and phone calls, visits in the field, and evaluation sessions in the home office. At different times, the sales manager acts as the salesperson's boss, companion, coach, and confessor.

Sales Quotas

Many companies set **sales quotas** for their salespeople—standards stating the amount they should sell and how sales should be divided among the company's products. Compensation is often related to how well salespeople meet their quotas.

Sales quotas are set when the annual marketing plan is developed. The company first decides on a sales forecast that is reasonably achievable. Based on this forecast, management plans production, workforce size, and financial needs. It then sets sales quotas for its regions and territories. Generally, sales quotas are set higher than the sales forecast to encourage sales managers and salespeople to their best effort. If they fail to make quotas, the company may still make its sales forecast.

Positive Incentives

Companies also use several incentives to increase salesforce effort. *Sales meetings* provide social occasions, breaks from routine, chances to meet and talk with "company brass," and opportunities to air feelings and identify with a larger group. Companies also sponsor *sales contests* to spur the salesforce to make a selling effort above what would normally be expected. Other incentives include honors, merchandise and cash awards, trips, and profit-sharing plans.

EVALUATING SALESPEOPLE

We have described how management communicates what salespeople should be doing and how it motivates them to do it. But this process requires good feedback. And good feedback means getting regular information from salespeople to evaluate their performance.

Sources of Information

Management gets information about its salespeople in several ways. The most important source is *sales reports*. Additional information comes from personal observation, customers' letters and complaints, customer surveys, and talks with other salespeople.

Sales reports are divided into plans for future activities and write-ups of completed activities. The best example of the first is the *work plan*, that salespeople submit a week or month in advance. The plan describes intended calls and routing. This report

Salesforce incentives: Many companies award cash, gift cheques, merchandise, or trips as incentives for outstanding sales performance.

leads the salesforce to plan and schedule activities, informs management of their where-abouts, and provides a basis for comparing plans and performance. Salespeople can then be evaluated on their ability to ''plan their work and work their plan.'' Sometimes, managers contact individual salespeople to suggest improvements in work plans.

Companies are also beginning to require their salespeople to draft *annual territory marketing plans* in which they outline their plans for building new accounts and increasing sales from existing accounts. Formats vary greatly. Some ask for general ideas on territory development and others ask for detailed sales and profit estimates. Such reports cast salespeople as territory marketing managers. Sales managers study these territory plans, make suggestions, and use them to develop sales quotas.

Salespeople write up their completed activities on *call reports*. Call reports keep sales management informed of the salesperson's activities, show what is happening with each customer's account, and provide information that might be useful in later calls. Salespeople also turn in *expense reports* for which they are partly or wholly repaid. Some companies also ask for reports on new business, reports on lost business, and reports on local business and economic conditions.

These reports supply the raw data from which sales management can evaluate salesforce performance. Are salespeople making too few calls per day? Are they spending too much time per call? Are they spending too much money on entertainment? Are they closing enough orders per hundred calls? Are they finding enough new customers and holding onto enough old customers?

Formal Evaluation of Performance

Using salesforce reports and other information, sales management formally evaluates members of the salesforce. Formal evaluation produces three benefits. First, management must develop and communicate clear standards for judging performance. Second, management must gather well-rounded information about each salesperson. Finally, salespeople know they will have to sit down one morning with the sales manager and explain their performance.

Comparing Salespeople's Performance

One type of evaluation compares and ranks the sales performance of different salespeople. Such comparisons, however, can be misleading. Salespeople may perform differently because of differences in such factors as territory potential, workload, level of competition, and company promotion effort. Furthermore, sales are not usually the best indicator of achievement. Management should be more interested in how much each salesperson contributes to net profits, a concern that requires looking at each salesperson's sales mix and sales expenses.

Comparing Current Sales With Past Sales

A second type of evaluation is to compare a salesperson's current performance with past performance. Such a comparison should directly indicate the person's progress. An example is shown in Table 18-1.

The sales manager can learn many things about Chris Smith from this table. Smith's total sales increased every year (line 3). This does not necessarily mean that Smith is doing a better job. The product breakdown shows that Smith has been able to push the sales of product B further than those of product A (lines 1 and 2). According to the quotas for the two products (lines 4 and 5), the success in increasing product B sales may be at the expense of product A sales. According to gross profits (lines 6 and 7), the company earns twice as much gross profit (as a ratio to sales) on A as it does on B. Smith may be pushing the higher-volume, lower-margin product at the expense

TABLE 18-1
Evaluating Salespeople's Performance

	TERRITORY: MIDLAND		SALESPERSON: CHRIS SMITH	
	1987	1988	1989	1990
1. Net sales product A	$251,300	$253,200	$270,000	$263,100
2. Net sales product B	$423,200	$439,200	$553,900	$561,900
3. Net sales total	$674,500	$692,400	$823,900	$825,000
4. Percent of quota product A	95.6	92.0	88.0	84.7
5. Percent of quota product B	120.4	122.3	134.9	130.8
6. Gross profits product A	$ 50,260	$ 50,640	$ 54,000	$ 52,620
7. Gross profits product B	$ 42,320	$ 43,920	$53,390	$56,190
8. Gross profits total	$ 92,580	$94,560	$109,390	$108,810
9. Sales expense	$ 10,200	$ 11,100	$ 11,600	$ 13,200
10. Sales expense to total sales (%)	1.5	1.6	1.4	1.6
11. Number of calls	1,675	1,700	1,680	1,660
12. Cost per call	$ 6.09	$ 6.53	$ 6.90	$ 7.95
13. Average number of Customers	320	324	328	334
14. Number of new customers	13	14	15	20
15. Number of lost customers	8	10	11	14
16. Average sales per customer	$ 2,108	$ 2,137	$ 2,512	$2,470
17. Average gross profit per customer	$ 289	$ 292	$ 334	$ 326

of the more profitable product. Although Smith increased total sales by $1,000 between 1989 and 1990 (line 3), the gross profits on these total sales actually decreased by $580 (line 8).

Sales expense (line 9) shows a steady increase, although total expense as a percentage of total sales seems to be under control (line 10). The upward trend in Smith's total dollar expenses does not seem to be explained by any increase in the number of calls (line 11), although it may be related to his success in acquiring new customers (line 14). However, there is a possibility that in prospecting for new customers. Smith is neglecting present customers, as indicated by an upward trend in the annual number of lost customers (line 15).

The last two lines on the table show the level and trend in Smith's sales and gross profits per customer. These figures become more meaningful when they are compared with overall company averages. If Chris Smith's average gross profit per customer is lower than the company's average, Chris may be concentrating on the wrong customers or may not be spending enough time with each customer. Looking back at the annual number of calls (line 11), Smith may be making fewer calls than the average salesperson. If distances in the territory are not much different, this may mean he is not putting in a full workday, he is poor at planning his routing or minimizing his waiting time, or he spends too much time with certain accounts.

Qualitative Evaluation of Salespeople

A *qualitative evaluation* usually looks at a salesperson's knowledge of the company, products, customers, competitors, territory, and tasks. Personal traits—general manner, appearance, speech, and temperament—can be rated. The sales manager can also review any problems in motivation or compliance. The sales manager should check to make sure that salespeople know the laws relating to personal selling (see Marketing Highlight 18–5). Each company must decide what would be most useful to know. It should communicate these criteria to salespeople so that they understand how their performance is evaluated and can make an effort to improve it.

PRINCIPLES OF PERSONAL SELLING

We now turn from designing and managing a salesforce to the actual personal selling process. Personal selling is an ancient art. It has spawned a large literature and many principles. Effective salespeople operate on more than just instinct—they are highly trained in methods of territory analysis and customer management.

The Personal Selling Process

Companies spend hundreds of millions of dollars on seminars, books, cassettes, and other materials to teach salespeople the "art" of selling. Millions of copies of books on selling are purchased every year, with such tantalizing titles as *How to Sell Anything to Anybody*, *How I Raised Myself from Failure to Success in Selling*, *The Four-Minute Sell*, *The Best Seller*, *The Power of Enthusiastic Selling*, *Where Do You Go from No. 1?*, and *Winning Through Intimidation*. One of the most enduring books on selling is Dale Carnegie's *How to Win Friends and Influence People*.

All of the training approaches try to convert a salesperson from a passive *order taker* to an active *order getter*. Order takers assume that customers know their own needs, that they would resent any attempt at influence, and that they prefer salespeople who are polite and reserved. An example of an order taker is a salesperson who calls on a dozen customers each day, simply asking if the customer needs anything.

There are two approaches to training salespeople to be order *getters*—a sales-oriented approach and a customer-oriented approach. The *sales-oriented approach* trains the salesperson in high-pressure selling techniques, such as those used in selling encyclopedias or automobiles. This form of selling assumes that the customers will not buy except under pressure, that they are influenced by a slick presentation, and that they will not be sorry after signing the order (and that, if they are, it no longer matters).

The *customer-oriented approach*—the one most often used in today's professional selling—trains salespeople in customer problem solving. The salesperson learns how to identify customer needs and find solutions. This approach assumes that customer needs provide sales opportunities, that customers appreciate good suggestions, and that they will be loyal to salespeople who have their long-term interests at heart. In one survey, purchasing agents described the following qualities as the ones they *most disliked* in salespeople: pushy, arrogant, unreliable, too talkative, fails to ask about needs. The qualities they *value most* included reliability and credibility, integrity, innovativeness in solving problems, and product knowledge.[17] The problem solver salesperson fits better with the marketing concept than the hard seller or order taker.

Steps in the Selling Process

Most training programs view the **selling process** as consisting of several steps that the salesperson must master. These steps are shown in Figure 18-3 and discussed below.[18]

Prospecting and Qualifying

The first step in the selling process is **prospecting**—identifying qualified potential customers. The salesperson must approach many prospects to get a few sales. In the insurance industry, only one out of nine prospects becomes a customer. In the computer business, 125 phone calls result in 25 interviews leading to 5 demonstrations and 1 sale.[19] Although

FIGURE 18–3
Major steps in effective selling

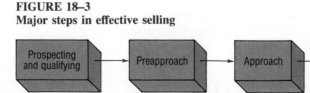

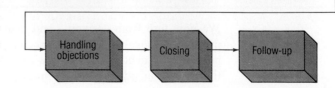

the company supplies some leads, salespeople need skill in finding their own. They can ask current customers for the names of prospects. They can build referral sources, such as suppliers, dealers, noncompeting salespeople, and bankers. They can join organizations to which prospects belong or can engage in speaking and writing activities that will draw attention. They can search for names in newspapers or directories and use the telephone and mail to track down leads. Or they can drop in unannounced on various offices (a practice known as "cold calling").

Salespeople need to know how to *qualify* leads—that is, how to identify the good ones and screen the poor ones. Prospects can be qualified by looking at their financial ability, volume of business, special needs, location, and possibilities for growth.

Preapproach

Before calling on a prospect, the salesperson should learn as much as possible about the organization (what it needs, who is involved in the buying) and its buyers (their characteristics and buying styles). This step is known as the **preapproach.** The salesperson can consult standard sources (*Moody's, Standard and Poor's, Dun and Bradstreet*), acquaintances, and others to learn about the company. The salesperson should set *call objectives*, which may be either to qualify the prospect, to gather information, or to make an immediate sale. Another task is to decide on the best approach, which might be a personal visit, a phone call, or a letter. The best timing should be thought out because many prospects are busiest at certain times. Finally, the salesperson should give thought to an overall sales strategy for the account.

Approach

During the **approach** step, the salesperson should know how to meet and greet the buyer and to get the relationship off to a good start. This step involves the salesperson's appearance, opening lines, and the follow-up remarks. The opening lines should be positive, such as "Mr. Johnson, I am Chris Anderson from the Alltech Company. My company and I appreciate your willingness to see me. I will do my best to make this visit profitable and worthwhile for you and your company." This opening might be followed by some key questions to learn more about the customer's needs or the showing of a display or sample to attract the buyer's attention and curiosity.

Presentation and Demonstration

During the **presentation** step of the selling process, the salesperson tells the product "story" to the buyer, showing how the product will make or save money. The salesperson describes the product features but concentrates on presenting customer benefits.

Companies use three styles of sales presentation. The oldest is the *canned approach*, which consists of a memorized or scripted talk covering the seller's main points. This approach has limited usefulness in industrial selling, but scripted presentations can be effective in some telephone selling situations. A properly prepared and rehearsed script should sound natural and move the salesperson smoothly through the presentation. With electronic scripting, computers can lead the salesperson through a sequence of selling messages tailored on the spot to the prospect's responses.

Using the *formula approach*, the salesperson first identifies the buyer's needs, attitudes, and buying style. Then the salesperson moves into a formula presentation that shows how the product will satisfy that buyer's needs. Although not canned, the presentation follows a general plan.

The *need-satisfaction approach* starts with a search for the customer's needs by

In the sales presentation, the salesperson tells the product story to buyers.

getting the customer to do most of the talking. This approach calls for good listening and problem-solving skills. One marketing director describes the approach this way:

> [High-performing salespeople] make it a point to understand customer needs and goals before they pull anything out of their product bag. . . . Such salespeople spend the time needed to get an in-depth knowledge of the customer's business, asking questions that will lead to solutions our systems can address.[20]

Any style of sales presentation can be improved with demonstration aids such as booklets, flip charts, slides, videotapes or videodiscs, and product samples. If buyers can see or handle the product, they will better remember its features and benefits.

Handling Objections

Customers almost always have objections during the presentation or when asked to place an order. The problem can be logical or psychological. And objections are often unspoken. In **handling objections,** the salesperson should use a positive approach, seek out hidden objections, ask the buyer to clarify any objections, take objections as opportunities to provide more information, and turn the objections into reasons for buying. Every salesperson needs training in the skills of handling objections.

Closing

The salesperson now tries to close the sale. Some salespeople do not get around to **closing** or do not handle it well. They may lack confidence, or feel guilty about asking for the order, or do not recognize the right moment to close the sale. Salespeople should know how to recognize closing signals from the buyer, including physical actions, comments, and questions. For example, the customer might sit forward and nod approvingly or ask about prices and credit terms. Salespeople can use one of several closing techniques. They can ask for the order, review points of agreement, offer to help write up the order, ask whether the buyer wants this model or that one, or note that the buyer will lose out if the order is not placed now. The salesperson may offer the buyer special reasons to close, such as a lower price or an extra quantity at no charge.

Follow-Up

The last step in the selling process—**follow-up**—is necessary if the salesperson wants to ensure customer satisfaction and repeat business. Right after closing, the salesperson should complete any details on delivery time, purchase terms, and other matters. The salesperson should schedule a follow-up call when the initial order is received to make sure there is proper installation, instruction, and servicing. This visit would reveal any problems, assure the buyer of the salesperson's interest, and reduce any buyer concerns that might have arisen since the sale.

Relationship Marketing

The principles of personal selling are *transaction oriented*—their aim is to help marketers close a specific sale with a customer. However, a larger concept should guide the seller's dealings with customers, that of *relationship marketing*. Sellers who know how to build and manage strong relationships with key customers will gain greater future sales from these customers. Thus, marketers need to master relationship marketing skills.

Relationship marketing is most appropriate with those customers who can most affect the company's future. For many companies, a small proportion of customers account for large share of the company's sales. Salespeople working with these key customers must do more than just call when they think a customer might be ready to place an order. They should monitor each key account, know its problems, and be ready to serve in a number of ways. They should call or visit frequently, make useful suggestions about how to improve the customer's business, take the customer to dinner, and take an interest in the customer as a person.

The importance of relationship marketing will no doubt increase in the future. Most companies are finding they earn a higher return from resources invested in getting repeat sales from current customers than from money spent to attract new customers. They are realizing the benefits gained from cross-selling opportunities with current customers. More companies are forming strategic partnerships, making skilled relationship marketing essential. And for customers who buy large, complex products—such as cement factories, robotic equipment, or large computer systems—the sale is only the beginning of the relationship. Thus, although it is not appropriate in all situations, relationship marketing continues to grow in importance (see Marketing Highlight 18–6).

MARKETING HIGHLIGHT 18–6

WHEN—AND HOW—TO USE RELATIONSHIP MARKETING

Although relationship marketing may not be effective in all situations, it works extremely well in the right situations. Transaction marketing, which focuses on one sales transaction at a time, is more appropriate than relationship marketing for customers who have short time horizons and who can switch from one supplier to another with little effort or investment. This situation often occurs in "commodity" markets, such as steel, where various suppliers offer largely undifferentiated products. A customer buying steel can buy from any of several steel suppliers and choose the one offering the best terms on a purchase-by-purchase basis. The fact that one steel supplier works at developing a longer-term relationship with a buyer does not automatically earn it the next sale; its price and other terms still have to be competitive.

On the other hand, relationship marketing can pay off handsomely with customers who have long time horizons and high switching costs, such as buyers of office automation systems. Such major system buyers usually research competing suppliers carefully and choose one from whom it can expect state-of-the-art technology and good long-term service. Both the customer and the supplier invest much money and time in building the relationship. The customer would find it costly and risky to switch to another supplier, and the seller would find that losing this customer would be a major loss. Thus, each seeks to develop a solid long-term working relationship with the other. It is with such customers that relationship marketing has the greatest payoff.

In these situations, the "in-supplier" and "out-supplier" face very different challenges. The in-supplier tries to make switching difficult for the customer. It develops product systems that are incompatible with those of competing suppliers and installs proprietary ordering systems that simplify inventory management and delivery. It works to become the customer's indispensable partner. Out-suppliers, on the other hand, try to make it easy and less costly to switch

suppliers. They design product systems that are compatible with the customer's system, that are easy to install and learn, that save the customer a lot of money, and that promise to improve through time.

Some marketers believe that the issue of transaction versus relationship marketing depends not so much on the type of industry as on the wishes of the particular customer. Some customers value a high-service supplier and will stay with that supplier for a long time. Other customers want to cut their costs and will readily switch suppliers to obtain lower costs. In this latter case, the company can still try to keep the customer by agreeing to reduce the price, providing that the customer is willing to accept fewer services. For example, the customer may forego free delivery, design assistance, training, or some other extra. However, the seller would be well advised to treat this type of customer on a transaction basis rather than on a relationship-building basis. As long as the company cuts its own costs by as much or more than its price reduction, the transaction-oriented customer will still be profitable.

Thus, relationship marketing is not the best approach in all situations—for some types of customers, heavy relationship investments simply don't pay off. But it can be extremely effective with the right types of customers, those who make hefty commitments to a specific system and then expect high-quality, consistent service over the long-term. To win and keep such accounts, the marketer will have to invest heavily in relationship marketing. But the returns will be well worth the investment.

Source: See Barbara Bund Jackson, *Winning and Keeping Industrial Customers: The Dynamics of Customer Relationships* (Lexington, Mass.: Heath, 1985); and James C. Anderson and James A. Narus, "Value-Based Segmentation, Targeting, and Relationship-Building in Business Markets," ISBM Report #12, 1989, The Institute for the Study of Business Markets, Pennsylvania State University, University Park, PA, 1989.

Here are the main steps in creating a relationship marketing program:

- *Identify the key customers deserving relationship marketing*—choose the five or ten largest customers and designate them for relationship marketing. Additional customers can be added who show exceptional growth or who pioneer new industry developments.

- *Assign a skilled relationship manager to each key customer*—the salesperson who is currently servicing the customer should receive training in relationship management or be replaced by someone more skilled in relationship management. The relationship manager should have characteristics that match or appeal to the customer.

- *Develop a clear job description for relationship managers*—it should describe their reporting relationships, objectives, responsibilities, and evaluation criteria. Make the relationship manager the focal point for all dealings with and about the client. Give each relationship manager only one or a few relationships to manage.

- *Appoint an overall manager to supervise relationship managers*—this person will develop job descriptions, evaluation criteria, and resource support to increase relationship manager effectiveness.

- *Have relationship managers prepare annual and long-range customer-relationship plans*—these plans should state objectives, strategies, specific actions, and required resources.

A properly implemented relationship marketing program will change many aspects of dealing with customers, replacing many of the ''bad things'' affecting relationships with ''good things'' (see Table 18-2). The organization will begin to focus as much on managing its customers as its products.

TABLE 18-2
Actions Affecting
Buyer-Seller
Relationships

| THINGS AFFECTING RELATIONSHIPS | |
Good Things	Bad Things
Initiate positive phone calls	Make only callbacks
Make recommendations	Make justifications
Candor in language	Accommodative language
Use phone	Use correspondence
Show appreciation	Wait for misunderstandings
Make service suggestions	Wait for service requests
Use ''we'' problem-solving language	Use ''owe-us'' legal language
Get to problems	Only respond to problems
Use jargon/shorthand	Use long-winded communications
Personality problems aired	Personality problems hidden
Talk of ''our future together''	Talk about making good on the past
Routinize responses	Fire drill/emergency responsiveness
Accept responsibility	Shift blame
Plan the future	Rehash the past

Source: Thedore Levitt, *The Marketing Imagination* (New York: Free Press, 1983), p. 119.

■ SUMMARY

Most companies use salespeople, and many companies assign them the key role in the marketing mix. The high cost of the salesforce calls for an effective *sales management process* consisting of six steps: setting *salesforce objectives*; designing *salesforce strategy*, *structure*, *size*, and *compensation*; *recruiting* and *selecting*; *training*; *supervising*; and *evaluating*.

As an element of the marketing mix, the salesforce is very effective in achieving certain marketing objectives and carrying on such activities as prospecting, communicating, selling and servicing, and information gathering. A market-oriented

salesforce needs skills in marketing analysis and planning, in addition to the traditional selling skills.

Once the salesforce objectives have been set, strategy answers the questions of what type of selling would be most effective (solo selling, team selling), what type of salesforce structure will work best (territorial, product, or customer structured), how large the salesforce should be, and how the salesforce should be compensated in terms of salary, commissions, bonuses, expenses, and fringe benefits.

To hold down the high costs of hiring the wrong people,

salespeople must be *recruited* and *selected* carefully. *Training* programs familiarize new salespeople not only with the art of selling, but with the company's history, its products and policies, and the characteristics of its market and competitors. All salespeople need supervision, and many need continuous encouragement because they must make many decisions and face many frustrations. Periodically, the company must evaluate their performance to help them do a better job.

The art of selling involves a seven-step *selling process*: *prospecting and qualifying*, *preapproach*, *approach*, *presentation and demonstration*, *handling objections*, *closing*, and *follow-up*. These steps help marketers close a specific sale. However, a seller's dealings with customers should be guided by the larger concept of *relationship marketing*—the company's salesforce should work to develop long-term relationships with key accounts.

■ QUESTIONS FOR DISCUSSION

1. Grocery stores require their suppliers' salespeople not only to sell, but also to serve as aisle clerks. These salespeople must arrange and restock shelves, build special displays, and set up point of purchase material. Is it important for a manufacturer to meet these demands? Are there creative ways to free the salesperson's time for more productive uses?

2. Describe the advantages each of the different salesforce structures would have for IBM. Which structure do you think would be most appropriate?

3. Some companies have installed computerized inventory tracking that automatically sends reorders to the supplier's computer as needed. Is this process likely to expand? Discuss the effects this could have on the role of the salesperson.

4. Why do so many salesforce compensation plans combine salary with bonus or commission? What are the advantages and disadvantages of using bonuses as incentives, rather than commissions?

5. What two personal characteristics do you think are most related to success in a sales career? What kinds of tests could be used to detect these characteristics in an applicant for a selling job?

6. Many people feel they do not have the ability to be a successful salesperson. What role does training play in helping someone develop selling ability?

7. How would you apply the different steps in the selling process to a summer job selling encyclopedias door to door? Would these steps be the same or different in selling copiers for Xerox?

8. What kinds of companies would find it worthwhile to have an inside salesforce? What major factors determine whether an inside salesforce is appropriate for a company?

9. The surest way to become a salesforce manager is to be an outstanding salesperson. What are the advantages and disadvantages of promoting top salespeople to management positions? Why might an outstanding salesperson refuse to be promoted?

10. Good salespeople are familiar with their competitors' products as well as their own. What would you do if your company expected you to sell a product that you thought was inferior to the competition's? Why?

■ KEY TERMS

Approach. The step in the selling process in which the salesperson meets and greets the buyer to get the relationship off to a good start.

Closing. The step in the selling process in which the salesperson asks the customer for an order.

Customer salesforce structure. A salesforce organization under which salespeople specialize in selling only to certain customers or industries.

Follow-up. The last step in the selling process in which the salesperson follows up after the sales to ensure customer satisfaction and repeat business.

Handling objections. The step in the selling process in which the salesperson seeks out, clarifies, and overcomes customer objections to buying.

Preapproach. The step in the selling process in which the salesperson learns as much as possible about a prospective customer before making a sales call.

Presentation. The step in the selling process in which the salesperson tells the product "story" to the buyer, showing how the product will make or save money.

Prospecting. The step in the selling process in which the salesperson identifies qualified potential customers.

Product salesforce structure. A salesforce organization under

which salespeople specialize in selling only a portion of the company's products or lines.

Salesforce management. The analysis, planning, implementation, and control of salesforce activities. It includes setting salesforce objectives; designing salesforce strategy; and recruiting, selecting, training, supervising, and evaluating the firm's salespeople.

Salesperson. An individual acting for a company by performing one or more of the following activities: prospecting, communicating, servicing, and information gathering.

Sales quotas. Standards set for salespeople stating the amount they should sell and how sales should be divided among the company's products.

Selling process. The steps that the salesperson follows when selling, which include prospecting and qualifying, preapproach, approach, presentation and demonstration, handling objections, closing, and follow-up.

Territorial salesforce structure. A salesforce organization that assigns each salesperson to an exclusive geographic territory in which that salesperson carries the company's full line.

Workload approach. An approach to setting salesforce size in which the company groups accounts into different size classes and then determines how many salespeople are needed to call on them the desired number of times.

■ REFERENCES

1. Adapted from Bill Kelley, "How to Sell Airplanes, Boeing Style," *Sales & Marketing Management*, December 9, 1985, pp. 32–34. Also see Anthony Ramirez, "Boeing's Happy, Harrowing Times," *Fortune*, July 17, 1989, pp. 40–45; and Dori Jones Yang, "How Boeing Does It," *Business Week*, July 9, 1990, pp. 46–49.

2. See Robert N. McMurry, "The Mystique of Super-Salesmanship," *Harvard Business Review*, March–April, 1961, p. 114. For a comparison of several classifications, see William C. Moncrief III, "Selling Activity and Sales Position Taxonomies for Industrial Salesforces," *Journal of Marketing Research*, August 1986, pp. 261–70.

3. See Rayna Skolnik, "Campbell Stirs Up Its Salesforce," *Sales & Marketing Management*, April 1986, pp. 56–58.

4. See Thayer C. Taylor, "Xerox's Sales Force Learns a New Game," *Sales & Marketing Management*, July 1, 1986, pp. 48–51; and Thayer C. Taylor, "Xerox's Makeover," *Sales & Marketing Management*, June 1987, p. 68.

5. For more on salesforce specialization, see Allan J. McGrath, "To Specialize or Not to Specialize," *Sales & Marketing Management*, June 1989, pp. 62–68.

6. See William Keenan, Jr., "Is Your Sales Pay Plan Putting the Squeeze on Top Performers?" *Sales & Marketing Management*, January 1990, pp. 74–75; and "1990 Survey of Selling Costs," *Sales & Marketing Management*, February 26, 1990, p. 75.

7. Survey of Selling Costs: 1987, "*Sales & Marketing Management*, 16, 1987, p. 55.

8. See Lynn G. Coleman, "Sales Force Turnover Has Managers Wondering Why," *Marketing News*, December 4, 1989, p. 6; and George H. Lucas, Jr., A. Parasuraman, Robert A. Davis, and Ben M. Enis, "An Empirical Study of Salesforce Turnover," *Journal of Marketing*, July 1987, pp. 34–59.

9. See Thayer C. Taylor, "Anatomy of a Star Salesperson," *Sales & Marketing Management*, May 1986, pp. 49–51; Bill Kelley, "How to Manage a Superstar," *Sales & Marketing Management*, November 1988, pp. 32–34; and "What Is the Best Advice on Selling You Have Ever Been Given," *Sales & Marketing Management*, February 1990, pp. 8–9.

10. See "'Pink Ghetto' in Sales for Women," *Sales & Marketing Management*, July 1988, p. 80; and "Women in Sales: Percentages by Industry," *Sales & Marketing Management*, February 26, 1990, p. 81.

11. See Richard Kern, "IQ Tests for Salesmen Make a Comeback," *Sales & Marketing Management*, April 1988, pp. 42–46.

12. See "1990 Survey of Selling Costs," *Sales & Marketing Management*, p. 81; and Patricia Sellers, "How IBM Teaches Techies to Sell," *Fortune*, June 6, 1988, pp. 141–46.

13. See Bill Kelley, "How Much Help Does a Salesperson Need?" *Sales & Marketing Management*, May 1989, pp. 32–35.

14. See "Computer-Based Sales Support: Shell Chemical's System" (New York: The Conference Board, Management Briefing: Marketing, April/May 1989), pp. 4–5.

15. See Jeremy Main, "Frito-Lay Shortens Its Business Cycle," *Fortune*, January 15, 1990, p. 11. Also see Thayer C. Taylor, "Make Way for the Salesman's New Friend," *Sales & Marketing Management*, February 1988, pp. 53–55; and Rowland T. Moriarty and Gordon S. Swartz, "Automation to Boost Sales and Marketing," *Harvard Business Review*, January–February 1989, pp. 100–108.

16. James A. Narus and James C. Anderson, "Industrial Distributor Selling: The Roles of Outside and Inside Sales," *Industrial Marketing Management*, Vol. 15, 1986, pp. 55–62.

17. "PAs Examine the People Who Sell to Them," *Sales & Marketing Management*, November 11, 1985, pp. 38–41.

18. Some of the following discussion is based on W. J. E. Crissy, William H. Cunningham, and Isabella C. M. Cunningham, *Selling: The Personal Force in Marketing* (New York: John Wiley & Sons, 1977), pp. 119–29.

19. Vincent L. Zirpoli, "You Can't 'Control' the Prospect, So Manage the Presale Activities to Increase Performance," *Marketing News*, March 16, 1984, p. 1.

20. Thayer C. Taylor, "Anatomy of a Star Salesperson," p. 50. Also see Harvey B. Mackay, "Humanize Your Selling Strategy," *Harvard Business Review*, March–April 1988, pp. 36–47.

MULTIFORM DESICCANTS: DESIGNING AN EFFECTIVE SALESFORCE

Steven Stepson, the new Director of Sales and Marketing at Multiform Desiccants, Inc. (MDI), knew when he accepted the job that he faced many hurdles in making MDI a top-notch sales and marketing organization. Sales were up—15 percent over last year. But company executives believed that a better organized and better managed salesforce could provide even greater sales growth. Stepson now faced the challenge of evaluating the current salesforce structure and recommending appropriate changes.

Most of us know desiccants as those little packets that you find in stereo equipment, cameras, and leather goods with the inscription "DO NOT EAT" on the wrapper. Desiccants absorb any moisture that could damage the product. More technically, however, desiccant applications are highly specialized and usually require a custom-blend of chemicals for each different use. MDI's safe, natural nontoxic products eradicate moisture and odors in containers and packages, while dramatically reducing the destructive effects of oxygen. Desiccants come in many forms—from gels to capsules of all shapes and sizes. These innovative products can be found in a variety of goods ranging from vitamin bottles to automotive air conditioning units, from photographic film packages to seagoing shipping containers. A typical MDI account is a pharmaceutical company that must keep moisture from products during shipment and storage. Other uses range from anti-fogging pellets for optical sensors on missiles to packets that keep orange juice crystals dry. In all, MDI manufactures 774 products for 23 different markets.

MDI started in the late 1960s as a garage-shop operation founded by a young entrepreneur with a dream. As a chemist working for a large bulk-desiccant manufacturer, he saw the need for formulating and packaging desiccants in small, single use packets. His employer had no desire to enter the packaging end of the business and so gave him permission to work on his ideas during nonworking hours. And although most technical companies require their employees to sign an agreement giving the company all rights to any business-related inventions, this company allowed him to retain all patent rights.

Before MDI took on the task, companies had to buy desiccants in bulk and then package them for their own specialized uses. Packaging desiccants in a variety of bagging materials—and labeling them for the customers—thus met the needs of a previously neglected market. That was 25 years ago. Today, with annual sales topping $15 million, MDI is a leader in packaged desiccants.

Nevertheless, believing that sales could be much higher, MDI hired Stepson to boost sales volume. As in any sales-management position, Stepson was under immediate pressure to increase sales quickly. The area likely to make the greatest immediate impact on MDI's sales

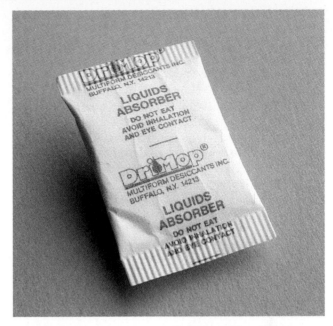

was its domestic salesforce. Thus, the new director first conducted a situation analysis to assess MDI's market position. This analysis included an external audit of competition and other market factors, a forecast of where market growth was likely to occur, and an internal audit of MDI's salesforce.

Salesforce design presented several problems and a challenge to Stepson, who discovered that frequent salesforce turnover had plagued MDI in the past. MDI had only three salespeople to cover the entire United States; each was paid a direct salary. Together, they serviced more than 3,850 accounts—although only 161 of these customers accounted for more than 80 percent of MDI's business. Therefore, it was important for the company to maintain this base while continuing to develop significant new accounts. Stepson found that three factors had influenced the salesforce's structure—the geographical location of customers, the technical skills needed to sell desiccants, and the long selling cycle dictated by the nature of the product.

Organizational markets tend to be geographically concentrated, and MDI's markets were typical in that regard. The majority of current and potential customers were located in large metropolitan areas east of the Mississippi River and along the West Coast, predominantly in California. MDI thus assigned sales representatives to geographically defined territories in order to take advantage of the clustering of its customers. Stepson realized that, unfortunately, geographical territory assignments created a situation in which sales representatives had to be knowledgeable in the assorted businesses of all their customers: One sales representative might call on customers in industries as diverse as automotives, pharmaceuticals, and aerospace.

Stepson also recognized a second problem. The complex nature of desiccants requires that salespeole have technical backgrounds. Sales representatives often had college degrees in engineering—either chemical or mechanical. Technical skills were thus essential to successful selling of the products. For example, to sell a desiccant product to a new customer, the sales representative had to analyze the customer's needs. How much moisture had to be absorbed? How fast must it be absorbed? In what environment (for example, temperature) will the desiccant be working? These are just some of the questions that sales representatives would need answered in order to solve the problem facing the customer. Naturally, the answers to these kinds of questions are very technical. The customer-oriented approach demanded that, in addition to having knowledge about the technical qualities of the product, sales representatives had to be innovative in solving problems.

Finally, working with an important customer to find the MDI product to satisfy a particular need often took many sales calls, meetings, and telephone conversations. Because each new application undergoes rigorous testing before it is finally accepted as a routine purchase by the customer, the process of nurturing an important account takes at least 12 to 18 months. Because it took so long to land a new account, MDI felt that paying its salesforce on a salary basis would provide them with an even income flow. However, although the salary-only compensation system provided even income, it gave salespeople little incentive to strive for increased sales. Moreover, with 161 accounts representing more than $15 million in annual revenue and the number of new accounts growing continuously, salespeople felt that they were not receiving their fair share of the revenues that they generated.

As Stepson discovered, travel and call planning were also problematic. Visits to various customers usually required air travel, car rental, and many overnight stays to service accounts properly. Travel accounted for at least three-quarters of a day per week. Salespeople usually spent two days per week in their offices to catch up on paper work and set up appointments for the following weeks. This schedule left only 2¼ days for customer visits. Thus, salespeople could on average make only five customer calls per week—an arrangement that did not provide the penetration necessary to meet projected sales. Moreover, salespeople kept busy serving existing accounts, allocating little time to prospect for new customers.

Stepson considered hiring additional salespeople, but the present salesforce balked at the idea. They felt that bringing in additional people at the same salary level would dilute their impact and diminish their importance and pay. The three current salespeople threatened to quit if such a policy were adopted.

Another problem was the background and training of the salesforce. Although the present salespeople had solid technical experience, Stepson felt that they lacked the sales skills required to sell MDI products effectively. For example, because there were a number of competitors selling substitutes, once a product was selected by the customer and purchased on a routine basis, the sales task turned from a technical issue to a pure price issue. Thus, making the initial sale and servicing the account in the future were very different kinds of selling activities requiring a variety of selling skills.

All in all, Stepson had his work cut out for him.

QUESTIONS

1. What objectives should Stepson set for MDI's salesforce?
2. Design a salesforce strategy for MDI which will accomplish its objectives. Be sure to address the issue of size, compensation, and structure.
3. Given the objectives and strategy you have developed, how should Stepson supervise and evaluate the salesforce?

Source: This case was written by Richard V. Resh, partner, DICRIS Company, Buffalo, New York.

TECHNIQUES FOR TRAINING SALESPEOPLE

Bob Spliz was hired as national sales manager for the Dorr Corporation after 25 years of sales experience. Although he had received sales management position offers before, he had always turned them down, but the Dorr Corporation's offer captured his interest because it would allow him to rebuild the entire sales program. Dorr's top management thought poor salesperson performance was a major contributing factor to the company's drastic declines in sales and profits. Therefore, they were committed to completely rebuilding their sales organization.

Bob is especially interested in improving the sales training program. As he put it, "I've seen many eager, talented young people enter the sales profession, only to leave it prematurely. Most of them were discouraged when, due to a lack of training, they made mistakes that cost them sales and the company customers. Their sales managers were not supportive or helpful. Therefore, rather than face more rejection in sales calls and reprimands at the sales office, they left selling. Training is the key to building and retaining a first-rate sales force."

In planning the new sales training program, Bob and his assistant sales manager, Julie Green, began by identifying the major topics to be covered. These are: product knowledge, market knowledge, company knowledge, selling techniques, record keeping and report writing, planning of activities, and time management. Then Bob asked Julie to determine what techniques are currently used in sales training programs and to send him a short report.

He received her report two days ago. In it, Julie provided the following brief descriptions of sales training techniques:

1. *Lectures*: These are formal oral presentations made in a classroom setting.
2. *Case studies*: These describe a selling problem and students develop ways to respond to the situation. Case studies generate interaction among students and can stimulate development of "solutions" not previously thought of.
3. *Role playing*: One trainee plays the role of a salesperson making a sales presentation and the instructor or another trainee plays the buyer. The "buyer" asks many questions and raises objections to various aspects of the product to provide the trainee playing the salesperson with realistic experience in handling sales calls. After the role play, everyone critiques it—pointing out good and poor performance aspects and discussing how the sales call should have been handled.
4. *Videotapes*: Some videotapes are prerecorded lectures used to provide information and to demonstrate selling techniques. Others are prerecorded enactment of sales calls that are shown in class to supplement lectures or to stimulate discussion of various selling techniques. Role-playing sessions can be recorded on videotape. When these are played back, trainees are able to view themselves in sales situations. They may watch these with only their instructor present or with the whole class. Discussion of the tapes gives the trainee valuable feedback.
5. *One-on-one*: This usually involves pairing a trainee with an experienced salesperson. By traveling with the salesperson, trainees can observe how to make sales calls and how to enter into a sales conversation before they actually conduct a sales call themselves. The experienced salesperson provides feedback on the trainee's performance, coaches the trainee, and encourages the trainee by being supportive and providing positive reinforcement for good work.
6. *Self study*: In this technique, sales trainees study printed or recorded materials and lessons at home or at work. Although self study has been around for a long time, it is increasing in importance because of the widespread use of computerized programmed instruction that lets trainees test and improve their recall of information.
7. *Discussion groups*: These are seminars organized around a preselected topic such as routing techniques or prospecting for new accounts. Usually, trainees have read information about the topic beforehand, so they are prepared to discuss the topic in depth.

Bob spent last evening reading Julie's report. In today's meeting they are discussing which techniques they want to use.

Bob begins by saying, "I remember sitting through a lot of lectures as a trainee. Sometimes they were boring, and some were so long that it was difficult to concentrate and my attention wandered. But, much as I hate to say it, they are probably the best technique for disseminating product, company, and market knowledge."

Julie responds, "I know what you mean about boring. Perhaps we could make them more interesting by combining them with—" The telephone interrupts Julie before she can complete her sentence.

QUESTIONS

1. What technique(s) do you think Julie was going to suggest when the telephone rang?
2. What technique(s) would you use to teach (a) selling techniques, (b) record keeping and report writing, (c) planning of activities, and (d) time management?

Sources: Gilbert A. Churchill, Neil M. Ford, and Orville C. Walker, Jr., *Sales Force Management: Planning, Implementation and Control* (Homewood, IL: Richard D. Irwin, 1985), Chap. 12; and Douglas J. Dalrymple, *Sales Management Concepts and Cases* (New York: Wiley, 1988), Chap. 8.

AT&T: PLAYING IT SMART WITH A NEW PRODUCT

Whatever happened, you may ask, to quadraphonic stereo, to videodiscs, and to videotext? Answer: The first is gone, the second has been forced into a narrower market, and the third is languishing. All three were new technologies that were literally supposed to change our lives; all three had millions of dollars invested in them by well-known corporations bent not only on being first in their niche but actually creating the niche.

The question and answer are of special interest to 40-year-old Joe Griffin, who is charged with the marketing of still another product based on a new technology—the AT&T smart card. It may look like a traditional credit card, but this little slice of plastic can do more things than you ever thought of. And although Joseph E. Griffin may look like a mild-mannered middle manager, he is supersalesman, gospel spreader, alliance maker, applications developer, corporate guerrilla, publicist, production maven—and above all, the "product champion," as he calls himself, of this very, very smart card.

Even with the AT&T name attached to it, the product looks as if it will need all the championing it can get—for several reasons. First, AT&T is a relative latecomer to the field. The earliest patents for the smart cards—which are essentially credit cards containing computer chips that provide processing power and electronic memory—were filed in France back in the early 1970s. Since then, the French have almost made smart cards a symbol of national honor. They've not only pushed the technology at home—there are more than 30 million smart cards in service in France—but they're making major inroads elsewhere in the world as well. Using the French technology, a number of U.S. companies have established a presence in this country.

Second, the AT&T card differs from traditional smart cards in that it has no electrical contact points (the points on the card's surface that come into contact with the points on the terminal during use). This absence of contact points gives the AT&T card several advantages: It has far greater durability, and it resists water, dirt, grease, and static electricity. These advantages come at a price, of course: Informed sources estimate that such a card will cost anywhere from $15 to $35—compared to about $5 for a traditional smart card and about 15¢ or less for a conventional magnetic-strip credit card.

These advantages also come at the price of broad acceptance. Because the AT&T technology is unique, its smart card cannot relate to other smart card technologies, which have their own standards and ways of doing things.

On the other hand, just because it comes from AT&T, it has a great deal going for it—including unrivaled experience with similar cards (AT&T has more than 40 million telephone calling cards in circulation) and a network and terminal system (telephones) already in place. AT&T is also arguably the premier communications company in the world.

So, what does it *do*, this unique AT&T card? Much as a PC runs a word-processing program along with a database application and spreadsheet, the AT&T card contains an operating system with a reusable memory that permits multiple applications to coexist with the same card. The user chooses from a "menu" to switch from one application to another. All the information on the card is protected by a security system to make unauthorized access extremely difficult, if not impossible.

Yes, but what does an individual *do* with such a portable information system in his or her wallet? Well, let's say you're a sales manager about to leave on a business trip. The card contains the cash value authorized for the trip; it also contains your business credit card numbers, your airline tickets, and confirmed reservations for your hotel and rental car. In addition, the card carries ID information that gains you admittance to your company's high-security field office. Oh, yes—it can also hold important phone numbers and an electronic notebook that lets you record expenses, customer calls, salespeople appraisals, or any other information vital to your job. Or let's say you've just finished a day of trouble-shooting in the field. By dialing a certain number, you can load your findings into your company's main database; at the same time, you can get an updated list of customers whom you should see the next day.

And there are still other potential uses for smart cards—a "smart dog tag," for instance, that would provide portable personnel and payroll files, training records, and medical histories. Smart employee badges are also being tested, using the card's capability to store video images, digitized fingerprints, or voice prints.

Innovative, yes—indeed, downright creative. But a jaded marketer might well ask: Is the world really waiting—or ready—for a card this brainy? Joe Griffin believes it is—if not exactly with open arms, then at least willing to embrace it given the right conditions. To create those conditions, he must first meet his key marketing challenge: focusing on customer needs. His second challenge is to get other people to play the game according to AT&T rules. Other players must be signed on—for instance, providers of financial, travel, and information service.

But the most immediate task, as Griffin sees it, is to spread the gospel of this new technology. His prime objective: to gain acceptance of common standards. "Remember quadraphonic sound, which was introduced in 1977?" he asks. "There were three different technologies competing with each other. Record manufacturers didn't know which one to support. The result: Quadraphonic disappeared. Another example: RCA's electromechanical videodisc versus the Philips/Pioneer optical laser disk. Their battle drew so much negative press the public didn't know which to support. Then along came home videotape, which was technically inferior but didn't have to overcome the market confusion and negative press. Griffin wants to make sure that this won't happen with his smart card: "My goal," he says, "is to sign up major players before they've made any commitments elsewhere."

But what about the problem of AT&T's smart card technology versus that of the rest of the world? Griffin answers with another question: "How can the AT&T card meet the criteria for contact cards when our cards have no contacts? I think that, for the time being at least, there are going to be two technologies—contact and noncontact—and both will be equally valid, just as there is a standard for VHS videotape and a standard for Beta." About the future of the AT&T technology, however, Griffin is confident: "The traditional smart card is like a steam engine compared to our gas turbine."

Besides finding new constituencies for his technology, Griffin must also defend smart card's turf *inside* AT&T. "Internal critics are often the most vocal," he explains. "They'll say things like, 'We've tried that before,' or 'That doesn't belong in your group,' or 'You're just product management, we're marketing.'

"Part of the problem," he points out, "is that it's never clear who's in charge of the product. That's why the product champion has to be a corporate guerrilla. There are very few people I can fire at AT&T. I don't have a factory under my control, or legal or accounting, or any other staff departments. I have to negotiate with each of them for their time and resources. I also have to go to top management to justify funding. Eventually," Griffin concludes, "we've got to make hard decisions. Do we build the factory or not—not bricks and mortar, necessarily, but, say, giving the project a certain amount of square footage or level of staffing."

The platform for smart card technology is the E-card (for *experimental*), recently tested by AT&T with the help of 1,000 frequent travelers. After the E-card is inserted into a specially equipped telephone (and an optional password entered), the names and phone numbers within the card's memory are displayed on a screen. When the user touches one or two keys, the number is speed-dialed and billed to one of eight designated sub-billing numbers. The card's "menu" allows the user to choose what he wants from among its contents.

Griffin describes the E-card test as successful but hedges when it comes to whether it holds the most immediate potential for the new technology: "You don't always test your best application," he explains. Certainly, he keeps plugging away at new markets for the smart card. After the so-called electronic dog tag which the military put out to bid in 1988, the next hottest market is medical systems. "Because of AIDS," Griffin explains, "this country is going to spend millions of dollars tracking our blood supply—the donor, date donated, tests performed, who administered to, and so on. People will insist that there be an information trail." Currently, he says, AT&T is meeting with several major national health care organizations on proposals to store medical information for rapid patient check-in as well as for use in emergencies.

The proportion of the gross national product devoted to health care is 10 percent and growing, and Griffin sees other opportunities for the smart card in this area. He points out that many people—the elderly in particular—often can't recall important medical events in their lives, the names of doctors who've treated them, or medications they've taken. Entire medical histories and medication data could be contained—and updated—on a smart card.

Still another promising market is corporate security badges. "Key locations within Bell Labs use them now," Griffin explains. "The smart badge tells who's in the building, for how long, and so on. In effect, the badge acts as a portable miniaturized time clock." But it goes beyond that, he says: "Access to databases can be limited and navigation quietly tracked within the computer system to monitor and permit only key individuals to gain access to certain files."

Probably the biggest market of all, however, is in financial services. Although both MasterCard and Visa have expressed varying degrees of interest in smart cards, in pilot tests both have opted for the traditional contact-point credit card. Visa, however, plans a step-by-step approach and intends by 1993 to introduce its so-called "super smart card" to upscale customers. MasterCard, on the other hand, opted for a 1989 worldwide rollout of its smart card terminals and claims banks are receptive despite the price tag of $275 to $325 per terminal. But there are doubters. Spencer Nilson, who writes a newsletter reflecting a bent for traditional magnetic-stripe technology, scoffs, "If MasterCard says they've gotten some banks to spring for the technology, they're full of baloney. In the crunch, the banks won't pay. And even if one does, so what? One bank doesn't make a technology."

Generally, experts in the smart card field are cautious. "There's not going to be any splashy application that will catch everybody's attention," comments James Kobielus of the International Center for Information Technologies, a Washington, D.C., think tank in the field of information technology. "I see two trends occurring simultaneously: first, the trend to smarts—smart toys, smart houses, smart cars, and so on; second, there's the trend to cards—ATM cards, office-admission cards, and the like. When these trends cross, and they will, we'll wind up with a collection of smart cards in our wallet, each dedicated to a different purpose. It's been said that the smart card technology is a solution looking for a problem.

What I'm saying," explains Kobielus, "is that there is no single problem but a whole range of problems that smart card technology will solve."

QUESTIONS

1. What will influence the movement of smart cards from the introductory stage of the product life cycle to the growth stage?

2. Suggest what the market for smart cards will be like for the remainder of its product life cycle.

3. The idea of storing an elderly person's medical history and medication data on a smart card is in the concept-development stage at AT&T. How should the company proceed?

4. Think of other problems that the smart card could be used to solve. Describe the consumer need, the target market, and a proposed marketing mix.

Source: Adapted from A. J. Vogl, "Marketing a New Technology," *Sales & Marketing Management*, July 1988, pp. 37–42.

Competitor Analysis and Competitive Marketing Strategies

Y ou've probably never heard of *Vernor's Ginger Ale*. And if you tried it, you might not even think it tastes like ginger ale. Vernor's is "aged in oak," the company boasts, and "deliciously different." The caramel-colored soft drink is sweeter and smoother than other ginger ales you've tasted. But to many people in Detroit who grew up with Vernor's, there's nothing quite like it. They drink it cold and hot; morning, noon, and night; summer and winter; from the bottle and at the soda fountain counter. They like the way the bubbles tickle their noses. And they'll say you haven't lived until you've tasted a Vernor's float. To many, Vernor's even has some minor medicinal qualities—they use warm Vernor's to settle a child's upset stomach or to soothe a sore throat. To most Detroit adults, the familiar green and yellow packaging brings back many pleasant childhood memories.

The soft-drink industry is headed by two giants—Coca-Cola leads with a 40 percent market share and Pepsi challenges strongly with about 30 percent. Coke and Pepsi are the main combatants in the "soft-drink wars." They wage constant and pitched battles for retail shelf space. Their weapons include a steady stream of new products, heavy price discounts, an army of distributor salespeople, and huge advertising and promotion budgets.

A few "second-tier" brands—such brands as Dr. Pepper, 7-Up, and Royal Crown—capture a combined 20 percent or so of the market. They challenge Coke and Pepsi in the smaller, non-cola segments. When Coke and Pepsi battle for shelf space, these second-tier brands often get squeezed. Coke and Pepsi set the ground rules, and if the smaller brands don't follow along, they risk being pushed out or gobbled up.

At the same time, a group of speciality producers who concentrate on small but loyal market segments fights for what's left of the market. While large in number, each of these small firms holds a tiny market share—usually less than one percent. Vernor's falls into this "all others" group, along with A&W root beer, Shasta sodas, Squirt, Faygo, Soho Natural Soda, Yoo-hoo, Dr. Brown's Cream Soda, A.J. Canfield's Diet Chocolate Fudge Soda, and a dozen others. Whereas Dr Pepper and 7-Up merely get squeezed in the soft-drink wars, these small fries risk being crushed.

When you compare Vernor's to Coca-Cola, for example, you wonder how Vernor's survives. Coca-Cola spends more than $200 million a year advertising its soft drinks; Vernor's spends less than $1 million. Coke offers a long list of brands and brand versions—Coke, Coke Classic, Cherry Coke, Diet Coke, Caffeine-Free Coke, Diet Cherry Coke, Caffeine-Free Diet Coke, Sprite, Tab, Mellow Yellow, Minute Maid soda, and others; Vernor's sells only two versions—original and diet. Coke's large distributor salesforce sways retailers with huge discounts and promotion allowances; Vernor's has only a small marketing budget and carries little clout with retailers. When you are lucky enough to find Vernor's at your local supermarket, it's usually tucked away on the bottom shelf with other specialty beverages. Even in Detroit, the company's stronghold, stores usually give Vernor's only a few shelf-facings, compared with 50 or 100 facings for the many Coca-Cola brands.

Yet Vernor's does more than survive—it thrives! How? Instead of going head-to-head with the bigger companies in the major soft-drink segments, Vernor's niches in the market. It concentrates on serving the special needs of loyal Vernor's drinkers. Vernor's knows that it could never seriously challenge Coca-Cola for a large share of the soft-drink market. But it also knows that Coca-Cola could never create another Vernor's ginger ale—at least not in the minds of Vernor's drinkers. As long as Vernor's keeps these special customers happy, it can capture a small but profitable share of the market. And "small" in this market is nothing to sneeze at—a one percent market share equals $380 million in retail sales! Thus, through *concentrated marketing*, Vernor's prospers in the shadows of the soft-drink giants.[1]

CHAPTER OBJECTIVES

After reading this chapter, you should be able to:

1. Explain the importance of developing competitive marketing strategies that position the company against competitors and give it the strongest possible competitive advantage.
2. Identify the steps companies go through in analyzing competitors.
3. Discuss the competitive strategies that market leaders use to expand the market and to protect and expand their market shares.
4. Describe the strategies market challengers and followers use to increase their market shares and profits.
5. Discuss how market nichers find and develop profitable corners of the market.

Today, understanding customers is not enough. In the fast-growth environment of the 1960s, companies could ignore their competitors because most markets were growing. But in the turbulent 1970s and flat 1980s, companies realized that sales gains would have to come from wresting market share away from competitors. The 1990s will be a decade of even greater competition, both foreign and domestic. Many foreign economies are deregulating and encouraging market forces to operate. The European Common Market is removing trade barriers between Western European countries. Multinationals are aggressively moving into new markets and practicing global marketing. The result is that companies have no choice but to cultivate "competitiveness." They must start paying as much attention to tracking their competitors as to understanding target customers.

Under the marketing concept, companies succeed by designing offers that satisfy target consumer needs better than competitors' offers. Thus, marketing strategies must consider not only the needs of target consumers, but also the strategies of competitors. The first step is **competitor analysis,** the process of identifying key competitors; assessing their objectives, strengths and weaknesses, strategies, and reaction patterns; and selecting which competitors to attack or avoid. The second step is developing **competitive strategies** that strongly position the company against competitors and that give the company the strongest possible competitive advantage.

COMPETITOR ANALYSIS

To plan effective competitive marketing strategies, the company needs to find out all it can about its competitors. It must constantly compare its products, prices, channels, and promotion with those of close competitors. In this way the company can find areas of potential competitive advantage and disadvantage. And it can launch more precise attacks on its competitors as well as prepare stronger defenses against attacks.

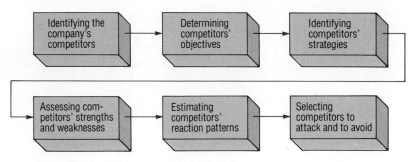

FIGURE 19-1
Steps in analyzing competitors

But what do companies need to know about their competitors? They need to know: Who are our competitors? What are their objectives? What are their strategies? What are their strengths and weaknesses? What are their reaction patterns? The major steps in analyzing competitors are shown in Figure 19-1 and discussed below.

Identifying the Company's Competitors

Normally, it would seem a simple task for a company to identify its competitors. Coca-Cola knows that Pepsi-Cola is its major competitor; and General Motors knows that it competes with Ford. At the most obvious level, a company can define its competitors as other companies offering a similar product and services to the same customers at similar prices. Thus, Buick might see Ford as a major competitor, but not Mercedes or Hyundai.

But companies actually face a much broader range of competitors. More broadly, the company can define competitors as all firms making the same product or class of products. In that case Buick would see itself as competing against all other automobile makers. Even more broadly, competitors might include all companies making products that supply the same service. In this case Buick would see itself competing against not only other automobile manufacturers but also against the makers of motorcycles, bicycles, and trucks. Finally, and still more broadly, competitors might include all companies that compete for the same consumer dollars. If that were so Buick would see itself competing with companies that sell major consumer durables, foreign vacations, new homes, or major home repairs.

Companies must avoid "competitor myopia." A company is more likely to be "buried" by its latent competitors than its current rivals. For example, Eastman Kodak, in its film business, has been worrying about the growing competition from Fuji, the Japanese film maker. But Kodak faces a much greater threat from the recent invention of the "filmless camera." This camera, sold by Canon and Sony, takes video still pictures that can be shown on TV set, turned into hard copy, and later erased. What greater threat is there to a film business than a filmless camera!

The Industry Point of View

Many companies identify their competitors from the *industry* point of view. An **industry** is a group of firms which offer a product or class of products that are close substitutes for each other. Examples are the auto industry, the oil industry, the pharmaceutical industry, or the beverage industry. In a given industry, if the price of one product rises, it causes the demand for another product to rise. In the beverage industry, for example, if the price of coffee rises, this leads people to switch to tea or lemonade or soft drinks. Thus coffee, tea, lemonade, and soft drinks are substitutes, even though they are physically different products. A company must strive to understand the competitive pattern in its industry if it hopes to be an effective "player" in that industry.

The Market Point of View

Instead of identifying competitors from the industry point of view, the company can take a *market* point of view. In that case, competitors are companies that are trying to satisfy the same customer need or serve the same customer group. From an industry point of view, Coca-Cola might see its competition as Pepsi, Dr. Pepper, 7-Up, and

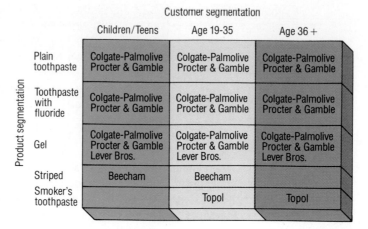

FIGURE 19-2
Product/market segments for toothpaste

Source: William A. Cohen. *Winning on the Marketing Front* (New York: John Wiley & Sons, 1986), p. 63.

other soft-drink manufacturers. From a market point of view, however, the customer really wants "thirst quenching." This need can be satisfied by iced tea, fruit juice, bottled water, or many other beverages. Similarly, Crayola might define its competitors as other makers of crayons and children's drawing supplies. But from a market point of view, the competitors are all firms that make recreational products for the children's market. In general, the market concept of competition opens the company's eyes to a broader set of actual and potential competitors, and it leads to better long-run market planning.

The key to identifying competitors is to link industry and market analysis by mapping product/market segments. Figure 19-2 shows the product/market segments in

Product/market segments: Procter & Gamble targets various versions of Crest at many different product/market segments, including children. Topol targets smokers and others who want a "stain-free smile."

the toothpaste market by product types and customer age groups. We see that P&G (with several versions of Crest and Gleam) and Colgate-Palmolive (with Colgate) occupy six of the segments. Lever Brothers (Aim), Beecham (Aqua Fresh), and Topol each occupy two segments. If Topol wanted to enter other segments, it would need to estimate the market size of each segment, the market shares of the current competitors, and their current capabilities, objectives, and strategies. Clearly each product/market segment would pose different competitive problems and opportunities.

Determining Competitors' Objectives

Having identified the main competitors, marketing management now asks: What does each competitor seek in the marketplace? What drives each competitor's behavior?

The marketer might at first assume that all competitors simply want to maximize their profits and choose their actions accordingly. But companies differ in the weights they put on short-term versus long-term profits. And some competitors might be oriented toward ''satisfying'' rather than ''maximizing'' profits. They have target profit goals and are satisfied in achieving them, even if more profits could have been produced by other strategies.

Thus, marketers must look beyond competitors' profit goals. Each competitor has a mix of objectives, each with differing importance. The company wants to know the relative importance that a competitor places on current profitability, market share growth, cash flow, technological leadership, service leadership, and other goals. Knowing a competitor's mix of objectives reveals whether the competitor is satisfied with its current situation and how it might react to different competitive actions. For example, a company that pursues low cost leadership will react much more strongly to a competitor's cost-reducing manufacturing breakthrough than to the same competitor's advertising increase. A company must also monitor its competitors' objectives for attacking various product/market segments. If the company finds that a competitor has discovered a new segment, this might be an opportunity. If it finds that competitors plan new moves into segments now served by the company, it will be forewarned and, hopefully, forearmed.

Identifying Competitors' Strategies

The more that one firm's strategy resembles another firm's strategy, the more the firms compete. In most industries, the competitors can be sorted into groups that pursue different strategies. A **strategic group** is a group of firms in an industry following the same or a similar strategy. For example, in the major appliance industry, General Electric, Whirlpool, and Sears all belong to the same strategic group. Each produces a full line of medium-price appliances supported by good service. Maytag and KitchenAid, on the other hand, belong to a different strategic group. They produce a narrow line of very high quality appliances, offer a high level of service, and charge a premium price.

Some important insights emerge from strategic group identification. For example, if a company enters one of the groups, the members of that group become its key competitors. Thus, if the company enters the first group against General Electric, Whirlpool, and Sears, it can succeed only if it develops some strategic advantages over these large competitors.

Although competition is most intense within a strategic group, there is also rivalry between groups. First, some of the strategic groups may appeal to overlapping customer segments. For example, no matter what their strategy, all major appliance manufacturers will go after the apartment and home builders segment. Second, the customers may not see much difference in the offers of different groups—they may see little difference in quality between Whirlpool and Maytag. Finally, members of one strategic group might expand into new strategy segments. Thus, General Electric might decide to offer a premium quality, premium price line to compete with KitchenAid.

The company needs to examine all of the dimensions that identify strategic groups within the industry. It needs to know each competitor's product quality, features, and mix; customer services; pricing policy; distribution coverage; sales force strategy; and advertising and sales promotion programs. And it must study the details of each competitor's R&D, manufacturing, purchasing, financial, and other strategies.

Expanding into a new strategy segment: General Electric offers a premium-quality, premium-price line of kitchen appliances.

Assessing Competitor's Strengths and Weaknesses

Can the various competitors carry out their strategies and reach their goals? This depends on each competitor's resources and capabilities. Marketers need to accurately identify each competitor's strengths and weaknesses.

As a first step, a company gathers important data on each competitor's business for the past few years. It wants to know about competitors' goals, strategies, and performance. Admittedly, some of this information will be hard to collect. For example, industrial goods companies find it hard to estimate competitors' market shares because they do not have the same syndicated data services that are available to consumer packaged goods companies. Still, any information they can find will help them form a better estimate of each competitor's strengths and weaknesses.

Companies normally learn about their competitors' strengths and weaknesses through secondary data, personal experience, and hearsay. But they can also increase their knowledge by conducting primary marketing research with customers, suppliers, and dealers. They can carry out a **customer value analysis,** asking customers what benefits they value and how they rate the company versus competitors on important attributes (see Marketing Highlight 19–1). This information shows which competitors are open to attack and in what ways. It also points out areas where the company is vulnerable to competitors' actions.

In searching for competitors' weaknesses, the company should try to identify any assumptions they make about their business and the market which are no longer valid. Some companies believe they produce the best quality in the industry when this is no longer true. Many companies are victims of rules of thumb such as ''customers prefer full line companies,'' ''the salesforce is the only important marketing tool,'' or ''customers value service more than price.'' If a competitor is operating on a major wrong assumption, the company can take advantage of it.

CUSTOMER VALUE ANALYSIS: THE KEY TO COMPETITIVE ADVANTAGE

In analyzing competitors and searching for competitive advantage, one of the most important marketing tools is *customer value analysis*. The aim of a customer value analysis is to determine what benefits target customers value and how they rate the relative value of various competitors' offers. The major steps in customer value analysis are described below.

1. *Identify the major attributes that customers value.* Various people in the company may have different ideas on what customers value. Thus, the company's marketing researchers must ask customers themselves what features and performance levels they look for in choosing a product or seller. Different customers will mention different features and benefits. If the list gets too long, the researcher can remove overlapping attributes. Still, the final list of things that customers value may run as high as ten or twenty items.

2. *Assess the importance of different attributes.* Customers are asked to rate or rank the importance of the different factors. If the customers differ very much in their ratings, they should be grouped into different customer segments.

3. *Assess the company's and competitors' performance on different customer values against their rated importance.* Next customers are asked where they rate each competitor's performance on each attribute. Ideally, the company's own performance will be high on the attributes the customers value most and low on the attributes which customers value least. Two pieces of bad news would be: (a) the company's performance

ranks high on some minor attributes—a case of "overkill"; and (b) the company's performance ranks low on some major attributes—a case of "underkill." The company must also look at how each competitor ranks on the important attributes.

4. *Examine how customers in a specific segment rate the company's performance against a specific major competitor on an attribute-by-attribute basis.* The key to gaining competitive advantage is to take each customer segment and examine how the company's offer compares to that of its major competitor. If the company's offer exceeds the competitor's offer on all important attributes, the company can charge a higher price and earn higher profits, or it can charge the same price and gain more market share. But if the company is seen as performing at a lower level than its major competitor on some important attributes, it must invest in strengthening those attributes or finding other important attributes where it can build a lead on the competitor.

5. *Monitor customer values over time.* Although customer values are fairly stable in the short run, they will probably change as competing technologies and features appear and as customers face different economic climates. A company that assumes that customer values will remain stable flirts with danger. The company must periodically review customer values and competitors' standings if it wants to remain strategically effective.

Estimating Competitors' Reaction Patterns

A competitor's objectives, strategies, and strengths and weaknesses go a long way toward explaining its likely actions, and its reactions to company moves such as a price cut, a promotion increase, or a new product introduction. In addition, each competitor has a certain philosophy of doing business, a certain internal culture and guiding beliefs. Marketing managers need a deep understanding of a given competitor's mentality if they want to anticipate how the competitor will act or react.

Each competitor reacts differently. Some do not react quickly or strongly to a competitor's move. They may feel their customers are loyal; they may be slow in noticing the move; they may lack the funds to react. Some competitors react to certain types of assaults but not others. They might always respond strongly to price cuts in order to signal that such moves will never succeed. But they might not respond at all to advertising increases, believing these to be less threatening. Other competitors react swiftly and strongly to any assault. Thus, P&G does not let a new detergent come easily into the market. Many firms avoid direct competition with P&G and look for easier prey, knowing that P&G will fight fiercely if challenged. Finally, some competitors show no predictable reaction pattern. They might or might not react on a given occasion, and there is no way to foresee what they will do based on their economics, history, or anything else.

In some industries, competitors live in relative harmony; in others, they fight constantly. Knowing how major competitors react gives the company clues on how best to attack competitors or how best to defend the company's current positions.[2]

Selecting Competitors to Attack and Avoid

Management has already largely determined its major competitors through prior decisions on customer targets, distribution channels, and marketing mix strategy. These decisions define the strategic group to which the company belongs. Management must now decide which competitors to compete against most vigorously. The company can focus its attack on one of several classes of competitors.

Strong or Weak Competitors
Most companies prefer to aim at weak competitors, which requires fewer resources and time. But in the process, the firm may gain little. The argument could be made that the firm should also compete with strong competitors in order to sharpen its abilities. Furthermore, even strong competitors have some weaknesses, and succeeding against them often provides greater returns.

Close or Distant Competitors
Most companies will compete with those competitors who resemble them the most. Thus, Chevrolet competes more against Ford than against Jaguar. At the same time, the company may want to avoid trying to "destroy" a close competitor. Here is an example of a questionable "victory":

> Bausch and Lomb in the late 1970s moved aggressively against other soft lens manufacturers with great success. However, this led one after another competitor to sell out to larger firms such as Revlon, Johnson & Johnson, and Schering-Plough, with the result that Bausch and Lomb now faced much larger competitors.[3]

In this case, the company's success in hurting its closest rival brought in tougher competitors.

"Well-Behaved" or "Disruptive" Competitors
A company really needs and benefits from competitors. The existence of competitors results in several strategic benefits. Competitors may help increase total demand. They share the costs of market and product development and help to legitimize new technology. They may serve less attractive segments or lead to more product differentiation. Finally, they lower the antitrust risk and improve bargaining power versus labor or regulators.

However, a company may not view all of its competitors as beneficial. An industry often contains "well-behaved" competitors and "disruptive" competitors.[4] Well-behaved competitors play by the rules of the industry. They favor a stable and healthy industry, set prices in a reasonable relation to costs, motivate others to lower costs or improve differentiation, and accept a reasonable level of market share and profits. Disruptive competitors, on the other hand, break the rules: They try to buy share rather than earn it, take large risks, invest in overcapacity, and in general shake up the industry. For example, IBM finds Cray Research to be a well-behaved competitor because it plays by the rules, sticks to its supercomputer segment, and doesn't attack IBM's core markets. But IBM finds Fujitsu a disruptive competitor because it attacks IBM in its core markets with subsidized prices and little differentiation. A company might be smart to support well-behaved competitors, aiming its attacks at disruptive competitors.

The implication is that "well-behaved" companies should try to shape an industry that consists of only well-behaved competitors. Through careful licensing, selective retaliation, and coalitions, they can shape the industry so that the competitors behave rationally and harmoniously, follow the rules, try to earn share rather than buy it, and differentiate somewhat to compete less directly.

Designing the Competitive Intelligence System

We have described the main types of information that company decision makers need to know about their competitors. This information must be collected, interpreted, distributed, and used. While the cost in money and time of gathering competitive intelligence is high, the cost of not gathering it is higher. Yet the company must design its competitive intelligence system in a cost-effective way.

The competitive intelligence system first identifies the vital types of competitive information and the best sources of this information. Then the system continuously collects information from the field (salesforce, channels, suppliers, market research firms, trade associations) and from published data (government publications, speeches, articles). Next the system checks the information for validity and reliability, interprets it, and organizes it in an appropriate way. Finally, it sends its best information to relevant decision makers, and responds to inquiries from managers about competitors.

With this system, company managers will receive timely information about competitors in the form of phone calls, bulletins, newsletters, and reports. In addition, managers can access the system when they need an interpretation of a competitor's sudden move, or when they want to know a competitor's weaknesses and strengths, or how a competitor will respond to a planned company move.

Smaller companies that cannot afford to set up a formal competitive intelligence office can assign specific executives to watch specific competitors. Thus, a manager who used to work for a competitor might follow closely all developments connected with that competitor, acting as the "in-house" expert on that competitor. Any manager needing to know the thinking of a given competitor could contact the assigned in-house expert.[5]

COMPETITIVE STRATEGIES

Having identified and evaluated the major competitors, the company must now design broad competitive marketing strategies that will best position its offer against competitors' offers in the minds of consumers—strategies that will give the company or its product the strongest possible **competitive advantage**.[6] But what broad marketing strategies might the company use? Which are best for a particular company, or for the company's different divisions and products?

No one strategy is best for all companies. Each company must determine what makes the most sense given its position in the industry and its objectives, opportunities, and resources. Even within a company, different strategies may be required for different businesses or products. Johnson & Johnson uses one marketing strategy for its leading brands in stable consumer markets and a different marketing strategy for its new high-tech health care businesses and products.

Competitive Positions

Firms competing in a given target market will, at any point in time, differ in their objectives and resources. Some firms will be large, others small. Some will have great resources, others will be strapped for funds. Some will be old and established, others new and fresh. Some will strive for rapid market share growth, others for long-term profits. And the firms will occupy different competitive positions in the target market.

Michael Porter suggests four basic competitive positioning strategies that companies can follow—three winners and one loser.[7]

- *Overall cost leadership.*—The company works hard to achieve the lowest costs of production and distribution so that it can price lower than its competitors and win a large market share. Texas Instruments is a leading practitioner of this strategy.
- *Differentiation.*—The company concentrates on creating a highly differentiated product line and marketing program so that it comes across as the class leader in the industry. Most customers would prefer to own this brand if its price is not too high. IBM and Caterpillar follow this strategy in computers and heavy construction equipment, respectively.
- *Focus.*—The company focuses its effort on serving a few market segments well rather than going after the whole market. Thus, glassmaker AFG Industries focuses on users of tempered and colored glass—it makes 70 percent of the glass for microwave oven doors and 75 percent of the glass for shower doors and patio table tops.[8]

Companies that pursue a clear strategy—one of the above—are likely to perform well. The firm that carries off that strategy best will make the most profits. But firms that do not pursue a clear strategy—*middle-of-the-roaders*—do the worst. Chrysler and International Harvester both came upon difficult times because neither stood out as the lowest in cost, highest in perceived value, or best in serving some market segment. Middle-of-the-roaders try to be good on all strategic counts, but end up being not very good at anything.

We adopt a different classification of competitive positions, based on the role firms play in the target market—that of leading, challenging, following, or niching.

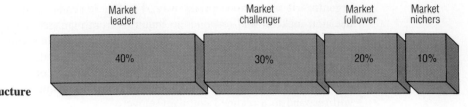

Market
leader
           Market
challenger
          Market
follower
      Market
nichers

FIGURE 19-3
Hypothetical market structure

Suppose that an industry contains the firms shown in Figure 19-3. Forty percent of the market is in the hands of the **market leader,** the firm with the largest market share. Another 30 percent is in the hands of a **market challenger,** a runner-up that is fighting hard to increase its market share. Another 20 percent is in the hands of a **market follower,** another runner-up that wants to hold its share without rocking the boat. The remaining 10 percent is in the hands of **market nichers,** firms that serve small segments not being pursued by other firms.

We now examine specific marketing strategies that are available to market leaders, challengers, followers, and nichers. In the sections that follow, you should remember that the classifications of competitive positions often do not apply to a whole company, but only to its position in a specific industry. For example, large and diversified companies such as IBM, Sears, or General Mills (or their individual businesses, divisions, or products) might be leaders in some markets and nichers in others. For example, IBM leads in the overall personal computer market and in the business segment, but it challenges Apple in the educational segment. Such companies often use different strategies for different business units, depending on the competitive situations of each.

Market-Leader Strategies

Most industries contain an acknowledged market leader, the firm with the largest market share. It usually leads the other firms in price changes, new product introductions, distribution coverage, and promotion spending. The leader may or may not be admired or respected, but other firms concede its dominance. The leader is a focal point for competitors, a company to challenge, imitate, or avoid. Some of the best-known market leaders are General Motors (autos), Kodak (photography), IBM (computers), Procter & Gamble (consumer packaged goods), Caterpillar (earth-moving equipment), Coca-Cola (soft drinks), Sears (retailing), McDonald's (fast food), and Gillette (razor blades).

A leading firm's life is not easy. It must maintain a constant watch. Other firms keep challenging its strengths or probing for its weaknesses. The market leader can easily miss a turn in the market and plunge into second or third place. A product innovation may come along and hurt the leader (as when Tylenol's nonaspirin painkiller took the lead from Bayer Aspirin, or when P&G's Tide, the first synthetic laundry detergent, beat out Lever Brothers' leading brands). Or the leading firm might grow fat and slow, losing against new and peppier rivals (Xerox's share of the world copier market fell from more than 80 percent to less than 35 percent in just five years when Japanese producers challenged with cheaper and more reliable copiers).

Leading firms want to remain number one. This calls for action on three fronts. First, the firm must find ways to expand total demand. Second, the firm must protect its current market share through good defensive and offensive actions. Third, the firm can try to expand its market share further, even if market size remains constant.

Expanding the Total Market

The leading firm normally gains the most when the total market expands. If Americans do more picture-taking, Kodak stands to gain the most because it sells more than 80 percent of this country's film. If Kodak can convince more Americans to take pictures, or take pictures on more occasions, or to take more pictures on each occasion, it will benefit greatly. In general, the market leader should look for new users, new uses, and more usage of its products.

NEW USERS.   Every product class can attract buyers who are still unaware of the product, or who are resisting it because of its price or its lack of certain features. A seller can usually find new users in many places. For example, Revlon might find new perfume users in its current markets by convincing women who do not use perfume to try it. Or it might find users in new demographic segments, say by producing cologne for men. Or it might expand into new geographic segments, perhaps by selling its perfume in other countries.

Johnson's Baby Shampoo provides a classic example of developing new users. When the baby boom had passed and the birth rate slowed down, the company grew concerned about future sales growth. But J&J's marketers noticed that other family members sometimes used the baby shampoo for their own hair. Management developed an advertising campaign aimed at adults. In a short time, Johnson's Baby Shampoo became a leading brand in the total shampoo market.

NEW USES.   The marketer can expand markets by discovering and promoting new uses for the product. Du Pont's nylon provides a classic example of new-use expansion. Every time nylon became a mature product, some new use was discovered. Nylon was first used as a fiber for parachutes; then for women's stockings; later as a major material in shirts and blouses; and still later in automobile tires, upholstery, and carpeting. Another example of new-use expansion is Arm & Hammer baking soda. Its sales had flattened after 125 years. Then the company discovered that consumers were using baking soda as a refrigerator deodorizer. It launched a heavy advertising and publicity campaign focusing on this use and persuaded consumers in half of America's homes to place an open box of baking soda in their refrigerators and to replace it every few months.

MORE USAGE.   A third market expansion strategy is to convince people to use the product more often or to use more per occasion. Campbell advertises that "Soup is

Expanding the total market: Johnson & Johnson develops new users (adults); Arm & Hammer promotes new uses.

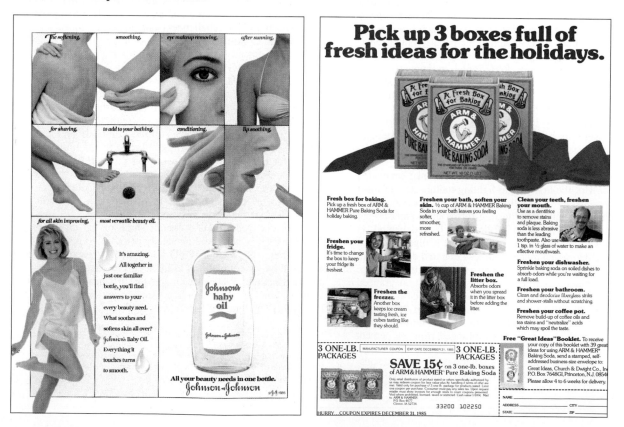

Good Food" to encourage people to eat soup more often. And it runs ads containing new recipes in *Better Homes and Gardens* and other home magazines to remind buyers that "soup *makes* good food." Procter & Gamble advises users that its Head and Shoulders shampoo is more effective with two applications instead of one per shampoo.

Some years ago, the Michelin Tire Company found a creative way to increase usage per occasion. It wanted French car owners to drive more miles per year, resulting in more tire replacement. Michelin began rating French restaurants on a three-star system. It reported that many of the best restaurants were in the south of France, leading many Parisians to take weekend drives south. Michelin also published guidebooks with maps and sights along the way to further entice travel.

Protecting Market Share

While trying to expand total market size, the leading firm must also constantly protect its current business against competitor attacks. Coca-Cola must constantly guard against

---

MARKETING HIGHLIGHT 19–2

PROCTER & GAMBLE LEADS WITH INNOVATION

P&G has always invested heavily to find innovative products that solve consumer problems. This constant innovation has made P&G the leader in the American consumer package goods industry. P&G markets the leading brand in 21 of the 40 product categories in which it competes. P&G spent years developing a toothpaste that would effectively reduce tooth decay. When introduced, Crest soon passed less effective brands, and with constant improvement, it remained the leading toothpaste for more than 30 years. In the same way, P&G looked at the shampoo market and found that no brand provided the dandruff control that consumers wanted. Years of research produced Head and Shoulders—an instant market leader. Then P&G looked at the paper products business. It found that new parents wanted relief from handling and washing diapers. Again, P&G found an innovative solution—Pampers—an affordable disposable paper diaper that immediately won market leadership. Thus, innovative marketing took P&G to the top in consumer products.

Yet in the early 1980s, P&G appeared to let up some of its pressure to innovate. More innovative competitors quickly challenged P&G's leadership in several product areas, especially toothpaste and disposable diapers.

Crest was hard hit. In 1983, Minnetonka innovated with Check-Up, the first plaque-fighting toothpaste packaged in a pump container. And Lever Brothers and Beecham introduced gels, clear and better tasting forms of toothpaste that appeal strongly to children. While P&G lagged behind on these innovations, its major competitor, Colgate, surged ahead. Colgate poured money into research and development and beat P&G to the market by many months with the pump, gels, and a plaque-fighting formula. Colgate soon grabbed 50 percent of the pump segment, and boosted its overall share of the $1 billion toothpaste market from 18 percent in 1979 to 28 percent by the end of 1984. During the last six months of 1984, Crest's share plunged from 36 percent to 30 percent.

Procter & Gamble took a similar beating in the disposable diaper market. Its Pampers brand created the disposables category, and for years P&G's Pampers and Luvs brands

dominated with a combined share exceeding 75 percent. But in 1984, while P&G coasted, Kimberly-Clark introduced Huggies, an innovative brand with greater absorbency, a contour shape, and refastenable tapes. By mid-1985, P&G found itself following rather than leading this market. Its overall share fell to 46 percent, and Pampers slid to second place behind Huggies. In 1985, P&G suffered its first income decline in 33 years.

P&G was down but far from out. It struck back hard with innovations in both product areas. In late 1985, P&G introduced a superior pump and extended its line to include gels. And it did the challengers one better by introducing Crest Tartar Control Formula paste and gel in pumps and tubes. More recently, it successfully introduced Crest Supergel for Kids. P&G also spent more than $500 million to create a new generation of Pampers and an improved Luvs. Competitors were left scrambling to match P&G's new Ultra Pampers, a super-thin, super-absorbent disposable diaper. In 1989, P&G again rocked the industry with its latest innovation, "gender-specific" diapers—Luvs for Girls and Luvs for Boys. And, again, competitors hurried to catch up.

Procter & Gamble's surge of fresh innovation produced amazing results. In less than six months, Crest's share of the toothpaste market jumped to 38 percent; Colgate's fell to 22 percent. Gender-specific Luvs met with astounding success—Luvs share climbed to 24 percent in 1990, up 9 points in one year. P&G's overall share of the disposable diaper market is now holding steady at about 50 percent.

Thus, the weapon P&G used to first reach the top was used by its competitors to threaten P&G's leadership—and used again by P&G to regain the lost ground. The weapon is innovation. The message is a simple one—to stay ahead, P&G must continue to lead.

Sources: See Nancy Giges and Laurie Freeman, "Wounded Tiger? Trail of Mistakes Mars P&G Record," *Advertising Age*, July 29, 1985, pp. 1, 50–51; Kenneth Labich, "The Innovators," *Fortune*, June 6, 1988, pp. 51–64; Brian Dumaine," P&G Rewrites the Marketing Rules," *Fortune*, November 6, 1989, pp. 34–48; and Freeman, "New Diaper Fight," *Advertising Age*, March 5, 1990, p. 4.

Pepsi-Cola; Gillette against Bic; Kodak against Fuji; McDonald's against Burger King; General Motors against Ford.

What can the market leader do to protect its position? First, it must prevent or fix weaknesses that provide opportunities for competitors. It needs to keep its costs down and its prices in line with the value the customers see in the brand. The leader should "plug holes" so that competitors do not jump in. But the best defense is a good offense, and the best response is *continuous innovation*. The leader refuses to be content with the way things are and leads the industry in new products, customer services, distribution effectiveness, and cost cutting. It keeps increasing its competitive effectiveness and value to customers. It takes the offensive, sets the pace, and exploits competitors' weaknesses (see Marketing Highlight 19–2).

Increased competition in recent years has sparked management's interest in models of military warfare.[9] Leader companies have been advised to protect their market positions with competitive strategies patterned after successful military defense strategies. Six defense strategies that a market leader can use are shown in Figure 19-4.[10]

POSITION DEFENSE.   The most basic defense is a position defense in which a company builds fortifications around its current position. But simply defending one's current position or products rarely works. Henry Ford tried it with his Model-T and brought an enviably healthy Ford Motor Company to the brink of financial ruin. Even such lasting brands as Coca-Cola and Bayer Aspirin cannot be relied upon to supply all future growth and profitability for their companies. These brands must be improved and adapted to changing conditions, and new brands must be developed. Coca-Cola today, in spite of producing more than a third of America's soft drinks, is aggressively extending its beverage lines and has diversified into desalinization equipment and plastics.

FLANKING DEFENSE.   When guarding its overall position, the market leader should watch its weaker flanks closely. Smart competitors will normally attack the company's weaknesses. Thus, the Japanese successfully entered the small car market because U.S. automakers left a gaping hole in that submarket. Using a flanking defense, the company carefully checks its flanks and protects the more vulnerable areas.

FIGURE 19-4 Defense strategies

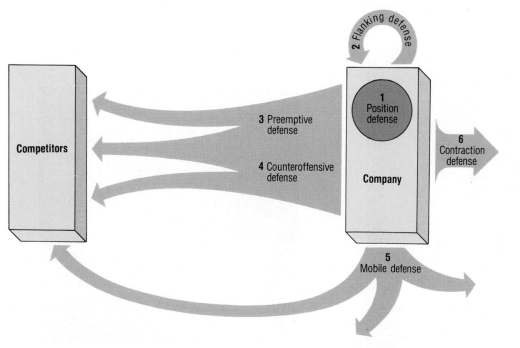

PREEMPTIVE DEFENSE.   The leader can launch a more aggressive preemptive defense, striking competitors before they can move against the company. A preemptive defense assumes that an ounce of prevention is worth a pound of cure. Thus, when threatened in the mid-1980s by the impending entry of Japanese manufacturers into the U.S. market, Cummins Engine slashed its prices by almost a third to save its No. 1 position in the $2 billion heavy-duty truck engine market. Today, Cummins claims a commanding 50 percent market share in North Amerca, and not a single U.S.-built tractor-trailer truck contains a Japanese engine.[11]

COUNTEROFFENSIVE DEFENSE.   When a market leader is attached despite its flanking or preemptive efforts, it can launch a counteroffensive defense. When Fuji attacked Kodak in the U.S. film market, Kodak counterattacked by dramatically increasing its promotion and introducing several innovative new film products. When attacked by UPS's low-price claims, Federal Express counterattacked by slashing its prices. Sometimes companies hold off for a while before countering. This may seem a dangerous game of "wait and see," but there are often good reasons for not barreling in. By waiting, the company can more fully understand the competitor's offense and perhaps find a gap through which a successful counteroffensive can be launched.

MOBILE DEFENSE.   A mobile defense involves more than aggressively defending a current market position. The leader stretches to new markets that can serve as future bases for defense and offense. Through *market broadening*, the company shifts its focus from the current product to the broader underlying consumer need. For example, Armstrong Cork redefined its focus from "floor covering" to "decorative room covering" (including walls and ceilings) and expanded into related businesses that were balanced for growth and defense. *Market diversification* into unrelated industries is the other alternative for generating "strategic depth." When U.S. tobacco companies R. J. Reynolds and Philip Morris faced growing curbs on cigarette smoking, they moved quickly into new consumer products industries.

When Fuji attacked, Kodak counterattacked with innovative new films and more promotion.

CONTRACTION DEFENSE.   Large companies sometimes find they can no longer defend all positions. Their resources are spread too thin and competitors are nibbling away on several fronts. The best action then appears to be a contraction defense (or strategic withdrawal). The company gives up weaker positions and concentrates its resources on stronger ones. During the 1970s, many companies diversified wildly and spread themselves too thin. In the slow-growth 1980s, ITT, Gulf & Western, Georgia Pacific, General Mills, Kraft, Quaker, and dozens of other companies pruned their portfolios to concentrate resources on products and businesses in their core industries. These companies now serve fewer markets but serve them much better.

Expanding Market Share
Market leaders can also grow by increasing their market shares further. In many markets, small market share increases result in very large sales increases. For example, in the coffee market, a one percent increase in market share is worth $48 million; in soft drinks, $380 million! No wonder normal competition turns into marketing warfare in such markets.

Many studies have found that profitability rises with increasing market share.[12] Businesses with very large relative market shares averaged substantially higher returns on investment. Because of these findings, many companies have sought expanded market shares to improve profitability. General Electric, for example, declared that it wants to be at least number one or two in each of its markets or else get out. GE shed its computer, air-conditioning, small appliances, and television businesses because it could not achieve top-dog position in these industries.

Other studies have found that many industries contain one or a few highly profitable large firms, several profitable and more focused firms, and a large number of medium-sized firms with poorer profit performance.

> The large firms . . . tend to address the entire market, achieving cost advantages and high market share by realizing economies of scale. The small competitors reap high profits by focusing on some narrower segment of the business and by developing specialized approaches to production, marketing, and distribution for that segment. Ironically, the medium-sized competitors . . . often show the poorest profit performance. Trapped in a strategic "No Man's Land," they are too large to reap the benefits of more focused competition, yet too small to benefit from the economies of scale that their larger competitors enjoy.[13]

Thus, it appears that profitability increases as a business gains share relative to competitors in its *served market*. For example, Mercedes holds only a small share of the total car market, but it earns high profit because it is a high-share company in its luxury car segment. And it has achieved this high share in its served market because it does other things right, such as producing high quality, giving good service, and holding down its costs.

Companies must not think, however, that gaining increased market share automatically improves profitability. Much depends on their strategies for gaining increased share. Many high-share companies endure low profitability, and many low-share companies enjoy high profitability. The cost of buying higher market share may far exceed the returns. Higher shares tend to produce higher profits only when unit costs fall with increased market share or when the company offers a superior quality product and charges a premium price that more than covers the cost of offering higher quality.

Market-Challenger Strategies

Firms that are second, third, or lower in an industry are sometimes quite large, such as Colgate, Ford, K mart, Avis, Westinghouse, Miller, and PepsiCo. These runner-up firms can adopt one of two competitive strategies. They can attack the leader and other competitors in an aggressive bid for more market share (market challengers). Or they can play along with competitors and not rock the boat (market followers). We now focus on competitive strategies for market challengers.

Defining the Strategic Objective and Competitor

A market challenger must first define its strategic objective. Most market challengers seek to increase their profitability by increasing their market shares. But the strategic objective chosen depends on the competitor. In most cases, the company can choose which competitors to challenge.

The challenger can attack the market leader, a high-risk but potentially high-gain strategy which makes good sense if the leader is not serving the market well. To succeed with such an attack, a company must have some sustainable competitive advantage over the leader—a cost advantage leading to lower prices or the ability to provide better value at a premium price. In the construction equipment industry, Komatsu successfully challenged Caterpillar by offering the same quality at much lower prices. And P&G grabbed a big share of the toilet tissue market by offering a softer and more absorbent product than the one offered by market leader Scott. When attacking the leader, a challenger must also find a way to minimize the leader's response. Otherwise its gains may be short lived.[14]

The challenger can avoid the leader and instead attack firms its own size, or smaller local and regional firms. Many of these firms are underfinanced and will not be serving their customers well. Several of the major beer companies grew to their present size not by attacking large competitors, but by gobbling up small local or regional competitors.

Thus, the challenger's strategic objective depends on which competitor it chooses to attack. If the company goes after the market leader, its objective may be to wrest a certain market share. Bic knows that it can't topple Gillette in the razor market—it simply wants a larger share. Or the challenger's goal might be to take over market leadership. IBM entered the personal computer market late, as a challenger, but quickly became the market leader. If the company goes after a small local company, its objective may be to put that company out of business. The important point remains: The company must choose its opponents carefully and have a clearly defined and attainable objective.

Choosing an Attack Strategy

How can the market challenger best attack the chosen competitor and achieve its strategic objectives? Five possible attack strategies are shown in Figure 19-5.

FIGURE 19-5 Attack strategies

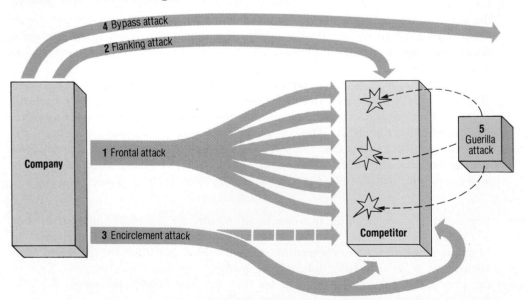

Unilever launched a frontal attack against P&G with Surf, Sunlight, and Snuggle.

FRONTAL ATTACK.   In a full frontal attack, the challenger matches the competitor's product, advertising, price, and distribution efforts. It attacks the competitor's strengths rather than its weaknesses. The outcome depends on who has the greater strength and endurance. Even great size and strength may not be enough to successfully challenge a firmly entrenched and resourceful competitor.

> Unilever is the world's largest packaged goods company. It has twice the worldwide sales of Procter & Gamble and five times the sales of Colgate-Palmolive. Yet its American subsidiary, Lever Brothers, trails P&G by a wide margin in the U.S. Lever recently launched a full frontal assault against P&G in the detergent market. Lever's Wisk was already the leading liquid detergent. In quick succession, it added a barrage of new products—Sunlight dishwashing detergent, Snuggle fabric softener, Surf laundry powder—and backed them with aggressive promotion and distribution efforts. But P&G spent heavily to defend its brands and held on to most of its business. And it counterattacked with Liquid Tide, which came from nowhere in just 17 months to run neck-and-neck with Wisk. Lever did gain market share, but most of it came from smaller competitors.[15]

If the market challenger has fewer resources than the competitor, a frontal attack makes little sense. GE and Xerox learned this the hard way when they launched frontal attacks on IBM, overlooking its superior defensive position.

FLANKING ATTACK.   Rather than attacking head on, the challenger can launch a flanking attack. The competitor often concentrates its resources to protect its strongest positions, but it usually has some weaker flanks. By attacking these weak spots, the challenger can concentrate its strength against the competitor's weakness. Flank attacks make good sense when the company has fewer resources than the competitor. PepsiCo flanked Coca-Cola when it created Slice, a soft drink with real fruit juice added. Coke's lemon-lime drink, Sprite, contained no fruit juice. Slice quickly replaced Sprite as the No. 2 lemon-lime drink behind 7-Up in most markets.

Another flanking strategy is to find gaps that are not being filled by the industry's products, fill them, and develop them into strong segments. German and Japanese automakers chose not to compete with American automakers by producing large, flashy, gas-guzzling automobiles. Instead they recognized an unserved consumer segment that wanted small, fuel-efficient cars and moved to fill this hole. To their satisfaction and Detroit's surprise, the segment grew to be a large part of the market.

ENCIRCLEMENT ATTACK. An encirclement attack involves attacking from all directions, so that the competitor must protect its front, sides, and rear at the same time. The encirclement strategy makes sense when the challenger has superior resources and believes that it can quickly break the competitor's hold on the market. An example is Seiko's attack on the watch market. For several years, Seiko has been gaining distribution in every major watch outlet and overwhelming competitors with its variety of constantly changing models. In the U.S. it offers about four hundred models, but its marketing clout is backed by the twenty-three hundred models it makes and sells worldwide.

BYPASS ATTACK. A bypass attack is an indirect strategy. The challenger bypasses the competitor and targets easier markets. The bypass can involve diversifying into unrelated products, moving into new geographic markets, or leapfrogging into new technologies to replace existing products. Technological leapfrogging is a bypass strategy used often in high-technology industries. Instead of copying the competitor's product and mounting a costly frontal attack, the challenger patiently develops the next technology. When satisfied with its superiority, it launches an attack where it has an advantage. Thus, Minolta toppled Canon from the lead in the 35mm SLR camera market when it introduced its technologically advanced autofocusing Maxxum camera. Canon's market share dropped toward 20 percent while Minolta's zoomed past 30 percent. It took Canon three years to introduce a matching technology.[16]

GUERRILLA ATTACK. A guerrilla attack is another option available to market challengers, especially the smaller or poorly financed challenger. The challenger makes small, periodic attacks to harass and demoralize the competitor, hoping eventually to establish permanent footholds. It might use selective price cuts, executive raids, intense promotional outbursts, or assorted legal actions. Normally, guerrilla actions are taken by smaller firms against larger ones. But continuous guerrilla campaigns can be expensive, and they must eventually be followed by a stronger attack if the challenger wishes to "beat" the competitor. Thus, guerrilla campaigns are not necessarily cheap.

Market-Follower Strategies

Not all runner-up companies will challenge the market leader. The effort to draw away the leader's customers is never taken lightly by the leader. If the challenger's lure is lower prices, improved service, or additional product features, the leader can quickly match these to diffuse the attack. The leader probably has more staying power in an all-out battle. A hard fight might leave both firms weakened. Thus, the challenger must think twice before attacking. Therefore, many firms prefer to follow rather than attack the leader.

A follower can gain many advantages. The market leader often bears the huge expenses involved with developing new products and markets, expanding distribution channels, and informing and educating the market. The reward for all this work and risk is normally market leadership. The market-follower, on the other hand, can learn from the leader's experience and copy or improve on the leader's products and marketing programs, usually at a much lower investment. Although the follower probably will not overtake the leader, it can often be as profitable.[17]

In some industries—such as steel, fertilizers, and chemicals—opportunities for differentiation are low, service quality is often comparable, and price sensitivity runs high. Price wars can erupt at any time. Companies in these industries avoid short-run grabs for market share because that strategy only provokes retaliation. Most firms decide against stealing each other's customers. Instead they present similar offers to buyers, usually by copying the leader. Market share show a high stability.

This is not to say that market followers are without strategies. A market follower must know how to hold current customers and win a fair share of new consumers. Each follower tries to bring distinctive advantages to its target market—location, services, financing. The follower is a major target of attack by challengers. Therefore the market follower must keep its manufacturing costs low and its product quality and services high. It must also enter new markets as they open up. Following is not the same as being passive or existing as a carbon copy of the leader. The follower must define a growth path, but one that does not create competitive retaliation.

The market-follower firms fall into one of three broad types. The *cloner* closely copies leader's products, distribution, advertising, and other marketing moves. The cloner originates nothing—it simply attempts to live off the market leader's investments. The *imitator* copies some things from the leader but maintains some differentiation in terms of packaging, advertising, pricing, and other factors. The leader doesn't mind the imitator as long as the imitator does not attack aggressively. The imitator may even help the leader avoid the charges of monopoly. Finally, the *adapter* builds on leader's products and marketing programs, often improving them. The adapter may choose to sell to different markets to avoid direct confrontation with the leader. But often the adapter grows into a future challenger, as many Japanese firms have done after adapting and improving products developed elsewhere.

Market-Nicher Strategies

Almost every industry includes firms that specialize in serving market niches. Instead of pursuing the whole market, or even large segments of the market, these firms target segments within segments, or niches. This is particularly true of smaller firms because of their limited resources. But smaller divisions of larger firms may also pursue niching strategies. EG&G provides a good example of a large company that profitably employs a niching strategy:

> EG&G is a $1.4 billion industrial equipment and components company consisting of over 175 distinct and independent business units, many with less than $10 million in sales in markets worth $25 million. Many EG&G business units have their own R&D, manufacturing, and salesforce operations. The company is currently the market or technical leader in eighty percent of its niche markets. More astonishing, EG&G ranked second in earnings per share and first in profitability in the *Fortune* 1000. EG&G illustrates how niche marketing may pay larger dividends than mass marketing.

The main point is that firms with low shares of the total market can be highly profitable through smart niching.

A recent study of highly successful midsize companies found that, in almost all cases, these companies niched within a larger market rather than going after the whole market.[18] An example is A. T. Cross, which niches in the high-price pen and pencil market. It makes the famous gold writing instruments that every executive owns or wants to own. By concentrating in the high-price niche, Cross has enjoyed great sales growth and profit. Of course, the study found other features shared by the successful smaller companies—offering high value, charging a premium price, and strong corporate cultures and vision.

Why is niching profitable? The main reason is that the market nicher ends up knowing the target customer group so well that it meets their needs better than other firms that casually sell to this niche. As a result, the nicher can charge a substantial markup over costs because of the added value. Whereas the mass marketer achieves *high volume*, the nicher achieves *high margins*.

Nichers try to find one or more market niches that are safe and profitable. An ideal market niche is big enough to be profitable and has growth potential. It is one that the firm can serve effectively. Perhaps most importantly, the niche is of little interest to major competitors. And the firm can build the skills and customer goodwill to defend itself against an attacking major competitor as the niche grows and becomes more attractive.

The key idea in nichemanship is specialization. The firm must specialize along market, customer, product, or marketing mix lines. Here are several specialist roles open to a market nicher:

- *End-use specialist.*—The firm specializes in serving one type of end-use customer. For example, a law firm can specialize in the criminal, civil, or business law markets.
- *Vertical-level specialist.*—The firm specializes at some level of the production-distribution cycle. For example, a copper firm may concentrate on producing raw copper, copper components, or finished copper products.

- *Customer-size specialist.*—The firm concentrates on selling to either small, medium, or large customers. Many nichers specialize in serving small customers who are neglected by the majors.
- *Specific-customer specialist.*—The firm limits its selling to one or a few major customers. Many firms sell their entire output to a single company, such as Sears or General Motors.
- *Geographic specialist.*—The firm sells only in a certain locality, region, or area of the world.
- *Product or feature specialist.*—The firm specializes in producing a certain product, product line, or product feature. Within the laboratory equipment industry are firms that produce only microscopes, or even more narrowly, only lenses for microscopes.
- *Quality-price specialist.*—The firm operates at the low or high end of the market. For example, Hewlett-Packard specializes in the high-quality, high-price end of the hand-calculator market.
- *Service specialist.*—The firm offers one or more services not available from other firms. An example is a bank that takes loan requests over the phone and hand delivers the money to the customer.

Niching carries a major risk in that the market niche may dry up or be attacked. That is why many companies practice *multiple niching*. By developing two or more niches, the company increases its chances for survival. Even some large firms prefer a multiple-niche strategy to serving the total market. One large law firm has developed a national reputation in the three areas of mergers and acquisitions, bankruptcies, and prospectus development, and does little else.

BALANCING CUSTOMER AND COMPETITOR ORIENTATIONS

We have stressed the importance of a company watching its competitors closely. Whether a company is a market leader, challenger, follower, or nicher, it must find the competitive marketing strategy that positions it most effectively against its competitors. And it must continually adapt its strategies to the fast-changing competitive environment.

The question now arises: can the company spend too much time and energy tracking competitors, damaging its customer orientation? The answer is yes! A company can become so competitor-centered that it loses even its more important customer focus. A **competitor-centered company** is one whose moves are mainly based on competitors' actions and reactions. The company spends most of its time tracking competitors' moves and market shares and trying to find strategies to counter them.

This mode of strategy planning has some pluses and minuses. On the positive side, the company develops a fighter orientation. It trains its marketers to be on a constant alert, watching for weaknesses in their own position, and watching for competitors' weaknesses. On the negative side, the company becomes too reactive. Rather than carrying out its own consistent customer-oriented strategy, it bases its moves on competitors' moves. As a result, it does not move in a planned direction toward a goal. It does not know where it will end up, because so much depends on what the competitors do.

A **customer-centered company,** in contrast, focuses more on customer developments in designing its strategies. Clearly, the customer-centered company is in a better position to identify new opportunities and set a strategy that makes long-run sense. By watching customer needs evolve, it can decide what customer groups and what emerging needs are the most important to serve, given its resources and objectives.

In practice, today's companies must be **market-centered companies,** watching both their customers and their competitors. They must not let competitor watching blind them to customer focusing. Figure 19-6 shows that companies have moved through four orientations. In the first stage, they were product-oriented, paying little attention to either customers or competitors. In the second stage, they became customer-oriented

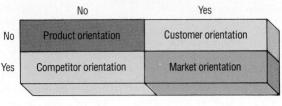

FIGURE 19-6
Evolving company orientations

and started to pay attention to customers. In the third stage, when they started to pay attention to competitors, they became competitor-oriented. Today companies need to be market-oriented, paying balanced attention to both customer and competitors.[19]

■ SUMMARY

In order to prepare an effective marketing strategy, a company must consider its competitors as well as its actual and potential customers. It must continuously analyze its competitors and develop competitive marketing strategies that effectively position it against competitors and give it the strongest possible competitive advantage.

Competitor analysis first involves identifying the company's major competitors, using both an industry and a market-based analysis. The company then gathers information on competitors' objectives, strategies, strengths and weaknesses, and reaction patterns. With this information in hand, it can select competitors to attack or avoid. Competitive intelligence must be collected, interpreted, and distributed continuously. Company marketing managers should be able to obtain full and reliable information about any competitor affecting their decisions.

Which *competitive marketing strategy* makes the most sense depends on the company's industry position and its objectives, opportunities, and resources. The company's competitive marketing strategy depends on whether it is a market leader, challenger, follower, or nicher.

A *market leader* faces three challenges: expanding the total market, protecting market share, and expanding market share. The market leader is interested in finding ways to expand the total market because it will benefit most from any increased sales. To expand market size, the leader looks for new users of the product, new uses, and more usage. To protect its existing market share, the market leader has several defenses: position defense, flanking defense, preemptive defense, counteroffensive

defense, mobile defense, and contraction defense. The most sophisticated leaders cover themselves by doing everything right, leaving no openings for competitive attack. Leaders can also try to increase their market shares. This makes sense if profitability increases at higher market-share levels.

A *market challenger* is a firm that aggressively tries to expand its market share by attacking the leader, other runner-up firms, or smaller firms in the industry. The challenger can choose from a variety of attack strategies, including a frontal attack, flanking attack, encirclement attack, bypass attack, and guerrilla attack.

A *market follower* is a runner-up firm that chooses not to rock the boat, usually out of fear that it stands to lose more than it might gain. The follower is not without a strategy, however, and seeks to use its particular skills to gain market growth. Some followers enjoy a higher rate of return than the leaders in their industry.

A *market nicher* is a smaller firm that serves some part of the market that is not likely to attract the larger firms. Market nichers often become specialists in some end use, vertical level, customer size, specific customer, geographic area, product or product feature, or service.

A competitive orientation is important in today's markets, but companies should not overdo their focus on competitors. Companies are more likely to be hurt by emerging consumer needs and new competitors than by existing competitors. Companies that balance consumer and competitor considerations are practicing a true market orientation.

■ QUESTIONS FOR DISCUSSION

1. Erol's is a chain of videotape rental stores with outlets in Washington, D.C., and other eastern cities. Who are its competitors? What product and market do Erol's and its competitors serve?

2. What different strategic groups can you identify in the automobile industry? Which groups compete with which other groups? Be sure to consider foreign manufacturers as well as domestic manufacturers.

3. Do a customer value analysis for Levi Strauss. Compare

Levi's strengths and weaknesses with those of its competitors.

4. "Well-behaved" companies prefer well-behaved competition. Should it make any different to consumers whether competition is "well-behaved" or "disruptive"? Why or why not?

5. Hewlett-Packard, a market leader in the high-priced end of the calculator market, has found itself in a squeeze between aggressively promoted portable computers and less expen-

sive calculators with increasingly sophisticated features. What market leader strategy would you recommend for Hewlett-Packard? Why?

6. How could Morton Salt expand the total market for table salt? Discuss the role sales promotion would play in getting new users, communicating new uses, or increasing usage of table salt.

7. After the initial success of California Cooler, more than one hundred wine coolers were introduced in the United States. What strategies did Bartles & Jaymes and Seagram's use to overtake California Cooler? Could California Cooler have used a defensive strategy to maintain its leadership?

8. Many medium-sized firms are in an unprofitable middle ground between large firms and smaller, more focused firms. Discuss how medium-sized firms could use market nicher strategies to improve their profitability.

9. Which will have more impact on a market-centered company's strategies—competitors or customers? Will the company do more research on customers or on competitors, or will research expenditures be balanced?

10. A small firm has developed a desktop copier using advanced technology for better—and more economical—performance. Suggest a strategy for this firm to use in entering the photocopier market. Justify your recommendation.

11. The goal of the marketing concept is to satisfy customer wants and needs. What is the goal of a competitor-centered strategy? Discuss whether the marketing concept and competitor-centered strategy are in conflict.

12. Assume you are the product manager in charge of Lysol Disinfectant or Woolite Fine Fabric Wash. Your brand has more than 60 percent of the market, and no competing brand has ever succeeded. What would your strategy be for growing your business?

■ KEY TERMS

Competitive advantage. An advantage over competitors gained by offering consumers lower prices than competitors for similar products or by providing more benefits that justify higher prices.

Competitive strategies. Strategies that strongly position the company against competitors and that give the company the strongest possible strategic advantage.

Competitor analysis. The process of identifying major competitors; assessing their objectives, strategies, strengths and weaknesses, and reaction patterns; and selecting which competitors to attack or avoid.

Competitor-centered company. A company whose moves are mainly based on competitors' actions and reactions; it spends most of its time tracking competitors' moves and market shares and trying to find strategies to counter them.

Customer-centered company. A company that focuses on customer developments in designing its marketing strategies.

Customer value analysis. Analysis conducted to determine what benefits target customers value and how they rate the relative value of various competitors' offers.

Industry. A group of firms which offer a product or class of products that are close substitutes for each other.

Market-centered company. A company that pays balanced attention to both customers and competitors in designing its marketing strategies.

Market challenger. A runner-up firm in an industry that is fighting hard to increase its market share.

Market follower. A runner-up firm in an industry that wants to hold its share without rocking the boat.

Market leader. The firm in an industry with the largest market share; it usually leads other firms in price changes, new product introductions, distribution coverage, and promotion spending.

Market nicher. A firm in an industry that serves small segments that the other firms overlook or ignore.

Strategic group. A group of firms in an industry following the same or a similar strategy.

■ REFERENCES

1. See Betsy Bauer, "Giants Loom Larger Over Pint-Sized Soft-Drink Firms," *USA Today*, May 27, 1986, p. 5B; Ford S. Worthy, "Pop Goes Their Profit," *Fortune*, February 15, 1988, pp. 68–83; and Patricia Winters, "Small Competitor Feels Coke's Ire," *Advertising Age*, February 20, 1989, p. 37.

2. For a good discussion of the underlying rules of competitive interaction and reaction, see Gloria P. Thomas and Gary F. Soldow, "A Rules-Based Approach to Competitive Interaction," *Journal of Marketing*, April 1988, 63–74.

3. See Michael E. Porter, *Competitive Advantage* (New York: The Free Press, 1985), pp. 226–27.

4. Ibid., Chapter 6.

5. For more discussion, see William L. Sammon, Mark A. Kurland, and Robert Spitalnic, *Business Competitor Intelligence* (New York: Ronald Press, 1984); Leonard M. Fuld,

Monitoring the Competition (New York: John Wiley & Sons, Inc., 1988); and Howard Schlossberg, "Competitive Intelligence Pros Seek Formal Role in Marketing," *Marketing News*, March 5, 1990, pp. 2, 28.

6. See Michael E. Porter, *Competitive Advantage*; Pankaj Ghemawat, "Sustainable Advantage," *Harvard Business Review*, September–October 1986, pp. 53–58; Michael E. Porter, "From Competitive Advantage to Corporate Strategy," *Harvard Business Review*, May–June 1987, pp. 43–59; and George S. Day and Robin Wensley, "Assessing Competitive Advantage: A Framework for Diagnosing Competitive Superiority," *Journal of Marketing*, April 1988, pp. 1–20.

7. Michael E. Porter, *Competitive Strategy: Techniques for Analyzing Industries and Competitors* (New York: Free Press, 1980), Ch. 2.

8. Stuart Gannes, "The Riches in Market Niches," *Fortune*, April 27, 1987, p. 228.

9. See Al Ries and Jack Trout, *Marketing Warfare* (New York: McGraw-Hill, 1986); and Gerald A. Michaelson, *Winning the Marketing War* (Lanham, MD: Madison Books, 1987).

10. For more discussion on defense and attack strategies, see Philip Kotler, *Marketing Management: Analysis, Planning, Implementation, and Control* (Englewood Cliffs, NJ: Prentice Hall, 1991), Ch. 14.

11. See Lois Therrien, "Mr. Rust Belt," *Business Week*, October 17, 1988, pp. 72–80.

12. See Robert D. Buzzell, Bradley T. Gale, and Ralph G. M. Sultan, "Market Share—the Key to Profitability," *Harvard Business Review*, January–February 1975, pp. 97–106; and Ben Branch, "The Laws of the Marketplace and ROI Dynamics," *Financial Management*, Summer 1980, pp. 58–65. Others suggest that the relationship between market share and profits has been exaggerated. See Carolyn Y. Woo and Arnold C. Cooper, "Market-Share Leadership—Not Always So Good," *Harvard Business Review*, January–February 1984, pp. 2–4; and Robert Jacobson and David A. Aaker, "Is Market Share All It's Cracked Up to Be?" *Journal of Marketing*, Fall 1985, pp. 11–22.

13. See John D. C. Roach, "From Strategic Planning to Strategic Performance: Closing the Achievement Gap," *Outlook*, published by Booz, Allen & Hamilton, New York, Spring 1981, p. 21. Michael Porter makes the same point in his *Competitive Strategy* (New York: The Free Press, 1980).

14. See Michael E. Porter, "How to Attack the Industry Leader," *Fortune*, April 19, 1985, pp. 153–166.

15. See Andrew C. Brown, "Unilever Fights Back in the U.S.," *Fortune*, May 26, 1986, pp. 32–38.

16. See Otis Port, "Canon Finally Challenges Minolta's Mighty Maxxum," March 2, 1987, pp. 89–90.

17. See Daniel W. Haines, Rajan Chandran, and Arvind Parkhe, "Winning by Being First to Market . . . Or Last?" *Journal of Consumer Marketing*, Winter 1989, pp. 63–69.

18. Donald K. Clifford and Richard E. Cavanagh, *The Winning Performance: How America's High- and Midsize Growth Companies Succeed* (New York: Bantam Books, 1985).

19. See Kenichi Ohmae, "Getting Back to Strategy," *Harvard Business Review*, November–December 1988, pp. 149–156.

GTE AND THE PAY-PHONE MARKET: COMPETITION COMES CALLING

As he drove into the parking lot at the Smile gas station on Route 70 in Durham, NC, Kevin Murphy, a salaried General Telephone and Electronics (GTE) Sales Consultant, thought about how the pay-phone business had changed since he joined the company in 1983. During those six years he had witnessed the impact of deregulation on the telephone industry, and he had seen about every kind of competitive move. He was now stopping to call on Jim Lewis, the manager of Smile Gas. Mr. Lewis had a relative in the private pay-phone business. Eight months ago, Mr. Lewis had agreed to install one of the relative's phones and had asked GTE to remove its phone. However, his relative's company had gone out of business and the new phone had never been installed.

Many of Smile's customers want to make only one stop to buy gas or food and to use a phone. Now, when Mr. Lewis' customers inquire about a pay phone, he has to send them across the intersection to the Wilco gas station. Mr. Lewis is angry about losing business to the competition, and he decided to call GTE.

Like Mr. Lewis' customers, you've probably used a pay telephone many times: in the dorm to call out for pizza; at the convenience store to see if a friend's at home; or at the airport to tell someone you've landed safely. They seem to be everywhere. But have you ever really paid much attention to the pay phones themselves? Probably not. Unfortunately, neither has GTE. And that's a real problem, given that GTE owns and operates 29,000 pay telephones in its franchised areas in nine southeastern states.

However, because of dramatic changes in its marketing environment, GTE is now starting to pay attention to its public communications operation instead of taking it for granted as it has traditionally done. Other companies *have* noticed the pay telephone market. Literally hundreds of small companies are racing to enter what promises to be a lucrative business, challenging the almost monopolistic grip GTE and other telephone companies have had on the pay-phone market.

THE PUBLIC COMMUNICATIONS MARKET

Although pay telephones may seem out of date amid the rapid technological advances in the modern telecommunications world, the approximately 2 million U.S. pay phones generated $6.3 *billion* in revenues in 1989. Callers deposited about 25 percent of this amount as "coins in the box." The remaining 75 percent consisted of credit card, collect, and other operator-assisted calls. GTE receives 100 percent of the cost of local calls (usually twenty-five cents each) made on its pay phones, 100 percent of the cost of long-distance calls made within GTE's franchise

area, and $.06 to $.10 per minute for long-distance calls going outside its area. In total, GTE's 29,000 pay phones produced about $56 million in total revenues in 1989.

Telephone companies generally segment the public communications market based on the number of pay phones installed at each location. Table 1 presents the overall breakdown of U.S. businesses by number of pay phones per location and gives the chief attributes of each segment. The table shows that 90 percent of all businesses have less than four pay phones per location and that these businesses account for 40 percent of the total number of pay phones installed. In contrast, only 4 percent of businesses have more than 10 pay phones installed, but these businesses account for 49 percent of all installed pay phones. Convenience stores, shopping centers, and fast food restaurants are the best locations. Generally, GTE wants to place its pay phones in safe, well-lighted locations with lots of car or foot traffic. GTE budgets $1,500 to $2,000 to install an outside pay-phone booth; wall-mounted units cost slightly less. GTE depreciates the booths over a seven-year period. The company estimates that the variable cost of a phone is $35 per month and that a phone must generate at least $90 per month to break even.

Prior to 1984, the telephone companies enjoyed a monopoly in the pay-telephone market. Only regulated telephone companies could install a pay phone that was connected to their telephone networks. Although customers paid to use the phones, the phone companies subsidized their pay-phone operations from general revenues. GTE did not even account for pay phones separately from its general telephone operations. If a business wanted a pay phone installed, it would file a request with the local telephone company, such as GTE. GTE would evaluate

TABLE 1
Pay Phone Market Segments

	0–4 PAY PHONES per LOCATION	5–9 PAY PHONES per LOCATION	10+ PAY PHONES per LOCATION
Businesses	90%	6%	4%
Pay phones	40	11	49
Revenues:			
Local	43	47	26
Coin	8	7	16
Non-coin	49	46	58

Source: GTE South

the request based on the revenue potential of the location and on the company's obligation as a regulated monopoly to provide public service. If the location looked profitable, GTE would install one or more *public* pay phones. The phone cost the owner nothing, but GTE made no payments to the owner. If a location did not justify a public pay phone, GTE could offer the customer a *semi-public* phone, for which the customer paid an installation fee and guaranteed GTE a fixed monthly revenue. In this process of receiving requests and evaluating locations, telephone companies did no "marketing." GTE either accepted requests or rejected them. In fact, it accepted only two out of every ten requests. GTE rarely searched for new places to install pay phones.

DEREGULATION STRIKES

However, in June 1984, everything changed. The Federal Communications Commission (FCC), as part of the general deregulation of the telecommunications industry, ruled that any person who purchased a coin-operated telephone had the right to connect it to the local telephone network. This ruling created a new product and a new market: the customer-owned, coin-operated telephone (COCOT). Many entrepreneurs set up businesses to develop and run private pay-phone networks. These firms included everything from one-person businesses operated out of the back of a pick-up truck to People's Telephone, the largest independent operator, with 6,500 phones in 15 states as of 1989.

Another aspect of deregulation further spurred the development of the COCOT industry. With deregulation, AT&T lost its monopoly over long-distance service. Because of a rule stipulating "equal access," local telephone companies had to furnish all long-distance carriers the same access to their networks that they had previously given only to AT&T. The local telephone company could no longer automatically select AT&T to provide long-distance service to its customers. Each customer would select one of the main carriers (AT&T, MCI, Sprint) or an alternative operator service (AOS) to provide long-distance service. AOS's buy blocks of long-distance service at wholesale rates from the main carriers and then resell the service at higher rates (sometimes even higher

than AT&T rates) to their customers. To attract the AOS business, the main carriers also began offering commissions to the AOSs. In turn, the AOSs began offering commissions to COCOTs who tied their pay-phone systems to the AOSs for long-distance service. These commissions provided an additional source of revenues to the COCOT business, making it profitable and competitive. Until December, 1988, these commissions also provided the CO-COTs with a competitive advantage, because GTE and the other telephone companies were required to use AT&T for their long-distance pay-phone service. AT&T paid them no commissions.

Prior to deregulation, once GTE installed a phone, it had a customer for life. GTE did not require any contracts for public phones, and it paid no commissions to the owner of the location in which the phone was installed. GTE could take customers for granted—and it usually did. The COCOTs, however, entered the business with a vengeance. Taking advantage of their low overhead and commissions, they began offering the location-owner a percentage of the coins in the box as a commission for allowing them to install a pay phone. Further, they targeted established pay phones. Because GTE had no contracts with location-owners, the COCOTs could suggest that the owner ask GTE to remove its phone. Then the COCOT would install a phone and pay the owner a commission, typically 20 to 30 percent of the coins in the box. To most owners, a pay phone is a pay phone—they were glad to dump GTE in order to make some extra money. Some COCOTs even hired college students to go door-to-door, signing up businesses for new pay phones and for removals of existing phones. COCOTs also targeted retail chains which operated in many locations. Whereas GTE can provide pay-phone service only in its franchised areas, COCOTs operate over large areas and can offer chains the ability to handle much or all of their pay-phone service with one contact.

GTE responded by offering a commission of 30 percent of the coins in the box over $60 a month and asking owners to agree to give 30 days notice before removing a phone. However, these actions did not slow the loss of customers. GTE then introduced a second contract which paid 15 to 20 percent of all coins in the box in return for the customer signing a 3- to 5-year contract.

The contract, however, allowed the owner to have the GTE phone removed if the owner paid the installation and removal costs, usually about $500 to $650.

Competitors responded to these moves in some cases by offering commissions of 30 to 50 percent of *net* profits (pay-phone revenues less maintenance and collection costs), including revenue on long-distance calls. GTE argued that this higher percentage of net might often be less than its 15 to 20 percent of gross. In some cases, competition had even offered to pay GTE's installation and removal costs for the location-owner in order to win the location.

BACK AT SMILE GAS

Kevin Murphy agreed to install a new pay phone at Smile Gas. He told Mr. Lewis that he would receive 20 percent of the coin-in-the-box revenue. Mr. Lewis asked about a commission on long-distance calls. Kevin indicated that the FCC does not allow GTE to recommend long-distance carriers and that Mr. Lewis would have to choose a carrier and negotiate with that carrier about commissions. When Mr. Lewis also asked about maintenance and repair service for the phone, Kevin assured him that GTE provided 24-hour, around-the-clock service.

Kevin left the meeting with Mr. Lewis to attend a sales meeting in GTE's Durham office. The 10 sales consultants for GTE South were gathering for the first time ever to begin sales training and to work with management to develop a new marketing strategy for GTE's public communications operations in the southeast. As he drove to the meeting, Kevin rehearsed the suggestions he wanted to make. Competitors' fierce moves had created trouble already, and Kevin knew that analysts predicted only a 1.5 percent annual market growth rate through 1994. This slow growth would fuel even more competitive challenges. GTE's market share in its franchised areas had already fallen from 100 percent to 85 percent. Kevin knew GTE had to improve its pay-phone strategy to stop the erosion.

QUESTIONS

1. What are the objectives, strategies, strengths, and weaknesses of GTE's competitors' in the pay-phone market?
2. What value does a pay phone provide for a location-owner? For a customer making a call? What features of telephone service are important to these two customer groups?
3. Are the COCOTs "well-behaved" or "disruptive" competitors?
4. How can GTE gather intelligence about competitors' moves?
5. GTE clearly serves as a market leader. Given the changing nature of competition, what changes should it make in its marketing strategy? Be certain to address each aspect of the marketing mix.
6. What market challenger strategies have the COCOTs been using? How might they respond to your recommended marketing strategy changes?

Source: We appreciate the support of GTE Telephone Operations in the development of this case.

SNEAKER WARS

Sneakers have become a national obsession. Everyone seems to have them and everyone likes them—from the sports enthusiast and the health conscious to the junior executive, the fashion conscious, and the active home-maker. Indeed, according to one analyst, one-third of all shoes sold in the United States today are sneakers.

Two giants dominate the athletic shoe industry: Nike from Oregon and Reebok from Boston control approxi-mately 50 percent of the sneaker business. Nike's success was based on creating a performance shoe for the fitness boom, specifically for the jogging craze of the 1970s, while Reebok made it on the new relaxed life-style of the 1980s, recognizing that 80 percent of all sneakers sold are for leisure use. Now both companies make hun-dreds of styles for both performance and recreational use.

Today in the battle to be number one, it has become Nike substance versus Reebok style. In the mid-1980s, by focusing on a special shoe for women, Reebok roared past Nike, unseating them from their position atop the athletic shoe industry. It was the aerobic shoe that propelled Reebok to number one. Although the wrinkled leather was originally a production mistake, management loved it and so did the consumer.

Paul Fireman, Reebok's CEO and founder of Reebok in the United States, was a salesman who once ran a small family sporting goods business. Because of the suc-cess of Reebok, he has become one of the highest-paid executives in the nation. Even he is surprised by the success of the business. But Fireman concedes that it is consumers who have made his company number one. Therefore, Ree-bok will continue to focus its efforts on satisfying the customer. A recent example of this customer orientation is the introduction of handpainted sneakers for the masses.

Nike was founded by Phil Knight, a runner from the University of Oregon. Knight and his former track coach, Bill Baumann, started the company and rode the running boom to instant success. Knight is the driving force, and remains immensely competitive. While Nike has made concessions to fashion, it is technology the com-pany is counting on to win the war against Reebok. A recent innovation is the Air Revolution, a plastic airbag

in the heel of the shoe that is visible. Reebok has developed its own system, called Energy Return, which involves the placement of plastic tubes in the shoes. It may ulti-mately include a window so that the tubes would be visible.

Both companies spend enormous amounts on adver-tising and endorsements. Nike has long favored prominent athletes like Salazar, McEnroe, and Jordan as spokesper-sons. Their strategy seems to be paying off. Their advertis-ing campaign with the slogan "Just Do It," coupled with the success of their Air Pocket shoes such as the Air Jordan, has allowed Nike to move past Reebok and recap-ture the number-one position in the industry. But Reebok is expected to rebound from its recent slump, which some analysis say was brought on by its avant-garde "Reeboks Let UBU" promotional campaign. This $25 million cam-paign with fairy godmothers, three-legged men, tuba-play-ing swimmers, and bobby-soxed twins was seen as too weird, and it failed to enhance sales.

The competition never ceases. An upstart company called L.A. Gear sneers at research, development, and technology—simply letting people wear their sneakers and then listen to what is said about them. L.A. Gear came from nowhere in 1987 to capture an 11 percent share of the market and $600 million in sales by 1990.

The industry is cyclical. Today's leaders could easily go the way of Keds, Converse, and Adidas—popular in the 1950s, 60s, and 70s, respectively, and still on the market, but nowhere near number one today.

QUESTIONS

1. Explain how Reebok has been both a market leader and a market challenger.
2. Explain why Nike should properly be classified as a market-centered company.
3. Discuss market-expansion strategies that Nike either has used or could use to enhance its market position.

Sources: "Sneaker Attack," *Advertising Age*, June 20, 1988, p. 2; "Treading on Air," *Business Month*, January 1934, pp. 29–34; "Foot's Parade," *Time*, August 28, 1989, pp. 54–55; "L.A. Gear Is Going Where the Boys Are," *Business Week*, June 19, 1989, p. 54; and "Reebok on the Rebound," *New York*, October 16, 1989.

20
Planning, Implementing, and Controlling Marketing Programs

During the 1970s, IBM became stodgy and bureaucratic. The highly structured and tradition-bound IBM organization was having trouble competing against smaller, more flexible competitors in fast-changing, high-growth segments. Thus, when IBM decided in the early 1980s to enter the personal computer market, industry analysts were skeptical. The strategy was sound enough—to carry the IBM name and reputation for quality and service into the fastest-growing segment of the computer market. But with personal computers, the company would be selling a very different product to very different customers—and against very different competition. Could large and slow-moving IBM successfully *plan* for and *implement* a new strategy so different from its previous strategies? Despite its great size and power, few analysts expected IBM to have much immediate impact in the personal computer market against more nimble competitors.

But the introduction of the IBM PC has become a classic story of smart marketing planning and innovative implementation. IBM pulled some big surprises, swept aside traditional methods, and broke many of its own long-held rules. It set up a "special operating unit" called the Entry Systems Division (ESD) with complete responsibility for the IBM PC. This independent "company within a company" developed a culture and operating style similar to those of its smaller competitors. Free of close IBM control, ESD ignored traditions and did many "non-IBM-like" things. For example:

- IBM had *always* built its computers from the ground up, using only IBM electronic components. But to get the PC to the market more quickly, ESD made it from readily available components bought from outside suppliers.
- IBM had *always* carefully guarded its computer designs and developed its own software. Not so for the PC! To increase acceptance and sales, ESD published the PC's technical specifications to show how the machine was built. This made it easier for outside companies to design PC-compatible software. The resulting wealth of available software made the PC even more attractive to consumers. IBM machines soon became the industry standard for software producers.
- IBM had *always* sold its products directly through its own salesforce. But for the PC, ESD used a network of independent retailers, including such large ones as Sears and Computerland.
- IBM had *always* been slow but sure in making product and price changes. But ESD spent millions to build modern production facilities that could turn out PCs at low cost, then used aggressive pricing to keep competitors off balance.

Thus, to plan and implement its strategy to enter the personal computer market, IBM made several tradition-shattering changes in its structure, operations, and tactics. And the new approach paid off. The IBM PC went from initial planning to market in 13 months. In less than three years, IBM claimed a 40 percent share of the overall personal computer market (60 to 70 percent in the company segment). Although using available parts and publishing designs later made it easier for copycat competitors to crank out IBM imitations, without these moves IBM would not likely have gotten to market so quickly or penetrated so deeply. And when IBM introduced its next generation PS/2 personal computers in 1987, even with a dozen low-priced "clones" on the market, the venerable old IBM PC still held a 30 percent market share, compared with only 7 percent shares for nearest competitors Apple and Compaq.

Entering the 1990s, the Entry Systems Division, which began as a 12-person team, has grown into a 10,000-employee division. IBM has now blended ESD into the rest of the $50 billion company. But the new approach worked so well that IBM set up more than a dozen other special business units to develop products for software, robotics, high-tech health care, and other fast-growing markets.[1]

CHAPTER OBJECTIVES

After reading this chapter, you should be able to:

1. Identify the sections of a marketing plan and what each section contains.
2. Explain why companies have trouble implementing marketing plans and programs.
3. Describe the elements of the marketing-implementation process.
4. Compare the four ways of organizing the marketing department.
5. Explain the three ways in which companies control their marketing activities.

In this chapter, we look more closely at each marketing management function—*analysis*, *planning*, *implementation*, and *control*. Figure 20-1 shows the relationship between these marketing activities. The company first develops overall strategic plans. These company-wide strategic plans are then translated into marketing and other plans for each division, product, and brand.

Through implementation, the company turns the strategic and marketing plans into actions that will achieve the company's strategic objectives. Marketing plans are implemented by people in the marketing organization working with others both inside and outside the company. Control consists of measuring and evaluating the results of marketing plans and activities, and taking corrective action to make sure objectives are being reached. Marketing analysis provides information and evaluations needed for all of the other marketing management activities.

To review all the factors that marketers must consider when designing marketing programs, we discuss planning first. But this does not mean that planning always comes

FIGURE 20-1
The relationship between analysis, planning, implementation, and control

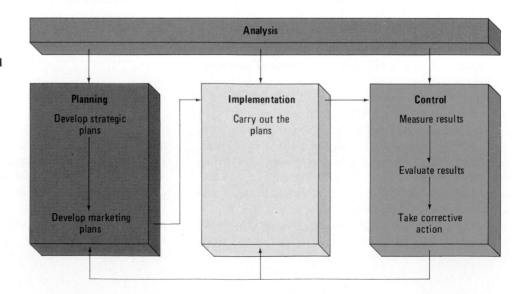

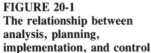

first, or that planning ends before marketers move on to the other activities. Figure 20-1 shows that planning and the other activities are closely related. Marketers must plan their analysis, implementation, and control activities; analysis provides inputs for planning, implementation, and control; control provides feedback for future planning and implementation.

Chapters 4 and 8 examine many of the tools used in marketing analysis. In this chapter we discuss marketing planning and how plans are implemented and controlled by people in the marketing department.

MARKETING PLANNING

The strategic plan defines the company's overall mission and objectives. Within each business unit, functional plans must be prepared, including marketing plans. If the business unit consists of many product lines, brands, and markets, plans must be drawn up for each. Marketing plans might include product plans, brand plans, or market plans.

The Components of a Marketing Plan

What does a marketing plan look like? Our discussion focuses on product or brand plans. A product or brand plan should contain the following sections: *executive summary*, *current marketing situation*, *threats and opportunities*, *objectives and issues*, *marketing strategies*, *action programs*, *budgets*, and *controls* (see Figure 20-2).

Executive Summary

The marketing plan should open with a short summary of the main goals and recommendations to be presented in the plan. Here is a short example:

> The 1992 Marketing Plan outlines an approach to attaining a significant increase in company sales and profits over the preceding year. The sales target is $240 million, a planned 20 percent sales gain. We think this increase is attainable because of the improved economic, competitive, and distribution picture. The target operating margin is $25 million, a 25 percent increase over last year. To achieve these goals, the sales promotion budget will be $4.8 million, or 2 percent of projected sales. The advertising budget will be $7.2 million, or 3 percent of projected sales . . . [More details follow]

The **executive summary** helps top management to find quickly the major points of the plan. A table of contents should follow the executive summary.

Current Marketing Situation

The first major section of the plan describes the target market and the company's position in it. In **current marketing situation** section, the planner provides information about the market, product performance, competition, and distribution. It includes a *market description* which defines the market, including major market segments. The planner shows market size in total and by segment for several past years, then reviews customer needs and factors in the marketing environment that may affect customer purchasing. Next the *product review* shows sales, prices, and gross margins of the major products in the product line. A section on *competition* identifies major competitors and each of their strategies for product quality, pricing, distribution, and promotion. It also shows

FIGURE 20-2
Components of a marketing plan

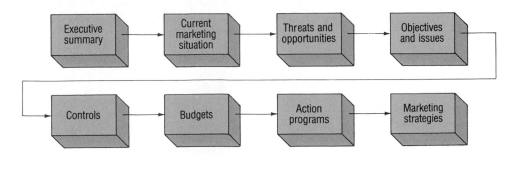

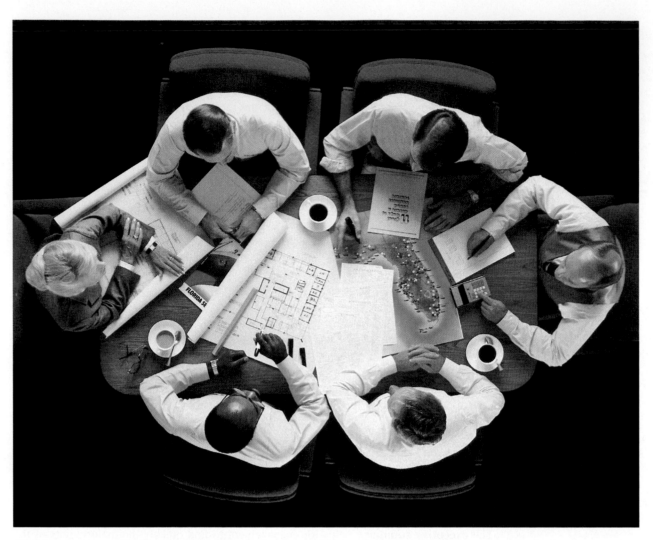

Marketers must continually plan their analysis, implementation, and control activities.

the market shares held by the company and each competitor. Finally, a section on *distribution* describes recent sales trends and developments in the major distribution channels.

Threats and Opportunities

This section requires the manager to look ahead for major threats and opportunities that the product might face. Its purpose is to make the manager anticipate important developments that can have an impact on the firm. Managers should list as many threats and opportunities as they can imagine. Suppose a major pet foods marketer comes up with the following list:

- A large competitor has just announced that it will introduce a new premium pet food line, backed by a huge advertising and sales promotion blitz.
- Industry analysts predict that supermarket chain buyers will face more than 10,000 new grocery product introductions next year. The buyers are expected to accept only 38 percent of these new products and give each one only five months to prove itself.
- Because of improved economic conditions during the past several years, pet ownership is increasing in almost all segments of the U.S. population.
- The company's researchers have found a way to make a new pet food that is low in fat and calories yet highly nutritious and tasty. This product will appeal strongly to many of today's pet food buyers, who are almost as concerned about their pets' health as about their own.

▪ Pet ownership and concern about proper pet care are increasing rapidly in foreign markets, especially in developing nations.

The first two items are *threats*. Not all threats call for the same attention or concern—the manager should assess the likelihood of each threat and the potential damage each could cause. The manager should then focus on the most probable and harmful threats and prepare plans in advance to meet them.

The last three items in the list are marketing opportunities. A **company marketing opportunity** is an attractive arena for marketing action in which the company could enjoy a competitive advantage. The manager should assess each opportunity according to its potential attractiveness and the company's probability of success. Figure 20-3 shows that the company should pursue only the opportunities that fit its objectives and resources. Every company has objectives based on its business mission. And each opportunity requires that the company have certain amounts of capital and know-how. Companies can rarely find ideal opportunities that exactly fit their objectives and resources. Developing opportunities involves risks. When evaluating opportunities, the manager must decide whether the expected returns justify these risks.

Objectives and Issues

Having studied the product's threats and opportunities, the manager can now set objectives and consider issues that will affect them. The objectives should be stated as goals the company would like to reach during the plan's term. For example, the manager might want to achieve a 15 percent market share, a 20 percent pre-tax profit on sales, and a 25 percent pre-tax profit on investment. Suppose the current market share is only 10 percent. This poses a key issue: How can market share be increased? The manager should consider the major issues involved in trying to increase market share.

FIGURE 20-3
Evaluating a company marketing opportunity in terms of company objectives and resources

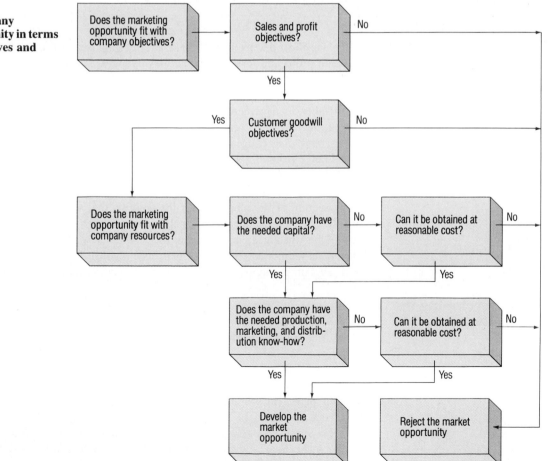

Marketing Strategies

In this section of the marketing plan, the manager outlines the broad marketing strategy or "game plan" for attaining the objectives. **Marketing strategy** is the marketing logic by which the business unit hopes to achieve its marketing objectives. It consists of specific strategies for target markets, marketing mix, and marketing expenditure level. Marketing strategy should detail the market segments the company will focus on. These segments differ in their needs and wants, responses to marketing, and profitability. The company would be smart to put its effort and energy into those market segments it can best serve from a competitive point of view. It should develop a marketing strategy for each targeted segment.

The manager should also outline specific strategies for such marketing mix elements as new products, field sales, advertising, sales promotion, prices, and distribution. The manager should explain how each strategy responds to the threats, opportunities, and critical issues spelled out earlier in the plan.

Finally, the manager should also provide a specific marketing budget that will be sufficient to carry out the planned strategies. The manager knows that higher budgets will produce more sales but is looking for the marketing budget that will produce the best profit picture.

Action Programs

Marketing strategies should be turned into specific action programs that answer the following questions: *What* will be done? *When* will it be done? *Who* is responsible for doing it? And *how much* will it cost? For example, the manager may want to increase sales promotion as a key strategy for winning market share. A sales promotion action plan should be drawn up to outline special offers and their dates, trade shows entered, new point-of-purchase displays, and other promotions. The action plan shows when activities will be started, reviewed, and completed.

Budgets

Action plans allow the manager to make a supporting **marketing budget** that is essentially a projected profit and loss statement. For revenues, it shows that forecasted number of units that would be sold and the average net price. On the expense side, it shows the cost of production, physical distribution, and marketing. The difference is the projected profit. Higher management will review the budget and approve or modify it. Once approved, the budget is the basis for materials buying, production scheduling, manpower planning, and marketing operations. Budgeting can be very difficult, and budgeting methods range from simple "rules of thumb" to complex computer models.[2]

Controls

The last section of the plan outlines the controls that will be used to monitor progress. Typically, goals and budgets are spelled out for each month or quarter. This practice allows higher management to review the results each period and to spot businesses or products that are not meeting their goals. The managers of these businesses and products have to explain problems and what corrective actions they will take.

Developing the Marketing Budget

We now look at how marketing managers construct a marketing budget to attain a given level of sales and profits. We first examine a common budget-setting approach, then describe some improvements.

Target Profit Planning

Suppose John Smith, the ketchup product manager at Heinz, has to prepare his annual marketing plan. He will probably follow the procedure shown in Table 20-1 called *target profit planning*.

John Smith first estimates the total household market for ketchup for the coming year. To make this estimate, he applies the recent market growth rate (6 percent) to this year's market size (23.6 million cases). This forecasts a market size of 25 million

TABLE 20-1
Target Profit Plan

1. *Forecast of total market* This year's total market (23,600,000 cases) × recent growth rate (6%)	25,000,000 cases
2. *Forecast of market share*	28%
3. *Forecast of sales volume* [(1) × (2)]	7,000,000 cases
4. *Price to distributor*	$4.45 per case
5. *Estimate of sales revenue* [(3) × (4)]	$31,150,000
6. *Estimate of variable costs* Tomatoes and spices ($0.50) + bottles and caps ($1.00) + labor ($1.10) + physical distribution ($0.15)	$2.75 per case
7. *Estimate of contribution margin to cover fixed costs, profits, and marketing* {[(4) − (6)] × (3)}	$11,900,000
8. *Estimate of fixed costs* Fixed charge $1 per case × 7 million cases	$7,000,000
9. *Estimate of contribution margin to cover profits and marketing* [(7) − (8)]	$4,900,000
10. *Estimate of target profit goal*	$1,900,000
11. *Amount available for marketing* [(9) − (10)]	$3,000,000
12. *Split of the marketing budget* Advertising Sales promotion Marketing research	$2,000,000 $ 900,000 $ 100,000

cases for next year. John assumes that Heinz's current 28 percent market share will continue and forecasts next year's sales at 7 million cases.

Next, based on expected increases in labor and material costs, John sets next years' distributor price at $4.45 per case and calculates that sales revenue will be $31.15 million. He then estimates next year's variable costs at $2.75 per case. This indicates that the contribution margin to cover fixed costs, profits, and marketing is $11.9 million. Suppose the company charges this brand with a fixed cost of $1 per case, or $7 million. This leaves a contribution margin of $4.9 million to cover profits and marketing.

John now brings in the target profit goal. Suppose higher management will be satisfied with a profit level of $1.9 million, a 10 percent increase over this year's profit. John then subtracts the target profit from what remains of the contribution margin, leaving $3 million available for marketing.

Finally, John allocates the marketing budget to some of the marketing mix elements, such as advertising, sales promotion, and marketing research. This year's split uses the same proportions as last year's. John spends two-thirds of the money on advertising, almost one-third on sales promotion, and the remainder on marketing research.

Although this method produces a workable budget, John could make improvements. He could estimate market size and share by examining past trends and considering changes in the marketing environment that would lead to a different demand forecast. Rather than assuming he would continue last year's marketing strategy, John could have considered one or several alternative strategies and their potential impact on sales, profits, and the budget. John set price mainly to cover expected costs but could have used a more market-oriented method. John allocated the budget to the marketing mix using ''more-of-the-same'' thinking but should have considered each marketing element's potential contribution given this year's marketing objectives and the product's current situation. Finally, John's plan and budget seek only satisfactory profits. Instead, John should look for a plan which optimizes profits.

Profit Optimization Planning

To optimize profits, the manager must first identify the relationship between sales and the various marketing mix elements. The *sales-response function* describes this relationship. Figure 20-4 shows a hypothetical sales-response function. This function shows that the more the company spends in a given period on marketing, the higher its sales are likely to be. This particular function is S-shaped, although other shapes are possible. The S-shaped function says that low levels of marketing expenditure are not likely to

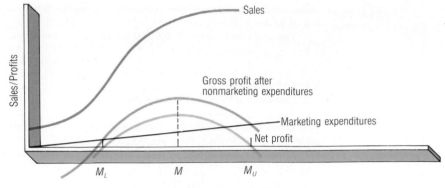

FIGURE 20-4
The sales-response function:
the relationship between sales,
marketing expenditures, and
profits

produce much sales. Too few buyers will be reached, or reached effectively, by the company's marketing. Higher levels of marketing spending during the period will produce much higher levels of sales. But very high spending might not add much more sales because of eventually diminishing returns.

Diminishing returns to increases in marketing expenditures occur because there is an upper limit to the total potential demand for any product. As demand approaches this upper limit, it becomes increasingly expensive to attract the remaining, more reluctant buyers. Also, as the company steps up its marketing effort, competitors tend to do the same, so that each company faces more sales resistance.

How can marketing managers estimate the sales-response functions for their businesses? They can use one of three methods. Using the *statistical method*, the manager gathers data on past sales and marketing mix levels and estimates the sales-response functions with statistical techniques. Using the *experimental method*, the manager varies the marketing mix levels in matched samples and notes the resulting sales responses. Finally, using the *judgmental method*, experts are asked to make intelligent guesses about the nccdcd relationships.[3]

Once estimated, how are sales-response functions used in profit optimization? Figure 20-4 shows the analysis for finding the optimal marketing expenditure. First, the marketing manager subtracts all nonmarketing costs from the sales-response function to find the gross-profit curve. Next, the marketing expenditures, shown by the straight line starting at the origin, are subtracted from the gross-profit curve to find the net-profit curve. The net-profit curve shows positive net profits with marketing expenditures between M_L and M_U, which could be defined as the range of rational marketing spending. The net-profit curve reaches a maximum of M. Therefore the marketing expenditure that would maximize net profit is M. The graphic solution can also be carried out mathematically; in fact, it has to be if sales volume is a function of more than one marketing mix variable.

This budgeting approach offers a good conceptual framework for studying relationships between marketing mix levels and the resulting sales and profits. Some marketers have developed complex models for estimating response curves and finding optimal budgets. Others prefer more practical, easier-to-use budgeting methods.

IMPLEMENTATION

Planning good strategies is only a start toward successful marketing. A brilliant marketing strategy counts for little if the company fails to implement it properly. **Marketing implementation** is the process that turns marketing strategies and *plans* into marketing *actions* in order to accomplish strategic marketing objectives. Implementation involves day-to-day, month-to-month activities that effectively put the marketing plan to work. Whereas marketing planning addresses the *what* and *why* of marketing activities, implementation addresses the *who*, *where*, *when*, and *how*.

Many managers think that "doing things right" (implementation) is as important, or even more important, than "doing the right things" (strategy):

> A surprisingly large number of very successful large companies . . . don't have long-term strategic plans with an obsessive preoccupation on rivalry. They concentrate on operating details and doing things well. Hustle is their style and their strategy. They move fast and they get it right. . . . Countless companies in all industries, young or old, mature or booming, are finally learning the limits of strategy and concentrating on tactics and execution.[4]

Yet implementation is difficult—it is often easier to think up good marketing strategies than to carry them out. And managers often have trouble diagnosing implementation problems. It is usually hard to tell whether poor performance was caused by poor strategy, poor implementation, or both.[5]

Reasons for Poor Implementation

What causes poor implementation? Why do so many companies have trouble getting their marketing plans to work effectively? Several factors cause implementation problems.

Isolated Planning

The company's strategic plans often are set by top management or high-level "professional planners" who have little direct contact with the marketing managers who must implement the plan. Central strategic planning can provide benefits—strong central leadership, better coordination of strategies across business units, and more emphasis on long-term strategic thinking and performance. But central planning also leads to several problems. Top-level managers and planners are concerned with broad strategy and may prepare plans that are too general. They may not understand the practical problems faced by line managers and many produce unrealistic plans. Or lower-level managers who did not prepare the plans may not fully understand them. Finally, managers who face day-to-day operations may resent what they see as unrealistic plans made up by "ivory-tower" planners.

Many companies have realized that high-level managers and planners cannot plan strategies *for* marketing managers. Instead, planners must help the marketing managers

Marketing plans and strategies are of little value until they are properly implemented.

find their *own* strategies. Many companies are cutting down their large central planning staffs and are giving more planning responsibility to lower-level managers. In these companies, top management and strategy planners are not isolated—they work directly with line managers to design more workable strategies.[6]

Tradeoffs between Long-Term and Short-Term Objectives

Company marketing strategies often address *long-run* activities for the next three to five years. But the marketing managers who implement these strategies are usually rewarded for *short-run* sales, growth, or profits. When choosing between long-run strategy and short-run performance, U.S. managers usually favor one of the more rewarding short-run results. One study found many examples of such harmful tradeoffs. For example, one company designed a marketing strategy that stressed product availability and customer service. But to increase short-term profit, operating managers cut costs by reducing inventories and service staff. These managers met short-run performance goals and received high evaluations, but their actions hurt the company's long-run strategy.[7]

Some companies are taking steps to attain a better balance between short- and long-run goals. They are making managers more aware of strategic goals, evaluating managers on both long-run and short-run performance, and rewarding managers for reaching long-run objectives.

Natural Resistance to Change

As a rule, the company's current operations have been designed to implement past plans and strategies. New strategies requiring new company patterns and habits may be resisted. And the more different the new strategy from the old, the greater the resistance to implementing it. For very different strategies, implementation may cut across traditional organization lines within the company. For example, when one company tried to implement a strategy of developing new markets for an old product line, its established salesforce resisted strongly. The company was forced to create an entirely new sales division in order to develop the new markets.

Lack of Specific Implementation Plans

Some marketing plans are poorly implemented because the planners fail to make detailed implementation plans. They leave the details to managers, and the result is poor implementation or no implementation at all. Planners cannot simply assume that their plans will be implemented. They must prepare a detailed implementation plan that shows the specific activities needed to put the plan into action. They must develop timetables and assign major implementation tasks to individual managers.

The Implementation Process

People at all levels of the marketing system must work together to implement marketing plans and strategies. People in the marketing department, in other company departments, and in outside organizations—all can help or hinder marketing implementation. The company must find ways to coordinate all these actors and their activities.

The implementation process is shown in Figure 20-5.[8] The figure shows that marketing strategy and marketing performance are linked by an implementation system consisting of five related elements: *action programs*, an *organization structure*, *decision and reward systems*, *human resources*, and *managerial climate and company culture*.

The Action Program

To implement marketing plans, people at all company levels make decisions and perform tasks. At Procter & Gamble, implementation of a plan to introduce a stream of high-quality new products requires day-to-day decisions and actions by thousands of people both inside and outside the organization. In the marketing organization, marketing researchers test new product concepts and scan the marketplace for new product ideas. For each new product, marketing managers make decisions about target segments, branding, packaging, pricing, promoting, and distributing. Salespeople are hired, trained and retrained, directed, and motivated.

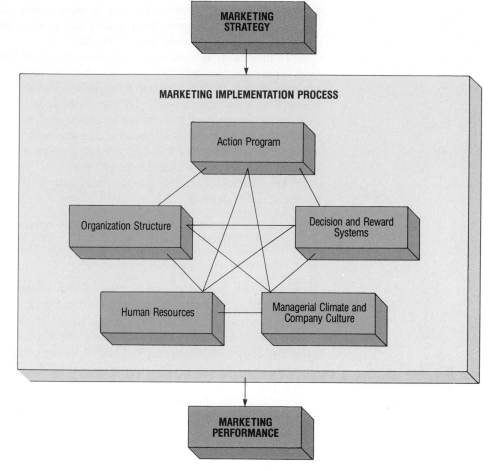

FIGURE 20-5
The marketing implementation process

Marketing managers work with other company managers to get support for promising new products. They talk with engineering about product design. They talk with manufacturing about production and inventory levels. They talk with finance about funding and cash flows, with the legal staff about patents and product-safety issues, and with personnel about staffing and training needs. Marketing managers also work with outside people. They meet with advertising agencies to plan ad campaigns and with the media to obtain publicity support. The salesforce urges retailers to advertise the new products, to provide ample shelf space, and to use company displays.

The **action program** pulls all of these people and activities together. It identifies the decisions and actions needed to implement the marketing program. It also gives responsibility for these decisions and actions to specific people in the company. Finally, the action program gives a timetable that states when decisions must be made and when actions must be taken. The action program shows what must be done, who will do it, and how decisions and actions will be coordinated to reach the company's marketing objectives.

The Organization Structure

The company's formal **organization structure** plays an important role in implementing marketing strategy. The structure breaks up the company's work into well-defined jobs, assigns these jobs to people and departments, and allows efficiency through specialization. The structure then coordinates these specialized jobs by defining formal ties between people and departments and by setting lines of authority and communication.

Companies with different strategies need different organization structures. A small firm developing new products in a fast-changing industry might need a flexible structure that encourages individual action—a *decentralized* structure with ample informal communication. A more established company in more stable markets might need a structure that provides more integration—a more *centralized* structure with well-defined roles and communication "through proper channels."[9]

In their study of successful companies, Peters and Waterman found that they had many common structural characteristics that led to successful implementation.[10] For example, their structures tended to be more *informal*—Hewlett–Packard's MBWA (management by wandering around), IBM's "open-door" policy, 3M's "clubs" to create small-group interaction. The successful companies' structures were *decentralized*, with small independent divisions or groups to encourage innovation. The structures also tended to be *simple and lean*. These simple structures are more flexible and allow the companies to adapt more quickly to changing conditions.

The excellent companies also have lean staffs, especially at higher levels. According to Peters and Waterman:

> Indeed, it appears that most of our excellent companies have comparatively few people at the corporate level, and that what staff there is tends to be out in the field solving problems rather than in the home office checking on things. The bottom line is fewer administrators, more operators.[11]

In recent years, many large companies—General Motors, Polaroid, Du Pont, General Electric, Lever Brothers, and others—have cut back unneeded layers of management and restructured their organizations to reduce costs and increase marketing flexibility.

Some of the Peters and Waterman's conclusions have been questioned because the study focused on high-technology and consumer goods companies operating in rapidly changing environments.[12] The structures used by these companies may not be right for other types of firms in different situations. And many of the study's excellent companies will need to change their structures as their strategies and situations change. For example, the informal structure that made Hewlett-Packard so successful at the time of the study later caused problems. The company has since moved toward a more formal structure (see Marketing Highlight 20–1).

Decision and Reward Systems

Decision and reward systems include formal and informal operating procedures that guide such activities as planning, information gathering, budgeting, recruiting and training, control, and personnel evaluation and rewards. Poorly designed systems can work against implementation; well-designed systems can help implementation. Consider a company's compensation system. If it compensates managers for short-run results, they will have little incentive to work toward long-run objectives. Many companies are designing compensation systems to overcome this problem. Here is an example:

> One company was concerned that its annual bonus system encouraged managers to ignore long-run objectives and focus on annual performance goals. To correct this, the company changed its bonus system to include rewards for both annual performance and for reaching "strategic milestones." Under the new plan, each manager works with planners to set two or three strategic objectives. At the end of the year, the manager's bonus is based on both operating performance and on reaching the strategic objectives. Thus, the bonus system encourages managers to achieve more balance of the company's long- and short-run needs.[13]

Human Resources

Marketing strategies are implemented by people, so successful implementation requires careful **human resources** planning. At all levels, the company must fill its structure and systems with people who have the needed skills, motivation, and personal characteristics. Company personnel must be recruited, assigned, trained, and maintained.

The selection and development of executives and other managers are especially important for implementation. Different strategies call for managers with different personalities and skills. New venture strategies need managers with entrepreneurial skills; holding strategies require managers with organizational and administrative skills; and retrenchment

HEWLETT-PACKARD'S STRUCTURE EVOLVES

In 1939, two engineers—Bill Hewlett and Dave Packard—started Hewlett-Packard in a Palo Alto garage to build test equipment. At the start, Bill and Dave did everything themselves, from designing and building their equipment to marketing it. As the firm grew out of the garage and began to build more and different types of test equipment, Hewlett and Packard could no longer make all the necessary operating decisions by themselves. They assumed roles as top managers and hired functional managers to run various company activities. These managers were relatively autonomous but still closely tied to the owners.

By the mid-1970s, Hewlett-Packard's 42 divisions employed more than 1,200 people. The company's structure evolved to support its heavy emphasis on innovation and autonomy. The structure was loose and decentralized. Each division operated as an autonomous unit and was responsible for its own strategic planning, product development, marketing programs, and implementation.

In 1982, Peters and Waterman, in their *In Search of Excellence*, cited HP's informal and decentralized structure as a major reason for the company's continued excellence. They praised HP's unrestrictive structure and high degree of informal communication (its MBWA style—management by wandering around). Peters and Waterman noted that the HP structure decentralized decision making and responsibility. In the words of one HP manager:

> Hewlett-Packard [should not] have a tight, military-type organization, but rather . . . give people the freedom to work toward [overall objectives] in ways they determine best for their own areas of responsibility.

The structure also decentralized authority and fostered autonomy:

The sales force does not have to accept a product developed by a division unless it wants it. The company cites numerous instances in which several million dollars of development funds were spent by a division, at which point the sales force said, "No thanks."

But in recent years, although still profitable, Hewlett-Packard has met with some problems in the fast-changing microcomputer and minicomputer markets. According to *Business Week*:

> Hewlett-Packard's famed innovative culture and decentralization spawned such enormously successful products as its 3000 minicomputer, the handheld scientific calculator, and the ThinkJet nonimpact printer. But when a new climate required its fiercely autonomous divisions to cooperate in product development and marketing, HP's passionate devotion to the "autonomy and entrepreneurship" that Peters and Waterman advocate became a hindrance.

Thus, Hewlett-Packard is finding that it must change its structure and culture to bring them in line with its changing situation. As *Business Week* puts it:

> To regain its stride, HP is being forced to abandon attributes of excellence for which it was praised. Its technology-driven, engineering-oriented culture, in which decentralization and innovation were a religion and entrepreneurs were the gods, is giving way to a marketing culture and growing centralization.

Sources: Based on information in Donald F. Harvey, *Business Policy and Strategic Management* (Columbus, OH: Charles E. Merrill, 1982), pp. 269–70; "Who's Excellent Now?" *Business Week*, November 5, 1984, pp. 76–78; and Thomas J. Peters and Robert H. Waterman, Jr., *In Search of Excellence: Lessons from America's Best-Run Companies* (New York: Harper & Row, 1982).

Hewlett-Packard began in this garage in 1939; now it operates around the world from this headquarters complex. Structure and culture changed with growth.

strategies call for managers with cost-cutting skills. Thus, the company must carefully match its managers to the needs of the strategies to be implemented.

In recent years, more and more companies have recognized the importance of good people planning. Systematic, long-run human resources planning can give the company a strong competitive advantage.[14]

Managerial Climate and Company Culture

The company's managerial climate and company culture can make or break marketing implementation. **Managerial climate** refers to the way company managers work with others in the company. Some managers take command, delegate little authority, and keep tight controls. Others delegate much, encourage their people to take initiative, and communicate informally. No one managerial style is best for all situations. Different strategies may require different leadership styles, and which style is best varies with the company's structure, tasks, people, and environment.[15]

Company culture is a system of values and beliefs shared by people in an organization. It is the company's collective identity and meaning. The culture informally guides the behavior of people at all company levels. Peters and Waterman found that excellent companies have strong and clearly defined cultures:

> Without exception, the dominance and coherence of culture proved to be an essential quality of the excellent companies. Moreover, the stronger the culture and the more it was directed toward the marketplace, the less need there was for policy manuals, organization charts, or detailed procedures and rules. In these companies, people way down the line know what they are supposed to do in most situations because the handful of guiding values is crystal clear. . . . Everyone at Hewlett-Packard knows that he or she is supposed to be innovative. Everyone at Procter & Gamble knows that product quality is the [norm].[16]

Marketing strategies that do not fit the company's style and culture will be difficult to implement. For example, a decision by Procter & Gamble to increase sales by reducing product quality and prices would not work well. It would be resisted by P&G people at all levels who identify strongly with the company's reputation for quality. Because managerial style and culture are so hard to change, companies usually design strategies that fit their current cultures rather than trying to change their styles and cultures to fit new strategies.[17]

TABLE 20-2
Questions about the Marketing Implementation System

Structure
What is the organization's structure?
What are the lines of authority and communication?
What is the role of task forces, committees, or similar mechanisms?

Systems
What are the important systems?
What are the critical control variables?
How do product and information flow?

Tasks
What are the tasks to be performed and which are critical?
How are they accomplished, with what technology?
What strengths does the organization have?

People
What are their skills, knowledge, and experience?
What are their expectations?
What are their attitudes toward the firm and their jobs?

Culture
Are shared values visible and accepted?
What are the shared values and how are they communicated?
What are the dominant management styles?
How is conflict resolved?

Fit
Does each component above support marketing strategy?
Do the various components fit together well to form a cohesive framework for implementing strategy?

Source: Adapted from David L. Aaker, *Strategic Market Management* (New York: Wiley, 1984), p. 151. © 1984, John Wiley & Sons, Inc.

Table 20-2 lists some questions companies should ask about each element of the implementation system. Successful implementation depends on how well the company blends the five activities into a cohesive program that supports its strategies.

MARKETING DEPARTMENT ORGANIZATION

The company must design a marketing department that can carry out marketing analysis, planning, implementation, and control. In this section, we focus on how marketing departments within companies are organized. If the company is very small, one person might do all the marketing work—research, selling, advertising, customer service, and other activities. As the company expands, a marketing department organization emerges to plan and carry out marketing activities. In large companies, this department contains many marketing specialists. Thus, General Mills has product managers, salespeople and sales managers, market researchers, advertising experts, and other specialists.

Modern marketing departments can be arranged in several ways. A company will set up its marketing department in the way which best helps it meet its marketing objectives.

Functional Organization

The **functional organization** is the most common form of marketing organization. Marketing specialists are in charge of different marketing activities, or functions. Figure 20-6 shows five specialists: marketing administration manager, advertising and sales promotion manager, sales manager, marketing research manager, and new products manager. Other specialists might include a customer service manager, a marketing planning manager, and a distribution manager.

The main advantage of a functional marketing organization is that it is simple to administer. On the other hand, this form by itself is less and less effective as the company's products and markets grow. First, to make plans for each different product or market becomes difficult, and products that are not favorites of the functional specialists may get neglected. Second, as the functional groups compete with each other to gain more budget and status, top management may have trouble coordinating all the marketing activities.

Geographic Organization

A company selling across the country often uses a **geographic organization** for its salesforce. Figure 20-7 shows 1 national sales manager, 4 regional sales managers, 24 zone sales managers, 192 district sales managers, and 1,920 salespersons. Geographic organization allows salespeople to settle into a territory, get to know their customers, and work with a minimum of travel time and cost.

Product Management Organization

Companies with many products or brands often create a **product management organization.** The product management organization is led by a products manager who supervises several product group managers. In turn, they supervise product or brand managers in charge of specific products or brands (see Figure 20-8). The product manager's job is to develop and implement a complete strategy and marketing program for a specific

FIGURE 20-6 Functional organization

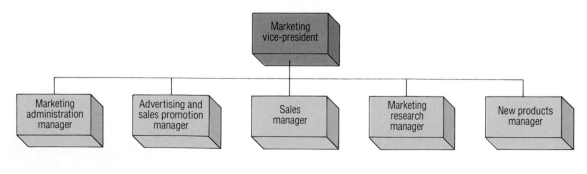

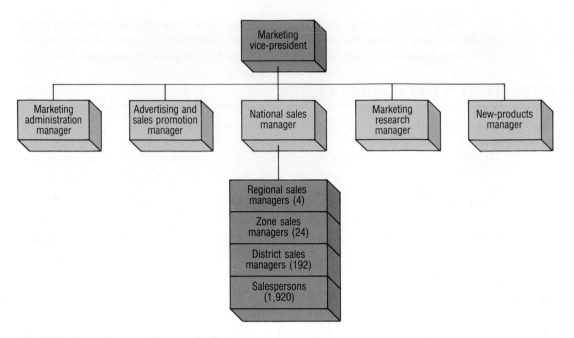

FIGURE 20-7   Geographic organization

product or brand. A product management organization makes sense if the company has many very different products.

Product management first appeared in the Procter & Gamble Company in 1929. A new company soap, Camay, was not doing well, and a young P&G executive was assigned to give his exclusive attention to developing and promoting this product. He was successful, and the company soon added other product managers.[18]

Since then, many firms, especially in the food, soap, toiletries, and chemical industries, have set up product management organizations. General Foods, for example, uses a product management organization in its Post Division. Separate product group managers are in charge of cereals, pet food, and beverages. Within the cereal product group, there are separate product managers for nutritional cereals, children's presweetened

FIGURE 20-8   Product management organization

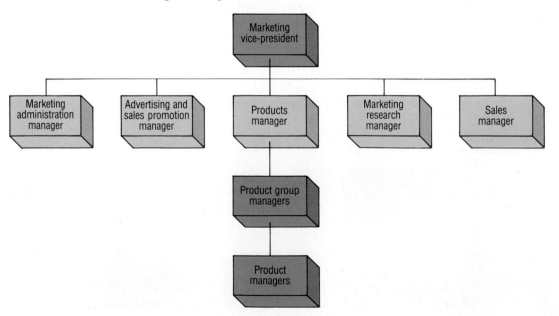

cereals, family cereals, and miscellaneous cereals. In turn, the nutritional cereal product manager supervises brand managers.

Product managers are found in both consumer and industrial products companies. However, their jobs differ somewhat. Consumer product managers typically manage fewer products than industrial product managers. They spend more time on advertising and sales promotion. They also spend more time working with others in the company and various agencies and little time with customers. They are often younger and more educated. Industrial product managers, by contrast, think more about the technical aspects of their products and possible design improvements. They spend more time with laboratory and engineering people. They work more closely with the sales force and key buyers. They pay less attention to advertising, sales promotion, and promotional pricing, and tend to emphasize rational product factors over emotional ones.

The product management organization has many advantages. The product manager coordinates the whole marketing mix for the product and can sense and react more quickly to product problems. Smaller brands get more attention because they have their own product manager. Finally, product management is an excellent training ground for young executives—it involves them in almost every area of company operations.

But a price is paid for these advantages. First, product management creates some conflict and frustration. Product managers are often not given enough authority to carry out their responsibilities effectively. They usually are told they are "mini-presidents" but often are treated as low-level coordinators. Second, product managers become experts in their product but rarely become experts in any functions. This hurts products which depend on a specific function, such as advertising. Third, the product management system often costs more than expected. Originally, one manager is assigned to each major product. Soon product managers are appointed to manage even minor products. Each product manager gets an assistant brand manager, then later a brand assistant. With all these personnel, payroll costs climb. The company becomes saddled with a costly structure of product management people. Although the product management system remains firmly entrenched, recent dramatic changes in the marketing environment have caused many companies to rethink the role of the product manager (see Marketing Highlight 20–2).

Market Management Organization

Many companies sell one product line to many different types of markets. For example, Smith Corona sells its electric typewriters to consumer, business, and government markets. National Steel sells its steel to the auto, railroad, construction, and public utility industries. When different markets have different needs and preferences, a **market management organization** might be best for the company.

A market management organization is similar to the product management organization shown in Figure 20-8. Market managers are responsible for developing long-range and annual plans for the sales and profits in their markets. They have to coax help from marketing research, advertising, sales, and other functions. This system's main advantage is that the company is organized around the needs of specific customer segments.

Many companies have reorganized along market lines. The Heinz Company split its marketing organization into three groups: groceries, commercial restaurants, and institutions. Each group contains further market specialists. For example, the institutional division contains separate market specialists who plan for schools, colleges, hospitals, and prisons.

Product Management/ Market Management Organization

Companies that produce many different products flowing into many different markets face a problem. They could use a product management system, which requires product managers to be familiar with highly diverse markets. Or they could use a market management system, which means that market managers would have to be familiar with the many diverse products bought by their markets. Or they could install both product and market managers in a *matrix organization*.

Figure 20-9 shows Du Pont's matrix organization. The product managers plan sales and profits for their respective fibers. They contact each market manager for estimates

RETHINKING BRAND MANAGEMENT

Brand management has become a fixture in most consumer packaged goods companies. Brand managers plan long-term brand strategy and watch over their brand's profits. Working closely with advertising agencies, they create national advertising campaigns to build market share and long-term consumer brand loyalty. The brand management system made sense in its earlier days, when the food companies were all-powerful, consumers were brand-loyal, and national media could reach mass markets effectively. Recently, however, many companies have begun to question whether this system fits well with today's radically different marketing realities.

Two major environmental forces are causing companies to rethink brand management. First, consumers and markets have changed dramatically. For one thing, consumers are becoming less brand loyal. Today's consumers face an ever-growing set of acceptable brands, and they are exposed to so much price promotion that they are now more deal-prone than brand-prone. As a result, companies are shifting away from national advertising in favor of pricing and other point-of-sale promotions. Also, with the recent swing toward regionalized marketing, emphasis is shifting toward local markets and shorter term strategies. Thus, whereas brand managers have traditionally focused on long-term, brand-building strategies targeting mass audiences, today's marketplace realities demand shorter-term, sales-building strategies designed for local markets.

A second major force affecting brand management is the growing power of retailers. Larger, more powerful, and better informed retailers are now demanding and getting more trade promotions in exchange for their scarce shelf space. The increase in trade promotion spending leaves fewer dollars for national advertising, the brand manager's primary marketing tool. Retailers are also demanding more customized "multi-brand" promotions that span many of the producer's brands and help them to compete better. Such promotions are beyond the scope of any single brand manager and must be designed at higher levels of the company. Yet each brand manager must chip in to support these deals. As a result, they are left with less control over their budgets and less money to invest in brand advertising.

Thus, changes in the marketplace have significantly altered the way companies market their products, causing marketers to rethink the brand management system that has served them so well for many years. Although it is unlikely that the brand managers will soon vanish, many companies are now groping for alternative ways to manage their brands.

One alternative is to change the nature of the brand manager's job. For example, some companies are asking their brand managers to spend more time in the field working with salespeople, learning what is happening in stores, and getting closer to the customer. Campbell Soup recently created "brand sales managers," combination product managers and salespeople charged with handling brands in the field, working with the trade, and designing more localized brand strategies.

As another alternative, Colgate-Palmolive, Procter & Gamble, Kraft, Nabisco, General Foods, and other companies have adopted *category management* systems. Under this system, brand managers report to a category manager, who has total responsibility for an entire product line. Category management offers many advantages. First, the category managers have broader planning perspectives than brand managers. Rather than focusing on specific brands, they shape the company's entire category offering. This results in a more complete and coordinated category offer. It also helps reduce internal brand conflicts—the category manager can allocate budgets, protect individual brand positions, and resolve disputes among brand managers. Perhaps the most important benefit of category management is that it better matches the buying processes of retailers. Recently, retailers have begun making their individual buyers responsible for working with all suppliers of a specific product category. A category management system links up better with these new retailer "category buying" systems.

Some companies are combining category management

---

of how much fiber can be sold in each market. The market managers, on the other hand, develop profitable markets for existing and future Du Pont fibers. They contact the product managers to find out about prices and availabilities of different fibers.

FIGURE 20-9
DuPont's product management/market management system

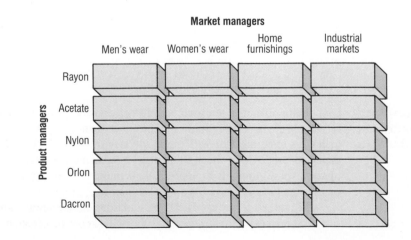

Rethinking the role of the product manager: Campbell set up "brand sales managers."

with another concept—*brand teams* or *category teams*. For example, instead of having several cookie brand managers, Nabisco has three cookie category management teams, one each for adult rich cookies, nutritional cookies, and children's cookies. Headed by a category manager, each category team includes several marketing people—brand managers, a sales planning manager, and a marketing information specialist—who handle brand strategy, advertising, and sales promotion. Each team also includes specialists from other company departments: a finance manager, a research and development specialist, and representatives from manufacturing, engineering, and distribution. Thus, category managers act as small businesspeople, with complete responsibility for the performance of an entire category and with a full complement of people to help them plan and implement category marketing strategies.

Thus, although brand managers are far from extinct, their jobs are changing. And such changes are much needed. The brand management system is product-driven, not customer-driven. Brand managers focus on pushing their brands out to anyone and everyone, and they often concentrate so heavily on a single brand that they lose sight of the marketplace. Even category management focuses on products—"cookies" if not "Oreos." But today, more than ever, companies must start not with brands, but with the needs of the consumers and retailers that these brands serve. Colgate recently took a new step forward. It moved from *brand management* (Colgate brand toothpaste) to *category management* (all Colgate-Palmolive toothpaste brands), to a new stage, *customer need management* (customers' oral health needs). This last stage finally gets the organization to focus on customer needs.

Sources: See Robert Dewar and Don Schultz, "The Product Manager: An Idea Whose Time Has Gone," *Marketing Communications*, May 1989, pp. 28–35; Kevin T. Higgins, "Category Management: New Tools Changing Life for Manufacturers, Retailers," *Marketing News*, September 25, 1989, pp. 2, 19; Ira Teinowitz, "Brand Managers: '90s Dinosaurs?" *Advertising Age*, December 19, 1988, p. 19; and Judann Dagnoli, "RJR Trying Brand 'Teams,' " *Advertising Age*, August 14, 1989, pp. 1, 46.

This matrix organization assures that each product and market receives its share of management attention. But this system also has disadvantages. It adds costly layers of management and reduces organizational flexibility. And it generates additional conflict. For example, at Du Pont, should the nylon product manager have final authority for setting nylon prices in all markets? What happens if the men's wear market manager feels that nylon will lose out in this market unless special price concessions are made on nylon?

Most managers believe that only the more important products and markets justify separate managers. Some are not upset about the conflicts and costs and believe that the benefits of product and market specialization outweigh the costs.[19]

MARKETING CONTROL

Because many surprises occur during the implementation of marketing plans, the marketing department must engage in constant marketing control. **Marketing control** is the process of measuring and evaluating the results of marketing strategies and plans, and taking corrective action to assure that marketing objectives are attained.

There are three types of marketing control (see Table 20-3). *Annual plan control*

TABLE 20-3
Types of Marketing Control

TYPE OF CONTROL	PRIME RESPONSIBILITY	PURPOSE OF CONTROL	APPROACHES
Annual plan control	Top management Middle management	To examine whether the planned results are being achieved	Sales analysis Market-share analysis Marketing expense-to-sales ratios Customer attitude tracking
Profitability control	Marketing controller	To examine where the company is making and losing money	Profitability by: Product Territory Market segment Trade channel Order size
Strategic control	Top management Marketing auditor	To examine whether the company is pursuing its best marketing opportunities and doing this efficiently	Marketing audit

involves checking ongoing performance against the annual plan and taking corrective action when necessary. *Profitability control* involves determining the actual profitability of different products, territories, markets, and channels. *Strategic control* involves looking at whether the company's basic strategies are well matched to its opportunities.

Annual Plan Control

The purpose of **annual plan control** is to ensure that the company achieves the sales, profits, and other goals set out in its annual plan. It involves the four steps shown in Figure 20-10. Management first sets monthly or quarterly goals in the annual plan. It then measures its performance in the marketplace and evaluates the causes of any differences between expected and actual performance. Finally, management takes corrective action to close the gaps between its goals and its performance. This may require changing the action programs or even changing the goals.

What specific control tools are used by management to monitor performance? The four main tools are *sales analysis*, *market-share analysis*, *marketing expense-to-sales analysis*, and *customer attitude tracking*.

Sales analysis consists of measuring and evaluating actual sales in relation to sales goals. This might involve finding out whether specific products and territories are producing their expected share of sales. Suppose the company sells in three territories where expected sales were 1,500 units, 500 units, and 2,000 units, respectively, totaling 4,000 units. The actual total was 3,000 units, 25 percent low. A breakdown by territory shows that territories one, two, and three had respective sales of 1,400 units, 525 units, and 1,075 units. Thus, territory one fell short by 7 percent; territory two had a 5 percent surplus; and territory three fell short by 46 percent! Territory three is causing most of the trouble. The sales vice-president will check into territory three.

However, company sales do not show how well the company is doing relative to *competitors*. A sales increase could be due to better economic conditions in which all companies gained, rather than to improved company performance in relation to its competitors. Management therefore needs to use **market-share analysis** to track the company's

FIGURE 20-10
The control process

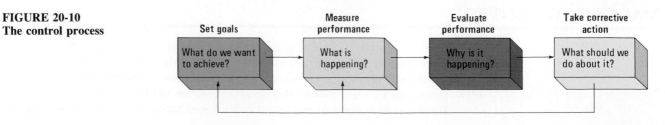

Keeping track of sales and expenses.

market share. If the company's market share goes up, it is gaining on competitors; if its market share goes down, it is losing to competitors.

Annual plan control requires assuring that the company is not overspending to achieve its sales goals. Thus, marketing control also includes **expense-to-sales analysis.** Watching the ratio of marketing expenses to sales will help keep marketing expenses in line.

Alert companies use **customer attitude tracking** to check the attitudes of customers, dealers, and other marketing system participants. By watching changes in customer attitudes before they affect sales, management can take preventive action. The main customer attitude tracking systems are complaint and suggestion systems, customer panels, and customer surveys.

Profitability Control

Besides annual plan control, companies also need **profitability control** to measure the profitability of their various products, territories, customer groups, channels, and order sizes. This information will help management determine whether any products or marketing activities should be expanded, reduced, or eliminated.

The following example illustrates the steps in marketing profitability analysis: A lawnmower company wants to determine the profitability of selling its lawnmower through three types of retail channels: hardware stores, garden supply shops, and department stores. Its profit and loss statement is shown in Table 20-4A.

TABLE 20-4A
A Simple Profit and Loss Statement

Sales		$60,000
Cost of goods sold		39,000
Gross margin		$21,000
Expenses		
Salaries	$9,300	
Rent	3,000	
Supplies	3,500	
		15,800
Net profit		$ 5,200

Step 1: *Identify functional expenses*. The company incurred the expenses listed in Table 20-4A to sell the product, advertise it, pack and deliver it, and bill and collect for it. Management must first measure the expense incurred for each activity. Suppose

that most of the $9,300 in salary expense went to salespeople ($5,100); the rest went to an advertising manager ($1,200), packing and delivery help ($1,400), and office accounting people ($1,600). Table 20-4B shows the allocation of the salary expense to these four activities.

Table 20-4B also shows how rent of $3,000 is allocated to the four activities. Because the sales representatives work away from the office, the company allocates none of the building's rent expense to selling. The advertising manager and accounting manager use a small portion of floor space, but most of the floor space and equipment are rented for packing and delivery. Finally, the supplies expense covers promotional materials, packing materials, fuel purchases for delivery, and home-office stationary. The $3,500 in this account is reassigned to the functions. Thus, Table 20-4B summarizes how the company translates total expenses of $15,800 into functional expenses.

<table>
<tr><td rowspan="2" style="text-align:right">TABLE 20-4B
Translating Natural Expenses
into Functional Expenses</td><td>NATURAL
ACCOUNTS</td><td>TOTAL</td><td>SELLING</td><td>ADVERTISING</td><td>PACKING
AND
DELIVERY</td><td>BILLING
AND
COLLECTING</td></tr>
<tr><td>Salaries
Rent
Supplies</td><td>$ 9,300
3,000
3,500
$15,800</td><td>$5,100
—
400
$5,500</td><td>$1,200
400
1,500
$3,100</td><td>$1,400
2,000
1,400
$4,800</td><td>$1,600
600
200
$2,400</td></tr>
</table>

Step 2: *Assign functional expenses to channels*. The company next measures the functional expense for selling through each type of channel. It first calculates the number of sales made in each channel. Altogether 275 sales calls were made during the period (see the Selling column of Table 20-4C). With a total selling expense of $5,500 (Table 20-4B), the selling expense per call averaged $20.

TABLE 20-4C
Allocating Functional Expenses to Channels

CHANNEL TYPE		SELLING	ADVERTISING	PACKING AND DELIVERY	BILLING AND COLLECTING
		No. of Sales Calls in Period	No. of Advertisements	No. of Orders Placed in Period	No. of Orders Placed in Period
Hardware		200	50	50	50
Garden supply		65	20	21	21
Department stores		10	30	9	9
		275	100	80	80
Functional expense	=	$5,500	$3,100	$4,800	$2,400
No. of units		275	100	80	80
Cost per unit	=	$20	$31	$60	$30

Similarly, the company allocates advertising expense according to the number of ads directed at each channel. With 100 ads, the average ad cost $31. Management allocates packing and delivery expense according to the number of orders placed by each channel; it uses the same basis for allocating billing and collection expense.

Step 3: *Prepare a profit and loss statement for each channel*. The company can now prepare a profit and loss statement for each channel (Table 20-4D). Because hardware stores accounted for one-half of total sales ($30,000 of $60,000), the company charges this channel with half the cost of goods sold ($19,500 of $39,000). This leaves a gross margin from hardware stores of $10,500. From this we must deduct the proportions of the functional expenses for hardware stores.

TABLE 20-4D
Profit and Loss Statements for
Channels

	HARDWARE	GARDEN SUPPLY	DEPT. STORES	WHOLE COMPANY
Sales	$30,000	$10,000	$20,000	$60,000
Cost of goods sold	19,500	6,500	13,000	39,000
Gross margin	$10,500	$ 3,500	$ 7,000	$21,000
Expenses				
Selling ($20 per call)	$ 4,000	$ 1,300	$ 200	$ 5,500
Advertising ($31 per advertisement)	1,550	620	930	3,100
Packing and delivery ($60 per order)	3,000	1,260	540	4,800
Billing ($30 per order)	1,500	630	270	2,400
Total expenses	$10,050	$ 3,810	$ 1,940	$15,800
Net profit (or loss)	$ 450	$ (310)	$ 5,060	$ 5,200

According to Table 20-4C, hardware stores received 200 of 275 total sales calls. At $20 a call, hardware stores must be charged with $4,000 selling expense. Hardware stores also received 50 ads. At $31 an ad, the hardware stores are charged with $1,550 of advertising. In the same way, the company computes the share of the other functional expenses to charge to hardware stores. In total, it allocates $10,050 of expenses to this channel. Subtracting this from the gross margin, the profit of selling through hardware stores is only $450.

The company repeats this analysis for the other channels. Management finds that it is losing money selling through garden supply shops and makes virtually all its profits in selling through department stores. Note that the gross sales through each channel do not reliably indicate the net profits from each channel.

What corrective action should the company take? To conclude that management should drop garden supply shops and hardware stores in order to concentrate on department stores would be naive. Several questions should be answered first. Would garden supply and hardware store buyers look for the brand in the remaining channel? What are the important trends regarding the three channels? Perhaps garden supply centers are growing while department stores are declining. Has the company used the proper marketing with each channel?

Based on the answers, the company might take a number of alternative actions. It might drop only the weakest retailers in each channel. Or it might offer a program to train people in hardware and garden supply stores to sell lawnmowers more effectively. Or it could cut channel costs by reducing the number of sales calls and promotional aids going to garden supply shops and hardware stores. As a last resort, it could drop the less profitable channels altogether.

Strategic Control

From time to time, companies need **strategic control** to critically review their overall marketing effectiveness. Marketing strategies and programs can quickly become out of date. Thus, each company should occasionally reassess its overall approach to the market-place, using a tool known as the marketing audit.[20] A **marketing audit** is a comprehensive, systematic, independent, and periodic examination of a company's environment, objectives, strategies, and activities to determine problem areas and opportunities and to recommend a plan of action to improve the company's marketing performance.

The marketing audit covers *all* major marketing areas of a business, not just a few trouble spots. It is normally conducted by an objective and experienced outside party who is independent of the marketing department. The marketing audit should be carried out periodically, not simply during a crisis. It promises benefits for the successful company as well as for the company in trouble.

The marketing auditor should be given freedom to interview managers, customers, dealers, salespeople, and others who might throw light on marketing performance. Table 20-5 shows the kinds of questions the marketing auditor might ask, although not all these questions are important in every situation. The auditor will develop a set of findings and recommendations based on the results. The findings may come as a surprise—and sometimes as a shock—to management. Management then decides which recommendations make sense and how and when to implement them.[21]

TABLE 20-5
Parts of the Marketing Audit

PART I—MARKETING ENVIRONMENT AUDIT

The Macroenvironment

A. Demographic
   1. What major demographic developments and trends pose opportunities or threats to this company?
   2. What actions has the company taken in response to these developments and trends?
B. Economic
   1. What major developments in income, prices, savings, and credit will impact the company?
   2. What actions has the company taken in response to these developments and trends?
C. Natural
   1. What is the outlook for the cost and availability of natural resources and energy needed by the company?
   2. What concerns have been expressed about the company's role in pollution and conservation, and what steps has the company taken?
D. Technological
   1. What major changes are occurring in technology? What is the company's position in technology?
   2. What major generic substitutes might replace this product?
E. Political
   1. What laws now being proposed could affect marketing strategy and tactics?
   2. What federal, state, and local actions should be watched? What is happening in pollution control, equal employment opportunity, product safety, advertising, price control, and other areas that affect marketing strategy?
F. Cultural
   1. What is the public's attitude toward business and toward the products produced by the company?
   2. What changes in consumer and business life styles and values might affect the company?

The Task Environment

A. Markets
   1. What is happening to market size, growth, geographic distribution, and profits?
   2. What are the major market segments?
B. Customers
   1. How do customers rate the company and its competitors on reputation, product quality, service, salesforce, and price?
   2. How do different customer segments make their buying decisions?
C. Competitors
   1. Who are the major competitors? What are their objectives and strategies, their strengths and weaknesses, their sizes and market shares?
   2. What trends will affect future competition for this product?
D. Distribution and Dealers
   1. What are the main channels for bringing products to customers?
   2. What are the efficiency levels and growth potentials of the different channels?
E. Suppliers
   1. What is the outlook for the availability of crucial resources used in production?
   2. What trends are occurring among suppliers in their patterns of selling?
F. Marketing Service Firms
   1. What is the cost and availability outlook for transportation services, warehousing facilities, and financial resources?
   2. How effectively is the advertising agency performing?
G. Publics
   1. What publics provide particular opportunities or problems for the company?
   2. What steps has the company taken to deal effectively with each public?

PART II—MARKETING STRATEGY AUDIT

A. Business Mission
   1. Is the business mission clearly stated in market-oriented terms? Is it feasible?
B. Marketing Objectives and Goals
   1. Are the corporate and marketing objectives stated in the form of clear goals to guide marketing planning and performance measurement?
   2. Are the marketing objectives appropriate, given the company's competitive position, resources, and opportunities?
C. Strategy
   1. What is the core marketing strategy for achieving the objectives? Is it sound?
   2. Are enough resources (or too many) budgeted to accomplish the marketing objectives?
   3. Are the marketing resources allocated optimally to market segments, territories, and products?
   4. Are the marketing resources allocated optimally to the major elements of the marketing mix—such as product quality, service, salesforce, advertising, promotion, and distribution?

TABLE 20-5 *(Continued)*

PART III—MARKETING ORGANIZATION AUDIT

A. Formal Structure
1. Does the marketing officer have adequate authority and responsibility over company activities that affect the customer's satisfaction?
2. Are the marketing activities optimally structured along functional, product, end user, and territorial lines?
B. Functional Efficiency
1. Are there good communication and working relations between marketing staff and sales?
2. Is the product management system working effectively? Are product managers able to plan profits or only sales volume?
3. Are there any groups in marketing that need more training, motivation, supervision, or evaluation?
C. Interface Efficiency
1. Are there any problems between marketing and manufacturing, R&D, purchasing, or financial management that need attention?

PART IV—MARKETING SYSTEMS AUDIT

A. Marketing Information System
1. Is the marketing intelligence system producing accurate, sufficient, and timely information about marketplace developments?
2. Is marketing research being adequately used by company decision makers?
B. Marketing Planning System
1. Is the marketing planning system effective?
2. Are sales forecasting and marketing potential measurement soundly carried out?
3. Are sales quotas set on a proper basis?
C. Marketing Control System
1. Are control procedures adequate to ensure that the annual plan objectives are being achieved?
2. Does management periodically analyze the profitability of products, markets, territories, and channels of distribution?
3. Are marketing costs being examined periodically?
D. New Product Development System
1. Is the company well organized to gather, generate, and screen new product ideas?
2. Does the company do adequate concept research and business analysis before investing in new ideas?
3. Does the company carry out adequate product and market testing before launching new products?

PART V—MARKETING PRODUCTIVITY AUDIT

A. Profitability Analysis
1. What is the profitability of the company's different products, markets, territories, and channels of distribution?
2. Should the company enter, expand, contract, or withdraw from any business segments, and what should be the short- and long-run profit consequences?
B. Cost-Effectiveness Analysis
1. Do any marketing activities seem to have excessive costs? Can cost-reducing steps be taken?

PART VI—MARKETING FUNCTION AUDITS

A. Products
1. What are the product line objectives? Are these objectives sound? Is the current product line meeting the objectives?
2. Are there products that should be phased out?
3. Are there new products that are worth adding?
4. Would any products benefit from quality, feature, or style modifications?
B. Price
1. What are the pricing objectives, policies, strategies, and procedures? To what extent are prices set on cost, demand, and competitive criteria?
2. Do the customers see the company's prices as being in line with the value of its offer?
3. Does the company use price promotions effectively?
C. Distribution
1. What are the distribution objectives and strategies?
2. Is there adequate market coverage and service?
3. Should the company consider changing its degree of reliance on distributors, sales representatives, and direct selling?
D. Advertising, Sales Promotion, and Public Relations
1. What are the organization's advertising objectives? Are they sound?
2. Is the right amount being spent on advertising? How is the budget determined?

(Continued)

TABLE 20-5   *(Continued)*

3. Are the ad themes and copy effective? What do customers and the public think about the advertising?
4. Are the advertising media well chosen?
5. Is sales promotion used effectively?
6. Is there a well-conceived public relations program?

E. Salesforce
1. What are the organization's salesforce objectives?
2. Is the salesforce large enough to accomplish the company's objectives?
3. Is the salesforce organized along the proper principles of specialization (territory, market, product)?
4. Does the salesforce show high morale, ability, and effort?
5. Are the procedures adequate for setting quotas and evaluating performances?
6. How is the company's salesforce rated in relation to competitors' salesforces?

■ SUMMARY

This chapter examines how marketing strategies are planned, implemented, and controlled.

Each business must prepare marketing plans for its products, brands, and markets. The main components of a *marketing plan* are: executive summary, current marketing situation, threats and opportunities, objectives and issues, marketing strategies, action programs, budgets, and controls. To plan good strategies is often easier than to carry them out. To be successful, companies must implement the strategies effectively. *Implementation* is the process that turns marketing strategies into marketing actions. Several factors can cause implementation failures—isolated planning, trade-offs between long- and short-term objectives, natural resistance to change, and failure to prepare detailed implementation plans.

The implementation process links marketing strategy and plans with marketing performance. The process consists of five related elements. The *action program* identifies crucial tasks and decisions needed to implement the marketing plan, assigns them to specific people, and establishes a timetable. The *organization structure* defines tasks and assignments and coordinates the efforts of the company's people and units. The company's *decision and reward systems* guide activities such as planning, information, budgeting, training, control, and personnel evaluation and rewards. Well-designed action programs, organization structures, and systems can encourage good implementation.

Successful implementation also requires careful *human resources planning*. The company must recruit, allocate, develop, and maintain good people. It must carefully match its managers to the requirements of the marketing programs being implemented. The company's managerial climate and company culture can make or break implementation. *Company climate and culture* guide people in the company—good implementation relies on strong, clearly defined cultures that fit the chosen strategy.

Each element of the implementation system must fit company marketing strategy. Moreover, successful implementation depends on how well the company blends the five elements into a cohesive program that supports its strategies.

Most of the responsibility for implementation goes to the company's marketing department. Modern marketing departments are organized in a number of ways. The most common form is the *functional marketing organization*, in which marketing functions are directed by separate managers who report to the marketing vice-president. The company might also use a *geographic organization* in which its salesforce or other functions specialize by geographic area. Another form is the *product management organization*, in which products are assigned to product managers who work with functional specialists to develop and achieve their plans. Another form is the *market management organization*, in which major markets are assigned to market managers who work with functional specialists.

Marketing organizations carry out three types of marketing control. *Annual plan control* involves monitoring current marketing results to make sure that the annual sales and profit goals will be achieved. The main tools are *sales analysis, market-share analysis, marketing expense-to-sales analysis*, and *customer attitude tracking*. If underperformance is detected, the company can implement several corrective measures.

Profitability control calls for determining the actual profitability of the firm's products, territories, market segments, and channels. *Strategic control* makes sure that the company's marketing objectives, strategies, and systems fit with the current and forecasted marketing environment. It uses the *marketing audit* to determine marketing opportunities and problems and to recommend short-run and long-run actions to improve overall marketing performance.

■ QUESTIONS FOR DISCUSSION

1. A junior member of your staff wonders how a one- or two-hundred page marketing plan can be condensed into a useful one-page executive summary. What should go into the executive summary? What should be left out?

2. Describe some of the threats and opportunities facing the fast-food restaurant business. How should McDonald's and other chains respond to these threats and opportunities?

3. Overall, which is the most important part of the marketing management process: planning, implementation, or control?

Discuss whether a company that "does things right" is more or less likely to succeed than a company that "does the right things?"

4. Many customers now demand long-range information about marketing programs, which locks these programs into place far in advance. How can managers keep enough flexibility to respond quickly to changes in the marketplace, but still give their customers the long-range plans they demand?

5. Which is easier to change, organization structure or company

culture? Which has a greater impact on how well plans are implemented?

6. IBM sells a wide range of information processing systems to individuals and organizations in the United States and around the world. What organization should IBM use for its marketing department—functional, geographic, product management, or market management? Why?

7. A friend of yours who owns a restaurant thinks that it is not as profitable as it ought to be. How could marketing control help your friend's restaurant be more successful?

8. Why should a public university conduct a periodic marketing audit of itself? Briefly describe how you would conduct an audit of your school and what you think the audit would reveal.

■ KEY TERMS

Action program. A detailed program that shows what must be done, who will do it, and how decisions and actions will be coordinated to implement marketing plans and strategy.

Annual plan control. Evaluation and corrective action to ensure that the company achieves the sales, profits, and other goals set out in its annual plan.

Company culture. A system of values and beliefs shared by people in an organization—the company's collective identity and meaning.

Company marketing opportunity. An attractive arena for marketing action in which the company would enjoy a competitive advantage.

Current marketing situation. The section of a marketing plan that describes the target market and the company's position in it.

Customer attitude tracking. Tracking the attitudes of customers, dealers, and other marketing system participants and their affects on sales.

Decision and reward systems. Formal and informal operating procedures that guide such activities as planning, information gathering, budgeting, recruiting and training, control, and personnel and rewards.

Executive summary. The opening section of the marketing plan which presents a short summary of the main goals and recommendations to be presented in the plan.

Expense-to-sales analysis. Analyzing the ratio of marketing expenses to sales in order to keep marketing expenses in line.

Functional organization. An organization structure in which marketing specialists are in charge of different marketing activities or functions such as advertising, marketing research, sales management, and others.

Geographic organization. An organization structure in which a company's national sales force (and perhaps other functions) specializes by geographic area.

Human resources. The people with needed skills, motivation, and personal characteristics who fill out the organization structure.

Managerial climate. The company climate resulting from the way managers work with others in the company.

Market management organization. An organization structure in which market managers are responsible for developing plans for sales and profits in their specific markets.

Market-share analysis. Analysis and tracking of the company's market share.

Marketing audit. A comprehensive, systematic, independent, and periodic examination of a company's environment, objectives, strategies, and activities to determine problem areas and opportunities and to recommend a plan of action to improve the company's marketing performance.

Marketing budget. A section of the marketing plan that shows projected revenues, costs, and profits.

Marketing control. The process of measuring and evaluating the results of marketing strategies and plans, and taking corrective action to assure that marketing objectives are attained.

Marketing implementation. The process that turns marketing strategies and plans into marketing actions in order to accomplish strategic marketing objectives.

Marketing strategy. The marketing logic by which the business unit hopes to achieve its marketing objectives. Marketing strategy consists of specific strategies for target markets, marketing mix, and marketing expenditure level.

Organization structure. A structure which breaks up the company's work into specialized jobs, assigns these jobs to people and departments, then coordinates the jobs by defining formal ties between people and departments and by setting lines of authority and communication.

Product management organization. An organization structure in which product managers are responsible for developing and implementing marketing strategies and plans for a specific product or brand.

Profitability control. Evaluation and corrective action to assure the profitability of various products, territories, customer groups, trade channels, and order sizes.

Sales analysis. Measuring and evaluating actual sales in relation to sales goals.

Strategic control. A critical review the company's overall marketing effectiveness.

■ REFERENCES

1. For more information, see "How the PC Project Changed the Way IBM Thinks," *Business Week*, October 3, 1983, pp. 86–90; Peter Nulty, "IBM, Clonebuster," *Fortune*, April 27, 1987, p. 225; and Geoff Lewis, "If the PS/2 Is a Winner, Why Is IBM So Frustrated?" *Business Week*, April 11, 1988, pp. 82–83.

2. For an interesting discussion of marketing budgeting methods and processes, see Nigel F. Piercy, "The Marketing Budgeting Process: Marketing Management Implications," *Journal of Marketing*, October 1987, pp. 45–59.

3. For more on estimating and using sales-response functions, see Philip Kotler, *Marketing Management: Analysis, Planning, Implementation, and Control*, 7th Edition (Englewood Cliffs, NJ: Prentice Hall, 1991), chapter 3.

4. Amar Bhide, "Hustle as Strategy," *Harvard Business Review*, September–October 1986, p. 59.

5. For more on diagnosing implementation problems, see Thomas V. Bonoma, "Making Your Marketing Strategy Work," *Harvard Business Review*, March–April 1984, pp. 70–71.

6. See "The New Breed of Strategic Planner: Number-Crunching Professionals Are Giving Way to Line Managers," *Business Week*, September 17, 1984, p. 62; and Michael Goold and Andrew Campbell, "Many Best Ways to Make Strategy," *Harvard Business Review*, November–December 1987, pp. 70–76.

7. See Ray Stata and Modesto A. Maidique, "Bonus System for Balanced Strategy," *Harvard Business Review*, November–December 1980, pp. 156–63.

8. This figure is styled after several models of organizational design components. For example, see Jay R. Galbraith, *Organizational Design* (Reading, MA: Addison–Wesley, 1977); Peter Lorange, *Implementation of Strategic Planning* (Englewood Cliffs, NJ: Prentice Hall, 1982), p. 95; David A. Aaker, *Strategic Market Management* (New York: John Wiley and Sons, 1988), Chap. 17; and Carl R. Anderson, *Management: Skills, Functions, and Organization Performance* (Dubuque, IA: Wm. C. Brown, 1984), pp. 409–13.

9. For an extensive discussion of the organizational structures and processes best suited for implementing different business strategies, see Orville C. Walker, Jr., and Robert W. Ruekert, "Marketing's Role in the Implementation of Business Strategies: A Critical Review and Conceptual Framework," *Journal of Marketing*, July 1987, pp. 15–33.

10. See Thomas J. Peters and Robert H. Waterman, *In Search of Excellence: Lessons from America's Best-Run Companies* (New York: Harper & Row, 1982). For an excellent summary of the study's findings on structure, see Aaker, *Strategic Market Management*, pp. 154–57.

11. Peters and Waterman, *In Search of Excellence*, p. 311.

12. See "Who's Excellent Now?" *Business Week*, November 5, 1984, pp. 76–78; and Daniel T. Carroll, "A Disappointing Search for Excellence," *Harvard Business Review*, November–December 1983, pp. 78–79.

13. This example is adapted from Robert M. Tomasko, "Focusing Company Reward Systems to Help Achieve Business Objectives," *Management Review* (New York: AMA Membership Publications Division, American Management Associations, October 1982), pp. 8–12.

14. For more on human resources planning, see D. Quinn Mills, "Planning With People in Mind," *Harvard Business Review*, July–August 1985, pp. 97–105; and John Hoerr, "Human Resources Managers Aren't Corporate Nobodies Anymore," *Business Week*, December 2, 1985, pp. 58–59.

15. For an interesting discussion of management styles, see J. S. Ninomiya, "Wagon Masters and Lesser Managers," *Harvard Business Review*, March–April, 1988, pp. 84–90.

16. Peters and Waterman. *In Search of Excellence*, pp. 75–76.

17. For more on company cultures, see Rohit Deshpande and Frederick E. Webster, Jr., "Organizational Culture and Marketing: Defining the Research Agenda," *Journal of Marketing*, January 1989, pp. 3–15; and Brian Dumaine, "Creating a New Company Culture," *Fortune*, January 15, 1990, p. 127–131.

18. Joseph Winski, "One Brand, One Manager," *Advertising Age*, August 20, 1987, pp. 86.

19. For a more complete discussion of marketing organization approaches and issues, see Robert W. Ruekert, Orville C. Walker, Jr., and Kenneth J. Roering, "The Organization of Marketing Activities: A Contingency Theory of Structure and Performance," *Journal of Marketing*, Winter 1985, pp. 13–25.

20. For details, see Kotler, *Marketing Management: Analysis, Planning, Implementation, and Control*, chapter 25.

21. For good discussions of broad conceptual issues in marketing control, see Bernard J. Jaworski, "Toward a Theory of Marketing Control: Environmental Context, Control Types, and Consequences," *Journal of Marketing*, July 1988, pp. 23–29; and Kenneth A. Merchant, "Progressing Toward a Theory of Marketing Control: A Comment," *Journal of Marketing*, July 1988, pp. 40–44.

CLARION COSMETICS: MAKING THE MASS MARKET BLUSH

Looking back on it, the idea was a natural. Noxell launched Clarion—a slick color cosmetic line of the sort one normally finds in department stores but which Noxell sold through mass-market outlets at moderate prices. And the plan has worked out beautifully. In one year, Clarion bounded into U.S. drug chains, enticed customers with personalized computer analysis, stunned competitors with an aggressive ad campaign, and emerged as the most successful cosmetic introduction in more than a decade. Now, however, Noxell faces adjustments in its marketing plans in order to ensure Clarion's continued success.

Initially positioned as a makeup line for those with sensitive skin, the high-flying Clarion ended 1987 with $50 million in sales and a 5 percent share of the mass cosmetics market. Thus, in only its first year, it almost caught up with Almay, the longtime leader in hypoallergenic makeup that claims a 5.2 percent share.

However, such dramatic success followed some early concerns. Although the wizardry of computers interacting with customers and providing advice on the individual customer's ideal look was popular in department stores, the concept might have proved unwieldy for other types of outlets. In drugstores and discount chains, for example, the shelf and counter space needed by the apparatus is scarce. In addition, Noxell managers initially worried about just who in such mass outlets could oversee Clarion's expensive product line and computer workings. At department stores, the sales staff had the motivation and skill to perform this complex role. But in the $3 billion mass-cosmetic market, the mode of sell is strictly "pegboard": Most products are selected by the customer from a display rack with little, if any, assistance from a salesperson. Finally, Noxell was concerned that Clarion might eat into the sales of its best-selling Cover Girl line. Although Clarion had a different positioning, a 25 percent higher price tag, and a supposed appeal to audiences older than Cover Girl's teen and young-adult buyers, the Clarion line still resembled Noxell's bread-and-butter brand in some ways.

Nevertheless, Noxell saw a marketing opportunity. The company already enjoyed a good reputation in the industry because of its Cover Girl cosmetics and Noxzema skin products. As yet, no one else was selling a slickly packaged and advertised line of color cosmetics for sensitive skin. Almay, the segment leader, seemed to be wandering, and its product line and marketing were dull. Moreover, Almay was experiencing internal turmoil: International Playtex, which had originally owned the brand, had undergone a restructuring and had finally sold Almay in 1986 to the Revlon Group—which itself had just changed hands. The market appeared ripe. Noxell had only to look at the amazing success of Clinique, a top-selling, pricey line of fragrance-free cosmetics sold through department stores, to see that there was a broad market for hypoallergenic products. With all this in mind, Noxell launched Clarion in 1987 as a "sensitive-skin makeup with a strong beauty image," says Peter M. Troup, Noxell's senior vice president of marketing.

The Clarion line of cosmetics was based on the four color groups (popularized by the book *Color Me Beautiful*) and Clarion's personalized computer. The computer—first in the mass market—lent a touch of science and reassured women that they were making the right purchases without a cosmetician's help. An exciting new merchandising technique, the Clarion Personalized Color System works as easily as a cash machine. Women answer questions about their skin type, complexion, hair, and eye color. The computer then recommends specific Clarion products and color groups from which they can choose.

Clarion's marketing strategy—"to look like an important, mainstream cosmetic immediately"—differed from strategies for previous new products. Instead of one product at a time, Noxell launched the 85-item Clarion collection all at once. It used aggressive advertising to help establish Clarion as an important brand. During the first nine months of 1987, Noxell spent about $15 million on advertising for Clarion, making it the third most heavily advertised brand (behind Cover Girl and Maybelline, both spending about $35 million per year). Noxell far outspent other competitors, including Revlon's Almay, Cosmair's L'Oréal, and Max Factor brands.

In addition, Clarion's message was dramatically and immediately communicated using prime-time television specials such as the *American Music* and *Emmy Awards* and high-rating, women-appeal programs such as *Dynasty*, *Dallas*, and *Family Ties*. Print ads ran in beauty and fashion magazines, such as *Mademoiselle*, *Glamour*, *Vogue*, and *Cosmopolitan*, which provided beauty and fashion authority, and in women's service magazines, such as *Good Housekeeping*, *McCall's*, *Redbook*, and *New Woman*, which allowed Noxell to reach the mass audience to which Clarion appealed. *Working Woman* was also used to capture the intelligent woman who appreciates a high-quality product in the mass marketplace.

Because the overall color cosmetic market grew only modestly in 1987, the new Clarion had to take market share away from competitors—and it did just that. The product became an immediate success. Sales soared. At the same time, the company insists that it did not cannibalize sales of its own Cover Girl line, which Noxell claims also gained substantial sales growth in the same year. Noxell's aim, says Troup, is now to make Clarion "the third or fourth largest brand behind Cover Girl" in the mass market. Based on units sold, Cover Girl leads with a 21 percent share, followed by Maybelline with 18 percent and Revlon with 17 percent.

Clarion's comely performance and Noxell's deep pockets have sent competitors back to powder their noses. As a direct reaction to Clarion, competitors have launched their own brands. For example, in late 1986, Maybelline introduced Ultra Performance Pure Makeup, a single foundation for sensitive skin. Even Revlon got into the act—in June 1987, it launched fragrance-free and non-irritating New Complexion makeup and press powder.

Many in the industry have dubbed Clarion "the mass-marketer's answer to Clinique"—a label that Noxell does not mind at all. However, while marketer Troup says he "admires" Clinique, he adds that Clarion is positioned at a "broader target than hypoallergenic." Noxell's research shows that more than half of all women identify with sensitive skin: "We fell that more women can relate to 'sensitive skin' than can relate to 'hypoallergenic,'" says Troup. In fact, Clarion never uses the word "hypoallergenic" in its advertising—instead, it uses "Ultra Pure," "fragrance-free," or "sensitivity-tested." The theme line—"Makeup so pure, even women with sensitive skin can wear it. And so beautiful, every woman will want to"—reaches women who want beauty as well as pure makeup.

Thanks to the good channel relations that Noxell has forged through close salesforce supervision of Cover Girl, Clarion has found ready acceptance in chain drugstores. Noxell designed a good looking display that would hold both Clarion products and the easy-to-use computer. Consumers such as Joni Dietrich of North Brunswick, N.J., found the computer worked as a "gimmick" to lure her to the brand and to make multiple purchases: "I thought it was rather clever," she says, "so I tried it, and I ended up buying more than just blush: I bought all the things that matched it."

In the first-ever award listing in Goldman Sach's winter 1988 *Fragrance and Cosmetic Buyer Survey*, Clarion and Noxell cleaned up. Clarion was named 1987's "Best New Product," Noxell was voted overwhelmingly as "Best All-Around Vendor," and the company won "Best Salesforce" by a landslide. Troup notes that "the sensitive-skin category in the cosmetic market is the fastest growing." And, he adds immodestly, "one of the reasons is because we're in there." As he puts it, "We're a beauty product first and foremost." And in 1987, at least, Clarion was a pretty sight, indeed.

For all of its success, however, Noxell detects some warning signs. Some analysts think that Clarion sales slowed when retailers moved the products from free-standing display units to traditional wall displays. Others believe that Clarion is missing some repeat purchases. Troup admits that with the initial heavy sell-in, "maybe there was some sluggishness" with repeat purchases. In addition, some buyers, in their enthusiasm, probably overpurchased. In hindsight, he says the company might have been better off controlling distribution more closely. The problem has been corrected, and, he adds, Clarion's sales in chain drugstores are now second only to Cover Girl.

The company also had some problems with Clarion's original ad campaign, which communicated a rather murky message. By urging buyers to "discover how pure beautiful color can be," Noxell promoted Clarion for both sensitive skin and cosmetic fashion, thereby diluting both positions.

Thus, despite its initial success, and perhaps because of that success, Clarion finds itself in need of a review of its marketing strategy.

QUESTIONS

1. What is Clarion's current marketing situation? Describe major market segments and competitors.
2. Evaluate Clarion's marketing plan.
3. What factors are most important in the successful implementation of the Clarion marketing plan?
4. What changes should Clarion make in its marketing strategy based on competitors' actions and other problems identified in the case? What threats or opportunities should it consider in making these changes?
5. What types of control should Clarion use to measure and evaluate its performance?

SATURN: GM'S BID FOR THE FUTURE

By the early 1980s, American automakers could not compete in the small-car market because they had much higher labor and manufacturing costs than foreign manufacturers. But the chairman of GM, Roger Smith, was not content to withdraw from the small-car market. He assigned some of GM's best engineers to work on a secret project, code-named Project Saturn, whose goal was to develop revolutionary production and marketing systems so that U.S. automakers could overtake the Japanese lead in small-car sales.

In 1985, GM converted Project Saturn to the Saturn Corporation, a GM subsidiary, and announced plans to inject $5 billion into the division in order to build 500,000 subcompact cars a year in 1990. These cars were intended to sell for $6,000 and get 60 mpg on the highway.

Initially, the Saturn operation differed from GM's other auto divisions in three ways. First, Saturn had a "clean sheet of paper," meaning it was not bound by existing GM designing, manufacturing, and marketing processes. Saturn engineers and managers were encouraged to find innovative, low-cost technologies because they were designing the manufacturing systems of GM's future. They were charged with developing a totally integrated, computerized production line manned mostly by robots.

Second, Saturn would be a "paperless" company where electronic data systems would replace mountains of paperwork and thousands of clerical workers. GM acquired Electronic Data Systems (EDS) for $2.5 billion in order to build a network that would hook together GM computers in design, engineering, and purchasing.

Third, Saturn personnel were given permission to devise a completely new marketing system. After lengthy deliberations, they decided to use a small number of existing dealers who would be carefully selected on the basis of a good service record. Each dealer would be given a regional franchise, which would permit economies of scale in marketing Saturns because only one marketing plan would be necessary in each area. Although the Saturn contract required that facilities be dedicated only to Saturns, dealers would be compensated for this exclusivity clause with multiple locations.

All dealerships would be hooked into the GM computer system so that customers could place orders directly to the factory. By pushing the appropriate computer buttons, prospective purchasers could specify the model, options, colors, and other features they desired. The plant would begin production of the car, which would be available within two weeks. Because of this fast turnaround, dealers would not need large showrooms or inventories. They could operate in electronic kiosks or small stores in shopping malls, with service facilities located elsewhere.

Saturn was an ambitious project. Has it lived up to its goals? By mid-1990, GM's Saturn investment had shrunk to roughly $3.5 billion and its production to 240,000 cars, while the car itself grew from a subcompact to a compact. It is not as fuel-efficient as originally planned, and costs more than anticipated—$10,000 to $12,000. It does have the aluminum engine originally planned, and early test drives indicate that it performs very well. But the Saturn is not revolutionary in style or design. However, GM seems to have finally produced a car that drives and handles like a Honda.

By June 1990, the production problems were solved, but the marketing plan was a source of concern. Fewer dealers than anticipated had applied for Saturn dealerships. Eventually, GM secured enough dealers, but as fall approached, some of them canceled their contracts. Why? They were nervous because their product and market had changed. GM's market share had declined from 46 percent in 1980 to 33 percent in 1989, and auto sales were down in the first half of 1990. Of major concern to dealers were the changes that upgraded the Saturn to a compact that would compete with cars such as the Honda Accord. To meet sales goals, 80 percent of Saturn buyers would have to be lured from their current ownership of Hondas, Toyotas, and Mazdas—a very difficult task without a strong nationwide marketing program.

Other elements of the marketing plan were not in place. Positioning of the product was still undecided. Company personnel were uncertain whether they should emphasize or downplay Saturn's domestic origin. The advertising theme for Saturns was not known, and GM had not undertaken heavy advertising to build interest in the product. The computer hookups that were to be a prominent feature of the marketing plan had not been installed in all the dealerships. Dealers believed that because GM had no clear, integrated marketing effort, it had failed to create the consumer excitement necessary to launch a new product successfully. Although all of the marketing problems might be solved eventually, dealers believed that Saturn's success depended on strong sales initially—not at some time in the future.

QUESTIONS

1. What was GM's market situation when it began the Saturn Project and how was that situation changed? What were the threats and opportunities that GM faced?

2. How would you characterize the planning process used in developing the Saturn? Evaluate this process.

3. Evaluate the implementation of the Saturn marketing plan. List all the problems with the implementation.

Sources: "GM Pits Saturn Against Japanese in a Big Gamble," *The Raleigh News and Observer*, July 12, 1990, p. D1; "Here Comes GM's Saturn," *Business Week*, April 9, 1990, pp. 56–62; "How GM's Saturn Could Run Rings Around Old-Style Carmakers," *Business Week*, January 28, 1985, pp. 126 and 128; "GM's New Baby," *Fortune*, February 4, 1985, p. 8; Anne B. Fisher, "Behind the Hype at GM's Saturn," *Fortune*, November 1, 1985, pp. 34–46; Michelle Krebs, "Saturn Puts Big Bang in Dealer Universe," *Advertising Age*, August 10, 1987, p. 8; Roger B. Smith, "A New Age of Almost Cosmic Industrial Achievement," *Journal of Business Strategy*, Summer 1985, pp. 78–80; and Alex Taylor III, "Back to the Future at Saturn," *Fortune*, August 1, 1988, pp. 63–68 and 72.

STEEL PRODUCTS COMPANY: STOPPING THE ALUMINUM SLIDE

Mike Smithson, branch general manager at one of Steel Product Company's (SPC) Chicago branches, looked across the conference table at Sam Jordan, a branch general manager in Atlanta. "I'll tell you, Sam," he said, "I don't know what *you* are going to do, but *our* branch won't sell aluminum. That's it."

Sam Jordan took a deep breath and pushed himself slowly away from the conference table. He glanced at Bill Olney, SPC's president, and then at each of the other five branch general managers seated around him at their March 1989 meeting. Sam was not certain what to do, but he knew that his actions during the next few seconds could make or break his efforts to get SPC to improve its aluminum sales. After a long, tense pause he turned to Bill Olney and said, "If Mike's branch won't sell aluminum, *our* branch will not sell *steel*!"

"What do you mean you won't sell steel?" Bill asked with an incredulous look. "We are a steel company! You can't just decide you aren't going to sell steel."

Sam replied, "We've been an aluminum company, too, although less and less so. And if Mike can decide that he's not going to sell any more aluminum, then I will decide that I'm not going to sell any more steel."

Bill Olney leaned back in his chair, raised his eyes briefly to the ceiling, and then returned his gaze to the branch general managers seated around him. He had not missed Sam Jordan's point. "Okay, Sam," he agreed. "We'll sell steel *and* aluminum. We will meet again in two weeks to discuss it further. At that meeting I want you to present a complete marketing strategy for revitalizing our aluminum business." Turning to the others, he declared, "I want each of you to cooperate as necessary with Sam in developing this plan."

BACKGROUND

Steel Products Company provides first-stage processing for steel and aluminum products and distributes them to industrial customers. In addition to its Chicago headquarters, the company has five other branches: two in the New York City area, two in the Atlanta area, and one other in the Chicago area. The company locates its branches in pairs because one branch in each pair handles only hot-rolled steel while the other handles only cold-rolled steel. A branch general manager oversees the sales, marketing, and operations of each branch. Each branch general manager reports directly to Bill Olney.

Bill and a group of investors purchased SPC in 1986

when the company's sales were about $120 million. During the past two years, Bill and the general managers had worked to shore up the steel business. When Bill took over, the company had been languishing with relatively flat sales and profits in both its steel and aluminum product lines. Because steel accounted for approximately 80 percent of total sales, Bill's first priority after the acquisition had been to get control of and improve SPC's steel operations.

By 1989, Bill had the steel business under control. Thus, he felt that he could turn his attention to the SPC's aluminum operations. Several weeks ago, he had invited Sam Jordan in to discuss the Atlanta branch's solid success in selling aluminum products. After a brief meeting, Bill had asked Sam to make a presentation on the company's position in aluminum products at the next branch general managers' meeting. That presentation led to the exchange with Mike Smithson.

THE STEEL SERVICE CENTER BUSINESS

Steel Products Company operates what the steel industry calls "steel service centers." These centers operate in the channel of distribution between steel mills and manufacturing firms. They perform several functions for their manufacturing customers. First, because the steel mills themselves cannot supply steel on a consistent or dependable basis, manufacturers have difficulty dealing directly with the steel mills. Steel service centers solve this problem by holding an inventory of steel for their customers and distributing it dependably when needed. Thus, the service centers function in a traditional "wholesaler" role. Second, some steel service centers perform first-stage processing for their customers. SPC, for example, buys steel from the steel mills in rolls that resemble large rolls of paper towels. These rolls are 12 to 48 inches wide, varying from 20 one-thousandths to one-eighth inch thick. Prior to delivery to the customer, SPC cuts these rolls into more narrow rolls or into steel sheets of various lengths. For example, one SPC customer, a manufacturer of drip coffee makers, orders 6-inch rolls. It feeds the steel from these rolls into stamping machines that stamp out the "hot plates" used in its coffee makers. Depending on how a service center customer uses the steel, it pays close attention to the steel's quality and the statistical control of any cutting operations. Steel that is not cut to proper width, that has improper thicknesses at some point, or that does not have the correct hardness can damage expensive equipment and even bring the customer's operations to a costly halt.

Segmentation. A steel service center can segment its markets in a number of ways. First, it can segment based on the *type* of metal used by the customer. "Hot-rolled" steel is steel that has been manufactured by a steel mill but has not been further processed. It has a rough finish and might vary in thickness or width. "Cold-rolled" steel is hot-rolled steel that has been processed further to tighten its dimensions and give it a smoother finish. Second, the service centers can segment based on the *form* of the metal delivered to the end customer, for example, rolls or sheets. Third, firms can segment based on the *quantity ordered* by customers. Some customers order in "truckload lots," defined as 40,000 pounds. Other customers order in "odd lots" that can be considerably less than truckload volume. Fourth, companies can group their customers by the nature of *delivery requirements*— some customers require next day delivery while others have long lead times. Finally, some customers order based on *contracts*, whereas others wish to order from general inventory without any minimum annual purchase requirements. Contract customers typically request quotations from several steel service centers once a year for the coming year's steel or aluminum requirements. They then award a contract committing them to purchase a certain quantity of product in certain amounts during the contracted time period.

By using different combinations of these segmentation variables, steel service centers shape the market niches they will serve. For example, one firm might focus on serving customers who need next-day delivery of uncut steel rolls from general inventory in odd lots. Steel Products Company focuses on high-tonnage (preferably truckloads), high-volume customers who need first-stage processing. Each of SPC's three cold-rolled steel branches has sophisticated equipment for cutting and controlling the dimensions and hardness of the steel. SPC provides customers with a computer printout showing the characteristics and dimensions of the steel they purchase. SPC also works with its customers to provide just-in-time delivery and electronic ordering via computer hook-ups. A recent customer survey showed that SPC has a strong, positive reputation with its customers. These customers know that SPC purchases high-quality steel and provides the statistical quality control necessary to assure that they will receive just what they request.

Price. Because steel is a commodity, steel service centers suffer from fierce price competition. Steel service centers must negotiate price with steel mills when they purchase their inventories. And, in turn, they must formally or informally negotiate prices with their customers. Thus, SPC competes on price with other steel service centers for almost every order. In 1988, SPC charged its customers an average price of 30 cents per pound for steel.

Promotion. Each of SPC's six branches has three "outside" and three "inside" salespeople. The outside salespeople visit customers in their territories to keep abreast of their needs and ordering requirements and to monitor the quality of incoming products. The outside salespeople work with inside salespeople in setting prices for quotations and in following up on delivery and service problems.

Under SPC's standard sales compensation plan, each *outside* salesperson receives a base salary plus a quarterly commission based on achieving a target gross profit on products sold by that salesperson. For example, SPC has set a current target gross profit percentage of 20 percent. SPC increases or decreases the salesperson's commission for every one-half percentage point that his or her quarterly performance falls above or below this target. SPC pays *inside* salespeople a base salary plus a bonus based on branch-level gross profit percentage.

In 1988, SPC had a weighted average gross profit percentage of about 20 percent on the six types of steel it sells. Some types of steel products have higher gross margin percentages and some have lower. SPC calculates gross margin by simply subtracting the cost of the steel sold in each order from the revenue from that order. Thus, if SPC buys a pound of steel for 23 cents from the steel mill and sells it for 30 cents, its gross margin is 7 cents and the gross profit percentage is 23.3 percent (7 cents/ 30 cents). SPC had an inventory turnover ratio of 4.26 for its steel products in 1988.

SELLING ALUMINUM

Sam Jordan came to SPC from a competitor in 1985 and assumed the position of general branch manager at one of the Atlanta branches. Sam had heard that, as recently as 1984, sales of aluminum products for the entire company had been almost $40 million. However, the "product champion" for aluminum had left the company that year. Since then, no one had paid careful attention to aluminum, and aluminum sales had begun to decline. Although he was responsible for all his branch's operations, Sam paid special attention to aluminum sales. He was very successful, and this success caught the attention of Bill Olney when he took over the company in 1986. Bill decided that the other cold-rolled branches should give greater emphasis to aluminum. As a result, the two other branches had hired aluminum product managers. These product managers had immediately purchased sizeable inventories of aluminum and had asked the salesforce to begin to push the aluminum. Sam watched in despair as these efforts at other branches had failed. Both aluminum product managers soon left the company, and one branch still had a large $2 million aluminum inventory on hand at the end of 1988.

SPC sells aluminum in much the same way that it sells steel. It buys the aluminum in rolls and provides the first-stage processing. Most of the company's aluminum sales have been to customers who also purchase steel. Whereas SPC charges an average price of 30 cents per pound for steel, it charges an average of $1.50 per pound for aluminum. However, SPC realizes only an average gross margin percentage of only 16 percent on aluminum as compared with steel's 20 percent average. SPC had an inventory turnover ratio of 6.15 for aluminum in 1988.

Although Sam's Atlanta branch continued to do well in aluminum sales, sales at other branches continued to decline. In 1988, total SPC aluminum sales reached only about $17 million. Sam realized without quick action the firm would continue to lose aluminum sales. In the face of the current flat or declining steel market, this would severely damage branch and company profits.

A CONVERSATION WITH MIKE

The day following the meeting, Sam sat in his office and considered his attack. He decided to take the bull by the horns and call Mike Smithson. He reached Mike on the first try.

"Hey, Sam," Mike volunteered, "I want to apologize if I was a little abrupt at the meeting yesterday. I know you're really big on selling aluminum, but I just don't think that we should be in that business. The other day, I was talking with one of our competitors who also sells aluminum. He told me that it's a really different business. And look at all the competitors we'd have," Mike continued. "You also know how much inventory I have sitting up here from our last shot at aluminum. Frankly, I don't think we'll do any better this time. After all, we are a steel company. And further, the salespeople are worried that always getting into and out of the aluminum business will hurt our strong reputation in steel."

"Well, Mike," Sam replied. "all I want you to do is to keep an open mind until I make my presentation. I think I can answer your objections and concerns. As you know, I think it is important that we be in both aluminum and steel. I'll try to show you a plan that will ensure success this time."

"Okay, Sam," Mike responded, "I'll try to keep an open mind. But it's going to be a tough sale for you. You'd better have all your facts together at the meeting."

QUESTIONS

1. Describe Steel Products Company's position in early 1989 relative to selling steel and aluminum.
2. What is SPC's business?
3. Why has SPC not been successful in selling aluminum? Of the problems it faces, which is the *central* marketing problem?
4. Evaluate the sales compensation plan. What improvements are needed in the plan?
5. Assume Sam Jordan's position and prepare an outline of a marketing strategy for presentation to the president and other branch general managers at the upcoming meeting. What can Sam recommend that will turn the situation around?

21

International Marketing

For more than 100 years, Eastman Kodak has been known for its easy-to-use cameras, high-quality film, and solid profits. But during the past decade, Kodak's sales have flattened and its profits have declined. Perhaps complacent after its century of success, the company has been outpaced by more innovative competitors. In many cases, the competitors have been Japanese. Kodak dragged its feet in the 35mm camera market and fell far behind Nikon, Canon, and Minolta. It lagged on video cameras and recorders and lost out to Sony, Matsushita, and Toshiba. And faster moving Japanese competitors grabbed the market for self-contained, one-hour film processing labs. So when another large Japanese competitor—Fuji Photo Film Company—moved in on Kodak's bread-and-butter color film business, Kodak took the challenge seriously.

When Fuji entered the U.S. film market, it offered high-quality color films at 10 percent lower prices and beat Kodak to the market with high-speed films. Fuji also pulled a major marketing coup by outbidding Kodak to become the official film of the 1984 Los Angeles Summer Olympic Games. Fuji's share of the huge U.S. color film market grew to more than 8 percent in 1984, and it announced its goal of winning a 15 percent market. Fuji's U.S. sales were growing at a rate of 20 percent a year—much faster than the overall market-growth rate.

Kodak fought back fiercely to protect its share of the U.S. film market. It matched Fuji's lower prices and unleashed a series of product improvements that culminated most recently in its Ektar 25, 125, and 1,000 films.

Kodak outspent Fuji by twenty to one on advertising and promotion and paid about $10 million to obtain sponsorship of the 1988 Summer Olympics in Seoul, South Korea. Through these and other moves, Kodak has successfully defended its U.S. market position. Fuji has not been able to entice many consumers to abandon Kodak's familiar yellow and black film box to reach for Fuji green. Going into the 1990s, Kodak's share of the U.S. market has stabilized at a whopping 80 percent.

But Kodak is taking the battle a step further—it's attacking Japan, Fuji's home turf. Kodak is no stranger to international marketing: 40 percent of its $17 billion in sales come from 150 countries outside the United States. In fact, Kodak has been selling film in Japan since 1889. But until a few years ago, it didn't give the Japanese market much attention. Recently, however, Kodak has taken several aggressive steps to increase its Japanese presence and sales. It set up a separate subsidiary—Kodak Japan—and tripled its Japanese staff. It bought out a Japanese distributor and prepared to set up its own Japanese marketing and sales staff. It invested in a new technology center and a large Japanese research facility. Finally, Kodak has greatly increased its Japanese promotion and publicity. Kodak Japan now sponsors everything from television talk shows to sumo wrestling tournaments.

Despite these strong efforts, it may be as hard for Kodak in Japan as for Fuji in the United States. Fuji, with more than $3 billion in annual sales, has the resources to blunt Kodak's attack. The Japanese giant is firmly entrenched with a 70 percent share of the Japanese market versus Kodak's 15 percent. Moreover, high tariffs on foreign film protect Fuji's interests. Still, Kodak will gain several benefits from its stepped-up attack on Japan. First, Japan offers big opportunities for increased sales and profits—its $1.5 billion film and photo paper market is second only to that of the United States. Second, much of today's new photographic technology originates in Japan, so a greater presence in Japan will help Kodak to keep up with the latest developments. Third, ownership and joint ventures in Japan will help Kodak to better understand Japanese manufacturing and to obtain new products for the U.S. and other world markets. Kodak already sells many Japanese-made products under its own name in the United States: Kodak video cameras are made by Matsushita, its video tape by TDK Electronics. Kodak owns 10 percent of Chinon Industries, which makes the company's 35mm cameras. Kodak sells film-processing labs made by Japanese manufacturers, and its medium-volume copiers are made by Canon.

Kodak reaps one more important benefit from its attack on the Japanese market: If Fuji must devote heavy resources to defending its Japanese home turf against Kodak's attacks, it will have fewer resources to use against Kodak in the United States.[1]

CHAPTER OBJECTIVES

After reading this chapter, you should be able to:

1. Discuss how foreign trade, economic, political-legal, and cultural environments affect a company's international marketing decisions.
2. Describe three key approaches to entering international markets.
3. Explain how companies might adapt their marketing mixes for international markets.
4. Identify the three major forms of international marketing organization.

In former times, American companies paid little attention to international trade. If they could pick up some extra sales through exporting, that was okay. But the big market was at home, and it teemed with opportunities. The home market was also much safer. Managers did not need to learn other languages, deal with strange and changing currencies, face political and legal uncertainties, or adapt their products to different customer needs and expectations.

Today, however, the situation is much different. The 1990s mark the first decade when companies around the world must start thinking globally. Time and distance have been rapidly shrinking with the advent of faster communication, transportation, and financial flows. Products developed in one country are finding enthusiastic acceptance in other countries.

True, many companies have been carrying on international activities for decades. IBM, Kodak, Nestle, Shell, Bayer, Toshiba, and other companies are familiar to most consumers around the world. But today global competition is intensifying. Foreign firms are aggressively expanding into new international markets. And home markets are no longer as rich in opportunity. Domestic companies that never thought about foreign competitors suddenly find these competitors in their own backyards. The firm that stays at home to play it safe not only might lose its chance to enter other markets but also risks losing its home market.

Daily headlines tell us about Japanese victories over U.S. producers in everything from consumer electronics to motorcycles, from cameras to copying machines. They talk of gains by Japanese, German, Swedish, and even Korean imports in the U.S. car market. They tell us about Bic's successful attacks on Gillette, Nestle's gains in the coffee and candy markets, and the loss of textile, furniture, and shoe markets to Third World imports. Such names as Sony, Toyota, Nestle, Perrier, Norelco, Mercedes, and Panasonic have become household words. Other products that appear to be produced by American firms are really produced by foreign companies: Bantam Books, Baskin-Robbins Ice Cream, Capital Records, Firestone Tires, Kiwi Shoe Polish, Lipton Tea, Carnation, Pillsbury, and Bloomingdales. America is also attracting huge foreign investments in basic industries such as steel, petroleum, tires, and chemicals and in tourist and real estate ventures—for example, Japanese land purchases in Hawaii and California, Kuwait's resort development off the South Carolina coast, and Arab and Japanese purchases of Manhattan office buildings. Few American industries are now safe from foreign competition.

Although some companies would like to stem the tide of foreign imports through protectionism, this response would be only a temporary solution. In the long run, it would raise the cost of living and protect inefficient U.S. firms. The answer is that more American firms must learn how to enter foreign markets and increase their global competitiveness. Several American companies have been successful at international marketing: General Motors, Coca-Cola, McDonald's, IBM, General Electric, Caterpillar, Dow, Ford, Kodak, 3M, Boeing, and dozens of other American firms have made the world their market. But there are too few like them. In fact, just five U.S. companies account for 12 percent of all exports; 1,000 manufacturers (out of 300,000) account for 60 percent.[2]

Every country is trying to get more of its firms to internationalize. Every country wants to export more and import less. Export promotion programs abound. For example, West Germany, the United Kingdom, and the Scandinavian countries are now subsidizing marketing programs to help their firms move into exporting.[3] Denmark pays more than

Many American companies have made the world their market.

half the salary of marketing consultants to help small and medium-size Danish companies move into exports. Many countries go further and subsidize companies by granting preferential land and energy costs—they even supply cash outright so that their companies can charge lower prices than foreign competitors.

The more that companies delay taking steps toward internationalizing, the more they risk being shut out of growing markets in Western Europe, Eastern Europe, the Far East, and elsewhere. Domestic businesses which thought they were safe now find companies from neighboring countries invading their home markets. All companies will have to answer some basic questions: What market position should we try to establish in our country, on our continent, and globally? Who will our global competitors be and what are their strategies and resources? Where should we produce or source our products? What strategic alliances should we form with other firms around the world?

Ironically, while the need for companies to go abroad is greater, so are the risks. Several major problems confront companies that go global. First, high debt, inflation, and unemployment in several countries have resulted in highly unstable governments and currencies, limiting trade and exposing U.S. firms to many risks. Second, governments are placing more regulations on foreign firms, such as requiring joint ownership with domestic partners, the hiring of nationals, and limiting profits that can be taken from the country. Third, foreign governments often impose high tariffs or trade barriers in order to protect their own industries. Finally, corruption is an increasing problem— officials in several countries often award business not to the best bidder but to the highest briber.

We might thus conclude that companies are doomed whether they stay at home or go abroad. But companies selling in global industries have no choice but to internationalize their operations. A **global industry** is one in which the strategic positions of competitors in given geographic or national markets are affected by their overall global positions. A **global firm,** therefore, is one that, by operating in more than one country, gains R&D, production, marketing, and financial advantages in its costs and reputation that are not available to purely domestic competitors.[4] The global company sees the world as one market. It minimizes the importance of national boundaries and manufactures, sources, raises capital, and markets wherever it can do the best job. For example, Ford's "world truck" sports a cab made in Europe and a chassis built in North America. It is assembled in Brazil and imported to the U.S. for sale. Thus, global firms gain advantages by planning, operating, and coordinating their activities on a worldwide basis.

Because firms around the world are globalizing at a rapid rate, domestic firms in global industries must act quickly before the window closes on them. This does not mean that small and medium-size firm must operate in a dozen countries to succeed. These firms can practice global nichemanship. But the world is becoming smaller, and every company operating in a global industry, whether large or small, must assess and establish its place in world markets.

As shown in Figure 21-1, a company faces six major decisions in international marketing.

FIGURE 21-1
Major decisions in international marketing

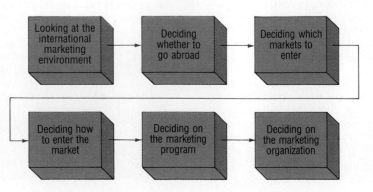

LOOKING AT THE INTERNATIONAL
MARKETING ENVIRONMENT

Before deciding whether to sell abroad, a company must thoroughly understand the international marketing environment. That environment has changed very much in the last two decades, creating both new opportunities and new problems. The world economy has globalized. World trade and investment have grown rapidly, with many attractive markets opening up in Western and Eastern Europe, China, the USSR, and elsewhere. There has been a growth of global brands in autos, food, clothing, electronics, and many other categories. The number of global companies has grown dramatically. Meanwhile, the United States's dominant position has declined. Other countries such as Japan and West Germany have increased their economic power in world markets (see Marketing Highlight 21–1). The international financial system has become more complex and fragile, and U.S. companies face increasing trade barriers erected to protect foreign markets against outside competition.

The International Trade System

The American company looking abroad must start by understanding the international *trade system.* When selling to another country, the American firm faces various trade restrictions. The most common is the **tariff,** which is a tax levied by a foreign government against certain imported products. The tariff may be designed either to raise revenue or

---

MARKETING HIGHLIGHT 21–1

THE WORLD'S CHAMPION MARKETERS: THE JAPANESE?

Few dispute that the Japanese have performed an economic miracle since World War II. In a very short time, they have achieved global market leadership in many industries: automobiles, motorcycles, watches, cameras, optical instruments, steel, shipbuilding, computers, and consumer electronics. They are now making strong inroads into tires, chemicals, machine tools, and even designer clothes, cosmetics, and food. Some credit the global success of Japanese companies to their unique business and management practices. Others point to the help they get from Japan's government, powerful trading companies, and banks. Still others say Japan's success is based on low wage rates and unfair dumping policies.

In any case, one of the main keys to Japan's success is certainly its skillful use of marketing. The Japanese came to the United States to study marketing and went home understanding it better than many U.S. companies do. They know how to select a market, enter it in the right way, build market share, and protect that share against competitors.

Selecting Markets. The Japanese work hard to identify attractive global markets. First, they look for industries that require high skills and high labor intensity but few natural resources. These include consumer electronics, cameras, watches, motorcycles, and pharmaceuticals. Second, they like markets in which consumers around the world would be willing to buy the same product designs. Finally, they look for industries in which the market leaders are weak or complacent.

Entering Markets. Japanese study-teams spend several months evaluating a target market, searching for market niches that are not being satisfied. Sometimes they start with a low-priced, stripped-down version of a product, sometimes with a product that is as good as the competitions' but priced lower, sometimes with a product with higher quality or new features. The Japanese line up good distribution channels in order to provide quick service. They also use effective advertising to bring their products to the consumer's attention. Their basic entry strategy is to build market share rather than early profits: The Japanese often are willing to wait as long as a decade before realizing their profits.

Building Market Share. Once Japanese firms gain a market foothold, they begin to expand their market share. They pour money into product improvements and new models so that they can offer more and better products than the competition. They spot new opportunities through market segmentation, develop markets in new countries, and work to build a network of world markets and production locations.

Protecting Market Share. Once the Japanese achieve market leadership, they become defenders rather than attackers. Their defense strategy is continuous product development and refined market segmentation. Their philosophy is to make "tiny improvements in a thousand places."

U.S. firms are now fighting back by adding new product lines, pricing more aggressively, streamlining production, buying or making components abroad, and forming strategic partnerships with foreign companies. Moreover, many U.S. companies are now operating successfully in Japan. American companies sell more than 50,000 different products in Japan, and many hold leading market shares—Coke leads in soft drinks (60 percent share), Schick in razors (71 percent), Polaroid in instant cameras (66 percent), and McDonald's in fast-food. Since the early 1980s, U.S. companies have increased their Japanese computer sales by 48 percent, pharmaceutical sales by 41 percent, and electronic parts sales by 63 percent.

Sources: See Philip Kotler, Liam Fahey, and Somkid Jatusripitak, *The New Competition* (Englewood Cliffs, NJ: Prentice Hall, 1985); Vernon R. Alden, "Who Says You Can't Crack Japanese Markets?" *Harvard Business Review,* January–February 1987, pp. 52–56; and Carla Rapoport, "You Can Make Money in Japan," *Fortune,* February 12, 1990, pp. 85–92.

---

to protect domestic firms. The exporter may also face a **quota,** which sets limits on the amount of goods that the importing country will accept in certain product categories. The purpose of the quota is to conserve on foreign exchange and protect local industry and employment. An **embargo** is the strongest form of quota, which totally bans some kinds of imports.

American firms may face **exchange controls** which limit the amount of foreign exchange and the exchange rate against other currencies. The company may also face **nontariff barriers,** such as bias against American company bids or product standards that go against American product features:

> One of the cleverest ways the Japanese have found to keep foreign manufacturers out of their domestic market is to plead "uniqueness." Japanese skin is different, the government argues, so foreign cosmetics companies must test their products in Japan before selling there. The Japanese say their stomachs are small and have room for only the *mikan,* the local tangerine, so imports of U.S. oranges are limited. Now the Japanese have come up with what may be the flakiest argument yet: Their snow is different, so ski equipment should be too.[5]

At the same time, certain forces *help* trade between nations—or at least between some nations. Certain countries have formed **economic communities**—a group of nations organized to work toward common goals in the regulation of international trade. The most important such community is the European Community (EC, also known as the European Common Market). The EC's members are the major Western European nations, with a combined population exceeding 320 million. The EC works to create a single European market by reducing physical, financial, and technical barriers to trade among member nations. Founded in 1957, the European Community has yet to achieve the true "common market" originally envisioned. In 1985, however, member countries renewed their push to integrate economically (see Marketing Highlight 21–2). Since the EC's formation, other economic communities have been formed, such as the Latin American Integration Association (LAIA), the Central American Common Market (CACM), and the Council for Mutual Economic Assistance (CMEA) in Eastern Europe.[6]

Each nation has unique features that must be understood. A nation's readiness for different products and services and its attractiveness as a market to foreign firms depend on its economic, political, legal, and cultural environments.

Economic Environment

The international marketer must study each country's economy. Two economic factors reflect the country's attractiveness as a market.

The first is the country's *industrial structure.* The country's industrial structure shapes its product and service needs, income levels, and employment levels. The four types of industrial structures are as follows:

- *Subsistence economies*—In a subsistence economy the vast majority of people engage in simple agriculture. They consume most of their output and barter the rest for simple goods and services. They offer few market opportunities.
- *Raw material-exporting economies*—These economies are rich in one or more natural resources but poor in other ways. Much of their revenue comes from exporting these resources. Examples are Chile (tin and copper), Zaire (copper, cobalt, and coffee), and Saudi Arabia (oil). These countries are good markets for large equipment, tools and supplies, and trucks. If there are many foreign residents and a wealthy upper class, they are also a market for luxury goods.
- *Industrializing economies*—In an industrializing economy, manufacturing accounts for 10 to 20 percent of the country's economy. Examples include Egypt, the Philippines, India, and Brazil. As manufacturing increases, the country needs more imports of raw textile materials, steel, and heavy machinery, and fewer imports of finished textiles, paper products, and automobiles. Industrialization typically creates a new rich class and a small but growing middle class, both demanding new types of imported goods.
- *Industrial economies*—Industrial economies are major exporters of manufactured goods and investment funds. They trade goods among themselves and also export them to other types of economies for raw materials and semifinished goods. The varied manufacturing activities of these industrial nations and their large middle class make them rich markets for all sorts of goods.

1992: RESHAPING THE EUROPEAN COMMUNITY

The European Community—or Common Market—was formed in 1957. It set out to create a single European market by reducing trade barriers among its member nations and developing European-wide policies on trade with nonmember nations. However, the dream of a true "common market" was quickly buried under heaps of regulations and nationalistic squabbling. Despite early common market initiatives, Europe remained a fragmented maze of insular and protected national markets, making it a difficult and confusing place to do business. Companies selling to or operating in Europe faced a hodgepodge of trade restrictions, economic conditions, and political tensions which varied widely by country. As a result, Europe lagged behind the U.S., Japan, and other far eastern countries in economic growth and technological innovation.

In 1985, however, the European Community countries renewed their push for a common market. They jointly enacted the Single European Act, which sets December 31, 1992, as the target date for completing the European economic unification process. The act calls for sweeping deregulation to eliminate barriers to the free flow products, services, finances, and labor among member countries. Thus, "1992" has come to symbolize the complete transformation of the European economy.

The European Community represents one of the world's largest markets. It contains 320 million consumers and accounts for 20 percent of the world's exports, compared to 14 percent for the U.S. and 12 percent for Japan. Thus, 1992 promises tremendous opportunities for U.S. firms—as trade barriers drop, lower costs will result in greater operating efficiency and productivity. European markets will grow and become more accessible. As a result, most U.S. companies are drafting new strategies for cultivating the invigorated European market. Yet, many American managers have mixed reactions: Just as 1992 creates many opportunities, it also poses threats. As a result of increased unification, European companies will grow bigger and more competitive. Thus, many companies from the U.S., Japan, and other non-European countries are bracing for an onslaught of new European competition, both in Western Europe and in other world markets. Perhaps an even bigger concern, however, is that lower barriers *inside* Europe will only create thicker *outside* walls. Some observers envision a "Fortress Europe," which heaps favors on firms from European Community countries but hinders outsiders by imposing such obstacles as stiffer import quotas, local-content requirements, and other nontariff barriers. Companies that already operate in Europe will be shielded from such protectionist moves. Thus, companies that sell to Europe but are not now operating there are rushing to become insiders before 1992 threatens to close them out. They are building their own operations in Europe, acquiring existing businesses there, or forming strategic alliances with established European firms.

1992 has created much excitement within the European Community, but it has also drawn critics. There is still confusion and disagreement among Europeans as to the scope and nature of the changes they want. Thus, many doubt whether Europe can complete its unification efforts by 1992—or ever. As of early 1990, about 60 percent of the 279 provisions in the original 1992 plan had been ratified. But the most difficult issues—those involving the free flow of money, people, and goods—were unresolved. Such actions as creating a common currency, standardizing taxes, setting up a common banking system, abolishing boarder checks, and forging other European-wide efforts will require changing the entire economic make-up of Europe. Individual countries will have to give up some of their independence for the common good, pushing aside the nationalism that has ruled European history for centuries. Thus, the odds are low that Europe will ever realize the full vision of 1992.

Even if the European Community does manage to standardize its general trade regulations, creating an economic community will not create a homogeneous market! With nine different languages and distinctive national customs, Europe will be anything but a "common market." Although economic and political boundaries may fall, social and cultural differences will remain. And although 1992 may create common general standards, companies marketing in Europe will still face a daunting mass of local rules. Take advertising, for example. One large advertising agency has prepared a 52-page book containing dense statistics on country-by-country restrictions. Ireland, for example, forbids ads for liquor but allows them for beer and wine—as long as they run after 7 P.M.; Spain allows ads only for drinks with less than 23 percent alcohol, and only after 9:30 P.M. and in Holland, ads for sweets must show a toothbrush in the corner of the television screen. The 1992 goals will have little effect on such local rules.

Thus, the European market will always be far more diverse than U.S. or Japanese markets. It is unlikely that the European Community will ever become the "United States of Europe." Nevertheless, great changes are occurring in Europe. Even if only partly successful, 1992 will make a more efficient and competitive Europe a global force to be reckoned with. The best prepared companies will benefit most. Thus, whether they cheer it or fear it, all companies must prepare now for the New Europe or risk being shut out later.

Sources: Chris Maynard, "Pop Goes Europe," *Business Today*, Winter 1990, pp. 24–25; Frank J. Comes and Jonathan Kapstein, "Reshaping Europe: 1992 and Beyond, *Business Week*, December 12, 1988, pp. 49–51; Richard I. Kirkland, Jr., "Outsider's Guide to Europe in 1992," *Fortune*, October 24, 1988, pp. 121–27; John F. Magee, "1992: Moves Americans Must Make," *Harvard Business Review*, May–June 1989, pp. 78–84; and Ronald Beatson, "The Americanization of Europe?" *Advertising Age*, April 2, 1990, p. 16.

The second economic factor is the country's *income distribution*. The international marketer might find countries with five different income distribution patterns: (1) very low family incomes, (2) mostly low family incomes, (3) very low/very high family incomes, (4) low/medium/high family incomes, and (5) mostly medium family incomes. Consider the market for Lamborghinis, an automobile costing $128,000. The market would be very small in countries with Type 1 or Type 2 income patterns. Most Lambor-

Income distribution: Expensive Lamborghinis sell well in small, wealthy countries like Saudi Arabia.

ghinis are sold in large markets like the United States, Europe, and Japan, which have large segments of high-income consumers, or in small but wealthy countries like Saudi Arabia.

Political-Legal Environment

Nations differ greatly in their political-legal environments. At least four political-legal factors should be considered when considering whether to do business in a given country.

Attitudes toward International Buying

Some nations are quite receptive to foreign firms, and others are quite hostile. For example, Mexico has been attracting foreign businesses for many years by offering investment incentives and site-location services. On the other hand, India has bothered foreign businesses with import quotas, currency restrictions, and limits on the percentage of the management team that can be non-nationals. IBM and Coca-Cola left India because of all the "hassles." Pepsi, on the other hand, took positive steps to persuade the Indian government to allow it to do business in that country on reasonable terms (see Marketing Highlight 21–3).

Political Stability

Stability is another issue. Governments change hands, sometimes violently. Even without a change, a government may decide to respond to new popular feelings. The foreign company's property may be taken, its currency holdings may be blocked, or import quotas or new duties may be set. International marketers may find it profitable to do business in an unstable country, but the situation will affect how they handle business and financial matters.

Monetary Regulations

Sellers want to take their profits in a currency of value to them. Ideally, the buyer can pay in the seller's currency or in other world currencies. Short of this, sellers might accept a blocked currency—one whose removal from the country is restricted by the buyer's government—if they can buy other goods in that country that they need or can sell elsewhere for a needed currency. Besides currency limits, a changing exchange rate also creates high risks for the seller.

Most international trade involves cash transactions. Yet many nations have too little hard currency to pay for their purchases from other countries. They want to pay with other items instead of cash, which has led to a growing practice called **countertrade,** which now accounts for about 25 percent of all world trade. Countertrade takes several forms. *Barter* involves the direct exchange of goods or services, as when the West Germans built a steel plant in Indonesia in exchange for oil. Another form is *compensation* (or *buy-back*), whereby the seller sells a plant, equipment, or technology to another country and agrees to take payment in the resulting products. Thus, Goodyear provided China with materials and training for a printing plant in exchange for finished labels. Another form is *counterpurchase*: The seller receives full payment in cash but agrees to spend some portion of the money in the other country within a stated time period. For example, Pepsi sells its cola syrup to the USSR for rubles and agrees to buy Soviet vodka for sale in the U.S.

Countertrade deals can be very complex. For example, Daimler-Benz recently agreed to sell 30 trucks to Romania in exchange for 150 Romanian jeeps, which it then sold to Ecuador for bananas, which were in turn sold to a West German supermarket chain for German currency. Through this round-about process, Daimler-Benz finally obtained payment in German money.[7]

Government Bureaucracy

A fourth factor is the extent to which the host government runs an efficient system for helping foreign companies: efficient customs handling, good market information, and other factors that aid in doing business. A common shock to Americans is how quickly barriers to trade disappear if a suitable payment (bribe) is made to some official.

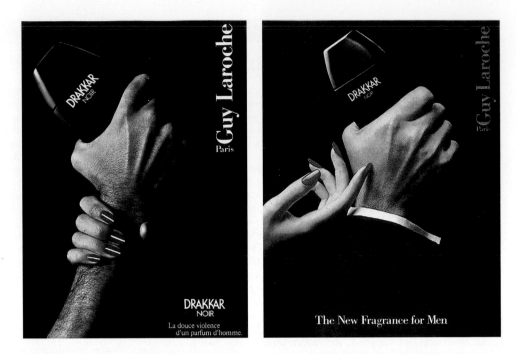

Adapting to the cultural environment: Compared with the European version of this ad (left), Guy Laroche tones down the sensuality in the Arab verison (right). The man is clothed and the woman barely touches him.

Cultural Environment Each country has its own folkways, norms, and taboos. The way foreign consumers think about and use certain products must be examined by the seller before planning a marketing program. There are often surprises. For example, the average French man uses almost twice as many cosmetics and beauty aids as does his wife. The Germans and the French eat more packaged, branded spaghetti than do Italians. Italian children like to eat chocolate bars between slices of bread as a snack. And women in Tanzania will not give their children eggs for fear of making them bald or impotent.

Business norms and behavior also vary from country to country. U.S. business executives need to be briefed on these factors before dealing in another country. Here are some examples of different foreign business behavior:

- South Americans like to sit or stand very close to each other when they talk business—in fact, almost nose-to-nose. The American business executive tends to keep backing away as the South American moves closer. Both may thus end up being offended.
- In face-to-face communications, Japanese business executives rarely say no to an American business executive. Americans tend to be frustrated and may not know where they stand. Americans come to the point quickly. Japanese business executives may find this behavior offensive.
- In France, wholesalers don't want to promote a product. They ask their retailers what they want and deliver it. If an American company builds its strategy around the French wholesaler's cooperating in promotions, it is likely to fail.
- When American executives exchange business cards, each usually gives the other's card a cursory glance and stuffs it in a pocket for later reference. In Japan, however, executives dutifully study each other's cards during a greeting, carefully noting company affiliation and rank. They hand their card to the most important person first.

Thus, each country and region has cultural traditions, preferences, and behaviors that the marketer must study.

DECIDING WHETHER TO GO ABROAD

Not all companies need to venture into foreign markets to survive. For example, many companies are local businesses that need to market well only in the local marketplace.

However, companies that operate in global industries, where their strategic positions in specific markets are strongly affected by their overall global positions, must think and act globally. Thus, IBM must organize globally if it is to gain purchasing, manufacturing, financial, and marketing advantages. Firms in a global industry must compete on a worldwide basis if they are to succeed.

Any of several factors might draw a company into the international arena. Global competitors might attack the company's domestic market by offering better products or lower prices. The company might want to counterattack these competitors in their home markets to tie up their resources. Or the company might discover foreign markets that present higher profit opportunities than the domestic market. The company's domestic market might be shrinking, or the company might need an enlarged customer base in order to achieve economies of scale. Or it might want to reduce its dependence on any one market so as to reduce its risk. Finally, the company's customers might be expanding abroad and require international servicing.

Before going abroad, the company must weigh several risks and answer many questions about its ability to operate globally. Can the company learn to understand the preferences and buyer behavior of consumers in other countries? Can it offer competitively attractive products? Will it be able to adapt to other country's business cultures and be able to deal effectively with foreign nationals? Do the company's managers have the necessary international experience? Has management considered the impact of foreign regulations and political environments?

Because of the risks and difficulties of entering foreign markets, most companies do not act until some situation or event thrusts them into the international arena. Someone— a domestic exporter, a foreign importer, a foreign government—asks the company to sell abroad. Or the company is saddled with overcapacity and must find additional markets for its goods.

DECIDING WHICH MARKETS TO ENTER

Before going abroad, the company should try to define its international *marketing objectives and policies*. First, it should decide what *volume* of foreign sales it wants. Most companies start small when they go abroad. Some plan to stay small, seeing foreign sales as a small part of their business. Other companies have bigger plans, seeing foreign business as equal to or even more important than their domestic business.

Second, the company must choose *how many* countries it wants to market in. The Bulova Watch Company decided to operate in many foreign markets and expanded into more than one hundred countries. However, it spread itself too thin, made profits in only two countries, and lost about $40 million. Generally, it makes better sense to operate in fewer countries with deeper penetration in each.

Third, the company must decide on the *types* of countries to enter. A country's attractiveness depends on the product, geographical factors, income and population, political climate, and other factors. The seller may prefer certain country groups or parts of the world.

After listing possible international markets, the company must screen and rank them. Consider the following example:

> Many mass marketers dream of selling to China's one billion people. Some think of the market less elegantly as two billion armpits. To PepsiCo, though, the market is mouths, and the People's Republic is especially enticing: it is the most populous country in the world, and Coca-Cola does not yet dominate it.[8]

PepsiCo's decision to enter the Chinese market seems fairly simple and straightforward. China is a huge market without established competition. In addition to selling Pepsi soft drinks, the company hopes to build many of its Pizza Hut restaurants there. Yet we can still question whether market size *alone* is reason enough for selecting China. PepsiCo must also consider other factors. Will the Chinese government be stable and supportive? Does China provide for the production and distribution technologies

Pepsi in China—a huge but risky market.

needed to produce and market Pepsi products profitably? Will Pepsi and pizza fit Chinese tastes, means, and life styles?

Possible foreign markets should therefore be ranked on several factors, including market size, market growth, cost of doing business, competitive advantage, and risk level. The goal is to determine the potential of each market, using indicators such as those shown in Table 21-1. Then the marketer must decide which markets offer the greatest long-run return on investment.

TABLE 21-1
Indicators of Market Potential

1. Demographic characteristics	**4. Technological factors**
Size of population	Level of technological skill
Rate of population growth	Existing production technology
Degree of urbanization	Existing consumption technology
Population density	Education levels
Age structure and composition of the population	**5. Socio-cultural factors**
2. Geographic characteristics	Dominant values
Physical size of a country	Life style patterns
Topographical characteristics	Ethnic groups
Climate conditions	Linguistic fragmentation
3. Economic factors	**6. National goals and plans**
GNP per capita	Industry priorities
Income distribution	Infrastructure investment plans
Rate of growth of GNP	
Ratio of investment to GNP	

Source: Susan P. Douglas, C. Samual Craig, and Warren Keegan, "Approaches to Assessing International Marketing Opportunities for Small and Medium-Sized Business," *Columbia Journal of World Business*, Fall 1982, pp. 26–32.

DECIDING HOW TO ENTER THE MARKET

Once a company has decided to sell in a foreign country, it must determine the best mode of entry. Its choices are *exporting*, *joint venturing*, and *direct investment*. These three market-entry strategies are shown in Figure 21-2, along with the options under each. As the figure shows, each succeeding strategy involves more commitment and risk but also more control and potential profits.

Exporting

The simplest way to enter a foreign market is through **exporting.** The company may passively export its surpluses from time to time, or it may make an active commitment to expand exports to a particular market. In either case, the company produces all its goods in its home country. It may or may not modify them for the export market. Exporting involves the least change in the company's product lines, organization, investments, or mission.

Companies typically start with *indirect exporting*, working through independent international marketing middlemen. Indirect exporting involves less investment because the firm does not require an overseas salesforce or set of contacts. It also involves less risk. International marketing middlemen—domestic-based export merchants or agents, cooperative organizations, export-management companies—bring know-how and services to the relationship, and so the seller normally makes fewer mistakes.

Sellers may eventually move into *direct exporting*, handling their own exports. The investment and risk are somewhat greater, but so is the potential return. A company can conduct direct exporting in several ways. First, it can set up a domestic export department that carries out export activities. Or it can set up an overseas sales branch that handles sales, distribution, and perhaps promotion. The sales branch gives the seller more presence and program control in the foreign market, and it often serves as a display center and customer service center. Or the company can send home-based salespeople abroad at certain times in order to find business. Finally, the company can do its exporting either through foreign-based distributors who buy and own the goods or through foreign-based agents who sell the goods on behalf of the company.

Joint Venturing

A second method of entering a foreign market is **joint venturing**—joining with foreign companies to produce or market the products or services. Joint venturing differs from exporting in that the company joins with a partner to sell or market abroad. It differs from direct investment in that an association is formed with someone in the foreign country. There are four types of joint ventures.

Licensing

Licensing is a simple way for a manufacturer to enter international marketing. The company enters into an agreement with a licensee in the foreign market, offering the right to use a manufacturing process, trademark, patent, trade secret, or other item of value for a fee or royalty. The company thus gains entry into the market at little risk; the licensee gains production expertise or a well-known product or name without having to start from scratch. Coca-Cola markets internationally by licensing bottlers around

FIGURE 21-2
Market entry strategies

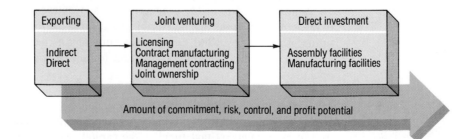

夜がきれい、君もきれい、スターライト★デート。

ゆったり、ふたりで、たっぷり5時間。東京ディズニーランド。お得なスターライト券発売中。

Licensing: TOKYO DISNEYLAND is owned and operated by the Oriental Land Co., Ltd. (a Japanese development company), under license from Walt Disney Company.

the world and supplying them with the syrup needed to produce the product. In Japan, Budweiser beer flows from Suntory breweries, Lady Borden ice cream is churned out at Meiji Milk products dairies, and Marlboro cigarettes roll off production lines at Japan Tobacco Inc.[9]

However, licensing has potential disadvantages. The firm has less control over the licensee than it would over its own production facilities. If the licensee is very successful, the firm has given up these profits, and if and when the contract ends, it may find it has created a competitor. To avoid these dangers, the company must create a mutual advantage for the licensee. One answer is to remain so innovative that the licensee continues to depend on the company.

Contract Manufacturing

Another option is **contract manufacturing**—contracting with manufacturers in the foreign market to produce its product or provide its service. Sears used this method in opening up department stores in Mexico and Spain. Sears found qualified local manufacturers to produce many of the products it sells. Contract manufacturing has the drawback of less control over the manufacturing process and the loss of potential profits on manufacturing. On the other hand, it offers the company a chance to start faster, with less risk, and with the later opportunity either to form a partnership with or buy out the local manufacturer.

Management Contracting

Under **management contracting,** the domestic firm supplies management know-how to a foreign company that supplies the capital. The domestic firm exports management services rather than products. Hilton uses this arrangement in managing hotels around the world.

Management contracting is a low-risk method of getting into a foreign market, and it yields income from the beginning. The arrangement is even more attractive if the contracting firm has an option to buy some share in the managed company later on. On the other hand, the arrangement is not sensible if the company can put its scarce management talent to better uses or if it can make greater profits by undertaking the whole venture. Management contracting also prevents the company from setting up its own operations for a period of time.

Joint Ownership

Joint ownership ventures consist of one company joining with foreign investors to create a local business in which they share joint ownership and control. A company may buy an interest in a local firm, or the two parties may form a new business venture. Joint ownership may be needed for economic or political reasons. The firm may lack the financial, physical, or managerial resources to undertake the venture alone. Or a foreign government may require joint ownership as a condition for entry.

Joint ownership has certain drawbacks. The partners may disagree over investment, marketing, or other policies. Whereas many American firms like to reinvest earnings for growth, local firms often like to take out these earnings. Whereas American firms give a large role to marketing, local investors may rely on selling.[10]

Direct Investment

The biggest involvement in a foreign market comes through **direct investment**—developing foreign-based assembly or manufacturing facilities. If a company has gained experience in exporting, and if the foreign market is large enough, foreign production facilities offer many advantages. The firm may have lower costs in the form of cheaper labor or raw materials, foreign government investment incentives, and freight savings. The firm may improve its image in the host country because it creates jobs. Generally, a firm develops a deeper relationship with government, customers, local suppliers, and distributors, letting it better adapt its products to the local market. Finally, the firm keeps full control over the investment and can therefore develop manufacturing and marketing policies that serve its long-term international objectives.

The main disadvantage is that the firm faces many risks, such as restricted or devalued currencies, falling markets, or government takeovers. In some cases, a firm has no choice but to accept these risks if it wants to operate in the host country.

DECIDING ON THE MARKETING PROGRAM

Companies that operate in one or more foreign markets must decide how much, if at all, to adapt their marketing mixes to local conditions. At one extreme are companies that use a **standardized marketing mix** worldwide. Standardization of the product, advertising, distribution channels, and other elements of the marketing mix promises the lowest costs because no major changes have been introduced. This thinking is behind the idea that Coca-Cola should taste the same around the world and that General Motors should produce a ''world car'' that suits the needs of most consumers in most countries.

At the other extreme is an **adapted marketing mix.** The producer adjusts the marketing mix elements to each target market, bearing more costs but hoping for a larger market share and return. Nestle, for example, varies its product line and its advertising in different countries. Many possibilities exist between the extremes of standardization and complete adaptation. For example, Coca-Cola sells the same beverage worldwide, and in most markets it uses television spots showing a thousand children singing the praises of Coke. For different local markets, however, it edits the commercials to include close-ups of children from those markets—at least 21 different versions of the spot are currently running. The question of whether to adapt or standardize the marketing mix has been much debated in recent years (see Marketing Highlight 21–4).

GLOBAL STANDARDIZATION OR ADAPTATION?

The marketing concept holds that consumers vary in their needs and that marketing programs will be more effective if tailored to each customer target group. If this concept applies within a country, it should apply even more in foreign markets where economic, political, and cultural conditions vary widely. Consumers in different countries have varied geographic, demographic, economic, and cultural characteristics—a fact that results in different needs and wants, spending power, product preferences, and shopping patterns. Because most marketers believe that these differences are hard to change, they adapt their products, prices, distribution channels, and promotion approaches to fit unique consumer desires in each country.

However, some global marketers are bothered by what they see as too much adaptation. Consider Gillette:

> Gillette sells over eight hundred products in more than two hundred countries. It now finds itself in a situation where it uses different brand names and formulations for the same products in different countries. For example, Gillette's Silkience shampoo is called Soyance in France, Sientel in Italy, and Silience in Germany; it uses the same formula in some cases but varies it in others. It also varies the product's advertising messages because each Gillette country manager proposes several changes that he or she thinks will increase local sales. These and similar adaptations for its hundreds of other products raise Gillette's costs and dilute its global brand power.

As a result, many companies have imposed more standardization on their products and marketing efforts. They have created so-called "world brands" that are manufactured and marketed in much the same way worldwide. These marketers believe that advances in communication, transportation, and travel are turning the world into a common marketplace. They claim that people around the world want basically the same products and life styles. Everyone wants things that make life easier and that increase both free time and buying power. Common needs and wants thus create global markets for standardized products.

Whereas traditional marketers cater to differences between specific markets and respond with a proliferation of highly adapted products, marketers who standardize globally sell more or less the same product the same way to all consumers. They agree that differences exist in consumer wants and buying behavior and that these differences cannot be entirely ignored. But they argue that wants are changeable. Despite what consumers say they want, all consumers want good products at lower prices:

> If the price is low enough, they will take highly standardized world products, even if these aren't exactly what mother said was suitable, what immemorial custom decreed was right, or what market research . . . asserted was preferred.

Thus, proponents of global standardization claim, international marketers should adapt products and marketing programs only when local wants cannot be changed or avoided. Standardization results in lower production, distribution, marketing, and management costs, letting the company offer consumers higher quality and more reliable products at lower prices. They would advise an auto company to make a world

Standardized advertising messages: Black & Decker uses about the same promotion

car, a shampoo company to make a world shampoo, and a farm-equipment company to make a world tractor. And, in fact, some companies have successfully marketed global products—for example, Coca-Cola, McDonald's hamburgers, A. T. Cross pens and pencils, Black & Decker tools, and Sony Walkmans. Some products are more global and require less adaptation. Yet, even in these cases, companies make some adaptations. Coca-Cola is less sweet or less carbonated in certain countries; McDonald's uses chili sauce instead of ketchup on its hamburgers in Mexico; and Cross pens and pencils have different advertising messages in some countries.

Moreover, assertions that global standardization will lead to lower costs and prices, causing more goods to be snapped up by price-sensitive consumers is debatable:

> Mattel Toys had sold its Barbie Doll successfully in dozens of countries without modification. But in Japan, it did not sell well. Takara, Mattel's Japanese licensee, surveyed eighth-grade Japanese girls and their parents and found that they thought the doll's breasts were too big and that its legs were too long. Mattel, however, was reluctant to modify the doll because this would require additional production, packaging, and advertising costs. Finally, Takara won out and Mattel made a special Japanese Barbie. Within two years, Takara had sold over two million of the modified dolls. Clearly, incremental revenues far exceeded the incremental costs.

Rather than assuming that their products can be introduced without change in other countries, companies should review all possible adaptation elements and determine which would add more revenues than costs. The adaptation elements include the following:

Product features	Colors	Advertising themes
Brand name	Materials	Advertising media
Labeling	Prices	Advertising execution
Packaging	Sales promotion	

One study showed that companies made adaptations in one or more of these areas in 80 percent of their foreign-directed products; the average product was adapted in 4 out of the 11 areas.

So which approach is best, global standardization or adaptation? Clearly, global standardization is not an all-or-nothing proposition, but rather a matter of degree. Companies are justified in looking for more standardization to help keep down costs and prices and to build greater global brand power. But they must remember that although standardization saves money, competitors are always ready to offer more of what consumers in each country want, and that they might pay dearly for replacing long-run marketing thinking with short-run financial thinking. Some international marketers suggest that companies should "think globally but act locally." The corporate level gives strategic direction; local units focus on the individual consumer differences. Global marketing, yes; global standardization, not necessarily.

Sources: See John A. Quelch and Edward J. Hoff, "Customizing Global Marketing," *Harvard Business Review*, May–June, 1986, pp. 59–68; Theodore Levitt, "The Globalization of Markets," *Harvard Business Review*, May–June 1983, pp. 92–102; and "Marketers Turn Sour on Global Sales Pitch Harvard Guru Makes," *The Wall Street Journal*, May 12, 1988, p. 1.

approach in many different countries.

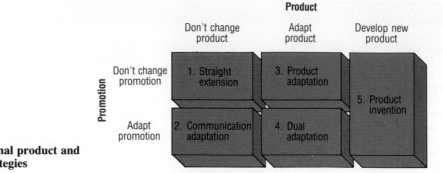

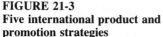

FIGURE 21-3
Five international product and promotion strategies

Product   Five strategies allow for adapting product and promotion to a foreign market (see Figure 21-3).[11] We discuss the three product strategies here and then look at the two promotion strategies.

Straight product extension means marketing a product in a foreign market without any change. Top management tells its marketing people: "Take the product as is and find customers for it." The first step, however, should be to find out whether foreign consumers use that product and what form they prefer.

Straight extension has been successful in some cases but a disaster in others. Coca-Cola, Kellogg cereals, Heineken beer, Black & Decker tools—all are sold in about the same form around the world. But General Foods introduced its standard powdered Jell-O in the British market only to find that British consumers prefer a solid-wafer or cake form. Likewise, Philips began to make a profit in Japan only after it reduced the size of its coffee makers to fit into smaller Japanese kitchens and its shavers to fit smaller Japanese hands. Straight extension is tempting because it involves no additional product-development costs, manufacturing changes, or new promotion. But it can be costly in the long run if products fail to satisfy foreign consumers.

Product adaptation involves changing the product to meet local conditions or wants. McDonald's serves beer in Germany and coconut, mango, and tropic mint shakes in Hong Kong. General Foods blends different coffees for the British (who drink their coffee with milk), the French (who drink their coffee black), and Latin Americans (who want a chicory taste). In Japan, Mister Donut serves coffee in smaller and lighter cups that better fit the fingers of the average Japanese consumer; even the doughnuts are a little smaller. IBM adapts its worldwide product line to meet local needs. For example, IBM must make dozens of different keyboards to match different languages, 20 for Europe alone.[12]

Product invention consists of creating something new for the foreign market. This strategy can take two forms. It might mean reintroducing earlier product forms that happen to be well-adapted to the needs of a given country. For example, the National Cash Register Company reintroduced its crank-operated cash register at half the price of a modern cash register and sold large numbers in the Orient, Latin America, and Spain. On the other hand, a company might create a new product to meet a need in another country. For example, an enormous need exists in less-developed countries for low-cost, high-protein foods. Companies such as Quaker Oats, Swift, and Monsanto are researching the nutrition needs of these countries, creating new foods, and developing advertising campaigns to gain product trial and acceptance. Product invention can be costly, but the payoffs are worthwhile.

Promotion   Companies can adopt the same promotion strategy they used in the home market or change it for each local market.

Consider the message. Some global companies use a standardized advertising theme around the world. Exxon used "Put a tiger in your tank" and gained international

WATCH YOUR LANGUAGE!

Many U.S. multinationals have had difficulty crossing the language barrier, with results ranging from mild embarrassment to outright failure. Seemingly innocuous brand names and advertising phrases can take on unintended or hidden meanings when translated into other languages. Careless translations can make a marketer look downright foolish to foreign consumers. We've all run across examples when buying products from foreign countries—here's one from a firm in Taiwan attempting to instruct children on how to install a ramp on a garage for toy cars:

> Before you play with, please fix the waiting plate by yourself as per below diagram. But after you once fixed it, you can play with as is and no necessary to fix off again.

Many U.S. firms are guilty of similar atrocities when marketing abroad.

The classic language blunders involve standardized brand names that do not translate well. When Coca-Cola first marketed Coke in China in the 1920s, it developed a group of Chinese characters that, when pronounced, sounded like the product name. Unfortunately, the characters actually translated to mean "bite the wax tadpole." Today, the characters on Chinese Coke bottles translate as "happiness in the mouth."

Several car makers have had similar problems when their brand names crashed into the language barrier. Chevy's Nova translated into Spanish as *no va*—"It doesn't go." GM changed the name to Caribe and sales increased. Ford introduced its Fiera truck only to discover that the name means "ugly old woman" in Spanish. And it introduced its Comet car in Mexico as the Caliente—slang for "streetwalker." Rolls-Royce avoided the name Silver Mist in German markets, where "mist" means "manure." Sunbeam, however, entered the German market with its Mist-Stick hair curling iron. As should have been expected, the Germans had little use for a "manure wand."

One well-intentioned firm sold its shampoo in Brazil under the name Evitol. It soon realized it was claiming to sell a "dandruff contraceptive." An American company reportedly had trouble marketing Pet milk in French-speaking areas. It seems that the word "pet" in French means, among other things, "to break wind."

Advertising themes often lose—or gain—something in the translation. The Coors beer slogan "get loose with Coors" in Spanish came out as "get the runs with Coors." Coca-Cola's "Coke adds life" theme in Japanese translated into "Coke brings your ancestors back from the dead."

Such classic boo-boos are soon discovered and corrected, and they may result in little more than embarrassment for the marketer. But countless other more subtle blunders may go undetected and damage produce performance in less obvious ways. The multinational company must carefully screen its brand names and advertising messages to guard against those that might damage sales, make it look silly, or offend consumers in specific international markets.

Sources: Some of these and many other examples of language blunders are found in David A. Ricks, "Products That Crashed into the Language Barrier," *Business and Society Review*, Spring 1983, pp. 46–50. Also see Marty Westerman, "Death of the Frito Bandito," *American Demographics*, March 1989, pp. 28–32.

recognition. Of course, the copy may be varied in minor ways to adjust for language differences. In Japan, where consumers have trouble pronouncing "snap, crackle, pop," the little Rice Crispies critters say say "patchy, pitchy, putchy." Colors are sometimes changed to avoid taboos in other countries. Purple is associated with death in most of Latin America; white is a mourning color in Japan; and green is associated with jungle sickness in Malaysia. Even names must be changed. In Sweden, Helene Curtis changed the name of Every Night Shampoo to Every Day because Swedes usually wash their hair in the morning. Kellogg also had to rename Bran Buds cereal in Sweden, where the name roughly translates as "burned farmer."[13] (See Marketing Highlight 21–5 for more language blunders in international marketing.)

Other companies fully adapt their advertising messages to local markets. The Schwinn Bicycle Company might use a pleasure theme in the United States and a safety theme in Scandinavia. Kellogg ads in the United States promote the taste and nutrition of Kellogg's cereals versus competitors' brands. In France, where consumers drink little milk and eat little for breakfast, Kellogg's ads must convince consumers that cereals are a tasty and healthful breakfast.

Media also need to be adapted internationally because media availability varies from country to country. TV advertising time is very limited in Europe, ranging from four hours a day in France to none in Scandinavian countries. Advertisers must buy time months in advance, and they have little control over air times. Magazines also vary in effectiveness. For example, they are a major medium in Italy and a minor one in Austria. Newspapers are national in the United Kingdom but only local in Spain.

Price Companies also face many problems in setting their international prices. For example, how might Coca-Cola set its prices globally? It could set a uniform price all around the world. But this amount would be too high a price in poor countries and not high enough in rich ones. Coca-Cola could charge what consumers in each country would bear. But this strategy ignores differences in the actual cost from country to country. Finally, the company could use a standard markup of its costs everywhere. But this approach might price Coca-Cola out of the market in some countries where costs are high.

Regardless of how companies go about pricing their products, their foreign prices will probably be higher than their domestic prices. A Gucci handbag may sell for $60 in Italy and $240 in the U.S. Why? Gucci must add the cost of transportation, tariffs, importer margin, wholesaler margin, and retailer margin to its factory price. Depending on these added costs, the product may have to sell for two to five times as much in another country to make the same profit. For example, a 1988 Chrysler automobile priced at $10,000 in the United States sold for more than $47,000 in South Korea.[14]

Another problem involves setting a *transfer price* for goods the company ships to its foreign subsidiaries. Consider the following example:

> The Swiss pharmaceutical company Hoffman-Laroche charged its Italian subsidiary only $22 a kilo for librium in order to make high profits in Italy where the corporate taxes were lower. It charged its British subsidiary $925 per kilo for the same librium in order to keep the profits at home instead of in Britain where the corporate taxes were high. The British government sued Hoffman-LaRoche for back taxes and won.

If the company charges too high a price to a foreign subsidiary, it ends up paying higher tariff duties although it may pay lower income taxes in that country. If the company charges too low a price to its subsidiary, it can be charged with *dumping*. Dumping occurs when a company either charges less than its costs or less than it charges in its home market. Thus, Harley-Davidson accused Honda and Kawasaki of dumping motorcycles on the U.S. market. The U.S. International Trade Commission agreed and responded with a special five-year tariff on Japanese heavy motorcycles, starting at 45 percent in 1983 and gradually dropping to 10 percent by 1988.[15] The commission also recently ruled that Japan was dumping computer memory chips in the U.S. and laid stiff duties on future imports. Various governments are watching for dumping abuses and often force companies to set the price charged by other competitors for the same or similar products.

Last but not least, many global companies face a *grey market* problem. For example: Minolta sold its cameras to Hong Kong distributors for less than it charged German distributors because of lower transportation costs and tariffs. Minolta cameras ended up selling at retail for $174 in Hong Kong and $270 in Germany. Some Hong Kong wholesalers noticed this price difference and shipped Minolta cameras to German dealers for less than the dealers were paying their German distributor. The German distributor couldn't sell its stock and complained to Minolta. Thus, a company often finds some enterprising distributors buying more than they can sell in their own country, then shipping goods to another country to take advantage of price differences. International companies try to prevent grey markets by raising their prices to lower-cost distributors, dropping those who cheat, or altering the product for different countries.

Distribution Channels The international company must take a **whole-channel view** of the problem of distributing products to final consumers. Figure 21-4 shows the three major links between the seller and the final buyer. The first link, the *seller's headquarters organization*, supervises the channels and is part of the channel itself. The second link, *channels between nations*, moves the products to the borders of the foreign nations. The third link, *channels within nations*, moves the products from their foreign entry point to the final consumers.

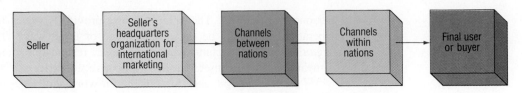

FIGURE 21-4   Whole-channel concept for international marketing

Some American manufacturers may think their job is done once the product leaves their hands, but they would do well to pay more attention to its handling within foreign countries.

Within-country channels of distribution vary greatly from nation to nation. First are the large differences in the *numbers and types of middlemen* serving each foreign market. For example, a U.S. company marketing in China must operate through a frustrating maze of state-controlled wholesalers and retailers. Chinese distributors often carry competitors' products and frequently refuse to share even basic sales and marketing information with their suppliers. Hustling for sales is an alien concept to Chinese distributors, who are used to selling all they can obtain. Working with or getting around this system sometimes requires substantial time and investment. When Coke and Pepsi first entered China, customers bicycled up to bottling plants to get their soft drinks. Now, both companies have set up direct-distribution channels, investing heavily in trucks and refrigeration units for retailers.[16]

Another difference lies in the *size and character of retail units* abroad. Whereas large-scale retail chains dominate the U.S. scene, most foreign retailing is done by many small independent retailers. In India, millions of retailers operate tiny shops or sell in open markets. Their markups are high, but the real price is lowered through price haggling. Supermarkets could offer lower prices, but they are difficult to build and open because of many economic and cultural barriers. Incomes are low, and people prefer to shop daily for small amounts rather than weekly for large amounts. They lack storage and refrigeration to keep food for several days. Packaging is not well developed because it would add too much to the cost. These factors have kept large-scale retailing from spreading rapidly in developing countries.

DECIDING ON THE MARKETING ORGANIZATION

Companies manage their international marketing activities in at least three different ways. Most companies first organize an *export department*, then create an *international division*, and finally become a *global organization*.

Export Department

A firm normally gets into international marketing by simply shipping out its goods. If its international sales expand, the company organizes an export department with a sales manager and a few assistants. As sales increase, the export department can then expand to include various marketing services so that it can go after business actively. If the firm moves into joint ventures or direct investment, the export department will no longer be adequate.

International Division

Many companies get involved in several international markets and ventures. A company may export to one country, license to another, have a joint venture in a third, and own a subsidiary in a fourth. Sooner or later it will create an international division or subsidiary to handle all its international activity.

International divisions are organized in a variety of ways. The international division's corporate staff consists of marketing, manufacturing, research, finance, planning, and personnel specialists. They plan for and provide services to various operating units. Operating units may be organized in one of three ways. They may be *geographical organizations*, with country managers who are responsible for salespeople, sales branches, distributors, and licensees in their respective countries. Or the operating units may be *world product groups*, each responsible for worldwide sales of different product groups. Finally, operating units may be *international subsidiaries*, each responsible for its own sales and profits.

Global Organization   Several firms have passed beyond the international division stage and become truly global organizations. They stop thinking of themselves as national marketers who sell abroad and start thinking of themselves as global marketers. The top corporate management and staff plan worldwide manufacturing facilities, marketing policies, financial flows, and logistical systems. The global operating units report directly to the chief executive or executive committee of the organization, not to the head of an international division. Executives are trained in worldwide operations, not just domestic *or* international. The company recruits management from many countries, buys components and supplies where they cost the least, and invests where the expected returns are greatest.

Major companies must go more global in the 1990s if they hope to compete. As foreign companies successfully invade the domestic market, U.S. companies must move more aggressively into foreign markets. They will have to change from companies that treat their foreign operations as secondary to companies viewing the entire world as a single borderless market.[17]

■ SUMMARY

Companies today can no longer afford to pay attention only to their domestic market, no matter how large it is. Many industries are global industries, and those firms that operate globally achieve lower costs and higher brand awareness. At the same time, *global marketing* is risky because of variable exchange rates, unstable governments, protectionist tariffs and trade barriers, and several other factors. Given the potential gains and risks of international marketing, companies need a systematic way to make their international marketing decisions.

As a first step, a company must understand the *international marketing environment*, especially the international trade system. It must assess each foreign market's *economic, political-legal*, and *cultural characteristics*. Second, the company must decide whether it wants to go abroad and consider the potential risks and benefits. Third, the company must decide the volume

of foreign sales it wants, how many countries it wants to market in, and which specific markets it wants to enter. This decision calls for weighing the probable rate of return on investment against the level of risk. Fourth, the company must decide how to enter each chosen market—whether through *exporting, joint venturing*, or *direct investment*. Many companies start as exporters, move to joint ventures, and finally make a direct investment in foreign markets. Companies must next decide how much their products, promotion, price, and channels should be adapted for each foreign market. Finally, the company must develop an effective organization for international marketing. Most firms start with an *export department* and graduate to an *international division*. A few become *global organizations*, with worldwide marketing planned and managed by the top officers of the company. They view the entire world as a single, borderless market.

■ QUESTIONS FOR DISCUSSION

1. With all the problems facing companies that "go global," why are so many companies choosing to expand internationally? What are the advantages of expanding beyond the domestic market?

2. When exporting goods to a foreign country, a marketer may be faced with various trade restrictions. Discuss the possible effects of the following restrictions on an exporter's marketing mix: (a) tariffs, (b) quotas, and (c) embargoes.

3. Which of these will have the greatest impact on a soft-drink manufacturer's appraisal of a foreign nation's attractiveness as a market: the economic environment, the political-legal environment, or the cultural environment? Why?

4. The first Honda automobile exported here was described by a U.S. car magazine as "a shopping cart with a motor;"

the first Subaru exported to the U.S. was voted "Worst New Car of the Year." Both companies, however, have become highly successful. Discuss the Japanese strategy of long-term commitment to international business objectives. Would the Japanese have left India, as IBM and Coca-Cola did, because of "hassles?"

5. Discuss the steps an advertising agency could take in entering a foreign market. What types of joint venture would be worth considering?

6. Which combination of product and promotion strategies would you recommend that Campbell Soup Company use in marketing canned soups in Brazil? Why?

7. Imported products are usually more expensive, but not always. A Nikon camera is cheaper in New York than in

Tokyo. Why are foreign prices sometimes higher and sometimes lower than domestic prices for exports?

8. "Dumping" leads to price savings to the consumer. Why do governments make dumping illegal? What are the *disadvantages* to the consumer of dumping by foreign firms?

9. Which type of international marketing organization would you suggest for the following companies? (a) Schwinn Bicycles, selling three models in the Far East; (b) a small U.S.

manufacturer of toys, marketing its products in Europe; and (c) Dodge, planning to sell its full line of cars and trucks in the Middle East.

10. As noted in Marketing Highlight 21–2, even after 1992 marketing in the European Community will not be like marketing in a single large country. In addition to those discussed in Marketing Highlight 21–2, what specific country to country differences are likely to remain?

■ KEY TERMS

Adapted marketing mix. An international marketing strategy for adjusting the marketing mix elements to each international target market, bearing more costs but hoping for a larger market share and return.

Contract manufacturing. Joint venturing to enter a foreign market by contracting with manufacturers in the foreign market to produce the product.

Countertrade. International trade involving the direct or indirect exchange of goods for other goods instead of cash. Forms include barter, compensation (buy-back), and counterpurchase.

Direct investment. Entering a foreign market by developing foreign-based assembly or manufacturing facilities.

Economic community. A group of nations organized to work toward common goals in the regulation of international trade.

Embargo. A ban on the import of a certain product.

Exchange controls. Limits placed by a government on the amount of its foreign exchange with other countries and on its exchange rate against other currencies.

Exporting. Entering a foreign market by exporting products and selling them through international marketing middlemen (indirect exporting) or through the company's own department, branch, or sales representatives or agents (direct exporting).

Global firm. A firm that, by operating in more than one country, gains R&D, production, marketing, and financial advantages in its costs and reputation that are not available to purely domestic competitors.

Global industry. An industry in which the strategic positions of competitors in given geographic or national markets are affected by their overall global positions.

Joint ownership. Entering a foreign market by joining with foreign investors to create a local business in which the company shares joint ownership and control.

Joint venturing. Entering foreign markets by joining with for-

eign companies to produce or market a product or service.

Licensing. A method of entering a foreign market in which the company enters into an agreement with a licensee in the foreign market, offering the right to use a manufacturing process, trademark, patent, trade secret, or other item of value for a fee or royalty.

Management contracting. A joint venture in which the domestic firm supplies the management know-how to a foreign company that supplies the capital; the domestic firm exports management services rather than products.

Nontariff trade barriers. Nonmonetary barriers to foreign products such as biases against foreign company's bids or product standards that go against foreign company's product features.

Product adaptation. Adapting a product to meet local conditions or wants in foreign markets.

Product invention. Creating new products or services for foreign markets.

Quota. A limit on the amount of goods that an importing country will accept in certain product categories; it is designed to conserve on foreign exchange and protect local industry and employment.

Standardized marketing mix. An international marketing strategy for using basically the same product, advertising, distribution channels, and other elements of the marketing mix in all the company's international markets.

Straight product extension. Marketing a product in the foreign market without any change.

Tariff. A tax, levied by a government against certain imported products, which is designed to raise revenue or protect domestic firms.

Whole-channel view. Designing international channels that take into account all the necessary links in distributing the seller's products to final buyers, including the seller's headquarters organization, channels between nations, and channels within nations.

■ REFERENCES

1. See James B. Treece, Barbara Buell, and Jane Sasseen, "How Kodak is Trying to Move Mount Fuji," *Business Week*, December 2, 1985, pp. 62–64; Bill Saporito, "Companies that Compete Best," *Fortune*, May 22, 1989, pp. 36–44; and Carla Rapoport, "You Can Make Money in Japan," *Fortune*, February 12, 1990, pp. 85–92.

2. See Edward C. Baig, "50 Leading U.S. Exporters," *Fortune*, July 18, 1988, pp. 70–71. Also see Edward Prewitt, "America's 50 Biggest Exporters," *Fortune*, July 17, 1989, pp. 50–51; and Alex Taylor III, "The U.S. Gets Back in Fighting Shape," *Fortune*, April 24, 1989, pp. 42–46.

3. See "European States Subsidize Marketing Aid," *Business Marketing*, November 1986, pp. 27–28.

4. For a good discussion of the differences between "international," "multinational," and "global" marketing, see Warren J. Keegan, *Global Marketing Management*, 4th ed. (Englewood Cliffs, NJ: Prentice Hall, 1989), pp. 6–11.

5. "The Unique Japanese," *Fortune*, November 24, 1986, p. 8. For more on nontariff barriers, see Rahul Jacob, "Export Barriers the U.S. Hates Most," *Fortune*, February 27, 1989, pp. 88–89.

6. See John A. Quelch, Robert D. Buzzell, and Eric R. Salama, *The Marketing Challenge of 1992* (Boston: Addison Wesley, 1990); "1992: Moves Americans Must Make," *Harvard Business Review*, May–June 1989, pp. 78–84; and Chris Maynard, "Pop Goes Europe," *Business Today*, Winter 1990, pp. 24–25.

7. For further reading, see John W. Dizard, "The Explosion of International Barter," *Fortune*, February 7, 1983; Leo G. B. Welt, *Trade Without Money: Barter and Countertrade* (New York: Harcourt Brace Jovanovich, 1984); Demos Vardiabasis, "Countertrade: New Ways of Doing Business," *Business to Business*, December 1985, pp. 67–71; and Louis Kraar, "How to Sell to Cashless Buyers," *Fortune*, November 7, 1988, pp. 147–54.

8. Louis Kraar, "Pepsi's Pitch to Quench Chinese Thirsts," *Fortune*, March 17, 1986, p. 58. Also see Maria Shao, "Laying the Foundation for the Great Mall of China," *Business Week*, January 25, 1988, pp. 68–69; and Alan Farnham, "Ready to Ride Out China's Turmoil," *Fortune*, July 3, 1989, pp. 117–18.

9. Larry Armstrong, "A Cheaper Dollar Doesn't Always Mean Cheaper American Goods," *Business Week*, May 5, 1986, p. 43.

10. For more on joint ventures, see Kenichi Ohmae, "The Global Logic of Strategic Alliances," *Harvard Business Review*, March–April 1989, pp. 143–54; and Louis Kraar, "Your Rivals Can Be Your Allies," *Fortune*, March 27, 1989, pp. 66–76.

11. See Keegan, *Global Marketing Management*, pp. 378–81.

12. For other examples, see Andrew Kupfer, "How to Be a Global Manager," *Fortune*, March 14, 1988, pp. 52–58.

13. See Kenneth Labich, "America's International Winners," *Fortune*, April 14, 1986, p. 44.

14. Dori Jones Yang, "Can Asia's Four Tigers Be Tamed?" *Business Week*, February 15, 1988, p. 47.

15. See Michael Oneal, "Harley-Davidson: Ready to Hit the Road Again," *Business Week*, July 21, 1986, p. 70.

16. See Maria Shao, "Laying the Foundation for the Great Mall of China," p. 69.

17. See Kenichi Ohmae, "Managing in a Borderless World," *Harvard Business Review*, May–June 1989, pp. 152–61.

SENECA COLD-DRAWN STEEL, INC.: DOING BUSINESS IN THE PEOPLE'S REPUBLIC OF CHINA

Jim Hoffmann, President of Seneca Cold-Drawn Steel, Inc., is considering possible ways to overcome the severe difficulty that his company has encountered in its domestic market. Seneca is a small cold-drawn precision-steel factory located in western New York. The company was founded in 1974 when a nearby large steel mill closed down its production line as part of a strategic contraction plan resulting from the oil crisis. Hoffmann seized the opportunity and set up Seneca three miles away from the larger mill.

In its first five years, Seneca's business involved buying hot-rolled steel bars from the large steel mill and "cold-drawing" them according to customers' required specifications, such as round, square, flat, or hexagonal bars. The cold-drawing process begins with the receipt of the "hot-rolled steel" in the form of bars or coils. The material is then shot-blasted to remove dirt, scale, and rust. Next, it is coated with a lime solution to prevent rust and improve lubrication when it is drawn through the dies used for cutting and shaping. The steel is then drawn through the dies, which size it to customer specifications. The steel bar is then straightened and cut to desired length. Whereas hot-rolled steel is usually dirty, rusty, and inconsistent in size, cold-drawn steel is sized within precise tolerances, stronger, and finished to a clean, semi-polished surface. Finished cold-drawn products are then supplied to industrial users, mainly in the automobile and machinery industries.

Seneca operated profitably in its first five years, primarily because of its ability to meet customers' fluctuating delivery and specification requirements. And because of its small scale, local market demand was sufficient to keep Seneca operating at full capacity. After 1980, however, increasing competition from Japanese automobiles and machinery-products manufacturers in Pacific Rim countries (principally Japan, Korea, and Taiwan) drove many of Seneca's customers out of business. Moreover, the supplier providing Seneca with raw steel was forced to reduce its production. In turn, this development forced Seneca to buy most of its raw steel from mills located more than 500 miles away, greatly increasing raw-material costs and reducing Seneca's ability to meet its customers' rapidly fluctuating requirements. Given these changing customer and supplier markets, Seneca faced an important turning point.

However, at the same time that Seneca encountered severe difficulties in its domestic market, many opportunities were developing in international markets. For example, China, a vast market and a land of great resources, was opening its long-closed doors and attempting to play a

role in the global economy. Recently, China had greatly increased its international trade. Since 1979—the year China implemented a new Open Door policy that allowed Western companies to establish joint ventures with Chinese investors—the Chinese government has encouraged direct foreign participation in order to develop its economy. Since then, the Chinese gross national product has grown at least 10 percent annually, and international trade has grown at an annual rate of 17 percent. By 1987, about 140 wholly foreign-owned enterprises were operating in China. There were also numerous other cooperative undertakings, including nearly 8,000 joint-venture companies—300 of them American. Today, American-owned enterprises or Chinese-American joint ventures include both large, well-known companies (Xerox, Union Carbide, IBM, and Occidental Chemical) and smaller, lesser-known companies (such as Mundi Westport Corp., Rochester Instruments, Pretolite Electric, and Kamsky Associates).

The Chinese government encourages such enterprises in order to secure the technology, financial resources, and management systems needed in such strategically important industries as communication and transportation, machinery, iron and steel, biochemicals, food production and processing. As a member of an industry being courted by the Chinese government, Seneca may face a great new opportunity. With a population of more than one billion people and a geographic territory exceeding that of the United States, China is a potential market that few companies can ignore. To tap this market, however, Seneca must be willing and able to transfer its production technology to China in a way that will enhance the Chinese steel industry.

In July 1988, Jim Hoffman had received a letter from an international management consulting firm asking that Seneca host a delegation of Chinese steel entrepreneurs. The Chinese delegation, known as the "China Entrepreneurs of Medium-Small Steel Plants Training and Studying Mission to U.S.A.," consisted of plant managers or directors of 45 medium to small steel plants located in 26 major Chinese steel-industry cities. Hoffman had decided to participate in the program.

During the delegation's visit that October, Seneca provided a tour of its plant and arranged visits to two large steel mills. In a series of open discussions with the Chinese plant managers and directors, Hoffman identified several business opportunities:

1. A *compensation-trading* opportunity: Because of the availability of less labor-intensive equipment, some production lines used to make small-sized products at Seneca's plant are obsolete in the United States. Seneca could sell these

production lines to interested Chinese firms. With easy access to suitable raw materials and lower labor costs, the Chinese may be in a better position to produce such small-sized products. Seneca could then buy back the finished products and resell them to its customers.

2. A *processing-and-assembling trade* opportunity: Seneca could acquire raw materials from Pacific Rim countries, send them to Chinese partners for cold-drawing, and then resell the finished products to its own U.S. customers.

3. A *joint-venture* opportunity: Seneca could enter a joint venture, using a Chinese partner's existing facilities to supply hot-rolled bars for its own U.S. plant. In addition, the joint-venture steel factory could further process hot-rolled bars into cold-drawn bars to serve the Chinese market.

4. A *wholly foreign-owned enterprise* opportunity: Seneca could set up a wholly-owned factory in China, taking advantage of the availability and lower price of Chinese raw materials and the huge potential market for cold-drawn bars in China.

After the Chinese delegation had left, Hoffman faced an important decision regarding which opportunity, if any, to pursue. To help with the decision, he hired a consulting company that specialized in U.S.-China trade. The consultants suggested that Seneca consider several factors before making a decision:

1. *Foreign exchange:* Foreign exchange is perhaps the most important factor in any China-development decision. Foreign exchange woes are common in developing countries that have not yet created an industrial base capable of producing exportable goods. This is particularly important in China, a regulated market and a country trying to balance its foreign exchange. Because Chinese currency, called "IMB," has no value on international currency markets, companies doing business in China insist on payment in a major international currency. The Chinese government, however, tightly controls the availability of foreign currency, ensuring that what little international currency it does possess is channeled to the payment of important strategic products. Such policies can result in great inefficiencies and hamper the growth of important enterprises. Thus, foreign companies must often develop counter-trade arrangements and negotiate guarantees for payment in their own currencies. These arrangements can be very complicated—the issue of foreign exchange should therefore be addressed early in contract negotiations.

2. *Labor practices:* Although China has abundant labor resources, the government is still wary of the foreign use of domestic labor, mainly because of memories of colonial exploitation. Foreign firms doing business in China do not pay workers directly: The money is paid to local governments that, in turn, pay the members of a particular "work unit." Thus, the Chinese labor force is neither cheap nor efficient. Although there have been recent signs of change toward more flexibility in hiring and firing practices, firms like Seneca must negotiate contracts that provide as much control over labor issues as possible.

3. *Legal considerations:* China has no history of an international-style legal system. Its laws are vague and arbitrary, and there is always the concept of *neibu*—bureaucrats are not sure if they should give information about laws to foreigners and so will not openly discuss many rules and regulations. Foreign firms must thus negotiate patiently and adhere to their own basic principles and goals. The Chinese political system also continues to be highly "personalistic" in nature—there is often no commonly agreed-upon legal system, and government officials seldom interpret rules consistently. Therefore, it would be important for Seneca to develop key contacts and become active on the Chinese banquet circuit.

However, with recent refinements in business law and the popularization of legal study among some of China's top leaders, the legal situation is slowly changing. Chinese leadership has traditionally been determined to maintain control over the political system, but this attitude has softened because of the remarkable recent turnover of leadership at all levels. Many younger, better-educated, professionally qualified leaders have reduced the bureaucracy that has for years been a major obstacle to foreign investment.

4. *Relationship with the Chinese Counter-Party:* The contractual relationship formed with a company's Chinese counter-party can be summarized as follows: Everything is negotiable. In general, the importance of *guaxi*—the building up of good favors—is perhaps the best strategy for negotiating. The negotiation process does not *end* with the signing of a contract—it simply *begins* there. In addition, it is important to consider carefully what *type* of Chinese counter-party is best for a given business: Firms should seek counter-parties with strong political affiliations—if indeed such affiliations can be determined.

5. *Selecting a Business Location:* Each area of China is unique. China is not homogeneous: Cities differ, provinces differ, and languages differ. Foreign firms are encouraged to locate in special economic zones where banking, transportation, and utility services are readily available. Some companies, for example, have made mistakes by trying to locate in areas where the cost of labor and materials were lower but the services necessary for doing business not sufficiently developed. A company entering China should carefully investigate the rules, regulations, and idiosyncrasies of different areas.

Armed with this advice from his consultants, Hoffmann planned a business trip to visit several potential counter-parties in China. On his return, he would make a decision about Seneca's first step into China.

QUESTIONS

1. Describe the marketing environment facing foreign firms in the People's Republic of China.

2. What criteria should be used to decide whether or not to pursue a business opportunity in China?

3. Evaluate the advantages and disadvantages of each business opportunity under consideration. Which opportunity would you recommend to Hoffmann?

Source: This case was written by Mr. Ben Liu, Research Assistant at the China Trade Center, School of Management, State University of New York at Buffalo. Although the case is based on an actual business situation, all names have been disguised to protect the interests of the company.

EC '92: OPPORTUNITY OR THREAT?

The excitement nowadays about Europe is "EC '92." It is constantly discussed in the press, on television and radio, in boardrooms and offices, and over lunches. What is the EC? And why is 1992 important?

The EC is the European Community—a union of 12 countries committed to moving toward a single common market in Europe. In such a market, there would be free movement of goods, persons, services, and capital because all internal frontiers and trade barriers would be abolished. The changes in trade that are necessary to make the EC a reality are due to be accomplished by 1992.

Because the EC is such an exciting prospect, many American firms are considering entering the European market. Before making this decision, however, they should carefully consider not only the advantages and disadvantages of the EC, but also their *own preparedness* for this move.

One of the EC's primary advantages will be its market size—320 million people, compared with 240 million in the United States and 122 million in Japan—most of whom are relatively well educated, affluent, cosmopolitan consumers living in a small geographic area. Their cultural heritage and consumption behavior patterns are similar to those of Americans. Sophisticated distribution and communications systems already exist to serve this market, facilitating the promotion and distribution of goods and services. For all of these reasons, EC '92 is an attractive and potentially lucrative opportunity for American firms.

Another advantage will be the establishment of one set of standards for the entire market instead of the multiple sets of standards that currently exist. Since manufacturers need only design one product for sale in the EC rather than multiple product versions, smaller markets will be aggregated into one large market. With economies of scale, manufacturers should be able to sell more goods at lower prices. When internal barriers are eliminated, manufacturers may need only one sales office and one distribution center for the EC rather than many offices located in various countries. In short, marketing in the EC will be easier and more efficient.

While most American firms are aware of the EC's advantages, they are not preparing for EC '92. A recent study of 350 top American executives indicated that only 45 percent thought their firms could compete in the EC after 1992. Of the remaining 55 percent, only a few are making preparations to enter the EC.

Why are American firms shying away from this enormous market? For one thing, there will be some serious disadvantages to competing in the EC. Most importantly, ways of doing business will change in Europe, and American firms will have to learn a formidable array of new procedures, policies, laws, and regulations—many of which relate to the marketing of products. Second, competition will become much more intense because firms will no longer have exclusive business rights in their home countries. Increased competition should exert a downward pressure on costs, prices to consumers, and firms' profits, thereby eliminating weak, marginal competitors. Only lean, mean firms will survive.

Besides the competitive difficulties, American firms might experience internal human resource problems if they enter the EC. Along with the obvious disruption in their normal life-styles, American managers and their families relocated abroad will experience difficulties in finding housing, schools, transportation, shopping, and entertainment in the language and currency of a foreign country. As a result, they may feel isolated and unhappy—feelings that can adversely affect job performance.

To minimize these effects, American companies should be preparing their employees for relocation, but few are doing so. Recent studies indicate that a startling 84 percent of the managers sent to Western Europe received no briefing about management practices in their host countries; 77 percent didn't get information about the host country; only 15 percent received language training; and only 25 percent of spouses received any company communications about the relocation. Clearly, these failures of communication will inhibit the job performance of employees. Furthermore, firms may lose the valuable investment they have in their managers if some of them are dissatisfied enough to leave the firm while they are still abroad or after they return to the United States.

If they compound these already existing human resource problems with the inevitable problems of entering the entirely new market structure of the EC, unprepared firms will be asking for disaster. Before committing millions of dollars and many corporate and human resources to EC participation, American firms should ask themselves if they are willing to invest the time and effort in the language, business, and life-style education necessary to prepare employees and their families for living and working abroad.

QUESTIONS

1. Suppose a small manufacturer of household table lamps wants to enter the EC. What mode of entry might be most practical for this firm? Would your answer change if this were a large firm?

2. Suppose a service firm such as Jiffy Lube wanted to enter the EC. What mode of entry could it use?

3. In marketing products abroad, manufacturers can use a standardized or an adaptation marketing mix. Which type of marketing mix is a manufacturer of a small appliance such as coffeemakers likely to use in the EC? Which type of marketing mix is a manufacturer of packaged foods such as cookies and cereals likely to use?

Sources: "But It Could Be Cold Comfort for U.S. Companies There," *Business Week*, January 22, 1990, p. 20; *Europe 1992*, published by the Department of Trade and Industry and the Central Office of Information of the United Kingdom, September 1989; Bill Orr, "Fortress Europe?", *ABA Banking Journal*, April 1989, pp. 68ff.; and "The Shape of Things to Come," *The Banker*, September 1988, pp. 31ff.

22

Marketing Services, Organizations, Persons, Places, and Ideas

The Walt Disney Company is a master service marketer. Its "product" is entertainment, and no company provides more of it. In fact, last year, Disney's movie studios (including Touchstone) led all other studios in box office receipts. But nowhere is the "Disney Magic" more apparent than at the company's premier theme park, Disney World. More than 25 million people flock to Disney World each year—ten times more than visit Yellowstone National Park—making it the world's number one tourist attraction. What brings so many people to Disney World? Part of the answer lies in its many attractions. Disney World is a true fantasyland—28,000 acres brimming with such attractions as Space Mountain, Journey into Imagination, Pirates of the Caribbean, and Typhoon Lagoon. But these attractions provide only part of the story. In fact, what visitors like even more, they say, is the park's sparkling cleanliness and the friendliness of Disney World employees. In an increasingly rude, dirty, and mismanaged world, Disney offers warmth and order. As one observer notes, "In the Magic Kingdom, America still works the way it is supposed to. Everything is clean and safe, quality and service still matter, and the customer is always right."

Thus, the real "Disney Magic" lies in the company's obsessive dedication to serving its customers. The company sets high standards of service excellence and takes extreme care to make every aspect of every customer's visit memorable. According to Michael Eisner, Disney's Chairman, "We are in the business of exceeding people's very high expectations." Disney works hard at getting every employee, from the executive in the corner office to the person stamping hands at the gate, to embrace its customer-centered company culture. And it appears to be succeeding splendidly. Even as the Disney World waiting lines get longer, the "satisfaction rate," as measured by surveys of consumers as they leave the park, gets higher and higher. Sixty percent of all Disney World visitors are repeaters.

How does Disney do it? How does it inspire such high levels of customer service? Beyond the 4*P*s of marketing, Disney has mastered *internal marketing*—motivating its employees to work as a team to provide top-quality service—and *interactive marketing*—teaching employees how to interact with customers to deliver satisfaction. On their first day, all new employees report for a three-day motivational course at Disney University in Orlando, where they learn how to do the hard work of helping other people have fun. They learn that they are in the entertainment business, that they are "cast members" whose job is to be enthusiastic, knowledgeable, and professional in serving Disney's "guests." Each cast member, they learn, plays a vital role in the Disney World "show," whether it's as a "security host" (police), "transportation host" (driver), "custodial host" (street cleaner), or "food and beverage host" (restaurant worker).

Before they can receive their "theme costumes" and go "on stage," cast members must learn how to deal effectively with guests. In courses titled Traditions I and Traditions II, they learn the Disney language, history, and culture. They are taught to be enthusiastic, helpful, and *always* friendly. They learn to do good deeds, such as volunteering to take pictures of guests, so that the whole family can be in the picture. They are taught never to say, "It's not my job." When a guest asks a question—whether it's, "Where's the nearest restroom?" or, "What are the names of Snow White's seven dwarves?"—they need to know the answer. If they see a piece of trash on the ground, they pick it up. So that cast members will blend in and promote whole show, not individuals, Disney enforces a strict grooming code: men cannot sport mustaches, beards, or long hair; women cannot have long, brightly-colored fingernails, large hair decorations, heavy eye make-up, or dangling earrings. Disney is so confident that its cast members will charm guests that it finds ways to force contact. For example, many items in the park's gift shops bear no price tags, requiring shoppers to ask the price.

Disney keeps its managers close to employees and customers. At least once in his or her career, every Disney World manager must spend a day prancing around the park in an 80- to 100-pound character costume. And all managers spend a week each year in "cross-utilization," leaving the desk and heading for the front line—taking tickets, selling popcorn, or loading and unloading rides. And the company works to keep employees at all levels motivated and feeling like an important part of the team. All managers and employees wear name badges and ad-

dress each other on a first-name basis, regardless of rank. Employees receive a Disney newspaper called *Eyes and Ears*, which features news of activities, employment opportunities, special benefits, and educational offerings. A recreational area—consisting of a lake, recreation hall, picnic area, boating and fishing facilities, and a large library—is set aside for the employees' exclusive use. All exiting employees answer a questionnaire on how they felt about working for Disney. In this way, Disney measures its success in producing employee satisfaction. Thus, employees are made to feel important and personally responsible for the "show." Their sense of "owning the organization" spills over to the millions of visitors. Employee satisfaction ultimately leads to customer satisfaction.

Disney has become so highly regarded for its ability to inspire employees to meet its exacting service standards that many of America's leading corporations—from General Electric and AT&T to General Motors and Pan Am—send managers to Disney University to find out how Disney does it. And Disney's dedication to outstanding service marketing has paid off handsomely. During the past six years, Disney's annual revenues have more than doubled—to $4.7 billion. Profits have *quintupled*. Revenues have grown at an average annual rate of 23 percent, net income at 50 percent. Thus, Disney has found that by providing outstanding service to its *customers*, it also serves *itself*.[1]

CHAPTER OBJECTIVES

After reading this chapter, you should be able to:

1. Define *service* and describe four characteristics that affect the marketing of a service.
2. Explain how organizations market themselves.
3. Explain how persons and places are marketed.
4. Define social marketing and explain how social ideas are marketed.

Marketing developed initially for selling physical products such as toothpaste, cars, steel, and equipment. But this traditional focus may cause people to overlook the many other types of things that are marketed. In this chapter, we look at the special marketing requirements for *services*, *organizations*, *persons*, *places*, and *ideas*.

SERVICES MARKETING

One of the major trends in America has been the dramatic growth of services. Service jobs now account for 77 percent of total employment and 70 percent of the GNP, and services will provide 90 percent of all new jobs in the next 10 years.[2] Service jobs include not only those in service industries—hotels, airlines, banks, and others—but also in providing services in product-based industries, such as corporate lawyers, medical staff, and sales trainers. As a result of rising affluence, more leisure time, and the growing complexity of products that require servicing, the United States has become

The convenience industry: Services that save you time—for a price.

the world's first service economy. This has led to a growing interest in the special problems of marketing services.

Service industries vary greatly. The *government sector* offers services through courts, employment services, hospitals, loan agencies, military services, police and fire departments, postal service, regulatory agencies, and schools. The *private nonprofit* sector offers services through museums, charities, churches, colleges, foundations, and hospitals. A large part of the *business sector* offers services through airlines, banks, hotels, insurance companies, consulting firms, medical and law practices, entertainment companies, real estate firms, advertising and research agencies, and retailers.

Not only are there traditional service industries, but also new types keep popping up all the time:

> Want someone to fetch a meal from a local restaurant? In Austin, Texas, you can call EatOutIn. Plants need to be watered? In New York, you can call the Busy Body's Helper. Too busy to wrap and mail your packages? Stop by any one of the 72 outlets of Tender Sender, headquartered in Portland, Oregon. "We'll find it, we'll do it, we'll wait for it," chirps Lois Barnett, the founder of Personalized Services in Chicago. She and her crew of six will walk the dog, shuttle the kids to Little League, or wait in line for your theater tickets. Meet the convenience peddlers. They want to save you time. For a price, they'll do just about anything that's legal.[3]

Some service businesses are very large, with total sales and assets in the trillions of dollars. Table 22-1 shows the five largest service companies in each of eight service categories. But there are also tens of thousands of smaller service providers. Selling services presents some special problems calling for special marketing solutions.[4]

Nature and Classification of Services

We define a **service** as an activity or benefit that one party can offer to another that is essentially intangible and does not result in the ownership of anything. Its production may or may not be tied to a physical product. Renting a hotel room, depositing money in a bank, traveling on an airplane, visiting a psychiatrist, getting a haircut, having a car repaired, watching a professional sport, seeing a movie, having clothes cleaned at a dry cleaner, getting advice from a lawyer—all involve buying a service.

Services can be classified in a number of ways. First, the service can be *people-based* or *equipment-based*. Equipment-based services vary depending on whether they are automated or monitored by unskilled or skilled operators. People-based services also vary by whether they are provided by unskilled, skilled, or professional workers. Figure 22-1 shows several industries that cluster in each group.

Some but not all services require the *client's presence*. A dental checkup involves the client's presence, but a car repair does not. If the client must be present, the service provider has to be considerate of his or her needs. Thus, hair stylists decorate their

TABLE 22-1		
The Largest U.S. Service Companies	**Diversified Services**	**Commercial Banking**
	AT&T	Citicorp
	Fleming Companies	Chase Manhattan
	Super Valu Stores	BankAmerica
	Enron	J. P. Morgan
	Marriott	Security Pacific
	Diversified Financial	**Life Insurance**
	American Express	Prudential
	Federal National Mortgage Association	Metropolitan
	Salomon	Equitable
	Aetna Life and Casualty	Aetna
	Merrill Lynch	Teachers Insurance and Annuity
	Retailing	**Transportation**
	Sears	United Parcel Service
	K mart	AMR
	Wal-Mart	UAL
	American Stores	Delta Air Lines
	Kroger	CSX
	Utilities	**Savings Institutions**
	GTE	H. F. Ahmanson
	BellSouth	Great Western Financial
	Bell Atlantic	Calfed
	NYNEX	Glenfed
	US West	Golden West Financial

Source: "The Service 500," *Fortune*, June 4, 1990, pp. 297–335.

shops, play background music, and talk pleasantly with customers, in order to make the service environment pleasant.

Services differ as to whether they meet a *personal* need (personal services) or a *business* need (business services). Doctors may price physical examinations for private patients differently from those for company employees on a retainer. Service providers typically develop different marketing programs for personal and business markets.

Finally, what about the *service provider's objectives* (profit or nonprofit) and *ownership* (private or public)? These characteristics may be combined to produce quite different types of service organizations. For example, the marketing programs of a private investor hospital differ sharply from those of a private charity hospital or a Veterans Administration hospital.[5]

FIGURE 22-1   Types of service business
Source: Adapted by permission of the *Harvard Business Review*. An exhibit from "Strategy Is Different in Service Business," by Dan R. E. Thomas (July–August 1978). Copyright © 1978 by the President and Fellows of Harvard College; all rights reserved.

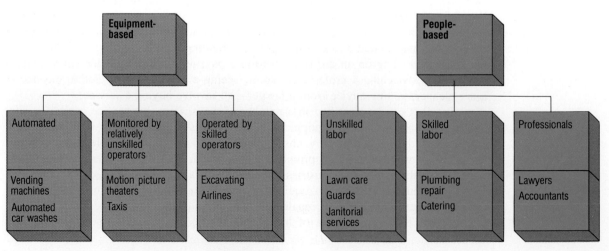

Characteristics of Services and Their Marketing Implications

Whether public or private, profit or nonprofit, services have four major characteristics that greatly affect the design of marketing programs: *intangibility*, *inseparability*, *variability*, and *perishability*.

Intangibility

Services are **intangible**—they cannot be seen, tasted, felt, heard, or smelled before they are bought. People undergoing cosmetic surgery cannot see the result before the purchase, and airline passengers have nothing but a ticket and the promise of safe delivery to their destinations.

To reduce uncertainty, buyers thus look for signs of service quality. They draw conclusions about quality from the place, people, equipment, communication material, and price that they can see. Therefore, the service provider's task is to make the service tangible in one or more ways. Whereas product marketers try to add intangibles to their tangible offers, service marketers try to add tangibles to their intangible offers.[6]

Consider a bank that wants to convey the idea that its service is quick and efficient. It must make this positioning strategy tangible in every aspect of customer contact. The bank's physical setting must suggest quick and efficient service: Its exterior and interior should have clean lines, internal traffic flow should be planned carefully, waiting lines should seem short, and background music should be light and upbeat. The bank's staff should be busy and properly dressed. Its equipment—computers, copy machines, desks—should look modern. The bank's ads and other communications should suggest efficiency, with clean and simple designs and carefully chosen words and photos that communicate the bank's positioning. The bank should choose a name and symbol for its service that suggest speed and efficiency. Its pricing for various services should be kept simple and clear.

Inseparability

Physical goods are produced, then stored, later sold, and still later consumed. But services are first sold, then produced and consumed at the same time. Thus, services are **inseparable** from their providers, whether the providers be people or machines. If a person provides the service, then the person is a part of the service. Because the client is also present as the service is produced, *provider-client interaction* is a special feature of services marketing. Both the provider and the client affect the service outcome.

In the case of entertainment and professional services, buyers care a great deal about *who* provides the service. It is not the same service at a Kenny Rogers concert if Rogers gets sick and is replaced by Billy Joel. A legal defense supplied by John Nobody differs from one supplied by F. Lee Bailey. When clients have strong provider preferences, price is used to ration the limited supply of the preferred provider's time. Thus, F. Lee Bailey charges more than do lesser-known lawyers, and only wealthy clients can afford his services.

Several strategies exist for getting around the problem of service-provider time limitations. First, the service provider can learn to work with larger groups. Some psychotherapists, for example, have moved from one-on-one therapy to small-group therapy to groups of more than 300 people in larger hotel ballrooms. Second, the service provider can learn to work faster—the psychotherapist can spend 30 minutes with each patient instead of 50 minutes and thus see more patients. Finally, the service organization can train more service providers and build up client confidence, as H & R Block has done with its national network of trained tax consultants.

Variability

Services are highly **variable**—their quality depends on who provides them and when, where, and how they are provided. For example, some hotels have reputations for providing better service than others. Within a given hotel, one registration-desk employee may be cheerful and efficient while another standing just a few feet away may be unpleasant and slow. Even the quality of single employee's service varies according to his or her energy and frame of mind at the time of each customer contact.

Service firms can take several steps toward quality control.[7] They can carefully select and train their personnel. Airlines, banks, and hotels spend large sums to train their employees to give good service. Consumers should find the same friendly and helpful personnel in every Marriott Hotel. Service firms can also provide employee incentives that emphasize quality, such as employee-of-the-month awards or bonuses based on customer feedback. They can make service employees more visible and accountable to consumers—auto dealerships can let customers talk directly with the mechanics working on their cars. A firm can regularly check customer satisfaction through suggestion and complaint systems, customer surveys, and comparison shopping. When poor service is found, it can be corrected. How a firm handles problems resulting from service variability can dramatically affect customer perceptions of service quality. Here is a good example:

> A while back, we had a Federal Express package that, believe it or not, absolutely, positively didn't get there overnight. One phone call to Federal Express solved the problem. But that's not all. Pretty soon our phone rang, and one of Federal Express' senior executives was on the line. He wanted to know what happened and was very apologetic. Now that's service. With that one phone call, he assured himself of a customer for life.[8]

Perishability

Services are **perishable**—they cannot be stored for later sales or use. Many doctors charge patients for missed appointments because the service value existed only at that point and disappeared when the patient did not show up. The perishability of services is not a problem when demand is steady. When demand fluctuates, however, service firms often have difficult problems. For example, public transportation companies are forced to own much more equipment because of rush hour demand that they would if demand were even throughout the day.

Service firms can use several strategies for producing a better match between demand and supply.[9] On the demand side, charging different prices at different times will shift some demand from peak to off-peak periods. Examples include low early-evening movie prices and weekend discount prices for car rentals. Or nonpeak demand can be increased, as when McDonald's offered its Egg McMuffin breakfast and hotels developed mini-vacation weekends. Complementary services can be offered during peak times to provide alternatives to waiting customers, such as cocktail lounges to sit in while waiting for a restaurant table and automatic tellers in banks. Reservation systems can help to manage the demand level—airlines, hotels, and physicians use them regularly.

On the supply side, part-time employees can be hired to serve peak demand. Colleges add part-time teachers when enrollment goes up, and restaurants call in part-time waiters and waitresses. Or peak-time demand can be handled more efficiently by having employees do only essential tasks during peak periods. Some tasks can be shifted

Services are perishable: Empty seats at slack times cannot be stored for later use during peak periods.

to consumers, as when consumers fill out their own medical records or bag their own groceries. Or providers can share services, as when several hospitals share an expensive piece of medical equipment. Finally, a firm can plan ahead for expansion, as when an amusement park buys surrounding land for later development.

Marketing Strategies for Service Firms

Until recently, service firms lagged behind manufacturing firms in their use of marketing.[10] Many service businesses are small (shoe repair shops, barbershops) and often consider marketing unneeded or too costly. Other service businesses (colleges, hospitals) once had so much demand that they did not need marketing until recently (see Marketing Highlight 22–1). Still others (legal, medical, and accounting practices) believed that it was unprofessional to use marketing.

Furthermore, service businesses are more difficult to manage when using only traditional marketing approaches. In a product business, products are fairly standardized and sit on shelves waiting for customers. In a service business, the customer interacts with a service provider whose service quality is less certain and more variable. The service outcome is affected not just by the service provider, but by the whole supporting production process. Thus, service marketing requires more than just the traditional external marketing using the 4*P*s. As shown in Figure 22-2, service marketing also requires both *internal marketing* and *interactive marketing*.[11]

Internal marketing means that the service firm must effectively train and motivate its customer-contact employees and all the supporting service people to work as a *team* to provide customer satisfaction. For the firm to deliver consistently high service quality, all employees must practice a customer orientation. It is not enough to have a marketing department doing traditional marketing while the rest of the company goes its own way. Marketers must also get everyone else in the organization to practice marketing. In fact, internal marketing must *precede* external marketing. It makes little sense to advertise excellent service before the company's staff is ready to provide it. This point is well-illustrated by a story about how Bill Marriott, Jr., chairman of Marriott hotels, interviews prospective managers:

> Bill Marriott tells the job candidate that the hotel chain wants to satisfy three groups: *customers*, *employees*, and *stockholders*. Although all of the groups are important, he asks in which order should the groups be satisfied? Most candidates say first satisfy customers. Marriott, however, reasons differently. First, employees must be satisfied. If employees love their jobs and feel a sense of pride in the hotel, they will serve customers well. Satisfied customers will return frequently to the Marriott. Moreover, dealing with happy customers will make employees even more satisfied, resulting in better service and still greater repeat business, all of which will yield a level of profits which will satisfy Marriott stockholders.

Interactive marketing means that perceived service quality depends heavily on the quality of the buyer-seller interaction. In product marketing, product quality often depends little on how the product is obtained. But in services marketing, service quality depends both on the service deliverer and on the quality of the delivery, especially in professional services. The customer judges service quality not just on *technical quality*

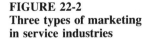

FIGURE 22-2
Three types of marketing in service industries

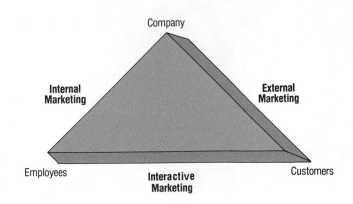

HOSPITAL MARKETING: CENTURY CITY'S EQUIVALENT OF A SUITE AT THE RITZ

Traditionally, hospitals had the problem of too many patients. But during the past decade, they began to face falling admissions and low occupancy. In the scramble to pull in new patients, many hospitals turned to marketing. The more they looked at the problem, the more complex the marketing challenges appeared. Most hospitals realized that they couldn't be all things to all people. Some began to focus on offering certain specialties—heart, pediatrics, burn treatment, psychiatry. Others focused on serving the special needs of certain demographic segments.

Century City Hospital in Los Angeles provides a good example of modern hospital marketing. It recently unveiled its "Century Pavilion"—the hospital equivalent of a suite at the Ritz. The Pavilion consists of six luxury suites in which the area's affluent can get some of the finer things along with their basic health care. Since it opened, a steady stream of celebrities and other wealthy patients have lined up to pay the $1,000 per night required to stay in a classy Pavilion suite. From the moment they are whisked to their rooms by private elevator, Pavilion guests are pampered.

Century City did not stumble across the Pavilion idea by chance. The service is the result of a solid marketing program headed by the hospital's marketing director. A research study of the hospital's primary market area showed that almost 50 percent of area residents were high-income, highly educated professionals. Thirty-seven percent of the area population lives in homes worth more than $200,000; more than 7 percent have household incomes above $75,000. And more than 40,000 millionaires live in the Los Angeles–Long Beach area. Century City set out to capture this segment of well-heeled residents who had come to expect the best in food, accommodations, and service.

While cost efficiency is the battle cry in most health-care corners, upscale patients want and can afford extras. Century City's research showed that this segment wanted privacy and exclusivity. So the hospital employed a noted interior-design firm to create suites with understated luxury and an elegant but quiet atmosphere. In these posh rooms, gourmet food is served on imported china and specially selected silver flatware. And because four of Pavilion's units come with guest suites (for family, friends, and bodyguards), each unit allows for gracious hospitality. The hospital has even catered parties in the suites. Finally, the units come with many other extras, such as secretarial services to help patients to keep up with their business tasks.

Century City decided against flashy institutional ads to promote the Pavilion. Instead, direct-mail pieces were sent to about 10,000 households in Brentwood, Bel Aire, Beverly Hills, and wealthy areas of West Los Angeles. Direct mail was also used to reach 800 staff physicians, each of whom received a rose one day, a fancy notepad another, and a chocolate truffle in a third mailing—each alerting them that the service was available for their prominent patients.

Century City uses a low-key approach to marketing. Other hospitals have used flashier, mass-selling tactics to drum up business. Sunrise Hospital in Las Vegas ran a large ad showing a ship with the caption: "Introducing the Sunrise Cruise. Win a Once-in-a-Lifetime Cruise Simply by Entering Sunrise Hospital Any Friday or Saturday: Recuperative Cruise for Two." St. Luke's Hospital in Phoenix introduced nightly bingo games for all patients (except cardiac cases), producing immense patient interest and an annual profit of $60,000. A Philadelphia hospital served candlelight dinners with steak and champagne to parents of newborn children. Republic Health Corporation hospitals offer eleven branded "products," including Gift of Sight (cataract surgery), Miracle Moments (childbirth), and You're Becoming (cosmetic surgery).

Whatever the approach, most major hospitals now use some form of marketing; many have become good at it. Last year, American hospitals spent $1.6 billion on marketing. According to Century City's director: "The Century Pavilion represents one element of what is happening in hospital marketing. Hospitals are becoming very sophisticated in defining who their patients are, what their needs are, and they're creating the kinds of services—whether it be luxury suites or same-day surgery—to meet those needs. In short, hospitals are definitely consumer oriented—a very large factor in health care today."

Sources: Portions adapted from Kevin T. Higgins, "Hospital Puttin' on the Ritz to Target High-End Market," *Marketing News*," January 17, 1986, p. 14. Also see Robert B. Kimmel, "Should Hospitals Advertise?" *Advertising Age*, June 13, 1988, p. 20.

Hospital marketing: Century City targets affluent consumers who want some of the finer things along with their health care.

(say, the success of the surgery) but also on its *functional quality* (whether the doctor showed concern and inspired confidence). Thus, professionals cannot assume that they will satisfy the client simply by providing good technical service. They must master interactive marketing skills or functions as well.

Today, as competition increases, as costs rise, as productivity drops, and as service quality falls off, more marketing sophistication will be needed. Service companies face three major marketing tasks. They want to increase their *competitive differentiation*, *service quality*, and *productivity*.

Managing Differentiation

In these days of intense price competition, service marketers often complain about the difficulty of differentiating their services from those of competitors. To the extent that customers view the services of different providers as similar, they care less about the provider than the price.

The solution to price competition is to develop a differentiated offer, delivery, and image. The *offer* can include *innovative features* to distinguish it from competitors' offers. For example, airlines have introduced such innovations as in-flight movies, advanced seating, air-to-ground telephone service, and frequent flyer award programs to differentiate their offers. Singapore Airlines once even added a piano bar. Unfortunately, most service innovations are easily copied. Still, the service company that regularly finds desired service innovations will usually gain a succession of temporary advantages, and may, by earning an innovative reputation, keep customers who want to go with the best.

The service company can differentiate its service *delivery* in three ways—through people, physical environment, and process. The company can distinguish itself by having more able and reliable customer contact people than its competitors. Or it can develop a superior physical environment in which the service product is delivered. Finally, it can design a superior delivery process. For example, banks might offer home banking as a superior way to deliver banking services to customers than having them drive, park, and wait in line.

Service companies can also work on differentiating their *images* through symbols and branding. The Harris Bank of Chicago adopted the lion as its symbol on its stationery, in its advertising, and even as stuffed animals offered to new depositors. The well-known "Harris Lion" confers an image of strength upon the bank. Humana, the nation's second largest investor-owned system of hospitals and services, has developed a successful branding strategy. It has standardized the names of all of its 90 hospitals with the "Humana" prefix and then built tremendous awareness and a reputation for quality around that name.[12]

Managing Service Quality

One of the major ways to differentiate a service firm is for the firm to deliver consistently higher quality than its competitors. Many companies are finding that outstanding service quality can give them a potent competitive advantage leading to superior sales and profit performance. Some firms have become almost legendary for their high-quality service (see Marketing Highlight 22–2). The key is to meet or exceed the customers' service-quality *expectations*. As the chief executive at American Express puts it, "Promise only what you can deliver and deliver *more* than you promise!"[13] These expectations are based on past experiences, word-of-mouth, and service firm advertising. Customers often compare the *perceived service* of a given firm to their *expected service*: If the perceived service meets or exceeds expected service, customers are apt to use the provider again.

The service provider thus needs to identify the expectations of target customers' concerning service quality. Unfortunately, service quality is harder to define and judge than product quality. It is harder to get agreement on the quality of a haircut than on the quality of a hair dryer. Moreover, although greater service quality results in greater customer satisfaction, it also requires higher costs. Thus, service firms cannot always

COMPETITIVE ADVANTAGE THROUGH CUSTOMER SERVICE

Some companies go to extremes to coddle their customers with service. Consider the following examples:

- An L. L. Bean customer says he lost all his fishing equipment—and nearly his life—when a raft he bought from the company leaked and forced him to swim to shore. He recovered the raft and sent it to the company along with a letter asking for a new raft and $700 to cover the fishing equipment he says he lost. He gets both.

- A woman visits a Nordstrom department store to buy a gift for a friend. She's in a hurry and leaves the store immediately after making her purchase. The Nordstrom salesclerk gift-wraps the item at no charge and later drops it off at the customer's home.

- At 11:00 P.M., a driver making a crucial delivery for Sigma Midwest is having electrical problems with his Ryder rental truck. He calls the company and within an hour the truck is fixed, yet the Ryder employee stays with the driver for the next five hours to help him make deliveries and remain on schedule.

- An American Express cardholder fails to pay more than $5,000 of his September bill. He explains that during the summer he'd purchased expensive rugs in Turkey. When he got home, appraisals showed that the rugs were worth half of what he'd paid. Rather than asking suspicious questions or demanding payment, the American Express representative notes the dispute, asks for a letter summarizing the appraisers' estimates, and offers to help solve the problem. And until the conflict is resolved, American Express doesn't ask for payment.

From a dollars-and-cents point of view, these examples sound like a crazy way to do business. How can you make money by giving away your products, providing free extra services, or letting customers get away without paying their bills on time? Yet studies show that good service, though costly, goes hand-in-hand with good financial performance. For example, despite its costly emphasis on service, or more likely *because* of it, American Express earns the *highest* profit margins of any credit card company. Similarly, Nordstrom enjoys the highest sales per square foot of any department store, about *double* the industry average. And L. L. Bean has grown at almost *twice* the industry growth rate over the last five years. These and other companies know that good service is good for business. In today's highly competitive marketplace, companies that take the best care of their customers have a strong competitive advantage.

Good customer service involves more than simply opening a complaint department, smiling a lot, and being nice to customers. It requires hard-headed analysis and an intense commitment to helping customers. Outstanding service companies set high service standards and often make seemingly outlandish efforts to achieve them. They take great care to hire the right service people, train them well, and reward them for going out of their way to serve customers.

But at these companies, exceptional service is more than a set of policies or actions—it's a company-wide attitude, an important part of the overall company culture. Concern for the consumer becomes a matter of pride for everyone in the company. American Express loves to tell stories about how its people have rescued customers from disasters ranging from civil wars to earthquakes, no matter what the cost. The company gives cash rewards of up to $1,000 to "Great Performers" such as Barbara Weber, who last year moved mountains of State Department and Treasury Department bureaucracy to refund $980 in stolen traveler's checks to a customer stranded in Cuba. Four Seasons Hotels, long known for its outstanding service, tells its employees the story of Ron Dyment, a doorman in Toronto who forgot to load a departing guest's briefcase in his taxi. The doorman called the guest, a lawyer, in Washington, D.C., and learned that he desperately needed the briefcase for a meeting the following morning. Without first asking for approval from management, Dyment hopped on a plane and returned it. The company named Dyment Employee of the Year. Similarly, Nordstrom thrives on stories about its service heroics—such as employees dropping off orders at customers' homes or warming up cars while customers spend a little more time shopping. There's even a story about a customer who got a refund on a tire—Nordstrom doesn't carry tires, but it prides itself on a no-questions-asked return policy!

There's no simple formula for offering good service, but neither is it a mystery. According to the president of L. L. Bean, "A lot of people have fancy things to say about customer service . . . but it's just a day-in, day-out, ongoing, never-ending, unremitting, persevering, compassionate type of activity." For the companies that do it well, it's also very rewarding.

Sources: Bill Kelley, "Five Companies that Do It Right—and Make It Pay," *Sales and Marketing Management*, April 1988, pp. 57–64; Joan O'C. Hamilton, "Why Rivals Are Quaking as Nordstrom Heads East," *Business Week*, June 15, 1987, pp. 89–90; Patricia Sellers, "Getting Customers to Love You," *Fortune*, March 13, 1989, pp. 38–49; and John Paul Newport, Jr., "American Express: Service that Sells, *Fortune*, November 20, 1989, pp. 80–94.

meet consumers' service-quality desires—they face trade-offs between customer satisfaction and company profitability. Whatever the level of service provided, it is important that the service provider clearly define and communicate that level so that its employees know what they must deliver and customers know what they will get.

Studies of well-managed service companies show that they share a number of common virtues regarding service quality. First, they have a history of *top management commitment to quality*. Management at companies such as Marriott, Disney, Delta, and McDonald's looks not only at financial performance but also at service performance. The best service providers *set high service quality standards*. Swissair, for example, aims to have 96 percent or more of its passengers rate its service as good or superior;

otherwise it takes action. The top service firms also *watch service performance closely*—both their own and that of competitors. They use such methods as comparison shopping, customer surveys, and suggestion and complaint forms. General Electric sends out 700,000 response cards each year to households who rate their service people's performance. Citibank takes regular measures of "ART"—accuracy, responsiveness, and timeliness—and sends out employees who act as customers to check on service quality. Finally, well-managed service companies *satisfy employees as well as customers*. They believe that good employee relations result in good customer relations. Management creates an environment of employee support, gives rewards for good service performance, and monitors employee job satisfaction.[14]

Managing Productivity

With their costs rising rapidly, service firms are under great pressure to increase productivity. Several ways exist to improve service productivity. First, the service providers can better train current employees or hire new ones who will work harder or more skillfully for the same pay. Or the service providers can increase the quantity of their service by giving up some quality. Doctors working for health maintenance organizations (HMO's) have moved toward handling more patients and giving less time to each. The provider can "industrialize the service" by adding equipment and standardizing production, as in McDonald's assembly-line approach to fast-food retailing. Commercial dishwashing, jumbo jets, multiple-unit movie theatres—all represent technological expansions of service.

Service providers can also increase productivity by designing more effective services. How-to-quit-smoking clinics and recommendations for exercise may reduce the need for expensive medical services later on. Hiring paralegal workers reduces the need for expensive legal professionals. Providers can also give customers incentives to substitute company labor with their own labor. For example, business firms that sort their own mail before delivering it to the post office pay lower postal rates.

Services marketing strategies: UPS claims that greater efficiency and productivity allow it to offer high quality service at a low price.

However, companies must avoid pushing productivity so hard that doing so reduces perceived quality. Some productivity steps help standardize quality, increasing customer satisfaction. But other productivity steps lead to too much standardization and rob consumers of customized service. In some cases, the service provider accepts reduced productivity to create more differentiation.

Organization Marketing

Organizations often carry out activities to "sell" the organization itself. **Organization marketing** consists of activities undertaken to create, maintain, or change the attitudes and behavior of target audiences toward an organization. Both profit and nonprofit organizations practice organization marketing. Business firms sponsor public relations or corporate advertising campaigns to polish up their images. Nonprofit organizations such as churches, colleges, charities, museums, and performing arts groups market their organizations in order to raise funds and attract members or patrons. Organization marketing calls for assessing the organization's current image and developing a marketing plan to improve it.

Image Assessment

The first step in image assessment is to research the organization's current image among key publics. The way an individual or a group sees an organization is called its **organization image.** Different people can have different images of the same organization. The organization might be pleased with its public image or might find that it has serious image problems.

For example, suppose a bank does some marketing research to measure its image in the community. Suppose it finds its image to be that shown by the red line in Figure 22-3. Thus, current and potential customers view the bank as somewhat small, non-innovative, unfriendly, and unknowledgeable. The bank will want to change this image.

Image Planning and Control

Next, the organization should decide what image it would like to have and can achieve. For example, the bank might decide that it would like the image shown by the blue line in Figure 22-3. It would like to be seen as a provider of more friendly and personal service, and as being more innovative, knowledgeable, and larger.

The firm now develops a marketing plan to shift its actual image toward the desired one. Suppose the bank first wants to improve its image as giving friendly and personal service. The key step, of course, is to actually provide friendlier and more personal service. The bank can hire and train better tellers and others who deal with customers. It can change its decor to make the bank seem warmer. Once the bank is certain that it has improved performance on important image measures, it can then design a marketing program to communicate that new image to customers. Using public relations, the bank can sponsor community activities, send its executives to speak to local business and civic groups, offer public seminars on household finances, and issue press releases on newsworthy bank activities. In its advertising, the bank can position itself as "your friendly, personal neighborhood bank."

Corporate image advertising is a major tool companies use to market themselves to various publics. Companies spend more than $785 million each year on image advertising.[15] They can use corporate advertising to build up or maintain a favorable

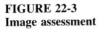
FIGURE 22-3
Image assessment

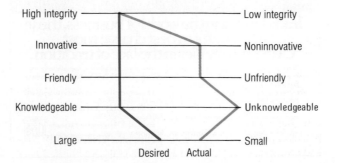

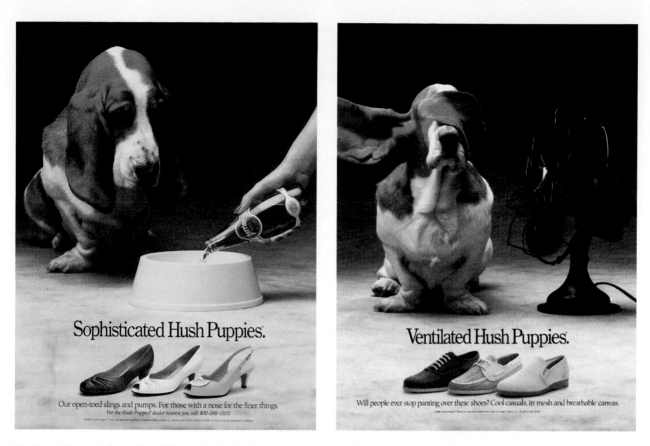

Corporate image advertising: These ads attempt to reposition Hush Puppies as a modern, stylish brand.

image over many years. Or they can use it to counter events that might hurt their image. For example, Chrysler hired an image consultant firm to tell it how to keep its positive image after Lee Iacocca moves on. Waste Management, the giant garbage disposal company, got into trouble a few years ago for dumping toxic wastes. So it countered with an advertising campaign telling how the company has worked with various government agencies to help save a threatened species of butterfly.

Such organization marketing efforts can work only if the actual organization lives up to the projected image. No amount of advertising and public relations can fool the public for long if the reality fails to match the image. Thus, Waste Management's image campaign worked only because the company has in fact worked to clean up toxic waste sites. Otherwise, even saving butterflies would not help the company's reputation.[16]

An organization must resurvey its publics once in a while to see whether its activities are improving its image. Images cannot be changed overnight: campaign funds are usually limited and public images tend to stick. If the firm is making no progress, either its marketing offer or its organization marketing program will have to be changed.

PERSON MARKETING

People are also marketed. **Person marketing** consists of activities undertaken to create, maintain, or change attitudes or behavior toward particular people. All kinds of people and organizations practice person marketing. Politicians market themselves to get votes and program support. Entertainers and sports figures use marketing to promote their careers and improve their incomes. Professionals such as doctors, lawyers, accountants, and architects market themselves in order to build their reputations and increase business.

Business leaders use person marketing as a strategic tool to develop their company's fortunes as well as their own. Businesses, charities, sports teams, fine arts groups, religious groups, and other organizations also use person marketing. Creating, flaunting, or associating with well-known personalities often helps these organizations to better achieve their goals.

Here are some examples of successful person marketing:

- Lee Iacocca, the heavily marketed chairman of Chrysler Corporation, is highly visible. His direct, dramatic, and blunt style commands attention and respect. In Chrysler ads, Iacocca levels with consumers, conveying confidence and trust. In a typical press conference, he might attack the timid U.S. trade policy toward Japan, praise Chrysler cars and workers, speak out on the federal deficit, advise broadly on how to tackle tomorrow's business problems, and again deny that he will run for president. Iacocca's visibility helps Chrysler sell cars and gain the support of important consumer, financial, employee, government, media, and other publics. Iacocca's visibility is no accident; his transformation into a celebrity was as deliberate as the manufacture of his cars. Creating the image of the confident chairman in a sixty-second TV ad requires days of filming, weeks of editing, and months of planning and research. Iacocca's image as an old-style street fighter—tough, decisive, in control—is the result of extensive planning and practice by Iacocca and careful image crafting by a team of policy planners, media advisors, ghostwriters, and ad agencies.[17]

- Michael Jordan, star of the Chicago Bulls, possesses remarkable basketball skills—great court sense with quick, fluid moves and the ability to soar above the rim for dramatic dunks. And he has an appealing, unassuming personality to go along with his dazzling talents. All of this makes Michael Jordan very marketable. After graduating from college, Jordan signed on with ProServ Inc., a well-known sports management agency. The agency quickly negotiated a lucrative five-year contract with the Bulls, paying Jordan some $4 million. But that was just the beginning. ProServ decided to market Jordan as the new Dr. J of basketball—a supertalented good guy and solid citizen. Paying careful attention to placement and staging, the agency booked Jordan into the talk-show circuit, accepted

Person marketing: Associating with well-known personalities can help organizations to better achieve their goals.

only the best products to endorse, insisted on only high-quality commercials, arranged appearances for charitable causes, and even had him appear as a fashion model. Jordan's market appeal soared, and so did his income. Person marketing has paid off handsomely for Michael Jordan, for his team, and for the products he represents. Jordan recently signed a new eight year, $25 million contract with the Bulls and current endorsements for Nike, Wilson, Coca-Cola, Johnson Products, McDonald's, and other companies earn Jordan an additional $4 million a year. In its first full year with Jordan as its representative, Nike sold $110 million worth of "Air Jordan" basketball shoes and apparel. And last year the Bulls sold out all but one of their home games—more sellouts than they've totaled in their 22 year history.[18]

- Former president Ronald Reagan's administration was unequaled in its use of marketing to sell the president and his policies to the American people. Every move made by Reagan during his eight years as president was carefully managed to support the administration's positioning and marketing strategy. An army of specialists—marketing researchers, advertising experts, political advisers, speech writers, media planners, press secretaries, even make-up artists—worked tirelessly to define political market segments, identify key issues, and strongly position Reagan and his programs. The administration used extensive marketing research. It regularly polled voter segments to find out what was "hot" and what was not. Using focus groups, it pretested important speeches and platforms. "Theming it" was an important element of marketing strategy—the administration packaged key benefits into a few highly focused themes, then repeated these basic themes over and over and over. This focus on basic marketable themes, coupled with careful planning and delivery of messages and media exposures, helped control what was reported by the press. Reagan even made careful use of "regional marketing," tailoring timely speeches to the special needs of regional or local audiences.[19]

The objective of person marketing is to create a "celebrity"—a well-known person whose name generates attention, interest, and action. Celebrities differ in the *scope* of their visibility. Some are very well known, but only in limited geographic areas (a town mayor, a local businessperson, an area doctor) or specific segments (the president of the American Dental Association, a company vice-president, a jazz musician with a small group of fans). Still others have broad national or international visibility (major entertainers, sports superstars, world political and religious leaders).

Celebrities also differ in their *durability*. Figure 22-4A shows a standard celebrity life cycle pattern. The person's visibility begins at a low level, gradually builds to a

FIGURE 22-4
Celebrity life cycles
Source: Adapted from Irving Rein, Philip Kotler, and Martin Stoller. *High Visibility* (New York: Dodd, Mead & Company, 1987), pp. 109–10. Used with permission.

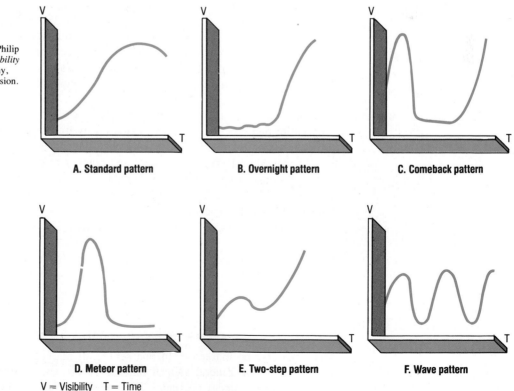

A. Standard pattern   B. Overnight pattern   C. Comeback pattern

D. Meteor pattern   E. Two-step pattern   F. Wave pattern

V = Visibility   T = Time

peak as the person matures and becomes well known, then declines as the celebrity fades from the limelight. But as the rest of Figure 22-4 shows, celebrity life cycle patterns can vary greatly. For example, in the *overnight* pattern (22-4B), a person acquires quick and lasting visibility because of some major deed or event (Charles Lindbergh, Neil Armstrong). In the *comeback* pattern (Figure 22-4C), a celebrity achieves high visibility, loses it, then gets it back again (Tina Turner, George Burns). In the *meteor pattern* (22-4D), someone gains fame quickly loses it suddenly. For example, William ''Refrigerator'' Perry, the overweight Chicago defensive lineman, became an instant ''hot property'' after he was used as a running back on Monday Night Football, made millions of dollars from product endorsements, and then sank back into obscurity—all within about a year.

The person marketing process is similar to the one used by product and service marketers. Person marketers begin with careful market research and analysis to discover consumer needs and market segments. Next comes product development—assessing the person's current qualities and image and transforming the person to better match market needs and expectations. Finally, the marketer develops programs to value, promote, and deliver the celebrity. Some people naturally possess the skills, appearances, and behaviors that target segments value. But for most, celebrity status in any field must be actively developed through sound person marketing.

PLACE MARKETING

Place marketing involves activities undertaken to create, maintain, or change attitudes or behavior toward particular places. Examples include business site marketing and vacation marketing.

Business Site Marketing

Business site marketing involves developing, selling, or renting business sites for such uses as factories, stores, offices, warehouses, and conventions. Large developers research companies' land needs and respond with real estate solutions, such as industrial parks, shopping centers, and new office buildings. Most states operate industrial development offices that try to sell companies on the advantages of locating new plants in their states (see Marketing Highlight 22–3). They spend large sums on advertising and offer to fly prospects to the site at no cost. Troubled cities, such as New York, Detroit, Dallas, and Atlanta, have appointed task forces to improve their images and draw new businesses to their areas. They may build large centers to house important conventions and business meetings. Even nations, such as Canada, Ireland, Greece, Mexico, and Turkey, have marketed themselves as good locations for business investment.

Vacation Marketing

Vacation marketing involves attracting vacationers to spas, resorts, cities, states, and even entire nations. The effort is carried on by travel agents, airlines, motor clubs, oil companies, hotels, motels, and governmental agencies.

Today almost every city, state, and country markets its tourist attractions. Miami Beach is considering making gambling legal in order to attract more tourists. Texas advertises ''It's Like a Whole Other Country,'' and Michigan touts ''YES M!CH!GAN.'' Philadelphia invites you to ''Get To Know Us!'' and Palm Beach, Florida, advertises ''The Best of Everything'' at low off-season prices. Some places, however, try to *demarket* themselves because they feel that the harm from tourism exceeds the revenues. Thus, Oregon has publicized its bad weather; Yosemite National Park may ban snowmobiling, conventions, and private cars; and Finland discourages tourists from vacationing in certain areas.

IDEA MARKETING

Ideas can also be marketed. In one sense, all marketing is the marketing of an idea, whether it be the general idea of brushing your teeth or the specific idea that Crest is the most effective decay preventer. Here, however, we narrow our focus to the marketing

"THE GOODLIEST LAND": BUSINESS SITE MARKETING IN NORTH CAROLINA

In 1584, when two English explorers returned to their homeland with news of "The Goodliest Land Under the Cope of Heaven," they were describing what is now North Carolina. In recent years, numerous American and foreign companies have come to share this opinion of the Tar Heel state. In three successive *Business Week* surveys, North Carolina was named as first choice of the nation's top business executives for new-plant location. The state does offer a number of economic and cultural advantages, but much credit for the state's popularity goes to the North Carolina Department of Commerce's Business/Industry Development Division. The division employs a high-quality marketing program—including advertising, publicity, and personal selling—to convince targeted firms and industries to come to North Carolina.

The division's 24 industrial development representatives coordinate efforts with development professionals in more than 300 individual North Carolina communities. And the division provides extensive information to firms considering locating in the state—in-depth profiles of more than 325 communities, a computerized inventory of available industrial sites and buildings, estimates of state and local taxes for specific sites, analyses of labor costs and fringe benefits, details of convenient transportation to sites, and estimates of construction costs.

But the Business/Industry Development Division does more than simply provide information—it aggressively seeks out firms and persuades them to locate in North Carolina. It invites groups of business executives to tour the state and hear presentations, and it sets up booths at industry trade fairs. Its representatives (sometimes including the governor) travel to other states to carry the North Carolina story to executives in attractive businesses and industries. The division also communicates and persuades through informational and promotional brochures delivered by mail and through mass-media advertising. Ads and brochures such as that shown here tout North Carolina's benefits: a large and productive labor force, numerous educational and technical training institutions, low taxes, a good transportation network, low energy and construction costs, a good living environment, and plentiful government support and assistance.

The division's total budget runs only about $6 million a year, but the returns are great. From 1975 through 1989, new and expanding business announced investments of more than $31 billion in North Carolina, creating more than 430,000 new jobs.

Source: Based on information supplied by the North Carolina Department of Commerce, Business/Industry Development Division.

North Carolina advertises to attract new business to the state.

SOCIAL MARKETING OF SAFE AND SOBER DRIVING

The Reader's Digest Foundation, in partnership with the National Association of Secondary School Principals (NASSP), recently launched a two-year, $1 million social marketing campaign to deliver a sober message to teen-agers all across America. As part of the "Don't Drink and Drive Challenge," *Reader's Digest* magazine invited teams from leading advertising agencies to create posters for the campaign, with the winners receiving a Paris trip for two. In the first year of the campaign, more than 1,000 teams from top agencies competed. Shown here are some of the outstanding posters created for the program.

The foundation then distributed copies of the winning posters to 20,000 high schools. Students were challenged to compete for college scholarships by devising programs to promote sober driving. More than 700 schools submitted entries ranging from rock videos to puppet shows to anti-drunk-driving awareness weeks. Scholarships totaling $500,000 went to 115 winning schools. The program was held a second year, with advertising agencies and schools again taking part and another $500,000 in scholarships awarded. Reader's Digest Foundation continues to offer copies of its posters and summaries of winning student programs as a resource to educators, the media, and community organizations.

Social marketing: Marketing safe and sober driving.

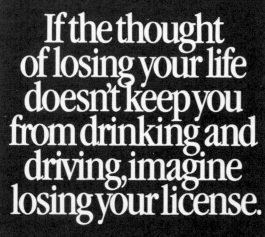

of *social ideas*, such as public health campaigns to reduce smoking, alcoholism, drug abuse, and overeating; environmental campaigns to promote wilderness protection, clean air, and conservation; and other campaigns such as family planning, human rights, and racial equality. This area has been called *social marketing*.[20] **Social marketing** is the design, implementation, and control of programs seeking to increase the acceptability of a social idea, cause, or practice among a target group.

Social marketers can pursue different objectives. They might want to produce understanding (knowing the nutritional value of different foods) or trigger a one-time action (joining in a mass immunization campaign). They might want to change behavior (discouraging drunk driving) or change a basic belief (convincing employers that handicapped people can make strong contributions in the workforce).

The Advertising Council of America has carried out dozens of social advertising campaigns, including "Smokey the Bear," "Keep America Beautiful," "Join the Peace Corps," "Buy Bonds," "Go to College," and "Say No to Drugs."[21] But social marketing is much broader than only advertising.[21] Many public marketing campaigns fail because they assign advertising the primary role and fail to develop and use all the marketing mix tools.

In designing effective social-change strategies, social marketers go through a normal marketing planning process. First, they define the social-change objective—for example, "to reduce the percentage of teenagers who drink and drive from 15 percent to 5 percent within 5 years." Next, they analyze the attitudes, beliefs, values, and behavior of teenagers and the forces that support teenage drinking. They consider communication and distribution approaches that might prevent teenagers from driving while drinking, develop a marketing plan, and build a marketing organization to carry out the plan (see Marketing Highlight 22–4). Finally, they evaluate and, if necessary, adjust the program to make it more effective.

Social marketing is fairly new, and its effectiveness relative to other social-change strategies is hard to evaluate. It is hard to produce social change with any strategy, let alone one that relies on voluntary response. Social marketing has been applied mainly to family planning, environmental protection, energy conservation, improved health and nutrition, auto driver safety, and public transportation—and there have been some encouraging successes. But more applications are needed before we can fully assess social marketing's potential for producing social change.

■ SUMMARY

Marketing has been broadened in recent years to cover "marketable" entities other than products—namely, services, organizations, persons, places, and ideas.

As the United States moves increasingly toward a *service economy*, marketers need to know more about marketing services. *Services* are activities or benefits that one party can offer to another that are essentially intangible and do not result in the ownership of anything. Services are *intangible*, *inseparable*, *variable*, and *perishable*. Each characteristic poses problems and requires strategies. Marketers have to find ways to make the service more tangible; to increase the productivity of providers who are inseparable from their products; to standardize the quality in the face of variability; and to improve demand movements and supply capacities in the face of service perishability.

Service industries have typically lagged behind manufacturing firms in adopting and using marketing concepts, but this situation is now changing. Services marketing strategy calls not only for external marketing but also for *internal marketing* to motivate employees and *interactive marketing* to create service delivery skills among service providers. To succeed, service marketers must create *competitive differentiation*, offer high service quality, and find ways to increase *service productivity*.

Organizations can also be marketed. *Organization marketing* is undertaken to create, maintain, or change the attitudes or behavior of target audiences toward an organization. It calls for assessing the organization's current image and developing a marketing plan for bringing about an improved image.

Person marketing consists of activities undertaken to create, maintain, or change attitudes or behavior toward particular persons. Two common forms are celebrity marketing and political candidate marketing.

Place marketing involves activities to create, maintain, or change attitudes or behavior toward particular places. Examples include business site marketing and vacation marketing.

Idea marketing involves efforts to market ideas. In the case of social ideas, it is called *social marketing* and consists of the design, implementation, and control of programs seeking to increase the acceptability of a social idea, cause, or practice among a target group. Social marketing goes further than public advertising—it coordinates advertising with the other elements of the marketing mix. The social marketer defines the social-change objective, analyzes consumer attitudes and competitive forces, develops and tests alternative concepts, develops appropriate channels for the idea's communication and distribution, and finally, checks the results. Social marketing has been applied to family planning, environmental protection, and antismoking campaigns and to other public issues.

◼ QUESTIONS FOR DISCUSSION

1. A "hot" concept in fast-food marketing is home delivery of everything from pizza to hamburgers to fried chicken. Why is demand for this service growing? How can marketers gain a competitive advantage by satisfying the growing demand for increased services?

2. Many banks have begun hiring marketing executives with experience in consumer packaged goods marketing. What benefits and problems might banks experience as a result of this hiring practice?

3. How can a theater deal with the intangibility, inseparability, variability, and perishability of the service it provides? Give examples.

4. Retail stores sell tangible products rather than services. Is interactive marketing an important concept to retailers? How can retailers use internal marketing to improve the quality of buyer-seller interactions in their stores?

5. Why do organizations want to "sell" themselves, and not just their products? List several reasons for organization marketing and relate them to promotional campaigns of companies you are familiar with.

6. Wendy's serves its hamburgers "fresh off the grill." This assures high quality but creates leftover burgers if the staff overestimates demand. Wendy's solves this perishability problem by using the meat in chili, tacos, and spaghetti

sauce. How do airlines solve the perishability of unsold seats? Give additional examples of perishability and how service firms address it.

7. Many people believe that too much time and money are spent marketing political candidates. They also complain that modern political campaigns overemphasize image at the expense of issues. What is your opinion of political candidate marketing? Would some other approach to campaigning help consumers make better voting decisions?

8. News reports of questionable, high-pressure tactics in the sale of vacation homes are common. For example, the "food processor" one marketer used as an incentive to attract prospects turned out to be a fork! Why do you think unethical practices appear to be so frequently used in place marketing?

9. Social marketing is one approach to achieving social change. What other methods are available? What advantages and disadvantages would social marketing have in attempting to reduce the amount of litter on the highways, compared with other approaches?

10. Marketing is defined as satisfying needs and wants through exchange processes. What exchanges occur in marketing nonprofit organizations such as a museum or the American Red Cross?

◼ KEY TERMS

Interactive marketing. Marketing by a service firm which recognizes that perceived service quality depends heavily on the quality of buyer-seller interaction.

Internal marketing. Marketing by a service firm to effectively train and motivate its customer-contact employees and all the supporting service people to work as a team to provide customer satisfaction.

Organization image. The way an individual or a group sees an organization.

Organization marketing. Activities undertaken to create, maintain, or change attitudes and behavior of target audiences toward an organization.

Person marketing. Activities undertaken to create, maintain, or change attitudes or behavior toward particular persons.

Place marketing. Activities undertaken to create, maintain, or change attitudes or behavior toward particular places.

Service. Any activity or benefit that one party can offer to another

that is essentially intangible and does not result in the ownership of anything.

Service inseparability. A major characteristic of services—they are produced and consumed at the same time and cannot be separated from their providers, whether the providers are people or machines.

Service intangibility. A major characteristic of services—they cannot be seen, tasted, felt, heard, or smelled before they are bought.

Service perishability. A major characteristic of services—they cannot be stored for later sale or use.

Service variability. A major characteristic of services—their quality may vary greatly, depending on who provides them and when, where, and how they are provided.

Social marketing. The design, implementation, and control of programs seeking to increase the acceptability of a social idea, cause, or practice among a target group.

◼ REFERENCES

1. See Paul Burka, "What They Teach You at Disney U.," *Fortune*, November 7, 1988, in a special advertising section following p. 176; Charles Leerhsen, "How Disney Does It," *Newsweek*, April 3, 1989, pp. 48–54; and Christopher Knowlton, "How Disney Keeps the Magic Going," *Fortune*, December 4, 1989, pp. 111–32.

2. See Norman Jonas, "The Hollow Corporation," *Business Week*, March 3, 1986, pp. 57–59; and Edward Prewitt and Sarah E. Morgenthau, "Flush Times for the Money Men," *Fortune*, June 8, 1987, pp. 192–94.

3. "Presto! The Convenience Industry: Making Life a Little Simpler," *Business Week*, April 27, 1987, p. 86.

4. See Leonard L. Berry, "Services Marketing Is Different," *Business*, May–June 1980, pp. 24–30; Eric Langeard, John E. G. Bateson, Christopher H. Lovelock, and Pierre Eiglier, *Services Marketing: New Insights from Consumers and Managers* (Cambridge, Mass.: Marketing Science Institute, 1981); Karl Albrecht and Ron Zemke, *Service America! Doing Business in the New Economy* (Homewood, IL: Dow-Jones-Irwin, 1985); Karl Albrecht, *At America's Service* (Homewood, Il: Dow-Jones Irwin, 1988); and William H. Davidow and Bro Uttal, *Total Customer Service: The Ultimate Weapon* (New York: Harper and Row, 1989).

5. Further classifications of services are described in Christo-

pher H. Lovelock, *Services Marketing* (Englewood Cliffs, NJ: Prentice Hall, 1984). Also see John E. Bateson, *Managing Services Marketing: Text and Readings* (Hinsdale, Il: Dryden Press, 1989).

6. See Theodore Levitt, "Marketing Intangible Products and Product Intangibles," *Harvard Business Review*, May–June, 1981, pp. 94–102.

7. For more discussion, see James L. Heskett, "Lessons in the Service Sector," *Harvard Business Review*, March–April 1987, pp. 122–124.

8. See Ray Lewis, "Whose Job Is Service Marketing?" *Advertising Age*, August 3, 1987, pp. 14, 20.

9. See W. Earl Sasser, "Match Supply and Demand in Service Industries," *Harvard Business Review*, November–December 1976, pp. 133–40.

10. See A. Parasuraman, Leonard L. Berry, and Valarie A. Zeithaml, "Service Firms Need More Marketing," *Business Horizons*, November–December 1983, pp. 28–31.

11. See Christian Gronroos, "A Service Quality Model and Its Marketing Implications," *European Journal of Marketing*, Vol. 18, No. 4, 1984, pp. 36–44.

12. For other examples, see Leonard Berry, Edwin F. Lefkowith, and Terry Clark, "In Services, What's in a Name?" *Harvard Business Review*, September–October 1988, pp. 28–30.

13. John Paul Newport, "American Express: Service that Sells," *Fortune*, November 20, 1989.

14. For more on service quality, see A. Parasuraman, Valarie A. Zeithaml, and Leonard L. Berry, "A Conceptual Model of Service Quality and Its Implications for Future Research," *Journal of Marketing*, Fall 1985, pp. 41–50; Valarie A. Zeithaml, Leonard L. Berry, and A. Parasuraman, "Communication and Control Processes in the Delivery of Service Quality," *Journal of Marketing*, April 1988, pp. 35–48; and Mary Jo Bitner, Bernard H. Booms, and Mary Stanfield Tetreault, "The Service Encounter: Diagnosing Favorable and Unfavorable Incidents," *Journal of Marketing*, January 1990, pp. 71–84.

15. Lori Kessler, "Corporate Image Advertising," *Advertising Age*, October 15, 1987, p. S1.

16. See Anne B. Fisher, "Spiffing Up the Corporate Image," *Fortune*, July 21, 1986, p. 69.

17. See Irving Rein, Philip Kotler, and Martin Stoller, *High Visibility* (New York: Dodd, Mead & Company, 1987), pp. 1–2.

18. See Michael Oneal, " 'Air' Jordan Has the Bulls Walking on a Cloud," *Business Week*, December 12, 1988, p. 124.

19. See Steven Colford, "Hail to the Image—Reagan Legacy: Marketing Tactics Change Politics," *Advertising Age*, June 27, 1988, pp. 3, 32; and Jack Honomichl, "How Reagan Took America's Pulse," *Advertising Age*, January 23, 1989, pp. 1, 25, 32.

20. See Philip Kotler and Gerald Zaltman, "Social Marketing: An Approach to Planned Social Change," *Journal of Marketing*, July 1971, pp. 3–12.

21. See Lenore Skenazy, "Ad Council Chief to Lure Media," *Advertising Age*, June 20, 1988, p. 37.

LIFELINE MAGAZINE: MARKET TARGETING
ON THE NONPROFIT FRONT

Sometimes target groups do not want to be reached. In that case, the only option is to communicate with those who can influence the target group. That's what the National Foundation for Alcoholism Communications, located in Seattle, plans to do with its new magazine, *Alcoholism-Codependency-Addiction Lifeline*.

The publication hit Waldenbooks' shelves in March of 1988. Billed as "America's answer book about alcoholism and addiction," the magazine focuses on prevention, treament, and recovery. "People and families in trouble with drugs and alcohol have many personal and pressing questions that are not being answered by public service announcements and government-sponsored campaigns," says Jerauld D. Miller, publisher and executive director of the foundation.

"Hundreds of thousands of Americans need help and answers and resources, not just political platitudes," he adds. "They need a publication with names and numbers and case histories from people who have successfully kicked their habits, and we intend to make this information available to every American who needs to know."

The magazine's difficulties rest in trying to reach some of these people—namely, the addicts or alcoholics themselves. Most people who have these dependencies either do not realize they have a problem or refuse to admit it exists, according to Bill Wipple, director of marketing and sales. "Our first marketing goal is to reach the addict," Wipple says. "But you can't reach the addict until he's reached the point of remorse."

This fact makes it almost impossible to reach most alcoholics or addicts when they need help the most. The foundation has thus decided to target *codependents* (those who live with addicts and alcoholics) and those recovering from the diseases. The principle is similar to the one adopted by Al-Anon in its relationship to Alcoholics Anonymous (AA), Wipple said. Once codependents know the facts about the diseases and how to deal with the people suffering from them, they can set the dependents on the road to recovery.

But the magazine has an edge on Al-Anon, he said. Many codependents will not attend the group's meetings for fear that the addict will find out. They can use a magazine in the privacy of offices or cars or when the dependent is not around. Besides providing education for codependents, the publishers hope that addicts will find the magazines and get the clue that at least somebody thinks all is not well, Wipple said.

However, codependents are not *Lifeline*'s only direct target audience. The publication is also designed with recovering alcoholics and addicts in mind, partly because these people can spot others suffering from the diseases. For those going through the recovery process, the magazine features "articles of hope" about people who have pulled themselves out of the drinking or drug-use cycle.

Wipple believes the magazine will sell, largely because of the way it looks. It's kind of like *People*, with the first issue displaying a picture of Elizabeth Taylor on the cover and her tales of addiction inside. Hopefully, once people are attracted to the celebrity cover, they will take note of the other articles within, including "10 Tips for Tempted Teens" and "Warning Signs of Relapse."

In addition to trying to sell the magazine to consumers, the foundation wants to sell it to ad agencies. To do so, the foundation emphasizes that recovering addicts and alcoholics are a strong target market, especially for health-oriented products. "These people have a new lease on life and usually become interested in other, more healthy habits after they've given up their addictions," Wipple explains.

More than 10 million books on alcoholism and other addictions were sold last year. Millions of phone calls are logged each year by hotlines, treatment programs, and self-help organizations. According to one Gallup survey, one out of every four American families has a member with a drug or drinking problem. Moreover, a survey conducted in 1987 by GMA Research Corp. indicated that among a sample of 100 recovering alcoholics and other dependents, more than 80 percent would buy *Lifeline*.

QUESTIONS

1. What are the target markets for *Lifeline* magazine? Are there other appropriate markets not mentioned in the case?

2. What are the objectives of the magazine? What are the objectives of the National Foundation for Alcoholism Communications?

3. If you were Bill Wipple, how would you approach advertising agencies and consumer-products companies to sell advertising space in *Lifeline*?

4. In what ways are *Lifeline*'s marketing challenges different from those faced by a profit-seeking firm in the private sector?

Source: Reprinted from Diane Schneidman, "New Magazine Targets A Segment That May Not Want to Be Reached," *Marketing News*, Vol. 21, Dec. 4, 1987, pp. 1, 24, published by the American Marketing Association.

Marketing and Society: Social Responsibility and Marketing Ethics

Generations of parents have trusted the health and well-being of their babies to Gerber baby foods. Gerber sells more than 1.3 billion jars of baby food each year, holding almost 70 percent of the market. But in 1986, the company's reputation was threatened when more than 250 customers in 30 states complained about finding glass fragments in Gerber baby food.

The company believed that these complaints were unfounded. Gerber plants are clean and modern, using many filters that would prevent such problems. No injuries from Gerber products were confirmed. Moreover, the Food & Drug Administration had looked at more than 40,000 jars of Gerber baby food without finding a single major problem. Gerber suspected that the glass was planted by the people making the complaints and seeking publicity or damages. Yet the complaints received widespread media coverage, and many retailers pulled Gerber products from their shelves. The state of Maryland forbade the sales of some Gerber baby foods, and other states considered such bans.

The considerable attention given to the complaints may have resulted from the "Tylenol scares," in which Tylenol capsules laced with cyanide had caused consumer deaths. At the time, product tampering was a major public issue and consumer concern.

Gerber wanted to act responsibly, but social responsibility issues are rarely clear-cut. Some analysts believed that, to ensure consumer safety, Gerber should quickly recall all its baby food products from store shelves until the problem was resolved. That was how the makers of such products as Tylenol, Contac, and Gatorade had reacted to tampering scares for their products. But Gerber executives did not think that a recall was best either for consumers or for the company. After a similar scare in 1984, the company had recalled some 700,000 jars of baby food and had advertised heavily to reassure consumers. The isolated incident turned out to be the result of normal breakage during shipment. The recall cost Gerber millions of dollars in expenses and lost profits; the advertising caused unnecessary alarm and inconvenience to consumers. The company concluded that it had overreacted in its desire to be socially responsible.

The second time, therefore, Gerber decided to do nothing, at least in the short-run. It refused to recall any products—in fact, it filed a $150 million suit against Maryland to stop the ban on the sales of Gerber products. It suspended its advertising, monitored sales and consumer confidence, reassured nervous retailers, and waited to see what would happen. This wait-and-see strategy could have been risky. If the complaints turned out to be well-founded and Gerber's failure to act quickly were to cause consumer injuries or deaths, Gerber's reputation would be seriously damaged.

Finally, when research showed that consumer concern was spreading, Gerber aired a few television ads noting its concern about "rumors you may have heard" and assuring buyers that Gerber products "meet the highest standards." The company also mailed letters to about two million new mothers, assuring them of Gerber's quality. In the end, the scare resulted in little long-term consumer alarm or inconvenience, and it caused only a temporary dip in Gerber's market share and reputation.

However, the question lingers: Should Gerber have immediately recalled its products to prevent even the remote chance of consumer injury? Perhaps. But in many matters of social responsibility, the best course of action is often unclear.[1]

Responsible marketers discover what consumers want and respond with the right products, priced to give good value to buyers and profit to the producer. The *marketing concept* is a philosophy of service and mutual gain. Its practice leads the economy by an invisible hand to satisfy the many and changing needs of millions of consumers.

Not all marketers, however, follow the marketing concept. In fact, some companies use questionable marketing practices. And some marketing actions that seem innocent in themselves strongly affect the larger society. Consider the sale of cigarettes. Ordinarily, companies should be free to sell cigarettes and smokers free to buy them. But this transaction affects the public interest. First, the smoker may be shortening his or her own life. Second, smoking places a burden on the smoker's family and on society at large. Third, other people around the smoker may have to inhale the smoke and may suffer discomfort and harm. This is not to say that cigarettes should be banned. Rather, it shows that private transactions may involve larger questions of public policy.

This chapter examines the social effects of private marketing practices. We look at several questions. What are the most frequent social criticisms of marketing? What steps have private citizens taken to curb marketing ills? What steps have legislators and government agencies taken to curb marketing ills? What steps have enlightened companies taken to carry out socially responsible and ethical marketing? Let's examine the effects of marketing on each of these.

SOCIAL CRITICISMS OF MARKETING

Marketing receives much criticism. Some of this criticism is justified; much is not.[2] Social critics claim that certain marketing practices hurt individual consumers, society as a whole, and other business firms.

Marketing's Impact on Individual Consumers

Consumers have many concerns about how well the American marketing system serves their interests. Surveys usually show that consumers hold slightly unfavorable attitudes toward marketing practices.[3] One consumer survey found that consumers are most worried about high prices, poor-quality and dangerous products, misleading advertising claims, and several other marketing related problems (see Figure 23-1). Consumer advocates, government agencies, and other critics have accused marketing of harming consumers through high prices, deceptive practices, high-pressure selling, shoddy or unsafe products, planned obsolescence, and poor service to disadvantaged consumers.

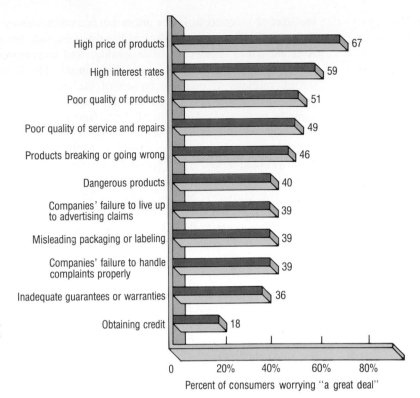

FIGURE 23-1
Survey of consumer concerns
Source: See Myrlie Evers, "Consumerism in the Eighties," reprinted with permission from the August 1983 issue of *Public Relations Journal*, copyright 1983, pp. 24–26. Also see "The Public Is Willing to Take on Business," *Business Week*, May 29, 1989, p. 29.

Figure content labels:
- High price of products — 67
- High interest rates — 59
- Poor quality of products — 51
- Poor quality of service and repairs — 49
- Products breaking or going wrong — 46
- Dangerous products — 40
- Companies' failure to live up to advertising claims — 39
- Misleading packaging or labeling — 39
- Companies' failure to handle complaints properly — 39
- Inadequate guarantees or warranties — 36
- Obtaining credit — 18

0   20%   40%   60%   80%
Percent of consumers worrying "a great deal"

High Prices

Many critics charge that the American marketing system causes prices to be higher than they would be under more "sensible" systems. They point to three factors—*high costs of distribution, high advertising and promotion costs,* and *excessive markups.*

HIGH COSTS OF DISTRIBUTION   A longstanding charge is that greedy middlemen mark up prices beyond the value of their services. Critics charge either that there are too many middlemen or that middlemen are inefficient and poorly run, provide unnecessary or duplicate services, and practice poor management and planning. As a result, distribution costs too much and consumers pay for these excessive costs in the form of higher prices.

How do retailers answer these charges? They argue as follows: First, middlemen do work that would otherwise have to be done by manufacturers or consumers. Second, the rising markup reflects improved services that consumers themselves want—more convenience, larger stores and assortment, longer store hours, return privileges, and others. Third, the costs of operating stores keep rising and force retailers to raise their prices. Fourth, retail competition is so intense that margins are actually quite low. For example, after taxes, supermarket chains are typically left with barely 1 percent profit on their sales.

HIGH ADVERTISING AND PROMOTION COSTS   Modern marketing is also accused of pushing up prices because of heavy advertising and sales promotion. For example, a dozen tablets of a heavily-promoted brand of aspirin sell for the same price as 100 tablets of less-promoted brands. Differentiated products—cosmetics, detergents, toiletries—include promotion and packaging costs that can amount to 40 percent or more of the manufacturer's price to the retailer. Critics charge that much of the packaging and promotion adds only psychological rather than functional value to the product. Retailers use additional promotion—advertising, displays, and sweepstakes—that add several cents more to retail prices.

Marketers answer these charges in several ways. First, consumers *want* more than the merely functional qualities of products. They also want psychological benefits such as feeling wealthy, beautiful, or special. Consumers can usually buy functional versions of products at lower prices but are often willing to pay more for products that also provide desired psychological benefits. Second, branding gives buyers confidence. A brand name implies a certain quality, and consumers are willing to pay for well-known brands even if they cost a little more. Third, heavy advertising is needed to inform millions of potential buyers of the merits of a brand. If consumers want to know what is available on the market, they must expect manufacturers to spend large sums of money on advertising. Fourth, heavy advertising and promotion are necessary for a firm when its competitors are doing it. The business would lose ''share of mind'' if it did not match competitive spending. At the same time, companies are cost-conscious about promotion and try to spend their money wisely. Finally, heavy sales promotion is needed from time to time because goods are produced ahead of demand in a mass-production economy. Special incentives have to be offered in order to sell inventories.

EXCESSIVE MARKUPS   Critics also charge that some companies mark up goods excessively. They point to the drug industry, where a pill costing 5 cents to make may cost the consumer 40 cents. They point to the pricing tactics of funeral homes that prey on the emotions of bereaved relatives. They point to the high charges of television repair and auto repair people.

Marketers respond that most businesses try to deal fairly with consumers because they want repeat business. Most consumer abuses are unintentional. When shady marketers do take advantage of consumers, they should be reported to Better Business Bureaus and other consumer protection groups. Marketers also respond that consumers often do not understand the reason for high markups. For example, pharmaceutical markups must cover the costs of purchasing, promoting, and distributing existing medicines plus the high research and development costs of finding new medicines.

Deceptive Practices

Marketers sometimes are accused of deceptive practices that lead consumers to believe they will get more value than they actually do. Deceptive practices fall into three groups. *Deceptive pricing* includes such practices as falsely advertising ''factory'' or ''wholesale'' prices or advertising a large price reduction from a phony high list price. *Deceptive promotion* includes such practices as overstating the product's features or performance, luring the customer to the store for a bargain that is out of stock, or running rigged

Some retailers use high markups, but the higher prices cover services that consumers want—assortment, convenience, personal service, and return privileges.

contests. *Deceptive packaging* includes exaggerating package contents through subtle design, not filling the package to the top, using misleading labeling, and describing size in misleading terms.

Deceptive practices have led to legislation and other consumer protection actions. In 1938, the Wheeler-Lea Act gave the FTC power to regulate "unfair or deceptive acts or practices." The FTC has published several guidelines listing deceptive practices. The toughest problem is defining what is "deceptive." Shell Oil advertised that Super Shell with platformate gave more mileage than the same gasoline without platformate. Now this was true, but what Shell did not say is that almost *all* gasoline includes platformate. Its defense was that it had never claimed that platformate was found only in Shell gasoline. But even though the message was literally true, the FTC felt that the ad's *intent* was to deceive.

Marketers argue that most companies avoid deceptive practices because such practices harm their business in the long run. If consumers do not get what they expect, they will switch to more reliable products. In addition, consumers usually protect themselves from deception. Most consumers recognize a marketer's selling intent and are careful when they buy, sometimes to the point of not believing completely true product claims. Theodore Levitt claims that some advertising puffery is bound to occur—and that it may even be desirable:

> There is hardly a company that would not go down in ruin if it refused to provide fluff, because nobody will buy pure functionality. . . . Worse, it denies . . . man's honest needs and values. . . . Without distortion, embellishment, and elaboration, life would be drab, dull, anguished, and at its existential worst. . . .[4]

High-Pressure Selling

Salespeople are sometimes accused of high-pressure selling that persuades people to buy goods they had no thought of buying. It is often said that encyclopedias, insurance, real estate, and jewelry are *sold*, not *bought*. Salespeople are trained to deliver smooth canned talks to entice purchase. They sell hard because sales contests promise big prizes to those who sell the most.

Marketers know that buyers can often be talked into buying unwanted or unneeded things. Laws require door-to-door salespeople to announce that they are selling a product. Buyers also have a "three-day cooling-off period" in which they can cancel a contract after rethinking it. In addition, consumers can complain to Better Business Bureaus or state consumer protection agencies when they feel that undue selling pressure has been applied.

Shoddy or Unsafe Products

Another criticism is that products lack the quality they should have. One complaint is that products are not made well. Automobiles bear the brunt of many such complaints— it seems that every new car has something wrong with it. Consumers grumble about rattles and pings, misalignments, dents, leaking, and creaking. Complaints have also been lodged against home and auto repair services, appliances, and clothing.

A second complaint is that some products deliver little benefit. Consumers got a shock on hearing that dry breakfast cereal may have little nutritional value. One nutrition expert told a Senate subcommittee: "In short, [cereals] fatten but do little to prevent malnutrition. . . . The average cereal . . . fails as a complete meal even with milk added."[5] The expert added that consumers could often get more nutrition by eating the cereal package instead of the contents.

A third complaint concerns product safety. For years, Consumers Union—the organization that publishes *Consumer Reports*—has reported various hazards in tested products: electrical dangers in appliances, carbon monoxide poisoning from room heaters, injury risks from lawn mowers, and faulty automobile design.[6] The organization's testing and other activities have helped consumers to make better buying decisions and businesses to eliminate product flaws (see Marketing Highlight 23–1). Product quality has been a

WHEN *CONSUMER REPORTS* TALKS, BUYERS LISTEN— AND SO DO COMPANIES

Whether they're buying automobiles or life insurance, drain cleaner or refrigerators—or practically anything else—millions of shoppers won't plunk down their money until they consult *Consumer Reports*. For 51 years, the publication of Consumers Union has been a fiercely independent arbiter of quality goods and an ardent advocate of consumer rights. It has published CU's ratings of thousands of products and services without ever losing a libel suit. And today its monthly circulation is at an all-time high of 3.8 million.

A 106-member technical team puts products through their paces at CU's headquarters in Mount Vernon, NY. When they can, they use the same tests industry uses. They check the laundering power of washing machines, for example, by washing presoiled fabric swatches and measuring their brightness with optical instruments. If no standard tests exist, *Consumer Reports* invents them. To rate facial tissues, CU's technical team built a "sneeze machine" that squirts a controlled spray of water and air through a tissue mounted on embroidery hoops.

CU describes its tests in detail when it rates products. But those explanations don't always placate the manufacturer whose product comes in last. If a company isn't happy with its rating, CU responds with an invitation to visit its labs.

Many companies have made changes in their products after getting a bad rating from CU. Although Whirlpool chafed at criticism that its washing-machine design made repair too difficult, on its new models the cabinet pops off to allow access to important parts.

In its April, 1973, issue, *Consumer Reports* rejected an entire category of products—microwave ovens—because doors on all 14 models tested were leaking radiation. Since then, ovenmakers have changed their designs. Today, "there's very little leakage around those doors," says CU technical director R. David Pittle.

Although *Consumer Reports* remains CU's major endeavor, the organization is branching out. In the past two years, it has launched a travel newsletter, produced six home videocassettes, spruced up its *Penny Power* children's magazine, and formed a book-publishing company. Since January, CU has been selling dealer's-cost listings for most auto models

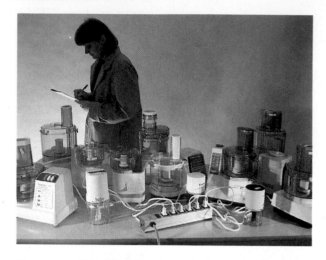

Consumers Union's 106-member technical team puts products through their paces.

and options. Its media push also includes a thrice-weekly syndicated newspaper column, plus radio and television spots. All this has helped CU's bottom line. Last year it earned $3.4 million.

Prosperity has not diluted CU's activism. Founded by labor unionists in the 1930s, it was among the first organizations to urge consumers to boycott goods made in Nazi Germany. Now *Consumer Reports* is alarmed that many Americans are slipping into poverty. So it is kicking off a three-part series on the working poor. But will the outspoken judge of what's good comment on how well U.S. manufacturers stack up against the Japanese? No way, says Pittle. "Our purpose is to provide an objective evaluation of a product—regardless of who made it."

Source: Mimi Bluestone, "When *Consumer Reports* Talks, Buyers Listen—and So Do Companies," *Business Week*, June 8, 1987, p. 135. Reprinted by permission.

problem for several reasons, including manufacturer indifference, increased production complexity, poorly trained labor, and poor quality control.

On the other hand, most manufacturers *want* to produce quality goods. Consumers who are unhappy with one of a firm's products may avoid their other products and talk other consumers into doing the same. The way a company deals with product-quality and safety problems can damage or help its reputation. Companies selling poor-quality or unsafe products risk damaging conflicts with consumer groups. Moreover, unsafe products can result in product-liability suits and large awards for damages.[7]

Planned Obsolescence

Critics have also charged that some producers follow a program of **planned obsolescence,** causing their products to become obsolete before they should actually need replacement. In many cases, producers have been accused of continually changing consumer concepts of acceptable styles in order to encourage more and earlier buying. An obvious example is constantly changing clothing fashions. Producers have also been accused of holding back attractive functional features, then introducing them later to make older models obsolete. Critics claim that this practice is found in the consumer electronics industry. Finally, producers have been accused of using materials and components that will break, wear, rust, or rot sooner than they should. For example, many drapery manufacturers are using a higher percentage of rayon in their drapes. They argue that rayon reduces the price of the drapes and has better holding power. Critics claim that using more rayon causes the drapes to fall apart sooner.

Marketers respond that consumers *like* style changes. They get tired of the old goods and want a new look in fashion or a new design in cars. No one has to buy the new look, and if too few people like it, it will simply fail. Companies frequently withhold new features when they are not fully tested, when they add more cost to the product than consumers are willing to pay, and for other good reasons. But they do so at the risk of having a competitor introduce the new feature and steal the market. Moreover, companies often put in new materials to lower their costs and prices. They do not design their products to break down earlier, because they do not want to lose their customers to other brands. Thus, much of so-called "planned obsolescence" is the working of the competitive and technological forces in a free society—forces that lead to ever-improving goods and services.

Poor Service to Disadvantaged Consumers

Finally, the American marketing system has been accused of poorly serving disadvantaged consumers. Critics claim that the urban poor often have to shop in smaller stores that carry inferior goods and charge higher prices. The former chairman of the Federal Trade Commission (FTC), Paul Rand Dixon, summarized a Washington, D.C., study as follows:

> The poor pay more—nearly twice as much—for appliances and furniture sold in Washington's low-income area stores . . . Goods purchased for $100 at wholesale sold for $225 in the low-income stores compared with $159 in the general market stores. . . . Installment credit is a major marketing factor in selling to the poor . . . some low-income market retailers imposed effective annual finance charges as high as 33 percent. . . .[8]

Yet the merchants' profits were not too high:

> Low income market retailers have markedly higher costs, partly because of bad debt expenses, but to a greater extent because of higher selling, wage, and commission costs. These expenses reflect in part greater use of home demonstration selling, and expenses associated with the collection and processing of installment contracts. Thus, although their markups are often two or three times higher than general market retailers, on the average low-income market retailers do not make particularly high profits.[9]

Clearly, better marketing systems must be built in low-income areas—one hope is to get large retailers to open outlets in low-income areas. Moreover, low-income people clearly need consumer protection. The FTC has taken action against merchants who advertise false values, sell old merchandise as new, or charge too much for credit. It is also trying to make it harder for merchants to win court judgments against low-income people who were wheedled into buying something.

Marketing's Impact on Society as a Whole

The American marketing system has been accused of adding to several "evils" in American society at large. Advertising has been a special target—so much so that the American Association of Advertising Agencies recently launched a campaign to defend advertising against what it felt to be common but untrue criticisms (see Marketing Highlight 23–2).

False Wants and Too Much Materialism

Critics have charged that the marketing system urges too much interest in material possessions. People are judged by what they *own* rather than by what they *are*. To be considered successful, people must own a suburban home, two cars, and the latest

ADVERTISING: ANOTHER WORD FOR FREEDOM OF CHOICE

During the past few years, the American Association of Advertising Agencies has run a campaign featuring ads such as these to counter common criticism of advertising. The association is concerned about research findings of negative public attitudes toward advertising. Two-thirds of the public recognizes that advertising provides helpful buying information, but a significant portion feels that advertising is exaggerated or misleading. The association believes that its ad campaign will increase general advertising credibility and make advertisers' messages more effective. Several media have agreed to run the ads as a public service.

The American Association of Advertising Agencies runs ads to counter common advertising criticisms.

clothes and appliances. And indeed, this drive for wealth and possessions appears to have increased in recent years:

> Money, money, money is the incantation of today. Bewitched by an epidemic of money enchantment, Americans wriggle in a St. Vitus's dance of materialism unseen since the Gilded Age of the Roaring Twenties. Under the blazing sun of money, all other values shine palely. . . . The evidence is everywhere. Open the scarlet covers of the Saks Fifth Avenue Christmas Catalog, for starters, and look at what Santa Claus offers today's young family, from Dad's $1,650 ostrich-skin briefcase and Mom's $39,500 fur coat to Junior's $4,000, 15-mph miniature Mercedes.[10]

In a recent survey of teenage girls, 39 percent listed shopping as their favorite pastime, far ahead of dating, which placed sixth. In another poll, 80 percent of college freshmen stated that it was very important for them to be quite well-off financially, against only 40 percent who said developing a meaningful philosophy of life was an important objective.[11] Although some social scientists are noting a return to more basic values and social commitment in the 1990s, our infatuation with material things will continue.[12]

Critics do not view this interest in things as a natural state of mind but rather as a matter of false wants created by marketing. Business hires Madison Avenue to stimulate people's desires for goods, and Madison Avenue uses the mass media to create materialistic models of the good life. People work harder to earn the necessary money. Their purchases increase the output of American industry, and industry in turn uses Madison Avenue to stimulate more desire for the industrial output. Thus, marketing is seen as creating false wants that benefit industry more than they benefit consumers.

These criticisms, however, overstate the power of business to create needs. People have strong defenses against advertising and other marketing tools. Marketers are most effective when they appeal to existing wants rather than when they attempt to create new ones. Furthermore, people seek information when making important purchases and do not often rely on single sources. Even minor purchases, which may be affected by advertising messages, lead to repeat purchases only if the product performs as promised. Finally, the high failure rate of new products shows that companies are not able to control demand.

On a deeper level, our wants and values are influenced not only by marketers, but also by family, peer groups, religion, ethnic background, and education. If Americans are highly materialistic, these values arose out of basic socialization processes that go much deeper than business and mass media could produce alone.

Too Few Social Goods

Business has been accused of overselling private goods at the expense of public goods. As private goods increase, they require more public services that are usually not forthcoming. For example, an increase in automobile ownership (private good) requires more highways, traffic control, parking spaces, and police services (public goods). The overselling of private goods results in "social costs." For cars, the social costs include excessive traffic congestion, air pollution, and deaths and injuries from car accidents.

A way must be found to restore a balance between private and public goods. Producers could be made to bear the full social costs of their operations. For example, the government could require automobile manufacturers to build cars with additional safety features and better pollution-control systems. Automakers would then raise their prices to cover extra costs. However, if buyers found the price of some cars too high, the producers of these cars would disappear, and demand would move to those producers that could support the sum of the private and social costs.

Cultural Pollution

Critics charge the marketing system with creating *cultural pollution*. People's senses are constantly being assaulted by advertising. Commercials interrupt serious programs; pages of ads obscure printed matter; billboards mar beautiful scenery. These interruptions continuously pollute people's minds with messages of materialism, sex, power, or status. Although most people do not find advertising overly annoying (some even think it is the best part of television programming), some critics call for sweeping changes.

Marketers answer the charges of "commercial noise" with these arguments: First, they hope that their ads reach primarily the target audience. But because of mass-communication channels, some ads are bound to reach people who have no interest in the product and are therefore bored or annoyed. People who buy magazines addressed to their interests—such as *Vogue* or *Fortune*—rarely complain about the ads because the magazines advertise products of interest. Second, ads make television and radio free media and keep down the costs of magazines and newspapers. Most people think commercials are a small price to pay.

Too Much Political Power

Another criticism is that business wields too much political power. There are "oil," "tobacco," and "auto" senators who support an industry's interests against the public interest. Advertisers are accused of holding too much power over the mass media, limiting their freedom to report independently and objectively. One critic has asked:

Cultural pollution: People's senses are sometimes assaulted by commercial messages.

"How can *Life* . . . and *Reader's Digest* afford to tell the truth about the scandalously low nutritional value of most packaged foods . . . when these magazines are being subsidized by such advertisers as General Foods, Kellogg's, Nabisco, and General Mills? . . . The answer is *they cannot and do not*."[13]

American industries do promote and protect their interests. They have a right to representation in Congress and the mass media, although their influence can become too great. Fortunately, many powerful business interests once thought to be untouchable have been tamed in the public interest. Standard Oil was broken up in 1911, and the meatpacking industry was disciplined in the early 1900s after exposures by Upton Sinclair. Ralph Nader caused legislation that forced the automobile industry to build more safety into its cars, and the Surgeon General's Report resulted in cigarette companies putting health warnings on their packages. Moreover, because the media receive advertising revenues from many different advertisers, it is easier to resist the influence of one or a few of them. Too much business power tends to result in counter forces that check and offset these powerful interests.

Marketing's Impact on Other Businesses

Critics also charge that a company's marketing practices can harm other companies and reduce competition. Three problems are involved: acquisitions of competitors, marketing practices that create barriers to entry, and unfair competitive marketing practices.

Critics claim that firms are harmed and competition reduced when companies expand by acquiring competitors rather than by developing their own new products. In the food industry alone during the past few years, R. J. Reynolds acquired Nabisco Brands, Philip Morris bought General Foods and Kraft, Procter & Gamble gobbled up Richardson-Vick and Noxell, Nestle absorbed Carnation, and Quaker Oats bought Stokely-Van Camp.[14] These and large acquisitions in other industries have caused concern that vigorous young competitors will be absorbed and that competition will be reduced.

Acquisition is a complex subject. Acquisitions can sometimes be good for society. The acquiring company may gain economies of scale that lead to lower costs and lower prices. A well-managed company may take over a poorly managed company and improve its efficiency. An industry that was not very competitive might become more competitive after the acquisition. But acquisitions can also be harmful and are therefore closely regulated by the government.

Critics have also charged that marketing practices adds barriers to the entry of new companies into an industry. Large marketing companies can use heavy promotion spending, patents, and tie-ups of suppliers or dealers to keep out or drive out competitors. People concerned with antitrust regulation recognize that some barriers are the natural result of the economic advantages of doing business on a large scale. Other barriers could be challenged by existing and new laws. For example, some critics have proposed a progressive tax on advertising spending to reduce the role of selling costs as a major barrier to entry.

Finally, some firms have in fact used unfair competitive marketing practices with the intention of hurting or destroying other firms. They may set their prices below costs, threaten to cut off business with suppliers, or discourage the buying of a competitor's products. Various laws work to prevent such predatory competition. It is difficult, however, to prove that the intent or action was really predatory. In the classic A&P case, this large retailer was able to charge lower prices than small "mom and pop" grocery stores. The question is whether this was unfair competition or the healthy competition of a more efficient retailer against the less efficient.

CITIZENS AND PUBLIC ACTIONS TO REGULATE MARKETING

Because some people have viewed business as the cause of many economic and social ills, grass-roots movements have arisen from time to time to keep business in line. The two major movements have been *consumerism* and *environmentalism*.

Consumerism   American business firms have been the target of organized consumer movements on three occasions. The first consumer movement took place in the early 1900s. It was fueled by rising prices, Upton Sinclair's writings on conditions in the meat industry, and scandals in the drug industry. The second consumer movement, in the mid-1930s, was sparked by an upturn in consumer prices during the Depression and another drug scandal.

The third movement began in the 1960s. Consumers had become better educated, products had become more complex and hazardous, and people were unhappy with American institutions. Ralph Nader appeared, forcing many issues, and other well-known writers accused big business of wasteful and unethical practices. President John F. Kennedy declared that consumers have the right to safety, to be informed, to choose, and to be heard. Congress investigated certain industries and proposed consumer-protection legislation. Since then, many consumer groups have been organized and several consumer laws have been passed. The consumer movement has spread internationally and has become very strong in Scandinavia and the Low Countries.[15]

But what is the consumer movement? **Consumerism** is an organized movement of citizens and government to improve the rights and power of buyers in relation to sellers. Traditional sellers' rights include:

- The right to introduce any product in any size and style, provided it is not hazardous to personal health or safety; or, if it is, to include proper warnings and controls.
- The right to charge any price for the product, provided no discrimination exists among similar kinds of buyers.
- The right to spend any amount to promote the product, provided it is not defined as unfair competition.
- The right to use any product message, provided it is not misleading or dishonest in content or execution.
- The right to use any buying incentive schemes, provided they are not unfair or misleading.

Traditional buyers' rights include:

- The right not to buy a product that is offered for sale.
- The right to expect the product to be safe.
- The right to expect the product to perform as claimed.

Nutrition information

Product freshness information

Ingredients

Consumer desire for more information led to putting ingredients, nutrition, and dating information on product labels.

Comparing these rights, many believe that the balance of power lies on the sellers' side. True, the buyer can refuse to buy. But critics believe that the buyer has too little information, education, and protection to make wise decisions when facing sophisticated sellers. Consumer advocates call for the following additional consumer rights:

- The right to be well-informed about important aspects of the product.
- The right to be protected against questionable products and marketing practices.
- The right to influence products and marketing practices in ways that will improve the "quality of life."

Each proposed right has led to more specific proposals by consumerists. The right to be informed includes the right to know the true interest on a loan (truth-in-lending), the true cost per unit of a brand (unit pricing), the ingredients in a product (ingredient labeling), the nutrition in foods (nutritional labeling), product freshness (open dating), and the true benefits of a product (truth-in-advertising). Proposals related to consumer protection include strengthening consumer rights in cases of business fraud, requiring greater product safety, and giving more power to government agencies. Proposals relating to quality of life include controlling the ingredients that go into certain products (detergents) and packaging (soft-drink containers), reducing the level of advertising "noise," and putting consumer representatives on company boards to protect consumer interests.

Consumers have not only the *right* but also the *responsibility* to protect themselves instead of leaving this function to someone else. Consumers who believe they got a bad deal have several remedies available, including writing to the company president or to the media; contacting federal, state, or local agencies; and going to small-claims courts.

Environmentalism While consumerists consider whether the marketing system is efficiently serving consumer wants, environmentalists are concerned with marketing's effects on the environment and at the costs of serving consumer needs and wants. They are concerned with damage to the ecosystem caused by strip mining, forest depletion, acid rain, loss of the ozone layer in the atmosphere, toxic wastes, and litter; with the loss of recreational areas; and with the increase in health problems caused by bad air, polluted water, and chemically treated food. These concerns are the basis for **environmentalism**—an organized movement of concerned citizens and government to protect and improve people's living environment.

Environmentalists are not against marketing and consumption; they simply want people and organizations to operate with more care for the environment. The marketing system's goal should not be to maximize consumption, consumer choice, or consumer satisfaction. The marketing system's goal should be to maximize life quality. And "life quality" means not only the quantity and quality of consumer goods and services, but also the quality of the environment. Environmentalists want environmental costs included in producer and consumer decision making.

Environmentalism has hit some industries hard. Steel companies and public utilities have had to invest billions of dollars in pollution-control equipment and costlier fuels. The auto industry has had to introduce expensive emission controls in cars. The packaging industry has had to find ways to reduce litter. The gasoline industry has had to create new low-lead and no-lead gasolines. These industries often resent environmental regulations, especially when imposed too rapidly to allow companies to make proper adjustments. These companies have absorbed large costs and have passed them on to buyers.

Thus, marketers' lives have become more complicated. Marketers must check into the ecological properties of their products and packaging. They must raise prices to cover environmental costs, knowing that the product will be harder to sell. Yet environmental issues have become so important in our society that there is no turning back to the time when few managers worried about the effects of product and marketing decisions on environmental quality. Many analysts view the 1990s as the "Earth Decade," in which protection of the natural environment will be the major issue facing people around the world. Companies have responded with "green marketing"—developing ecologically safer products, recyclable and biodegradable packaging, better pollution controls, and more energy-efficient operations (see Marketing Highlight 23-3).

Public Actions to Regulate Marketing

Citizen concerns about marketing practices will usually lead to public attention and legislative proposals. New bills will be debated—many will be defeated, others will be modified, and a few will become workable laws.

FIGURE 23-2
Major marketing decision areas that may be called into question under the law

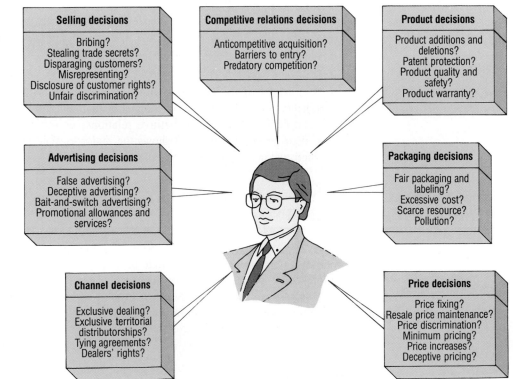

Selling decisions

Bribing?
Stealing trade secrets?
Disparaging customers?
Misrepresenting?
Disclosure of customer rights?
Unfair discrimination?

Competitive relations decisions

Anticompetitive acquisition?
Barriers to entry?
Predatory competition?

Product decisions

Product additions and deletions?
Patent protection?
Product quality and safety?
Product warranty?

Advertising decisions

False advertising?
Deceptive advertising?
Bait-and-switch advertising?
Promotional allowances and services?

Packaging decisions

Fair packaging and labeling?
Excessive cost?
Scarce resource?
Pollution?

Channel decisions

Exclusive dealing?
Exclusive territorial distributorships?
Tying agreements?
Dealers' rights?

Price decisions

Price fixing?
Resale price maintenance?
Price discrimination?
Minimum pricing?
Price increases?
Deceptive pricing?

THE NEW ENVIRONMENTALISM AND "GREEN MARKETING"

On Earth Day, 1970, a newly emerging environmentalism movement made its first large-scale effort to educate Americans about the dangers of pollution. This was a tough task: At the time, most Americans weren't all that interested in environmental problems. Although the environmental activism of the 1960s produced some important results—such as the Environmental Protection Act and the Clean Air and Clean Waters Acts—most of the public still viewed environmentalists as a fringe group and environmentalism as a "counterculture" movement. And many corporations strongly opposed what they saw as unrealistic environmental regulations, restrictions, deadlines, and penalties proposed by "special interest loonies."

Earth Day, 1990, however, was an entirely different proposition. Today, environmentalism has broad public support. Polls show that 76 percent of all Americans consider themselves to be environmentalists. Some 62 percent of Americans believe that environmental pollution is a very serious threat, up from 44 percent in 1984; 82 percent think that air and water pollution will plague us more than any other problem during the next 25 to 50 years. People hear and read daily about a growing list of environmental problems—global warming, acid rain, depletion of the ozone layer, air and water pollution, hazardous waste disposal, the buildup of solid wastes—and they are now calling for solutions.

Thus, Earth Day, 1990, became a nationwide cause, punctuated by articles in major magazines and newspapers, prime time television extravaganzas, and countless events in large cities and small towns around the country. Major companies, eager to show their corporate concern, ran special Earth Day advertisements and contributed dollars, equipment, and manpower to support Earth Day events. Many trend spotters believe that Earth Day, 1990, was just the start of an entire "Earth Decade" in which environmentalism will become a massive worldwide force.

The new environmentalism is causing many consumers to reconsider the products they buy and from whom they buy them. Several recent polls show that consumers are willing to spend more and to give up convenience in order to buy environmentally safe products. These changing consumer attitudes have sparked a major new marketing thrust—*green marketing*—the rush by companies to develop and market "environmentally friendly" products. Green marketing began in the early 1980s in Europe with the sale of "green" products—new types of disposable diapers, detergents, batteries, aerosols, and other products that cause less damage to the environment. The movement grew quickly and is now catching on in the U.S.

Procter & Gamble, whose products alone account for about 1 percent of the nation's solid wastes, provides a good example of the new wave of green marketing. It now packages Tide, Bold, Cheer, Dreft, Dash, Bounce, and Downy in recycled paper and has redesigned Crisco Oil bottles so that 28 percent less plastic holds the same amount of oil. P&G now makes its diapers without the chlorine-bleached paper pulp that causes pollution during production, and it will soon offer phsophate-free detergents. The company is also introducing many of its cleaning products in "Enviro-paks"—refill containers that are less bulky and use 70 to 80 percent less plastic.

McDonald's is also "turning green." It used to purchase Coca-Cola syrup in plastic bags encased in cardboard, but now the syrup is delivered like gasoline, pumped directly from tank trucks into storage vats at restaurants—the change saves 68 million pounds of packaging a year. All napkins in McDonald's restaurants are made from recycled paper, as is the paper in its carry-out drink trays and even the stationary used at headquarters. For a company the size of McDonald's, even small changes can make a big difference—making its drinking straws 20 percent lighter saves the company 1 million pounds of waste per year. Finally, McDonald's has also mounted a consumer education campaign to convince consumers that its polystyrene packaging, which is 100 percent recyclable, is better for the environment than paper.

Retailers are jumping onto the "green" bandwagon. For example, Wal-Mart is pressuring its 7,000 suppliers to provide it with more recycled or recyclable products. In its stores, it runs videos to help educate customers and flags environmentally friendly products with green and white shelf tags. Loblaw, the $10 billion Canadian grocery-store chain,

---

Many of the laws that affect marketing are listed in Chapter 3. The task is to translate these laws into the language that marketing executives understand as they make decisions about competitive relations, products, price, promotion, and channels of distribution. Figure 23-2 shows the major legal issues facing marketing management when making decisions.

BUSINESS ACTIONS TOWARD SOCIALLY RESPONSIBLE MARKETING

At first, many companies opposed consumerism and environmentalism. They thought the criticisms were either unfair or unimportant. But by now, most companies have grown to accept the new consumer rights in principle. They might oppose some pieces of legislation as inappropriate ways to solve certain consumer problems, but they recognize the consumer's right to information and protection. Many of these companies have

WE'VE GOT
TO STOP
TREATING
OUR GARBAGE
LIKE
GARBAGE.

The bottle may be empty, yet
it's anything but trash. In fact, this
empty bottle is actually full of
potential. Thanks to recycling.

Over 20% of all plastic soft
drink containers are already
being recycled into additional
consumer and industrial products
and the demand for recycled
plastic is growing.

At Du Pont, we're making sure
this growth continues. Together
with Waste Management Inc.,
we've pioneered the country's
largest and most comprehensive
plastic recycling program. In this,
its first year, the operation will
recycle more than 80 million
pounds of plastic.

With recycling, we believe that
plastic will be increasingly appre-
ciated for filling valuable human
needs instead of valuable land.

At Du Pont, our dedication to
quality makes the things that make
a difference.

DU PONT
BETTER THINGS FOR BETTER LIVING

Corporate environmentalism: Enlightened companies are taking action not because someone is forcing them to, but because it is the right thing to do.

recently introduced a "Green" line of environmentally safe products, backed by a $3 million promotional campaign. The 100 item line includes biodegradable diapers, bathroom tissue made from recycled paper, and foam plates made without ozone-destroying gasses. In its Ontario stores alone, the chain sold $5 million worth of Green products in a single month. It's now thinking of introducing the line in its U.S. stores, too.

Thus, promoting environmentally safe products has ballooned into a big business. In fact, some environmentalists

and regulators are concerned that companies may be going overboard with their environmental pitches. Terms like "re-cyclable," "degradable," and "environmentally friendly" are not yet well defined, and such environmental claims might be exploited or distorted in the same way that food health claims have recently been abused. Overeager green-marketing campaigns have already been attacked in Britain and Canada by environmentalists for making unproven or improper claims.

Many companies have responded to the new environmentalism by doing whatever is required to avert new regulations or to keep environmentalists quiet. Others are rushing to make money by catering to the public's mounting concern for the environment. But enlightened companies are taking action not because someone is forcing them to, or to reap short-run profits, but because it is the right thing to do. They believe that environmental farsightedness today will pay off tomorrow. For example, Edgar Woolard, chief executive of Du Pont, believes that companies should do more than merely comply with the laws. He states, "The real environmental challenge is not one of responding to the next regulatory proposal. Nor is it making the environmentalists see things our way. Nor is it educating the public to appreciate the benefits of our products and thus to tolerate their environmental impacts . . . I'm calling for *corporate environmentalism*, which I define as an attitude and a performance commitment that places corporate environmental stewardship fully in line with public desires and expectations." Woolard is backing his beliefs with actions. Since joining Du Pont, he has met at least once a month with leading environmentalists, and under his leadership the company is making some dramatic moves. In 1988, Du Pont announced that it would pull out of its $750 million-a-year chlorofluorocarbon (CFC) business by the year 2000, or sooner if possible, because it *might* harm the earth's atmosphere. And Du Pont is prepared to spend as much as $1 billion to find a replacement.

Source: Joe Schwartz, "Earth Day Today," *American Demographics*, April 1990, pp. 40–41; David Kirkpatrick, "Environmentalism: The New Crusade," *Fortune*, February 12, 1990, pp. 44–54; Jeremy Main, "Here Comes the Big New Cleanup," *Fortune*, November 21, 1988, pp. 102–118; Brian Bremner, "A New Sales Pitch: The Environment," *Business Week*, July 24, 1989, p. 50; and Marketers Rush Earth Day Ads," *Advertising Age*, April 23, 1990, p. 83.

responded positively to consumerism and environmentalism in order to better serve consumer needs.

A Concept of Enlightened Marketing

The concept of **enlightened marketing** holds that a company's marketing should support the best long-run performance of the marketing system. Enlightened marketing consists of five principles: *consumer-oriented marketing*, *innovative marketing*, *value marketing*, *sense-of-mission marketing*, and *societal marketing*.

Consumer-Oriented Marketing

Consumer-oriented marketing means that the company should view and organize its marketing activities from the consumers' point of view. It should work hard to sense, serve, and satisfy the needs of a defined group of customers. Consider the following example:

> Barat College, a women's college in Lake Forest, Illinois, published a college catalog that openly spelled out Barat College's strong and weak points. Among the weak points it

shared with applicants were the following: "An exceptionally talented student musician or mathematician . . . might be advised to look further for a college with top faculty and facilities in that field. . . . The full range of advanced specialized courses offered in a university will be absent. . . . The library collection is average for a small college, but low in comparison with other high-quality institutions."

The effect of "telling it like it is" is to build confidence so that applicants really know what they will find at Barat College and to emphasize that Barat College will strive to improve its consumer value as rapidly as time and funds permit.

Innovative Marketing

The principle of **innovative marketing** requires that the company continuously seek real product and marketing improvements. The company that overlooks new and better ways to do things will eventually lose to a company that has found a better way. One of the best examples of an innovative marketer is Procter & Gamble:

> Wisk, a Lever Bros. product, has dominated liquid detergents for a generation, and liquids have been taking a growing share of the $3.2-billion-a-year detergent market. P&G tried to topple Wisk with run-of-the-laundry-room liquids called Era and Solo, but couldn't come close. Then it developed a liquid with 12 cleaning agents, twice the norm, and a molecule that traps dirt in the wash water. P&G christened it Liquid Tide and put it in a bottle colored the same fire-bright color as the ubiquitous Tide box. After just 18 months on the market, Liquid Tide is washing as many clothes as Wisk in the U.S., and the two are locked in a fierce battle for the No. 2 position, after powdered Tide, among all detergents.[16]

Value Marketing

According to the principle of **value marketing,** the company should put most of its resources into value-building marketing investments. Many things marketers do—one-shot sales promotions, minor packaging changes, advertising puffery—may raise sales in the short run but add less *value* than would actual improvements in the product's quality, features, or convenience. Enlightened marketing calls for building long-run consumer loyalty by continually improving the value consumers receive from the firm's marketing offer.

Sense-of-Mission Marketing

Sense-of-mission marketing means that the company should define its mission in broad *social* terms rather than narrow *product* terms. When a company defines a social mission, company people feel better about their work and have a clearer sense of direction. For example, defined in narrow product terms, International Minerals and Chemical Corporation's mission might be "to sell fertilizer." But the company states its mission more broadly:

> We're not merely in the business of selling our brand of fertilizer. We have a sense of purpose, a sense of where we are going. The first function of corporate planning is to decide what kind of business the company is in. Our business is *agricultural productivity.* We are interested in anything that affects plant growth, now and in the future.[17]

Reshaping the basic task of selling fertilizer into the larger mission of improving agricultural productivity in order to feed the world's hungry gives a new sense of purpose to employees.

Societal Marketing

Following the principle of **societal marketing,** an enlightened company makes marketing decisions by considering consumers' wants, the company's requirements, consumers' long-run interests, and society's long-run interests. The company is aware that neglecting the latter two factors is a disservice to consumers and society. Alert companies view societal problems as opportunities.

A societally oriented marketer wants to design products that are not only pleasing but also beneficial. The difference is shown in Figure 23-3. Products can be classified according to their degree of immediate consumer satisfaction and long-run consumer

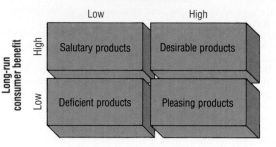

Immediate satisfaction

Low   High

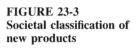

| | Salutary products | Desirable products |
| Long-run consumer benefit | Deficient products | Pleasing products |

FIGURE 23-3
Societal classification of new products

benefit. **Desirable products** give both high immediate satisfaction and high long-run benefits. A desirable product with immediate satisfaction and long-run benefits would be a tasty *and* nutritious breakfast food. **Pleasing products** give high immediate satisfaction but may hurt consumers in the long run. An example is cigarettes. **Salutary products** have low appeal but benefit consumers in the long run. Seat belts and air bags in automobiles are salutary products. Finally, **deficient products,** such as bad-tasting and ineffective medicine, have neither immediate appeal nor long-run benefits.

The challenge posed by pleasing products is that they sell very well but may end up hurting the consumer. The product opportunity, therefore, is to add long-run benefits without reducing the product's pleasing qualities. For example, Sears developed a phosphate-free laundry detergent that was very effective. The challenge posed by salutary products is to add some pleasing qualities so that they will become more desirable in the consumers' minds. For example, synthetic fats and fat substitutes, such as Procter & Gamble's Olestra and NutraSweet's Simplesse, promise to improve the appeal of more healthful low-calorie and low-fat foods.

Marketing Ethics

Conscientious marketers face many moral dilemmas. The best thing to do is often unclear. Because not all managers have fine moral sensitivity, companies need to develop *corporate marketing ethics policies*—broad guidelines that everyone in the organization must follow. These policies should cover distributor relations, advertising standards, customer service, pricing, product development, and general ethical standards.

The finest guidelines cannot resolve all the difficult ethical situations the marketer faces. Table 23-1 lists some difficult ethical situations marketers could face during their careers. If marketers choose immediate sales-producing actions in all these cases, their marketing behavior might well be described as immoral or amoral. If they refuse to go along with *any* of the actions, they might be ineffective as marketing managers and unhappy because of the constant moral tension. Managers need a set of principles that will help them figure out the moral importance of each situation and how far they can go in good conscience.

But *what* principle should guide companies and marketing managers on issues of ethics and social responsibility? One philosophy is that such issues are decided by the free market and legal system. Under this principle, companies and their managers are not responsible for making moral judgments. Companies can in good conscience do whatever the system allows.

A second philosophy puts responsibility not in the system, but in the hands of individual companies and managers. This more enlightened philosophy suggests that a company should have a "social conscience." Companies and managers should apply high standards of ethics and morality when making corporate decisions, regardless of "what the system allows." History provides an endless list of examples of company actions that were legal and allowed but were highly irresponsible. Consider the following example:

Prior to the Pure Food and Drug Act, the advertising for a diet pill promised that a person taking this pill could eat virtually anything at any time and still lose weight. Too good to be true? Actually the claim was quite true; the product lived up to its billing with frightening

TABLE 23-1
Some Morally Difficult Situations in Marketing

1. You work for a cigarette company and up to now have not been convinced that cigarettes cause cancer. A report comes across your desk that clearly shows the link between smoking and cancer. What would you do?
2. Your R&D department has changed one of your products slightly. It is not really "new and improved," but you know that putting this statement on the package and in advertising will increase sales. What would you do?
3. You have been asked to add a stripped-down model to your line that could be advertised to pull customers into the store. The product won't be very good, but salespeople will be able to switch buyers up to higher-priced units. You are asked to give the green light for this stripped-down version. What would you do?
4. You are thinking of hiring a product manager who just left a competitor's company. She would be more than happy to tell you all the competitor's plans for the coming year. What would you do?
5. One of your top dealers in an important territory has had recent family troubles and his sales have slipped. It looks like it will take him a while to straighten out his family trouble. Meanwhile you are losing many sales. Legally, you can terminate the dealer's franchise and replace him. What would you do?
6. You have a chance to win a big account that will mean a lot to you and your company. The purchasing agent hints that a "gift" would influence the decision. Your assistant recommends sending a fine color television set to the buyer's home. What would you do?
7. You have heard that a competitor has a new product feature that will make a big difference in sales. The competitor will demonstrate the feature in a private dealer meeting at the annual trade show. You can easily send a snooper to this meeting to learn about the new feature. What would you do?
8. You have to choose between three ad campaigns outlined by your agency. The first (A) is a soft-sell, honest information campaign. The second (B) uses sex-loaded emotional appeals and exaggerates the product's benefits. The third (C) involves a noisy, irritating commercial that is sure to gain audience attention. Pretests show that the campaigns are effective in the following order: C, B, and A. What would you do?
9. You are interviewing a capable woman applicant for a job as salesperson. She is better qualified than the men just interviewed. Nevertheless, you know that some of your important customers prefer dealing with men, and you will lose some sales if you hire her. What would you do?
10. You are a sales manager in an encyclopedia company. Your competitor's salespeople are getting into homes by pretending to take a research survey. After they finish the survey, they switch to their sales pitch. This technique seems to be very effective. What would you do?

efficiency. It seems that the primary active ingredient in this "diet supplement" was tapeworm larvae. These larvae would develop in the intestinal tract and, of course, be well fed; the pill taker would in time, quite literally, starve to death.[18]

Each company and marketing manager must work out a philosophy of socially responsible and ethical behavior. Under the societal marketing concept, each manager must look beyond what is legal and allowed and develop standards based on personal integrity, corporate conscience, and long-run consumer welfare. A clear and responsible philosophy will help the marketing manager deal with the many knotty questions posed by marketing and other human activities. Many industrial and professional associations have suggested codes of ethics, and many companies are now adopting their own codes of ethics and developing programs to teach managers about important ethics issues and help them find the proper responses (see Marketing Highlight 23–4).[19]

Yet, written codes and ethics programs do not assure ethical behavior. Ethics and social responsibility require a total corporate commitment. They must be a component of the overall corporate culture:

> In the final analysis, "ethical behavior" must be an integral part of the organization, a way of life that is deeply ingrained in the collective corporate body. . . . In any business enterprise, ethical behavior must be a tradition, a way of conducting one's affairs that is passed from generation to generation of employees at all levels of the organization. It is the responsibility of management, starting at the very top, to both set the example by personal conduct and create an environment that not only encourages and rewards ethical behavior, but which also makes anything less totally unacceptable.[20]

Marketing executives of the 1990s will face many challenges. They will have abundant marketing opportunities because of technological advances in solar energy, home computers, robots, cable television, modern medicine, and new forms of transportation, recreation, and communication. However, forces in the socioeconomic, cultural, and natural environments will increase the limits under which marketing can be carried out. Companies that are able to create new values and practice societally responsible marketing will have a world to conquer.

THE GENERAL DYNAMICS ETHICS PROGRAM

The General Dynamics ethics program is considered the most comprehensive in the industry. And little wonder—it was put together as generals from the Pentagon looked on. The program came about after charges that the company had deliberately overbilled the government on defense contracts.

Now at General Dynamics, a committee of board members reviews its ethics policies, and a corporate ethics director and steering group execute the program. The company has set up hot lines that let any employee get instant advice on job-related ethical issues and has given each employee a wallet card listing a toll-free number to report suspected wrongdoing. Nearly all employees have attended workshops; those for salespeople cover such topics as expense accounts and supplier relations.

The company also has a 20 page code of ethics that tells employees in detail how to conduct themselves. Here are some examples of rules for salespeople:

- If it becomes clear that the company must engage in unethi-

cal or illegal activity to win a contract, it will not pursue that business further.

- To prevent hidden interpretations or understandings, all information provided relative to products and services should be clear and concise.

- Receiving or soliciting gifts, entertainment, or anything else of value is prohibited.

- In countries where common practices indicate acceptance of conduct lower than that to which General Dynamics aspires, salespeople will follow the company's standards.

- Under no circumstances may an employee offer or give anything to customers or their representatives in an effort to influence them.

Source: Adapted from "This Industry Leader Means Business," *Sales & Marketing Management*, May 1987, p. 44; and Stewart Toy, "The Defense Scandal," *Business Week*, July 1, 1988, pp. 28–30.

General Dynamics has developed a model ethics program.

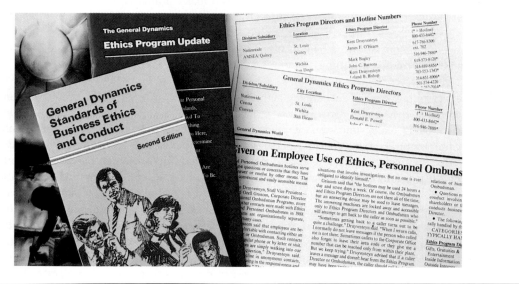

PRINCIPLES FOR PUBLIC POLICY TOWARD MARKETING

Finally, we want to propose several principles that might guide the formulation of public policy toward marketing. These principles reflect assumptions underlying much of modern American marketing theory and practice.

The Principle of Consumer and Producer Freedom

As much as possible, marketing decisions should be made by consumers and producers under relative freedom. Marketing freedom is important if a marketing system is to deliver a high standard of living. People can achieve satisfaction in their own terms rather than in terms defined by someone else. This leads to greater fulfillment through a closer matching of products to desires. Freedom for producers and consumers is the cornerstone of a dynamic marketing system. But more principles are needed to implement this freedom and prevent abuses.

The Principle of Curbing Potential Harm

As much as possible, transactions freely entered into by producers and consumers are their private business. The political system curbs producer or consumer freedom only to prevent transactions that harm or threaten to harm the producer, consumer, or third parties. Transactional harm is a widely recognized grounds for government intervention. The major issue is whether there is sufficient actual or potential harm to justify the intervention.

The Principle of Meeting Basic Needs

The marketing system should serve disadvantaged consumers as well as affluent ones. In a free-enterprise system, producers make goods for markets that are willing and able to buy. Certain groups who lack purchasing power may go without needed goods and services, causing harm to their physical or psychological well-being. While preserving the principle of producer and consumer freedom, the marketing system should support economic and political actions to solve this problem. It should strive to meet the basic needs of all people, and all people should share to some extent in the standard of living it creates.

The Principle of Economic Efficiency

The marketing system strives to supply goods and services efficiently and at low prices. The extent to which a society's needs and wants can be satisfied depends on how efficiently its scarce resources are used. Free economies rely on active competition and informed buyers to make a market efficient. To make profits, competitors must watch their costs carefully while developing products, prices, and marketing programs that serve buyer needs. Buyers get the most satisfactions by finding out about different competing products, prices, and qualities and choosing carefully. The presence of active competition and well-informed buyers keeps quality high and prices low.

The Principle of Innovation

The marketing system encourages authentic innovation to bring down production and distribution costs and to develop new products to meet changing consumer needs. Much innovation is really imitation of other brands, with a slight difference to provide a talking point. The consumer may face ten very similar brands in a product class. But an effective marketing system encourages real product innovation and differentiation to meet the wants of different market segments.

The Principle of Consumer Education and Information

An effective marketing system invests heavily in consumer education and information to increase long-run consumer satisfaction and welfare. The principle of economic efficiency requires this investment, especially in cases involving products that are confusing because of their numbers and conflicting claims. Ideally, companies will provide enough information about their products. But consumer groups and the government can also give out information and ratings. Students in public schools can take courses in consumer education to learn better buying skills.

The Principle of Consumer Protection

Consumer education and information cannot do the whole job of protecting consumers. The marketing system must also provide consumer protection. Modern products are so complex that even trained consumers cannot evaluate them with confidence. Consumers do not know whether a microwave oven gives off too much radiation, whether a new automobile has safety flaws, or whether a new drug product has dangerous side effects. A government agency must review and judge the safety levels of various foods, drugs, toys, appliances, fabrics, automobiles, and housing. Consumers may buy products but fail to understand the environmental consequences, so consumer protection also covers production and marketing activities that might harm the environment. Finally, consumer protection prevents deceptive practices and high-pressure selling techniques that leave consumers defenseless.

These seven principles are based on the assumption that marketing's goal is not to maximize company profits or total consumption or consumer choice, but rather to maximize life quality. Life quality means meeting basic needs, having available many good products, and enjoying the natural and cultural environment. Properly managed, the marketing system can help create and deliver a higher quality of life to people around the world.

■ SUMMARY

A marketing system should sense, serve, and satisfy consumer needs and improve the quality of consumers' lives. In working to meet consumer needs, marketers may take some actions that are not to everyone's liking or benefit. Marketing managers should be aware of the main *criticisms of marketing*.

Marketing's *impact on individual consumer welfare* has been criticized for high prices, deceptive practices, high-pressure selling, shoddy or unsafe products, planned obsolescence, and poor service to disadvantaged consumers. Marketing's *impact on society* has been criticized for creating false wants and too much materialism, too few social goods, cultural pollution, and too much political power. Critics have also criticized marketing's *impact on other businesses* for harming competitors and reducing competition through acquisitions, practices that create barriers to entry, and unfair competitive marketing practices.

Concerns about the marketing system have led to *citizen action movements*—consumerism and environmentalism. *Consumerism* is an organized social movement to strengthen the rights and power of consumers relative to sellers. Alert marketers view it as an opportunity to serve consumers better by providing more consumer information, education, and protection. *Environmentalism* is an organized social movement seeking to minimize the harm done to the environment and quality of life by marketing practices. It calls for curbing consumer wants when their satisfaction would create too much environmental cost. Citizen action has led to the passage of many laws to protect consumers in the area of product safety, truth-in-packaging, truth-in-lending, and truth-in-advertising.

Many companies originally opposed these social movements and laws, but most of them now recognize a need for positive consumer information, education, and protection. Some companies have followed a policy of *enlightened marketing* based on the principles of *consumer orientation, innovation, value creation, social mission*, and *societal orientation*. Increasingly, companies are responding to the need to provide company policies and guidelines to help their managers deal with questions of *marketing ethics*.

Future public policy must be guided by a set of principles that will improve the marketing system's contribution to the quality of life. These principles call for consumer and producer freedom, intervention only to prevent potential harm, arrangements to meet basic consumer needs adequately, the practice of economic efficiency, emphasis on authentic innovation, and the provision of consumer education, information, and protection.

■ QUESTIONS FOR DISCUSSION

1. Was Gerber right or wrong not to recall its baby food after customers complained of finding glass fragments in bottles? Without considering what you know about how things turned out, analyze the situation facing Gerber in 1986 and describe the action you would have recommended.

2. If regulators limited the allowable number of levels in a channel of distribution or set a cap on the maximum markup a middleman could add to the price of a product, would the cost of distribution increase or decrease? What impact would these regulations have on consumers?

3. Does advertising add an excessive amount to the price of products? Give evidence to support your answer.

4. Does marketing *create* barriers to entry or *reduce* them? Describe how a small manufacturer of household cleaning products could use advertising to compete with Procter & Gamble.

5. If you were a marketing manager at Dow Chemical Company, which would you prefer: government regulations on acceptable levels of air and water pollution, or a voluntary industry code suggesting target levels of emissions? Why?

6. Does Procter & Gamble practice the principles of enlightened marketing? Does your school? Give examples to support your answers.

7. Compare the marketing concept with the principle of societal marketing. Do you think marketers should adopt the societal marketing concept? Why or why not?

8. Choose three of the situations described in Table 23-1 and describe what you would do in each case. Would you make the same decision if your company were having severe financial troubles or if it did not have a stated policy supporting high ethical standards?

9. Do you think marketing has a tarnished image? If so, what are the reasons for this image problem? Are these reasons legitimate?

10. If you had the power to change our marketing system in any way feasible, what improvements *would* you make? What improvements *can* you make as a consumer or entry-level marketing practitioner?

■ KEY TERMS

Consumerism. An organized movement of citizens and government to improve the rights and power of buyers in relation to sellers.

Consumer-oriented marketing. A principle of enlightened marketing which holds that the company should view and organize its marketing activities from the consumers' point of view.

Deficient products. Products that have neither immediate appeal nor long-run benefits.

Desirable products. Products that give both high immediate satisfaction and high long-run benefits.

Enlightened marketing. A marketing philosophy holding that a company's marketing should support the best long-run performance of the marketing system; its five principles include consumer-oriented marketing, innovative marketing, value marketing, sense-of-mission marketing, and societal marketing.

Environmentalism. An organized movement of concerned citizens and government to protect and improve people's living environment.

Innovative marketing. A principle of enlightened marketing which requires that a company seek real product and marketing improvements.

Planned obsolescence. A strategy of causing products to become obsolete before they actually need replacement.

Pleasing products. Products that give high immediate satisfaction but may hurt consumers in the long run.

Salutary products. Products that have low appeal but benefit consumers in the long run.

Sense-of-mission marketing. A principle of enlightened marketing which holds that a company should define its mission in broad social terms rather than narrow product terms.

Societal marketing. A principle of enlightened marketing which holds that a company should make marketing decisions by considering consumers' wants, the company's requirements, consumers' long-run interests, and society's long-run interests.

Value marketing. A principle of enlightened marketing which holds that a company should put most of its resources into value-building marketing investments.

■ REFERENCES

1. See Patricia Strnad, "Gerber Ignores Tylenol Textbook," *Advertising Age*, March 10, 1986, p. 3; Felix Kessler, "Tremors from the Tylenol Scare Hit Food Companies," *Fortune*, March 31, 1986, pp. 59–62; and Wendy Zellner, "Gerber's New Chief Doesn't Take Baby Steps," *Business Week*, November 7, 1988, pp. 130–32.

2. See Steven H. Star, "Marketing and Its Discontents," *Harvard Business Review*, November–December 1989, pp. 148–54.

3. See John F. Gaski and Michael Etzel, "The Index of Consumer Sentiment Toward Marketing," *Journal of Marketing*, July 1986, pp. 71–81; and "The Public Is Willing to Take Business On," *Business Week*, May 29, 1989, p. 29.

4. Excerpts from Theodore Levitt, "The Morality (?) of Advertising," *Harvard Business Review*, July–August 1970, pp. 84–92.

5. "The Breakfast of Fatties?" *Chicago Today*, July 24, 1970.

6. See Jim Treece, "If It Has Wheels and Carries People, Shouldn't It Be Safe?" *Business Week*, June 20, 1988, p. 48.

7. For more on product safety, see "Unsafe Products: The Great Debate Over Blame and Punishment," *Business Week*, April 30, 1984, pp. 96–104; Michael Brody, "When Products Turn," *Fortune*, March 3, 1986, pp. 20–24; and Marisa Manley, "Product Liability: You're More Exposed Than You Think," *Harvard Business Review*, September–October 1987, pp. 28–40.

8. A speech delivered at Vanderbilt University Law School, reported in *Marketing News*, August 1, 1968, pp. 11, 15. For more discussion, see Louis W. Stern and Adel I. El-Ansary, *Marketing Channels*, 4th ed. (Englewood Cliffs, NJ: Prentice Hall, 1988), pp. 480–83.

9. Ibid.

10. Myron Magnet, "The Money Society," *Fortune*, July 6, 1987, p. 26.

11. Ibid., p. 26.

12. See Bill Barol, "The Eighties Are Over," *Newsweek*, January 4, 1988, pp. 40–48; "*Business Week*'s 1988 Hip Parade: Goodbye Greed, Hello Heartland," *Business Week*, January 18, 1988, p. 31; and Ronald Henkoff, "Is Greed Dead?" *Fortune*, August 14, 1989, pp. 40–49.

13. From an advertisement for *Fact* magazine, which does not carry advertisements.

14. See Michael Oneal, "The Best and the Worst Deals of the '80s," *Business Week*, January 15, 1990, pp. 52–57.

15. For more details, see Paul N. Bloom and Stephen A. Greyser, "The Maturing of Consumerism," *Harvard Business Review*, November–December 1981, pp. 130–39, Robert J. Samualson, "The Aging of Ralph Nader," *Newsweek*, December 16, 1985, p. 57; and Douglas A. Harbrecht, "The Second Coming of Ralph Nader," *Business Week*, March 6, 1989, p. 28.

16. Faye Rice, "The King of Suds Reigns Again," *Fortune*, August 4, 1986, p. 131.

17. Gordon O. Pehrson, quoted in "Flavored Algae from the Sea?" *Chicago Sun-Times*, February 3, 1965, p. 54.

18. Dan R. Dalton and Richard A. Cosier, "The Four Faces of Social Responsibility," *Business Horizons*, May–June 1982, pp. 19–27.

19. For examples, see the American Marketing Association's code of ethics, discussed in "AMA Adopts New Code of Ethics," *Marketing News*, September 11, 1987, p. 1; and John A. Byrne, "Businesses Are Signing Up for Ethics 101," *Business Week*, February 15, 1988, pp. 56–57.

20. From "Ethics as a Practical Matter," a message from David R. Whitman, Chairman of the Board of Whirlpool Corporation, as reprinted (in Ricky E. Griffin and Ronald J. Ebert) *Business* (Englewood Cliffs, NJ: Prentice Hall, 1989, pp. 578–79. For more discussion, see Shelby D. Hunt, Van R. Wood, and Lawrence B. Chonko, "Corporate Ethical Values and Organizational Commitment in Marketing," *Journal of Marketing*, July 1989, pp. 79–90.

NESTLÉ: UNDER FIRE AGAIN

Questionable marketing techniques by a unit of Nestlé are raising the concerns of consumer products activists. And this is not the first time that Nestlé has been scrutinized by the public eye.

Nestlé S.A., headquartered in Vevey, Switzerland, is the world's largest food company, with annual worldwide sales of more than $25 billion. The company's products are produced in 383 factories operating in 50 countries. Many Nestlé products are quite familiar—Nestlé's chocolates, Nescafé, Taster's Choice, and Hills coffees, Libby and Contadina foods, Beech-Nut baby products, Stouffer foods, and Friskies, Fancy Feast, and Mighty Dog pet foods. In 1985, the company acquired Carnation Company, makers of Evaporated Milk, Hot Cocoa Mix, Instant Breakfast Mix, Coffee-Mate, and other familiar brands.

In the late 1970s and early 1980s, Nestlé came under heavy fire from health professionals who charged the company with encouraging Third World mothers to give up breast feeding and use a company-prepared formula. Critics accused Nestlé of using sophisticated promotional techniques to persuade hundreds of thousands of poverty-stricken, poorly educated mothers that formula feeding was better for their children. Unfortunately, formula feeding is not usually a wise practice in such countries. Because of poor living conditions and habits, people cannot or do not clean bottles properly and often mix formula with impure water. Furthermore, income level does not permit many families to purchase sufficient quantities of formula.

In 1977, two American social-interest groups spearheaded a worldwide boycott against Nestlé. The boycott ended in 1984, when the company complied with infant formula marketing codes adopted by the World Health Organization (WHO). The code adopted by the WHO eliminates all promotional efforts, requiring companies to serve primarily as passive "order takers." It prohibits advertising, samples, and direct contact with consumers. Contacts with professionals (such as doctors) are allowed only if professionals seek such contact. Manufacturers can package products with some form of visual corporate identity, but they cannot picture babies. In effect, then, the WHO code allows almost no marketing. However, the code contains only *recommended* guidelines. They become *mandatory* only if individual governments adopt national codes through their own regulatory mechanisms.

In addition to the formula controversy, Nestlé has had other public-relations difficulties in recent years. In contrast to the Third-World baby formula debacle, the next incident involved top-management ethics at a Nestlé subsidiary. Beech-Nut Nutrition Corp., one of Nestlé's U.S. baby-products units, found itself in hot water in 1987, when it was forced to admit to selling adulterated and mislabeled apple juice intended for babies. The product contained little if any apple juice and was made from beet sugar, cane sugar syrup, corn syrup, and other ingredients. After pleading guilty to federal charges, Beech-Nut agreed to pay a $2 million fine and $140,000 for Food & Drug Administration investigative costs. Two company executives were fined and imprisoned.

Nestlé may once again be in the limelight with a recent new-product entry in the U.S. infant formula market. To maintain its growth and profitability, Nestlé is planning to enter the U.S. baby formula market, a market that it dominates in Europe. In the $1.6 billion U.S. market, however, it faces several large, well-established competitors—Abbott Laboratories (with Similac and Isomil brands) has a 53 percent market share, followed by Bristol-Myers (Enfamil and ProSobee brands) with 36 percent, and American Home Products (SMA brand) with 11 percent. Despite the competition, formula sales are predicted to grow at 8 or 9 percent annually. Although there has been a trend toward breast feeding in recent years, this trend has been partially offset by the number of working mothers who have less time to breast-feed.

Nestlé's new infant formula, named Good Start, will be introduced by its Carnation unit—a company with a pure and sparkling reputation in the baby business. Nestlé claims that its product offers important benefits over current infant formulas. The new formula is a whey-based product designed for infants allergic to standard milk-based and soy-based formulas. The company estimates that 15 to 20 percent of all infants are allergic to the protein in standard formulas. By contrast, the Pediatric Academy's Committee on Nutrition says that the number is closer to 1 to 2 percent. Nevertheless, Carnation has declared the product a medical breakthrough. Good Start is "hypoallergenic"—a claim made in bold type on the can. The company claims that the product can prevent or reduce

fussiness, sleeplessness, colic, rash, and other problems. Pediatricians, however, caution that although the formula is easier to digest than common milk-based formulas, it should be used only under recommendation from the child's physician.

Although the U.S. has not adopted the WHO marketing code for infant formula, most U.S. manufacturers abide, at least in part, by the code. The U.S. infant formula business is governed largely by relationships between marketers and health professionals. Except for hospital giveaway programs, Abbott and Bristol-Myers market their infant formula products mainly to physicians. Neither company promotes directly to consumers. Consequently, there is little consumer brand loyalty in the infant formula market. In addition, because pediatricians tell mothers what to buy, infant formula products are largely price-insensitive.

Observers expect Carnation to break from industry tradition by promoting Good Start directly to new mothers by using mass-media advertising. Carnation is certain to take advantage of its long association with such milk products as Evaporated Milk. The company is expected to spend $50 to $100 million with its first entry in the infant formula market.

Some leading pediatricians, however, suggest that Nestlé's marketing is misleading—Good Start may not be mild enough for the small number of babies severely allergic to cow's milk. The danger, pediatricians argue, is that direct marketing to consumers may attract mothers of these high milk-allergic babies. These mothers would thus unknowingly expose their babies to a dangerous formula without physician supervision. Consumer groups, meanwhile, watch the situation carefully. A new citizen-action movement may renew criticisms of Nestlé's marketing practices.

QUESTIONS

1. Think through the traditional buyers' and sellers' rights listed in Chapter 23. Which rights were violated in the Third World infant formula situation? Which rights were violated in the Beech-Nut apple juice situation? Does Carnation have the right to promote Good Start infant formula in whatever way it wants?

2. Will Nestlé be practicing socially responsible marketing with its Good Start product?

3. What marketing plan would you recommend for Good Start?

BIODEGRADABLE DIAPERS

Some marketers have been criticized for being so concerned about their own interests that they ignore all other interests. High prices, deceptive practices, high-pressure selling, and poor service to disadvantaged customers are some of the practices critics bring up when charging that some firms are socially irresponsible. But now several firms have developed what appears to be the correct product for the 1990s—biodegradable disposable diapers.

Almost 4 million babies are born each year in the United States. They are part of the "baby boom echo"—children of the postwar baby boomers. A baby in the house means bottles, baby food, and lots and lots of diapers. The average baby goes through between 8,000 and 10,000 diapers between birth and toilet training. For the country, that means 18 billion used diapers a year, which converts to 4.5 million tons of waste filling up landfills and taking 2 to 500 years to dissolve. Concern about the impact of all these diapers has led to a different kind of boom—biodegradable diapers.

Biodegradable diapers are made with advanced plastics, most involving the binding of cornstarch polymers—molecules made up of repeating, identical subunits—with plastic molecules. The newly formed plastic is supposed to be readily broken down in the soil by a variety of microorganisms, such as fungi and bacteria that feed on the starch. As the cornstarch is eaten, the plastic's polymeric chains are broken down into smaller and smaller units, leaving behind only a plastic dust.

So far, most of the diapers have been sold to well-educated parents who are willing to help the environment by paying an extra 5 to 10 percent for a disposable diaper that actually does dispose of itself. Even though the industry is still in its infancy, brands such as Rocky Mountain, Tender Cares, Dove Tails, Nappies, and Bunnies are starting to challenge major brands for supermarket shelf space.

But recently, some people have begun to question just how much disposable biodegradable diapers will do to alleviate our landfill problem. One researcher found that the average landfill contains 36 percent paper, 20 percent yard wastes, 9 percent metal, 9 percent food, 8 percent glass, 7 percent plastic, and 11 percent other materials. And these proportions of materials do not change appreciably over time. Research also indicates that once material is placed in a landfill, it remains virtually unchanged. Decades after it was buried, paper, metal, glass, and plastic remain. Even yard waste and food do not easily decay. It seems that in order for biodegradation to take place, water, oxygen, and sunlight must be present so that the microorganisms can break down the materials. Unfortunately, these conditions are not typically present in modern landfills.

Also, the problem with landfills is not so much the *type* of material placed in them as the *volume* of that material.

Some researchers suggest that the benefits of biodegradable plastics are illusory and that the solution to our waste problem is a combination of recycling, incineration, composition, and landfills.

QUESTIONS

1. Explain why firms that make biodegradable disposable diapers, such as Rocky Mountain Medical Corporation, could be said to be following a philosophy of societal marketing.
2. What impact, if any, will biodegradable disposable diapers have on landfills?
3. How are environmentalists likely to view biodegradable disposable diapers?

Sources: "Biodegradable Plastics?" *Country Journal*, May/June 1990, p. 25; "The World of Crumbling Plastics," *U.S. News and World Report*, November 24, 1986, p. 76; "Biodegradables That Don't Make Degrade," *U.S. News and World Report*, March 26, 1990, p. 14; "Bagging It," *Scientific America*, August 1987, p. 22; "The Perils of Plastic," *Health*, June 1990, p. 36; and "Natural Plastic," *Natural History*, May 1990, pp. 82–84.

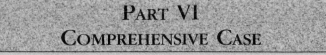

PART VI
COMPREHENSIVE CASE

SMITH'S HOME FOODS: BRINGING HOME THE BACON

Ronald Smith, President of Smith's Country Hams, walked into his daughter's office and plopped down in one of the chairs across from her desk. "Christy," he said, "I've just been looking at last month's numbers, and they are pretty discouraging. We've got to find a way to get the home foods business moving. I'm not sure what's wrong, but I think we've somehow got the cart before the horse. I'm convinced that if we could just find the right button, and push it, everything would work well."

Christy Smith looked across the desk at her casually dressed father. Meeting him on the street, one would never guess that he was president of a highly successful meat wholesaling operation in Smithfield, North Carolina. "Dad, I am just as frustrated as you are," she replied. "Nothing we try seems to work right. Even when we do attract new customers, they are the wrong kind."

Christy was a very busy person. In addition to her duties at Smith's, she commuted daily to a major university located in a neighboring city where she was a senior business major. Although she had worked in the family business for as long as she could remember, she had been pleased and surprised when her father had asked her to take over the newly-formed Smith's Home Foods operation. Glancing at the calendar on her desk, she noted the date—April 4, 1990. She could hardly believe that five months had passed since taking on the assignment. Although pleased with her father's confidence in her, she knew that he felt frustrated about the slow development of the Smith's Home Foods business.

As Christy and her father talked, Sonny Jones, one of Home Foods' two full-time salespeople, entered the office and joined the conversation. He seemed upset. "We just got two more turn-downs from the finance company," he grumbled. "They rejected both of the families I sold plans to last night. We just can't seem to get onto the right side of the street."

"What do you mean?" Christy asked.

"It's the same old story," Sonny replied. "Both families I called on last night live in Dogwood Acres—they're nice people and all, but they don't have very high incomes. We have to find a way to attract the higher-income folks who live across the road in Smithfield Estates."

Ronald Smith rose to leave. "Whatever the problem is, I'm depending on the two of you to figure it out and tell me what we need to do. And you need to get moving quickly."

BACKGROUND

Smith's Country Hams, a 25-year-old family business which focuses on wholesale meat products such as ham, bacon, and other pork products, sells to restaurants and fast food operations in Eastern North Carolina. In July, 1989, seeking growth opportunities, Ronald Smith started a new division—Smith's Home Foods. He got the idea from an employee who had previously worked for another home-delivered foods company. Ronald, who is always looking for new ways to make money, believed the idea had potential. He knew that people these days are seeking more convenience. Therefore, a service which provides home-delivered meats, vegetables, and fruits should be in considerable demand. He also realized that he could use his own meat products in the business, thereby providing new sales for Smith's Country Hams.

Ronald reconditioned an old production facility which had been idle and set up offices there for Smith's Home Foods. He put the employee who had the idea in charge of the business. However, by October, 1989, the employee had failed to meet Ronald's expectations and had resigned. Ronald then asked Christy to take over. He knew this would be a challenging assignment for her. She was still a full-time university student. As a result, she could devote only afternoons and whatever time she could squeeze from her evenings to managing Smith's Home Foods.

THE HOME FOODS BUSINESS

The home-delivered foods business centers on providing families with prearranged assortments of foods which are delivered to their homes. Smith's Home Foods offers 11 standard packages which contain varying combinations of frozen meats, vegetables, and fruits. The packages vary in size and cost, but each provides a four-month food supply. Table 1 shows the items in a typical package. Table 2 summarizes the characteristics of each of the 11 packages.

When Christy first assumed management of the operation, she wondered why everything was sold in four-month packages. According to Sonny Jones, who had once worked with a competitive food service, most competitors also offer similar four-month packages. As a result, the quantity of food delivered with each package would require that customers own a freezer or purchase one. Therefore, Smith's Home Foods, like other home-foods companies, also sells a 21-cubic foot freezer on an install-

650 PART VI ■ EXTENDING MARKETING

TABLE 1
Contents of a Typical Smith's Home Foods Package

```
107#  NET WEIGHT BEEF
   6    CHUCK ROASTS 2# AVG
   4    SHOULDER ROASTS 2# AVG
   1    SIRLOIN TIP ROAST 3# AVG
   1    EYE OF ROUND ROAST 3# AVG
   1    BOTTOM ROUND ROAST 3# AVG
  20    RIBEYE STEAKS 8 OZ
  12    T–BONE STEAKS 12 OZ
  8#    CUBE STEAK
 10#    BLS STEW BEEF
  18    CHOPPED BEEF STEAK 8 OZ 9# CASE
 32#    GROUND BEEF (1# ROLL/4 OZ PATTIES)
  6#  PORK CHOPS
  6#  BLS PORK CHOPS
  5#  DINNER HAM
  30    MISC. MEATS
  20    FRYERS
   1    SEAFOOD
  60    VEGETABLES (16 OZ)
  12    FRUITS
  32    JUICES (12 OZ)
  6#  CHEESE
  6#  MARGARINE
```

BANK	$1,094.38
TAX	54.71
	1,149.09
DEPOSIT	35.00
AMOUNT FINANCED	1,114.09
FINANCE CHARGE	56.23
DEFERRED PAYMENT	1,170.32
TOTAL PRICE	1,205.32

4 PAYMENTS AT $292.58
$68.04 PER WEEK

TABLE 2
Characteristics of Smith's Home Foods Packages

FOOD PACKAGE NUMBER	POUNDS OF MEAT Per WEEK	MINIMUM FREEZER SIZE	FAMILY SIZE	PACKAGE PRICE*
1	14	21 cu ft	3–4	$1,205
2	12	18	3–4	1,088
3	12	18	3	1,070
4	10	15	2–3	940
5	17	21	4–5	1,532
6	6.5	12	2	655
7	8	15	2–3	1,093
8	9.5	12	2–3	825
9	11	15	2–3	809
10	11	15	2–3	834
11	13	21	4–5	958

* Price for four-month package, including tax and finance charges.

ment payment plan. In general, the requirement of having a freezer does not appear to be a barrier to food-package sales.

Christy believes that customers gain many benefits from the home delivery of food. First, it's convenient—customers can make fewer trips to the store because Smith's Home Foods packages make a large variety of foods readily available in the home. And the person who does the cooking has fewer worries about whether enough food is available. Second, Christy feels that Smith's offers superior quality products, especially meats, compared with what consumers typically find at grocery stores. She and her father carefully select the meat offered in the packages. Of course, they supply their own high-quality Smith's Country Ham products. All other meats are purchased from other quality wholesalers, either in individually wrapped portions such as eight-ounce T-bone steaks or in "family portions" such as five pound rib roasts. The wholesalers vacuum pack the meats with plastic shrink wrap to protect their freshness and flavor. Smith's Home Foods packages feature brand name meats such as Morrell, Armour, Jimmy Dean, and Fishery Products. The packages also include brand-name fruits and vegetables, such as Dulany and McKenzie, which are purchased from wholesalers. Smith's guarantees the quality of its food, stating that it will replace any food that fails to completely satisfy the customer.

Finally, Christy argues, purchasing food through a home food service saves consumers money. Because customers buy in large quantities, they receive lower prices. And they escape any price increases which occur during the four-month period covered by their food packages. Making fewer trips to the store also helps customers avoid expensive impulse purchases.

SMITH'S HOME FOODS' MARKETING PROGRAM

Smith's food packages are priced at $655 to $1,532, including tax and finance charges, with an average price of $1,000. Smith's cost of goods sold averages 48 percent for the 11 packages, not including a variable cost of $30 per package for delivery. Customers can pay cash, or they can charge or finance their purchases. Although Smith's accepts Visa and Mastercard, customers seldom use these cards to purchase the food packages. Another option allows customers to pay one-half in cash upon signing the contract and the final half within 30 days without an interest charge.

Smith's provides credit to qualified customers through the Fair Finance Company of Akron, Ohio, one of the few finance companies which finances food purchases. Customers who opt for financing make a $35 down payment and fill out a credit application. If Fair approves the application, the customer makes the first payment—one-fourth of the amount financed—thirty days after the delivery of the food. Thus, on a $1,200 food package financed by Fair, the customer makes four $300 payments. Because the first payment is not due until a month after delivery, the financing plan allows this customer to save $65 a week for food in each of the four weeks leading up to the first payment, and so forth for the remaining three payments. Although the finance company absorbs the risks of the purchase, Smith's assumes the risk until the first payment is made. That is, if a customer receives the food but does not make the first payment, Smith's accepts responsibility for the entire amount financed and must take whatever action it can to obtain payment or reclaim the food.

When a salesperson submits an order for a food package, if the customer wants to finance it, Smith's faxes a copy of the order to Fair Finance Company. Typically, the finance company approves or rejects the application within one business day. If credit is approved, a clerk completes a "pull sheet" which tells warehouse employees which package the customer purchased and what items are included. Typically, the warehouse manager holds orders until five or six are ready to be pulled and then sets a delivery date with the customer.

For customers who want to purchase freezers, Smith's sells a 21-cubic-feet freezer for approximately $800, with a cost of goods sold of $435. This freezer can also be financed through a separate finance company—consumers pay $12.95 down and make 24 monthly payments of about $43. When a customer orders a freezer and credit is approved, Smith's calls a local appliance store which then delivers the freezer to the customer and installs it. Once installed, the freezer must run for about 3 days before it reaches the appropriate temperature to receive the food. Therefore, food delivery must be coordinated with delivery of the freezer.

At this time, Smith's Home Foods stores its inventory in the Smith's Country Hams warehousing and cold storage facilities. It has a one-ton pickup truck equipped with a freezer box to make the delivery to customers. Two Smith's Country Hams employees make the deliveries, personally placing the food in the customer's freezer.

Smith's Home Foods uses both personal and mass selling techniques to promote its service. Its two full-time salespeople, Sonny Jones and Barbara Johnson, both earn salaries plus commission on their own sales. Sonny and Barbara have also recruited four other part-time, commission-only salespeople. Smith's pays its salespeople a $100 commission on each package sold. It also pays an additional $25 commission to both Sonny and Barbara for each sale made by the part-time salespeople. The same commissions are paid on each freezer sold.

When the salespeople make a call, they must often meet with the customer in the evening, spending as long as two hours discussing the service and completing the applications. Each salesperson carries a three-ring binder which contains all the information needed for a sales presentation. The binder includes twelve pages of beef and pork product pictures, six pages of poultry and fish product pictures, three pages of vegetable and fruit product pictures, and one page of dessert pictures. Additional pages describe the costs and terms for each of the 11 packages. The binder also contains pictures of freezers which can be purchased and lists substitutions allowed in the packages.

To generate leads for the salesforce, Smith's uses several mass selling techniques. First, it has advertised three times recently in the local Smithfield paper, which also serves the small adjoining community of Wolfsburg and the surrounding county with a total population of about 100,000. Each insert costs about $.04. The inserts stress the money-saving features of the service and include a detachable postcard that can be mailed, postage paid, to the company.

More recently, the company has contracted with the local Welcome Wagon to distribute a $10-off coupon for Smith's products along with the other promotions that it gives to newlyweds, families who have just had babies, and new arrivals to the community. Finally, Christy also prepared a flyer which outlines the service. Salespeople place these flyers in various locations around the community, such as beauty parlors.

Christy does not feel that Smith's Home Foods faces any direct competition in the Smithfield area. Another large, well-established company, Southern Foods of Greensboro, NC, operates a home foods service very similar to Smith's. However, although Southern Foods also operates in some other states and has customers throughout North Carolina, it does not directly target the Smithfield area. In fact, Christy feels that Southern Foods has probably helped her business—it has developed the market generally and acquainted potential customers with the kinds of services that Smith's offers.

When Christy took over, she made a number of immediate changes in an effort to improve performance of the home foods operation. She redesigned the food packages to make them more attractive and developed the newspaper insert, flyer, and sales book. Despite these efforts, however, the business has developed very slowly. As Sonny noted, the people responding most to Smith's advertisements are lower-income families who do not have the money to pay cash and who cannot qualify for financing. Smith's has had trouble attracting the middle- to upper-income families for which Christy believes the service is ideally suited.

Although only about eight families had contracted for the service when Christy took over, customers now totaled 60. However, many of the families who had signed up since she arrived would soon be finishing their first package. Christy was concerned about how many of these customers would reorder. She was also worried about how long her father's patience would last. He had told her that he would invest as much as $250,000 to get this business going. He had already invested $25,000 in inventory. Further, she estimated that Smith's Home Foods annual fixed costs amounted to $57,000, including salaries, rent and utilities, and other overhead. Christy wondered about the business' profitability and about how many customers she needed to reach to break even.

QUESTIONS

1. Outline Smith's Home Foods marketing strategy. What is Smith's Home Foods really selling?
2. What problems, if any, do you see with each element of the strategy?
3. Using information given in the case, calculate the average contribution per food package and the number of customers Smith's Home Foods needs to break-even.
4. Based on your analysis, what steps would you recommend that Christy take to improve her marketing strategy and Smith's performance?

Marketing Arithmetic

One aspect of marketing not discussed within the text is marketing arithmetic. The calculation of sales, costs, and certain ratios is important for many marketing decisions. This appendix describes three major areas of marketing arithmetic: the *operating statement*, *analytic ratios*, and *markups and markdowns*.

OPERATING STATEMENT

The operating statement and the balance sheet are the two main financial statements used by companies. The **balance sheet** shows the assets, liabilities, and net worth of a company at a given time. The **operating statement** (also called **profit and loss statement** or **income statement**) is the more important of the two for marketing information. It shows company sales, cost of goods sold, and expenses during a specified time period. By comparing the operating statement from one time period to the next, a firm can spot favorable or unfavorable trends and take appropriate action.

Table A1-1 shows the 1990 operating statement for Dale Parsons Men's Wear, a specialty store in the Midwest. This statement is for a retailer; the operating statement for a manufacturer would be somewhat different. Specifically, the section on purchases within the "cost of goods sold" area would be replaced by "cost of goods manufactured."

The outline of the operating statement follows a logical series of steps to arrive at the firm's $25,000 net profit figure:

Net sales	$300,000
Cost of goods sold	−175,000
Gross margin	$125,000
Expenses	−100,000
Net profit	$ 25,000

The first part details the amount received for the goods sold during the year. The sales figures consist of three items: *gross sales*, *returns and allowances*, and *net sales*.

Gross sales			$325,000
Less: Sales returns and allowances			25,000
Net sales			$300,000
Cost of goods sold			
Beginning inventory, January 1, at cost		$ 60,000	
Gross purchases	$165,000		
Less: Purchase discounts	15,000		
Net purchases	$150,000		
Plus: Freight-in	10,000		
Net cost of delivered purchases		$160,000	
Cost of goods available for sale		$220,000	
Less: Ending inventory, December 31, at cost		$ 45,000	
Cost of goods sold			$175,000
Gross margin			$125,000
Expenses			
Selling expenses			
Sales, salaries, and commissions	$ 40,000		
Advertising	5,000		
Delivery	5,000		
Total selling expenses		$ 50,000	
Administrative expenses			
Office salaries	$ 20,000		
Office supplies	5,000		
Miscellaneous (outside consultant)	5,000		
Total administrative expenses		$ 30,000	
General expenses			
Rent	$ 10,000		
Heat, light, telephone	5,000		
Miscellaneous (insurance, depreciation)	5,000		
Total general expenses		$ 20,000	
Total expenses			$100,000
Net profit			$ 25,000

Gross sales is the total amount charged to customers during the year for merchandise purchased in Parsons's store. As expected, some customers returned merchandise because of damage or a change of mind. If the customer gets a full refund or full credit on another purchase, we call this a *return*. Or the customer may decide to keep the item if Parsons will reduce the price; this is called an *allowance*. By subtracting returns and allowances from gross sales, we arrive at net sales—what Parsons earned in revenue from a year of selling merchandise:

Gross sales	$325,000
Returns and allowances	−25,000
Net sales	$300,000

The second major part of the operating statement calculates the amount of sales revenue Dale Parsons retains after paying the costs of the merchandise. We start with the inventory in the store at the beginning of the year. During the year, Parsons bought $165,000 worth of suits, slacks, shirts, ties, jeans, and other goods. Suppliers gave the store discounts totaling $15,000, so that net purchases were $150,000. Because the store is located away from regular shipping routes, Parsons had to pay an additional $10,000 to get the products delivered, giving the firm a net cost of $160,000. Adding the beginning inventory, the cost of goods available for sale amounted to $220,000. The $45,000 ending inventory of clothes in the store on December 31 is then subtracted to come up with the $175,000 **cost of goods sold.** Here again we have followed a logical series of steps to figure out the cost of goods sold:

Amount Parsons started with (beginning inventory)	$ 60,000
Net amount purchased	+150,000
Any added costs to obtain these purchases	+ 10,000
Total cost of goods Parsons had available for sale during year	$220,000
Amount Parsons had left over (ending inventory)	− 45,000
Cost of goods actually sold	$175,000

The difference between what Parsons paid for the merchandise ($175,000) and what he sold it for ($300,000) is called the **gross margin** ($125,000).

In order to show the profit Parsons "cleared" at the end of the year, we must subtract from the gross margin the *expenses* incurred while doing business. *Selling expenses* included two sales employees, local newspaper and radio advertising, and the cost of delivering merchandise to customers after alterations. Selling expenses totaled $50,000 for the year. *Administrative expenses* included the salary for an office manager, office supplies such as stationery and business cards, and miscellaneous expenses including an administrative audit conducted by an outside consultant. Administrative expenses totaled $30,000 in 1990. Finally, the general expenses of rent, utilities, insurance, and depreciation came to $20,000. Total expenses were therefore $100,000 for the year. By subtracting expenses ($100,000) from the gross margin ($125,000), we arrive at the net profit of $25,000 for Dale Parsons Men's Wear during 1990.

ANALYTIC RATIOS

The operating statement provides the figures needed to compute some crucial ratios. Typically these ratios are called **operating ratios** the ratio of selected operating statement items to net sales. They let marketers compare the firm's performance in one year with that in previous years (or with industry standards and competitors in the same year). The most commonly used operating ratios are the *gross margin percentage*, the *net profit percentage*, the *operating expense percentage*, and the *returns and allowances percentage*.

RATIO		FORMULA	COMPUTATION FROM TABLE A1-1
Gross margin percentage	=	$\dfrac{\text{gross margin}}{\text{net sales}}$	$= \dfrac{\$125{,}000}{\$300{,}000} = 42\%$
Net profit percentage	=	$\dfrac{\text{net profit}}{\text{net sales}}$	$= \dfrac{\$\ 25{,}000}{\$300{,}000} = 8\%$
Operating expense percentage	=	$\dfrac{\text{total expenses}}{\text{net sales}}$	$= \dfrac{\$100{,}000}{\$300{,}000} = 33\%$
Returns and allowances percentages	=	$\dfrac{\text{returns and allowances}}{\text{net sales}}$	$= \dfrac{\$\ 25{,}000}{\$300{,}000} = 8\%$

Another useful ratio is the *stockturn rate* (also called *inventory-turnover rate*). The stockturn rate is the number of times an inventory turns over or is sold during a specified time period (often one year). It may be computed on a cost, selling, or unit price basis. Thus, the formula can be:

$$\text{Stockturn rate} = \frac{\text{cost of goods sold}}{\text{average inventory at cost}}$$

or

$$\text{Stockturn rate} = \frac{\text{selling price of goods sold}}{\text{average selling price of inventory}}$$

or

$$\text{Stockturn rate} = \frac{\text{sales in units}}{\text{average inventory in units}}$$

We use the first formula to calculate the stockturn rate for Dale Parsons Men's Wear:

$$\frac{\$175,000}{\dfrac{\$60,000 + \$45,000}{2}} = \frac{\$175,000}{\$52,500} = 3.3$$

That is, Parson's inventory turned over 3.3 times in 1990. Normally, the higher the stockturn rate, the higher the management efficiency and company profitability.

Return on investment (ROI) is frequently used to measure managerial effectiveness. It uses figures from the firm's operating statement and balance sheet. A commonly used formula for computing ROI is:

$$\text{ROI} = \frac{\text{net profit}}{\text{sales}} \times \frac{\text{sales}}{\text{investment}}$$

You may have two questions about this formula: Why use a two-step process when ROI could be computed simply as net profit divided by investment? And what exactly is "investment"?

To answer these questions, let's look at how each component of the formula can affect the ROI. Suppose Dale Parsons Men's Wear has total investment of $150,000. Then we can compute ROI as follows:

$$\text{ROI} = \frac{\$25,000 \text{ (net profit)}}{\$300,000 \text{ (sales)}} \times \frac{\$300,000 \text{ (sales)}}{\$150,000 \text{ (investment)}}$$

$$8.3\% \quad \times \quad 2 \quad = 16.6\%$$

Now suppose that Parsons had worked to increase its share of the market. The firm could have had the same ROI if sales doubled while dollar profit and investment stayed the same (accepting a lower profit ratio to get a higher turnover and market share):

$$\text{ROI} = \frac{\$25,000 \text{ (net profit)}}{\$600,000 \text{ (sales)}} \times \frac{\$600,000 \text{ (sales)}}{\$150,000 \text{ (investment)}}$$

$$4.16\% \quad \times \quad 4 \quad = 16.6\%$$

Parsons might have increased its ROI by increasing net profit through more cost cutting and more efficient marketing:

$$\text{ROI} = \frac{\$50,000 \text{ (net profit)}}{\$300,000 \text{ (sales)}} \times \frac{\$300,000 \text{ (sales)}}{\$150,000 \text{ (investment)}}$$

$$16.6\% \quad \times \quad 2 \quad = 33.2\%$$

Another way to increase ROI is to find some way to get the same levels of sales and profits while decreasing investment (perhaps by cutting the size of Parson's average inventory):

$$\text{ROI} = \frac{\$25{,}000 \text{ (net profit)}}{\$300{,}000 \text{ (sales)}} \times \frac{\$300{,}000 \text{ (sales)}}{\$75{,}000 \text{ (investment)}}$$

$$8.3\% \quad \times \quad 4 \quad = 33.2\%$$

What is "investment" in the ROI formula? *Investment* is often defined as the total assets of the firm. But many analysts now use other measures of return to assess performance. These measures include *return on net assets* (*RONA*), *return on stockholders' equity* (*ROE*), or *return on assets managed* (*ROAM*). Because investment is measured at a specified point in time, we usually compute ROI as the average investment between two time periods (say, January 1 and December 31 of the same year). We can also compute ROI as an "internal rate of return" by using discounted cash flow analysis (see any finance textbook for more on this technique). The objective in using any of these measures is to determine how well the company has been using its resources. As inflation, competitive pressures, and cost of capital increase, such measures become increasingly important indicators of marketing and company performance.

MARKUPS AND MARKDOWNS

Retailers and wholesalers must understand the concepts of **markups** and **markdowns.** They must make a profit to stay in business, and the markup percentage affects profits. Markups and markdowns are expressed as percentages.

There are two different ways to compute markups—on *cost* or on selling *price*:

$$\text{Markup percentage on cost} = \frac{\text{dollar markup}}{\text{cost}}$$

$$\text{Markup percentage on selling price} = \frac{\text{dollar markup}}{\text{selling price}}$$

Dale Parsons must decide which formula to use. If Parsons bought shirts for $15 and wanted to mark them up $10, the markup percentage on cost would be $10/$15 = 66.7%. If Parsons based markup on selling price, the percentage would be $10/$25 = 40%. In figuring markup percentage, most retailers use the selling price rather than the cost.

Suppose Parsons knew the cost ($12) and desired markup on price (25%) for a man's tie and wanted to compute the selling price. The formula is:

$$\text{Selling price} = \text{cost} \div (1 - \text{markup})$$
$$\text{Selling price} = \$12 \div .75 = \$16$$

As a product moves through the channel of distribution, each channel member adds a markup before selling the product to the next member. This "markup chain" is shown for a suit purchased by a Parsons customer for $200:

		$ AMOUNT	% OF SELLING PRICE
Manufacturer	Cost	$108	90%
	Markup	12	10%
	Selling price	$120	100%
Wholesaler	Cost	$120	80%
	Markup	30	20%
	Selling price	$150	100%
Retailer	Cost	$150	75%
	Markup	50	25%
	Selling price	$200	100%

The retailer whose markup is 25 percent does not necessarily enjoy more profit than a manufacturer whose markup is 10 percent. Profit also depends on how many items with that profit margin can be sold (stockturn rate) and on operating efficiency (expenses).

Sometimes a retailer wants to convert markups based on selling price to markups based on cost, and vice versa. The formulas are:

$$\text{Markup percentage on selling price} = \frac{\text{markup percentage on cost}}{100\% + \text{markup percentage on cost}}$$

$$\text{Markup percentage on cost} = \frac{\text{markup percentage on selling price}}{100\% - \text{markup percentage on selling price}}$$

Suppose that Dale Parsons found that a competitor was using a markup of 30 percent based on cost and wanted to know what this would be as a percentage of selling price. The calculation would be:

$$\frac{30\%}{100\% + 30\%} = \frac{30\%}{130\%} = 23\%$$

Because Parsons was using a 25 percent markup on the selling price for suits, he believed that the markup was suitable compared with that of the competitor.

Near the end of the summer Parsons still had an inventory of summer slacks in stock. Therefore, he decided to use a *markdown*, a reduction from the original selling price. Before the summer he had purchased 20 pairs at $10 each and had since sold 10 pairs at $20 each. Parsons marked down the other pairs to $15 and sold 5 pairs. We compute the *markdown ratio* as follows:

$$\text{Markdown percentage} = \frac{\text{dollar markdown}}{\text{total net sales in dollars}}$$

The dollar markdown is $25 (5 pairs at $5 each) and total net sales are $275 (10 pairs at $20 + 5 pairs at $15). The ratio, then, is $25/$275 = 9%.

Larger retailers usually compute markdown ratios for each department rather than for individual items. The ratios provide a measure of relative marketing performance for each department and can be calculated and compared over time. Markdown ratios can also be used to compare the performance of different buyers and salespeople in a store's various departments.

■ KEY TERMS

Balance sheet. A financial statement that shows the assets, liabilities, and net worth of a company at a given time.

Cost of goods sold. The net cost to the company of all goods sold during a given time period.

Gross margin. The difference between net sales and cost of goods sold.

Gross sales. The total amount that a company charges customers during a given period of time for merchandise purchased.

Markdown. A percentage reduction from the original selling price.

Markup. The percentage of the cost or price of a product added to the cost in order to arrive at a selling price.

Operating ratios. Ratios of selected operating statement items to net sales that allow marketers to compare the firm's performance in one year with that in previous years (or with industry standards and competitors in the same year).

Operating statement (or **profit and loss statement** or **income statement**). A financial statement that shows company sales, cost of goods sold, and expenses during a given period of time.

Return on investment (ROI). A common measure of managerial effectiveness—the ratio of net profit to investment.

Careers in Marketing

Now that you have completed your first course in marketing, you have a good idea of what the field entails. You may have decided that you want to pursue a marketing career because it offers constant challenge, stimulating problems, the opportunity to work with people, and excellent advancement opportunities. Marketing is a very broad field with a wide variety of tasks involving the analysis, planning, implementation, and control of marketing programs. You will find marketing positions in all types and sizes of institutions. This appendix describes entry-level and higher-level marketing opportunities and lists steps that you might take to select a career path and better market *yourself*.

DESCRIPTION OF MARKETING JOBS

Almost a third of all Americans are employed in marketing-related positions. Thus, the number of possible marketing careers is enormous. Because of the knowledge of products and consumers gained in these jobs, marketing positions provide excellent training for the highest levels in an organization. A recent study by one executive recruiting firm found that more top executives have backgrounds in marketing than any other field—31 percent of the *Fortune* 1000 chief executives spent the bulk of their careers in marketing.[1]

Marketing salaries vary by company and position. Beginning salaries usually rank only slightly below those for engineering and chemistry but equal or exceed those for economics, finance, accounting, general business, and the liberal arts. If you succeed in an entry-level marketing position, you will quickly be promoted to higher levels of responsibility and salary.

Marketing has become an attractive career for some people who have not traditionally considered the field. One trend is the growing number of women entering the marketing field. Women have historically been employed in the retailing and advertising areas of marketing. But they have now moved into all types of sales and marketing positions. Women now pursue successful sales careers in pharmaceutical companies, publishing companies, banks, consumer products companies, and an increasing number of industrial selling jobs. Their ranks are also growing in product and brand manager positions.

Another trend is the growing acceptance of marketing by nonprofit organizations. Colleges, arts organizations, libraries, and hospitals are increasingly applying marketing to their problems. They are beginning to hire marketing directors and marketing vice-presidents to manage their varied marketing activities.

Here are brief descriptions of some important marketing jobs.

Advertising

Advertising is an important business activity that requires skill in planning, fact gathering, and creativity. Although compensation for starting advertising people tends to be lower than that in other marketing fields, opportunities for advancement are usually greater because of less emphasis on age or length of employment. Typical jobs in advertising agencies include the following positions.[2]

Copywriters help find the concepts behind the written words and visual images of advertisements. They dig for facts, read avidly, and borrow ideas. They talk to customers, suppliers, and *anybody* who might give them clues about how to attract the target audience's attention and interest.

Art directors constitute the other part of the creative team. They translate copywriters' ideas into dramatic visuals called "layouts." Agency artists develop print layouts, package designs, television layouts (called "storyboards"), corporate logotypes, trademarks, and symbols. They specify the style and size of typography, paste the type in place, and arrange all the details of the ad so that it can be reproduced by engravers and printers. A superior art director or copy chief becomes the agency's creative director and oversees all its advertising. The creative director is high in the ad agency's structure.

Account executives are liaisons between clients and agencies. They must know a great deal about marketing and its various components. They explain client plans and objectives to agency creative teams and supervise the development of the total advertising plan. Their main task is to keep the client happy with the agency! Because "account work" involves many personal relationships, account executives are usually personable, diplomatic, and sincere.

Media buyers select the best media for clients. Media representatives come to buyers' offices armed with statistics to prove that *their* numbers are better, *their* costs per thousand are less, and *their* medium delivers more ripe audiences than competitive media. Media buyers must evaluate these claims. In addition, they must bargain with the broadcast media for best rates and make deals with the print media for good ad positions.

Large ad agencies have active marketing research departments that provide the information needed to develop new ad campaigns and assess current campaigns. People interested in marketing research should consider jobs with ad agencies.

Brand and Product Management

Brand and product managers plan, direct, and control business and marketing efforts for their products. They are concerned with research and development, packaging, manufacturing, sales and distribution, advertising, promotion, market research, and business analysis and forecasting. In consumer goods companies, the newcomer—who usually needs a Masters of Business Administration (MBA) degree—joins a brand team and learns the ropes by doing numerical analyses and watching senior brand people. This person eventually heads a team and later moves on to manage a larger brand. Many industrial goods companies also have product managers. Product management is one of the best training grounds for future corporate officers.

Customer Affairs

Some large consumer goods companies have customer affairs people who act as liaisons between customers and firms. They handle complaints, suggestions, and problems concerning the company's products, determine what actions to take, and coordinate the activities required to solve problems. The position requires an empathetic, diplomatic, and capable person who can work with a wide range of people both inside and outside a firm.

Industrial Marketing People interested in industrial marketing careers can go into sales, service, product design, marketing research, or one of several other positions. They sometimes need a technical background. Most people start in sales and spend time in training and making calls with senior salespeople. If they stay in sales, they may advance to district, regional, and higher sales positions. Or they may go into product management and work closely with customers, suppliers, manufacturing, and sales engineering.

International Marketing As U.S. firms increase their international business, they need people who are familiar with foreign languages and cultures and who are willing to travel to or relocate in foreign cities. For such assignments, most companies seek experienced peole who have proved themselves in domestic operations. An MBA often helps but is not always required.

Marketing Management Science and Systems Analysis People who have been trained in management science, quantitative methods, and systems analysis can act as consultants to managers who face such difficult marketing problems as demand measurement and forecasting, market structure analysis, and new-product evaluation. The most career opportunities exist in larger marketing-oriented firms, management consulting firms, and public institutions concerned with health, education, or transportation. An MBA or a Master of Science (MS) degree is often required.

Marketing Research Marketing researchers interact with managers to define problems and identify the information needed to resolve them. They design research projects, prepare questionnaires and samples, analyze data, prepare reports, and present their findings and recommendations to management. They must understand statistics, consumer behavior, psychology, and sociology. A master's degree helps. Career opportunities exist with manufacturers, retailers, some wholesalers, trade and industry associations, marketing research firms, advertising agencies, and governmental and private nonprofit agencies.

New-Product Planning People interested in new-product planning can find opportunities in many types of organizations. They usually need a good background in marketing, marketing research, and sales forecasting; they need organizational skills to motivate and coordinate others, and they may need a technical background. Usually, these people work first in other marketing positions before joining the new-product department.

Physical Distribution Physical distribution is a large and dynamic field, with many career opportunities. Major transportation carriers, manufacturers, wholesalers, and retailers all employ physical-distribution specialists. Coursework in quantitative methods, finance, accounting, and marketing provides the necessary skills for entering the field.

Public Relations Most organizations have a public relations person or staff to anticipate public problems, handle complaints, deal with media, and build the corporate image. People interested in public relations should be able to speak and write clearly and persuasively, and they should have a background in journalism, communications, or the liberal arts. The challenges in this job are highly varied and very people-oriented.

Purchasing Purchasing agents are playing a growing role in firms' profitability during periods of rising costs, materials shortages, and increasing product complexity. In retail organizations, working as a ''buyer'' can be a good route to the top. Purchasing agents in industrial companies play a key role in holding down costs. A technical background is useful in some purchasing positions, along with a knowledge of credit, finance, and physical distribution.

Retailing Management Retailing provides people with an early opportunity to take on marketing responsibilities. Although retail starting salaries and job assignments have typically been lower than those in manufacturing or advertising, the gap is narrowing. The major routes to top management in retailing are merchandise management and store management. In merchandise management, a person moves from buyer trainee to assistant buyer to buyer to merchandise division manager. In store management, an individual moves from management trainee to assistant department (sales) manager to department manager to store (branch) manager. Buyers are primarily concerned with merchandise selection and promotion; department managers are concerned with salesforce management and display. Large-scale retailing lets new recruits move in only a few years into the management of a branch or part of a store doing as much as $5 million in sales.

Sales and Sales Management Sales and sales-management opportunities exist in a wide range of profit and nonprofit organizations and in product and service organizations, including financial, insurance, consulting, and government. Individuals must carefully match their backgrounds, interests, technical skills, and academic training with available sales jobs. Training programs vary greatly in form and length, ranging from a few weeks to two years. Career paths lead from salesperson to district, regional, and higher levels of sales management and, in many cases, the top management of a firm.

Other Marketing Careers Many other marketing-related jobs exist in areas such as sales promotion, wholesaling, packaging, pricing, and credit management. Information on these positions can be gathered from sources such as those listed in the following discussion.

CHOOSING AND GETTING A JOB

To choose and obtain a job, you must apply marketing skills, particularly marketing analysis and planning. Here are eight steps for choosing a career and finding that first job.

Make a Self-Assessment Self-assessment is the most important part of a job search. It involves honestly evaluating your interests, strengths, and weaknesses. What are your career objectives? What kind of organization do you want to work for? What do you do well or not so well? What sets you apart from other job seekers? Do the answers to these questions suggest which careers you should seek or avoid? For help in self-assessment, you might look at the following books, each of which raises many questions you should consider:

1. *What Color Is Your Parachute?*, by Richard Bolles
2. *Three Boxes in Life and How to Get Out of Them*, by Richard Bolles
3. *Guerrilla Tactics in the Job Market*, by Tom Jackson

Also consult the career counseling, testing, and placement services at your school.

Examine Job Descriptions Now look at various job descriptions to see what positions best match your interests, desires, and abilities. Descriptions can be found in the *Occupation Outlook Handbook* and the *Dictionary of Occupational Titles* published by the U.S. Department of Labor. These volumes describe the duties of people in various occupations, the necessary specific training and education, the availability of jobs in each field, possibilities for advancement, and probable earnings.

Develop Job-Search Objectives Your initial career shopping list should be broad and flexible. Look broadly for ways to achieve your objectives. For example, if you want a career in marketing research, consider the public as well as the private sector and regional as well as national firms. Only after exploring many options should you begin to focus on specific industries and initial jobs. You need to set down a list of basic goals. Your list might say: "a job in a small company, in a large city, in the Sunbelt, doing marketing research, with a consumer products firm."

Examine the Job Market and Assess Opportunities You must now look at the market to see what positions are available. For an up-to-date listing of marketing-related job openings, refer to the latest edition of the *College Placement Annual* available at school placement offices. This publication lists current job openings for hundreds of companies seeking college graduates for entry-level positions. It also lists companies seeking experienced or advanced-degree people. At this stage, use the services of your placement office to the fullest extent in order to find openings and set up interviews. Take the time to analyze the industries and companies in which you are interested. Consult business magazines, annual reports, business reference books, faculty members, school career counselors, and fellow students. Try to analyze the future growth and profit potential of the company and industry, chances for advancement, salary levels, entry positions, amount of travel, and other important factors.

Develop Search Strategies

How will you contact companies in which you are interested? There are several possible ways. One of the best ways is through on-campus interviews. But not all the companies that interest you will visit your school. Another good way is to phone or write the company directly. Finally, you can ask marketing professors or school alumni for contacts and references.

Develop Résumé and Cover Letter

Your résumé should persuasively present your abilities, education, background, training, work experience, and personal qualifications—but it should also be brief, usually one page. The goal is to gain a positive response from potential employers.

The cover letter is, in some ways, more difficult to write than the résumé. It must be persuasive, professional, concise, and interesting. Ideally, it should set you apart from other candidates for the position. Each letter should look and sound original— that is, it should be individually typed and tailored to the specific organization being contacted. It should describe the position you are applying for, arouse interest, describe your qualifications, and tell how you can be contacted. Cover letters should be addressed to an individual rather than a title. You should follow up the letter with a telephone call.

Obtain Interviews

Here is some advice to follow before, during, and after your interviews.

Before the Interview

1. Interviewers have extremely diverse styles—the ''chit chat,'' let's-get-to-know-each-other style; the interrogation style of question after question; the tough-probing why, why, why style; and many others. Be ready for anything.
2. Practice being interviewed with a friend and ask for a critique.
3. Prepare to ask at least five good questions that are not readily answered in the company literature.
4. Anticipate possible interview questions and prepare good answers ahead of time.
5. Avoid back-to-back interviews—they can be exhausting.
6. Dress conservatively and tastefully for the interview. Be neat and clean.
7. Arrive about ten minutes early to collect your thoughts before the interview. Check your name on the interview schedule, noting the name of the interviewer and the room number.
8. Review the major points you intend to cover.

During the Interview

1. Give a firm handshake when greeting the interviewer. Introduce yourself using the same form the interviewer uses. Make a good initial impression.
2. Retain your poise. Relax. Smile occasionally. Be enthusiastic throughout the interview.
3. Good eye contact, good posture, and distinct speech are musts. Don't clasp your hands or fiddle with jewelry, hair, or clothing. Sit comfortably in your chair. Do not smoke, even if asked.
4. Have extra copies of your résumé with you.
5. Have your story down pat. Present your selling points. Answer questions directly. Avoid one-word answers but don't be wordy.
6. Most times, let the interviewer take the initiative, but don't be passive. Find good opportunities to direct the conversation to things you want the interviewer to hear.
7. To end on a high note, the latter part of the interview is the best time to make your most important point or to ask pertinent questions.

8. Don't be afraid to "close." You might say, "I'm very interested in the position and I have enjoyed this interview."
9. Obtain the interviewer's business card or address and phone number so that you can follow up later.

After the Interview

1. After leaving the interview, record the key points that arose. Be sure to record who is to follow up on the interview and when a decision can be expected.
2. Objectively analyze the interview with regard to questions asked, answers given, your overall interview presentation, and the interviewer's response to specific points.
3. Send a thank-you letter mentioning any additional items pertinent to your application and your willingness to supply further information.
4. If you do not hear within the time specified, write or call the interviewer to determine your status.

Follow-Up If you are successful, you will be invited to visit the organization. The in-company interview will run from a few hours to a whole day. The company will examine your interest, maturity, enthusiasm, assertiveness, logic, and company and functional knowledge. You should ask questions about things that are important to you. Find out about the environment, job role, responsibilities, opportunity, current industrial issues, and the firm's personality. The company wants to know if you are the right person for the job; just as importantly, you want to know if this is the right job for you.

■ REFERENCES

1. See E. S. Ely, "Room at the Top: American Companies Turn to Marketers to Lead Them Through the Eighties," *Madison Avenue*, September 1984, p. 57.

2. This description of advertising positions is based on Jack Engel, *Advertising: The Process and Practice* (New York: McGraw-Hill, 1980), pp. 429–34.

Glossary

Accessibility The degree to which a market segment can be reached and served.

Actionability The degree to which effective programs can be designed for attracting and serving a given market segment.

Action program A detailed program that shows what must be done, who will do it, and how decisions and actions will be coordinated to implement marketing plans and strategy.

Actual product A product's parts, styling, features, brand name, packaging, and other attributes that combine to deliver core product benefits.

Adapted marketing mix An international marketing strategy for adjusting the marketing mix elements to each international target market, bearing more costs but hoping for a larger market share and return.

Administered VMS A vertical marketing system that coordinates successive stages of production and distribution, not through common ownership or contractual ties but through the size and power of one of the parties.

Adoption The decision by an individual to become a regular user of the product.

Adoption process The mental process through which an individual passes from first hearing about an innovation to final adoption.

Advertising Any paid form of nonpersonal presentation and promotion of ideas, goods, or services by an identified sponsor.

Advertising objective A specific communication *task* to be accomplished with a specific *target* audience during a specific period of *time*.

Advertising specialties Useful articles imprinted with an advertiser's name given as gifts to consumers.

Affordable method Setting the promotion budget at a level management thinks the company can afford.

Age and life-cycle segmentation Dividing a market into different age and life-cycle groups.

Agent A wholesaler who represents buyers or sellers on a more permanent basis, performs only a few functions, and does not take title to goods.

Allowance Promotional money paid by manufacturers to retailers in return for an agreement to feature the manufacturer's products in some way.

Alternative evaluation The stage of the buyer decision process in which the consumer uses information to evaluate alternative brands in the choice set.

Annual plan A short-range marketing plan that describes the current marketing situation, company objectives, the marketing strategy for the year, the action program, budgets, and controls.

Annual plan control Evaluation and corrective action to ensure that the company achieves the sales, profits, and other goals set out in its annual plan.

Approach The step in the selling process in which the salesperson meets and greets the buyer to get the relationship off to a good start.

Aspirational group A group to which an individual wishes to belong.

Atmospheres Designed environments that create or reinforce the buyer's leanings toward consumption of a product.

Attitude A person's consistently favorable or unfavorable evaluations, feelings, and tendencies toward an object or idea.

Augmented product Additional consumer services and benefits built around the core and actual products.

Automatic vending Selling through vending machines.

Available market The set of consumers who have interest, income, and access to a particular product or service.

Baby boom The major increase in the annual birth rate following World War II and lasting until the early 1960s. The "baby boomers," now moving into middle age, are a prime target for marketers.

Barter transaction A marketing transaction in which goods or services are traded for other goods or services.

Basing-point pricing A geographic pricing strategy in which the seller designates some city as a basing point and charges all customers the freight cost from that city to the customer location, regardless of the city from which the goods are actually shipped.

BCG growth-share matrix A portfolio planning method that evaluates a company's strategic business units in terms of their market growth rate and relative market share. SBUs are classified as stars, cash cows, question marks, or dogs.

Behavior segmentation Dividing a market into groups based on their knowledge, attitude, use, or response to a product.

Belief A descriptive thought that a person holds about something.

Benefit segmentation Dividing the market into groups according to the different benefits that consumers seek from the product.

Brand A name, term, sign, symbol, or design, or a combination of these intended to identify the goods or services of one seller or group of sellers and to differentiate them from those of competitors.

Brand extension A new or modified product launched under an already successful brand name.

Brand image The set of beliefs consumers hold about a particular brand.

Brand mark That part of a brand which can be recognized but is not utterable, such as a symbol, design, or distinctive coloring or lettering. Examples are the Pillsbury doughboy, the Metro-Goldwyn-Mayer lion, and the red K on the Kodak film box.

Brand name That part of a brand which can be vocalized—the utterable, such as Avon, Chevrolet, Tide, Disneyland, American Express, and UCLA.

Breakeven pricing (target profit pricing) Setting price to break even on the costs of making and marketing a product, or to make the desired profit.

Broker A wholesaler who does not take title to goods and whose function is to bring buyers and sellers together and assist in negotiation.

Business analysis A review of the sales, costs, and profit projections for a new product to determine whether these factors satisfy the company's objectives.

Business portfolio The collection of businesses and products that make up the company.

Buyer The person who makes an actual purchase.

Buyer-readiness states The stages consumers normally pass through on their way to purchase, including awareness, knowledge, liking, preference, conviction, or purchase.

Buying center All the individuals and units who participate in the organizational buying decision process.

By-product pricing Setting a price for by-products in order to make the main product's price more competitive.

Capital items Industrial goods that enter the finished product partly, including installations and accessory equipment.

Captive-product pricing The pricing of products that must be used along with a main product, such as blades for a razor and film for cameras.

Cash cows Low-growth, high-share businesses or products—established and successful units that generate cash which the company uses to pay its bills and support other business units that need investment.

Cash discount A price reduction to buyers who pay their bills promptly.

Cash refund offers (rebates) Offers to refund part of the purchase price of a product after the purchase to consumers who send a "proof of purchase" to the manufacturer.

Catalog marketing Direct marketing through catalogs mailed to a select list of customers or made available in stores.

Catalog showroom A retail operation that sells a wide selection of high-markup, fast-moving, brand-name goods at discount prices.

Chain stores Two or more outlets that are commonly owned and controlled, have central buying and merchandising, and sell similar lines of merchandise.

Channel conflict Disagreement among marketing channel members on goals and roles—on who should do what and for what rewards.

Channel level A layer of middlemen that perform some work in bringing the product and its ownership closer to the final buyer.

Closed-end questions Questions that include all the possible answers and allow subjects make choices among them.

Closing The step in the selling process in which the salesperson asks the customer for an order.

Cognitive dissonance Buyer discomfort caused by post-purchase conflict.

Combination stores Combined food and drug stores.

Commercialization Introducing a new product into the market.

Company culture A system of values and beliefs shared by people in an organization—the company's collective identity and meaning.

Company marketing opportunity An attractive arena for marketing action in which the company would enjoy a competitive advantage.

Comparison advertising Advertising that compares one brand directly or indirectly to one or more other brands.

Competitive advantage An advantage over competitors gained by offering consumers greater value—either through

lower prices or by providing more benefits that justify higher prices.

Competitive-parity method Setting the promotion budget to match competitors' outlays.

Competitive strategies Strategies that strongly position the company against competitors and that give the company the strongest possible strategic advantage.

Competitor analysis The process of identifying major competitors; assessing their objectives, strategies, strengths and weaknesses, and reaction patterns; and selecting which competitors to attack or avoid.

Competitor-centered company A company whose moves are mainly based on competitors' actions and reactions; it spends most of its time tracking competitors' moves and market shares and trying to find strategies to counter them.

Concentrated marketing A market-coverage strategy in which a firm goes after a large share of one or a few submarkets.

Concept testing Testing new product concepts with a group of target consumers to learn whether the concepts have strong consumer appeal.

Consumer franchise-building promotions Sales promotions that promote the product's positioning and include a selling message along with the deal.

Consumer goods Those bought by final consumers for personal consumption.

Consumerism An organized movement of citizens and government to improve the rights and power of buyers in relation to sellers.

Consumer market All the individuals and households who buy or acquire goods and services for personal consumption.

Consumer-oriented marketing A principle of enlightened marketing which holds that a company should view and organize its marketing activities from the consumers' point of view.

Consumer promotion Sales promotion designed to stimulate consumer purchasing, including samples, coupons, rebates, prices-off, premiums, patronage

rewards, displays, contests, and sweepstakes.

Containerization Putting the goods in boxes or trailers that are easy to transfer between two transportation modes. They are used in "multimode" systems commonly referred to as piggyback, fishyback, trainship, and airtruck.

Contests, sweepstakes, and **games** Promotional events that give consumers the chance to win something—such as cash, trips, or goods—by luck or through extra effort.

Continuity Scheduling ads evenly within a given period.

Contract manufacturing Joint venturing to enter a foreign market by contracting with manufacturers in the foreign market to produce the product.

Contractual VMS A vertical marketing system in which independent firms at different levels of production and distribution join together through contracts to obtain more economies or sales impact than they could achieve alone.

Convenience goods Consumer goods that the customer usually buys frequently, immediately, and with the minimum of comparison and buying effort.

Convenience store A small store, located near a residential area, open long hours, seven days a week, and carrying a limited line of high-turnover convenience goods.

Conventional distribution channel A channel consisting of one or more independent producers, wholesalers, and retailers, each a separate business seeking to maximize its own profits even at the expense of profits for the system as a whole.

Copyright The exclusive legal right to reproduce, publish, and sell the matter and form of a literary, musical, or artistic work.

Copy testing Measuring the communication effect of an advertisement before or after it is printed or broadcast.

Core product The problem-solving services or core benefits that consumers are really buying when they obtain a product.

Corporate VMS A vertical marketing system which combines successive stages of production and distribution under single ownership—channel leadership is established through common ownership.

Cost-plus pricing Adding a standard markup to the cost of the product.

Countertrade International trade involving the direct or indirect exchange of goods for other goods instead of cash. Forms include barter, compensation (buy-back), and counterpurchase.

Coupons Certificates that give buyers a saving when they purchase a product.

Cultural environment Institutions and other forces that affect society's basic values, perceptions, preferences, and behaviors.

Culture The set of basic values, perceptions, wants, and behaviors learned by a member of society from family and other important institutions.

Current marketing situation The section of a marketing plan that describes the target market and the company's position in it.

Customer attitude tracking Tracking the attitudes of customers, dealers, and other marketing system participants and their effects on sales.

Customer-centered company A company that focuses on customer developments in designing its marketing strategies.

Customer salesforce structure A salesforce organization in which salespeople specialize in selling only to certain customers or industries.

Customer value analysis Analysis conducted to determine what benefits target customers value and how they rate the relative value of varius competitors' offers.

Decider The person who ultimately makes a buying decision or any part of it—whether to buy, what to buy, how to buy, or where to buy.

Decision and reward systems Formal and informal operating procedures that guide such activities as planning, information gathering, budgeting, recruiting and training, control, and personnel and rewards.

Decline stage The product life-cycle stage at which a product's sales decline.

Deficient products Products that have neither immediate appeal nor long-run benefits.

Demand curve A curve that projects the number of units the market will buy in a given time period at different prices that might be charged.

Demands Human wants that are backed by buying power.

Demarketing Marketing in which the task is to temporarily or permanently reduce demand.

Demographic segmentation Dividing the market into groups based on demographic variables such as age, sex, family size, family life cycle, income, occupation, education, religion, race, and nationality.

Demography The study of human populations in terms of size, density, location, age, sex, race, occupation, and other statistics.

Department store A retail organization that carries a wide variety of product lines—typically clothing, home furnishings, and household goods; each line is operated as a separate department managed by specialist buyers or merchandisers.

Derived demand Organizational demand that ultimately comes from (derives from) the demand for consumer goods.

Descriptive research Marketing research to better describe marketing problems, situations, or markets—such as the market potential for a product or the demographics and attitudes of consumers.

Desirable products Products that give both high immediate satisfaction and high long-run benefits.

Differentiated marketing A market-coverage strategy in which a firm decides to target several market segments and designs separate offers for each.

Direct investment Entering a foreign market by developing foreign-based assembly or manufacturing facilities.

Direct-mail marketing Direct marketing through single mailings that include letters, ads, samples, foldouts, and other "salespeople on wings" sent to prospects on mailing lists.

Direct marketing Marketing through various advertising media that interact directly with consumers, generally calling for the consumer to make a direct response.

Direct-marketing channel A marketing channel that has no intermediary levels.

Discount A straight reduction in price on purchases during a stated period of time.

Discount store A retail institution that sells standard merchandise at lower prices by accepting lower margins and selling at higher volume.

Discriminatory pricing Selling a product or service at two or more prices; the difference in prices is not based on differences in costs.

Distribution center A large and highly automated warehouse designed to receive goods from various plants and suppliers, take orders, fill them efficiently, and deliver goods to customers as quickly as possible.

Distribution channel (marketing channel) A set of interdependent organizations involved in the process of making a product or service available for use or consumption by the consumer or industrial user.

Distribution programming Building a planned, professionally managed, vertical marketing system that meets the needs of both the manufacturer *and* the distributors.

Diversification A strategy for company growth by starting up or acquiring businesses outside the company's current products and markets.

Dogs Low-growth, low-share businesses and products that may generate enough cash to maintain themselves, but do not promise to be a large source of cash.

Door-to-door retailing Selling door-to-door, office-to-office, or at-home sales parties.

Durable goods Consumer goods that are usually used over an extended period of time and that normally survive many uses.

Economic community A group of nations organized to work toward common goals in the regulation of international trade.

Economic environment Factors that affect consumer buying power and spending patterns.

Electronic shopping Direct marketing through a two-way system that links consumers with the seller's computerized catalog by cable or telephone lines.

Embargo A ban on the import of a certain product.

Emotional appeals Message appeals that attempt to arouse negative or positive emotions that will motivate purchase; examples include fear, guilt, shame, love, humor, pride, and joy appeals.

Engel's laws Differences noted more than a century ago by Ernst Engel in how people shift their spending across food, housing, transportation, health care, and other goods and services categories as family income rises.

Enlightened marketing A marketing philosophy holding that a company's marketing should support the best long-run performance of the marketing system; its five principles include consumer-oriented marketing, innovative marketing, value marketing, sense-of-mission marketing, and societal marketing.

Environmentalism An organized movement of concerned citizens and government to protect and improve people's living environment.

Environmental management perspective A management perspective in which the firm takes aggressive actions to affect the publics and forces in its marketing environment rather than simply watching and reacting to them.

Events Occurrences staged to communicate messages to target audiences, such as news conferences, grand openings, or others.

Exchange The act of obtaining a desired object from someone by offering something in return.

Exchange controls Limits placed by a government on the amount of its foreign exchange with other countries and on its exchange rate against other currencies.

Exclusive distribution Giving a limited number of dealers the exclusive right to distribute the company's products in their territories.

Executive summary The opening section of the marketing plan which presents a short summary of the main goals and recommendations to be presented in the plan.

Expense-to-sales analysis Analyzing the ratio of marketing expenses to sales in order to keep marketing expenses in line.

Experience curve (learning curve) The drop in the average per-unit production costs that comes with accumulated production experience.

Experimental research The gathering of primary data by selecting matched groups of subjects, giving them different treatments, controlling related factors, and checking for differences in group responses.

Exploratory research Marketing research to gather preliminary information that will help to better define problems and suggest hypotheses.

Exporting Entering a foreign market by exporting products and selling them through international marketing middlement (indirect exporting) or through the company's own department, branch, or sales representatives or agents (direct exporting).

Extensive problem solving Buyer behavior in cases in which buyers face complex buying decisions for more expensive, less frequently purchased products in an unfamiliar product class. Buyers engage in extensive information search and evaluation.

Factory outlets Off-price retailing operations that are owned and operated by manufacturers and that normally carry the manufacturer's surplus, discontinued, or irregular goods.

Fads Fashions that enter quickly, are adopted with great zeal, peak early, and decline very fast.

Family life cycle The stages through which families might pass as they mature over time.

Fashion A currently accepted or popular style in a given field.

Financial intermediaries Banks, credit companies, insurance companies, and other businesses that help finance transactions or insure against the risks associated with the buying and selling of goods.

Fixed costs Costs that do not vary with production or sales level.

FOB origin pricing A geographic pricing strategy in which goods are placed free on board a carrier, and the customer pays the freight from the factory to the destination.

Focus-group interviewing Personal interviewing which consists of inviting six to ten people to gather for a few hours with a trained interviewer to talk about a product, service, or organization. The interviewer "focuses" the group discussion on important issues.

Follow-up The last step in the selling process in which the salesperson follows up after the sales to ensure customer satisfaction and repeat business.

Forecasting The art of estimating future demand by anticipating what buyers are likely to do under a given set of conditions.

Franchise A contractual association between a manufacturer, wholesaler, or service organization (a franchiser) and independent business people (franchisees) who buy the right to own and operate one or more units in the franchise system.

Franchise organization A contractual vertical marketing system in which a channel member called a franchiser links several stages in the production-distribution process.

Freight absorption pricing A geographic pricing strategy in which the company absorbs all or part of the actual freight charges in order to get the business.

Frequency The number of times the average person in the target market is exposed to an advertising message during a given period.

Full-service retailers Retailers that provide a full range of services to shoppers.

Full-service wholesalers Wholesalers that provide a full set of services such as carrying stock, using a salesforce, offering credit, making deliveries, and providing management assistance.

Functional discount A price reduction offered by the seller to trade channel members who perform certain functions such as selling, storing, and recordkeeping.

Functional organization An organization structure in which marketing specialists are in charge of different marketing activities or functions such as advertising, marketing research, sales management, and others.

GE strategic business-planning grid A portfolio planning method that evaluates a company's strategic business units using indexes of industry attractiveness and the company's strength in the industry.

General need description The stage in the industrial buying process in which the company describes the general characteristics and quantity of a needed item.

Geographic organization An organization structure in which a company's national sales force (and perhaps other functions) specializes by geographic area.

Geographic segmentation Dividing a market into different geographical units such as nations, states, regions, counties, cities, or neighborhoods.

Income segmentation Dividing a market into different income groups.

Global firm A firm that, by operating in more than one country, gains R&D, production, marketing, and financial advantages in its costs and reputation that are not available to purely domestic competitors.

Global industry An industry in which the strategic positions of competitors in given geographic or national markets are affected by their overall global positions.

Going-rate pricing Setting price based largely on following competitors' prices rather than on company costs or demand.

Government market Governmental units—federal, state, and local—that purchase or rent goods and services for carrying out the main functions of government.

Gross margin The difference between net sales and the cost of goods sold.

Gross sales The total amount that a company charges customers for merchandise purchased during a given time period.

Growth-share matrix A tool used in strategic planning to classify a company's strategic business units according to market-growth rate and market share.

Growth stage The product life cycle stage at which a product's sales start climbing quickly.

Handling objections The step in the selling process in which the salesperson seeks out, clarifies, and overcomes customer objections to buying.

Horizontal marketing systems A channel arrangement in which two or more companies at one level join together to follow a new marketing opportunity.

Human need A state of felt deprivation.

Human resources The people with needed skills, motivation, and personal characteristics who fill out the organization structure.

Human want The form that a human need takes as shaped by culture and individual personality.

Hypermarkets Huge stores that combine supermarket, discount, and warehouse retailing; in addition to food, they carry furniture, appliances, clothing, and many other things.

Idea generation The systematic search for new-product ideas.

Idea screening Screening new product ideas in order to spot good ideas and drop poor ones as soon as possible.

Independent off-price retailers Off-price retailers that are either owned and run by entrepreneurs or are divisions of larger retail corporations.

Industrial goods Goods bought by individuals and organizations for further processing or for use in conducting a business.

Industrial market All the individuals and organizations acquiring goods and services which enter into the production of other products and services that are sold, rented, or supplied to others.

Industry The set of all sellers of a product. A group of firms which offer a product or class of products that are close substitutes for each other.

Inelastic demand Total demand for a product that is not much affected by price changes, especially in the short run.

Influencer A person whose views or advice carries some weight in making a final buying decision.

Information search The stage of the buyer decision process in which the consumer is aroused to search for more information; the consumer may simply have heightened attention or may go into active information search.

Informative advertising Advertising used to inform consumers about a new product or feature and to build primary demand.

Initiator The person who first suggests or thinks of the idea of buying a particular product or service.

Innovative marketing A principle of enlightened marketing which requires that a company seek real product and marketing improvements.

Integrated direct marketing Direct marketing campaigns which use multiple vehicles and multiple states to improve response rates and profits.

Interactive marketing Marketing by a service firm which recognizes that perceived service quality depends heavily on the quality of buyer-seller interaction.

Internal marketing Marketing by a service firm to effectively train and motivate its customer-contact employees and all the supporting service people to work as a team to provide customer satisfaction.

Internal records information Information gathered from sources within the company to evaluate marketing performance and to detect marketing problems and opportunities.

Introduction stage The product life cycle stage when the new product is first distributed and made available for purchase.

Joint ownership Entering a foreign market by joining with foreign investors to create a local business in which the company shares joint ownership and control.

Joint venturing Entering foreign markets by joining with foreign companies to produce or market a product or service.

Leading indicators Time series that change in the same direction but in advance of company sales.

Learning Changes in an individual's behavior arising from experience.

Licensing A method of entering a foreign market in which the company enters into an agreement with a licensee in the foreign market, offering the right to use a manufacturing process, trademark, patent, trade secret, or other item of value for a fee or royalty.

Lifestyle A person's pattern of living as expressed in his or her activities, interests, and opinions.

Limited problem solving Buying behavior in cases in which buyers are aware of the product class but not familiar with all the brands and their features. Buyers engage in limited information search and evaluation.

Limited-service retailers Retailers that provide only a limited number of services to shoppers.

Limited-service wholesalers Wholesalers that offer only limited services to their suppliers and customers.

Long-range plan A marketing plan that describes the major factors and forces affecting the organization over the next several years and outlines long-term objectives, the major marketing strategies that will be used to attain them, and the resources required.

Macroenvironment The larger societal forces that affect the whole microenvironment—demographic, economic, natural, technological, political, and cultural forces.

Management contracting A joint venture in which the domestic firm supplies the management know-how to a foreign company that supplies the capital; the domestic firm exports management services rather than products.

Managerial climate The company climate resulting from the way managers work with others in the company.

Manufacturer's brand (or national brand) A brand created and owned by the producer of a product or service.

Manufacturers' sales branches and offices Wholesaling by sellers or buyers themselves rather than through independent wholesalers.

Market The set of actual and potential buyers of a product.

Market challenger A runner-up firm in an industry that is fighting to increase its market share.

Market development A strategy for company growth by identifying and developing new market segments for current company products.

Market follower A runner-up firm in an industry that wants to hold its share without rocking the boat.

Market leader The firm in an industry with the largest market share; it usually leads other firms in price changes, new product introductions, distribution coverage, and promotion spending.

Market management organization An organization structure in which market managers are responsible for developing plans for sales and profits in their specific markets.

Market nicher A firm in an industry that serves small segments that the other firms overlook or ignore.

Market penetration A strategy for company growth by increasing sales of current products to current market segments without changing the product in any way.

Market penetration pricing Setting a low price for a new product in order to attract a large number of buyers and a large market share.

Market positioning Formulating competitive positioning for a product and a detailed marketing mix. Arranging for a product to occupy a clear, distinctive, and desirable place relative to competing products in the minds of target consumers.

Market segment A group of consumers who respond in a similar way to a given set of marketing stimuli.

Market segmentation Dividing a market into distinct groups of buyers who might require separate products or marketing mixes. The process of classifying customers into groups with different needs, characteristics, or behavior.

Market-skimming pricing Setting a high price for a new product to skim maximum revenue from the segments willing to pay the high price; the company makes fewer by more profitable sales.

Market targeting Evaluating each market segment's attractiveness and selecting one or more segments to enter.

Market-centered company A company that pays balanced attention to both customers and competitors in designing its marketing strategies.

Market-share analysis Analysis and tracking of the company's market share.

Marketing A social and managerial process by which individuals and groups obtain what they need and want through creating and exchanging products and value with others.

Marketing audit A comprehensive, systematic, independent, and periodic examination of a company's environment, objectives, strategies, and activities to determine problem areas and opportunities and to recommend a plan of action to improve the company's marketing performance.

Marketing budget A section of the marketing plan that shows projected revenues, costs, and profits.

Marketing concept The marketing management philosophy which holds that achieving organizational goals depends on determining the needs and wants of target markets and delivering the desired satisfactions more effectively and efficiently than competitors.

Marketing control The process of measuring and evaluating the results of marketing strategies and plans, and taking corrective action to assure that marketing objectives are attained.

Marketing database An organized set of data about individual customers or prospects that can be used to generate and qualify customer leads, sell products and services, and maintain customer relationships.

Marketing environment The actors and forces outside marketing that affect marketing management's ability to develop and maintain successful transactions with its target customers.

Marketing implementation The process that turns marketing strategies and plans into marketing actions in order to accomplish strategic marketing objectives.

Marketing information system (MIS) People, equipment, and procedures to gather, sort, analyze, evaluate, and distribute needed, timely, and accurate information to marketing decision makers.

Marketing intelligence Everyday information about developments in the marketing environment that helps managers prepare and adjust marketing plans.

Marketing intermediaries Firms that help the company to promote, sell, and distribute its goods to final buyers; they include middlemen, physical distribution firms, marketing-service agencies, and financial intermediaries.

Marketing management The analysis, planning, implementation, and control of programs designed to create, build, and maintain beneficial exchanges with target buyers for the purpose of achieving organizational objectives.

Marketing management process The process of (1) analyzing marketing opportunities, (2) selecting target markets, (3) developing the marketing mix, and (4) managing the marketing effort.

Marketing mix The set of controllable marketing variables that the firm blends to produce the response it wants in the target market.

Marketing research The function that links the consumer, customer, and public to the marketer through information—information used to identify and define marketing opportunities and problems; to generate, refine, and evaluate marketing actions; to monitor marketing performance; and to improve understanding of the marketing process.

Marketing services agencies Marketing research firms, advertising agencies, media firms, marketing consulting firms, and other service providers that help a company to target and promote its products to the right markets.

Marketing strategy The marketing logic by which the business unit hopes to achieve its marketing objectives. Marketing strategy consists of specific strategies for target markets, marketing mix, and marketing expenditure level.

Marketing strategy development Designing an initial marketing strategy for a new product based on the product concept.

Marketing strategy statement A statement of the planned strategy for a new product that outlines the intended target market, the planned product positioning, and the sales, market share, and profit goals for the first few years.

Materials and parts Industrial goods that enter the manufacturer's product completely, including raw materials and manufactured materials and parts.

Maturity stage The stage in the product life cycle where sales growth slows or levels off.

Measurability The degree to which the size and purchasing power of a market segment can be measured.

Media Nonpersonal communications channels including print media (newspapers, magazines, direct mail), broadcast media (radio, television), and display media (billboards, signs, posters).

Media impact The qualitative value of an exposure through a given medium.

Media vehicles Specific media within each general media type, such as specific magazines, television shows, or radio programs.

Membership groups Groups that have a direct influence on a person's behavior and to which a person belongs.

Merchandising conglomerates Cor-porations that combine several different retailing forms under central ownership and that share some distribution and management functions.

Merchant wholesaler An independently owned business that takes title to the merchandise it handles.

Microenvironment The forces close to the company that affect its ability to serve its customers—the company, market channel firms, customer markets, competitors, and publics.

Micromarketing A form of target marketing in which companies tailor their marketing programs to the needs and wants of narrowly defined geographic, demographic, psychographic, or benefit segments.

Middlemen Distribution channel firms that help the company find customers or make sales to them.

Mission statement A statement of the organization's purpose, what it wants to accomplish in the larger environment.

Modified rebuy An industrial buying situation in which the buyer wants to modify product specifications, prices, terms, or suppliers.

Monetary transaction A marketing transaction in which goods or services are exchanged for money.

Monopolistic competition A market in which many buyers and sellers trade over a range of prices rather than a single market price.

Moral appeals Message appeals that are directed to the audience's sense of what is right and proper.

Motive (or **drive**) A need that is sufficiently pressing to direct the person to seek satisfaction of the need.

Multibrand strategy A strategy under which a seller develops two or more brands in the same product category.

Multichannel marketing Multichannel distribution, as when a single firm sets up two or more marketing channels to reach one or more customer segments.

Natural environment Natural resources which are needed as inputs by marketers or which are affected by marketing activities.

New product A good, service, or idea that is perceived by some potential customers as new.

New-product development The development of original products, product improvements, product modifications, and new brands through the firm's own R&D efforts.

New task An industrial buying situation on which the buyer purchases a product or service for the first time.

Nondurable goods Consumer goods that are normally consumed in one or a few uses.

Nonpersonal communication channels Media that carry messages without personal contact or feedback, including media, atmospheres, and events.

Nontariff trade barriers Nonmonetary barriers to foreign products such as biases against foreign company's bids or product standards that go against foreign company's product features.

Objective-and-task method Developing the promotion budget by (1) defining specific objectives, (2) determining the tasks that must be performed to achieve these objectives, and (3) estimating the costs of performing these tasks; the sum of these costs is the proposed promotion budget.

Observational research The gathering of primary data by observing relevant people, actions, and situations.

Occasion segmentation Dividing the market into groups according to occasions when buyers get the idea, make a purchase, or use a product.

Off-price retailers Retailers that buy at less than regular wholesale prices and sell at less than retail, usually carrying a changing and unstable collection of higher-quality merchandise, often leftover goods, overruns, and irregulars obtained from manufacturers at reduced prices. They include factory outlets, independents, and warehouse clubs.

Oligopolistic competition A market with only a few sellers, who are highly sensitive to each other's pricing and marketing strategies.

Open-end questions Questions that allow respondents to answer in their own words.

Opinion leaders People within a reference group who, because of special skills, knowledge, personality, or other characteristics, exert influence on others.

Optional-product pricing The pricing of optional or accessory products along with a main product.

Order routine specification The stage of the industrial buying process in which the buyer writes the final order with the chosen supplier(s) listing the technical specifications, quantity needed, expected time of delivery, return policies, warranties, and so on.

Organization image The way an individual or a group sees an organization.

Organization marketing Activities undertaken to create, maintain, or change attitudes and behavior of target audiences toward an organization.

Organization structure A structure which breaks up the company's work into specialized jobs, assigns these jobs to people and departments, then coordinates the jobs by defining formal ties between people and departments and by setting lines of authority and communication.

Organizational buying The decision making process by which formal organizations establish the need for purchased products and services, and identify, evaluate, and choose among alternative brands and suppliers.

Packaging The activities of designing and producing the container or wrapper for a product.

Packaging concept What the package should *be* or *do* for the product.

Patronage rewards Cash or other awards for the regular use of a certain company's products or services.

Penetrated market The set of consumers who have already bought a particular product or service.

Perceived-value pricing Setting price based on buyers' perceptions of value rather than on the seller's cost.

Percentage-of-sales method Setting the promotion budget at a certain percentage of current or forecasted sales or as a percentage of the sales price.

Perception The process by which people select, organize, and interpret information to form a meaningful picture of the world.

Performance review The stage of the industrial buying process in which the buyer rates its satisfaction with suppliers, deciding whether to continue, modify, or drop them.

Person marketing Activities undertaken to create, maintain, or change attitudes or behavior toward particular persons.

Personal communication channels Channels through which two or more people communicate directly with each other, including face-to-face, person-to-audience, over the telephone, or through the mail.

Personal influence The effect of statements made by one person on another's attitude or probability of purchase.

Personal selling Oral presentation in a conversation with one or more prospective purchasers for the purpose of making sales.

Personality A person's distinguishing psychological characteristics that lead to relatively consistent and lasting responses to his or her own environment.

Persuasive advertising Advertising used to build selective demand for a brand by persuading consumers that it offers the best quality for their money.

Physical distribution The tasks involved in planning, implementing, and controlling the physical flow of materials and final goods from points of origin to points of use to meet the needs of customers at a profit.

Physical distribution firms Warehouse, transportation, and other firms that help a company to stock and move goods from their points of origin to their destinations.

Place marketing Activities undertaken to create, maintain, or change attitudes or behavior toward particular places.

Planned obsolescence A strategy of causing products to become obsolete before they actually need replacement.

Pleasing products Products that give high immediate satisfaction but may hurt consumers in the long run.

Point-of-purchase promotions (POP) Displays and demonstrations that take place at the point of purchase or sale.

Political environment Laws, government agencies, and pressure groups that influence and limit various organizations and individuals in a given society.

Portfolio analysis A tool by which management identifies and evaluates the various businesses that make up the company.

Postpurchase behavior The stage of the buyer decision process in which consumers take further action after purchase based their satisfaction or dissatisfaction.

Potential market The set of consumers who profess some level of interest in a particular product or service.

Preapproach The step in the selling process in which the salesperson learns as much as possible about a prospective customer before making a sales call.

Premiums Goods offered either free or at low cost as an incentive to buy a product.

Presentation The step in the selling process in which the salesperson tells the product "story" to the buyer, showing how the product will make or save money.

Price The amount of money charged for a product or service, or the sum of the values consumers exchange for the benefits of having or using the product or service.

Price elasticity A measure of the sensitivity of demand to changes in price.

Price packs (cents-off deals) Reduced prices that are marked by the producer directly on label or package.

Primary data Information collected for the specific purpose at hand.

Primary demand The level of total demand for all brands of a given product or service—for example, the total demand for motorcycles.

Private brand (or middleman, distributor, or dealer brand) A brand created and owned by a reseller of a product or service.

Problem recognition The first stage of the buyer decision process in which the consumer recognizes a problem or need.

Problem recognition   The stage of the industrial buying process in which someone in the company recognizes a problem or need that can be met by acquiring a good or a service.

Product   Anything that can be offered to a market for attention, acquisition, use, or consumption that might satisfy a want or need. It includes physical objects, services, persons, places, organizations, and ideas.

Product adaptation   Adapting a product to meet local conditions or wants in foregin markets.

Product-bundle pricing   Combining several products and offering the bundle at a reduced price.

Product concepts   The idea that consumers favor products that offer the most quality, performance, and features and that the organization should therefore devote its energy to making continuous product improvements. A detailed version of the new-product idea stated in meaningful consumer terms.

Product design   The process of designing a product's style and function: creating a product that is attractive; easy, safe, and inexpensive to use and service; and simple and economical to produce and distribute.

Product development   A strategy for company growth by offering modified or new products to current market segments. Developing the product concept into a physical product in order to assure that the product idea can be turned into a workable product.

Product idea   An idea for a possible product that the company can envison offering to the market.

Product image   The way consumers perceive an actual or potential product.

Product invention   Creating new products or services for foreign markets.

Product life cycle (PLC)   The course of a product's sales and profits during its lifetime. It involves five distinct stages: product development, introduction, growth, maturity, and decline.

Product line   A group of products that are closely related either because they function in a similar manner, are sold to the same customer groups, are marketed through the same types of outlets, or fall within given price ranges.

Product-line featuring   Selecting one or a few items in a product line to feature.

Product-line filling   Increasing the product line by adding more items within the present range of the line.

Product-line pricing   Setting the price steps between various products in a product line based on cost differences between the products, customer evaluations of different features, and competitor's prices.

Product line-stretching   Increasing the product line by lengthening it beyond its current range.

Product management organization   An organization structure in which product managers are responsible for developing and implementing marketing strategies and plans for a specific product or brand.

Product and market expansion grid   A portfolio planning tool for identifying company growth opportunities through market penetration, market development, product development, or diversification.

Product mix (or **product assortment**)   The set of all product lines and items that a particular seller offers for sale to buyers.

Product position   The way the product is defined by consumers on important attributes—the place the product occupies in consumers' minds relative to competing products.

Product quality   The ability of a product to perform its functions; it includes the product's overall durability, reliability, precision, ease of operation and repair, and other valued attributes.

Product salesforce structure   A salesforce organization in which salespeople specialize in selling only a portion of the company's products or lines.

Product specification   The stage of the industrial buying process in which the buying organization decides on and specifies the best technical product characteristics for a needed item.

Product-support services   Services that augment actual products.

Production concept   The philosophy that consumers favor products that are available and highly affordable and that management should therefore focus on improving production and distribution efficiency.

Profitability control   Evaluation and corrective action to assure the profitability of various products, territories, customer groups, trade channels, and order sizes.

Promotion mix   The specific mix of advertising, personal selling, sales promotion, and public relations a company uses to pursue its advertising and marketing objectives.

Promotional allowance   A payment or price reduction to reward dealers for participating in advertising and sales-support programs.

Promotional pricing   Temporarily pricing products below the list price, and sometimes even below cost, to increase short-run sales.

Proposal solicitation   The stage of the industrial buying process in which the buyer invites qualified suppliers to submit proposals.

Prospecting   The step in the selling process in which the salesperson identifies qualified potential customers.

Psychographic segmentation   Dividing a market into different groups based on social class, life style, or personality characteristics.

Psychographics   The technique of measuring life styles and developing lifestyle classifications; it involves measuring the major AIO dimensions (activities, interests, opinions).

Psychological pricing   A pricing approach which considers the psychology of prices and not simply the economics—the price is used to say something about the product.

Public   Any group that has an actual or potential interest in or impact on an organization's ability to achieve its objectives.

Public relations   Building good relations with the company's various publics by obtaining favorable publicity, building up a good "corporate image," and handling or heading off unfavorable rumors, stories, and events. Major PR tools include press relations, product publicity, corporate communications, lobbying, and counseling.

Publicity Activities to promote a company or its products by planting news about it in media not paid for by the sponsor.

Pull strategy A promotion strategy that calls for spending a lot on advertising and consumer promotion to build up consumer demand; if successful, consumers will ask their retailers for the product, the retailers will ask the wholesalers, and the wholesalers will ask the producers.

Pulsing Scheduling ads unevenly in bursts during a specified time period.

Purchase decision The stage of the buyer decision process in which the consumer actually buys the product.

Pure competition A market in which many buyers and sellers trade in a uniform commodity—no single buyer or seller has much affect on the going market price.

Pure monopoly A market with a single seller—it may be a government monopoly, a private regulated monopoly, or a private nonregulated monopoly.

Push strategy A promotion strategy that calls for using the salesforce and trade promotion to push the product through channels; the producer promotes the product to wholesalers, the wholesalers promote to retailers, and the retailers promote to consumers.

Qualified available market The set of consumers who have interest, income, access, and qualifications for a particular product or service.

Quantity discount A price reduction to buyers who buy large volumes.

Question marks A low-share business unit in a high-growth market which requires much cash to hold its share or build into a star.

Quota A limit on the amount of goods that an importing country will accept in certain product categories; it is designed to conserve on foreign exchange

and protect local industry and employment.

Rational appeals Message appeals that relate to the audience's self-interest and show that the product will produce the claimed benefits; examples include appeals of product quality, economy, value, or performance.

Reach The percentage of people in the target market exposed to an ad campagin during a given period.

Reference groups Groups that have a direct (face-to-face) or indirect influence on the person's attitudes or behavior.

Reference prices Prices that buyers carry in their minds and refer to when they look at a given product.

Reminder advertising Advertising used to keep consumers thinking about a product.

Reseller market All the individuals and organizations that acquire goods for the purpose of reselling or renting them to others at a profit.

Retailer cooperatives Contractual vertical marketing systems in which retailers organize a new, jointly owned business to carry on wholesaling and possibly production.

Retailers Businesses whose sales come *primarily* from retailing.

Retailing All activities involved in selling goods or services directly to final consumers for their personal, non-business use.

Role The activities a person is expected to perform according to the people around him or her.

Routine response behavior Buying behavior in cases in which buyers face simple buying decisions for low-cost, low-involvement, frequently purchased items in familiar product classes. Buyers do not give much thought, search, or time to the purchase.

Sales analysis Measuring and evaluating actual sales in relation to sales goals.

Sales promotion Short-term incentives to encourage purchase or sales of a product or service.

Sales quotas Standards set for salespeople stating the amount they should

sell and how sales should be divided among the company's products.

Salesforce management The analysis, planning, implementation, and control of salesforce activities. It includes setting salesforce objectives; designing salesforce strategy; and recruiting, selecting, training, supervising, and evaluating the firm's salespeople.

Salesforce promotion Sales promotion designed to motivate the salesforce and make salesforce selling efforts more effective, including bonuses, contests, and sales rallies.

Salesperson An individual acting for a company by performing one or more of the following activities: prospecting, communicating, servicing, and information gathering.

Salutary products Products that have low appeal but benefit consumers in the long run.

Sample A segment of the population selected for marketing research to represent the population as a whole.

Samples Offers of a trial amount of a product to consumers.

Sealed-bid pricing Setting price based on how the firm thinks competitors will price rather than on its own costs or demand—used when a company bids for jobs.

Seasonal discount A price reduction to buyers who buy merchandise or services out of season.

Secondary data Information that already exists somewhere, having been collected for another purpose.

Selective demand The demand for a given brand of a product or service—for example, the demand for a *Honda* motorcycle.

Selective distortion The tendency of people to adapt information to personal meanings.

Selective distribution The use of more than one but less than all the middlemen who are willing to carry the company's products.

Selective exposure The tendency of people to screen most of the information to which they are exposed.

Selective retention The tendency of

people to retain only part of the information to which they are exposed, usually information that supports their attitudes and beliefs.

Self-concept Self-image, or the complex mental pictures people have of themselves.

Self-service retailers Retailers that provide few or no services to shoppers; shoppers perform their own locate-compare-select process.

Selling concept The idea that consumers will not buy enough of the organization's products unless the organization undertakes a large-scale selling and promotion effort.

Selling process The steps that the salesperson follows when selling, which include prospecting and qualifying, pre-approach, approach, presentation and demonstration, handling objections, closing, and follow-up.

Sense-of-mission marketing A principle of enlightened marketing which holds that a company should define its mission in broad social terms rather than narrow product terms.

Sequential product development A new-product development approach in which one company department works individually to complete its stage of the process before passing the new product along to the next department and stage.

Served market (or **target market**) The part of the qualified available market the company decides to pursue.

Service Any activity or benefit that one party can offer to another that is essentially intangible and does not result in the ownership of anything.

Service inseparability A major characteristic of services—they are produced and consumed at the same time and cannot be separated from their providers, whether the providers are people or machines.

Service intangibility A major characteristic of services—they cannot be seen, tasted, felt, heard, or smelled before they are bought.

Service perishability A major characteristic of services—they cannot be stored for later sale or use.

Service variability A major character-istic of services—their quality may vary greatly, depending on who provides them and when, where, and how they are provided.

Sex segmentation Dividing a market into different groups based on sex.

Shopping center A group of retail businesses planned, developed, owned, and managed as a unit.

Shopping goods Consumer goods that the customer, in the process of selection and purchase, characteristically compares on such bases as suitability, quality, price, and style.

Simultaneous product development An approach to developing new products in which various company departments work closely together, over-lapping the steps in the product-development process to save time and increase effectiveness.

Single-source data systems Electronic monitoring systems that link consumers' exposure to television advertising and promotion (measured using television meters) with what they buy in stores (measured using store checkout scanners).

Social classes Relatively permanent and ordered divisions in a society whose members share similar values, interests, and behaviors.

Social marketing The design, implementation, and control of programs seeking to increase the acceptability of a social idea, cause, or practice among a target group.

Societal marketing A principle of enlightened marketing which holds that a company should make marketing decisions by considering consumers' wants, the company's requirements, consumers' long-run interests, and society's long-run interests.

Societal marketing concept The idea that the organization should determine the needs, wants, and interests of target markets and deliver the desired satisfactions more effectively and efficiently than competitors in a way that maintains or improves the consumer's and society's well-being.

Specialty goods Consumer goods with unique characteristics or brand identifi-cation for which a significant group of buyers is willing to make a special purchase effort.

Specialty store A retail store that carries a narrow product line with a deep assortment within that line.

Standardized marketing mix An international marketing strategy for using basically the same product, advertising, distribution channels, and other elements of the marketing mix in all the company's international markets.

Stars High-growth, high-share businesses or products, which often require heavy investment to finance their rapid growth.

Statistical demand analysis A set of statistical procedures used to discover the most important real factors affecting sales and their relative influence; the most commonly analyzed factors are prices, income, population, and promotion.

Status The general esteem given to a role by society.

Straight product extension Marketing a product in the foreign market without any change.

Straight rebuy An industrial buying situation in which the buyer routinely reorders something without any modifications.

Strategic business unit (SBU) A unit of the company that has a separate mission and objectives, and that can be planned independently of other company businesses. An SBU can be a company division, a product line within a division, or sometimes a single product or brand.

Strategic control A critical review of the company's overall marketing effectiveness.

Strategic group A group of firms in an industry following the same or a similar strategy.

Strategic planning The process of developing and maintaining a strategic fit between the organization's goals and capabilities and its changing marketing opportunities. It relies on developing a clear company mission, supporting objectives, a sound business portfolio, and coordinated functional strategies.

Style A basic and distinctive mode of expression.

Subculture A group of people with shared value systems based on common life experiences and situations.

Substantiality The degree to which a market segment is large or profitable enough.

Supermarkets Large, low-cost, low-margin, high-volume, self-service stores that carry a wide variety of food, laundry, and household products.

Superstore A store almost twice the size of a regular supermarket carrying a large assortment of routinely purchased food and nonfood items, and offering such services as dry cleaning, post offices, photo finishing, check cashing, bill paying, lunch counters, car care, and pet care.

Supplier search The stage of the industrial buying process in which the buyer tries to find the best vendors.

Supplier selection The stage of the industrial buying process in which the buyer reviews proposals and selects a supplier or suppliers.

Suppliers Firms and individuals that provide the resources needed by the company and its competitors to produce goods and services.

Supplies and services Industrial goods that do not enter the finished product at all.

Survey research The gathering of primary data by asking people questions about their knowledge, attitudes, preferences, and buying behavior.

Systems buying Buying a packaged solution to a problem and not making all the separate decisions involved.

Target market A set of buyers sharing common needs or characteristics that the company decides to serve.

Tariff A tax, levied by a government against certain imported products, which is designed to raise revenue or protect domestic firms.

Technological environment Forces that create new technologies, creating new product and market opportunities.

Telemarketing Using the telephone to sell directly to consumers.

Territorial salesforce structure A salesforce organization that assigns each salesperson to an exclusive geographic territory in which that salesperson carries the company's full line.

Test marketing The stage of new-product development in which the product and marketing program are tested in more realistic market settings.

Time-series analysis Breaking down past sales into its trend, cycle, season, and erratic omponents, then recombining these components to produce a sales forecast.

Total costs The sum of the fixed and variable costs for any given level of production.

Total market demand The total volume of a product or service that would be bought by a defined consumer group in a defined geographic area in a defined time period in a defined marketing environment under a defined level and mix of industry marketing effort.

Trade-in allowance A price reduction given for turning in an old item when buying a new one.

Trade promotion Sales promotion designed to gain reseller support and to improve reseller selling efforts, including discounts, allowances, free goods, cooperative advertising, push money, and conventions and trade shows.

Trademark A brand or part of a brand that is given legal protection—it protects the seller's exclusive rights to use the brand name or brand mark.

Transaction A trade between two parties that involves at least two things of value, agreed upon conditions, a time of agreement, and a place of agreement.

Two-part pricing A strategy for pricing services in which price is broken into a fixed fee plus a variable usage rate.

Undifferentiated marketing A market-coverage strategy in which a firm decides to ignore market segment differences and go after the whole market with one market offer.

Uniform delivered pricing A geographic pricing strategy in which the company charges the same price plus freight to all customers regardless of their location.

Unsought goods Consumer goods that the consumer either does not know about or knows about but does not normally think of buying.

User The person who consumes or uses a product or service.

Value analysis An approach to cost reduction in which components are carefully studied to determine if they can be redesigned, standardized, or made by cheaper methods of production.

Value marketing A principle of enlightened marketing which holds that a company should put most of its resources into value-building marketing investments.

Variable costs Costs that vary directly with the level of production.

Vertical marketing system (VMS) A distribution channel structure in which producers, wholesalers, and retailers act as a unified system—either one channel member owns the others, or has contracts with them, or has so much power that they all cooperate.

Warehouse clubs (or **wholesale clubs**) Off-price retailers that sell a limited selection of brand-name grocery items, appliances, clothing, and a hodgepodge of other goods at deep discounts to members who pay annual membership fees.

Wheel of retailing concept A concept of retailing which states that new types of retailers usually begin as low-margin, low-price, low-status operations but later evolve into higher-priced, higher-service operations, eventually becoming like the conventional retailers they replaced.

Whole-channel view Designing international channels that take into account all the necessary links in distributing the seller's products to final buyers, including the seller's headquarters organization, channels between nations, and channels within nations.

Wholesalers Firms engaged *primarily* in wholesaling activity.

Wholesaler-sponsored voluntary chains Contractual vertical marketing systems in which wholesalers organize voluntary chains of independent retailers to help them compete with large corporate chain organizations.

Wholesaling All activities involved in selling goods and services to those buying for resale or business use.

Word-of-mouth influence Personal communication about a product between target buyers and neighbors, friends, family members, and associates.

Workload approach An approach to setting salesforce size in which the company groups accounts into different size classes and then figures out how many salespeople are needed to call on them the desired number of times.

Zone pricing A geographic pricing strategy in which the company sets up two or more zones—all customers within a zone pay the same total price, and this price is higher in the more distant zones.

Acknowledgment
of Illustrations

Chapter 11

284 clockwise: Michael L. Abramson, 3M Corporation; **291** Pillsbury Company; **293** Donald Dietz/Stock, Boston; **296** Dole Packaged Food Companies; **301** Ford Motor Company; **302** Kikkoman International, Inc.; **304** Sony Corporation of America; **309** Page Poore.

Chapter 12

312 Sears; **316** Sub-Zero Freezer Co., Inc.; **317** Jaguar Cars Inc.; **321** Stanley Hardware Division of The Stanley Works, New Britain, CT 06052; **323** Mazda Information Bureau; **330** Waterford Wedgwood.

Chapter 13

336 Caterpillar, Inc.; **339** Polaroid Corporation; **340** Snapper Power Equipment; **342** Hyatt Hotels Corporation; **344** AT&T; **346** top: Laima Druskis, bottom: Page Poore; **349** Jean Patou, Inc.

Chapter 14

356 Winn-Dixie Stores; **359** clockwise: The Coca-Cola Company, Michael S. Yamashita/West Light, John Zoiner/International Stock Photo, Smith/Garner/The Stock Market; **367** Toys Я Us; **368** Sears and McDonald's; **370** left: Michael Rizza/Stock Boston; right: Lee Lockwood/Black Star; **371** left: Dario Perla/International Stock Photo, right: Christina Mufson/Comstock; **377** Xerox Corporation; **379** clockwise: CSX Creative Services, CSX Creative Services, American Airlines, Conrail.

Chapter 15

386 IKEA Inc.; **390** Athletic Attic; **392** Biggs, Cincinnati; **394** 47th Street Photo; **396** Minneapolis Convention and Visitors Center; **399** Teri Stratford; **403** Fingerhut; **406** Ted Hardin; **409** Fleming Companies, Inc., Oklahoma City, OK; **412** Foremost-McKesson.

Chapter 16

420 The Quaker Oats Company; **426** Procter & Gamble Company; **429** PepsiCo, Inc.; **433** Blake Little; **435** McGraw-Hill, Inc.; **439** PepsiCo, Inc.

Chapter 17

442 Eveready Battery Company, Inc.; **446** Kraft, Inc.; **451** left: Cunard Line, right: Heinz Pet Products; **452** Federal Express/K·H·B·B; **454** left: John M. Roberts, right: Ted Kappler; **456** left: Parking Meter Advertising, right: Procter & Gamble; **460** Jayne Conte; **462** PepsiCo, Inc.; **466** Coleco; **468** 3M Commercial Graphics Division.

Chapter 18

476 Boeing Corporation; **479** left: Bill Brewer, right: Gabe Palmer/The Stock Market; **485** Wilson Learning Corporation; **487** left: Welton Doby, right: Carol Fatta; **488** Frito-Lay; **489** Comstock; **491** Princess Cruises, right: American Express Travel Related Services Company, Inc.; **496** Lawrence Migdale/Photo Researchers; **501** Multiform Desiccants, Inc.

Chapter 19

508 Teri Stratford; **512** left: Procter & Gamble Company, right: DEP Corporation; **514** GE Appliances; **519** left: Johnson & Johnson Baby Products Company, right: Church & Dwight Co., Inc.; **522** left: Fuji Photo Film USA, Inc. right: Eastman Kodak Company © Eastman Kodak Company; **525** Teri Stratford, **532** GTE Telephone Operations.

Chapter 20

536 IBM; **540** State of Florida, Division of Economic Development, based on an original photographic concept by Arnold Zann/Black Star; **545** Ken Lax; **549** Hewlett-Packard; **555** Mark Seliger; **557** Carol Lee/West Stock.

Chapter 21

572 background: Eastman Kodak Company, top right: David H. Durland, bottom right: David H. Durland; **575** clockwise: IBM Corp., Caroline Parsons, Ted Morrison, Greg Davis/The Stock Market; **580** Thomas Zimmermann/FPG International; **582** Guy Laroche; **584** Pepsi-Cola International; **586** Tokyo Disneyland is owned and operated by the Oriental Land Co., Ltd (a Japanese development company) under license from The Walt Disney Company © 1986 The Walt Disney Company; **588-89** Black & Decker Corp.

Chapter 22

600 Joseph MacNally/Sygma; **603** left: Robert Holmgren, right: John S. Hillery; **606** Reuben E. Lee/The Stock Shop; **608** Century City Hospital; **611** United Parcel Service of America; **613** Hush Puppies Division of Wolverine World Wide, Inc.; **614** Coca-Cola and Coca-Cola Classic are registered trademarks of the Coca-Cola Company, permission for their use is granted by the Coca-Cola Company/ProServ Incorporated/Nike, Inc.; **617** North Carolina Department of Commerce; **618** MADD, Mothers Against Drunk Driving, Milwaukee County, Wisconsin/*Readers Digest*.

Chapter 23

624 Marty Katz © Marty Katz 1985; **628** Paolo Koch/Photo Researchers, Inc.; **630** Rob Kinmonth; **632** American Association of Advertising Agencies; **634** Tom McHugh/Photo Researchers; **636** Campbell Soup Company; **639** E. I. Dupont de Nemours & Company; **643** Ken Lax; **647** Nestlé.

Author Index

Giges, Nancy, 520
Gillette, King, 163
Gilley, Mary C., 157
Gollub, James, 62, 81n3
Goold, Michael, 546, 564n6
Gould, Peter, 362, 381n4
Graham, John L., 169, 190n6
Graham, Judith, 128, 138n10, 399, 407, 415n16
Gray, Daniel H., 35, 51n5
Greenhouse, Steven, 286, 307n1
Greyser, Stephen A., 635, 646n15
Griffin, Joseph E., 505–6
Griffin, Ricky E., 642, 646n20
Gronroos, Christian, 607, 621n11
Guelzo, Carl M., 380
Gutenberg, Johann, 445
Gwynne, S.C., 323

H

Hafner, Katherine M., 374, 382n18
Haines, Daniel W., 48, 51n12, 526, 531n17
Haley, Russell I., 227, 244n10
Hamel, Gary, 366, 382n12
Hamel, Ruth, 391, 415n5
Hamermesh, Richard G., 35, 51n4
Hanna, Sherman, 127
Hansen, Richard W., 157
Harbrecht, Douglas A., 635, 646n15
Harper, Marion, Jr., 90, 112n2
Harris, Brian F., 262
Harris, Catherine L., 93, 112n7
Harvey, Donald F., 549
Haspeslagh, Philippe, 33, 51n3
Hatten, Mary Louise, 349, 352n7
Hawkins, Del I., 92, 102, 109, 112n6, 113n14, 207, 208, 210, 212nn6, 7, 9
Haywood, K. Michael, 428, 438n4
Heatherington, Ray, 309
Helvar, John, 140
Hemmes, Thomas M.S., 266, 280n18
Henkoff, Ronald, 76, 82n21, 632, 646n12
Hermann, Paul, 479
Heskett, James L., 606, 621n7
Hewlett, Bill, 549
Higgins, Kevin, 297, 308n13, 555, 608
Hill, Richard M., 182, 185, 190n28
Hills, Gerald E., 404
Hite, Robert, 463, 471n29
Hoerr, John, 550, 564n14
Hoff, Edward J., 589
Hoffman, Jim, 597–98
Hogan, Catherine, 486
Homer, Pamela, 128, 138n13
Honomichl, Jack, 90, 112n1, 615, 621n19
Hope, Bob, 78
Horton, Cleveland, 118, 138n1, 225, 244n8
Horton, Raymond L., 129, 138n14, 172, 190n10
Houston, Franklin S., 7, 14, 21nn9, 12
Howard, John A., 146, 152, 161nn2, 6
Huey, John, 377, 382n20
Hughes, James W., 120, 138n4

Hulin-Salkin, Belinda, 391, 415n3
Hume, Scott, 15, 448, 460, 471nn5, 23
Hunt, D., 642, 646n20
Hutchins, Dexter, 338, 352n1
Hutchinson, Norman E., 379, 382n23

I

Iacocca, Lee, 466, 467, 613, 614
Ivey, Mark, 228, 244n12

J

Jackson, Barbara Bund, 172, 190n7, 497
Jackson, Bo, 143
Jackson, Donald W., 175, 190n13
Jackson, Tom, 664
Jacob, Rahul, 578, 595n5
Jacobson, Robert, 258, 279n4, 523, 531n12
Jatusripitak, Somkid, 577
Jaworski, Bernard J., 559, 564n21
Jeanes, William, 301
Jereski, Laura, 144, 161n1
Joel, Billy, 605
Johansson, Johny K., 344, 352n5
Johnson, Wesley J., 176, 190n15
Jonas, Norman, 602, 620n2
Jones, Michael H., 169, 190n6
Jordan, Michael, 144, 428, 614–15
Jordan, Sam, 568–70

K

Kahle, Lynn R., 128, 138n13
Kaia, Ernest, 179
Kaikati, Jack G., 393, 415n9
Kanuk, Leslie Lazar, 120, 126, 128, 138nn3, 7, 11, 147, 159, 161n3, 162n16, 205, 225, 244n7, 427, 428, 438nn3, 5
Kapstein, Jonathan, 579
Kardes, Frank R., 427, 438n3
Kassarjian, Harold H., 129, 138n14
Keegan, Warren, 576, 584, 595n4
Keenan, William, Jr., 483, 500n6
Keller, Kevin L., 265, 280n14
Kelley, Bill, 154, 162n9, 272, 280n25, 338, 352n1, 388, 399, 415nn1, 18, 478, 483, 485, 500nn1, 9, 13
Kellogg, Will, 55
Kelly, Kevin, 392, 415n6
Kennedy, John F., 69, 635
Kern, Richard, 62, 65, 81n4, 81n10, 203, 212n3
Kerr, Janet E., 175, 190n13
Kessler, Felix, 297, 308n12, 449, 462, 471nn9, 27, 626, 646n1
Kessler, Lori, 612, 621n15
Key, Wilson Bryan, 135
Kiechel, Walter, III, 38
Kimmel, Robert B., 608
Kinnear, Thomas C., 100, 112n11, 154, 161n7
Kirkland, Richard I., Jr., 579
Kirkpatrick, David, 69, 81n16

Kneale, Dennis, 449, 471n9
Knowlton, Christopher, 602, 620n1
Knutson, Ted, 109
Kobielus, James, 506
Koeppel, Dan, 282
Kohli, Ajay, 180, 190n21
Konrad, Walecia, 64, 81n7, 120, 138n4, 446
Kornakovich, Ron J., 169, 190n5
Koschnick, Wolfgang, J., 20, 22n18
Koten, John, 148
Kotler, Philip, 18, 19, 22nn16, 17, 79, 82n25, 109, 113n14, 206, 212n5, 237, 244n20, 259, 279n9, 306, 308n17, 362, 381n5, 521, 531n10, 577, 581, 614, 615, 619, 621nn17, 20
Kraar, Louis, 581, 583, 587, 596nn7, 8, 10
Kroc, Ray, 14
Kupfer, Andrew, 393, 415n8, 590, 596n12
Kurland, Mark A., 517, 530n5

L

LaBarbara, Priscilla A., 154, 161n8
Labich, Kenneth, 520, 591, 596n13
Landler, Mark, 241, 244n23
Lane, Ronald, 461, 471n25
Langeard, Eric, 602, 620n4
Larson, Jan, 460, 471n24
Lavitz, Harold, 62, 81n3
Lawrence, Jennifer, 77, 436
Lawrence, Steve, 224, 244n4
Lawton, Leigh, 90, 307n4
Lazarsfeld, P.F., 428, 438n5
Leerhsen, Charles, 602, 620n1
Lefkowith, Edwin F., 609, 621n12
Legg, Donna, 115
Lehmann, Donald R., 182, 190n24
Lekashman, Raymond, 375
Lele, Milind, M., 4, 21n3
Leon, Carol Boyd, 399, 415n16
Leonard, Stew, 4
Lepisto, Lawrence, 127, 138n8
Letterman, David, 443
Levine, Jonathan B., 62, 81n5
Levine, Joshua, 422, 438n1
Levitt, Theodore, 6, 14, 21nn8, 12, 253, 498, 589, 605, 621n6, 629, 646n4
Levy, Sidney, J., 132
Lewis, Geoff, 538, 563n1
Lewis, Jim, 532
Lewis, Ray, 606, 621n8
Lewyn, Mark, 224, 244n2
Lieberman, David, 38
Lieblich, Julia, 120, 138n4
Lilien, Gary L., 109, 113n14
Lincoln, Abraham, 69
Lindbergh, Charles, 616
Linden, Fabian, 65, 81n12
Lipman, Joanne, 101, 282
Little, John D. C., 109, 113n14
Liu, Ben, 598
Lodish, Leonard M., 101
Lopez, Edwin, 84

Company/Brand Index

March of Dimes, 426, 450
Market Research Corporation of America, 95
Marlboro, 139
Marriott Hotels, 4, 13, 94, 156, 275, 461, 604, 606, 607, 610
Marriott Marquis line, 275
Marshall Field, 389
Mary Kay Cosmetics, 124, 401
Maryland Club, 217
MasterCard, 77, 455, 505–6
Matsushita, 87, 573, 574
Mattel Toys, 238, 589
Max, 245
Max Factor, 566
Maxwell House, 3, 129, 219
Maxxum camera, 526
Maybelline, 565–66
Maytag Corporation, 86–87, 271, 513
Mazda, 301
Mazda MX-T Miata, 323
Mead Paper, 93
Meiji Milk, 586
Mellow Yellow, 509
Mercedes, 6, 43, 48, 117, 126, 235, 240, 511, 522, 574
Mercedes-Benz 300 E, 323
Merck, 239
Mercury Sable, 95, 301
Merrill Lynch, 128, 604
Mervyn's, 390
Metro-Goldwyn-Mayer, 260
Metropolitan Insurance, 604
Metropolitan Museum of Art, 3
MGA, 323
Michelin Tire Company, 520
Michelob beer, 17, 263
Midas Muffler, 272, 358
Midcal Aluminum Co., 364
Middlebrook Park, 418
Mighty Dog pet food, 647
Miller Brewing Company, 266, 522
Miller High Life, 281, 305
Miller Lite, 228, 281
Milliken & Company, 239
Minnetonka, 520
Minolta, 326, 455, 526, 573, 592
Minute Maid, 3, 218, 296
Minute Maid soda, 509
Mister Donut, 590
Model-T, 521
Monet, 38
Monsanto Corporation, 170, 590
Montgomery Ward, 86
Morrell, 652
Motel 6, 254, 315
Motorola, 94
Mountain Dew Sport, 245
Mr. Clean, 217
Mr. P's, 474
MRB Group (Simmons Market Research Bureau), 99
MRCA Information Services, 99
Mueslix, 55
Multiform Desiccants, Inc. (MDI), 501
Mundi Westport Corporation, 597

Murjani, 264
My Classic, 474

N

Nabisco Brands, 287, 554, 634
Nacho Cheese soup, 220
NAPA, 358
National Association of Secondary School Principals (NASSP), 618
National Cash Register Company (NCR), 479, 590
National Dairy Board, 450
National Foundation for Alcoholism Communications, 622
National Steel, 290
Nature Valley, 264
Nautilus Fitness Center, 3
Navistar (International Harvester), 44–45, 48, 337, 517
Neiman-Marcus, 3, 156, 224, 398, 399
Nemo, 367
Nescafé, 647
Nestlé, 19, 287, 473, 574, 634, 647–48
Nestle's New Cookery, 287
New Coke, 89
New Complexion, 566
NFO Research, 99
Nike, 3, 8, 143–44, 428, 451, 615
Nikon, 127, 130, 134, 135, 152, 326, 573
9-Lives, 465, 469
Nintendo Entertainment System (NES), 238–39
Nissan, 43, 118
Nissan Foods, 83
Noodle-a-Roni, 38
Nordstrom, 610
Norelco, 574
Norge, 86
Northwest Airlines, 477
Nova, 591
Noxell, 287, 444, 634
NutraSweet Company, 170, 641
Nutri-Grain, 55
NYNEX, 604
Nyquil, 287

O

Obsession (perfume), 251, 287
Occidental Chemical, 597
Oh!s, 421
Old Spice After-Shave Lotion, 264, 267
Olestra, 641
Olivetti, 581
100% Natural, 421
Opium (perfume), 251, 287
Orange Crush, 270
Oscar de la Renta, 251
Oshkosh Truck Corporation, 44–45, 233
Outback Red, 263
Oxydol, 217, 218

P

Pace Membership Warehouse, 393
Pampers, 217, 264, 265, 520

Pan Am, 461
Panasonic, 260, 417, 574
Pantene, 217
Paper Mate, 164
Parker Brothers, 38
Passion (perfume), 240, 251
Pathmark, 263
Pathmark Super Centers, 391
Pay Less Drug Stores, 407
Peerless Paper Company, 345–46, 347
Pennsylvania House furniture, 87
Pentax, 326
Pepperidge Farm, 83
Pepsi-Cola Company (PepsiCo), 4, 199, 439–40, 444, 511–12, 521, 522, 525, 580, 581, 583
Pepsi (drink), 89, 236, 245, 249, 287, 428, 455, 461, 509–10, 581, 584, 593
Pepto-Bismol, 287
Perdue, 237
Perrier, 240, 574
Personalized Services, 603
Personal label, 418
Personal System/2 (PS/2) Computers, 383, 538
Pert, 217
Pet milk, 591
Pfizer Corporation, 71
Philip Morris, 287, 444, 522, 634
Philips, 300
Philips/Pioneer, 505
Picturevision phones, 241
Pierre Cardin, 8, 264
Pillsbury Co., 240, 260, 290, 295, 357, 366, 450, 454, 473–74, 574
Pillsbury Microwave Pizza, 474
Pillsbury's French Bread Pizza, 474
Piper Aircraft, 277
Pizza Hut, 583
Pizza Inn, 363
Plax, 429
Polaroid Corporation, 5, 144, 241, 277, 288, 338–39, 341, 373, 453, 461, 548, 581
Polarvision instant home movie system, 144, 241
Pontiac, 43, 135, 224
Popov vodka, 345
Porsche, 48, 117–18, 235
Porsche 911 Carrera, 323
Post Division, 552
Post-It Notes, 286
Potato Board, The, 469
Power-Burst, 245
PowerBurst Corporation, 245
Prego, 83
Prell shampoo, 217
Premier (cigarette), 139–40
Premier Cruise Lines, 27
Pretolite Electric, 597
Price Club, 393
Princess Cruises, 491
Procter & Gamble Company (P & G), 4, 13, 18, 76, 122, 148, 156, 172, 217–18, 222, 223, 233, 237, 262, 263, 264, 265, 272, 276–77, 281, 287, 295, 305, 357, 366, 429,

Subject Index

Clutter:
    advertising, 447, 449
    promotion, 458
CMSAs (Consolidated Metropolitan Statistical Areas), 81n10
Cognitive dissonance, 154–55
Cold calling, 495
College Placement Annual, 664
Collusion, price, 327
Colors, international promotion and, 591
Combination stores, 391
Commerce Business Daily, 188
Commerce Department, 188, 207
Commercial data, 99
Commercialization, 298
Commission merchants, 411
Commission system, 446
Committees, new-product, 289
Communicability, product, 160
Communication, 421–30
    corporate, 465
    elements in process, 423–24
    marketing communication system, 422
    of position, 242
    responsibility for planning, 437
    steps in developing effective, 423–30
        determining response sought, 424–26
        feedback, collecting, 430
        identifying target audience, 424
        media choice, 427–28
        message choice, 426–27
        message source selection, 428–30
    See also Promotion
Communication effect of advertising, measuring, 457–58
Community shopping center, 396
Company:
    as actor in microenvironment, 57–58
    alternative views of marketing's role in, 38–40
    channel design decisions and, 369
    culture of, 550
Company marketing opportunity, 541
Comparison advertising, 447
Compatibility, product, 160
Compensation, 548
    salesforce, 482–83, 490
Compensation (buy-back), 581
Competition:
    advertising budget and, 447
    fair, 493
    marketing plan on, 539–40
    monopolistic, 321–22
    oligopolistic, 322
    price, 609
    pure, 321
    unfair, 72, 635
Competition-based pricing, 330–31
Competitive advantage, 517
    customer value analysis and, 515
    identifying possible, 237–40
    selecting right, 240–42
Competitive intelligence system, 94–96, 516–17

Competitive-parity promotion budget method, 431
Competitive strategies, 47–48, 517–28
    competitive positioning, 517–18
    market-challenger strategies, 47, 518, 523–26
    market-follower strategies, 47–48, 518, 526–27
    market-leader strategies, 47, 518–23
    market-nicher strategies, 48, 518, 527–28
Competitor(s), 60
    channels of, 370
    choosing market-coverage strategy and, 235
    intelligence gathering on, 94–96, 516–17
    of market challenger, 524
    new-product ideas from, 290
    positional strategy based on, 236
    prices and offers of, 326
    reactions to price changes, 350
Competitor analysis, 47, 510–17
    assessing strengths and weaknesses, 514
    competitors to attack or avoid, selecting, 515–16
    defined, 510
    determining competitor objectives, 513
    estimating reaction patterns, 515
    identification of competitors, 511–13
    identifying competitor strategies, 513
Competitor myopia, 511
Competitor-centered company, 528
Complaints, handling customer, 155–57
Complex salesforce structures, 482
Complexity, product, 160
Computer Assisted Telephone Interviewing (CATI), 104
Computers:
    expert-system programs for shoppers, 152
    personal, salesforce use of, 487–89
Concentrated marketing, 232, 233–34, 510
Concept development and testing, 292–93
Conference selling, 481
Confidence, consumer, 207
Conflict:
    channel, 363
    between departments, 40–41
Confused positioning, 241
Conglomerates, 38, 395–96
Congress, 186
Conjunctive model of consumer choice, 152
Constraints, channel, 369–70
Consulting services, 238
Consumer(s):
    disadvantaged, poor service to, 631
    marketing's impact on individual, 626–31
    target, selecting, 41, 42–45
Consumer and producer freedom, principle of, 643–44

Consumer behavior, 118–36
    factors affecting, 119–36
        cultural, 120–23
        personal, 126–30
        psychological, 130–36
        social, 121–26
    model of, 118–19
Consumer buyer-decision processes, 143–66
    buying roles in, 145
    for new products, 158–60
    stages in, 147–58
        evaluation of alternatives, 150–52
        information search, 149–50
        postpurchase actions, 155–58
        postpurchase behavior, 154–55
        problem recognition, 149
        purchase decision, 152–54
    surveys of buyers' intentions, 207
    types of behavior, 146–47
Consumer confidence measure, 207
Consumer cooperative, 395
Consumer education and information, principle of, 644
Consumer franchise, 260
Consumer franchise building, 459
Consumer goods, 254–55
Consumer Goods Pricing Act (1975), 74
Consumer market(s), 59
    defined, 118
    market segmentation of, bases for, 219–28
        behavior, 220, 225–28
        demographic, 220, 221–25
        geographic, 219–21
        psychographic, 220, 225
    organizational markets vs., 169–72
    relative importance of promotion tools in industrial vs., 434
Consumer marketing channels, 361
Consumer-oriented marketing, 639–40
Consumer perceptions of price and value, 322–23
Consumer product managers, 553
Consumer Product Safety Act (1972), 73, 277
Consumer Product Safety Commission, 72, 74, 277
Consumer promotion, 436, 458, 459
    tools, 460–62
Consumer protection, 72, 644
Consumer Reports, 152, 629, 630
Consumer rights, 636
Consumer satisfaction, maximization of, 17
Consumer sentiment measure, 207
Consumer service needs, analyzing, 369
Consumer spending patterns, 66–67
Consumerism, 74, 635–36
Consumers Union, 629, 630
Consumption, maximization of, 17
Contact methods in market research, 100, 102–4
Containerization, 379
Contests, 462
    sales, 463, 490
Continuity, 456

Contract:
  blanket, 182
  long-term, 178
  negotiated, 188
Contract manufacturing, 586
Contracting, management, 586–87
Contraction defense, 523
Contractual sales force, 481
Contractual vertical marketing system, 364–66
Control, marketing, 48, 555–62
  annual plan control, 555–57
  defined, 555
  evaluation of channel alternatives and, 373
  image control, service marketing and, 612–13
  in marketing plan, 542
  of outlets in store retailing, 394–96
  profitability control, 556, 557–59
  strategic control, 556, 559–62
Controlled test markets, 297, 298
Convenience goods, 254–55
Convenience sample, 105
Convenience stores, 391
Conventions, 463
Conviction, buyer, 425
Cooperative advertising, 185
Cooperatives:
  consumer, 395
  retailer, 365, 395
Copy testing, 456
Copywriters, 662
Core beliefs and values, 74
Core products, 252–53
Corporate chain, 395
Corporate communications, 465
Corporate environmentalism, 639
Corporate identity materials, 467
Corporate image advertising, 612–13
Corporate marketing ethics policies, 641
Corporate responsibility research, 96
Corporate vertical marketing system, 364
Cost-based pricing, 327–29
Cost leadership, 517
Cost-plus pricing, 327–28
Costs:
  advertising and promotion, 627–28
  advertising media, 453
  distribution, 627
  of energy, 68
  evaluation of channel alternatives based on, 372
  of information, calculating, 92–93
  markup percentage on, 659–60
  pricing and, 318–20
  of product in decline stage, 305
  types of, 318–20
Council for Mutual Economic Assistance (CMEA), 578
Counseling, 466
Counteroffensive defense, 522
Counterpurchase, 581
Countertrade, 581
County and City Data Book, 99
Coupons, 460, 465

Cover letter, 665
Creative phrasing, 451
Creative selling, 480
Credible sources, 428–29
Credit department, 40
Criticisms of marketing, social, 626–35
Cues, 134
Cultural environment, 74–79, 582
Cultural pollution, 633
Cultural shifts, 120
Culture:
  company, 550
  consumer behavior and, 120–23
Current marketing situation, 539–40
Customer affairs, jobs in, 662
Customer attitude tracking, 557
Customer complaints, handling, 155–57
Customer markets, types of, 59–60
Customer need management, 555
Customer salesforce structures, 482
Customer satisfaction, 155–58
Customer Service Department, 93, 272
Customer targets, developing, 485
Customer training service, 238
Customer value analysis, 514, 515
Customer-centered company, 528
Customer-oriented approach to personal selling, 494
Customers:
  getting information about competitors from, 94
  new-product ideas from, 290
Customer-segment pricing, 343
Customized marketing, 219

D

Data:
  primary, 99, 100–107
  secondary, 99–100
Data collection, 100–107, 108
Database, marketing, 95, 401, 402
Dealer brand, 263–64
Dealers' rights, 374
Dealing, exclusive, 374
Death of a Salesman (Miller), 478
Decentralized exchange, 8, 9, 21n10
Decentralized structure, 547–48, 549
Decentralizing of marketing information system, 110, 111
Deceptive practices, 327, 457, 628–29
Deciders, 145, 175
Decision and reward systems, 548
Decisions:
  brand, 259–67
  industrial buyer behavior in making, 180–83
  labeling, 270
  organizational vs. consumer decision process, 171–72
  packaging, 267–70
  product attributes, 257–59
  product-line, 273–76
  product-support services, 271–72
  retailer marketing, 402–6
  wholesalers marketing, 411–12
  See also Consumer buyer-decision

processes; International marketing; Marketing information system (MIS)
Decline stage in product life cycle, 299, 305–6
Decoding in communication process, 426
Defense Department, 185
Defense Logistics Agency, 185
Defense strategies, 521–23, 577
Deficient products, 641
Defining Advertising Goals for Measured Advertising Results (Colley), 445–47
Delivery, 238, 609
Delphi method, 208
Demand, 197–216
  analyzing price-demand relationship, 323–24
  consumer vs. organizational, 169–71
  defined, 6
  defining market and, 199–200
  derived, 169, 170
  fluctuating, 170–71
  forecasting future, 42, 206–10
  inelastic, 170
  measuring current, 42, 200–206
    actual sales and market shares, 206
    area market demand, 203–6
    total market demand, 200–203
    types of measurement, 198–99
  price elasticity of, 170, 325
  primary, 201
  selective, 201
  states of, 10
  and supply of services, 606–7
Demand curve, 323–24
Demand management, 10
Demarketing, 10
Demassification of mass markets, 397
Demographic environment, 62–66
Demographic markets, 36
Demographic segmentation, 220, 221–25, 229
Demography, defined, 62
Demonstration aids, 496
Department store, 389–90
Departments, conflict between, 40–41
Deregulation, 343–44, 379
Derived demand, 169, 170
Descriptive research objectives, 98
Design:
  distribution channel, 368–73
  product, 259
Design for manufacturability and assembly (DFMA), 294
Designer labels, 264
Desirable products, 641
Dictionary of Occupational Titles, 664
Differentiated marketing, 232, 233
Differentiation:
  as competitive positioning strategy, 517
  image, 240
  market positioning by, 44
  personnel, 239–40
  product, 237, 448
  services, 238–39, 609

Impulse goods, 255
In Search of Excellence (Peters and Waterman), 4, 549
IN WATS, 399
Incentive programs, 463
Incentives, salesforce effort, 490
Income:
    changes in, 66
    consumer spending patterns and, 67
    distribution of, 66, 579–80
Income segmentation, 224
Income statement, 655–57
Independent off-price retailers, 393
Independent service firms, 272
India, 580, 593
Indirect exporting, 585
Individual differences in innovativeness, 158–59
Individual factors in industrial buying, 180
Individual interviewing, 103
Industrial buyer behavior, 172–83
    intention surveys of, 207
    major influences on buyers, 176–80
    methods of decision making, 180–83
    participants in buying process, 175–76
    types of buying decisions, 173–75
Industrial distributors, 371, 409
Industrial economies, 578
Industrial goods, 255–57
    test marketing, 297–98
Industrial market, 59, 169
    relative importance of promotion tools in consumer vs., 434
    segmentation of, bases for, 229–30
Industrial marketing, careers in, 663
Industrial marketing channels, 361
Industrial product managers, 553
Industrial structure of country, 578
Industrializing economies, 578
Industry:
    defined, 199, 511
    global, 576
    strategic groups within, 513
Industry attractiveness, 34
Inelastic demand, 170
Inflation, price increases and, 348
Influencers, 145, 175
Information:
    principle of consumer education and, 644
    for salesforce evaluation, 490–91
    See also Marketing information system (MIS)
Information analysis, 109
Information-based economy, 90–91
Information distribution, 110–11
Information networks, 110, 111
Information search, consumer, 149–50
Information sources, consumer, 149
Informative advertising, 447
In-home shopping, 397
Initiator, 145
Innovation:
    characteristics influencing rate of adoption, 160

continuous, 520, 521
    pricing innovative product, 338–39
    principle of, 644
    See also New-product development strategy
Innovative marketing, 640
Innovativeness, individual differences in, 158–59
Innovators, 158–59
Inseparability of services, 605
Inside salesforces, 481, 489
Inside-out perspective, 13
Installation, 238, 256
Institutional markets, 36
In-supplier, 497
Intangibility of services, 605
Integrated direct marketing, 400–401
Intelligence, marketing, 94–96, 516–17
Intensive distribution, 371
Intentions, purchase, 152–54
    surveys of buyers', 207
Interactive marketing, 601, 607–9
Intermediaries, marketing, 58–59
    See also Distribution channels
Internal marketing, 601, 607
Internal publics, 61
Internal records information, 93
Internal sources, new-product ideas from, 290
Internal stimuli, 149
International division, 593–94
International marketing, 573–600
    careers in, 663
    decisions faced in, 582–94
        choosing markets to enter, 583–84
        to go abroad, 582–83
        marketing organization, 593–94
        marketing program, 587–93
        mode of entry, 585–87
    environment, 577–82
        cultural, 582
        economic, 578–80
        political-legal, 580–81
        trade system, 577–78
    risks in, 576
International markets, 59
International sector, rapid adoption of marketing in, 19–20
International subsidiaries, 594
Interpersonal factors in industrial buying, 178–80
Interpretation phase of marketing research, 108–9
Interstates Commerce Commission, 74
Interviewing:
    job, 665–66
    personal, 102, 103–4
    telephone, 102, 103
Introduction stage in product life cycle, 299, 303, 306, 338–40
Inventory, 377
Inventory department, 40
Inventory-turnover rate, 657–58
Investment:
    direct, 587
    return on (ROI), 658–59

Irregular demand, 10
Isolated planning, 545–46

J

Japanese marketing skill, 577
Job descriptions, 664
Job market, 664–65
Jobs, marketing, 661–66
    choosing and getting, 664–66
    description of, 661–64
Job-search objectives, 664
Joint ownership, 587
Joint venturing, 585–87
Journal of the American Medical Association, 429
Journals, 99
Judgment sample, 105
Judgmental method of sales-response estimation, 544
Justice Department, 172
Just-in-time production systems, 178, 179

K

Knowledge, buyer, 425

L

Labeling, 270, 636
Labor market, 9
Laboratory tests, 456
Laggards, 158
Language in international promotion, 591
Lanham Trademark Act (1946), 73
Last Supper, 581
Late majority, 158
Late middle age population, 64
Latent demand, 10
Latin American Integration Association (LAIA), 578
Lead time, 464
Leaders:
    loss, 345
    market, 47, 518–23
    opinion, 125, 428
Leading indicators, 209–10
Learning, consumer behavior and, 134
Learning curve, 320
Leasing, 172
Legislation, 72–74, 327
    See also specific laws
Liability, product, 277
Licensing, 585–86
    of brand names for royalties, 264
Life cycle:
    celebrity, 615–16
    family, 126–27
    product. *See* Product life-cycle (PLC) strategies
Life-cycle segmentation, 221–22
Life expectancy, 62
Life quality, maximization of, 18
Life style:
    consumer behavior and, 127–29
    linking census with, 205
    market segmentation based on, 225

Life style advertising, 450
Likability of message source, 430
Liking, buyer, 425
Limited-line store, 389
Limited problem solving, 146
Limited-service retailers, 389
Limited-service wholesalers, 408, 409–10
Lobbying, 465
Local publics, 60
Location:
    retailing, 405, 406
    wholesaler, 412
Location pricing, 343
Long-range plan, 29
Long-run average cost (LRAC) curve, 318, 319
Long-term contracts, 178
Long-term objectives, tradeoff between short-term and, 546
Loss leaders, 345
Low-involvement goods, 146
Loyalty status, market segmentation based on, 228

M

McGuire Act (1952), 73
Macroenvironment, 56, 61–79
    cultural environment, 74–79, 582
    defined, 56
    demographic environment, 62–66
    economic environment, 66–67, 177, 578–80
    natural environment, 67–69
    political environment, 72–74, 580–81
    technological environment, 69–71
Magazines, 453, 455–56
Magnuson-Moss Warranty Act (1973), 277
Magnuson-Moss Warranty/FTC Improvement Act (1975), 74
Mail-order wholesalers, 410
Mail questionnaires, 102, 103
Maintenance and repair service, 257, 271–72
Malls, factory outlet, 393
Management contracting, 586–87
Managerial climate, 550
Managers:
    assessing information needs of, 91–92
    brand, 662
    brand sales, 554
    new-product, 289
    product, 289, 551–55, 662
Manufactured materials and parts, 256
Manufacturers' agents (manufacturers' representatives), 370, 410
Manufacturer's brand (national brand), 263–64
Manufacturer-sponsored retailer franchise system, 366
Manufacturer-sponsored wholesaler franchise system, 366
Manufacturer's sales agency, 372
Manufacturers' sales branches and offices, 411

Manufacturing, contract, 586
Manufacturing department, 40, 58, 93
March of Dimes, 76
Markdown ratio, 660
Market(s):
    concepts of, 8–9
    customer, types of, 59–60
    definitions of, 199
    entering, 577
      barriers to, 634–35
      mode of, 585–87
    as factor in setting promotion mix, 434
    foreign. *See* Foreign markets; International marketing
    job, 664–65
    pricing in different types of, 321–22
    selecting, 577
    See also Consumer market(s); Organizational markets
Market broadening, 522
Market-buildup method, 203–4
Market-centered companies, 528–29
Market-challenger strategies, 47, 518, 523–26
Market-coverage strategies, 232–35
Market demand. *See* Demand
Market description in marketing plan, 539
Market development, 36–37
Market diversification, 522
Market expansion strategies, 518–20
Market-factor index method, 204–6
Market-follower strategies, 47–48, 518, 526–27
Market fragmentation, 288
Market-leader strategies, 47, 518–23
Market management, 538–39
    See also Analysis; Control, marketing; Implementation; Planning, marketing
Market management organization, 553
Market minimum, 201
Market modification, 304–5
Market-nicher strategies, 48, 518, 527–28
Market opportunities, analyzing, 41, 42
Market-oriented mission statement, 30
Market penetration, 35–36
Market-penetration pricing, 339
Market pioneer, 303
Market positioning, 235–42
Market potential, 201, 584
Market rollout, 298
Market segmentation, 44–45, 219–31
    of consumer markets, bases for, 219–28
      behavior, 220, 225–28
      demographic, 220, 221–25, 229
      geographic, 219–21
      psychographic, 220, 225
    defined, 43, 219
    evaluating segments, 231–32
    example of, 217–18
    of industrial market, bases for, 229–30
    requirements for effective, 230–31
    selecting segments, 232–35

Market share:
    advertising budget and, 447
    analysis, 556–57
    building, 577
    estimating, 206
    expanding, 523
    leadership, 316
    strategies for protecting, 520–23
Market-skimming pricing, 338–39
Market structure, consumer vs. organizational, 169–71
Market targeting, 43, 44–45, 231–35
Market variability, 234–35
Marketing:
    core concepts of, 5–9
    defining, 5, 9, 21n5
    as key factor in business success, 4
    other business functions and, 38–40
    rapid adoption of, 18–20
    role in company, alternative views of, 38–40
    role in strategic planning, 28, 37–38
    social criticism of, 626–35
Marketing audit, 48, 559–62
Marketing concept, 12–15, 626
Marketing database, 95, 401, 402
Marketing department organization, 551–55
Marketing effort, managing, 41, 47–48
Marketing environment. *See* Environment, marketing
Marketing Information Guide, 99
Marketing information system (MIS), 42, 91–115
    assessing information needs, 91–93
    decentralizing, 110, 111
    defined, 91
    developing information, 93–109
      information analysis, 109
      marketing intelligence, 94–96, 516–17
      marketing research. *See* Marketing research
    distributing information, 110–11
Marketing intelligence, 94–96, 516–17
Marketing intermediaries, 58–59
    See also Distribution channels
Marketing management, 9–16
    defined, 10
    functions, 48
    philosophies, 10–16
Marketing management process, 41–49
    analyzing market opportunities, 41, 42
    defined, 41
    marketing effort, managing, 41, 47–48
    marketing mix, developing, 41, 45–47
    selecting target consumers, 41, 42–45
Marketing management science career, 663
Marketing mix:
    adapted, 587–93
    defined, 45
    developing, 41, 45–47
    modification of, 305
    positioning strategy and, 242

Noise in communication process, 426
Nondurable goods, 254
Non-family households, 64
Nonpersonal communication channels, 428
Nonprobability samples, 105
Nonprofit organizations:
    marketing by, 18–19, 662
    marketing research in, 97–98
Nonprofit sector, private, 603
Nonrenewable resources, 68
Nontariff barriers, 578
Norms:
    call, developing, 485, 486
    cultural, 582
North Carolina, business site marketing in, 617
NutraSweet, 170
Nutritional labeling, 270, 636

O

Objections, handling, 496
Objective-and-task promotion budget method, 432
Objectives:
    advertising, setting, 445–47
    call, 495
    channel, setting, 369–70
    competitors', determining, 513
    evaluating market segment and company, 231–32
    job-search, 664
    of market challenger, 524
    in marketing plan, 541
    of physical distribution, 375–76
    pricing and marketing, 315–17
    public relations, setting, 467–68
    research, 97–98
    sales promotion, setting, 459
    salesforce, setting, 480
    strategic planning and setting company, 31–32
    tradeoffs between long-term and short-term, 546
Observational research, 100–101
Obsolescence, planned, 630–31
Occasion segmentation, 225–26
Occupation, consumer behavior and, 127
Occupation Outlook Handbook, 664
Offer, differentiating service, 609
Office of Consumer Affairs, 74
Office of Management and Budget, 187
Office-party selling, 124
Off-invoice, 462
Off-list, 462
Off-price retailers, 393, 394
Oil prices, 68
Oligopolistic competition, 321–22
Open-bid buying, 188
Open dating, 270
Open-end questions, 105–6, 107
Operating expense percentage, 657
Operating ratios, 657–59
Operating statement, 655–57
Operating variables, industrial market segmentation by, 229
Opinion leaders, 125, 428

Opportunities, 540–41
    market, analyzing, 41, 42
    technological, 69–70
Optimal-product pricing, 341
Order processing, 376
Order routine specification, 182
Organization:
    distribution channel, 363–68
    international marketing, 593–94
    marketing department, 551–55
    marketing organization audit, 561
Organization image, 612–13
Organization marketing, 612
Organization structure, 289, 547–48, 549
Organizational buying, defined, 168
Organizational climate, 490
Organizational factors in industrial buying, 178
Organizational markets, 169–72
    characteristics of, 169–72
    government buyer behavior, 185–88
    industrial buyer behavior, 172–83
        major influences on buyers, 176–80
        methods of decision making, 180–83
        participants in buying process, 175–76
        types of buying decisions, 173–75
    model of buying behavior in, 172–73
    reseller buyer behavior, 183–85
    types of, 169
Organizations, people's views of, 77
Orientation, family of, 125
Others, people's views of, 76–77
Others self-concept, 130
OUT WATS, 399
Outdoor advertising, 453, 454–55
Outlets, control of, 394–96
Outside salesforces, 489
Outside-in perspective, 13
Out-supplier, 497
Overfull demand, 10
Overhead, 318
Overpositioning, 241
Ozone layer, 67

P

Pack peddlers, 479
Packaging, 267–70, 627, 629
Packaging concept, 268
Parts and materials, 256
Patent protection, 277
Patronage rewards, 461
Peak Performance-Mental Training Techniques of the World's Greatest Athletes (Garfield), 484
Penetration, market, 35–36, 200
Penetration pricing, 339
Penny Power (children's magazine), 630
Pentagon, 294
People meters, 100
People-based services, 603, 604
People's Republic of China, 583–84, 593
Perceived risk, 154
Perceived-value pricing, 329–30

Percentage labeling, 270
Percentage-of-sales promotion budget method, 431
Perception:
    consumer behavior and, 131–34
    defined, 132
    of price and value, consumer, 322–23
    subliminal, 135
Performance evaluation:
    of salesforce, 492–93
    of suppliers, 182–83
Periodicals, 99
Perishability of services, 606–7
Peristroika (economic restructuring), 20
Person marketing, 362, 613–16
Personal characteristics, industrial market segmentation by, 229, 230
Personal communication channels, 427–28
Personal influence, role of, 159
Personal interviewing, 102, 103–4
Personal selling, 493–97
    defined, 425
    nature of, 433
    process, 494
    public policy and, 493
    relationship marketing, 496–97
    steps in selling process, 494–96
Personal services, 604
Personality:
    consumer behavior and, 129–30
    market segmentation based on, 225
Personality symbol, 450
Personnel differentiation, 239–40
Persuasive advertising, 447
Philosophies, marketing management, 10–16
Physical distribution, 374–80
    careers in, 663
    defined, 375
    inventory, 377
    nature of, 375
    objective of, 375–76
    order processing, 376
    organizational responsibility for, 379–80
    transportation, 377–79, 380
    warehousing, 376–77
Physical distribution firms, 59
Physical evidence, information from, 94–95
Physiological needs, 131, 133
Pioneer, market, 303
Pipelines, 378
Place in marketing mix, 45–46
    See also Location
Place marketing, 616, 617
Planned obsolescence, 630–31
Planning, marketing, 48, 539–44
    approaches to, 29
    benefits of, 29
    budget development, 542–44
    components of marketing plan, 539–42
    distributor relations, 373–74
    human resources, 548–50

image, services marketing and, 612–13
isolated, problem of, 545–46
kinds of plans, 29
research plan, developing, 98–107
See also Strategic planning
Pleasing products, 641
PMSAs (Primary Metropolitan Statistical Areas), 81*n*10
Point-of-purchase (POP) promotions, 461
Political-legal environment, 72–74, 580–81
Political power of business, 633–34
Pollution, 69, 270
cultural, 633
Poor, service to the, 631
Population, U. S.:
changing age structure of, 62–64
geographic shifts in, 64–65
white-collar, 65
Portfolio, designing business, 32–37
Portfolio tests, 456
Position defense, 521
Positioning:
competitive, 517–18
market, 235–42
product, 44–45
Positioning errors, 241
Postpurchase actions, consumer, 155–58
Postpurchase behavior, consumer, 154–55
Posttesting of ads, 457
Potential market, 199
Power:
of buyers, 231
political, of business, 633–34
of retailers, 554
of suppliers, 231
Preapproach, 495
Preemptive defense, 522
Preference, buyer, 425
Premiums, 461, 463–64
Presentation step of selling process, 495–96
Press relations, 465
Pretesting, 456, 464
Preticketing, 185
Price, pricing, 313–36
consumer perceptions of, 322–23
deceptive, 327, 628
defined, 315
factors to consider in, 315–26
external, 321–26
internal, 315–20
general approaches to, 326–31
buyer-based pricing, 329–30
competition-based pricing, 330–31
cost-based pricing, 327–29
international, 592
marketing and high, 627–28
in marketing mix, 45, 46
markup percentage on, 659–60
names for price, 314
during product life-cycle stages, 303, 304
public policy and, 327
in retailing, 392–94, 405–6
transfer, 592

unit, 270, 636
wholesaler, 411
Price changes, 347–51
increases, 327
initiating, 347–50
responding to, 350–51
Price competition, 609
Price discrimination, 327, 343–44
Price elasticity of demand, 170, 325
Price fixing, 327
Price packs, 461
Price points, 341
Price-demand relationship, analyzing, 323–24
Price-off, 462
Pricing department, 320
Pricing strategies, 337–56
new-product, 338–40
price changes, 327, 347–51
price-adjustment strategies, 342–47, 462
product-mix, 340–42
Pricing structure, 338
Primary data, 99
collection, 100–107
Primary demand, 201
Principle-oriented people, 129
Print media, 428
Private and public goods, balance between, 633
Private brand, 263–64
Private nonprofit sector, 603
PRIZM, 205
Probability sample, 105
Problem, defining, 97–98
Problem recognition:
by consumer, 149
by industrial buyer, 180
Problem solving:
extensive, 146–47
limited, 146
Procreation, family of, 125
Producer and consumer freedom, principle of, 643–44
Producers' cooperatives, 410
Product(s), 251–83
channel design decisions and, 369
classifications, 254–57
core, 252–53
defining, 7, 252–54
as factor in setting promotion mix, 434
group influence on choice of, 124–25
individual product decisions, 257–72
brand, 259–67
labeling, 270
packaging, 267–70
product attributes, 257–59
product-support services, 271–72
influence on rate of adoption, 159–60
levels of, 252–53
in marketing mix, 45, 46
placing. *See* Distribution channels; Retailing; Wholesaling
planned obsolescence of, 630–31
product line decisions, 273–76

product-mix decisions, 276–77
public policy and, 277
reviving old, 287
shoddy or unsafe, 629–30
societal classification of new, 640–41
strategy in foreign market, 590
substitute, 231
See also New-product development strategy; Product life-cycle (PLC) strategies
Product adaptation, 590
Product assortment. *See* Product mix (assortment)
Product attributes, 150–51, 236, 257–59
Product-bundle pricing, 341
Product choice set, 7
Product class, 237, 300
Product concept, 12, 292–93
Product design, 259
Product development, 37, 294, 299
Product differentiation, 237, 448
Product-form pricing, 343
Product forms, 300
Product idea, 292
Product image, 292
Product invention, 590
Product liability, 277
Product life-cycle (PLC) strategies, 299–306
advertising budget and, 447
characteristics and responses, 306
promotion mix and, 436–37
sales-profits patterns and, 299–300
stages and, 299, 303–6
choosing market-coverage strategy and, 234
decline stage, 299, 305–6
growth stage, 299, 303–4, 306
introduction stage, 299, 303, 306, 338–40
maturity stage, 299, 304–5, 306
Product line:
decisions, 273–76
sold in store retailing, 389–92
Product-line featuring, 276
Product-line filling, 275
Product-line length, 273–74
Product-line modernization, 275–76
Product-line pricing, 340–41
Product-line stretching, 274
Product management organization, 551–55
Product management/market management organization, 553–55
Product managers, 289, 551–55, 662
Product mix (assortment), 276–77
pricing strategies for, 340–42
retailers', 404–5
wholesaler, 411
Product modification, 305
Product positioning, 44–45
Product publicity, 465
Product quality, 257–59, 277, 316
Product-quality leadership, 316
Product research, 96
Product review, 539
Product safety, 268, 277, 629–30
Product salesforce structure, 481–82

Product specification, 181
Product-support services decisions, 271–72
Product tampering, 625
Product-use tests, 297–98
Product variability, 234
Product-variety marketing, 218
Product warranties, 277
Production:
    costs at different levels of, 318–19
    just-in-time, 178, 179
Production concept, 12
Production experience, costs as function of, 319–20
Productivity audit, marketing, 561
Productivity, service, 611–12
Product/market expansion grid, 35–37
Professionals:
    adoption of marketing by, 18
    promoting products through, 429
Profit and loss statement, 557, 558–59, 655–57
Profit maximization, current, 316
Profit optimization planning, 543–44
Profitability control, 556, 557–59
Profits:
    expected, 331
    over product life-cycle, 299–300, 304
    target profit planning, 542–43
Promotion, 421–22, 430–37
    consumer, 436
    costs, 627–28
    deceptive, 628–29
    in foreign market, 590–92
    in marketing mix, 46
    during product life-cycle, 203, 303
    promotion mix:
        defined, 422–23
        setting, 432–37
    retailer, 406
    setting total budget for, 431–32
    tools, 423, 432–34
    trade, 436
    wholesaler, 411–12
    See also Advertising; Personal selling; Public relations; Salesforce management; Sales promotion
Promotion clutter, 458
Promotional allowances and services, 343, 457
Promotional pricing, 345
Proposal solicitation, 181
Prospecting, 486, 494–95
Protectionism, 575
Prototype, 294
Psychographic segmentation, 220, 225
Psychographics, 127
Psychological factors affecting consumer behavior, 130–36
Psychological pricing, 344–45
Public actions to regulate marketing, 637–38
Public Citizen group, 74
Public documents, getting information from, 94
Public goods, balance between private and, 633
Public interest groups, 74

Public policy:
    advertising and, 457
    distribution decisions and, 374
    toward marketing, principles for, 643–45
    packaging and, 270
    personal selling and, 493
    price decisions and, 327
    product decisions and, 277
Public relations, 464–69
    careers in, 663
    decisions in, 467–69
    defined, 425, 464
    nature of, 434
    tools, 465–66, 467
Public service activities, 467
Publicity, 465
Publics:
    goals of, 17
    types of, 60–61
Published materials, getting information from, 94
Pull strategy, 421, 435
Pulsing, 456
Purchase, 425
Purchase decision, consumer, 152–54
Purchase intentions, 152–54
Purchase probability scale, 207
Purchasing:
    careers in, 663
    centralized, 178
    stockless, 185
    upgraded, 178
Purchasing agents, 410–11
Purchasing approaches, industrial market segmentation by, 229–30
Purchasing department, 40, 57–58
Purchasing offices, 411
Purchasing performance evaluation, 178
Pure competition, 321
Pure Food and Drug Act, 641
Pure monopoly, 321–22
Push money, 463
Push-strategy, 421, 434–35, 436

Q

Qualified available market, 199
Qualifying leads, 495
Qualitative evaluation of salespeople, 493
Quality:
    audience, 456
    product, 257–59, 277, 316
    service, 607–11
Quality control, 179, 606
Quality improvement, 305
Quality of life, maximization of, 18
Quantity discounts, 342–43
Question marks (SBU classification), 33–34
Questionnaire, 105–6
    mail, 102, 103
Questions, types of, 105–6, 107
Quota sample, 105
Quotas:
    import, 578
    sales, 490

R

Racial diversity, 66
Rack jobbers, 410
Radio, 453
Railroads, 378
Rational appeals, 426
Ratios, analytic, 657–59
Raw-material-exporting economies, 578
Raw materials, 67–68, 256
Reach, advertising, 452–53
Readiness states, buyer, 228, 424–26, 436
Rebates, 345, 461
Rebuy:
    modified, 174
    straight, 173
Recall tests, 457
Receiver in communication process, 426
Reciprocity, 172
Recognition tests, 457
Records, internal, 93
Recruitment of salespeople, 483–84
Recruits, getting information from, 94
Redbook magazine, 225
Reference groups, 122–25
Reference prices, 344–45
Regional shopping center, 396
Regionalization, 222
Regulation:
    increased, 72
    legislation, 72–74, 327
    of marketing, 635–38
    monetary, 580–81
    purposes of, 72
Reinforcement, 134
Relationship marketing, 496–97
Relative advantage, 160
Reminder advertising, 447
Renewable resources, 68
Repair services, 238
Reports, sales, 490–91
Repositioning, 55
    brand, 266
Resale price maintenance, 327
Research & development (R&D), 40, 57, 70–71, 294
Research instruments, 100, 105–7
Research. See Marketing research
Reseller buyer behavior, 183–85
Reseller market, 58–59, 169, 326
Resident buyers, 411
Resistance to change, 546
Resources, company:
    choosing market-coverage strategy and, 234
    evaluating market segment and, 231–32
Resources, natural, 67–69
Response in communication process, 426
Response sought, determining, 424–26
Responsibilities of channel members, 371–72
Responsibility, organizational:
    for marketing communications planning, 437
    for physical distribution, 379–80
    social, 625, 638–43